Seventh Edition

MANAGERIAL ACCOUNTING

Geraldine F. Dominiak
Texas Christian University

Joseph G. Louderback III
Clemson University

COLLEGE DIVISION South-Western Publishing Co.
Cincinnati Ohio

AQ63GA

ISBN: 0-538-82534-0

2 3 4 5 6 7 K 9 8 7 6 5 4

Printed in the United States of America

Vice President/Publisher: Mark Hubble
Developmental Editor: Tom Bormann
Production Editor: Nancy Ahr
Associate Editor: M. R. Cline
Editorial Assistant: Holly Knoechel
Internal Design: Tom Hubbard
Cover Design and Cover Illustration: Graphica
Director of Marketing: Martin Lewis

Library of Congress Cataloging-in-Publication Data

Dominiak, Geraldine F.
Managerial accounting / Geraldine F. Dominiak, Joseph G. Louderback III -- 7th ed.
p. cm.
Includes index
ISBN 0-538-82534-0
1. Managerial accounting. I. Louderback, Joseph G. II. Title.
HF5657.4.D66 1993
658.15--dc20 93-8305
CIP

I(T)P

International Thomson Publishing
South-Western Publishing Co. is an ITP Company. The ITP trademark is under license.

brief contents

contents

preface

This book is designed for an introductory course in managerial accounting. Though we wrote the book with the undergraduate student in mind, we have had many reports of its successful use in both graduate and management development courses. One reason is that the wide variety of assignment material allows instructors to select assignments consistent with their students' backgrounds.

The book emphasizes the *uses* of managerial accounting information. It is therefore appropriate not only for accounting majors but also for nonaccounting business majors (marketing, management, finance, etc.), and majors in nonbusiness areas such as engineering, mathematics, and the physical sciences.

We assume that a reader has had one or two terms of financial accounting or a working exposure to basic financial statements. We expect that a reader has some understanding of the most basic principles on which financial statements are based. The journal-entry/T-account framework appears only in Chapter 15 and is not, with the exception of that chapter, critical to understanding the concepts.

Most discussions in the book focus on the functions of management: planning, decision making, controlling, and performance evaluation. This emphasis is apparent even in the chapters on product costing (Chapters 13-15), a topic that accounting textbooks seldom discuss with the nonaccountant in mind. Those chapters approach product costing from the standpoint of analyzing results under different costing systems, rather than concentrating on cost-accumulation procedures or the accounting problems related to those procedures.

Our objectives in this edition remain essentially the same as those for the first six editions:

1. To present clearly and understandably the most important conceptual and practical aspects of managerial accounting;
2. To order the material in a way that allows the reader to build from elementary concepts to more complex topics and thus to integrate and expand early understanding;

3. To illustrate some of the interrelationships between managerial accounting and other courses in a normal business curriculum;
4. To show the reader, through discussion, illustration, and assignment material, the almost infinite number of applications of managerial accounting principles to decision making in economic entities of all types (including personal decisions);
5. To encourage the reader to recognize that *people*, not entities, make decisions and are responsible for the results of those decisions.

We use several means to achieve these objectives. First, we use examples and illustrations liberally. Second, we proceed through the text (and its increasingly complex concepts) in a building-block fashion. We begin with the principles of cost behavior and cost-volume-profit analysis, which underlie virtually all of managerial accounting, and use this basis to approach the more complex problems encountered in decision making, comprehensive budgeting, responsibility accounting, and product costing. A reader will see the continued reliance on previously developed concepts by the regularity of references to earlier chapters.

The applicability of managerial accounting concepts to a wide variety of economic entities is most obvious in sections of the text that specifically refer to nonbusiness situations. But both the examples used in other parts of the text and the decision situations posed in assignment material also reflect our efforts to demonstrate the opportunities for using managerial accounting concepts in a nonbusiness context.

We regularly draw attention to qualitative and difficult-to-quantify aspects of a topic. As part of the qualitative considerations, we discuss behavioral problems and point out the implications of such problems. We raise these qualitative issues to emphasize that decisions are made by individuals with beliefs and feelings. We expect readers to recognize that accounting data provide relevant information but do not dictate courses of action.

Throughout the book we emphasize that decisions are made on the basis of estimates and that some factors important to a decision are difficult to quantify. Our intentions are to underscore (1) the presence of uncertainty, and (2) the importance of recognizing all the available alternatives and all the factors relevant to each alternative. Both the text and many of the problems emphasize that a major problem in managing any enterprise is determining the right questions to ask and, concomitantly, what kinds of information to seek. In our opinion, students should learn that real-world problems do not present themselves in the form of schedules to be filled in and manipulated. Indeed, sometimes a manager's most difficult task is to discern, from the mass of economic activity taking place all around, exactly what the problem is that requires investigation and resolution.

NEW FEATURES

1. *More Real-World Examples and More Activity-Based Costing.* The most comprehensive changes reflected in this edition are the increased number of references to actual companies and the increased coverage

and integration of the terminology and techniques of the just-in-time (JIT) philosophy and of activity-based costing. These ideas are incorporated throughout the book, consistent with its overall plan, so that almost every chapter is affected.

- Activity-based costing (ABC) is now an integral part of virtually every chapter after Chapter 3. This important topic should not be treated in a separate chapter as if it were an add-on.
- More complete integration of the new manufacturing environment is evident and nearly every chapter refers to the just-in-time (JIT) operating philosophy. As with ABC, this subject should be integrated and not treated as an add-on.
- More examples from the real world are included with more references to actual companies.

The assignment material in various chapters has been revised or expanded to reflect the integration described above. In addition, we have incorporated in the text the reported experiences of some companies that have adopted advanced manufacturing techniques.

2. *More International Coverage.* More attention is given to international matters, such as cultural differences as well as currency translation.
3. *More Ethics.* Material on ethics has been expanded and includes a reprint of the IMA Standards for Professional Conduct. Most chapters have assignments dealing with ethical issues.
4. *Guidelines for Preparing Memoranda.* Virtually all chapters have assignments that require preparing memoranda with regard to the Accounting Education Change Commission. A new appendix gives guidelines for preparing memoranda.
5. *New Appendix A.* Former Chapter 16 on quantitative methods is now an appendix.
6. *Statement of Cash Flows and Analyzing Finanacial Statements Chapters on Disk.* Former Chapters 17 and 18 are on disk and available for reproduction.

ALTERNATIVE CHAPTER SEQUENCING

The text contains more material than is needed for a one-term course, and we expect most users to omit one or more chapters. Several users have found alternative sequencing to be practical. We recommend, however, that whatever chapters are used, they should be covered in the order presented. The text does offer considerable flexibility in the order of coverage.

Appendix A, which discusses several quantitative methods of analysis, can be covered separately at any time after Chapter 12. Or, individual segments of that chapter can be assigned in conjunction with earlier chapters. The section on statistical decision theory has illustrations that use materials from Chapters 6, 8, and 12. The illustrations, while concentrating on applying the quantitative methods, draw on topics discussed in these earlier chapters. (The concept of expected value can be introduced as early as Chapter 5.) The section on inventory control models is particularly relevant to Chapter 6, which covers production and purchases budgets. The linear programming section extends the material in Chapter 5 on alternative uses of limited resources. Similarly, the section on learning curves can supplement the discussion in Chapter 3 on cost prediction methods.

Instructors desiring an earlier and greater emphasis on product costing can move to Chapters 12 through 15 after Chapter 3. (Note that giving early emphasis to product costing requires incorporating Chapter 12 in the coverage of that topic rather than as part of the study of responsibility accounting, because some understanding of standard costs is assumed in Chapters 14 and 15.) Some users increase the time available to cover product costing by omitting Chapters 10 and 11. Alternatively, some users omit all product-costing material, or omit all or parts of Chapter 14 and 15. Chapter 4 can be omitted without loss of continuity. Also, one or both chapters on capital budgeting (Chapters 8 and 9) can be omitted without serious loss of continuity.

Appendix C, which deals with present values, was designed to be used with Chapters 8 and 9 on capital budgeting. It assumes no previous exposure to the general idea of the time value of money, but those who have had such exposure are likely to find this material useful for review.

ASSIGNMENT MATERIAL

One of the strongest features of this book is the assignment material, because of its integration with the text, its volume, and its variety with respect to degree of difficulty and economic entities. Users of previous editions have told us that these factors make it possible to teach this course, and the individual topics therein, at various levels of difficulty. Users cite the same factors in successful offerings of the course to students with widely different backgrounds. (Comments in the Solutions Manual aid in judicious choice of assignment items to accommodate different objectives.)

End-of-chapter material includes questions for discussion, exercises, problems, and cases. There are no review questions that can be answered by referring to a sentence or two in the chapter. Discussion questions are designed to increase students' understanding of concepts, and many have no clearly correct answers. Exercises are usually short and cover basic applications of one or two key concepts. Problems tend to be longer than exercises, and are more challenging, sometimes contain irrelevant information, and often ask the student to state reservations about whatever solutions are proposed. Both exercises and problems are generally arranged in order of increasing difficulty.

Cases normally contain less information than is needed to develop a single solution; our intention is to emphasize this inconvenient characteristic of real-life situations. For most cases, the student must propose an analytical approach appropriate to the available, relevant information. Cases, and the later problems, require the student to determine what principles are relevant and how those principles apply in a given situation. That is, these assignments are designed to encourage the student to think, since a manager must do so.

SUPPLEMENTARY MATERIAL

Test Bank, which contains true-false and multiple-choice questions and short problems, is available in both printed and microcomputer versions.

Solutions Manual contains solutions for all assignment material and suggested times for completing assignments. It also provides notes to the instructor regarding class use of the material. These notes offer (1) alternative approaches for arriving at solutions; (2) suggestions for eliciting class discussion; and (3) suggestions for expanding individual assignments to cover new issues, pursuing existing issues in more depth, or highlighting relationships between managerial accounting concepts and concepts studied in other business disciplines. Also, the Solutions Manual contains suggested time allocations for alternative course lengths and chapter sequencing. For each chapter, it provides a brief statement of the topical coverage, suggestions of assignment items for coverage of basic concepts, and a brief commentary about concepts or approaches that students find difficult to understand.

Transparencies are available upon adoption for many solutions.

Lotus 1-2-3 templates for various assignments are complimentary to instructoras who adopt this text.

Study Guide is designed to help students obtain full value from the study of this text. This supplement, which offers key statements to use as guides in reading the chapters, includes not only objective questions but also a variety of short and medium-length problems (solutions included) to test understanding. The final section of the Guide for each chapter identifies those concepts, practices, or approaches that cause the most difficulty or greatest misunderstanding for students.

Videos assist in classroom presentations of new manufacturing environment techniques, such as continuous-flow manufacturing and activity-based costing.

ACKNOWLEDGMENTS

We wish to thank the many instructors and students whose comments and suggestions have helped us significantly in the preparation of all seven editions of this book. In particular, we want to thank the reviewers of the revised material for the seventh edition:

Wagdy Abdallah
Seton Hall University

Larry N. Bitner
University of Richmond

Wayne G. Bremser
Villanova University

Linda M. Campbell
University of Toledo

Al Chen
North Carolina State University

Ted R. Compton
Ohio University

John M. Cucka
Northwest State University of Louisiana

Timothy A. Farmer
University of Missouri—St. Louis

David F. Fetyko
Kent State University

Charles F. Grant
Skyline College

Rosalie C. Hallbauer
Florida International University

Jay S. Holmen
University of Wisconsin—Eau Claire

Robert E. Jensen
Trinity University

David A. Kunz
Southeast Missouri State University

Fred Nordhauser
University of Texas at San Antonio

P. Merle Maddocks
Memphis State University

Gerald M. Myers
Pacific Lutheran University

Ginger G. Parker
Creighton University

Manash R. Ray
Lehigh University

Barbara W. Scofield
University of Kentucky

Steven V. Senge
Western Washington University

Douglas Sharp
Wichita State University

Alex EC. Yuen
San Francisco State University

Special thanks goes to Donald Lucy for verifing the solutions manual and test bank.

We also express our appreciation to the American Institute of Certified Public Accountants and Institute of Management Accountants for their generous permission to use problems adapted from past CPA and CMA examinations, respectively.

Finally, we thank our respective institutions, and our colleagues at those institutions, without whom the development of this volume, in its current and prior editions, would have been a much less pleasant task.

Geraldine F. Dominiak
Joseph G. Louderback

1 introduction

Accountants develop and communicate much of the economic information used by managers of businesses and other economic organizations and by external parties, such as creditors, stockholders, and governmental agencies. Providing information to outsiders is **financial accounting. Managerial accounting**, on the other hand, provides information to help meet the needs of internal parties, the organization's managers.

Managers make decisions about acquiring and using economic resources and need information to help them make those decisions. Managerial accounting generates much of that information, and also includes some of the techniques managers use in performing their jobs. No reasonably concise definition of managerial accounting captures all of its aspects. The subject constantly changes to adapt to technological changes, changes in managers' needs, and new approaches to other functional areas of business—marketing, production, finance, organizational behavior, and management. Managerial accounting is an indispensable part of the system that provides information to managers—the people whose decisions and actions determine the success or failure of an organization.

Managerial accounting obviously applies to businesses since it deals with economic information, and businesses seek profits and other economic goals. Managerial accounting also applies to organizations that do not seek profits—government units, universities, hospitals, churches—because those organizations, like businesses, use economic resources to meet their objectives. Hence, an understanding of the concepts of managerial accounting is important to managers in any organization. Therefore, in this book, we do not assume that you plan to major in accounting or to become an accountant; we assume only that you are interested in managing.

FUNCTIONS OF MANAGEMENT

Two important functions of management are planning and control. **Planning** is setting goals and developing ways to achieve those goals. Planning includes the important process of budgeting. **Budgeting** is the relating of goals to the specific means for achieving them. For example, if a goal is to obtain a particular level of profit, the budgeting process determines what machinery, cash, labor force, and other resources will be needed to achieve that goal and how to acquire the necessary amount of each resource.

Managing requires **decision making**. A plan for a year, for example, requires deciding what products or services to sell, what prices to charge, what machinery to acquire, how many people to hire, whether to borrow money or issue stock, and so on.

Planning often uses an important managerial method—**management by objectives**. A management-by-objectives program requires that managers set objectives and then try to achieve them. On occasion, the objectives of some departments within the firm conflict, and the managerial accountant may gather relevant information to help resolve the conflict. To illustrate, the sales manager might want increased production of a particular product to meet a sales objective. The production manager might argue that it would be prohibitively expensive—preventing him or her from meeting cost and production objectives—to shift production away from other products to meet this request. The managerial accountant might analyze the effects of the changed production schedule and recommend what to do.

Control is determining whether goals are being met, and if not, what can be done. What changes might be made to achieve existing goals? Should the existing goals be changed? Managerial accounting is used extensively in control because many goals are expressed in dollar terms—so much sales, so much cost—and because managerial accountants use analytical tools to help managers understand the reasons for not achieving goals. Implicit in control is **performance evaluation**—managers reviewing the accomplishments of their employees and weighing them against standards. Many such evaluations use managerial accounting information.

At its simplest, control is achieved through close, physical supervision, but the size of most modern corporations precludes close contact among persons who are several levels apart in the organizational hierarchy. Even in relatively small companies, managers usually cannot exercise constant oversight of the activities of their staffs. The principle of **management by exception** helps managers to control operations. Applying this principle, managers rely on *reports* to keep informed. Reports reduce the need for minute-by-minute, physical supervision and allow managers time to perform their other functions. If reports show that results are not in accordance with plans—that is, if there are exceptions—investigation and action might follow. Thus, accounting reports partially substitute for managers' personal supervision of activities.

TYPES OF MANAGERS

It is common practice to distinguish between *line* and *staff* functions in an organization. The manager of a **line function** is concerned with the primary operating activities of the organization—usually, acquiring and selling a physical product or performing a service. A staff manager manages a department that serves other departments. For example, financial managers are concerned with obtaining sufficient cash to keep operations running smoothly. The manager of the legal department advises other managers regarding the legal ramifications of actions.

Accounting is a **staff function**, with the managerial accountant providing information to other managers. The information can relate to financial statements, tax problems, dealings with governmental authorities, and other matters. The managerial accountant, like other staff managers, often recommends courses of action to those using the information. But neither the managerial accountant, nor any other staff manager, can impose recommendations on line managers. Nevertheless, because of their expertise, staff managers can influence decisions. In fact, in some organizations "management accountants have votes on some line decisions, and, on certain decisions, their prior approval is sought."[1] Staff managers, like all managers, must also make decisions about the activities in their own departments.

MANAGERIAL ACCOUNTING AND FUNCTIONS OF MANAGEMENT

Managers require information to plan and control. The managerial accountant is the primary, though not the only, provider of information. This information includes such historical data as the prices of materials, wages paid to employees, rents on leased facilities or equipment, costs of fringe benefits, and various taxes. Also, managerial accountants provide information about the probable effects of proposed actions. For example, managerial accountants will tell other managers what profit is likely if a proposed advertising program works as planned. Managers also use information originating outside the firm. For example, statistics on the state of the economy are helpful in forecasting sales; studies of patterns of population growth are relevant to decisions about locations for new stores, warehouses, and manufacturing plants; statistics on the state of each industry in which a company operates are useful in forecasting both sales and related expenses.

PLANNING AND BUDGETING

Without careful planning, a company achieves its goals only by accident. Managerial accounting is important in planning because it provides information for decision making and because the entire budgeting process is developed around accounting-related reports.

A firm that sets a target profit for a year must also determine how to reach that target. For example, what products are to be sold at what prices? Managerial accountants develop data that help managers identify the more profitable products. Often, managerial accountants are asked to determine the effects of alternative prices and selling efforts. (What will profit be if we cut prices 5% and increase volume 15%? Would spending $250,000 on adver-

1 *Gerald H. Lander, James R. Holmes, Manuel A. Tipgos, and Marc J. Wallace, Jr.,* Profile of the Management Accountant *(New York: National Association of Accountants, 1983), 10.*

The importance of planning is underscored by the way that outside investors respond to public announcements of plans. R. H. Macy, the giant retailer, went into bankruptcy in early 1992. In late 1992, it submitted a plan to its creditors detailing how it expected to return to profitable operation. The plan included such elements as reducing advertising from 4% of sales to 3%, having fewer one-day sales, rebuilding its business in moderate-priced women's apparel, improving customer service, and installing a sophisticated inventory-management system. Macy forecast sales, expenses, profits, and cash flow for several years into the future and the details allowed creditors to evaluate the likelihood that the company could achieve its goals.

Responses by representatives of Macy's creditors paid considerable attention to the point that Macy was taking an important step simply by developing a sound, realistic plan. While some of Macy's creditors and securities analysts voiced concern about some aspects of the plan, they generally applauded the company for producing a plan that could serve as a basis for action.*

*The Wall Street Journal, *November 6, 1992, B2/, and "Prudence on 34th Street,"* Business Week, *November 6, 1992, 44.*

tising, or offering a 10% sales commission, be wise if it led to a 20% increase in sales?)

As part of the budgeting process, managerial accountants prepare budgeted financial statements, often called **pro forma statements.** Among the most important statements is the budget of cash receipts and disbursements. The finance department uses forecasts of cash requirements to determine whether borrowing will be necessary. The *management* of cash is extremely critical; more companies fail because they run out of cash as a result of inadequate planning than because they are unable to make a profit. Making profits and maintaining adequate cash are two very different things, and managers must understand that profitability does not guarantee generating enough cash to pay the bills.

DECISION MAKING

Much of the information provided by managerial accountants is used in decision making, which is an important part of planning. Some decision making is carried on continually. For example, managers decide daily or weekly how many units of a product to buy or make, or how much advertising to place in specific newspapers or on specific radio stations. Often, they also must decide what prices to charge for products or services. Timeliness is critical for reports that are needed for such decisions. It is equally important that the information in the reports be relevant to the decision at hand. Sales managers need, among other data, information about product costs and margins, trends of sales, and inventories. These same managers probably do not need *detailed* information about the cost to make a particular product. On the other hand, production managers *do* need detailed information about product costs, so that their reports might show 20 or more categories of costs.

Some decisions are made infrequently, such as whether to build a new factory, buy a new warehouse, introduce a new product line, or enter a foreign market. Developing the information managers need for such decisions requires that the managerial accountant do special analyses. The data for such analyses probably are not readily available. The managerial accountant determines what data are needed, presents those data in an understandable way, and explains the analysis to the managers making the decisions.

Managerial accountants assist managers in making decisions not only by providing information, but also by using analytical techniques that help managers understand the implications of a decision. For example, managerial accountants can tell managers how many units of a new product they must sell to earn a desired profit or what cost savings are necessary to justify buying new machinery. We discuss many of these techniques in this book.

Although managers use accounting data extensively in making decisions, such data do not *answer* the questions that managers face. *People* make decisions, and people bring to decision making their experience, values, and knowledge that usually cannot be incorporated into quantitative analyses. An action based on an analysis of the accounting data might not be taken because of some qualitative factor not captured in those data. For example, if the managers of a company want to maintain technological leadership, they might launch a new product that they *expect* to be unprofitable. Quantifying the benefits of such leadership is not easy. Such a quantification is unlikely to be included in the managerial accountant's analysis of the desirability of bringing out the new product. However, a report of that analysis quite likely would include a comment about the benefits and the inability to quantify them. That is, reports from managerial accountants recognize factors whose financial implications are not incorporated in the quantitative analyses.

CONTROLLING

For many managers, the most common contact with managerial accounting information comes through **control reports**, which detail costs incurred by them and their staffs and usually relates those costs to budgeted costs. Managers use such reports to determine whether some aspect of their areas of responsibility requires special attention and corrective action. The use of control reports follows the principle of management by exception. As a rule, when budgeted and actual results are very close, managers conclude that operations are going according to plan and that no special investigation is needed. When significant differences between budgeted and actual results arise, managers usually will investigate to determine what is going wrong and who might need help.

Control reports do not tell managers what to do. The fact that actual results differ greatly from planned results does not tell managers why the results differed. Control reports provide feedback to help managers determine where attention might be required. They do not tell managers how to correct any problems that might exist or which people performed satisfactorily or unsatisfactorily. Substandard performance could result from conditions outside a manager's control.

Control reports should be timely and relevant. A manager might receive one report daily, another weekly, and others monthly, the frequency depending on the manager's position. The closer the manager is to actual operations, the more frequent the reports. For example, some factory supervisors receive daily reports on production and costs, but higher-level managers need production reports at less frequent intervals.

Advances in computers and in the ability to store and retrieve large amounts of information sometimes have been accompanied by an unfortunate side effect called *information overload*. Some managers receive far more information than they can possibly use. One of the challenges in managerial accounting is to develop ways to determine what information is relevant for particular managers, summarize the information, and present it in a usable form. The general manager of a factory employing 500 people cannot effectively use weekly reports showing the actual amounts incurred for 800 cost categories. The general manager could, however, use a report showing which costs differed significantly from their budgeted amounts. Communication between managers and managerial accountants is important so that managers receive the information they need and need the information they receive.

EVALUATING

Evaluating and controlling are very closely related. Managers usually are evaluated partly on the basis of how well they control their operations: whether they achieve budgeted sales volume, meet budgeted cost levels, or produce budgeted quantities of product. Higher-level managers who are not involved directly in day-to-day activities rely on the information reported by management accountants about the performance of lower-level managers.

Developing suitable measures of performance for a given manager can be difficult. For example, if sales managers are evaluated on the basis of total sales dollars, they might concentrate on obtaining the highest dollar sales without regard to the profitability of the items sold. The result might be very high sales volume but very low overall profit. Similarly, if production managers are evaluated on the basis of whether they meet budgeted costs, they might be tempted to ignore the quality of the product, postpone preventive maintenance, or take other actions that harm the firm in the long run. Selecting appropriate measures of performance is a constant concern to both managers and managerial accountants.

ILLUSTRATION — MANAGEMENT AND ACCOUNTING

Exhibit 1-1 diagrams some managerial processes and related accounting activities. Usually the topmost level of management sets overall objectives that are then formalized into profit plans. Objectives such as 10% growth in sales, 12% growth in profits over the next three or five years, a 20% return on total investment, and a 35% return on stockholders' equity can be put into profit plans. The costs of achieving other objectives, such as those related to product quality, pollution abatement, and employee satisfaction, are also described formally in profit plans.

Managers set broad objectives and strategies, then make detailed plans to realize them. What new products can we introduce? What can existing products contribute to future profits and sales? What will foreign competitors do? Can some of our products be marketed more widely? Should we stress

Exhibit 1-1 Management and Accounting

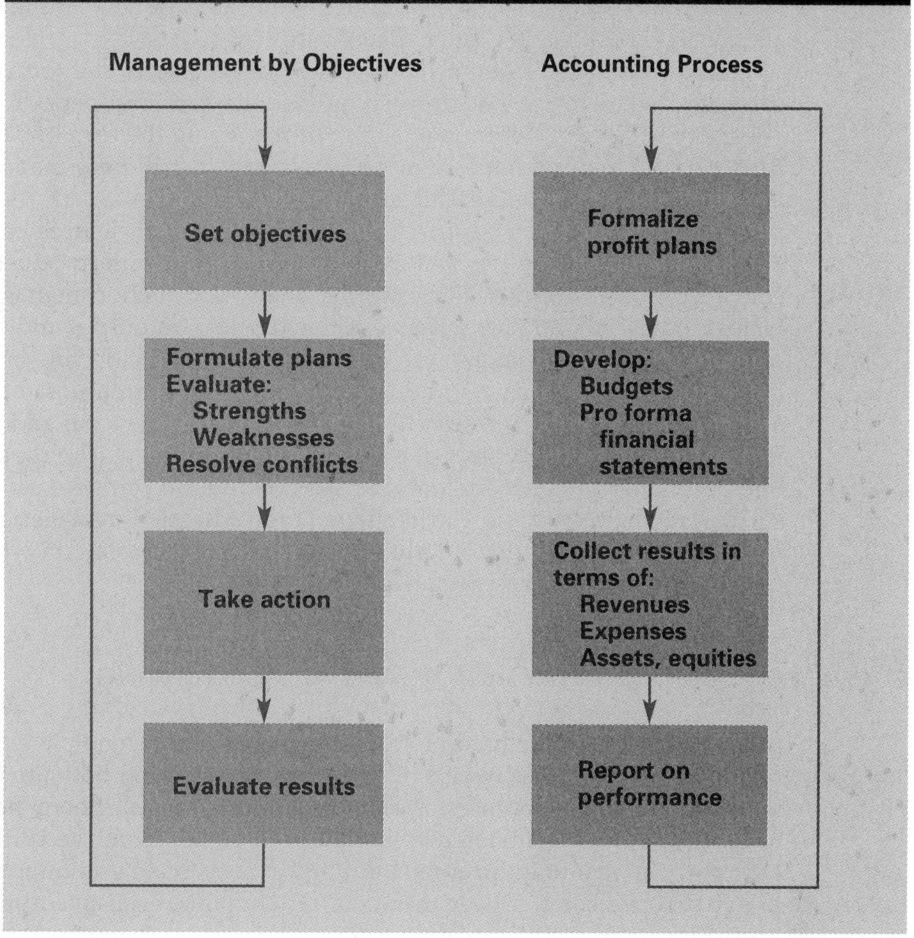

overseas operations or pay more attention to domestic business? Strategic and tactical questions like these and others are thrashed out, and planning is based then on the company's strengths and weaknesses and the opportunities and threats that it faces. These plans are expressed in budgets and pro forma financial statements.

Having established plans that are consistent with the broad objectives of the firm, managers implement these designs. They direct research programs on new products, advertising, and other sales efforts, add plant capacity to meet anticipated demand, and fill requirements for workers, managers, and other personnel. Many results of these actions show up within the framework of the accounting system. The results of sales efforts show up as revenues, while the firm's efforts show up as expenses and assets. The financing aspects of the various efforts are reflected in equities—long-term debt, common stock issuances, and increases in retained earnings.

In Exhibit 1-1, we have shown the boxes labeled "Take action" and "Evaluate results" as independent, but there is usually continual feedback. Managers evaluate results quickly so that corrective action can be taken if necessary. Evaluations of results can also lead to reconsidering the original objectives or the plans formulated to meet them. Thus, the cycle shown rarely runs a complete course without any modifications. Plans and budgets are not static; managers change them continually.

Periodically the results of management decisions, in the form of formal financial statements, are distributed outside the firm. But periodic reporting does not change the continuous nature of managing the firm. Indeed, by the time periodic reports have been prepared and distributed, managers have already made more plans and decisions.

Effective evaluation requires that performance measures capture the essential aspects of the job. Failure to do so can be counterproductive to the company's best interests. For example, many production managers in the United States for years have been evaluated solely on output and cost. Some observers believe that such measures contributed to the decline in quality of many American products and have hurt those companies. Managerial accountants continue to research the ways in which the form and content of reports influence the actions of those who receive them. The reports developed by managerial accountants should continue to improve as a result of such research. In any case, the likelihood of misdirected managerial efforts is reduced when a manager is fully informed about the bases on which his or her performance will be evaluated.

MANAGERIAL ACCOUNTING AND FINANCIAL ACCOUNTING

Both managerial and financial accounting deal with economic events. Both require quantifying the results of economic activity, and both are concerned with revenues and expenses, assets, liabilities, and cash flows. Both, therefore, involve financial statements, and both suffer from the difficulties of capturing, in quantitative terms, the many aspects of an economic event. The major differences between financial and managerial accounting arise because they serve different audiences.

Financial accounting serves persons outside the firm, such as creditors, customers, government units, and investors. Hence, financial accounting reports are concerned mostly with the firm as a whole. In contrast, managerial accounting reports usually deal with segments of a firm; managers receive information related to their own responsibilities rather than to the entire firm.

The different audiences for accounting information use information for different purposes. Creditors and investors use information to decide whether or not to extend credit to the firm, whether to buy, sell, or hold its stock. People inside the firm use accounting information to make decisions such as which of several products to sell, whether to issue bonds or stock, which employees to reward for good performance, and what prices to charge.

The classification schemes used in managerial accounting reports usually differ from those in financial accounting reports. In financial accounting, costs are usually classified by the *object* of the expense (salaries, taxes, rent, repairs) or by the *function* of the expense (cost of goods sold, selling expenses, administrative expenses, financing expenses). In contrast, reports for managerial accounting purposes often follow other cost classification schemes. Some reports are based on the *behavior* of costs, separating costs that change when activity levels change, from costs that do not change regardless of the level of activity. Other managerial accounting reports concentrate on the concepts of *responsibility* and *controllability*; costs are classified according to whether or not a particular manager is responsible for the cost and can control it. These classification schemes—behavior, responsibility, and controllability—underlie much of the material in this book and are critical to almost all aspects of planning, control, and evaluation.

Information in financial accounting reports might also differ in source and nature from that in managerial accounting reports. Financial accounting reports are developed from the basic accounting system, which captures data about completed transactions. Some managerial accounting reports incorporate information that is not found in the financial accounting system. Such information might relate primarily to future transactions or even to alternatives to past transactions. For example, financial accounting reports from the accounting system include depreciation for buildings. A managerial accounting report might include, instead, the rent that would have to be paid for the buildings if they were not owned (information not obtainable from the accounting system).

Managerial accounting reports are specifically designed for a particular user or a particular decision; whereas, financial accounting reports are general purpose reports. For this reason, a particular cost may appear on one internal report and not on another; the cost might be relevant for some internal decisions and not for others. We can illustrate this point with an example from everyday life. Suppose you own a car and pay $450 for insurance per year. That cost is part of the total cost of owning the car, but it is irrelevant if you are trying to determine how much it will cost to take a 200-mile trip. Because you pay the same $450 for insurance whether you take the trip or not, you can ignore it in determining the cost of the trip. The phrase "different costs for different purposes" describes the idea that relevance depends on the specific purpose.

Financial and managerial accounting information differ in that the former is primarily historical while the latter is concerned more with the future. Although many items in financial statements incorporate expectations (e.g., estimated useful life and residual value in the computation of depreciation, estimated warranty work to be done on items sold, and so on), financial accounting reports concentrate more on the results of past decisions. Internal reports to managers, on the other hand, very often concentrate on what is likely to happen in the future.

Managerial accounting has no restrictions such as the generally accepted accounting principles (GAAP) that govern financial accounting. For managerial purposes, relevance is the important concern, and managerial accountants respond to specific information requirements. For example, market price (replacement cost, fair market value, or some other measure) will be used in a managerial accounting report if it will help the manager make a better decision. Such alternatives are usually not allowed in financial accounting.

In summary, managerial accounting is different from financial accounting in purpose, orientation, and constraints. In addition, as we noted earlier, a difference in the timing and timeliness aspects of internal and external reporting exists. Formal financial statements are prepared less often than reports for managers and therefore include information that is less current than that received by managers.

ADVANCED MANUFACTURING

Although managerial accounting deals with all types of economic enterprises, a significant number of them are manufacturers. One of the driving forces behind many recent developments in managerial accounting is profound changes in manufacturing. At various points throughout this text we use the term **advanced manufacturing environment,** or, more often, **advanced manufacturing,** to describe such developments. To help you better understand these references, we discuss those changes and some of their implications in this introductory chapter.

CONVENTIONAL MANUFACTURING: ITS BACKGROUND AND ITS PROBLEMS

Practices that have come to be called conventional manufacturing originated in conditions facing U.S. manufacturing firms for more than two decades after World War II. American companies were the unchallenged world leaders in manufacturing. They had long leads in product quality, in capacity, and in distribution facilities, and, exaggerating only a little, they could sell nearly anything they made. Production was the critical activity.

In this environment, many U.S. manufacturers adopted practices that reflected a "just-in-case" philosophy. As insurance against production delays caused by defects in components or the unavailability of materials, companies routinely purchased more than required to meet production needs. (They inspected all incoming shipments, though they often adopted sophisticated statistical techniques to cope with this growing task.) To avoid production shortfalls caused by manufacturing errors (or by delays because of defects in materials), companies produced more and also scheduled production much earlier than required to meet shipping schedules. As a result, **lead time** or **cycle time**—the period that begins with the arrival of materials and ends with shipment of a finished unit—extended well beyond the time needed for the manufacturing process alone. (A product that could be manufactured in a day or two might have a lead time of one, two, or even three months.)

Not surprisingly, significant costs were associated with these manufacturing practices. The high inventories of materials and finished units increased the risk of spoilage and obsolescence, as well as the costs of storage, insurance, financing, and handling. Inspecting more incoming raw materials or component parts and more finished units was also costly. Inevitably, prices rose to cover the increased costs. An unfortunate outcome of striving to meet output requirements on a timely basis was that waste, scrap, and the reworking of defective units came to be thought of as normal. Such an attitude did not encourage high quality and may even have discouraged quality-control efforts. Thus, practices that might have been wise *if* quality was suspect often contributed to lowering quality.

Philosophies and practices that characterize the new manufacturing environment surfaced as overseas companies began to compete with U.S. manufacturers. In searching for a competitive edge, overseas manufacturers concentrated on the weaknesses of conventional manufacturing practices, particularly mediocre quality and high inventories. The term often used to describe a manufacturing environment that would eliminate those weaknesses is just-in-time manufacturing.

JUST-IN-TIME MANUFACTURING

Just-in-time (JIT) manufacturing is probably the most familiar aspect of advanced manufacturing. JIT is a philosophy that focuses on timing, efficiency, and quality in meeting commitments. Companies that employ JIT strive for continual improvement in their operations. One major aspect of this philosophy is to increase customer satisfaction by reducing lead time. (How would you like to be told that you must wait two months for something you are ready to order? A commitment to reducing cycle time was thought important enough at IBM to be mentioned by the chair of its Board of Directors at an annual stockholders meeting.) Advocates of the JIT philosophy continually strive to promote a smooth and rapid flow of materials and products.

The term "just in time" refers to one way of characterizing the goals of such techniques. Under ideal conditions, purchased materials and components arrive *just in time* to be used, partly assembled units arrive at work stations *just in time* for the next step in production, and finished units emerge from production *just in time* to meet the shipping date requested by the customer. Of course, the ideal conditions are virtually impossible to achieve, but they serve as goals against which to measure progress, and progress has been dramatic in many cases. As examples, some factories receive deliveries of some items several times a day, and some have eliminated loading docks in favor of entrances allowing trucks to deliver materials directly to work stations. The delivery system reduced space requirements and eliminated the steps of putting materials in storage and then later taking them to work stations when needed. The trucks also carry away finished products so that they do not have to go into storage and then be taken out again for delivery to customers. (Allen-Bradley reports that its "factory within a factory" can take an order one day, produce the required units, and ship the order the following day, with only a small amount of material, and no finished or unfinished units, on hand at the end of the day.[2]) Progress toward achieving just-in-time goals means shortened lead times, as well as reduced inventories and inventory costs.

The JIT philosophy is concerned with all aspects of cycle time, not just inventory reduction. So managers continually scrutinize each step in the production process itself, trying to determine which cost-producing and time-consuming activities add value to the final product and which do not. For example, moving partially finished units from one work station to another is a non-value-adding activity. Hence, work stations in a JIT environment are often adjacent, rather than being spread throughout a factory, so that as much work as possible is done in a small cluster of machinery and workers, called a manufacturing cell. Coupling the use of cells with reduced needs for space to store inventories of various types, JIT operations use less space than conventional operations. Exhibit 1-2 illustrates production flows in a conventional operation and a JIT operation.

2 *Robert A. Howell and Stephen R. Soucy, "Cost Accounting in the New Manufacturing Environment,"* Management Accounting, *August 1987, 5.*

Exhibit 1-2 Material and Product Flow

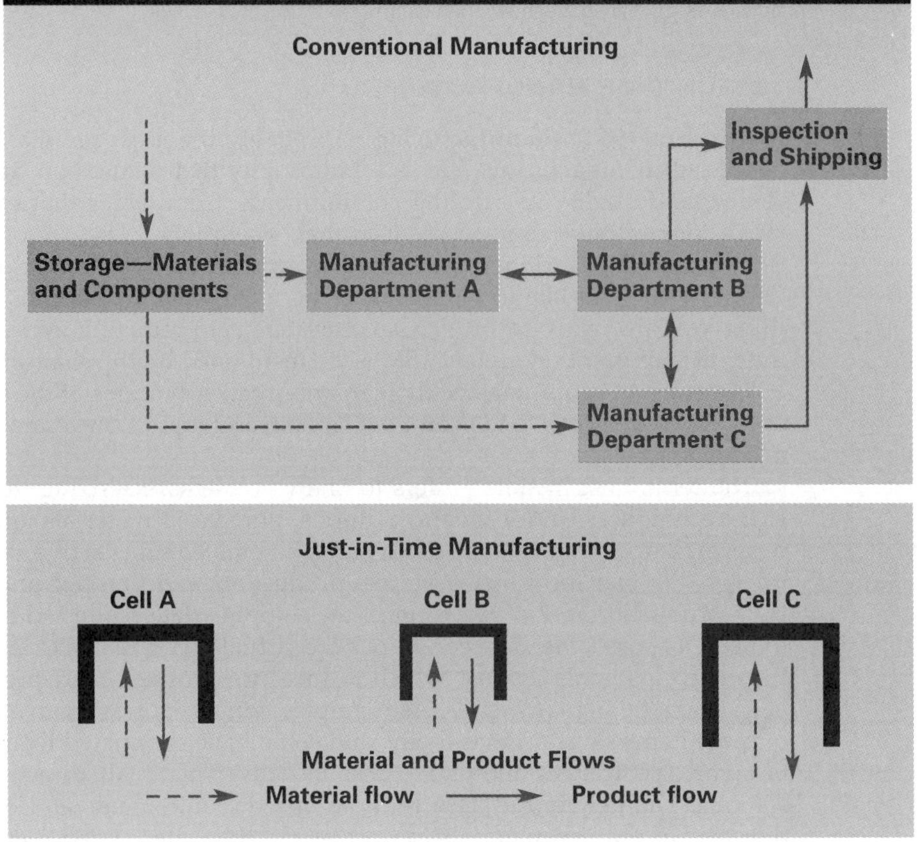

In their efforts to reduce production time, JIT managers also have emphasized reducing *set-up time*, the time required to change machine settings from making one product to making another. Conventional manufacturers often make long production runs of each product which result in set-up times measured in hours. The term *flexible manufacturing system* describes a JIT operation with a set-up time of a few minutes, that can respond quickly to customer orders. For example, some modern plants for the manufacture of wearing apparel, which often has a high risk of obsolescence, can make and ship an order of ten pairs of Bermuda shorts, in various sizes, colors, and patterns, within 24 hours of receiving the order. A manufacturer's ability to achieve flexible manufacturing depends partly on the available technology. But the goal of a flexible manufacturing system is to produce by units, rather than by batches.

Of course, total quality control is critical to the success of JIT operations. If virtually no inventories of purchased raw materials and components of finished units exist, everything received must be without defects or production could be delayed. Also, manufacturing errors leading to defective units cannot be tolerated. Several practices have evolved to achieve this condition, which is often referred to as *zero defects*. To illustrate, companies that make use of JIT stop inspecting incoming shipments when they are assured that a supplier is providing components of the desired quality, and they stop buy-

JIT principles apply also to merchandising and service operations. Wal-Mart, the giant retailer, uses cash registers that send sales data to a computer that in turn places orders with suppliers. Orders are filled quickly and go right to stores without sitting in warehouses. Wal-Mart's products are said to be "either in the store or on the truck." Another example demonstrating JIT principles is Southwest Airlines' ground crews having an airplane back in the air only 15 minutes after it lands, compared to 45 minutes or more for other airlines. Southwest's theory is that airplanes do not make money sitting on the ground. Its speed translates into fewer aircraft needed to maintain schedules, as well as other cost savings. Southwest also flies only one type of aircraft, so it stocks spare parts and trains its mechanics for only that aircraft.

ing from suppliers who do not meet that standard. Similarly, JIT operations pinpoint problems early because workers inspect units throughout production instead of only at a few points. Moreover, to reduce costs and increase quality, JIT manufacturers design quality and ease of manufacturability into products. At conventional manufacturers, product designers rarely talk with production people. Production engineers develop a manufacturing process to accommodate the design specifications, though a minor design change might greatly simplify production. And, often, design flaws show up in manufacturing difficulties or in customer dissatisfaction.

The following schedule contrasts JIT and conventional manufacturing.

JIT Manufacturing	Conventional Manufacturing
1. Manufacturing cells concentrating on one product	Departments working on all products
2. Multiskilled workers	Single-skilled workers
3. Small batches, smooth flows	Large batches, erratic flows
4. Total quality control	Some defects seen as inevitable
5. Short production cycle	Long production cycle
6. Zero or trivial inventories	Large inventories held as buffers
7. Daily delivery of materials and components	Large deliveries
8. Relentless search to improve, eliminate all waste	Achieve acceptable performance
9. Integrate design and manufacturing	Design and manufacturing separate

ACTIVITIES OF MANAGERIAL ACCOUNTANTS

At the beginning of the chapter, we stated that accountants within an organization perform functions related to both financial and managerial accounting. We concentrate here on those aspects of the internal accountant's activities that involve serving the needs of internal information users. The major activities of managerial accountants consist of (1) aiding in the design of the firm's information system; (2) gathering data; (3) ensuring that the system performs according to plan; (4) undertaking special analyses for management; (5) interpreting accounting data based on a particular manager's requirements.

The organization's information system must meet the needs of all people who require information to perform their jobs. For example, managers responsible for the sales of a particular product might need weekly sales reports for each territory. Their supervisor, who also supervises other managers, might need a weekly report for a group of products. The chief sales executive might want monthly reports of sales by product groups and sales territories. The managerial accountant must ensure that the system meets these varying needs.

Computers usually record transactions in journals and ledgers. The accountant is responsible for supervising the gathering of data and for monitoring the system, making sure it functions as intended. The accountant also must make sure that the output of the information system is understood and used appropriately. Suppose that a particular report designed for the sales manager to identify sales trends by geographic area subsequently was used as the basis for computing commissions to salespeople. The report is inappropriate for this second use if it fails to reflect customer returns on which no commissions should be paid.

Special analyses are required when managers consider nonroutine actions. In some cases, such as the possibility of building a new plant, relevant data might not be available in a form that enables managers to decide on the best course of action. Accountants must develop relevant information to serve such special purposes.

Finally, the accountant frequently explains accounting data and reports to other managers. A manager may be unable to understand a report, or the data in a report might not be appropriate for the manager's particular purpose. The latter situation indicates that some change in the system might be appropriate.

Managerial accountants have gained status in recent years as their activities have become concerned more with analysis of the firm's operations and less with the problems of recording and computing costs of products. The Institute of Management Accountants (IMA), the principal organization of managerial accountants in the United States, has instituted a program to provide certification for managerial accountants. The **Certified Management Accountant** (CMA) examination was first given in 1972. More than 10,000 people successfully completed the examination by the end of 1992. A listing of the required subject areas in the CMA examination indicates the breadth of knowledge expected of the professional managerial accountant. The examination consists of the following four parts: Economics, Finance and Management; Financial Accounting and Reporting; Management Reporting, Analysis and Behavioral Issues; and Decision Analysis and Information Systems. The IMA also promulgated a code of ethics for management accountants, which is discussed further in the next section.

Further evidence of the increasing importance and status of managerial accountants appeared in an article on 3M, which is one of the most admired corporations in America according to a *Fortune* magazine study. At 3M, divisional controllers are seen as "business advisors and financial consultants who are part of the operating/decision-making team."[3] This attitude was

3 *Kathy Williams, "The Magic of 3M, Management Accounting Excellence,"* Management Accounting, *February 1986, 20-27.*

not prevalent 20 years ago. Controllers and other management accountants were then viewed as "bean counters" whose only purpose was to harass operating managers with trifling reports.

The role of the controller is expanding in many ways, in many companies. For example, the controller at Adolph Coors Company is an important manager who participates in management meetings and is consulted on all major decisions. However, this was not always so. In 1981, many managers at Coors thought of accountants as bean counters. A new controller came in with a plan to "transform 'accounting' reports into management reports, and place more emphasis on a forward financial perspective rather than on historical reporting of the company's financial results." Now, Coors' "accounting system produces management reports that present a combination of financial and nonfinancial data important for performance evaluation, forecasting, and strategic planning."[4]

ETHICS

In 1983, the Institute of Management Accountants published Standards of Ethical Conduct for Management Accountants. The Institute also established an Ethics Committee and an Ethics Counseling Service. Unlike certified public accountants, who must be independent of the companies they audit, management accountants are employees of the companies they serve; they are not independent of their employers. Nevertheless, management accountants are expected to abide by the Standards, which are reproduced in Exhibit 1-3.

Should you work as controller or work in some other managerial accounting position, you will be expected to comply with the Standards. Even if you are not subject to the code, there are two reasons why it is important that you know something about why the code exists. First, as a manager you have the right to expect ethical behavior from the managerial accountants with whom you work. Second, you should be aware that managerial accountants are prohibited from committing unethical acts on behalf of managers of the company by which they are employed.

The Standards have four main sections: competence, confidentiality, integrity, and objectivity. The *competence* provisions require management accountants to develop their knowledge and skills and to do their tasks in accordance with relevant laws, regulations, and standards. The *confidentiality* provisions forbid them to act on, or even appear to act on, confidential information they acquire in doing their work. This provision thus forbids "insider" actions such as selling the company's stock upon learning that it is likely to lose a major lawsuit. The *integrity* provisions cover avoidance of conflicts of interest, improprieties of accepting gifts or favors, and other matters generally associated with professional behavior. The *objectivity* provisions require management accountants to "communication information fairly and objectively" and to "disclose fully all relevant information. . . ."

Management accountants ethically cannot ignore relevant data or use wildly optimistic projections to justify a course of action. Managers in charge of a product line that is not doing well, who fear for their job, might

4 *Kenton B Walker, "Coors, Brewing a Better Controllership,"* Management Accounting, *January 1988, 23.*

Exhibit 1-3 Standards of Ethical Conduct

Standards of Ethical Conduct for Management Accountants

Management accountants have an obligation to the organizations they serve, their profession, the public, and themselves to maintain the highest standards of ethical conduct. In recognition of this obligation, the Institute of Management Accountants, formerly the National Association of Accountants, has promulgated the following standards of ethical conduct for management accountants. Adherence to these standards is integral to achieving the *Objectives of Management Accounting.*[1] Management accountants shall not commit acts contrary to these standards nor shall they condone the commission of such acts by others within their organizations.

COMPETENCE
Management accountants have a responsibility to:

- Maintain an appropriate level of professional competence by ongoing development of their knowledge and skills.
- Perform their professional duties in accordance with relevant laws, regulations, and technical standards.
- Prepare complete and clear reports and recommendations after appropriate analyses of relevant and reliable information.

CONFIDENTIALITY
Management accountants have a responsibility to:

- Refrain from disclosing confidential information acquired in the course of their work except when authorized, unless legally obligated to do so.
- Inform subordinates as appropriate regarding the confidentiality of information acquired in the course of their work and monitor their activities to assure the maintenance of that confidentiality.
- Refrain from using or appearing to use confidential information acquired in the course of their work for unethical or illegal advantage either personally or through third parties.

INTEGRITY
Management accountants have a responsibility to:

- Avoid actual or apparent conflicts of interest and advise all appropriate parties of any potential conflict.
- Refrain from engaging in any activity that would prejudice their ability to carry out their duties ethically.
- Refuse any gift, favor, or hospitality that would influence or would appear to influence their actions.
- Refrain from either actively or passively subverting the attainment of the organization's legitimate and ethical objectives.
- Recognize and communicate professional limitations or other constraints that would preclude responsible judgment or successful performance of an activity.
- Communicate unfavorable as well as favorable information and professional judgments or opinions.
- Refrain from engaging in or supporting any activity that would discredit the profession.

OBJECTIVITY
Management accountants have a responsibility to:

- Communicate information fairly and objectively.
- Disclose fully all relevant information that could reasonably be expected to influence an intended user's understanding of the reports, comments, and recommendations presented.

RESOLUTION OF ETHICAL CONFLICT

In applying the standards of ethical conduct, management accountants may encounter problems in identifying unethical behavior or in resolving an ethical conflict. When faced with significant ethical issues, management accountants should follow the established policies of the organization bearing on the resolution of such conflict. If these policies do not resolve the ethical conflict, management accountants should consider the following course of action:

- Discuss such problems with the immediate superior except when it appears that the superior is involved, in which case the problem should be presented initially to the next higher managerial level. If satisfactory resolution cannot be achieved when the problem is initially presented, submit the issues to the next higher managerial level.

  If the immediate superior is the chief executive officer, or equivalent, the acceptable reviewing authority may be a group such as the audit committee, executive committee, board of directors, board of trustees, or owners. Contact with levels above the immediate superior should be initiated only with the superior's knowledge, assuming the superior is not involved.
- Clarify relevant concepts by confidential discussion with an objective advisor to obtain an understanding of possible courses of action.
- If the ethical conflict still exists after exhausting all levels of internal review, the management accountant may have no other recourse on significant matters than to resign from the organization and to submit an informative memorandum to an appropriate representative of the organization.

Except where legally prescribed, communication of such problems to authorities or individuals not employed or engaged by the organization is not considered appropriate.

[1] Institute of Management Accountants, formerly National Association of Accountants, *Statements on Management Accounting: Objectives of Management Accounting,* Statement No. 1B, New York, N.Y., June 17, 1982.

pressure management accountants to use exceedingly optimistic sales projections in an analysis. For management accountants to do so would compromise their professionalism. Moreover, management accountants could not ethically recommend buying office equipment from a company owned by a family member, unless they disclosed the family member's interest to the persons making the decision.

The Standards require professional behavior, especially in avoiding conflicts of interest. They require management accountants to bring bad news to the attention of their supervisors, and to work competently. They also recognize that management accountants faced with a serious ethical conflict might have to resign and explain why to "an appropriate representative of the organization." Periodically, the Standards are reprinted in *Management Accounting,* the monthly magazine to the Institute, and the magazine's monthly column on ethics contains case studies and other materials that serve to remind management accountants of their ethical responsibilities.

Evidence indicates that pressure to violate the code is a serious problem. One study showed that a third to nearly half of management accountants felt pressured to achieve a specific income and that pressure was more common in companies that had formal codes of conduct.[5]

INTERNATIONAL ASPECTS OF MANAGERIAL ACCOUNTING

In today's global economy, managers face new and more complex decisions. Should capital be raised in the U.S. or elsewhere? Where should the company

5 *Anne J. Rich, Carl S. Smith, and Paul H. Mihalek, "Are Corporate Codes of Conduct Effective?"* Management Accounting, *September, 1990, 34.*

manufacture the products it sells to customers in and outside of the U.S.? What products should the company make and in which countries? Should the company make some parts for its products in one country and complete the manufacturing process in others? Would it be profitable to change some products to accommodate differences among countries in tastes and culture? These new and more complex decisions expand the information needs that must be met by managerial accountants. At various points in this text we consider some of the special issues raised when analyzing the decisions confronting managers of international companies.

One example of the special problems that arise with international operations is changing currency values. The Toronto Blue Jays, World Series winners in 1992, pay their players in U.S. dollars, but collect gate receipts in Canadian dollars. (They pay some expenses in Canadian dollars, but player salaries are the major expense.) Suppose the Canadian dollar is worth 0.90 U.S. dollars ($0.90). Then the U.S. dollar is worth $1.111 Canadian dollars ($1.00/$0.90). Paying each dollar of salary requires 1.111 Canadian dollars. If the value of the Canadian dollar drops to $0.80, is the team better off or worse off? It is worse off because each U.S. dollar in salary now requires 1.25 Canadian dollars ($1.00/$0.80). The team must take more of its Canadian dollars to the bank to exchange for U.S. dollars than it previously did. Of course, if the Canadian dollar rises to $0.95, the team is better off. The Blue Jays and other organizations with similar dealings can take some actions to guard against such possibilities.

SUMMARY

Managerial accounting and financial accounting both deal with economic events and reports about them. But the two areas of accounting differ in many ways, primarily because they serve different audiences. Managerial accounting serves internal managers in organizations. In businesses, managers in sales, production, finance, and accounting, and top executives use accounting data for planning and control, including decision making and performance evaluation. Managers of not-for-profit organizations perform many of these same functions and use much of the same accounting data as managers in businesses.

As you study managerial accounting, you will be introduced to some of the activities managers carry out in several areas of a business firm or other economic organization. Changes in the manufacturing environment are prompting changes in managerial accounting as well as in related disciplines. Some managerial accounting concept or type of report relates to almost every area of managerial activity, and managerial accounting draws heavily on the concepts from related business disciplines. Management accountants are expected to carry out their activities in a manner consistent with their ethical responsibilities.

KEY TERMS

advanced manufacturing
advanced manufacturing environment
budgeting
Certified Management Accountant
control
control reports
cycle time
decision making
financial accounting
just-in-time (JIT) manufacturing
lead time
line function
management by exception
management by objectives
managerial accounting
performance evaluation
planning
pro forma statement
staff function

ASSIGNMENT MATERIAL

QUESTIONS FOR DISCUSSION

1-1 Everyday planning and control For each of the following activities, find an analogy to the planning and control process described in the chapter. Describe the process to be undertaken in these activities and compare with the process described in the chapter.

(a) Taking a course in college, including preparation and study, taking examinations, and evaluating test results.
(b) Taking a long automobile trip.
(c) Decorating your own room or apartment.
(d) Coaching an athletic team.

1-2 Financial versus managerial accounting information The chapter illustrates that financial and managerial accounting overlap to some extent, but that managerial accounting uses information not normally used in financial accounting. For financial accounting purposes, the information needed about a particular automobile is its cost, its expected useful life, its residual value at the end of that life, and the method of depreciation to be applied. What other information about a particular business automobile might be important for managerial accounting purposes?

1-3 Who needs financial accounting? The chapter points out that differences between financial and managerial accounting relate to differences in the decisions made by managers and those made by parties external to the firm. If managerial accounting is supposed to serve the information needs of managers, why should managers know and understand financial accounting?

PROBLEMS

1-4 Review of financial statement preparation Following is the balance sheet for Illustrative Company as of December 31, 19X4 and selected information relating to activities in 19X5.

Illustrative Company Balance Sheet as of December 31, 19X4

Assets		
Current assets:		
Cash	$ 10,000	
Accounts receivable	40,000	
Inventory	65,000	
Total current assets		$115,000
Property, plant, and equipment:		
Cost	250,000	
Less: Accumulated depreciation	100,000	
Net		150,000
Total assets		$265,000
Equities		
Current liabilities:		
Accounts payable	$ 10,000	
Taxes payable	12,000	
Total current liabilities		$ 22,000
Long-term debt:		
Bonds payable, 7% , due 19X8		100,000
Total liabilities		122,000
Stockholders' equity:		
Common stock, no par value, 10,000 shares issued and outstanding	90,000	
Retained earnings	53,000	
Total stockholders' equity		143,000
Total equities		$265,000

During 19X5 the following events occurred.

(a) Sales on account were $350,000.
(b) Collections on receivables were $360,000.
(c) Credit purchases of inventory were $180,000.
(d) Cost of goods sold was $150,000.
(e) Payments to suppliers for inventory were $165,000.
(f) Cash paid for operating expenses was $80,000; interest on bonds was also paid.
(g) Plant and equipment were bought for $70,000 cash.
(h) Taxes payable at December 31, 19X4, were paid.
(i) Depreciation expense was $30,000.
(j) Income taxes are 40% of income before taxes. No payments were made on 19X5 taxes in 19X5.
(k) A dividend of $10,000 was declared and paid.

Required

1. Prepare an income statement for Illustrative Company for 19X5.
2. Prepare a balance sheet for Illustrative Company as of December 31, 19X5.

1-5 Review of the cash flow statement Using the information from 1-4, prepare a cash flow statement for 19X5 for Illustrative Company.

1-6 ***Review of financial statement preparation*** Below is the balance sheet for Example Company as of December 31, 19X4, followed by selected information relating to activities in 19X5.

Example Company
Balance Sheet
as of December 31, 19X4

Assets		
Current assets:		
Cash	$ 20,000	
Accounts receivable	50,000	
Inventory	120,000	
Prepaid expenses	8,000	
Total current assets		$198,000
Property, plant, and equipment:		
Cost	350,000	
Less: Accumulated depreciation	130,000	
Net		220,000
Total assets		$418,000
Equities		
Current liabilities:		
Accounts payable	$ 40,000	
Taxes payable	25,000	
Accrued expenses	12,000	
Total current liabilities		$ 77,000
Long-term liabilities:		
Bond payable, 6%, due 19X7		200,000
Total liabilities		277,000
Stockholders' equity:		
Common stock, $10 par value, 5,000 shares issued and outstanding	50,000	
Retained earnings	91,000	
Total stockholders' equity		141,000
Total equities		$418,000

Other data relating to activities in 19X5 were as follows.

(a) Sales on account were $480,000.
(b) Collections on accounts receivable were $430,000.
(c) Credit purchases of goods for resale were $220,000.
(d) Cost of goods sold was $240,000.
(e) Payments of accounts payable were $210,000.
(f) Interest expense on bonds payable was paid in cash.
(g) Prepaid expenses at the beginning of the year expired and new prepayments in the amount of $6,000 were made in 19X5.
(h) Accrued taxes payable at the beginning of the year were paid.
(i) Accrued expenses payable are for wages and salaries. Total cash payments for wages and salaries during 19X5 were $95,000. At the end of 19X5, $7,000 was owed to employees.
(j) Other cash payments for expenses during 19X5 were $65,000, not including the $6,000 prepayments in (g).

(k) Common stock was sold for $40,000 (4,000 shares).
(l) Plant and equipment were purchased for $30,000 cash.
(m) Depreciation expense was $40,000.
(n) The income tax rate is 40%. Income taxes for 19X5 were unpaid at year end.
(o) A dividend of $5,000 was declared and paid.

Required

1. Prepare an income statement for Example Company for 19X5.
2. Prepare a balance sheet for Example Company as of December 31, 19X5.

1-7 Review of the cash flow statement Using the information from 1-6, prepare a cash flow statement for 19X5 for Example Company.

1-8 Different costs for different purposes Suppose you are going to drive home this weekend, a round trip of 180 miles. Your car gets 30 miles per gallon of gas and you expect gas to cost $0.80 per gallon. Insurance and depreciation are $1,000 per year. You usually drive 10,000 miles per year. A friend asks you to take her along. She lives a block from your home.

Required

1. What are the costs of taking your friend along, as opposed to going by yourself?
2. Suppose now that you are not planning on going home. Your friend asks for a ride and you are willing to go. What are the costs of going, as opposed to not going?

1-9 JIT You have been telling your fellow managers about the potential benefits of adopting the JIT philosophy, but some remain unconvinced. A couple of them seem not to hear what you have been saying. Manager A says, "Look, we just can't hit production right on the nose so that stuff arrives just when a guy finishes the last batch. We need some extra units so that our people aren't waiting around for the guys before them to finish." Manager B chimes in, "It all sounds great, but we're doing fine the way we work now. Some of our problems are caused by bad design of products, but we have to please our customers."

The quality control manager says, "We use the latest techniques to inspect both incoming shipments of parts and components and outgoing shipments of finished product. We are sure our quality is good on what goes out the door. And we catch plenty of stuff before we ship it, maybe 10%-15% defectives that have to be reworked or scrapped. So we earn our keep around here." The production manager argues that the functional factory arrangement, with all machines of a given type in the same area, makes the company more efficient because the workers " . . . can really learn how to operate that one machine they're responsible for."

Required

Comment on each of the statements and indicate how JIT could help the company.

1-10 Ethics You are the newly hired controller of TM Enterprises, a large manufacturer of industrial products. Yesterday morning the president of the company called you and other senior executives to her office where she stated that a competitor was about to file suit against TM for patent infringement.

Regardless of the merits of the case, it will tie up company talent for a long while and will be quite costly to fight. The effects on the company's prospects cannot be measured, but it is possible that they will be severe.

This evening your father called from Florida, where he and your mother have lived in retirement for a few years. You chatted about the weather, the children, dad's golf game, and other such things. Then he told you that he had just bought shares of stock in TM Enterprises because he knew that any company you worked at would do well.

Required

What do you say to your father?

1-11 Ethics You work as the data processing manager of Acme Products, a manufacturer of various consumer products. You recently asked for bids on new microcomputers and asked the controller's office to assist you in evaluating the costs and benefits of the suppliers' proposals. Eventually, you settled on systems offered by Micron Technologies, a relatively new company with a good reputation. The decision was based partly on a favorable analysis by Larry Bowman, an assistant controller.

A week or so after deciding on the Micron systems, you happen to see Bowman eating lunch with Paul Coleman, one of the Micron sales engineers. You later ask Bowman about it and he says that he and Paul were college classmates. He says that he didn't mention their friendship because it wasn't relevant; he did his analysis strictly on the facts.

Required

1. Has Bowman violated the IMA Standards for Ethical Conduct? If so, which standard?
2. Suppose instead of seeing Bowman and Coleman at lunch, you saw them at the airport. Bowman waved to you and said Coleman was paying for a weekend of sun and surf in the Bahamas. Has Bowman violated the Standards now? If so, which?

1-12 Conventional and JIT manufacturing Jason Company manufactures five or six basic products that are similar and relatively standard. That is, they are not made-to-order. Product design and features are updated periodically in response to customer suggestions. Product designers come up with improvements and production is responsible for re-tooling and other activities required to implement the re-design.

Jason receives orders from customers, then fills the orders from stock or manufactures the required units. The company has a warehouse where it keeps finished units, raw materials, and components. The Quality Control Department inspects all incoming shipments of raw materials and components and rejects those with defects above a certain percentage. The percentage differs for different items. For instance, a relatively high percentage, say 10%, of defectives is considered acceptable for sophisticated, hard-to-manufacture components, while a low percentage, say 1%, is acceptable for mass-produced items like simple valves.

The company usually buys a two or three month supply of high-volume raw materials. Jason receives a 1% average discount on prices by buying in large quantities. Jason's purchasing manager is responsible, and rewarded, for obtaining raw materials and components at the lowest possible cost and so scours the country looking for the best deals. Jason therefore deals with a great many suppliers.

Production begins by withdrawing the necessary raw materials and components from the warehouse, inspecting them for possible deterioration during storage, and transporting them to the first station that will work on the batch of product. No job begins until all raw materials and components are available. Each station does one function, such as drilling, planing, welding, and various assembly operations.

Each station has an area to store raw materials and components for work that has not started yet. The raw materials wait there until the station is ready to begin the job. Significant setup time is required in changing over from one product to another at some stations. After the workers at the station have finished their part of the job, they send the semi-completed units along with the raw materials and components not yet installed to the next station. At that station the same process is repeated and so on until all work is complete. In some cases, a job will go to the same station more than once during production because it requires the same operation at different stages of production.

At the conclusion of the process, the finished units go to the Quality Control Department where they are tested and inspected. They then are sent to the warehouse to await shipment. The company usually makes 10% more units than needed for an order to allow for defects. Any spare good units are held in the warehouse until another order arrives. Defective units are sometimes reworked or sometimes sold as scrap. Reworked units are stored in the warehouse. If the work station that produced the defective part has been determined, the work station's manager is held responsible. (Bonuses for station managers are based largely on total good output.) In many cases, determining the source of the defect is not possible, so no one is held responsible.

The factory manager has said that "it gets pretty hectic at the end of each month when we're trying to finish up jobs and get the stuff out to the warehouse."

The cycle time varies among types of products, but spans from 10 days to 45 days depending on various factors.

Required

Prepare a memorandum describing how Jason differs from a JIT company and what changes in its operations you would recommend. Use the guidelines in Appendix B at the back of the book.

PART ONE

cost-volume-profit analysis and decision making

The first part of this book discusses the basic principles of decision making, the principles of cost-volume-profit analysis. These principles underlie the chapters in Part One and most of the material in the rest of the book. Much planning and decision making depends on classifying costs according to their behavior. An understanding of cost behavior is essential if a manager is to have the best information for making rational decisions.

The principles and techniques developed in this section are discussed and illustrated primarily in a business context. But nearly all are applicable to not-for-profit economic entities, such as hospitals, universities, charitable institutions, and government units.

2 profit planning

Companies must earn profits to stay in business. Managers want to take actions to increase profitability and therefore need to predict how their actions will affect profits. For example, what will happen to profits if increasing promotional efforts by $250,000 increases sales by 50,000 units? Managers also are concerned with such questions as: How many units must we sell to earn $50,000? What selling price should we set? Should we hire another salesperson? Would staying open another two hours each day be profitable?

Cost-volume-profit analysis helps managers to plan for change and to answer questions such as those posed above. **Cost-volume-profit (CVP) analysis** is a method for analyzing the relationships among costs, volume, and profits.[1] Managers use these relationships to plan, budget, and make decisions. The first step in CVP analysis is classifying costs according to behavior.

Classifying costs according to behavior is distinctive to managerial use of accounting information. In financial accounting reports prepared for external use, costs normally are grouped according to the functional areas of business: production (cost of goods sold); marketing (selling expenses); administration (general and administrative expenses); and financing (interest expense).[2] A functional classification does not provide the necessary information to predict what likely is to happen to costs and profits if circum-

1 *Other terms you may encounter that mean essentially the same thing as CVP analysis are* breakeven analysis *and* profit-volume analysis.

2 *In financial accounting the term* cost *denotes the expenditure for an asset and* expense *denotes expired costs—costs assigned to the income statement for a period of time. We shall generally use the more general term* cost.

stances change, and a manager must plan for change and take actions to make changes.

COST BEHAVIOR

A cost is classified as either fixed or variable, according to whether the *total* amount of the cost changes as activity changes. *Activity* is a general term denoting anything that the company does; examples of activity include units of product sold or produced, hours worked, invoices prepared, and parts inspected. *Volume* is, for many purposes, virtually synonymous with activity, and both terms are used throughout this book. In this chapter, sales is used as the measure of volume and costs are classified as either fixed or variable with sales. Not all costs fall into these categories and other measures of activity are often important. Other measures of activity are considered in Chapter 3.

VARIABLE COSTS

A **variable cost** changes, in total, in direct proportion to changes in volume. To illustrate this concept, consider Ted's Threads, a retail store.

Ted buys shirts for $9.80 each from a wholesaler and sells them for $20 each. He also incurs a $0.20 cost for wrapping materials for each shirt sold. Ted rents a store in a mall and the monthly rent is 10% of sales. At a selling price of $20 per shirt, the cost of rent is $2 per shirt ($20 × 10%).

Rent differs from the other two costs. The per-unit cost of rent changes if Ted changes his selling price, while the per-unit amounts of the other two costs do not. But all three costs vary with the volume of sales. That is, the costs are incurred each time a shirt is sold, and the *total* of each increases or decreases in proportion to changes in sales. For our purposes, we can treat these three costs as a single variable cost of $12 per shirt ($9.80 + $0.20 + $2.00).

CONTRIBUTION MARGIN

Contribution margin is the difference between selling price per unit and variable cost per unit. Also, often the term is used to denote *total contribution margin*, the difference between total sales and total variable costs. In some cases, expressing contribution margin as a percentage is useful and convenient. The **contribution margin percentage** is per-unit contribution margin divided by selling price, or total contribution margin divided by total sales dollars.

The term *contribution* is used because what is left from a sale after variable costs are covered *contributes* to covering other costs and producing profit. In Ted's case, contribution margin per unit is $8 ($20 – $12) and contribution margin percentage is 40% ($8/$20).

FIXED COSTS

Fixed costs remain the same in *total* over a wide range of volume. Suppose that Ted spends $4,800 per month to pay a salesperson and utilities, and to rent display counters, cash registers, and other equipment. These costs will be the same whether he sells 600 or 800 shirts; they even might be the same if he sells no shirts at all. Note that the rent on equipment is a fixed cost, while store rent is a variable cost. As discussed in Chapter 3, the behavior of a cost cannot be determined necessarily by its name.

We can determine total costs as

Total costs = fixed costs + (variable cost per unit × unit volume)

As you can see, fixed costs are a part of total cost but remain the same regardless of volume. The following income statements for Ted's Threads show the effects of fixed costs and of changes in sales. Unlike financial accounting income statements, these statements group costs only as variable or fixed and show contribution margin as a subtotal.

Ted's Threads
Income Statements at Various Sales Levels

	749 Units	750 Units	751 Units
Sales ($20 per unit)	$14,980	$15,000	$15,020
Variable costs ($12 per unit)	8,988	9,000	9,012
Contribution margin	5,992	6,000	6,008
Fixed costs	4,800	4,800	4,800
Income	$ 1,192	$ 1,200	$ 1,208

Notice that the $8 difference in contribution margin at 749, 750, and 751 units is also the difference in incomes for those levels. It is important to realize that income can be calculated by multiplying per-unit contribution margin by unit sales and then subtracting total fixed costs.

Thus, to calculate Ted's income for sales of 750 shirts, we can multiply the $8 contribution margin by 750 shirts. This gives total contribution margin of $6,000, and when we subtract fixed costs of $4,800, we find income of $1,200. We could also determine total contribution at that level of sales by multiplying sales of $15,000 (750 × $20) by the 40% contribution margin percentage, giving $6,000. Again, income is total contribution margin minus fixed costs.

An important use of CVP analysis is to help managers predict how income will *change* if volume changes. If Ted wonders what will happen to his income if sales increase by 50 shirts per month, CVP analysis can tell him that income will increase by $400, the 50-shirt increase multiplied by the $8 per-shirt contribution margin. The $400 change in income also can be determined by computing the increase in sales revenue (50 units × $20 = $1,000) and multiplying by the contribution margin percentage of 40%. Note that the increase in income is $400 no matter what the current level of sales.

EMPHASIS ON EXPECTATIONS

At this early stage we are dealing with a simplified case, looking at the costs in a single period (a month, a quarter, or perhaps a year) and predicting costs and income for the following period. The important point is that predictions are about the future. To expect either per-unit variable costs or total fixed costs to remain the same month after month, or year after year, is unreasonable. Total fixed costs, per-unit variable costs, and selling prices can change for many reasons.

Inflation is a major cause of changes in both fixed and variable costs—suppliers might raise their prices, lessors might raise rents, salaries might rise, and so on. Profit planning must take into account *expected* changes in costs. Based on expectations, CVP analysis does not assume that costs remain constant over time. Thus, if Ted expected the price that he pays for shirts to go up by $0.80 next month, he would use $10.60 (instead of $9.80) in his planning for next month. Rapid inflation is a serious problem for managers in many countries and forces them to be creative. In Russia, for example, a manufacturer of shirts raised prices 15-20 times per month to cover rising costs. Having a good idea of how cost increases affect fixed and variable costs is necessary to make such adjustments.

Because of inflation, competition, or for other reasons, managers might change selling prices. For example, if Ted expects an increase in the price he pays for shirts, he might raise his price to $21. (Of course, an increase in his selling price will *also* increase Ted's per-unit cost for rent, so Ted would use both the new price and the new variable costs in his plans.)

Managers can themselves change some of their costs. Ted could hire another employee at a monthly salary, increasing his fixed costs, or he could advertise (also increasing fixed costs). In a more complex firm, many cost changes are the result of managerial actions. A large company could increase (or decrease) its office staff or change its level of spending on such items as travel and employee training. Thus, fixed costs might change during a period. But they are still fixed because they do not change with the level of activity. For planning purposes, then, managers predict fixed costs based on what they *expect* for the coming period, knowing they might change costs to meet changing conditions.

As a general rule, managers can change some fixed costs more easily than they can change per-unit variable costs, especially over short periods of time (more about this in Chapter 3). Some accountants, therefore, use the term **nonvariable costs** instead of *fixed costs*. Their point is that fixed costs are not fixed in the sense that they cannot be changed, but rather that, unlike per-unit variable costs, fixed costs do not change *automatically* when volume changes. In this book, such costs are called *fixed* because that term is more common. Regardless of terminology, the emphasis in planning is on expectations. If actual conditions (selling prices, prices from suppliers, etc.) do not coincide with expectations, or if managers later change decisions, differences will occur between actual and predicted costs and profit. Such differences between actuality and expectations are inherent in business but do not reduce the need to plan.

INCOME STATEMENT FORMATS—FINANCIAL ACCOUNTING AND CONTRIBUTION MARGIN

The format used for income statements in this chapter differs from that used in financial accounting. As stated earlier, in financial accounting costs are usually classified by function or by object. The income statements in Exhibit 2-1 highlight the differences between the two approaches. Notice that the sales and income figures are the same under both approaches, but the costs

Exhibit 2-1 Comparison of Income Statements Using the Financial Accounting and the Contribution Margin Approaches

Financial Accounting Format (Functional)		Contribution Margin Format (Behavioral)	
Sales	$15,000	Sales	$15,000
Cost of sales (750 × $9.80)	7,350	Variable costs:	
		Cost of shirts (750 × $9.80)	7,350
Gross profit	7,650	Wrapping (750 × $0.20)	150
		Store rent (750 × $2, or 10% of $15,000)	1,500
		Total	9,000
Operating expenses:			
Wrapping (750 × $0.20)	150	Contribution margin	6,000
Store rent (750 × $2, or 10% of $15,000)	1,500		
Salary, utilities and equipment rent	4,800	Fixed costs:	
Total operating expenses	6,450	Salary, utilities and equipment rent	4,800
Income	$ 1,200	Income	$ 1,200

are classified in different ways. The statements are for a month when Ted sells 750 shirts.

The obvious differences between the statements are in terminology and the placement of the costs of store rent and wrapping materials. The principal difference is that a manager who receives a statement in the financial accounting format cannot perform CVP analysis, because the financial accounting format tells little about cost behavior. The manager determines how much of each cost is fixed and variable, which is not possible without additional analysis. One unfortunate result is the tendency of some managers to treat fixed costs as if they were variable and to use average total cost per unit for planning.

UNIT COSTS AND PLANNING

You should see that, because total fixed costs remain the same at different levels of activity, the *average* fixed cost per unit changes whenever volume changes. Thus, the average fixed cost per unit when Ted sells 750 units is $6.40 ($4,800/750), while the average when he sells 800 units is $6 ($4,800/800). The **average total cost per unit,** then, depends on the level of activity, with the average total per-unit cost for Ted being $18.40 ($6.40 fixed plus $12 variable) when he sells 750 units, and $18 ($6 fixed plus $12 variable) when he sells 800 units.

Failing to recognize that average total per-unit cost changes as activity changes creates problems for managers who—unwisely—use averages to predict future costs. Managers should not use the average total per-unit cost for one level of activity to predict total costs at another level.

To illustrate this point, suppose Ted uses the $18.40 average total cost per unit (at a volume of 750 shirts) to predict total costs at a volume of 800 shirts. He would predict costs of $14,720 ($18.40 × 800 shirts). But Ted's income statements at volumes of 750 and 800 shirts are

	750 Shirts	800 Shirts
Sales	$15,000	$16,000
Variable costs	9,000	9,600
Contribution margin	6,000	6,400
Fixed costs	4,800	4,800
Income	$ 1,200	$ 1,600
Average cost per unit	$ 18.40	$ 18
Profit per unit	$ 1.60	$ 2

Total costs at sales of 800 shirts are $14,400 ($9,600 + $4,800), not $14,720. What *appears* to be additional profit per unit at the higher level of activity is simply the result of spreading the fixed costs over a larger number of units. The behavior of Ted's costs has not changed at all; variable costs remain at 60% of sales ($12 per unit) and fixed costs remain at $4,800. Using average total cost per unit to predict total costs works *only if all costs are variable.*

In the preceding example, notice that income *as a percentage of sales* (called **return on sales**, or **ROS**) differs at the two levels of volume. At sales of 750 units, income is 8% of sales, while at sales of 800 units, income is 10% of sales. Perhaps the most common mistake managers make is to use the ROS percentage at one level of volume to predict income at another volume level. If a company has *any* fixed costs, its income, as a percentage of sales, increases as volume increases. Additionally, the percentage increase in income is greater than the percentage increase in sales. In the income statements just shown, a mere 6 2/3% increase in sales ($1,000/$15,000) produced a 33 1/3% increase in income (from $1,200 to $1,600).

RELEVANT RANGE

As stated earlier, per-unit variable costs and total fixed costs might not remain the same for very long. Per-unit variable costs and total fixed costs cannot be expected to be the same at all possible levels of activity. That is, the per-unit variable cost and total fixed cost can be expected to behave as predicted only over some range of activity.

For example, Ted might be able to handle the store with only one helper as long as he sells no more than 900 shirts per month. At some point around that level of sales, he will have to hire additional help. If he pays a new employee a commission on each shirt sold, his variable cost per unit will increase; if he pays the new employee a salary, his fixed costs will increase. Another possibility is that if Ted sells a great many shirts, he will get a discount on the purchase price, thus reducing his per-unit variable costs.

The foregoing illustrates an important assumption underlying CVP analysis: that the company will operate within a **relevant range**, a range of volume over which it can reasonably expect selling price, per-unit variable cost, and total fixed costs to be constant.[3] The width of the range varies among companies. When operating outside the relevant range, managers cannot expect these factors to remain constant. Also possible is that a company might have more than one relevant range, within each of which a particular price/cost combination prevails. For planning purposes, managers forecast the approximate range of activity and use the selling price and costs they believe will hold within that range.

A special case of operating outside the relevant range occurs when a business shuts down for a short period. A company that closes for a week or a month should find its total costs for that period to be less than its normal total fixed costs. For instance, a company closing for a month would turn out the lights, turn down the heat, and probably not advertise. The company might also lay off some employees. Thus, to think of *fixed costs* as the costs that the firm would incur at zero activity is not appropriate. Fixed costs are better thought of as the planned costs that will not change in total as volume changes *within the relevant range.* To recap, relevant range is a range of volume over which price, fixed costs in total, and variable costs per unit are expected to remain the same.

COST-VOLUME-PROFIT GRAPH

Exhibit 2-2 gives a graphical representation of the CVP picture for Ted's Threads. The revenue line shows total sales dollars at any volume which is simply the selling price per unit multiplied by the level of unit volume. At any volume, the vertical distance between total costs and fixed costs is total variable costs at that volume.

Although we have extended the lines on the graph far to the right and back to the vertical axis on the left, it is not legitimate to do so because of the relevant range. As suggested earlier, Ted's fixed costs should be less than $4,800 if the store is closed for the month (zero activity), and either per-unit variable or total fixed costs, or both, are likely to change if volume exceeds 900 shirts per month. We extend the lines to zero volume and beyond 900 shirts to make it easier to read the graph.

The graph highlights an important point. As long as selling price exceeds variable cost (contribution margin is positive), selling more units will benefit the firm, either by increasing profits or by *decreasing losses*. Thus, the firm would do better to stay open and incur losses than to shut down and incur larger losses. Such is often the case with *seasonal* businesses. For example, businesses in summer resort areas *expect* losses during the winter. Similarly, toy companies expect losses after the Christmas season. Many seasonal businesses continue to operate in the off-season because they recognize that the contribution margin from the additional, though lower, sales reduces their losses. Chapter 3 considers this point in more detail.

---

3 The problem of changing selling prices is considered in Chapter 4.

Exhibit 2-2 Cost-Volume-Profit Chart

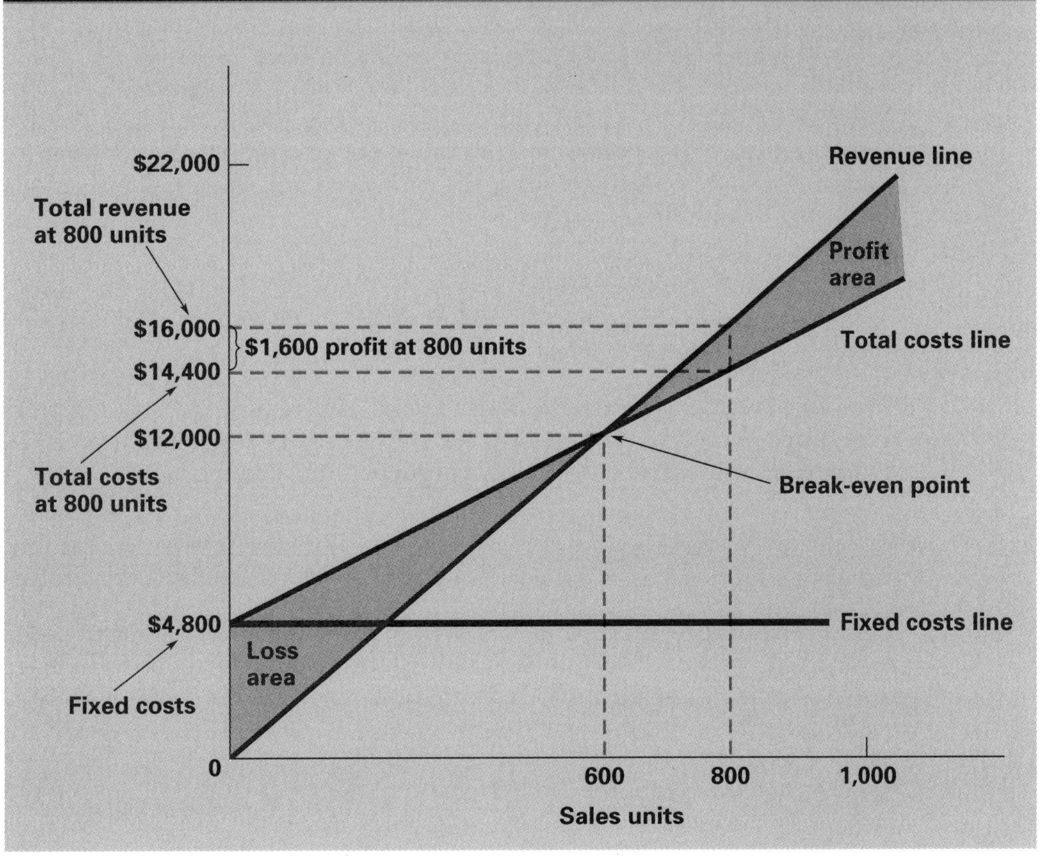

At any volume, the vertical distance between the revenue line and the total cost line is the amount of profit or loss (shaded areas) at that volume. The graphical presentation directs attention to the **break-even point**—the point at which profits are zero because total revenues equal total costs. A firm operating above the break-even point makes profits; below that point, it incurs losses.

Knowing the break-even point is useful for many purposes. Managers of not-for-profit organizations frequently seek to break even, or show only a small profit or loss, on some of their activities. Managers of business firms do not want to break even—they want to earn profits. But they still want to know how low volume can be before losses appear. Using relationships we already know, we can derive an equation to find this point. Again, profit equals total sales minus total variable costs minus total fixed costs. That is,

$$\textit{Total sales dollars} - \textit{total variable costs} - \textit{total fixed costs} = \textit{profit}$$

Using Q to denote the quantity of units sold, we can restate the formula as

$$\left(\begin{matrix}\textit{Per unit}\\ \textit{selling}\\ \textit{price}\end{matrix} \times Q\right) - \left(\begin{matrix}\textit{per-unit}\\ \textit{variable}\\ \textit{cost}\end{matrix} \times Q\right) - \textit{fixed} = \begin{matrix}\textit{total}\\ \textit{profit}\\ \textit{costs}\end{matrix}$$

Knowing that selling price minus variable cost per unit equals contribution margin per unit, we can combine the first two components. We then add fixed costs to both sides, and get

$$\left(\begin{matrix}\textit{Contribution}\\ \textit{margin}\\ \textit{per unit}\end{matrix} \times Q\right) = \begin{matrix}\textit{total}\\ \textit{fixed}\\ \textit{costs}\end{matrix} + \textit{profit}$$

Since we are looking for the break-even point (where profit is *zero*), the profit term drops out. Now we can solve for Q (the break-even point in units) by dividing both sides by contribution margin per unit, producing

$$Q\ \textit{(break-even sales in units)} = \frac{\textit{total fixed costs}}{\textit{contribution margin per unit}}$$

Ted can interpret this formula as saying: "How many units must I sell to cover fixed costs of $4,800, if each unit contributes $8 to cover those fixed costs?" Applying the formula, Ted can determine that his break-even point is 600 shirts.

$$\begin{matrix}\textit{Break-even sales}\\ \textit{in units}\end{matrix} = \frac{\$4{,}800}{\$20 - \$12} = \frac{\$4{,}800}{\$8} = \textit{600 shirts}$$

Both the graph in Exhibit 2-2 and the break-even formula derived above show sales in units. We could just as well state the break-even point in sales dollars, which would be $12,000 (600 × $20). Sometimes computing the break-even point in sales dollars by working with the contribution margin percentage is more convenient. The following equation shows this alternative applied to Ted's situation.

$$\begin{matrix}\textit{Break-even sales}\\ \textit{in dollars}\end{matrix} = \frac{\textit{total fixed costs}}{\textit{contribution margin percentage}} = \frac{\$4{,}800}{40\%} = \$12{,}000$$

Ted can interpret this version of the break-even formula as saying: "How many dollars of sales must I have to cover fixed costs of $4,800, *given* that each sales dollar yields $0.40 of contribution margin (the 40% contribution margin percentage)?" The *units* required to break even are still 600 ($12,000/$20 selling price per unit), and both formulas give the same answer for the break-even point, 600 units or $12,000.

For a single-product company, either of the ways of stating contribution margin (and of determining the break-even point) can be used; the choice depends on computational convenience. The contribution-margin-percentage approach especially is useful to companies that sell several products. For instance, managers of a department store that sells thousands of items cannot easily work with unit sales. (It makes little sense to speak of sales of 12,500,000 units when the units are as diverse as handkerchiefs, shoes, refrigerators, and television sets.) They prefer to work with sales dollars because their experience allows them to interpret numbers such as $4,000,000 of sales. Chapter 4 discusses multiproduct companies in more detail.

Firms that sell services, rather than goods, often charge their clients for the hours that they work. CPA firms, law firms, and consulting firms are examples. For these firms, chargeable hours (the number of hours worked that are chargeable to client business) is an appropriate and useful measure of activity, and works well as the horizontal axis of a CVP graph. Still other companies use percentage of capacity as the measure of volume. Airlines use seat-miles or passenger-miles to measure volume. (A seat-mile is one seat flown one mile. A passenger-mile is a seat-mile occupied by a paying passenger.) Annual reports of airlines cite various statistics regarding seat-miles and passenger-miles. For example, Delta Airlines stated that its break-even point in 1992 was 63% of available seat-miles. American Airlines' break-even was 61.6% of available seat-miles in 1991.

ACHIEVING TARGET PROFITS

The break-even point is of interest, but managers of profit-seeking organizations are concerned more with meeting a desired or **target profit**. The target could be expressed as an absolute dollar amount or as an ROS percentage. The technique for determining the volume needed to achieve a target profit is a simple variation of the break-even case. The break-even point reveals what sales are required to make no profit and incur no loss; by incorporating the amount or rate of profit desired, we can determine the sales volume required to achieve that profit.

TARGET DOLLAR PROFIT

In break-even calculations we found the number of units or the sales dollars required to provide total contribution margin equal to total fixed costs. Finding the volume required to achieve a target profit is essentially the same thing. We now want to know what sales are required, in units or dollars, to earn total contribution margin equal to the *sum* of total fixed costs and the target profit.

Suppose Ted wishes to earn a profit of $2,000 per month. How many shirts must he sell? We know that total contribution margin must be equal to fixed costs of $4,800 for Ted to break even. Hence, to achieve a profit of $2,000, total contribution margin must be $2,000 greater than fixed costs, or $6,800. To achieve total contribution margin of $6,800 when the contribution margin per unit is $8 ($20 – $12), he must sell 850 units. Expressed in general terms

$$\left(\begin{array}{c}\textit{Sales, in units,}\\ \textit{to achieve}\\ \textit{target profit}\end{array} \times \begin{array}{c}\textit{contribution}\\ \textit{margin}\\ \textit{per unit}\end{array}\right) - \begin{array}{c}\textit{fixed}\\ \textit{costs}\end{array} = \begin{array}{c}\textit{target}\\ \textit{profit}\end{array}$$

Restating this equation to solve for the needed level of sales yields

$$\textit{Sales, in units, to achieve target profit} = \frac{\textit{fixed costs + target profit}}{\textit{contribution margin per unit}}$$

Applying this formula in Ted's case, we have

$$\textit{Sales, in units, to achieve target profit} = \frac{\$4{,}800 + \$2{,}000}{\$20 - \$12} = \frac{\$6{,}800}{\$8} = 850 \textit{ units}$$

Notice that the numerator of the formula is the total contribution margin required to earn the target profit. The numerator consists of the $4,800 contribution margin required for break-even plus the $2,000 required for the target profit.

The same technique applies if contribution margin percentage is used rather than per-unit contribution margin. Substituting the contribution margin percentage in the above formula, and recognizing that the switch to a percentage yields sales dollars rather than sales in units, the formula is

$$\textit{Sales, in dollars, to achieve target profit} = \frac{\textit{fixed costs + target profit}}{\textit{contribution margin percentage}}$$

Applying the formula to Ted's situation yields required sales of $17,000.

$$\textit{Sales, in dollars, to achieve target profit} = \frac{\$4{,}800 + \$2{,}000}{40\%} = \frac{\$6{,}800}{40\%} = \$17{,}000$$

Once again, the answer is the same regardless of approach. Target sales in units are 850 units, whether computed directly or as a result of the computation of target sales dollars ($17,000/$20), and target sales in dollars are $17,000 (850 × $20).

TARGET RETURN ON SALES

Occasionally, managers state their profit target as an ROS (profit divided by sales). Managers with such a profit target are saying that their desired dollar profit varies with sales.

Suppose that Ted wishes to earn a 15% ROS. We already know that his variable costs are 60% of sales ($12/$20). Therefore, he wants 75% of his sales to go to variable costs and profit, leaving 25% to cover fixed costs. We use a variation of the break-even formula based on contribution margin percentage to find target sales.

$$\textit{Sales, in dollars, to achieve target ROS} = \frac{\textit{fixed costs}}{\textit{contribution margin percentage} - \textit{target ROS}}$$

To achieve a target ROS of 15%, Ted needs sales of

$$\textit{Sales, in dollars, to achieve target ROS} = \frac{\$4{,}800}{40\% - 15\%} = \frac{\$4{,}800}{25\%} = \$19{,}200$$

Again, because Ted needs 75% of sales for variable costs and profit, 25% is left to cover fixed costs. Ted's income statement shows that logic.

Sales	$19,200	100%
Variable costs (60% of sales)	11,520	60%
Contribution margin	7,680	40%
Fixed costs	4,800	25%
Income	$ 2,880	15%

Warning: Don't forget that the percentages of fixed costs and profit to sales are valid *only* at this volume. To achieve sales of $19,200, Ted has to sell 960 shirts ($19,200/$20).

We could also translate Ted's goal of a 15% ROS into a $3 profit per shirt ($20 × 15%). Subtracting the variable costs of $12 *and* the $3 profit from the $20 selling price leaves $5 to cover fixed costs. In a variation of the basic break-even formula (fixed costs/contribution margin), we could determine the sales volume needed for a target 15% ROS as 960 units ($4,800/$5). Note that this answer agrees with the one computed earlier.

CHANGING PLANS

The concepts of contribution margin, break-even analysis, and target profit are useful when managers are contemplating changes in plans in the hope of increasing profits. A typical example is an increase in advertising, with the expectation of increased sales.

Note that the advertising does not increase profits by the increase in units sold multiplied by the per-unit contribution margin. Why? Although *total contribution margin* increases by that amount, total fixed costs also increase by the cost of the advertising. Thus, the change in profit is the change in total contribution margin *minus* the change in fixed costs.

Consider a company with a per-unit contribution margin of $10 and a $50,000 proposed advertising campaign that is expected to increase sales by 4,000 units. Total contribution margin will increase by $40,000 (4,000 × $10), but fixed costs will be $50,000 higher, so that profit will be $10,000 less than it would have been without the extra advertising. Using the break-even formula and the concept of contribution margin, we can determine that it will take a sales increase of 5,000 units just to cover the increase in fixed costs ($50,000 fixed costs/$10 per-unit contribution margin). Total profit will increase only if the advertising can increase sales by more than 5,000 units.

The preceding analysis does not require knowing what sales the firm expected without the advertising campaign. That is, knowing if sales expected without the additional advertising were 0, 50,000, or 2,000,000 units does not matter. As long as the increase in volume is greater than 5,000 units, taking the proposed action increases profits over what they would have been.

TARGET SELLING PRICES

CVP analysis also can be used to determine the selling price to charge to earn a target profit *given* expected unit sales. Determining a target selling price requires separating *variable* costs into those that are constant amounts *per unit* and those that are a constant *percentage of selling price.*

VARIABLE COSTS AS A CONSTANT PER-UNIT AMOUNT

If all variable costs are a constant amount per unit, determining target selling price is relatively simple. Ted's Threads has a variable cost that is a constant percentage of sales. So, to illustrate how a target price is determined, consider another retailer. Joan's Jeans' per-unit variable costs are $12, none of which depends on selling price, and monthly fixed costs are $4,800. Suppose Joan wishes to earn $1,500 per month and believes she can sell 900 pairs of jeans. What price must she charge?

The easiest way to answer this question is to prepare an income statement from the bottom up. Start with the required profit of $1,500, add the $4,800 of fixed costs, and arrive at a total required contribution margin of $6,300. At a volume of 900 units, Joan's total variable costs are $10,800 ($12 × 900). The following is Joan's income statement as far as we know it.

Joan's Jeans
Income Statement at Monthly Volume of 900 Units

Sales	$?
Variable costs ($12 × 900)	10,800
Contribution margin	6,300
Fixed costs	4,800
Income	$ 1,500

Sales must be $17,100, the amount necessary to provide $6,300 of contribution margin when variable costs are $10,800. The unit selling price has to be $19 ($17,100/900 units).

Another approach is to determine the desired contribution margin per unit—by dividing the total required contribution margin by unit volume ($6,300/900 = $7 in Joan's case)—and add that amount to the per-unit variable cost to arrive at the required selling price. Adding the $7 to the $12 per-unit variable cost yields, again, a price of $19.

Of course, a manager's analysis does not end with determining a required selling price. Suppose that Joan set a target profit of $6,000 per month on expected sales of 900 units. The required selling price is $24. (Prove this for yourself.) If other stores sell similar jeans for $20, monthly sales of 900 units at $24 probably are unachievable. The analysis gives only the price required to reach a particular profit goal and does not mean that the assumed sales volume can be realized at that price.

MIXTURE OF VARIABLE COSTS

For a firm with some variable costs that are a constant amount per unit and others that are a constant percentage of selling price, the required price is determined most easily by using a formula. To illustrate, let's return to Ted's Threads.

Assume that Ted's target, like Joan's, is $1,500 per month and that he expects to sell 900 shirts. Remember that Ted's variable costs are $9.80 to purchase a shirt and $0.20 for wrapping material, plus rent at 10% of sales. Thus, his per-unit variable cost is $10 plus 10% of selling price. Instead of an income statement, the following formula describes an income statement.

$$
\begin{array}{llcrl}
\textit{Sales} & - \textit{ variable costs} & - & \textit{fixed costs} & = \textit{profit} \\
S & - [(900 \times \$10) + 10\% S] & - & \$4{,}800 & = \$1{,}500 \\
S & - \$9{,}000 - 10\% S & - & \$4{,}800 & = \$1{,}500 \\
 & & & 90\% S & = \$15{,}300 \\
 & & & S & = \$17{,}000
\end{array}
$$

Dividing the required sales of $17,000 by the expected volume of 900 shirts yields a target price of $18.89 (rounded).

Again, whatever the basis used for setting a target profit, the manager must then ask: Is the assumed sales volume likely to be achieved at the calculated selling price? CVP analysis cannot answer this question. The more competitive the market, the less control a company has over its selling price. Most companies have some discretion in pricing, but the amount of discretion can change as market conditions change. Personal computers used to be high-priced because people needed support and wanted to be able to call someone when they could not get the computer to work correctly. Now users are more sophisticated, so many buy from mail-order companies or from large retailers who offer little or no support, but charge very low prices.

TARGET COSTING

Some companies use a planning technique called target costing to help them decide whether to enter a new market or bring out a new product. The essence of **target costing** is to determine how much the company can spend to manufacture and market a product, given a target profit. That is, the price and volume are estimated first, then the costs. Target costing is useful especially in deciding whether to enter an established market where selling prices are relatively stable. Proponents of target costing argue that its use increases the involvement of manufacturing, designing, and engineering people in planning because they have a cost to aim at, and will be encouraged to be creative in reaching the target cost.

Analytically, the technique simply requires solving the basic CVP equation for total cost, variable cost, or fixed cost. For instance, if the managers agree on a target profit of $300,000 and that unit volume of 100,000 is achievable at a $20 price, the total allowable cost is

Revenue (100,000 × $20)	*$2,000,000*
Target profit	*300,000*
Total allowable cost	*$1,700,000*

If managers expect total fixed costs to be $1,200,000, total variable costs can be $500,000, or $5 per unit. The $5 then, along with the $1,200,000 fixed cost, becomes an objective for the managers responsible for designing and manufacturing the product. Note, however, that as with target pricing, the answer given by the analysis might not be achievable with existing manufacturing techniques. The managers responsible for manufacturing might be unsuccessful in reaching the target cost objective. In such cases, the top managers might decide against introducing the new product or entering the new market. Or they might decide to re-examine their profit target and estimates of price and volume. For example, reconsidering the profit target is more likely when the new product (or market) is one the managers believe is especially important for, say, the company's reputation as an innovator, or for pursuing a long-range strategy.

A major world-wide maker of motion control components and systems, with $2.25 billion sales, uses target costing at the design stage to enable management to emphasize cost even before product is ready. The company's managers believe that competition has increased the pressure to shorten development time, but they recognize that most cost is built in at the design/development stage. So they look at costs over the life cycle of the product.[4]

COST STRUCTURE AND MANAGERIAL ATTITUDES

Businesses can operate in different ways. A company can use a great deal of labor and little machinery or vice versa. Salespeople might be on salary, commission, or a combination of the two. When making choices, managers must consider the effects of their decisions on the cost structure—the relative proportions of fixed and variable costs. For example, a company might take on higher fixed costs to reduce variable costs and thereby increase contribution margin. (Automation does exactly that.) Such an action increases potential profitability, but also increases *risk*. The break-even point will probably rise, and if volume drops, profits will fall more rapidly with the higher contribution margin.

To illustrate, consider Benson Company. Suppose its managers decide to introduce a new product. They expect to sell 20,000 units at $10. They can make the product in either of two manufacturing processes. Process A uses a great deal of labor and has variable costs of $7 per unit and annual fixed costs of $40,000. Process B uses more machinery, with unit variable costs of $4 and annual fixed costs of $95,000. Given these estimates, Process B yields more profit, as shown in the following income statement.

	Process A	Process B
Sales (20,000 × $10)	$200,000	$200,000
Variable costs at $7 and $4	140,000	80,000
Contribution margin at $3 and $6	60,000	120,000
Fixed costs	40,000	95,000
Profit	$ 20,000	$ 25,000

If the managers are certain that the numbers are correct, they will choose Process B. But, the numbers are estimates, so the managers should do some additional analysis before deciding which process to use. One item the managers should look at is the break-even point for each process:

Process A: $40,000/$3 = 13,333 units
Process B: $95,000/$6 = 15,833 units

4 *John P. Campi, "Total Cost Management at Parker-Hannifin,"* Management Accounting, *January 1989, 51.*

Process B's higher break-even point is one indication that it is riskier, but that analysis ignores sales expectations. To incorporate those expectations in their assessment of the alternatives, managers often express risk by referring to the margin of safety.

MARGIN OF SAFETY

The decline in volume from the expected level of sales to the break-even point is called the **margin of safety (MOS).** As the name suggests, the MOS is the difference between expected sales and the break-even point. The MOS can be expressed as a unit amount, dollar amount, or percentage. In our example, the MOS for Process A is 6,667 units (20,000 expected – 13,333 break-even), or $66,670 (6,667 units at $10 each), or 33.3% (6,667/20,000). For Process B it is 4,167 units (20,000 – 15,833), $41,670 (4,167 units at $10), or 20.8% (4,167/20,000). Generally, the higher the MOS, the lower the risk. Our illustration involved computing the MOS for a single product, but the concept can be applied to a group of products or to an entire company.

INDIFFERENCE POINT

Another tool that managers use to help them choose between alternative cost structures is the indifference point. The **indifference point** is the level of volume at which total costs, and hence profits, are the same under both cost structures. If the company operated at that level of volume, which alternative was used would not matter because income would be the same either way.

We calculate the indifference point by setting up an equation where each side represents total cost under one of the alternatives. (If selling price is the same under both alternatives, profits will be the same when total costs are the same.) At unit volumes below the indifference point, the alternative with the lower fixed cost gives higher profits; at volumes above the indifference point, the alternative with the higher fixed cost is more profitable. The indifference point for Benson's new product is 18,333 units, calculated as follows, with Q equal to unit volume.

Total Cost for Process A				Total Cost for Process B		
Fixed cost	+	variable cost		Fixed cost	+	variable cost
$40,000	+	7Q$	=	$95,000	+	4Q$
		3Q$	=	$55,000		
		Q	=	18,333 (rounded)		

At volumes below 18,333 units, Process A gives lower total costs (and higher profits); above 18,333 units, Process B gives higher profits.

The line 3Q$ = $55,000 gives a clue to the tradeoff between the alternatives: Benson gains $3 per unit in reduced variable costs by increasing fixed costs $55,000. The indifference point shows that the company needs 18,333 units to make the tradeoff desirable; that volume is only 1,667 units (or 8%) below the estimated volume of 20,000. If Benson's managers believe that a high likelihood exists that volume will be lower than their estimate of 20,000 units, they might decide to use Process A.

Exhibit 2-3 shows Benson's choices in a variation of the CVP graph shown earlier. As in the earlier graph, the axes represent volume and dollars. Each line represents profit at each level of volume for the associated alternative. Notice that the line for each process begins at a negative point equal to fixed costs for that process and crosses zero at the break-even point for that process. Where profit is the same under both alternatives, the two lines cross. This form of the graph is useful especially in examining alternatives because it reduces the number of lines needed to represent an alternative.

Benson's managers have no correct answer in their choice of cost structure. Analytical tools such as the indifference point, margin of safety, and the CVP graph, help them evaluate alternatives, but the decision depends on their attitudes about risk and return. If they want to avoid risk, they will choose Process A, foregoing the potential for higher profits from Process B. If they are venturesome, they probably will be willing to take some risk for the potentially higher returns and choose Process B.

ASSUMPTIONS AND LIMITATIONS OF CVP ANALYSIS

We have already mentioned some of the conditions necessary for CVP analysis to give useful predictions. It must be possible to graph both revenues and total costs as straight, rather than curved, lines within the relevant range. This requirement means that selling price, per-unit variable cost, and total fixed costs must be constant throughout the relevant range. We introduce two other assumptions here, but we discuss them in detail in later chapters.

First, CVP analysis assumes either (1) that the company sells only one product or (2) that the sales of each product in a multiproduct company are

Exhibit 2-3 Benson's Alternatives

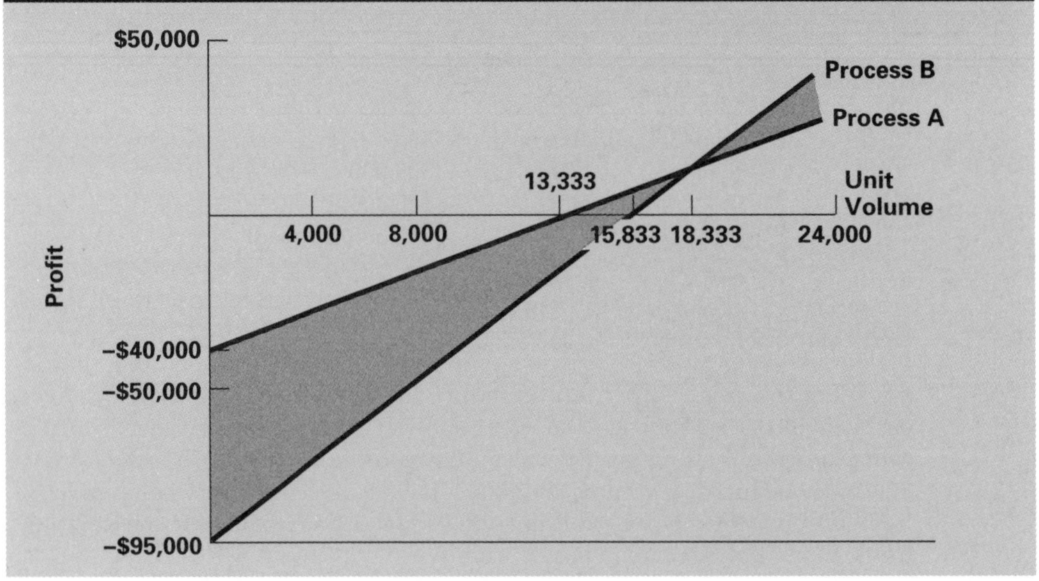

a constant percentage of total sales. The term **sales mix** describes the percentage of each product's sales to total sales. If a change in sales mix occurs, the contribution margin percentage probably will change. Chapter 4 discusses multiproduct CVP analysis.

The second assumption is relevant only to manufacturing companies, not to merchandising and service companies. To apply CVP analysis to a manufacturing firm, *production must equal sales.* (That assumption was implicit in the analysis of Benson Company's alternative cost structure.) Because of certain requirements of financial accounting (and tax laws) for manufacturing companies, income reported for financial accounting (or tax) purposes usually does not agree with income predicted by CVP analysis. Chapter 13 explains how those requirements cause differences between reported income and income predictions using CVP analysis.

Our illustrations, Ted's Threads, its counterpart Joan's Jeans, and even Benson Company, are relatively simple operations compared with most companies today. Bigger, more diverse companies are more difficult to analyze. Yet CVP analysis is a tool that can be and *is* used, in various forms, by managers of the largest and most complex organizations.

SUMMARY

Cost-volume-profit analysis is critical to planning and requires classifying costs by behavior. A cost is either fixed or variable depending on whether the total amount of the cost changes as activity changes. Contribution margin, the difference between price and variable cost, is important in CVP analysis. Contribution margin can be expressed as a per-unit amount, a total, or a percentage of selling price. The critical points in the chapter are the recognition of the fixed/variable cost classification scheme, the analytical value of this classification, and the usefulness of contribution margin.

Cost-volume-profit analysis answers such questions as: What profits are earned at different levels of sales? What sales are needed to earn a particular profit? What are the effects of changes in selling prices? What price must we charge to earn a particular profit?

With varying degrees of ease, managers can change both costs and prices. Within limits, managers also can control the relative proportions of fixed and variable costs in their cost structure. The usefulness of CVP analysis as a planning tool depends, therefore, on managers' estimates about future conditions, not those prevailing in the past. A basic CVP graph presents a single set of conditions that mangers expect. The indifference point, margin of safety, and a variation of the basic CVP graph help managers assess the risks and returns of alternative cost structures. Managers' attitudes toward risk-return relationships influence decisions about cost structure.

Managers in multiproduct and/or manufacturing companies usefully can apply CVP analysis if they recognize that certain assumptions underlie that analysis.

KEY TERMS

average total cost per unit
break-even point
contribution margin
contribution margin percentage
cost-volume-profit (CVP) analysis
fixed costs
indifference point
margin of safety (MOS)
nonvariable costs
relevant range
return on sales (ROS)
sales mix
target costing
target profit
variable costs

KEY FORMULAS

$$\text{Break-even sales, in units} = \frac{\text{total fixed costs}}{\text{contribution margin per unit}}$$

$$\text{Break-even sales, in dollars} = \frac{\text{total fixed costs}}{\text{contribution margin percentage}}$$

$$\text{Profit} = \text{sales} - \text{variable costs} - \text{fixed costs}$$

$$\text{Margin of safety} = \text{expected sales} - \text{break-even sales}$$

$$\text{Sales, in dollars, to achieve target profit} = \frac{\text{fixed costs} + \text{target profit}}{\text{contribution margin percentage}}$$

$$\text{Sales, in units, to achieve target profit} = \frac{\text{fixed costs} + \text{target profit}}{\text{contribution margin per unit}}$$

$$\text{Sales, in dollars, to achieve target return on sales} = \frac{\text{fixed costs}}{\text{contribution margin percentage} - \text{target return on sales}}$$

$$\text{Total costs} = \text{fixed costs} + (\text{variable cost per unit} \times \text{unit volume})$$

REVIEW PROBLEM

Cost-volume-profit analysis assumes that important variables (selling price, variable cost per unit, total fixed costs) do not change within the relevant range. Nevertheless, as we saw in the section on price determination, a manager may want to know what value for one of these variables is consistent with a particular target profit. Moreover, because prices and costs can change quickly, a manager must be alert to the effects of such changes. The following problem tests your basic understanding of CVP analysis. Solve the problem, one part at a time, and check your answers with those provided. Consider each question independently of the others.

Glassman Company sells its one product at \$20 per unit. Variable costs are \$12 per unit and fixed costs are \$100,000 per month.

Required

1. If Glassman can sell 15,000 units in a particular month, what will its income be?
2. What is its break-even point in units?
3. What is its break-even point in sales dollars?
4. What sales, in units, are required to earn $40,000 for the month?
5. What sales, in dollars, are required to earn $40,000 for the month?
6. Suppose Glassman reduces its selling price to $18 because competitors are charging that amount. What is its new break-even point (a) in units? (b) in dollars?
7. Suppose that fixed costs are expected to increase by $10,000 (to $110,000 per month). What is the new break-even point (a) in units? (b) in dollars? Price is $20.
8. Suppose that the firm is currently selling 10,000 units per month. The marketing manager believes that sales would increase if advertising were increased by $5,000. How much would sales have to increase, in units, to give the firm the same income or loss that it is currently earning? (Although you know how many units are now being sold, you do not need this fact to solve the problem.)
9. Suppose Glassman is selling 20,000 units per month at $20. What is its margin of safety?
10. Glassman currently pays its salespeople salaries that total $40,000 per month, but no commissions. The vice-president for sales is considering a plan whereby the salespeople would receive a 5% commission, but their salaries would fall to a total of $25,000 per month (a drop of $15,000). At what sales level is the company indifferent between the two compensation plans?

ANSWER TO REVIEW PROBLEM

1. The firm will earn $20,000. An income statement is shown below.

Sales (15,000 × $20)	$300,000
Variable costs (15,000 × $12)	180,000
Contribution margin (15,000 × $8)	120,000
Fixed costs	100,000
Income	$ 20,000

   A shortcut is to multiply contribution margin per unit of $8 by 15,000 units (which gives $120,000 in contribution margin), then subtract fixed costs of $100,000 to get $20,000 income.
2. 12,500 units. The break-even point in units is the result of dividing fixed costs ($100,000) by the $8 contribution margin per unit.
3. $250,000. This amount can be determined either by multiplying the break-even point in units (from question 2) by the selling price per unit (12,500 × $20) or by applying the break-even formula using the contribution margin percentage ($100,000/40%). The contribution margin percentage is determined by dividing the selling price of $20 into the contribution margin of $8 (from question 2).
4. 17,500 units. The profit of $40,000 is added to the fixed costs of $100,000, and the target profit formula is then applied. Thus, the total to be obtained from sales is $40,000 plus $100,000 in fixed costs. If Glassman gets $8 per unit and desires total contribution margin of $140,000, it must sell 17,500 units ($140,000/$8).

5. $350,000. This amount can be determined either by multiplying the 17,500 units (from question 4) by the $20 selling price per unit or by applying the formula using the contribution margin percentage. To return the fixed costs of $100,000 plus a profit of $40,000, when the contribution margin percentage is 40%, requires sales of $350,000 ($140,000/40%).
6. (a) 16,667 units. If fixed costs of $100,000 must be covered when each unit carries a contribution margin of $6 ($18 selling price – variable cost of $12), a total of 16,667 units must be sold ($100,000/$6).
   (b) $300,000. This amount can be determined either by multiplying the number of units (16,667) computed in part (a) by the selling price of $18 or by using the formula with the contribution margin percentage. Thus, 16,667 × $18 is $300,000 (rounded) or $100,000/[($18 – $12)/$18] = $300,000.
7. (a) 13,750 units. With fixed costs of $110,000 and a contribution margin per unit of $8, the number of units to produce a contribution margin equal to the fixed costs is 13,750 ($110,000/$8). Another approach is to determine what additional sales volume (beyond that required to break even with the current cost structure) provides sufficient contribution margin to cover the additional fixed costs. It will take the contribution margin from an additional 1,250 units ($10,000/$8 per unit) to cover the added fixed costs, and the break-even point is already 12,500 units, so the total number of units required to break even with the new cost structure is 13,750 (12,500 + 1,250).
   (b) $275,000. The most direct approach to this answer is to multiply the number of units (13,750) computed in part (a) by the selling price per unit ($20). Or, the answer could be determined by dividing the fixed costs ($110,000) by the contribution margin percentage (40%).
8. 625 units. Income will not be affected as long as the contribution margin from the additional units sold is sufficient to offset the expenditure for advertising. Hence, we need to determine only what additional sales will produce contribution margin sufficient to cover the cost of the advertising. Because contribution margin per unit is $8, the number of units needed to cover the $5,000 advertising campaign is $5,000/$8 or 625 units. (Note that the current level of sales is irrelevant to the decision of whether or not to undertake the advertising campaign. As long as the campaign will increase sales by 625 units, Glassman will be neither better nor worse off than it would have been without it.)
9. 7,500 units, or 37.5%. At sales of 20,000 units Glassman earns $60,000 (20,000 × $8 – $100,000) and the break-even point is 12,500 units (from question 2).
10. 15,000 units. Fixed costs fall to $85,000 under the proposal and variable costs increase to $13 ($12 + .05 × $20).

Total Costs Now		Total Costs Under Proposal
$100,000 + $12*Q*	=	$85,000 + $13*Q*
$1*Q*	=	$15,000
Q	=	15,000

Below 15,000 units the proposed method is more profitable for Glassman, while above 15,000 units the existing method gives higher profit. Note that this situation differs from one in which the company was changing the way it manufactures a product. The method of manufacture probably does not affect the sales of the product (quality remaining constant). But for Glassman motivational questions might arise. The salespeople might sell more units under one method than they would under the other. We cannot be certain which method would better motivate the salespeople.

This review problem has emphasized the possibility of changes in the structure of costs and selling prices. Managers must be alert for changes from outside (for example, a supplier raising prices) and should understand their effects on profits. Additionally, managers can analyze changes that they propose to see if they will increase profits. Question 8 of this problem gave an important practical example: an increase in a fixed cost was expected to lead to some increase in volume. If the marketing manager believes that the added cost will generate additional sales in excess of 625 units, the proposal for additional advertising would be wise.

APPENDIX: INCOME TAXES AND PROFIT PLANNING

Income taxes are a cost of doing business and should be considered, as should all costs, in the planning process. Income taxes are based on the amount of income before taxes. For our purposes, it is reasonable to assume that income taxes are a constant percentage of income before taxes. In most large corporations, this assumption is reasonable, but we hasten to point out that tax law is exceedingly complex, not all businesses are incorporated, and generalizations are risky.

Income taxes must be considered if managers seek an *after-tax* target profit. An after-tax target requires a revision of the basic target-profit formula. The revision requires converting the after-tax target profit to a pretax profit, which is accomplished by dividing the after-tax target profit by the quantity 1 minus the income tax rate. For example, suppose Ted wants to earn an after-tax profit of \$2,100 and his tax rate is 30%. To earn \$2,100 after taxes, Ted must earn \$3,000 before taxes (\$2,100/70%). Of the pretax income of \$3,000, \$900 goes to the government (\$3,000 × 30%), leaving \$2,100 (\$3,000 – \$900). Accordingly, when the target is an after-tax profit, the basic formula for calculating the volume needed to achieve the target is as follows:

$$\textit{Sales to achieve target after-tax profit} = \frac{\textit{fixed costs} + \dfrac{\textit{after-tax profit}}{1 - \textit{tax rate}}}{\textit{contribution margin percentage} \text{ or } \textit{contribution margin per unit}}$$

We already know that Ted's fixed costs are \$4,800 and that his contribution margin percentage is 40%. Solving the above formula for sales dollars to achieve a \$2,100 profit after taxes gives

$$\textit{Sales} = \frac{\$4{,}800 + \dfrac{\$2{,}100}{70\%}}{40\%} = \frac{\$4{,}800 + \$3{,}000}{40\%} = \frac{\$7{,}800}{40\%} = \$19{,}500$$

We could calculate the unit sales required either by dividing $19,500 sales by the $20 selling price, or by dividing the $8 contribution margin per unit into the $7,800 (fixed costs plus required pretax profit). Either way, the answer is 975 shirts.

You needn't concern yourself with any formulas beyond those in the chapter if you recognize that the key step in both of the above calculations was converting an after-tax target ($2,100) to a before-tax target ($3,000). That conversion is the key whether the target is an absolute dollar amount of profit or a specific ROS.

To demonstrate, suppose Ted's target is an after-tax ROS of 14%. Once again, his after-tax target is 70% (1 minus the 30% income tax rate) of a before-tax target; so his *before-tax* ROS target is 20% (14%/70%). Using the formula on page 36, the sales target is $24,000, as shown below.

$$\textit{Sales, in dollars, to achieve target ROS} = \frac{\$4{,}800}{40\% - 20\%} = \$24{,}000$$

The income statement below, with both dollar amounts and percentages of sales, shows that sales of $24,000 will produce the after-tax ROS target of 14%.

Sales	$24,000	100%
Variable costs	14,400	
Contribution margin	9,600	40%
Fixed costs	4,800	
Income before taxes	4,800	20%
Income taxes, at 30%	1,440	
Net income	$ 3,360	14%

One final reminder. Planning for income taxes is important if the entity is subject to income taxes and if there is income to tax. Therefore, income taxes do not affect the determination of the break-even point, at which there is no income to tax.

ASSIGNMENT MATERIAL

QUESTIONS FOR DISCUSSION

2-1 ***CVP assumptions*** You have been trying to convince a friend to use CVP analysis in planning her business, a clothing store. She has come up with the following objections to using the analysis and asks you to explain how to overcome them, if possible.

1. Inflation makes it likely that she will have to pay successively higher prices for the utilities, clothing she buys, the salaries she pays employees, and other operating costs. In addition, she will raise her selling prices as her costs rise. Therefore, she cannot use the current prices and costs to plan operations.
2. She sometimes advertises heavily, sometimes lightly. Because she can alter advertising cost almost at will, she wonders how you can treat it as fixed.

3. On occasion, she must sell clothes at greatly reduced prices to make room for new merchandise. Therefore, the percentage of the purchase price to the selling price is not always constant, and she is unsure whether that can be worked into the analysis.

Required
Respond to these objections.

2-2 ***Misconceptions about CVP analysis*** A classmate is having trouble with CVP analysis and asks for your help. He has the following questions.

1. "How can CVP analysis work when you really don't know what's going to happen? You might have to change your selling price. Your suppliers might change their prices. You might not sell the number of units you need to sell in order to earn a target profit. All sorts of things can happen that will invalidate your calculations."
2. "When I took economics, I learned that the higher the price, the less you sell. So how can you draw a straight revenue line?"
3. "I don't see how you can say that some costs are fixed. I'll accept depreciation and a few others, but salaries can be raised or lowered easily, your insurance premiums can go up or down, you can spend more or less on advertising, travel, and all sorts of other elements that you would call fixed."

Required
Answer your classmate's questions.

2-3 ***Will Sears' stockholders understand?*** The following statement appeared in the Sears, Roebuck and Co. report to stockholders for the first quarter of a recent year.

Traditional buying patterns in the merchandise business generally result in the lowest sales of the year in the first quarter, producing a relatively high ratio of fixed costs to sales and lower ratio of income to sales.

Required
Discuss this statement in relation to the concepts introduced in Chapter 2 and the traditional, late-January "white sales" at most department stores.

EXERCISES

2-4 ***Income statement and CVP analysis*** The following data are available for Abbot Company's one product.

Unit selling price	$10
Unit variable cost	$8
Total fixed costs	$80,000
Unit volume	60,000

Required

1. Prepare an income statement using the contribution margin format.
2. Determine the break-even point in (a) units and (b) sales dollars.

3. Determine the (a) unit volume and (b) dollar volume required to earn a 10% return on sales.
4. Determine the price that the company must charge to double the profit you determined in item 1, still selling 60,000 units.

2-5 Income statement and CVP analysis The following data relate to Barton Company.

Sales	$800,000
Variable cost percentage	40%
Total fixed costs	$450,000

Required
1. Prepare an income statement using the contribution margin format.
2. Determine the break-even point in sales dollars.
3. Determine the dollar volume required to double the profit you determined in item 1.

2-6 Income statement and CVP analysis with taxes (related to Appendix) Use the data from 2-4 for this assignment. Also assume a 30% income tax rate.

Required
1. Prepare an income statement.
2. Determine the (a) unit volume and (b) dollar volume required to double the after-tax profit you determined in item 1.
3. Determine the selling price that will double the before-tax profit at the original volume.

2-7 Income statement and CVP analysis with taxes (related to Appendix) Use the data from 2-5 for this assignment. Also assume a 40% income tax rate.

Required
1. Prepare an income statement.
2. Determine the dollar volume required to double the after-tax profit you determined in item 1.

2-8 Basic CVP analysis Sea-Crest Company sells frozen fish dinners to supermarkets for $30 per case. Variable cost is $12 per case and annual fixed costs are $600,000.

Required
1. Determine the break-even point in (a) units and (b) dollars.
2. Determine the volume required to earn a $120,000 profit in (a) units and (b) dollars.
3. Determine the volume required to earn a 15% return on sales in (a) units and (b) dollars.
4. If Sea-Crest can sell 30,000 cases, what price would it have to charge to earn a $100,000 profit?
5. Redo item 4 assuming that the variable cost of $12 consists of $9 related to the case and a 10% commission on sales ($3 per case at the $30 price).

2-9 Basic CVP relationships, with income taxes (related to Appendix) In one of its factories, M&J Company manufactures a single type of water pump sold to auto parts dealers throughout the country. M&J sells the pump for $30. Variable costs are $12 and annual fixed costs are $2,000,000. The tax rate is 40%.

Required

1. Determine the volume required to earn a $300,000 after-tax profit in (a) units and (b) dollars.
2. If M&J can sell 150,000 pumps, what price would it have to charge to earn a $300,000 after-tax profit?
3. Redo item 2 assuming that the variable cost of $12 consists of $9 for manufacturing and a 10% commission on sales ($3 per pump at the $30 price).

2-10 Relationships among variables Fill in the blanks for each of the following independent situations.

Case	(a) Selling Price per Unit	(b) Variable Cost Percentage	(c) Number of Units Sold	(d) Contribution Margin	(e) Fixed Costs	(f) Income (Loss)
1.	$80	—	4,000	$80,000	—	($10,000)
2.	40	60%	—	—	$60,000	18,000
3.	25	—	15,000	—	25,000	50,000

2-11 Relationships among variables Fill in the blanks for each of the following independent situations.

	1	2	3
Selling price per unit	$ 5	—	—
Variable cost per unit	$ 3	$ 6	$ 6
Number of units sold	—	4,000	1,000
Total contribution margin	$4,000	$16,000	$2,000
Total fixed costs	$1,500	$ 8,000	—
Income	—	—	$1,200

2-12 CVP graph The graph on the next page portrays the operations of Richmond Company.

Required

Using the graph, determine the following.

1. Sales dollars at the break-even point.
2. Fixed costs at 4,500 units sold.
3. Total variable costs at 4,000 units sold.
4. Variable cost per unit at 2,000 units sold.
5. Variable cost per unit at 5,000 units sold.
6. Selling price per unit.
7. Total contribution margin at 3,000 units sold.
8. Profit (loss) at sales of 3,000 units.
9. Profit (loss) at sales of 5,000 units.
10. Break-even sales, in units, if fixed costs were to increase by $500.

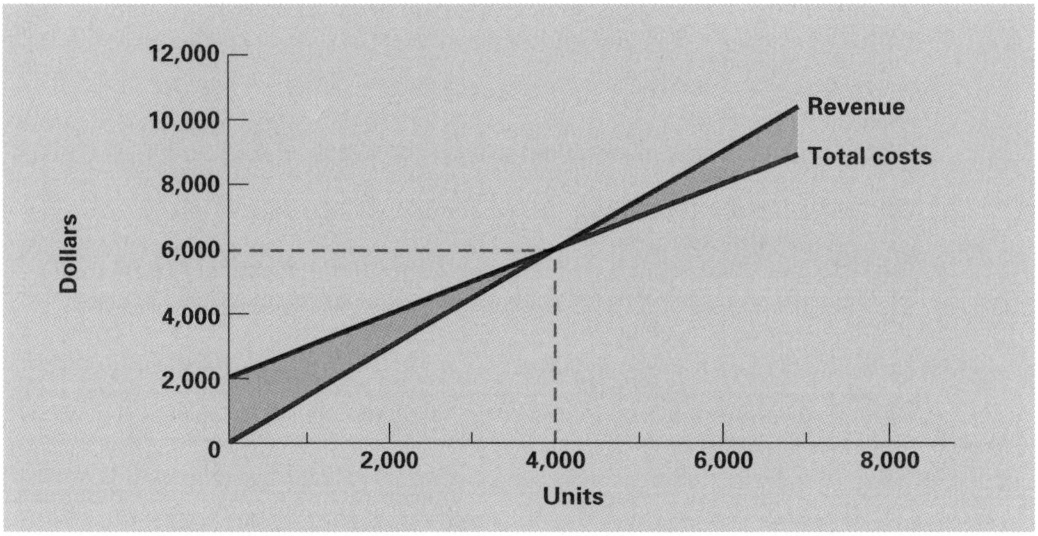

2-13 Graphs of cost behavior The graphs below depict the behavior of costs in relation to volume.

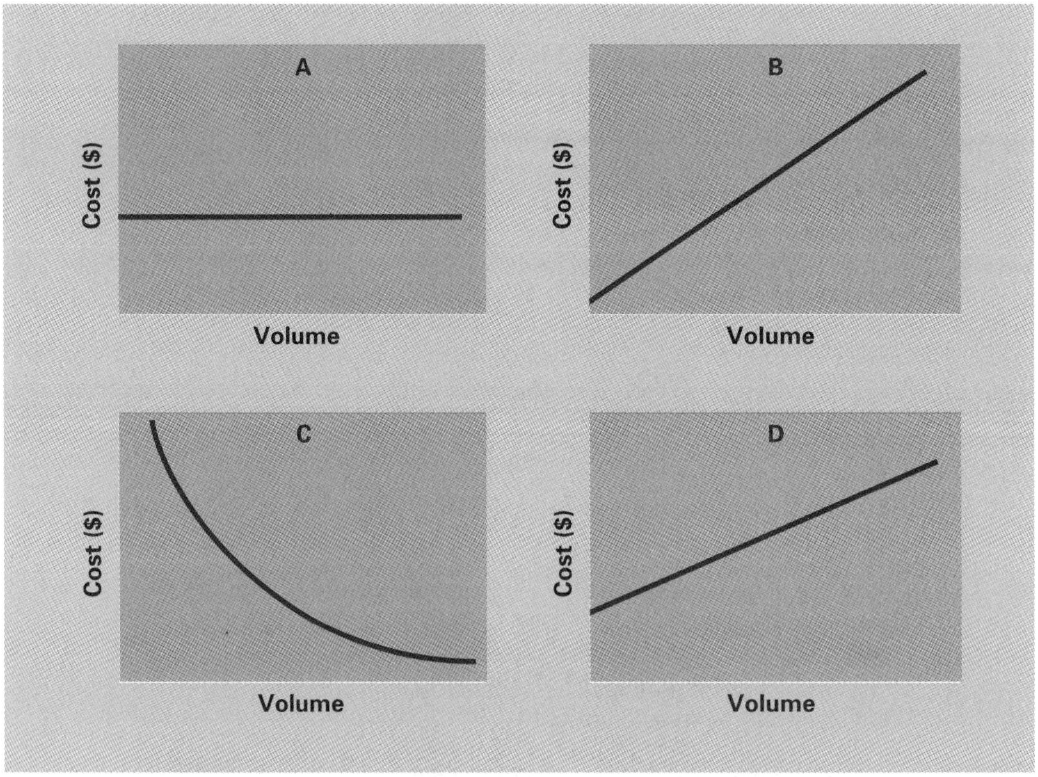

Required

Fill in the blanks using the letters from the graphs (A-D). One letter may be the answer to more than one question.

1. Which graph shows the behavior of total variable costs? ______
2. Which graph shows the behavior of total fixed costs? ______
3. Which graph shows the behavior of variable costs per unit? ______

4. Which graph shows the behavior of fixed costs per unit? ______
5. Which graph shows the behavior of total costs? ______

2-14 ***CVP chart*** The chart below portrays the operations of Weyand Company.

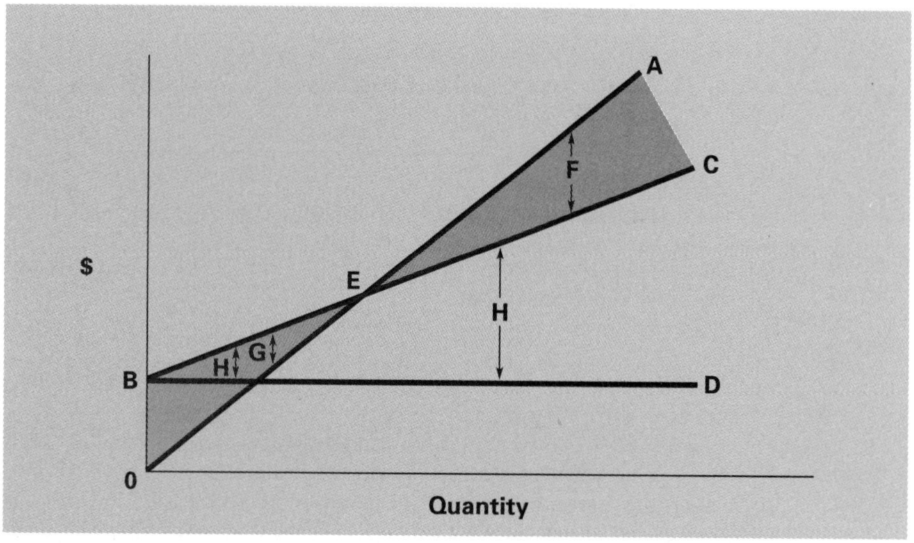

Required
Fill in the blanks with the appropriate letter(s) from the chart. You may have to indicate additions or subtractions.

1. Revenue line ______
2. Variable costs ______
3. Fixed costs ______
4. Profit area ______
5. Loss area ______
6. Total cost line ______
7. Break-even point ______
8. Contribution margin ______

2-15 ***Margin of safety*** Trivia Inc. plans to market a new electronic game. The game would sell for $120, and Trivia expects sales to be 11,000 units. Per-unit variable manufacturing cost is $82. The only other variable cost is a 15% sales commission. The fixed costs associated with this game are $160,000.

Required
Compute the margin of safety at the expected sales volume.

2-16 ***Alternative CVP graph (extension of previous assignment)*** The managers of Trivia Inc. have determined that the new game could also be brought out using a different combination of production and marketing strategies. The alternative strategies would reduce per-unit variable manufacturing cost to $71, but annual fixed costs would increase to $175,000 and the sales commission would be raised to 20%.

Required
In a CVP graph like Exhibit 2-3, plot the results of the two alternatives that Trivia is considering.

2-17 CVP graph, analysis of changes You have prepared a CVP graph for NMA Shoes. It reflects the following expectations.

Selling price	$50
Unit variable cost	$30
Total fixed costs	$400,000

NMA's managers are wondering what the effects will be on operations if some changes take place, either by management decision or by some outside force such as the prices charged by a supplier. The following specific changes are the most likely possibilities.

a. A decrease in the selling price resulting from greater-than-expected competition.
b. A decrease in unit variable cost arising from a decision to use less expensive leather in the shoes.
c. An increase in total fixed costs accompanied by a decrease in unit variable cost from introducing labor-saving machinery.
d. A decrease in the number of units expected to be sold.
e. An increase in the selling price combined with an increase in unit variable cost resulting from a decision to increase the quality of the product.

Required
Treat each change independently of the others. For each, state the effects on (a) the revenue line, (b) the total cost line, and (c) the break-even point. Some changes will have no effect on one or more of the items. In at least one case, the effect on the break-even point cannot be determined without additional information. Note that both the intercept and slope of the total cost line could be affected by a set of changes.

2-18 Converting an income statement Sandy Goode, president of SG Enterprises, has given you the following income statement for a recent month.

Sales		$250,000
Cost of goods sold		150,000
Gross profit		100,000
Operating expenses:		
Salaries and commissions	$42,000	
Utilities	11,200	
Rent	13,300	
Other	23,000	89,500
Profit		$ 10,500

SG sells one product, an exercise glove, at $20 per pair. Cost of goods sold is variable. A 10% sales commission, included in salaries and commissions, is the only other variable cost. Goode tells you that the income statement is not helpful, for she cannot determine such things as the break-even point or the price that will achieve a target profit.

Required

1. Redo the income statement using the contribution margin format.
2. Determine the break-even point in (a) units and (b) dollars.
3. Determine the price that would give a $15,000 profit at 12,500 units. The cost of the product is a constant $12 per unit.

2-19 Target costing Managers of TNC Enterprises are thinking about a new product in the industrial electronics area. TNC has considerable technical expertise in the field but has never entered the segment of the market in which the new product would compete. Before writing specifications for performance, the managers want to determine what costs are allowable. They estimate sales of 200,000 units per year at a $100 selling price. They also want a profit of $6,000,000.

Required

1. Determine the total costs that TNC can incur and meet its profit objective.
2. Suppose that the designers, engineers, and manufacturing managers estimate that annual fixed costs will be about $9,000,000 per year. Find the maximum per-unit variable cost that TNC can incur and meet its profit objective.

2-20 Profit planning Tinney Company, a wholesaler of jeans, had the following income statement in 19X5.

Sales (40,000 pairs at $15)		$600,000
Cost of sales		300,000
Gross margin		300,000
Selling expenses	$150,000	
Administrative expenses	90,000	240,000
Income		$ 60,000

Mr. Tinney informs you that the only variable costs are cost of sales and $2 per-unit selling costs. All administrative expenses are fixed. In planning for the coming year, 19X6, Mr. Tinney expects his selling price to remain constant, with unit volume increasing by 20%. He also forecasts the following changes in costs.

Variable costs:	
Cost of goods sold	up $0.50 per unit
Selling costs	up $0.10 per unit
Fixed costs:	
Selling costs	up $10,000
Administrative costs	up $15,000

Required

1. Prepare an income statement for 19X6 using the contribution margin format and assuming that all forecasts are met.
2. Determine the number of units that Tinney will have to sell in 19X6 to earn the same profit it did in 19X5.

3. If 19X6 volume is 48,000 units, what selling price will earn $60,000? All variable costs are constant per unit.

2-21 Basic income taxes (related to Appendix) Mayes Company is introducing an electronic printer that will sell for $140. Unit variable manufacturing cost is $106, and Mayes pays a 10% sales commission. Fixed costs for the printer are $150,000 per year. The tax rate is 40%.

Required

1. Determine the profit after taxes that Mayes would earn selling 12,000 printers.
2. Determine the number of units that Mayes has to sell to earn an after-tax profit of $75,000.
3. Determine the price that Mayes has to charge to earn a $100,000 pretax profit selling 11,000 units.

PROBLEMS

2-22 Indifference point Travelco sells one of its products, a piece of soft-sided luggage, for $40. Variable cost per unit is $20, and monthly fixed costs are $60,000. A combination of changes in the way Travelco produces and sells this product could reduce per-unit variable cost to $16 but would increase monthly fixed costs to $84,000.

Required

1. Determine the monthly break-even points under the two available alternatives.
2. Determine the indifference point of the two alternatives.

2-23 Cost structure Ben Skove, the owner of SKE Company, is trying to decide which of two machines to rent. He needs a machine to sand the surfaces of a picnic table that SKE manufactures. Data related to the two alternatives are

	Hand-Fed Machine	Automatic Machine
Annual rental payments	$12,000	$36,000
Other annual fixed costs	88,000	92,000

Skove expects the variable cost per table to be $34 using the hand-fed machine and $27 using the automatic machine. He also expects annual volume of about 3,000 tables.

Required

1. Determine the total annual cost to manufacture 3,000 tables under each alternative.
2. Determine the annual volume of tables at which total manufacturing cost would be the same for each machine.

2-24 Changes in contribution margin Mr. Pahl, owner of Jeantown, a specialty clothing store, asks you for some advice. Last year, his business had the following income statement.

Sales (10,000 units at $20)	$200,000
Variable costs	100,000
Contribution margin	100,000
Fixed costs	50,000
Income	$ 50,000

Mr. Pahl expects variable costs to increase to $11 per unit in the coming year.

Required

1. Determine the volume that Mr. Pahl needs to earn $50,000 in the coming year.
2. Mr. Pahl decides to increase his selling price so that he can earn $50,000 next year with the same unit volume he had last year. (a) What price will achieve that objective? (b) What dollar sales will he have?
3. Suppose now that Mr. Pahl raises his price so that the contribution margin percentage is the same as it was last year. (a) What price will he set? (b) What dollar volume will give a $50,000 profit? (c) What is the unit volume?

2-25 Pricing and return on sales Rogers Construction Company builds steel structures for commercial and industrial customers. The buildings are various shapes and sizes, with the average price being $30 per square foot and the average variable cost $18 per square foot. Annual fixed costs are $5,000,000.

Required

Answer each of the following items independently.

1. Determine the volume that will give Rogers a 20% return on sales in (a) sales dollars and (b) square feet of construction.
2. If Rogers can sell 600,000 square feet of construction in the coming year, what selling price will give a $400,000 profit?
3. If Rogers can sell 600,000 square feet of construction in the coming year at $30, how high could variable cost per square foot rise and still allow Rogers to earn a $280,000 profit?
4. If variable cost increases to $22 per square foot and Rogers can sell 500,000 square feet, what price will give a $280,000 profit?

2-26 Per-unit data The controller of Walker Company provides the following per-unit analysis, based on a volume of 50,000 units.

Selling price		$20
Variable costs	$8	
Fixed costs	7	
Total costs		15
Profit		$ 5

Required

Answer each of the following questions independently of the others.

1. What total profit does Walker expect to earn?
2. What total profit should the company earn at 60,000 units?

3. What is its break-even point in units?
4. Walker's managers expect to increase volume to 55,000 units by spending an additional $40,000 on salaries for more salespeople. What total profit will Walker earn?
5. The managers expect to sell 60,000 units and want a $280,000 profit. What price per unit must the firm charge? Variable costs are constant per unit.
6. Redo item 5 assuming that the variable cost of $8 consists of a $6 purchase price and a 10% sales commission ($2 at the $20 price).

2-27 CVP analysis for a CPA firm Bret McConnell, a certified public accountant, has estimated the following fixed costs of operation for the coming year.

Office salaries	$42,000
Rent, utilities	21,000
Other	14,000
Total	$77,000

There are no variable costs as McConnell currently plans operations. He charges clients $70 per hour for his time.

Required
1. How many hours must McConnell work to earn a profit of $50,000?
2. McConnell is thinking about hiring one or two senior accounting majors from a local university for $8 per hour to do some routine work for his clients. He expects each to work about 300 hours, but about 30 of those hours (training and temporary idle time) will not be chargeable to clients. McConnell wants each student to provide at least $3,000 profit. What hourly rate must he charge for their time to achieve his objective?

2-28 Pricing decision—nursery school The Board of Directors of First Community Church is considering opening a nursery school. Members of the board agree that the school, which would be open to all children, should operate within $100 of the break-even point.

The school would be open for nine months each year, with two classes, one in the morning and one in the afternoon. The treasurer prepares an analysis of the expected costs of operating the school, based on conversations with members of other churches that run similar programs.

Salaries—teacher and assistant	$16,400 for nine months
Utilities	$800 for nine months
Miscellaneous operating costs	$300 for nine months
Supplies, paper, paint	$2 per child per month
Snacks, cookies, juice	$4 per child per month

The best estimate of enrollment is 20 children in each of the two classes, which is all that the teacher and assistant can handle and still achieve the quality that the board feels is essential.

Required
1. Determine the monthly fee per child that would have to be charged for the school to break even (round to nearest dollar) with its maximum enrollment.
2. If the monthly fee is $60, what is the break-even point in enrollment?

2-29 *Sensitivity of variables* Cranston Jellies expects the following results in 19X5.

Planned sales in cases—19X5	40,000
Selling price	$20
Variable costs	$14
Total fixed costs	$200,000

Required
Answer the following questions, considering each independently.

1. Which of the following would reduce planned profit the most:
   (a) A 10% decrease in selling price?
   (b) A 10% increase per case in variable costs?
   (c) A 10% increase in fixed costs?
   (d) A 10% decrease in sales volume?
2. Which of the following would increase planned profit the most:
   (a) A 10% increase in selling price?
   (b) A 10% decrease per case in variable costs?
   (c) A 10% increase in sales volume?
   (d) A 10% decrease in fixed costs?
3. If the selling price declined by 10%, how many cases would have to be sold to achieve the planned profit?
4. If the selling price increased by 20%, by how much could variable cost per case increase and the planned profit be achieved?

2-30 *CVP analysis—changes in variables* During two recent months the Thompson Company had the following income statements.

	March	April
Sales	$200,000	$216,000
Variable costs	130,000	120,600
Contribution margin	70,000	95,400
Fixed costs	40,000	40,000
Income	$ 30,000	$ 55,400

You learn that the price of the product Thompson sells generally changes each month, though its purchase cost is stable at $11 per unit. The only other variable cost is a 10% commission paid on all sales.

Required
Determine the selling price, unit volume, and variable cost per unit in each of the two months.

2-31 *Changes in cost structure* Manfred Company makes a product with variable production costs of $6 per unit. The production manager has been approached by a salesperson from a machinery maker. The salesperson offers a machine for rent for five years on a noncancelable lease at $24,000 per year. The production manager expects to save $0.40 per unit in variable manufacturing costs using the machine.

Required

1. Determine the annual unit production that would make renting the machine and continuing with current operations yield the same profit to the firm.
2. Suppose that the expected volume is 80,000 units per year. Determine the change in the firm's annual profit that would occur if the firm were to rent the machine.
3. Would you be more likely or less likely to rent the machine if the lease were cancelable at your option rather than noncancelable for a five-year period? Explain your answer.

2-32 ***Cost structure*** Michael Cooper owns a beauty parlor. He has some space and wants to install a tanning bed. His estimates below are based on observations and discussions with knowledgeable people.

Annual volume, 2 hour sessions	800
Price per session	$6.00
Variable cost per session, mostly electricity	$0.80

Michael can lease a suitable bed from a manufacturer for $2,000 per year. He can also lease one for $1,200 per year plus $1.50 per two hours session. The beds have instruments to verify use. There are no other fixed costs.

Required

1. Suppose that Michael leases the bed for $2,000. (a) Determine the expected profit from the bed. (b) What is break-even volume in number of sessions?
2. Redo item 1 assuming that Michael elects the $1,200 plus $1.50 per session option.
3. Which lease arrangement would you prefer? Write a memorandum using the guidelines of Appendix B to support your position.

2-33 ***CVP analysis on new business*** Some managers of Harter Enterprises, a medium-sized manufacturer of dress gloves, want to branch out from the company's traditional business into exercise gloves. Doing so requires leasing additional equipment for $550,000 per year. Other fixed costs associated with the new venture—including new personnel, advertising, and promotion—are estimated at $380,000 annually.

The variable cost of the new glove is expected to be about $7 per pair and the selling price about $15 per pair. The managers are reluctant to try the new gloves unless they can be fairly confident of earning $150,000.

Required

1. Determine how many pairs Harter must sell to earn the target profit on the new gloves.
2. The marketing people believe that unit sales will be 120,000 units. What selling price will yield the target profit at that volume?
3. Suppose again that 120,000 units is the best estimate of volume and that Harter will stick with the $15 price. How much must Harter reduce the expected variable cost to meet the profit target?

2-34 ***CVP analysis for a hospital*** The administrator of the Caldwell Memorial Hospital is considering methods of providing X-ray treatments to patients. The hospital now refers about 200 patients per month to a nearby private clinic, and each treatment costs the patient $65. If the hospital provides the treatment, a machine will be rented for $2,200 per month and technicians will be hired for $3,600 per month. Variable costs are $10 per treatment.

Required

1. The administrator considers charging the same fee as the clinic. By how much will the hospital increase its income if it provides the service?
2. How much must the hospital charge to break even on the treatments?

2-35 CVP in a service business Microprog develops microcomputer programs to customer order, primarily for business applications. The company charges its customers $40 per hour for programming time. The managers are planning operations for the coming year and have developed the following estimates.

Total estimated chargeable hours	80,000
Total fixed costs, salaries, rent, etc.	$1,750,000

Microprog employs 15 full-time programmers at an average salary of $30,000. These salaries are included in the cost figure given above. Each programmer works about 2,000 chargeable hours per year. The company does not wish to hire additional programmers, but rather wants to use free-lancers to meet demand. Free-lancers charge an average of $25 per hour.

Required

1. If the company meets its goal of 80,000 chargeable hours, what profit will it earn?
2. How many chargeable hours must it obtain from free-lancers, in addition to the hours its full-time programmers work, to earn a $300,000 profit?

2-36 Developing CVP information The manager of Sans Flavour Food Store, a franchise operation, is confused by the income statements she has received from her accountant. She asks you to help her with them. She is especially concerned that her return on sales dropped much more than sales from April to May.

	April	May
Sales	$100,000	$80,000
Cost of sales	40,000	32,000
Gross profit	60,000	48,000
Operating expenses:		
Rent	1,200	1,200
Salaries, wages, commissions	34,500	30,500
Insurance	1,100	1,100
Supplies	2,000	1,600
Utilities	1,500	1,500
Miscellaneous expenses	6,000	6,000
Total operating expenses	46,300	41,900
Income	$ 13,700	$ 6,100
Return on sales	13.7%	7.6%

The manager informs you that the salaries, wages, and commissions account includes the salaries of several clerks and himself, as well as commissions. All salespeople earn commissions of 20% of sales. Supplies are primarily wrapping paper and tape and vary directly with sales. The manager had expected the $20,000 decline in sales, but expected income of $10,960, 13.7% of expected sales. She is now concerned that income will continue to be 7.6% of sales.

Required
Prepare income statements using the contribution margin format for April and May, and explain to the manager the advantages of this alternative format.

2-37 Margin of safety Nelson Wallet Company is considering two new wallets for introduction during the coming year. Because of a lack of production capacity, only one will be brought out. Data on the two wallets are given below.

	Model 440	Model 1200
Expected sales	$200,000	$250,000
Expected contribution margin	60,000 (30%)	150,000 (60%)
Expected fixed costs for production, advertising, promotion, etc.	39,000	120,000
Expected annual profit	$21,000	$30,000

Required
1. Determine the margins of safety for each wallet, in dollars and as percentages of expected sales.
2. Suppose that the firm is relatively conservative; its top managers do not like to take significant risks unless the potential profits are extremely high. Which wallet would you recommend be introduced? Why? Explain in a memorandum using the guidelines of Appendix B in the back of the book.

2-38 Changes in operations Bart Packard operates the 15th Street Parking Lot, leasing the lot from the owner at $12,000 per month plus 10% of sales. Packard is thinking about staying open until midnight. He now closes at 7:00 P.M. Keeping the lot open requires paying an additional $800 per week to attendants, with increases in utilities and insurance being another $100 per week. The lot must pay a 5% city tax on its total revenue. The parking charge is $0.80 per hour.

Required
1. Suppose that Packard expects additional business amounting to 2,000 hours per week. Should he stay open until midnight?
2. How much additional business, stated in hours, does Packard need to break even on the additional hours of operation?

2-39 Converting income statement to contribution margin basis Clarkston Manufacturing Company has been profitable over the past few quarters and the top managers are taking steps to continue the increased profitability. The most recent quarterly income statement appears on the next page. All amounts are in thousands.

Sales		$3,882.6
Cost of sales:		
Materials and parts	$763.3	
Labor	588.1	
Fringe benefits	69.0	
Repairs and maintenance	322.1	
Depreciation	189.2	
Supplies	56.1	
Power	118.6	
Miscellaneous	47.8	2,154.2
Gross margin		1,728.4
Operating expenses:		
Sales, salaries, and commissions	$489.2	
Sales expenses	112.7	
Advertising	377.4	
Administrative expenses	541.3	1,520.6
Income before taxes		$ 207.8
Unit volume		415.3

The controller is concerned about the format of the income statement, which has been in use for several years. The controller, relatively new to the job, prefers income statements that use the contribution margin format. After talks with the relevant managers, she determines the following.

	Variable Amount per Unit	Quarterly Fixed Amount
Materials and parts	$1.838	$ 0
Labor	1.416	0
Fringe benefits	0.166	0
Repairs and maintenance	0.323	188.0
Depreciation	0.000	189.2
Supplies	0.135	0
Power	0.131	64.2
Miscellaneous	0.032	34.5
Sales salaries and commissions	0.789	161.5
Sales expenses	0.124	61.2
Advertising	0.000	377.4
Administrative expenses	0.022	532.2

Required

1. Prepare a new income statement using the contribution margin format.
2. Comment on the differences between your statement and the one above. For example, what decisions are easier, or more difficult, to make with your statement?

2-40 ***Unit costs*** Carl Murphy owns a chain of shoe stores. He recently opened a store in a shopping mall and was not pleased with the results for the first month.

Sales		$80,000
Cost of sales		40,000
Gross margin		40,000
Salaries and wages	$23,000	
Utilities, insurance, rent	3,500	
Commissions at 15% of sales	12,000	38,500
Profit		$ 1,500

Noting that sales were 4,000 pairs at an average price of $20, Murphy calculates the per-pair cost at $19.625 ($78,500/4,000), leaving only a $0.375 profit per pair. He did expect sales to rise to 5,000 pairs at an average price of $20 over the next month or two, but he figured that profit would increase only to about $1,875 (5,000 × $0.375), which was still not adequate.

Murphy asks for your advice, and, in response to your questions, says that even with the increase in sales additional salaried personnel will not be needed and that utilities, insurance, and rent will remain about the same. The cost of sales percentage will also remain at 50%.

Required

Prepare an income statement based on sales of 5,000 pairs of shoes. If profit is different from Mr. Murphy's estimate, explain the fallacy in his reasoning.

2-41 CVP analysis and break-even pricing—municipal operation Gardendale operates a municipal trash collection service. Analyses of costs indicate that monthly fixed cost is $15,000 and variable cost is about $0.80 per pickup per customer. The city collects trash in the business district 12 times a month and in the residential districts four times a month. The difference in frequency results from the much larger volume of trash in the business district. There are 250 businesses and 1,500 residences served by trash collection.

Required

1. The city manager is aware that other cities charge business customers $20 per month and residential customers $6 per month. What profit or loss would the operation generate at these prices?
2. The city manager would like to break even or show a small profit on trash collection. She believes it is fair to charge businesses three times as much as residences because the businesses get three times as much service. What monthly prices would make the operation break even?

2-42 CVP analysis for a service business Walker Associates is a market research firm. Companies contact Walker Associates for various types of studies regarding consumers' preferences, and Walker develops a plan for the study. If the company approves the plan, Walker does the job.

Walker's business involves interviewing people near supermarkets, drugstores, and department stores. Walker hires part-timers to do the interviews for $9 per hour and pays such expenses as mileage and meals. These expenses average $11 per day per person. Each person works about six hours per day. Fixed costs associated with Walker's operation consist largely of salaries to the permanent staff. These, along with rent and utilities, total $400,000 per year.

Walker wants to develop a pricing policy based on an hourly rate, that is, charging the client company an amount per hour that Walker's part-time employees spend interviewing.

Required

1. Walker's managers expect enough business to require about 10,000 six-hour days of interviewing. What hourly charge will give a $75,000 profit?
2. Suppose that Walker sets the charge at $17 per hour. How many six-hour days must it achieve to earn a $75,000 profit?
3. Walker is considering using full-time, salaried interviewers rather than part-time people. What are some of the implications of such a change?

2-43 Alternative cost behavior—a movie company (continued in Chapters 3 and 4) Blockbusters Incorporated, a leading producer of movies, is currently negotiating with Sky Kirkwalker, the biggest box-office attraction in the movie industry, to star in *War Trek,* a science fiction film. For a starring role, Sky normally receives a salary of $1,500,000 plus 5% of the receipts-to-the-producer. (The producer normally receives 40% of the total paid admissions wherever the movie is shown.) However, Sky is quite optimistic about the prospects for *Trek* and has expressed some interest in a special contract that would give him only 25% of his normal salary but increase his portion of the receipts-to-the-producer to 20%. Other than Sky's pay, costs of producing the picture are expected to be $2,500,000.

Required

Answer the following questions, calling the alternative compensation schemes *N* (for the normal contract) and *S* (for the special contract).

1. What are the break-even receipts-to-the-producer under each of the compensation schemes?
2. If total paid admissions in theaters are expected to be $14,000,000, what will be the income to the producer under compensation schemes *N* and *S*?
3. At what level of receipts-to-the-producer would Sky earn the same total income under compensation schemes *N* and *S*?

2-44 Conversion of income statement to contribution margin basis The following income statement is prepared by the controller of Wassenich Company. Materials and labor are variable costs of manufacturing the product.

Wassenich Company
Income Statement for 19X4

Sales (10,000 units)		$120,000
Cost of goods sold:		
Materials	$30,000	
Labor	35,000	
Other manufacturing costs:		
Variable	16,000	
Fixed	14,000	95,000
Gross profit		25,000
Selling and administrative expenses:		
Variable	9,000	
Fixed	22,000	31,000
Loss		($ 6,000)

Required

1. Prepare a new income statement using the contribution margin format.
2. What is the break-even point in units?

3. The president believes that spending an additional $7,000 on advertising will increase sales by 4,000 units. His son, the general manager, says that would be silly because the firm is losing enough already. Is the son right?

2-45 Occupancy rate as measure of volume Norman Motels is a chain operating in small cities throughout the Midwest. Its most relevant measure of volume is the occupancy rate, the percentage of available rooms rented to guests. Monthly revenue is $100,000 per percentage point of occupancy. (For example, at 40% occupancy, revenue is $4,000,000.) Contribution margin is 70%, monthly fixed costs $4,200,000.

Required

1. Find the monthly break-even point in (a) dollars and (b) occupancy rate.
2. Determine Norman's profit at a 75% occupancy rate.
3. Determine the occupancy rate Norman needs to earn $700,000 per month.
4. Determine whether Norman should increase advertising $100,000 per month if doing so increases the occupancy rate by two percentage points.

2-46 Assumptions of CVP analysis Last year you were engaged as a consultant to Thompson Products Company and prepared some analyses of its CVP relationships. Among your findings was that the contribution margin percentage was 40% at the planned selling price of $20. The firm expected to sell 10,000, which you estimated would yield a $46,000 income. You told Ms. Thompson, the owner, that profit would change at the rate of $0.40 per $1 change in sales.

Ms. Thompson has just called to tell you that the results did not come out as you had said they would. The firm earned $63,200 on sales of $226,800. Variable costs per unit were incurred as expected, as were total fixed costs. Ms. Thompson was very pleased at the results. However, she asks you why profit did not increase by 40% of the added sales volume of $26,800, but rather by somewhat more.

Required

1. Prepare an income statement for the year, based on the actual results.
2. Determine (a) the number of units sold and (b) the selling price per unit.
3. Write a memorandum to Ms. Thompson explaining why the results were not as you had forecast. Use guidelines in Appendix B at the back of the book.

2-47 Cost structure Wink Company manufactures replacement parts for automobiles and sells them to distributors in the northeastern United States. The president of the firm wishes to begin selling in the Southeast but is uncertain how to expand most profitably. Two alternatives have been selected for final consideration. Under the first, Wink would use the services of independent sales representatives who would sell to distributors for a 15% commission. This plan would increase the clerical costs at the company's central office by $20,000 per year. Under the second alternative, Wink would hire its own salespeople to work on straight salary. Salaries for salespeople are estimated to be $100,000 per year; additionally, an office would be opened in the region and would cost $25,000 per year to operate.

The variable cost on parts is now 35%. The president is uncertain about demand in the Southeast and asks that you analyze profitability under both plans at various volumes. He selects $500,000, $700,000, $1,000,000, and $1,200,000 as the sales volumes to be used for comparison.

Required

Prepare a memorandum using the guidelines in Appendix B at the back of the *book.* Choose an alternative and defend your choice. Identify the nonquantified factors that are related to the alternatives.

CASES

2-48 A concessionaire Ralph Newkirk is considering a bid for the hot dog and soft drink concession at the 14 football games for the season. There will be seven college games and seven professional games. Average attendance at college games is 20,000, at professional games, 50,000. Ralph estimates that he sells one hot dog and one soft drink for each two persons attending a game.

Revenue and cost data are as follows.

	Hot Dogs	Soft Drinks
Selling price	$0.50	$0.30
Variable costs:		
Hot dog	0.080	
Roll	0.040	
Mustard, onion, etc.	0.005	
Soft drink and ice		0.125

In addition, salespeople earn a 15% commission on all sales. Fixed costs per game are $4,000 for rentals of heating, cooking, mixing, and cooling equipment.

The stadium management requests that bids be made in the form of royalties on sales. The highest percentage of sales bid will win the contract.

Required

1. What percentage of sales can Ralph pay as royalty to the stadium and earn $20,000 for the season? (Round to nearest one tenth of a percentage point.)
2. If Ralph bids 12% of sales, what income can he expect if operations go according to plan? (Is this consistent with your answer in item 1?)
3. Assuming a royalty of 12% of sales, what is Ralph's break-even point for the season, based on total attendance?
4. What kinds of information does Ralph need if he is also deciding to bid for the concession at baseball games at the same stadium?
5. Ralph has forecast attendance for football games. He then learns that the star quarterback of the local professional team will retire before the coming season. What effect does this information have on Ralph's planning?

2-49 Soccer camp Since Jean Longhurst has been head soccer coach at Oldberne College, she has enjoyed considerable success. Longhurst has coached at summer camps for children and now is considering a summer camp for Oldberne. The college would provide room and board for the campers at a price (see the next page) and would also take 10% of revenue. Longhurst asks you for advice. You say that some of the important factors are setting a price, estimating enrollment, and estimating costs. After a few weeks, Longhurst returns with the following information, gathered from various sources.

Average enrollment	90 campers
Average price for one-week camp	$ 190
Costs:	
Food, charged by college	$ 50 per camper
Insurance and T-shirts	$ 12 per camper
Room rent charged by college	$ 15 per camper
Coaches' salaries	$ 450 per coach
Brochures, mailing, miscellaneous	$2,800 total

Longhurst also says that other camps have typically employed one coach for each 15 campers, excluding the director (Longhurst in this case). One problem is that you generally need to engage the coaches before you know the enrollment, although it is usually possible to find one or two at the last minute. It is, however, necessary to engage some of the coaches early so that you can use their names in brochures. Furthermore, while the enrollment and price given above are averages, wide variations exist, with enrollments ranging from 40 to 120 and prices ranging from $160 to $230. As might be expected, the better-known camps have higher enrollments at higher prices, but they also pay better, as high as $800 per week for a well-known coach. Longhurst will keep the profits and suffer the losses, and so she wants to be fairly confident before proceeding.

Required

1. If Longhurst hires enough coaches to meet the average enrollment and achieves all of the averages given above, what will her profit be?
2. If she wants to earn $4,000 and expects 100 campers, what price must she set?
3. The college offers to take over the cost of brochures, mailing, and miscellaneous ($2,800 estimated) in exchange for a higher share of the revenue. If Longhurst achieves the results from item 1 (meets the averages), what percentage of revenue will she be able to pay the college and earn the same profit expected in item 1?
4. Write a memorandum to Longhurst explaining the advantages and disadvantages to her and to the college of the proposed arrangements. Use the guidelines in Appendix B at the back of the book.

3 cost analysis

In Chapter 2 we knew how much cost was variable and how much was fixed and that variable costs varied only with sales. In practice, costs do not come with labels describing their behavior, so we must study them to determine their behavior and estimate their amounts. Some costs do not vary with sales, but with some other activity. For example, costs of materials and labor needed to manufacture a product vary with production, while some costs of the purchasing department vary with the number of vendors that the company uses and the number of parts and components the company buys. Some costs have both fixed and variable components. An example is the cost of water, which typically includes a minimum charge for being connected to the water system plus a charge that varies with the volume of water used. Analyzing such costs occupies a major portion of this chapter.

Identifying and analyzing the activities that cause costs is also important in cost management, and the chapter discusses a range of issues related to this topic. The chapter also introduces some other categories of costs that are useful for various purposes and refines the concepts of Chapter 2.

OBJECTIVES OF ANALYZING COSTS

From Chapter 2 you already know that managers must understand the behavior of costs to plan and make decisions. To plan income for a future period, managers must be able to predict costs for that period, which requires estimates of fixed and variable costs. Managers also need good estimates of variable cost so they can compute contribution margin. Much important planning and decision-making activity requires knowledge of contribution margin.

COST MANAGEMENT

Managers also must understand cost behavior to manage and control operations. Chapter 1 described some recent changes in the competitive environment, especially the emergence of companies that compete world-wide. That discussion showed that reducing costs and increasing quality have been critical to the success of many modern companies. Cost reduction is one key to increasing competitiveness and profitability *if* reduction can be achieved without sacrificing product quality; prompt delivery; technological superiority; and quick response to changing conditions, style, and fashion.

There are two basic aspects to managing costs: One is managing the cost itself—for instance, buying the needed raw materials at good prices. This aspect has traditionally been the principal focus of managerial accounting. The second, and often more important, aspect is managing the *activity* that causes the costs—for instance, finding ways to reduce the material content of a product without sacrificing quality. Managers are now paying much more attention to this aspect.

MANAGING ACTIVITIES—COST DRIVERS AND COST POOLS

To manage costs effectively, managers first identify the activities that *cause* specific costs. These activities are **cost drivers** and include sales, production, and various other activities such as the number of products the company makes and the number of customers served. A group of costs driven by the same activity is a **cost pool**. A cost pool might consist of all of the costs incurred by a department, such as the assembly department in a factory. A pool also could consist of only some of the costs of a department. For instance, some costs of the purchasing department are driven by the number of purchase orders, while other costs have other drivers, such as the number of vendors the company uses. A pool also could consist of some of the costs of more than one department. Some costs of payroll and personnel departments are driven by the number of employees.

As later sections of this chapter show, identifying cost drivers and their associated cost pools is an important step in estimating the behavior of the cost. Identifying cost drivers also enables managers to focus their attention where it is likely to do the most good.

For example, an activity such as setting up machines to run particular products drives a pool of $250,000 annual costs; and another activity such as storing materials and components drives a pool of only $30,000 annual costs. Managers are likely to reduce costs more by concentrating on doing fewer machine setups, or doing them faster, than by trying to streamline storage procedures. Of course, all cost savings are helpful, but managers should concentrate their attention where the payoff will probably be the highest. Even if most of the costs of setups are fixed, large reductions in setups almost certainly will reduce the costs in the related pool.

After identifying a cost driver, managers estimate the fixed and variable components of each cost that is driven by that activity. The methods they use are explained throughout this chapter. But, even if managers fail to estimate successfully how much of a cost is fixed and and how much is variable, they can still manage costs better when they know what drives the cost.

For many years, labor activity—measured in hours or dollars—was the dominant driver of most other manufacturing costs. As manufacturing became more sophisticated, machines and computers took over many of the tasks that people had performed, and the labor required to make a product declined. Now, more costs are driven by such activities as procurement, machine setup, and recordkeeping than was once the case. This newer environment therefore has more cost drivers.

VALUE-ADDING AND NON-VALUE-ADDING ACTIVITIES

As managers came to understand the changed environment and identified some of the new cost drivers, they also looked harder at *why* cost-driving activities occur and whether they add value to the product. Some activities, such as acquiring materials, are clearly necessary to making the product. These activities are *value-adding activities.* Activities such as storing materials before they are needed and moving them into and out of warehouses are *non-value-adding activities* because they do not make the product more valuable to the customer. Of course, disagreements will occur about activities at the margin. Classifying activities as value-adding or non-value-adding is not always easy.

Non-value-adding activities are prime targets for cost-reduction efforts. Chapter 1 showed that companies utilizing JIT organize manufacturing cells to minimize movement of goods which reduces costs of that activity. Similarly, many companies now inspect for defects at each stage of production as a matter of course instead of making a separate, final inspection that was a non-value-adding activity. From efforts to avoid the non-value-adding activity of reworking defective units came the emphasis on quality work—doing things right the first time. The hallmark of JIT operations, minimal inventory, is a product of cost-reduction efforts directed at the non-value-adding storage activity.

Consider the different views taken by U.S. and Japanese auto makers. American auto makers try to keep cars on their assembly lines moving at all times. In contrast, Japanese companies try to have work being done on the cars at all times. Japanese companies want to be adding value to the cars at all times, rather than moving them more rapidly. In another example, a few years ago, Hewlett-Packard, the highly successful electronics company, simplified its accounting system in one plant. The company had been collecting considerable information about labor, but stopped after it went to a highly mechanized manufacturing process. As the company stopped collecting detailed information about labor, it was able to cut out some 100,000 journal entries per month and thereby experienced ". . . significant savings in staff time and costs . . ."[1]

1 *R. Hunt, L. Garrett, and C. M. Merz, "Direct Labor Not Always Relevant at H-P,"* Management Accounting, *February 1985, 58-62.*

Nonmanufacturing firms also have benefited from identifying non-value-adding activities. For example, many service companies discovered that the activity of following up on customers' complaints seldom added to customers' perception of value received. Such firms determined that improving the quality of the service initially provided was less costly than following up complaints.

In sum, identifying cost drivers is an important part of managing costs as well as estimating cost behavior for planning purposes. As illustrated later in this book, the increased attention to identifying cost drivers also has contributed to the development of activity-based costing, a relatively new approach to assigning costs to products.

ESTIMATING COST BEHAVIOR

Managers use several ways to determine the behavior of costs. The methods range from simple to sophisticated. Each method has advantages and disadvantages, and managers in most companies will use more than one method.

A **mixed** (or **semivariable**) cost has both a fixed component and a variable component. For example, maintenance costs are likely to have a fixed component related to normal preventive maintenance carried out more or less routinely every month. There is also likely to be a variable component related to the amount of machine use. Exhibit 3-1 shows the behavior of a mixed cost; the pattern is like that of total costs when both fixed and variable costs are present.

ACCOUNT ANALYSIS

A simple, yet sometimes effective, method of classifying the behavior of a cost is **account analysis**. Applying this method, the manager decides how to classify a cost by looking at its name and then checking this judgment by scanning the account for that cost for several periods. For instance, costs such as rent, depreciation, salaries, and advertising are generally fixed. If the amounts in the account for a cost vary only a little from month to month, it is likely that the cost is fixed. If the cost varies considerably from month to month, it is probably variable or mixed.

Exhibit 3-1 Mixed Cost Behavior

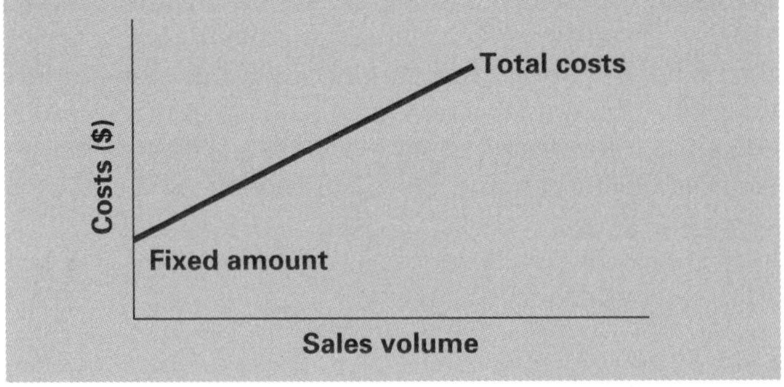

One weakness of account analysis is that the usefulness of the results depends heavily on the analyst's knowledge of the company. For example, Ted's rent in Chapter 2 was a variable cost (a percentage of sales); but it could be erroneously classified as fixed if sales changed little over the most recent months and the person doing the analysis didn't know the terms of the rental contract. The analyst's knowledge of the company is also critical because this method looks only at what cost *has been*, not at what cost *will be* in the periods being planned. But perhaps the most important weakness of this method is that the importance of identifying the cost-driving activity is ignored. Hence, account analysis is, at best, of limited usefulness.

ENGINEERING APPROACH

Another widely used method of ascertaining cost behavior is the *engineering approach*, which has been used most successfully to determine per-unit variable costs in manufacturing firms. Under this method, engineers study the material and labor requirements of products and related operations, then make per-unit estimates of the costs that should vary with production. The engineering approach has not been used as successfully when applied to nonmanufacturing costs.

An advantage of the engineering approach is that it indicates what costs *should be* rather than what they have been. This is important because simply knowing that, for instance, labor cost per unit of product has been $3.50 does not tell you that the labor is being used efficiently. For example, it could be that the company should be using a good deal less labor and that a cost of $2.80 is readily achievable if workers make changes in the way they do their jobs.

INTERVIEWS

A simple tool that has proven useful in determining what drives many costs is interviewing managers to determine what is likely to happen to particular costs, given specific actions. For instance, the purchasing manager probably could estimate what increase in workload might follow the introduction of a new product that requires parts not used in any other products. Using such parts would require evaluating new vendors, establishing testing procedures, doing paperwork, and so on. The new parts also could require additional personnel in purchasing, and perhaps in receiving and inspection.

Interviewing does not help determine how much of a particular cost is fixed or variable. But, it does help to identify cost drivers, which is an important part of applying the methods discussed in the remainder of this section. Interviewing might be useful in developing ballpark estimates of the effects of various decisions. For instance, a manufacturing manager might be able to tell a cost analyst how many additional people might be needed to speed up the introduction of a new product. The analyst could then put dollar amounts on the additional needs.

To aid the presentation of the remaining methods, we will use the following data related to maintenance costs of RFC Manufacturing Co. In this situation, we assume RFC already has identified hours of machine use as the cost-driving activity, *and* that all of the observations are within the relevant range.

Machine Hours	Maintenance Cost
5,000	$14,800
10,800	28,200
12,200	27,300
7,300	19,100
10,000	25,400
8,100	24,900
18,000	40,800
13,400	31,800
5,400	18,100
14,100	31,900
15,100	36,100
17,300	35,900

TWO-POINT (HIGH-LOW) METHOD

A relatively unsophisticated, yet widely used, method of estimating the components of a mixed cost is the **two-point** (or **high-low**) **method**. This method uses two past levels of activity and the amounts of the cost incurred at those levels. The high and low points of the name are the highest and lowest levels of activity (as opposed to the highest and lowest costs) within the relevant range. To find the variable component of the cost, divide the difference in cost at the two levels by the difference in volumes of the cost-driving activity. The formula for finding the variable cost factor in a mixed cost is

$$\textit{Variable cost component of mixed cost} = \frac{\textit{change in cost}}{\textit{change in activity}}$$

Using our example,

$$\begin{aligned}\textit{Variable cost component of mixed cost} &= \frac{\$40{,}800 - \$14{,}800}{18{,}000 - 5{,}000} \\ &= \$26{,}000/13{,}000 \\ &= \$2 \textit{ per machine hour}\end{aligned}$$

Because the total cost at *any* volume equals total variable cost at that volume plus total fixed cost, the fixed component of the total cost equals the difference between the total cost and the total variable cost at that volume. In formula notation this becomes, using the high volume:

$$\textit{Fixed cost component of mixed cost} = \textit{total cost at high volume} - \left(\textit{high volume} \times \textit{variable cost component}\right)$$

At 18,000 machine hours,

Total cost	$40,800
Less variable portion (18,000 × $2)	36,000
Fixed component	$ 4,800

We get the same answer using the low volume, at 5,000 machine hours.

Total cost	\$14,800
Less variable portion (5,000 × \$2)	10,000
Fixed component	\$ 4,800

The formula that RFC can then use to predict maintenance cost is:

Total maintenance cost = \$4,800 + (\$2 × machine hours)

The rationale for the method is best understood if you recognize that your goal—a cost prediction formula—is nothing more than a formula to describe a straight line such as that in Exhibit 3-1. The *general* formula for a straight line is: $y = a + bx$, with b being the slope of the line and a the point where the line intercepts the y axis. The formula given above for determining the variable component of a mixed cost computes b, the slope of the line. The formula given for determining the fixed component is equivalent to solving the general formula for a when you know b (the slope), x (a level of the cost-driving, independent, activity represented by the x axis), and y (the value of the dependent variable, total cost, at that activity-level).[2]

At this point remember that the volume levels used when applying the high-low method must be within the relevant range if the resulting cost prediction formula is to be useful. (Remember from Chapter 2 that the relevant range is that over which per-unit variable cost and total fixed cost can be expected to remain constant.) The two-point (high-low) method has some serious disadvantages, which will become clearer as we discuss the next method of analyzing costs.

SCATTER-DIAGRAM METHOD

Like the high-low method, the **scatter-diagram** (or **graphical**) **method**, requires cost and volume data from prior periods, and derives an equation (cost prediction formula) based on those data. Again, the goal is a cost prediction formula of the form: $y = a + bx$.

The first step is to plot points that represent total cost at various levels of activity within the relevant range. The dots in Exhibit 3-2 show the maintenance cost that RFC incurred at various levels of machine hours. The second step is to draw a line as close to all the points as possible. (Exhibit 3-2 shows such a line.) The placement and slope of the line are matters of judgment; the manager "eyeballs" the data and fits the line visually.

Once the line is drawn, the fixed and variable components of the cost are found in the following manner. The fixed component (a in the formula) is simply that point at which the line hits the vertical axis, about \$7,200 in this case. To find the variable component (b), determine the *total* cost at some point on the line and subtract the fixed cost to obtain the total variable cost at that level of volume. Then, divide total variable cost by the level of volume associated with that point. For example, along the line drawn in Exhibit

2 *Using the same approach, the cost prediction formula for a fixed cost is* $y = a$ *(because the line has a slope of 0) and for a variable cost is* $y = bx$ *(because the line intercepts the y axis at* $y = 0$*).*

Exhibit 3-2 Scatter Diagram

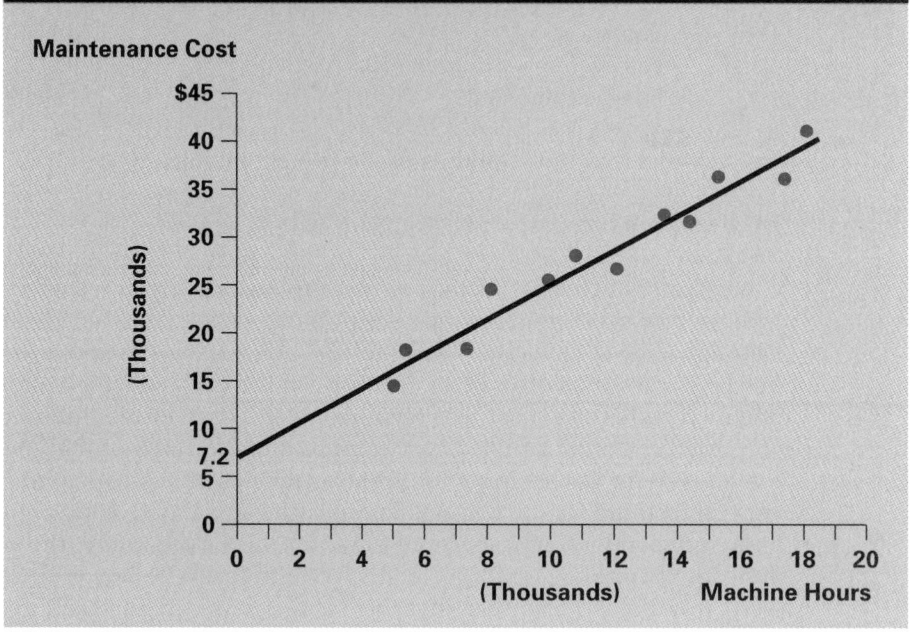

3-2, the total cost is $25,400 at 10,000 machine hours. Of that total cost, about $7,200 is fixed cost, so total variable cost is $18,200. Dividing the total variable cost of $18,200 by 10,000 machine hours yields $1.82, which is the variable cost per dollar of sales. Thus, the scatter-diagram method gives RFC the following formula to predict maintenance cost:

Total maintenance cost = $7,200 + ($1.82 × machine hours)

We now have two formulas for predicting RFC's maintenance cost. Which formula should RFC use? Like the high-low method, the scatter-diagram method suffers from its reliance on what costs *have been*, rather than what they *are likely to be* in the future. But for two reasons the scatter diagram method generally is preferable. First, because the high-low method relies on only two observations, it carries the risk that a random oddity or unusual event occurred in one of the periods. If the company did a great deal of preventive maintenance in the low-activity month, the resulting prediction formula could be useless. (See Exhibit 3-7 in the Appendix.) Because the scatter-diagram method uses more observations and permits the manager to see the pattern of costs, the formula derived by using that method is less likely to be influenced by such events and oddities. The second advantage of the scatter-diagram method is that by looking at the plotting of costs at various levels of the activity, a manager will get some idea of how closely the cost follows changes in the perceived cost-driving activity. (This issue is discussed in more detail later.)

Whichever formula RFC uses, note that it cannot expect to predict maintenance costs exactly. The number of points on the scatter diagram that do *not* fall on the line shows that differences can be expected. Several reasons exist for these differences. One reason is that factors other than machine hours (e.g, dry, dusty conditions) might affect maintenance costs. Or, perhaps there are simply random elements in the cost, just as there are in an automobile's gas mileage, which varies with each tank of gas.

REGRESSION METHOD

A more sophisticated method for estimating the fixed and variable components of a mixed cost is **regression analysis** (or just **regression**). Like the two-point and scatter-diagram methods, this statistical method uses cost and volume data from prior periods and provides an equation of the form: $y = a + bx$, or Total cost = fixed cost + (variable cost per unit of activity × level of activity). In contrast to the high-low method, regression uses more than two observations. And in contrast to the scatter-diagram method, regression relies on statistical concepts, rather than on the judgment of the manager drawing the line, to fit the mathematically best line to the data.

In recent years, accountants have increased their efforts to find techniques for planning administrative costs, partly because managers have noted that such costs have increased more rapidly than many others. A tool that has been employed with some success in analyzing administrative and other costs is *multiple regression analysis*—which uses two or more independent variables to predict the behavior of a cost. Knowledge of some important statistical principles is required before you can understand and apply either simple or multiple regression analysis. But you should be aware that advanced techniques such as these are available for solving cost estimation problems. A discussion of the basic terms and procedures of simple and multiple regression analysis appears in the appendix to this chapter.

PROBLEMS AND PITFALLS IN COST BEHAVIOR ANALYSIS

The methods we have discussed for estimating the behavior of mixed costs are all subject to problems that could decrease the usefulness of cost prediction formulas derived from their use.

HISTORICAL DATA

The common thread in the high-low, scatter-diagram, and regression methods is that they all use past (historical) information about both the dependent variable (the cost to be predicted) and the independent variable (the measure of activity). Though easy to gather, historical information should be used carefully, because formulas based on historical data can give useful predictions only if conditions that prevailed in the past will also prevail in the future. For example, observations from months before a company installed new machinery are suspect because having the new machinery will probably change the cost structure. Similarly, the usefulness of a formula for predicting electricity cost will be reduced if rates have changed since the observations were collected. (The cure in the latter example is to develop the equation using electricity consumption in kilowatt hours, and then apply the *expected* rates to the predicted use of kilowatt hours.)

The usefulness of a cost-prediction formula can be impaired by nonrepresentative historical data. We've already warned that the analyst should consider only observations within the relevant range. But other observations might be unrepresentative of normal circumstances, such as the cost and activity data for a period when a company used temporary, perhaps less efficient, workers. Formulas developed using nonrepresentative data can lead to major misestimates of costs. Hence, managers should apply the cost estimation methods we have discussed only after they review and understand the operating conditions under which cost and activity data were gathered. Because the plotting phase of the scatter-diagram method highlights out-of-line points, managers often plot data even when they use regression analysis. An out-of-line observation (called an *outlier*) often can be ignored.

Finally, an analyst should understand that, whatever the method used to derive the cost prediction formula, it is based on observations within the range of activity over which the observations were gathered. Hence, predicting costs at activity levels outside that range is unwise.

Apart from the problems created by using historical data, analysts must consider the possibility that their predictions will be ineffective because they collected the wrong data. Some of the flaws of data collection are discussed in the next section.

CORRELATION AND ASSOCIATION

If the equation is to be useful for planning, the relationship between the cost and the activity must be fairly close. The closeness of the relationship is called **correlation** or **association**. Consider, for example, the costs of preparing invoices to bill customers. The scatter diagram in Exhibit 3-3, relates the total costs of a firm's billing department to sales activity measured by sales dollars. It shows a wide spread of costs around the cost-prediction line, which suggests that sales dollars is not the driver of invoice preparation costs and that using sales dollars to predict the cost is unlikely to be successful. (Considering the facts should suggest some reasons why this might be so. Does it take more time or more people to prepare an invoice for $100,000

Exhibit 3-3 Scatter Diagram of Invoice Preparation Costs Plotted Against Sales Dollars

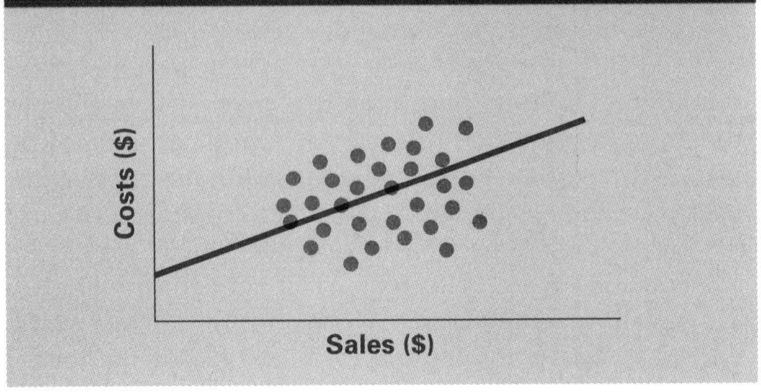

than one for $10,000?) Some other measure of activity might give better results.

Exhibit 3-4 shows invoice preparation costs plotted against another measure of sales activity, the number of sales orders processed. Because preparing one invoice for each sales order is common, and because individual sales orders are likely to vary in dollar value, it is not surprising that the total cost for invoice preparation varies more closely with the number of sales orders than with the dollars of sales represented by the orders. Finding this better correlated activity measure could be important for cost management as well as cost prediction. For example, with this information on the cost driver, managers will investigate whether salespeople write separate sales orders for reasons not related to servicing the customer. Then they might devise ways to reduce the number of orders written (and the processing costs) without affecting customer satisfaction.

As stated earlier, the visual aspect of the scatter-diagram method is an important advantage; it allows the manager to see whether the activity chosen as the independent variable is likely to be a good predictor of the dependent variable (cost). Virtually all computer programs for regression analysis also provide information about correlation. The high-low method, because it includes only two points, does not provide this important information.

SPURIOUS CORRELATION

We stated earlier that an important objective of cost analysis was to determine what activity drives the cost, so that both the cost *and the activity* could be monitored and controlled. Computers make it possible to analyze an incredible number of combinations of cost and activity very quickly. It is quite possible that computer analyses will show a high correlation between a cost and an activity even though no causal relationship exists. Such a correlation is called *spurious* and presents problems for the unwary.

For example, some electric utilities have a relatively high correlation between the number of kilowatt hours they generate and the cost of outside maintenance of their property (cutting the grass, etc.). Outside maintenance costs obviously cannot be driven by producing electric power (or vice versa),

Exhibit 3-4 Scatter Diagram of Invoice Preparation Costs Plotted Against Sales Orders

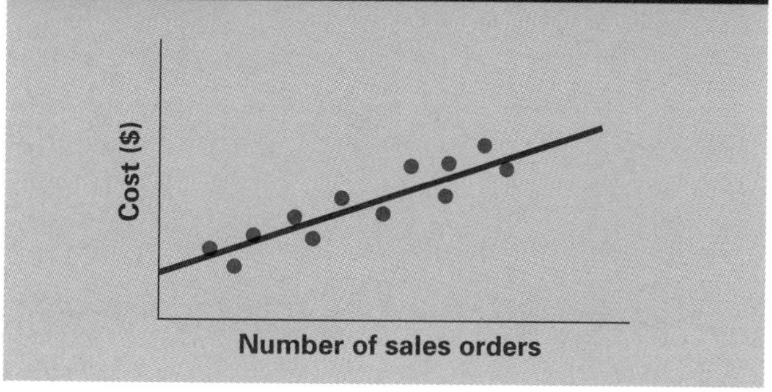

so why the high correlation? The logical reason for the high correlation is that both depend on another factor: the weather. (Both electric power output and outside maintenance are highest in the summer; both are also low in the winter.) Because both are related to the same factor, they *appear* to be related to one another. The key, then, in seeking a relationship that will provide useful predictions and enhance cost management is to question high correlations that seem to have no causal basis. The measure of activity used to predict a cost must make sense.

A more subtle example of an unwarranted conclusion about the relationship between a cost and a particular activity occurs when managers plan the level of a *fixed* cost on the basis of the expected level of some activity. This situation occurs when, for example, a firm's managers decide that its advertising expenditures will be some particular percentage of its expected sales. Such a planned correlation, which is discussed later in the chapter when we explain how managerial actions can influence the classification of costs, may mislead an unknowing analyst about the nature of the cost being studied.

STEP-VARIABLE COSTS

Exhibit 3-5 shows a pattern of cost behavior that fits neither the fixed-variable classification scheme nor the pattern of a typical mixed cost. A cost exhibiting such behavior is commonly called a **step-variable cost**. It is fixed over a range of volume, then jumps to a new level and remains fixed at that level until the next jump. The width of the range of volume over which the cost remains fixed depends on the particular cost but is usually smaller than the relevant range.

Most step-variable costs exist because of the indivisibility of resources; that is, many resources cannot be acquired in infinitely divisible increments. For instance, an airline can make a flight or cannot; it can't use fractions of planes to provide exactly as many seats as passengers demand. Similarly, space needed for storage seldom can be obtained one cubic foot at a time.

In some cases, step-variable behavior occurs because of management decisions. A company might establish a policy of having one production

Exhibit 3-5 Step-Variable Cost

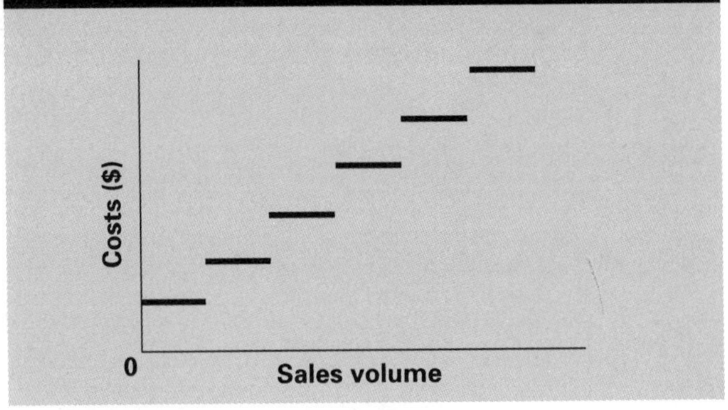

supervisor for every 20 workers, or one inventory clerk for every 1,000 items of inventory. As individual workers and inventory items are added, adding fractional supervisors or inventory clerks is not possible.

In greater or lesser degree, all companies incur step-variable costs. How should a firm plan step-variable costs? Should the cost be planned as if it were mixed, though the fixed component changes within the relevant range? Should it be considered as variable, even though it does not vary between steps? Both approaches are used in practice, which means that actual costs differ from cost predictions under either alternative. Managers are more likely to treat a cost as variable if the steps are relatively short and as a fixed cost if the steps are relatively long (measured horizontally).

Step-variable costs are particularly troublesome to predict and manage when, as in the examples of production supervisors and inventory clerks, the point at which the cost jumps is a matter of managerial choice. Is one supervisor per 20 workers the best decision? Should a supervisor be added and responsibilities reshuffled when some supervisors are responsible for more than 20 people, only when all have at least 20 people, or perhaps when the average span of responsibility is, say, 18 people?

Predicting and managing step-variable costs are also difficult if the cost analyst fails to identify the activity driving the cost. (If the analyst misidentifies the cost-driving activity, the real cost-driving activity is less likely to be carefully monitored and controlled.) Isolating the activity that drives a step-variable cost often is difficult because many such costs do not change in direct proportion to *short-term* changes in activity, but are only likely to respond to changes in activity over longer periods. Often, interviewing is helpful in analyzing step-variable costs. Many companies have reported success in controlling some types of step-variable costs only after interviewing provided clues to the cost-driving activity, enabling managers to concentrate on reducing the level of that activity. For example, companies that have worked closely with suppliers to achieve a high level of quality in purchased materials have been able to reduce inspection and rework costs after recognizing that those costs were driven by the quality, rather than the quantity, of incoming shipments.

COST BEHAVIOR AND MANAGERIAL ACTIONS

Understanding cost behavior goes beyond developing cost prediction formulas. Managers have learned that planning—particularly in decision making—requires that they understand how their actions affect cost behavior. At a minimum, managers and cost analysts must recognize that behavior patterns can be *dictated* by planning decisions.

For example, many companies plan to incur fixed costs such as advertising, employee training, charitable contributions, and research and development, at some percentage of sales. When plotted in a scatter diagram, such costs *appear* to be variable, when in reality, managerial action creates that appearance. In this section we discuss three cost classification schemes that contribute to managers' understanding of the relationships between their actions and their costs.

COMMITTED AND DISCRETIONARY FIXED COSTS

Recall from Chapter 2 that classifying a cost as "fixed" does not imply that the cost cannot be changed, only that it is nonvariable. Because some fixed costs can be changed more easily and quickly than others, it is sometimes useful to classify them using this criterion.

Fixed costs that can be quickly altered by managerial action are **discretionary costs**. Managers decide whether to incur the cost at all and how much to incur at relatively frequent intervals. Advertising, employee training, and research and development are examples of discretionary fixed costs. (Ted probably decides each month whether to advertise and how much to spend.) Fixed costs that cannot be changed fairly rapidly are **committed costs**, so called to express the idea that managers have made some prior commitment that cannot be readily changed. Depreciation is an example of a committed fixed cost. Like other committed fixed costs, depreciation arises from past managerial decisions—some made several years ago—and cannot be changed without disposing of the asset to which the depreciation applies.

Deciding whether a cost is committed or discretionary is not always possible just by knowing what the cost is for (rent, salaries, research and development, etc.). For example, rent might or might not be a committed cost depending on the terms of the rental agreement. Or suppose part of the cost of research and development is depreciation and property taxes on a building used only by the research and development department. Regardless of the building's use, the depreciation and property taxes are committed as long as the company owns it.

Some costs are on the borderline between committed and discretionary in the sense that a past decision committed the firm to incurring the cost but did not dictate its level. For example, a decision to carry on research and development activities implies a commitment to incur *some* salary cost for employees fulfilling that purpose, but management can exercise discretion over the number of such employees and the level of their salaries. On a broader scale, the very existence of the company embodies a commitment to employ people to manage it. But to a great extent the number and compensation of those people are subject to the discretion of current managers.

Do not misinterpret the discretionary-committed classification as distinguishing between unnecessary and necessary costs, respectively. Advertising is a discretionary fixed cost, but *some* type of advertising—a sign, a Yellow Pages listing, whatever—is probably necessary for most enterprises. Similarly, depreciation is a committed fixed cost; yet most companies could probably operate successfully without one or more of several cash registers, telephone lines, or display racks.

Discretionary costs present unique problems in cost management because managers must determine whether the level of the discretionary activity—the cost driver—is appropriate. For example, should the company hire another research scientist? Should it reduce the number of pages in the annual report? Should it discontinue a particular training program? Should it stop distributing certain management reports? Then there is the large question of whether the company should even be performing the activity at all. Should the company support in any way its employees' pursuit of additional education? Should the company make charitable contributions, given that managers would be following their own preferences rather than those of the company's stockholders?

Unfortunately, discretionary costs are often the first to be cut in cost-reduction programs. Such cuts reflect a misunderstanding of the classification. Consider the long-run effect of cutting the following discretionary costs: research and product development, management training programs, programs to upgrade worker skills, advertising and maintenance.

Research and product development are crucial to the success of companies in such high technology fields as drugs, computers, aircraft, and some consumer products. Reducing expenditures for personnel development can lead to reduced morale, high turnover, and lessened productivity. A decline in advertising can influence buyer-recognition of the company's name and, hence, weaken prospects for future acceptance of new products. Deferring routine maintenance might result in high repair costs, as well as interruptions of production when machines finally break down.

Managers treat discretionary and committed fixed costs differently when analyzing day-to-day operations. We already have noted that, perhaps unwisely, discretionary costs are often the first targets of cost-reduction programs. Recognizing that little, if anything, can be done to change committed costs over short periods, managers often are inclined to watch committed costs less closely than discretionary costs. It should be obvious, however, that failure to monitor committed costs can also prove unwise, if only because every commitment that begins must have an end and so must be evaluated for its continuing importance. Possibly, a major change has occurred in the conditions that made the commitment appear wise at an earlier time.

AVOIDABLE AND UNAVOIDABLE COSTS

Another useful subdivision of fixed costs hinges on whether the company could avoid the cost by dropping or curtailing some activity. The amount by which a cost can be reduced is **avoidable**, the amount that cannot be reduced is **unavoidable**. Thus, the ideas of avoidability and unavoidability apply only when a decision is at hand. Avoidable if we do what?

At first glance, the avoidable-unavoidable categories might seem to parallel the discretionary-committed categories. This is sometimes so, but significant exceptions may exist, and determining whether or not a cost is avoidable typically requires a case-by-case analysis. Consider the following monthly income statement for a regional sales office of a large company. Upper-level managers might close the office. They expect the results to continue at the same level indefinitely if the office remains open.

Sales		$100,000
Variable costs		80,000
Contribution margin		20,000
Fixed costs:		
Salaries	$15,000	
Rent	1,000	
Other fixed costs	7,000	23,000
Loss		($ 3,000)

The decision about the future of the office requires more information about the fixed costs. Because the company cannot have an office without having space and some people, the rent and *some* salaries are certainly unavoidable costs. But, some of these costs might be avoidable *if the company were to close the office.* Perhaps all or some salaries could be avoided if the firm let the people go or could use them elsewhere, thus avoiding having to hire others. Let's suppose that the entire $15,000 is salaries of salespeople who can either be let go or transferred to openings elsewhere. In that case, the $15,000 is avoidable. Suppose, however, that the rent and $4,000 of the other fixed costs are unavoidable. If the company closed the office, it would still be paying $5,000 per month. The company should keep the office open and lose only $3,000 rather than close it and still pay $5,000. In general, the question is not whether the office is unprofitable but whether the unavoidable costs are greater than the loss incurred by keeping the office open.

Even if the analysis indicated that closing the office would save money, compelling reasons might support keeping it open. For example, the managers might believe that the firm's reputation requires having offices in certain geographical areas and that closing this office could hurt that reputation. Analyzing costs does not *tell* managers what to do: policy considerations might override financial concerns.

DIRECT AND INDIRECT (COMMON) COSTS

In some situations where a manager wants to determine whether a cost is avoidable or unavoidable, a refinement of our basic cost classification scheme is often useful. Costs may be classified as direct or indirect.

A **direct cost**, also called a **separable cost**, is incurred specifically because of a particular activity of the firm, like a product, product line, or geographical area. (All costs are direct to *some* activity, if only to the company as a whole.) An **indirect cost**, also called a **common** or **joint cost**, does not relate to one specific activity, but rather to several.

Variable costs are direct to a particular product or activity. Some fixed costs are direct to particular products or activities, and some are not. Consider a company that makes several models of lawn mowers. One department in the factory does some work on every model. The fixed costs of that department are direct to the lawn mower business as a whole, but not to any particular model. For another example, salaries of salespeople who cover particular geographical regions are direct to those regions. But if the salespeople sell several products, their salaries are indirect to each of the products. Thus, to classify a cost as direct or indirect, it is necessary first to specify the activity in which the manager is interested.

Direct costs usually are avoidable, although there certainly are exceptions. If a company rents a sales office and the lease has 10 years to run, the rent is direct to the office, but is unavoidable. Indirect costs generally are unavoidable; by definition, they are incurred to support two or more activities, so they will continue to be incurred if only one of the activities is discontinued. Even here, though, the individual circumstances determine the classification. Consider a large company with six major production departments in a single factory building. Dropping one department could enable the company to reduce such indirect costs as those of operating the payroll and personnel functions, even though no one person in either of those departments works exclusively on the production department being dropped. Thus, some portion of the indirect cost is avoidable.

MANUFACTURING COSTS

A manufacturer incurs costs to make its products before it sells them. For this reason, the behavioral classification and management of manufacturing costs concentrates on activities having to do with production.

A typical manufacturing company has three general types of manufacturing costs: materials and purchased components, direct labor, and manufacturing overhead. The cost of **materials** (sometimes called **raw materials** or **direct materials**) and components that the company buys and transforms into its products (steel, wood, etc.), normally varies with the volume of production. The cost of **direct labor** (those employees who work *directly* on the product) is also normally variable with the volume of production. In some European countries it is difficult, even impossible, to lay off workers in slow times, so labor becomes a fixed cost. Many U.S. companies also follow no-layoff policies as well. **Manufacturing overhead** (which consists of all production costs other than materials and direct labor) includes costs that are fixed, variable, and mixed. Many such costs also vary with production, but many others vary with other cost drivers. Activity-based costing (discussed in the next section) is concerned with analyzing these costs, determining their drivers, and relating the costs to products. Some examples of manufacturing overhead costs are

Costs of acquiring materials and components, including evaluating vendors and carrying out routine purchasing functions

Wages of indirect laborers (those who do not work directly on the products), such as maintenance workers, materials handlers, and cleaners

Costs of data processing related to manufacturing activities

Salaries of production supervisors

Costs of changing machinery over from making one product to another (setup costs)

Accounting and recordkeeping related to manufacturing operations

Salaries of workers responsible for inspecting incoming shipments of materials and components

Wages of workers responsible for the storage and control of materials

Heat, light, and power costs for production

Depreciation and property taxes on factory buildings and factory machinery

Salary and office expenses of plant managers (and their personnel)

From this brief listing you should see that companies have several pools of manufacturing overhead costs, each driven by a different activity. Some pools of manufacturing overhead will be mixed costs, with variable components based on activities such as labor hours or machine hours. Some pools will be fixed in the short-term because they are driven by factors that do not change significantly over short periods. (One example is the costs of some administrative functions that change only as the factory increases the number of products it makes.)

In a multiproduct company it is seldom possible to relate the behavior of many manufacturing overhead costs to a broad measure of output such as the number of units produced. For example, a company that makes refrigerators, ovens, and toasters could not expect each type of manufacturing overhead cost to vary with the total number of units produced because the units are so different. (Making a toaster does not cause as much overhead as making a refrigerator because a refrigerator requires more labor and machine time, has many more parts and is much more complex.) For overhead cost pools that are associated with non-volume activities such as the number of parts in a product or the number of recordkeeping entries the product generates, managers determine an overhead cost per unit of product of each type. But for other pools, managers relate costs to *input* factors such as number of hours worked by direct laborers or the number of machine hours, and determine a variable overhead rate per hour. Then, the variable component of overhead cost *per unit of product* is computed by multiplying the variable overhead rate by the number of hours a unit of product requires.

For example, suppose that a manager determined that one cost pool of manufacturing overhead cost is well described by the equation:

$$\textit{Total cost} = \$40{,}000 + (\$8 \times \textit{machine hours})$$

Suppose further that a toaster requires 0.20 machine hours and, a refrigerator requires 6.0 hours. The variable manufacturing overhead for each product is as follows:

	Toaster	Refrigerator
Machine hours	0.20	6.00
Variable overhead per machine hour	$8.00	$ 8.00
Variable manufacturing overhead per unit	$1.60	$48.00

The manager adds this variable overhead to the variable overhead component of other pools to determine the total variable manufacturing overhead. The total variable manufacturing overhead plus the direct labor and material cost per unit gives the total variable manufacturing cost for each product.

ACTIVITY-BASED COSTING

Activity-based costing (ABC) refers to assigning costs to products (or other segments such as customers or geographical areas) by referring to the activities that each product requires. ABC also relates to identifying cost drivers. Because activities cause costs, to understand cost behavior fully requires understanding those activities (cost drivers). Managers who understand activities can determine what costs the activities drive.

For instance, a design engineer revising the specifications of a product might incorporate a component the company does not now use. Introducing that component might require that the purchasing department find vendors who supply it, and then evaluate each potential vendor's prices, quality control, and ability to meet delivery schedules. Finally, purchasing managers will decide which vendor(s) to use. The storeroom will set aside space for the component, add the component to its list of stocked items, and probably generate other paperwork. Until the vendor has satisfied the company that the quality of the component is acceptable, the company will inspect incoming shipments. The data processing department must incorporate the component into whatever computer files are used by various departments. The accounts payable section will have a new vendor, process more invoices, and pay more bills. The company's internal auditors will have to count the component. In short, a seemingly simple change might send ripples of cost through many areas of the company, which, though relatively small, can accumulate as more and more such changes occur.

All of the costs described above must be considered in making such decisions, as well as in other areas. Evaluating the profitability of products or of geographical areas is one example where ABC is helpful in classifying activities as value-adding or non-value-adding and thereby plays a role in cost reduction and continuous improvement which JIT operations pursue.

A company using ABC still assigns some costs based on labor or machine time. Analysts examine activities such as those noted above and determine an average cost per unit of activity. This average is then used to assign overhead from that pool to each product that uses the activity.

MANUFACTURING COST ACCOUNTING

Managers in manufacturing companies often face a problem when analyzing cost behavior to apply CVP analysis. For financial accounting purposes, manufacturers must calculate cost of goods sold using fixed manufacturing costs. From Chapter 2 you know that per-unit fixed costs are of little use in planning (because they are different at every level of volume). Hence, to analyze the cost structure of the manufacturing company requires eliminating the effect of fixed costs from the per-unit manufacturing costs computed for financial accounting purposes. That task can become extremely complicated, and we defer a complete discussion of it to Chapters 13 and 14. At this point, we shall simply show how a manufacturer calculates the per-unit cost of product and prepares its income statement.

Assume the following data for MFG Manufacturing Company. MFG makes a single product. It produced 25,000 units and sold them all at $20 per unit. There was no beginning inventory.

Total variable manufacturing cost per unit	$6
Total variable manufacturing cost (25,000 × $6)	$150,000
Total fixed manufacturing overhead	$200,000
Total manufacturing costs	$350,000
Variable selling expenses per unit	$2
Total fixed selling and administrative expenses	$60,000

Fixed manufacturing cost per unit is $8 ($200,000/25,000), so the total manufacturing cost per unit is $14, $6 variable plus $8 fixed. (The total cost per unit also could be determined by dividing the $350,000 total manufacturing cost by 25,000 units.) Accordingly, Cost of Goods Sold will be $14 per unit on the income statement for financial reporting purposes. That income statement appears on the left side of Exhibit 3-6, along with one prepared using the contribution margin approach for comparison.

The incomes shown under the two approaches are the same, but the contribution margin format allows the manager to understand the company's cost structure and facilitates the use of CVP analysis. For these reasons, the contribution margin format often is used in reports prepared for managers even when such managers also receive copies of the reports prepared for persons outside the company.

Exhibit 3-6 MFG Manufacturing Company Income Statement for the Year

Financial Accounting Format		Contribution Margin Format		
Sales (25,000 × $20)	$500,000	Sales (25,000 × $20)		$500,000
Cost of sales (25,000 × $14)[a]	350,000	Variable costs:		
		Manufacturing		
Gross margin	150,000	(25,000 × $6)	$150,000	
		Selling (25,000 × $2)	50,000	
Selling and administrative				200,000
expenses[b]	110,000			
		Contribution margin		300,000
		Fixed costs:		
		Manufacturing	200,000	
		Selling and		
		administrative	60,000	
				260,000
Income	$ 40,000	Income		$ 40,000

a Variable cost of $6 per unit + fixed cost of $8 per unit ($200,000/25,000 units) = $14 manufacturing cost per unit.
b Variable cost of $2 per unit + fixed cost of $60,000 = $110,000.

SUMMARY

Costs do not always fit into fixed or variable classifications, and not all variable costs vary with sales. Some manufacturing costs vary with the number of units manufactured, some selling costs vary with the number of orders placed by customers, and so on. It is not always easy to find an appropriate measure of activity to use in planning a given cost, but finding close relationships is important to the manager both for planning and for cost management.

Some costs are mixed and contain both fixed and variable elements. Step-variable costs are fixed over small ranges of activity but at different levels for different ranges. Scatter diagrams, high-low estimates, and regression analysis are useful tools for analyzing cost behavior, but must be used with care.

Whatever the method used to analyze cost behavior, actual costs will probably differ from planned costs.

Several other classifications of costs exist: discretionary or committed, avoidable or unavoidable, direct or indirect. Discretionary fixed costs may be changed on relatively short notice. Committed fixed costs cannot normally be changed quickly. In general, only future levels of committed costs may be affected by present management.

Costs are classified as avoidable or unavoidable only in relation to specific decisions, such as closing an office. Direct costs relate to a specific activity, while indirect (or common) costs benefit more than one activity. Generally speaking, direct costs, other than committed fixed costs, are avoidable, and indirect costs are unavoidable if the activity is to be stopped. Activity-based costing uses the notions of cost pools and cost drivers to arrive at costs of products for decision making purposes.

KEY TERMS

account analysis
activity-based costing (ABC)
association
avoidable cost
committed cost
common (joint) cost
correlation
cost driver
cost pool
direct (separable) cost
direct labor
discretionary cost
indirect cost
manufacturing overhead
materials (raw or direct)
mixed (semivariable) cost
regression analysis
scatter-diagram (graphical) method
step-variable cost
two-point (high-low) method
unavoidable cost

KEY FORMULAS

$$\text{Total costs} = \text{fixed costs} + (\text{variable cost per unit of sales} \times \text{number of units sold})$$

$$\text{Total costs} = \text{fixed costs} + (\text{variable cost as \% of sales} \times \text{dollars of sales})$$

$$\text{Variable cost component of mixed cost} = \frac{\text{change in cost}}{\text{change in activity}}$$

$$\text{Fixed cost component of mixed cost} = \text{total cost at high volume} - \left(\text{high volume} \times \text{variable cost component}\right)$$

REVIEW PROBLEM

SwanCo operates several stores in three cities. One of the stores is expected to show the following annual results for the next few years.

Sales		$600,000
Variable costs		360,000
Contribution margin		240,000
Fixed costs:		
Salaries	$150,000	
Rent	36,000	
Insurance and utilities	12,000	
Other	67,000	265,000
Loss		($25,000)

SwanCo has a 10-year lease on the space occupied by the store, and the lease cannot be canceled. Other fixed costs include $4,000 in charges the home office makes to the store for services such as general advertising (advertising the company name, not any particular store). These home office costs would not decline if the store were closed.

Required
Determine the change that would occur in the firm's total profit if the store were closed.

ANSWER TO REVIEW PROBLEM

Considering only the facts as given, total profit would drop by at least $15,000 per year if the store were closed. The $36,000 rent is an unavoidable cost; it would not be eliminated if the store were closed. Also, the $4,000 indirect cost charged by the home office would not be eliminated if the store were closed. That is, the loss for the store would be $40,000 ($36,000 + $4,000) if it were closed, compared with the current loss of $25,000, because no revenues and thus no contribution margin is generated. If the store were closed, the loss might even exceed $40,000 if, as part of the rental agreement, SwanCo were required to insure the premises, or if some type of fixed-term employment agreement existed with the store's manager such that he or she could not be transferred to another location.

APPENDIX: REGRESSION ANALYSIS

Regression analysis is a technique for fitting a straight line to a set of data. In contrast to the high-low method, regression analysis can use many observations, not just two. In contrast to the scatter-diagram method, regression analysis fits a mathematically precise line, rather than one that depends on the judgment of the manager drawing the line to fit the data. The procedures for developing a regression equation are laborious if done by hand, but you can easily set up and solve a regression using a computer spreadsheet. Some hand-held calculators can also solve regressions.

Although regression analysis is used for many different purposes, our main interest here is predicting cost behavior—determining the fixed and variable components of a cost or pool of costs associated with a cost driver.

Regression provides an equation of the same form as do the high-low and scatter-diagram methods.

Total cost = fixed component + (variable rate × activity)

Regression analysis also provides measures that indicate how well the costs are associated with the measure of activity (cost driver) used. Thus, you can test several drivers to determine which seems to predict costs best. The first step, then, in using regression analysis is deciding which cost driver to use—sales dollars, production in units, number of sales invoices prepared, hours worked by direct laborers, or number of parts and components in a product. Once a possible driver has been selected, the procedures for developing the regression equation are relatively mechanical.

We present two techniques, simple and multiple regression, in this appendix. In simple regression, we develop an equation that uses one cost driver (independent variable) to explain costs (the dependent variable). The procedures for developing the equation will be explained at some length. Using multiple regression, we develop an equation that uses more than one independent variable to explain the dependent variable. We do not require the use of multiple regression in this text and discuss it only briefly.

SIMPLE REGRESSION

Developing a regression equation requires the solving of two equations simultaneously. These equations, which are given below, are called the normal equations.

$$(1)\ \Sigma XY = a\Sigma X + b\,\Sigma X^2$$
$$(2)\ \Sigma Y = na + b\,\Sigma X$$

where

X = *measure of activity*
Y = *total cost*
a = *total fixed cost*
b = *variable cost per unit of activity*
n = *number of observations*
Σ = *sum of (e.g., ΣX^2 = sum of the squares of the volumes)*

As in the high-low and scatter diagram method, in regression analysis, the letter *Y* designates the dependent variable, the one that we are trying to predict. The letter *X* designates the independent variable, the one that we believe drives the dependent variable.

We shall use the data from the example in the chapter to illustrate regression analysis. For convenience, we repeat the data below, along with the calculations of X^2 and XY.

X	Y	X^2	XY
5,000	14,800	25,000,000	74,000,000
10,800	28,200	116,640,000	304,560,000
12,200	27,300	148,840,000	333,060,000
7,300	19,100	53,290,000	139,430,000
10,000	25,400	100,000,000	254,000,000
8,100	24,900	65,610,000	201,690,000
18,000	40,800	324,000,000	734,400,000
13,400	31,800	179,560,000	426,120,000
5,400	18,100	29,160,000	97,740,000
14,100	31,900	198,810,000	449,790,000
15,100	36,100	228,010,000	545,110,000
17,300	35,900	299,290,000	621,070,000
136,700	334,300	1,768,210,000	4,180,970,000

Substituting the values in normal equations gives the following.

$$(1)\ 4{,}180{,}970{,}000 = 136{,}700a + 1{,}768{,}210{,}000b$$
$$(2)\ 334{,}300 = 12a + 136{,}700b$$

With two equations and two unknowns, we can solve the equations in several ways. One simple way is to eliminate *a* and solve for *b*. Multiplying equation 1 by 12 (the coefficient of *a* in equation 2) and equation 2 by 136,700 (the coefficient of *a* in equation 1) will allow us to eliminate *a* from both equations.

$$(1)\ 50{,}171{,}640{,}000 = 1{,}640{,}400a + 21{,}218{,}520{,}000b$$
$$(2)\ 45{,}698{,}810{,}000 = 1{,}640{,}400a + 18{,}686{,}890{,}000b$$

Subtracting equation 2 from equation 1

$$4{,}472{,}830{,}000 = 2{,}531{,}630{,}000b$$
$$b = 1.7668$$

Substituting the value for *b* into equation 1 and solving for *a*,

$$4{,}180{,}970{,}000 = 136{,}700a + 1{,}768{,}210{,}000b$$
$$4{,}180{,}970{,}000 = 136{,}700a + 3{,}124{,}073{,}428$$
$$a = 7{,}732 \text{ (rounded)}$$

The value for *a*, the fixed component, is $7,732. The formula for total cost is then,

Total maintenance cost = $7,732 + $1.7668 × machine hours

The results are not significantly different from those using the scatter-diagram (*a* = $7,200, *b* = $1.82). This is to be expected because the scatter-diagram uses all of the observations that regression does. However, regression also gives us formal measures of the likely accuracy of our predictions using the regression equation.

CORRELATION AND THE STANDARD ERROR

Because managers use the regression equation and the estimates of *a* and *b*, they want to have some idea about the accuracy of the predictions. There are several measures of goodness of fit, how well the regression line fits the data, that suggest to managers how good their predictions are likely to be. The two measures we discuss are the **coefficient of determination,** often called r^2 and the **standard error of the estimate.**

The coefficient of determination is a measure of how well the regression line accounts for the changes in *Y*, the dependent variable. It can have values from zero through 1. The value is the percentage of the variation in *Y* that is "explained" by the movement of *X*. A value of 1 means that the regression line is perfect: all points fall on it. A value near zero means that the values of *Y* are randomly scattered with no relationship to the values of *X*. Exhibit 3-7 shows a scatter diagram for two cases.

Using machine hours as the independent variable, it is clearly easier to predict Cost W than Cost T. Perhaps you could better predict Cost T using some other measure of activity, or perhaps Cost T is not driven by any activity, but is just random.

The coefficient of determination is calculated in the following way.

$$r^2 = 1 - \frac{\Sigma (Y - Yc)^2}{\Sigma (Y - \bar{Y})^2}$$

The differences, $Y - Yc$ are the differences between the actual values of *Y* and those predicted by the regression equation. The differences, $Y - \bar{Y}$ are the differences between the actual values of *Y* and the mean, or average of the values of *Y*. (The differences are squared for reasons that we shall not discuss here.) Roughly speaking, if you had no values for *X* and had to predict *Y* using only the past values of *Y*, your best prediction is the average of previous costs. The variation around that mean is the denominator of the equation. The numerator of the equation is the unexplained variation, which is zero if the regression line was perfect and all observations fell on it. The schedule below shows the calculations.

The mean of maintenance costs ($\bar{Y}$) is $27,858.

Exhibit 3-7 High and Low Correlations

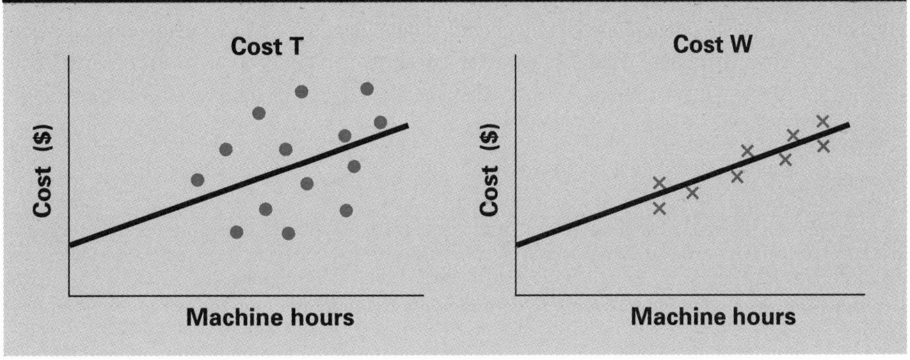

Yc	Y	$(Y - Yc)^2$	$(Y - \bar{Y})^2$
16,566	14,800	3,118,756	170,511,364
26,813	28,200	1,923,769	116,964
29,287	27,300	3,948,169	311,364
20,630	19,100	2,340,900	76,702,564
25,400	25,400	0	6,041,764
22,043	24,900	8,162,449	8,749,764
39,534	40,800	1,602,756	167,495,364
31,407	31,800	154,449	15,539,364
17,273	18,100	683,929	95,218,564
32,644	31,900	553,536	16,337,764
34,411	36,100	2,852,721	67,930,564
38,298	35,900	5,750,404	64,673,764
Totals		31,091,838	689,629,168

Therefore,

$$R^2 = 1 - (31{,}091{,}838/689{,}629{,}168)$$
$$= 0.955$$

The result indicates an excellent fit of the line to the data, so predictions using the regression equation should be good. Again, however, we have only twelve observations to keep down the calculations. Using more observations, say 20 to 30, would make us more confident of the equation.

The standard error of the estimate (S_e) is a measure of the variation around the regression line as is shown by its calculation.[3]

$$S_e = \sqrt{\frac{\Sigma\,(Y - Yc)^2}{n - 2}}$$

The lower the standard error of the estimate, the better. A standard error of zero, like an r^2 of 1, indicates that all observations fall on the regression line.

In our example,

$$S_e = \sqrt{\frac{31{,}091{,}838}{12 - 2}}$$
$$= 1{,}763$$

Statistical theory tells us that roughly 68% of the actual values of cost lie within one standard error of their predicted values, about 95% within two standard errors.[4] With the standard error of $1,763, about 68% of the time,

---

3 *The divisor is actually the number of observations minus the number of coefficients estimated in the equation. We estimate* a *and* b *here. In multiple regression, we could have four or more coefficients and the divisor would decrease accordingly.*

4 *The following is very rough, but is given to illustrate the principle of the standard error of the estimate. The actual intervals within which predicted costs are likely to fall are wider than the standard error of the estimate.*

actual cost will be within \$1,763 of its predicted value, and within \$3,526 (2 × \$1,763) about 95% of the time. Assuming a cost prediction at the average of about \$28,000, 95% of the time actual cost should differ by no more than 12.6% (\$3,526/28,000). Thus, the standard error of the estimate, like r^2, suggests a good fit of the regression line to the data.

Problems and pitfalls

A basic assumption in using regression analysis is that the data that have been collected are representative. That is, it is assumed that the conditions under which the cost-volume observations were assembled were about the same and can be expected to continue. As we suggested in the chapter, if one or more of the observations used in the analysis are not representative of normal conditions, the regression line would not be as useful a prediction tool as desired.

Consider the scatter diagram in Exhibit 3-7 for Cost W. Suppose Cost W is maintenance and repairs plotted against machine hours. Picture an observation of a very high cost at a very low volume, well up the left-hand part of the scatter diagram. Such an observation, called an outlier, would have a disproportionate effect on a regression equation. Such an observation is clearly unusual and might best be ignored in developing the equation. That observation might have been from a month in which the plant was shut down for a considerable period for extensive repair work. The high cost of repairs combined with the low volume of machine hours makes the observation nonrepresentative. Great care must be taken in "throwing out" observations, but if a particular observation occurred for unusual reason, it is best to ignore it.

One final caution. As is the case with both the high-low and scatter-diagram methods, the predictions resulting from regression analysis depend for their validity on observations over a particular range of activity, *viz.*, the range over which the observations were gathered. Care must be taken in using any of these methods to predict costs for levels of activity not included within the range over which the observations were gathered. For example, if costs of power to operate machines have been analyzed in a range from 500 to 800 hours of machine time per week, there is no reason to assume that the relationships that held over that range will hold also at 350 hours or 1,100 hours.

MULTIPLE REGRESSION

Multiple regression analysis is a technique for developing a prediction equation using more than one independent variable. In a modern business, many costs depend on more than one activity. The cost of heating a factory depends both on the number of hours it is open and on the outside temperature. Shipping costs depend on both the weight of the goods and the distance over which they must travel. As indicated in the chapter, the costs to prepare invoices to customers are affected not only by the number of sales orders received but also by the number of items covered by each sales order.

A multiple regression equation has the following general form.

$$Y = a + b_1X_1 + b_2X_3 \ldots b_nX_n$$

where

Y = *the dependent variable to be predicted*
$X_1 \ldots X_n$ = *the values of the various independent variables influencing the value of* Y
$b_1 \ldots b_n$ = *the coefficients of the various independent variables*
a = *the fixed component (as in simple regression)*

Suppose the manager of a factory that makes a number of different products has requested an analysis of manufacturing overhead costs. The managerial accountant, working in conjunction with a statistician, came up with the following analysis.

Fixed component of manufacturing overhead cost	\$32,500 per month (a)
Variable components (independent variables):	
Direct labor hours (X_1)	\$2.40 per hour (b_1)
Machine-hours (X_2)	\$1.80 per hour (b_2)
Weight of materials put into production (X_3)	\$0.30 per pound (b_3)

The accountant and the statistical consultant have found that variations in three variables (direct labor hours, machine-hours, and weight of materials processed) better describe variations in total overhead costs than do variations in any one or combination of two such variables. Such a conclusion is reasonable when one considers that many overhead costs (fringe benefits, for example) are related to labor time, that some (like power, supplies, and lubricants) are readily associated with machine time, and that still others (like materials handling and storekeeping costs) depend on the quantity of materials being used.

Suppose, now, that the factory manager expects the following activity in the coming month.

Direct labor hours	20,000
Machine-hours	15,000
Pounds of materials processed	70,000

The manager could predict total manufacturing overhead of \$128,500.

Total manufacturing overhead = *\$32,500 + (\$2.40 × 20,000) + (\$1.80 × 15,000) + (\$0.30 × 70,000)*

= *\$32,500 fixed cost* + *\$48,000 variable with direct labor hours* + *\$27,000 variable with machine-hours* + *\$21,000 variable with pounds of materials*

The cautions associated with simple regression also apply here, plus one more. Multiple regression analysis requires the assumption that the independent variables are not correlated *with each other*. In our example, for instance, knowing whether direct labor hours and machine-hours (or some other combination of the three independent variables) are closely associated is important. If two (or more) of the independent variables are highly correlated, the results of multiple regression analysis must be used with care and the underlying statistical problems must be understood. Such problems will be presented in depth in your statistics courses.

A multiple regression equation also has a coefficient of determination and a standard error of the estimate, but the calculations are somewhat different than they are for simple regression and we shall omit them.

In summary, when using either simple or multiple regression analysis, you must understand the statistical principles that underlie these approaches. Critical to the production of useful results under either approach is the need for the observations to be representative of conditions expected to prevail during the period for which predictions are being made.

REVIEW PROBLEM—APPENDIX

The controller of Tuscany Products has just received the following results from the company's statistics department.

$$Y = \$326{,}389 + \$8.625X,\ r^2 = 0.712,\ S_e = \$16{,}352$$
$$Y = \textit{monthly factory power cost},\ X = \textit{machine hours}$$

The statistician collected the data in a range of 20,000 to 30,000 machine hours.

Required

1. Calculate the expected power cost at 22,000 machine hours.
2. Explain the meaning of the equation and of each component of the equation and the measures of goodness of fit. Also indicate the usefulness of each item in cost analysis.

ANSWER TO REVIEW PROBLEM

1. \$516,139; \$326,389 + \$8,625 × 22,000
2. The equation itself tells us that factory power cost has a fixed component of \$326,389 per month and a variable component of \$8.625 per machine hour. We can therefore predict power cost by using the equation, as we did in part 1.

   Because the slope is the variable component of the cost, we can use it to estimate the total variable cost of power for a product or component that we manufacture by multiplying \$8.625 by the number of machine hours the manufactured item requires.

   The coefficient of determination, r^2 of 0.712, or 71.2%, tells us the percentage of the variation in power cost that is associated with changes in machine hours. The relatively high value for r^2 indicates that the fit is good.

   The standard error of the estimate, S_e, tells us how close our predictions are likely to be to the actual results. In this case, we expect predictions to be within \$16,352 about 68% of the time, within \$32,704 (2 × \$16,352) about 95% of the time.

   It is also helpful to understand what the results do *not* tell you. The equation is not necessarily the best available. Some other factor might predict better. Multiple regression with some other factors might give better results, higher r^2, lower standard error.

The intercept, $326,389, is *not* the estimate of total cost at zero machine hours. The data were collected in the range of 20-30 thousand hours and it is unsafe to extrapolate outside that range.

ASSIGNMENT MATERIAL

QUESTIONS FOR DISCUSSION

3-1 Cost classification Indicate whether each of the following items of cost is likely to be discretionary or committed. If in doubt, describe the circumstances under which the cost would fall into one or the other category. If the cost is mixed, consider only the fixed portion.

(a) Straight-line depreciation on building.
(b) Sum-of-years-digits depreciation on a machine.
(c) Salaries of salespeople.
(d) Salaries of president and vice-presidents for production, sales, and finance.
(e) Fees for consultants on long-range planning.
(f) Utilities for factory—heating and lighting.
(g) Management development costs—costs of attending seminars, training programs, etc.

3-2 High-low method The controller of your firm recommends the following approach to estimating the fixed and variable components of manufacturing overhead costs such as supervision, indirect labor, and supplies.

Estimate the total cost that the firm would incur if it shut down, and treat that amount as fixed cost. Then estimate the total cost if the firm worked at 100% of capacity, stated in machine hours. Divide the difference in the two cost figures by the difference in machine hours and treat that as the variable component.

Required

Comment on the procedure. Would the formula derived from it work well for the firm if it normally operated between 75% and 90% of capacity?

3-3 Take or pay contract Boulder Chemical Company has a contract that requires it to buy 100,000 tons of raw materials each month. The materials are perishable, and if Boulder cannot sell the products that use the materials, the unused materials must be discarded. In most firms, raw materials costs are variable. Is that so in this case?

3-4 Committed fixed costs Analyze each of the following statements, explaining what is wrong with it.

(a) The controller tells you that the units-of-production method is used for depreciation of machinery and that depreciation is therefore a variable cost, not a committed fixed cost.
(b) The same controller tells you that, since the firm nearly always operates at full capacity, all fixed costs cannot be reduced and are therefore committed.
(c) A sales manager tells you that the firm cannot operate without salespeople and that therefore salespeople's salaries are committed fixed costs.
(d) Another controller says that if committed costs are those necessarily incurred because the firm is in business, there are no such costs because the firm could reduce its costs to zero by simply closing up.

3-5 Cost classification Melton Company sells a variety of industrial products. It operates eight regional sales offices. State whether each of the following costs is likely to be (a) avoidable or unavoidable and (b) direct or indirect to the South-Central office.

(a) Salaries of salespeople in the South-Central region.
(b) Rent on the South-Central office. The lease has five years left.
(c) Rent on equipment used in the South-Central regional office. The equipment can be returned with one week's notice.
(d) Salaries of the national vice-president for sales and her staff.
(e) National advertising.
(f) Travel expenses of salespeople working in the South-Central region.

3-6 ***Cost classification*** Talley Industries makes small fiberglass boats. It has two production departments, the Forming Department and the Finishing Department. State whether each of the following costs is likely to be (a) avoidable or unavoidable and (b) direct or indirect to the Forming Department.

(a) Wages of workers in the Forming Department.
(b) Property taxes on the factory building.
(c) Depreciation on machinery used only in the Forming Department.
(d) Salaries of the plant controller and her staff.
(e) Salary of the Forming Department manager.
(f) Wages of maintenance workers who take care of all machinery in the factory.

EXERCISES

3-7 ***Accuracy of predictions*** The scatter diagrams below show two costs plotted against production. Which cost can you predict and plan for more easily? Explain.

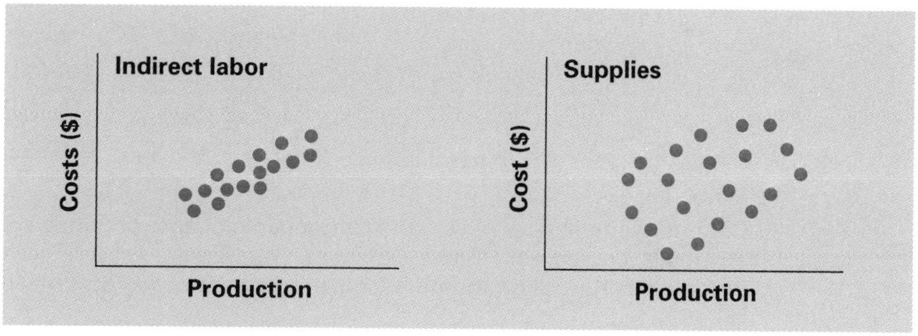

3-8 ***Mixed costs*** The president of Gorman Company has asked you to develop a behavioral classification for indirect labor cost. You have the following data from two recent months.

Direct Labor Hours	Indirect Labor Cost
19,000	$63,600
27,000	80,800

Required

Compute the fixed and variable portions of indirect labor cost based on direct labor hours.

3-9 ***Cost behavior*** A study of office supplies used in the regional sales offices of a large manufacturer shows that the cost is mixed. A record of sales and corresponding supply costs in one of the offices is as follows.

Monthly Sales	Cost of Supplies
$43,000	$2,164
48,000	2,486
34,000	2,115
52,000	2,521
37,000	2,315
38,000	2,464
45,000	2,728
56,000	2,984
50,000	2,652

Required
Determine the variable cost percentage of sales and the fixed costs using the high-low method.

3-10 ***Revenue and cost analysis—high-low method*** The controller of your firm, a retail store, is attempting to develop CVP relationships to be used for planning and control. He is not sure how this might be done and asks your assistance. He has prepared two income statements from monthly data.

	October	November
Sales	$50,000	$60,000
Cost of goods sold	30,000	36,000
Gross profit	20,000	24,000
Operating expenses:		
Selling expenses	7,400	7,700
Administrative expenses	6,200	6,400
Total expenses	13,600	14,100
Income	$ 6,400	$ 9,900

Required
1. Determine the fixed and variable components of cost of goods sold, selling expenses, and administrative expenses.
2. Prepare a contribution margin income statement based on sales of $70,000.

3-11 ***Explaining regression analysis (related to Appendix)*** The controller of ARCON, Inc. has received the following regression results from the industrial engineering department.

Y = monthly manufacturing supplies cost, X = machine hours
$Y = \$89{,}234 + \$0.8765X$, $r^2 = .6781$, $S_e = \$9{,}289$

The data were collected in a range of 30,000 to 50,000 monthly machine hours for the company's only plant. The controller wants your assistance in explaining these results to a group of managers.

Required
Write a memorandum that explains the meaning and significance of each of the items in the regression results. Use the guidelines in Appendix B.

3-12 Interpretation of scatter diagram The graph below depicts the costs experienced by Magma Enterprises.

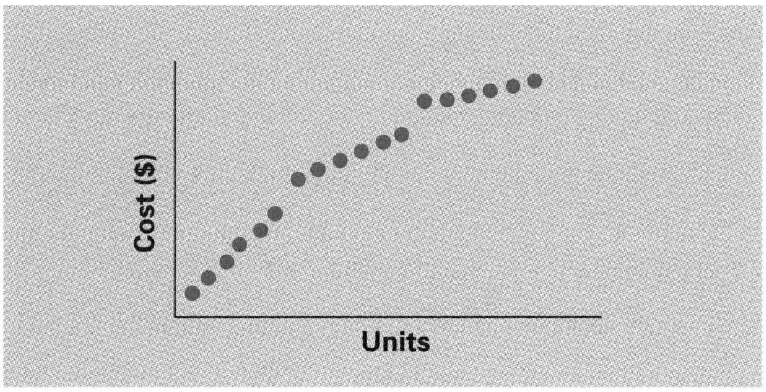

Required

1. Give some possible reasons for the observed behavior of costs.
2. How would you plan for costs that exhibited this type of behavior?

3-13 High-low method for manufacturing company The chief accountant of Blackman Industries prepared the following income statements.

	June	July
Sales	$420,000	$450,000
Cost of sales	216,000	225,000
Gross margin	204,000	225,000
Selling and administrative expenses	105,000	108,000
Income before taxes	$ 99,000	$117,000

Blackman produces a single product.

Required

1. Determine the fixed and variable components of cost of sales and of selling and administrative expenses.
2. Prepare income statements for June and July using the contribution-margin format. Comment on the differences between the statements above and the ones that you prepared.

3-14 Relationships Answer the following questions, considering each situation independently. You may not be able to answer the questions in the order they are asked.

1. A firm earns $40,000, selling 50,000 units at $5 per unit. Its fixed costs are $180,000.
   (a) What are variable costs per unit?
   (b) What is total contribution margin?
   (c) What would income be if sales increased by 5,000 units?
2. A firm has return of sales of 10%, income of $30,000, selling price of $10, and a contribution margin of 30%.
   (a) What are fixed costs?
   (b) What are variable costs per unit?
   (c) What are sales in units?
   (d) What are sales in dollars?

3. A firm has return of sales of 15% at sales of $300,000. Its fixed costs are $75,000, and variable costs are $6 per unit.
   (a) What are sales in units?
   (b) What is contribution margin per unit?
   (c) What is income?

3-15 Using per-unit data Nimmer Company expects the following per-unit results at a volume of 80,000 units.

Sales		$4.00
Variable costs	$1.40	
Fixed costs	2.25	3.65
Profit		$0.35

Required

Answer the following questions independently of one another.

1. How many units must the company sell to earn a profit of $90,000?
2. If Nimmer could sell 70,000 units, what selling price will yield a $60,000 profit?
3. Nimmer can undertake an advertising campaign for $6,000. Volume will increase by 3,000 units at the $4 selling price. By how much and in which direction (increase or decrease) will the company's profit change if it takes the action?

3-16 Percentage income statement The president of Fillmore Industries has developed the following income statement showing expected percentage results at sales of $800,000.

Sales	100%
Cost of sales	60%
Gross margin	40%
Other expenses	30%
Income	10%

The president tells you that cost of sales is all variable and that the only other variable cost is commissions, which are 10% of sales.

Required

1. Determine the profit that the company expects to earn.
2. Determine the break-even point and the margin of safety.
3. If sales are $700,000, what will profit be?
4. The president wants a $120,000 profit. Expected unit volume is the same as for the statement above. By what percentage must the company increase its selling price to achieve the goal? Assume the *per-unit* cost of sales remains constant.

3-17 Cost behavior graphs (AICPA adapted) Graphs and descriptions of cost elements are given on the next page. For each description, select the letter of the graph that best shows the behavior of the cost. Graphs may be used more than once. The zero point for each graph is the intersection of the horizontal and vertical axes. The vertical axis represents *total* cost for the described cost

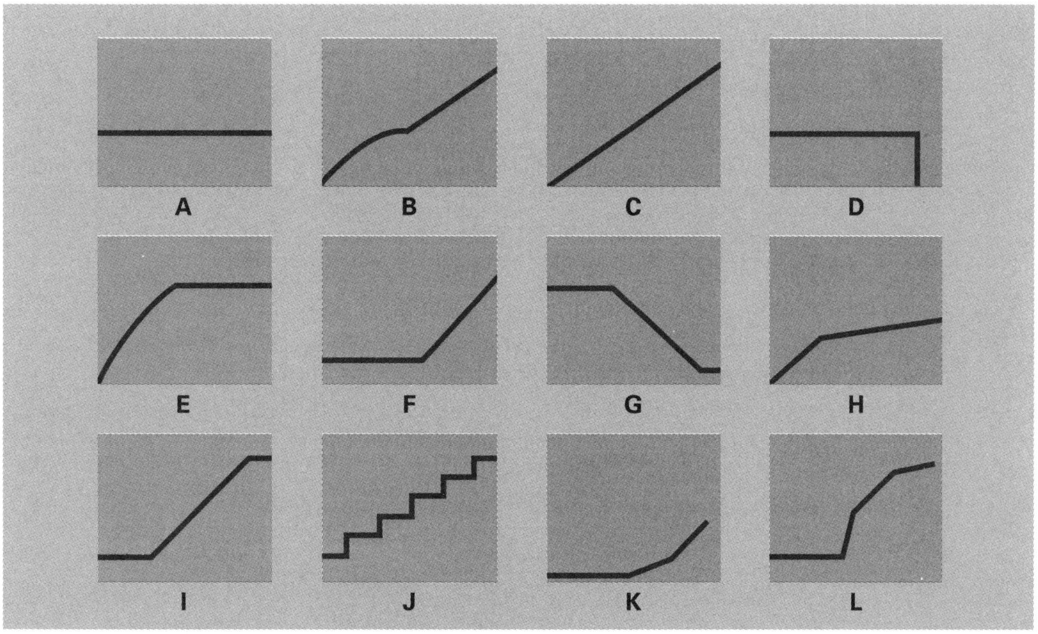

and the horizontal axis represents production in units. Be prepared to discuss any assumptions you might have to make in selecting your answers.

1. Depreciation of equipment, using the units-of-production method.
2. Electricity bill, a flat charge plus a variable cost after a certain number of kilowatt-hours are used.
3. City water bill, computed as follows:

First 1,000,000 gallons or less	$1,000 flat fee
Next 10,000 gallons	0.003 per gallon used
Next 10,000 gallons	0.006 per gallon used
Next 10,000 gallons	0.009 per gallon used
etc., etc., etc.	

4. Cost of lubricant for machines, where cost per unit decreases with each pound of lubricant used (for example, if one pound is used, the cost is $10.00; if two pounds are used, the cost is $19.98; if three pounds are used, the cost is $29.94; with a minimum cost per pound of $9.25).
5. Depreciation of equipment, using the straight-line method.
6. Rent for a factory building donated by the city, where the agreement calls for a fixed-fee payment unless 200,000 person-hours are worked, in which case no rent need be paid.
7. Salaries of repairpeople, where one repairperson is needed for every 1,000 hours of machine-time or less (i.e., 0 to 1,000 hours requires one repairperson, 1,001 to 2,000 hours requires two repairpeople, etc.).
8. Federal unemployment compensation taxes, where the labor force is constant in number throughout the year and the average annual wage is $16,000. The tax is levied only on the first $8,500 earned by each employee.

9. Rent for production machinery, computed as follows:

First 10,000 hours of use	$20,000 flat fee
Next 2,000 hours of use	$1.90 per hour
Next 2,000 hours of use	$1.80 per hour
Next 2,000 hours of use	$1.70 per hour
etc., etc., etc.	

10. Rent for a factory building donated by the county, where the agreement calls for rent of $100,000 less $1 for each hour laborers worked in excess of 200,000 hours, but a minimum rental payment of $20,000 is required.

3-18 Cost behavior—regression analysis (related to Appendix) The following data have been collected for the purpose of determining the behavior of factory costs.

Month	Units Produced	Factory Costs
January	112	$1,820
February	154	2,296
March	98	1,568

Required

1. Determine the fixed and variable components of factory costs using the high-low method.
2. Repeat part 1 using regression analysis.

3-19 Target profits and unit prices Tina's Handicrafts sells handmade sweaters at $50 apiece. The firm acquires the sweaters from Ms. Posey at $30 apiece, but the agreement with her also requires an extra fee of 10% (of selling price) for each sweater sold. Monthly fixed costs are $3,000.

Required

Answer each of the following questions independently.

1. If the firm wants to earn profit of $3,000 a month before taxes, how many sweaters must it sell?
2. The firm wants a before-tax profit of $5,000 and expects to sell 500 sweaters. What price must be charged per sweater to obtain the desired level of profit?
3. Suppose the firm is selling 500 sweaters per month at $50 and making a before-tax profit of $4,500. Ms. Posey offers to renegotiate the buying agreement so that there would be a charge of $24 per sweater plus a 20% (based on selling price) fee per sweater sold. How many sweaters must the firm sell under the new agreement to earn the same $4,500 in before-tax profits?

PROBLEMS

3-20 Profit improvement alternatives Following is the income statement for Meriwether Company for 19X6.

Sales (100,000 × $10)	$1,000,000
Variable costs (100,000 × $7)	700,000
Contribution margin	300,000
Fixed costs	250,000
Profit	$ 50,000

Leslie Meriwether, president of the company, was not happy with the 19X6 results and stated that a profit of $100,000 was a reasonable target for 19X7. She instructed the controller to analyze each component of the statement separately and determine the change in each component that would allow the firm to earn the target profit of $100,000. (For example, what change in per-unit selling price would produce the target profit if sales volume, fixed costs, and per-unit variable costs remained constant; or what change in sales volume would be needed, assuming that prices and costs did not change?)

Required
Write a memorandum to Ms. Meriwether that summarizes your findings and indicates what changes might be easier to achieve. Use the guidelines in Appendix B.

3-21 Interpretation of data Your assistant used the scatter diagram below to separate maintenance expenses into the fixed and variable components. She derived the following equation: Monthly total cost = $350 + ($0.80 × machine-hours), which is represented by the line drawn on the diagram.

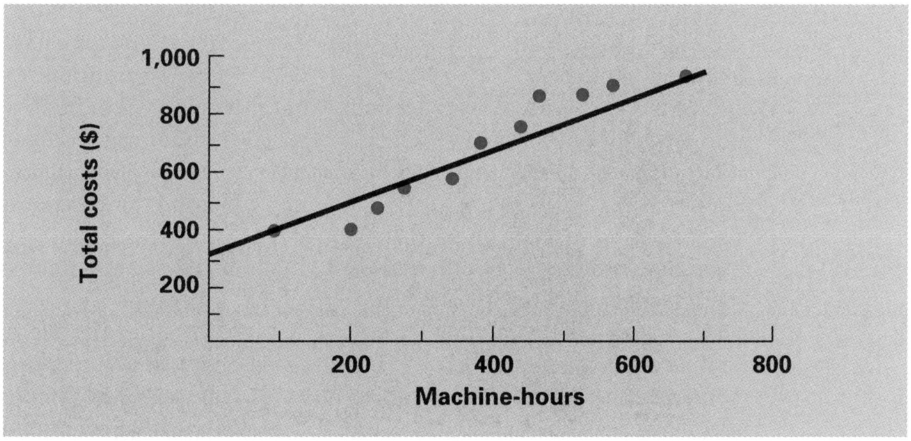

Required
Comment on the way in which your assistant fitted the line to the data and make an alternative recommendation.

3-22 Activity-based cost analysis The controller of the Wellcome Plant of RKD Industries has been analyzing costs of support departments to identify the major cost drivers and seek ways to reduce costs. He has just finished analyzing the costs and activity of the production scheduling department. The schedulers determine when particular products will be made, what machinery will be used, and how large the batch will be. Scheduling has come under increasing pressure as the number of products the plant manufactures has increased. The controller has assembled the following information regarding scheduling costs and the number of different products being made. All amounts are in thousands.

Quarter	Number of Products	Costs of Production Scheduling Department
19X6 Q4	5.2	$93.0
19X6 Q3	5.2	84.0
19X6 Q2	4.2	83.8
19X6 Q1	4.1	82.3
19X5 Q4	4.0	75.1
19X5 Q3	3.2	74.0
19X5 Q2	3.2	67.0
19X5 Q1	2.7	66.0

Required

Analyze the scheduling department costs using a scatter diagram or regression analysis. Comment on the usefulness of the results for pursuing cost reduction.

3-23 ***Cost drivers*** For each of the following costs, indicate which activity of those listed below might drive it. Some activities might drive more than one cost, some might drive none of the listed costs. You might also suggest activities not listed below.

Costs	Activities
Machine maintenance	Direct labor hours
Wages of workers who reset machinery when products change	Number of parts in a product
Costs of inspecting incoming materials and components	Number of employees
Costs of keeping records on workers—how much they produce, what they earn	Number of products
Costs of inspecting finished products	Number of sales orders
Costs to rework defective units	Number of customers
Building maintenance	Number of components/parts stocked
Personnel department costs, including payroll processing costs	Number of suppliers
Purchasing department costs, including soliciting bids from vendors and preparing, reviewing, and auditing purchase orders	Number of incoming shipments
Customer billing	Number of outgoing shipments
	Number of production runs of individual products
	Production in units
	Sales in dollars
	Machine hours
	Space in factory

3-24 ***Delta Airlines cost structure*** The 1990 annual report of Delta Airlines contained the following data, in millions of dollars.

Operating revenues	$8,582.2
Operating expenses	$8,162.7
Operating income	$ 419.5
Load factor (percentage of available seat-miles occupied)	61.15%
Break-even load factor	57.96%

Required

1. Determine the variable cost as a percentage of revenue for Delta Airlines in 1990. (Hint: Find total revenue and total cost at break-even then use the high-low method.)
2. Determine fixed operating costs for Delta Airlines for 1990.
3. Determine what operating income Delta Airlines would have earned had it flown its aircraft 62.15% full (one percentage point higher than it actually did.)
4. What does your answer to part 3 tell you about how to be successful in the airline industry?

3-25 Multiple regression analysis (related to Appendix) Your boss at AJK Company has just handed you the following results of a regression analysis.

$$Y = \$32{,}450 + \$2.44L + \$1.10M$$

where

Y = total monthly manufacturing overhead cost
L = labor hours
M = machine hours

AJK plans to use 12,000 labor hours and 2,000 machine-hours next month.

Required

1. Determine the total manufacturing overhead cost that AJK should incur next month.
2. AJK makes a product that has $3.50 in materials cost. It requires two hours of labor time and 30 minutes of machine time. Laborers earn $7.50 per hour. What is the product's per-unit variable manufacturing cost?
3. Suppose that AJK could reduce the labor time for the product described in item 2 by 30 minutes, to 1.50 hours. Machine time will remain the same. By how much would the per-unit variable manufacturing cost fall?

3-26 Understanding regression results (related to Appendix) The controller of the Cromwell Plant of TAYCO Enterprises has the following regression results prepared by the plant's statistician.

$$Y = \$57{,}528 + \$2.3561X,\ r^2 = .8243,\ S_e = \$11{,}356$$
$$Y = \text{monthly power cost},\ X = \text{machine hours}$$

The results are based on the past 30 months of operations during which monthly machine hours ranged from 80,000 to 140,000. The controller wants you to explain the results to some of her staff.

Required

1. If the plant will work 100,000 machine hours next month, what is the predicted power cost?
2. If the plant shuts down next month, should power cost be $57,528?
3. The company is considering a new product that requires 45 machine hours per batch of 100 units. What is the variable cost of power for the product?
4. How close are your predictions of power costs likely to be to the actual results? For example, can you state the range within which actual cost should be some specified percentage of the time?
5. Can you tell whether this equation is the best available to predict power costs?

3-27 Review problem, including income taxes, Chapters 2 and 3 (continued in Chapter 4) After reviewing its cost structure (variable costs of $7.50 per unit and monthly fixed costs of $60,000) and potential market, Forecast Company established what it considered to be a reasonable selling price. The company expected to sell 50,000 units per month and planned its monthly results as follows.

Sales	$500,000
Variable costs	375,000
Contribution margin	125,000
Fixed costs	60,000
Income before taxes	65,000
Income taxes (at 40%)	26,000
Net income	$ 39,000

Required

On the basis of the preceding information, answer the following questions independently. Items with an asterisk involve income taxes.

1. What selling price did the company establish?
2. What is the contribution margin per unit?
3. What is the break-even point in units?
4. If the company determined that a particular advertising campaign had a high probability of increasing sales by 3,000 units, how much could it pay for such a campaign without reducing its planned profits?
5. If the company wants a $60,000 before-tax profit, how many units must it sell?
6. If the company wants a 10% before-tax return on sales, what level of sales, in dollars, does it need?

*7. If the company wants a $45,000 after-tax profit, how many units must it sell?

*8. If the company wants an after-tax return on sales of 9%, how many units must it sell?

*9. If the company wants an after-tax profit of $45,000 on its expected sales volume of 50,000 units, what price must it charge?

10. If the company wants a before-tax return on sales of 16% on its expected sales volume of 50,000 units, what price must it charge?
11. The company is considering offering its salespeople a 5% commission on sales. What would the total sales, in dollars, have to be in order to implement the commission plan and still earn the planned pretax income of $65,000?

3-28 Cost formula, high-low method The owner of Bed and Bath Boutique regularly uses part-time help in addition to the full-time employees. Some part-time help is needed every day for miscellaneous chores and the owner arranges for additional hours based on estimates of sales for the following week. The following is a record of the wages paid to part-time employees at recent monthly sales volumes.

Sales	Wages Paid to Part-Time Help
$ 9,600	$ 874
2,000	600
6,400	730
17,000	1,260
18,000	1,350
12,800	1,030
15,000	1,362
6,000	710
11,000	960

The owner considers these months to be relatively normal; however, in the month with volume of $2,000, the Boutique was closed for about two weeks for repainting and the installation of new carpeting.

Required
Determine the variable cost rate and fixed costs using the high-low method.

3-29 Fixed costs in decision making Warren Keith owns a restaurant in a suburb of a large city. The restaurant does not do very much business during August, and Keith is considering closing down and taking a vacation for the month. He develops the following income statement based on planned operations for August.

Sales		$24,860
Cost of sales		9,740
Gross margin		15,120
Wages to part-time help	$4,500	
Utilities	1,500	
Rent on building	1,500	
Depreciation on fixtures	750	
Supplies and miscellaneous	6,450	14,700
Income		$ 420

Keith believes it is not worthwhile to stay open unless he can net at least $2,000 for the month. He works hard when the restaurant is open and believes that he deserves at least that much to compensate him for the work he does.

He also tells you that if he closes, he will have to pay a minimum utility bill of $350. Supplies and miscellaneous expenses are fixed, but avoidable if he closed.

Required
Write a memorandum that advises Mr. Keith about the desirability of staying open for August. Use the guidelines in Appendix B.

3-30 Alternative cost structures—a movie company (continuation of 2-43) Lois Lane, the president of Blockbusters Incorporated, has reviewed the preliminary analysis of the two contract alternatives and wishes to give further consideration to the arrangements with Kirkwalker. Kirkwalker's agent is also having second thoughts about the alternatives and is wondering what is best for his client.

Required

Answer the following questions.

1. If total paid admissions are expected to be between $9 and $10 million, which compensation scheme is best for (a) Blockbusters and (b) Kirkwalker? (*Hint:* Refer to your answers in 2-43 regarding break-even points.)
2. If total paid admissions are expected to be about $20 million, which scheme is better for (a) Blockbusters and (b) Kirkwalker?

3-31 Regression analysis (related to Appendix) Your new assistant has just handed you the following results of a regression analysis.

Factory overhead = \$262,203 + (\$13.19 × units produced)

You are surprised because your company makes several models of lawn mowers and you had not thought it possible to express factory overhead so simply. Your assistant assures you that the results are correct, giving you the following data.

Month	Units Produced	Factory Overhead
January	1,700	$260,000
February	1,100	280,000
March	2,800	300,000
April	2,300	260,000
May	2,000	360,000
June	1,800	320,000
July	2,400	320,000
August	2,000	200,000
September	2,100	300,000

Required

Comment on your assistant's results. You may assume the mathematical accuracy of your assistant's work.

3-32 Alternative CVP graph Below are data for three alternatives being considered by the managers of Sanders Company. Each represents a particular strategy for one of its products. The differences result from alternatives such as salaries versus commissions and different levels of product quality, advertising, and promotion.

Alternative	Price	Variable Cost	Fixed Costs
1	$20	$12	$180,000
2	$20	$ 8	$240,000
3	$18	$10	$120,000

When evaluating alternative strategies, the firm's managers prefer the alternative graphical approach presented on page 111. It represents a graph with Alternative 1 already plotted.

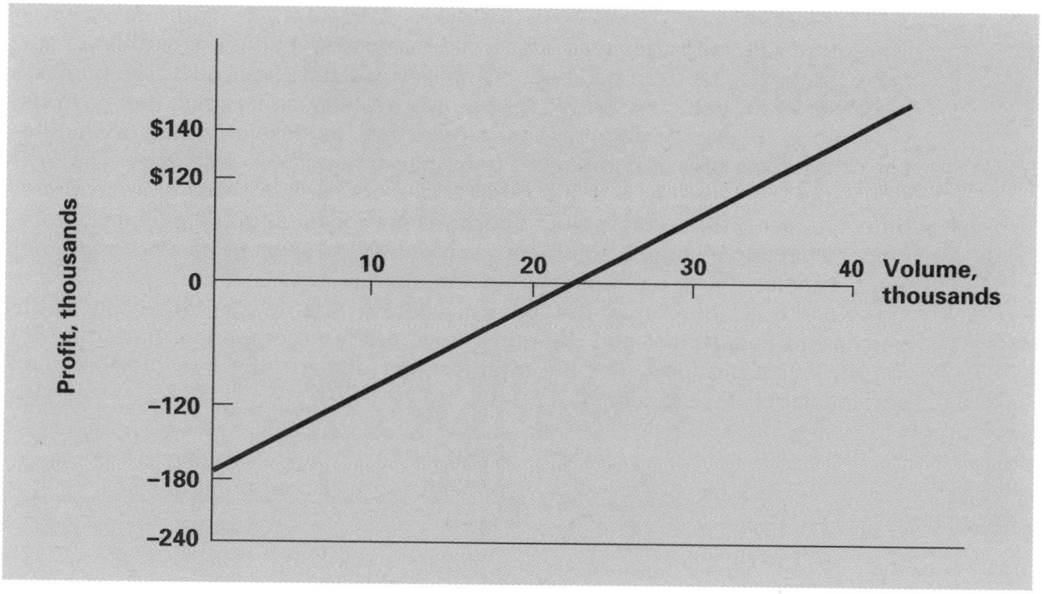

Required

1. Plot the profit lines for alternatives 2 and 3.
2. What general conclusions can you draw from the completed graph? Could you select the best alternative based on the graphical results?

3-33 ***Changes in costs*** Stoneham Company manufactures a complete line of toiletries. The average selling price per case is $20 and cost data appear below.

Variable costs per case:	
Materials	$4.00
Labor	2.00
Other variable costs	2.00
Total variable costs	$8.00
Annual fixed costs:	
Manufacturing	$1,500,000
Selling and administrative	$2,500,000

Art Stoneham, the president, expects to sell 350,000 cases in the coming year. After gathering the above data, Stoneham learned that materials costs will increase by 25% because of shortages.

Required

1. Determine the profit that Stoneham expected before the increase in materials prices.
2. Given the increase in materials costs, determine the price that Stoneham has to charge to earn the profit you calculated in item 1.
3. Suppose that Stoneham decided to raise the price enough to maintain the same contribution margin percentage it had before the cost increase.
   (a) Determine the price.
   (b) Would Stoneham earn more or less than your answer to item 2 if it charged that price and sold 350,000 cases?

3-34 Cost drivers, activity-based analysis The controller of the Summerton Division of KPL Industries was concerned that costs of some departments normally thought to be fixed had been rising over the past few years. The purchasing department had come in for special review because its costs had been rising rapidly. The purchasing manager argued that the division's increasing number of products and of component parts had strained his resources. The division's products are similar, but product designers use parts that differ in size or other characteristics. Purchasing is responsible for finding and evaluating vendors, inspecting incoming shipments, reordering parts when needed, and other tasks associated with managing component parts.

The controller developed the following data related to quarterly costs of the purchasing department and the number of different component parts used in the division's products (not the total number of parts put into products). All amounts are in thousands.

Quarter	Number of Parts	Purchasing Department Costs
19X6 Q4	14.2	$123.1
19X6 Q3	14.1	115.1
19X6 Q2	12.8	111.7
19X6 Q1	11.0	109.0
19X5 Q4	10.9	106.7
19X5 Q3	10.8	106.6
19X5 Q2	10.1	104.6
19X5 Q1	10.1	100.1

Required

Analyze the purchasing department's costs using a scatter diagram or regression analysis. What do your results tell about cost reduction?

3-35 Negative fixed costs The managers of Kooper Company have observed the following costs and activity.

Month	Direct Labor Hours	Overhead Costs
1	2,200	$3,590
2	2,500	4,210
3	2,800	4,830
4	2,300	3,780
5	3,100	5,400
6	3,200	5,650

Required

1. Find the fixed and variable components of overhead costs using either a scatter diagram or regression analysis.
2. Does the pattern make sense to you? Is it possible to have negative fixed costs? Can you suggest an explanation?
3. How would you handle the negative fixed cost for planning purposes?

3-36 Cost structures and average costs At a dinner meeting of a local association of company accountants, the following conversation took place.

Ruth Hifixed: "My firm has enormous fixed costs, and volume is our critical problem. My cost per unit is now $6, at 100,000 units, but if I could get 200,000 units, cost per unit would drop to $4. My selling price is also too low, only $6."

Jim Lofixed: "You are lucky. My cost per unit is $5 at 200,000 units, but we can't produce any more than 200,000. At least we're now better off than we were when sales were 80,000 units. At that volume we lost $0.50 per unit at our $6 price. We kept the same selling price at all volumes."

Required

1. Compute the profit earned by each firm at its current level of sales.
2. Determine fixed costs, variable cost per unit, and contribution margin per unit for each firm.
3. Compute the break-even point for each firm.
4. Which firm earns more at 150,000 units?
5. Which firm earns more at 100,000 units?

3-37 Cost classification Halton's Flower Shop buys and sells floral arrangements. The average selling price is $25, and average purchase cost is $5. Weekly fixed costs are $4,000. Because the arrangements are perishable, the shop cannot sell any units after they have been in inventory for one week. The shop must order a full week's supply at one time.

Mr. Halton, the owner, would like to earn $1,000 per week from the business. A friend has explained CVP analysis to him and made the following calculation.

$$\text{Unit volume required for \$1,000 profit} = \frac{\$4,000 + \$1,000}{\$25 - \$5}$$
$$= 250 \text{ arrangements}$$

Required

1. Is the above equation correct in the sense that if Mr. Halton orders 250 arrangements per week, he will earn $1,000? Why or why not?
2. Is the purchase cost fixed or variable? Explain.
3. Can you tell Mr. Halton how many arrangements he must sell to earn $1,000 if he purchases 300? If he purchases 400?

3-38 Cost estimation—service business William Jarvis operates his own firm of Certified Public Accountants. For planning purposes, he is interested in developing information about the cost structure of the firm. At times, he hires part-time employees, usually accounting majors from the nearby university.

The best measure of activity for the firm is chargeable hours, the number of hours that employees work on client business. The firm charges the clients for these hours at hourly rates. Jarvis has the following data regarding wages of part-time employees from recent months.

Total Chargeable Hours	Part-Time Wages
3,000	$3,000
3,500	3,100
2,800	2,990
3,200	3,090
4,800	5,400
5,200	6,180
5,600	6,900

Required

Plot the data on a scatter diagram and comment on the results. Can Mr. Jarvis use your results for planning? What reasons might there be for the pattern that you observe?

3-39 Labor policies—cost behavior In conversation with the president of Hirsch Industries, you hear the following: "We employ 40 skilled workers and guarantee them 80 hours of work per month even if production doesn't keep them busy. When we crank up production beyond a 40-hour week for all of our employees, we work overtime and pay $6 per hour instead of the usual $4. Each of our workers produces two units of product per hour."

Required

1. Determine the firm's total labor cost at the following monthly volumes of production in units. Assume that a month has four weeks.
   (a) 5,000
   (b) 6,000
   (c) 7,000
   (d) 10,000
   (e) 14,000
   (f) 16,000
2. Graph the firm's labor costs, with clearly marked points on the horizontal axis for the volumes where the cost behavior changes.
3. What is the range, if any, over which labor cost per unit behaves like a true variable cost?

3-40 Understanding regression results (related to Appendix) Your assistant in the Cost Management Office has just brought in some regression results sent over by the plant's operations analysis group. The group tried several regressions to analyze power costs. The first equation used direct labor hours as the independent variable.

$$Y = \$182{,}938 + \$0.5612X,\ r^2 = .2691,\ S_e = \$79{,}982$$
$$Y = \text{monthly power costs},\ X = \text{labor hours}$$

The second equation used machine hours as the independent variable.

$$Y = \$61{,}122 + \$1.4651X,\ r^2 = .7314,\ S_e = \$8{,}982$$
$$Y = \text{monthly power costs},\ X = \text{machine hours}$$

The number of labor hours per month runs between 15,000 and 25,000. The number of machine hours between 70,000 and 125,000, depending on the mix of products being made.

The controller has requested that your office do a study to help her planning and you are to discuss the results with her shortly.

Required

Write a memorandum to the controller. Justify your recommendation. Use the guidelines in Appendix B.

3-41 CVP analysis for an airline Icarus Airlines flies a number of routes in the southwestern United States. The firm owns six airplanes, each of which can hold 150 passengers. All routes are about the same distance, and all fares are $66 one way. The line is obligated to provide 250 flights per month. Each flight costs $4,000 for gasoline, crew salaries, and so on. Variable costs per passenger are $6, to cover a meal and a head tax imposed for each passenger at every airport to which Icarus flies. Other costs, all fixed, are $130,000 per month.

Required

1. How many passengers must Icarus carry on its 250 flights in order to earn $70,000 profit per month? What percentage of capacity is this number?

2. If the firm could cut its flights to 200 per month, how many passengers are required to earn $70,000 per month? What percentage of capacity does this number represent (using 200 flights as capacity)?
3. Is the $4,000 cost per flight fixed or variable?
4. What is the chief problem faced by a firm with this type of cost structure?

3-42 Promotional campaign Ajax Publishers sells magazine subscriptions. Its managers are considering a large promotional campaign in which it will award prizes of $10,000,000. Other costs associated with the campaign appear below.

Television time	$ 4,400,000
Fee to Fred Mahon, TV spokesperson	700,000
Mailing	5,300,000
Total	$10,400,000

Ajax plans to mail 20,000,000 packages containing entry blanks and forms for subscribing to magazines. Ajax receives 25% of total subscription revenue. Experience indicates that about 15% of those receiving a package take out one or more subscriptions. The average subscription revenue from a respondent is $35.

Required

1. What profit will Ajax earn if the campaign meets all expectations?
2. What is the break-even point for the campaign expressed as a response rate, assuming that each respondent orders $35 in magazine subscriptions?

3-43 Calculating contribution margin percentage Bell Company has a 25% margin of safety. Its after-tax return on sales is 6%, and its tax rate is 40%.

Required

1. Determine Bell's contribution margin percentage.
2. Assuming that current sales are $120,000, determine total fixed costs.

3-44 Committed versus discretionary cost Gladack Company makes a number of products and uses a great deal of machinery. A new product this coming year will require the acquisition of a new machine. The machine can only be leased, not purchased. There are two alternative leasing arrangements: (1) a month-to-month lease that can be canceled on 30-days' notice by either Gladack or the lessor, at a monthly rental of $6,000, and (2) a five-year noncancelable lease at $5,200 per month. The new product is expected to have a life of five years, during which annual revenues will be $250,000 and annual variable costs $100,000. There are no new fixed costs other than the lease payments. The president is concerned that the five-year lease removes a great deal of flexibility; if the product does not pan out as expected, the company is stuck with the machine and there are no other uses for it. He does, however, like the idea of saving $800 per month.

Required

1. Are the rentals, under each alternative, discretionary or committed fixed costs?

2. Why would the president hesitate between the choices? What could happen to make him regret choosing (a) the five-year lease? (b) the month-to-month lease?
3. Suppose Gladack takes the monthly lease option. It is now the end of the fourth year, and management expects the sales of the product will be $90,000 in year five, evenly spread over the year. Should the firm use the machine for the fifth year?
4. Answer item 3 again assuming that the firm had signed the five-year lease.

3-45 Loss per unit A firm had a loss of $3 *per unit* when sales were 40,000 units. When sales were 50,000 units, the firm had a loss of $1.60 *per unit.*

Required

1. Determine contribution margin per unit.
2. Determine fixed costs.
3. Determine the break-even point in units.

3-46 CVP analysis—measures of volume Acme Foam Rubber Company buys large pieces of foam rubber (called "loaves") and cuts them into small pieces that are used in seat cushions and other products. A loaf contains 5,000 board feet of foam rubber (a "board foot" is one foot square and one inch thick), of which 10% becomes scrap during the process of cutting up the loaf. A loaf costs $700, including freight, and the firm is currently processing 100 loaves per month.

The firm charges $0.22 per board foot for its good output, $0.07 per board foot for the scrap. Variable costs of cutting the loaf are $100, for labor and power to run the cutting machines. Fixed costs are $18,000 per month.

The president of the firm has asked for your assistance in developing CVP relationships.

Required

1. Determine the firm's income when it processes 100 loaves per month.
2. Determine the firm's break-even point expressed as number of loaves processed.
3. The president tells you that your analyses in items 1 and 2 are not what he had in mind. He says that he is accustomed to thinking in terms of board feet of good output sold. He would like to know how many board feet he would have to sell to earn $6,000 per month. Determine the firm's contribution margin per board foot of good output sold and sales required to earn $6,000 per month.

CASES

3-47 Measures of volume The controller of Throckton Company has been to a seminar on CVP analysis and wants to use some of the techniques she learned. She gives you the following data and asks that you analyze each cost into its fixed and variable components. She plans to use the information for profit planning. You prepare the following schedules of costs and measures of activity for the previous 6 months.

Sales	Labor Hours	Production Costs	Selling Expenses	Administrative Expenses
$12,000	500	$ 9,100	$3,250	$3,200
10,000	700	11,000	2,980	3,300
21,000	1,200	14,300	4,130	4,100
30,000	1,300	15,300	4,950	4,500
33,000	900	11,980	5,370	4,300
35,000	800	11,200	5,560	4,800

Required

Analyze the cost behavior patterns in accordance with the request of the controller. Indicate weaknesses and suggest possible improvement.

3-48 Value-adding and non-value-adding activities and costs MUL Company manufactures six types of products. The products are relatively standard, not made-to-order. MUL takes orders from customers, then fills the orders from stock or manufactures the required units. The company keeps finished units in a warehouse that it also uses for materials and components. The Quality Control Division inspects all shipments of materials and components, as well as all finished products before they are shipped.

The company holds a two- to three-month supply of parts and components that it uses to make high-volume products. MUL's purchasing manager is responsible for obtaining materials and components at the lowest possible cost and so scours the country looking for the best deals. MUL therefore uses a good many vendors.

Production begins by withdrawing the necessary materials and components from the warehouse, inspecting them for possible deterioration during storage, and transporting them to the first station that works on the product. Each station does one function, such as drilling, planing, welding, and various assembly operations.

Each station has an area to store materials and components for jobs that it has not yet started. The materials wait in the area until the station is ready to begin the job. Setup time in going from one product to another is often substantial at some stations. After the workers at the station have finished with their part of the job, they send the semi-completed units along with the materials and components not yet installed to the next station. There the same process is repeated and so on until all work is completed. In some cases, a job will go to the same station more than once because it requires the same operation at different stages of production.

At the conclusion of production, units go the Quality Control Division to await testing and inspection. They then go to the warehouse for shipment. The company usually makes 10% more units than needed for an order to allow for defects. Any spare good units are held in the warehouse until another order arrives. Defective units are sometimes reworked, sometimes sold as scrap. Reworked units are stored in the warehouse. If it is possible to determine which work station caused the defect, its manager is held responsible. (Bonuses for station managers are based largely on total good output.) In cases where it is not possible to determine the source of the defect, no one is held responsible.

The factory manager has said that "it gets pretty hectic at the end of each month when we're trying to finish up jobs and get the stuff out to the warehouse."

The cycle time varies among types of products, but runs from 10 days to 45 days depending on various factors.

Required
What activities described above do not add value to products? What changes in operations can you recommend?

3-49 Determining variable costs of products—activity-based analysis Mel Teague, controller of Rothman Industries, has not been satisfied with the cost analysis that the staff has been doing. Predictions of total costs have been well off the mark and other managers have complained about poor information on which to base their decisions. The staff has used direct labor hours to develop regression equations for all manufacturing overhead costs.

Teague believed that the staff had failed to recognize that drivers other than direct labor hours are at work. She therefore conducted a study of cost pools and drivers and developed the following analysis, showing the fixed and variable components of various cost pools and drivers.

Cost Driver	Variable Amount
Direct labor hours (DLH)	$ 3.00 per DLH
Machine hours (MH)	$18.00 per MH
Number of parts/components	$ 0.05 per part
Total processing time	$ 3.00 per hour

Teague has instructed you to determine the variable cost of two products using the data she has developed. Variable costs for materials and labor and other data for the products are:

	Product 816	Product 389
Materials cost	$13.00	$11.00
Direct labor cost at $14 per DLH	7.00	14.00
Other data:		
Machine hours	0.50	0.20
Number of parts	120	185
Total processing time	10.0 hours	5.0 hours

Required
1. Determine the total variable cost of each product.
2. Suppose that the staff had estimated variable overhead cost at $40.00 per direct labor hour. Determine the cost of each product using that estimate.
3. Comment on the differences between your answers to parts 1 and 2.

4 additional aspects of cost-volume-profit analysis

Planned and actual results usually differ, and managers analyze these differences, called variances. This chapter illustrates techniques for analyzing variances. (Chapter 12 continues the discussion.) This chapter also treats some aspects of CVP analysis that we have not yet discussed, with special attention to multiproduct companies. Finally, we discuss the use of CVP analysis by not-for-profit entities.

ANALYZING VARIANCES

Income depends on several factors, including selling price, sales volume, and the firm's costs. Planned and actual incomes rarely coincide because prices, volume, and costs can (and do) vary from expectations. To plan and to evaluate previous decisions, managers need to know the sources of variances.

The analytical approach in this chapter concentrates on variances in contribution margin, specifically those that arise because of differences between (1) planned and actual sales volume and (2) planned and actual selling prices. (Managers often use the same analysis to explain differences between the actual results of two periods, such as the current and the prior month.) Of course, planned and actual contribution margin also can differ because of changes in variable costs. Analysis of cost variances requires a full chapter (Chapter 12). The analyses in this chapter are nevertheless important and provide useful information for planning and control.

Suppose Horton Company expected to sell 20,000 units at $20 with unit variable costs of $12. Horton actually sold 21,000 units at $19. These results and the differences appear in Exhibit 4-1.

Exhibit 4-1 Horton Company, Planned and Actual Results

	Actual	Planned	Difference
Units sold	21,000	20,000	1,000
Sales	$399,000	$400,000	$ 1,000
Variable costs	252,000	240,000	12,000
Contribution margin	$147,000	$160,000	$13,000

We want to explain the $13,000 unfavorable variance, the difference between planned and actual contribution margin. Total revenues were $1,000 less than planned, while total variable costs were $12,000 more than planned. But notice that actual variable cost per unit was $12 ($252,000/21,000), the same as planned. So the difference in total variable costs is due to the increase in volume, not to a difference between planned and actual per-unit variable cost.

Two factors caused the difference between planned and actual contribution margin: a variance in selling price and a variance in sales volume. To isolate the effect of each factor, we hold one of them (price or volume) constant and look at the effect of the other. One simple way to do this is to prepare a statement that shows what would have happened if the firm had sold the actual volume, but at the planned price, as shown in Exhibit 4-2.

SALES VOLUME VARIANCE

The $8,000 difference in total contribution margin in Exhibit 4-2 is called the **sales volume variance**. The variance is the 1,000 additional units sold times the $8 planned contribution margin per unit. Thus, the sales volume variance can also be computed as

$$\textit{Sales volume variance} = \textit{planned contribution margin per unit} \times \left(\textit{actual sales, in units} - \textit{planned sales, in units}\right)$$

$$\$8{,}000 = \$8 \times (21{,}000 - 20{,}000)$$

Exhibit 4-2 Horton Company, Expected Results at Planned Price and Actual Volume

	Actual Results		Actual Volume at Planned Price		Planned Results
Units sold	21,000		21,000		20,000
Sales	$399,000		$420,000		$400,000
Variable costs	252,000		252,000		240,000
Contribution margin	$147,000		$168,000		$160,000
Differences		$21,000		$ 8,000	

If a company sells more units than planned, the variance is favorable. If it sells fewer units than planned, the variance is unfavorable. In this example, the variance is favorable. Again, please notice that we are holding selling price and per-unit variable cost constant because we want to determine the effect on total contribution margin of selling more (or fewer) units than planned. Holding selling price and per-unit variable cost constant is, by definition, holding contribution margin per unit constant.

Even if unit variable cost changed, we still would use the planned unit variable cost for this analysis, because we want to isolate the effects of sales volume *apart* from changes in variable costs or selling prices. We now can look at the variance in total contribution margin that is attributable only to the difference between the planned and actual selling price.

SALES PRICE VARIANCE

If unit cost does not change, a change in selling price changes unit contribution margin by the same amount and in the same direction. Horton sold its product for $19, or $1 less than planned. The $21,000 difference between the $168,000 contribution margin that would have been earned selling 21,000 units at the $20 price (Exhibit 4-2) and the actual contribution margin of $147,000 is the **sales price variance.** In this case, the variance is unfavorable, because the actual selling price was less than planned.

We can also calculate the sales price variance by multiplying the difference between the actual and planned prices by the actual unit volume.

Sales price variance = units sold × (actual price – planned price)
$21,000 = 21,000 × ($19 – $20)

The $1 difference between the planned and actual selling prices is also the difference between planned and actual unit contribution margin.

A word of caution. An "unfavorable" variance, either sales price or sales volume, is not *necessarily* bad, nor is a "favorable" variance *necessarily* good. The *total* variance in contribution margin is more important than either variance taken separately. The two variances are often related. A manager might lower prices to obtain a large increase in volume. The wisdom of such a decision depends on the overall results, not on either variance considered separately. Pricing policy is discussed in more detail later in the chapter. Also, it is important to know whether conditions were as expected when the original plans were developed. For instance, suppose the planned volume was based on forecasts of rapid growth for the industry and that growth failed to materialize. The company probably could not meet its planned volume, but the managers are not at fault because they cannot control industry sales. (The managers are responsible for accepting the inaccurate forecast, however.)

MULTIPLE PRODUCTS

Chapter 2 stated that CVP analysis assumes either a single product or a constant sales mix. (Recall that **sales mix** is the percentage of each product to total sales.) The reason for the assumption is that if the products have widely differing contribution margins, and if the mix changes, the company's contribution margin percentage will change and results could be much different from those predicted. Multiple-product firms can easily use CVP analysis for each individual product or for groups of products where the contribution margins (per-unit or percentage) are about equal. Also, they can use CVP analysis where contributions differ greatly, provided that the sales mix remains constant.

Many companies have a constant sales mix. Several reasons exist for firms having the same sales mix over several periods. Some firms sell products that are used together, so that the sales of one affect the sales of the other. Common examples are cameras and film, gasoline and motor oil, ice cream and toppings, and wallpaper and paste. Such products are called **complementary products**.

Even with no apparent complementary relationship among the firm's products, the sales mix still might remain fairly constant. A department store might consistently derive 40% of its sales from clothing, 25% from furniture and housewares, and 35% from its other departments. These percentages might be relatively constant over time despite the absence of obvious causes. Whatever the reasons for the predictability of sales mix, managers of a multiple-product firm can apply CVP analysis by using a weighted-average contribution margin.

WEIGHTED-AVERAGE CONTRIBUTION MARGIN PERCENTAGE

As its name suggests, the **weighted-average contribution margin percentage** is the overall contribution margin percentage. It consists of the individual products' percentages weighted by their relative sales. The weighted-average contribution margin percentage is used just as the contribution margin percentage is used for a single product.

Suppose that Ted of Ted's Threads (in Chapter 2) has expanded his business. He now sells shoes and jeans, as well as shirts. His fixed costs are now $30,000 per month because he has added employees and moved to a larger store. Data for the individual products appear below.

	Shirts	Shoes	Jeans
Selling price	$20	$50	$30
Variable cost	12	25	12
Contribution margin	$ 8	$25	$18
Contribution margin percentage	40%	50%	60%
Percentage in sales mix	60%	10%	30%

The percentages shown for sales mix are the proportions of total sales dollars coming from each product. (These percentages must total 100 percent.)

Ted has the same questions he had in Chapter 2: What is the break-even point? What sales are required to achieve a particular profit target? When Ted had only one product, he could probably work equally well with either dollars or units. With multiple products, it might be more convenient, and simpler, to work with sales dollars, so long as Ted looks at the business as a whole. In that case, Ted would measure volume by sales dollars instead of units, using the weighted-average contribution margin percentage.

We can calculate the weighted-average contribution margin percentage in several ways. One way is to prepare a hypothetical income statement, such as the one below, which assumes total sales of $100,000 and the sales mix that he expects.

	Shirts	Shoes	Jeans	Total	Percentage
Sales	$60,000	$10,000	$30,000	$100,000	100%
Variable costs	36,000	5,000	12,000	53,000	53%
Contribution margin	$24,000	$ 5,000	$18,000	$ 47,000	47%
Total fixed costs				30,000	
Profit				$ 17,000	

The weighted-average contribution margin percentage is 47%.

A more direct way to find the weighted-average contribution margin percentage is to multiply the contribution margin percentage for each product by its percentage in the sales mix and add the results. This calculation appears below.

	Shirts		Shoes		Jeans		Total
Contribution margin percentage	40%		50%		60%		
Percentage in sales mix	60%		10%		30%		100%
Weighted average	24%	+	5%	+	18%	=	47%

Let's look at the logic of this calculation. With the 60%, 10%, 30% sales mix, the *average* sales dollar is composed of $0.60 from shirts, $0.10 from shoes, and $0.30 from jeans. The $0.60 sales from shirts provides $0.24 in contribution margin because the contribution margin percentage on shirts is 40%. The contribution margin of $0.24 is the 24% in the shirts column. Similarly, the $0.30 sales of jeans in the average sales dollar provides $0.18 contribution margin because the rate on jeans is 60%. The following schedule shows the calculations in dollars.

	Shirts		Shoes		Jeans		Total
Average sales dollar	$0.60		$0.10		$0.30		$1.00
Contribution margin percentage	40%		50%		60%		
Contribution margin	$0.24	+	$0.05	+	$0.18	=	$0.47

Because the average sales dollar yields $0.47 in contribution margin, the weighted-average contribution margin percentage is 47%.

Using the 47% weighted-average contribution margin percentage, Ted now can do the same analyses he did in Chapter 2. His break-even point is $63,830, $30,000 fixed costs divided by 47% weighted-average contribution margin percentage. To earn a $20,000 target profit requires sales of $106,383 [($30,000 + $20,000)/47%].

CHANGES IN SALES MIX

Sales mix is very important when the contribution margin percentages differ greatly among products. (If all products have the same contribution margin percentages, that percentage *is* the weighted-average contribution margin percentage.) Suppose that Ted sees a trend that is likely to change his sales mix to 40% shirts, 30% shoes, and 30% jeans (a shift from shirts to shoes). His new weighted-average contribution margin percentage is 49%, an increase of two percentage points.

	Shirts		Shoes		Jeans		Total
Contribution margin percentage	40%		50%		60%		
Percentage in sales mix	40%		30%		30%		100%
Weighted average	16%	+	15%	+	18%	=	49%

Exhibit 4-3 shows Ted's CVP chart. Note that the horizontal axis shows sales in dollars rather than in units because we are working with contribution margin percentage. The chart shows two total cost lines to represent two sales mixes. The dotted line shows the 53% variable cost percentage, which holds when the weighted-average contribution margin percentage is 47% (as originally computed when the sales mix was 60% shirts, 10% shoes, and 30% jeans). The solid total cost line uses a 51% variable cost percentage, which holds when the weighted-average contribution margin is 49% (the second computation, when the sales mix was 40% shirts, 30% shoes, and 30% jeans).

The break-even point is lower and profits are higher, at any level of sales, when contribution margin is 49% than when it is 47%. *Other things equal,* a richer sales mix—one with a higher overall contribution margin percentage—is better, which explains why managers routinely try to enrich sales mix. Under some circumstances, if a firm can increase its total sales by some dollar amount, or shift a dollar in sales from one product to another, the product that should be emphasized is the one with the higher contribution margin percentage. Accordingly, managers might shift the emphasis in their regular advertising among products with higher contribution margin per-

Exhibit 4-3 CVP Chart for Ted's Threads

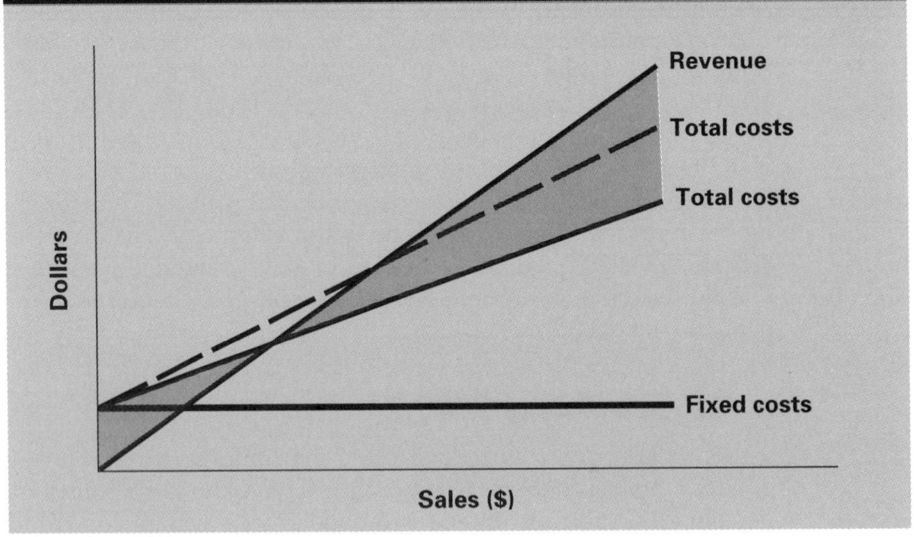

centages, while regularly devoting a minimum of advertising space to products carrying lower percentages.

Note, however, that some efforts to enrich sales mix might make "other things" *unequal*. For example, *increasing* advertising to enrich sales mix also increases fixed costs. In such cases, the indifference analysis described in Chapter 2 can be useful. Too, if two (or more) of the firm's products are substitutes, shifting sales from one to the other might *not* be profitable. That case is best considered in the next section, which deals with contribution margin per unit.

WEIGHTED-AVERAGE CONTRIBUTION MARGIN PER UNIT

Some multiple-product companies use units, rather than dollars, to measure volume. For instance, managers of an automobile manufacturer usually talk about the number of cars sold, rather than dollars of sales. (They are concerned, of course, about dollar sales, but most of the analyses they perform use units—cars—instead of dollars.) Similarly, managers of service businesses, such as CPA firms, law firms, and consulting firms, discuss their sales volumes in terms of chargeable hours, the hours that personnel spend on client business. Like cars, chargeable hours is a measure of unit volume. These managers also discuss sales mix in unit percentages, not dollar percentages. While Ted says that 40% of dollar sales are from shirts, a manager of an automaker says that 40% of the cars it sells are sedans.

Such companies could calculate weighted-average contribution margin percentages, but they often find it more useful to calculate a weighted-average contribution margin per unit. Consider the following data for Corbin Company, a manufacturer of three models of desks.

	President	Senior VP	Junior VP
Selling price	$1,000	$800	$500
Unit variable cost	600	500	250
Unit contribution margin	$ 400	$300	$250
Percentage in mix, in units	20%	30%	50%

The **weighted-average contribution margin per unit** is calculated in basically the same way as the weighted-average contribution margin percentage. The per-unit contribution margin of each product (in *dollars*, not as a *percentage*) is multiplied by its percentage in the sales mix.

	President		Senior VP		Junior VP		Total
Unit contribution margin	$400		$300		$250		
Mix percentage, in units	20%		30%		50%		
Weighted-average unit contribution margin	$ 80	+	$ 90	+	$125	=	$295

So long as the sales mix holds, managers can use the weighted-average unit contribution margin of $295 just as they would if the company made a single product. Thus, if Corbin's fixed costs are $500,000, its break-even point is about 1,695 desks (fixed costs of $500,000 divided by the weighted-average per-unit contribution margin of $295). To prove that the per-unit calculation works, suppose that Corbin sells 1,000 desks in the expected mix. Its income statement, through contribution margin, is:

	President	Senior VP	Junior VP	Total
Sales in units*	200	300	500	1,000
Sales	$200,000	$240,000	$250,000	$690,000
Variable costs	120,000	150,000	125,000	395,000
Contribution margin	$ 80,000	$ 90,000	$125,000	$295,000

* 1,000 × 20%, 30%, 50%

Total contribution margin is $295,000, which is exactly $295 times 1,000 total units. We also might note that the weighted-average contribution margin percentage is about 42.8% ($295,000/$690,000). Corbin's managers could use either form of contribution margin in their analyses.

Note that the contribution margin percentages of Corbin's three models, the President, Senior VP, and Junior VP, are 40%, 37.5%, and 50%, respectively. Would Corbin's profits increase if its managers tried to shift the sales mix toward the Junior VP, the model with the highest contribution margin percentage? The answer is: It depends. Unlike Ted's products, which might be complementary to some extent. Corbin manufactures **substitute products**. That is, for some customers, buying a desk of one model is likely to preclude buying a desk of another model. Because Corbin receives the contribution margin on only one desk, its managers would certainly prefer to receive the highest contribution margin possible on the one desk sold. (That is, they would not want to sell one more Junior VP if by doing so they lost a sale of one of the other models.) Hence, to the extent they can do so, Corbin's managers would try to attract customers by emphasizing the Junior VP, and then encourage those customers to consider the other models. Such a strategy is often associated with automobile and appliance dealers. (An extreme, and illegal, implementation of this strategy is called bait and switch, where the available supply of the product being promoted could not possibly meet the demand generated by the promotion.)

OVERALL PLANNING

Historical trends often provide clues to the expected sales mix, and managers can use the weighted-average contribution margin for planning. As suggested above, managers can also influence sales mix. For example, they might undertake special advertising campaigns or sales promotions aimed at one product. They can encourage salespeople to concentrate on certain products, either through direct instructions or special commissions. If, as we discussed earlier, some products are substitutes or complementary, managers should not adopt strategies to influence the volume of one product unless they have considered the effects on sales of the related products.

Before proposing a program that could influence sales mix, a manager needs to know price and cost data for each product as well as the current sales mix. These data give the manager some idea of profitability by product and how the sales mix might be enriched. Managers often study sales and cost data for various products and evaluate alternative strategies by assuming different mixes of sales. *Simulation* is a technique used in this type of study. Simulation is a computer-based technique in which a manager inputs sets of assumptions and the computer calculates the profit for each combination. Alternative assumptions could relate to different selling prices, variable costs, total volumes, and sales mixes.

In planning sales mix, managers should continually evaluate individual products or product lines. A **product line** is a group of similar products. An example is a hair-care line, consisting of shampoos, conditioners, colorings, creams, tonics, and restorers. In many cases, managers will treat the entire line as a single "product." There are many reasons for taking this simplified approach for analytical purposes.

First, the products might have such similar contribution margin percentages that little is gained by examining them individually. After all, planning does involve estimates; moreover, minor differences that may result from grouping products with slightly different contribution margins are not likely to affect decisions. Another reason is that the sheer number of products might make analyzing them individually very difficult and time consuming.

A third reason for grouping products relates to the level of the manager for whom an analysis is being prepared. Different managers make different decisions and therefore need different kinds of information. The president of a full-line department store does not look at sales and cost details for every product stocked by the store. However, a lower-level manager—one in charge of sporting goods—does look at individual products in that line. That manager is concerned about each product and makes decisions about adding and dropping individual products. The store's president is more concerned with the product line as a whole and makes decisions about adding or dropping entire departments.

An important factor in analyzing either an individual product or a product line is an understanding of the nature of the fixed costs associated with that product or line. The next section applies principles from Chapter 3 to multiproduct companies.

FIXED COSTS AND MULTIPLE-PRODUCT FIRMS

Chapter 3 introduced the concepts of committed/discretionary, direct/indirect, and avoidable/unavoidable fixed costs. These concepts are important in evaluating products, product lines, geographical areas, and other activities, or segments, of a company. The classification of a particular cost depends on the segment being examined. Nationwide advertising (for example, on network television) for a product line is discretionary, avoidable, and direct to the line. But the cost is indirect and unavoidable to any particular geographical region. Thus, so long as the company advertises nationally, no discretionary component to this cost is created from the standpoint of any geographical region. Similarly, regional advertising promoting several product lines is discretionary, direct, and avoidable to the region, but indirect and unavoidable to any single line.

The importance of a particular classification, such as direct or avoidable, depends on the purpose of the analysis. If a manager is trying to decide whether to drop a segment (drop a product or line or stop selling in a particular region), the important issue is whether a cost is avoidable. If the manager is assessing a segment's profitability, then avoidability is important, but it is also important to know whether a cost is direct or indirect. Decisions to drop segments are multifaceted and are discussed in detail in Chapter 5. Our focus here is on developing information that will help managers evaluate segments.

Exhibit 4-4 shows a segmented income statement with two important subtotals: **short-term margin** and **long-term margin**. Generally speaking, a segment with a negative short-term margin is unprofitable. A segment with a negative long-term margin is not profitable in the long-term, and it might be wise for the company to liquidate the segment gradually by not renewing the commitments represented by direct, committed fixed costs.

Exhibit 4-4 shows that Sundries has a $120,000 short-term margin. This means that Davis's total profit would fall by $120,000 if it dropped Sundries *and* if there were no effects on the sales of other lines. Because Sundries has a

Exhibit 4-4 Davis Department Store Product-Line Income Statement for 19X5 (thousands of dollars)

	Clothing	Housewares	Sundries	Total
Sales	$2,400	$1,800	$1,300	$5,500
Variable costs:				
Cost of goods sold	1,050	900	910	2,860
Commissions	240	180	130	550
Other variable costs	150	120	90	360
Total variable costs	1,440	1,200	1,130	3,770
Contribution margin	960	600	170	1,730
Avoidable fixed costs:				
Salaries and expenses of department managers	80	65	40	185
Other	30	15	10	55
Total avoidable fixed costs	110	80	50	240
Short-term product margin	850	520	120	1,490
Direct committed fixed costs:				
Depreciation on fixtures	80	40	35	155
Other	45	30	20	95
Total direct committed fixed costs	125	70	55	250
Long-term margin	$ 725	$ 450	$ 65	$1,240
Common fixed costs:				
Rent on store				250
Salaries of administrative staff				365
Utilities				130
Other				300
Total common fixed costs				1,045
Profit				$ 195

relatively low long-term margin, Davis might be wise to phase it out by not renewing the commitments that underlie the direct, committed fixed costs. Before taking any actions to phase out Sundries, though, Davis should consider what other lines it might substitute for Sundries.

ACTIVITY-BASED COSTING

Activity-based costing, which we described briefly in Chapter 3, is especially useful in assigning fixed costs to products based on their use of resources. Exhibit 4-5 shows data for such an example and illustrates the process. Fixed costs common to more than one product or segment are not included in the pools to be assigned.

Managers could use the costs in Exhibit 4-5 to prepare income statements such as the one in Exhibit 4-4, even though no costs are classified as avoidable in the short-term. The income statement would not show separate short-term and long-term margins, only a single product margin. Of course, common fixed costs would appear only in the total column.

Exhibit 4-5 Activity-Based Cost Analysis

Analysis of Fixed Overhead Cost Pools

Cost Driver	Total Overhead Cost in Pool
Direct labor hours	$ 400,000
Machine hours	600,000
Number of machine setups	150,000
Number of design changes	60,000
Total fixed overhead	$1,210,000

Product Data

	Standard Model		Deluxe Model	
	Amount	Percentage of Total	Amount	Percentage of Total
Direct labor hours	9,000	75%	3,000	25%
Machine hours	15,000	60%	10,000	40%
Number of machine setups	900	50%	900	50%
Number of design changes	100	40%	150	60%

Activity-based Cost

Overhead Cost from Activity	Standard Model	Deluxe Model	Total
Direct labor hours	$300,000	$100,000	$ 400,000
Machine hours	360,000	240,000	600,000
Number of machine setups	75,000	75,000	150,000
Number of design changes	24,000	36,000	60,000
Total cost assigned	$759,000	$451,000	$1,210,000

Activity-based-costing has a role in analyzing and evaluating products and lines. Among the many reported instances of its use is in a company that had long maintained a very broad product line because the company believed its customers wanted to deal with a full-line supplier. One result of having so many products was very long lead times. After the company began using ABC it made major changes. The company raised prices on some products and dropped some products altogether when it found that customers actually did not require the company to maintain a broad product line. (Customers favored shorter delivery times).*

* *Michael O'Guin, "Focus the Factory with Activity-Based Costing,"* Management Accounting, *February 1990, 36.*

Tracing as much cost as possible to segments is important because it improves the analysis of product profitability. If little cost is directly traceable to products, they will probably all look very profitable, making it difficult to distinguish among them. IBM seeks to identify as much fixed overhead as possible with specific products, calling its practice *direct charging.* One thing that makes this tracing possible is that assembly lines in some plants are dedicated to one product, so that relatively little use of common facilities occurs.[1]

Increasing the traceability of costs is an advantage of JIT manufacturing, especially using cells that each specialize in one product. The more work done on each product in a dedicated area, the more the traceable cost. Moreover, because the people in the cells do the inspection, the materials-handling, and much of the required maintenance, less factory-wide cost is incurred for these support activities. Were these support activities performed by centrally managed departments, much of their cost would be common to production departments and products.

ABC and Ethics

Some costs are on the borderline between being direct or indirect to a product or line. And because managerial accountants use some judgment in assigning costs to products, they become open to potential ethical conflicts. Managers responsible for products want to keep their costs low and might pressure accountants to leave particular costs off the income statements of their products. Suppose a product manager, who is also a friend, argues that you should not include a particular cost in the line's income statement because the cost cannot be controlled. You then have an ethical conflict: should you exclude the cost even though you believe it does belong on the income statement?

1 *Robert H. Kelder, "Era of Cost Accounting Changes," in* Cost Accounting, Robotics, and the New Manufacturing Environment, *ed. Robert Capettini and Donald K. Clancy (Sarasota, FL.: American Accounting Association, 1987), 3.18.*

PRICE-VOLUME RELATIONSHIPS

We have assumed that selling price was constant, or changed only by managerial action. We also briefly discussed whether a company could sell a given volume of product at a given price. It is, of course, true that a company can sell more units at a lower price than it can at a higher price. This price-volume relationship is reflected in the **law of demand,** which states that as prices increase the quantity sold decreases, and vice versa. In most realistic situations, *some* price-volume interdependence exists and managers must recognize such interdependence in developing plans.

Consider a company that currently sells 10,000 units of product at $15 per unit. Variable costs are $10 per unit. The sales manager believes that if the price were increased to $16, volume would fall to 9,000 units. The firm can evaluate its alternatives by considering only contribution margin. The existing price yields $50,000 of contribution margin ($5 × 10,000), whereas the proposed price is expected to yield $54,000 ($6 × 9,000). If fixed costs stay the same, the $16 price increases income by $4,000.

COST-VOLUME-PROFIT ANALYSIS IN NOT-FOR-PROFIT ENTITIES

The term *not-for-profit* describes many kinds of economic entities, including governmental units, universities, churches, charitable organizations such as the Red Cross and American Cancer Society, and clubs and fraternal groups. Though some call such organizations *nonprofit,* we prefer the term *not-for-profit* because it better describes the *intent* of such organizations. (Many businesses turn out to be "nonprofit," but not by choice!)

Income is one measure of how well a business is doing. Although profit is not the only objective of a business firm (survival, growth, product quality, good corporate citizenship are others), earning profits sufficient to attract capital investment is necessary to its survival. How, then, is CVP analysis relevant to entities that do not intend to earn profits?

First, many not-for-profit entities try to earn profits (or at least try to break even) on some activities. College bookstores and food services often operate profitably and help to defray other costs of the college. Municipalities run parking lots or utilities that operate at a profit. A not-for-profit entity that operates a service that benefits only a portion of its constituents might try to break even on that service. For instance, not everyone in a city will use a municipal golf course. Hence, the city's elected officials might believe that the course should "pay its own way" and, therefore, require that the prices charged provide enough revenue to cover the costs.

Second, not-for-profit entities almost always must choose from among alternative ways to accomplish some task. Making these choices requires an understanding of cost behavior. For instance, a city can do its own trash collection or contract the task to a private firm. If the outside firm charges on the basis of the volume of trash collected, the cost is variable. If the city has its own trucks and personnel, a large portion of the cost is fixed. Recognizing the implications of the different types of behavior, city officials need information about the likely volumes of trash, including estimates about probable growth in volume.

The examples mentioned so far are relatively straightforward applications of cost analysis or CVP analysis. As a rule, however, the major activities of not-for-profit entities are not amenable to such straightforward applications because there is often no objective way to determine the value of the services—there is no revenue. Of course, not-for-profit entities do get revenues—taxes, donations, tuition—but not necessarily from the specific services that they provide. Cities have police forces, but the people do not pay for this service on the basis of use; they pay for it in taxes that also support the other activities of the government.

Despite the difficulties of measuring the results of activities of not-for-profit entities, some evaluations are always being made. Essentially, not-for-profit entities are concerned with analyzing the benefits and costs of activities, not so much with the revenues, costs, and profits. Accordingly, many use **benefit-cost analysis**.

BENEFIT-COST ANALYSIS

Managers of not-for-profit entities take many actions based on analyses that incorporate some kind of monetary measurement of both benefits and costs. For instance, governmental studies relating to the construction of a new dam are likely to include both construction costs and estimates of benefits from flood control and new recreational opportunities. Opponents of the dam might offer alternative analyses that measure benefits using different assumptions, attempt to quantify the cost of displacing people who live near the dam site, and state that the proposed dam would do irreparable, unquantifiable harm to various species of wildlife. Interested parties on both sides will dispute each other's figures on quantified points and argue about how to evaluate the unquantified ones.

In other situations, especially those relating to ongoing activities such as public education or police and fire protection, measuring benefits and costs might be even more difficult. Most people believe that a better-educated citizen is more beneficial to a community than one less well-educated. But how much more beneficial? Is the difference between the income taxes that the two would pay a reasonable measure, or, perhaps, the difference between their incomes?

Benefit-cost analysis often uncovers inefficiencies. The General Accounting Office, often called watchdog of the Congress, discovered that costs of filing information returns for state income tax refunds exceeded benefits by $2 million. Pennsylvania used benefit-cost analysis to evaluate vocational rehabilitation programs.[2]

As a practical matter, responsible decision makers approach many public service problems in one of two basic ways:

1. Decide on the amount of money to spend on a particular activity and concentrate on getting the most benefit from that level of expenditure.
2. Decide on the level of service to be provided and concentrate on providing that level of service at the most reasonable cost.

2 *G. Stevenson Smith and M. S. Tseng, "Benefit-Cost Analysis as a Performance Indicator,"* Management Accounting, *June 1986, 44.*

As an example of the first approach, a city council might decide to spend $500,000 on police protection. The chief of police then decides how best to spend the allotted money. Should the chief increase the number of patrol cars and cut down on police officers walking beats, or the reverse? Should the department send officers to training programs on advanced crime-fighting techniques, and if so, how many officers and which programs? Unfortunately, establishing the level of expenditure does not avoid the problems of measuring the benefits of public services. The chief must find ways to measure the benefits from alternative plans to provide police protection. Meanwhile, the council must decide whether the city is getting its money's worth, which means finding ways to measure the accomplishments for the approved expenditure. Were the funds well spent if the number of arrests increased? (Not necessarily, because arrests for minor offenses count as much as ones for major crimes.) Are the funds being better used this year if the crime rate has dropped? (Possibly, but many factors besides the quality and quantity of the police force affect the level of crime.)

The second approach—deciding first on the level of service and then trying to achieve that level at reasonable cost—presents many of the same problems as the first. For example, a state legislature might decide that all high school graduates should have the opportunity to attend college whether or not they can afford it. A number of alternatives, with differing costs, are available. Should there be branches of the state university in large population centers? Should the state establish community colleges to prepare students for work at senior colleges? Might it be better to provide money for tuition assistance directly to the students, who could use the funds to attend colleges of their choice? (Should the choices include private colleges? Colleges outside the state?) How does one evaluate whether the stated level of service has been provided at reasonable cost? Choosing among the alternatives involves not only determining the costs but also developing some measures of the benefits of each alternative. Thus, trying to achieve a specified level of service at a reasonable cost does not avoid the problems of measuring the benefits of a public service or evaluating the performance of that service.

In sum, analyzing public service activities is exceedingly difficult because of the lack of objective, unarguable measures of services and performance. Analyzing costs, especially if one is trying to determine whether or not money is spent wisely, is also difficult, but usually less difficult than analyzing activities. The problems are not limited to not-for-profit entities. Businesses spend a great deal of money on employee training, research and development, and other activities where the benefits are not readily measurable in monetary terms. Finding ways to make useful measurements is a constant concern of managers and a goal of much research in universities, business, and government.

SUMMARY

The techniques of CVP analysis are helpful in analyzing the results of operations. Differences between planned and achieved contribution margin and income may be attributed to differences in volume, price, and mix. Managers then concentrate on those products or strategies (pricing, promotion, etc.) that are expected to yield the best results. Managers also use contribution margin information to identify profitable products.

Multiproduct companies need to compute a weighted-average contribution margin to do CVP analysis. This computation requires information about the sales mix, stated either in dollars or units, as well as price and cost data.

Not-for-profit entities use benefit-cost analysis, a counterpart of CVP analysis. Defining and measuring benefits of a particular expenditure in a not-for-profit entity are difficult. Despite these difficulties, more and more managers in such entities are finding that adaptations of the concepts of managerial accounting can be helpful in their organizations.

KEY TERMS

benefit-cost analysis
complementary products
law of demand
long-term margin
product line
sales mix
sales price variance
sales volume variance
short-term margin
substitute products
weighted-average contribution margin percentage
weighted-average contribution margin per unit

KEY FORMULAS

$$\text{Sales volume variance} = \text{planned contribution margin per unit} \times \left(\text{actual sales, in units} - \text{planned sales, in units}\right)$$

$$\text{Sales price variance} = \text{units sold} \times (\text{actual price} - \text{planned price})$$

REVIEW PROBLEM

Data on the three types of can openers that are sold by McMichael Company are given below. Monthly fixed costs are $90,000.

	Regular	Deluxe	Super
Selling price	$2.00	$3.00	$5.00
Variable costs	1.20	1.50	2.00
Contribution margin	$ .80	$1.50	$3.00
Contribution margin percentage	40%	50%	60%

Required

Consider each part independently.

1. Suppose the sales mix in *dollars* is Regular, 60%; Deluxe, 30%; and Super, 10%.
   (a) Determine the weighted-average contribution margin percentage and the monthly sales to break even.

(b) Determine how many units of each model are sold at the break-even point.

(c) Prepare an income statement by product line for sales of $250,000. Assume that, of the $90,000 fixed costs, avoidable fixed costs for each model are $10,000 and direct committed fixed costs are $5,000, $7,000, and $3,000 for the Regular, Deluxe, and Super models, respectively.

2. Suppose now that the sales mix in *units* is Regular, 50%; Deluxe, 30%; and Super, 20%.
   (a) Determine the weighted-average contribution margin per unit.
   (b) Determine the total sales dollars required to earn $26,000 profit per month.
3. Suppose that in one month the firm expected to sell 40,000 Regular openers at $2 each. It actually sold 42,000, but the average selling price was $1.85. Compute the sales price variance and sales volume variance.

ANSWER TO REVIEW PROBLEM

1. (a) The weighted-average contribution margin percentage is 45%, computed as follows:

	Regular		Deluxe		Super		Total
Contribution margin percentage	40%		50%		60%		
multiplied by sales mix percentage	60%		30%		10%		
equals contribution margin per sales dollar	24%	+	15%	+	6%	=	45%

The sales required to break even are $200,000 per month (fixed costs of $90,000/45%).

(b) Sales are 60,000 units, 20,000 units, and 4,000 units of the Regular, Deluxe, and Super models, respectively. Unit sales for each model are computed by multiplying the sales mix percentage by total sales, to get dollar sales for each model, and then dividing by the selling price per unit.

Regular:($200,000 × 60% = $120,000)/$2 = 60,000 units
Deluxe: ($200,000 × 30% = $ 60,000)/$3 = 20,000 units
Super: ($200,000 × 10% = $ 20,000)/$5 = 4,000 units

(c)

	Regular	Deluxe	Super	Total
Sales[a]	$150,000	$75,000	$25,000	$250,000
Variable costs[b]	90,000	37,500	10,000	137,500
Contribution margin	60,000	37,500	15,000	112,500
Avoidable fixed costs	10,000	10,000	10,000	30,000
Short-term margin	50,000	27,500	5,000	82,500
Direct committed fixed costs	5,000	7,000	3,000	15,000
Long-term margin	$ 45,000	$20,500	$ 2,000	67,500
Common fixed costs				45,000
Income				$ 22,500

a Based on the stated sales mix of 60%, 30%, and 10%. $250,000 × 60% = $150,000; $250,000 × 30% = $75,000; $250,000 × 10% = $25,000.

b These figures can be determined by using the variable cost percentages, which are 60%, 50%, and 40% (all are 1 – contribution margin percentages). Or, the number of units of each product can be determined by dividing sales for the product by selling price per unit as given in the problem. Then, the results are multiplied by variable cost per unit as given in the problem. For example, sales of the Regular model are 75,000 units ($150,000/$2). Variable costs are given as $1.20 per unit, so total variable costs are $90,000 for 75,000 units ($1.20 × 75,000).

2. (a) The weighted-average contribution margin per unit is $1.45.

	Regular		Deluxe		Super		Total
Unit contribution margin	$0.80		$1.50		$3.00		
Sales mix, percentage in units	50%		30%		20%		
Weighted-average contribution margin	$0.40	+	$0.45	+	$0.60	=	$1.45

(b) Unit sales required for $26,000 profit, computed using the target profit formula from Chapter 2, are 80,000 units [(fixed costs of $90,000 + target profit of $26,000)/$1.45 weighted-average contribution per unit]. Dollar sales are computed by using the sales mix to determine the number of units sold of each type and then multiplying by the selling price per unit.

Regular:	(80,000 × 50% = 40,000 units) × $2 =	$ 80,000
Deluxe:	(80,000 × 30% = 24,000 units) × $3 =	72,000
Super:	(80,000 × 20% = 16,000 units) × $5 =	80,000
Total		$232,000

3. Because of the way the information is given, the easiest way to solve the problem is to deal with only the price and volume differences, as follows.

Sales price variance = quantity sold × (actual price – planned price)
= 42,000 × ($1.85 – $2.00)
= $6,300 unfavorable (unfavorable because actual price was lower than planned)

Sales volume variance = planned contribution margin × (actual volume – planned volume)
= $0.80 × (42,000 – 40,000)
= $0.80 × 2,000
= $1,600 favorable (favorable because actual volume was greater than planned)

Alternatively, we could prepare the following schedule.

	Actual Results	Actual Volume at Planned Selling Price	Planned Results
Sales	$77,700 (42,000 × $1.85)	$84,000 (42,000 × $2.00)	$80,000
Variable costs	50,400 (42,000 × $1.20)	50,400 (42,000 × $1.20)	48,000
Contribution margin	$27,000 (42,000 × $0.65)	$33,600 (42,000 × $0.80)	$32,000

$6,300 unfavorable sales price variance

$1,600 favorable sales volume variance

ASSIGNMENT MATERIAL

QUESTIONS FOR DISCUSSION

4-1 ***Price determination—postal service*** What do you think is the major problem in determining prices to be charged for the various classes of mail handled by the postal service? What ethical issues might arise for an accountant studying the question and making recommendations?

4-2 ***CVP chart*** Explain how preparation of a CVP graph differs between (a) a firm that sells only one product, and (b) one that sells several products.

4-3 ***Unit costs and governmental performance*** The manager of a medium-sized city was quoted as saying that trash collection service in her city was better than that in many neighboring cities because the unit cost was lower. The unit cost was the total cost of collections divided by the number of tons collected. Does having a low unit cost mean that the city is doing a good job?

EXERCISES

4-4 ***Basic variance analysis*** Tartan Mills expected to sell 40,000 of its Style 105 knit sweaters at $30 each. It actually sold 38,000 at $31. Variable cost is $14 per sweater.

Required

1. Determine the sales volume variance.
2. Determine the sales price variance.

4-5 ***Basic sales mix*** The general manager of Lo-Price Grocery Stores reviewed the following data. Fixed costs are $1,110,000 per month.

	Produce	Meat/Dairy	Canned Goods
Contribution margin percentage	40%	50%	30%
Sales mix percentage, in dollars	30%	20%	50%

Required

1. Determine the weighted-average contribution margin percentage.
2. Determine the break-even sales volume per month.
3. Determine the sales necessary to earn $250,000.

4-6 ***Improving sales mix*** Davis Exterminating Company performs a wide variety of pest control services. George Davis, the owner, has been examining the following forecasts for 19X6.

Type of Service	Expected Dollar Volume for 19X6	Contribution Margin Percentage
Termites	$120,000	60%
Lawn pests	90,000	50%
Interior pests	90,000	70%

Total fixed costs are expected to be $140,000 in 19X6.

Required

1. What is the weighted-average contribution margin percentage?
2. What profit should Davis earn?
3. The actual sales mix turned out to be 20% termites, 30% lawn pests, and 50% interior pests. Total actual sales were $300,000 and total fixed costs were

$140,000. Determine (a) the actual weighted-average contribution margin percentage and (b) profit.

4-7 *Relationships* Bruton Syrup sold 11,000 cases of Light Maple. It had a $3,000 unfavorable sales volume variance and a $3,300 favorable sales price variance. It had a budgeted selling price of $10 and variable cost of $7.

Required
1. Determine the number of cases that Bruton had budgeted to sell.
2. Determine the actual price per case that Bruton received.
3. Determine Bruton's budgeted and actual contribution margins.

4-8 *Price and volume variances* Klaxton Company makes large plastic wastebaskets. Planned results for March were as follows.

Sales (30,000 units)	$210,000
Variable costs	75,000
Contribution margin	$135,000

Actual results were as follows.

Sales	$212,350
Variable costs	77,500
Contribution margin	$134,850

Variable costs were incurred as expected, per unit.

Required
1. How many wastebaskets did the firm sell?
2. What was the actual selling price?
3. What were the volume variance and price variance?

4-9 *Product line income statements* Campus Laundromat is two years old. Sales have been $3,000 per week, contribution margin is 75% of sales, and weekly fixed costs are $1,200. Jill Owens, its owner, recently began to sell beer and also installed stereo equipment. She is now selling 800 bottles per week at $1.00 each. Variable cost is $0.40 per bottle. Additional fixed costs associated with the beer and stereo equipment are $300 per week. The laundry business has also increased to $3,600 per week. Jill's accountant has prepared the following income statement.

	Beer	Laundry	Total
Sales	$800	$3,600	$4,400
Variable costs	320	900	1,220
Contribution margin	480	2,700	3,180
Fixed costs	380	1,120	1,500
Income	$100	$1,580	$1,680

The accountant assigned the $300 fixed costs added by the beer business to beer. He also allocated $80 in building rent, light, and heat to beer, based on the relative space occupied by the bar and the laundry equipment.

Required

1. Prepare an income statement for Jill's business before she sold beer.
2. Prepare a new product-line income statement for Jill's business after she started selling beer. Show the $300 fixed costs as direct to beer and the original $1,200 as direct to the laundry business.
3. Does the income statement you prepared for item 2 better show the results of the two lines? Why or why not?

4-10 ***Basic sales mix*** Allen Cosmetics makes two facial creams, Allergy-free and Cleansaway. Data are as follows.

	Allergy-Free	Cleansaway
Price per jar	$10	$8
Variable cost per jar	$ 5	$2

Monthly fixed costs are $90,000.

Required

1. If the sales mix in dollars is 60% for Allergy-free and 40% for Cleansaway, what is the weighted-average contribution margin percentage? What dollar sales are needed to earn a profit of $30,000 per month?
2. If the sales mix is 50% for each product in units, what is the weighted-average unit contribution margin? What unit sales are needed to earn $30,000 per month?
3. Suppose that the firm is operating at the level of sales that you calculated in item 1, earning a $30,000 monthly profit. The sales manager believes that it is possible to persuade customers to switch to Cleansaway from Allergy-free by increasing advertising expenses. He thinks that $8,000 additional monthly advertising would change the mix to 40% for Allergy-free and 60% for Cleansaway. Total dollar sales will not change, only the mix. What effect would the campaign have on profit?

4-11 ***Weighted-average contribution margin*** Blue-Room Products sells three types of simulated brass soap dishes, the Necessary, the Frill, and the Luxury. Detailed selling price and cost data for the products appear below.

	Necessary	Frill	Luxury
Selling price	$10	$20	$25
Variable cost	$ 4	$12	50% of selling price

Fixed costs for these products are $286,000.

Required

1. If the company has a choice of selling one more unit of any one of its products, which product should it choose?
2. If the company could sell $1,000 more of any one of its products, which product should it choose?
3. Assume that the sales dollar volume of the company is distributed 40% from Necessary, 20% from Frill, and 40% from Luxury.
   a. What is the weighted-average contribution margin percentage?
   b. What is the break-even point for the company in sales dollars?
   c. At the break-even point, how many units of Luxury are sold?

4. Assume, instead, that the company's sales in units are 40% for Necessary, 20% for Frill, and 40% for Luxury.
   a. What is the weighted-average unit contribution margin?
   b. What is the break-even point in units?
   c. At the break-even point, how many units of Luxury would be sold?

4-12 Variance analysis The controller of MHA Inc. is examining the following budgeted and actual income statements for its principal product for 19X5. All amounts are in thousands of dollars.

	Budget	Actual
Sales	$4,800.0	$4,958.3
Variable costs	1,680.0	1,780.8
Contribution margin	$3,120.0	$3,177.5

The budgeted unit selling price is $8.00. Actual unit volume is 6% over budget, but the actual selling price is below budget. Per-unit variable costs are incurred as budgeted.

Required
Determine the sales price variance and sales volume variance.

4-13 Pricing policy—public service Speebus, the city-owned bus service of Middleville, charges $0.75 for all rides. The city has many retired citizens, whose incomes are generally lower than those of working citizens. A member of the city council has proposed that Speebus reduce its fares for persons over 65 to $0.40.

At the present time, about 1,200,000 rides per month are made on Speebus buses, about 30% of which are by citizens over 65. Buses are rarely crowded. The council member estimates that the decrease in fares to older persons would increase their use of the bus service by 50%. The number of other users would remain the same. Even with the expected increase in riders, buses rarely would be crowded.

Required
1. How much will it cost per month for Speebus to reduce fares to riders over 65?
2. Suppose that the bus service is breaking even. By how much would regular fares have to increase to get back to break-even if the reduction is granted?

4-14 Product profitability and mix The sales manager of Worthem Company has been looking at the following extracts from the monthly marketing plan for the coming year. Worthem distributes scented bath oils.

	Paree	Enchanté	Whisper
Selling price	$20	$16	$8
Variable cost	6	4	4
Contribution margin	$14	$12	$4
Expected monthly volume, in bottles	5,000	12,000	16,000

Required
1. Determine which product is most profitable (a) per unit sold and (b) per dollar sold.

2. The sales manager would like to achieve a better mix and believes that an advertising campaign could result in buyers of 3,000 bottles of Enchanté switching to Paree and buyers of 8,000 bottles of Whisper switching to Paree. The campaign would cost $80,000 per month. Determine whether Worthem should undertake the campaign.

4-15 *Price-volume relationships* Watson Brothers manufactures two models of shelving. The standard model sells for $20 and has variable costs of $7. The deluxe model sells for $50 and has variable costs of $35. Unit volume for each model is 8,000 per month. The sales manager believes that a 10% price reduction for either model would increase its unit volume by 25%. Referring to the following schedule, which shows that sales of the deluxe model would increase more than those of the standard model, the sales manager suggests reducing the price for the deluxe model.

	Standard Model	Deluxe Model
Sales after reduction:		
10,000 × $18	$180,000	
10,000 × $45		$450,000
Current sales:		
8,000 × $20	160,000	
8,000 × $50		400,000
Increase in sales	$ 20,000	$ 50,000

Required

1. Determine the total contribution margin that each model currently earns.
2. Determine the total contribution margin that each model would earn after the proposed price reduction.
3. Would you reduce the price of either model?

4-16 *Pricing to break even* The Student Senate at Western University sponsors programs for students and faculty. Among the programs is a monthly movie in an auditorium that holds 3,200 people. The movies selected ordinarily would not be shown in the one theater in the small town in which the university is located. Attendance at the university showings is high; a one-evening showing is invariably sold out. When shown on two evenings, attendance at each showing averages 2,375.

Movies are rented at a cost of $2,400 for one showing, $3,200 for two showings. Other fixed costs per showing are $600, and variable costs are $0.40 per person for chair rentals, tickets, and miscellaneous items. The Senate wants to break even for the year on the movie program.

Required

1. Determine the prices that must be charged so that the Senate can break even on the movie showings for the year assuming (a) one showing of each movie and (b) two showings of each movie.
2. Write a memorandum that makes a recommendation to the Senate regarding the number of times a movie should be shown. Explain the factors that influenced your decision. Use the guidelines in Appendix B.

4-17 *Market share* MBT Company produces and sells consumer products. It recently hired a new vice president for sales who is a great believer in increasing the market share of a product. One of the first proposals was to reduce the price of Kleenbrite, a toothpaste that had a 15% share of the total market of 2,000,000 tubes.

The current price is $1.60 per tube, variable costs $0.50. The new vice president reduced the price by $0.10, and Kleenbrite increased its share of the market to 16% of the 2,000,000 tube market.

Required

1. Was reducing the price to gain market share a wise move? Show separately the effects of the change in price and the change in volume.
2. What share of the market did Kleenbrite need to achieve in order to justify the $0.10 price reduction?
3. Suppose that the firm could increase the market share of Kleenbrite at the $1.60 price by increasing advertising and promotion expenses. What additional expenditures would MBT be able to make to increase market share by one percentage point without reducing its overall profit?

4-18 Variances from plans (extension of 3-27) Competitive pressures late in February prompted the managers of Forecast Company to reduce its selling price for March to $9.80. Per-unit variable costs, total fixed costs, and income tax rates continued to behave as planned, and total variable costs for March were $420,000.

Required

1. How many units were sold in March?
2. What was the total contribution margin for March?
3. Was the March sales volume variance favorable or unfavorable?
4. What was the sales volume variance?
5. Was the March sales price variance favorable or unfavorable?
6. What was the sales price variance?
7. What income did the company earn in March?

4-19 Product profitability Wrynn Company sells three kinds of tobacco jars. The controller has prepared the following analysis of profitability of each of the jars.

	Flavorsaver	Shagholder	Burleykeeper
Selling price	$5.00	$8.00	$11.00
Variable costs	2.00	4.00	6.40
Fixed costs	3.00	3.00	3.00
Total costs	5.00	7.00	9.40
Profit	—	$1.00	$ 1.60
Profit percentage to selling price	0%	12.5%	14.5%
Annual volume	22,000	15,000	13,000

The firm has total fixed costs of $150,000 per year. The controller obtained the fixed cost per unit figure of $3 by dividing $150,000 by 50,000 units (22,000 + 15,000 + 13,000). On the basis of the analysis, the controller suggests that the Flavorsaver model be discontinued if a more profitable substitute can be found. This conclusion upsets the sales manager, who has planned a $10,000 promotional campaign for Flavorsavers. He estimates that the $10,000 expenditure on any product would increase its volume by 25%. Sales of the other products would be unaffected, as would existing fixed costs.

Required

Determine which product should be selected for the special promotion.

4-20 Variances in a service business Earl Torgeson, the managing partner of Torgeson, Watts, and Gold, Certified Public Accountants, is comparing planned and actual results for 19X1. Because all employees are on salary, there are no variable costs associated with chargeable hours (hours worked on client business).

	Planned			Actual		
Employee Category	Hourly Rate	Total Hours	Revenue	Hourly Rate	Total Hours	Revenue
Junior staff	$20	40,000	$800,000	$19	38,000	$722,000
Senior staff	40	12,000	480,000	38	13,000	494,000

Required

For each category, determine the price (rate) and volume variances.

PROBLEMS

4-21 Segmented income statements—costs of activities Claxton Industries makes three principal product lines: sporting goods, housewares, and hardware. The company has suffered reduced profitability in the past few quarters, and the top managers have taken a number of actions to try to improve the situation. The most recent quarterly income statement, segmented by product line, appears below. Common fixed costs are allocated to the lines based on relative sales or labor content.

Claxton Industries
Income Statement, Second Quarter, 19X9
(in thousands of dollars)

	Total	Sporting Goods	Housewares	Hardware
Sales	$3,337.0	$650.0	$921.0	$1,766.0
Cost of sales	1,928.8	357.3	545.7	1,025.8
Gross margin	1,408.2	292.7	375.3	740.2
Operating expenses:				
Selling expenses	787.6	157.1	225.9	404.6
Administrative expenses	514.6	94.2	135.6	284.8
Total operating expenses	1,302.2	251.3	361.5	689.4
Income before taxes	$ 106.0	$ 41.4	$ 13.8	$ 50.8

The managers are still not happy with the 3.2% return on sales, but the $106 thousand pretax profit was a bit higher than the previous quarter's profit. The consensus of the managers is that they should concentrate on sporting goods and hardware because their ROS's are higher than that of housewares. One manager even wants to ignore housewares because its ROS was only 1.5%. "If we only keep a cent and a half from a dollar's sales, why even bother with it?"

When asked to confirm the judgments about relative profitabilities, the controller points out that some common costs are allocated to the product lines and that some distortions might result from those allocations. Therefore, her assistant has been asked to prepare an alternative income statement without making allocations. The assistant's analysis of Claxton's cost structure reveals the following, dollars in thousands.

	Sporting Goods	Housewares	Hardware
Variable Costs, Percentage of Sales			
Cost of sales	28.00%	32.00%	35.00%
Selling expenses	2.00%	1.50%	1.80%
Administrative expenses	0.90%	0.70%	2.00%
Direct Fixed Costs			
Cost of sales	$158	$141	$197
Selling expenses	56	87	133
Administrative expenses	13	22	43

The assistant evaluates the costs by examining the activities that generate them. For example, sporting goods require relatively more attention from manufacturing support personnel, such as engineers, than hardware and so is assigned relatively higher direct fixed manufacturing costs. By the same token, hardware consumes considerably more relative administrative time than sporting goods, giving it relatively more direct cost.

Required

1. Prepare a new segmented income statement using the assistant's findings. Show common costs only in the total column, as in Exhibit 4-4.
2. Write a memorandum to the controller that comments on the differences between your statement and the one above. Indicate for example, what decisions are easier, or more difficult, to make with your statement. Use the guidelines in Appendix B.
3. Each line is controlled by a manager. From an ethics standpoint, what can these managers expect from the people who develop the information and prepare the reports. Refer to Exhibit 1-3.

4-22 Costs and profits per unit Managers of Hylman Company, which manufactures a packaged beverage-sweetener, have been trying to decide what price to charge for the product next year. One manager has come up with the following analysis.

	Likely Results		
Price per Case	Case Volume	Average Total Per-Case Cost	Per-Case Gross Margin
$260	60,000	$225.00	$35.00
$250	70,000	$218.00	$32.00
$240	80,000	$212.75	$27.25

"It seems to me," the manager says, "that we should go with the $260 price, since the per-case gross margin is highest at that price."

Required

Determine the price that yields the highest total profit to the firm.

4-23 CVP analysis—product mix Happy Times Brewery produces and sells two grades of beer: regular and premium. Premium sells for $9.50 per case, regular for $7.20. Variable brewing costs per case are $4.80 (premium) and $3.75 (regular). Sales of regular beer, in cases, are double those of premium. Fixed brewing costs are $120,000 monthly and fixed selling and administrative costs are $75,000 monthly. The only variable cost besides variable brewing costs is a 10% sales commission.

Required

1. Compute the break-even point in total cases per month.
2. How many cases of each kind of beer are sold at break-even?
3. The brewery is now selling about 90,000 cases per month. The advertising manager believes that sales of premium beer could be increased by 20% if an extensive advertising campaign were undertaken. The campaign would cost $24,000 per month. However, sales of regular beer are expected to fall by about 5% because some customers now buying the regular grade would merely switch to premium. Should the campaign be undertaken?
4. If the campaign were undertaken, what is the weighted-average unit contribution margin?
5. What is the new break-even point in unit sales?

4-24 Pricing a product Watson Camera Company makes cameras and film. The firm is introducing a new camera this year, the Super-90. Variable costs are $20 per unit. Associated fixed costs are $2,000,000 per year for production, advertising, and administration. The sales manager of Watson believes that if the camera is priced at $40, about 250,000 units per year will be sold. If the price is $50, about 200,000 units per year would be sold.

Required

1. Determine which price would yield the higher profit.
2. Suppose that for each camera sold, the firm usually sells eight packages of film per year. Film sells for $6 per package and the variable cost is $1.20 per package. Would this information affect your analysis in part 1?

4-25 Pricing decision and average costs The sales manager for Markham Pen Company has been trying to decide what price to charge for a pen the firm is introducing this year. His staff has prepared a research report that indicates the following price-volume relationships.

Price	Volume (millions)
$3.25	1.6 units
3.10	1.8
2.95	2.0
2.80	2.2
2.65	2.4

The variable cost per pen is $1.50, and total annual fixed costs are estimated at $1.5 million. The sales manager believes that any product should be priced at 150% of total cost. He decides to use 2.2 million units as the volume to determine the average unit cost and computes the cost at $2.182 per pen. He intends to set the price at $3.25.

Required

1. Assuming that the predictions of the staff are correct, determine what profit would be earned if the pen is priced at $3.25.

2. Again assuming the correctness of the staff's predictions, determine which price would yield the highest profit.
3. Suggest what might be wrong with the sales manager's method of setting prices.

4-26 ***Product profitability*** Immediately on graduation from State University, Jan Wilks took the position of assistant controller with Crow Clothing Company. The controller has given her the following information based on expected operations for the coming year.

	T-Shirts	Sweatshirts	Jeans
Selling price	$6	$15	$20
Variable costs	3	6	12
Contribution margin	$3	$ 9	$ 8
Sales mix percentage, in dollar sales	40%	40%	20%

Total fixed costs are $840,000.

Required

1. The marketing manager believes that the company could increase sales of any of the three products by one unit for each $4 in additional advertising expenditures. Which product would it be most profitable to advertise?
2. Determine the weighted-average contribution margin percentage.
3. Determine the break-even point.
4. The president wants a profit of $210,000. Determine the sales dollars needed to achieve this goal.
5. After extensive discussions with the sales manager and marketing department, the controller believes that the sales mix will probably change to 20%, 30%, and 50% for T-shirts, sweatshirts, and jeans, respectively.
   (a) Determine the new break-even point.
   (b) Determine the sales needed to earn $210,000.

4-27 ***Sales promotion*** Sales of pizza and beer at Bob's Pizza & Pub have been averaging about $3,000 per week. The weighted-average contribution margin is 60% and weekly fixed costs are $1,200. To attract more business, Bob has hired a local band to play on Saturday nights. The band charges $450 per night. Other costs associated with having the band are $60 per night. Bob charges each person a $1 entry fee when the band is playing. Sales on Saturday nights had been about $600 before the band was hired. Since Bob hired the band, Saturday night attendance has averaged 300 people.

Required

1. Determine the income or loss attributable to having the band. For the moment, ignore the effects that the band might have had on sales of pizza and beer.
2. Determine the increase in sales of pizza and beer that Bob needs to maintain his weekly income at the same level it was before he hired the band.
3. Sales of beer and pizza on Saturday nights actually increased to $1,100, raising total weekly sales to $3,500. Determine the overall effect on Bob's weekly income of hiring the band.
4. Item 3 stated that the entire increase in weekly sales came on Saturday nights. Suppose that weekly sales increased by $500, but that $300 of the increase came on Saturday nights and $200 on other nights. Would your analysis from item 3 still hold? Why or why not?

4-28 Product-line report Karen Bell is president of Bell & Company, which distributes consumer products to supermarkets. Ms. Bell has been trying to analyze the profitability of her lines. She has available the following information.

Line	Annual Sales	Gross Profit Percentage	Direct Fixed Costs
Paper products	$2,000,000	30%	$110,000
Detergents	1,200,000	40%	150,000

The only variable cost, besides cost of goods sold, is a 10% commission paid on all sales. Bell incurs $350,000 in fixed costs that are common to both lines. All direct fixed costs listed above are discretionary.

Required

Answer each item independently.

1. Prepare an income statement using the format shown in Exhibit 4-4.
2. Ms. Bell believes that she could increase the volume of either line by 10% by increasing promotion of the line by $30,000. Which, if either, line should she select? She cannot select both.
3. Ms. Bell believes that she could increase the volume of either line by 10% if she raised the commission rate on that line to 12%. Which, if either, line should she select? She cannot select both.
4. How does the report format you used for item 1 provide better information than would an income statement showing only combined results for the two lines?

4-29 Sales interdependencies (AICPA adapted) Breezway Company operates a resort complex on an offshore island. The complex consists of a 100-room hotel, shops, a restaurant, and recreational facilities. Mr. Blenem, manager of the complex, has asked for your assistance in planning the coming year's operations. He is particularly concerned about the level of profits the firm is likely to earn.

Your conversation with Mr. Blenem reveals that he expects the hotel to be 80% occupied during the 300 days that it is open. All rooms rent for $40 per day for any number of persons. In virtually all cases, two persons occupy a room. Mr. Blenem also tells you that past experience, which he believes is an accurate guide to the future, indicates that each person staying at the hotel spends $10 per day in the shops, $20 in the restaurant. There are no charges for use of the recreational facilities. All sales in the shops and restaurant are made to guests of the hotel, which is isolated from the only large town on the island.

After talking with Mr. Blenem, you obtain the following data from the firm's controller.

	Shops	Restaurant
Variable costs, as a percentage of sales dollars:		
Cost of goods sold	40%	30%
Supplies	10	15
Other	5	5

For the hotel, variable costs are $6 per day per occupied room, for cleaning, laundry, and utilities. Fixed costs for the complex are $1,200,000 per year.

Required

1. Prepare an income statement for the coming year based on the information given.
2. Mr. Blenem tells you he believes that the occupancy rate would increase to 90% if the room rate were reduced to $35 per day. Determine the effect on planned income if the rate were reduced.

4-30 Variance analysis—brain teaser Mack Bolend, controller of AMH Industries, received the following budgeted and actual income statements for one of its major products for a recent month. Not having time to analyze them, he requests that you determine why the company did not achieve its budgeted results. All dollar amounts are in thousands.

	Budget	Actual
Sales	$2,350.0	$2,197.8
Variable costs	1,527.5	1,405.3
Contribution margin	$ 822.5	$ 792.5

Per-unit variable costs were incurred as budgeted.

Required

Determine the sales price variance and sales volume variance.

4-31 Product profitability and pricing Jackson Confections makes three flavors of jelly: grape, strawberry, and peach. Price and cost data are as follows.

	Grape	Strawberry	Peach
Selling price per case	$10	$12	$14
Variable cost per case	6	9	7

Monthly fixed costs are $250,000.

Required

1. The sales mix, in dollars, is 40%, 40%, 20% for grape, strawberry, and peach jelly, respectively. Determine the sales dollars that will yield a monthly profit of $50,000.
2. The president would like to earn $50,000 on sales of $800,000. He proposes to do this by increasing the price of strawberry jelly. He expects the mix to remain the same after the price of strawberry jelly increases. What price must Jackson charge for strawberry jelly to achieve the president's goal?

4-32 Product line reporting, activity analysis Kelly Company is a retail store specializing in men's clothing. The firm has three major product lines: suits, sport clothes, and accessories. The most recent monthly income statement is given on the next page.

Kelly Company
Income Statement for April 19X7
(thousands of dollars)

Sales		$800.0
Cost of sales		572.0
Gross profit		228.0
Operating expenses:		
Commissions	$48.0	
Salaries	71.4	
Rent	21.4	
Shipping and delivery	15.2	
Insurance	14.0	
Miscellaneous	20.8	190.8
Income before taxes		$ 37.2

The president wants a product-line income statement. She gives you the following additional data:

1. The sales mix in April was 30% suits, 50% sport clothes, and 20% accessories, expressed in dollars of total sales.
2. The cost of sales percentages are 80% for suits, 75% for sport clothes, and 50% for accessories.
3. Sales commissions are 6% for all product lines.
4. Each product line is the responsibility of a separate manager, and each manager has a small staff. The salaries that are directly related to each product line are $12,000 for suits, $8,000 for sport clothes, and $5,200 for accessories. These salaries are avoidable. All other salaries are common to the three lines.
5. Rent is for both office and warehouse space, all of which is in a single building.
6. Shipping and delivery costs are for operating expenses and depreciation on the firm's three trucks. Each truck serves a particular geographical area and delivers all three product lines.
7. Insurance includes a $6,000 fixed amount for basic liability coverage. The rest is for coverage of merchandise at the rate of one percent of the selling price of the average inventory on hand during the month. In April, the average inventories at selling prices were equal to sales for each product line.
8. Miscellaneous expenses are committed, but direct. The amounts are $6,000 to suits, $8,800 to sport clothes, and $6,000 to accessories.

Required

Prepare an income statement by product, using the format shown in Exhibit 4-4.

4-33 Product profitability Messorman Company produces three models of pen and pencil sets, regular, silver, and gold. Price and cost data are as follows.

	Regular	Silver	Gold
Selling price	$10	$20	$30
Variable costs	6	8	15

Monthly fixed costs are $200,000.

Required

1. Which model is most profitable per unit sold?

2. Which model is most profitable per dollar of sales?
3. Suppose the sales mix in dollars is 40% Regular, 20% Silver, and 40% Gold.
   (a) What is the weighted-average contribution margin?
   (b) What is the monthly break-even point?
   (c) What sales volume is necessary to earn a profit of $30,000 per month?
4. Suppose the sales mix in dollars is 30% Regular, 30% Silver, and 40% Gold.
   (a) What is the break-even point?
   (b) What sales volume is necessary to earn $30,000 per month?
5. Suppose that the sales mix in units is 40% Regular, 20% Silver, and 40% Gold.
   (a) What is the weighted-average unit contribution margin?
   (b) What is the break-even point in total units?
   (c) How many total units must Messorman sell to earn $30,000 per month?

4-34 ***What is profitability?*** Kimbell Company sells three products. Data are as follows.

	Product		
	A	B	C
Selling price	$30	$50	$100
Variable cost	20	25	60
Contribution margin	$10	$25	$ 40
Annual unit volume	50,000	10,000	5,000

Required

1. Rank the products in order of profitability as measured by (a) total annual profit, (b) profitability per unit sold, and (c) profitability per dollar of sales.
2. Explain what the rankings mean and how Kimbell's managers might use the information.

4-35 ***Product line income statements*** The president of Mifflan Tool Company has just received the firm's income statement for January 19X8. He is puzzled because you had told him last year, when working as a consultant to the firm, that sales of $500,000 should produce a profit of about $46,500 before income taxes.

Mifflan Tool Company
Income Statement for January 19X8

Sales		$500,000
Cost of sales		307,500
Gross profit		192,500
Operating expenses:		
Rent	$40,000	
Salaries	70,000	
Shipping and delivery	23,000	
Other expenses	30,000	163,000
Income before taxes		$ 29,500

The firm sells three lines of power tools, and your analysis assumed the following sales mix in dollars: saws, 30%; drills, 20%; and sanders, 50%. The actual mix in dollars in January was 40%, 30%, 30%. The firm does not manufacture its products. Cost of sales and shipping and delivery are variable costs. All others are fixed. Data per unit for each product are on the next page.

	Saws	Drills	Sanders
Selling price	$50	$20	$40
Cost of sales	30	15	20
Shipping and delivery	2	1	2
Total variable costs	32	16	22
Contribution margin	$18	$ 4	$18

None of the fixed costs is directly associated with any particular product line. All costs were incurred as expected, per unit for variable costs, in total for fixed costs. Selling prices were as expected.

Required

1. Prepare a new income statement by product, based on actual results in January. Show both gross profit and contribution margin for each product.
2. Prepare an income statement by product for January, assuming that the expected sales mix had been achieved.
3. Explain the reasons for the differences between the two statements.

4-36 Revenue variances for an airline Big Sky Airline had planned for $22 million revenue in March, expecting a 60% load factor (percentage of seat-miles occupied). Actual revenue was $22.8 million. The load factor was 66%. Variable cost per seat-mile is negligible.

Required

Determine the difference between planned and actual revenue attributable to (a) price and (b) volume (load factor). Round to the nearest $100,000.

4-37 Decision making for student programs The Speaker Committee at a large university invites distinguished persons to address students, faculty, and members of the public. Students and faculty are admitted free; members of the public pay $2. Students and faculty must pick up tickets in advance; any tickets left on the day of the speech are sold to the public. The speaker program is expected to break even for the year.

The committee is trying to decide whether to invite Marvin Gardens, a noted environmentalist, or Cayuga Waters, a famous industrialist. One student member of the committee argues that Marvin Gardens is an ideal speaker. His fee is $800. The student states that the auditorium, which holds 2,000 people, will be almost completely filled with students and faculty if Garden speaks. He believes that only about 500 tickets would be available to members of the public and that all available tickets could be sold. Another member, an administrative officer of the university, says that Waters would be a better speaker. She believes that only 500 students and faculty would show up, leaving 1,500 tickets which could easily be sold to the public. Waters charges a fee of $2,000.

Required

1. Assuming that both committee members are correct in their assessments of demand for tickets, which speaker would be more profitable?
2. What other factors should be considered in reaching a decision?
3. What do you recommend?

4-38 Cost analysis in a university The School of Management at State University currently has 500 students and 25 faculty members. The school's students are juniors and seniors who take all their courses in the school, an average of five courses per semester. The school offers 75 sections per semester, with each faculty member teaching three sections.

Following are the data for the number of sections, average number of students per section, and "student-sections," which is the total number of enrollments in all sections. Since 500 students take five courses each semester, there are 2,500 student-sections.

Number of Sections	×	Average Enrollment	=	Student-Sections
20		20		400
30		35		1,050
25		42		1,050
75				2,500

The university's administration is considering increasing the enrollment in the School of Management to 1,000 students. One university officer objects that the cost would be prohibitive. He states that faculty salaries are now $950,000 per year and would double if enrollment were to double because twice the number of teaching faculty would be required.

Another officer points out that doubling the size of the faculty would not be necessary because the size of the sections could be increased. However, university policy is that no more than 45 students be enrolled in a single section.

You are assigned the task of determining the additional cost of faculty salaries required to support enrollment of 1,000 students. You estimate that demand for the classes now averaging 20 students per section is such that each section would go up to 25 students if enrollment went to 1,000. All other sections would be increased to the 45-student maximum. A faculty member would be hired for each three sections per semester added, at a salary of $30,000 per year.

Required

1. How many sections are needed if enrollment increases to 1,000 students? (*Hint:* Because 1,000 students will take five courses per semester, you must account for 5,000 individual enrollments.)
2. How much additional cost will be incurred for faculty salaries?
3. After you performed the analyses in items 1 and 2, the chancellor of the university became concerned about the large class sizes. You are asked to redo the analysis of required additional faculty salaries assuming that only 40 sections would hold 45 students, 20 would still hold 25 students, and the rest would have a maximum of 36 students.

4-39 Multiple products—movie company (continuation of 2-43 and 3-30)
Both the producing company and prospective star have given further thought to the contract terms and concluded that some provision probably should be made for revenues to be earned from contracts authorizing showings of the movie on television. After lengthy negotiations, Kirkwalker's agent proposed the following terms: (a) a payment of $1,000,000, plus (b) 15% of the receipts-to-the-producer from theater admissions, plus (c) 10% of the revenues from sales of television rights. Blockbusters' negotiating team leaves the negotiations to study the potential effect of the new offer.

A study of past productions indicates that the producer can expect revenues from sales of television rights to be approximately one eighth (12.5%) of producer's revenues from theater admissions. Ms. Lane is pleased with the opportunity to lower the fixed-payment part of the contract but is concerned about the magnitude of the two off-the-top percentages.

Required

1. At what level of receipts-to-the-producer will Blockbusters break even under the new contract proposal?
2. Considering the additional information about the sale of television rights, at what level of receipts-to-the-producer will Blockbusters break even under Kirkwalker's normal contract terms ($1,500,000 plus 5% of the producer's receipts)?
3. Assume that, because of Blockbusters' delay in accepting the contract offer, Kirkwalker's agent decides that his client should also receive a percentage of the revenues Blockbusters will derive from the sale of screening rights in foreign countries, which revenues typically amount to 10% of domestic receipts. If the agent proposes a 5% cut of those revenues for Kirkwalker, what is the break-even point for Blockbusters Incorporated?

4-40 Interrelationships between products Rapidcal Company manufactures hand-held calculators. The industry is highly competitive and pricing is critical to sales volume. Warren James, sales manager of Rapidcal, has been trying to set a price for a model that the firm will introduce shortly. The new model, the RC-89, is somewhat more sophisticated than the RC-63, which has been successful in recent years. The RC-63 now sells at retail for $20, of which 30% goes to the dealer and 70% to Rapidcal. Variable costs for the RC-63 are $8 per unit. The variable costs for the RC-89, exclusive of dealer share, are $18 per unit.

James is especially concerned about the effects on sales of RC-63 following the introduction of the RC-89. He believes that if the RC-89 is priced at $44 retail, no loss in sales of the RC-63 would occur. However, if the RC-89 were sold at $42, he thinks that some people will buy the RC-89 instead of buying the RC-63. At the $44 price, James expects sales of 150,000 RC-89s per year. For each $2 price cut for RC-89s, sales would increase by about 30,000 units, but about 40% of the increased sales of RC-89 would be at the expense of sales of the RC-63. At any price for the RC-89, Rapidcal receives 70%, the retailer 30%.

Also, James believes that a $38 retail price is rock-bottom for the RC-89. He therefore instructs you to determine the effects on the income of the firm of pricing the RC-89 at $44, $42, $40, and $38.

Required

Comply with the sales manager's request and determine the price that should be set for the RC-89.

4-41 Multiple products (extension of 3-27) The planned data for Forecast Company, as shown in 3-27, represent the combined plans for three products: a platter, a cup, and a saucer. The expected sales mix of the three products, in sales dollars, is 40%, 30%, and 30%, for the platter, cup, and saucer, respectively.

Required

1. What are the expected sales, in dollars, for each product?
2. If the contribution margin percentage for cups is 10% and that for saucers is 30%, what is the contribution margin percentage for platters?
3. The normal sales mix is one platter for every two cup-and-saucer sets, and the planned results reflect that mix. If the expected sales of 50,000 units count each platter, cup, and saucer as a separate unit, what are the planned selling prices and per-unit variable costs for each of the three products?
4. Assume that the actual sales for April were $450,000 and that the sales mix, in dollars, was 60% platters and 20% each for cups and saucers.
   (a) What was the actual total contribution margin earned for April?

(b) What was the actual weighted-average contribution margin percentage for April?

5. B. J. Douglas, sales manager for Forecast Company, considers the April results to be unusual and not likely to be repeated. That is, she believes that sales and cost data reflected in the original plans are appropriate as long as there are no changes in costs or selling prices. But she is convinced that the price of plates (in relation to those charged for the other two products) is too high and not in the firm's best interest. Accordingly, she has developed several plans for improving sales, all involving price reductions for plates. These plans, together with Douglas's best estimates of their effects on sales, are summarized below.

Plan A: Reduce the price of a plate to $19. Douglas estimates that unit sales of plates will increase by 10% and that the price reduction will have no effect on the sales of the other two products.

Plan B: Reduce the price of a plate to $16. Douglas estimates that unit sales of plates will increase 20% and that the price reduction will result in more customers buying cups and saucers so that three of each of the other products will be sold for every plate sold.

Plan C: Reduce the price of a plate to $18. Douglas estimates that unit sales of plates will increase 20% and that the present sales mix of two cups and two saucers sold for every plate sold will not change.

Which, if any, of the proposed plans should be adopted?

4-42 Personnel policies and decisions Patterson Company operates a chain of hardware stores in a metropolitan area. Each store has a manager, several salespeople, and one or two clerks. The vice president has reviewed the performance of each store and is considering closing the Middleton store. The income statement shows the following for 19X8 and future results are expected to be about the same.

Middleton Store
Income Statement for 19X8

Sales		$500,000
Cost of sales	$350,000	
Salaries	85,000	
Commissions, 10% of sales	50,000	
Rent on building	20,000	
Rent on store equipment	4,000	
Miscellaneous expenses	7,000	516,000
Net loss		($ 16,000)

If Patterson closes the Middleton store, it will transfer all personnel to other stores. The firm is opening several new stores and needs to hire additional people even if the ones from the Middleton store are transferred. The miscellaneous expenses are fixed, but avoidable if the store is closed. If the store closes, none of its former business would go to any of the existing stores.

Required

1. Assume that the leases on building and equipment have 12 years to run. Patterson has no other use for the building and equipment and could not sublease them to another firm. Determine whether the firm should close the store.
2. Assume now that the leases are month-to-month and can be canceled at any time. Determine whether the store should be closed.

3. Assume that the leases are unavoidable, as in item 1. However, suppose now that the Middleton store has been losing business because the firm has two newer stores relatively close by. The vice president believes that closing the Middleton store will increase total sales in its other stores by $80,000 per year. Cost of sales and commissions, as percentages of sales dollars, are the same in all stores. Fixed costs in the other stores would not be affected by the increases in sales. Determine whether the Middleton store should be closed.

4-43 Line of business reporting (CMA adapted) Riparian Company produces and sells three products. Each is sold domestically and in foreign countries. The foreign market has been disappointing to management because of poor operating results, as evidenced by the income statement for the first quarter of 19X8.

	Total	Domestic	Foreign
Sales	$1,300,000	$1,000,000	$300,000
Cost of goods sold	1,010,000	775,000	235,000
Gross profit	290,000	225,000	65,000
Selling expenses	105,000	60,000	45,000
Administrative expenses	52,000	40,000	12,000
	157,000	100,000	57,000
Income	$ 133,000	$ 125,000	$ 8,000

Management decided a year ago to enter the foreign market because of excess capacity, but is now unsure whether to continue devoting time and effort to developing it. The following information has been gathered for consideration of the alternatives that management has identified.

	Products		
	A	B	C
Sales:			
Domestic	$400,000	$300,000	$300,000
Foreign	100,000	100,000	100,000
Variable manufacturing costs (percentage of sales)	60%	70%	60%
Variable selling expenses (percentage of sales)	3%	2%	2%

Of the $190,000 total fixed manufacturing costs, $30,000, $40,000, and $70,000 are direct to products A, B, and C, respectively. These amounts are not avoidable in the short-term. Additionally, $90,000 in fixed manufacturing costs are direct to the domestic market, $20,000 to the foreign market. These amounts are also unavoidable.

All administrative expenses are fixed and common to the three products and to the two markets. Fixed selling expenses are direct and avoidable by market. Some $40,000 of fixed selling expenses are direct to products, and also avoidable. The percentages of the $40,000 applicable to each product are 30% to A, 30% to B, and 40% to C.

Management believes that if the foreign market were dropped, sales in the domestic market could be increased by $200,000. The increase would be divided 40%, 40%, 20% among products A, B, and C, respectively.

Management also believes that a new product, D, could be introduced by the end of the current year. The product would replace product C and would increase fixed costs by $30,000 per quarter.

Required

1. Prepare an income statement for the quarter by product, using the format of Exhibit 4-4.
2. Prepare an income statement for the quarter by market, using the format of Exhibit 4-4.
3. Determine whether the foreign market should be dropped.
4. Assume that the foreign market would not be dropped. Determine the minimum quarterly contribution margin that product D would have to produce in order to make its introduction desirable.

4-44 Price and volume variances (AICPA adapted) Bay City Gas Company supplies liquefied natural gas to residential customers. Below are the results, both planned and actual, for the month of November 19X7. Although he knows that the price of gas per 1,000 cubic feet drops with increases in purchases by a customer, the operations manager is having difficulty interpreting the report.

	Planned	Actual	Difference
Number of customers	26,000	28,000	2,000
Sales in thousands of cubic feet	520,000	532,000	12,000
Revenue	$1,300,000	$1,356,600	$56,600
Variable costs	$ 416,000	$ 425,600	($ 9,600)

Required

Compute the sales price variance and sales volume variance.

4-45 Sales strategies Nova Company sells cosmetics through door-to-door salespeople who receive 25% commissions. Nova's national sales manager has been evaluating alternative selling strategies for the coming season. She is trying to decide whether any products should be discounted in price by 30%, receive increased promotional efforts, or be left alone. She is now considering four products, data for which are given below.

	Mascara	Eyeliner	Lipstick	Cologne
Normal selling price	$2.50	$2.20	$2.00	$12.00
Variable cost	0.90	1.00	0.80	5.00
Contribution margin	$1.60	$1.20	$1.20	$ 7.00
Expected volumes:				
Without discount or special promotion (units)	800,000	750,000	2,000,000	200,000
With 30% discount	1,650,000	1,350,000	3,200,000	380,000
With special promotion	950,000	920,000	2,150,000	240,000

If the special promotion is chosen for a particular product, its price and variable cost will remain the same. Additional fixed costs are $200,000 for each product selected, primarily for advertising and incentive payments to salespeople.

If a product is selected for a 30% price cut, variable costs will remain the same, per unit, because Nova pays sales commissions on the basis of the normal selling price even during such special sales.

Required

1. For each product, determine which of the following should be done: reduce price, do a special promotion, or do nothing.

2. Discuss some additional factors that might influence the sales manager's decisions about each product.

4-46 *CVP for a hospital—patient-days* The administrator of Brookwood Memorial Hospital has developed the following estimate of costs.

Total annual cost = \$39,000,000 + (\$28 × P1) + (\$40 × P2)

where

P1 = patient-days on medical wards
P2 = patient-days on surgical wards

A *patient-day* is one patient occupying a bed for one day. The administrator expects contribution margins, other than from room charges, to be about \$25 per day from each medical patient and \$60 per day from each surgical patient. These come from pharmacy, blood bank, operating room charges, and other such sources.

Required

1. Suppose that patient-days on medical wards generally run twice the number of those on surgical wards. The room charges are tentatively set at \$75 per day for medical patients and \$100 for surgical patients. How many patient-days must the hospital achieve to break even?
2. Suppose now that the administrator forecasts 250,000 medical patient-days and 150,000 surgical patient-days. He wants to set room rates so that the hospital breaks even and also wants each type of patient-day to provide the same dollar contribution margin. What room rates will achieve these objectives? (The \$25 and \$60 miscellaneous contributions should be included in determining the contribution margins from room charges.)
3. Repeat item 2 assuming that the administrator wants both types of patient-day to provide the same contribution margin percentage.

4-47 *Comprehensive review of Chapters 2, 3, and 4* Tacky Company makes three products and sells them in about the same mix each month. Below are income statements for two recent months.

Tacky Company Income Statements
(in thousands of dollars)

	April	May
Sales	\$80	\$60
Costs	60	52
Income	\$20	\$ 8

Selling price and cost data by product are as follows.

	A	B	C
Selling price	\$20	\$10	\$5
Variable costs	8	3	3
Contribution margin	\$12	\$ 7	\$2
Contribution margin percentage	60%	70%	40%
Percentage of total sales dollars (mix)	40%	40%	20%

Required

1. Using the income statements for April and May, find total fixed cost and variable cost as a percentage of sales dollars.

2. Determine the break-even point in sales dollars.
3. Which product is most profitable per unit sold?
4. Which product is most profitable per dollar of sales?
5. What sales dollars are needed to earn $35,000 per month, and how many units of each product will be sold at that sales level if the usual mix is maintained?
6. The sales manager believes that he could increase sales of C by 10,000 units per month if more attention were devoted to it and less to B. Sales of B would fall by 2,000 units per month. What change in income would occur if this action were taken?
7. June sales were $100,000 with a mix of 40% A, 30% B, and 30% C. What was income?
8. July sales were $90,000 and income was $22,000.
   (a) What was the contribution margin percentage?
   (b) Which product would you think was sold in a higher proportion than in the usual mix?
9. Suppose the firm is currently selling 6,000 units of C. Because this is the least profitable product, management believes it should be dropped from the mix. If C is dropped, it is expected that sales of B would remain the same and those of A would rise. By how much would sales of A have to rise to maintain the same total income?

4-48 Segmented income statements, activity analysis Vic Kemp, executive vice president of Taylor, Inc., is examining the most recent monthly income statements, which are segmented by geographical area. Each area is the responsibility of a regional manager. Taylor, a distributor of products used by paper manufacturers, began operations in the western part of the United States 20 years ago and expanded into the southern and eastern markets only a year ago. Taylor does not manufacture its products, but rather buys them for resale to its customers.

Because Taylor has a good reputation and strong product lines, it has done well in the new markets, or at least Kemp thinks it has. Other than salespeople,

Taylor, Inc.
Income Statement, October 19X9
(in thousands of dollars)

	Total	Eastern	Southern	Western
Sales	$2,896.0	$589.0	$752.0	$1,555.0
Cost of sales	1,231.9	200.3	300.8	730.8
Gross margin	1,664.1	388.7	451.2	824.2
Selling expenses:				
Salaries and commissions	754.2	156.2	192.6	405.4
Shipping and warehousing	187.3	43.2	67.1	77.0
Other selling expenses	84.5	12.1	27.6	44.8
Total selling expenses	1,026.0	211.5	287.3	527.2
Administrative expenses:				
Salaries	147.2	42.6	36.8	67.8
Building occupancy	61.7	22.7	26.5	12.5
Other	56.1	12.3	22.1	21.7
Total administrative expenses	265.0	77.6	85.4	102.0
Total operating expenses	1,291.0	289.1	372.7	629.2
Income before taxes	$ 373.1	$ 99.6	$ 78.5	$ 195.0

Taylor has relatively few people and other assets in the market areas. The bulk of expenses are incurred at the home offices in Corvallis, Oregon.

Kemp is happy with the results in the new territories, but at the same time mistrusts them, not really knowing how the statements are prepared. Kemp is also concerned that the push into the new territories has caused managers to neglect the western territory, which seems to be slipping from past levels of profitability. He is quite concerned that the income statements do not give him the kind of information he needs to make judgments and decisions. He has asked the chief accountant for an explanation of the income statements, but to little avail. The chief accountant usually puts him off by saying that it is very complicated and that he does not have the time to explain every number.

Taylor's chief accountant has been allocating costs to the markets using a set of formulas based on relative sales volume in both unit and dollar terms. No one else quite knows how the chief accountant prepares the statements. Kemp finally goes to the controller and asks for a special study to help him get the information he feels is needed. The controller has been concerned with the allocation methods for some time and has collected the following information based on analyses of the activities in each territory.

	Eastern	Southern	Western
Variable Costs,			
Percentage of Sales			
Cost of sales	34.00%	40.00%	47.00%
Selling expenses	14.00%	13.00%	16.00%
Administrative expenses	0.00%	0.00%	0.00%
Direct Fixed Costs			
Cost of sales	$ 0	$ 0	$ 0
Selling expenses	152	155	207
Administrative expenses	9	12	19

The controller explains that she has developed the information by analyzing the cost driving activities associated with each category. For instance, the eastern territory has relatively heavy direct fixed selling expenses for several reasons. First, there are more established competitors in that region, and new customers are harder to cultivate. Second, shipping costs tend to be higher because orders from the east are smaller than those from the other regions, thus losing economies of large shipments. Other reasons contribute to the differences between the activity-based direct costs and the costs as allocated in the income statement on the previous page.

Required

1. Prepare a segmented income statement using the contribution margin format. Work with totals only for selling expenses and administrative expenses. Ignore the individual components of those cost categories.
2. Write a memorandum to Mr. Kemp telling him how each territory is doing. Use the guidelines in Appendix B.
3. Write a memorandum indicating the ethical issues that might arise from your analysis, such as what the regional managers have a right to expect from you or another managerial accountant. Refer to Exhibit 1-3.

4-49 Comprehensive problem on CVP analysis You are presented with the following information about Gammon Sales Company, based on plans for the year 19X1.

Sales ($1 per unit)		$100,000
Variable costs:		
Cost of goods sold	$67,000	
Other operating costs	15,000	
Total		82,000
Contribution margin		18,000
Fixed costs		13,140
Planned income before taxes		$ 4,860

Required

1. What is Gammon's break-even sales volume?
2. The company's officers have analyzed anticipated cash flows for the year and have determined that it could afford to spend $3,600 on a special advertising campaign. They are not sure, however, that the expenditure would be worthwhile. What is the break-even point if the campaign is undertaken?
3. If, as a result of the advertising campaign, the number of units sold could be expected to increase in an amount equal to the change in the break-even point in units, would the campaign be financially advisable? Explain.
4. Assume that Gammon has decided not to undertake the advertising campaign and is looking for other ways to improve the financial outlook for 19X1. The purchasing agent determines that there is a supplier (other than the one with which the company now deals) that will allow the company to buy at a price 10% below the anticipated purchase price. The sales manager believes that the new supplier does not provide a product of equal quality, and he estimates that sales volume will decrease by about 15% if the new supplier were used. The controller has determined that the switch in suppliers will necessitate minor changes in the administrative procedures, which will increase fixed costs by approximately $1,000. Would the change of suppliers be wise? Explain your answer with supporting computations.
5. Are there some qualitative considerations that might influence the decision on the change in suppliers?
6. After further investigation, you determine that Gammon has not one, but three separate products in its line, each of which has the same selling price. The planned activity for 19X1 in more detail is as follows.

	Product			
	1	2	3	Total
Sales ($1 per unit)	$50,000	$30,000	$20,000	$100,000
Variable costs:				
Cost of goods sold	30,000	21,000	16,000	67,000
Other operating costs	7,500	4,500	3,000	15,000
Total	37,500	25,500	19,000	82,000
Contribution margin	$12,500	$ 4,500	$ 1,000	18,000
Fixed costs				13,140
Planned income before taxes				$ 4,860

Gammon has decided not to dilute the impact of a special advertising campaign by trying to promote more than one product. Which product should the company probably choose to promote in the $3,600 advertising campaign? Explain.

7. The company has found an alternative supplier for each of its products. Each supplier is willing to sell to the company at a price 10% lower than is currently being paid. In each case, however, the product from the new supplier will probably reduce the total sales of that product by 15%. However, the company can change suppliers for only one of the products at a time. Ignoring any qualitative considerations, decide for which product, if any, Gammon should change suppliers. Support your answer.
8. Assume that Gammon's directors decide to postpone the advertising campaign and continue doing business with current suppliers. At the end of 19X1, despite sales of $110,000, income before taxes was only $360. Analysis of sales by product showed the following.

Sales of Product 1	$ 30,000
Sales of Product 2	20,000
Sales of Product 3	60,000
Total	$110,000

These results surprised the board of directors because operating managers assured the directors that variable and fixed costs had behaved exactly as expected and sales were in excess of the forecast. Explain the reason or reasons for the disappointing results.

4-50 ***Explaining revenue differences for a motel*** Great Eastern Inns, a large motel chain, had revenue of $60 million in 19X5, operating at a 70% occupancy rate. In 19X6, Great Eastern raised its room rates by 5%, and its occupancy rate fell to 65%. Variable costs are negligible.

Required

1. Determine Great Eastern's revenue for 19X6.
2. Determine how much of the difference in revenue, from 19X5 to 19X6, is attributable to (a) room rates and (b) room occupancy. You can treat 19X5 in the same way you usually do "planned results," and 19X6 as you do "actual results." Round to the nearest $100,000.

CASES

4-51 ***Product mix, profit planning, taxes*** Michael Monte, the new assistant controller of Remley Company, has prepared a CVP analysis for the firm based on sales of the firm's three products from 19X7. He will present the analysis to a group of managers later in the week. Data per unit are given below.

	Products		
	101	102	103
Selling price	$3.50	$4.00	$5.00
Variable costs	1.50	3.00	2.00
Contribution margin	$2.00	$1.00	$3.00

On the basis of the sales mix in 19X7, Michael believed that of every ten units sold, four would be 101s, four 102s, and two 103s. Total fixed costs were predicted to be $90,000. Total sales were expected to be 100,000 units, based on a projection of trends in recent years, and Michael had prepared the following planned income statement for the year 19X8.

	101	102	103	Total
Sales	$140,000	$160,000	$100,000	$400,000
Variable costs	60,000	120,000	40,000	220,000
Contribution margin	$ 80,000	$ 40,000	$ 60,000	180,000
Fixed costs				90,000
Income before tax				90,000
Income taxes (40%)				36,000
Net Income				$ 54,000

At the meeting, Michael demonstrated that his analysis could be used to predict changes in profits that would be expected to follow changes in sales. As an example, he said that the break-even point for the firm is $200,000 in sales, because the contribution margin percentage is 45% and fixed costs are $90,000. He showed the other managers that target profits can also be computed, although the presence of income taxes makes it a bit more complicated than computing the break-even point. He said that if an after-tax profit figure were desired, it was necessary to divide it by 60%, the percentage of net income to income before taxes. The resulting before-tax profit could be added to fixed costs and the sum divided by 45%. Thus, the sales required for profits of $90,000 are about $533,300, since before-tax profits have to be $150,000, and ($90,000 + $150,000)/45% is $533,333.

Some of the managers were becoming restless as Michael explained his analysis. Finally, the production manager said that it was all very interesting, but irrelevant. She told the group that labor costs, which are 50% of variable costs, would increase by 20% under a new union contract.

The controller was somewhat disappointed with Michael's analysis because it had failed to provide for a $40,000 dividend to stockholders that the president of the firm had said should be a target. The firm has a policy of not allowing dividends to be more than one-third of after-tax profits. The controller had thought that Michael would incorporate the desired dividend into his analysis to show the other managers what had to be done to meet the president's goal.

As the managers began to mumble among themselves about the irrelevance of the analysis, the sales manager announced that the assumed sales mix was no good. "I don't know how this will affect the analysis, but we expect that each product will be sold in equal amounts during this coming year. The demand for 103s is increasing substantially."

The production manager commented that the firm was going to rent some additional equipment to increase production of 103s. The rental would be $10,000 per year. She wondered what effect that news would have on Michael's figures.

As he left the meeting, Michael chastised himself for not having obtained more information before going in and looking ill-prepared.

Required

Prepare a new analysis for Remley, incorporating the goals and changed assumptions learned at the meeting. Show the sales necessary to (a) break even and (b) meet the profit required to pay the $40,000 dividend without violating the firm's dividend policy.

4-52 ***Explaining territorial differences*** Barkman Company sells various types of jams and jellies all across the country. The following income statement shows results for two territories for a recent month, in thousands of dollars.

	Northwest	Southeast
Sales	$2,800	$2,400
Variable costs	840	600
Contribution margin	1,960	1,800
Fixed costs, discretionary	920	920
Territory income	$1,040	$ 880

Variable costs per case are the same in both territories. The territorial managers have wide discretion over setting prices and incurring advertising and promotion expenses.

Required

Compare the pricing strategies of the managers of the territories. Show why the Northwest territory is more profitable than the Southeast.

4-53 ***Variance analysis (CMA adapted)*** Handler Company distributes two power tools to hardware stores: a heavy-duty hand drill and a table saw. Handler buys the tools from a manufacturer that attaches the Handler label to them.

The 19X4 planned and actual results appear below. The plan was adopted in late 19X3 based on Handler's estimates of market share for each tool. During the first quarter of 19X4 it seemed likely that the total market for the tools would be 10% less than Handler had estimated. In an attempt to prevent planned unit sales from declining by 10%, Handler's managers instituted a marketing program consisting of price reductions and increased advertising. The table saw was emphasized over the drill in this program.

Handler Company
Income Statement for 19X4
(all data in thousands)

	Drill		Table Saw		Total	
	Plan	Actual	Plan	Actual	Plan	Actual
Unit sales	120	86	80	74	200	160
Revenue	$7,200	$5,074	$9,600	$8,510	$16,800	$13,584
Variable costs	6,000	4,300	6,400	5,920	12,400	10,220
Contribution margin	$1,200	$ 774	$3,200	$2,590	4,400	3,364
Unallocated costs:						
Selling					1,000	1,000
Advertising					1,000	1,060
Administration					400	406
Total unallocated costs					2,400	2,466
Income					$ 2,000	$ 898

Required

1. For each product, determine the sales price variance and sales volume variance.
2. Write a memorandum to the president assessing the success, or lack thereof, of the marketing program (price reductions and increased advertising). Use the guidelines in Appendix B.

5 short-term decisions and accounting information

Making decisions is choosing from alternatives. Even continuing to do what we have been doing is a decision, if there is some other alternative available. (When no alternatives are available, no decision can be made because you have no choice.) Should we raise the price of our product? Should we drop a particular product? Should we add a new product? Should we compensate salespeople by salary (a fixed cost) or by commission (a variable cost)? Should we make a component in our factory or buy it? Managers are continually concerned about such sets of alternatives.

Another critical characteristic of decisions is that they relate to future actions; they cannot be made retroactively. (You cannot decide in August, after the price of a particular stock has increased, to buy that stock the previous February.) This characteristic has two important implications. First, because managers must base their decisions on estimates, a decision is not necessarily bad just because some unpredictable change in circumstances caused results to differ markedly from expectations. Second, managers can never be *sure* that a particular decision was wise, because they cannot know what would have happened if they had selected different courses of action. But managers can have a reasonable degree of confidence if the decision is based on the best available information, *and* if they understand the significance of the information.

Consider a relatively simple example where a company experienced much improved results after a decision. The Toronto Argonauts of the Canadian Football League paid Rocket Ismail, the Heisman Trophy winner from Notre Dame, $18 million for four years. The Argonauts' average attendance increased from 15,000 to 36,000 and television ratings went up 40%.

These improvements are worth a great deal more than $18 million. Can we conclude that the team made a wise decision? It certainly looks good, but we cannot be sure how much of the increased interest is attributable to Ismail. We can certainly argue that if the team had made no other major changes, Ismail may have made a great deal of difference, but we can never know. Evaluating decisions where the consequences are not nearly so clear-cut is much more difficult.

This chapter focuses on short-term decisions; Chapters 8 and 9 focus on long-term decisions. Most managers and accountants consider a decision to be short-term if it involves a period of one year or less. The cutoff is arbitrary but commonly used. Perhaps a better distinction between short- and long-term decisions is that the former normally do not require large capital investments. For this reason, short-term decisions are more easily reversible than long-term ones. (You can almost always change prices or the method of compensating salespeople, but you cannot so simply sell a factory or even a large piece of equipment.) The basic principles that apply to short-term decisions also apply to long-term ones, but long-term decisions require some additional considerations. In general, the long-term decisions discussed in later chapters require the commitment of money for a fairly long period.

One final matter before we proceed. Almost every decision has both quantitative and qualitative aspects, and managers must understand both. In this chapter, we often mention qualitative issues associated with specific decisions, but our analytical approaches concentrate on the quantitative, economic aspects. In practice, qualitative considerations sometimes override quantitative factors; that is, in some cases, managers select an alternative that is not as economically sound as others because of company policy or a belief that an action just is not right for the company. For example, some manufacturers of name-brand products sell unlabeled products to discount stores. However, some manufacturers do not because their managers believe that the company's reputation for quality could suffer if people learned that discount stores were carrying the merchandise under another name. Such managers cannot be called wrong. But it is critical that they be aware of the costs, in the form of lost profits. The techniques described in this chapter help the managers to determine the cost of having such a policy.

Additionally, companies will often sacrifice short-term results in the expectation of better long-term results. In late 1992, the Ford Taurus was neck-and-neck with the Honda Accord to be the best-selling automobile in the U.S. The Accord had held the honor for several years. The business press widely reported that Ford was practically giving Tauruses away in late December, through rebates and special offers, to gain the sales lead. Taurus did outsell Accord and Ford immediately began capitalizing on its victory in its advertising. Obviously, Ford's managers expected to recoup what they had lost through earlier price reductions and rebates.

THE CRITERION FOR SHORT-TERM DECISIONS

The economic criterion for making short-term decisions is simple: *Take the action that you expect will give the highest income (or least loss) to the firm.* Applying this rule is not always simple, and two subrules might be helpful:

1. The only revenues and costs that are *relevant* in making decisions are the expected future revenues and costs that will *differ* among the choices that are available. These are called **differential revenues and costs.** (Because many decisions result in increases in revenues and costs, some use the terms **incremental revenues and costs.**)
2. Revenues and costs that have already been earned or incurred are *irrelevant* in making decisions. Their only use is that they might aid in predicting future revenues and costs.

DIFFERENTIAL (INCREMENTAL) REVENUES AND COSTS

The term *differential* is more inclusive than *incremental.* The latter term suggests increases, and some decisions result in decreases in both revenues and costs. But the terms used are not as important as what they denote. Differential costs are *avoidable* costs, which we introduced in Chapters 3 and 4. If the firm can change a cost by taking one action as opposed to another, the cost is avoidable and therefore is differential. Suppose a firm could save $50,000 in salaries and other fixed costs if it stopped selling a product in a particular geographical region. The $50,000 is avoidable (differential) because it will be incurred if the firm continues to sell in the region and will not be incurred if the firm stops selling in that region. Of course, the company will lose revenue if it discontinues sales in the region. Hence, the lost revenue is differential in a decision to stop selling in the region.

SUNK COSTS AND OPPORTUNITY COSTS

The emphasis on differential revenues and costs gives rise to two other, related concepts that you may have already encountered in your study of economics: *sunk costs* and *opportunity costs.* A **sunk cost** is one that has already been incurred and therefore will be the same no matter which alternative a manager selects. Sunk costs are *never* relevant for decision making because they are not differential.

Suppose a company has spent $500,000 developing a new product. Problems have arisen and the managers must now decide whether or not to market it. The $500,000 is irrelevant to the decision because it is not differential; that is, the cost will be the same whether or not the firm markets the product. Similarly, depreciation on a machine is irrelevant in deciding which products to make with that machine. *All* historical costs, whether original cost or book value (cost minus accumulated depreciation), are sunk costs.

Even though the historical cost of a resource is sunk, it can have a cost for decision-making purposes. If a resource can be used in more than one way, it has an opportunity cost. In general terms, an **opportunity cost** is the benefit lost by taking one action as opposed to another. The "other" action is the best alternative available other than the one being contemplated.

Suppose PPF Company owns a warehouse and can either use it to store products or rent it to another company for $8,000 per year. Using the space for storage requires that PPF forego the opportunity to rent it, which means that there *is* a difference to PPF if it chooses to take one action rather than another. When PPF considers any action that requires using the space for storage, the relevant cost of the space is its opportunity cost, the $8,000 rent

PPF will not collect. What if PPF would have to pay $1,000 per year for a license to rent the warehouse? The opportunity cost of using the space for storage falls to $7,000, the net sacrifice that PPF makes by foregoing the rental opportunity.

As another example, suppose PPF owns a machine that can be used to produce either of two products, X and Y. The products require the same amount of machine time, but the contribution margin of X is greater than that of Y. When PPF considers a decision to use the machine to produce X, the cost of using the machine is its opportunity cost, the contribution margin sacrificed by not using it to produce Y. If PPF is considering using the machine to produce Y, the cost is the contribution margin sacrificed by not using it to produce X. As you can see, opportunity cost depends on what action is being considered.

The example described in the next section incorporates the concepts of differential revenues and costs, sunk costs, and opportunity costs. As you read, look for examples of these concepts.

Basic Example

Walters Company manufactures clothing. Walters has in stock 5,000 shirts that it cannot sell through normal channels and a chain store has approached Walters with an offer to buy the shirts for $12,000. The cost to manufacture these shirts was $17,000. The president says he'd rather throw the shirts away than sell them at a loss of $5,000 ($17,000 manufacturing costs – $12,000 revenue). Is he correct? If there is no likelihood of getting a better offer, he is not, and the chain's offer should be accepted.

Walters has two alternatives: (1) throw the shirts away or (2) sell them to the chain. Throwing the shirts away yields no revenue and requires no additional costs. The chain's offer should be accepted because the difference in profit is $12,000. The differential revenues and costs for selling to the chain *as opposed to* throwing out the shirts are shown below.

Sell to Chain *Rather* than Throw Shirts Away	
Differential revenues	$12,000
Differential costs	0
Profit	$12,000

The opportunity cost of throwing the shirts away is $12,000, the benefit lost by not taking the best available alternative course of action. What is the opportunity cost of selling the shirts to the chain? Nothing, because Walters would obtain no benefit from that alternative, which is to throw the shirts away. Thus, opportunity cost depends on which alternative is being considered.

But what of the $17,000 cost to make the shirts? You understand the concepts of differential and sunk costs if you saw that the $17,000 is sunk. That cost has already been incurred and will not change regardless of which alternative is chosen. True, Walters will have a $5,000 loss if it sells the shirts to the chain ($17,000 – $12,000). But if the shirts are simply thrown out, Walters will have a loss of $17,000. (Note that Walters is better off selling the shirts for $12,000, whether the cost to manufacture them was $2,000, $17,000, or even $50,000, if the only other alternative is to throw them away.)

Let's add another alternative: Another chain store has offered to pay $20,000 for the shirts provided that Walters puts on two more pockets and dyes them a different color. The production manager estimates the incremental cost to do the work at $5,000. The president isn't happy about this alternative either, because the total cost ($17,000 + $5,000) is greater than the $20,000 offer.

Although three alternatives are now available, we already know that the as-is sale is preferable to throwing the shirts away. Therefore, we need only compare the new alternative with the as-is sale. Which of those two alternatives should Walters choose? It should do the work and sell the shirts for $20,000. To understand why, consider the differential revenues and costs.

Rework and Sell, *Rather* than Sell As Is	
Differential revenues ($20,000 – $12,000)	$8,000
Differential costs ($5,000 – $0)	5,000
Differential profit	$3,000

Walters would be $3,000 better off by reworking the shirts rather than selling them as is.

What is the opportunity cost of an as-is sale of the shirts? The best available alternative is now the rework option, which has a profit of $15,000 ($20,000 revenue minus $5,000 cost). Thus, the opportunity cost of the as-is sale is the $15,000 sacrificed by not accepting the rework option. What is the opportunity cost of accepting the rework offer? The opportunity cost is $12,000, the benefit foregone by rejecting the as-is sale.

Some decision makers prefer to incorporate opportunity costs directly into their analysis of an alternative. Using this approach, the analysis of the as-is alternative would show a $3,000 loss (revenues of $12,000 and the $15,000 opportunity cost noted above). A similar analysis of the rework option would show a $3,000 profit (revenues of $20,000 and $17,000 of costs, consisting of $5,000 for the extra work plus the $12,000 opportunity cost of using the shirts for this option). Analyzing the alternatives separately but incorporating opportunity costs in each analysis indicates the same choice as does the comparative analysis: Accept the rework option because its $3,000 profit is preferable to the $3,000 loss from the as-is sale.

As before, the $17,000 cost of manufacturing the shirts is irrelevant. To emphasize the irrelevance of this sunk cost, consider Walters' income statement for each of the alternatives.

	Throw Out Shirts	Sell Shirts As Is	Rework Shirts
Revenues	$ 0	$12,000	$20,000
Costs:			
Manufacturing	(17,000)	(17,000)	(17,000)
Rework			(5,000)
Profit (loss)	($17,000)	($ 5,000)	($ 2,000)

Reworking the shirt produces the smallest loss, confirming the results of the differential analyses, which showed that alternative to be the best of the three. The loss incurred by selling the shirts as-is is $12,000 less than that from throwing them out, which is equal to the $12,000 differential profit shown in the first analysis. The $2,000 loss reported for reworking the shirts is $3,000 less than the loss from the as-is sale, which is equal to the $3,000 differential profit we found when comparing those choices.

Let us revise our example one last time. The unchanged fact is that Walters has on hand 5,000 shirts that were manufactured at a cost of $17,000. But now assume that the shirts can be sold at regular prices, so that Walters will have to produce similar shirts to meet future sales if it sells the on-hand shirts. The production manager says that the cost of manufacturing 5,000 shirts has risen to $20,000. A discount outlet offers Walters $18,000 for the shirts on hand. What should the firm do under these conditions? The key to the analysis is to understand that, *whatever* Walters decides to do, it must have 5,000 shirts available to meet the expected future demand at the regular price. (Everything that happens after that point, including the expected regular sales, will be the same no matter what Walters decides to do about the 5,000 shirts on hand.)

Walters has two alternatives. First, it can hold the shirts until they can be sold at regular prices, which is to say it can choose to "do nothing." If Walters chooses that alternative, it receives no revenues and incurs no costs between now and the time the shirts are needed for regular sales, for a net of zero. Second, Walters can sell the shirts now and make others to meet regular sales needs. If this alternative is chosen, Walters receives $18,000 revenue and incurs a cost of $20,000 (to produce the shirts needed for regular sales), for a loss of $2,000. The better choice is to "do nothing"; Walters will be $2,000 better off by choosing that action.

The opportunity cost of choosing to sell the shirts now is $20,000, the cost of replacing them later. This is their value because selling them now requires replacing them at a $20,000 cost. Opportunity cost is replacement cost in some situations. In our previous examples, the opportunity cost was always a selling price (less additional costs to complete).

DEVELOPING RELEVANT INFORMATION

Managers make many decisions that affect a relatively small segment of the company: a product, a product line, a factory, even a single component of a finished product. Often, the segment (individual activity) that managers are reviewing for possible change is not large enough to warrant separate reporting.

For example, consider a company that makes office equipment. The company might make several models each of typewriters, calculators, and copiers; sell them in several regions to different types of customers (businesses, hospitals, governmental agencies, etc.); and operate several factories, some of which make only one product or line and others of which make several products. Normal accounting reports might not show information by model of product, by region, by type of customer, and by factory.

An existing accounting report, such as the product-line income statement in Exhibit 4-4, is a good base from which to analyze a product line because it highlights avoidable costs. But information in past accounting reports is of interest only if it helps to predict the future. Other sources are often more important. Engineers provide information about materials needs and labor requirements for a new product. From the marketing department come estimates of future sales of a product. Thus, even the availability of a regular accounting report on the segment for which some change is contemplated does not mean that the report contains the information needed for making a decision about that change.

The availability of computers helps managers more easily develop some types of information, like the number of units of a particular product sold in each region to each type of customer. But a computer cannot determine whether or not costs are avoidable. Making these determinations requires a great deal of work and close cooperation between the managerial accountant and other managers.

For example, consider the office equipment company described above. Suppose salespeople are paid salaries, concentrate on specific types of customers, *and* sell all of the firm's products. Neither sales salaries nor travel costs are avoidable costs when analyzing a particular *model* of copier; if a model is dropped, the salespeople will still call on the same customers. On the other hand, if the segment is a particular type of customer, some sales salaries and related expenses might well be avoidable. Similarly, if salespeople cover specific geographical regions, their salaries and other expenses are avoidable in a segment analysis by region.

The most important point about decisions relating to segments is that the analyses will differ with the decisions. There is no magic formula for identifying the costs and revenues relevant to decisions. Costs that are avoidable, and therefore differential, when one segment is under review might be unavoidable when looking at a different segment. *In general, the smaller the segment is, the less the avoidable cost.* Avoidable costs of a model of typewriter sold in a particular region are probably limited to the variable costs of producing that model. Those associated with the entire line of typewriters in the same region include variable production costs and perhaps some selling expenses. Some fixed manufacturing costs might also be saved, especially if typewriters sold in that region are made in a factory that does not make other product lines. But even that conclusion depends on the specific circumstances of that plant. As the segment under study expands to an entire product line, more and more costs become avoidable.

ALLOCATED COSTS

The task of identifying the costs relevant to a particular decision is often complicated by the accounting practice of allocating **joint (common) costs** to segments. For example, firms regularly allocate fixed manufacturing costs to units of product, because they are required to do so for financial accounting and tax purposes. For reasons discussed in Chapter 10, cost allocations are often incorporated into internal reports that serve as a starting point for decision making.

Earlier in this chapter we emphasized that the basis for decision making was information about the future. In Chapter 2, we showed that per-unit fixed costs—the result of allocations—are not useful in predicting future costs. Hence, per-unit fixed costs are not relevant for decision making. By definition, common costs are unavoidable to individual segments to which they are common. Allocating such costs to individual segments does not make the allocated amount avoidable in the future. Hence, for making decisions about a segment, common costs allocated to that segment are not relevant; the only relevant costs are those that will change (be differential) if a firm chooses one course of action rather than another.

Although there is a strong presumption that an allocated cost is unavoidable, it is sometimes possible to reduce common costs if a large enough segment is eliminated. For example, suppose that each of the 20 employees of a payroll department works on some part of the payrolls of all six factories that the company operates. The salaries of all of the employees in the payroll department are then common to the six factories. But if one large factory closes, the payroll department might be able to reassign work and people, reducing the staff to 17 or 18 and so reducing *some* of the common cost. Determining these types of changes in costs is part of analyzing costs in an activity framework, activity-based costing. Again, analyzing costs for decisions requires very careful attention to the specific situation.

The appearance of allocated costs on segment reports raises an important point about providing information within a firm. An information system must provide data for preparing financial statements, completing tax and other government forms, and making decisions. The system is usually designed around the needs of financial accounting and taxation, because the specific information required for these purposes is well-known and is needed regularly. Because the information system and resulting segment reports serve several purposes, a manager using such reports should take care to include only relevant costs in analyzing a particular decision.

ACTIVITY-BASED ALLOCATIONS

Companies (or not-for-profit organizations) that use activity-based-costing (ABC) allocate costs only after making careful studies of cost pools and related cost drivers. These companies should have fewer problems with allocations getting in the way of good decisions. If companies only allocate those costs that are clearly driven by activities of the segments, then significant amounts of such allocated costs might be avoidable. Managers who can determine how *activities* will change as a result of taking particular courses of action should be better able to estimate the effects of the changes on costs. Good estimates are especially likely if the company will cease doing certain activities. However, the company might not be able to reduce costs immediately. Moreover, changing the level of an activity might not have a direct, proportional effect on costs, so ABC does not automatically determine how much cost is avoidable in any given situation. Activity-based allocations do not substitute for careful analyses of the likely effects of decisions, but they should make those analyses less difficult.

Most of the remainder of this chapter is devoted to typical examples of short-term decisions. Although the situations appear to be quite different, the same principle applies to all: Find the most profitable alternative by analyzing the differential revenues and costs. In some cases, it will be relatively easy to determine the differentials and choose among the alternatives. In others, you might find it easier to make your choice by preparing complete income statements for the alternatives. But the two approaches should lead to the same decision.

TYPICAL SHORT-TERM DECISIONS

DROPPING A SEGMENT

You already know there are many ways to segment a firm. Determining the best mix of segments is a continual problem for managers, who sometimes have to decide whether to drop a segment, or perhaps to replace one segment with another.

Consider Moorehead Department Store, which uses its available space for three product lines. Below is the income statement for a recent month, and Moorehead's managers expect these results to continue in the foreseeable future.

	Clothing	Appliances	Housewares	Total
Sales	$45,000	$40,000	$15,000	$100,000
Variable costs	25,000	18,000	11,000	54,000
Contribution margin	20,000	22,000	4,000	46,000
Fixed costs:				
Direct—all avoidable	(4,000)	(3,400)	(1,500)	(8,900)
Indirect (common), allocated on sales revenues	(9,450)	(8,400)	(3,150)	(21,000)
Income (loss)	$ 6,550	$10,200	($ 650)	$ 16,100

Should the store drop the housewares line because it shows a loss? To answer that question we must know what would change if the line were dropped.

Obviously, the $4,000 contribution margin for housewares would be lost, and the $1,500 avoidable direct fixed costs could be saved if the housewares line were dropped. A careful analysis of the cost drivers for the various common (indirect) fixed costs would show Moorehead's managers how much, if any, of those costs would probably be avoided by dropping the line. (Remember the example of the payroll department.) Suppose such an analysis showed that dropping any one segment would reduce common costs by $1,000, so that common costs would drop to $20,000. The changes (differentials) are summarized below.

Differential contribution margin—decrease		$4,000
Differential costs:		
Direct fixed costs saved	$1,500	
Indirect fixed costs saved	1,000	
Total cost saving		2,500
Differential loss from dropping housewares		$1,500

Assuming only the two alternatives, keep housewares or drop them, keeping them seems the best choice because dropping them would *reduce* income by $1,500. The above analysis shows the differential contribution margin, but the lost revenues and the savings of variable costs could be shown separately. The decline in income could also be determined by preparing a new income statement that included only the remaining product lines and the lower common costs. (Income would drop from $16,100 to $14,600, a $1,500 difference.)

Of course, a company considering dropping a segment often has other alternatives. For example, if Moorehead drops housewares, the company probably could use the freed-up space in some other way, such as to expand one of the other lines, add another line, or even to rent to another company. The preceding analysis can help managers evaluate other alternatives. Suppose the space could be rented to another company. Because dropping housewares would reduce profits by $1,500, managers know it would take at least $1,500 in rental income to offset the loss. That is, if renting is the only alternative, the opportunity cost of using the space to sell housewares is the rental income foregone by using the space to sell housewares.

Let's examine a more complicated situation. Suppose Moorehead could substitute a shoe department in the space now occupied by housewares. Moorehead's managers estimate that a shoe department would generate contribution margin of $12,000 (revenues of $20,000 and variable costs of $8,000) and would have $2,700 of direct fixed costs. Note, however, that if the shoe department is substituted for housewares, Moorehead will not reduce common costs because it will still have three departments. Should Moorehead make the substitution?

Let's look at what will change if the substitution is made. Contribution margin will increase $8,000 ($12,000 from shoes vs. $4,000 from housewares), but direct fixed costs will increase $1,200 ($2,700 for shoes vs. $1,500 for housewares). Hence, the substitution would increase income by $6,800 ($8,000 – $1,200). The differential analysis of the substitution option appears as follows.

Differential contribution margin—increase ($12,000 – $4,000)	$8,000
Differential costs—increase in	
direct fixed costs ($2,700 – $1,500)	1,200
Differential profit favoring substitution	$6,800

If you prepared a complete income statement for the new sales mix, income would be $22,900 ($16,100 + $6,800).

We must emphasize that the decision being considered is whether to substitute shoes for housewares. The purpose of that decision is to find the best way to use *existing* resources. The analysis would be different if Moorehead was considering adding shoes to its existing product lines. Adding a line is likely to require some investment in new resources (e.g., display equipment, furniture and fixtures, etc.), a characteristic that generally distinguishes long-term from short-term decisions.

Finally, the alternatives considered thus far serve to remind you that whether a cost is avoidable depends on the decision being considered. If the decision is whether to drop housewares altogether, the $1,000 potential reduction in common costs is relevant because it is avoidable, and, therefore, differential. But if the decision is whether to substitute shoes for housewares, none of the common costs are relevant because they are all unavoidable.

Complementary Effects

The facts associated with the preceding example did not include any likelihood that dropping or adding a segment (product line, in this case) might affect the sales of continuing segments. But as noted in the discussion of sales mix in Chapter 4, a change in the sales of one product might be accompanied by a change in the sales of another. When such a relationship exists, a decision about the one product is said to have **complementary effects.** Marketing studies of shopping habits can often help to quantify the effects of such suspected complementary relationships,

Let's return to Moorehead Department Store, whose managers are considering dropping housewares and adding shoes. Suppose the managers believe that some people coming to shop for shoes are also likely to buy clothing, and that some people coming to shop for housewares also buy appliances at the same time. After authorizing and reviewing the results of market studies, the managers estimate that appliance sales will drop 10% and clothing sales increase 7% if shoes are substituted for housewares. Considering this new information should the substitution be made?

You should see that a differential analysis of the substitution decision includes everything in the previous analysis *plus* the impact of the complementary effects. Below is such an analysis.

Differential contribution margin:	
Increase due to selling shoes vs. housewares	$8,000
Increase due to higher clothing sales	
(7% × $20,000 contribution margin on current sales)	1,400
Decrease due to lower sales of appliances	
(10% × $22,000 contribution margin on current sales)	(2,200)
Net increase in contribution margin	7,200
Differential costs—increase in direct fixed costs	
($2,700 – $1,500)	1,200
Differential profit favoring substitution	$6,000

The advantage of the substitution is less than computed earlier ($6,000 vs. $6,800), but the substitution is still profitable. Again, the outcome of the substitution could have been determined by preparing an income statement to reflect the new sales mix including the complementary effects. (You might want to prepare such a statement to confirm the answer reached using only differentials.) The statement should show income of $22,100, which is $6,000 greater than income with the current mix.

Loss Leader

A particularly interesting case of complementary effects is the **loss leader,** a product or line that shows a negative profit in the sense that its contribution margin does not cover its avoidable fixed costs. In an extreme case, the product might even have a negative contribution margin! If the complementary effects between the loss leader and the firm's other products are large enough, even such an extreme pricing policy could be beneficial.

Consider the manager of a local pizza parlor who is dismayed by a lack of business at lunchtime. He attributes this to the specials of competing restaurants and is eager to change the situation. He has prepared the following income statement, based on a normal week, for the 11:00 a.m. to 2:00 p.m. period. The costs shown are all incremental.

Computer information service is but one example of an industry that depends on loss leaders. Prodigy, a prominent company in the industry, loses money on its $12.95 monthly charge for basic services. The company counts on advertising and extra services to earn profits. Of course, Prodigy could not provide those extra services without having people signed up for the basic service, so the motivation for the loss leader is obvious.*

* *"Prodigy Installs a New Program,"* Business Week, *September 14, 1992, 96.*

	Pizza	Soft Drinks	Total
Sales (200 pizzas @ $1.80)	$360	$100	$460
Variable costs	120	40	160
Contribution margin	$240	$ 60	300
Part-time employee salaries			80
Income			$220

He is thinking about offering his own luncheon special; with each pizza comes all the free soft drinks a customer can drink. He believes that the offer could double his lunchtime pizza sales. On the basis of his experience and judgment, he anticipates that soft drink consumption will increase to two and one-half times the present level. To take care of the additional business, he estimates that he will have to hire additional part-time help at an additional cost of $40 per week. Soft drinks will generate no revenue, but the costs will continue, so he will obviously lose money on beverages. Can he gain enough on the sales of pizza to offset the loss? Using his estimates of the effects of the special (which are the best information available), he can prepare the following expected income statement for the lunchtime period.

	Pizza	Soft Drinks	Total
Sales	$720	$ 0	$720
Variable costs	240 [a]	100 [b]	340
Contribution margin	$480	($100)	380
Part-time employee salaries			120
Income			$260

a Variable costs computed at the same rate as before, one-third or 33 1/3% of selling price.
b Variable costs computed as two and one-half times the previous costs.

Soft drinks show a *negative* contribution margin. Yet if expectations about increased sales are realized, total income increases by $40 per week ($260 – $220).

The potential for complementary effects is more obvious in some cases than in others. For example, one can readily see the relationship between sales of gasoline and motor oil. But the loss-leader rationale is behind many low prices that are expected to encourage sales of products that are not complementary. Examples include supermarket offers of extremely inexpensive name-brand items in return for a newspaper coupon and the sale of well-known products for a few pennies to any customer purchasing a specific dollar amount of other merchandise.

Emphasizing the total profit picture is important in evaluating any product. A product that is selling at a loss (that is, negative contribution or product margin) might be so essential to the sales of other products that it should not be dropped. A manager contemplating the elimination of a specific product should consider the potential for complementary effects.

MAKE-OR-BUY DECISIONS

Most manufactured products consist of several components that are assembled into a finished unit. Many of these components can be bought from an outside supplier or made by the assembling firm. For each of these components, the firm's managers must decide: make or buy. As with other decisions, the quantitative factors are the differential costs to make and to buy.

Suppose XYZ Company now makes a component. A manager has prepared the following estimates of costs at the expected volume of 20,000 units.

Materials at $2 per unit	$ 40,000
Direct labor at $5 per unit	100,000
Variable overhead at $3 per unit	60,000
Allocated indirect fixed costs (building depreciation, heat and light, etc.)	120,000
Total costs	$320,000

An outside supplier offers to supply the component at $14 per unit or $280,000 for 20,000 units. Should the offer be accepted?

Because XYZ will sell the same quantity of product whether the component is made internally or purchased from an outside supplier, revenues are the same either way. Hence, the decision depends on which alternative results in the lower cost. Now we must determine whether alternative uses can be found for the space and equipment now used to make the component. If no alternative use were available, then the analysis is quite straightforward. The fixed costs that are now being allocated to making the component will not change if the component is bought from the outside supplier. Hence, they are not relevant. The following schedule focuses on the relevant costs for each available course of action.

	Decisions	
	Make	Buy
Materials	$ 40,000	0
Direct labor	100,000	0
Variable overhead	60,000	0
Purchase price	0	$280,000
Total	$200,000	$280,000

The firm saves $80,000 by making the component. Note that including the fixed overhead of $120,000 under *both* alternatives would not change the

$80,000 advantage of making the component. Of course, if XYZ could actually reduce the indirect fixed costs by outside purchase of the component, the avoidable cost should be part of the total cost of making the component internally.

The firm is better off making the component unless it can obtain more than $80,000 by using the space and equipment in some other way. Considering only the quantitative data, XYZ should use the available space and equipment to make the component until some other opportunity arises such that the opportunity cost—the benefit to be gained by using the space and equipment for that other purpose—exceeds the $80,000 cost savings available by using those resources to make the component. Such a benefit could come from renting the space and equipment or using them to make a product that would bring more than $80,000 in incremental profit.

Several qualitative factors must be considered when deciding whether to purchase or make a component. Will the quality of purchased components be as good as the firm can achieve? Will the supplier meet delivery commitments? Will the supplier who now quotes a low price later raise it, thinking that you are a captive customer? The make-or-buy decision is especially important in an advanced manufacturing environment. A just-in-time manufacturer is extremely concerned with quality and delivery schedules and will not buy a component unless both are guaranteed. Such a company will make a component, even at a cost disadvantage, rather than risk compromising quality or delivery schedules.

JOINT PRODUCTS

When a single manufacturing process invariably produces two or more separate products, the products are called **joint products**. The process that makes the joint products is called a **joint process.** Refining crude petroleum yields a number of products, such as gasoline, various grades of oil, and kerosene. Processing cattle results in hides, hoofs, various cuts of meat, and other items (fat, organs). Some joint products are quite valuable; some have little or no value. Some can be sold just as they emerge from the joint process or can be processed further. For example, a meat packer might sell hides to a tanner, or if the meat packer has the expertise and the facilities, it could tan the hides and make shoes, gloves, and other products.

Manufacturers of joint products must decide whether to sell them at the **split-off point**—the point at which they emerge from the joint process—or to process them further into another saleable product. This decision cannot be based on the total costs of the individual final products or even on the total variable costs. To produce *any* of the joint products, the firm must undertake the joint process, incurring all the costs to perform that process. For example, a meat packer might pay $300 per animal. This cost does not relate to particular cuts of meat, to hides, or to by-products. To get *any* of those products, the packer must buy the entire animal. The $300 varies with the number of animals entering the joint process, but it cannot be identified with any specific cut of meat or even with all cuts of meat yielded by the joint process. The $300 cost per animal is the same whether any or all of the joint products is sold immediately or processed further. Hence, the costs incurred prior to split-off are irrelevant to decisions about the joint products.

The costs of the joint process are relevant only in determining whether that process should be carried on at all. In determining whether to sell a product at the split-off point or process it further, *all* costs—fixed and variable—incurred prior to the split-off are sunk.

Consider the following example. A chemical company makes two products, Alpha and Omega, in a joint process. Each 1,000 pounds of materials yields 600 pounds of Alpha and 400 pounds of Omega. Both Alpha and Omega can be sold at the split-off point or processed further. Selling price and cost data per batch (1,000 pounds of materials) are given below.

	Alpha	Omega
Selling price at split-off	$1,200 ($2 per pound)	$1,600 ($4 per pound)
Selling price after additional processing	$3,600 ($6 per pound)	$2,000 ($5 per pound)
Costs of additional processing, all variable	$900 ($1.50 per pound)	$500 ($1.25 per pound)

What should be done with each product? We can analyze the results of both alternatives for each product. Alpha is analyzed as follows:

Decision on Alpha		
	Sell at Split-Off	Process Further
Sales value	$1,200	$3,600
Incremental cost	0	900
Incremental profit	$1,200	$2,700

Alpha should be processed further because profit will be $1,500 higher ($2,700 – $1,200). We can reach the same conclusion by examining just the revenues and costs that differ by processing Alpha further.

Differential revenue ($3,600 – $1,200)	$2,400
Differential costs	900
Profit	$1,500

Similar analysis reveals that Omega should be sold at split-off, not processed further.

Differential revenues ($2,000 – $1,600)	$400
Differential costs	500
Loss	($100)

The firm would be $100 worse off if it processed Omega further.

The preceding analytical approaches are appropriate when all incremental costs of additional processing are variable, an unlikely situation. The additional processing will almost surely require some space, equipment, and people; some of the associated costs might be avoidable. Let us assume that further processing Alpha requires avoidable fixed costs of $10,000 per month and that the company usually processes ten batches per month. When the additional processing requires fixed costs, a slightly different approach is necessary. Note that the $10,000 is *joint* to all pounds of Alpha further processed during the month and cannot be identified with any one batch. Hence, to compare costs and revenues, the focus must be on the monthly output of 6,000 pounds (10 × 600 pounds per batch). The analysis below indicates a $5,000 advantage ($17,000 – $12,000) to processing Alpha beyond split-off.

Decision on Alpha

	Sell at Split-Off	Process Further
Sales: 10 × $1,200 per batch	$12,000	
10 × $3,600 per batch		$ 36,000
Incremental costs:		
Variable (10 × $900 per batch)		(9,000)
Fixed and avoidable		(10,000)
Incremental profit	$12,000	$ 17,000

A differential analysis would show the $24,000 additional revenue from selling after further processing ($36,000 – $12,000) and the additional costs of further processing ($19,000), giving the same $5,000 difference in favor of a decision to process Alpha beyond the split-off point. Another way to look at the decision is to say that the opportunity cost of processing further is the $12,000 given up by not selling at split-off. Incorporating the opportunity cost into the analysis of the decision to process further gives total costs of $31,000 ($9,000 + $10,000 + $12,000). Subtracting $31,000 from $36,000 revenue also gives the $5,000 advantage.

One of two conditions is critical to the legitimacy of analyzing the decision considered here as short term. Either the firm already has the facilities and expertise to carry out the additional processing, or it can acquire them without additional capital (long-term) investment. Under either condition, the firm has the flexibility to respond quickly to changes in selling prices of a joint product, either at the split-off point or after further processing. If an additional, long-term investment is required, the decision about further processing becomes long-term. Similarly, a decision about reducing the firm's short-term flexibility by eliminating the facilities needed for the additional processing of one (or more) of the joint products is a long-term decision. Chapter 8 introduces several techniques for analyzing long-term decisions.

The joint products case exemplifies a critical point made earlier: the relevance or irrelevance of a cost depends on the specific decision at hand. The variable costs of the joint process are relevant in deciding whether to operate that process at all, because they are avoidable if the joint process is not operated. But they are irrelevant in deciding whether to sell a given joint product at the split-off point or to process it further. Thus, the managerial accountant cannot respond to the question "What does it cost?" without knowing why the manager wants the answer to that question.

SPECIAL ORDERS

Companies that make products to be sold under their own brand names often also make nearly identical products that are sold at lower prices under the brand names of chain stores (called *house brands*). The manufacturer normally sells to chains at lower prices than to dealers who sell the products under the manufacturer's brand name. Manufacturers also sometimes accept special one-time orders at lower prices than usual. Let's examine the analysis managers need in order to make such decisions.

Griffith Company's income statement for 19X8 is based on planned production and sales of 60,000 units, with sales at $15 per unit. Griffith has just been approached by a chain store wanting to buy 20,000 units at $10. Griffith has the physical capacity to produce 100,000 units, and could hire additional hourly workers to achieve production in excess of 60,000. The variable portion of selling and administrative costs is $12,000 for sales commissions, which Griffith would not have to pay on the special order. The president is hesitant to accept the order because the average manufacturing cost of $13 per unit ($780,000/60,000) is greater than the $10 price offered.

Griffith Company, Planned Income Statement

	Per Unit		Total
Sales (60,000 units)	$15		$900,000
Manufacturing costs:			
Materials	4	$240,000	
Direct labor	3	180,000	
Overhead (one-third variable)	6	360,000	
Total	13		780,000
Gross margin			120,000
Selling and administrative expenses			80,000
Operating income			$ 40,000

As always, only the differential elements should be considered in making a decision. Below is a summary of the differentials.

	Per Unit		Total
Differential revenues (20,000 units)	$10		$200,000
Differential costs:			
Materials	4	$80,000	
Direct labor	3	60,000	
Variable overhead	2	40,000	180,000
Incremental profit from the order			$ 20,000

Accepting the special order increases income by $20,000; therefore, Griffith should accept it unless its managers believe that unquantifiable factors outweigh that benefit.

In this example, the only differential costs for the order were variable manufacturing costs. In another situation, variable selling and administrative expenses and perhaps some incremental fixed costs might apply to the order. For example, where a special order requires a large increase in production, additional fixed costs might be incurred because the higher production level involves one or more steps in step-variable manufacturing or administrative costs. Those costs, too, should be incorporated in the analysis.

Special orders, either one-shot or continuing (like the house-brand arrangement mentioned above), require careful study because of the potential effect of the orders on sales at regular prices. For instance, an appliance manufacturer deciding whether to supply a discount chain with 100,000 washing machines must consider whether its sales to regular dealers will fall because some customers buy from the chain instead of from regular dealers. Or perhaps the special order is larger than available capacity, or causes production delays, so that accepting the order requires foregoing some of the sales planned at regular prices. And even if the firm's capacity can accommodate both the planned sales and the special order, accepting the order carries the potential for lost sales if actual demand is greater than planned. The analysis of a special order should incorporate the potential for lost sales at regular prices. Examples abound of real companies harming their regular sales by offering some product at lower prices. The Big-Three U.S. automakers sell many cars to fleets, such as Hertz and Avis. The automakers used to buy these cars back within 4-6 months, then sell them to dealers as "program cars." Dealers in turn sold them to retail customers. Many analysts believed that these sales both hurt new car sales and also depressed prices of used cars.[1]

Gucci, the purveyor of high-fashion, high-priced shoes, luggage, and other products, gives a different kind of example. In the 1980's, Gucci licensed its logo to appear on over 10,000 items. The prestige that Gucci had enjoyed dissipated rapidly as customers saw its logo all over and no longer felt the sense of exclusivity.[2] We can illustrate the problem of lost sales, and a basic approach for dealing with it, by continuing the example of Griffith Company.

Suppose that because of a shortage of labor, Griffith can expect to produce only 75,000 units despite its physical capacity for 100,000 units. *If* Griffith accepts the special order, Griffith won't be able to fill orders for 5,000 of the 60,000 planned sales at the regular price because filling the order leaves capacity to make only 55,000 units for sale at the regular price (capacity of 75,000 – 20,000 units on the special order). A differential analysis that includes the new information appears below. (Remember that there is a commission, a variable selling cost, on regular sales.)

Differential revenues:		
New revenues from the order (above)	$200,000	
Lost revenues on regular sales (5,000 × $15)	75,000	
Total differential revenues		$125,000
Differential costs:		
Costs for the special order (above)	180,000	
Costs saved by not making regular sales:		
Variable manufacturing cost		
5,000 units × $9 ($4 + $3 + $2)	(45,000)	
Commissions		
5,000 × $0.20 ($12,000/60,000)	(1,000)	
Total differential costs		134,000
Differential loss from accepting the order		$ (9,000)

Another approach is to compare the contribution margin obtained from the special order with the contribution margin lost on regular sales.

1 *Neil Templin, "Sales of Rental Cars by Big Three Depress Other Second-Hand Auto Prices,"* The Wall Street Journal, *January 6, 1992, B1.*
2 *"At Gucci La Vita Is No Longer So Dolce,"* Business Week, *November 2, 1992, 60.*

New contribution margin—special order	
20,000 × ($10 – $9 variable manufacturing cost)	$20,000
Lost contribution margin—regular sales	
5,000 × ($15 – $9 – $0.20 = $5.80)	29,000
Loss from accepting order	$(9,000)

Both analyses show the special order to be unprofitable under the revised conditions (total output of 75,000 units).

The capacity constraint aside, if Griffith's managers believed the firm would lose *some* sales at the regular price through customers buying from the chain, they could use the differential analysis to determine the maximum sales the firm could lose before accepting the special order became unprofitable. At a $5.80 per-unit contribution margin for regular sales (shown above), Griffith could lose sales of up to 3,448 units ($20,000 incremental profit/$5.80 contribution margin) at regular prices without hurting overall profits. The question the managers must then answer is whether lost sales are likely to approach that critical number.

Because managers view special-order decisions as short term, they tend to focus on variable costs when quoting a price. Many managers do understand, however, that these decisions can have long-term consequences. For example, a company might accept so much private branding that it must acquire additional manufacturing capacity to meet the continuing growth of its regular sales. Another long-term effect of accepting special orders has to do with a company's prospects for survival, because a company cannot continue indefinitely without covering *all* of its costs. Smaller companies, especially, must be careful not to devote too much capacity to special orders that could turn out to dominate their business. These companies are often delighted to acquire large customers such as Sears or JC Penny. But, as *The Wall Street Journal* has reported, they often become captives as their large customers demand more and more of their capacity. Large customers often squeeze prices of small suppliers, resulting in many bankruptcies. The *Journal* cited Victor V. Coppola, Director of National Emerging Business Services for Coopers & Lybrand, the international firm of Certified Public Accountants, as saying that there are no success stories of captive suppliers.[3]

Even when managers know that the difference between the price and the variable costs of a special order should depend on the firm's cost structure, they must still decide what contribution margin is adequate. For a firm in which variable costs predominate, the contribution from a special order must be sufficient to allow for errors in computing or forecasting variable costs. (A 3% underestimate in a $49 variable cost for an order with a $50 price would change the contribution margin from positive to negative.) Where fixed costs predominate, the managers' determination of an adequate contribution margin must consider all special orders rather than a single order, lest the contribution from all orders and regular business still be insufficient to cover fixed costs. Unfortunately, we have no rules for determining an adequate contribution margin for a single special-order opportunity.

3 The Wall Street Journal, *June 10, 1988, 36R.*

FACTORS IN LIMITED SUPPLY

In the special-order example, Griffith's production was limited to 75,000 units because of a shortage of labor. A shortage of some other factor, such as space, machine time, or some critical material might also restrict operations. The term *constraint* is often used to describe a shortage of an input factor.

A firm with two or more products faces the additional problem of deciding how to use the limited quantity of the constraining factor. Consider Neal Company, which makes a desk tray and a box for computer diskettes. Neal can sell all it can make of either product. Both products require processing on a machine that can operate only 100 hours per week. Data relating to these two products appear below.

	Desk Tray	Diskette Box
Selling price	$10	$ 6
Variable cost	6	4
Contribution margin	$ 4	$ 2
Number of units that can be made per machine-hour	60	150

Looking only at contribution margin, Neal's managers will conclude that it should make trays, each of which brings twice the contribution margin of a diskette box. However, Neal can make (and sell) more boxes than trays. If the managers are to make the best possible use of the available machine time, they must consider both the difference in contribution margin and the difference in the production demands on the scarce input factor, machine time. Two approaches are available to combine these differences. The first approach compares total contribution margin from the products over some specific period, such as a week (100 machine hours available).

	Desk Tray	Diskette Box
Maximum weekly production		
(60 × 100)	6,000	
(150 × 100)		15,000
Contribution margin per unit	$ 4	$ 2
Total weekly contribution margin	$24,000	$30,000

The analysis shows that producing boxes is the more profitable use of the machine time. (You should see that the same answer follows whether the period used for the analysis is an hour, a day, a week, or a month.)

The second approach also shows differences in contribution margin but concentrates on a unit of the scarce input. That is, the second approach determines the *contribution margin per unit of the scarce factor.* In Neal's case, the scarce factor is machine time, so the second analysis compares contribution per machine hour.

	Desk Tray	Diskette Box
Number of units that can be made per machine-hour	60	150
Contribution margin per unit	$ 4	$ 2
Contribution margin per hour	$240	$300

The second analysis, like the first, shows that it is more profitable to produce boxes; boxes contribute more than trays, *per hour of machine time used*. Thus, the opportunity cost of using an hour of machine time making trays is the $300 you give up by not using that hour to make boxes. (If the machine time could be used to make some third product, say a drawer organizer, the opportunity cost of choosing to make that product is $300, the benefit gained from the best available alternative use of the limited resource.)

Information derived from the preceding analyses can be useful for decisions about product pricing as well as about the use of available facilities. For example, suppose Neal is considering raising the price of its desk tray. You already know that producing diskette boxes is the more profitable use of the available machine time. What price must Neal charge for the desk tray to make using machine time for it as profitable as using the time to make boxes? The contribution margins per machine-hour have to be equal, which means that the margin for making trays has to be $300 per hour. Since Neal can make 60 trays per hour, the contribution per tray has to be $5 ($300/60). Adding the $5 desired margin to the $6 variable cost per tray gives a required selling price of $11 per tray. At that price, devoting machine time to making trays yields the same contribution margin as spending the time making boxes.

At the start of the example, we stated that Neal could sell all that it could produce of either product. Even if that were not so, the preceding analyses are important in deciding how to use the limited supply of machine hours. Suppose that Neal could sell only 9,000 boxes per week (though it could make 15,000). The previous analyses show that Neal should make as many boxes as it can sell and devote the remaining hours of machine time to making trays. Thus, Neal should spend 60 hours of machine time making boxes (9,000 boxes/150 boxes per hour) and use the remaining 40 hours (100 – 60) making trays.

The importance of understanding cost and contribution margin data when evaluating the effects of constraints was recently illustrated in an article in *Management Accounting*.[4] A plant of the very successful Latex Division of GenCorp Polymer Products faced a problem in analyzing product profitability because it had reached capacity and was unable to supply the demand for all of its products. The constraining factor was the capacity of reactors, vessels in which the ingredients for each product are cooked. Any product can be made in any reactor, but the reactors differ in size, and the time required to process a product depends on the size of the reactor. Hence, a product's contribution margin per unit of processing time, and any ranking of product profitability based on such a contribution, would only apply to reactors of a particular size. The managers wanted to choose products independent of the reactor size, so they selected a single size reactor and stated the processing time for each product in *relative* terms (calling the result "product standard processing time"). These standardized times were incorporated into a measure called the Product Profit Velocity (PPV), which was used to analyze product profitability. The measure is calculated as follows (materials and freight-out are the only variable costs).

---

4 *Gary B. Frank, Steven A. Fisher, and Allen R. Wilkie, "Linking Cost to Price and Profit,"* Management Accounting, *June 1989, 22-26.*

$$PPV = \left(\textit{revenue per reactor run} - \textit{materials and freight-out} = \textit{contribution margin}\right) \div \textit{product standard processing time}$$

The products were then ranked, and the lower-ranked products were cut back when capacity was reached. Because of concerns about customer ill-will, the plant manager chose to increase prices rather than drop lower-ranking products. The rankings were also used to highlight products to study for ways to reduce costs (for example, by changing the materials mix).

This section suggests analytical approaches for making decisions when the firm faces a single constraint. Appendix A at the back of this book extends the analysis to situations where there are two or more constraints. Chapter 8 suggests techniques for dealing with decisions to relieve a constraint by making a long-term investment in additional capacity.

A Word of Caution

The approaches that we have presented have many things in common, including the need for the manager to understand CVP relationships and the concepts of common/joint and avoidable/unavoidable costs. But perhaps the most important commonality is that each approach requires the manager, and hence the managerial accountant, to use estimates. Decisions require estimates of future sales volumes, future costs, future cost savings, lost sales, and so on.

Estimates about the future are not certainties. Managers often say that the only thing they can be certain about is the uncertainty of the future and of the information used in decision making. At this point in your study of decision making and the use of accounting information, you should recognize the extent to which estimates, and the associated uncertainties, influence decision-making. We discuss some formal methods of dealing with uncertainty in Appendix A, and the typical collegiate program of study presents those and other methods in courses in statistics and management science.

DECISION MAKING UNDER ENVIRONMENTAL CONSTRAINTS

The United States has laws that managers must be aware of when deciding among various courses of action. Antitrust laws forbid actions that might substantially reduce competition. Environmental protection laws restrict actions that could harm wildlife or increase pollution. At various times controls on wages and prices have restricted price increases. We shall limit our discussion to the major laws dealing with pricing practices.

The Sherman Act, Clayton Act, and Robinson-Patman Act prohibit "predatory pricing," which is pricing below cost in the short-term to drive competitors out of business and eventually to raise prices. The question is what cost is appropriate. Courts have held that prices below average variable costs are predatory. However, on occasion, courts have used incremental costs as the standard, particularly when companies have excess capacity. No matter what version of cost is employed, management accountants must be able to justify the costs that their companies use in defense.

Robinson-Patman forbids charging different prices to different customers *unless* there are intrinsic cost differences in serving the different customers;

in other words, this act forbids discriminatory pricing. The Federal Trade Commission (FTC) is the regulatory agency responsible for enforcing the act. The passing of the act was partially stimulated by the practice of selling to large customers (such as grocery chains) at lower prices than to corner grocery stores, enabling the large chains to charge their customers lower prices and endangering the existence of smaller firms.

Defendants charged with discriminatory pricing under Robinson-Patman can avoid liability by showing that the differences in prices from one customer to another emanate from different methods of manufacturing, different quantities purchased, or attempts to meet competition in good faith. The last is not a cost issue. Justifications based on different methods of manufacture must show that the company sold different products to different customers. Companies that sell private brands usually modify the products to meet this criterion. Companies that custom-make products for different customers can also use this defense. Pittsburgh Plate Glass successfully defended itself against a price discrimination suit by showing that it sold a nonstandard size of glass to the plaintiff, which therefore costs more to make. PPG also showed that the plaintiff bought smaller quantities than other customers.[5]

One key to a successful defense against price discrimination or predatory pricing is for the company's management accountants to have a thorough understanding of costs. They must be able to amass cost data that support the company's position. Of course, potential ethical problems arise in developing cost studies. Management accountants' objectivity and competence are put at risk if they falsify, or even shade data to meet the company's needs. The IMA Standards expressly forbid such acts.

SUMMARY

Managerial accountants supply information for short-term decision making. The essential quantitative factors influencing such decisions are differential revenues and costs, including opportunity costs. Costs and revenues that will be the same whatever action is taken can be ignored. Historical costs are sunk and are irrelevant for current decisions because they cannot be changed by some current action. Avoidable fixed costs are relevant. Whether a cost is relevant to a particular decision does not always depend on whether the cost is variable or fixed.

Typical examples of short-term decisions are whether to drop a product or product line, whether to produce a component internally or purchase it from an outside supplier, whether to further process joint products, whether to accept a special order, and how best to use the limited supply of some critical input factor.

5 *Arnold I. Barkman and John David Jolley II, "Cost Defenses for Antitrust Cases,"* Management Accounting, *April, 1986, 37-41.*

As a general rule, the action that is expected to result in the highest income for the firm should be pursued. This decision rule considers only the quantifiable factors in a given situation. Most decisions involve some factors that can have monetary effects but for which no reliable estimates can be made. Still other factors, such as a company policy prohibiting certain types of products, may not lend themselves to quantification at all. These qualitative factors should not be ignored.

KEY TERMS

complementary effects
differential revenue and cost
incremental revenue and cost
joint (common) costs
joint process
joint products
loss leader
opportunity cost
split-off point
sunk cost

REVIEW PROBLEM

Andrews Company makes three products. Below are revenue and cost data for a typical month.

	Product			
	X	Y	Z	Total
Sales	$300	$500	$800	$1,600
Variable costs	100	200	400	700
Contribution margin	200	300	400	900
Fixed costs:				
Avoidable	80	100	120	300
Common, allocated on sales dollar basis	60	100	160	320
Total fixed costs	140	200	280	620
Profit	$ 60	$100	$120	$ 280

Required

Answer each of the following questions independently.

1. If product X were dropped, what will total profit be?
2. Andrews is considering a new product P, to take the place of X. Product P will sell for $7 per unit, have variable costs of $5 per unit, and have avoidable fixed costs of $130. How many units of P would have to be sold to maintain the existing income of $280?
3. The firm charges $10 per unit for product Z. A chain store has offered to buy 40 units of Z per month at $8 per unit. Total fixed costs and variable costs per unit would not be affected by the sale. Andrews has the capacity to produce 110 units of Z per month. If Andrews accepts the offer, what will its total monthly income be?

4. Closer analysis reveals that X, Y, and Z are joint products of a single raw material and are all now being processed beyond the split-off point. The cost of the joint process, including raw material, is the $320 joint allocated fixed cost. All other costs are incurred to process the three products beyond the split-off point. If the sales values of X, Y, and Z are $110, $220, and $230, respectively, at split-off, could Andrews increase its profits by selling one or more products at split-off? If so, which product or products should be sold at split-off and what will the increase in total profit be?
5. Unit sales of X and Z are 100 and 200, respectively. Both products are made on a single machine that has a limited capacity. The machine can make five units of X per hour, or eight units of Z.
   (a) If Andrews can sell all that it can make of either product, should it continue to make both products? If not, which product should Andrews make?
   (b) Assuming that the machine is being operated at its capacity of 45 hours per month, what will happen to monthly profits if the firm makes only the more profitable product as determined in part (a)? Give the dollar increase in profits. (Hint: Remember that if only one product is made, the firm will save the avoidable fixed costs on the product that it drops.)

ANSWER TO REVIEW PROBLEM

1. $160. Andrews would lose the contribution margin from the sale of X but would save the $80 avoidable fixed costs. Subtracting the net reduction in profit of $120 ($200 – $80) from the current profit of $280 gives $160. The $120 drop is the incremental profit on X.
2. 125 units. To achieve the same profit, the new product must provide the same incremental profit that is lost by dropping X. Incremental profit from X is $120 (see item 1). The sale of P must provide contribution margin sufficient to cover both the new avoidable fixed costs and the $120 profit. Since the new fixed costs are $130, the contribution margin needed is $250 ($130 fixed costs plus the desired profit). P carries a contribution margin of $2 per unit ($7 – $5), so a total of 125 units ($250/$2) have to be sold.
3. $350. It is important to see that if this special order is accepted, the company will lose sales at the regular price. Capacity is 110 units and planned sales are 80 units ($800/$10 selling price). If Andrews sells 40 units to the new customer, regular sales will fall by 10 units. The analysis might proceed as follows.

Gain from contribution margin on special order ($8 – $5 [a]) × 40 units	$120
Lost contribution margin because of loss of sales of 10 units at regular price ($10 – $5) × 10 units	50
Gain on special order	70
Planned profit	280
New monthly income	$350

a Variable cost per unit ($400/80 units = $5 per unit).

4. The firm could increase its profits by $20 per month by selling product Y at split-off, as shown by the following analysis.

	X	Y	Z
Sales with further processing	$300	$500	$800
Additional processing costs:			
Variable costs	100	200	400
Avoidable fixed costs	80	100	120
Total additional processing costs	180	300	520
Profit if further processed	120	200	280
Split-off values	110	220	230
Advantage (disadvantage) of further processing	$ 10	($ 20)	$ 50

5. (a) The company should concentrate on product Z rather than product X. This can be shown even without knowing the number of hours available; the contribution margin per hour of machine time spent on product Z is the higher.

	X	Z
Contribution margin per unit	$2 ($200/100)	$2 ($400/200)
Units that can be made in 1 hour	5	8
Contribution margin per hour	$10	$16

As long as the company can sell all the units it makes of either product, total contribution margin will be greater by making only product Z.

(b) Profit will increase by $200. If Andrews used its capacity of 45 hours to produce only Z, it could make 360 units (45 × 8) for total contribution margin of $720 (360 × $2 per unit). This is an increase of $320 ($720 – $400 contribution margin already anticipated). However, Andrews loses the current *incremental profit* from product X, which is $120 (see item 1). Thus, if the firm concentrated on product Z it would gain $200 ($320 additional contribution margin from Z – $120 incremental profit lost from not producing X).

ASSIGNMENT MATERIAL

QUESTIONS FOR DISCUSSION

5-1 "Where do you start?" One of your classmates, who believes that he thoroughly understands the principle of incremental costs, placed the following advertisement in the school paper.

Wanted—Ride to Linville

I will pay all of the extra costs involved in taking me to Linville. Call Bob at 555-6202.

Linville is 1,200 miles from the university. Did your classmate make a mistake in wording the advertisement the way he did?

5-2 Cost analysis While standing in line to use a telephone, you hear the following part of a conversation. "No dear, I'm going to play golf today." (Pause) "Look, sweetie, I know it costs $6 for a caddy and $3 for drinks after the round, but it really does get cheaper the more I play. Look, the club dues are $1,000 per year, so if I play 50 times it costs, ah, let's see, $29 per round. But if I play

100 times it only costs, um, just a second, yeah, about $19 per round." (Pause) "I knew you'd understand, see you at dinner, bye." How did the golfer figure the cost per round? Comment on her analysis.

5-3 The generous management Several years ago, a leading newspaper ran an advertisement for itself. The advertisement stated that the paper, which cost the customer $0.40, cost the publisher $0.53 for paper, $0.09 for printers' labor, $0.05 for ink, $0.15 for salaries of editorial employees (reporters, editors, etc.), and $0.18 for other operating expenses such as executives' salaries, rent, depreciation, and taxes. Thus, the opportunity to buy a paper for $0.40 that had a cost of $1.00 was presented as a great bargain. Is the buyer actually paying less than cost? What assumptions did you make to arrive at your answer? How can the management be so generous to its readers?

5-4 Pricing policy At Washington National Airport you enter the departure area of an airline just before a flight to Los Angeles is to take off. The plane is about 80% full, and the regular fare for the flight is $300. You have neither a ticket nor a reservation for the flight, but you offer to pay $50 to take the flight. Assume there are no variable costs associated with the number of passengers. Do you think the airline would accept your offer? Explain.

5-5 Unit costs The B-2, or Stealth bomber, was much in the news in the late 1980's, partly because of its cost. The consensus seemed to be that buying 132 of the aircraft would cost $70 billion, or about $530 million per plane. At that time the total cost already incurred for development and a couple of prototypes was about $23 billion, which is included in the $70 billion total cost. Opponents of the program argued that we could not afford to spend $530 million for each aircraft, while proponents said that the amount already spent was wasted unless we did produce the bomber.

Required

Would it have cost $530 million per plane to continue the program? If not, what is your estimate of the future per-plane cost if 132 are built? Assume that the $70 billion figure holds.

EXERCISES

5-6 Special order Watt, Inc. manufactures lamps and expects to sell 350,000 units in 19X0 at a price of $21 per unit. Planned per-unit manufacturing costs at that level of production are as follows.

Variable manufacturing costs	$9
Fixed manufacturing costs	$5

Early in 19X0, a new customer approaches Watt offering to buy 15,000 lamps at $11 each. Watt can produce additional units with no change in fixed manufacturing cost or per-unit variable cost. The only additional fixed cost for this order is for packing and shipping, estimated at $3,800.

Required
Determine the effect of accepting the special order on planned profit for the year. Assume that filling the special order will not affect regular sales.

5-7 ***Joint products*** Rox Company produces two families of chemicals, orides and octines. The production phase of each chemical group begins with a joint process. Below are production, sales and cost data for the products that result from each 100-gallon batch of materials going through the joint process that produces orides.

	Boride	Doride	Foride
Gallons produced	40	50	10
Selling price per gallon at the split-off point	$ 6	$ 5	$ 0
Selling price per gallon after further processing	$10	$ 9	$ 4
Per-gallon variable cost of further processing	$ 5	$ 2	$ 3

Required
Determine which of the joint products should be sold at the split-off point and which should be processed further.

5-8 ***Joint products (extension of 5-7)*** Rox normally processes 120,000 gallons of oride mixture per month. You have determined that, in addition to the variable costs of the additional processing of boride, doride, and foride, there are monthly fixed costs associated with such added processing, as listed below.

	Boride	Doride	Foride
Avoidable fixed costs of additional processing	$40,000	$55,000	$20,000
Unavoidable fixed costs of additional processing, allocated	$25,000	$60,000	$ 4,000

Required
1. Does the information about the fixed costs of additional processing of the joint products change your answer from 5-7, as to whether any of those products should be processed after the split-off point?
2. Assume that Rox takes the most profitable course of action with respect to each of the joint oride products. Ignoring the costs of the joint process, what will be the total monthly profit from orides?

5-9 ***Product selection—capacity constraint*** Winston Company makes three products, all of which require the use of a special machine. Only 200 hours of machine time are available per month. Data for the three products are as follow. Winston can sell as much of any product as it can make.

	Gadgets	Supergadgets	Colossalgadgets
Selling price	$12	$16	$20
Variable cost	4	11	11
Contribution margin	$ 8	$ 5	$ 9
Machine time required in minutes	10	6	12

Required

1. If all products required the same amount of machine time, which product should be made?
2. Given the capacity constraint, determine which product should be made and the total monthly contribution margin that would be earned if only that product was made.
3. How much would the selling price of the next most profitable (per machine-hour) product have to rise to be as profitable, per machine-hour, as the product that you selected in item 2?

5-10 ***Dropping a segment*** Colbert Company expects the following results for the coming year.

	Hats	Belts	Jeans	Total
Sales	$100,000	$150,000	$470,000	$720,000
Variable costs	$ 52,000	$ 50,000	$190,000	$292,000
Fixed costs	80,000	50,000	240,000	370,000
Total costs	132,000	100,000	430,000	662,000
Profit (loss)	($ 32,000)	$ 50,000	$ 40,000	$ 58,000

Required

Answer each of the following questions independently.

1. Suppose that all fixed costs are allocated based on the floor space each segment occupies and are all unavoidable. What will total profit be if Colbert drops the hat segment?
2. Suppose that $55,000 of the fixed costs shown for the hat segment are avoidable. What will the firm's total profit be if Colbert drops the hat segment?
3. Suppose that Colbert could avoid $55,000 in fixed costs by dropping the hat segment (as in item 2). However, the managers believe that if they do drop hats, sales of each of the other lines will fall by 5%. What will profit be if Colbert drops hats and loses 5% of the sales of each of the other segments?

5-11 ***Make or buy*** GFA Company is introducing a new product. The managers are trying to decide whether to make one of its components, part #A-3, or to buy it from an outside supplier. Making the part internally requires using some machinery that has no other use and no resale value. The space that could be used to make the part also has no alternative use.

The outside supplier will sell the part for $5 per unit. An estimate of costs to make the part appears below.

	Cost to Make Part #A-3
Materials	$1.50
Direct labor	2.00
Variable manufacturing overhead	.50
Fixed manufacturing overhead	2.50
Total cost	$6.50

The above estimate reflects expected volume of 10,000 units of the part. The fixed manufacturing overhead consists of depreciation on the machinery and a share of the costs of the factory (heat, light, building depreciation, etc.) based on the floor space that manufacturing the part would occupy.

Required
Determine whether GFA should make or buy part #A-3.

5-12 Special order Devio Company produces high-quality golf balls. A chain of sporting goods stores would like to buy 25,000 dozen balls at $15 per dozen. The chain would sell the balls for $20, which is $5 less than usually charged by dealers. The chain would obliterate the Devio name so that customers would not be able to tell who had made the balls.

Devio can produce 200,000 dozen balls per year. Planned results for the coming year, without considering the order from the chain, are given below.

Sales (150,000 dozen at $18 per dozen)	$2,700,000
Cost of goods sold	1,110,000
Gross profit	1,590,000
Selling and administrative expenses, all fixed	600,000
Income	$ 990,000

Cost of goods sold contains variable costs of $7 per dozen balls. The rest of the cost is fixed.

Required
1. Determine whether Devio should accept the order.
2. Might your answer to item 1 change if the Devio name were to appear on the balls sold in the chain stores?

5-13 Short-term decisions Nickolai Company expects the following results in 19X5.

	Product A	Product B	Total
Sales	$500	$300	$800
Variable costs	200	150	350
Contribution margin	300	150	450
Fixed costs	150	90	240
Profit	$150	$ 60	$210

Fixed costs, all unavoidable, are allocated based on relative sales dollars.

Required
Answer each question independently, unless otherwise told.
1. The managers are considering increasing advertising for product B by $18. They expect to achieve a 30% increase in volume for product B with no change in selling price, but some of that increase will be at the expense of product A. Sales of A are expected to decline by 5%. What will the firm's total profit be if it takes the action?
2. What is the maximum percentage decline in volume of product A that would leave the action in item 1 just barely desirable?

3. The firm is considering dropping product B and replacing it with product C. Introducing product C would increase total fixed costs by $24. Its contribution margin percentage is 40%. What dollar sales of product C are needed to maintain the original profit of $210?

5-14 ***Analyzing data for decisions*** The expected results for the coming year for Porter Company, which manufactures two lines of products, appear below, in thousands of dollars.

	Kitchenwares	Officewares	Total
Sales	$3,300	$2,700	$6,000
Variable costs	1,650	810	2,460
Contribution margin	1,650	1,890	3,540
Avoidable fixed costs	650	1,300	1,950
Incremental profit	$1,000	$ 590	1,590
Common, unavoidable fixed costs			900
Profit			$ 690

Required

Suppose that Porter uses the same production facilities for both products. Demand is such that the firm could sell $500,000 more of either product line but it would have to reduce output and sales of the other line by the same amount. Which line should the firm make more of and what is the effect on total profit?

5-15 ***Changing product lines (extension of 5-14)*** Suppose Porter could introduce a new line that is much more profitable than either of the existing ones. To introduce the new line, however, Porter must drop one of the existing lines entirely. The other line—the one not dropped—will continue as originally planned. Which line should Porter drop?

5-16 ***Joint products*** TAB Company produces four joint products at a joint cost of $80,000. All products are currently processed beyond the split-off point, and the final products are sold as follows.

Products	Sales	Additional Processing Costs
M	$160,000	$120,000
N	180,000	60,000
O	45,000	40,000
P	30,000	25,000

The firm could sell the products at the split-off point for the following amounts: M, $80,000; N, $50,000; O, $15,000; and P, zero.

Required

1. Determine which products the firm should sell at the split-off point.
2. Determine what TAB's profit would be if it took the most profitable action with respect to each of its products.

5-17 ***Dropping a product—complementary effects*** Kaiser Face Care Company makes three products in the same factory. Revenue and cost data for a typical month follow, in thousands.

	Razors	After-Shave	Shaving Cream	Total
	Product			
Sales	$400	$600	$400	$1,400
Variable costs	300	240	120	660
Contribution margin	100	360	280	740
Fixed costs				
Avoidable	120	150	70	340
Unavoidable, allocated on basis of relative sales dollars	80	120	80	280
Total fixed costs	200	270	150	620
Income (loss)	($100)	$ 90	$130	$ 120

Required

1. Determine total income if razors were dropped from the product line.
2. Suppose that if razors were dropped, the sales of after-shave would decline by 20% and those of shaving cream by 10%. Determine income for the firm if razors were dropped.

5-18 ***Inventory values*** James Company has 300 pounds of a chemical compound called bysol, bought at $3.20 per pound several months ago. Bysol now costs $3.80 per pound. The firm could sell it for $3.50 per pound (shipping costs account for the $0.30 difference between the cost to buy and the selling price).

Required

Answer each of the following questions independently.

1. Suppose the firm has stopped making the product for which it used bysol and will sell it or use it to make a special order. The special order has a price of $2,000. Incremental costs, excluding the bysol, are $900. What is the relevant cost of using the bysol in the special order? Should the firm accept the order?
2. Suppose the firm has alternative uses for bysol so that if it accepts the special order it will have to buy more for its regular production. What is the relevant cost of using the bysol in the special order? Should the firm accept the order?

5-19 ***Make or buy (AICPA adapted)*** MTZ Company manufactures 10,000 units of part Z-101 annually, using the part in one of its products. The controller has collected the following data related to the part.

Materials	$ 20,000
Direct labor	55,000
Variable overhead	45,000
Fixed overhead	70,000
Total costs	$190,000

Vortan Company has offered to supply the part for $18 per unit. If MTZ accepts the offer, it will be able to rent some of the facilities it devotes to making the part to another firm for $15,000 annually and will also be able to reduce its fixed overhead costs by $40,000.

Required

1. Should MTZ accept the offer based on the available information?
2. What is the maximum price that MTZ is willing to pay for the part—the price that would give it the same income it would have if it continued making it?
3. Assuming the $18 price from Vortan, at what annual unit volume will MTZ earn the same income making the part as it would buying it?

5-20 Joint products Grevel Company slaughters cattle and processes the meat, hides, and bones. It tans the hides and sells them to leather manufacturers. The bones are made into buttons and other sundries. In a typical month, it processes about 3,000 cattle. An income statement for such a month follows, in thousands of dollars.

	Totals	Meat	Hides	Bones
Sales	$500	$300	$120	$80
Cost of cattle [a]	300	180	72	48
Gross profit	200	120	48	32
Additional processing costs, avoidable	80 [b]	40 [b]	20 [b]	20 [b]
Allocated costs [c]	60 [b]	30 [b]	15 [b]	15 [b]
Income (loss)	$ 60	$ 50	$ 13	($ 3)

a Allocated on the basis of relative sales value (60% of sales).
b Deduction.
c Allocated on the basis of additional processing costs, all unavoidable.

Required

1. Is the firm losing money by processing the bones into buttons and sundry items?
2. A tanner has offered to buy the hides as they are sheared off the cattle for $7 each. He contends that income from hides would be $21,000 if hides were sold directly to him (3,000 hides × $7). Should Grevel accept his offer?
3. If the bones could be sold without further processing, how much would have to be received per month to keep total profits the same as they are now?

5-21 Opportunity cost pricing Boyett Company makes three products. Data are as follows.

	Product		
	Wallet	Belt	Hat
Current selling price	$10	$15	$25
Variable cost	3	6	10
Contribution margin	$ 7	$ 9	$15
Machine time required, in minutes	15	10	20

Boyett has 40,000 minutes of machine time available per week. It can sell all of any of the three products that it can make.

Required

1. Determine which product the firm should make.
2. Determine the selling prices that the firm would have to charge for each of the other two products to make them equally profitable per minute of machine time as the one you selected in item 1.

5-22 *Comprehensive review of short-term decisions* The data below relate to the planned operations of Kimble Company before considering the changes described later.

	Product		
	Chair	Table	Sofa
Selling price	$ 120	$ 400	$ 600
Variable costs	40	160	360
Fixed costs	30	120	180
Total costs	70	280	540
Profit per unit	$ 50	$ 120	$ 60
Annual volume	8,000	3,000	4,000

All fixed costs are direct, but unavoidable.

Required

Answer each of the following items independently of the others unless otherwise instructed.

1. What is total profit expected to be?
2. What will happen to profit if the company drops sofas?
3. What will happen to profit if the company drops chairs, but is able to shift the facilities to making more sofas so that volume of sofas increases to 7,000 units? (Total fixed costs remain constant.)
4. Variable cost per sofa includes $60 for parts that the company now buys outside. The company could make the parts at a variable cost of $45. It would also have to increase fixed costs by $35,000 annually. What would happen to profit if the company took the proposed action?
5. The company has received a special order for 1,000 tables at $245. Capacity is sufficient to make the units, and sales at the regular price would not be affected. What will happen to profit if the firm accepts the order?
6. Repeat item 5 assuming now that the order is for 1,500 tables and that capacity is limited to 4,000 tables.

5-23 *Using per-unit data* The managers of Ferrara Company expect the following per-unit results at a volume of 200,000 units.

Sales		$10
Variable costs	$6	
Fixed costs	3	9
Profit		$ 1

Required

Answer each of the following parts independently of the others.

1. The company has the opportunity to sell 20,000 units to a chain store for $8 each. The managers expect that sales at the regular price will drop by about 8,000 units as some customers will buy from the chain store instead of from the regular outlets. What will happen to the company's profit if it accepts the order?
2. Of the total unit variable cost of $6, $2.80 is for a part that the company now buys from an outside supplier. The company could make the part for $2.25 variable cost plus $100,000 per year fixed costs for renting additional machinery. What will happen to annual profit if it makes the part?

3. The company is considering a new model to replace the existing product. The new model has a $6 unit variable cost and the same total fixed costs as the existing product. The new model has expected sales of 100,000 units per year. At what selling price per unit will the new model give the same total profit as the existing one?

PROBLEMS

5-24 Product pricing—off-peak hours Marie Angelo, owner of Gino's Pizzeria, is considering a luncheon special to increase business during the slow time from 11:00 a.m. to 1:00 p.m. on weekdays. For $2.20 on any weekday, she will give customers all the pizza they can eat. Marie has prepared the following data for weekly business during those hours.

	Pizza	Beverages	Total
Sales (average pizza price, $2.80)	$420	$84	$504
Variable costs	120	24	144
Contribution margin	$300	$60	360
Avoidable fixed costs—wages of students hired			180
Current incremental profit, lunch period			$180

She estimates that at the special price she will serve about 300 pizzas per week to about 250 customers. (Some customers will eat more than one pizza, given the lower price.) She also anticipates that variable costs per unit will be about 20% higher because people will want more toppings than they now order. Beverage sales will bear the same relationship to the number of customers that they do now when each customer eats one pizza. The increase in the number of customers will entail an increase in personnel during the hours of the special, increasing wage cost by 15%.

Required

Evaluate the monetary effects of the proposed luncheon special.

5-25 Just-in-time, costs of activities Racine Machinery recently began to change one of its plants to a just-in-time operation. So far, Racine has set up one manufacturing cell to make a product that had formerly been made in large batches. The following analysis of April operations for the cell was disappointing to the controller who had expected dramatic improvements with JIT.

Operations for April	
Units Produced	20,000
Costs:	
Materials	$ 55,000
Labor	67,000
Overhead	35,000
Total	$157,000
Per-unit	$7.85

The overhead cost shown is mostly allocated costs. Roughly $9,000 is incremental, avoidable cost. The per-unit cost to manufacture the product under the old system follows.

Materials	$2.90
Labor	2.80
Overhead	1.80
Total	$7.50

Overhead is based on 22,000 units and is 40% variable, 60% fixed at that level. Under the old system, quality control was weak so that the company had to produce about 22,000 units to obtain 20,000 good units. With the JIT cell, workers do their own inspection during production, and only 20,000 total units are produced to obtain 20,000 good units.

Under the old system, manufacturing the product required the following people in addition to direct laborers. The costs given include fringe benefits such as health insurance.

Two inspectors, each earning	$2,000 per month
One production scheduler earning	$2,500 per month
Two maintenance people each earning	$1,800 per month

When setting up the cell Racine reassigned the people described above and other support personnel who had worked on the product. The other support people earned about $11,000 per month, including fringes.

Required

Determine the incremental cost to produce 20,000 good units in a month under the old method and using the JIT cell. Using the guidelines in Appendix B, prepare a memorandum explaining your results.

5-26 ***Choosing a product*** Hare Company operates a cannery. It buys raw carrots from farmers and can produce three types of canned carrots: sliced, mashed, and pickled. Hare's fixed production costs for a season are $20,000. This season, Hare has contracted to purchase 100,000 pounds of raw carrots at $0.25 per pound and will not be able to purchase any more. Price and other data for Hare's three products are below.

	Sliced	Mashed	Pickled
Selling price per case	$3.50	$3.00	$4.25
Variable processing cost per case	$1.50	$1.75	$2.00
Pounds of raw carrots per case	5 lbs.	2.5 lbs.	5 lbs.

Required

1. Assuming Hare can sell as many cases as it makes of all types of product, which type should it produce?
2. Assuming Hare has no costs other than those already mentioned and that it follows the advice you offered in part 1, what is the maximum profit Hare can make this season?
3. Assume that, despite your advice in part 1, Hare's managers really want to produce and sell pickled carrots and are convinced that they can slightly reduce the volume of carrots in each can of pickled carrots without affecting the selling price. How many pounds of carrots would Hare have to use in

each case of pickled carrots to make that product as profitable as the type you selected in part 1?

5-27 ***Car pool*** You and your neighbor carpool to work, driving on alternate days. A colleague at work has injured his hand and will not be able to drive for the next three months. He inquires about riding with you and your neighbor. He could ride a bus for $2 per day and offers to pay you a "fair price."

From your house it is a 10-mile round trip to work. If you pick up your injured colleague, the round trip is 14 miles. Last year, your car cost you the following for 15,000 miles. (Your neighbor's car cost the same for the same number of miles.)

Gasoline and oil	$1,350
Maintenance	450
New tires (life of 30,000 miles)	300
Insurance and registration	600
Decline in market value	3,000
Total	$5,700

Required
1. Quote a daily price to your colleague that seems fair to you.
2. What do you think your colleague would say is a fair price?

5-28 ***Sales premiums*** Mrs. Nelson's Coffee Company has been experiencing difficulties in achieving sales goals because of increased competition. The sales manager has proposed the following to stimulate sales: The firm will place a coupon in each one-pound can of coffee. A customer who returns ten coupons will receive merchandise that costs the firm $1. In addition, mailing and handling costs will be $0.20 for each $1 of merchandise. The sales manager expects an increase in sales of about 50,000 one-pound cans per month and further predicts that only about 40% of the coupons will be redeemed. The firm currently sells 350,000 one-pound cans per month at $1.50, with variable costs being $0.90.

Required
Should the firm adopt the plan?

5-29 ***Joint products—changes in mix*** Brewer Company makes three products in a joint process. The process is set up to yield the following quantities of each product from ten pounds of raw material: Nyron, three pounds; Xylon, three pounds; and Krylon, four pounds. Each product can be further processed; price and cost data are given below.

	Nyron	Xylon	Krylon
Selling price at split-off, per pound	$2	$4	$ 6
Additional processing costs, per pound	$1	$3	$ 8
Selling price after additional processing, per pound	$8	$6	$12

Required
1. Determine which products the firm should sell at split-off.
2. Assume that Brewer is now operating in accordance with your answer to

item 1. Suppose that by changing the production process the firm could get eight pounds of Nyron and one pound each of Xylon and Krylon from ten pounds of raw material. The change will increase fixed costs by $60,000 per month. The firm generally processes 100,000 pounds of raw material each month. Should Brewer change the process?

3. At what level of output per month, expressed in pounds of raw material processed, would Brewer have the same income under the existing process and under the changed process as described in item 2?

5-30 Hours of operation Bronson Book Store is normally open 12 hours per day, six days per week. As an experiment, the owner kept the store open for six hours one Sunday and had sales of $750. The payroll was $110.

In an effort to determine whether staying open on Sundays was worthwhile, the owner collected the following additional information on annual results.

Sales		$361,400
Cost of sales		162,700
Gross margin		198,700
Operating expenses:		
Salaries	$88,300	
Rent	36,000	
Utilities	11,500	
Insurance	6,500	
Other	17,200	159,500
Profit		$ 39,200

Doing a few calculations, the owner came up with $511 as the estimated daily cost of operations, exclusive of cost of sales. He therefore concluded that about $930 in sales was necessary to justify staying open.

Required

1. Try to determine just what calculations the owner made to get his figures of $511 and $930.
2. With the information available, does it appear profitable to stay open Sundays?
3. Prepare a memorandum, using the guidelines in Appendix B, that describes other information you wish to have before making a final decision.

5-31 Special order—alternative volumes Woolen Products Company makes heavy outdoor shirts. Data relating to the coming year's planned operations appear below.

Sales (230,000 shirts)	$4,140,000
Cost of sales	2,760,000
Gross profit	1,380,000
Selling and administrative expenses	805,000
Income	$ 575,000

The factory has capacity to make 250,000 shirts per year. Fixed costs included in cost of goods sold are $690,000. The only variable selling, general, and administrative expenses are a 10% sales commission and a $0.50 per shirt licensing fee paid to the designer.

A chain store manager has approached the sales manager of Woolen Products offering to buy 15,000 shirts at $14 per shirt. These shirts would be sold in areas where Woolen's shirts are not now sold. The sales manager believes that accepting the offer would result in a loss because the average total cost of a shirt is $15.50 {($2,760,000 + $805,000)/230,000}. He feels that even though sales commissions would not be paid on the order, a loss would still result.

Required

1. Determine whether the company should accept the offer.
2. Suppose that the order was for 40,000 shirts instead of 15,000. What would the firm's income be if it accepted the order?
3. Assuming the same facts as in item 1, what is the lowest price that the firm could accept and still earn $575,000?
4. How many units at the regular price could the company lose before it became profitable to accept the order in part 2?

5-32 ***Make or buy*** Christensen Appliance Company is bringing out a new washing machine. The machine requires a type of electric motor not used for the current line of products. The purchasing manager has received a bid of $29 per motor from Wright Motor Company for any number the firm would need. Delivery is guaranteed within two weeks after order.

Christensen's production manager believes the firm could make the motor by extensively converting an existing model. Additional space and machinery would be required if the firm were to make the motors. The firm currently leases, for $39,600 per year, space that could be used to make the motors. However, the space is now used to store vital materials, so the firm would have to lease additional space in an adjacent building to store the materials. That space could be rented for $48,000 per year. It is suitable for storage, but not for converting the motors. The equipment needed to convert the motors could be rented for $45,000 per year.

The treasurer has developed the following unit costs based on the expected demand of 18,000 units per year.

Materials	$11.80
Direct labor	10.60
Rent for space	2.20
Machinery rental	2.50
Other overhead	8.20
Total cost	$35.30

The "other overhead" figure includes $5.40 in fixed overhead that would be allocated to conversion of the motors.

Required

1. Determine whether the motors should be bought or made.
2. Determine the volume of motors at which Christensen would show the same total income whether it bought or made the motors.
3. Suppose that the firm had decided to make the motors, however wisely or unwisely according to your analysis in item 1. One-year contracts have been signed for the additional space and for the equipment. These contracts can-

not be canceled. Determine the price that Wright Motor would have to offer Christensen to induce it to buy the motors.

5-33 Dropping a product—opportunity costs Grothe Company has three product lines. Data for the coming year's operations that reflect the managers' best estimates appear below.

	Cabinets	Shelves	Bureaus
Sales	$450,000	$320,000	$200,000
Variable costs	200,000	180,000	125,000
Contribution margin	250,000	140,000	75,000
Avoidable fixed costs	110,000	60,000	40,000
Product margin	$140,000	$ 80,000	$ 35,000
Investment in receivables and inventories	$350,000	$300,000	$320,000

Unallocated joint costs total $130,000 and plant and equipment is $560,000.

The managers are not happy with the expected results of the bureau line and are considering dropping it. If they did so, the firm could recover the investment in receivables and inventory related to the line and pay off debt of $320,000 that bears 14% interest.

Required

Determine whether Grothe should drop the bureau line.

5-34 Joint process (extension of 5-8) Rox's production manager for orides is following the advice you gave in your answer to 5-8. The vice president of manufacturing is satisfied with the results but is now wondering whether Rox should continue competing in the oride market. The controller has provided the following information about the joint process that is the first phase in producing the chemicals in the oride family.

Variable costs per 100 gallon batch	$ 180
Monthly fixed costs:	
Avoidable	$92,000
Unavoidable	$50,000

Required

Assume that Rox has no alternative uses for the facilities now devoted to operating the joint process that starts the production of orides. Determine whether the firm should continue to operate the joint process.

5-35 Salesperson's time as scarce resource Lombard Company sells to both wholesalers and retailers. The firm has 30 salespeople and cannot easily increase the size of the sales force. An analysis has shown that a salesperson's call on a wholesale customer yields an average order of $400, on a retailer $180. However, prices to wholesalers are 20% less than those to retailers. Cost of goods sold (all variable) is 60% of prices charged to retailers, 75% of prices charged to wholesalers. A salesperson can call on 7 wholesalers or 12 retailers per day. (The greater number of retailers reduces travel time between calls.)

Required

1. Should salespeople concentrate on wholesalers or retailers? Provide an analysis based on one salesperson for one week showing the difference.

2. Using the guidelines in Appendix B, write a memorandum describing other factors that require consideration.

5-36 *Special order—capacity limitation* Weston Tire Company has been approached by a large chain store that offers to buy 80,000 tires at $17. Delivery must be made within 30 days. Weston can produce 320,000 tires per month and has an inventory of 10,000 tires on hand. Expected sales at regular prices for the coming month are 300,000 tires. The sales manager believes that about 60% of sales lost during the month would be made up in later months. Price and cost data are as follows.

Selling price		$24
Variable costs:		
Production	$12	
Selling	3	15
Contribution margin		$ 9

Variable selling costs on the special order are $2 per unit.

Required

1. Determine whether the firm should accept the special order.
2. Determine the lowest price Weston could charge on the special order and not reduce its income.
3. Suppose now that the chain offers to buy 50,000 tires per month at $17. The offer is for an entire year. Expected sales are 300,000 tires per month without considering the special order. Assume also that there is no beginning inventory and that any sales lost during the year would *not* be made up in the following year. Determine whether the offer should be accepted and determine the lowest price that Weston could accept.

5-37 *Special orders and qualitative factors* Robinson Company has had a reputation for high-quality phonograph products for many years. The firm is owned by descendants of its founder, Allan Robinson, and continues the policy of producing and selling only high-quality, high-priced stereo components.

Recently James Giselle, president of a chain of discount stores, proposed that Robinson make and sell him a cheaper line of components than it currently produces. Giselle knows that Robinson has excess capacity and that many other firms produce lower-quality lines for sale in discount stores. Giselle believes that buyers will become aware that Robinson makes the components even though the Robinson name will not appear on them. Giselle tries to convince the management that its only potential for growth lies in the private-brand field, because Robinson now sells only to devoted aficionados who would not settle for less than Robinson components.

Giselle proposes that Robinson sell to the chain at 60% of its current selling price to other outlets. Variable costs are now about 60% of normal selling price but would be reduced by 20% per unit if the cheaper components were made. The first-year order is to be $1,260,000, for which Robinson has enough excess capacity.

Required

1. Evaluate the monetary effects of the proposed deal.
2. Using the guidelines in Appendix B, write a memorandum that evaluates qualitative factors such as the attitudes of the management and the family owners and the reputation of the firm.

5-38 *Cost of being your own boss* Martha and Jim Crain own a leather goods store in a large city. Their most recent year's income statement showed the following results.

Sales		$123,000
Cost of sales		55,000
Gross profit		68,000
Other expenses:		
Rent (monthly lease)	$3,600	
Utilities	2,450	
Advertising	1,000	
Supplies	700	
Insurance	1,150	
Licenses and fees	380	
Miscellaneous	720	
		10,000
Income		$ 58,000

In discussing the results, Martha said that it was nice to own one's own business and not have to work for someone else, and Jim agreed. He commented that he had been earning $28,000 per year before the store had been opened and that she had been earning $35,000. She replied that their hours were much longer working in the store than in their previous jobs. "Of course," she went on, "we have $50,000 invested in the business, which is a lot, but we also don't have to fight the traffic to get there."

Required

Assume that the Crains could sell the business for $50,000, invest the proceeds at 12% interest, and go back to their former jobs. Should they do so?

5-39 *Pricing policy and excess capacity* Electric utilities face several problems in achieving optimal use of their facilities. First, because electricity cannot be stored economically, utilities must be able to generate enough electricity to meet demand at all times. Second, the use of electricity is seasonal, especially in warmer climates where air conditioning produces high-peak requirements in the summer months.

Executives of Southern Electric Company are evaluating a proposal by the sales manager to offer discounts on electrical service to customers who will use electrical heating equipment. The controller has amassed the following data at the request of the sales manager.

Current generating capacity—monthly	$20 million kilowatt-hours (kwh)
kwh sold—typical winter month	7 million
kwh sold—typical summer month	18 million
Price per 1,000 kwh	$35
Variable cost per 1,000 kwh	$19

The proposal is to reduce the price of electricity to $29 per 1,000 kwh if the customer uses electrical heating equipment. It is anticipated that about 5 million additional kwh per month could be sold in the winter, a total of about 22 million additional hours per year. Total annual sales are now 120 million kwh. Users expected to convert to electrical heating now consume a total of about 30 million kwh per year. Sales to customers currently using electrical heating equipment, who would also qualify for the discount, are about 10 million kwh per year.

Required

Evaluate the monetary effects of the proposed decision.

5-40 Processing decisions Ayers Sawmill buys pine logs and saws them into boards of two grades, A and B. The grade is determined by factors such as the number of knotholes and quality of the grain. Bark and sawdust also emerge from the sawing operation. Each log usually produces, by volume, about 35% A-grade boards, 55% B-grade boards, and 10% bark and shavings. Charles Ayers, the owner, has just received the income statement for a typical month's operations. Ayers expects much the same results in the foreseeable future.

	Total	Grade A	Grade B	Bark/Shavings
Sales	$80,000	$36,000	$41,000	$3,000
Costs:				
Logs	$42,000	$14,700	$23,100	$4,200
Sawing	17,000	5,950	9,350	1,700
Trimming	3,200	2,340	860	
Sanding	7,700	4,320	3,380	
Shipping	4,500	1,550	2,430	520
Total costs	74,400	28,860	39,120	6,420
Income (loss)	$ 5,600	$ 7,140	$ 1,880	$(3,420)

Sawing costs include wages, depreciation, and other nonitemized costs of running the sawmill. The cost of logs and of sawing are allocated based on volume (35%, 55%, 10%). Trimming, sanding, and shipping costs are direct and avoidable. Ayers was disturbed at the results. He told an employee, "The bark and shavings are really hurting me. I might as well throw the stuff out rather than sell it."

Required

1. Tell Ayers whether he should continue selling bark and shavings or throw it out. Explain the reasons for your decision.
2. A chain of lawn and garden stores has offered to buy Ayers's output of bark and shavings if Ayers will grind it into mulch. The grinding would cost about $1,500 per month for wages and equipment rental. The chain will pick the mulch up at the mill, so Ayers will not incur shipping costs. What monthly revenue does Ayers need to make it profitable to do the grinding?
3. A furniture manufacturer has approached Ayers with an offer to buy all of the sawmill's output of grade B lumber for $30,000 per month as it comes out of the sawing operation. Ayers would not have to trim or sand the lumber. Shipping costs would be $1,200. Determine whether Ayers should accept the offer.

5-41 Evaluating a decision—costs of activities Six months ago the marketing manager of Arcon Company approved the sale of sizable quantities of the company's principal product to a chain store in a geographical region where the company's products are not currently sold. The sales were made monthly.

The sales manager recently asked the controller for an analysis of the business to see whether it should be renewed for another six months as the chain wants to do. The controller prepares the following income statement related to the special order.

Sales	$320,000
Cost of sales	247,000
Gross margin	73,000
Operating expenses	61,000
Profit	$ 12,000

The controller concludes that a $12,000 profit over six months is not enough to justify the added time and effort, as well as the risk of being unable to supply regular customers. Although the company has not operated at capacity during the period, it has come close on occasion.

The sales manager is surprised at the results and asks for more information. The controller provides the following additional data regarding the income statement.

(a) Cost of sales includes the following.

Materials	$ 86,000
Labor	41,000
Overhead, 60% variable	120,000
Total	$247,000

(b) Operating expenses:

Sales salaries	$ 27,000
Clerical	12,000
Other	22,000
Total	$ 61,000

The sales manager is confused about some items and receives the following additional explanation. The sales salaries are for the time of a sales representative who services the account. The representative spends about 80% of her time on the account, and the $27,000 is 80% of her six-month salary. The clerical costs are for a part-time clerk who works exclusively on this account. The bulk of the "other" category is a $16,000 administrative charge. This charge, equal to 5% of sales, is levied on all products to cover administrative expenses of the company. The remaining $6,000 are all incremental costs of various activities as estimated by the controller.

The sales manager seeks your help in understanding the statement and evaluating the order. He is confused and wonders whether to bother discussing renewal of the arrangement.

Required

Prepare a new income statement that will assist the sales manager in evaluating the business.

5-42 *Relevant range* The president of Ipswick Company has received an offer to purchase 20,000 of the tables made by his firm. The offer is to be filled any time during the coming year, and the offer price per table is $60. The planned income statement for the year without this order is as follows.

Sales (45,000 tables at $100)		$4,500,000
Cost of goods sold:		
Materials	$ 900,000	
Direct labor	810,000	
Overhead	1,340,000	
Total cost of goods sold		3,050,000
Gross profit		1,450,000
Selling, general, and administrative expenses		1,220,000
Income		$ 230,000

The president believes that the order should be rejected because the price is below average production cost of $67.78 per table. He asks you to check the matter further because he knows that some costs are fixed and would not be affected by the special order.

In your analysis you find that $800,000 in overhead is fixed and that a 10% commission is the only variable selling, general, and administrative expense.

Required

Answer the following questions, considering each situation separately.

1. Assume the relevant range for the firm is between 30,000 and 70,000 tables, that existing sales would not be affected, and that the 10% sales commission would not have to be paid on the special order. What effect would there be on income if the order were accepted? Should it be accepted?
2. The relevant range is the same as in item 1, and existing sales would be unaffected, but the 10% sales commission would have to be paid. Should the order be accepted?
3. The relevant range is now 30,000 to 55,000 tables. If the special order is accepted, sales at regular prices would fall to 35,000 units. The 10% sales commission would not be paid on the special order. Should the order be accepted?
4. The relevant range is the same as in item 3, but production could be increased to meet the special order as well as regular planned sales. For all units produced above 55,000, labor cost per unit and per-unit variable overhead would be 20% higher than planned. Fixed production overhead would increase by $47,000. No sales commission would be paid on the order, and other selling, general, and administrative expenses would remain the same as planned. Should the order be accepted?

5-43 *Value of new products—complementary effects* Jackman's Grocery is a medium-sized operation in a suburb of a large city. Joe Jackman, the owner, is contemplating the addition of a department to sell either hardware or beer and wine. He has talked to owners of several similar stores and has reached the following conclusions.

1. A hardware department would generate sales of $40,000 per year with a gross profit of 60%. No other variable costs would be added. Fixed costs added would be $12,000. Sales of groceries would increase 5% because of increased traffic through the store.

2. A beer and wine department would generate sales of $60,000 per year with gross profit of 40%. No other variable costs would be added, and additional fixed costs would be $18,000. Sales of groceries would increase by 8%.

The income statement for a typical year for grocery sales alone is as follows.

Sales	$600,000
Cost of goods sold (variable)	240,000
Gross profit	360,000
Other variable costs	120,000
Contribution margin	240,000
Fixed costs	140,000
Income	$100,000

Required

1. Ignore the effects on sales of groceries for the moment. Compute the change in income that would result from adding (a) the hardware department and (b) the beer and wine department.
2. Recompute the effects on income of adding each department, considering the effects on sales of groceries. Which department should be added and why?
3. What can be learned from this problem?

5-44 Special orders—effects on existing sales Hunt Company makes high-quality calculators that are sold only by department stores and office equipment dealers. A large discount chain has offered to buy 30,000 calculators this year at an average price of $30. The income statement expected for the coming year shows the following without considering the special order.

Sales (90,000 units at average price of $50)	$4,500,000
Variable production costs (average of $20)	1,800,000
Contribution margin	2,700,000
Fixed costs (production and selling, general, and administrative)	2,200,000
Income	$ 500,000

The 30,000 units to be bought by the chain are in the same mix as Hunt currently sells. The firm has the capacity to produce 140,000 units per year.

Required

1. Should the order be accepted if there would be no effect on regular sales?
2. Suppose that accepting the order will result in a 10% decline in sales at regular prices because some current customers would recognize the chain store's product and make their purchases at the lower price. The sales mix would remain unchanged. Should the special order be accepted?
3. By how much could sales at regular prices decline before it became unprofitable to accept the order?
4. Assuming the same facts as in item 2, what other factors should be considered before the order is accepted?

5-45 Alternative uses of product (CMA adapted) So-Clean Corporation manufactures a variety of cleaning compounds and solutions for both industrial and household use. Some of its products share ingredients and some can be refined into others.

Grit 337 is a coarse, industrial cleaning powder that sells for $2.00 per pound and has variable costs of $1.60 per pound, all for manufacturing costs. The firm currently uses a portion of Grit 337 in making a silver polish that sells for $4.00 per jar. Each jar requires one quarter pound of Grit 337. Other variable production costs for the silver polish are $2.50 per jar and variable selling expenses are $0.30 per jar. Monthly avoidable fixed costs of making the silver polish are $5,600.

Required

1. Assuming that the firm cannot sell all of the Grit 337 it can produce, how many jars of silver polish must So-Clean sell monthly to justify continuing to sell it?
2. Suppose now that the firm can sell all of the Grit 337 that it can make. How many jars of silver polish must the firm sell per month to justify further processing Grit 337 into silver polish?

5-46 Services of an athlete—jumping leagues The Fort Bluff Titans of the Cross Continental Football League have been approached by Flinger Johnson, the star quarterback of the Snidely Whips, a team in the other major football league—the Nationwide Football League. Johnson is unhappy with his current salary and wants to jump leagues if a satisfactory arrangement can be made. His contract has run out, so he is free to negotiate with the opposing league.

The owner of the Titans believes that acquiring Johnson would be a boon to attendance, estimating that he would be worth 10,000 additional admissions in every game he played. No team in the Cross Continental League comes close to filling its stadium, and even with Johnson, no sellouts would occur. Six teams are in the league, each playing each of the others twice, for a total of ten games. Each team plays every opponent once at home and once away. Tickets sell for $10 per game and variable costs are about $2 per ticket. The home team collects $7 per admission; the visiting team collects $3. The home team pays the variable costs.

Required

1. What is the additional annual income to the Titans from acquiring Johnson?
2. What is the additional annual income to *all* teams in the Cross Continental League?
3. Why is it necessary to state that no sellouts would occur even if Johnson were playing? If there were, how would it affect your analysis?
4. Suppose that Johnson demands $500,000. Should the Titans meet his demand?
5. Suppose that the other teams in the league agree to pay part of Johnson's salary. How much could each team pay without reducing its profits below the current level? (Include the Titans and each of the other five teams.)
6. Johnson is now being paid $300,000 per year. Suppose that the teams in the Nationwide League decide to try to keep Johnson. The member teams estimate that if Johnson jumps, 8,000 admissions will be lost for each game in which he would have played. Ticket prices are $12, with $2 variable costs, and each team plays 12 games.
   (a) How much would the total profits of the teams in the league fall if Johnson did jump leagues?
   (b) How much of a raise could be given to Johnson to yield the same total profit that would be earned if he jumped leagues?

(c) Assume the same facts except that each team has 50% of its games sold out. There are usually 3,000 more requests for tickets than seats available for the sellouts. If Johnson were to jump, the total number of requests for tickets per game in which his old team plays would drop by 8,000. How would this additional information affect your analysis?

5-47 ***Product processing*** Taylor Plywood company makes wall paneling used in homes and offices. The firm buys walnut logs and processes them into thin sheets of veneer that are glued to sheets of plywood to make the paneling. The firm makes plywood from various kinds of wood. Taylor has enough capacity to make 1,000,000 square feet of veneer per month and 1,200,000 square feet of plywood. Capacity in the gluing operation is 1,300,000 square feet per month.

At the present time, the firm can sell its paneling for $178 per 1,000 square feet. Veneer and plywood can be sold separately for $74 and $81, respectively, per 1,000 square feet. Cost data developed by the controller are given below, per 1,000 square feet.

	Plywood	Veneer	Paneling
Materials	$18	$16	$ 34
Direct labor	25	20	55
Overhead	32	29	93
Total	$75	$65	$182

The figures shown for paneling are cumulative. They are the sums of the costs of veneer and plywood plus the additional costs associated with the gluing operation. Thus, no new materials are added in the gluing operation because the paneling cost for materials is equal to the sum of the veneer and plywood costs for materials. Direct labor in the gluing operation is $10 per 1,000 square feet, $55 total minus $25 for plywood operation and $20 for veneer operation.

The controller stated that Taylor should stop making paneling because it is unprofitable, and instead make and sell veneer and plywood.

You learn that the overhead figures contain both fixed and variable overhead. The variable portion of overhead is 80% of direct labor cost. All fixed overhead is unavoidable.

Required

1. Determine how much of each product should be produced and sold.
2. Determine what the firm should do if the price of paneling drops to $164 per 1,000 square feet.
3. Assume that paneling can be sold for $178 and veneer for $74, as in item 1. At what price for plywood would Taylor earn the same profit selling all of its plywood and veneer separately as it would combining them into paneling?
4. Assume the prices in item 1. Suppose Taylor could increase capacity in any operation by renting equipment on a month-to-month lease. Determine the maximum monthly cost the firm could incur to increase capacity by 100,000 square feet in each of the three operations, considered independently.

5-48 ***Special order (CMA adapted)*** Anchor Company manufactures jewelry cases. The firm is currently operating at 80% of its capacity of 7,500 direct labor hours per month. Its sales manager has been looking for special orders to increase the use of capacity. JCL Company has offered to buy 10,000 cases at $7.50 per case provided that delivery is within two months. Per-case cost data for the order are as follows.

Materials	$2.50
Direct labor (1/2 hour at $6)	3.00
Manufacturing overhead	2.00
Total unit cost	$7.50

Variable overhead is $1.50 per direct labor hour and the firm allocates fixed manufacturing overhead to units of product based on their direct labor time. Without the order, Anchor has enough business to operate at 6,000 direct labor hours (7,500 × 80%) in each of the next two months. The normal selling price of the jewelry case is $10.50. JCL would put its own label on the case.

The production manager is concerned about the labor time that 10,000 cases require. She cannot schedule more than 7,500 labor hours per month because Anchor has a policy against overtime. Thus, the firm will have to reduce some regular-price sales of the jewelry case if it accepts the order. JCL will not take fewer than 10,000 cases.

Required

1. Determine whether or not Anchor should accept the order.
2. Determine the price per case for the order that would make Anchor indifferent between accepting and rejecting the order (the price that would give Anchor the same profit under both alternatives).

5-49 Processing decision Most beef bought in stores comes from cattle that have been fattened on feedlots. A feedlot is an area consisting mainly of pens and barns in which cattle are closely packed and fed diets designed to increase their weight rapidly. The cattle are bought from ranchers when they weigh about 500 pounds, at a cost of $260, including freight. After the cattle are fattened, their selling price is $0.50 per pound and the buyer pays the freight.

The average animal gains weight in the pattern shown below.

First month	140 pounds
Second month	130
Third month	120
Fourth month	100
Total potential gain	490 pounds

For each month that an animal is on the feedlot, it eats $52 worth of feed. The lot can hold 5,000 head of cattle at a time.

Required

1. Assume that there is a shortage of animals available for fattening. The lot is only able to buy 600 head per month. Determine the number of months that each animal should be kept on the lot before being sold.
2. Suppose the supply of animals is very high so that the lot is operating at full capacity. Determine the number of months each animal should be kept.

CASES

*5-50 Peanuts for peanuts**

The Time Hopefully never, but then everybody knows the outcome of wishful thinking.

The Scene: A small neighborhood diner in a small New Jersey town about 25 miles from New York City. The operator-owner, Mr. Joseph Madison, is preparing to open for the day. He has just placed a shiny new rack holding brightly colored bags of peanuts on the far end of the counter. As he stands back to admire his new peanut rack, his brother-in-law, Harry, a self-styled efficiency expert, enters from the back door.

Harry. Morning Joe. What're you looking so pleased about?

Joe. I jus' put up my new peanut rack—the one I tole you about the other night.

Harry. Joe, you told me that you were going to put in these peanuts because some people asked for them. But I've been thinking about it and I wonder if you realize what this rack of peanuts is costing you.

Joe. It ain't gonna cost. Gonna be a profit. Sure, I hadda pay $25 for a fancy rack to hol' the bags, but the peanuts cost 6¢ a bag and I sell 'em for 10¢. I figger I can sell 50 bags a week to start. It'll take twelve and a ha'f weeks to cover the cost of the rack and after that I make a clear profit of 4¢ a bag. The more I sell, the more I make.

Harry (shaking his finger at Joe). That is an antiquated and completely unrealistic approach. Fortunately, modern accounting procedures permit a more accurate picture which reveals the complexities involved.

Joe. Huh?

Harry. To be precise, those peanuts must be integrated into your entire operation and be allocated their appropriate share of business overhead. They must share a proportionate part of your expenditures for rent, heat, light, equipment depreciation, decorating, salaries for counter help, cook . . .

Joe. The cook? What's he gotta do wit' the peanuts? He don't even know I got 'em yet.

Harry. Look, Joe. The cook is in the kitchen; the kitchen prepares the food; the food is what brings people in; and while they're in, they ask to buy peanuts. That's why you must charge a portion of the cook's wages, as well as a part of your own salary to peanut sales. Since you've talked to me I've worked it all out. This sheet contains a carefully calculated cost analysis which clearly indicates that the peanut operation should pay exactly $1,278 per year toward these general overhead costs.

Joe (unbelieving). The peanuts? $1,278 a year for overhead? That's nuts!

Harry. It's really a little more than that. You also spend money each week to have the windows washed, to have the place swept out in the mornings, to keep soap in the washroom and provide free cokes to the police. That raises the actual total to $1,313 per year.

Joe (thoughtfully). But the peanut salesman said I'd make money—put 'em on the end of the counter, he said—and get 4¢ a bag profit.

Harry (with a sniff). He's not an accountant. And remember, he wanted to sell you something. Do you actually know what the portion of the counter occupied by the peanut rack is worth to you?

Joe. Sure. It ain't worth nuttin'. No stool there—just a dead spot at the end.

Harry. The modern cost picture permits no dead spots. Your counter contains

* *Used with the permission of Rex H. Anderson, Senior Vice-President, INA Reinsurance Company.*

60 square feet and your counter business grosses $15,000 a year. Consequently, the square foot of space occupied by the peanut rack is worth $250 per year. Since you have taken that area away from general counter use, you must charge the value of the space to the occupant. That's called opportunity cost.

Joe. You mean I gotta add $250 a year more to the peanuts?

Harry. Right. That raises their share of the general operating costs to $1,563 per year. Now then, if you sell 50 bags of peanuts per week, these allocated costs will amount to 60¢ per bag.

Joe (incredulously). What?

Harry. Obviously, to that must be added your purchase price of 6¢ a bag, which brings the total to 66¢. So you see, by selling peanuts at 10¢ per bag, you are losing 56¢ on every sale.

Joe. Something's crazy!!

Harry. Not at all. Here are the figures. They prove your peanut operation just can't stand on its own feet.

Joe (brightening). Suppose I sell lotsa peanuts—1,000 bags a week mebbe, 'stead of 50?

Harry (tolerantly). No. Joe, you just don't understand the problem. If the volume of peanut sales increased, your operating costs will go up—you'll have to handle more bags, with more time, more general overhead, more everything. The basic principle of accounting is firm on that subject: "The bigger the operation the more general overhead costs must be allocated." No, increasing the volume of sales won't help.

Joe. Okay, you so smart, you tell me what I gotta do.

Harry (condescendingly now). Well—you could first reduce operating expenses.

Joe. Yeah? How?

Harry. You might take smaller space in an older building with cheaper rent. Maybe cut salaries. Wash the windows biweekly. Have the floor swept only on Thursdays. Remove the soap from the washrooms. Cut out the cokes for the cops. This will help you decrease the square-foot value of the counter. For example, if you can cut your expenses 50%, that will reduce the amount allocated to peanuts from $1,563 down to $781.50 per year, reducing the cost to 36¢ per bag.

Joe. That's better?

Harry. Much, much better. Of course, even then you'd lose 26¢ per bag if you charged only 10¢. Therefore, you must also raise your selling price. If you want a net profit of 4¢ per bag, you would have to charge 40¢.

(Harry is looking very confident, now, but Joe appears flabbergasted.)

Joe. You mean even after I cut operating costs 50%, I still gotta charge 40¢ for a 10¢ bag of peanuts? Nobody's that nuts about nuts! Who'd buy 'em?

Harry. That's a secondary consideration. The point is, at 40¢, you'd be selling at a price based upon a true and proper evaluation of your then reduced costs.

(Joe does not look convinced; then, he brightens.)

Joe. Look! I gotta better idea. Why don't I jus' throw the nuts out—so I lost $25 on the rack. I'm outa this nutsy business and no more grief.

(Harry is shaking his head vigorously.)

Harry. Joe, it just isn't that simple. You are in the peanut business! The minute you throw those peanuts out, you are adding $1,563 of annual overhead to the rest of your operation. Joe—be realistic—can you afford to do that?

Joe (by now completely crushed). It's unbelievable! Last week I wuz makin' money. Now I'm in trouble—jus' becuz I think peanuts on the counter is gonna bring me some extra profit. Jus' becuz I believe 50 bags of peanuts a week is easy.

Harry (by now smiling and satisfied that his brother-in-law will not be so quick to argue with him in the future). That is the reason for modern cost studies, Joe—to dispel those false illusions.

Curtain falls.

Required

1. Who's nuts?
2. Write a memorandum that evaluates the position(s) that Harry takes.

5-51 Dropping a segment Tom Johnson, owner of Johnson's Drugstore, is opposed to smoking and wants to drop the tobacco counter from the store. He has determined from industry statistics and opinions of other drugstore managers that the tobacco counter creates a good deal of other business because many people who come in just for cigarettes, cigars, and pipe tobacco buy other articles. Moreover, some people will go elsewhere for drugs and sundries if they know that tobacco is not being sold.

The manager estimates that sales of drugs would drop by 5% and sundries by 10% if the tobacco counter were removed. The space now occupied by the tobacco counter would be devoted to greeting cards, which Johnson does not now sell. Estimated annual sales for greeting cards are $8,000, with cost of sales of $3,000.

If the tobacco counter is dropped, one clerk earning $4,000 could be dropped. But a pharmacist would have to handle the greeting card sales which would result in a further drop in drug sales of 2% (from the current level).

Carrying costs of the inventory of greeting cards are expected to be about $300 less per year than those associated with tobacco products.

The manager has asked you to advise him in this decision. He has provided you with an income statement for the coming year showing his expectations if tobacco products are retained.

Johnson's Drugstore
Expected Income Statement for the Coming Year

	Tobacco	Drugs	Sundries	Total
Sales	$27,000	$120,000	$33,000	$180,000
Cost of goods sold	9,000	50,000	11,000	70,000
Gross profit	18,000	70,000	22,000	110,000
Operating expenses:				
Salaries	6,700	36,000	7,300	50,000
Occupancy costs (rent, utilities, maintenance, etc.)	3,000	7,000	4,000	14,000
Miscellaneous	1,500	6,700	1,800	10,000
Total operating expenses	11,200	49,700	13,100	74,000
Income before taxes	$ 6,800	$ 20,300	$ 8,900	$ 36,000

You learn that occupancy costs are allocated to each product group based on percentages of space occupied for display of those products. These costs will not change in total if greeting cards are substituted for tobacco. The manager's salary, $18,000, is arbitrarily allocated to departments and included in the salaries amount in the income statement. Miscellaneous expenses are allocated based on relative sales volume and would be unaffected by the change except for the cost of carrying inventory.

Required

Comment on the cost to Mr. Johnson of implementing his convictions about smoking.

5-52 Alternative uses of space Several years ago the Star Department Store began leasing space to Clothes Horse, Inc., a chain of boutiques specializing in high-priced women's clothing and accessories. The boutiques are usually separate stores in shopping centers, but the management of Clothes Horse wished to experiment with an operation in a department store and Star was willing, as the space was not then needed for its own operations.

Clothes Horse pays Star a monthly rental of $3,000 plus 5% of its gross sales, and the arrangement has been profitable for both parties. Star pays all electricity, gas, and other costs of occupancy, which are negligible when considered incrementally because the space would have to be lighted and heated anyway. The lease is about to expire, and Clothes Horse is eager to renew it for another year on the same terms. However, some of Star's department heads have indicated a desire to take over the operation of the boutique, and others have requested the use of the space to expand their selling areas.

After reviewing all the requests, Ron Stein and Margot Miller, Star's executive vice president and general manager, respectively, have narrowed the range of choices to the following: (1) renew the lease with Clothes Horse; (2) keep the boutique, but place it under the women's wear department head, Bill Rausch; (3) use the space to expand the shoe department, which is located next to the boutique.

The boutique had total sales of $400,000 in the first ten months of the current year, and the monthly rate is expected to double for the last two months, which come at the height of the Christmas season. Stein and Miller expect a 10% increase in sales in the coming year if Clothes Horse continues to operate the boutique. Mr. Rausch has presented the following expected income statement for the coming year, which he believes he could achieve if he took over the operation of the boutique.

Sales		$380,000
Cost of sales		171,000
Gross profit		209,000
Salaries	$75,000	
Advertising and promotion	14,000	
Supplies	7,000	
Miscellaneous	8,000	
		104,000
Profit		$105,000

Mr. Stein commented that Mr. Rausch is generally too optimistic and that his estimate of sales volume was probably about 10% too high. He noted that he had provided for fewer salespeople than were employed by Clothes Horse and that the somewhat reduced level of service would not help business. He felt that expenses other than cost of sales would probably be about as he had estimated, even at the lower volume that he thought would be achieved.

The manager of the shoe department believed that if the space were used to expand his department his sales would increase by about $200,000 with a gross profit rate of 45%. He would need to add one salesperson, who would work on a 10% commission, like the other employees in that department. Virtually all other store employees work on salary, not commission.

Miller and Stein both brought up the subject of traffic through the store and both agreed that traffic had increased since Clothes Horse opened the boutique. They were uncertain about the effects of the increased traffic on sales in the store's own departments, and so Miller said that she would investigate the matter.

Miller instructed several of her assistants to interview people in the store, particularly in the boutique, regarding their shopping habits. Several days later, the results were in, and she went to Stein's office to discuss them. The following major conclusions were contained in the reports Miller had received.

1. About 40% of sales made in the boutique are to people who come especially to shop there. These people have to walk through parts of the store to get to the boutique and spend about 20% as much in the store as they do in the boutique.
2. The remainder of the boutique's sales are to people who come for other reasons. Many drop in on their way in or out of the store; some plan to shop in the store's other departments as well as in the boutique. These people spend about twice as much in the store's own departments as they do in the boutique.

After a discussion lasting nearly an hour, Stein and Miller decided that the people who came in especially to shop in the boutique would not patronize the store at all if Clothes Horse did not operate it. The executives believed that only the popularity of the Clothes Horse name induced these people to come in.

Of the other group, they believed that about 10% of the patronage would be lost if Clothes Horse did not operate the boutique. This loss of sales would be spread fairly evenly throughout the store. The average gross profit rate in the store is 45%, and other variable costs are an additional 8% of sales.

Required

Determine the best course of action for the store. Write a memorandum supporting your position.

PART TWO

budgeting

Economic enterprises engage in a myriad of activities. These activities require not only planning but also coordination of plans. We explore the relationships among those activities in this part.

The comprehensive budget is a tool to make planning effective and provides a means for monitoring whether activities are going according to plan. In a formal and integrated way, the budget captures and reflects the results of planning decisions, from decisions about prices, product mix and cost structure, to those about dividends and major new investments.

CVP analysis and knowledge of cost behavior are important in budgeting for the relatively near future—the coming year. Those concepts are also important in analyzing the potential of longer-term projects, the expenditures for which might have to be made in the near future. In addition, some of the principles from financial accounting are important in budgeting because a comprehensive budget includes financial statements normally prepared for external reporting.

Budgeting is more than a technical or mechanical exercise. Because it is people who plan and people who act (according to or contrary to plans), the ways that budgets are developed and used can affect people's behavior and vice versa. In this part we introduce some behavioral problems entailed in the budgeting process. A more comprehensive treatment of these problems is given in Part Three.

6 operational budgeting

The functional areas of a business (marketing, production, personnel, finance, administration) are interdependent and must work in harmony to achieve profit goals. Production must make enough units for marketing to achieve its sales objectives, but must not overproduce because having too much inventory causes excessive costs for storage, insurance, taxes, and interest. For the same reason, the purchasing manager must not overpurchase, yet must ensure that enough material is available to meet production schedules. Finance must make cash available to pay for materials, labor, and other operating costs, as well as for dividends, acquisitions of assets, and debt repayments. But the timing and amount of those cash needs depend on the plans of other managers.

The overall plans of the business must be so specified that the manager of each functional area knows what must be done to ensure smooth performance for other areas and for the firm as a whole. Firms use comprehensive budgets to coordinate all of these activities.

According to one study, companies that use budgets effectively do four principal things.[1]

1. generate commitment to budgets
2. connect short-term, mid-term, and long-term plans
3. adopt detailed, comprehensive procedures to prepare budgets
4. analyze budget variances and take corrective action

We treat each of these at various points in the chapter.

---

1 *Srinivasan Umapathy, "How Successful Firms Budget,"* Management Accounting, *February, 1987, 25.*

COMPREHENSIVE BUDGETS

A **comprehensive budget** is a set of financial statements and other schedules showing the *expected,* or pro forma, results for a future period. A comprehensive budget normally contains an income statement, a balance sheet, a statement of cash receipts and disbursements, and schedules of production, purchases, and fixed asset acquisitions. The budget package might have other components, depending on the needs of the firm.

Comprehensive budgeting requires careful studies of cost behavior patterns. The income statements developed for CVP analysis and short-term decision making are very similar to budgeted income statements. But budgeting involves more than CVP analysis. For instance, budgeting cash collections requires both predicting sales *and* estimating the pattern of cash collections (how much do we collect within 30 days? within 60 days?). Predicted cash collections from sales combine with cash receipts from planned borrowing to become a cash receipts budget.

Comprehensive budgeting is also more complex than CVP analysis because a change in a single assumption affects the whole set of budgets, not just one or a few items in an income statement. For example, changing forecasted sales for a particular month affects not only cost of sales, other variable costs, and profit, but also plans for purchasing the items to be sold, and the timing and amounts of expected cash receipts, payments for purchases, and perhaps even loans that must be negotiated. The ripple effects of changes in budgets make budgeting ideal for computer spreadsheets. Spreadsheet users can develop sophisticated budgeting models.

All levels of management are involved in putting together some part of the interrelated statements and schedules that make up the comprehensive budget. However, individual managers deal only with segments of the total package, and the degree of detail in the schedules they use varies with the breadth of the manager's responsibilities. Thus, while top managers are interested in overall results, the production manager might deal only with schedules of production data. In general, most managers have budgets showing what is expected of *them*—what objectives *they* are to achieve and at what costs.

BUDGETS AND PLANNING

The comprehensive budget is part of a formal strategy and overall plan, in contrast to an intuitive ad hoc approach to operations. A major benefit of formal planning is that it requires explicit statements not only of objectives (such as sales volume and profit) but also of the means required to achieve those objectives. Some of the objectives initially considered feasible may prove not so in light of the budget. Suppose the budget specifies high sales in the early part of the year. When the production manager tries to plan production on the basis of the initial sales budget, he or she may recognize that productive capacity is insufficient to meet the budgeted level of sales. Or perhaps the financial manager will see that sufficient production and inventory to meet the budgeted level of sales are possible *only* if the firm obtains a

Viewing budgets as an integral part of managing is important for managers. As with many other companies, Elgin Sweeper's accounting department had prepared its budgets without participation by the affected managers. Consequently, managers were not committed to meeting the budget and no one "owned the budget." Elgin made a number of changes, but it was a long process to get front-line people to prepare budgets. Now, its managers believe that the " . . . key to a successful cost management program was to educate and entrust responsibility to those front-line managers who made the decisions that drive costs."*

John P. Callan, Wesley N. Tredup, and Randy S. Wissinger, "Elgin Sweeper Company's Journey Toward Cost Management," Management Accounting, *July, 1991, 24.*

great deal of short-term financing. If securing the necessary financing is undesirable (or even impossible), the budgets have to be modified to be consistent with the amount of cash available.

Exhibit 6-1 shows how the budgeting process coordinates the financial statements and other schedules into a comprehensive system. Chapter 5 shows that decision making, which is considered part of the overall planning process, relies on estimates about future results under alternative courses of action. One of the alternatives in virtually all decisions is maintaining the status quo. In making their short-term decisions, such as special orders, managers use the information in carefully prepared budgets as the status quo, the baseline for determining incremental revenues and costs. Moreover, the comprehensive budget incorporates the current effects of plans for long-term financing and for acquisitions of major assets. The development of those long-term plans, and the related decision making, are discussed in Chapters 7, 8, and 9.

Exhibit 6-1 Relationships Among Financial Statements in Budgeting

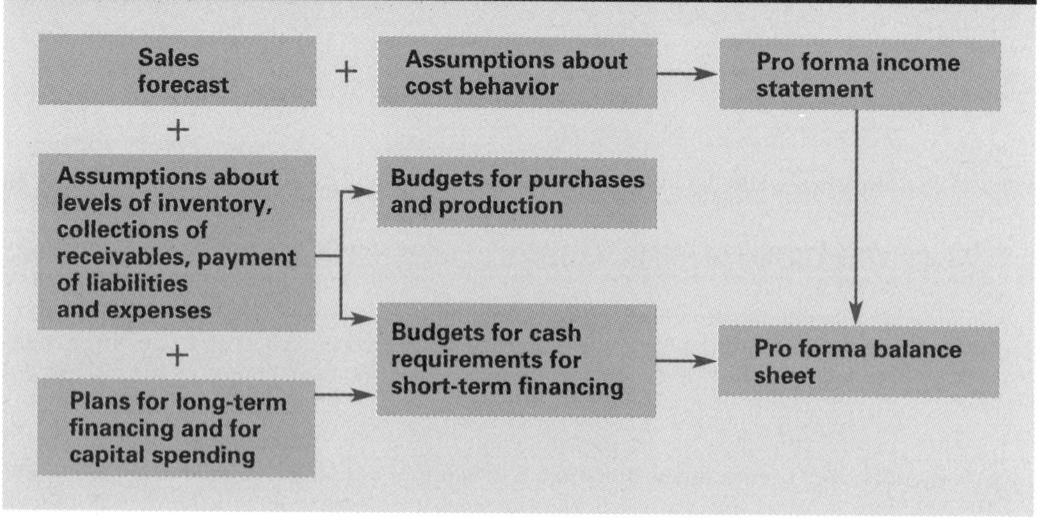

BUDGETS AND CONTROL

Budgets express targets or goals; actual results express achievements. Thus, a comparison of budgeted and actual results is a basis for evaluating performance and helps control future operations. Problems that show up in the comparisons prompt managers to take corrective action.

The preceding statements are oversimplified but fair statements of the role of budgets in control and performance evaluation. If expectations are reasonable and based on all available information, it is better to judge actual performance by comparison with expected, rather than past, performance. Using past performance to judge current performance is inappropriate because circumstances change. Moreover, comparisons with past performance cannot reveal whether current performance is as good as it should have been. (A student who gets 38% on one examination and 42% on the next has improved, but is still not performing adequately.)

The budgeting process incorporates all the managerial functions that are associated with managerial accounting. Planning, control, decision making, and performance evaluation are integrated in the budgeting cycle.

ORGANIZATION OF BUDGETS

Budgets usually cover specific time periods. Virtually all companies prepare budgets for the fiscal year, and the annual budget is normally broken down into shorter periods—quarters, months, or even weeks. Budgets are also prepared for periods longer than a year, usually for three, four, or five years, which are broken down into one-year units. Because forecasting several years into the future is difficult, longer-term budgets tend to be less detailed than annual budgets.

An annual budget is normally broken down into shorter periods for several reasons. Monitoring progress toward meeting the goals in the annual budget is easier for managers if benchmarks are available during the year. More important, what actually happens is often different from even the most sophisticated plans, so managers might need to make changes in operating plans for the remainder of the period.

Consider the following situation. Suppose actual sales for the first month of the year are higher than budgeted. The sales manager must try to determine whether the additional sales in this month will be offset by lower sales later, or whether the high sales are an indication that the *total* expectations were too low. Suppose the sales manager concludes that expectations for the rest of the first quarter, or even for the year, are too low. If the *original* production plan for future months is followed, inventory will be less than budgeted at the end of the first month and shortages may develop. The sales manager might then want production increased to meet the expected increases in sales. An increase in production means acquiring greater quantities of materials and components and perhaps hiring more employees, actions that involve other managers. Changes in plans—such as increased production—will go more smoothly and more effectively if the need for them is recognized well in advance of the point at which a crisis develops. This is true even with the flexibility provided by a true JIT environment.

Even if the sales manager concludes that sales for the full year will not be significantly greater than budgeted, the higher-than-expected sales in the first month could mean that inventory will be lower than budgeted. It might then be necessary to plan a temporary increase in production sufficient to maintain the desired level of inventory. Thus, whether sales in excess of expectations are a temporary or a longer-lasting phenomenon, new plans must be made, with implications for production and cash flows.

Seasonal businesses must make or buy large quantities of goods in advance of the selling season, thus creating a need for funds prior to the receipt of cash from customers. But even without seasonality, cash requirements vary over the year because some costs fluctuate throughout the year. For example, property taxes can normally be paid in two installments, some insurance premiums are due only annually, interest payments might be required quarterly, semiannually, or annually, and dividends are seldom paid monthly. (It makes a big difference whether a $100,000 payment for taxes or dividends must be made in January or July, because the funds must be available when the payment falls due.) Cash budgets are an important part of the total budget package. Budgets prepared for the year as a whole fail to reveal these irregular funds requirements and so are not useful for monthly planning.

Continuous Budgets

Most managers like to have plans for at least a year in advance. If budgets are prepared only for fiscal years, as the year goes by the period for which a budget is available will shorten until the budget for the next year is prepared. To alleviate this problem some firms use **continuous budgets,** which add a budget for a month (or quarter) as one of these periods goes by. Thus, there is a 12-month budget at all times, so managers are aware of the needs for the next 12 months, regardless of the time of the year.

Project Budgets

Some kinds of budgets are not oriented to time periods but to stages in completing specific projects. For example, a firm building a new plant will have a time schedule (finish the exterior by June, the interior by November, begin production by March). The periods selected, which may be of unequal length, depend on the project and are of no importance in themselves. The focus is on completing each stage of the project. Project budgets have implications for periodic budgeting because cash expenditures for projects must be incorporated in the cash budget. Therefore, project budgets supplement, rather than replace, regular periodic budgets.

Capital Budgeting

Virtually all firms prepare a budget of expenditures for long-lived assets, often for many years into the future. This is called a **capital budget.** Forecasted expenditures from this budget must be incorporated into the cash budgets for the appropriate periods. Chapters 8 and 9 treat capital budgeting in detail.

DEVELOPING THE COMPREHENSIVE BUDGET

The development of the comprehensive budget begins well in advance. The earliest discussions of prospects for the coming year normally focus on some overall goals relating to profit or growth (such as a 10% increase in income, a 2% increase in return on sales or on assets, a 15% increase in sales, or perhaps a 2 point increase in market share). At least at the outset, most budgets are driven by desired results. But whatever the initial concerns, in every case the budget for the coming period begins with a sales forecast, because expected sales determine production requirements, needs for labor, for materials and other operating costs, cash flows, and financing requirements. The interrelationships among these various elements depend on managerial policies (how much inventory to keep, what credit terms to offer to customers) and operating characteristics (cost structure, cycle time).

The preparation of income statements based on sales forecasts and cost behavior should be familiar. With minor exceptions, preparing a budgeted income statement is an extension of CVP analysis. Other budgets, especially the pro forma balance sheet and statement of cash flows, present some technical difficulties because of the leads and lags involved. For example, revenue is generally *recorded* at the point of sale, though cash may not be collected for some time after the sale. Similarly, while cost of goods sold is recognized when revenue is recorded, the costs to purchase or produce the inventory are normally incurred *before* the sale. Cash payments of incurred costs might be required immediately or might be delayed for varying periods. These leads and lags give rise to the critical technical problems in comprehensive budgeting.

In the remainder of this chapter we discuss and illustrate sales forecasts, purchases budgets, and expense budgets. These budgets are usually called **operating budgets.** In Chapter 7 we complete the process by considering **financial budgets** (pro forma balance sheet and cash budget).

SALES FORECASTING

The **sales forecast** is critical to budgeting because virtually everything else depends on it. For a large company, developing the sales forecast is a complex and time-consuming task. For example, when the seven-member forecasting team at Xerox adopted a sophisticated computer program, developing the forecast took 50% less time—but it still took three months. Firms use many methods to forecast sales. Not all firms use all of the methods we discuss, but most firms use one or more.

INDICATOR METHODS

The sales of many industries are closely associated with one or more factors in the economy. Sales of long-lasting consumer goods (cars, washing machines) generally correlate well with indicators of economic activity like the Gross Domestic Product (GDP) and personal income. Sales of baby food are associated with the number of births and housing units with the formation of new households. A firm in such an industry might first use an economic indicator (e.g., GDP) to predict total sales for the industry and *then* forecast its own sales by estimating its share of the total market. Scatter diagrams and regression analysis are widely used in forecasting sales, just as they are in predicting costs.

Sales in many industries depend to a great extent on sales of some *other* industries. For example, makers of cans and bottles look at forecasts for sales of beer and soft drinks, and steel companies and tire companies keep abreast of developments affecting the auto industry. In these situations, too, a firm tries to develop a forecast for its industry and then for itself, but the indicator is a forecast from *another* industry.

To be useful for sales forecasting, the indicator itself must be known (or predictable) in advance. Suppose that the sales in an industry correlate well with GDP. It can be used to predict industry sales—and then a company's—sales *only* if a prediction of GDP can be obtained. Thus, once the relationships have been determined as well as possible (probably using regression equations) *and* a forecast of GDP is available, the relationships can be used to forecast sales for the industry or firm.

The scatter-diagram in Exhibit 6-2 shows sales of residential carpeting plotted against housing starts. Not surprisingly, the correlation is imperfect, partly because replacement sales do not depend on housing starts. The managers using the data would use either regression analysis or a visual fit of a line to develop a sales-forecasting equation.

Sometimes managers can obtain predictions of their industry's sales directly. Many trade associations publish studies that provide guidance in sales forecasting. For example, an association of appliance dealers might conduct studies to determine what kinds of appliances are likely to sell, and in what quantities. Forecasting the sales of washing machines could take into account the overall economic outlook, previous sales of washing machines, the average age of machines currently in use, and forecasts for new housing units. Although the study would not indicate how these factors affect the sales of any single dealer, individual dealers have a picture of what is likely to happen to industry sales and can apply it to their own sales forecasts.

HISTORICAL ANALYSIS

Some firms analyze their sales of previous years and project the trend to arrive at a forecast. Thus, if sales have been rising at 10% per year, the firm

Exhibit 6-2 Carpet Sales and Housing Starts

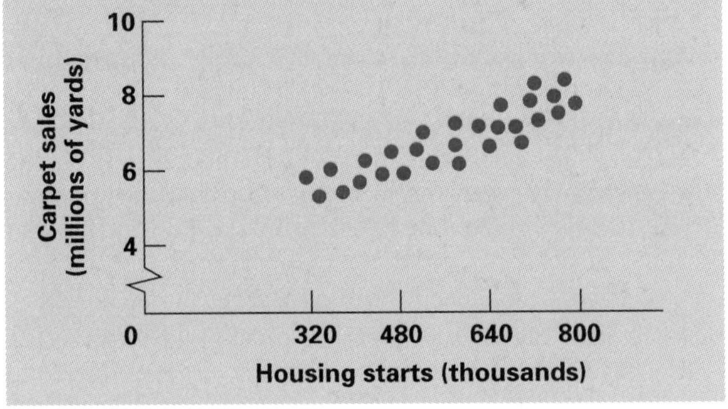

will start with a forecast based on last year's sales plus 10%. Then they will look for factors that suggest higher or lower sales. Were last year's sales abnormally high or low because of a strike or unusual weather conditions (ice cream, beer, golf balls, and many other products sell better in hot weather)? Are there discernible changes in taste that could affect sales? The past can be used for guidance on what might happen, but differences in conditions can cause the future to differ from the past.

Several sophisticated statistical techniques are available for making predictions from historical data. These techniques are beyond the scope of this book, but you may learn about some of them in other courses.

JUDGMENTAL METHODS

Some firms forecast sales using judgment based on experience with the company's customers and products. Each regional sales manager, in consultation with the sales staff, will estimate sales in that area, by customer or product line. The chief sales executive reviews and discusses the forecasts with the regional managers and develops a forecast for the entire company.

The analysis underlying judgment-based forecasts follows the lines of the other methods described here, but is less formal. Instead of using regression analysis or some other mathematical tool, managers will rely on their own experience and perceptions of changing circumstances to develop a forecast of the prospects for the industry and for the firm. For example, a manager may notice several newspaper and magazine articles about the decreasing length of the work week and reason that people will have increased leisure time. If the firm's products are used for leisure-time activities, a manager is likely to forecast increased sales for the industry and for the firm.

WHICH METHOD TO USE

The applicability of any of the methods discussed depends on the characteristics of the firm. Most firms use a combination of methods. Forecasts using judgmental methods alone might reflect unwarranted optimism of the sales manager and sales force. For some firms, no reliable—or predictable—indicators may exist. Even where indicators are available and used, there is danger in relying exclusively on them, because current conditions may differ from those in force when the relationships among the indicators and the sales of the firm or industry were first developed. Successful forecasting results from combining sound and experienced business judgment with the judicious use of quantitative tools.

Whatever methods are used to forecast, the sales budget for the firm as a whole is likely to evolve from several forecasts made on a smaller scale. The original forecasts may be by product, product line, geographical area, department, or some combination of these. The scope of the original forecasts and the methods used depend on the organization of the firm.

EXPECTED VALUES AND FORECASTING

Some firms generate several forecasts by using different indicators or methods or consulting several managers. When different methods are used, or different persons are preparing forecasts, the resulting forecasts are likely to differ. Even a single manager might come up with several forecasts based on different assumptions and judgments about conditions for the coming period. With several forecasts at hand, the concept of expected value is sometimes used to reach a single forecast figure to use in budgeting.

To determine an **expected value,** managers assign probabilities to each alternative forecast. The probabilities reflect the managers' judgments of the likelihood of each forecast actually coming about. For example, suppose the vice president for sales and the regional managers believe there is a 30% probability of sales being $4,500,000 next year, a 50% probability that they will be $5,000,000, and a 20% probability that they will be $6,000,000. The following schedule shows the calculation of the expected value of $5,050,000.

(1) Forecast	(2) Assigned Probability	(1) × (2) Expected Value
$4,500,000	0.30	$1,350,000
5,000,000	0.50	2,500,000
6,000,000	0.20	1,200,000
Expected value	1.00	$5,050,000

The probabilities must add up to 1, or 100%, because there must be *some* value for sales. The vice president would use the $5,050,000 expected value in the budget but would recognize that sales could run from $4,500,000 to $6,000,000. The vice president would monitor actual results and be prepared to revise the budget if conditions warranted. (Although we have introduced the expected-value concept in connection with forecasting sales, it also applies to budgeting costs.)

Probability assignments are usually based on the manager's judgment and experience, sometimes refined by other statistical techniques. The probabilities are, therefore, said to be *subjective:* different managers might assign different probabilities. As with any managerial tool, the quality of the final information or decision rests heavily on the quality of a manager's judgment.

INTERIM PERIOD FORECASTS

The forecasting methods discussed apply to sales forecasts of three distinct types: (1) annual forecasts, (2) longer-term forecasts (three to five years), and (3) quarterly or monthly forecasts. Once a forecast for the year has been approved as a basis for planning, it is necessary to break it down into shorter periods, called *interim periods.*

Often the data used to forecast annual sales (economic indicators, sales for other industries) are also available for quarters. In such cases, managers can base quarterly forecasts on the same indicator used for the annual forecast. Many firms have developed other reliable ways for breaking down annual forecasts. For example, their experience may show that consistent percentages of yearly sales occur in particular quarters or months (15% of annual sales are concentrated in March, 40% in the first quarter, and so on).

Whatever the methods used to develop the sales forecast, and whatever the length of the forecast period, managers revise budgets when they obtain more information. A budget is a plan, not a straitjacket; changing it in the face of changing conditions is sound practice.

EXPENSE BUDGETS

Each manager is responsible for specific tasks and expenses. Hence, each manager should have a budget allowance, or **expense budget,** stating the acceptable limits for expenses the manager may incur in accomplishing assigned tasks.

There are two general ways to develop budget allowances. One approach sets the budget for a particular cost at a single amount without considering the level of activity. An allowance set this way is called a **static budget.** This approach is used with fixed costs. The other approach sets a variable, or **flexible budget allowance,** based on volume of activity. Budgets are set in this fashion for variable costs and mixed costs.

Budget allowances for committed costs can generally be set by referring to existing obligations (because costs to be incurred have largely been set by actions already taken). Discretionary cost allowances are generally set by managerial policy. For example, a flexible budget allowance would be appropriate if the firm's policy is to spend an amount equal to some percentage of sales on advertising, research and development, bonuses, and other discretionary costs. The manager responsible for controlling the discretionary cost will participate with higher management in determining the amount to be allowed. (Some problems relating to the budgeting of discretionary costs are discussed later in the chapter.)

ALTERNATIVE MEASURES OF ACTIVITY

As shown in Chapter 3, the amount of a particular cost may vary with some activity other than sales. The amounts originally budgeted for such costs, and the subsequent flexible budget allowances, must be based on the activity determined to be the best in predicting the amounts of the cost in question.

Production managers are the most obvious example of those who use an activity other than sales to predict costs. The production budget for the period must be related to production activity rather than sales. Whether units are sold or not, the cost to make them is incurred at the time of production. Unless, as in an ideal JIT operation, production exactly coincides with sales shipments, the production manager incurs costs before they become expenses in the income statement. Hence, the budget allowance for production costs is some fixed amount *plus* the variable costs of production times the number of units produced.

Suppose a department manager and supervisor have agreed on the following flexible budget allowances for the listed components of factory overhead in the department.

Cost	Fixed Amount per Month	Variable Amount per Hour of Direct Labor
Indirect labor	$1,200	$0.50
Supplies	200	0.40
Maintenance	2,400	0.10
Depreciation	1,200	0
Miscellaneous	700	0.05
Total	$5,700	$1.05

Suppose further that 1,000 direct labor hours are budgeted for the coming month. The original budget allowances for the month will be determined and reported as in the first column of Exhibit 6-3. Budgeted amounts for each cost element are computed by using the following formula:

$$\text{Flexible budget allowance} = \text{fixed cost per month} + \left(\text{direct labor hours} \times \text{variable cost per hour}\right)$$

For example, the budget amount for indirect labor is computed as $1,200 + (1,000 × $0.50) or $1,700. Note that the formula for a flexible budget allowance is equivalent to the cost prediction formula introduced in Chapter 3. The equivalence is logical, because a flexible budget allowance is a prediction of the cost to be incurred at a particular level of activity.

Exhibit 6-3 is actually the beginning of a performance report that will be completed later when actual labor hours are known.

As you know from Chapter 3, the budget allowances (cost predictions) for 1,000 hours represent expected costs *only* for 1,000 hours. If actual hours are higher (or lower), the production manager should be *expected* to incur more (or less) cost. That is the idea of flexible budgets: to give the manager a budget allowance based on the actual level of activity.

Suppose the department actually works 1,300 hours. To be useful for evaluating the manager's performance in controlling costs, the budget allowance for each cost element should be revised to take into consideration the higher production. For example, the flexible budget allowance for indirect labor would be revised to $1,850 [$1,200 + (1,300 hours × $0.50)]. The final budget allowances represent goals for the manager's performance. In Exhibit 6-4, we have completed the performance report by inserting the flexible budget allowances for the achieved level of production, inserted some assumed actual costs, and computed a variance between the *revised* budget and the actual costs. When actual costs are less than the budget allowance, the variance is *favorable;* when the reverse is true, the variance is *unfavorable.* Hence, the variances for supplies, maintenance, and total costs were favorable. In Chapter 12 we discuss methods for analyzing variances.

Exhibit 6-3 Production Performance Report

Month *March* Department *Mixing*

Manager *E. Jones*

	Budget Allowances			
	Budgeted Hours	Actual Hours	Actual Costs Incurred	Variance
Direct labor hours	1,000			
Indirect labor	$1,700			
Supplies	600			
Maintenance	2,500			
Depreciation	1,200			
Miscellaneous	750			
Total	$6,750			

Exhibit 6-4 Production Performance Report

Month *March* Department *Mixing*
Manager *E. Jones*

	Budget Allowances			Variance
	Budgeted Hours	Actual Hours	Actual Costs Incurred	Favorable (Unfavorable)
Direct labor hours	1,000	1,300		
Indirect labor	$1,700	$1,850	$1,870	($20)
Supplies	600	720	705	15
Maintenance	2,500	2,530	2,470	60
Depreciation	1,200	1,200	1,200	—
Miscellaneous	750	765	780	(15)
Total	$6,750	$7,065	$7,025	$40

Of course, a budget allowance must be based on *whatever* variable is determined to have a predictable relationship with actual cost. In many cases, important cost-driving activities are not related directly to sales, labor hours, or production volume. For example, activities such as the number of vendors from whom the company buys materials and components, the number of employees in a department, the number of different types of products manufactured, or the number of design changes made to a product often generate significant costs. The analytical methods discussed in Chapter 3 help managers identify activities that are useful for budgeting purposes. Of course, the usefulness of the identified relationships for budgeting purposes depends on the availability of estimates or predictions of the level of the cost-driving activities.

BUDGETING DISCRETIONARY COSTS

Establishing budget allowances for discretionary costs presents some of the most difficult problems in budgeting because no one really knows the optimal amount to spend on most discretionary activities. What *is* optimal spending for employee development? for improving current products? for research on potential products?

Expenditures for discretionary items seldom produce immediately measurable output. Research and development activities and employee training might not show results for several years. In some cases, budgets for discretionary items are related to some variable input factor, such as the number of employees being given training or the number of products being studied by research scientists and engineers. (But, note that the number of employees to be trained or products to be studied is *also* a matter of managerial choice for which there is no right answer.) In some cases, a manager might be able to specify, at least qualitatively, what benefits could come from a particular level of spending on a discretionary item. For example, the data processing manager might be able to say that leasing a certain software package would speed customer billing by one or two days. (Getting bills out quicker could mean that payments would come in sooner. But there remains the question whether the benefits of faster collections—the opportunity cost of money tied up in accounts receivable—exceed the cost of leasing the software package.)

Because optimal spending levels for discretionary items cannot be determined, budget allowances for them are often set through negotiations between the affected managers and the budget director, or perhaps between those managers and upper levels of management. In many instances, budgets for these areas are established by specific policy decisions of top management. "We shall increase spending on research and development by 10% per year for the next five years" is an example of such a policy statement. Such a statement is likely to be the result of top managers having set a particular goal for the firm, such as the goal to be an innovator in the industry. Whatever the goal accepted by top management, managers of the affected areas must understand the reason behind a stated policy, so that they authorize actions (and the related expenditures) consistent with the goal.

Discretionary costs are often the first to be cut in hard times, but sometimes companies cut costs that will harm the firm in the long run. Cuts in research and development, employee training, and quality enhancement are often unwise. In the difficult economic times of the early 1990s, Toyota instituted a cost-cutting program. Wisely, rather than reduce its budgets for research, development, and automation, Toyota attacked the budgets for entertainment, overtime for white-collar employees, and travel. These cuts helped the company keep its no-layoff policy intact.

BUDGETING AND HUMAN BEHAVIOR

Budgeting necessarily entails behavioral problems. These problems include the following: conflicting views, imposed budgets, budgets as checkup devices, and unwise adherence to budgets.

CONFLICTS

We can illustrate the problem of conflicts in budgeting by considering a matter of importance to almost any firm—inventory policy. The sales manager of a retail firm wants inventory to be as high as possible because it is easier to make sales if the goods are available to the customer immediately. For the same reason, the sales manager in a manufacturing firm also wants inventory immediately ready for delivery. A financial manager wants low inventories because of the costs associated with having inventory (storage, insurance, taxes, interest, and so on). In a manufacturing firm, the production manager is not interested in inventory per se, but in steady production, no interruptions for rush orders, no unplanned overtime, and other conditions that minimize production costs. Thus, three managers have different views on the desirable level of inventory. They will be evaluated by reference to how well they do their job, so each has an interest in the firm's inventory policy. In a conventional manufacturing environment, the conflict is resolved with great difficulty, if at all, and the managerial accountant might be called in to help determine the best inventory level for the firm. Note that a manufacturing firm committed by its top management to the just-in-time philosophy has already established a policy or goal for the level of its materials and finished products: little or none. The firm-wide commitment to this common goal not only drops the financial manager's concerns from the conflict, but also encourages the other managers to work together to achieve the maximum sales at the minimum cost.

IMPOSED BUDGETS

Unfortunately, it is not uncommon for higher levels of management to *set* performance goals (budgets) for the individuals below them. When such is the case, the budgets are said to be imposed, and serious behavioral problems can arise (or be avoided) depending on the attitudes of the managers imposing the performance goals.

Some managers believe that performance goals should be set very high (budgeted costs very low)—so high that almost no one could be expected to meet the budget. This position is sometimes justified on the grounds that it "keeps people on their toes" and is based on the assumption that people will be lax in their performance if they can easily meet a budget. Other managers say that budgets should be achievable given a good, but not exceptional, performance.

Significant problems can result from the imposition of unachievable budgets. Managers can become discouraged and feel no commitment to meeting budgeted goals. Or perhaps they will take actions that *seem* to help achieve goals (such as scrimping on preventive maintenance to achieve lower costs in the short run) but are really harmful in the longer run (when machinery breaks down and production must be halted altogether).

A major problem with imposed budgets is that, if unrealistic, they are not useful for planning, when planning is one of a budget's primary purposes. Consider the implications of setting unrealistically high sales goals. Based on the unrealistic sales budget, production plans will be made, including perhaps commitments for materials and components and the hiring and training of factory workers. Based on the sales budget, cash receipts will be planned, and the firm will estimate and perhaps negotiate short-term financing.[2] Now what if the sales goals are not realized? Unless the firm operates under the JIT philosophy, inventory will be higher than expected, and additional space may have to be acquired at unfavorable rates. And, whatever the firm's operating philosophy, cash receipts will not materialize as planned, and additional short-term financing may have to be negotiated on terms unfavorable to the firm. If subsequent production schedules are adjusted to bring them into line with lower sales (and to reduce inventory), employee relations may suffer as workers are laid off, and relations with suppliers may be harmed as delays in delivery of materials are requested.

2 One of the advantages of the cash portion of the comprehensive budget is that it allows the firm to identify financing needs before they occur, so the managers have time to seek the best financing sources. More on this in Chapter 7.

At their worst, unrealistic budgets can have serious financial effects on the firm. At the very least, unrealistic budgets will probably be ignored by those whose actions they were intended to guide.

As stated earlier, it is possible for imposed budgets to reflect achievable, realistic performance goals. There are, however, at least two reasons to adopt a budgeting approach that involves participation by the individuals expected to meet the performance goals reflected in the budget. First, managers can never be as knowledgeable about the costs to perform specific tasks as are the persons actually performing them. Second, a considerable body of empirical evidence suggests that allowing individuals a say in their expected levels of performance is conducive to better performance than when those individuals are not consulted.

BUDGETS AS "CHECKUP" DEVICES

Behavioral problems do not arise solely because of the procedure followed for developing budget allowances. Comparisons of budgeted and actual results and subsequent evaluation of performance also introduce difficulties. In ideal circumstances managers use actual results to evaluate their own performance, to evaluate the performance of others, and to correct elements of operations that seem to be out of control. The budget serves as a feedback device; it lets managers know the results of their actions. Having seen that something is wrong, they can take steps to correct it.

Unfortunately, budgets are often used more for checking up on managers; that is, the feedback function is ignored. Where this is the case, managers are constantly looking over their shoulders and trying to think of ways to explain unfavorable results. The time spent on thinking of ways to defend the results could be more profitably used to plan and control operations. Some evaluation of performance is necessary, but the budget ought not to be perceived as a club to be held over the heads of managers. More attention is given to behavioral problems of performance evaluation in Chapters 10, 11, and 12.

UNWISE ADHERENCE TO BUDGETS

As we said earlier, the budget sets limits on cost incurrence, allowances beyond which managers are not expected to go. However, if managers view budgeted amounts as strict limits on spending, they may spend either too little or too much. For example, there are times when exceeding the budget benefits the firm. Suppose a sales manager believes that a visit to several important customers or potential customers will result in greatly increased sales. The sales manager will be reluctant to authorize the visit if it will result in exceeding the travel budget.

At the other extreme, a manager who has kept costs well under budget might be tempted to spend frivolously so that expenditures will reach the budgeted level. The manager may fear that the budget for the following year will be cut because of the lower costs for the current year. Not wishing to be given a lower budget next year, the manager might take an undesirable action—authorize an unnecessary trip—in order to protect personal interests.

Because the activities carried on in a typical company are interrelated, managerial actions influenced by budget concerns in one area are likely to affect the actions taken by managers in other areas. A recently reported example of this interrelationship involved a manufacturing supervisor who was running a machine at 50% of its rated capacity.[3] Asked why, the supervisor said that the machine needed new bearings and would produce only scrap if run faster. A request for maintenance had been ignored for several months because the maintenance supervisor had been controlling costs by not replacing employees who left, and that practice had been going on for several years.

INTERNATIONAL ASPECTS

Companies with foreign operations face several problems that their domestic counterparts do not. One technical problem is translating budgets and actual results from the local currency to the currency of the company's home base. Chapter 11 discusses this issue. Of equal, or greater, importance are the beliefs and behavior of the people.

In extreme cases, such as in formerly communist countries, the very ideas of budgeting and profit are unknown, and teaching managers about these and other aspects of business is necessary. Managers in such countries have long been accustomed to doing what a central authority says—produce so much of this, so many of that. They find it very difficult to make the transition to responding to the market. Moreover, just getting local managers thinking in terms of profit is a formidable task.

People in some cultures have fatalistic attitudes and see little reason to plan anything. After all, if certain things are going to happen no matter what you do, why bother? In such cultures it is difficult, even impossible, to motivate managers to budget at all. Increased contact with foreigners usually reduces some of the opposition to budgeting, but it can be a long, slow process.

In other cultures people uncritically accept authority. Here, the problem is that anything upper-level managers say is fine with lower-level managers. Lower-level managers will not question their managers, nor will they take active roles in developing budgets. Instead, they will wait for clues as to what their managers are looking for and respond only then. Home office managers might also receive the same deferential treatment. As a result, the company loses the benefit of the lower-level managers' insights and understanding.

BUDGETING AND ETHICS

Budgeting is a fertile field for ethical problems and for violations of the IMA Standards. Each of the items we have discussed offers considerable opportunity for questionable practices. Management accountants could be pressured by their immediate managers to assist in preparing budgets with a great deal of slack, so that the managers will be able to meet them without

3 *Robert D'Amore, "Just-in-Time Systems,"* Cost Accounting, Robotics, and the New Manufacturing Environment, *ed. Robert Capettini and Donald K. Clancy (Sarasota, Fl.: American Accounting Association, 1987).*

great effort. They might also be pressured by upper-level managers to submit extremely tight budgets, so tight that there is little chance of achieving them.

Management accountants might be ethically uncomfortable if their role is to act as enforcers for upper-level management. Such a budgetary climate fosters distrust and manipulation, so some responses are likely to violate personal ethical codes as well as the IMA Standards. The check-up device view of budgets encourages such behavior. Downright misstatement is a potential problem in several contexts. A manager might ask for a misclassification of a cost to stay within a line budget.

ILLUSTRATION OF A COMPREHENSIVE BUDGET

We illustrate the preparation of a comprehensive budget by working with Cross Company, a retailing firm. The illustration will be done in two parts. In this chapter we prepare the sales forecast, purchases budget, and tentative pro forma income statement. In Chapter 7 we prepare the cash budget, which requires some of the data in the budgets developed here. We shall then see how the operating and financial budgets are related, especially how the results in the tentative cash budget could prompt managers to look again at the operating budgets and possibly make changes in them.

The managers of Cross Company are developing its comprehensive budget for the first six months of 19X4. As the first step, they have developed the following sales budget, which extends to August 19X4. (As we shall see shortly, a firm must budget sales beyond the six-month period in order to complete the purchases budget for June.)

Month	Sales Budget	Month	Sales Budget
Jan.	$ 400	May	$1,200
Feb.	600	June	800
Mar.	800	July	700
Apr.	1,000	Aug.	800

Sales are obviously seasonal; they increase through May and then drop off, with May sales budgeted at three times those of January.

BUDGETED INCOME STATEMENT

First, we develop a budgeted or pro forma income statement. To do so, additional assumptions are necessary, and we shall assume that the managers of Cross believe that the following assumptions about cost behavior will provide a good basis for planning.

Cost of goods sold will be 60% of sales dollars.

Other variable costs will be 15% of sales.

Total fixed costs will be $240, of which $120 is depreciation expense.

With this information we can develop the budgeted income statements for the six months, as shown in Exhibit 6-5. Separate income statements for each month are not needed; a statement for the six-month period will suffice. However, the other budgets have to be broken down by month, and the monthly income statements will facilitate the preparation of those budgets.

PURCHASES BUDGET—MERCHANDISING FIRM

Our next step is to prepare a **purchases budget**, which requires us to decide on a desirable level of inventory. As we have already suggested, this determination can be extremely complex. We assume here that the interested managers agreed that inventory should be kept at a level of two months' budgeted sales. That is, the managers have adopted an *inventory policy* requiring that at the end of each month the firm should have enough inventory on hand to cover the sales of the following two months. Relating inventory policy to expected sales levels is in keeping with the fact that a firm stocks goods in anticipation of sales. Following the lead of modern manufacturing firms, some retailers, notably Wal-Mart, have worked with suppliers to obtain more frequent deliveries with shorter notice. But retailers must have stock on hand, and if sales are expected to increase in the next period, inventory should also increase.

As you move from budgeting sales to budgeting inventory and purchases, you must also move from using selling prices to using costs. (Remember that inventory is carried at cost.) We can determine purchasing requirements for the six months by using the general formula for cost of goods sold (from financial accounting):

$$\begin{array}{c}\textit{Cost of}\\\textit{goods sold}\end{array} = \begin{array}{c}\textit{beginning}\\\textit{inventory}\end{array} + \textit{purchases} - \begin{array}{c}\textit{ending}\\\textit{inventory}\end{array}$$

Exhibit 6-5 Cross Company Budgeted Income Statements, for the Six Months Ending June 30, 19X4

	Jan.	Feb.	Mar.	Apr.	May	June	Six-Month Period
Sales	$400	$600	$800	$1,000	$1,200	$800	$4,800
Cost of goods sold (60% of sales)	240	360	480	600	720	480	2,880
Gross profit	160	240	320	400	480	320	1,920
Other variable costs (15% of sales)	60	90	120	150	180	120	720
Contribution margin	100	150	200	250	300	200	1,200
Fixed costs (depreciation, rent, etc.)	40	40	40	40	40	40	240
Income	$ 60	$110	$160	$ 210	$ 260	$160	$ 960

Adding ending inventory and subtracting beginning inventory from both sides, we obtain

$$\textit{Purchases} = \begin{matrix}\textit{cost of}\\ \textit{goods sold}\end{matrix} + \begin{matrix}\textit{ending}\\ \textit{inventory}\end{matrix} - \begin{matrix}\textit{beginning}\\ \textit{inventory}\end{matrix}$$

Exhibit 6-6 shows the purchases budget by month for the period. The format follows the revised formula, above. Note that the sum of the cost of sales for two consecutive months is the inventory required at the beginning of that two-month period. For example, the inventory required at the end of January ($840) is the sum of the cost of sales for February ($360) and March ($480). The circled items show the derivations of the ending inventory for January and April. Note also that the ending inventory in one month *is* the beginning inventory in the following month.

The total requirement for any one month is the amount needed to cover that month's sales plus what the company has determined must be on hand at the end of that month. The total requirement can be met from two sources: goods already on hand (beginning inventory) and purchases during the month. Thus, purchase requirements are total requirements less beginning inventory. Work through the budget to be sure you understand the calculations.

The rows for cost of sales and purchases add across to the totals, but the inventory rows and total requirements row do not. The beginning inventory in the total column is the beginning inventory for the six-month period. The ending inventory is the required ending inventory for the last month being budgeted. The final column is the result you would obtain if you were budgeting *only* for the six-month period as a whole. The ending inventory balance, derived as part of the purchases budget, will appear on the June 30 pro forma balance sheet. As you will see in Chapter 7, the purchases budget is also important in preparing the cash budget.

Exhibit 6-6 Purchases Budget for the Six Months Ending June 30, 19X4

	Jan.	Feb.	Mar.	Apr.	May	June	Six Months
Cost of sales for month (Exhibit 6-5)	$ 240	$ 360	+ $ 480	$ 600	$ 720	+ $ 480	$2,880
Ending inventory required	840	1,080	1,320	1,200	900[a]	900[b]	900
Total requirements	1,080	1,440	1,800	1,800	1,620	1,380	3,780
Beginning inventory	600[c]	840	1,080	1,320	1,200	900	600
Purchases required	$ 480	$ 600	$ 720	$ 480	$ 420	$ 480	$3,180

a *June and July cost of sales, 60% × ($800 + $700).*
b *July and August cost of sales, 60% × ($700 + $800).*
c *Inventory at January 1 is assumed to be consistent with company policy.*

PURCHASES BUDGET—A MANUFACTURING FIRM

A retailer must budget purchases to meet sales goals and adhere to inventory policy. A manufacturer must prepare a **production budget** in keeping with expected sales and inventory policy. That is, the manufacturer must *produce* sufficient units to meet the sales goals, while the retailer must *purchase* those units. Moreover, the manufacturer must purchase sufficient materials and components to meet production goals. Thus, both types of firms must plan purchases, and the basic idea of such planning is the same. But developing the final budget is somewhat more complex for the manufacturer because such a firm must first develop a budget for production in units before developing a purchases budget in dollars. Units must be used first because both variable and fixed costs are associated with the production process, and the presence of the former makes the use of dollars difficult without an intermediate budget in units.

Suppose that Brandon Company, a conventional manufacturer, wishes to keep an inventory of the firm's product equal to the budgeted sales for the following two months (much like the retailer in the earlier example). Brandon's managers have gathered the following budgeted data for 19X8.

Units of product on hand at December 31, 19X7				200 units
Pounds of material on hand, December 31, 19X7				3,000 pounds
Budgeted sales for the next five months:				
January	120 units	April	280 units	
February	180 units	May	336 units	
March	240 units			
Variable costs of production per unit:				
Materials (8 lbs. at $0.50)				$ 4.00
Labor				3.00
Manufacturing overhead:				
Fringe benefits				0.40
Power				0.30
Supplies				0.30
Total				$ 8.00
Fixed costs of production per month:				
Rent of machinery				$ 400
Supervisory salaries				600
Insurance				100
Managerial salaries				800
Total				$1,900

Brandon has identified its costs as variable or fixed, as did the retailer. But for Brandon, the variable production costs will vary with the number of units produced, not with the number of units sold. A production budget shows the number of units that must be produced each period to meet sales and inventory requirements. Brandon's budget appears in Exhibit 6-7. Note that even though a sales forecast is available for the first five months of 19X8, we can prepare a production budget for only the first three months. This is true because the firm's inventory policy for finished units is based on the expected sales for the following two months, and we do not know the expected sales beyond May.

Exhibit 6-7 Production Budget for the Three Months Ended March 31, 19X4 (in units)

	Jan.	Feb.	Mar.	Three Months
Expected sales	120	180	240	540
Ending inventory required	420	520	616	616
Total units required	540	700	856	1,156
Beginning inventory	200	420	520	200
Required production	340	280	336	956

Just-in-time operations allow manufacturers to buy materials and components only as needed. Conventional manufacturers buy materials well in advance of production because their operations require a buffer. A conventional manufacturer usually has a policy regarding how much material should be on hand, just as it has a policy about a desired inventory of finished units. Referring to the original data, we see that the $4 material cost per unit of product consists of eight pounds of material at $0.50 per pound. Let us assume further that Brandon's managers desire to keep materials inventory equal to 150% of the coming month's budgeted production needs. (An inventory policy for materials is based on production, not on sales, because materials are needed when the product is made, not when it is sold.)

Exhibit 6-8 shows a budget for materials purchases in January and February. Brandon's inventory policy for materials makes it impossible to budget purchases for March because such purchases depend on an unknown, the budgeted production for April. This example offers further evidence of the problem that lead times can create, and of the need for planning if the firm is to operate efficiently.

Exhibit 6-8 Purchases Budget—Materials, January and February, 19X4

	January	February	March
Budgeted production (from Exhibit 6-7)	340	280	336
Needed for current production (budgeted production × 8)	2,720	2,240	2,688
Ending inventory, 150% of coming month's production needs (280 × 8 × 1.5) and (336 × 8 × 1.5)	3,360	4,032	?
Total pounds of materials needed	6,080	6,272	
Beginning inventory	3,000	3,360	
Required purchases, in pounds	3,080	2,912	
Required purchases at $0.50	$1,540	$1,456	

In a retailing firm, the purchases budget is important in developing a cash budget, because the payments for purchased units are not likely to be made at exactly the time of purchase. In a manufacturing firm, both the production and the materials and components purchases budgets are important for budgeting cash, because payments for materials and components purchases are not likely to be required at the same time as the payments for other costs associated with production. The development of a cash budget, one of the most important of the schedules included in a comprehensive budget, is discussed in detail in Chapter 7.

SUMMARY

Comprehensive budgeting is vital to effective planning and control. The comprehensive budget is the major near-term planning document developed by the firm and consists of a set of financial statements and other schedules showing the expected results for a future period. The development of a comprehensive budget formalizes management objectives and helps coordinate the many activities performed within a single firm.

Sales forecasting is critical to budgeting because the sales budget drives all other budgets. Several approaches are used for forecasting sales. The approach adopted depends on the reliability of available data, the nature of the product, and the experience and sophistication of the managers. The sales forecast and assumptions about cost behavior and inventory policy are needed to prepare the purchases and expense budgets and a pro forma income statement. Flexible budget allowances are recommended for most types of costs because they are useful in identifying problems that require managerial action and in evaluating performance. In a manufacturing firm, the production budget is the equivalent of the purchases budget in a retailing firm. The production budget is the basis for determining the purchases budget of a manufacturer.

Budgeting entails numerous behavioral problems, which can be particularly severe if managers do not participate in the development of the budget, or if budget goals are perceived as unachievable.

KEY TERMS

capital budget
comprehensive budget
continuous budget
expected value
expense budget
financial budgets
flexible budget allowance
operating budgets
production budget
purchases budget
sales forecast
static budget

KEY FORMULAS

$$\text{Budgeted purchases}^{a} = \text{cost of current sales} + \text{desired ending inventory} - \text{beginning inventory}$$

$$\text{Budgeted production, in units} = \text{units needed for current sales} + \text{desired ending inventory} - \text{beginning inventory}$$

a For budgeting purchases in a manufacturing firm, "cost of current sales" becomes "cost of units of materials and components needed for current production."

REVIEW PROBLEM

Using the following data for Exempli Company, prepare a budgeted income statement and a purchases budget in units and dollars for January 19X4.

Budgeted sales for January	5,000 units at $20	$100,000
Budgeted sales for February	6,000 units at $20	$120,000
Cost data:		
Purchase price of product		$5 per unit
Commission to salespeople		10% of sales
Depreciation		$2,000 per month
Other operating expenses		$40,000 per month plus 5% of sales

Exempli's policy is to maintain inventory at 150% of the coming month's sales requirements. Inventory at December 31, 19X3, is $30,000 (6,000 units at $5), which is less than budgeted.

ANSWER TO REVIEW PROBLEM

Budgeted Income Statement for January 19X4

Sales		$100,000
Cost of sales (5,000 units at $5)		25,000
Gross profit		75,000
Variable costs:		
Commissions (10% × $100,000)	$10,000	
Variable operating expenses (5% × $100,000)	5,000	15,000
Contribution margin		60,000
Fixed costs:		
Depreciation	2,000	
Other operating expenses	40,000	42,000
Income		$ 18,000

Purchases Budget for January 19X4

	Units	Dollars
Cost of sales	5,000	$25,000
Desired ending inventory (6,000 × 150%)	9,000	45,000
Total requirements	14,000	70,000
Beginning inventory	6,000	30,000
Purchases required for the month	8,000	$40,000

ASSIGNMENT MATERIAL

QUESTIONS FOR DISCUSSION

6-1 ***"Why Bother With Budgets?"*** Evaluate the following statement: "Budgets are fine for firms that can plan ahead, but I can't. Things are too uncertain for me to make plans. And besides, I have to spend my time looking after day-to-day operations and trying to figure out what is wrong."

6-2 ***Expense budgeting*** What are the major factors in setting budgeted amounts for the following?

(a) Commissions to salespeople
(b) Electricity
(c) Taxes on land and buildings
(d) Taxes on personal property (physical assets other than land and buildings)
(e) Charitable contributions

6-3 ***Sales forecasting—effects of external events*** Indicate what effect, if any, each of the following events or changes in expected conditions would have on the sales forecast that you have already prepared. Explain your reasoning.

(a) Your firm makes building materials. The federal government just announced a new program to assist low-income families to buy their own homes.
(b) Your firm makes toys. The government announces that the economic outlook is better than had been thought. Personal income is likely to increase and unemployment decrease.
(c) You make parts for the automobile industry. A strike against your major customer is announced by the head of the union.
(d) You make heating and air conditioning equipment. The prices of electricity, heating oil, and natural gas are expected to rise rapidly.
(e) You make insulation for houses and other buildings. The prices of electricity, heating oil, and natural gas are expected to rise rapidly.
(f) Your firm publishes college textbooks. Recent statistics show that the numbers of high school seniors and juniors have fallen off from previous years.
(g) Your firm makes plumbing pipe from copper. Chile, the major source of copper, has just gone to war with one of its neighbors.

6-4 ***Budget requests*** Some organizations follow the practice of cutting all budget requests by some set percentage, ignoring the merits of the specific requests. For example, the total budget for each department might be reduced by 5%, or each line item in each department reduced by 5%. Explain how this practice could be beneficial. Is there any way in which this practice could be harmful?

6-5 *Production budgets* From its sales budget, a manufacturing company prepares a production budget in units and then prepares budgets for production costs. Explain why the company must first prepare a production budget in units.

6-6 *Sales forecasting—value of indicators* The following conversation took place between two company presidents.

Grant: "We hired a consultant to help us with our sales forecasting and he has really done a good job. As you know, we make ballpoint pen refills, and he found that our sales are very closely correlated with sales of refillable pens from four months previous. He says that four months seems to be the average life of the cartridges used in most pens. Of course, we don't make pens, but our refills fit the pens that nearly every firm makes."

Harrison: We did the same thing. Our major product is baby bottles, and our consultant found that the number of bottles we sell is very closely related to the number of births about a month later. People seem to buy bottles about a month before the baby is born."

Required

State which firm seems to be in the better position to forecast its sales and explain your answer.

6-7 *What's happening here?* Jack Rolland, the assistant to the controller of Upton Company, was looking at the following report for the marketing department. Upton's fiscal year ends December 31.

		Expenditures Through	
Cost Category	Annual Budget	November	December
Salaries	$240,000	$220,000	$240,000
Travel	36,000	24,000	36,000
Other	96,000	87,000	96,000

Rolland said to you: "I wonder why Cal, the marketing department manager, waited so long to spend his travel money. Maybe a lot of his business is concentrated in December."

Required

Give at least one other explanation for Cal's December spending on travel.

EXERCISES

6-8 *Purchases budget (continued in 6-9 and Chapter 7)* Gentry Sporting Goods has budgeted sales as follows: May, $250,000; June, $220,000.

Gentry's cost of sales is 60%. Its policy is to have inventory equal to budgeted sales needs for the following month. Gentry began May with inventory of $105,000.

Required
Prepare a purchases budget for May.

6-9 Budgeted income statement (continuation of 6-8, continued in Chapter 7) Gentry's variable costs other than cost of sales are 10% of sales, and its monthly fixed costs are $20,000, including $3,000 depreciation.

Required
Prepare budgeted income statements for May and for June.

6-10 Budgeted income statement and purchases budget (continued in Chapter 7) Jordan Clothing has the following sales forecast for the first four months of 19X9.

January	$70,000
February	70,000
March	90,000
April	80,000

Jordan's cost of sales is 60% of sales. Its fixed costs are $10,000 per month. Jordan maintains inventory at 150% of the coming month's budgeted sales requirements and has $45,000 inventory at January 1.

Required
1. Prepare a budgeted income statement for the first three months of 19X9.
2. Prepare a purchases budget for the first three months of 19X9, in total and by month.

6-11 Budgeted income statement and purchases budget (continued in Chapter 7) The following data relate to the operations of Thomas Company, a retail store.

Sales Forecast—19X4	
January	$100,000
February	120,000
March	150,000
April	160,000

1. Cost of sales is 40% of sales. Other variable costs are 30% of sales.
2. Inventory is maintained at twice budgeted sales requirements for the following month. The beginning inventory is $80,000.
3. Fixed costs are $25,000 per month.

Required
1. Prepare a budgeted income statement for the first quarter of 19X4.
2. Prepare a purchases budget, by month, for the first quarter.

6-12 Expected values You have received the following data from the marketing department, regarding the expected unit sales of a new type of coffee maker that your company will introduce in a few months.

Sales	Probability
20,000	0.20
25,000	0.40
28,000	0.30
30,000	0.10

Required
Determine the expected value of sales.

6-13 Budgeting labor costs Kramwer Company's policy is to have a supervisor for every nine workers; whenever the number of supervisors divided into the number of workers is greater than nine, a supervisor is hired. The firm is expanding output and has budgeted production in units as follows.

January	4,800	April	6,800
February	5,400	May	7,300
March	6,100	June	7,500

A production worker can produce 100 units per month. Both workers and supervisors are hired at the beginning of the month in which they are to be added. Workers are paid $1,500 per month, supervisors, $2,800.

Required
Prepare a budget of requirements for workers and for supervisors, by month, in number and dollar cost.

6-14 Purchases budget—units and dollars Warner Company expects the following unit sales.

	Feb.	Mar.	Apr.	May	June
Sales	1,900	2,200	2,300	2,100	1,700

The firm maintains inventory equal to budgeted sales for the following two months. The beginning inventory is 3,700 units. Each unit costs $4.

Required
1. Prepare purchases budgets for as many months as you can in (a) units and (b) in dollars.
2. Explain why you had to stop where you did.

6-15 Budgeted income statement for a manufacturer (continued in 6-16, 6-17 and Chapter 7) HMA Company manufacturers a single product, a small cabinet for cassette tapes. Its sales budget for the first three months of 19X0 is as follows.

January	$2,000 (50 units)
February	$2,200 (55 units)
March	$1,800 (45 units)

Variable manufacturing costs are $26 per unit, of which $12 is for materials. HMA's fixed manufacturing costs are $150 per month, including $40 of depreciation. Its only variable selling cost is a 15% sales commission. Fixed selling and administrative costs are $70 per month. HMA maintains no inventory of finished cabinets.

Required

Prepare a budgeted income statement for HMA for January.

6-16 Production budget for a manufacturer (continuation of 6-15) Because HMA carries no inventory of finished cabinets, its production, in units, is the same as its sales. HMA's $12 per-unit material cost is for 4 pounds of material at a price of $3 per pound.

Required

Prepare HMA's production budget for January, in dollars, showing as much detail as the facts permit.

6-17 Purchases budget for a manufacturer (continuation of 6-15 and 6-16) HMA's company's policy is to maintain an inventory of material at 20% of what is needed to cover production in the upcoming month. At December 31, 19X9, HMA had 34 pounds of material that had cost $102.

Required

Prepare a materials purchases budget for HMA for January, in units and in dollars.

6-18 Expense budgets and variances Burnside Company has found the following formula helpful in predicting the monthly cost of utilities for its factory:

$$\text{Total utilities cost} = \$300{,}000 + \$4X$$

where X is the number of machine hours worked.

Based on budgeted production of 14,000 units in July, Burnside budgeted the use of 42,000 machine hours. Actual production in July was 15,000 units, each requiring 3 machine hours. Actual utilities costs for July were $410,000.

Required

1. Determine the amount Burnside budgeted for utilities for July.
2. Determine the amount and direction of the July budget variance for utilities based on Burnside's original budget for utilities.
3. Determine the amount and direction of the July budget variance for utilities assuming that Burnside uses a flexible budget for utilities.

6-19 Budgeted income statements Weinstock Building Supply operates a chain of lumberyards in a large metropolitan area. The sales manager has retained an economist to develop sales forecasting methods to enable the firm to plan better. The economist reports that the following equation will forecast sales quite well based on past patterns of behavior.

$$\text{Monthly sales in dollars} = \$136{,}000 + \left(\$0.052 \times \begin{array}{c}\text{dollar value of building}\\ \text{permits issued in prior}\\ \text{month}\end{array}\right)$$

The sales manager shows you the following data regarding building permits. The forecasts were developed by the Association of Builders in the area and have generally been accurate.

March	$3,000,000 (actual)
April	4,750,000 (forecast)
May	6,900,000 (forecast)
June	7,100,000 (forecast)

It is now April 3, and the sales manager would like forecasts of sales and income for as many months as you can prepare. She tells you that cost of goods sold, which is all variable, is 45% of sales, other variable costs are 8% of sales, and fixed costs are $140,000 per month.

Required
Prepare budgeted income statements for as many months as you can, given the data available. Round to the nearest $100.

6-20 Flexible budget and variances Adams Company makes a single product. Materials for a unit of the product cost $4, labor is $3, and manufacturing overhead is $20,000 per month fixed, plus $5 per unit variable (with production). In one month, production was 18,000 units and costs incurred were as follows: materials, $71,800; labor, $56,100; variable overhead, $89,000; and fixed overhead, $20,000.

Required
1. Prepare a flexible expense budget formula for total production cost.
2. What should costs have been to produce 18,000 units? (Consider each element of cost separately.)
3. What were the variances between actual and budgeted costs for each element of cost?

6-21 Flexible and static budgets You just became the supervisor of the grinding department of GHJ Company. The production manager has expressed concern to you about the use of supplies in the grinding department and has, after discussions with you, come up with the following monthly budget formula

$$\text{Budgeted supplies expense} = \$13{,}400 + (\$1.85 \times \text{units produced})$$

Budgeted production for April was 10,000 units, giving a budget allowance of $31,900. You actually produced 11,500 units and incurred $33,950 in supplies expense. The production manager attached a note to your monthly report saying that you needed to get better control of supplies because you exceeded the budget by $2,050.

Required
Using the guidelines in Appendix B, write a memorandum to the production manager showing that you did control the use of supplies in April.

PROBLEMS

6-22 Production budget StillWare Pottery manufactures various products. It has the following sales budget, in sets, for its Mexicali line of dishes: April, 18,000; May, 24,000; and June, 25,000. It keeps its inventory at twice the coming month's budgeted sales. At April 1, its inventory is expected to be 41,000 sets.

Required

Prepare production budgets for April and for May.

6-23 Purchases budget (extension of 6-22) Making one set of StillWare's Mexicali dishes requires 12 pounds of materials that costs $2.50 per pound. StillWare keeps its inventory of materials at 150% of the coming month's budgeted production. At the beginning of April, StillWare expects to have 540,000 pounds of materials on hand.

Required

Prepare a materials purchases budget for April in (a) pounds and (b) dollars.

6-24 JIT Manufacturing (extension of 6-22 and 6-23) StillWare Pottery is considering the adoption of just-in-time and flexible manufacturing principles. Some of its managers have studied other companies and believe that StillWare can implement some aspects of JIT now. They believe the company could very quickly cut its finished goods inventory to a constant 800 sets of Mexicali dishes and its materials inventory to a two day supply (1/15th of a month). They believe the company can achieve even greater reductions, with zero inventories the objective.

Required

1. Prepare production budgets for April and May, and a purchases budget for April. Assume that April's beginning inventories conform to the new policies.
2. Using the guidelines in Appendix B, write a memorandum to Jan Brown, the factory manager, about the advantages you see in reducing inventory as indicated here.

6-25 Budgeting production and purchases The production manager of Cram Company wishes to maintain an inventory of materials equal to budgeted production needs for the next two months. Each unit of product takes five pounds of materials. Inventory of finished goods is usually maintained at 150% of the following month's budgeted sales. The sales budget for the first five months of the coming year, given in units, is as follows.

January	12,000	April	16,000
February	14,000	May	20,000
March	10,000		

As of December 31, there were 170,000 pounds of materials on hand and 17,000 units of finished product.

Required

Prepare budgets of production and purchases of materials in units and pounds, respectively, for as many months as possible.

6-26 *JIT manufacturing (extension of 6-25)* Cram Company's managers have begun to use some principles of just-in-time manufacturing. They have been able to reduce finished goods inventory to a ten-day supply (one-third of the coming month's budgeted sales requirements) and materials inventory to a three-day supply (one-tenth of the coming month's budgeted production). Inventories at August 31 reflect these policies. The sales budget for the coming few months, in units, is: September, 14,000; October, 15,000; November, 15,500; December, 16,000.

Required

Prepare budgets of production and purchases of materials for as many months as you can. (Round all items to the nearest hundred units or pounds.) Comment on the differences between these budgets and those in the preceding assignment and on the advantages of the JIT operation.

6-27 *Production and purchases budgets* Bordan Products makes sets of plastic kitchen containers. For one of its lines, it has the following sales forecast for the first four months of 19X8: January, 1,500; February, 1,800; March, 2,200; and April, 1,900. Company policy is to keep inventory of finished sets equal to budgeted sales for the following two months. Each set requires five pounds of material that costs $0.60 per pound. Bordan maintains materials inventory at 150% of the following month's production requirements. At December 31, 19X7, Bordan has 2,200 sets of finished containers and 10,500 pounds of materials.

Required

1. Prepare a production budget for January and for February.
2. Prepare a purchases budget for January in (a) units and (b) dollars.

6-28 *Preparing flexible budgets* As a new assistant to the controller of GHJ Company, you have been assigned the task of preparing a set of flexible budget allowances for overhead costs. You have the following data available.

Cost	Variable Amount per Direct Labor Hour	Fixed Amount
Supplies	$0.70	$17,000
Repairs	0.12	9,200
Power	1.10	15,600
Depreciation		18,800

Supervision, the only other overhead item, is a step-variable cost. It is expected to be $7,000 at 10,000 direct labor hours and to rise by $1,000 for each additional 1,000 direct labor hours.

Required

Prepare a schedule showing the budgeted amount of each cost element, and of total budgeted overhead cost, at 10,000, 12,000, and 14,000 direct labor hours.

6-29 *Relationships* The following income statement relates to Habib Company's budgeted operations for April. No change in inventories is planned.

Sales (900 units at $50)		$45,000
Variable costs:		
Materials ($5 per unit)	$4,500	
Labor ($7 per unit)	6,300	
Overhead—manufacturing ($4 unit)	3,600	
Selling expenses ($2 per unit)	1,800	16,200
Contribution margin		28,800
Fixed costs:		
Manufacturing	8,000	
Selling and administrative	9,600	17,600
Income		$11,200

Required

Fill in the blanks.

1. Budgeted production for April is __________ units?
2. Total variable manufacturing costs for April are $__________?
3. The sale of an additional 10 units would increase income by $__________?
4. Total costs and expenses if 910 units were sold would be $__________?
5. Break-even volume in units is __________?
6. If variable manufacturing costs increased by $2 per unit, income at 900 units sold would be $__________?
7. If fixed costs increased by $4,800, and the firm wanted income of $11,200, sales in units would have to be __________?
8. If ending inventory were to be 30 units higher than beginning inventory, manufacturing costs incurred during the period would be $__________?

6-30 *Multiple materials—manufacturing firm* Williams Company expects the following sales by month, in units, for the first five months of the coming fiscal year.

	February	March	April	May	June
Budgeted sales	1,800	1,900	2,500	1,900	2,100

The company's one product, the Tow, requires two raw materials: Tics and Tacs. Each Tow requires three Tics and two Tacs. Williams follows the policy of having finished goods equal to 50% of budgeted sales for the following two months. Raw materials inventories are maintained at 150% of budgeted production needs for the coming month. Inventories at January 31, 19X8, reflect these policies.

Required

1. Prepare a production budget for Tows for as many months as you can.
2. Prepare purchases budgets for Tics and Tacs for as many months as you can.

6-31 *Budgeted income statements—expected values* Burke Company is preparing its comprehensive budget for 19X7. The sales manager does not wish to pin down a single estimate of sales, but would prefer to give three forecasts, along with his estimates of the probabilities he attached to them.

Sales Forecast	Probability
$ 500,000	0.5
800,000	0.3
1,000,000	0.2

Variable costs are 60% of sales and total fixed costs are budgeted at $240,000.

Required

1. Prepare budgeted income statements based on each of the three forecasts.
2. Prepare a budgeted income statement based on the expected value of sales.

6-32 Smoothing production Maynard Company makes bathing suits, with its sales falling heavily in the April-June period, as shown by the sales budget (in thousands of units).

	January	February	March	April	May	June
Sales	100	100	110	160	200	250

Maynard's normal inventory policy has been to have a two-month supply of finished product. The production manager has criticized the policy because it requires wide swings in production, which add to costs. He estimates that per-unit variable manufacturing cost is $3 higher than normal for each unit produced in excess of 180,000 units per month. Maynard's treasurer is concerned that increasing production in the early months of the year would lead to high costs of carrying inventory. He estimates that it costs the firm $0.80 per unit per month in ending inventory, consisting of insurance, financing, and handling costs. He emphasizes that these costs are incremental.

All of the managers agree that the firm should have 450,000 units on hand by the end of April. The production manager wants to spread the required production equally over the four months, while the treasurer believes that the firm should stick to its current policy unless it turns out to be costlier.

Required

1. Prepare a budget of production for January through April following the firm's current policy. Inventory at January 1 is 200,000 units.
2. Prepare a production budget using the production manager's preference.
3. Determine which budget gives lower costs.

6-33 Relationships among sales and production budgets Partially completed sales and production budgets for Firmin Company are shown below. The firm maintains an inventory equal to 150% of the budgeted sales for the coming month.

Required

Fill in the blanks.

Sales Budget in Units

Jan.	Feb.	Mar.	Apr.	May	June	July
3,000	3,400	_____	_____	_____	5,800	_____

Production Budget (in units)

	Jan.	Feb.	Mar.	Apr.	May	June
Ending inventory	_____	6,300	_____	_____	8,700	_____
Sales	3,000	_____	_____	_____	_____	5,800
Total requirements	_____	_____	_____	13,900	_____	_____
Beginning inventory	_____	5,100	_____	6,900	_____	_____
Production	3,600	_____	_____	7,000	_____	5,200

6-34 Budgeting in a CPA firm Takoski Inoe is a certified public accountant practicing in a large city. He employs two staff accountants and two clerical workers. He pays the four employees a total of $8,800 per month. His other expenses, all fixed, for such items as rent, utilities, subscriptions, stationery, and postage are $4,700 per month.

Public accounting is, for most firms, highly seasonal, with about four months (January through April) that are extremely busy, eight months of less activity.

The most relevant measure of volume in a CPA firm is charged hours—the hours worked on client business for which the clients are charged. Mr. Inoe expects his two staff accountants to work an average of 120 charged hours each month during the eight slower months, and 200 hours each per month during the January-April busy season. Clerical personnel work about 600 charged hours each per year, and Mr. Inoe works about 1,400. For both the clerical personnel and Mr. Inoe, approximately 40% of their charged hours fall in the four-month busy season.

Mr. Inoe charges his clients $75 per hour for his time, $35 for the time of a staff accountant, and $15 for the time of clerical personnel.

Required

Prepare a budget of revenues and expenses for a year for Mr. Inoe's firm. Separate the budgets for the periods January-April and May-December.

6-35 Sales forecasting—scatter diagram and regression Ridley Carpet Company has engaged you as a consultant to help in its sales forecasting. After a long discussion with Roberta Ridley, president of the firm, you develop the following data.

Year	Housing Units Built (in thousands)	Sales of Ridley Company (in thousands)
19X1	1,300	$2,440
19X2	1,400	2,610
19X3	1,900	3,380
19X4	1,500	2,760
19X5	2,000	3,520
19X6	1,600	2,875

Required

1. Develop an equation to be used to forecast sales for Ridley Company. Use a scatter diagram and regression analysis.
2. Ms. Ridley has learned that housing units to be built in 19X7 will be about 1.8 million. What is your forecast for Ridley's sales? Are you relatively confident about your forecast? Why or why not?

6-36 Comprehensive budget (continued in Chapter 7) The managers of Calco Products Company have been developing information for the comprehensive budget for the coming year. They have decided to use the following estimates and policies for planning.

Sales forecast, in units:	
January	20,000
February	24,000
March	30,000
April	25,000
May	22,000
Selling price	$30 per unit
Material cost	$8 per unit of product
Direct labor and variable overhead	$6 per unit of product
Variable selling expenses	$2 per unit sold
Fixed manufacturing costs	$120,000 per month
Fixed S, G, & A expenses	$60,000 per month

The managers plan to keep inventory of finished goods equal to budgeted sales for the following two months, and inventory of materials equal to twice budgeted production for the coming month. The December 31 inventories are: finished goods, 35,000 units and materials, 66,000 units (one unit of materials per unit of product).

Required

1. Prepare budgeted income statements for January, February, and the two-month period, using the contribution margin format.
2. Prepare production budgets for January, for February, and for March.
3. Prepare purchases budgets for materials for January and for February.

6-37 Indicators for sales forecasting The following economic indicators and other data might be useful in forecasting sales for certain kinds of firms: income per capita, population, car sales, and rate of unemployment.

For each of the types of firms listed below, state which, if any, of the listed indicators you think would be relevant in forecasting sales. Indicate briefly why you think each indicator is relevant or irrelevant.

(a) food company
(b) maker of outboard motors
(c) home construction firm
(d) tire maker
(e) textbook company
(f) jewelry maker
(g) maker of nonprescription drugs

6-38 Budgeting for a hospital (AICPA adapted) The administrator of Taylor Memorial Hospital, Dr. Gale, has asked for your help in preparing the budget for 19X7, which must be presented at the next meeting of the hospital's board of trustees. The hospital obtains its revenues through two types of charges: charges for use of a hospital room and charges for use of the operating room. Use of the basic rooms depends on whether the patient undergoes surgery during the stay in the hospital. Estimated data as to the types of patients and the related room requirements for 19X7 are as follows:

Type of Patient	Total Expected	Average Stay in Days	Percentages Selecting Kinds of Rooms		
			Private	Semiprivate	Ward
Surgical	2,400	10	15%	75%	10%
Medical only	2,100	8	10%	60%	30%

Basic room charges are $100, $80, and $40 for private, semiprivate, and ward, respectively.

Charges for use of the operating room are a function of the length of the operation and the number of persons required to be involved in the operation. The charge is $0.40 per person-minute. (A person-minute is one person for one minute; if an operation requires three persons for 40 minutes, there would be a charge for 120 person-minutes at $0.40 per person-minute, or $48.) Based on past experience the following is a breakdown of the types of operations to be performed.

Type of Operation	Number of Operations	Average Number of Minutes per Operation	Average Number of Persons Required
Minor	1,200	30	4
Major—abdominal	400	90	6
Major—other	800	120	8
	2,400		

Required

1. Prepare a schedule of budgeted revenues from room charges by type of patient and type of room.
2. Prepare a schedule of budgeted revenues from operating room charges by type of operation.

6-39 ***Inventory policy—carrying costs*** The managers for production, sales, and finance of the Steele Company are discussing production and inventory policies. The sales manager would like the firm to stock more units in inventory. The production manager is willing to do so. The financial manager argues that the cost of storing, insuring, and financing the additional inventory would be prohibitive; it costs the firm $4 per month per unit to cover these costs and they are variable with the number of units on hand.

The sales manager believes that if inventory were increased by 5,000 units, sales would be 2,000 units per month higher. Contribution margin per unit is $7.

Required

1. What is the value (per month) of the additional sales that would be generated by the increased inventory?
2. What additional monthly costs are associated with carrying the additional 5,000 units in inventory?
3. Using the guidelines in Appendix B, write a memorandum to the three managers giving and supporting your recommendation regarding production and inventory.

6-40 ***Flexible budget, multiple drivers*** The controller of Ames Industries has analyzed the costs of the Linden Plant. She comes up with the following cost drivers. Data are quarterly.

	Fixed Component	Variable Component	Cost Driver
Inspection	$ 72,500	$120.00	Shipments
Maintenance	61,200	2.40	Machine hours
Data processing	9,700	0.25	Transactions
Purchasing	63,600	180.00	Number of vendors
Other	278,800	2.20	Labor hours

Some of these costs are step-variable, so the variable components do not apply to small changes in activity, but only to relatively large movements. You may assume for this assignment that all changes are large.

Required
Develop flexible budget allowances for each element of cost, and for total cost, for the following two cases.

	Case	
	A	B
Shipments	110	75
Machine hours	15,000	22,000
Transactions	220,000	360,000
Number of vendors	120	40
Labor hours	7,000	11,000

6-41 Flexible and static budget Wilkinson Company prepares budgets for each month. Budgeted amounts, along with actual results, are shown in reports that are circulated to the managers whose operations are being reported on *and* to their supervisors. Excerpts from the report of the latest two months for one production department are given below.

	April			May		
	Budget	Actual	Variance	Budget	Actual	Variance
Production in units	8,000	7,000	1,000	10,000	10,500	(500)
Costs:						
Material	$16,000	$14,600	$1,400	$20,000	$20,800	($ 800)
Direct labor	24,000	21,600	2,400	30,000	31,300	(1,300)
Indirect labor	4,000	3,900	100	5,000	5,300	(300)
Power	7,000	6,700	300	8,000	8,400	(400)
Maintenance	5,200	4,700	500	6,000	6,200	(200)
Supplies and other	4,600	4,580	20	5,000	5,050	(50)
Total costs	$60,800	$56,080	$4,720	$74,000	$77,050	($3,050)

Required
1. Using the budgeted amounts, determine the fixed and variable components of each cost.
2. Using the guidelines in Appendix B, write a memorandum to R. James, the controller, about the usefulness of Wilkinson's current method of providing information to its managers.

6-42 Manufacturing cost budget Horton Company makes a variety of household products, usually in about the same mix. On the average, each unit requires $3 in materials and $2 in variable manufacturing overhead. Direct labor averages $4 per unit up to 100,000 units per month. Direct labor rises to $6 per unit for units over 100,000, because of overtime premium. The remainder of manufacturing overhead is step-variable, with the following pattern.

Monthly Unit Production	Other Costs
Up to 100,000	$230,000
100,001-120,000	245,000
120,001-140,000	275,000

The pattern of these costs reflects increased supervision, utilities, and other costs associated with operating beyond the normal eight-hour day.

Budgeted unit production for the next few months is

March	90,000
April	115,000
May	130,000
June	105,000
Total	440,000

Required

1. Prepare budgets for manufacturing costs for each month, and in total.
2. What would total production costs be for the four-month period if the company could equalize production at 110,000 units per month?
3. If Hornton needs only to produce 440,000 units for the entire four-month period, how should it produce by month to obtain the lowest possible total production cost?
4. What reasons might there be for the company to stick to the original monthly production budget despite its higher costs?

6-43 Budgeting and behavior Rydell Company sets sales budgets for its salespeople, who are evaluated by reference to whether they achieve budgeted sales. The budget is expressed in total dollars of sales and is $200,000 per salesperson for the first quarter of 19X3. The firm makes two products, for which price and cost data are given below.

	Wiffers	Trogs
Selling price	$10	$15
Variable costs	4	10
Contribution margin	$ 6	$ 5

Wiffers are a new product that the firm's president thinks should become a big seller. Trogs have been popular for some years. Customers who have been buying Trogs for years are not expected to buy Wiffers. Customers for Wiffers must be sought out by the salespeople and convinced of the high quality of the product.

The $200,000 budgeted sales per person is a fairly high goal, but is attainable. During the first quarter of 19X3, all salespeople met the $200,000 sales budget.

Required

1. Which product should salespeople stress?
2. Under the circumstances described, which product do you think sold most?

3. If your answers to items 1 and 2 conflict, what changes would you suggest for the firm's budgeting process?

6-44 ***Production and purchases budgets—units and dollars*** Drummond Company manufactures several products, including a frying pan with a wooden handle. Sales forecasts for the frying pan for the next five months are given below, in units.

	April	May	June	July	August
Budgeted sales	2,500	3,100	2,800	3,500	2,400

Each frying pan requires a blank sheet of iron that Drummond buys from a single supplier at $2 per sheet and molds into the appropriate shape. Handles are purchased in ready-to-use condition from another supplier at $0.40 each. The firm's policy is to keep finished goods inventory at twice the coming month's budgeted sales, blank iron sheets at budgeted production requirements for the coming two months, and handles at budgeted production requirements for the coming month.

Labor costs for shaping the iron and putting on a handle are $1.50 and variable manufacturing overhead costs are $0.80. Fixed manufacturing costs are $4,500 per month.

At the end of March the firm expects to have the following inventories.

Finished pans	5,300
Blank iron sheets	5,600
Handles	4,600

Required

1. Prepare production budgets for April through July, by month, in units and in dollar costs.
2. Prepare purchases budgets in units and dollars for blank iron sheets and handles for April and for May.

6-45 ***Conflicts in policy*** Timmons Fashions has the following sales budget, in units, for its best-selling line of women's wear.

January	65,000	April	60,000
February	90,000	May	100,000
March	60,000	June	80,000

Timmons manufactures the line in a single plant. Because of union agreements and employment policies, the only feasible amounts of monthly production are 72,000 and 90,000 for a four-day week and five-day week, respectively.

Timmons's policy is to keep inventory of at least 15,000 units at the end of each month to serve as a buffer in case of slow deliveries by suppliers or other problems that could lead to lost sales. Storage is limited, such that having inventory greater than 40,000 units results in abnormally high costs. The inventory at January 1 is 20,000 units.

Required

Develop a production budget for the six months. If you cannot keep inventory within the limits stated, be prepared to defend the reasoning you used in making your selection.

6-46 Budgeting administrative expenses The controller of Kaufman Company has asked you to prepare a flexible budget for costs in the purchasing department. The normal volume of work in the department is 800 purchase orders per week.

Typists in the department can type about 100 lines per hour and the average purchase order has 10 lines. Typists are paid $5 per hour and work a 35-hour week. When not busy typing, the typists file and perform other work. Order clerks prepare the purchase orders to be typed. They are paid $6 per hour for a 35-hour week and generally take 20 minutes to prepare an order for typing. They also work at other tasks when purchase orders are slack. The purchasing agent is paid $300 per week. Supplies, stationery, etc. average $0.40 per purchase order.

Required

1. Under normal circumstances, how many order clerks and typists are required and how much slack time do clerks and typists have available to perform other duties?
2. If salaries for clerks and typists, and costs for supplies and stationery are to be budgeted as variable costs, what is the flexible budget formula for total purchasing costs for each week, and what variance would you expect for a normal week?
3. What is the per-week capacity of the purchasing department given the personnel requirement derived in item 1?
4. What is the flexible budget formula for total weekly purchasing costs if the personnel requirements in item 1 are treated as fixed costs?

6-47 Sales forecasting, budgeted income, and budgeted production (continued in Chapter 7) Richards Company makes ignition systems for automobile engines. The firm has developed the following equation that has been successful in predicting the firm's annual sales, in units:

$$\text{Sales} = 80{,}000 + (0.009 \times \text{automobile sales}).$$

This coming year's automobile sales are expected to be 8,000,000 cars.

Each system sells for $80 and contains materials costing $5. Direct labor is $10 per unit and variable manufacturing overhead is $12. The firm's only other variable cost is its sales commission of 10% of dollar sales. Fixed manufacturing costs are $1,200,000 per year; fixed selling and administrative expenses are $1,800,000 per year. Both are incurred evenly over the year.

Sales are seasonal; about 60% of sales are in the first six months of the fiscal year, which begins June 1. The sales forecast for the first six months, in percentages of annual sales, is as follows.

June	5%	September	12%
July	8	October	14
August	9	November	12

Richards has a policy of keeping inventory of finished product equal to budgeted sales for the next two months. Materials are bought and delivered daily, so no inventory is kept. The inventory of finished product at May 31 is expected to be 19,000 units.

Required

1. Prepare a budgeted income statement for the coming year and for the first six months of the year.
2. Prepare a production budget by month for the first three months, in units.
3. Determine the firm's break-even point (in units) for a year. How might the firm's managers interpret that information in light of their successful sales predictions using the given formula?

6-48 Comprehensive budget (adapted from a problem prepared by Professor Maurice L. Hirsch, and continued in Chapter 7) Banana City is a wholesaler of bananas and nuts. Mr. Bertram A. Nana, the president of the firm, has asked for your assistance in preparing budgets for fiscal year 19X7, which begins on September 1, 19X6. The following information has been gathered for your use.

1. Sales are expected to be $880,000 for the year, of which bananas are expected to be 50%, nuts 50%.
2. Sales are somewhat seasonal. Banana sales are expected to be $77,000 in November, with the rest spread evenly over the remaining eleven months. Sales of nuts are expected to be $40,000 per month except in October and November, when they are expected to be $25,000 per month, and in April and May, when they are expected to be $35,000 per month.
3. Cost of sales, the only variable cost, is 40% for both products.
4. Inventory of bananas is generally kept equal to a one-month supply. Inventory of nuts is usually held at a two-month supply.
5. Income taxes are 40% of income before taxes.
6. Annual fixed costs, all incurred evenly throughout the year, are expected to be as follows.

Rent	$ 24,000	Depreciation	$ 36,000
Insurance	12,000	Interest	6,000
Wages and salaries	120,000	Other fixed costs	156,000

7. Inventories expected at August 31, 19X6 are: bananas, $14,300 and nuts, $27,500.
8. The firm expects to sell some land that it owns. The sale, which is expected to have a price of $6,000, will take place in October. The cost of the land on the balance sheet is $8,000.

Required

1. Prepare a budgeted income statement for the fiscal year ending August 31, 19X7.
2. Prepare a budgeted income statement for the first quarter of the fiscal year, by month, and in total.
3. Prepare a purchases budget by product for each month of the first quarter of the fiscal year and for the quarter as a whole.

CASES

6-49 Constraints on scheduling production Robertson Company experiences some seasonality in its sales. Its sales forecasts (in units) for the first eight months of 19X5 are shown below.

January	3,000	March	4,200	May	5,400	July	4,800
February	3,800	April	5,000	June	5,900	August	4,200

The inventory of finished units at January 1 is expected to be 6,800 units and Robertson's policy is to keep inventory equal to a two-month supply.

Robertson's current work force of 100 people is organized into 20 five-member teams. Each team takes responsibility for the product throughout the production process, so that workers can be hired only in groups of five. The 20 teams can produce 4,000 units per month, but overtime can be used to increase output by 10%.

Unlike some firms facing seasonality in sales, Robertson is not constrained by union contracts requiring some guaranteed level of employment for its employees. However, Robertson's top managers prefer not to hire and lay off workers when only moderate changes in production are contemplated. As explained to you by M.A. Martinez, Robertson's president, this preference is based partly on a perceived responsibility to provide regular employment and partly on a concern about a potential decline in the available work force if skilled workers leave the community due to unstable employment conditions.

Required

Using the guidelines in Appendix B, write a memorandum to M.A. Martinez about production and labor needs for the first six months of 19X5. Include in the memorandum a production budget, in units, a budget of worker requirements, and any assumptions you made and any reservations you have about the budgets you propose.

6-50 Budgeting step-variable costs Corman Company manufactures several products using a great deal of machinery. Since it is critical to keep the machines running well, Corman pays a good deal of attention to maintenance. The chief engineer has determined that routine maintenance requires a complete shutdown and cleaning every 200 hours a machine has been running. This job costs $250. Excluding these major cleanings, maintenance costs for ten machines have been as follows for the past eight months. Each machine runs about the same amount of time each month as every other machine.

Month	Hours for Ten Machines	Maintenance Costs
1	2,200	$1,400
2	2,100	1,380
3	1,950	1,260
4	2,000	1,290
5	1,700	1,190
6	2,400	1,505
7	2,300	1,455
8	1,800	1,200

Required

1. Using the high-low method, prepare a flexible budget formula for maintenance costs, excluding the major cleaning at 200 hours.
2. Determine the budgeted cost levels for 1,600 hours and at 100-hour intervals up to 2,500 hours. Include maintenance cost using the formula you developed in item 1 and the major cleaning costs.
3. Discuss your reservations about the use of flexible budgets when such costs are present.

7 financial budgeting

Chapter 6 discussed comprehensive budgeting and illustrated the operating budgets of the total budget package. Financial budgets are equally important to the package. In this chapter we complete the illustration by developing the cash budget and pro forma balance sheet.

We also show how financial statement data are used in the preparation of annual budgets and long-term budgets. Finally, we look at the special issues associated with budgeting in not-for-profit entities.

ILLUSTRATION OF CASH BUDGET

We prepared the budgeted income statement and purchases budget for Cross Company and can now proceed to the **cash budget** and **pro forma balance sheet.** Following are the balance sheet as of December 31, 19X3, and the budgeted income statement for the six-month period after that date (from Exhibit 6-5).

Cross Company
Balance Sheet as of December 31, 19X3

Assets		Equities	
Cash	$ 60	Accounts payable (merchandise)	$ 360
Accounts receivable	576	Accrued expenses	50
Inventory	600	Common stock	1,000
Plant and equipment, net	600	Retained earnings	426
Total	$1,836	Total	$1,836

Cross Company Budgeted Income Statement, January 1, 19X4 to June 30, 19X4	
Sales	$4,800
Cost of goods sold (all variable, at 60% of sales)	2,880
Gross profit	1,920
Other variable costs (15% of sales)	720
Contribution margin	1,200
Fixed costs (including $120 of depreciation)	240
Income	$ 960

We need the balance sheet at the beginning of the budget period because it shows both resources (assets) that are already available for use during the period and liabilities that must be paid during the period. For example, we used the inventory figure at December 31 in preparing the purchases budget.

CASH RECEIPTS

To develop the budgeted income statement we relied on the following sales forecast:

	Jan.	Feb.	Mar.	Apr.	May	June
Sales	$400	$600	$800	$1,000	$1,200	$800

To budget cash receipts we need more information. Does the company sell on credit or for cash only? How soon do credit customers pay their accounts? Assume that experience (adjusted for any *expected* changes in conditions) indicates that 20% of sales are collected in the month of sale, 48% in the month after sale, and the remaining 32% in the second month after sale. The beginning Accounts Receivable consists of $400 of December sales and $176 of November sales.

We can now determine cash inflows for the six-month period. Exhibit 7-1 is a good general format for budgeting cash receipts from sales. The circled items show the pattern of collection of January sales; the total is given below the schedule. Notice that an increase in cash receipts accompanies the increase in sales. But there is a lag. Except for January, the cash receipts for a month do not equal or exceed sales until June, when sales have already declined. By that time, collections are being made from the prior months in which sales were considerably higher. If it pays cash to stock goods in advance of sales, but collects cash well after the point of sale, a firm can run out of cash while its sales are rapidly increasing. This situation will be more obvious when we examine cash disbursements.

CASH DISBURSEMENTS

The major cash disbursement for Cross Company is for purchases. To determine cash disbursements for purchases, we use the purchases budget developed in Chapter 6 (Exhibit 6-6) and the timing of disbursements for those purchases. If the company pays for goods on delivery, cash disbursements for purchases equal purchases in each month. Suppose, however, that Cross

Exhibit 7-1 Cash Receipts

	Jan.	Feb.	Mar.	Apr.	May	June	Total
Sales for the month	$400	$600	$800	$1,000	$1,200	$ 800	$4,800
Collections from Sales							
20% of total sales for the month	$ 80	$120	$160	$ 200	$ 240	$ 160	$ 960
48% of prior month's sales	240	192	288	384	480	576	2,160
32% of second prior month's sales	176	160	128[a]	192	256	320	1,232
Total cash collections	$496	$472	$576	$ 776	$ 976	$1,056	$4,352

a $400 = total January sales, collected in January, February, and March ($80 + $192 + $128).

Company takes advantage of the 30-day credit terms extended by its suppliers so that it pays for purchases in the month after purchase. (If Cross used 60-day credit, it would pay in the second month after purchase, and so on.)

To derive cash disbursements, it is necessary only to lag payments a month behind purchases, as in Exhibit 7-2. The January payment is for December purchases, which are Accounts Payable at December 31, 19X3. The other amounts come from the purchases budget developed in Chapter 6 and summarized here. Purchases are paid for in the month after purchase. Accordingly, Accounts Payable at the end of any month equal that month's purchases, and cash disbursements (for purchases) in any month equal Accounts Payable at the end of the prior month.

Two parts of the cash budget are now complete: receipts from sales and disbursements for purchases. Other disbursements may be determined more easily than those for purchases. You will remember that variable expenses other than cost of sales are 15% of sales. Assume that one-third is paid in the month of incurrence, and two-thirds in the following month. (The portion paid in the month after incurrence could be for commissions to salespersons, who are paid in one month the commissions they earned in the previous month.) Thus, in each month, cash disbursements related to variable costs are 5% of that month's sales, plus 10% of the sales of the previous month. A schedule of disbursements, by month, for those variable costs appears in Exhibit 7-3.

Exhibit 7-2 Cash Disbursements for Purchases

	Jan.	Feb.	Mar.	Apr.	May	June	Total
Budgeted purchases	$480	$600	$720	$480	$420	$480	$3,180
Payments	$360	$480	$600	$720	$480	$420	$3,060

Exhibit 7-3 Cash Disbursements—Variable Costs

	Jan.	Feb.	Mar.	Apr.	May	June	Total
5% current month's sales	$20	$30	$ 40	$ 50	$ 60	$ 40	$240
10% previous month's sales	50 [a]	40	60	80	100	120	450
Total	$70	$70	$100	$130	$160	$160	$690

a December accrued expenses, from December 31, 19X3, balance sheet.

Total cash disbursements for variable costs ($690) do not correspond to variable costs on the income statement ($720) because of the timing of the payments. We can explain this difference by considering accrued expenses. Of the January disbursements, $50 was accrued in December. This payment is not an expense in 19X4. At June 30, 19X4, Cross owes $80 for commissions on June sales of $800. The cash payment for June commissions is made in July. The $80 to be paid in July appears as a liability on the balance sheet at June 30.

Suppose that the cash component of fixed costs is paid evenly over the six-month period. Depreciation, a noncash expense, is $120 out of the $240 fixed costs, so the cash portion is $120 ($240 – $120), or $20 per month. The complete cash disbursements budget is shown in Exhibit 7-4.

CASH BUDGET

The data developed above are combined in the tentative cash budget, shown in Exhibit 7-5. The budget is tentative because we will not know, until after preparing this schedule, whether revisions might be necessary because of potential cash shortages.

The total column in Exhibit 7-5 covers the six-month period, so the beginning balance is the balance at December 31, 19X3. Although Cross will complete the period with *much* more cash than it had at the start, the budget reveals that there will be cash deficits in March and April (and a balance of

Exhibit 7-4 Cash Disbursements—All Costs

	Jan.	Feb.	Mar.	Apr.	May	June	Total
For purchases (Exhibit 7-2)	$360	$480	$600	$720	$480	$420	$3,060
Variable costs (Exhibit 7-3)	70	70	100	130	160	160	690
Fixed costs	20	20	20	20	20	20	120
Total	$450	$570	$720	$870	$660	$600	$3,870

Exhibit 7-5 Tentative Cash Budget

	Jan.	Feb.	Mar.	Apr.	May	June	Six Months
Beginning balance	$ 60[a]	$106	$ 8	($136)	($230)	$ 86	$ 60
Collections (Exhibit 7-1)	496	472	576	776	976	1,056	4,352
Total available	556	578	584	640	746	1,142	4,412
Disbursements (Exhibit 7-4)	450	570	720	870	660	600	3,870
Ending balance (deficit)	$106	$ 8	($136)	($230)	$ 86	$ 542	$ 542

a From December 31, 19X3, balance sheet.

only $8 at the end of February) if all goes according to plan. If Cross had prepared a budget only for the entire six-month period, its managers would not have known of the deficits in advance, and would not have been on notice to make plans for dealing with the problem. Cash budgets should therefore be broken down into relatively short periods.

What could Cross do now? It could consider borrowing cash to tide it over the period during which the deficits appear. It could reconsider its inventory policy, reduce its purchases, and consequently reduce its needs for cash. It could also consider policy changes that would accelerate cash collections. But note that both types of policy changes might adversely affect sales.

Assume Cross can borrow cash at 12% interest, and that the firm decides to borrow to offset the expected cash deficits. The cash budget must be revised to incorporate the borrowings and the repayments (including interest). For simplicity, assume that borrowings must take place at the beginning of the month in which they are needed, and that repayments are made at the earliest possible time, which is at the end of a month with a budgeted surplus of cash. (Under these circumstances, a loan must be outstanding for at least two months.) Suppose further that borrowings must be in multiples of $10 and that interest is paid at the time of repayment. Assume also that the firm has a policy of maintaining a minimum cash balance of $50 at all times. (More about such policies later.) A revised cash budget appears in Exhibit 7-6.

Note that the revision of the cash budget requires us to revise the original budgeted income statement because that statement did not include interest expense.

REVISED FINANCIAL STATEMENTS

A revised budgeted income statement for the six-month period is shown in Exhibit 7-7. The income statement shows the interest expense necessary to finance the budgeted level of operations. The exhibit includes a separate pro forma income statement for the first three months of the period so that you may check your understanding, and because a firm ordinarily prepares pro forma statements more frequently than once every six months.

Exhibit 7-6 Revised Cash Budget

		Jan.	Feb.	Mar.	Apr.	May	June	Six Months
	Beginning balance	$ 60	$106	$ 58	$ 54	$ 50	$ 78	$ 60
	Collections	496	472	576	776	976	1,056	4,352
	Total available	556	578	634	830	1,026	1,134	4,412
	Disbursements	450	570	720	870	660	600	3,870
(1)	Indicated balance	106	8	(86)	(40)	366	534	542
(2)	Minimum required cash	50	50	50	50	50	50	50
1 − 2 = (3)	Excess (deficit)	56	(42)	(136)	(90)	316	484	492
(4)	Borrowings		50	140	90			280
(5)	Repayments					(280)		(280)
	Interest					(8)[a]		(8)
4 + 1 − 5 = (6)	Ending balance	$106	58	54	50	78	534	$ 534
	Cumulative borrowing		$ 50	$190	$280	$—0—	$—0—	

a 12% × 4/12 (four months) × $ 50 = $2.00
12% × 3/12 (three months) × $140 = 4.20
12% × 2/12 (two months) × $ 90 = 1.80
$8.00

Exhibit 7-7 Cross Company, Budgeted Income Statements

	Three Months Ending March 31, 19X4	Six Months Ending June 30, 19X4
Sales	$1,800	$4,800
Cost of goods sold (60% of sales)	1,080	2,880
Gross profit	720	1,920
Other variable costs (15% of sales)	270	720
Contribution margin	450	1,200
Fixed operating costs	120	240
Operating income	330	960
Interest expense	2.40[a]	8
Income	$ 327.60	$ 952

a At March 31, loans were outstanding for $190. Accrued interest was:
$ 50 × 2/12 × 12% = $1.00
$140 × 1/12 × 12% = 1.40
Total accrued interest and interest expense $2.40

A pro forma balance sheet for June 30 is shown in Exhibit 7-8. Here again, a pro forma balance sheet at an interim date—March 31—is included to facilitate your understanding and to recognize normal practice. In this instance, one important reason for having pro forma statements (income statement and balance sheet) prior to the end of the six-month period is that the firm has to obtain a short-term loan. A potential lender will want information to help it decide whether Cross can repay the loan and will be interested in whether its managers make good use of budgets. The lender will want to see monthly cash budgets and pro forma statements at least each quarter, if not each month. Later, managers (and lenders) can compare the actual balance sheets at March 31 and June 30 with the pro forma ones to see whether operations are proceeding as planned. For example, suppose the sales forecast proves accurate, but Accounts Receivable are higher than budgeted. This could be a danger signal; if customers pay later than anticipated, the firm could run into a cash shortage. Increasing receivables might also be a sign that the firm is extending credit to less worthy customers in order to meet its sales goals. This could be a costly move; bad debts might result, and the need for financing might increase as well.

MINIMUM-CASH-BALANCE POLICIES

Many companies adopt a policy of maintaining a **minimum cash balance** at all times. The minimum cash balance in our illustration ($50) is assumed.

Exhibit 7-8 Cross Company, Pro Forma Balance Sheets

Assets	As of March 31, 19X4	As of June 30, 19X4
Cash (from cash budget, Exhibit 7-6)	$ 54	$ 534
Accounts receivable (credit sales for month plus 32% of prior month's credit sales)	832	1,024
Inventory (from purchases budget, Exhibit 6-6)	1,320	900
Plant and equipment (beginning balance less depreciation for 3 and 6 months)	540	480
Total assets	$2,746	$2,938
Equities		
Accounts payable (from purchases budget, Exhibit 6-6)	$ 720	$ 480
Accrued expenses (10% of the month's sales)	80	80
Short-term loan (from cash budget, Exhibit 7-6)	190	0
Accrued interest on loan (Exhibit 7-7)	2.40	0
Common stock (beginning balance sheet, page 263)	1,000	1,000
Retained earnings (beginning balance plus income for period)	753.60	1,378
Total equities	$2,746	$2,938

Financial managers devote considerable attention to determining this amount. As with almost all decisions, a tradeoff between two conflicting factors is involved. The lower the minimum required balance, the greater the probability the firm will run out of cash. Remember we are budgeting—dealing with the future and with estimates. If customers pay more slowly than expected, or cash outflows are higher than expected, the firm could run out of cash.

Conflicting with the need to have sufficient cash to pay bills is the concern that idle cash earns no return. The higher the minimum cash balance, the higher the opportunity cost because the firm *could* be investing the cash elsewhere to earn additional income or, perhaps, saving interest costs by retiring outstanding debt. In deciding on a reasonable compromise, the financial manager must weigh carefully the conflicting objectives.

There are some sophisticated techniques, as well as some generally accepted rules, for approaching the problem of determining an optimal minimum cash balance. You will study the topic of determining minimum cash balances in your financial management course(s). For now it is enough to say that many firms set a policy of carrying cash equal to, for example, budgeted cash disbursements for the coming two weeks or month. Under such a policy, the minimum required balances change, depending on budgeted disbursements.

CONCLUDING COMMENTS

You have seen the statements and schedules that make up the comprehensive budget, so now we can point out other advantages of budgeting.

The cash budget and pro forma balance sheets are a basis for asset management. Managers can see that a large amount of cash becomes available at the end of June and they can begin to look for profitable uses for this cash. At the very least, the firm can buy marketable securities like government bonds and earn safe, though low, returns.

Knowing well in advance that extra cash will be needed, the firm is more likely to be able to find financing to carry it over the months in which deficits are budgeted. The firm will be able to explain to potential lenders not only why it needs the money, but also how a loan will be repaid. A firm that does not seek a loan until its cash balance is precariously low may have to pay a higher interest rate—or may not get a loan on any terms.

Our example is much simpler than is the case in practice. If some portion of a company's credit sales will never be collected (become bad debts), the receipts budget must reflect only the expected collections. There could, and probably would, be other receipts and disbursements. For example, many companies receive interest or dividends on investments, and many expenses, such as property taxes and insurance, are not paid monthly. In addition, a firm may be obligated to make periodic interest payments and repayments of outstanding debt and perhaps to pay quarterly dividends.

Perhaps the single most commonly found item missing from our example is expenditures for new, long-lived assets. Because such expenditures are usually relatively large, their inclusion is critical if the budget is to fulfill its functions of identifying the timing of financial needs and providing a realistic picture of planned activities. It is simple to incorporate the expenditures for major investments into the cash budget once managers have decided what investments are to be made. Making those decisions is not quite so simple, and the next two chapters consider the analyses that managers use to make them. At this point, you need only recognize that a firm's budget is not complete without including budgeted expenditures for new assets, as well as the means for financing those expenditures.

Cross Company, the firm in the illustration, is a retailer. Chapter 6 showed that developing a budget for a manufacturer is more complex than for a nonmanufacturer, but that the principles are virtually the same. For example, as we showed in Chapter 6, the production budget for Brandon Company, a manufacturer, is very similar to the purchases budget for a retailer. If we know when the costs of production are paid, we can easily compute cash requirements for production. Let us continue the example started on page 239 with Brandon showing a production budget as follows.

Month	No. of Units Produced
January	340
February	280
March	336

Production costs are as follows: materials at $4 per unit, other variable costs at $4 per unit, and fixed costs of $1,900.

Suppose Brandon is a JIT manufacturer, rather than a conventional manufacturer and so acquires materials as it needs them and keeps no material inventory. Neither the just-in-time philosophy, nor having zero inventory implies anything about the timing of payments for purchases. So, let us assume also that materials are paid for in the month after purchase and that Brandon pays other cash production costs in the month incurred. Assume further that December production was 300 units. (Why must we make some assumption about December production?) The cash disbursements budget for manufacturing costs appears below.

	Jan.	Feb.	Mar.
Units produced	340	280	336
Cash disbursements:			
Materials ($4 × prior month's production)	$1,200	$1,360	$1,120
Other variable costs ($4 × current production)	1,360	1,120	1,344
Fixed costs	1,900	1,900	1,900
Total	$4,460	$4,380	$4,364

The totals from the above schedule will be included in the computation of total disbursements for Brandon's cash budget, and the remainder of the budget package will be completed accordingly.

In principle, there is little difference between the budgets for the retailer and the manufacturer. In practice, the manufacturer's budget is likely to be more complicated. For example, individual production costs can have different payment schedules, and the materials used for production may have to be purchased in advance of production needs. Normally, a separate materials-purchases budget, such as the one in the example on page 240, is the basis for scheduling cash disbursements for materials.

ANNUAL AND LONG-TERM BUDGETS

Managers use some of the techniques of financial statement analysis to assist them in budgeting for longer periods and in assessing long-term asset requirements and financing requirements—long-term debt and stockholders' equity. Long term usually means more than one year.

ASSET REQUIREMENTS

We have shown how operating and financing budgets relate to each other in the short term. Using budgeted sales and expected relationships of certain assets to sales, we developed budgets of purchases and pro forma balance sheets showing budgeted amounts of cash, accounts receivable, and inventory. What was shown on the asset side of those balance sheets was essentially a statement of *asset requirements*—the amounts of various assets required to enable the firm to meet its goals of sales and income. We also said that a firm might have to reconsider its sales and profit goals if it could not obtain the financing needed to carry its planned levels of assets.

Managers make similar analyses when developing **long-term budgets.** If the firm forecasts increasing sales, it must also plan for the assets needed to support those planned levels of sales. Sales can seldom be increased significantly without providing additional production capacity and allowing receivables to increase. In many situations, significantly higher sales cannot be achieved without stocking more inventory. Moreover, the desired minimum cash balance will probably increase with higher sales volume.

In the long term, expected sales levels usually dictate the necessary levels of assets. Hence, firms normally use ratios of various assets to sales to determine the required amounts of those assets. Recognize, however, that the analyses undertaken and numbers used for long-term budgeting are less precise than when budgeting for the shorter term. Moreover, there is more opportunity for circumstances to change. When developing long-term plans, managers try to allow for changes in selling prices, purchase costs, and general economic conditions, but such changes are extremely hard to predict over relatively long periods. Hence, the predictions are fairly general, with managers trying to see what the firm's needs will be in broad terms. As time passes, managers refine their budgets of asset needs.

FINANCING REQUIREMENTS

A firm requires financing, in the form of liabilities or stockholders' equity, because it needs assets to generate sales. The need for assets creates *financing requirements*—the need for the items listed on the equity side of the balance sheet. Items on the equities side of the balance sheet are often referred to as the *sources* of the assets. As the need for assets increases because of increased sales, so does the need for sources to finance them. A few sources of financing are available almost automatically. For example, few firms pay cash on delivery of merchandise; most buy on credit. A vendor who extends credit is, in effect, providing a short-term loan—a source of financing. Similarly, when a firm earns income and does not distribute assets to its owners in an amount equal to net income, retained earnings increase. Thus, increases in retained earnings are also sources of financing.

Few firms can meet all their financing needs through funds provided by operations and trade creditors. If firms use short-term loans too liberally, and the current ratio (current assets/current liabilities) gets too low, creditors will be reluctant to lend to the firm. Thus, growing firms will need to seek long-term financing.

For long-term financing, firms issue long-term debt or additional stock. They can also lease assets. A growing firm generally requires higher and higher levels of assets to support its increased sales and so needs more financing than a firm that is not growing. We have already noted that a firm not able to obtain the loan needed to support its short-term requirements might have to scale down its purchases of goods, and that this could, in turn, reduce sales and profits. The same situation occurs in long-term budgeting. A firm might not be able to obtain the long-term financing to support the asset levels necessary to reach the projected sales levels.

Managers know that advance planning is needed to obtain both short- and long-term financing. We noted earlier that the balance of current assets and current liabilities was important to potential providers of short-term loans. The focus of interest for potential long-term lenders is the balance between long-term debt and equity capital. Those lenders are likely to expect a borrower to maintain some minimum ratio of long-term debt to equity (long-term liabilities/stockholders' equity), with the magnitude of the ratio dependent on various characteristics of the borrower. Hence, a firm must first study its long-term financing needs as a whole, and then pursue specific types and sources of long-term financing with those expectations in mind.

ILLUSTRATIONS OF ANNUAL AND LONG-TERM BUDGETS

Two types of procedures are used in budgeting for long periods: those that are used for a one-year period and those that are more appropriate for three- to five-year periods broken down into annual periods. Differences between the two types are primarily matters of detail; the composition of assets and equities for a one-year budget is more detailed than that for longer periods.

ANNUAL BUDGETS

Strand Company, a manufacturer of electrical equipment, had the following income statement for 19X3.

Sales	$800,000
Variable costs at 60%	480,000
Contribution margin	320,000
Fixed costs	240,000
Income	$ 80,000

Strand's balance sheet at the end of 19X3 follows. We include the percentages of current assets and current liabilities to sales because we will use them to develop the December 31, 19X4, pro forma balance sheet.

Increasing globalization has multiplied business opportunities and available sources of lending, both short-term and long-term. Choices are becoming more complicated and bring with them additional questions. Foreign operations present special problems in financing. Should they borrow locally or in their home country? The financial managers' expectations about exchange rates and inflation and their willingness to take on risk are important factors. High inflation in the foreign country makes borrowing cheaper than the interest rate indicates. Of course, lenders who expect inflation will build it into interest rates, so the combination of interest rate and expected inflation is important. Thus, we cannot say it is better to borrow in the U.S. at a 10% interest rate than in Argentina at a 40% rate. High inflation in Argentina could well make it cheaper to borrow there.

Currency translation is another problem common to all businesses that operate in foreign countries. One aspect of the problem is that changes in exchange rates cause gains and losses in the home currency. Another is that translating financial statements and other performance reports from one currency to another can distort performance. For example, Monsanto, the giant chemical company, found that currency shifts distorted decisions and hurt its allocations of capital. The company now uses hedges and options to reduce its exposure.*

*Gregory J. Millman, "Currency Risk at Monsanto," Management Accounting, April, 1991, 43.

Assets			Percentage of Sales
Cash		$ 40,000	5.0%
Accounts receivable		120,000	15.0%
Inventory		60,000	7.5%
Total current assets		220,000	27.5%
Plant and equipment, net		600,000	
Total assets		$820,000	
Equities			
Current liabilities		$ 80,000	10.0%
Long-term liabilities		100,000	
Total liabilities		180,000	
Common stock	$500,000		
Retained earnings	140,000	640,000	
Total equities		$820,000	

Strand's managers forecast a 10% increase in sales for 19X4. They expect current assets and current liabilities at the end of 19X4 to bear the same percentage relationships to sales that they did at the end of 19X3. They also expect variable costs to be the same percentage of sales as they were in 19X3 and total fixed costs to increase to $260,000. They budget net plant and equipment at $720,000 at the end of 19X4. They do not expect to pay a dividend in 19X4.

The budgeted income statement for 19X4 is necessary for us to determine retained earnings, a significant source of financing, at the end of 19X4.

Sales ($800,000 × 110%)	$880,000
Variable costs at 60%	528,000
Contribution margin	352,000
Fixed costs	260,000
Income	$ 92,000

We now determine the asset requirements at the end of 19X4. The current assets are simply the percentages of sales from the 19X3 balance sheet multiplied by 19X4 budgeted sales.

Assets		Percentage of Sales
Cash	$ 44,000	5.0%
Accounts receivable	132,000	15.0%
Inventory	66,000	7.5%
Total current assets	242,000	27.5%
Plant and equipment, net	720,000	
Total asset requirements	$962,000	

The following schedule shows the available financing to support the asset requirements. Current liabilities are at the same percentage of sales as they were in 19X3. Long-term liabilities and common stock are at their 19X3 levels. Retained earnings is the $140,000 beginning balance plus the $92,000 income budgeted for 19X4.

Equities			Percentage of Sales
Current liabilities		$ 88,000	10.0%
Long-term liabilities		100,000	
Total liabilities		188,000	
Common stock	$500,000		
Retained earnings	232,000	732,000	
Total available equities		$920,000	

The $42,000 difference between Strand's asset requirements ($962,000) and its available equities ($920,000) is called a **financing gap.** What can Strand do about the gap?

Strand has several options. If it makes no plans to cover the gap, cash at the end of 19X4 will be $2,000 (the budgeted $44,000 - $42,000), and Strand might be unable to pay a bill when due or to meet a payroll. Alternatively, Strand might plan some actions to reduce its current asset requirements. For example, Strand might require speedier payment of receivables or carry a smaller inventory. It might also decide to pay current liabilities more slowly or to postpone some of its capital expenditures. Strand could also decide to cover all or part of the financing gap by using additional financing, either debt or equity.

Each of these actions has potential problems. Reducing asset requirements could hamper the company's ability to generate sales and profits. Slower payment of liabilities could harm the company's credit rating.

Obtaining additional financing might be very costly because of unfavorable conditions in the economy. Strand's managers must evaluate all of the options and decide what risks they are willing to accept.

It is possible, of course, that an analysis of expectations and plans for asset requirements and available equities will reveal that available equities exceed asset requirements. In such cases, managers should plan how to use the excess cash. Some possibilities are paying dividends, reducing long-term debt, and making other investments.

LONG-TERM PLANNING

In the previous section we prepared a pro forma balance sheet to see whether Strand could meet its objectives for the year. Doing the same for a longer term usually involves preparing a series of schedules containing summary information about asset requirements and available financing.

Long-term planning is mostly concerned with developing plans for expanding long-term debt and equity capital to meet financing requirements. The choice between debt and equity can be critical for the company, and most companies adopt some policy about how much debt they will allow. The policy is often stated as a maximum percentage of long-term liabilities to stockholders' equity, or to total long-term financing (long-term liabilities and stockholders' equity). The advantages and disadvantages of particular kinds of financing are studied in managerial finance. Here, we say only two things: (1) debt can be risky because failing to meet the periodic interest payments can cause bankruptcy; (2) equity financing is less risky but can lead to lower returns.

We illustrate long-term planning by using the following data, assumptions, and policies of Klep Company.

Sales forecast in 19X4	$ 800,000
19X5	$1,000,000
19X6	$1,300,000
19X7	$1,700,000
19X8	$2,100,000
Stockholders' equity 12/31/X3	$ 412,000

Net income is expected to be 10% of sales over the period of the forecast.

Dividends of 40% of net income will be paid each year.

Current asset requirements are expected to be 30% of sales budgeted for the following year.

Net fixed assets expected to be required to meet budgeted sales are 75% of sales budgeted for the following year.

Desired current ratio of 3 to 1, so that current liabilities cannot exceed one-third of current assets.

Desired ratio of long-term debt to equity of 0.5 to 1 (long-term liabilities cannot exceed 50% of stockholders' equity).

These data are the bases of Exhibits 7-9 and 7-10, which determine year-by-year financing requirements. Exhibit 7-9 shows the analysis for 19X4 and 19X5 and how the numbers were derived. See if you can complete the rest of the table. (Answers appear in Exhibit 7-10.) Such a schedule gives the manager an idea of future financing needs.

Exhibit 7-9 Financing Requirements for Klep Company (in thousands of dollars)

		19X4	19X5	19X6	19X7
	(1) Sales	$800	$1,000	$1,300	$1,700
(1) × 10%	(2) Net income	80	100		
(2) × 40%	(3) Dividends	32	40		
(2) − (3)	(4) Add to stockholders' equity	$ 48	$ 60		
(1) for next year × 30%	(5) Current assets required	$300	$ 390		
(5) ÷ 3	(6) Permissible current liabilities	100	130		
(5) − (6)	(7) Working capital to be financed from long-term sources	200	260		
(1) for next year × 75%	(8) Net fixed assets required	750	975		
(7) + (8)	(9) Total long-term financing required	950	1,235		
	(10) Stockholders' equity [prior year plus (4)]	460	520		
(10) × 50%	(11) Permissible long-term debt	230	260		
(10) + (11)	(12) Total available long-term financing	690	780		
(9) − (12)	(13) Additional requirements	$260	$ 455		

Klep's managers can now direct their efforts to devising a plan for obtaining the financing to satisfy line (13), Additional requirements. For several reasons it is generally expensive and undesirable to obtain equity financing frequently. Therefore, the firm might plan to obtain enough funds from issuing common stock in 19X4 to enable it to finance without additional debt until 19X8. Funds received in excess of current needs might be invested or used to retire existing debt. As needs become more pressing, additional debt could be issued up to the limit prescribed by the 0.5 to 1 debt/equity ratio.

BUDGETING IN NOT-FOR-PROFIT ENTITIES

Not-for-profit entities, especially governmental units, make extensive use of budgeting, but the budgeting process is not usually of the type described earlier. First, such entities are likely to budget only for cash flows (expenditures and receipts), not for revenues and expenses. Second, the process is more likely to begin with expenditures rather than receipts. That is, in most cases, the problem is to determine what receipts are required to support the budgeted level of expenditures, as opposed to what costs will be incurred as a result of the budgeted level of revenues.

Exhibit 7-10 Financing Requirements for Klep Company (in thousands of dollars)

		19X4	19X5	19X6	19X7
	(1) Sales	$800	$1,000	$1,300	$1,700
(1) × 10%	(2) Net income	80	100	130	170
(2) × 40%	(3) Dividends	32	40	52	68
(2) − (3)	(4) Add to stockholders' equity	$ 48	$ 60	$ 78	$ 102
(1) for next year × 30%	(5) Current assets required	$300	$ 390	$ 510	$ 630
(5) ÷ 3	(6) Permissible current liabilities	100	130	170	210
(5) − (6)	(7) Working capital to be financed from long-term sources	200	260	340	420
(1) for next year × 75%	(8) Net fixed assets required	750	975	1,275	1,575
(7) + (8)	(9) Total long-term financing required	950	1,235	1,615	1,995
	(10) Stockholders' equity [prior year plus (4)]	460	520	598	700
(10) × 50%	(11) Permissible long-term debt	230	260	299	350
(10) + (11)	(12) Total available long-term financing	690	780	897	1,050
(9) − (12)	(13) Additional requirements	$260	$ 455	$ 718	$ 945

Budgets for not-for-profit entities are less geared to activity levels than are budgets for businesses. Nevertheless, budget allowances for some cost categories can be determined by activity analysis. For example, a university might budget faculty positions by applying some formula based on student enrollment. Thus, an academic department might be given one position for each 300 credit hours expected to be taught. If the department is expected to teach 2,800 credit hours during the coming year, it will be authorized 9 1/3 positions (2,800/300). The one-third position would probably be filled by part-time instructors.

Budgeting cash receipts for not-for-profit entities can be relatively simple or quite complex. School districts and some municipalities like towns and cities rely chiefly on property taxes. Property taxes are levied based on the assessed valuation of real property (land and buildings) in the area. Once the total assessed valuation is known, the entity can set the tax rate simply by dividing the required revenues by the assessed valuation. If a school district requires $4,580,000 in revenues and the assessed valuation of property in the district is $54,000,000, the rate is 0.08482 ($4,580,000/$54,000,000), which is usually reported as $84.82 per $1,000 of assessed value. Because the required revenue is determined on the basis of the budgeted expenditures, careful planning and monitoring of budgeted expenditures is especially important in not-for-profit entities. A legal requirement that limits the tax-rate increase in any year can trigger the same reconsideration of plans forced on business enterprises whose asset requirements exceed available financing.

For government units that depend heavily on income and sales taxes, as do most states, determining required tax rates is more complex because revenue estimates require estimates of total incomes subject to the income tax and of transactions subject to the sales tax. Forecasting methods such as those described in Chapter 6 may be used, and states have developed and used very sophisticated forecasting models.

The problems of developing receipts budgets for nongovernmental not-for-profit entities are more related to those of business entities. The variety of such entities rivals the variety of business entities, and the need for forecasts of revenue-related factors is at least as important. For example, tuition charges in a private school are set based on forecasts of enrollments and contributions, and a hospital sets charges for its various services by forecasting expected utilization. All the forecasting methods discussed in Chapter 6 are used in making such forecasts.

Government units like towns, states, school districts, and the federal government usually require voter or legislative approval of their budgets. Once adopted, the budget must be strictly adhered to and overspending may even be illegal. In addition, budget authorizations tend to be on a line-by-line basis. That is, specific amounts are authorized for specific categories of expenditures, such as salaries, equipment, supplies, travel, and postage. (The detail in such budgets can be overwhelming, with specified amounts for categories such as Grade II Typists and Grade IV Carpenters.) A budgeting process that includes a line-by-line approval procedure tends to have two major disadvantages in practice.

One problem with the line-by-line approval process is that a manager often cannot exercise discretion in using the total budgeted funds to achieve the expected objectives. This inflexibility can lead to actions inconsistent with the entity's objectives. For example, suppose that an accounting instructor in a public university is invited to a seminar on a contemporary accounting topic. The dean and faculty are in favor of the trip, but the travel budget is exhausted. Even if funds remain in the budget allowances for supplies, or telephone or secretarial help, the trip cannot be authorized. The problem lies in the concentration on individual budget items rather than on the objectives to be accomplished.

Another problem associated with line-by-line approval is that it tends to encourage the setting of current budget allowances based on prior year's (or an average of prior years') budget allowances or actual expenditures for each item. This general approach is called **incremental budgeting.** Under this approach, each department might be given a 5% increase (or decrease) in one or more of its line items. In a somewhat broader application of incremental budgeting, each department might be given a 5% increase (or decrease) and allowed to spread the total increase (or decrease) over whatever items are available. Either variation ignores the question of objectives. More important, either variation assumes that the increased (or decreased) benefits of changes in one segment of the total entity are equal to the increased (or decreased) benefits of any other segment. Further, when the current budget allowance is based on prior expenditures, there is a tendency for budget units to spend right up to the allowance in order to avoid cuts in the next period's budget. With some regularity, the media have reported particularly interesting examples, such as an end-of-year purchase of a five-year supply of toilet tissue or wastebaskets.

We hasten to point out that neither line-item budgeting nor incremental budgeting is unique to not-for-profit entities. Many businesses also use these techniques, especially in areas of discretionary spending, like employee training, and some general and administrative areas.

Recent years have seen increasing attention focused on the problems of budgeting in government and other not-for-profit entities. The next section discusses two alternative budgeting approaches, zero-based budgeting and program budgeting, which have been suggested as possible means of alleviating some of the problems.

ZERO-BASED BUDGETING

Strictly interpreted, **zero-based budgeting** means that managers must justify every dollar they request in a budget proposal for a given year. Past budget allowances are irrelevant, and managers must start from scratch to convince higher-level managers that the current request is necessary. In a strict but practical application of the zero-base concept, each budget unit develops its budget request as a series of **decision packages.** The most basic of the unit's services constitutes the first package, and incremental packages represent higher levels of service and/or additional services. A critical aspect of the decision packages is that each is associated with a *definable* level or quantity of services.

Higher-level managers perform cost-benefit analysis and exercise their judgment about the organization's needs, to evaluate and rank the packages from all units. The final budget might include the basic packages from all budget units, plus some incremental packages. This approach helps to circumvent any assumption that increased (or decreased) expenditures in all units are equally beneficial (or harmful) to the entire organization. Moreover, forcing managerial review of even the most basic functions of a budget unit may help to show that some budget unit has outlived its usefulness. (That is, managers might conclude, after reviewing all the decision packages and considering the quantity of potentially available resources, that the most basic service level of a particular budget unit contributes less to achieving desired goals than do higher-than-basic service levels in other units.)

Because a full review of each and every budget request every year is incredibly time-consuming, most organizations require such a review of some, or all, budget units only every few years. But the goals of these periodic reviews are the same as under the more strict application of the zero-base concept: to make sure that there is still a need to spend money for a particular service, and that the money being spent is being spent wisely. Sunset legislation, which requires that each program or regulatory agency approved by the legislature receive a full, regular review and be dropped if it has served its purpose, is a variation of this second approach to the implementation of zero-based budgeting.

PROGRAM BUDGETING

Program budgeting requires that a budget indicate not only how the requested funds are to be spent, but also *why* the funds are to be spent. A program budget emphasizes the desired results of the unit's efforts and normally provides the unit's manager with considerable discretion in shifting expenditures from one category to another as long as the shift will increase the likelihood of achieving the desired results. For instance, a traditional budget for a school district shows the objects of the expenditures, such as teachers' salaries, textbooks, and supplies. A program budget for the district shows expenditures by such categories as reading, mathematics, remedial work, student activities, and support services. Similarly, a program budget for a police department might show amounts requested for crime prevention, juvenile work, and detection.

Budgeting by program should permit the people who supervise the spending (the citizens, the contributors, etc.) to make better decisions about the use of resources. One feature of program budgeting that should be particularly beneficial is that managers making budget requests are expected to be able to state clearly what would happen if their requests were cut by, say, 10%. Thus, the director of parks and recreation for a city should be in a position to say that such a cut would reduce the hours that a swimming pool would be open or require that grass be cut every ten days instead of once a week. This feature of program budgeting is, in its result, similar to what can be accomplished with zero-based budgeting, in that different levels of service are associated with each level of requested funding.

The interest in and use of program and zero-based budgeting probably owes much to an increasing public demand for accountability from not-for-profit organizations. Taxpayers appear to have become dissatisfied with the performance of some government units, and donors to charitable causes have expressed concern about the proportion of contributed funds devoted to administrative expenses. Program budgets that specify goals allow people to see where their money is going and, eventually, to see whether it was spent effectively. (If a school district requests money "to raise the average reading levels of its pupils," board members can later see whether the levels rose.)

Both program and zero-based budgeting are applicable to business entities as well as not-for-profit organizations. Corporate executives have, for example, adopted variations of these alternative budgeting approaches for all or some portions of their organizations because of their increasing concern with the productivity of research and development, general administration, and other such activities. In the typical business use, however, program budgets are developed *in addition to,* rather than as a substitute for, more traditional budgets.

SUMMARY

Comprehensive budgeting brings together and coordinates the plans of many managers and many levels of management. A comprehensive budget is the most conspicuous process of communication within a firm, and facilitates the coordination of major functional areas—production, sales, finance, and administration.

Like operating budgets, financial budgets use forecasts and assumptions about the behavior of the various factors incorporated in them. Financial budgeting involves developing detailed budgets of cash receipts and cash disbursements and a pro forma balance sheet. The cash budgets use data from purchases and expense budgets and from the pro forma income statement. Hence, effective financial budgeting depends on good operational budgeting.

Once the preliminary cash budget is completed, it may become apparent that additional financing is needed. Managers can then plan in advance to meet this need.

Financial budgets are often prepared for relatively long periods. Such budgets are less precise than those prepared for the short term, but they can still assist managers in assessing long-term asset and financing requirements.

Budgeting takes place in not-for-profit entities as well as businesses. Although many of the same principles apply, there are some differences. The most significant difference is that not-for-profit entities normally budget receipts based on budgeted expenditures, while business entities budget expenditures based on budgeted receipts. Two additional budgeting approaches, program and zero-based budgeting, have been introduced for government units, to help offset the tendency in not-for-profit budgeting to concentrate on detailed expenditures rather than on objectives. Businesses also use variations of these approaches.

KEY TERMS

- cash budget
- decision package
- financing gap
- incremental budgeting
- long-term budget
- minimum cash balance
- pro forma balance sheet
- program budgeting
- zero-based budgeting

REVIEW PROBLEM

This problem continues the review problem from Chapter 6. Using the following additional data, prepare a cash budget for January 19X4 and a pro forma balance sheet for January 31, 19X4. Prepare supporting budgets for cash receipts and cash disbursements.

Exempli Company
Balance Sheet at December 31, 19X3

Assets		Equities	
Cash	$ 20,000	Accounts payable	
Accounts receivable	30,000	(for merchandise)	$ 12,000
Inventory (6,000 units)	30,000	Common stock	200,000
Building and equipment, net	200,000	Retained earnings	68,000
Total	$280,000	Total	$280,000

1. Sales are collected 40% in month of sale, 60% in the following month.
2. Purchases are paid 40% in month of purchase, 60% in the following month.
3. All other expenses requiring cash are paid in the month incurred.
4. The board of directors plans to declare a $3,000 dividend on January 10, payable on January 25.
5. The budgeted income statement and purchases budget from the solution in Chapter 6 are given below for convenience.

Exempli Company
Budgeted Income Statement for January 19X4

Sales		$100,000
Cost of sales		25,000
Gross profit		75,000
Variable costs:		
Commissions	$10,000	
Other variable expenses	5,000	15,000
Contribution margin		60,000
Fixed costs:		
Depreciation	2,000	
Other operating expenses	40,000	42,000
Budgeted income		$ 18,000

Purchases Budget for January 19X4

Cost of sales	$25,000
Desired ending inventory	45,000
Total requirements	70,000
Beginning inventory	30,000
Budgeted purchases	$40,000

ANSWER TO REVIEW PROBLEM

Cash Budget

Beginning balance	$20,000
Receipts (see below)	70,000
Cash available	90,000
Disbursements	86,000
Ending balance	$ 4,000

Cash Receipts Budget

Collection from December sales	$30,000
Collection from January sales ($100,000 × 40%)	40,000
Total	$70,000

December sales will all be collected by the end of January. Because sales are collected in full by the end of the month following sale, all accounts receivable at the end of a month are expected to be collected in the coming month.

Cash Disbursements Budget

Merchandise ($40,000 × 40%) + $12,000	$28,000
Commissions	10,000
Various operating expenses	45,000
Dividend	3,000
Total	$86,000

Pro Forma Balance Sheet as of January 31, 19X4			
Assets		Equities	
Cash (cash budget)	$ 4,000	Accounts payable [c]	$ 24,000
Accounts receivable [a]	60,000	Common stock	200,000
Inventory (purchases budget)	45,000	Retained earnings [d]	83,000
Building and equipment [b]	198,000		
Total	$307,000	Total	$307,000

a 60% of January sales of $100,000 (40% was collected in January).
b $200,000 beginning balance less $2,000 depreciation expense.
c 60% of January purchases of $40,000 (40% was paid in January).
d Beginning balance of $68,000 plus budgeted income of $18,000 minus dividend of $3,000.

Notice that cash declined by $16,000 (from $20,000 to $4,000), even though income was $18,000. The budgeted cash balance of $4,000 might be too low in management's judgment, and the firm might wish to seek a short-term bank loan.

ASSIGNMENT MATERIAL

QUESTIONS FOR DISCUSSION

7-1 Cash budgeting—effects of new information You are controller of a large manufacturer and have recently completed your cash budget for the coming year. Knowledgeable managers have now provided you with new information. Considering each item of information independently, indicate (1) whether you expect it to influence your budgets for cash receipts, cash disbursements, or both, and (2) in which direction each budget would be affected. Explain your answers.

1. The credit manager informs you that customers are not paying their bills as quickly as usual because of high interest rates.
2. The sales manager informs you that, due to a strike at the plant of a competitor, your firm's sales should be higher than budgeted.
3. The purchasing manager informs you that suppliers, who have been giving your firm 45-day credit, are now requiring payment in 30 days.
4. The vice president of marketing informs you that inventory policy is being changed from the carrying of the next two months' requirements to 80% of the next month's requirements.

7-2 Publication of budgets In financial accounting you learned that a firm's balance sheet and income statement are usually distributed to persons outside the company. A comprehensive budgeting program involves the preparation of the same statements using budgeted data, but budgeted financial statements are not normally made available to persons outside the organization. Do you see any advantages to publishing these budgeted statements as part of the annual reports? Do you see any disadvantages?

7-3 "Something is enough" The owner of a small chain of shoe stores is dissatisfied with the request from his budget director that he establish a policy regarding a minimum acceptable cash balance. "I see no reason for such a policy," he said. "As long as the monthly budgets show that we can expect to have some cash on hand at the end of the month, why put still another assumption into the budget? There are far too many assumptions in the budget already." Comment on the owner's position.

7-4 ***Philanthropy or business sense?*** Many public utilities offer "level-payment plans" for their customers. For example, individuals purchasing natural gas for heating purposes from Consumers Power in Michigan, and individuals purchasing electricity from Texas Electric Service Companies, have the opportunity to spread the payments for their purchases over the entire year. The normal plan is for a given month's payment to be 1/12 of the total cost of service provided in the 12 months ending with the current month.

Required

Discuss the reasons for a company to offer a level-payment plan.

7-5 ***Impact of policy changes on comprehensive budgets*** For many years, advertisements for VanZandt Foods, a grocery chain, have emphasized the high quality of its produce and the firm's top managers have required that local store managers either trash day-old produce or sell it to the highest bidder in the local area. After studying a proposal submitted by the national council of community food banks, VanZandt's top managers decided that directing store managers to donate day-old produce to a local food bank would be in the firm's best interests. What aspects of the firm's comprehensive budget would be affected by this change in policy?

7-6 Behavior of cash balances and profit Randolph Growing and Harry Declining were talking about the performances of their respective companies in recent months.

Growing: We are making profits hand over fist because of rapid increases in monthly sales. We expected growth and have been keeping our inventories up to meet the increasing demand. But, our cash balances have been a problem and we have borrowed a lot of money lately.

Declining: Things have not been going as well for us. We have entered our slow season, and sales have been falling. Of course, we knew it would happen and planned accordingly. We are not making much profit, but do we have cash. Our balance has risen every month.

Required

Explain why cash is going in the opposite direction from profit for each of these companies.

EXERCISES

7-7 ***Cash receipts budget (continuation of 6-8 and 6-9)*** Gentry Company collects 40% of its sales in the month of sale and 60% in the following month. Receivables at the end of April were $122,000.

Required

Prepare cash receipts budgets for May and for June.

7-8 *Cash budget (extension of 7-7)* Gentry Company pays for its purchases in the month after purchase. Accounts payable for merchandise at the end of April were $185,000. Variable costs other than for cost of sales are paid as incurred, as are fixed costs requiring cash disbursement. The cash balance at the beginning of May is $30,000.

Required

1. Prepare cash disbursements budgets for May and for June.
2. Prepare cash budgets for May and for June.

7-9 *Cash receipts budget* Jasica Company expects the following sales for the first six months of 19X7, in thousands of dollars.

	Jan.	Feb.	Mar.	Apr.	May	June
Budgeted sales	$1,600	$2,200	$1,100	$900	$1,600	$2,900

Cash collections expectations are as follows: 2% of sales become bad debts, 30% of sales are collected in the month of sale, 40% in the first month after sale, and 28% in the second month after sale. Sales in November 19X6 were $800,000 and in December, $1,200,000.

Required

Prepare a cash receipts budget for the five-month period ending May 31, 19X7, by month.

7-10 *Production and cash disbursements budgets* The following data relate to Corr Company and its single product, a desk lamp.

(a) Sales forecast, January through April, 19X9 (in units): 1,300; 1,600; 2,100; and 2,400.
(b) Inventory policy: inventory is maintained at 150% of budgeted sales needs for the coming month.
(c) Cost data: materials, $6 per unit; direct labor, $10 per unit; and variable overhead, $5 per unit. Monthly fixed costs are $15,000, including $3,000 depreciation.
(d) Corr uses some JIT principles. It purchases materials daily and pays for them as delivered; all other costs requiring cash disbursements are also paid as incurred.
(e) The beginning inventory for January is 1,800 units.

Required

1. Prepare a production budget for each of the first three months of 19X9.
2. Prepare a cash disbursements budget for each of the first three months of 19X9.

7-11 *Cash receipts and cash budget (continuation of 7-10)* The lamp sells for $40 per unit. All sales are on account with 30% collected in the month of sale, 70% in the month after sale. Receivables at December 31, 19X8 were $41,000.

Required

1. Prepare a schedule of budgeted cash receipts for each of the first three months of 19X9.
2. Prepare a cash budget for each of the first three months of 19X9. Cash at January 1 is $18,000.

7-12 *Cash budget (continuation of 6-10)* Jordan Clothing pays for its purchases 40% in the month of purchase and 60% in the following month. Its accounts payable at December 31, 19X8, were $18,000. It collects 60% of its sales in the month of sale and 40% in the following month. Receivables at December 31, 19X8, to be collected in January, were $30,000. All of its fixed costs require cash disbursements and are paid as incurred. Its cash balance at December 31, 19X8, was $20,000.

Required

1. Prepare a cash receipts budget for each of the first three months of 19X9 and for the quarter as a whole.
2. Prepare a cash disbursements budget for each of the first three months of 19X9 and for the quarter as a whole.
3. Prepare a cash budget for each of the first three months of 19X9 and for the quarter as a whole.

7-13 *Pro forma balance sheet (continuation of 7-12)* Jordan Clothing's balance sheet at December 31, 19X8, appears below.

Assets		Equities	
Cash	$20,000	Accounts payable	$18,000
Receivables	30,000		
Inventory	45,000	Stockholders' equity	77,000
Total	$95,000	Total	$95,000

Jordan rents all of its fixed assets.

Required

Prepare a pro forma balance sheet as of March 31, 19X9.

7-14 *Cash budget (continuation of 6-11)* Thomas Company pays for its purchases in the month after purchase. Its accounts payable at December 31, 19X3, were $35,000. It collects 30% of its sales in the month of sale and 70% in the following month. Receivables at December 31, 19X3, to be collected in January, were $63,000. Depreciation is $5,000 per month. All of its other costs require cash disbursements and are paid as incurred. Its cash balance at December 31, 19X3, was $25,000.

Required

1. Prepare a cash receipts budget for each of the first three months of 19X4 and for the quarter as a whole.
2. Prepare a cash disbursements budget for each of the first three months of 19X4 and for the quarter as a whole.
3. Prepare a cash budget for each of the first three months of 19X4 and for the quarter as a whole. If budgeted cash would go below $10,000 assume borrowing and repayments in multiples of $5,000 to maintain at least $10,000. Ignore interest.

7-15 *Pro forma balance sheet (continuation of 7-14)* Thomas Company had the following balance sheet at December 31, 19X3.

Assets		Equities	
Cash	$ 25,000	Accounts payable	$ 35,000
Receivables	63,000		
Inventory	80,000		
Fixed assets, net	150,000	Stockholders' equity	283,000
Total	$318,000	Total	$318,000

Required
Prepare a pro forma balance sheet as of March 31, 19X4.

7-16 Cash budget for a manufacturer (continuation of 6-15, 6-16 and 6-17 and continued in 7-17) HMA Company sells only on credit, collecting 70% in the month after sale and 30% the second month after sale. The company pays for its purchases of materials 60% in the month of purchase and 40% in the following month. It pays other cash manufacturing costs as incurred. Monthly fixed selling and administrative costs, all cash, are also paid as incurred, but sales commissions are paid in the month after a sale occurs. In December of 19X9 HMA declared a $220 dividend that it must pay in January of 19X0.

Required (NOTE: You may need to refer to the data in 7-17 below.)
1. Prepare a cash receipts budget for HMA for January, 19X0.
2. Determine HMA's budgeted accounts receivable at January 31, 19X0.
3. Prepare a cash disbursements budget for HMA for January, 19X0. (See balance sheet in 7-17.)
4. Determine HMA's budgeted accounts payable at January 31, 19X0 for materials purchases.
5. Assuming that HMA has $1,500 cash on hand at December 31, 19X9, prepare a cash budget for January, 19X0.

7-17 Budgeted balance sheet for a manufacturer (continuation of 7-16) Below is HMA's balance sheet at December 31, 19X9.

HMA Company, Balance Sheet as of December 31, 19X9

Assets		Liabilities and Owners' Equity	
Cash	$1,500	Accounts payable for materials	$ 216
Accounts receivable for:		Accrued commissions payable	360
November sales	660	Dividend payable	220
December sales	2,400		
Inventory, materials (34 lbs.)	102	Common stock	5,000
Building, net of depreciation	1,680	Retained earnings	546
Total	$6,342	Total	$6,342

Required
Prepare HMA's budgeted balance sheet at January 31, 19X0.

7-18 Cash budget—quarters Walton Company expects the following results by quarters in 19X4, in thousands of dollars.

	1	2	3	4
Sales	$2,400	$3,000	$3,600	$2,100
Cash disbursements:				
Production costs	1,800	2,800	2,200	1,700
Selling and general costs	400	600	200	320
Acquisitions of fixed assets	0	300	700	400
Dividends	30	30	30	40

The beginning balance in accounts receivable is $700,000. Cash on hand at the beginning of the year is $120,000, and the desired minimum balance is $100,000. Accounts receivable at the end of a quarter are one-third of sales for the quarter. Any borrowings are made at the beginnings of quarters in which the need will occur, in $10,000 multiples, and are repaid at the ends of quarters. Ignore interest.

Required

1. Prepare a cash budget by quarters for the year.
2. What is the loan outstanding at the end of the year?

7-19 ***Pro forma balance sheet*** The controller of Lamb Industries is developing an analysis to see what financing requirements will be at the end of the current year. So far the controller has come up with the following data.

Budgeted Income Statement for Year (in thousands of dollars)

Sales	$2,300
Cost of sales	1,100
Gross profit	1,200
Operating expenses	980
Income	$ 220

Outline of Pro Forma Balance Sheet as of Year End (in thousands of dollars)

Assets		Equities	
Cash	$ 50	Current liabilities	$?
Accounts receivable	?		
Inventory	?	Stockholders' equity	2,590
Plant, net	2,400		
Total	$?	Total	$?

Lamb's experience has been that accounts receivable are typically about 20% of sales and inventory about 40% of cost of sales. The firm expects to have about the same income-statement results for the next few years.

The controller would like to hold current liabilities to about one-half of current assets. The stockholders' equity figure given in the pro forma statement reflects expected profit and dividends for the year.

Required

Determine total asset requirements, total available equities, and the financing gap.

7-20 ***Comprehensive budgeting—selected elements*** Below is BLD Company's pro forma balance sheet at December 31, 19X3.

Balance Sheet Data, 12/31/X3

Assets		Equities	
Cash	$ 35,000	Accounts payable	$ 12,000
Receivables	16,000	Expenses payable	5,000
Inventory	63,000	Bank loan payable	20,000
Property, plant		Common stock	160,000
and equipment, net	116,000	Retained earnings	33,000
Total	$230,000	Total	$230,000

The following information is also available about BLD's plans and operations for 19X4.

- Expected sales for January through May are shown below.

Jan.	$50,000	Mar.	$70,000	May	$65,000
Feb.	$60,000	Apr.	$66,000		

- All sales are on credit and collected 70% in the month of sale and 30% in the month after sale.
- Cost of sales is expected to be 55% of sales.
- BLD's policy is to maintain inventory equivalent to sales requirement expectations for the following two months.
- Variable costs other than cost of sales are 15% of sales, with 40% being paid in the month the costs are incurred, and the remainder paid in the following month.
- Fixed costs are $7,000 per month, including depreciation of $1,000. Cash fixed costs are paid in the month they are incurred.
- BLD plans to declare a $1,800 cash dividend in January, to be paid in February.
- Purchases are all on credit and paid 80% in the month of purchase and 20% in the month after purchase.
- BLD plans to pay $2,200 to its bank in January, representing $2,000 of principal on its loan and $200 of interest.

Required

1. What are BLD's budgeted cash receipts for January of 19X4?
2. What are BLD's budgeted accounts receivable at January 31, 19X4?
3. What is BLD's budgeted inventory for January 31, 19X4?
4. What are BLD's budgeted purchases for January of 19X4?
5. What is BLD's budgeted income for January of 19X4?
6. What balance would BLD report for retained earnings in its pro forma balance sheet for January 31, 19X4?
7. List the purposes and budgeted amounts of all BLD's expected cash disbursements for January of 19X4? (Give supporting computations, if any computations are necessary.)
8. List the names and budgeted amounts of all BLD's budgeted liabilities at January 31, 19X4? (Give supporting computations for your answers, if any computations are necessary.)

PROBLEMS

7-21 ***Basic cash budget*** Before being called out of town on urgent company business, Sandy Banks, the controller of Zonar, Inc., developed the following information for the company's cash budget for the next few months.

	Unit Sales	Unit Production	Materials Purchases
January	1,000	1,400	$130,000
February	1,200	1,600	150,000
March	1,400	1,300	110,000

Zonar's one product, a stereo unit, sells for $600. Customers pay 40% in the month of sale, 60% in the following month. Materials purchases are paid for in the month after purchase. Variable production costs, excluding materials, are $150 per unit of product. Fixed production costs are $150,000 per month, including $30,000 depreciation. Selling and administrative expenses are $40,000 per month, all cash, paid as incurred. Production costs other than those for materials are paid as incurred.

At January 1, the company had $360,000 in accounts receivable from December sales and owed suppliers of materials $500,000. Cash at January 1 was $35,000.

Required

Prepare budgets of cash receipts and disbursements and a cash budget for January and for February. If you show a negative cash balance, assume borrowing to bring it to zero. Ignore any interest.

7-22 ***Comprehensive budget*** Borden Hardware Store is preparing its budgets for 19X7.

Forecasted Sales		Balance Sheet Data December 31, 19X6	
January	$60,000	Cash	$ 8,000
February	80,000	Accounts receivable	24,000
March	70,000	Inventory	54,000
April	90,000	Accounts payable (merchandise)	42,000

Other data are as follows:

(a) Sales are on credit with 40% of sales collected in the month of sale and 60% in the month after sale.
(b) Cost of sales is 60% of sales.
(c) Other variable costs are 10% of sales, paid in the month incurred.
(d) Inventories are to be 150% of next month's budgeted sales requirements.
(e) Purchases are paid for in the month after purchase.
(f) Fixed expenses are $3,000 per month; all require cash.

Required

1. Prepare budgets of purchases for each of the first three months of 19X7.
2. Prepare separate budgets of cash receipts and disbursements and a cash budget for each of the first three months of 19X7.
3. Prepare a budgeted income statement for the three-month period ending March 31, 19X7.

7-23 ***Understanding budgets*** Following are the Blaisdel Company balance sheet at December 31, 19X0, and information regarding the company's policies and past experiences.

Balance Sheet, 12/31/X0

Cash	$ 41,000	Accounts payable	$ 12,000
Inventory	63,000	Income taxes payable	5,000
Receivables	17,000	Common stock	170,000
Fixed assets, net	89,000	Retained earnings	23,000
Total	$210,000	Total	$210,000

Additional information:

1. All sales are on credit and are collected 70% in the month of sale and 30% in the month after sale.
2. Expected sales for January, February, March, April, and May are $50,000, $60,000, $70,000, $66,000, and $65,000, respectively.
3. Inventory is maintained at a level equivalent to the sales requirements for the following two months.
4. Purchases are all on credit and are paid 80% in the month of purchase and 20% in the month after purchase.
5. Other variable costs are 15% of sales and are paid in the month incurred.
6. Fixed costs are $7,000 per month, including $1,000 of depreciation. Cash fixed costs are paid in the month incurred.
7. The firm's income tax rate is 40%, with taxes being paid in the month after they are accrued.
8. Cost of goods sold is expected to be 60% of sales.

Required

1. What are budgeted cash receipts for January 19X1?
2. What is the budgeted inventory at January 31, 19X1?
3. What are budgeted purchases for January 19X1?
4. What is budgeted net income for January 19X1?
5. What is the budgeted cash balance at the end of January 19X1?
6. What are budgeted accounts receivable at February 28, 19X1?
7. What is the budgeted book value of fixed assets at March 31, 19X1?
8. What are budgeted accounts payable at March 31, 19X1?
9. If the company declared a cash dividend of $1,200 during January, payable in February, what would be the balance reported for retained earnings in a pro forma balance sheet as of January 31, 19X1?
10. What amount would show as the liability for income taxes as of March 31, 19X1?

7-24 ***Cash budget for a student*** Bo Phelps is a junior majoring in mathematics at a large university. At the beginning of the school year Bo wants to develop a cash budget for the fall term, which runs from September 1 through November 30. He has collected the following information.

Cash at September 1	$1,250
Tuition, due September 15	2,200
Room rent, due September 15 (for entire term)	800
Cost of meals, per month	250
Clothing expenditures, per month	50
Textbook purchases, due September 15	280

Phelps has been awarded a scholarship of $2,000; the check should arrive by the end of the first week of September. He estimates that expenditures for dates and miscellaneous other items should total about $300 for the term, spread about evenly over each month. He also expects that he can get a part-time job that pays $8 per hour. For the most part, he will be able to set the hours he will work each month. The employer, a local business, must withhold 10% of Phelps' earnings for income and social security taxes.

Required

Determine how many hours Phelps must work each month to be able to maintain a $100 cash balance for emergencies.

7-25 Pro forma financial statements and cash budget for a retailer The expected balance sheet at December 31, 19X1 for Bob's Foods, a specialty retail food store in an affluent suburban area, appears below.

Assets		Liabilities and Owners' Equity	
Cash	$ 42,000	Accounts payable	$ 48,000
Accounts receivable	4,500		
Inventory	14,000	Owners' equity	142,000
Equipment, net	95,000		
Other	34,500		
Total	$190,000	Total	$190,000

Robert Granger, owner of Bob's, has regularly permitted about 4% of the customers to place orders on credit and pay for them in the following month. (These customers account for about 10% of dollar sales.) Late in 19X1, Granger decided to increase the number of customers permitted to order on credit. He made no formal analysis of the likely effects of the decision, but he believes that the store would benefit from expanding credit privileges to include a total of 15% of his customers who account for about 40% of the store's sales. Under Granger's new policy, sales would be 60% for cash and 40% on credit, with credit sales being collected in the month after sale.

Granger has developed or collected the following information to help him prepare a budget for the first quarter of 19X2.

- Estimated sales:

January	$40,000	March	$60,000
February	45,000	April	50,000

- Cost of sales is 70%. Vendors are paid in the month after purchase.
- Variable selling costs are 10% of sales.
- Administrative costs are fixed at $8,000 per month, including $2,500 depreciation.
- Cash operating costs other than for inventory items are paid in the month incurred.

Many suppliers of inventory items deliver at least weekly, but Granger wants to maintain his overall inventory at a 15-days' supply (50% of the next month's sales needs). Because the new credit policy will have a fairly immediate impact on the store's cash balance, Granger is concerned that his cash balance may fall below the $20,000 he considers necessary.

Required

1. Prepare a budgeted income statement for the first quarter of 19X2.
2. Prepare a pro forma balance sheet as of March 31, 19X2.
3. Prepare the firm's cash budget for the first quarter of 19X2. If you prepare a cash budget for each month, do not assume any borrowing should the cash balance fall below $20,000.
4. What time frame do you believe Bob's Foods should use to prepare its cash budget? Explain your answer.

7-26 Comprehensive budget The following data pertain to Elgin's, a specialty store in a large shopping mall.

Sales Forecasts—19X8	
January	$ 80,000
February	90,000
March	110,000
April	120,000
May	100,000

Balance Sheet at December 31, 19X7

Cash	$ 15,000	Accounts payable	$ 28,000
Accounts receivable	60,000	Accrued sales commissions	7,000
Inventory	102,000	Common stock	160,000
Net fixed assets	200,000	Retained earnings	182,000
Total	$377,000	Total	$377,000

Other data are as follows.

(a) All sales are on credit with 40% collected in the month of sale, and 60% in the month after sale.
(b) Cost of sales is 60% of sales.
(c) The only other variable cost is a 7% commission to salespeople that is paid in the month after it is earned. All sales are subject to the commission.
(d) Inventory is kept equal to sales requirements for the next two months' budgeted sales.
(e) Purchases are paid for in the month after purchase.
(f) Fixed costs are $10,000 per month, including $4,000 depreciation.

Required

1. Prepare a budgeted income statement for the three-month period ending March 31, 19X8.
2. Prepare a cash budget for each of the first three months of 19X8 and all necessary supporting budgets.
3. Prepare a pro forma balance sheet as of March 31, 19X8.

7-27 Investing idle cash (extension of 7-26; adapted from a problem prepared by Professor Robert W. Koehler) The president of Elgin's was pleased with the cash budget you prepared, but felt that the firm might be able to invest some of its available cash and thereby earn an additional return. He knows that if the funds are invested in a money market fund the firm will be able to earn 1% per month interest and to withdraw the money at any time. He believes that a $10,000 cash balance is sufficient and asks you to redo the cash budget to reflect the investing of excess cash at 1% per month. (Thus, you can invest $5,000 on January 1, because the $15,000 balance is $5,000 over the required minimum.) Assume that you invest at the ends of months (except for January 1).

Required

Respond to the president's request.

7-28 Municipal budgeting—revenues The City of Wentworth is preparing its budget for 19X9. Total required revenues are $36,000,000. The city has two major sources of revenue, sales taxes and property taxes. The sales tax is 2% of taxable retail sales, which includes virtually all sales except for food and medicine. The assessed valuation of taxable property is $560,000,000. An economist hired by the city has forecast total taxable retail sales at $860,000,000 for 19X9.

Required

1. Determine the property tax rate needed to meet the city's revenue objective, assuming that the estimate of retail sales is correct.
2. The city council is considering a proposal to reduce property taxes on homes owned by people over 65 years of age. It is proposed that the rate on such homes be set at $30 per $1,000 assessed valuation. The total assessed valuation of homes owned by people over 65 is $45,000,000. Determine the rate that would have to be set on the remaining taxable property in order to meet the revenue objective if the proposal is adopted.

7-29 ***Manufacturer's cash budget—three months*** Tompkins Company produces a single product that sells for $15 per unit. Data are:

(a) Variable manufacturing costs, all requiring cash, are $7 per unit.
(b) Variable selling and administrative expenses are $1 per unit.
(c) Fixed manufacturing costs requiring cash are $50,000 per month. Depreciation is $12,000 per month. Fixed selling and administrative expenses are $40,000 per month, all requiring cash.
(d) Tompkins maintains a two-month supply of finished goods. The beginning inventory (January 1) is 42,000 units.
(e) Tompkins has partially implemented JIT principles and therefore buys raw materials as needed, maintaining no inventory. The cost of raw materials is included in the variable manufacturing cost of $7.
(f) Tompkins makes all sales on credit, collecting 30% in the month of sale and 70% in the month after sale. The beginning balance in accounts receivable is $140,000.
(g) All cash manufacturing costs are paid for in the month of production.
(h) Tompkins pays 80% of selling and administrative expenses in the month of sale, 20% in the following month. At January 1 the firm owed $14,000 from December expenses.
(i) The minimum desired cash balance is $40,000, which is also the amount on hand at the beginning of January. If the firm needs to borrow, it does so in multiples of $10,000. It must borrow at the beginning of the month and repay at the end, if sufficient cash is available. The monthly interest rate is 1%, and Tompkins pays interest when it repays loans, or a portion of them.
(j) The sales budget for the first six months is, in units, January, 20,000; February, 26,000; March, 30,000; April, 32,000; May, 30,000; June, 28,000.

Required

1. Prepare a cash budget and any necessary supporting schedules for the first three months of the year, by month and in total.
2. Given your results in item 1, does the firm appear to be profitable? Explain.
3. Suppose that sales stabilized at 25,000 units per month. What will monthly cash collections be? What will monthly cash disbursements for manufacturing costs and for selling and administrative expenses be?

7-30 ***One-month cash budget—discounts*** Stony Acres Department Store makes about 20% of its sales for cash. Credit sales are collected 20%, 30%, 45% in the month of sale, month after, and second month after sale, respectively. The remaining 5% become bad debts. The store tries to purchase enough goods each month to maintain its inventory at 2 1/2 times the following month's budgeted sales needs. All purchases are subject to a 2% discount if paid within ten days and the store takes all discounts. Accounts payable are then equal to one-third of that month's net purchases. Cost of goods sold, without considering the 2% discount, is 60% of selling prices. The firm records inventory net of the discount.

The general manager of the store has asked you to prepare a cash budget for August and you have gathered the following data.

Sales:		
May (actual)	$220,000	
June (actual)	260,000	
July (actual)	300,000	
August (budgeted)	340,000	
September (budgeted)	300,000	
Inventory at July 31, net of discount	455,700	
Cash at July 31	73,000	
Purchases in July (gross)	210,000	
Selling, general, and administrative expenses budgeted for August	102,000	(includes $21,000 depreciation)

The firm pays all of its other expenses in the month incurred.

Required
Prepare a cash budget for August.

7-31 ***Long-range financial budget*** Millard Company has retained you to develop a financing plan for the next few years. You collect the following information about the firm's expectations, goals, and policies. All dollar amounts are in thousands.

Sales Forecasts	
19X4	$ 800
19X5	1,000
19X6	1,250
19X7	1,500

Millard expects a return on sales of 12%. The firm's directors would like to maintain the policy of distributing dividends in an amount equal to 60% of net income each year. The directors would also like to have a current ratio of at least 3 to 1 and do not want long-term liabilities to exceed 60% of stockholders' equity.

Current asset requirements are 30% of expected sales in the coming year, and net fixed assets are 75% of budgeted sales for the coming year. At the end of 19X3, stockholders' equity is $500.

Required
Prepare a schedule showing financing requirements for 19X4, 19X5, and 19X6.

7-32 ***Budgeting equations (CMA adapted)*** Your firm has just acquired a new computer, and one of the first things the president wants to use it for is preparing the comprehensive budget. He assigns you the task of formulating a set of equations that can be used to write a program to perform the computations required for the budgets. You consult with the chief programmer, and the two of you decide that the following notation should be used, which will make it easy for the programmer to prepare the necessary programs.

S_0 = sales in current month (units)
S_1 = sales in coming month (units)

S_{-1} = sales in prior month (units)
S_{-2} = sales in second prior month (units)
P = selling price per unit
CGS = cost of goods sold per unit (purchase price)
OVC = other variable costs per unit
FC = total fixed costs per month
FCC = fixed costs per month requiring cash disbursements
PUR = purchases in current month (units)
PUR_{-1} = purchases in prior month (units)

You examine the records of the firm and decide that the firm's policies or experienced relationships are as follows.

1. Collections on sales are 30% in the month of sale, 50% in the month after sale, and 20% in the second month after sale.
2. Inventory is maintained at twice the coming month's budgeted sales volume.
3. Purchases are paid for 60% in the month after purchase and 40% in the month of purchase.
4. All other costs are paid as incurred.

Required

Prepare equations that can be used to budget for the following.

1. Income for the current month.
2. Cash receipts in current month.
3. Purchases in current month in units.
4. Purchases in current month in dollars.
5. Cash disbursements in current month.

7-33 Comprehensive budget (continuation of 6-48; adapted from a problem prepared by Professor Maurice L. Hirsch) The following additional information about Banana City is available.

1. Sales of bananas are for cash only. Sales of nuts are on credit and are collected two months after sale.
2. Banana City's suppliers give terms of 30 days for payment of accounts payable. Banana City takes full advantage of the 30-day payments. (Assume all months have 30 days.)
3. The firm must make quarterly payments on its income taxes. The payment for the first quarter of fiscal year 19X7 is due on January 15, 19X7. The liability for taxes payable shown on the balance sheet below is to be paid on October 15.
4. Fixed expenses that require cash disbursement are paid as incurred with the following exceptions: (a) insurance premiums are all paid on November 1 in advance for the next 12 months and (b) interest payments are all made on January 1. The $156,000 "other fixed expenses" shown in item 6 of 6-48 all require cash disbursements evenly over the year.
5. The balance sheet at August 31, 19X6 is given below.

Assets		Equities	
Cash	$ 15,000	Accounts payable (merchandise)	$ 26,000
Accounts receivable	75,000	Taxes payable	31,000
Inventories	41,800	Accrued interest	4,000
Prepaid insurance	2,000	Long-term debt, 6%	100,000
Land	8,000	Common stock	150,000
Equipment (net)	210,000	Retained earnings	40,800
Total	$351,800	Total	$351,800

6. Sales in the last part of fiscal year 19X6 are given below.

	June	July	August
Bananas	$31,000	$34,000	$32,500
Nuts	37,000	41,000	34,000

7. The firm expects to pay a dividend of $12,000 in October.

Required
1. Prepare budgets of cash receipts and disbursements for each of the first three months of fiscal year 19X7 and for the quarter as a whole.
2. Prepare a cash budget for the quarter, by month and in total.
3. Prepare a pro forma balance sheet for November 30, 19X6.

7-34 ***Pro forma balance sheet and financing requirements*** Jill Eyre, treasurer of Caldwell Company, has collected the following information as part of her planning. She believes the company will have to issue long-term debt during the year, but she is unsure how much.

Budgeted Income Statement for 19X6	
Sales	$300,000
Cost of goods sold	210,000
Gross profit	90,000
Selling, general, and administrative expenses	36,000
Income before taxes	54,000
Income taxes (40% rate)	21,600
Net income	$ 32,400

Balance Sheet Data, December 31, 19X5	
Common stock	200,000
Retained earnings	83,000

Asset requirements, December 31, 19X6	
Cash—minimum desired balance	$ 25,000
Accounts receivable	30% of sales
Inventory	40% of cost of sales
Plant and equipment—net	$210,000
Equities available:	
Accounts payable	50% of inventory
Income taxes payable	50% of income tax expense

A dividend of $22,000 will be paid during 19X6.

Required
Prepare a statement of asset requirements and available equities as of the end of 19X6. Determine the amount of long-term debt that Caldwell will need at the end of 19X6.

7-35 ***Financing growth*** The controller and treasurer of GlenCo Manufacturing have engaged you to assist them in long-term budgeting.

GlenCo's board of directors has approved a long-term plan that envisions about a 15% annual rate of growth in sales, as reflected in the following sales forecasts, in millions of dollars.

Sales Forecasts	
19X5	$40.0
19X6	46.0
19X7	52.9
19X8	60.8

The best information available indicates that net income will run at 10% of sales.

The directors have imposed some restrictions regarding financing. They wish to continue paying dividends of 40% of net income and want the current ratio to be at least 3 to 1. They also believe that long-term liabilities should not exceed 30% of stockholders' equity.

Current asset requirements generally are about 40% of forecasted sales for the coming year, and net fixed assets are usually about 110% of forecasted sales for the coming year. Stockholders' equity is $32.0 million at the beginning of 19X5.

Required

Prepare a schedule to show the controller and treasurer the financing requirements that GlenCo faces from 19X5 through 19X7. Round to the nearest tenth of a million dollars.

7-36 Comprehensive budget Shown below are the balance sheet of your firm, Arcon Industries, at December 31, 19X5, and its projected income statement for the first three months of 19X6. Happy with the projection, you gloat about it to your banker at lunch. The banker asks if you will need any cash to get through the first quarter. "Of course not" is your reply. Later, back at your office, the chief accountant informs you of the following:

1. Sales are all on credit and are collected 50% in the month of sale, 50% in the month after sale.
2. Although company policy is to maintain inventory equal to the next two months' sales in units, inventory at December 31, 19X5 does not conform to policy because of a recent dock strike.
3. Arcon pays for purchases 50% in the month of purchase, 50% in the following month.
4. Arcon is committed to paying the recorded cash dividend of $2,000 in March.
5. All cash expenses are paid in the month incurred, except for purchases.
6. The monthly breakdown of projected sales is as follows: January, $20,000; February, $30,000; and March, $50,000. In addition, April sales are expected to be $20,000, and May sales, $20,000.
7. Cash should not go below $5,000.

Balance Sheet at December 31, 19X5

Cash	$ 5,000		Accounts payable	$16,000	
Accounts receivable	10,000		Dividend payable	2,000	$18,000
Inventory	24,000	$39,000	Owners' equity		61,000
Plant and equipment, net of accumulated depreciation		40,000			
Total		$79,000	Total		$79,000

Budgeted Income Statement
for the Three Months Ending March 31, 19X6

Sales (10,000 units × $10)		$100,000
Cost of sales (10,000 units × $6)		60,000
Gross profit		40,000
Operating expenses:		
Wages and salaries	$9,000	
Rent	3,000	
Depreciation	3,000	
Other expenses	1,500	16,500
Income		$ 23,500

Required
Do you regret your reply to your banker? Explain by preparing the appropriate schedules. (If borrowings are necessary, assume that they are in $1,000 multiples at the beginning of the month and that repayments are at the ends of months with 12% annual interest on the amount repaid.)

7-37 ***Comprehensive budget (continuation of 6-36)*** The managers of Calco Products Company have the following additional information.

Sales should be collected 30% in the month of sale and 70% in the following month. Purchases are paid 40% in the month of purchase and 60% in the following month. Fixed manufacturing costs include $20,000 per month depreciation. All manufacturing costs requiring cash disbursements are paid as incurred. All selling and administrative expenses require cash disbursements, with 80% paid as incurred, and the remaining 20% paid in the following month. The balance sheet at December 31 appears below.

Balance Sheet as of December 31, 19X5

Assets	
Cash	$ 75,000
Accounts receivable	280,000
Finished goods (35,000 × $14)	490,000
Materials (66,000 × $8)	528,000
Plant and equipment, net	1,200,000
Total assets	$2,573,000
Equities	
Accounts payable	$ 96,000
Accrued expenses	18,000*
Stockholders' equity	2,459,000
Total equities	$2,573,000

* *$12,000 of the total relates to fixed costs.*

Required

1. Prepare cash budgets for January and for February assuming the company desires a minimum cash balance of $60,000 at the end of each month. If operating projections show that borrowing is necessary to meet the minimum balance and cover a month's cash activity, such borrowings occur at the beginning of the month, in multiples of $10,000. Assume that repayments, in multiples of $10,000, are made at the end of the month, as soon as

cash balances permit them. The bank charges interest at 1% per month, but interest payments need to be made only at the time a repayment occurs, and then only for the interest due on the amount being repaid.

2. Prepare a pro forma balance sheet as of the end of February. (Remember that interest accrues on loans outstanding, and that the income statement prepared for 6-36 does not yet reflect interest expense on any borrowed funds.)

7-38 ***Cash budget (continuation of 6-47)*** Richards Company collects its sales 30% in the month of sale, 30% in the next month, and 40% in the second month after sale. Fixed production costs not requiring cash are $40,000 per month. All selling, general, and administrative expenses require cash and are paid in the month incurred, except for sales commissions, which are paid in the month after incurrence.

All production costs requiring cash are paid 80% in the month of production and 20% in the month after production. This includes payments for materials, of which no inventory is kept since they are delivered daily.

Selected balance sheet data at May 31 are as follows.

Cash	$120,000	(equals the desired minimum balance)
Accounts receivable:		
From May sales	336,000	
From April sales	120,000	
Liabilities:		
Sales commissions	48,000	
Production costs	66,000	

Required

Prepare a cash budget for Richards Company for the first three months of the fiscal year, by month. If the need arises, show borrowings required to maintain the desired minimum balance of cash, in multiples of $10,000. Repayments are made at the ends of months and interest at 1% per month is paid when a repayment is made.

7-39 ***Analysis of budgets of a manufacturing firm*** Budgets for Simpson Company appear below for the first three months of 19X6.

Budgeted Income Statements
for the Three Months Ending March 31, 19X6

Sales (10,000 units)		$30,000
Variable costs:		
Production	$8,000	
Selling and administrative	7,500	15,500
Contribution margin		14,500
Fixed costs:		
Production	1,800	
Selling and administrative	2,400	4,200
Income		$10,300

Production Budget (in units)

	January	February	March
Desired ending inventory	4,500	7,500	6,000
Units sold	2,000	3,000	5,000
Total requirements	6,500	10,500	11,000
Beginning inventory	2,500	4,500	7,500
Production	4,000	6,000	3,500

Cash Receipts Budget

	January	February	March
Collections:			
December sales	$ 750		
January sales	1,500	$4,500	
February sales		2,250	$6,750
March sales			3,750
Total collections	$2,250	$6,750	$10,500

Cash Disbursements Budget

	January	February	March
Production costs:			
Variable	$3,200	$4,800	$2,800
Fixed	600	600	600
Selling and administrative:			
Variable—current month	600	900	1,500
—prior month	150	900	1,350
Fixed	800	800	800
Totals	$5,350	$8,000	$7,050

Required

Answer the following questions about the assumptions and policies used in formulating the budgets.

1. What are variable manufacturing costs per unit?
2. What are monthly fixed manufacturing costs requiring cash disbursements?
3. What are the firm's expectations about cash collections from receivables? (All sales are on account.)
4. What were sales in December 19X5?
5. What are accounts receivable at March 31, 19X6?
6. What proportion of variable selling and administrative expenses is paid in the month incurred, and what proportion is paid the following month? (*Hint:* Variable selling costs are 25% of sales.)
7. What are accrued expenses payable for selling and administrative expenses at March 31, 19X6?
8. How much cash does the firm expect to have at March 31, 19X6? (The balance at January 1 is $1,800.)
9. If the firm could sell 2,000 additional units in the three-month period, what would income be? (Ignore interest expense.)
10. Look at the production budget. From comparisons of inventories, sales, and so on, determine the firm's inventory policy.
11. Does the beginning inventory for January reflect the firm's policy? Show why or why not.
12. What are budgeted sales for April?

7-40 ***Variable minimum cash balance*** John Lock, chief financial officer of Bland Company, has asked for your help in preparing a cash budget. He plans to maintain a minimum balance based on the budgeted disbursements for the coming month and is unsure how to proceed. He tells you the following about his policy. "If the coming month's budgeted receipts are greater than budgeted disbursements, I want to hold a balance equal to 10% of budgeted disbursements and invest any excess cash in short-term government notes. If budgeted disbursements are greater than budgeted receipts, I want to have enough cash to make up the budgeted deficit and have 20% of budgeted disbursements on hand to begin the month. We will borrow if the indicated balance is less than required."

The budgets for sales and purchases in the coming months are as follows.

	Sales	Purchases
April	$500,000	$470,000
May	780,000	550,000
June	900,000	560,000
July	600,000	480,000
August	650,000	600,000

Sales are collected 30% in the month of sale and 70% in the following month. Purchases are paid for 50% in the month of purchase and 50% in the following month. Sales in March were $450,000 and accounts payable for merchandise at March 31 were $185,000. Cash at March 31 was $140,000. Fixed expenses requiring cash disbursements are $110,000 per month.

Required

1. Prepare a schedule by month for the April-July period indicating the amounts that would have to be borrowed, or would be available for investment, in each month. Borrowings would be repaid as soon as possible and are not included in the determination of disbursements for the purpose of setting the desired balance. Borrowings would be repaid before investments were made and investments would be sold before borrowings are made. Ignore interest.
2. Using the guidelines in Appendix B, write a memorandum to Mr. Lock describing the advantages and disadvantages of his policy in comparison with a policy of having a specific number of dollars as the minimum cash balance.

CASES

7-41 ***Qualifying for a loan*** The president of Stern's Department Store has requested your assistance. He will be seeking a large bank loan in a couple of months for the purpose of opening a new store and has been told by his banker that the March 31, 19X8 balance sheet should look good if the loan is to be granted. The banker said specifically that working capital should be at least $500,000 and that the current ratio should be at least 2.5 to 1.

The end of January is now approaching and the president is becoming anxious. He asks you to prepare a cash budget for February and March and a pro forma balance sheet as of March 31. The balance sheet at the end of January is expected to be about as follows, in thousands of dollars.

Assets		Equities	
Cash	$ 110	Accounts payable (merchandise)	$ 410
Accounts receivable	240	Notes payable	40
Inventory	680	Common stock	2,000
Building and equipment (net)	1,830	Retained earnings	410
Total	$2,860	Total	$2,860

The sales forecasts for the months of February, March, April, and May are, respectively, $780,000; $650,000; $600,000; and $820,000. Cost of sales averages 60% of sales. Receivables are collected 60% in the month of sale, 40% in the following month. Inventory is normally maintained at budgeted sales requirements for the following two months. Purchases are paid for in 30 days.

The notes payable shown in the balance sheet are due on March 15. Although the firm normally keeps a minimum cash balance of $80,000, the president asks you to disregard this for purposes of the budgets. He also informs you that monthly fixed costs are $265,000, of which $30,000 is depreciation. All fixed costs requiring cash are paid as incurred.

Required

1. Prepare the cash budget and pro forma balance sheet that the president wants. Use thousands of dollars.
2. Determine whether the firm will be likely to meet the criteria set by the bank.

7-42 Financing requirements Larsen Company makes fertilizer in a midwestern state. The firm has nearly completed a new plant that will produce twice as much as the old plant, which is being scrapped. Swen Larsen, the owner, has consulted you about his financing requirements for the coming year. He knows he will require additional financing because of the doubling of production, and he intends to obtain a loan as soon as possible. He is on good terms with local bankers and anticipates no difficulty in obtaining the loan, but he is anxious that the loan not be too large or too small.

The production process in the new plant is highly automated and can be carried out with a work force of the same size as that used last year in the old plant. The income statement for last year and the year-end balance sheet are as follows:

Income Statement for 19X4	
Sales	$1,600,000
Cost of goods sold	1,040,000
Gross profit	560,000
Selling, general, and administrative expenses	390,000
Income	$ 170,000

Balance Sheet at December 31, 19X4

Assets		Liabilities and Owners' Equity	
Cash	$ 40,000	Accounts payable	$ 20,000
Accounts receivable	80,000	Common stock	900,000
Inventory of materials	250,000	Retained earnings	150,000
Plant and equipment—old plant	0		
—new plant	700,000		
Total	$1,070,000	Total	$1,070,000

You learn that depreciation expense on the old plant was $80,000 per year, all of which was included in cost of goods sold. The new plant will be depreciated at $120,000 per year. Wages paid last year to production workers were $280,000. Materials purchases were $400,000, which is also the amount of materials cost included in cost of goods sold (the beginning and ending inventories of materials were the same). Factory overhead, other than depreciation, was $280,000 last year. It is expected that factory overhead, other than depreciation, will be $360,000 in the coming year.

Selling, general, and administrative expenses are expected to be $430,000 during the coming year. Sales will be only 120% of last year's sales because it will take some time to reach the full output of the new plant. Mr. Larsen expects to spend $250,000 buying new equipment to complete the plant. This expenditure will be made as soon as he obtains the new loan. The factory will be operating at full capacity the last few months of the year, so ending requirements for current assets should be double the beginning amounts. Accounts payable are closely related to the amount of inventory carried. The firm ships its products on completion so that all inventory is raw materials.

Required

Prepare a budgeted income statement for 19X5 and a pro forma balance sheet (as far as possible) for December 31, 19X5. State any assumptions you have to make and indicate how much Mr. Larsen must borrow from the bank.

7-43 Cash budgeting—a lender's viewpoint You are the chief assistant to Mr. Barnes, the loan officer of Metropolitan National Bank. In December 19X4 Mr. Barnes discussed a loan with Mr. Johnson, manager-owner of a local dry goods store. Mr. Johnson has requested a loan of $250,000 to be repaid at June 30, 19X5. The store is being expanded and additional inventory is needed. From the proceeds of the loan, $200,000 will be spent on remodeling and new fixtures. The rest will be spent for additional inventory. At Mr. Barnes' request, Mr. Johnson submitted a budgeted income statement for the six months ending June 30, 19X5.

Sales	$900,000
Cost of goods sold	360,000
Gross profit	540,000
Selling and administrative expenses, including $15,000 interest	310,000
Income	$230,000

Mr. Johnson said that, since $50,000 in depreciation was included in selling and administrative expenses, his firm would generate more than enough cash to repay the loan with $15,000 in interest (12% annual rate). Mr. Barnes asks you to check out the forecast with Mr. Johnson. From Mr. Johnson you obtain the following information:

1. Sales are expected to be $100,000 in January, $140,000 in February, and $165,000 in each of the rest of the months of the entire year.
2. Merchandise is held equal to two months' budgeted sales.
3. Accounts payable are paid in 30 days.
4. About half of sales are for cash. The rest are collected in the second month after sale (60 days).

5. Cost of goods sold is variable, and 15% of sales is the variable portion of selling, general, and administrative expenses. All selling, general and administrative expenses, except depreciation, are paid in the month incurred.
6. At December 31, 19X4, the following balance sheet is expected.

Pro Forma Balance Sheet as of December 31, 19X4

Cash (desired minimum)	$ 20,000	Accounts payable	$ 30,000
Accounts receivable	40,000	Common stock	200,000
Inventory	60,000	Retained earnings	115,000
Building and equipment	375,000		
Accumulated depreciation	(150,000)		
Total	$ 345,000	Total	$345,000

Required

Using the guidelines in Appendix B, write a memorandum to Mr. Barnes giving and supporting your conclusions regarding the likelihood that Mr. Johnson's firm can repay the loan and interest at the end of the first six months of 19X5.

7-44 Budgeting and industry data Ralph Robertson is considering opening a menswear store in a new shopping center. He has had a great deal of experience in men's stores and is convinced that he can make a success of his own store. He plans to invest $10,000 of his own money in the business and has asked you to develop a plan he can take to a bank to obtain a loan to cover the remainder of the needed financing because he knows that a loan officer will be more receptive to an applicant who has made careful plans of his needs.

Ralph gives you the following data obtained from a trade association's study of stores of the kind and size he plans to open (1,200 square feet of selling space).

Average sales per square foot	$70 per year
Average rent	$500 per month plus 5% of sales
Average gross profit	45% of sales
Average annual operating expenses (excluding rent and depreciation):	
At $60,000 sales annually	$19,200
At $90,000 sales annually	$26,700
Inventory requirements	four-month supply
Investment in fixtures and equipment (useful life of five years)	$22,000

Ralph plans to sell for cash only. He will have to pay cash for his first purchase of inventory, but he expects to get 30 days' credit from suppliers for further purchases. His other operating expenses, including rent, will be paid in the month incurred.

Ralph expects to have a steady growth in sales for the first four months of operation (January—April 19X8) and to reach the monthly average for the industry in May. His projections for the first four months are as follows: $4,000; $4,500; $5,200; and $6,100.

Required

Using the guidelines in Appendix B, write a memorandum to Mr. Robertson showing his financing requirements through April and a budgeted income statement for 19X8. Include in your memorandum brief comments about the assumptions you used to develop the financial data you are providing.

8 capital budgeting, part I

This chapter and the next require that you understand the principles of the time value of money. Before you begin this chapter, read Appendix C at the back of the book and work through the review problems to be sure that you understand these principles.

The comprehensive budget, the unifying topic of Chapters 6 and 7, reflects the results expected from a wide variety of planning decisions, such as those about product mix, cost structure, and pricing. Most of those decisions were aimed at achieving the best possible results given the firm's existing resources. That is, the decisions did not require large commitments of cash to investments in land, plant, machinery, or other long-lived assets. A comprehensive budget must also incorporate the planning decisions that *do* involve such long-term commitments, called **capital budgeting decisions.** Planned expenditures for new, long-lived assets are often the largest items in the cash disbursements budget.

Capital budgeting decisions are the subject of this and the next chapter. Such decisions can entail sizable commitments of cash. For example, *Business Week* reported that Gilette's investment in bringing out its Sensor razor involved $75 million in research and development, $125 million for a new plant, and $110 million for first-year advertising.[1] Such decisions are expected to generate returns (normally, income or cost savings) that will last for more than one year. Capital budgeting decisions are therefore also called *long-term decisions.*

1 Business Week, *January 29, 1990, 44.*

As Chapter 5 pointed out, the usual rule for determining whether a decision is short-term or long-term is whether its effects will be completed within one year. This rule, while arbitrary, provides a good basis for distinguishing the two types of decisions. Capital budgeting decisions are like short-term decisions in that they both use *differential revenues and costs*. Therefore, these concepts remain relevant to capital budgeting decisions.

For two reasons, capital budgeting decisions are generally more risky than short-term ones. First, the firm will recoup its investment, if at all, over a longer period. That is, more time expires between making the expenditure and receiving the cash. Second, reversing a capital budgeting decision is much more difficult than reversing a short-term decision. For example, suppose a firm raises its prices expecting to improve its profits, but sales fall so much that profits fall. Usually the firm can simply lower its prices. The firm may suffer a decline in profits for a short time, but it can recover fairly quickly once the managers see their error. But suppose a company buys land and constructs and equips a building especially to make a particular product. The plant may have little value in any other use (a low opportunity cost). If the product is unsuccessful, the firm will have made a large, nearly worthless investment. Du Pont and Waste Management Inc. spent $25 million to build plastic-recycling plants.[2] With the growing national interest in recycling, the invention of a substitute material or a plastic-variant material that the plant cannot process is an important risk of this joint venture.

Managers use the analytical techniques discussed in this and the following chapter to decide whether to undertake specific long-term projects. The expenditures on those projects selected by management are incorporated into short-term and long-term budgets such as those presented in the preceding chapter. We cover only briefly the issues surrounding decisions about how to *finance* long-term investments. In managerial finance you will study in more detail the problems of selecting from among financing alternatives.

CAPITAL BUDGETING AND RESOURCE ALLOCATION

Considering only quantifiable factors, in short-term decision making an action is desirable if incremental revenues exceed incremental costs. In capital budgeting decisions, the company must include as a relevant cost the **time value of money,** because capital budgeting decisions require investing money now to bring in more money in the future. The time value of money is an opportunity cost; by making a particular investment now, we give up the opportunity to make other investments.

Managers incorporate the time value of money into capital budgeting decisions by determining whether the expected rate of return on the investment is greater than the rate that must be paid to suppliers of capital. The latter rate is called *cost of capital*. The study of cost of capital is the province of managerial finance. Thus, we include only a brief introduction to the concept.

---

2 Business Week, *March 5, 1990, 50.*

COST OF CAPITAL

Cost of capital is the cost, expressed as a percentage, of obtaining the capital resources to operate the firm. Capital is obtained from two sources, creditors and owners, whose interests correspond to the divisions of liabilities and owners' equity on the balance sheet. The cost of capital supplied by creditors is the effective interest rate on borrowings. For example, if the firm has to make annual interest payments of $80,000 to obtain $1,000,000 from a sale of bonds with that face value, the effective interest rate is 8% ($80,000/$1,000,000).[3]

The cost of equity capital is more difficult to determine, for it is based on how much investors expect the firm to earn. In a simple situation, this cost may be approximated by dividing the expected earnings by the market value of the stock. Thus, if a firm is expected to earn $3 per share and the market price of the stock is $30 per share, the cost of equity capital is 10% ($3/$30).

We are interested in cost of capital because it is the minimum acceptable rate of return on investment. It serves as a **cutoff rate of return.** If the expected rate of return is greater than cost of capital, the investment is desirable; if the expected rate is less than cost of capital, the investment is not desirable.

Determining a firm's cost of capital is usually a complex task. Because of the practical difficulties of the task, managers might simply use their judgment to set a minimum acceptable rate. This rate is often called a **target rate of return,** and the firm will use this rate in deciding which projects to accept. In this and the next chapter, we assume that cost of capital has been estimated and is to be used in the decision to accept or reject a project.

CAPITAL BUDGETING TECHNIQUES

In a typical investment situation, a manager authorizes an investment with the intention of receiving returns sufficient both to recoup the original investment and to reward the company adequately for the risk taken. But the returns come in the future, often over many years. That is, the manager must wait for both the return *of* the investment and the return *on* it. Hence, when making an investment decision, the manager tries to determine, considering the time value of money, whether the rate of return associated with the investment is greater or less than the minimum acceptable rate—cost of capital. There are two ways to do this: (1) find the rate of return associated with the project and compare that rate with the cost of capital, or (2) use the cost of capital to find the present value of the future returns and compare that value with the cost of the investment.

The second method is usually easier to apply. Using this approach, called the **net present value (NPV)** method, we compare the present value of future returns from an investment with the cost of obtaining those returns—the required investment. The alternative approach, finding the rate of return on a project and comparing it with a specified minimum acceptable rate, is usually called the **internal rate of return (IRR)** method. It uses the same basic concepts as the net present value approach. Later in this chapter, we consider

3 *You may recall the determination of bond prices and effective interest rates from financial accounting. There are complications if bonds are issued at prices other than face value, but these problems are not important for our purposes.*

two other commonly used techniques for analyzing long-term investments. These additional techniques are conceptually inferior to either the NPV or the IRR method because neither considers the time value of money.

In three of the four analytical approaches to capital budgeting decisions discussed in this chapter, returns are defined as **cash flows,** not as income. Given the emphasis on income in prior chapters, and probably in your first course in accounting, we will briefly explain why cash flows are so important in capital budgeting.

CASH FLOWS AND BOOK INCOME

The criterion for acceptance for the short-term decisions covered in Chapter 5 was whether the decision would increase the company's income. If incremental revenues exceeded incremental costs, income would increase and the decision would be wise. We did not speak of cash flows in Chapter 5 because, in short-term decisions, incremental revenues and incremental costs are the same as incremental cash inflows and incremental cash outflows. Hence, incremental profit is also incremental cash flow. In the short-term, cash flows come in and go out within relatively short periods (during the year), so that the *time value of money is not significant.*

Capital budgeting decisions usually require investments in depreciable assets. In those cases incremental incomes and incremental cash flows will *differ* in the individual years of the life of the investment because of depreciation. When a depreciable asset is acquired, a cash outlay occurs in the year of acquisition. For accounting and tax purposes, the cost of that asset is allocated over the years in which the asset is used, so the incomes of those years are reduced by the depreciation expense. But no associated outlay of cash occurs in those years. Hence, the change in incomes of year 19X5 or 19X6 as a result of a long-term investment decision in 19X1 will not be the same as the change in cash flows of years 19X5 and 19X6 as a result of that same decision. The change in income will be less than the change in cash flow because income will be reduced by depreciation expense, which requires no cash flow. For this reason, we must be more specific in our analyses of decisions that involve depreciable assets and future incomes. We cannot use income as a substitute for cash flows (as we did in Chapter 5), because income will not equal cash flow when there is depreciation expense.

Depreciation *does affect* cash flows because it is a legitimate deduction for income and tax purposes, and income taxes *are* a cash outflow. Hence, to determine the incremental cash flow from an investment for a particular year, we must know the depreciation expense for that year. Later in this chapter we show how to deal with depreciation and income taxes.

Bear in mind one final and important point. As with all management decisions that deal with the future, the numbers used (for cash flows, useful lives, etc.) are *estimates.* They are almost never known with certainty at the time a decision must be made. Chapter 9 illustrates some techniques managers use to allow for this uncertainty.

ILLUSTRATION OF CAPITAL BUDGETING METHODS

As stated earlier, the principle introduced in Chapter 5—that the only relevant data for decisions are differential revenues and costs—also governs capital budgeting decisions. The relevant data for capital budgeting decisions are the incremental (or differential) cash flows expected from a decision. The following example illustrates the main points.

A firm with cost of capital of 12% has an opportunity to introduce a new product. The best available estimates indicate that the firm will be able to sell 3,000 units per year for the next five years at $14 each. Variable costs should be $5 per unit. To make the product, the firm will have to buy machinery that costs $60,000, has a five-year life with no salvage value, and requires annual fixed cash operating costs of $5,000 for maintenance, insurance, and property taxes. (Notice that we have not included depreciation as a cost because it does not require a cash payment. We also ignore income taxes for now.)

The annual *incremental* cash inflows appear below.[4]

	Annual Cash Flows Years 1-5
Revenues ($14 × 3,000)	$42,000
Variable costs ($5 × 3,000)	15,000
Contribution margin ($9 × 3,000)	27,000
Cash fixed costs	5,000
Expected increase in net cash inflows	$22,000

Using this information, we analyze the proposed investment in two basic ways.

NET PRESENT VALUE (NPV) METHOD

When using the NPV method the question is whether it is wise to invest $60,000 today to receive $22,000 per year for the next five years. The investment is worthwhile if the present value of the $22,000 per year to be received for five years is greater than the $60,000 outlay required today (which, obviously, has a present value of $60,000). The present value of the future cash flows of $22,000 minus the $60,000 required investment is called the *NPV* or the *excess present value*. If it is positive (present value of the future cash flows exceeds the required investment), the investment is desirable. If it is negative, the investment is undesirable.

To determine the NPV we must first find the present value of $22,000 per year for five years at 12%. In the appropriate present value table (Table B in Appendix C), we see that the factor for a series of payments of $1 for five years at 12% is 3.605. Multiplying this factor by $22,000, we obtain $79,310 as the present value of the future cash flows. This means that if you desire a 12% return and expect annual payments of $22,000 for five years, you would be willing to pay up to $79,310 for this investment. Therefore, you are more than happy to pay only $60,000, and the investment is desirable. The NPV is $19,310 ($79,310 – $60,000). Below is a summary of the analysis.

Present value of future cash flows ($22,000 × 3.605)	$79,310
Investment required	60,000
Net present value	$19,310

4 *Notice that income, using straight-line depreciation of $12,000 per year ($60,000/5), is $10,000 per year.*

INTERNAL RATE OF RETURN (IRR) METHOD

Another approach to analyzing investment opportunities is to find the expected IRR. This method poses the question "What return are we earning if we invest $60,000 now and receive $22,000 annually for five years?" The investment is desirable if the IRR is higher than the cost of capital. The IRR is also called the **time-adjusted rate of return** or the **discount rate.**

If net cash flows are equal in each year, the IRR is not difficult to find. The rate *equates* the present value of the future cash flows with the amount to be invested now. Consider that the computation of the present value of the future flows is as follows:

$$\textit{Present value of future flows} = \textit{annual cash flows} \times \textit{factor for the discount rate and the number of periods}$$

To compute the IRR, we use the cost of the investment as the present value, and try to determine the discount rate associated with the factor that, when multiplied by the annual flows, equals the cost of the investment. In effect, we are answering the question, "What discount rate gives the investment a net present value of zero?"

The first step is to find the factor related to both the discount rate and number of periods. Rearranging the preceding equation yields

$$\frac{\textit{Present value of future flows}}{\textit{annual cash flows}} = \textit{factor for the discount rate and the number of periods}$$

In our example

$$\frac{\$60{,}000}{\$22{,}000} = 2.727$$

The second step is to relate this factor, 2.727, to the factor for some discount rate and five periods. We can find the discount rate by looking at the factors listed in the five-period row in Table B. In the five-period row under the 24% column, the factor is 2.745; in that row, under the 25% column, the factor is 2.689. Hence, the IRR on this project is between 24% and 25%. (You should have been able to tell that the IRR on this project was greater than 12% because the NPV computed in the previous section is positive.)

Although we could use a financial calculator or spreadsheet to find the rate, we know it falls between 24% and 25% and is higher than cost of capital. Hence, the investment is desirable. Because we are dealing with estimates of future cash flows, greater precision is unwarranted.

GENERALITY OF THE ANALYSIS

Our example uses a new product, but the facts and numbers could just as well relate to an opportunity to expand the productive capacity for an existing product, or to an opportunity to reduce costs. Companies responding to changes prompted by the new manufacturing environment are continually evaluating investments that they expect will reduce costs. Suppose that instead of introducing a new product, the $60,000 investment is for labor-saving machinery that would cut $9 from the per-unit variable production costs of an existing product. (The reduction in variable costs increases the contribution margin on the existing product by $9, which is equal to the contribution margin expected to result from the new product in the original example.) Assume further that the sales volume on the product is 3,000 units per year, and that the additional cash fixed costs for the new machinery are $5,000 (the same as in the original example). The incremental cash flows are then

Savings in variable costs ($9 × 3,000)	$27,000
Less incremental cash fixed costs	5,000
Net increase in annual cash flows (savings)	$22,000

Thus, the pattern of analysis is the same whether the cash flows result from selling new products, expanding output of existing products, or saving on operating expenses. Find the incremental cash flows and then apply one of the methods described. *How* the cash flows come about is irrelevant. The important thing is to estimate what the cash flows will be.

Not-for-profit entities can also use the basic techniques when they confront decisions involving the acquisition of long-lived assets. For example, a city might want to decide whether to build a new municipal building or convention center. Because cities are not subject to income taxes, the analysis we have illustrated is adequate. As we noted earlier, however, managers in businesses must also consider the cash outflow for income taxes, which is affected by depreciation. The next section refines the analytical process to recognize the effects of taxes.

TAXES AND DEPRECIATION

Calculating after-tax cash flows is slightly more complex. Continuing with the example of the new product, assume a 40% income tax rate and straight-line depreciation for income tax calculations.[5] The initial outlay is still $60,000, but the annual incremental cash flows are different because the added income from the project is now subject to income taxes. The net cash inflow for each of the five years is computed below.

Net Incremental Cash Flow for Each Year

	Tax Computation	Cash Flow
Revenues	$42,000	$42,000
Cash expenses (variable and fixed)	20,000	20,000
Cash inflow before taxes	22,000	22,000
Depreciation ($60,000/5)	12,000	
Increase in taxable income	$10,000	
Tax at 40% (cash outflow)	$ 4,000	4,000
Net increase in annual cash inflow		$18,000

5 *Our purpose in discussing the tax effect of depreciation in this chapter is to emphasize that such an effect exists, not to explain the details of the tax law. Accordingly, in this chapter we do not consider such technical issues as the Accelerated Cost Recovery System or the requirement to abide by the half-year, mid-quarter, or mid-month conventions if straight-line depreciation is chosen for tax purposes.*

The tax deduction for depreciation on the asset reduces taxes. Without the deduction, taxes would be $8,800 ($22,000 × 40%). Thus, the $12,000 in depreciation expense saves $4,800 (40% × $12,000). This important saving is called the **tax shield,** or **tax effect of depreciation.**

We do not show net income in the above schedule because we want to emphasize that we are concerned with cash flows, not net income. However, you might find it easier, and more understandable, to develop an income statement and then add back depreciation to get net cash flow. (Accountants and financial managers frequently use this calculation.) The income statement converted to a cash basis appears below.

Revenues (cash inflow)	$42,000
Cash expenses	20,000
Cash inflow before taxes	22,000
Depreciation	12,000
Income before taxes	10,000
Tax at 40%	4,000
Increase in net income	6,000
Add back depreciation	12,000
Net increase in annual cash inflow	$18,000
Present value factor for 5 years at 12%	3.605
Present value of future cash inflows	$64,890
Investment required	60,000
Net present value	$ 4,890

The above approach to computing the increase in net annual cash flow is equivalent to the two-column approach used earlier. Using either approach, you must remember that taxes are determined by tax law, which does not always correspond to financial reporting principles. Chapter 9 discusses some of the differences.

Using either approach, annual incremental cash inflows are now $18,000 per year (rather than $22,000), which, when discounted at 12%, have a present value of $64,890. The NPV is $4,890; the investment is still desirable. To compute the IRR, we find the present value factor that, when multiplied by $18,000, equals $60,000. The factor is 3.333 ($60,000/$18,000). The factor closest to this in the five-year row in Table B is 3.274, the factor for 16%. The IRR is therefore between 14% and 16%, but closer to 16%. (You should have expected an IRR greater than 12%, since the NPV is positive at a 12% cost of capital.)

UNEVEN CASH FLOWS

The basic example has equal annual net cash inflows, but it is not unusual for revenues, or cash expenses, or both, to vary from year to year. For example, revenues from a new product might grow in the early years and decline in later years, or might take several years to reach a particular, expected level. Too, depreciation is seldom taken on a straight-line method for tax purposes. Accordingly, the cash outflow for taxes each year will vary. Or, the investment might have a salvage value that increases cash flow in the last year. We postpone to Chapter 9 a discussion of the somewhat more complex case of uneven cash flows for investments involving changes in inventory. (Remember that a goal of companies committed to the JIT philosophy is to reduce inventory levels to zero.) Uneven cash flows complicate the mathematics of the analysis but do not affect the basic principles of the analysis. We illustrate below two situations involving uneven cash flows.

SALVAGE VALUES

The cash flows from most projects involving the acquisition of depreciable assets could be uneven because of the salvage values of the assets at the ends of their useful lives. The simplest way to incorporate this factor into the analysis is to find the after-tax cash flow from the salvage value and discount it separately.

Assume, for example, that the new asset purchased in the basic example has an expected salvage value of $5,000 at the end of its useful life. How would this expectation affect the analysis of the investment? Your knowledge of financial accounting might lead you to expect the salvage value to change the depreciation of this asset. Such is not usually the case. Remember that the cash outflow for taxes depends on what is on the firm's tax return. Hence, your interest is in tax-return depreciation, and the tax law specifies that salvage values be ignored. For this reason, *any* proceeds received from selling a depreciable asset at the end of its useful life probably will be taxed.

Using straight-line depreciation and incorporating the expected salvage value into the basic example, we get the following analysis.

Incremental Cash Flows Years 1-5

	Tax Computation	Cash Flow
Revenues	$42,000	$42,000
Cash expenses	20,000	20,000
Cash inflow before taxes	22,000	22,000
Depreciation ($60,000/5)	12,000	
Increase in taxable income	$10,000	
Tax at 40%	$ 4,000	4,000
Net cash inflow per year, as before		$18,000

Summary of Present Value of Investment

Operating cash flows ($18,000 × 3.605)		$64,890
Salvage value:		
Total salvage value	$5,000	
Tax on salvage value at 40%	2,000	
After-tax cash inflow from salvage value	$3,000	
Times present value factor for 5 years hence at 12%	0.567	
Present value of salvage value		1,701
Total present value		66,591
Investment required		60,000
Net present value		$ 6,591

NPV was $4,890 when taxes were first considered. The new NPV ($6,591) is higher by the $1,701 present value of the salvage value. We could use a financial calculator or spreadsheet to find the IRR. Note that we cannot simply look up a value in Table B because we no longer have equal cash flows in every year.

VARIATIONS IN REVENUES

We said earlier that cash flows vary if sales vary during the life of a project. The uneven flows change the analysis only in that we need to discount the flows individually, instead of as an annuity. To illustrate, let us return to the basic example of a new product. Assume that sales are expected to be 2,000, 3,000, 3,000, 4,000, and 3,000 in years one through five, respectively. (The total is still 15,000 units for the five years.) *Before* any formal analysis, can you tell whether the investment will be more, or less, desirable than it was when sales were spread evenly over the five years? That is, will NPV be higher or lower than the $4,890 determined earlier? If you decided that the investment will be less desirable (lower NPV) you are correct; sales will be later, so cash will be received later. The present value of a cash receipt declines the longer you must wait to receive it.

The schedule below shows the calculations. For brevity, we use the $9 per-unit contribution margin instead of showing both revenues and variable costs. As expected, NPV is now lower ($3,502 vs $4,890), but the investment is still desirable because NPV is still positive. Notice that the totals are the same as they were before, which you can verify by multiplying the numbers in the previous schedule by five. Thus, total cash flow before taxes is $110,000 ($22,000 × 5), total income taxes are $20,000 ($4,000 × 5), and so on. The difference arises when the cash flows are converted to present values. The delay in the cash flows reduces the present value of those flows.

Cash Flows and Present Values

	Year					
	1	2	3	4	5	Total
Unit sales	2,000	3,000	3,000	4,000	3,000	15,000
Contribution margin at $9	$18,000	$27,000	$27,000	$36,000	$27,000	$135,000
Less cash fixed costs	5,000	5,000	5,000	5,000	5,000	25,000
Pretax cash inflow	13,000	22,000	22,000	31,000	22,000	110,000
Less depreciation	12,000	12,000	12,000	12,000	12,000	60,000
Income before taxes	1,000	10,000	10,000	19,000	10,000	50,000
Income taxes at 40%	400	4,000	4,000	7,600	4,000	20,000
Net income	600	6,000	6,000	11,400	6,000	30,000
Add depreciation	12,000	12,000	12,000	12,000	12,000	60,000
Net cash flow	$12,600	$18,000	$18,000	$23,400	$18,000	$ 90,000
Present value factor (Table A)	0.893	0.797	0.712	0.636	0.567	
Present value	$11,252	$14,346	$12,816	$14,882	$10,206	$ 63,502
Less investment						60,000
Net present value						$ 3,502

Finding the IRR can be difficult when there are uneven cash flows. Trial-and-error and interpolation will give a close approximation of the rate, and financial calculators and spreadsheets can make such calculations. Because the NPV is positive, the IRR *must* be greater than the 12% discount rate used in calculating the present values. (The IRR is about 14.2%.)

DECISION RULES

Looking only at the quantitative aspects of an investment opportunity, the decision rules for the two methods of analysis we describe are simple. Under the NPV method, a project having a positive NPV should be accepted; others should be rejected. Under the IRR method, a project having an IRR greater than the firm's cost of capital should be accepted. The relationship of the two criteria is as follows.

1. If IRR is less than cost of capital (or cutoff rate), NPV is negative.
2. If NPV is positive, IRR is greater than cost of capital (or cutoff rate).

When analyzing any single project for acceptance or rejection, both methods lead to the same decision. The problem of multiple investment opportunities is discussed in Chapter 9.

QUALITATIVE CONSIDERATIONS

Chapter 5 stated that qualitative, or hard-to-quantify, concerns often override quantitative analyses in short-term decisions. The same is true with capital budgeting decisions.

Toyota Motor Company has an explicit qualitative goal that investments in plant automation should improve working conditions, make employees more comfortable and put them under less stress. The company expects these better conditions to reduce worker turnover, which in turn will save on training costs. However, the company is committed to such investments even if the tangible, quantifiable benefits are insufficient to justify the investment. Some automated operations now cost more than they would if people were still doing them. One such operation is sanding auto bodies before painting, a dirty, difficult job now done robotically at greater cost than using people.[6]

Strategic considerations should also play an important part in major capital investment decisions. Companies usually commit themselves to following particular strategies and must be able to look past purely quantitative analyses to pursue those strategies.

When General Electric modernized its appliance complex in Louisville, Kentucky in the early 1980s, it achieved considerable reductions in costs of scrap, rework, and service calls. But GE had not aimed at cost reduction in undertaking the modernization. Rather, it sought higher product quality because it had adopted the strategy of being the highest-quality producer, not the lowest cost producer.[7]

Qualitative concerns are becoming increasingly important as companies adopt advanced manufacturing techniques. Some of the advantages of such techniques are difficult to quantify and might therefore be overlooked. For instance, while managers agree that increasing the quality of a product is desirable, the monetary effect is not easy to estimate. Similar considerations

6 *Alex Taylor III, "How Toyota Copes with Hard Times,"* Fortune, *January 25, 1993, 78-81.*
7 *Tony Baer, "Cost Justification is Possible,"* Managing Automation, *August, 1986, 57.*

International Paper concentrated on diversification in the 1970s. it then adopted the strategy of becoming the lowest-cost producer in the industry and devoted its capital budget to achieving that objective. Chrysler Corporation paid $25 million for Lamborghini, the famous maker of fast sports cars. It is unlikely that Chrysler will make high profits from the investment. Rather, Chrysler sought the acquisition to help its regular business in Europe by giving the company more credibility. Similarly, Ford paid over $2.5 billion to buy Jaguar PLC, the prestigious, but financially troubled British car maker. Ford also faced the need to spend another $1 billion to expand capacity, add new models, and improve productivity. The reason given for Ford's costly acquisition was to "round out the top end of its lineup." Both of these companies could have approached their objectives in other ways. Ford might have introduced its own luxury line or formed a new company to do so, as several Japanese companies have done. Chrysler could have developed its own sports car line.*

* Business Week, *February 12, 1990, 44.*

arise with such benefits as reducing cycle time. Chrysler Corporation has cut the technical staff needed to develop a new car from 2,000 to 740, and reduced the development time from 54 months to 39 months. These improvements mean that new models get to the market faster and cash inflows come in sooner.

Having emphasized the importance of qualitative considerations, we must also point out that ignoring quantitative measures of profitability is also unwise. It is not correct to say that companies should relentlessly pursue objectives that entail many large, unprofitable investments. At some point, reality must intrude and managers must pay attention to profitability or else the company could go under. Where qualitative factors are important, managers should still perform quantitative analyses so they will have a better idea of the *cost* to the company of accepting a particular qualitative goal as paramount.

OTHER METHODS OF CAPITAL BUDGETING

Although the NPV and IRR methods are theoretically sound, some managers argue that they are not practical because of the many estimates involved (cost of capital, cash flows, useful lives, etc.). Interestingly, the methods advocated by these managers, payback and book rate of return, require most of the same estimates which NPV and IRR require.

PAYBACK

One of the most commonly used methods of capital budgeting is the **payback** technique. This method poses the question "How long will it take to recover the investment?" If, as in our basic example, a project requires an outlay of $60,000 and will generate annual net cash inflows of $18,000, it has a payback period of 3.3 years ($60,000/$18,000). If the annual cash inflows are equal,

$$\textit{Payback period} = \frac{\textit{investment required}}{\textit{annual cash returns}}$$

Payback evaluates the rapidity with which an investment is recovered. As a practical matter, the payback period is automatically computed in the process of calculating IRR on an investment with equal annual cash flows. The investment required was $60,000, and annual cash inflows were $18,000. When computing IRR on this project, we determined that the investment divided by the annual cash inflows was 3.333, which is the payback period for the investment, as well as the present value factor for the discount rate and number of periods covered by the investment.

Decision rules when using the payback technique may be stated in different ways by different firms. Some firms set a limit on the payback period beyond which an investment will not be made. Others use payback to pick one of several investments, selecting the one with the shortest payback period.

Advantages

The payback period can be particularly important to a firm especially concerned about liquidity. Payback also can be used as a rough screening device for investment proposals. A long payback period usually means a low rate of return and an *extremely* short payback period very often suggests a good investment. For example, a division of General Electric expected a *four-month* payback period on an investment in a Pitney-Bowes Star system that determines the cheapest way to send a parcel.[8] Because the system could readily accommodate rate changes by available vendors, its useful life far exceeds the payback.

Some firms use payback as a measure of risk, because, in general, the longer it takes to get your money back, the greater the risk that the money will not be returned. As the time horizon lengthens, more uncertainties arise. Inflation might ease, or it might get worse; interest rates could rise, or they could fall; new techniques might be developed that would make the investment obsolete. Because of the increased uncertainty, a manager might prefer a project that pays back its investment in two years to one that takes ten years, even if the one with the ten-year payback period has a higher expected NPV and IRR.

An admittedly extreme example illustrates this point. Suppose you have $1,000,000 to invest and are considering two possibilities, both of which involve buying a cargo of merchandise and shipping it to a distant country. One voyage will take a year to complete, the other five years. The expected after-tax cash returns at the ends of the periods are $1,160,000 for the one-year voyage and $3,713,000 for the five-year voyage. The expected IRRs on the voyages are 16% and 30%, respectively, and, when a cost of capital of 10% is used, the NPVs are $54,545 and $1,305,481. A lot can happen to a ship on a long voyage—storms, piracy, or collisions with icebergs or rocks. Considering the hazards, who wouldn't feel that it was a lot safer tying up his or her money for one year rather than five despite the advantage of the

8 Business Week, *March 5, 1990, 50.*

longer voyage as determined under the normal techniques of analysis? Whether you would choose to invest in the one-year or the five-year opportunity depends on your attitude about risk and return. Because of its emphasis on the rapidity of return *of* investment, the payback method of evaluation gives higher priority to the one-year voyage. Payback is a common way to evaluate risk. There are other ways as well. One is to use higher discount rate to determine NPV, another is to raise the acceptable IRR on risky projects.

Flaws of Payback

The payback method has two very serious faults. The first is that it tells nothing about the profitability of the investment. Payback emphasizes the return *of* the investment but ignores the return *on* the investment. The life of the project after the payback period is ignored altogether.

Consider the two investment possibilities shown below.

	A	B
Cost	$10,000	$10,000
Useful life in years	5	10
Annual cash flows over the useful lives	$ 2,500	$ 2,000

Investment A has a payback period of four years ($10,000/$2,500), and B a payback period of five years ($10,000/$2,000). Using only the payback criterion, investment A is better than investment B because its payback period is shorter. Yet it should be obvious that investment B is superior; the returns from A cease one year after the payback period, while B continues to return cash for five more years.

The second serious fault of payback method is that it ignores the *timing* of the expected future cash flows and so ignores the time value of money. This fault, like the method's failure to consider years after the payback period, can lead to poor decisions. Consider two investments, X and Y, as described below.

	X	Y
Cost	$10,000	$10,000
Cash inflows by year:		
1	$ 2,000	$ 6,000
2	6,000	3,000
3	2,000	1,000
4-8	3,000	3,000

Both X and Y have payback periods of three years. They also show equal total returns. But the equal payback periods are misleading because the investment in Y will be recovered much more quickly than that in X. For the same reason, even if the two investments promise equal *total* returns, the one that generates the returns more quickly is the more desirable. (IRR on investment X is approximately 29%, whereas that on investment Y is about 31%.)

BOOK RATE OF RETURN

Another commonly used capital budgeting method is the **book-rate-of-return** technique. Under this method, the average annual expected *book* income is divided by the average *book* investment in the project. That is,

$$\textit{Average book rate of return} = \frac{\textit{average annual expected book income}}{\textit{average book investment}}$$

To illustrate, consider again the $60,000 investment opportunity in our basic example. The book net income for each of the five years of the project's life would be $6,000. The average book investment in this project will be $30,000 ($60,000/2). With an annual net income of $6,000, and an average book investment of $30,000, the average book rate of return is 20% ($6,000/$30,000). This return is an *average* rate of return because we have used the average book investment. The book rate of return for each year will be different because the average book investment in the project will change with each year's depreciation. For example, using the average book investment in year one, the book rate of return is 11.1% ($6,000/$54,000); in the last year, the book rate of return is 100% ($6,000/$6,000).

Let us compare these results with those obtained using the IRR method. The IRR on this project is something less than 16%. *If* the firm's cost of capital is 16% or more, both the NPV and the IRR methods of analysis suggest that the investment should be rejected. Use of the book rate of return as the criterion for evaluating investments could mislead managers to accept this investment opportunity.

To emphasize the deficiencies of the book-rate-of-return method, consider another, simpler example. As shown in the analysis below, investments A and B require identical investments ($10,000) and produce identical total net incomes, identical average net incomes, and identical book rates of return of 26.7%. Investment A is clearly superior to investment B; the flows come in faster for A. (Assuming straight-line depreciation, IRR on investment A is about 23%, whereas that on investment B is only about 15%.)

	A	B
Pretax cash flows by year:		
1	$10,000	$ 2,000
2	5,000	5,000
3	1,666	9,666
Totals	16,666	16,666
Depreciation	10,000	10,000
Income before taxes	6,666	6,666
Income taxes (40%)	2,666	2,666
Total net income	$ 4,000	$ 4,000
Average net income	$ 1,333	$ 1,333
Average book rate of return ($1,333/$5,000)	26.7%	26.7%

The book-rate-of-return method almost always misstates the internal rate of return because it ignores the timing of the cash flows and, therefore, the time value of money. This flaw makes it an unsatisfactory method of capital budgeting.

SUMMARY EVALUATION OF METHODS

Of course, qualitative factors can prevail over the decision rules for all of the methods previously discussed. The critical difference between the NPV and

IRR methods and the payback and book-rate-of-return methods is the attention given to the timing of the expected cash flows. The first two methods, called **discounted cash flow (DCF) techniques,** consider the timing of the cash flows; the last two methods do not. Their recognition of the time value of money makes DCF techniques conceptually superior, but payback is often used in conjunction with those techniques.

As stated earlier, some managers argue that DCF techniques are too complex or that they require too many estimates to make them useful in practice. We see little merit in these charges. All four methods require about the same estimates. DCF methods require estimates of future cash flows and the timing of those flows. The book-rate-of-return method requires estimates of future net incomes, which means making essentially the same estimates as those required to estimate cash flows. The payback method requires estimating cash flows but not useful lives. One point in favor of the payback method is that it emphasizes near-term cash flows, which are usually easier to predict than flows in later years. However, as we pointed out, unless consideration is given to useful life, the payback method could lead to very poor decisions.

The NPV, IRR, and book-rate-of-return methods all require an estimate of the cost of capital, or at least a decision as to a minimum acceptable rate of return. The payback method requires a decision regarding the minimum acceptable payback period. Thus, DCF techniques are no less realistic or practical than the other two approaches. The conceptual superiority of DCF techniques argues strongly for their use, though the payback period should probably not be ignored.

INVESTING DECISIONS AND FINANCING DECISIONS

Perhaps you've noticed that none of the examples in this chapter considered how the company will finance the project in question. That is, we did not say that the company plans to issue debt, common stock, some combination of the two, or finance the investment using cash flows from ongoing operations. The omission was deliberate. The investing decision nearly always should be kept separate from the financing decision.

It might be tempting to argue that if the firm *plans* to finance an investment with 9% debt, this rate should be used to discount the expected cash flows. Also, it might be tempting to subtract the interest payments as part of the cash flow computation. Resist these temptations!

A firm should not accept projects that will return less than the cost of capital, because it must earn a satisfactory return for *all* investors in the firm—both creditors and stockholders. Both types of capital suppliers are concerned about the safety of their investments and therefore monitor firm solvency by watching such factors as the ratio of debt to equity. If a firm makes too liberal use of debt and earns returns that exceed the interest rate but not cost of capital, it will find itself unable to raise *any* capital except at exorbitant rates. (Stockholders will sell their stock, which reduces the price and thus raises the cost of equity capital. Lenders will insist on higher interest rates, thus raising the cost of debt capital.)

Including interest payments as part of the cash flow computation reflects a misunderstanding of the concept of discounting. Using the cost of capital as the discount rate *automatically* provides for not only the recovery *of* the investment, but also a return *on* the investment at least equal to the cost of capital. Hence, subtracting interest payments to arrive at the net cash flow provides for the cost of debt twice—once by subtracting the interest payments, and again by using a discount rate that includes the cost of obtaining both the debt and equity capital.

INTERNATIONAL ASPECTS OF CAPITAL BUDGETING

Investing in foreign countries entails special problems and opportunities. On the positive side, many countries eagerly seek foreign investment and will offer tax and other concessions to make them more attractive to foreign companies. The U.S. is certainly amenable to foreign investment. Several states offered concessions to attract a BMW plant a few years ago. The plant went to South Carolina, which, along with some local governments, offered a package of tax abatement and other concessions reported to total $100 million. China has made many such concessions in recent years, as have some of the formerly communist countries in Eastern Europe.

Capital budgeting for foreign operations is much more complicated and much less precise. Some factors that can be critical in making investments in foreign countries follow.

- The risk of nationalization (a country seizes the property of foreign companies with limited or no compensation) is very great in some countries.
- Instability in economic, social, and political conditions can cause serious losses. Foreign companies can run into political problems in the U.S., as well. In 1992, the U.S. Department of Transportation thwarted a bid by British Airways to invest in U.S.Air. Other U.S. carriers also opposed the investment and it was widely reported that political considerations were paramount in the final decision.
- Astronomical inflation can wipe out the value of an investment.
- Restrictions on trade and on repatriation of cash can limit the company's ability to return its investment to its home country.
- Exchange rate fluctuations increase risk because overseas investments might be profitable in the local currency, but unprofitable when translated back to the home currency.

SUMMARY

Decisions to commit resources for periods longer than a year are capital budgeting decisions. Evaluating such decisions requires determining the investment and its resulting cash flows. Future cash flows may occur because of additional revenues and costs, or because of cost savings. Critical to capital budgeting is that most, if not all, of the numbers used in the analyses are estimates. The effects of depreciation on income taxes must also be recognized.

Effective evaluation of capital budgeting decisions requires consideration of the time value of money. The two approaches recommended, called discounted cash flow techniques, are the net present value (NPV) and the internal rate of return (IRR) methods. Two other methods—payback and book rate of return—are often used, but are conceptually inferior because they fail to consider the time value of money. Nevertheless, such methods, particularly payback, may be useful as rough screening devices for investment opportunities.

Discounted cash flow methods are used to decide on undertaking an investment. An important factor in the successful use of these methods is understanding the firm's cost of capital. The expected source for financing a particular investment is not relevant to the analysis of that investment.

KEY TERMS

book rate of return
capital budgeting decisions
cash flows
cost of capital
cutoff rate of return
discounted cash flow (DCF) techniques
discount rate
internal rate of return (IRR)
net present value (NPV)
payback
target rate of return
tax effect of depreciation
tax shield
time-adjusted rate of return
time value of money

KEY FORMULAS

$$\text{Present value of future flows} = \text{annual cash flows} \times \text{present value factor}$$

$$\text{Net present value} = \begin{matrix}\text{present value}\\ \text{of future flows}\end{matrix} - \begin{matrix}\text{required current}\\ \text{investment}\end{matrix}$$

$$\text{Payback period} = \frac{\text{investment required}}{\text{annual cash returns}}$$

$$\text{Average book rate of return} = \frac{\text{average annual expected book income}}{\text{average book investment}}$$

REVIEW PROBLEM

Dwyer Company has the opportunity to market a new product. The sales manager believes the firm could sell 10,000 units per year at $14 per unit for five years. The product requires machinery costing $100,000, having a five-year life and no salvage value. Variable costs per unit are $8. The machinery has fixed operating costs requiring cash disbursements of $20,000 annually. Straight-line depreciation will be used for both book and tax purposes. The tax rate is 40% and cost of capital is 14%.

Required

1. Determine the increase in annual net income and in annual cash inflows expected from the investment.

2. Determine the NPV of the investment.
3. Determine the payback period.
4. Determine the approximate IRR of the investment.
5. Determine the book rate of return on the average investment.
6. Suppose the machinery has salvage value of $5,000 at the end of its useful life, which is not considered in determining depreciation expense. The tax rate on the gain at the end of the asset's life is 40%. How will your answer to item 2 change?

ANSWER TO REVIEW PROBLEM

1.

	Tax Computation	Cash Flow
Sales (10,000 × $14)	$140,000	$140,000
Variable cost (10,000 × $8)	80,000	80,000
Contribution margin (10,000 × $6)	60,000	60,000
Fixed cash operating costs	20,000	20,000
Cash inflow before taxes	40,000	40,000
Depreciation ($100,000/5)	20,000	
Increase in taxable income	20,000	
Income tax at 40% rate	8,000	8,000
Increase in net income	12,000	
Add depreciation	20,000	
Net cash inflow per year	$ 32,000	$ 32,000

2. $9,856, calculated as follows:

Net cash inflow per year	$ 32,000
Present value factor, 5-year annuity at 14% (Table B)	3.433
Present value of future net cash flows	$109,856
Less investment	100,000
Net present value	$ 9,856

3. The payback period is 3.125 years, which is $100,000 divided by $32,000.
4. IRR is just barely over 18%. The factor to seek is 3.125, which is the payback period calculated in item 3. The closest factor in the five-year row of Table B is 3.127, which is the 18% factor. Because 3.125 is less than 3.127, the rate is greater than 18%. (Remember, the higher the rate, the lower the factor.)
5. The book rate of return on the average investment is 24%, which is annual net income of $12,000 divided by the average investment of $50,000 ($100,000/2).
6. The only change required is the determination of the present value of the salvage value less tax on the gain.

Salvage value	$ 5,000
Tax at 40%	2,000
Net cash inflow, end of year 5	$ 3,000
Present value factor for single payment, 5 years at 14% (Table A)	.519
Present value of salvage value	$ 1,557
Net present value from part 2	9,856
Net present value	$11,413

Notice that we did not have to recompute annual net cash flows. The firm still used $12,000 for depreciation expense. Therefore, at the end of five years, the machinery will have a book value of zero and the gain on disposal will equal the salvage value.

ASSIGNMENT MATERIAL

QUESTIONS FOR DISCUSSION

8-1 *Rental payments and installment purchase* Is there any difference between the cost of (a) renting a car for $60 per month and (b) buying a car for $3,600? To buy the car you will make payments of $60 per month for five years. You expect the car to have no value at the end of five years.

8-2 *Interest rates and economic activity* The federal government is concerned with regulating the level of economic activity, especially with encouraging production and investment to maintain high employment while not allowing excessive inflation. The government attempts to do this partly by changing interest rates through the Federal Reserve Board. How can the ability to influence interest rates be used to stimulate or discourage investment?

8-3 *Capital budgeting—effects of events* A capital expenditure proposal for a new machine has been evaluated. In what way(s) do each of the following events, not anticipated in the original analysis, affect the evaluation? Consider each event independently.

1. The interest rate on long-term debt increases.
2. The company signs a new contract with its union. The negotiated wage rate for all categories of workers is higher than the prevailing rate.
3. The company raises the selling prices of its products.
4. Congress approves the use of a depreciation rate that provides much faster recognition of depreciation expense than was previously available.

8-4 *Exceptions to decision rules* Using its 14% cost of capital, GSA Toy Company determines that the investment required to bring out a new product, a model tank, has an NPV of $100,000. Suggest at least four reasons why GSA's top managers might reject the project despite its positive NPV.

8-5 *Exceptions to decision rules* The top managers of J&G Products, Inc., a manufacturer of high quality electronic equipment have established a minimum IRR for investment projects at 30%. The analysis of one project prepared for the J&G board to consider shows an IRR of 25%. Suggest at least four reasons why J&G's board might accept the project despite its failure to meet its 30% minimum IRR.

EXERCISES

8-6 *Discounting*

1. Find the approximate IRR for each of the following investments.
   (a) Investment of $30,000 with annual cash flows of $5,000 for 14 years.

   (b) An investment of $90,000 with a single return of $120,000 at the end of three years.
2. Find the NPVs of the following investments at a 12% discount rate.
   (a) Annual flows of $30,000 for ten years are produced by an investment of $160,000.
   (b) An investment of $30,000 with annual flows of $8,000 for four years and a single return of $6,000 at the end of the fifth year.

8-7 NPV and IRR methods Jones Secretarial Service is thinking of buying some new word-processing equipment that promises to save $6,000 in cash operating costs per year. The equipment will cost $16,800. Its estimated useful life is four years. It will have no salvage value. (Ignore taxes.)

Required

1. Compute NPV if the minimum desired rate of return is 10%.
2. Determine IRR.

8-8 Discounting Solve each of the following independent problems.

1. Harry Smith starts college in one year. His father wishes to set up a fund for Harry to use for the $8,400 he will need each year for four years. Harry will make withdrawals at the beginning of each school year. If Mr. Smith can invest at 9%, how much must he invest today to provide for Harry's college expenses?
2. Henry Jackson is about to retire from his job. His pension benefits have accumulated to the point where he could receive a lump-sum payment of $250,000 or $40,000 per year for ten years, paid at the ends of years. Jackson has no dependents and fully expects to live ten years after he retires. If he can invest at 8%, which option should he take?
3. You have just won the $5,000,000 grand prize in a magazine sweepstakes. The prize will be paid in $167,000 installments for 30 years. If your interest rate is 6%, how much would you take now, instead of accepting the annuity?

8-9 Time value of money relationships Answer the following questions.

1. A person received a single payment of $6,440 as a result of having invested some money five years ago at an interest rate of 10%. How much did the person invest?
2. An investment of $2,000 returned a single payment of $5,400. The interest rate was 18%. How many years elapsed between the investment and the return?
3. A person received seven annual payments of $1,000 from an investment. The interest rate was 12%. What was the amount of the investment?
4. An investment of $1,000 returned $343 annually for some years. The rate of interest was 14%. How many payments were received?
5. A $12,000 investment made today will provide a 12% return. The returns will be paid in equal amounts over 12 years. What is the amount of the annual payment?

8-10 Basic capital budgeting without taxes Crestline Inc. produces custom paper boxes. Its managers have been trying to decide whether to buy a new folding machine for $100,000. It will last for four years, have no salvage value, and be depreciated using the straight-line method. The managers anticipate savings in cash operating costs of $40,000 in each of the four years. Cost of capital is 10%.

Required

1. Calculate the NPV of the investment.
2. Calculate the approximate IRR on the investment.
3. Determine the payback period for the investment.
4. Determine the book rate of return on the average investment.

8-11 Basic capital budgeting—taxes (extension of 8-10) Redo 8-10 with Crestline Inc. now being subject to a 30% income tax rate.

8-12 Basic cost savings Grove City Pottery currently makes 200,000 large strawberry jars per year at a variable cost of $9.75. Equipment is available for $500,000 that will reduce the variable cost to $7.50, while increasing cash fixed costs by $200,000. The equipment will have no salvage value at the end of its four-year life and will be depreciated using the straight-line method. Norton faces a 40% income tax rate and a 12% cost of capital.

Required

1. Determine the NPV of the investment.
2. Determine the change in NPV if the equipment has a $25,000 residual value.

8-13 Basic capital budgeting Boston Globes has an opportunity to reduce its annual cash operating costs by $20,000 by acquiring equipment that costs $60,000, has a five-year life, and has no salvage value. Boston uses straight-line depreciation. Cost of capital is 14%. Ignore taxes.

Required

1. Determine the NPV of the investment.
2. Determine the approximate IRR.
3. Determine the payback period.
4. Determine the book rate of return on the average investment.

8-14 Basic capital budgeting with taxes Redo 8-13 with a 40% income tax rate.

8-15 Comparison of methods (continued in Chapter 9) Jason Company has three investment opportunities, summarized below.

	A	B	C
Cost	$70,000	$ 70,000	$ 70,000
Cash inflows by year:			
Year 1	35,000	35,000	4,000
Year 2	35,000	10,000	8,000
Year 3	0	45,000	10,000
Year 4	5,000	20,000	98,000
Total	$75,000	$110,000	$120,000
Average annual income	$ 1,250	$ 10,000	$ 12,500

Required

1. Rank the investment opportunities in order of desirability using (a) payback period, (b) average book rate of return (use average net book value of the investment as the denominator), and (c) NPV using a 16% discount rate.
2. Comment on the results.

8-16 NPV Wilson Crocker owns a driving range. He presently pays several high school students $0.60 per bucket to pick up the golf balls that his customers hit. A salesperson has shown him a machine that will pick up balls at an annual cash cost of $6,600 plus $0.05 per bucket. The machine costs $8,000 and has a four-year life. Crocker would use straight-line depreciation. Volume for the driving range is about 18,000 buckets per year. Crocker's combined state and federal tax rate is 30%. He believes that the appropriate discount rate is 16%.

Required

Determine the NPV of the investment and identify one or more nonquantitative factors that might influence the decision in one or the other direction.

8-17 Capital budgeting for a hospital San Lucia Hospital has the opportunity to acquire a used CAT scanner for $200,000. It will last for ten years and have no salvage value. Estimated revenue is $110,000 per year, and estimated annual cash costs are $66,000. The hospital uses a 14% discount rate for capital budgeting decisions.

Required

For this project determine (a) NPV, (b) payback period, and (c) approximate IRR.

8-18 NPV and IRR Morison Company makes high-quality wallpaper. Its managers believe that the company can increase productivity by acquiring some new machinery but are unsure whether it would be profitable.

The machinery costs $800,000, has a four-year life with no salvage value, and should save about $350,000 in cash operating costs annually. The company uses straight-line depreciation, has a 40% income tax rate, and a 12% cost of capital.

Required

1. Calculate the NPV of the investment.
2. Calculate the approximate IRR.

8-19 Relationships Fill in the blanks for each of the following independent cases. In all cases the investment has a useful life of ten years and no salvage value.

	(a) Annual Net Cash Inflow	(b) Investment	(c) Cost of Capital	(d) Internal Rate of Return	(e) Net Present Value
1.	$ 45,000	$188,640	14%	______	$ ______
2.	$ 75,000	$______	12%	18%	$ ______
3.	$ ______	$300,000	______	16%	$ 81,440
4.	$ ______	$450,000	12%	______	$115,000
5.	$100,000	$______	______	14%	($ 38,300)

8-20 Comparison of book return and NPV (continued in Chapter 9) Welton Company is introducing a product that will sell for $10 per unit. Annual volume for the next four years should be about 200,000 units. The company can use either a hand-fed or a semiautomatic machine to make the product. Data are as follows.

	Hand-fed Machine	Semiautomatic Machine
Per unit variable cost	$ 4	$ 2
Annual cash fixed cost	$725,000	$ 850,000
Cost of machine	$800,000	$1,400,000

Both machines have four-year lives and no anticipated salvage value. Welton uses straight-line depreciation, has a 40% income tax rate, and has a 14% cost of capital.

Required

1. Determine which machine has the higher book rate of return on average investment.
2. Determine which machine has the higher NPV.
3. Determine which alternative has the highest IRR.

PROBLEMS

8-21 New product decision Cavala Company has the opportunity to introduce a new radio with the following expected results.

Annual unit sales volume	250,000	Selling price per unit	$60
Annual cash fixed costs	$3,800,000	Variable cost per unit	$35

The product requires equipment costing $4,500,000 and having a three-year life with no salvage value. The company has a 12% cost of capital. The income tax rate is 40% and Cavala uses straight-line depreciation.

Required

1. Determine the expected increase in future annual after-tax cash flows for this project.
2. Determine the NPV of the investment.
3. Determine the approximate IRR of the investment.
4. Suppose the equipment has a $600,000 salvage value. Cavala will still depreciate the full cost of the equipment, so there would be a tax on whatever proceeds are received from its sale. By how much and in what direction will the NPV of the project change because of the expected salvage value?

8-22 Meaning of IRR You want to withdraw $10,000 from a bank account at the end of each of the next three years. The interest rate is 10%.

Required

1. How much must you have in the bank at the beginning of the first year to be able to make the subsequent $10,000 withdrawals?
2. Schedule the activity in the bank account for the three years. Set up columns for Beginning Balance, Interest, Withdrawal, and Ending Balance. Interest is earned at 10% of the beginning balance of each year.

8-23 Investing in JIT Robson Industries operates several plants, one of which is moving toward JIT manufacturing. One of the first investments the plant will make is roughly $3.5 million to rearrange the factory into manufacturing cells. This cost is tax-deductible over five years using the straight-line method. The managers expect to save about $600,000 in annual manufacturing costs for the foreseeable future as a result of using cells. The tax rate is 40% and cost of capital is 10%.

Required

Determine the NPV of the investment. Use a 30-year period for the annual cost savings. It will be easier to discount the two types of flows separately.

8-24 Installing a sprinkler system Walton Company operates several factories, one of which was built some 30 years ago and is not in good condition. That factory has a fire insurance policy covering machinery, inventory, and the building itself. Premiums on the policy are $17,000 per year.

Recently, a fire inspector from the insurance company recommended that the premium be increased to $45,000 per year because the factory's fire protection has diminished. Its existing sprinkler system no longer works and cannot be repaired at a reasonable cost. The inspector told the plant manager, Jane Spring, that a new system, costing $120,000 and with a 10-year life and no salvage value, would be needed to continue the existing premium of $17,000 per year.

The system would be depreciated on a straight-line basis. The tax rate is 40% and Walton's cost of capital is 14%.

Required

1. Determine the NPV of the investment using only the data provided.
2. Using the guidelines in Appendix B, write a memorandum to Ms. Spring making a recommendation. Include support for your recommendation and suggest relevant factors not mentioned above.

8-25 Employment options Bob Wiblek is a college senior and an All-American football player. Drafted by the Bay City Beasts of the Tri-Continental League, he has been pondering two alternatives the team has offered. The first is that Bob receives $500,000 per year for ten years, the second is that he receives $300,000 per year for 30 years. Either way, Bob and the team both expect his playing career to be over in ten years. Under either alternative, he would get the prescribed amounts whether or not he plays.

Bob would have an income tax rate of 30%. The team has a 40% income tax rate. Bob believes that a 10% discount rate is appropriate. The team has a 14% cost of capital.

Required

1. Which offer should Bob take?
2. Which offer is better for the owners of the team?
3. If your answers to items 1 and 2 differ, explain why. You need not make any calculations.

8-26 Importance of depreciation period Your company has the opportunity to buy machinery for $100,000. It will last for five years, be depreciated using the straight-line method, and save $30,000 in cash operating costs per year. Cost of capital is 10% and the tax rate is 40%.

Required

1. Determine the NPV of the investment.
2. Suppose now that you could depreciate the machinery over two years for tax purposes instead of five years. Determine the NPV of the investment.

8-27 Bringing out a new product BDR is considering adding a new product with a contribution margin of $68 per unit. It expects to sell 5,000 units per year. To make the product, BDR must acquire a new machine costing $550,000 and having a useful life of five years. The machine will have no residual value at the end of its life. Managers estimate cash fixed costs to make the product at $150,000 per year. BDR's cost of capital is 14% and its tax rate is 30%. It uses straight-line depreciation for both financial reporting and tax purposes.

Required

1. What is the expected after-tax annual cash flow from the project?
2. What is the payback period for the project? (Round your answer to three decimal places.)
3. What is the IRR for the project?
4. What is the NPV for this project?
5. Assume BDR has determined that this project could be financed by an 11% loan from a bank. Explain your answer to each of the following.
   a. Should BDR use 11%, instead of 14%, to compute the project's NPV?
   b. Should BDR incorporate the annual interest payments on the note into its computation of the project's annual net cash flows?
6. Assume BDR could, for tax purposes only, depreciate the new machine using one of the accelerated methods of depreciation. Explain your answers to each of the following.
   a. Would BDR pay less total taxes on the income from the project?
   b. Would the project's payback period be different?

8-28 Manufacturing cells, JIT Some of the plant managers of Efron Manufacturing Company are trying to switch to JIT manufacturing. The manager of the Wilson Plant has developed the following data on the effects of introducing JIT, mainly from talks with managers whose plants have adopted JIT principles.

(all amounts in thousands)

	Current Cost	Estimated JIT Cost
Materials	$1,876.4	$1,692.0
Direct labor	2,845.2	2,312.0
Supervision	434.6	88.3
Maintenance	493.2	23.6*
Inspection, incoming and outgoing	256.3	32.8*
Other	673.9	569.5
Totals	$6,579.6	$4,718.2

* *Most costs of maintenance and inspection will be carried out by workers in their cells, thus greatly reducing the centrally administered amounts.*

Moving to cellular manufacturing requires investments of $7.5 million for rearranging and for new machinery more suited to cellular manufacturing. All of these costs can be deducted for tax purposes over ten years. None of the depreciation and amortization of these costs is included in the figures above. The company has a 40% tax rate and a 12% cost of capital. The horizon for discounting the after-tax savings in operating flows is 20 years.

Required

Determine the NPV of the proposed change. You will find it easier to discount the two types of flows separately.

8-29 Retirement option Mr. Ralph Mathews will retire in a few months, on reaching his 65th birthday. His firm's pension plan offers two options: (1) a lump-sum payment of $150,000 on the day of retirement and (2) annual payments of $20,000 per year beginning on the date of retirement and ending at death. Mr. Mathews is not sure which option he should select and asks for your assistance. He tells you that he has no savings now, that he could earn a 14% return if he invested part of the lump-sum payment, and that he would like to spend $25,000 per year during his retirement. He has no relatives or other heirs and is not concerned about leaving an estate. He tells you that he could live on $20,000 per year but would much prefer to spend $25,000 and be more comfortable.

If he chooses the lump-sum payment, he will take out $25,000 to live on during the first year of retirement and invest the remainder. He will then draw $25,000 at the beginning of every year until the money runs out.

Required

Determine how long Mathews could afford to keep up a $25,000 per year standard of living.

8-30 Expanding a product line Kiernan Company makes office equipment of various sorts, such as tables, desks, chairs, and lamps. The sales manager is trying to decide whether to introduce a new model of desk. The desk will sell for $400 and have variable costs of $220. Volume is expected to be 5,000 units per year for five years. To make the desks, the firm will have to buy additional machinery that will cost $1,500,000, have a five-year life, and no salvage value. Straight-line depreciation will be used. Fixed cash operating costs will be $400,000 per year.

The firm is in the 40% tax bracket and its cost of capital is 10%.

Required

1. Determine, using the NPV method, whether the new desk should be brought out.
2. Compute the payback period.
3. Determine the approximate IRR that the firm expects to earn on the investment.

8-31 Buying air pumps Magnum Mart is a chain of convenience stores that sells food, beverages, household products, and gasoline. Its product-development manager, Juanita Cortez, is trying to decide how to acquire coin-operated air pumps that customers can use to fill their tires. One choice is to lease pumps for $850 per year, renewable annually. The other is to buy them for $1,500. Pumps have about a three-year life. For each pump, revenue should average $2,100 per year and operating costs, exclusive of lease payments or depreciation, $250 per year.

Magnum is in the 40% tax bracket, uses a 12% cutoff rate of return, and straight-line depreciation.

Required

Using the guidelines in Appendix B, write a memorandum to Ms. Cortez giving and supporting your recommendation about which acquisition method to select.

8-32 Capital budgeting and reported earnings The president of Wallco Industries has been disturbed by published reports that the firm's stock is not a good buy. Wallco has been growing rapidly in a field that stresses swift technological advances. Wallco has an extensive research program and an ambitious building schedule, with $10 million plant and equipment expenditures planned for next year. The firm's stock is currently selling at $125, about 25 times earnings per share of $5 last year. Continued growth in earnings per share is viewed as necessary to sustain the price of the stock.

Wallco has a cutoff rate of return of 20% after taxes, using discounted cash flow techniques. The president wonders whether to add another capital spending constraint. By the second year of operations, a project must be expected to increase earnings per share by at least $0.40 for each $1,000,000 invested. She feels that such a requirement would help to keep the price of the stock from falling because of disenchantment of stockholders and financial analysts.

She shows you the following proposal.

Investment	$2,000,000
Cash inflows by year (before taxes):	
1	$ 600,000
2	800,000
3	1,050,000
4	1,110,000
5	1,500,000

The tax rate is 40%. There are 500,000 shares of common stock outstanding. Straight-line depreciation is used for both tax and book purposes.

Required

1. Determine whether the investment meets the 20% rate of return criterion.
2. Determine the effects of the investment on earnings per share.
3. What suggestions can you make to resolve the conflict?

8-33 Charitable donation Jan Williamson is a wealthy entrepreneur who wishes to make a substantial donation to her alma mater, Arkwright University. She is considering two alternatives, a $6,000,000 gift now or an equal annual amount in each of the next ten years.

From discussions with the president of Arkwright University, she has learned that the university, which pays no income taxes, earns a 10% return on its endowment fund. The president would be happy with either the $6,000,000 now or with equal annual amounts having a present value of $6,000,000. Mrs. Williamson is able to earn a 9% after-tax return investing in tax-free securities. She faces a combined state and federal tax rate of 35%.

Required

1. Determine the annuity that would yield a $6,000,000 present value to the university.
2. Should Mrs. Williamson make the lump-sum donation or pay the annuity that you determined in item 1?

8-34 Increasing capacity (continued in Chapter 9) Pitcairn Manufacturing Company has regularly been selling out its complete stock of its most popular style of men's socks, Heather. The production and marketing managers have investigated ways to increase capacity and have determined they could produce another 250,000 pairs annually if they bought equipment costing $1,200,000. The equipment has a five-year life with no salvage value. Pitcairn uses straight-line depreciation. The equipment would add $200,000 to annual cash fixed costs. The socks sell for $4 and have $1 per-pair variable cost. The variable cost would not be affected by using the equipment. The managers are confident of selling 200,000 more pairs annually. Cost of capital is 14% and the tax rate is 40%.

Required

1. Determine whether Pitcairn should acquire the equipment.
2. Suppose that additional volume is likely to be 250,000 pairs. Determine whether Pitcairn should acquire the equipment.

8-35 ***Funding a pension plan*** Knowles Company has an agreement with the labor union that represents its workers. The agreement calls for Knowles to pay $25,000 per year for the next ten years into a pension fund. Payments would begin one year from now.

Knowles has excess cash on hand from the sale of some of its assets, so the treasurer approaches the head of the union and asks if it would be all right to make a single, lump-sum payment to discharge the ten-year obligation. Before receiving the union leader's reply, the treasurer decided to determine the maximum amount that Knowles could pay right now. The company is in the 40% tax bracket and has cost of capital of 16%. The annual payments would be deductible for tax purposes in the years in which they were made and the single payment would be deductible in the current year.

Required

Determine the maximum amount that Knowles could pay in a lump-sum settlement of the obligation.

8-36 ***Bond refunding*** Expost Company has outstanding a $1,000,000 (par value) issue of bonds bearing a 14% interest rate. The bonds mature in ten years. Interest rates are lower than they were when this issue was sold, and the firm can now raise cash on a ten-year bond at 10%. The firm's directors are considering retiring the outstanding issue and replacing the old bonds with 10%, ten-year bonds. The firm would have to pay a premium of 12% over par value to buy back the currently outstanding issue. It would also have to spend $60,000 in legal fees and other costs to market the new issue. The premium is tax deductible in the year of refunding, but the costs of issuing the new bonds must be amortized evenly over ten years. The tax rate is 40%, and the company's cost of capital is 18%.

Required

Should the old issue be replaced?

8-37 ***Capital budgeting by a municipality*** The City Council of Alton is considering constructing a convention center in the downtown area. The city has been losing employment to surrounding suburbs, and tax revenues have been falling. The proposed center would cost $22,000,000 to build, and the city would incur annual cash operating costs of $500,000. The city controller estimates that the annual receipts from the center will be approximately $1.8 million. He estimates the center's useful life at 30 years.

The controller's estimate of revenues is based on total annual convention attendance of 200,000 persons. He reports that at 8% interest, the rate the city would have to pay on bonds to build the center, it would be a losing proposition. The present value of $1,300,000 ($1,800,000 − $500,000) annually for 30 years at 8% is $14,635,400, well below the cost of the center. (Assume this computation is correct.)

One member of the council comments that the rentals are not the only source of revenues to the city. To support this position, she offers studies showing that the average person attending a trade show or convention spends $500 in the city in which the event is being held. Because of the various taxes in effect, the city receives, on average, about 1% of all of the money spent in it.

Required

1. Prepare a new analysis, incorporating the additional tax receipts expected if the center is built.
2. Why is 8% used as the discount rate when it is the interest rate, not cost of capital? (Is the interest rate the same as the cost of capital to a city?)

8-38 Comparison of NPV and profit Graham Auto Products is bringing out a new heavy-duty battery and has two choices with respect to the manufacturing process. No matter which choice it makes, it expects to sell 100,000 units per year for four years at $50 per unit. Data on the two processes are

	Labor-Intensive Process	Capital-Intensive Process
Per-unit variable cost	$ 20	$ 10
Annual fixed cash operating costs	$ 400,000	$ 600,000
Investment in equipment	$4,000,000	$6,000,000

Neither set of equipment is expected to have salvage value at the end of four years. The firm uses straight-line depreciation. Cost of capital is 16% and the tax rate is 40%.

Required

1. Which process will give the higher annual profit?
2. Which process will give the higher book rate of return on average investment?
3. Which process will give the higher NPV?
4. Using the guidelines in Appendix B, write a memorandum to Morton Brown, Graham's factory manager, giving and supporting your recommendation regarding which process should be selected.

8-39 Capital budgeting for a computer service firm Many firms are in the business of selling computer time to others. Customers include other business firms, universities, hospitals, and so on. One such computer service firm, Compuservice, Inc., currently has a Whizbang 85, a high-speed machine that it rents from the manufacturer for $18,000 per month. The firm is considering the purchase of a Zoom 125, which is the fastest machine of its type available. The Whizbang 85 would be kept even if the Zoom were bought. Cal Kulate, president of Compuservice, believes that a number of new customers would be attracted if the firm acquired the Zoom 125. He estimates additional revenues of $40,000 per month. Additional costs requiring cash would be $4,000 per month for maintenance and salaries for added operators. The Zoom sells for $1,200,000 and has a useful physical life of about 15 years. However, computer experts have estimated that the Zoom will probably be technologically obsolete in six years.

The firm would use straight-line depreciation of $225,000 per year in order to depreciate the computer to its estimated salvage value of $300,000 at the end of four years. The firm's tax rate is 40% and its cost of capital is 16%.

Required
Using the guidelines in Appendix B, write a memorandum to Mr. Kulate giving and supporting your recommendation regarding the proposal.

8-40 Investing in quality Pellum Company manufactures a number of products in a relatively old plant. Parts of the manufacturing process are outmoded. One result is that about 10 percent of output is spoiled in production and must be scrapped. The manufacturing managers have been looking at new machinery and equipment that would reduce the rate of rejects to near zero. Outfitting the plant will cost about $6.5 million. The new machines have five-year lives and no salvage value. The company uses straight-line depreciation. The existing machinery is fully depreciated and has no sales value.

The total manufacturing costs of the plant under current conditions are about $94.6 million, with $58.0 million variable, the rest fixed. Cash fixed operating costs will increase by about $2.2 million annually if the new machinery were acquired. The tax rate is 40% and cost of capital is 12%.

Required
1. Determine the NPV of reducing spoiled output to zero while maintaining the current level of good output.
2. Annual revenue under existing conditions is $117.8 million. Suppose that demand is far above capacity so that the plant could increase sales by 10% if it acquired the new equipment. Determine the NPV of the investment.

8-41 Reevaluating an investment Ten years ago the Kramer Company, of which you are the controller, bought some machinery at a cost of $200,000. The purchase was made at the insistence of the production manager. The machinery is now worthless, and the production manager believes that it should be replaced. He gives you the following analysis, which he says verifies the correctness of the decision to buy the machinery ten years ago. He bases his statement on the 27% return he calculated, which is higher than the firm's cutoff rate of return of 20%.

Annual cost savings:	
Labor	$ 36,000
Overhead	29,000
Total	65,000
Less straight-line depreciation ($200,000/10)	20,000
Increase in pretax income	45,000
Income taxes at 40%	18,000
Increase in net income	$ 27,000
Average investment ($200,000/2)	$100,000
Return on investment	27%

Required
Do you agree that the investment was wise? Why or why not?

8-42 Purchase commitment Ralston Company buys copper from a number of suppliers, including the Boa Copper Company. The president of Boa has offered to sell Ralston up to 1,000,000 pounds of copper per year for five years at $0.80 per pound if Ralston will lend Boa $2,000,000 at 8% interest. The loan would be repaid at the end of five years; the interest would be paid annually.

Ralston uses at least 1,800,000 pounds of copper per year and expects the price to be $1.00 per pound over the next five years. The tax rate is 40% and Ralston's management considers the relevant discount rate to be 12%.

Required

1. Determine whether Ralston Company should accept the offer.
2. Determine the minimum price at which copper would have to sell, per pound, over the next five years to make accepting the offer worthwhile.

8-43 New product—complementary effects Elmendorf Company makes a variety of cleaning products. The firm's research and development department has recently come up with a new glass cleaner that is superior to all of the products on the market, including the one that Elmendorf currently makes. The new cleaner would be priced at $6 per case and would have variable costs of $2 per case. Elmendorf would have to buy additional machinery costing $8,000,000 to make the new cleaner. The machinery would have a ten-year life. Expected volume of the new cleaner is 800,000 cases per year for ten years. In addition to the variable costs, cash fixed costs will increase $200,000 per year.

The machinery would be depreciated using the straight-line method with no provision for salvage value. There is about $100,000 expected salvage value at the end of ten years. The tax rate is 40% and cost of capital is 14%.

One disadvantage of making the investment is that sales of the firm's existing cleaner would be affected. Volume of the existing cleaner is expected to fall by 300,000 cases per year. A case of the existing cleaner sells for $5 and has variable costs of $3.

Required

Determine the NPV of the proposed investment.

8-44 Uses of space (AICPA adapted) Lansdown Company manages office buildings in the downtown area of a major city. One of the buildings it manages has a large, unused lobby area. A manager of the firm believes that a newsstand should be placed in the lobby. She has talked to managers of several other office buildings and has projected the following annual operating results if Lansdown establishes a newsstand.

Sales	$49,000
Cost of sales	40,000
Salaries of clerks	7,000
Licenses and payroll taxes	200
Share of heat and light bills on the building	500
Share of building depreciation	1,000
Advertising for the newsstand	100
Share of Lansdown's administrative expense	400

The investment required would be $2,000, all for equipment that would be worthless in ten years. Before presenting the plan to her superiors, the manager learned that the space could be leased to an outside firm that would operate the same kind of newsstand. The other firm would pay $750 rent per year for each of the ten years. Because the lobby is heated and lighted anyway, Lansdown would supply heat and light at no additional cost. Lansdown's cost of capital is 12%. (Ignore taxes.)

Required

1. Determine the best course of action for Lansdown.
2. Determine how much annual rent Lansdown would have to receive to equalize the attractiveness of the alternatives.

8-45 Magazine subscriptions The managers of *PC Journal*, a magazine for computer users, are working on a campaign to get extended subscriptions. The magazine's base one-year rate is $23 for 12 issues. The rate for a two-year subscription is tentatively set at $40. Both amounts would be payable in advance. The variable cost per subscription per year is $10.00. Cost of capital is 12%. The company pays no income taxes.

Required

1. Suppose that all one-year subscribers will renew at the end of the year. Therefore, the company will either (a) collect $23 now and $23 in one year or (b) collect $40 now. Determine whether the magazine should offer the $40 rate for a two-year subscription.
2. Again, assuming that all subscribers taking one-year subscriptions would renew at the end of one year, determine the lowest two-year rate that the magazine should offer.
3. Suppose now there is about a 40% attrition rate in subscriptions. That is, of every ten 1-year subscribers, four will not renew next year. Determine whether the magazine should offer the $40 rate. Assume that the variable costs are paid at the *beginning* of each year. You might find it convenient to work with a hypothetical batch of ten subscribers.
4. Using the facts from item 3, determine the lowest two-year rate that the magazine should offer.

8-46 Long-term special order Nova Company makes indoor television antennae that sell for $12 and have variable costs of $7. The firm has been selling 200,000 units per year and expects to continue at that rate unless it accepts a special order from the Acme Television Company. Acme has offered to buy 40,000 units per year at $9, provided that Nova agrees to make the sales for a five-year period. Acme will not take fewer than 40,000 units.

Nova's current capacity is 230,000 units per year. Capacity could be increased to 260,000 units per year if new equipment costing $100,000 were purchased. The equipment would have a useful life of five years, have no salvage value, and add $20,000 in annual fixed cash operating costs. Variable costs per unit would be unchanged.

Nova would use straight-line depreciation for tax purposes. The tax rate is 40% and cost of capital is 14%.

Required

Using the guidelines in Appendix B, write a memorandum to Nova's vice president of manufacturing, Bjorn Hansen, giving and supporting your recommendation about the best course of action.

CASE

8-47 ***Introduction of new product*** Jerry Dollink, controller of Radsiville Industries, Inc., tells you about a meeting of several top managers of the firm. The topic discussed was the introduction of a new product that had been undergoing extensive research and development. Jerry Dollink had thought the product would be brought out in the coming year, but the managers decided to give it further study.

The product is expected to have a market life of ten years. Sales are expected to be 30,000 units annually at $90. The following unit costs were presented by Jamie Barker, manager of the division that would produce and sell the product.

Materials	$10
Direct labor	17
Overhead (manufacturing)	30
Selling and administrative expenses	12
Total costs	$69

Barker went on to point out that equipment costing $3,000,000 and having an expected salvage value of $100,000 at the end of ten years would have to be purchased. Adding the $900,000 that had already been spent on research and development brought the total outlay related to the new product to $3,900,000.

Depreciation of $300,000 per year would reduce taxes by $120,000 (40% rate). The $21 per-unit profit margin would produce $630,000 before taxes and $378,000 after taxes. The net return would then be $498,000 annually, which is a rate of return of about 4%, far below the firm's cost of capital at 14%. Barker concluded that the product should not be brought out.

Dollink tells you that Barker is a strong believer in "having every product pay its way." The calculation of the manufacturing overhead cost per unit includes existing fixed costs of $600,000 allocated to the new product. Additional cash fixed costs are $200,000 per year. Selling and administrative expenses were also allocated to the product on the basis of relative sales revenue. Commissions of $4 per unit will be the only incremental selling and administrative expenses.

Required

1. Prepare a new analysis.
2. Explain the fallacies in Barker's analysis.

9 capital budgeting, part II

The capital budgeting decisions discussed in Chapter 8 required the purchase of new productive assets. In this chapter we consider other kinds of decisions, but the basic principles of analysis remain the same. The new features require somewhat different methods of computing the net cash flows or the required investment, but the analyses still concentrate on cash flows and consider the time value of money.

Because of the many estimates in a capital budgeting decision, we introduce an analytical technique to help managers identify the most critical estimates. We also give attention to a few additional aspects of income tax law that affect capital budgeting decisions. Finally, because budgets reflect planning decisions and many of those decisions have social consequences, we conclude the chapter (and Part Two) with a discussion of the social consequences of decision making and a brief look at the special problem of decision making in the public sector.

COMPLEX INVESTMENTS

For many investment opportunities, the required investment is not a single cash payment for some new depreciable asset. Some opportunities require a change in the entity's investment in working capital or the replacement of existing assets. These features complicate the determination of the required investment.

CHANGES IN INVESTMENT IN WORKING CAPITAL

A capital budgeting decision involves an investment with a life of more than one year. Such investments usually involve plant assets. Often such investment opportunities also require a change in working capital (current assets – current liabilities). An analysis of a capital budgeting decision that necessitates a change in working capital must incorporate that change in the decision. The most common change is an increase in working capital, and we present that situation first. Later we discuss the less common and less analytically complex decisions requiring a decrease in working capital.

An investment that involves increased sales usually leads to an increase in accounts receivable. Supporting a higher level of sales also requires a higher level of inventory for both retail firms and manufacturers that are not pursuing the zero-inventory goal of the JIT philosophy. (When you followed the development of a comprehensive budget for Cross Company in Chapter 6, you saw the impact on inventory levels of a short-term increase in sales.) Moreover, even if no increase in inventory is necessary, sales-increasing opportunities also increase the firm's current liabilities (payables for purchases of product, materials and components, labor, commissions, etc.).

The increase in payables is likely to be smaller than the increase in receivables, and most surely would be smaller than the combined increase in receivables and inventory. Hence, undertaking the sales-increasing investment requires that the company carry a higher level of working capital or **working capital investment.** Investments in working capital are just as important as investments in plant assets, and a capital budgeting opportunity must provide an acceptable return on *all* of the investment that it requires.

There is one difference between investments in working capital and in plant assets. At the end of its useful life, a tangible asset is almost always worth less than it cost. In contrast, working capital investments are typically recovered *in full,* or nearly so, because the larger receivables and inventory will be turned into cash during the final operating cycle in the life of the project. Remember the time lags, discussed in Chapters 6 and 7, between making a purchase and paying for it, and between making a sale and collecting for it. In the final year of a project, the expectation of reduced sales reduces the required inventory, thereby reducing the required purchases, which in turn reduces the amount of cash needed to pay for purchases and frees such cash for other uses. Similarly, cash collections in that final year should exceed sales related to the project, because of the delay in collecting for sales made in the previous year.[1]

Dealing with projects that require investment in working capital is not particularly difficult. It is, however, important to recognize that *there are no tax effects* associated either with the initial increase in working capital or with its recovery at the end of the useful life of the project. (Remember that taxes are normally levied on income computed on the accrual basis.)

Consider an investment in a new product that is expected to have a useful life of five years. Revenues from the product are estimated to be $20,000 annually, with additional annual cash costs of $6,000. The investment is

1 As a practical matter, the return of the net investment in current asset items may extend one or two months after the end of a project because of the lags in (1) collections for sales (through accounts receivable) and (2) payments for purchases (through accounts payable). When discounting cash flows several years hence, a difference of a month or two is not usually significant and can be ignored.

$30,000 in equipment and $35,000 in working capital. Straight-line depreciation is used, the equipment has no salvage value, cost of capital is 12%, and the tax rate is 40%. The cash flows and NPV of the project are computed below.

Incremental Cash Flows Years 1-5

	Tax Computation	Cash Flow
Revenues	$20,000	$20,000
Cash expenses	6,000	6,000
Pretax cash inflow	14,000	14,000
Depreciation ($30,000/5)	6,000	
Increase in taxable income	$ 8,000	
Tax at 40%	$ 3,200	3,200
Net cash inflow per year		$10,800

End of Year 5

Recovery of working capital investment	$35,000

Summary of Net Present Value of Investment

Operating cash inflows ($10,800 × 3.605)	$38,934
Recovery of working capital investment ($35,000 × 0.567)	19,845
Total present value	58,779
Investment required ($30,000 + $35,000)	65,000
Net present value	($ 6,221)

The investment is undesirable. If only the noncurrent asset investment is considered, the investment appears desirable because it shows a positive NPV of $8,934 ($38,934 – $30,000). Failure to consider the working capital requirements would lead to a bad decision.

Some investments decrease working capital. A computerized billing system enables a company to collect its accounts receivable faster. For such a project, we would show a reduction of investment in working capital (accounts receivable) at the beginning of the life, and a cash outflow at the end of the useful life of the system. For, if the company does not recommit to the system (or one like it), receivables will increase.

By far the most common type of investment that reduces working capital investment comes from companies that are moving toward the JIT ideal of zero inventories. General Electric Appliances reduced the cycle time from receipt of an order to delivery of a finished product from 80 days to under 20 days. In the process, the segment reduced inventory by $200 million and significantly increased profitability.[2]

In the first year of such a project, the company will draw units from existing inventory to meet its earliest sales needs, but will not purchase materials or incur other production costs to replace those units until the units are needed to meet sales delivery deadlines. Delaying purchases and production has the effect of freeing up, fairly early in that first year, cash that can be used for other purposes.

The cash flow implications of inventory-reducing projects are different from those of projects requiring a build-up of inventory. A company committed to the JIT philosophy does not expect to return to its prior inventory

2 *"Jack Welch's Lessons for Success,"* Fortune, *January 25, 1993, 89.*

levels at the end of the project's life. The company expects a cash saving in the first year of a project's life but does *not* expect a cash outflow in the final year. Accordingly, the only unusual aspect of the analysis of an inventory-reducing decision is that the cash saving from reducing inventory in the first year shows as a reduction of the investment required for the decision. (As an alternative, the cash saving could simply be added to the present value of the future cash flows.) The second case of a complex investment to be considered, the replacement decision, is different from investments involving working capital because it involves additional calculations to determine future cash flows.

REPLACEMENT DECISIONS

Businesses frequently face the problem of whether to replace an asset currently in use. Such a question is called a **replacement decision.** Replacement decisions are made when economic or technological factors make it possible to perform tasks at lower cost. Faster and more efficient machines and labor-saving devices enable the firm to earn higher returns. Typically, replacement decisions involve essential operations. The focus is on how to perform those operations.

Determining cash flows for replacement decisions is more complex than for decisions about whether to purchase new assets because (1) there are tax differences if depreciation on the replacement is different from that on the existing assets, and (2) determining the net cost to purchase the replacement requires more steps. We illustrate two methods for evaluating replacement decisions: the incremental approach and the total-project approach.

The **incremental approach** focuses on the differences between the cash flows, given the alternatives of keeping the existing assets or replacing them. The **total-project approach** looks at the total cash flows and total present values under each alternative and compares the present values. The two approaches give the same results, so selecting one or the other is a matter of computational convenience.

Your firm now owns a machine for which it paid $100,000 five years ago. Other data relating to the machine are as follows.

Remaining useful life	5 years
Current book value	$50,000
Annual depreciation	$10,000
Expected sales value—now	$20,000
—in 5 yrs.	$10,000
Annual cash operating costs	$30,000

If you continue to use the machine for the next five years, there will be a tax (at an expected rate of 40%) on the expected salvage value, because that value was not included in the depreciation calculation. If you sell the machine now, the loss for tax purposes will be $30,000 ($50,000 book value – $20,000 sales price).

Suppose a new machine comes on the market that sells for $60,000, has an estimated useful life of five years with no salvage value, and costs only $15,000 per year to operate. The new machine can be depreciated over five years using the straight-line method. Suppose further that cost of capital is 16%. Is it wise to replace the old machine now?

As with any capital project, two considerations exist: initial investment and future cash flows. In a replacement decision, the computation of each of these is different from the computations we have made previously. First we determine the initial investment as shown below.

	Tax Computation	Cash Outlay
Purchase price of new asset		$60,000
Book value of old machine	$50,000	
Sale price, which is a cash inflow	20,000	(20,000)
Loss for taxes, which can be offset against regular income	$30,000	
Tax saved (40% × $30,000)	$12,000	(12,000)
Total cash benefit from sale		(32,000)
Net outlay for new asset		$28,000

The book value or cost of an existing asset is sunk and irrelevant to decisions. However, book value *does* affect taxes if the asset is sold and so must be considered in determining those taxes.[3] The sale of the old asset reduces the outlay for the new one by $32,000, because the firm will receive $20,000 from the sale and the loss on the sale produces a $12,000 saving in income taxes. Hence, a net outlay of only $28,000 is required to buy the new asset. Lest it appear that sales at a loss are desirable because they reduce taxes, consider that if the old asset could be sold for $60,000, creating a taxable gain of $10,000 and additional taxes of $4,000, the sale would bring in $56,000, substantially more than the $32,000 shown above.

Incremental Approach

Below is the computation of future cash flows, using the incremental approach.

Annual Cash Savings Years 1-5

		Tax Computation	Cash Flow
Pretax cash savings:			
Cash cost of using old asset		$30,000	
Cash cost of using new asset		15,000	
Difference in favor of replacement, cash inflow	(1)	15,000	15,000
Additional depreciation:			
Depreciation on new asset ($60,000/5)		12,000	
Depreciation on old asset		10,000	
Additional tax deduction for depreciation with replacement	(2)	2,000	
Increase in taxable income (1) – (2) =	(3)	$13,000	
Additional tax ($13,000 × 40%), cash outflow	(4)	$ 5,200	(5,200)
Additional net cash inflow favoring replacement (1) – (4)			$ 9,800

3 *In practice, the book value of an asset might not be the same as its carrying value for tax purposes (called its* tax basis*). For simplicity, in this section and in most of the assignment material, the book value and tax basis of the asset in question are equal. If there is a difference between the two, the tax effect of the gain or loss on disposition of an asset is computed using its tax basis. But the principles of the calculation remain unchanged: the carrying value of the asset is relevant only to the extent that it affects the cash flow for taxes.*

Salvage Values—End of Year 5	Tax Computation	Cash Flow
Old asset	$10,000	
New asset	0	
Difference in favor of not replacing	$10,000	$10,000
Tax on difference, cash outflow	$ 4,000	(4,000)
Difference in favor of not replacing (decrease in cash flow)		$ 6,000

The $9,800 per year for five years is then discounted at 16%, yielding a present value of $32,085 ($9,800 × 3.274). The $6,000 difference in cash flows from salvage values is discounted at 16%, yielding $2,856 ($6,000 × 0.476). The difference is subtracted from the present value of the $9,800 annual flows because you must give up the salvage value of the old asset in order to obtain the increased annual flows.

Summary of Present Values of Investment—Incremental Approach	
Present value of savings from using new machine	$32,085
Less: Present value of unfavorable difference in salvage values	2,856
Present value of future net savings	29,229
Required investment	28,000
Net present value of replacing machine	$ 1,229

The present value of future net savings from making a replacement now ($29,229) is greater than the net outlay required ($28,000), so the replacement is desirable. The decision rule, then, using the incremental approach, is to replace when the NPV of the replacement alternative is positive.

Total-Project Approach

A replacement decision can also be analyzed using a total-project approach. In the total-project approach we calculate, individually, the present values of the future outflows using the existing asset and using the replacement asset. The decision rule, using the total-project approach, is to accept the alternative with the *lower present value of future outflows.* This is because the analysis of both alternatives deals with costs (cash outflows), not revenues (cash inflows); the alternative with the lower present value minimizes costs.

For the example just given, the present value of the total outflows if the *existing* machine is used is calculated as follows.

Decision—Operate Existing Machine	Tax Computation	Cash Flow
Annual operating costs	$30,000	$30,000
Depreciation	10,000	
Total tax-deductible expenses	$40,000	
Tax savings expected (40%)	$16,000	16,000
Net cash outflow expected per year		$14,000
Present value factor for 5 years at 16%		3.274
Present value of future operating outflows		$45,836
Less: Present value of salvage value ($6,000 × 0.476)		2,856
Present value of future cash outflows on existing machine		$42,980

Consider, now, the present value of the total cash flows if the new machine is purchased.

Decision—Sell Existing Machine, Buy New Machine

	Tax Computation	Cash Flow
Annual operating costs	$15,000	$15,000
Depreciation	12,000	
Total tax-deductible expenses	$27,000	
Tax savings expected (40%)	$10,800	10,800
Net cash outflow expected per year		$ 4,200
Present value factor for 5 years at 16%		3.274
Present value of future operating outflows		$13,751
Net outlay required for the new machine		28,000
Present value of total cash outflows of buying new machine		$41,751

Comparing the two alternatives, we find

Present value of using existing machine	$42,980
Present value of buying and using new machine	41,751
Difference in favor of replacing machine	$ 1,229

The present value of the total outlays associated with using the existing machine is greater than that of the total outlays associated with acquiring and using the new machine. Note that the $1,229 difference is equal to the NPV we computed using the incremental approach. The two approaches give the same results, and the choice between them is a matter of convenience.

In the replacement decision considered here, it was possible to continue using the currently owned asset. The same two analytical approaches can be used if an essential asset has reached the end of its useful life and alternatives exist as possible replacements. For example, suppose that a firm needs a new fork-lift truck because one of its existing trucks is about to be scrapped. Perhaps two different models are available as replacements, each with a different acquisition cost and associated annual operating costs. Because the firm is committed to replacing the old forklift, the decision becomes how to minimize the future costs, which either the incremental or the total-project approach could be used.

MUTUALLY EXCLUSIVE ALTERNATIVES

The decision rules presented in this chapter and the preceding one classify investments as wise or unwise. They do not consider whether the company has enough money to make the investments. Of course, no firm has unlimited resources. Investments that are wise under the decision rules already presented remain so even when resources are limited. But when resources are limited, all of the firm's investment opportunities are *competing* for the available money. In some cases, the competition among opportunities is even more specific, as when the firm has two or more ways of accomplishing the same goal so that selecting one alternative precludes selecting the others. We call such competing proposals **mutually exclusive alternatives.**

Some of the decisions already considered fit this definition, such as the replacement decision. If the firm keeps its present equipment, the newer model is not acquired and vice versa. Mutual exclusivity can also arise as a matter of policy. For example, a firm might have a policy of introducing no more than one new product in any one year.

Whether exclusivity is inherent in the proposals or is the result of management policy, it is not unusual for competing alternatives to have unequal lives. Some analysts suggest that another evaluation technique, the profitability index, can be particularly useful in ranking and deciding among alternatives. These two special topics are discussed in the next sections.

UNEQUAL LIVES

Alternative investment opportunities often have different useful lives. For example, both a conveyor belt and a fork-lift truck might meet the need to move semifinished units from one place to another, but the life of the conveyor is likely to exceed that of the truck. Our techniques for evaluating investments can be used in such a case only if we find some way to make the alternatives comparable. One commonly used method of doing so is to assume a chain of replacements such that the analysis of each alternative covers the same number of years.

To illustrate this method, assume the following facts about two mutually exclusive investment opportunities involving a machine, versions Model G-40 and Model G-70, that is essential to the firm's operations.

	Model G-40	Model G-70
Purchase price	$40,000	$70,000
Annual cash operating costs	$ 8,000	$ 6,000
Expected useful life	4 years	8 years

Neither machine has any expected salvage value at the end of its useful life. The firm's cost of capital is 14%. So, as to concentrate on the specific problem at hand—the unequal lives of the alternatives—we ignore income taxes and, therefore, need not be concerned with depreciation.

The time period selected for the evaluation is eight years because that is the lowest common denominator for the lives of the two investments. (If the alternatives had lives of, say, four and six years, we would use a 12-year period to compare the two.) Evaluating first the alternative with the longer life (Model G-70), the present value of the expected cash outflows is $97,834, as shown below.

Annual operating costs	$ 6,000
Present value factor for 14% and 8 years	4.639
Present value of operating costs	$27,834
Investment required	70,000
Present value of total cash outflows for G-70	$97,834

To provide *comparable* information about the alternative of using Model G-40, we assume replacement at the end of four years at a cost of $44,000 but no change in annual operating costs. The present value of total cash outflows assuming a choice of Model G-40 is $103,168, as shown below.

Annual operating costs, years 1-4	$ 8,000
Present value factor for 14% and 4 years	2.914
Present value of operating cash outflows, years 1-4	$ 23,312
Present value of purchase of replacement Model G-40 at the end of year 4 ($44,000 × .592)	26,048
Present values of cash outlays in years 5-8:	
Year 5 $8,000 × .519	4,152
Year 6 $8,000 × .456	3,648
Year 7 $8,000 × .400	3,200
Year 8 $8,000 × .351	2,808
Present value of future cash outlays	63,168
Investment required now	40,000
Present value of total cash outflows for G-40	$103,168

Because we are dealing with cash *out*flows for the two alternatives, we are interested in the lower present value, which is $97,834 for selecting Model G-70 (compared with $103,168 for selecting Model G-40). However, the firm's managers should consider how confident they are in the forecast of the replacement cost of the G-40 as well as the likelihood of a significant change in technology. These and other unquantified factors influence the final decision.

RANKING INVESTMENT OPPORTUNITIES

In Chapter 8 we stated that the two discounted cash flow techniques (NPV and IRR) were conceptually superior to other methods presented in that chapter (payback period and book rate of return). It is possible, however, that if two or more proposals are *ranked* using each of the two conceptually superior methods, the *rankings* might not be the same. That is, the proposals ranking first and second using NPV might rank second and first using IRR. If the proposals are mutually exclusive there is now a conflict; the decision rule for NPV argues acceptance of one proposal, while the decision rule for IRR argues acceptance of the other.

To deal with such situations, some accountants and financial specialists prefer a third discounted cash flow technique, the profitability index, which, they argue, is as useful as NPV and IRR in most situations but more useful than those approaches in evaluating mutually exclusive alternatives. The **profitability index (PI)** is the *ratio* of the present value of the future cash flows to the investment. In general terms,

$$\textit{Profitability index} = \frac{\textit{present value of future cash flows}}{\textit{investment}}$$

Thus, a $100,000 investment with present value of future cash flows of $118,000 has a PI of 1.18.

The decision rule for this third approach to evaluating investments is to accept projects with a PI greater than 1.0. In the case of acceptance/rejection decisions, the decision rule for using PI produces the same results as the rules covering NPV and IRR. An investment with a positive NPV and an IRR greater than cost of capital also has a PI greater than 1.0.

However, except under very special circumstances, NPV is preferable to either IRR or PI when it comes to ranking competing alternatives. Let us see how the three criteria perform in an example, and explain those special circumstances.

Below are data for two mutually exclusive investment opportunities confronting a firm with a 10% cost of capital.

	Investment Opportunities	
	X	Y
Investment required	$50,000	$10,000
Life of investment	1 year	1 year
Cash flows, end of year 1	$55,991	$11,403
Present value of cash flows at 10% cost of capital (.909 × cash flow)	$50,896	$10,365
Net present value of project	$ 896	$ 365
Internal rate of return:		
Discount rate associated with factor .893 ($50,000/$55,991)	12%	
Discount rate associated with factor .877 ($10,000/$11,403)		14%
Profitability index:		
$50,896/$50,000	1.018	
$10,365/$10,000		1.037

Project Y has both a higher IRR and a higher PI than does project X, which is higher using only the NPV criterion. *However, provided that the 10% cost of capital is the rate at which other alternative investments can be made,* project X should be selected. The simplest way to show this is as follows.

A company considering both opportunities X and Y must have at least $50,000 (the investment required for X) available for investment. If the company accepts project Y (outlay of $10,000), it will have $40,000 available for other projects. Now assume that another, hypothetical project, Z, is available that requires an investment of $40,000 and shows an expected return of 10%, the cost of capital. What cash would the company have at the end of the year if it selected Y and invested the additional funds in Z? The cash position is summarized below.

Cash provided by investment in project Y		$11,403
Cash provided by investment in Z:		
Investment returned	$40,000	
Earnings on the investment (10%)	4,000	44,000
Total cash available to company at end of year		$55,403

At the end of the year, the company has $55,403 from the two projects. But, had it invested the entire $50,000 in project X, the company would have had $55,991 at the end of the year. Thus, accepting project Y and using the excess funds for another project produces less cash than accepting only project X.

The only time that the project with the higher PI or higher IRR should be chosen in preference to the one with the higher NPV is when investing in the former enables the firm to invest additional cash at a rate *greater* than the cost of capital *and* that opportunity is not available if the firm chooses the project with the higher NPV. Thus, in our example situation, we would choose project Y only if there were additional available investments with returns that were in excess of 10%, which investments would have to be foregone if the extra $40,000 were invested in project X.

SENSITIVITY ANALYSIS

In Chapter 5 we emphasized that decision analysis involves many estimates, errors in one or more of which could lead to an unwise decision. Because of the importance of estimates in decision making, managers analyze the sensitivity of decisions to changes in one or more variables. This testing of the estimates, called **sensitivity analysis,** involves trying to find out how much the value of a variable can rise or fall before a different decision is indicated. Although sensitivity analysis applies to all types of decisions, it is especially beneficial when applied to capital budgeting decisions.

A misestimate of annual cash flow is magnified because it applies to several years and is multiplied by a present value factor. For a project with a ten-year life where cost of capital is 20% (present value factor of 4.192), a $1 drop in annual cash flow produces a drop of $4.192 in the present value of those flows.

A capital budgeting decision also works out over an extended time, which is not true of short-term decisions, so a misestimate of useful life could be important. Suppose an investment of $12,000 is expected to generate cash flows of $3,000 per year for ten years and that the discount rate is 12%. The project has a positive NPV. But considering the uncertainties surrounding estimates for years far into the future, a manager might wonder just how long the investment must continue producing an annual flow of $3,000 in order to earn at least the required 12% return. Dividing the investment by the annual cash flow gives a present value factor (also the payback period) of 4 ($12,000/$3,000). Knowing the discount rate (12%) and the present value factor (4.0) we can consult Table B of Appendix C, look down the 12% column, and see that 3.605 is the factor for five years, 4.111 for six years. Hence, the project must yield its annual flows of $3,000 for nearly six years in order to earn the required 12% return. In this case then, the estimated useful life of the project has to be in error by 40% (from ten to six years), a large error in the original estimate, before the decision changes; so, the decision is not very sensitive to the estimate of useful life.

The outcome of analyzing a capital budgeting decision can also be affected significantly by differences in estimates of sales volumes, selling prices, and per-unit variable costs. (The effect of each such difference is magnified in the analysis, because each unit of volume is multiplied by contribution margin per unit.) Hence, managers might want to determine how sensitive a decision is to estimates of volume, selling price, or variable costs. For example, suppose a firm with a cost of capital of 14% and a 40% tax rate can bring out a new product priced at $22. Variable costs of the product are expected to be $4 per unit, fixed costs requiring cash outlays are estimated at $100,000 annually, and the estimated annual sales volume is 10,000 units. Bringing out the new product requires an investment of $200,000, all for depreciable assets with a five-year life and no salvage value, and the firm uses straight-line depreciation. The initial analysis for this decision follows.

		Tax	Cash Flow
Expected contribution margin (10,000 × $18)		$180,000	$180,000
Fixed costs:			
Cash	$100,000		(100,000)
Depreciation	40,000		
		140,000	
Increase in taxable income		$ 40,000	
Tax at 40% (cash outflow)		$ 16,000	(16,000)
Net cash inflow per year			$ 64,000
Present value factor, 5-year annuity at 14%			3.433
Present value of annual cash inflows			$219,712
Investment required			200,000
Net present value			$ 19,712

Based on the available estimates, the project has a positive NPV and should be accepted. But how far can volume fall before the investment becomes only marginally desirable?

Because NPV is now $19,712, we shall find how much a decline in volume will reduce NPV to zero. We can find the decrease in volume that will reduce NPV by $19,712 as follows.

Net present value	$19,712
Divided by 14% present value factor for 5 years	3.433
Equals change in annual net cash flows to make investment yield 14%	$ 5,742
Divided by (1 minus the tax rate) gives decrease in pretax cash flow	$ 9,570
Divided by $18 contribution margin gives decrease in sales	532 units
Volume required for 14% return (10,000 – 532)	9,468

The following schedule shows that NPV is virtually zero at a volume of 9,468 units.

Contribution margin, 9,468 × $18	$170,424
Fixed costs	140,000
Income before taxes	30,424
Income taxes at 40%	12,170
Net income	18,254
Plus depreciation	40,000
Net cash flow	$ 58,254
Present value factor, 5-year annuity at 14%	3.433
Present value of annual flows	199,986
Investment	200,000
NPV, difference from zero because of rounding	($ 14)

Managers can perform this analysis with other variables, such as selling price, unit variable cost, or total fixed costs. To test the sensitivity of selling price or unit variable cost, simply divide the allowable decrease in *total* contribution margin by unit volume to determine the allowable decrease in *unit* contribution margin. For our example, $9,570/10,000 = $0.957. A drop in selling price or increase in variable cost of $0.957 will bring the NPV to zero. You might wish to verify this result by doing an analysis as shown on the preceding page. Please see that we analyze only one variable at a time, holding the others constant. There are ways of allowing several variables to change simultaneously, but these are beyond our scope.

Sensitivity analysis gives managers an idea about how unfavorable occurrences like lower volumes, shorter useful lives, or higher costs affect the profitability of a project. It is used because of the uncertainty that prevails in almost any real-life situation. Some other ways to deal with uncertainty are introduced in Appendix A.

MORE ON INCOME TAXES

Throughout this book we have treated income taxes rather generally. In particular, we have assumed that a single tax rate applies to all of a company's revenues and expenses, that only revenues and expenses of the current year affect taxes, and that the depreciation rules of financial accounting govern tax deductions for depreciation. None of these assumptions is always true. However, tax law is far too complex to be treated in depth in an introductory text in managerial accounting. We therefore point out only a few aspects of the law that bear on capital budgeting decisions (and warn you at the outset that the details are subject to change virtually every time Congress meets.)

First, no single tax rate applies to all incomes. Rates are graduated (progressively higher) and depend on whether the business is incorporated. Federal tax rates for corporations begin at 15% for income up to $50,000 and increase to 34% for income over $75,000 (as of December 1992). However, above $100,000, the corporation loses the benefit of the lower rates, so that the rate on some incremental income can be as high as 39%. The federal rates on incomes of unincorporated businesses depend on, among other things, the incomes of their individual owners from sources other than the business. These rates are 15%, 28%, and 31% (in early 1993). Most states levy income taxes on individuals and on corporations, which further increases the rates. Because large businesses are likely to be in the top brackets for both federal and state tax purposes, it is reasonable for them to use a single combined federal and state rate for analyzing capital budgeting decisions.

Second, income taxes do not depend solely on revenues and expenses for a given tax year. One feature of tax law, called the operating loss carryback/carryforward, allows businesses to offset losses in one year against profits in another. For example, if a qualifying company lost $200,000 in 19X4, then earns $50,000 in 19X5, it does not have to pay any taxes on the $50,000 because of the loss in 19X4. In fact, with some restrictions, the company does not have to pay income taxes until it earns over $200,000 cumulatively after 19X4.

The segment of the tax law that introduces the greatest difference between our general approach and the specifics of tax law relates to the treatment of depreciation. As pointed out in Chapter 8, determining the cash outflow for taxes requires considering the tax deduction for depreciation. Because the rules governing depreciation for tax purposes differ considerably from those governing depreciation for financial accounting purposes, we now consider, in some detail, the major factor in producing that difference, the **Modified Accelerated Cost Recovery System (MACRS)**.

MACRS

For many years prior to 1981, business entities were allowed to use a different, and faster, depreciation method for tax purposes than was used for financial accounting purposes. An entity could start using one of the accelerated methods of depreciation, and then switch to the straight-line method when that method would produce higher depreciation charges for tax purposes. The life over which an asset could be depreciated for tax purposes was generally its *Asset Depreciation Range (ADR)* life. (ADR lives were developed by the Internal Revenue Service.) The schedule of ADR lives relieved a business from having to estimate useful lives for its assets for tax purposes.

The Economic Recovery Tax Act (ERTA) of 1981 continued to provide benefits from accelerated depreciation, but narrowed the options by introducing **Accelerated Cost Recovery System (ACRS).** ACRS specified much shorter depreciation periods than had previously been allowed. The Tax Reform Act of 1986 made some changes in ACRS and introduced Modified Accelerated Cost Recovery System (MACRS). (Both Acts allow businesses to use straight-line depreciation under the ADR lives, but that is usually less advantageous than MACRS.) Under MACRS, the business places individual assets into various classes according to their ADRs. For most industrial and service companies, four classes of property are important:

> 5-Year Class: This class includes automobiles, light trucks, typewriters, copiers, personal computers, and certain other enumerated items.
>
> 7-Year Class: This class includes office furniture and equipment, most types of machinery, and any property not designated by law as being in some other class.
>
> 10-Year Class: This class contains property with IRS specified lives of at least 16 years and less than 20 years, including certain types of transportation equipment.
>
> 31.5-Year Class: This class includes nonresidential real property such as factory buildings.

Exhibit 9-1 gives the percentages (rounded to the nearest 1%) of cost to be depreciated in each year for the three classes of most relevance to capital budgeting.[4] Depreciation under MACRS for 3-, 5-, 7-, and 10-year classes reflects the 200% declining balance method, with a switch to straight-line depreciation when it benefits the business. (The 150% declining balance method is used for other classes.) Salvage value is not recognized under MACRS. Also, MACRS uses the "half-year convention," which means that assets are assumed to be put in service halfway through the year. Its practical effect is that, as the exhibit shows, assets are depreciated over one year

---

4 The exact percentage from IRS publications must be used for tax returns.

Exhibit 9-1 Percentages of Cost Depreciated Under MACRS

Year	5-Year Class	7-Year Class	10-Year Class
1	20%	14%	10%
2	32	25	18
3	19	18	14
4	12	12	12
5	12	9	9
6	5	9	7
7		9	7
8		4	7
9			7
10			6
11			3

more than their class lives; that is, 5-Year assets over six years, 7-Year assets over eight years, and so on.

MACRS is usually advantageous because it concentrates depreciation deductions in the earlier years of an asset's life. MACRS class lives are much shorter than ADR lives and so write-offs are considerably faster than they were previously. Tax payments in the early years are less than under the straight-line method. Payments in later years are higher, but remember that the present value of the tax payments is lower the later they are made.

Calculating depreciation under MACRS can be tedious. Exhibit 9-2 provides a shortcut method for finding the *present value of tax savings* for 5- and 7-Year property at various discount rates. To use the table, multiply the cost

Exhibit 9-2 Present Value of MACRS Tax Shields[a]

Discount Rate	5-Year Assets	7-Year Assets
.08	.811	.766
.10	.774	.722
.12	.738	.681
.14	.706	.645
.16	.675	.611
.18	.647	.580
.20	.621	.552
.22	.597	.526
.24	.574	.502

a Factors in this table are the sums of the percentages of depreciation for each period multiplied by the present value factors. For example, the factor for 10% for a 5-Year asset is .774 or (20% × .909) + (32% × .826) + (19% × .751) + (12% × .683) + (12% × .621) + (5% × .564). There is some rounding.

of the asset by the factor for the life and discount rate, then multiply by the tax rate.

Let us look at an example to see how the table works. Suppose a company expects pretax cash flows of $3,000 per year from an asset costing $10,000. The asset is in the 5-Year class and, to reduce calculations, has a useful life of six years. The tax rate is 40% and cost of capital is 12%. A year-by-year analysis is below.

	Year					
	1	2	3	4	5	6
Pretax inflow	$ 3,000	$3,000	$3,000	$3,000	$3,000	$3,000
MACRS deduction [a]	2,000	3,200	1,900	1,200	1,200	500
Taxable income	1,000	(200)	1,100	1,800	1,800	2,500
Tax at 40%	400	(80)	440	720	720	1,000
Net cash inflow [b]	$ 2,600	$3,080	$2,560	$2,280	$2,280	$2,000
Present value factors	.893	.797	.712	.636	.567	.507
Present values	$ 2,322	$2,455	$1,823	$1,450	$1,293	$1,014
Total present value	$10,357					

a From the 5-year column of Exhibit 9-1.
b Pretax inflows minus tax, year 1, $3,000 – $400 = $2,600.

It is much easier to determine this present value of the operating inflows net of tax, and *then* to add the present value of the MACRS tax shield.

Present value of operating flows	
$3,000 × (1 – .40) × 4.111 (from Table B)	$ 7,400
Present value of MACRS shield	
$10,000 × .40 × .738 (from Exhibit 9-2)	2,952
Total present value (rounding difference)	$10,352

We needed only two calculations. The operating flow, net of tax, is an annuity of $1,800 [$3,000 × (1 – .40)] for six years, and is discounted using the Table B factor for six years at 12%. Exhibit 9-2 gives the factor for a 5-Year asset at 12% as .738, which, when multiplied by the cost of the asset *and* by the tax rate, gives the present value of the tax shield.

As noted earlier, the depreciation deductions mandated under MACRS are almost always more advantageous than those available prior to 1981, because of the relatively short lives now acceptable for tax purposes. Note, however, that the shorter lives are unlikely to be used to compute depreciation for financial reporting purposes because they are unlikely to coincide with the useful life of the property. An important result of MACRS is that the tax basis of an asset (cost minus *tax* depreciation) seldom equals its book value, and it is the tax basis that must be considered in calculating the taxable gain (or deductible loss) when the asset is sold. For capital budgeting decisions involving replacements of existing assets, the analysis of both current cash outlay and cash inflow from salvage value requires a calculation of the tax basis of the asset at the time of disposition.

Recent criticisms of DCF methods center on fears that they make it too difficult to justify investments that increase product quality, reduce cycle time, and have other benefits besides cost savings. Critics argue that many companies are not investing enough because they consider only the readily calculable, monetary benefits of investments and ignore more qualitative factors. Many companies do evaluate qualitative factors in making capital budgeting decisions. For instance, about 98% of companies responding to one survey considered increases in product quality, with 61% considering it only qualitatively, with no numerical justification. Almost two-thirds of the companies considered whether an investment was consistent with corporate strategy.*

* *James A. Hendricks, "Applying Cost Accounting to Factory Automation,"* Management Accounting, *December, 1988, 24-28.*

CRITICISMS OF DCF METHODS

Chapter 8 gave several examples of companies that explicitly downplayed quantitative analyses because of overriding qualitative, or hard-to-quantify, concerns. Companies are much more likely to approve investments that enhance their ability to carry out their strategies than those with no such discernible effect.

Many companies, especially those using JIT principles, include subjective factors in evaluating capital budgeting decisions. For example, projects that show negative NPVs are more likely to be accepted if they improve one or more of the following factors: cycle time, product quality, competitive position, manufacturing flexibility, and delivery time.

Some criticize the application of DCF methods because of too-high discount rates and the comparison of expected results against the status quo. The issue of discount rates is best left to courses in finance. The question of comparison is whether the company will be able to maintain the status quo. Managers might erroneously believe that if they do nothing to increase quality or reduce cycle time they will continue selling as much as they do now. But in many cases the company that fails to invest in a product will lose sales to competitors who *are* investing in their products. The comparison should consider realistic sales expectations if the company falls behind its competitors.

SOCIAL CONSEQUENCES OF DECISION MAKING

Throughout most of this book we have assumed that the consequences of an action were limited to the entity taking that action. Such an assumption is not always warranted. The action of a single entity may have many effects, desirable or detrimental, for other entities.

For example, a company might find that using a machine that saves labor is justified on economic grounds. But the decision to use the machinery might put people out of work. The workers who lose their jobs will suffer if they cannot find other jobs fairly quickly. If they do not find work, they will receive unemployment compensation or some other type of payment that is borne by taxpayers. If they move away from the area to find work, they must incur moving costs, and there may be problems in uprooting their families. The reduced payroll of the plant may adversely affect the community through declines in economic activity such as retail sales. Other jobs may be lost as a result of the layoffs. Some of these implications have been referred to in previous discussions of "qualitative considerations" of decision making; they were not specifically incorporated into the analyses. Costs that are not borne directly by the entity making a decision and taking an action are called **social costs,** or *externalities*.

Social benefits (also called externalities) are benefits not accruing directly to the entity making a decision. A company that hires workers who are currently unemployed (as opposed to hiring them away from other firms) provides benefits to the workers in the form of income and increased self-esteem, to the community in the form of increased economic activity and higher taxes, and to the taxpayers in the form of reduced expenditures for unemployment compensation and other social services. The firm does not benefit directly from these other benefits, even though its action caused them. Though business managers may not give direct and monetary recognition to externalities, they should at least try to recognize the existence of externalities as individual decisions are studied.

Social benefits and costs are particularly critical in decisions made by government units like municipalities, states, and the federal government. Decision making in these and other not-for-profit entities is, like that in business firms, based on estimates of discounted benefits and costs. There are several major differences between the analyses used by business firms and government units. One difference is that government units do not pay income taxes, which makes their decision making somewhat simpler than that of businesses. But other factors in the government decision-making process make decisions much more difficult. These special factors fall into three general categories: (1) measurement problems; (2) problems in determining whether a particular effect is a benefit or a cost; and (3) problems in the distribution of benefits and costs.

Measurement problems arise in decisions of government units because, as mentioned in Chapter 4, not all benefits and costs are monetary. If an unemployed person obtains a job, the government benefits from additional taxes paid by the employed worker. But other benefits like the worker's increased self-esteem are not readily measurable. Cleaner air is economically beneficial because of fewer deaths from respiratory ailments, less sickness, and reduced cleaning bills for clothing and buildings. But the monetary value of these benefits and of the increased pleasantness that accompanies cleaner air is not readily measurable.

The second factor, determining whether an effect is beneficial or costly, often depends on one's point of view. The government has sanctioned actions to reduce the populations of wolves and coyotes in sheep and cattle-raising states. These programs have been favorably received by ranchers but deplored by conservationists. Programs that result in growth in population of a particular area may also receive mixed reviews. Some states and towns seek industrial development, while others discourage it.

The problem of the distribution of benefits and costs has been a difficult social question since the beginning of government. Suppose a city or town is considering the construction of a municipal golf course and analyses show that the fees received will be insufficient to earn the minimum desired rate of return. If the project is accepted, the taxpayers will subsidize those who use the golf course. The town government might still decide to build the golf course because it feels that the people who would use it deserve some inexpensive recreation, even if the general taxpayers must pay some of the costs. Similar reasoning could apply to more widely used municipally owned facilities such as zoos, libraries, and parks.

The criterion that is most generally advocated for decision making by governmental units is the maximizing of "social welfare." Because of the many problems in identifying and quantifying social benefits and costs, this decision rule has generally meant the maximizing of economic benefits—those subject to monetary estimates. To the extent that this can be done, the same general analytical approaches proposed for business decision making can be used in the public sector. And, like the business manager, the decision maker in the public sector must make an effort to at least identify and consider the unquantified but relevant factors before reaching a final decision.

SUMMARY

Proper analyses of investment requirements and future cash flows are critical if a manager is to make good decisions about investing available funds. Required investment should include any required changes in the firm's working capital. Where the decision involves a replacement, the analysis may be particularly complex.

Mutually exclusive investment alternatives involve special problems. A third DCF technique, the profitability index, has been suggested to assist in choosing from among such alternatives. This technique can be useful, but the firm's circumstances in terms of available funds and investment opportunities should be considered before selecting a single capital budgeting technique for general use.

Whatever technique is used, managers find it helpful to perform sensitivity analysis. The use of sensitivity analysis is prompted by the number of estimates used in a typical capital budgeting situation.

Computations of cash flows for an investment opportunity require knowing the many special features of income tax laws, particularly the Modified Accelerated Cost Recovery System (MACRS). But other factors, such as differing tax rates for different levels of income in different types and sizes of businesses, can influence both the amounts and the timing of cash flows from a particular investment opportunity.

Qualitative issues are associated with almost every investment opportunity. This is true in both the private and the public sectors. Decision makers in both sectors should make every effort to identify and quantify as many factors as possible and to consider factors that remain unquantified.

KEY TERMS

accelerated cost recovery system (ACRS)
incremental approach
modified accelerated cost recovery system (MACRS)
mutually exclusive alternatives
profitability index (PI)
replacement decision
sensitivity analysis
social benefits
social costs
total-project approach
working capital investment

KEY FORMULAS

$$\text{Profitability index} = \frac{\text{present value of future cash flows}}{\text{investment}}$$

Working capital = current assets − current liabilities

REVIEW PROBLEM—INVESTMENT IN WORKING CAPITAL

Chapman Products is considering a new product that will sell for $10 and will have variable costs of $6. Expected sales volume is 22,000 units per year. Bringing out the new product requires a $30,000 increase in working capital, as well as the purchase of new equipment costing $150,000 and having a five-year useful life with no salvage value. The new equipment has cash operating costs of $20,000 per year and will be depreciated using the straight-line method, ignoring the half-year convention. Chapman is in the 40% tax bracket and has 12% cost of capital.

Required
Determine the net present value of this investment opportunity.

ANSWER TO REVIEW PROBLEM
The investment appears to be wise, as indicated by the following analysis.

Cash Flow, Years 1-5

	Tax Computation	Cash Flow
Additional contribution margin [22,000 × ($10 − $6)]	$88,000	$88,000
Cash operating costs of new machine	20,000	(20,000)
Additional pretax cash flow	68,000	
Depreciation ($150,000/5)	30,000	
Increase in taxable income	$38,000	
Income taxes, at 40%	$15,200	(15,200)
Net cash flow per year		$52,800

Cash Flow, End of Year 5	
Recovery of working capital investment ($30,000 × .567)	$17,010

Summary of Net Present Value of Investment	
Operating cash flows, years 1-5 ($52,800, from above, × 3.605)	$190,344
Recovery of working capital investment, as above	17,010
Total present value of future cash flows	207,354
Investment ($150,000 for machine + $30,000 for working capital)	180,000
Net present value of investment	$ 27,354

Note that the analysis shows the $30,000 increase in working capital as part of the investment required for the project, and then includes the recovery of that investment at the end of the project's life as part of the future cash flows. Note also that there is no tax effect of the working capital increase in either part of the analysis.

REVIEW PROBLEM—SENSITIVITY ANALYSIS

Refer to the facts in the first review problem.

Required

1. Determine the annual unit volume required to give Chapman Products a 12% return.
2. With unit volume at 22,000, what selling price will give Chapman a 12% return?

ANSWER TO REVIEW PROBLEM

1. Annual sales must be about 18,838 units. The previous Review Problem shows that the NPV of the investment is $27,354 when the annual sales are 22,000 units and the discount rate is 12%. If the project earned exactly 12%, its NPV would be zero. So, one way to solve the problem is to determine what *change*—in this case, what decline—in annual volume would reduce NPV of $27,354 to zero. That change is 3,162, as shown below.

Change in NPV	$27,354
Divided by the factor for an annuity of five years at 12%	3.605
Equals the equivalent change in annual after-tax cash flow	$ 7,588
Divided by 1 – 40% tax rate	.60
Equals the equivalent change in annual before-tax cash flow, which is also the change in contribution margin	$12,647
Divided by contribution margin per unit ($10 – $6)	$4
Equals the change in sales volume	3,162 units

Hence, the firm could sell 3,162 units fewer than its original expectation of 22,000, or 18,838 units, and earn exactly 12% on its investment.

2. We can use the allowable decrease in total contribution margin calculated above.

Allowable decrease in annual total contribution margin	$12,647
Divided by 22,000 unit volume	22,000
Allowable decrease in unit contribution margin	$0.5749

A decrease in selling price, or increase in unit variable cost of $0.5749 will bring NPV to zero. Thus a price of $9.4251 or variable cost of $6.5749, or any combination that reduces unit contribution margin by $0.5749 will give a 12% return.

REVIEW PROBLEM—REPLACEMENT DECISION AND REDUCTION IN WORKING CAPITAL

Eamon Company, which has a cost of capital of 14% and a tax rate of 40%, owns a machine with the following characteristics.

Book value (and tax basis)	$55,000
Current market value	$40,000
Expected salvage value at end of its 5-year remaining useful life	0
Annual depreciation expense, straight-line method	$11,000
Annual cash operating costs	$18,000

Eamon's managers look for opportunities consistent with their desire to create a JIT manufacturing environment. The managers believe that by replacing the old machine and rearranging part of the production area, the company could reduce its investment in inventory by $20,000 as well as save on operating costs. The replacement machine has the following characteristics.

Purchase price	$80,000
Useful life	5 years
Expected salvage value	$ 5,000
Annual cash operating costs	$ 3,000
Annual depreciation expense, straight-line, which ignores salvage value	$16,000

Rearrangement costs are expected to be $12,000 and can be expensed immediately for both book and tax purposes. By the end of the life of the new machine, Eamon's managers expect to be further advanced in their implementation of the JIT philosophy and so do not anticipate returning to the prior, higher level of inventory.

Required

Determine whether Eamon should purchase the new machine and undertake the plant rearrangement.

ANSWER TO REVIEW PROBLEM

The project should be accepted. The investment of $21,200 is less than the present value of the future cash flows of $39,320.

Investment Required

	Tax	Cash Flow
Purchase price of new machine		$80,000
Selling price of existing machine	$40,000	(40,000)
Book value of existing machine	55,000	
Loss for tax purposes	$15,000	
Tax saving at 40%	$ 6,000	(6,000)
Cost of plant rearrangement	$12,000	12,000
Tax savings at 40%	$ 4,800	(4,800)
Reduction of working capital requirements		(20,000)
Net required investment		$21,200

Notice that the reduction in working capital is treated as a reduction of the required investment. Because the company does not expect to return to its prior inventory policies at the end of the life of this project, the calculation of cash flows from the project will *not* include a corresponding outflow in the project's final year. We calculate the annual cash flows and present values for this replacement decision using first the incremental approach and then the total-project approach.

Incremental Approach—Annual Cash Flows

	Tax	Cash Flow
Savings in cash operating costs ($18,000 – $3,000)	$15,000	$15,000
Additional depreciation ($16,000 – $11,000)	5,000	
Increase in taxable income	$10,000	
Increased tax at 40%	$ 4,000	(4,000)
Net annual cash inflow		$11,000
Present value factor for 5-year annuity at 14%		3.433
Present value of annual cash inflows		$37,763
Add present value of after-tax recovery of salvage value ($5,000 × 60% × .519, factor from Table A)		1,557
Present value of future cash inflows		39,320
Required investment		21,200
Net present value		$18,120

Because depreciation was computed without regard to salvage value, the new asset will have no book value at the end of its life and the proceeds from its sale will be taxable.

Total-Project Approach—Keep Existing Machine

	Tax	Cash Flow
Cash operating costs	$18,000	$18,000
Depreciation	11,000	
Total expenses	$29,000	
Tax savings at 40%	$11,600	(11,600)
Net cash outflow		6,400
Present value factor for 5-year annuity at 14%		3.433
Present value of annual operating flows		$21,971

Buy New Machine		
Cash operating costs	$ 3,000	$ 3,000
Depreciation	16,000	
Total expense	$19,000	
Tax saving at 40%	$ 7,600	7,600
Net cash inflow		4,600
Present value factor for 5-year annuity at 14%		3.433
Present value of annual inflows		15,792
Add present value of salvage value (above)		1,557
Net present value of future inflows		17,349
Net outlay required for machine		21,200
Net present value of future outflows		$ 3,851

The existing machine has a present value of outflows of $21,971, while the new machine has a present value of outflows of $3,851. The NPV in favor of replacing the existing machine is $18,120 ($21,971 – $3,851), as computed under the incremental approach.

Using the new machine will result in new annual cash inflows rather than outflows. This happens because depreciation is so high that the tax saving is greater than the annual cash operating costs. Do *not* conclude that if a replacement asset yields a positive cash flow, it is automatically a wise investment. In the example used here, if the project had not included the expectation of a reduction in inventory the replacement would not be wise.

REVIEW PROBLEM—MACRS

Strock Company is considering investing in a new machine that costs $100,000, has an eight-year expected life, and no salvage value. The machine is expected to save about $35,000 per year in cash operating costs and falls in the 7-Year MACRS class. Cost of capital is 14% and the tax rate is 40%.

Required

Determine the NPV of the investment, discounting the operating flows and the tax shield of depreciation separately. Use Exhibit 9-2 to find the present value of the tax shield.

ANSWER TO REVIEW PROBLEM

Operating flows $35,000 × (1 – 0.40) × 4.639	$ 97,419
Tax shield of depreciation ($100,000 × 0.40 × 0.645)	25,800
Total present value	123,219
Less investment	100,000
Net present value	$ 23,219

ASSIGNMENT MATERIAL

QUESTIONS FOR DISCUSSION

9-1 Returns and income If all the forecasts for a capital project turn out as estimated, will the reported annual net income for the project equal the returns used in analyzing the project?

9-2 Factors in capital budgeting Governments frequently take actions that alter the economic climate. For each of the events listed below, state how it would change companies' capital spending—increase, decrease, or have no effect. Comment on what particular kinds of companies would be affected and how. Consider each independently.

1. Outlawed gasoline engines for automobiles; only electric cars are approved.
2. Discontinued long-standing price supports that have kept the price of cotton artificially high.
3. Levied high tariff on foreign automobiles.
4. Raised the tax rate on corporate income from 34% to 40%.
5. Authorized cash grants for attending college to persons with low incomes.

9-3 Capital budgeting—effects of events A proposal to acquire a new machine has been analyzed, based on earlier information. How might each of the following events (not anticipated at the time the analysis was done) affect the analysis? Consider each event independently.

1. An increase in taxes on real property (land and buildings) is approved by the voters of the city in which the firm has its manufacturing plant.
2. A new tax law provides for a credit against income taxes; the credit is a specified percentage of the investment in new long-lived assets.
3. The *Wall Street Journal* carries a report of a new product that is likely to be a good substitute for the product made by the machine being considered.

9-4 Comparing types of decisions The replacement decision is discussed separately in the chapter though it obviously involves mutually exclusive alternatives which are also discussed. In what ways do replacements differ from the general case of mutually exclusive alternatives?

9-5 Capital budgeting for a specific firm Suggest some of the circumstances under which a particular firm would evaluate its capital investments projects using straight-line depreciation rather than MACRS.

EXERCISES

9-6 Comparison of methods (extension of 8-15) Determine the profitability index for each opportunity in 8-15 and rank the investments based on these values.

9-7 Basic investment analysis Cunningham Company can buy a machine that will reduce annual cash operating costs by $50,000. The cost of the machine is $200,000. After its useful life of ten years, it is expected to have no salvage value. The tax rate is 40% and cost of capital is 14%. The company uses straight-line depreciation.

Required

1. What is the NPV for the project?
2. What savings in annual cash-operating costs make this project return exactly 14%?
3. Assuming that operating savings are $50,000, what useful life must the machine have to make the investment worthwhile?

4. Suppose the project is not really a new investment but rather a replacement for a machine that has a remaining life of ten years and a current book value of $66,000. The old machine can be sold now for $12,000 and will have no residual value if retained to the end of its useful life. Annual depreciation is $6,600. Should the company replace the old machine with the new one?

9-8 Basic replacement decision Rohn Company manufactures gear assemblies and has the opportunity to replace one of its existing lathes with a new model. The existing lathe has a book value of $20,000 and a market value of $12,000. It has an estimated remaining useful life of four years, at which time it will have no salvage value. The firm uses straight-line depreciation of $5,000 per year on the lathe, and its annual cash operating costs are $53,000.

The new model costs $80,000 and has a four-year estimated life with no salvage value. Its annual cash operating costs are estimated at $22,000. The firm will use straight-line depreciation. The tax rate is 40% and cost of capital is 16%.

Required

1. Determine the investment required to obtain the new lathe.
2. Determine the present value of the net cash flows expected from the investment and the NPV of the investment.
3. Suppose that the new lathe has a salvage value of $5,000. The firm will ignore the salvage value in determining annual depreciation and so will have a gain that will be taxed at 40%. Determine the NPV of the investment.

9-9 Relationships Miller Company invested $180,000 in depreciable assets and earned a 14% internal rate of return. The life of the investment, which had no salvage value, was five years.

Required

1. Determine the net cash flow that Miller earned in each year, assuming that each year's flow was equal.
2. Assume that the tax rate is 40% and that Miller used straight-line depreciation for the investment. Determine the annual pretax cash flow that Miller earned.
3. The investment related to a new product that had a selling price of $10, variable costs of $4, and cash fixed costs of $25,000 per year. Assuming a 40% tax rate and straight-line depreciation, determine how many units had to be sold to earn an 18% internal rate of return.

9-10 Basic working capital investment Managers of DeCosmo Enterprises are considering a new high-performance videotape. They expect to sell 50,000 units annually for the next five years at $8 each. Variable costs are expected to be $3 per unit, annual cash fixed costs $140,000. The product requires machinery costing $150,000 with a five-year life and no salvage value. The firm uses straight-line depreciation. Additionally, accounts receivable will increase about $60,000, inventory about $40,000. These amounts will be returned in full at the end of the five years. The tax rate is 40% and cost of capital is 16%.

Required

Determine the NPV of the investment.

9-11 Replacement decision—working capital Reynolds Company has the opportunity to replace a large drill press. The replacement press would cost $90,000, have a useful life of 2 years, and have annual cash operating costs of $20,000. Data on the existing press follows.

	Existing Press
Current book value and tax basis	$50,000
Annual cash operating costs	$80,000
Current market value	$30,000
Annual depreciation	$25,000
Remaining useful life	2 years

The company uses straight-line depreciation. Neither press is expected to have salvage value at the end of its useful life. Using the proposed press will require increased inventories of $40,000. The company has a 20% cost of capital and a 40% income tax rate.

Required
Determine the NPV of the proposed investment.

9-12 Basic MACRS (continued in 9-26) ORM Company has the opportunity to buy a machine for $1,500,000. It is expected to save $400,000 annually in cash operating costs over its ten-year life. For tax purposes, the company will use a 5-Year MACRS period. ORM has a 14% cost of capital and a 40% tax rate.

Required
Determine the NPV of the proposed investment.

9-13 Mutually exclusive alternatives (continuation of 8-20) In 8-20, Welton Company has a choice between a hand-fed machine and a semiautomatic machine to perform a function essential to bringing out a new product.

Required
1. Compute the PI for each alternative.
2. Using the guidelines in Appendix B, write a memorandum to J. Kratz, the production manager. Give and support your recommendation regarding which machine to acquire.

9-14 Investing to reduce inventory, JIT Park Mills manufactures several products in its relatively modern factory. Park currently maintains considerable inventories of materials, purchased components, and work-in-process as buffer stock to offset slow incoming deliveries and production bottlenecks.

Park's managers have been working on ways to reduce the investment in inventory. They have plans that include working with suppliers to have deliveries made right to the production areas instead of to an outside loading dock, revamping the flow of goods through the plant, and coordinating production activities better. Rearranging and outfitting the plant will cost about $8.5 million. The new assets have five-year lives and no salvage value. The company uses straight-line depreciation.

The best estimates are that cash operating costs will increase by about $0.8 million per year if the investment is made, while inventories will be reduced from about $25.7 million to about $1.2 million. The tax rate is 40% and cost of capital is 12%.

Required
Determine the NPV of the proposed investment.

9-15 New product decision—sensitivity analysis Bee Company is considering adding a new product to its Big Bear line of pure honey products. The product will sell for $8 and have per-unit variable costs of $5 and annual cash fixed costs of $60,000. Equipment to make the product costs $210,000 and is expected to last six years with no residual value. Bee estimates annual sales of the product will be 50,000 units. Bee's income tax rate is 45% and its cost of capital is 14%. Straight-line depreciation would be used.

Required

1. What is the expected annual increase in future after-tax cash flows if the project is accepted?
2. What are (a) NPV, (b) IRR, and (c) PI for this project?
3. How much could annual cash fixed costs on the project be before the project would have an NPV of zero (IRR of 14%)?
4. Approximately how long must the life of the project be to earn an IRR of 16%?
5. How many units of the product must Bee sell each year to have an IRR equal to the 14% cost of capital?
6. How much could variable cost per unit be before the project would have IRR of 14%?

9-16 Working capital The sales manager of Watlin Tools has received an offer from an overseas company to buy 10,000 power saws for $20 per unit, well below the usual $35 price. Watlin's sales manager believes that no domestic sales would be lost if the offer is accepted. Unit variable cost of the saw is $18. The only drawback the sales manager sees is that, while Watlin must make the units now and incur $180,000 in cash costs, the customer will pay for the saws one year from now because of restrictions on taking money out of the foreign country. Watlin's cost of capital is 16%. Ignore taxes.

Required

Determine whether Watlin should accept the order.

9-17 Mutually exclusive investments Miro Manufacturing Company needs additional productive capacity to meet greater demand for its products. Two alternatives are available. The firm can choose either one, but not both.

	Hand-Fed Machine	Semiautomatic Machine
Required investment in depreciable assets	$1,000,000	$2,000,000
Annual cash operating costs	$1,450,000	$1,230,000
Useful life	10 years	10 years

Under either alternative Miro expects additional revenues of $1,750,000. Additional variable costs are included in the cash costs given above. Straight-line depreciation will be used for either investment. Neither is expected to have any salvage value. The tax rate is 40% and cost of capital is 10%.

Required

1. For each alternative, compute: (a) NPV, (b) approximate IRR, (c) PI.
2. Make a recommendation on which alternative should be chosen.

9-18 Sensitivity analysis (extension of 9-17) The cost behavior under each alternative in 9-17 is as follows:

	Hand-Fed Machine	Semiautomatic Machine
Variable cost as percentage of revenue	70%	40%
Fixed cash operating costs	$225,000	$530,000

Required

Determine the volume, in dollar sales, that will bring each alternative to an IRR of 10%. Does this new information affect the decision you made in 9-17?

9-19 Basic MACRS Johnstone Manufacturing Company is considering a new machine that is expected to save $135,000 per year in scrap costs because of greater efficiency. The machine costs $500,000 and has a ten-year life with no expected salvage value. Johnstone has a 16% cost of capital and 40% tax rate.

Required

1. Determine the NPV of the investment using straight-line depreciation.
2. Determine the NPV of the investment using 7-Year MACRS depreciation. Use Exhibit 9-2 to determine the present value of the MACRS tax shield.

9-20 Review of chapters 8 and 9 Bullmark Company is considering a new product, the Super Bull, that will sell for $8 per unit, have variable costs of $5 per unit, and annual cash fixed costs of $60,000. Equipment required to produce the Super Bull costs $210,000, is expected to last, and be depreciated on a straight-line basis, for six years, with no expected salvage value. Bullmark estimates that sales of the new product will be 50,000 units per year for six years. Bullmark is subject to an income tax rate of 40% and has cost of capital of 14%.

Required

1. What is the expected increase in future annual after-tax cash flows if the project is accepted?
2. What is the NPV of the project?
3. *For this question only,* suppose the project also involves an increase in inventories and receivables totaling $40,000. What is the NPV of the project?
4. What is the PI for the project? (Round to two decimal places.)
5. What is the payback period for the project? (Round to two decimal places.)
6. What is the approximate IRR for the project?
7. What is the total annual contribution margin the firm must show to earn a return equal to the 14% cost of capital?
8. Approximately how long must the life of the project be to earn a return of exactly 16%?

9-21 Relationships Fill in the blanks for each of the following independent cases. There are no salvage values for the investments.

	(a)	(b)	(c)	(d)	(e)	(f)	(g)
Case	Years of Project Life	Annual Aftertax Cash Flows	Initial Investment	Cost of Capital	Internal Rate of Return	Net Present Value	Profitability Index
1	15	$40,000	______	__%	14%	______	1.109
2	8	______	$224,235	16%	18%	______	______
3	12	______	$215,292	16%	__%	$36,762	______
4	__	$80,000	$361,600	12%	__%	______	1.25

9-22 Review of Chapters 8 and 9 Hand Division of Hand-and-Glove Co. is considering acquiring an asset that has a cost of $141,000, a useful life of 4 years, and would reduce labor costs by $50,000 per year. Hand is assessed income taxes at a 30% rate, requires a 12% IRR on all investments, and uses straight-line depreciation.

Required

1. What is the IRR of this project?
2. What is the NPV of this project?
3. What is the PI on this project?
4. What would annual labor savings have to be for the project to have exactly a 16% IRR?
5. For this part only, assume that Hand could depreciate the asset evenly over 3 years for tax purposes, though the life of the project and the asset are still 4 years. What would the NPV of this project be?
6. For this part only, assume that undertaking this project means Hand must increase its working capital by $12,000. What effect would this new information have on the NPV of this project?
7. Assume that the asset in this project is actually a replacement for one now in use that has a remaining life of 4 years, a book value (and tax basis) of $25,000, and a current market value of $40,000. What is the NPV of the project?

9-23 Asset acquisition and MACRS Peyton Company is considering a new asset that costs $800,000. Peyton's managers expect to reduce cash operating costs by $230,000 per year over its ten-year estimated life. The asset qualifies for 7-Year recovery under MACRS. Cost of capital is 16% and the tax rate is 40%.

Required

Determine the NPV of the investment.

PROBLEMS

9-24 Working capital investment (without income taxes) Rawson Company, a wholesaler of paper products, has been approached by Clark Paper Products Company. Clark has offered Rawson exclusive rights to distribute its products in the Denver area. The contract runs for three years, after which time either company can terminate the arrangement.

Rawson's managers expect revenue from Clark's products to be about $200,000 per month, with variable costs (all cost of goods sold) about 85% of revenue. Incremental monthly fixed costs should be about $11,000. Additionally, Rawson must carry inventory approximating a two-month supply and accounts receivable of about three months' sales. Rawson will pay cash on delivery of Clark's products. Cost of capital is 20%.

Required

Determine whether Rawson should accept Clark's offer.

9-25 Replacement decision Charles Company, a maker of gardening products, is considering replacing a machine. Charles uses straight-line depreciation, has an 18% cost of capital, and a 40% income tax rate. Neither machine is expected to have salvage value at the end of its useful life. If the firm makes the replacement, it will finance the investment with debt bearing 10% interest. The existing machine could be sold now for $35,000.

Existing Machine	
Book value	$60,000
Remaining useful life	3 years
Annual cash operating costs	$80,000
Annual depreciation	$20,000 each of next 3 years

Proposed Machine	
Price	$150,000
Useful life	3 years
Annual cash operating costs	$20,000

Required
Determine the NPV of the proposed investment.

9-26 Sensitivity analysis and MACRS (extension of 9-12) The managers of ORM Company are not sure of the annual savings in cash operating costs that the machine will generate. One manager has asked how low the savings could be and the company still earn the 14% target rate of return.

Required
Determine the annual cash-operating savings that yield a 14% return.

9-27 Comparison of alternatives Stanley Company must choose between two machines that will perform an essential function. Machine A costs $40,000, has a ten-year life with no salvage value, and costs $12,000 per year to operate (cash costs). Machine B costs $80,000, has a ten-year life with no salvage value, and costs $3,000 per year to operate. The tax rate is 40% and cost of capital is 10%. Straight-line depreciation will be used for either machine.

Required
Using the guidelines in Appendix B, write a memorandum to Stanley's vice president of manufacturing, Frank Cousins, giving and explaining your recommendation regarding which machine should be purchased.

9-28 Unit costs Ramor Company manufactures running shoes. Its managers are considering entering the low-priced market and are looking at several alternatives. The model they wish to introduce will, they believe, sell 200,000 pairs annually at $22. Estimates of unit costs for two alternative production methods are as follows:

	Use Existing Facilities	Buy New Machinery
Materials	$ 3.50	$ 3.40
Direct labor	7.50	6.45
Variable overhead	2.50	2.15
Fixed overhead	3.75	4.225
Total unit costs	$17.25	$16.225

Company policy is to charge each product with both fixed and variable overhead. The basic charge for fixed overhead is $0.50 per direct labor dollar. The amount of fixed overhead shown for the new machinery includes $1.00 per unit for depreciation of $200,000 per year ($600,000 cost) on the new machinery, which has a three-year life. Thus, the $4.225 is $1.00 plus the normal overhead charge of $0.50 times $6.45 direct labor cost. One of the managers points out that the $1.025 difference in unit cost works out to $205,000 per year, a significant savings. He also points out that the after-tax savings is $123,000 (the tax rate is 40%), which gives a rate of return of 41% on the average investment of $300,000. Cost of capital is 18%.

Required

1. Determine the NPV of the investment.
2. Determine the approximate IRR on the investment.

9-29 JIT, Inventory The Anderson Plant of Benson Industries is moving toward JIT principles. So far it has been setting up manufacturing cells and smoothing the flow of work. The next phase involves a multitude of changes related to reducing the number of vendors, ensuring the quality of the parts provided by the remaining vendors, opening walls so that trucks can make deliveries straight to the cell where the parts are used, and teaching new skills to workers.

All of these activities are estimated to cost about $4.5 million, of which $2.9 million can be expensed immediately for income tax purposes. The remaining $1.6 million is for changes in physical plant that must be depreciated over the next 10 years, using the straight-line method. The estimated annual cash savings before taxes over the next ten years are $230,000. Based on conversations with other plant managers, the Anderson Plant manager expects inventory to fall to about $120,000 from the current $2.7 million. The tax rate is 40% and cost of capital is 12%.

Required

Determine the NPV of the investment.

9-30 Pollution control and capital budgeting Craft Paper Company operates a plant that produces a great deal of air pollution. The local government has ordered that the polluting be stopped or the plant will be closed. Craft does not wish to close the plant and so has sought to find satisfactory ways to remove pollutants. Craft has found two alternatives, both of which will reduce the outflow of pollutants to levels satisfactory to the government. One, called Entrol, costs $1,000,000, has a ten-year life with no salvage value, and has annual cash operating costs of $180,000. The other, Polltrol, costs $2,000,000, has a ten-year life with no salvage value, and has cash operating costs of $210,000 annually. However, Polltrol compresses the particles it removes into solid blocks of material that can be sold to chemical companies. Annual sales of the material are estimated at $250,000.

Either device will be depreciated on a straight-line basis. Cost of capital is 16% and the tax rate is 40%.

Required

Using the guidelines in Appendix B, write a memorandum to Paula Graves, Craft's vice president of manufacturing, giving and explaining your recommendation about which device to acquire.

9-31 Replacement decision and sensitivity analysis (without income taxes) Hutson Company owns data processing equipment that cost $80,000 five years ago, now has a book value of $40,000 and a market value of $18,000. The equipment costs $45,000 per year to operate and will have no value at the end of five more years.

Hutson can buy equipment that costs $65,000, will last five years with no salvage value, and cost $20,000 per year to operate. It performs the same functions as the existing equipment.

The firm has a cost of capital of 14%.

Required

1. Determine whether the new equipment should be purchased.
2. Determine the approximate IRR on the investment.
3. Suppose the data processing manager knows that the new machine is more efficient than the old, but not how much more. What annual cash savings are necessary for the firm to earn 14%?
4. Suppose that the estimate of annual cash flows is reliable, but that the useful life of the new equipment is in question. About how long must the new equipment last in order that the firm earn 14%?

9-32 ***Alternative production method*** Lizmith Co. is considering a change in its manufacturing process, from a labor-intensive to a highly automated method. Information about the current method appears below.

Book value of existing equipment	$20,000
Remaining useful life of existing equipment	5 years
Annual tax depreciation of existing equipment	$ 4,000
Current market value of existing equipment	$25,000
Annual cash operating costs, existing method	$64,000

The alternative method requires a machine that costs $100,000 and has a useful life of five years with no salvage value. The new machine can accomplish the same task with annual cash operating costs of $40,000. Straight-line depreciation will be used for tax purposes for the new machine. The tax rate is 40% and cost of capital is 12%.

Required

1. What is the net investment associated with acquiring the new equipment?
2. What is the total present value of the future after-tax cash flows of a *switch* to the new equipment?
3. What is the NPV of the investment?

9-33 ***Sensitivity analysis*** The managers of Boston Products Company have been trying to decide whether or not to introduce a new deluxe birdfeeder. They expect it to sell for $30 and to have unit variable costs of $14. Fixed costs requiring cash disbursements should be about $250,000 per year. The feeder also requires machinery costing $600,000 with a four-year life and no salvage value. The company uses straight-line depreciation. Cost of capital is 16%.

The one point of which the managers are unsure is the annual unit volume. Estimates made by individual managers range from 30,000 to 55,000 units.

Required

1. Ignoring income taxes, determine the number of feeders per year the company must sell to make the investment yield just 16%.
2. Redo item 1 assuming a 40% income tax rate.

9-34 *Determining required cost savings* Grunch Company can buy a machine that will reduce variable production costs of a product that sells 10,000 units annually. The machine costs $80,000, has no salvage value, and should last for five years. Annual fixed cash operating costs are $16,000. Cost of capital is 16%.

Required

1. Ignoring taxes, what reduction in unit variable production costs is necessary to make the investment desirable?
2. Answer item 1 assuming a tax rate of 40% and straight-line depreciation.
3. Suppose now that the machine will reduce unit variable production costs by $4, but that annual volume is in doubt. What annual volume is needed to make the investment desirable? Consider income taxes.

9-35 *Benefit-cost analysis* The Department of Health has made studies regarding treatment for two diseases, a type of kidney disease and a type of heart disease. The following data have been assembled.

	Kidney Disease	Heart Disease
Cost to save one life	$100,000	$150,000
Average age of victim at death	40 years	50 years
Average annual income of victims	$ 15,000	$ 25,000

The heart disease appears to be caused partly by stresses that affect higher-income people, which accounts in part for the difference in incomes between the two types of victims.

The department believes that a discount rate of 10% is appropriate. It also assumes that a person will work until age 70 (30 additional years for persons cured of kidney disease, 20 for those cured of heart disease).

Required

1. Compute the NPV of saving a single life from each disease. The cost to save the life is incurred immediately, and the annual incomes are assumed to be received at the ends of years.
2. Suppose that a lack of trained personnel makes it impossible to pursue treatment for both diseases and that the same amount will be spent regardless of which disease is selected for treatment. Which disease do you prefer to see treated and why?

9-36 *When-to-sell decisions* Smooth Scotch Company has a large quantity of Scotch whiskey that is approaching its sixth anniversary. When it reaches age six it can be sold for $700 per barrel. If it is held until it is ten years old it can be sold for $1,170 per barrel. Cost of capital is 12%.

Required

1. Determine the IRR that would be earned if the Scotch were held until it was ten years old.
2. Suppose that the price of six-year-old Scotch is $700 per barrel, but that the projected price of ten-year-old Scotch in four years is in doubt. What is the minimum price per barrel that the firm would have to receive four years hence to justify keeping the Scotch until it is ten years old?
3. Suppose now that the following schedule of prices is expected. Determine the point at which the Scotch should be sold using the criterion of highest IRR. (Assume that the cutoff rate of return is low enough so that all of the rates you compute would be acceptable. That is, the best decision is not to sell now.)

Years of Age	Expected Price
6	$ 700
7	800
8	950
9	1,200
10	1,400

4. Redo item 3 using the NPV criterion to make the decision.

9-37 Increased sales and working capital Baker Company now makes several products in a labor-intensive fashion. The products average $4.50 in variable costs, of which labor is $2.25. Fixed costs are $100,000 annually. The firm has had difficulty in expanding production to meet increased demand and is considering a large machine that will enable a production increase to 105,000 with the same size work force. Sales are currently 80,000 units at $8 average selling price. The firm expects to sell all its production at $7 per unit if the machine is bought.

Variable costs per unit other than labor will remain the same, and fixed costs will increase by the amount of depreciation on the new machine. The machine costs $80,000 and has a useful life of ten years. There will be increased working capital requirements of $80,000. Straight-line depreciation will be used for tax purposes. The tax rate is 40% and cost of capital is 14%.

Required
Determine whether Baker should buy the machine.

9-38 Sensitivity analysis (extension of 8-34) The managers of Pitcairn Company believe that volume will be 250,000 pairs, but are concerned about that estimate. They wish to know how many pairs of socks they must sell to earn an IRR of 14%.

Required
1. Determine the unit volume that will yield an IRR of 14%.
2. How does the calculation for item 1 change your attitude about the investment from your solution to 8-34?

9-39 Backing a play Kent Clark, a famous playwright, wants your company to back his forthcoming play, *I'll Fly Tomorrow.* He has prepared the following analysis.

Investment:	
Sets and other depreciable assets (straight-line basis)	$ 300,000
Working capital	100,000
Total investment	$ 400,000
Annual gross receipts, expected to continue for 4 years	$1,000,000
Annual salaries of actors and other personnel	$ 500,000
Rent, $20,000 + 5% of gross receipts	
Royalty to Clark, 10% of gross receipts	
Other cash expenses	$ 140,000

Your company has a cost of capital of 14% and a tax rate of 40%.

Required

1. Should your firm back the play on the basis of the information given?
2. At what level of annual gross receipts does the play yield a 14% IRR?

9-40 Replacement decision The management of Bettel Metals Inc. is considering a new machine. The new machine is more efficient than the one currently in use and would save the firm $6,000 annually because of greater operating speed. To keep the old machine operating at the present level of efficiency requires immediate repairs costing $5,000. The repair cost is tax deductible this year. Annual depreciation on the old machine, which is expected to last ten years, is $1,800. No scrap value is expected at that time.

The new machine costs $37,300, including freight and installation charges. It has an expected useful life of ten years and no expected scrap value. Straight-line depreciation would be used on the new machine. The old machine has a book value of $18,000 and a market value of $12,000. The tax rate is 40%.

Required

1. Compute the net cash outlay if the new machine is purchased.
2. Evaluate the proposal, assuming a minimum required rate of return of 10%.

9-41 Buying an athletic team A large portion of the purchase price of an athletic team is allocated to the value of the players' contracts. This amount can be amortized for income tax purposes. Some have argued that the principal value of a franchise is the monopoly right to operate and earn revenues from television, ticket sales, and so on. The amount allocated to the monopoly right is not amortizable for tax purposes, much as the cost of land is not depreciable.

Suppose you are in the 28% tax bracket and are considering buying the Midlands Maulers of the Transam Football League. You expect the operations of the team to generate pretax cash inflows of $4,000,000 annually. You also expect the league to fold in ten years, at which time your investment will be worthless. Your discount rate is 14%.

Required

1. Determine the maximum that you are willing to pay for the team assuming that the investment can be amortized evenly over ten years for tax purposes.
2. Determine the maximum that you are willing to pay for the team if you could not amortize the cost. (You then have a lump-sum tax deduction at the end of year 10 equal to your original investment.)

9-42 Investing in quality, JIT Roush, Inc. manufactures a variety of products in a relatively old plant. Parts of the manufacturing process are very outmoded and the quality of the output is slipping. The company is coming to be viewed as a low-quality producer, which is expected to affect future sales adversely. The manufacturing managers have been looking at new machinery and equipment that would increase quality to the point where the company could enjoy a favorable reputation. They have also been looking at employing JIT principles. Outfitting the plant for the new machinery and to accommodate JIT will cost about $5.5 million. The entire investment can be depreciated over its ten-year useful life. It has no salvage value. The company uses straight-line depreciation. The new machinery will not affect variable costs, but will increase cash fixed costs by $0.7 million per year.

The managers do not expect sales to increase markedly if they fail to make the investment. Rather, they expect sales to fall by about $1.5 million per year if they do not make the investment. The contribution margin ratio is about 60%

on the normal product mix. The managers also expect to reduce inventory by $4.8 million if they make the investment. The tax rate is 40% and cost of capital is 12%.

Required

Determine the NPV of the proposed investment.

9-43 Attracting industry Minerla is a small town with little industry and high unemployment. The mayor and members of the town council have been trying to interest businesses in locating factories in Minerla. Newman Industries has agreed to the following proposal of the town government. The town will build a $4.3 million plant to Newman's specifications and rent it to Newman for its estimated useful life of 20 years at $150,000 per year provided that Newman employs at least 600 currently unemployed citizens of Minerla.

The mayor expects some increases in the cost of town government to result from the additional employees that Newman would transfer to the new factory.

Additional fire and police protection	$ 35,000
Additional school costs	50,000
Additional general governmental costs	20,000
Total additional annual costs	$105,000

An economist from the state university has projected the following annual results if the plant is built.

Increases in retail sales in Minerla	$6,000,000
Increase in property tax base	$4,400,000

The town levies a 1% tax on all retail sales and taxes property at a rate of $80 per $1,000. The state spends about $2,000 per year in direct support for each unemployed person. The economist said that total unemployment is likely to fall by about 1,500 persons because the factory would help to create other jobs.

The council believes that the factory should be built provided that the benefits to the town government do not exceed the costs. The relevant discount rate is 9%.

Required

1. Determine whether the additional receipts to the town, less the additional costs, justify the building of the factory.
2. Assuming that your answer to item 1 is no, list and discuss other factors that might be considered and other actions that might be taken.

9-44 Modification of equipment Pride Company has several machines that have been used to make a product that the firm has phased out of its operations. The equipment has a book value of $600,000 and remaining useful life of four years. Depreciation is being taken using the straight-line method at $150,000 per year. No salvage value is expected at the end of the useful life.

Pride can sell the equipment for $320,000 now. Or, at a cost of $400,000, the equipment can be modified to produce another product. The modifications will not affect the useful life or salvage value and will be depreciated using the straight-line method. If the firm does not modify the existing equipment, it will have to buy new equipment at a cost of $800,000. The new equipment also has a useful life of four years with no salvage value, and would be depreciated using the straight-line method. The product to be made with the new equipment or modified existing equipment is essential to Pride's product line.

Cash operating costs of new equipment are $50,000 per year less than with the existing equipment. Cost of capital is 16% and the tax rate is 40%.

Required

Using the guidelines in Appendix B, write a memorandum to the company's president, Lee Pride, giving and supporting your recommendation about which alternative should be selected.

9-45 Dropping a product Stracke Company makes a variety of products in several factories throughout the country. The sales manager is unhappy with the results shown by Quickclean, a spray cleaner for household use. Quickclean is made in only one factory. A typical income statement appears below.

Sales	$4,400,000
Variable costs	3,800,000
Contribution margin	600,000
Fixed costs	775,000
Loss	($ 175,000)

The production manager tells the sales manager that about $480,000 of the fixed costs shown above require cash disbursements. These are all avoidable. The remaining $295,000 in fixed costs consists of $100,000 in depreciation on equipment used only to make Quickclean and $195,000 in allocated costs. The equipment used to make Quickclean has a useful life of five more years, and no salvage value is expected at the end of five years. The book value is $500,000 and straight-line depreciation is being used.

Stracke has a cost of capital of 16% and the tax rate is 40%.

Required

1. Assume that the machinery used to make Quickclean has no resale value. If the product is dropped, the machinery will be scrapped. The loss is immediately tax deductible. Determine whether Quickclean should be dropped.
2. Assume that the machinery could be sold for $320,000. Redo item 1.

9-46 New product—complementary effects Latona Jaxon, general manager of the McKeown Division of Standard Enterprises, Inc., is considering a new product. It will sell for $20 per unit and have variable costs of $9. Volume is estimated at 120,000 units per year. Fixed costs requiring cash disbursements will increase by $300,000 annually, mainly in connection with operating machinery that would be purchased for $2,000,000. The machinery has a useful life of ten years with no salvage value, and would be depreciated using the straight-line method.

The new product would be made in a section of the factory that is physically separate from the rest of the factory and is now leased to another firm for $120,000 per year. The lease expires this month, but the other firm has expressed an interest in renewing the lease for an additional ten years.

Jaxon expects inventories to increase by $500,000 if the new product is brought out. She also expects customers to pay for their purchases two months after purchase, but she is uncertain how to consider these factors.

Cost of capital is 20% and the tax rate is 40%.

Required

1. Determine whether the new product should be introduced.
2. Suppose that if the new product were brought out, the sales of an existing product would increase by 30,000 units per year. The existing product sells for $10 and has variable costs of $6. The increase in sales of this product will lead to increases in inventories and receivables of $60,000. Determine whether the new product should be brought out.

9-47 Closing a plant—externalities Fisher Manufacturing Company operates a plant in Vesalia, a small city on the Platte River. The firm has been notified that it must install pollution control equipment at the plant at a cost of $4,000,000, or else close the plant. The plant employs 400 people, virtually all of whom will lose their jobs if the plant were to close. Fisher will make a lump-sum payment of $80,000 to the people put out of jobs if the plant closes.

A buyer is willing to purchase the plant for $400,000, which equals its book value. Fisher could shift production to the Montclair plant if it closed the Vesalia plant, with no increase in total cash production costs. (The increase in Montclair's cash production costs equals the cash operating costs of the Vasalia plant.) However, shipping costs will increase by $900,000 annually because the Montclair plant is much farther away from customers than the Vesalia plant.

The new equipment has a ten-year useful life with no salvage value. Straight-line depreciation is used for tax purposes. The tax rate is 40% and cost of capital is 14%.

Required

1. Considering only monetary factors, determine whether Fisher should install the pollution control equipment or close the plant.
2. What other factors might be considered by those interested in the decision?

CASES

9-48 Mutually exclusive investments Seagle Company requires machinery for an essential task that will be carried out for the next ten years. Two available machines meet the firm's needs.

	Rapidgo 350	Rapidgo 600
Purchase cost	$50,000	$90,000
Annual operating expenses, exclusive of depreciation	$12,000	$15,000
Useful life	5 years	10 years

Either machine will be depreciated using the straight-line method. The firm expects to pay $60,000 to replace the Rapidgo 350 at the end of five years, if that machine is selected. The other data applicable to the Rapidgo 350 given above are applicable to the replacement model as well.

Cost of capital is 16% and the tax rate is 40%.

Required

Determine the course of action the firm should take.

9-49 Replacement decision, MACRS (CMA adapted) Lamb Company manufactures several lines of machine products. One valve stem requires special tools that must soon be replaced. The tools are fully depreciated and have no resale value. Management has decided that the only alternative to replacing these tools is to buy the stem from an outside supplier at $20 per unit.

Lamb has been using 80,000 stems over the past few years and this volume is expected to continue, although there could be some decline over the next few years. Cost records show the following at 80,000 units.

Material	$ 3.80
Labor	3.70
Variable overhead	2.20
Fixed overhead	4.50
Total unit cost	$14.20

Replacing the specialized tools will cost $2,500,000. The new tools have a life of eight years and $100,000 residual value. Lamb will use MACRS. The tools qualify for a five-year recovery period. Cost of capital is 12% and the tax rate is 40%.

Lamb's managers have had discussions with the toolmaker's sales engineers and with another manufacturer that uses similar tools. Indications are that labor and variable overhead will drop, but that material cost will increase because the new tools require higher-quality material than the ones currently used. The best estimates appear below.

Material	$ 4.50
Labor	3.00
Variable overhead	1.80
Fixed overhead	5.00
Total unit cost	$14.30

Cash fixed costs associated with the new tools are $100,000 per year; with the existing tools these costs are $50,000 per year. There will be no such costs if Lamb buys the stem from the outside supplier.

Required

1. Determine whether Lamb should buy the stem or manufacture it using the new tools.
2. Lamb's managers are concerned about making such a large investment when there is a possibility that the volume of the part might drop. Determine the volume of parts that makes Lamb indifferent between making it and buying it.

9-50 Evaluating an investment proposal Your new assistant has just brought you the following analysis of an investment you are considering. The investment relates to a new manufacturing process for making one of the firm's major products.

Required Investment	
New machinery (10-year life, no salvage value)	$350,000
Research and development	60,000
Administrative time	10,000
Total investment	$420,000

Annual Cash Flows (10 Years)	
Savings in cost over old process:	
Labor	$ 75,000
Materials	80,000
Variable overhead	40,000
Depreciation	(35,000)
Total operating savings	160,000
Less: Interest on debt to finance investment	35,000
Net savings before taxes	125,000
Less: Income taxes at 40% rate	50,000
Net cash flow after taxes	$ 75,000

Your assistant tells you that the new machinery would replace old machinery that has a ten-year remaining useful life with no salvage value. The old machinery will be scrapped if the new machinery is bought, and the salvage value equals the cost of having it removed. The old machinery has a book value of $110,000. The company uses straight-line depreciation for all machinery.

Your assistant also tells you that the listed costs for research and development and for administrative time relate solely to this project and contain no allocations. The costs have been incurred already, so their amounts are certain. The item in the analysis for interest on debt is for $350,000 at 10%, which will be borrowed if the new machinery is acquired.

Based on his analysis and the 16% cost of capital, he recommends that the project be rejected.

Required

Determine whether the investment should be made.

9-51 Alternative uses of assets (AICPA adapted) Miller Manufacturing Company has been producing toasters and blenders in its Syracuse plant for several years. The rent for the Syracuse factory building is $80,000 per year. Miller's directors have decided to cease operations at that location and scrap the equipment when the lease expires at the end of four years.

Blender production is approximately 50,000 per year and the company expects to continue production at that level. However, because of intense competition and price erosion, the company has decided to stop making toasters.

Two areas of the Syracuse plant, making up about 30% of the total floor space, are devoted to toasters. The equipment used to make toasters has a book value of $140,000 and is depreciated at $35,000 per year. The company has received an offer of $20,000 for all the equipment now used in toaster production, and the buyer is not interested in anything less than all of it. If the equipment were sold, the space now used for toaster production could be subleased for $12,000 per year.

Because the production of blenders is to be continued, the production manager, Hiroko Sagura, was asked if she needed the space and/or equipment now devoted to toaster production. She said that though she had no need for additional productive capacity for tasks currently undertaken at the plant, she is interested in using the space and equipment to manufacture a blender part now being purchased from an outside firm. The part is a blade assembly that the firm purchases for $5. The contract with the vendor runs for four more years and requires that Miller buy at least 5,000 assemblies per year.

Either of the two areas now used for toaster production could be converted to produce the blade assemblies. Sagura estimates the variable cost to produce an assembly at $3.60 and no additional fixed costs requiring cash would be incurred. However, the equipment now used has to be converted. She estimates the cost at $40,000 to convert enough of the equipment to make 35,000 assemblies per year and $80,000 to convert enough to make 60,000 assemblies. Because the prospective buyer of the equipment wants all or none of it, conversion of any of it means the company must forego the sale.

The company's tax rate is 40% and its cost of capital is 14%. Straight-line depreciation will be used on costs of converting equipment.

Required

Using the guidelines in Appendix B, write a memorandum to Ms. Sagura giving and explaining your recommendation as to the best course of action.

9-52 Expanding a factory Fisher Company needs more space and machinery to increase production. The production manager and president have been trying to decide which of two plans to accept.

	Plan A	Plan B
Investment required	$4,000,000	$5,500,000
Additional fixed cash operating costs per year	$ 600,000	$ 800,000
Additional capacity in machine-hours per year	200,000	280,000

The company uses straight-line depreciation. No salvage value is expected for either investment at the end of their ten-year useful lives.

The production manager prefers Plan B because the cost per machine-hour and investment per machine-hour are lower than those for Plan A. The president, E. J. Alvarez, is unsure about this and asks the sales manager whether the capacity would be fully utilized. The sales manager provides the following data.

	Product		
	101-X	201-X	305-X
Potential increased sales, in units	30,000	40,000	30,000
Contribution margin per unit	$18	$24	$40
Machine-hours required per unit	2	4	5

Fisher pays income taxes at a 40% rate and has cost of capital of 12%.

Required

Using the guidelines in Appendix B, write a memorandum to E. J. Alvarez giving and supporting your recommendation about expanding capacity and how the expanded capacity should be used.

PART THREE

control and performance evaluation

Part Three concentrates on the management functions of control and performance evaluation. To perform these functions more effectively, managers apply the principles and techniques of responsibility accounting. An essential step in the development of a responsibility accounting system is fixing responsibility for each cost. Fixing responsibility for costs is also important to derive the fullest advantage from comprehensive budgeting. In this part, the emphasis shifts from planning to control, and to evaluating actual results in relation to planned or budgeted results.

The major thrust of responsibility accounting is behavioral; the critical factor in its success is the extent to which the system encourages or discourages behavior consistent with the organization's best interests. Human behavior and the ways in which accounting methods encourage particular kinds of behavior are treated extensively in the three chapters in this part.

10 responsibility accounting

Thus far we have concentrated on applying the concepts of managerial accounting to the management functions of planning and decision making. We now look more closely at managerial control, particularly performance evaluation. Managers exercise control through a management control system, a set of policies and procedures used to determine whether or not operations are going as planned, and if not, to suggest corrective action. **Responsibility accounting** is the gathering and reporting of information that is used to control operations and evaluate performance. The responsibility accounting system is the formal, financial communication system within the overall management control system. Systems use both financial and nonfinancial information.

Nonquantifiable factors are even more important to effective control and evaluation than they are to planning and decision making. Of particular concern is the potential for accounting reports to influence the actions of managers. The problem of cost allocation from Chapter 5 is also relevant here. We shall see later that there *are* good reasons for allocating costs—to encourage particular kinds of behavior and to assist in evaluating performance. But there are also good reasons *not* to allocate costs, so that the issue is less clear than it was in decision making, where allocation was undesirable.

GOAL CONGRUENCE AND MOTIVATION

Managers and other employees work to achieve their own goals, which can include salary, promotion, and recognition. In pursuit of those goals, they

A particularly grating example of misplaced incentives was documented in *The Wall Street Journal.* A school district was offered the use of an interactive video system that could reduce by 30% the time required for sub-literate adults to complete an educational program. The director of the program turned the system down because his budget was based on average daily attendance; getting students through the program faster would reduce his budget. He commented that "The district pays us for attendance, not achievement." His position not only illustrates extremely poor performance criteria, but also spotlights ethical blindness. Presumably, the people to be served would be better off finishing the program faster.*

* The Wall Street Journal, *September 10, 1990, A14.*

attempt to perform well on the measures by which they are evaluated. The important question is whether they are also acting to achieve the goals of the company. A major objective of management control is to encourage **goal congruence,** where people work to achieve the goals of the company as *well* as their own goals. People must have *incentives* to work toward the company's goals. The responsibility accounting system should encourage managers to work toward goals that are in their best interests as well as the company's best interests.

Because reports generated by the responsibility accounting system influence behavior, they must be carefully designed and thoroughly understood. A good responsibility accounting system reports only on factors that managers can, in a broad sense, control. Thus, uncontrollable costs either should not appear in performance reports or should be carefully segregated and labeled. An example of a noncontrollable cost is the salary of the plant manager that is not controllable by any lower-level manager. Moreover, the system should give sufficient feedback for the manager to be aware of what has been happening, what trends might be expected, and, to the extent possible, why things happened the way they did.

Most of the major problems in developing an effective responsibility accounting system are behavioral. Managers must trust the system; they must believe that it accurately depicts performance. They must also believe the system is fair. Accordingly, the evaluation system should use performance evaluation criteria that are under the control of the managers. But if the system is to perform its function for the company as a whole, the feedback provided to the managers and the criteria used to evaluate them should also motivate them to act in such a way as to advance the goals of the firm. The first step in implementing responsibility accounting is to establish responsibility centers.

RESPONSIBILITY CENTERS

To be held accountable for performance, managers must have clearly defined areas of responsibility—activities they control. A **responsibility cen-**

ter is an activity, such as a department, that a manager controls. You might think it is relatively easy to identify activities with specific managers. A plant manager is in charge of a plant and is usually responsible for producing budgeted quantities of specific products within budgeted cost limits. A sales manager is responsible for getting orders from customers, and so on. In many cases, however, isolating the responsibilities of managers is no simple task.

The performance of one manager can be affected by the performance of others. The best salespeople in the world will have difficulty selling poorly made products. By the same token, no production manager can minimize costs if production schedules change daily to accommodate rush orders. Such interdependencies cannot be eliminated entirely, but their effects can be minimized by careful selection of responsibility centers, appropriate use of rewards and penalties, and proper use of performance reports by managers who understand the information that they receive.

For example, to reduce the potential for conflict between sales and production because of the quality of the output produced, the production manager should be responsible for the quality of output as well as for production costs. Some companies, including the publisher of this book, collect and study measures of customer satisfaction. Each situation where conflicts might arise must be considered by itself, and appropriate procedures and responsibilities assigned to the managers potentially in conflict; few general rules exist to which one can turn for guidance.

There are three types of responsibility centers: cost centers, profit centers, and investment centers. The type of responsibility center depends on the breadth of control of the manager.

COST CENTERS

A **cost center** is a segment whose manager is responsible for costs but not for revenues. A cost center can be relatively small, like a single department with a few people, but can also be quite large, such as an entire factory or the administrative area for a large firm. Some cost centers are composed of a number of smaller cost centers. For example, a factory may be segmented into many work stations, each of which is a cost center with several stations combined into departments that are also cost centers.

PROFIT CENTERS AND INVESTMENT CENTERS

A **profit center** is a segment whose manager is responsible for revenues as well as costs. For such a center, a type of profit figure is used to measure performance. In some cases, only direct costs are used to determine the center's profit figure; in others, the profit calculation includes some (or all) indirect costs. An **investment center** is a segment where the manager controls, not only revenues and costs, but also investment in assets. For such a center, it is possible to calculate return on investment as well as profit. In practice, both types of segments are often referred to as profit centers. Later in this chapter, and in parts of Chapter 11, we discuss various questions about how profit and investment might be measured.

Large companies usually have many profit/investment centers. Typically, managers of such segments have wider responsibilities than do managers of cost centers. Accordingly, managers of profit centers act, and are evaluated, much as if they were chief executives of autonomous companies.

A major reason for using profit and investment centers is that profit and return on investment are more comprehensive measures of success than is cost. To survive, a company must earn profits, not just control costs. When a manager is held responsible for revenues and investment, as well as costs, responsibility is pinpointed. This is not possible when a manager is responsible only for revenues, or costs, or investment. JKL Advertising provides an example of a company that increased profitability and control by isolating responsibility. The agency had grown rapidly, then began to show losses because it failed to control costs and to evaluate the profitability of accounts. Because managers were responsible either for revenues or costs, but not both, none were in charge of ensuring that each account was profitable. The agency changed its operations. Account managers must now set up budgets for profitability of every new account, so they consider themselves responsible for profitability. Account managers are motivated by and committed to profitability, not simply to revenues or costs taken separately.[1]

The idea that profit is a more comprehensive measure of performance than is cost has led some firms to create *artificial profit centers,* segments that do not deal with outsiders, but rather "sell" goods or services within the company. For instance, a data processing department might "charge" the segments that use its services. The department could then have an income statement, instead of just a statement of costs. The department's failure to show a profit—or to earn a satisfactory return on its investment—*might* indicate that it is inefficient. (A loss might even indicate that the company would be better off to buy the services from an outside company.) We emphasize *might* because factors outside the control of the data processing manager could affect the results and cause the department to appear inefficient. A common example of such a confounding factor occurs when a growing company acquires more equipment and personnel than it currently needs because of higher expected use in the future. (Current costs are higher than necessary, but it might have been a wise decision to acquire the higher capacity in anticipation of increased use in the future.)

CRITERIA FOR EVALUATION

Selecting criteria to measure and evaluate performance is important because the criteria influence managers' actions. (How might a student's day-to-day actions be influenced by knowing that part of a course grade depended on neatness of dress and timeliness of arrival?) The most common deficiencies in performance measurement are (1) using a *single* measure that emphasizes only one objective of the organization and (2) using measures that either misrepresent or fail to reflect the organization's objectives or the employee's responsibilities.

Managers want a single, comprehensive measure of performance, but the search for such a measure is seldom successful. Consider an example report-

1 *William B. Mills, "Drawing Up a Budgeting System for an Ad Agency,"* Management Accounting, *December, 1983, 46-51.*

ed from the former Soviet Union. Reportedly, the government was unhappy with the output of nails and decided to evaluate managers of nail factories by the weight of the nails produced. The managers could produce much greater weight by making only large spikes, and they did. Once the government saw that its performance measure was not working, it changed the basis of evaluation to the number of nails produced—and the factories began to pour out carpet tacks and small brads.

Although profit is a common measure of performance, it too can suffer from overemphasis. For example, managers *know* that emphasizing profits in the current period might be detrimental to profits in future periods. But a responsibility accounting system that emphasizes short-run profits can tempt managers to take actions that increase short-run profits at the expense of the long run. Many commentators have suggested that the failure to take a longer-term view was the principal factor in making many U.S. businesses less competitive in world markets than, say, the Japanese.

Linking performance measures to the goals and objectives at a given time is important. For example, a young company in a rapidly-growing industry does not need to be overly concerned with cost control because its early success depends on gaining customer acceptance and building a high market share. Prices and profit margins are high during the growth phase, so costs are not critical. But as the company and its industry mature, cost control becomes much more important. Many companies in the computer industry have begun to pay more attention to costs. Companies such as Apple, Sun Microsystems, and Compaq that used to have gross margins of 70% are now finding it hard to achieve 40% because of falling prices and cut-throat competition.[2]

Whether dealing with a cost, profit, or investment center, performance can only be evaluated by comparing results *with* something. Probably the best way to encourage managers to act in the firm's best interests is to measure their performance in relation to *budgeted* results. Managers of production departments are evaluated on whether they produce budgeted quantities of product at budgeted costs. (Product-quality expectations would, of course, be considered in establishing budgeted output and costs.) Managers of nonmanufacturing departments, such as a computer center or market research group, could be evaluated on whether they performed their assigned tasks and met budgeted costs. Managers of profit centers are normally evaluated by comparisons of actual and budgeted profit, and investment centers might be evaluated on the basis of return on investment. (The special problems of evaluating investment centers are taken up in the next chapter, but most of the comments on profit centers apply to investment centers also.)

Of course, the legitimacy of evaluating a manager's performance by comparing budgeted and actual results depends on (1) how the budgeted amounts were determined and (2) to what extent the comparisons consider the controllability of differences. As discussed in Chapters 6 and 7, budgeted amounts must reflect *attainable* performance if managers are to take them seriously and try to meet them. We also noted that managers tend to react

2 *"Deconstructing the Computer Industry,"* Business Week, *November 23, 1992, 90.*

more favorably to an evaluation based on a budget *they* helped to set. But even with budgets that are agreed upon in advance as attainable, an uncontrollable change in conditions can influence results, and managers do not react favorably to a reporting and evaluation system that fails to allow for variations due to circumstances beyond their control. For example, consider the impact of a major, unexpected road-repair project on the operating results of retail stores along the road.

There are other bases for evaluating performance. Some companies evaluate managers on the basis of improvement over some prior period, or by comparison with other segments of the same firm. (Did the factory manager produce at a lower cost than he or she did last year? Did this segment earn more profit this year than did the others?) Whatever bases are used for evaluation, both the evaluator and the evaluatee must understand the bases and the implications of using them.

Whatever the type of responsibility center, and whatever the basis used to compare with actual results, evaluating a *segment* is different from evaluating its *manager*. A manager might be doing an excellent job even though the segment is performing poorly. For example, the manager of a segment doing business in a declining industry might be doing an excellent job if segment profits are steady or decline more slowly than those of the industry as a whole. Similarly, a segment operating in a growing market might look healthy even if its manager is not doing as good a job as another manager could. The question in both cases is the standard for comparison: what *should* the segment be able to accomplish? The performance of each segment is important to those corporate managers who are concerned with allocating resources to their best uses.

ORGANIZATIONAL STRUCTURE

The way a company is organized influences its reporting system. Different organizational structures result in different groupings of responsibilities. That is, the way a company is structured affects the areas controlled by individual managers. For instance, in one firm a factory manager might also have responsibility over the sales force that sells the products from that factory and so is in charge of a profit center. Another firm, similar to the first in product lines, factories, and other physical aspects, might assign the responsibility for the sales force to a corporate vice president of sales. Factory managers in such a firm manage cost centers. The reporting requirements for the two firms are quite different.

In general terms, an organization is characterized as *centralized* or *decentralized* depending on the extent of the responsibilities granted to its managers. If managers have a good deal of responsibility and authority and can make many types of decisions without the approval of higher levels of management, the organization has a **decentralized organization structure**. Where managers can act less freely, a **centralized organization structure** exists. We take up the question of decentralization more fully in Chapter 11. For now it is sufficient to note that, in general, profit and investment centers are more commonly associated with decentralization than are cost centers. This is because managers of profit and investment centers have broader responsibility than do managers of cost centers. (Note, though, that managers of all three types of responsibility centers might have a number of cost centers reporting to them.) As we explore the basics of responsibility accounting, the issue is not so much whether an organization is centralized or decentralized but how the structure affects the reports developed for whatever responsibility centers there may be.

The organizational structure depicted in Exhibit 10-1 shows a great many cost centers. The structure follows functional lines (production, sales, administration, finance). Exhibit 10-2 shows an alternative organizational structure, with many profit or investment centers in which managers of each region are responsible for both production and sales. Note that the finance function is not delegated to individual operating managers in *either* structure. The responsibility for financing the entity is rarely assigned to anyone other than the highest level of management. One reason for not delegating financing decisions to lower levels is a legal consideration: the issuance of bonds and/or stock commits the entire entity and so must be approved by managers with commensurate responsibilities. For multinational firms, the choice of financing sources is also influenced by currency restrictions in specific countries. Legal issues aside, a firm's capital requirements can normally be met at less cost if the needs of its segments are consolidated and filled as a unit.

Exhibit 10-1 Sample of Organizational Structure

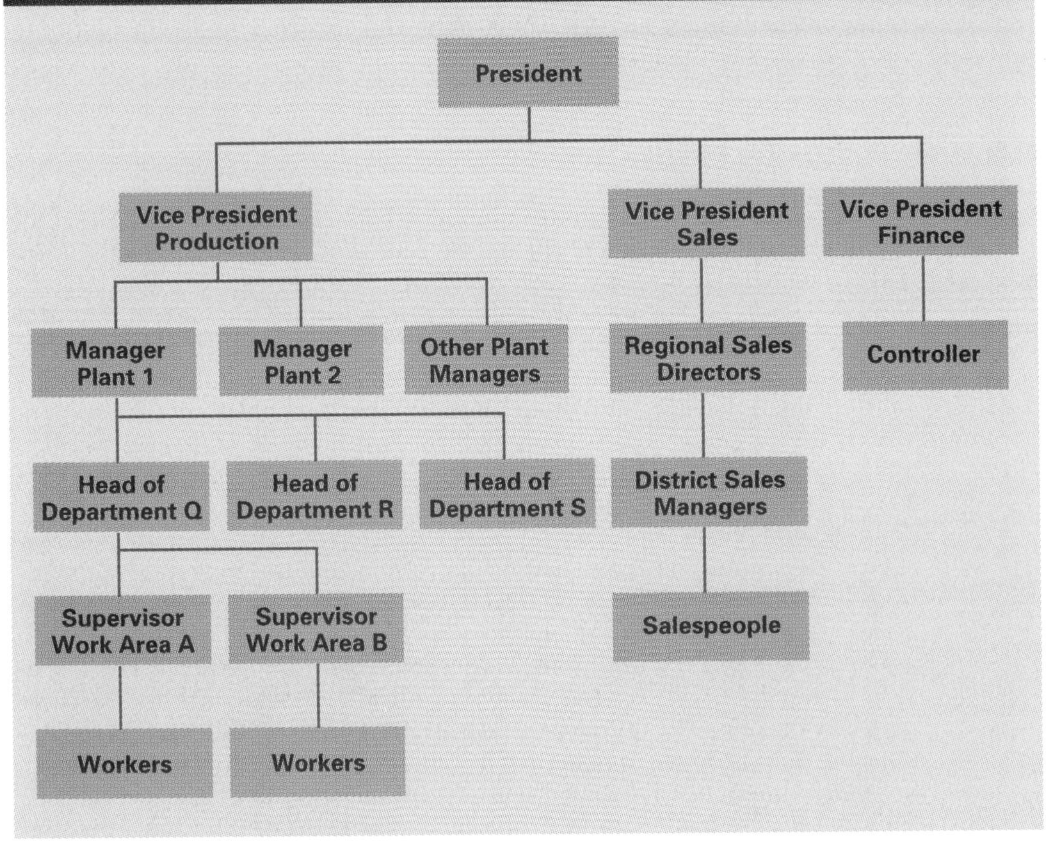

Exhibit 10-2 Sample of Organizational Structure

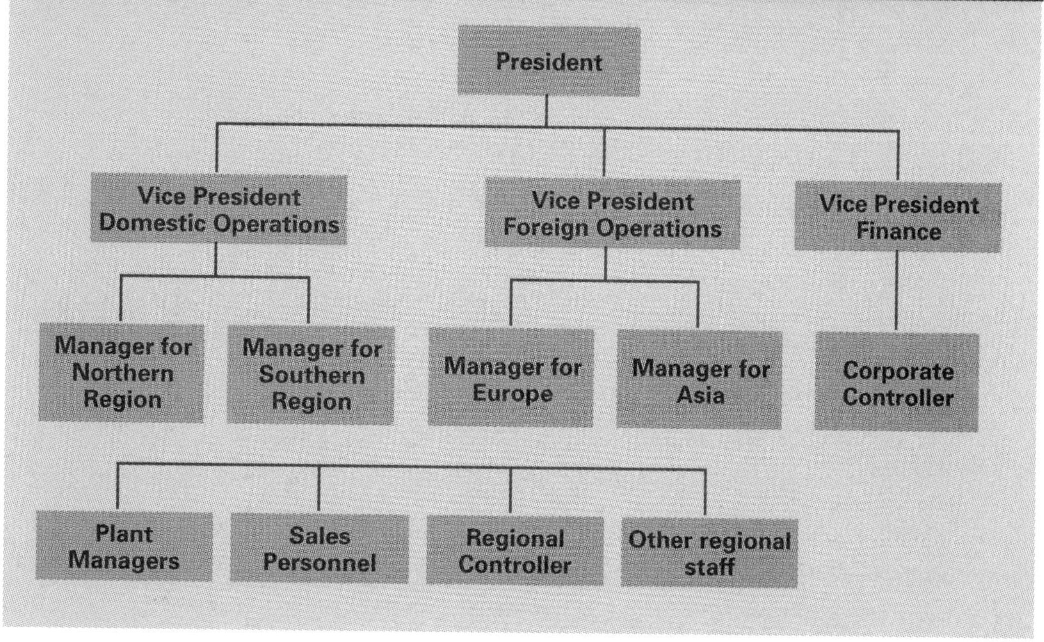

RESPONSIBILITY REPORTING FOR COST CENTERS

Exhibit 10-3 shows the interrelationships among reports for cost centers. Reports for a real company show more detail, more itemizations of individual costs. We restricted the number of items for simplicity.

The company whose reports are exhibited operates a factory that has three levels of supervision: (1) work stations, which are relatively small units under the control of supervisors; (2) departments, which are collections of work stations under the control of departmental supervisors; and (3) the factory as a whole, which is under the control of the factory manager. In addition, though not reflected in the reports, the factory manager is under the direction of the vice president of manufacturing.

A noteworthy feature of the sample reports is that they are not additive. That is, the total cost on the report to a manager is not the sum of the costs on the reports to the managers under her or his supervision. For example, Exhibit 10-3 shows that the total cost reported to the fabrication department supervisor is *greater* than the sum of the costs reported to the supervisors of the work stations. As stated earlier, an important characteristic of good responsibility reporting is that reports include only controllable costs. Whether a particular cost is controllable—and hence includable in the report to a particular manager—depends on the manager's level in the hierarchy. In the example company, the department supervisor is responsible for all costs that are direct to the work stations under his or her supervision. But she or he is also responsible for those costs that are common to the work stations within the group. In the exhibit, such common costs are general supervision (which probably includes the salary of the department supervisor), cleaning, and "other." Similarly, the plant manager is responsible for some

Exhibit 10-3 Responsibility Reports for Cost Centers

	Current Month		Year to Date	
	Budget	Over (Under)	Budget	Over (Under)
Report to Supervisor of Work Station 106—Drill Press				
Materials	$ 3,200	$ (80)	$ 12,760	$ 110
Direct labor	14,200	170	87,300	880
Supervision	1,100	(50)	4,140	(78)
Power, supplies, miscellaneous	910	24	3,420	92
Totals	$ 19,410	$ 64	$ 107,620	$1,004
Report to Supervisor of Fabrication Department				
Station 106—Drill Press	$ 19,410	$ 64	$ 107,620	$1,004
Station 107—Grinding	17,832	122	98,430	(213)
Station 108—Cutting	23,456	876	112,456	1,227
Total work stations	60,698	1,062	318,506	2,018
Departmental costs (common to work stations):				
General supervision	12,634	0	71,234	0
Cleaning	6,125	324	32,415	762
Other	1,890	(67)	10,029	(108)
Totals	$ 81,347	$ 1,319	$ 432,184	$2,672
Report to Manager of Factory				
Fabrication department	$ 81,347	$ 1,319	$ 432,184	$2,672
Milling department	91,234	(2,034)	405,190	(4,231)
Assembly department	107,478	854	441,240	1,346
Casting department	78,245	(433)	367,110	689
Total departments	358,304	(294)	1,645,724	476
General factory costs (common to departments):				
Engineering	14,235	261	81,340	842
Heat and light	8,435	178	46,221	890
Building depreciation	3,400	0	20,400	0
General administration (includes accounting, travel, plant manager's office, etc.)	23,110	340	126,289	776
Total factory costs	$407,484	$ 485	$1,919,974	$2,984

costs that the departmental supervisors are not: engineering, heat and light, building depreciation, and general administration.

Another important feature exhibited by the sample reports is that the amount of detail decreases as reports reach higher and higher levels of management. Managers cannot make effective use of information that is too detailed and voluminous. (Picture the president of IBM reading reports of several thousand cost centers.) Managers are usually concerned most with the performance of those who are directly under them. Departmental managers do not routinely receive reports detailing all of the costs of the work stations. Managers who *want* such detailed information can get it, and might well seek it, if they are concerned about some particular elements of cost.

One other aspect of the sample reports in Exhibit 10-3 deserves discussion. Two of the three reports show some costs as common to work stations or to departments. There are always *some* costs that are common to two or more segments within an organization, but the managerial level at which a particular cost is controllable varies from firm to firm. For example, the sample reports show heating and lighting costs as common to departments, which suggests that individual departmental supervisors cannot control these costs. In another firm, each department might have a meter to monitor the consumption of utilities, in which case the cost might well be controllable at the departmental level. Similarly, one company might require that requests for operating supplies identify the work station at which they are to be used, while another might require only that the operating department be noted on the request. Thus, a cost is not always common by its nature, but may be so because the organization does not produce information by segments below a certain level.

Large amounts of costs that cannot be assigned (and controlled) at lower levels can be frustrating to managers who evaluate the performance of their staffs. This is true because it is likely that the *actions* of staff could influence common costs that appear only on reports to higher levels of management. (To use the earlier example, the manager of a work station may be able to control the use of operating supplies even if existing procedures do not identify costs at that level.) Whether it is worthwhile to adopt procedures to assign responsibility for a particular cost to lower levels of management depends not only on the significance of the cost but also on the benefits to be gained by doing so. Benefits might include savings from lower-level managers being more careful in using particular items (supplies, repair services, whatever). But the benefits must be weighed against the cost of obtaining the additional information (meters, time required to fill out more detailed requisition forms and to produce more detailed reports, etc.). In any case, the facts in a particular case determine whether a cost is controllable at a given level of management, and the responsibility reporting system should follow, as closely as possible, the principle of including only controllable items.

RESPONSIBILITY REPORTING FOR PROFIT CENTERS

The principle of controllability also applies to responsibility reporting for profit centers (and for investment centers, which we consider in more detail in Chapter 11). Exhibit 10-4 provides sample reports for a firm that organizes profit centers around product lines and geographical areas. Managers at the lowest level of profit centers are responsible for product lines. They are responsible to the managers of the geographical areas, who are in turn, responsible to the executive vice president.

The unallocated costs—regional expenses common to product lines, or corporate expenses common to regions—consist of many items. For instance, regional expenses include the salaries of people at regional headquarters, including those in accounting, personnel, finance, and other functions administered from regional headquarters. These costs are not direct to prod-

Exhibit 10-4 Responsibility Reports for Profit Centers (thousands of dollars)

	Current Month		Year to Date	
	Budget	Over (Under)	Budget	Over (Under)
Report to Product Manager—Appliances, European Region				
Sales	$122.0	$ 1.5	$ 387.0	$ 3.2
Variable costs:				
Production	47.5	2.8	150.7	5.9
Selling and administrative	12.2	1.8	38.7	1.9
Total variable costs	59.7	4.6	189.4	7.8
Contribution margin	62.3	(3.1)	197.6	(4.6)
Direct fixed costs	36.0	(1.2)	98.5	(3.1)
Product margin	$ 26.3	($ 1.9)	$ 99.1	($ 1.5)
Report to Manager—European Region				
Product margins:				
Appliances	$ 26.3	($ 1.9)	$ 99.1	($ 1.5)
Industrial equipment	37.4	3.2	134.5	7.3)
Tools	18.3	1.1	59.1	(2.0)
Total product margins	82.0	2.4	292.7	3.8
Regional expenses (common to all product lines)	18.5	0.8	61.2	(1.3)
Regional margin	$ 63.5	$ 1.6	$ 231.5	$ 5.1
Report to Executive Vice President				
Regional margins:				
European	$ 63.5	$ 1.6	$ 231.5	$ 5.1
Asian	78.1	(4.3)	289.4	(8.2)
North American	211.8	(3.2)	612.4	(9.6)
Total regional margins	353.4	(5.9)	1,133.3	(12.7)
Corporate expenses (common to all regions)	87.1	1.4	268.5	3.1
Corporate profit	$266.3	($ 7.3)	$ 864.8	($15.8)

uct lines, and product managers cannot control them. In addition, image-building advertising not aimed at particular product lines, could also be under the control of a regional manager. At the total-firm level there are similar kinds of common costs.

For simplicity, the sample report for the regional manager shows only product margins for each of the product groups. In some companies, such managers receive more detail, such as sales, costs, contribution margin, and perhaps some expenses of special concern, such as advertising and promotion. Exhibit 10-5 shows an approach that provides more detail on individual components of the appliance segment in the European region and draws attention to costs that are common to the different categories of appliances. To focus attention on the format, we have omitted budgeted figures. The critical point in responsibility reporting is conveying the best information; the selection of the elements to include and the format are secondary. Notice that the amount of detail is greater in the alternative format and that some costs shown as direct to product lines in Exhibit 10-4 are shown as common to the individual products in the line in Exhibit 10-5.

In both Exhibit 10-4 and Exhibit 10-5, the sample reports to the manager of appliance sales for the European region include production costs. The implication is that the manager for the region can control, and is responsible for, production costs, but control of production is not necessary to justify this type of reporting. From earlier chapters you know that decisions about individual products or product lines are based on profitability. For decision-making purposes, then, regional sales managers must be *aware* of the costs of manufacturing the products being sold. Accordingly, reports to managers who are responsible only for sales and regional selling costs often include some charge for the products, even though such reporting does not follow strictly the principle of controllability.

Exhibit 10-5 Alternate Responsibility Reporting Format Report to Product Manager—Appliances, European Region (thousands of dollars)

	Total	Small Home Appliances	Large Home Appliances	Commercial Appliances
Sales	$390.2	$126.3	$109.5	$154.4
Variable costs:				
Production	156.6	41.1	31.2	84.3
Selling and administrative	40.6	14.2	18.1	8.3
Total variable costs	197.2	55.3	49.3	92.6
Contribution margin	193.0	71.0	60.2	61.8
Direct fixed costs	27.4	9.5	11.2	6.7
Margin	165.6	$ 61.5	$ 49.0	$ 55.1
Costs common to products in the appliance line	68.0			
Product margin	$ 97.6			

CHOOSING AN ORGANIZATIONAL STRUCTURE

Should a firm organize into profit and investment centers or into cost centers? Should it centralize or decentralize decision making? An important factor that influences answers to these questions is the attitudes and philosophies of top managers. Company presidents who are uncomfortable delegating critical decisions tend to centralize decision making; others who are comfortable delegating such decisions, tend to decentralize. Wal-Mart wants its managers, and other employees, to have a "bias for action" so it does not punish managers who take chances and fail. Managers receive the information and support required to allow them to act entrepreneurially. Managers use income statements, data on inventory turnover, and other information to increase profitability. For an international firm, communication time and type of operation carried on in each country (sales offices, manufacturing) would also be influential factors, as would the ability of on-site managers.

Even after a firm decides to use profit centers, there remains the question of how to make the separations. Should the segmentation be along product lines, geographical areas, types of customers (industrial, government), or markets (leisure, household products, mining)? The choice should be influenced by whether the segmentation facilitates evaluation, and that depends to some extent on the amount of common costs associated with each alternative structure. If each factory serves a particular region and makes many products, segmenting by region is more reasonable than segmenting by product line. If each factory produces a single product (or line) and serves all regions, to segment by product or line is more reasonable. (Even if there is a sales manager in each region, the profit centers could be product lines. Costs incurred by regional managers would be common to product lines.)

Setting up an organizational structure is difficult. Rarely does only one structure make sense for a given firm. Moreover, a structure found useful at one time, by one set of managers, will not remain useful forever. Managers, including top managers, change; products and product lines are dropped, added, or regrouped; manufacturing activities are transferred among plants or otherwise changed, perhaps because of technological innovations. Hence, the structure of the organization, for both responsibility reporting and for operating purposes, requires regular review and reconsideration.

CONTROL, EVALUATION, AND COST ALLOCATION

Responsibility centers that work on the company's products are usually called **operating departments.** Virtually all responsibility centers use services provided by other centers. The terms **service department** and **service center** are used to describe centers that provide services to operating departments and other service departments. Examples of service departments are personnel, accounting, building security, and data processing.

In Chapter 3 we introduced the term *direct cost* to describe a cost that is specifically identifiable with a particular activity. (Another term that refers to the same concept is **traceable cost.**) Managerial accountants also use the term to refer to a cost that is *controlled* by the manager receiving a report. In contrast, then, the term *indirect cost* refers to a cost that the manager receiving a report cannot control directly. Such costs are *common* to several responsibility centers. Many such costs are incurred by service departments for the benefit of other departments. (Of course, not all indirect costs are incurred in service departments, as, for example, depreciation on a factory building that houses both operating and service departments.)

A compelling reason to establish a service department is that having such a department can be cheaper than having each responsibility center perform or acquire the service on its own. (If there is no personnel department, each department must screen and hire its employees, maintain their records, and do all the other tasks that a personnel department performs.) In addition, companies sometimes establish a service department because their managers believe that a qualitative issue, such as a need for confidentiality, makes it wise to perform a particular service inside rather than have outsiders do it.

Because the responsibility centers that use the services of a service department benefit from those services, it seems natural that the users should "pay" for those services. The method most commonly used to reflect a "payment" for such services in reports to managers of service-using departments is to *allocate* the costs of the service department to the using departments. You have encountered allocations before. In Chapter 2 you saw that a total cost per unit gives misleading information because it requires allocating fixed costs to units of product. In Chapter 5 you saw that the only costs relevant for decision making are incremental costs and that allocated costs are not incremental and therefore not relevant.

Virtually all managerial accountants reject the use of cost allocations for decision making. Moreover, increased efforts to identify the activities that drive fixed costs—the costs most commonly thought of as indirect—have reduced the magnitude of untraceable costs that might be allocated. But accountants *disagree* about whether to allocate indirect costs for control and performance evaluation. (The allocation issue has become increasingly important because the indirect costs of operating modern factories are growing rapidly as direct laborers are replaced by robots and the corresponding need for computer operators and maintenance workers.) Thus, while users unquestionably benefit from the activities of service departments, there are serious questions about whether to charge users for the services and, if so, how.

REASONS FOR NOT ALLOCATING COSTS

There is general agreement that the variable costs of a service center should be allocated to service-using departments because the managers of those departments can cause an increase in such costs. For example, a manager who orders 1,000 copies of a document from the Central Copying Center should pay for, perhaps in the form of an allocation, at least the incremental cost of the copies, which probably approximates their variable cost. Where managerial accountants disagree is on the matter of allocating indirect *fixed* costs. There are two principal arguments against allocating indirect fixed costs, both of which stress the potential for adverse behavioral consequences.

First, because indirect fixed costs are not controllable by the users, allocating them violates the principle of controllability. Managers charged with costs they cannot control might come to distrust the whole system of control and evaluation. Worse, they might attempt to "beat the system" and so take actions not congruent with the company's objectives. Even with *variable* indirect costs, the using manager might control the use of the service, but cannot control the cost of providing the service. For instance, in a variation of an earlier example, suppose a firm establishes its own power-generating department to provide electricity to the factory. Managers of power-using departments influence the volume of power generated, thus influencing *total* variable costs in the service department. But such managers cannot control the per-unit variable cost.

The second reason has to do with making decisions. Because indirect fixed costs are common to several users, they are not differential to those users. As shown in Chapter 5, making sound decisions requires using differential revenues and costs. Managerial accountants who oppose including cost allocations in reports prepared for control and evaluation purposes argue that showing allocations in such reports could lead managers to make poor decisions.

REASONS FOR ALLOCATING COSTS

There are several reasons to allocate fixed indirect costs for control and performance evaluation. We have already mentioned that users benefit from the costs incurred by service departments and should have to pay for them. Failing to allocate also understates the full cost of operating the using centers. As we show in later chapters, the full-cost idea is important in product costing—determining the unit cost of products so as to determine inventory and cost of goods sold for financial reporting and income tax purposes. Because allocations *must* be made for financial reporting, there is a tendency also to use them in internal reporting.

Another reason for allocating is to remind managers of the existence of indirect costs and the need to cover them. If the company as a whole is to make a profit, its revenues must cover not only the direct costs of its profit centers, but also the indirect costs of the company as a whole. The Financial Services Department of Weyerhauser, a large integrated paper company charges each department a fee for processing each salaried employee. Managers of using departments who are considering adding salaried personnel know what the costs will be.[3]

Probably the most appealing reasons for showing allocated costs in reports are behavioral. For one, proponents of allocations argue that if indirect costs are not allocated, managers might overuse services because they view the services as "free." For example, if a company does not allocate its computer costs, managers might use more computer time than is economically justified, thus straining capacity and perhaps leading to an unwise purchase of additional capacity. Allocating computer costs could discourage overuse and help prevent incurring unnecessary costs. For a somewhat different example of using cost allocation to control costs, consider a sales manager who controls credit terms offered to customers and the level of inventory maintained. Sales managers normally want to carry a high inventory and offer liberal credit terms, with the firm incurring costs to carry the invest-

---

3 *H. Thomas Johnson and Dennis A. Loewe, "How Weyerhauser Controls Overhead Costs",* Management Accounting, *August, 1987, 20-26.*

ment in inventory and receivables. Sales managers are less likely to allow those assets to increase excessively if they are charged a financing cost based on the investments in those assets. (Note, however, that if the major objective of a relatively new firm is to establish a strong demand for its products by getting as much market penetration as possible, allocating financing costs to the sales manager works against achieving the firm's objective.)

Interestingly, some proponents of using cost allocations on performance reports offer a conflicting argument, also behavioral. They suggest that allocations are helpful when a service is, in the opinion of upper-level managers, *underused.* The reasoning behind this suggestion is that managers will use the service more because they are already paying for it through the cost allocation. For proponents of cost allocations, resolution of the apparent contradiction about how managers will respond to allocations lies in the *way* the costs are allocated, not in the *fact* of allocation.

Another behavior-oriented reason for allocating indirect costs is that the managers to whom costs are allocated will encourage the managers of service departments to keep the cost of the service under control. For example, suppose the manager of computer services wants to buy newer, faster equipment. The manager must convince the users that it is economically sound for them. In the absence of allocations, users have no reason to object to decisions that increase computer costs.[4]

The behavior-influencing aspects of cost allocations can be significant in a number of ways. A realistic example was reported by the Portables Group of Tektronix Company.[5] The Group had been allocating overhead based on direct labor, but its design and process engineers had driven direct labor costs down to less than 7% of total manufacturing cost (just over 3% on some of its newer products). Because overhead costs were high and rising, the overhead allocation rate per direct labor hour was extremely high. Thus, though direct labor cost was fairly low, the high overhead cost allocated on the basis of direct labor made the total cost that *seemed* to be labor-related very high. Many managers interpreted the situation as encouraging efforts to further reduce direct labor, but labor-reducing efforts that *also* increased overhead simply raised the overhead allocation rate. Fortunately, the Group undertook an internal study that showed that costs related to materials and components—purchasing, receiving, inspecting, storage, and recordkeeping—constituted roughly half of overhead costs. Follow-up of this study showed that design and process engineers often recommended using more parts when their use reduced direct labor because, there being no overhead charge on parts, there was no incentive either to reduce the number of components or to standardize those in use.

After its study of overhead costs, the Group began to allocate its material-related overhead based on the number of component parts needed and their annual use. A sample calculation of the two-step allocation process is shown on the next page.

---

4 *A major study found that the most common reasons for allocating corporate indirect service costs to profit centers for purposes of evaluating performance are: (1) to remind managers of the existence of indirect costs; (2) to make the sum of profit-center profits equal total company-wide profit; (3) to fairly reflect each center's use of services; (4) to encourage profit-center managers to pressure service managers to control costs; (5) to encourage use of services. See James M. Fremgen and Shu S. Liao,* The Allocation of Corporate Indirect Costs, *New York: National Association of Accountants, 1981.*

5 *John W. Jonez and Michael A. Wright, "Material Burdening,"* Management Accounting, *August, 1987, 27-31.*

Total material-related overhead	$5,000,000
Total number of parts needed, all types	6,250
Annual cost to carry a part	$800
Cost per part (example):	
Part A, annual use, 20,000 units	$800/20,000 = $0.04
Part B, annual use, 500 units	$800/500 = $1.60

The first step in the allocation process is to determine a cost per part, regardless of the annual volume of use of that part. The next step uses the annual volume of the part to determine a cost per unit, which cost is *then* allocated to the product based on the quantity of each part used in the product. Adopting the new cost-allocation plan influenced behavior in three important ways. First, it encouraged engineers to reduce the number of parts in existing products. Second, it encouraged standardization of parts for use in several products. Third, it encouraged use of fewer, and more standardized, parts in new products.

Whatever the reasons for allocating, remember that virtually all allocations are arbitrary. By *arbitrary* we mean that there is no way to prove that one allocation method is better than another. Nevertheless, some allocation methods are more reasonable than others. Also, as stated earlier, different allocation methods might influence managers differently. We shall, therefore, discuss further how allocations are made and the potential behavioral effects of various allocation methods.

ALLOCATION METHODS AND EFFECTS

Once managers decide to allocate indirect costs, they must select a basis for making the allocations. The basis is usually some measure of activity or use of the service. For instance, some companies use the number of employees in each department as the basis for allocating the costs of its personnel department. Similarly, costs related to a building (such as depreciation, property taxes, and insurance) are probably allocated on the basis of the space occupied by the departments.

The best allocation basis is the cost driver—the activity that reflects the causal relationship of use to cost. That is, if the users' actions cause the cost to increase, then the costs should be charged accordingly. The next best basis is one that reflects the benefits that the user receives. For instance, it is reasonable to allocate heating expense based on the space that each department occupies—a measure of the benefits received. Even if the managers of using departments cannot control heating expense, they must have heated space to operate.

When neither a use nor a benefit basis is available, allocations are often made on the basis of a department's "ability to bear" indirect costs. For example, there is no reasonable measure of how much each segment benefits from costs such as the salary of the president or the annual audit fee. Therefore such costs are often allocated based on sales or assets, with the idea that these measures reflect the segment's ability to bear them. (Or they might not be allocated at all.) Finally, sales is often used as the allocation basis when no measure of benefits received is available.

Assuming a decision to allocate on the basis of use, there are still several approaches to allocating indirect costs (both fixed and variable) and it is not easy to select a method that will work, in the sense of accomplishing goal congruence. Using the following information, we shall illustrate and comment on a few common methods.

Raleigh Company has one service department, the Maintenance Department, and two operating departments, Fabrication and Assembly. Data for the departments follow.

Operating Department	Hours of Maintenance Service Used
Fabrication	20,000
Assembly	10,000
Total	30,000

Maintenance Department Costs for Year	Budgeted	Actual
Fixed	$ 75,000	$ 79,500
Variable:		
$5 per hour	150,000	
$5.10 per hour		153,000
Total	$225,000	$232,500

Allocating Actual Costs Based on Actual Use

The simplest (and worst) allocation method is to allocate the *actual* total cost of the Maintenance Department based on the operating departments' relative use of the service. We can make the necessary calculations in two ways, both of which give the same result. First, we can calculate the actual per-hour rate of providing the service, which is $7.75 ($232,500 actual cost divided by 30,000 hours). The allocations are below.

Fabrication (20,000 × $7.75)	$155,000
Assembly (10,000 × $7.75)	77,500
Total maintenance cost allocated	$232,500

The other calculation uses the relative shares of the two operating departments. The Fabrication Department used two thirds of the maintenance time (20,000/30,000), so it is allocated two thirds of the total cost, or $155,000. The Assembly Department used one third (10,000/30,000) and is allocated $77,500.

This method is poor because: (1) it allocates actual costs rather than budgeted costs and (2) it allocates fixed costs based on use. Allocating actual costs passes the inefficiencies (or efficiencies, if actual costs are less than budgeted costs) of the Maintenance Department on to the operating departments. Operating managers are responsible for the *use* of the service, but not for the cost. The maintenance manager is responsible for maintenance costs.

Allocating fixed costs based on actual use is bad because the amount allocated to one department is affected by the actions of managers in other departments. To see this, suppose that each of Raleigh's operating departments *budgeted* 20,000 hours of maintenance for the year. The budgeted rate is $6.875, computed as follows.

Variable rate	$5.000
Fixed rate ($75,000/40,000)	1.875
Total rate (per hour)	$6.875

Budgeted total maintenance costs would have been $275,000 [$75,000 + ($5.00 × 40,000)], and each operating manager would have budgeted $137,500 in maintenance cost. Allocating on the basis of actual use, the manager of the Assembly Department looks good because $60,000 less than budget is charged ($137,500 budget minus the actual allocation of $77,500, as computed earlier). But the manager of Fabrication looks bad. The Fabrication Department is charged $155,000 (as computed above), $17,500 over budget, *even though it used exactly the budgeted amount for this service.* The additional charge arose partly because the Maintenance Department was over its budget, but more importantly because the Assembly Department used less of the service than it had budgeted. If an allocation is to be used in evaluation, the allocation to a given department should not be affected by the actions of other departments. In general, allocating fixed costs based on actual use encourages managers to underuse the service because the allocation depends not only on how much service a particular manager uses, but also on how much the other managers use.

Another serious problem of allocating fixed costs based on actual use is that an operating manager might interpret allocated amounts as incremental costs and use these irrelevant costs in making decisions. Suppose the manager of the Assembly Department is considering a decision requiring an additional ten hours of maintenance service. Even if actual use and costs had been as budgeted, so that the actual allocation rate equalled the budgeted rate of $6.875, the manager of the Assembly Department might estimate the amount to be charged at about $68.75 (10 × $6.875). Yet the *incremental* cost to Raleigh is the variable cost for ten hours, and only incremental costs are relevant to the decision. Note, however, that a decision involving a very large number of additional hours might well also involve incremental fixed costs in the Maintenance Department. Such costs would be relevant to the decision.

Allocating Budgeted Costs Using Dual Rates

A better allocation method is to allocate only *budgeted* costs, which prevents passing the efficiencies (or inefficiencies) of the service department on to operating departments. In addition, this method employs the concept of flexible budgeting by treating fixed and variable costs separately. Budgeted variable costs are allocated based on actual use (because total variable costs change as use changes); fixed costs are allocated based on long-term expected use. The term *dual rates* refers to allocating fixed costs and variable costs differently.

The use of dual rates overcomes the problems associated with allocating fixed costs based solely on actual use because each department's allocated fixed cost is a lump sum determined before the year begins. The idea supporting this approach is that service departments incur fixed costs to provide the capacity to serve, and the decisions that determined the capacity of the Maintenance Department were based, at least in part, on estimates made earlier by the managers of the operating departments. The argument is that if the manager of the Assembly Department has *requested* some amount of capacity, he or she should pay for it.

Suppose the estimated long-term use is 60% for the Fabrication Department and 40% for the Assembly Department. We then have the following allocations, which assign variable costs at the budgeted rate of $5 per hour of use and fixed costs at the budgeted total of $75,000.

	Fixed	Variable	Total
Fabrication	(60% × $75,000) $45,000	$100,000	$145,000
Assembly	(40% × $75,000) 30,000	50,000	80,000
Total	$75,000	$150,000	$225,000

This method has several advantages. One is that operating managers do not absorb the inefficiencies of the Maintenance Department because only budgeted costs ($225,000) are allocated. Consistent with the concept of flexible budgeting, operating managers are charged a budgeted lump sum and a budgeted variable rate. Another advantage is that operating managers probably will not overuse the service because there is a charge for use. The managers probably will not underuse the service because the hourly charge and the lump-sum charge are known in advance. Notice also that the amount charged to a department depends only on that department's use, not on the use made by other departments. Moreover, operating managers are less likely to consider the allocated fixed costs in making decisions because the amount of allocated fixed cost is independent of the actual use of the service.

Allocating Through Transfer Prices

An entirely different approach to allocating the costs of a service department to using departments is to use a transfer price. A **transfer price**, which we cover in more depth in Chapter 11, is a charge for services (or for goods) that one segment renders to another segment of the same firm.[6] As mentioned earlier, using transfer prices can transform a cost center, such as a service department, into an artificial profit center. Transfer prices are not cost allocations in the strict sense of the term because the charge is not necessarily related to the costs of the service department. Often, the transfer price approximates the market price for the services, which is the price that operating departments would have to pay to obtain the services from an outside company. Because the transfer price is set in advance, the using manager knows exactly how much will be charged to employ another ten hours of maintenance time. In this respect, the transfer price shares the advantage of the dual-rate method of allocation.

Suppose that in our example the transfer price for maintenance services was set at $8 per hour—a price management considered to be the best estimate of the cost to acquire maintenance services from another company. The amounts charged to each department are as below.

Fabrication(20,000 × $8)	$160,000
Assembly(10,000 × $8)	80,000
Total maintenance cost charged	$240,000

6 Transfer prices are also commonly used when profit centers "sell" goods to sister segments within the company. Chapter 11 discusses this use of transfer prices.

The Maintenance Department will show revenues of $240,000, actual costs of $232,500, and, therefore, a profit of $7,500. *Using a transfer price does not change the actual cost incurred.* The actual total cost was $232,500. Operating departments show maintenance costs of $240,000, and the Maintenance Department a $7,500 profit. The *net*, $232,500, is the actual cost incurred.

Using transfer prices to create artificial profit centers is not a simple task, as evidenced by the experience of Weyerhauser Company.[7] All of Weyerhauser's corporate-level service departments are required to charge for their services. The Financial Services Department, mentioned earlier, provides general accounting and payroll services, and its charges are based on a variety of factors. For example, charges to account for receivables are based on invoice volume and number of customers and are adjusted for situations that require hand-processing. In developing its charges for general accounting work, the Department used separate rates for employees of three types: analytical, clerical, and systems. A critical factor in Weyerhauser's system is that users are free to acquire services from outside the company. Consistent with comments made earlier, one result of the transfer-pricing system (called "charge-backs" at Weyerhauser) was that service department managers became profit-conscious, seeking to provide better services to the company *and* seeking outside customers for their services.

Another important advantage to using transfer prices is that the transfer price can be increased or decreased to encourage less or more use of the service, respectively. It is probably easier to encourage or discourage use through transfer pricing than it is by using the cost-allocation methods described earlier.

Not all transfer-pricing systems include the freedom to purchase services from, or sell services to, outsiders. As we said earlier, upper-level managers might conclude that confidentiality or other qualitative concerns override the benefits of permitting outside dealings. Permitting outside sales can also create problems, because the manager of a service department must establish priorities for the work-flow in the department. (As a part of a larger entity, should the service department give special consideration to the needs of internal customers? Does the "hard money" available from external customers justify assigning a lower priority to either anticipated or unanticipated needs of internal customers?)

One difficulty with trying to use a transfer price that approximates the outside cost for the service is that the outside cost for an equivalent service is often very difficult to determine. But if reliable outside prices are available, there is a significant advantage to using that price as a transfer price and treating a service department as a profit center. If a department consistently shows losses under such a pricing system, upper-level managers are alerted to the possibility that the firm could benefit from shutting down the department and buying outside. Such a decision must consider the structure of fixed costs (avoidable and unavoidable) and would be made along the lines described in Chapter 5 in connection with make-or-buy decisions.

7 *H. Thomas Johnson and Dennis A. Loewe, "How Weyerhauser Manages Corporate Overhead Costs,"* Management Accounting, *August, 1987, 20-26.*

WHAT TO DO?

Managers should be charged with at *least* the incremental costs associated with carrying out their functions. Thus, an amount of cost of a service department, or portion of cost of a joint activity that is attributable to a particular department, should be charged to the department.

If allocations are to be made, amounts allocated should be budgeted, rather than actual, costs. Charges should be for the quantity of the service received based on budgeted variable costs of providing the services. If fixed costs are allocated, the allocation should be budgeted fixed costs and should be based on the *long-run* percentages of the service capacity required by each operating department. In any case, the allocation to a particular department should not be affected by the actions of other departments.

Compromises are possible. Performance reports can show controllable and allocated costs separately. If the higher-level managers who use the reports to evaluate the performance recognize the distinction, there is less likelihood of misunderstanding and complaining from the lower-level managers. Elgin Sweeper, mentioned in Chapter 6, is an example of a company whose reports show only controllable costs. It changed its reports to show only controllable costs as part of a campaign to get front-line managers more involved in developing budgets.

We emphasize that performance reports and their content are specific to the circumstances that a particular company faces and to the preferences of its managers. No set of simple rules governs all conceivable situations or leads to reports that satisfy all managers.

ROLE OF ACTIVITY-BASED COSTING AND JIT

In conventional allocation schemes, costs might be allocated on any number of bases. Companies that allocate costs using ABC principles should find that operating managers are more apt to accept the allocations because they are charged for activities that drive costs. A benefit of adopting JIT principles is that managerial accountants and other managers who find non-value-adding activities in the course of analyzing centrally-performed activities will try to eliminate those costs. Operating managers can then be more confident that they are not being charged with inefficiencies or with costs that are driven by activities irrelevant to their operations.

Examples of activities driving costs for a corporate treasury department might include collecting delinquent accounts and managing cash, debt, and foreign currency. After determining the appropriate driver for each, the managers of the operating units are then charged the costs of meeting their requirements as expressed in their shares of the cost-driving transactions. As a manager of Westinghouse put it, "Managers will feel they are better able to manage their businesses when they know what they are being charged with. Furthermore, when it is clear that services are performed efficiently, it will add value to their businesses."[8]

---

8 *Thomas E. Steimer, "Activity-Based Accounting for Total Quality,"* Management Accounting, *October, 1990, 39-42.*

EFFECTS ON COMPANY INCOME

Allocations and transfer prices are managerial accounting devices, not economic activities. Hence, changes in allocations and transfer prices cannot, by themselves, change the firm's total income. Changes in the firm's income *can* occur if a change in an allocation or transfer price induces managers to act differently. But so long as the managers of the individual segments continue to operate as they have, the firm's total income will not be affected. The transfer price of the goods or services is revenue to the selling division and cost to the buying division. Therefore, an increase in the transfer price increases income to the seller, but reduces income to the buyer by a like amount.

OTHER USES OF ALLOCATIONS

In discussing why allocations might appear on performance reports, we pointed out that allocations are needed for product costing (for financial reporting and income tax purposes). Allocations are also necessary for other purposes. For instance, public utilities like electric and telephone companies are required to justify rate (price) increases to state commissions. Part of the justification for a rate increase is increases in costs, and many of the costs of public utilities are allocated among different classes of customers (residential, commercial, industrial). Too, reimbursements to hospitals under Medicaid are based on costs that include allocations, as are payments to cities, counties, and states under some federal grants and payments to universities for contract research.

The Cost Accounting Standards Board (CASB) was a potent force in support of making allocations. The CASB specified rules for allocating costs by firms that do certain kinds of business with the federal government. The Board issued a number of regulations regarding many aspects of allocation, including the bases to use for allocations and the costs to include in or exclude from the pool of costs to be allocated. (CASB pronouncements use the terms *allowable* and *not allowable* to indicate which types of costs—direct or allocated—may be included in reports for reimbursement.)

When organizations allocate costs for one or more of the purposes that demand such allocations, they are trying to develop a "full cost," with each activity or segment bearing its "fair share" of the indirect costs. The allocations may have to be made for the purpose of reporting on a particular contract, for preparing external financial statements, or in order to abide by some law. For example, society's interests may be served by reimbursing a hospital for an operation on the basis of the full cost of the operation (including the costs to provide and maintain an operating room). But the fact that a contract, GAAP, some regulatory agency, or a legislative mandate demands the allocation of joint costs does not make that allocation any the less arbitrary.

ETHICS AND ALLOCATIONS

Allocation schemes for indirect costs do not change a company's total operating costs. In a variety of circumstances, however, allocation schemes *can* influence a company's profits by affecting its revenue or its taxes. Such circumstances present ethical problems for a company's managers, including its managerial accountants.

Some governmental units, especially the Department of Defense, contract with businesses to do work on a cost-plus basis. Such contracts permit the company to be reimbursed for its costs, including an allocation of indirect costs, plus a specified profit. The temptations for a business involved in such contracts would be (1) to include as much costs as possible in the cost pool subject to allocation to government work, and (2) to allocate large amounts of the cost pools to such work. Less than careful attention in determining the costs to be included in a pool had serious consequences for Stanford University, which does a great deal of research for agencies of the U.S. government. In an address to alumni, Stanford's then-president conceded that the cost pool allocated to government research had mistakenly included, among other things, the cost of flowers, furniture, and repairs for the president's house and the cost of a yacht.

State regulation of rates charged by public utilities presents another opportunity for allocations to affect revenues, because regulators are expected to approve rates that cover a utility's costs. When utility companies engage in other, nonregulated, activities the temptation is to allocate large amounts of indirect costs to regulated services. Because public utilities provide, and usually seek differing rates for, services to various classes of customers (residential, commercial, industrial), utility companies must allocate costs to the classes of customers. A major charge in the litigation leading to the breakup of AT&T was that long-distance service was allocated so much cost that it heavily subsidized local-service customers.

Companies operating in more than one state and/or country often must allocate indirect costs among the jurisdictions within which they operate. If tax rates differ among those jurisdictions, the temptation is to assign larger amounts of costs to those jurisdictions with higher tax rates. Agents of taxing authorities are aware of the temptation and tend to give special attention to allocation methods that could affect the tax base.

In recent years, some charitable organizations have come under fire for questionable allocations. Donors naturally prefer charities that devote the bulk of their resources to charitable purposes and spend a relatively small portion of their money on fund-raising and administrative activities. A number of organizations have been accused of painting a false picture of their activities by including a few pieces of educational material with their fundraising communications and then allocating and reporting significant amounts of the costs of those communications (as well as administrative costs) as public education programs.

SUMMARY

Managers need accounting information to control operations, and their efforts must be evaluated on bases that are consistent with the goals of the firm. Responsibility accounting should assist in achieving goal congruence and in motivating managers. No single responsibility accounting system is appropriate for all firms, or for the same firm over its lifetime. The responsibility accounting system must parallel the structure of the organization. The structure of the organization depends on the nature of its operations and on the attitudes and management styles of top managers.

The reporting segments of a responsibility accounting system may be cost centers, profit centers, or investment centers. Most firms use all three types of responsibility centers. Whatever the plan for segmenting the firm for reporting purposes, individual managers can be held responsible for only that which they can control.

Cost allocations can be troublesome in responsibility accounting, as they have been shown to be in decision making. Conflicting objectives of cost allocation are charging managers for benefits they receive and reporting on the controllable aspects of the managers' operations in order to increase their motivation. Transfer prices, the selling prices established for artificial profit centers, can alleviate some of the problems of cost allocations. Pervasive behavioral considerations in responsibility accounting make it difficult to draw general conclusions about the best or most useful approaches to follow.

KEY TERMS

centralized organization structure
cost center
decentralized organization structure
goal congruence
investment center
operating departments
profit center
responsibility accounting
responsibility center
service center
service department
traceable cost
transfer price

REVIEW PROBLEM

Wolfert Company makes and sells air conditioners and operates in three regions: the Northeast, Southeast, and Southwest. Data for 19X5 are given below, in thousands of dollars.

	Northeast	Southeast	Southwest
Sales	$2,400	$5,600	$3,800
Variable cost of sales	1,220	2,200	1,700
Variable selling costs	170	330	240
Direct fixed costs:			
Production	310	810	440
Selling	240	400	280
Administrative	320	440	380

Common fixed costs were $450,000 for administration and $110,000 for selling.

Required

Prepare a performance report by region, showing contribution margin and regional profit. Show common costs as lump-sum deductions in the total column.

ANSWER TO REVIEW PROBLEM

Performance Report for 19X5
(in thousands of dollars)

	Northeast	Southeast	Southwest	Total
Sales	$2,400	$5,600	$3,800	$11,800
Variable costs:				
Production	1,220	2,200	1,700	5,120
Selling	170	330	240	740
Total variable costs	1,390	2,530	1,940	5,860
Contribution margin	1,010	3,070	1,860	5,940
Direct fixed costs:				
Production	310	810	440	1,560
Selling	240	400	280	920
Administration	320	440	380	1,140
Total direct traceable fixed costs	870	1,650	1,100	3,620
Regional profit	$ 140	$1,420	$ 760	$ 2,320
Common fixed costs:				
Selling				110
Administration				450
Total common costs				560
Income				$ 1,760

APPENDIX: OTHER ALLOCATION SCHEMES

As indicated in the chapter, common costs *must* be allocated for some purposes and allocations can be useful for influencing behavior. Allocation schemes are, therefore, of considerable interest. The chapter illustrated the **direct method.** The direct method ignores the fact that service departments provide services to other service departments, as well as to operating departments. This appendix describes two techniques that many managerial accountants believe to be superior to the direct method: the **step-down method,** and the **reciprocal method.**

STEP-DOWN METHOD

A distinguishing feature of many allocation schemes, particularly those specified under cost-reimbursement contracts, is the use of a multistep allocation. The process is called **step-down allocation,** the **step method,** or simply, **step-down.** It is seen in the legislated or regulated methods for determining how much to reimburse hospitals for services performed for citizens.

The idea behind the step-down method is to recognize that service departments provide services for other service departments as well as for operating departments. The costs of service departments are allocated one department at a time. As a result, the costs of all service departments, except the first to be allocated, will reflect their shares of the costs of *some* of the other service departments. An example should make this clear.

Consider GNL Manufacturing Company, which has, for simplicity, two operating departments and two service departments. The operating departments, Forging and Machining, receive services from Personnel and

Administration. Personnel keeps all employee records and handles payrolls; Administration handles all other administrative tasks. Each service department provides services to the other service department as well as to the two operating departments. Data for the most recent month follow.

Department	Direct Costs	Number of Employees
Personnel	$ 200,000	10
Administration	500,000	30
Forging	1,800,000	100
Machining	3,000,000	300
Total costs	$5,500,000	440

As with any allocation situation, we must select the bases for making the allocations. Suppose that GNL's managers decide to allocate Administration costs based on the direct costs of the departments and Personnel costs based on the number of employees.

Because the step-down method allocates the costs of one service department at a time, we must decide which service department's costs to allocate first. Several guidelines can be used to determine the sequence. One is to start with the department that serves the most other service departments. Another is to order the departments based on the percentage of their services that go to other service departments. Suppose GNL's managers decide to allocate Administration costs first.

The following schedule shows the allocation of the $500,000 of Administration costs, using direct costs as the basis.

	Personnel	Forging	Machining	Total
Direct costs	$200,000	$1,800,000	$3,000,000	$5,000,000
Percentage of total	4%	36%	60%	100%
Allocation	$ 20,000	$ 180,000	$ 300,000	$ 500,000
Previous totals	200,000	1,800,000	3,000,000	5,000,000
New total cost	$220,000	$1,980,000	$3,300,000	$5,500,000

Total costs are still $5,500,000, the total direct costs before allocation. But the total is spread differently, with the $500,000 from Administration now in the other three departments.

We are now ready to allocate the costs for Personnel on the basis of the number of employees. Notice that we allocate $220,000, the *new* total of costs in Personnel. Under the step-down method, a service department's costs build up through successive allocations to it. Note also that no Personnel costs are allocated to Administration. Once you allocate costs *from* a department, you do not allocate any back *to* the department. Below is the allocation of the Personnel costs and the final totals allocated to the operating departments.

	Forging	Machining	Total
Number of employees	100	300	400
Percentage of total	25%	75%	100%
Allocation of personnel	$ 55,000	$ 165,000	$ 220,000
Previous totals	1,980,000	3,300,000	5,280,000
New total cost	$2,035,000	$3,465,000	$5,500,000

By their nature, allocations are arbitrary no matter how sophisticated the method used to calculate them. The results are always influenced by the allocation basis chosen. Had we selected different bases for allocating the costs of either of the service departments, the final results would be different. Also, the results are influenced by the order in which allocations were made. That is, had we chosen to allocate Personnel first, the final total costs for each operating department would have been different. In summary, the allocation process succeeds in *assigning* the costs of service departments to the operating departments, but does not change the fact that the costs of service departments are common to the departments serviced. All of the reservations stated in the chapter about allocations and decision making apply regardless of the allocation scheme used.

The following schedule summarizes the procedures and explicitly shows the step-down feature as each department's costs are allocated.

	Administration	Personnel	Forging	Machining	Total
Direct costs	$500,000	$200,000	$1,800,000	$3,000,000	$5,500,000
Administration	(500,000)	20,000	180,000	300,000	
Personnel		(220,000)	55,000	165,000	
Total			$2,035,000	$3,465,000	$5,500,000

The total costs of the two operating departments ($5,500,000) are, of course, the same as the total costs of all departments before the allocation procedure began. As stated many times, allocations do not, by themselves, change total costs.

RECIPROCAL METHOD

The reciprocal, or **simultaneous,** method of allocation recognizes, more fully than does the step method, the services that each service department renders to other service departments. This means, in terms of the example used above, that not only are Administration costs allocated to Personnel, but Personnel costs are also allocated to Administration. To accomplish this reciprocal allocation we first find the percentages that each service department *receives* from the other. The original data from the example are presented below, in somewhat modified form, to facilitate the calculations.

Services Provided By	Services Provided To				
	Personnel	Administration	Forging	Machining	Total
Administration:					
Direct Costs	$200,000		$1,800,000	$3,000,000	$5,000,000
Percentages	4%		36%	60%	100%
Personnel:					
No. of employees		30	100	300	430
Percentages		6.98%	23.25%	69.77%	100%

The next step in the reciprocal method is to calculate what are called the **adjusted costs** of the service departments, to recognize that the departments provide services to each other. To accomplish this we set up simultaneous equations, letting P = the adjusted costs for Personnel and A = the adjusted costs for Administration. The equations are

$$P = \$200{,}000 + 0.04A$$
$$A = \$500{,}000 + 0.0698P$$

One approach to solving these equations is to substitute the equation for A in that for P, as below. (You could use other approaches, of course.)

$$P = \$200{,}000 + 0.04(\$500{,}000 + 0.0698P)$$

Simplifying and rearranging this equation yields

$$P = \$220{,}616$$

and substituting for P in the equation for A yields

$$A = \$515{,}399$$

The final step is to allocate these adjusted costs to the two operating departments using the percentages computed above. (That is, we do *not* adjust the percentages as was done using the step-down method.)

Service Departments	Operating Departments: Forging	Operating Departments: Machining	Total Costs
Allocations			
Personnel			
$220,616 × 23.25%	$ 51,293		
$220,616 × 69.77%		$ 153,924	
Administration			
$515,399 × 36%	185,544		
$515,399 × 60%		309,239	
Total allocated	236,837	463,163	700,000
Direct costs	1,800,000	3,000,000	4,800,000
Total cost	$2,036,837	$3,463,163	$5,500,000

Notice that the total costs allocated equal the direct costs of the two service departments ($500,000 for Administration and $200,000 for Personnel). The final total cost is still $5,500,000, the sum of the direct costs of the four departments, showing once again that the method of allocating costs does not, by itself, change the total cost incurred.

Those who favor the reciprocal method claim it is more "accurate" than other methods (including step-down). That is true in the sense that the reciprocal method recognizes all reciprocal services. But the results still depend on the choice of an allocation basis for each department. Moreover, the method is subject to the same objection as is any other allocation method. It is arbitrary and so cannot be said to yield a "true" or "correct" cost for an operating department (especially if the costs of one or more of the service departments are largely fixed).

In this case, the choice between the step-down and reciprocal methods does not produce a significant difference in the total costs finally assigned to individual operating departments. (The difference is $1,837, which is less than 1% of the final total cost for each department.) In other cases, the difference could be much larger, and the need for managers to understand the potential impact of alternative allocation methods is much greater.

ASSIGNMENT MATERIAL

QUESTIONS FOR DISCUSSION

10-1 Responsibility versus control The manager of a store of a large chain of supermarkets said the following to the controller of that chain.

My son is taking a managerial accounting course at CU, and he's been telling me about something called responsibility accounting and how it can help to motivate employees. How come we don't have responsibility accounting in our stores? I've got a meat manager who pretty much keeps that department in my store going. My son says the meat department would be a good candidate for what he calls a profit center.

What do you think?

10-2 Responsibility centers—universities What problems do you see in establishing and evaluating responsibility centers in the following: (a) universities, (b) colleges or schools within universities, and (c) departments within colleges?

10-3 Responsibility reporting The annual report of a major manufacturer carried the following paragraph (paraphrased).

Specialization also continues within each marketing force as we increase the number of personnel. We are experiencing a steady rise in the number of customers as well as in the variety and complexity of products and equipment. As a result, an increasing proportion of our salespeople concentrate on just one or a few industries—or on certain product categories.

Suppose that in the past, the salespeople sold all products to all kinds of customers in different industries. What effects will the new method of directing the efforts of the individual salespeople have on the responsibility reporting system?

10-4 Change in organizational structure During 1992, popular business periodicals carried many stories about decentralization of major companies that were viewed previously as centralized, and vice versa. Suggest some of the factors likely to affect the ease or difficulty of implementing change in each direction.

10-5 What's being centralized? Consider the following comments of executives of companies that had made changes in the way they operated.

Executive A: We centralized the purchasing function because so many of the stores that buy a broad range of our products complained about the extra cost to them of having to deal with a variety of purchasing procedures.

Executive B: After we centralized our recruiting function we had a 25% drop in the cost to recruit a new college-graduate to our company.

Executive C: We let people go in the field when we set up a home-office with an 800 number to handle the processing of and questions about insurance claims. But our employees say they are more satisfied with the new system because they get better answers to their questions and faster results to complaints.

Explain what the functions centralized by the companies above have in common and how "centralization," as discussed in the chapter, might differ from the centralization noted by the executives.

10-6 Evaluating a performance measure The top-level administrators of Mid-State University announced that, henceforth, the major factor in evaluating the performance of a faculty member will be the number of students who enroll in classes taught by that faculty member. Discuss how the proposed performance evaluation measure does or does not (a) reflect application of the principle of controllability, and (b) contribute to goal congruence.

10-7 Pricing, timing, allocations, and public relations For many years telephone companies did not charge for directory assistance (calling an operator to get a number). When they did begin to charge (usually 20 cents per request after three free requests per month), a commentator said: "This is ridiculous. They have operators on duty anyway, so there is no additional cost for their giving out a number. Ma Bell has just found another way to get into our pockets."

Required

Comment on the quotation.

10-8 Artificial profit centers A national trade association held a seminar for chief executives where one of the topics discussed was responsibility accounting and the profit-center concept as a means of evaluating departments. Two executives who attended the conference made the following statements to their respective chief accounting officers.

Executive A: I want you to set up as many profit centers as possible, beginning with the legal department. From now on, departments using legal services will be charged at $40 per hour. That's about twice the average lawyer's salary and ought to cover the nonsalary costs of the legal department. We haven't even allocated the costs of the legal department up to now, and we might as well do something to let our managers know that when they ask for legal advice they can expect to pay for it.

Executive B: Well, you accountants have done it again. Like all the other high-priced professionals, you insist on coming up with special names for something that everyone already understands. For years now we've been allocating the costs of the legal department, like all other corporate departments, to the operating units in our company. Now I'm told that what we need to do is set up a 'transfer price.' That's just a fancy name for allocating the costs.

Do you foresee any problems with the first executive's intentions? Do you agree with the position taken by the second executive?

EXERCISES

10-9 Alternative allocation bases The following data refer to the three departments of ABC Company.

	A	B	C
Sales	$400,000	$200,000	$400,000
Square feet of space occupied	8,000	7,000	5,000

Total common costs are $100,000.

Required
Allocate the common costs to the departments on the bases of (a) sales dollars and (b) square feet of space occupied.

10-10 Basic allocation methods Mighty Mart Stores has three profit centers and one service center, a central purchasing department. Data appear below.

	Profit Centers		
	Groceries	Meat	Canned Goods
Percentage of central purchasing services used in current year	40%	25%	35%
Expected long-term use of central purchasing services	30%	30%	40%

Budgeted central purchasing costs were $400,000 fixed and $200,000 variable. Actual fixed costs were $390,000, and actual variable costs were $220,000.

Required
1. Allocate the actual central purchasing costs to the profit centers based on actual use of the services.
2. Allocate the budgeted variable central purchasing costs to the profit centers based on actual use of the services and the budgeted fixed costs based on expected long-term use.
3. Which of the two methods do you prefer? Why?

10-11 Performance report York Tool Company operates six departments in its main plant. Each department manager is responsible for materials, direct and indirect labor, supplies, small tools, and equipment maintenance. The factory manager is responsible for buying equipment and for all other costs. The manager of the Stamping Department received the following performance report last month. The costs of building occupancy have been allocated to the department.

	Budget	Actual	Over (Under)
Materials	$ 31,900	$ 32,800	$900
Direct labor	36,200	36,500	300
Indirect labor	14,250	13,220	(1,030)
Supplies	6,600	6,450	(150)
Small tools	4,200	4,340	140
Equipment:			
Depreciation	12,800	12,800	0
Maintenance	5,700	4,950	(750)
Building:			
Depreciation	2,200	2,200	0
Maintenance	980	950	(30)
Property taxes	760	770	10
Total	$115,590	$114,980	($610)

Required

Prepare a new performance report that shows only the costs for which the manager of the Stamping Department is responsible.

10-12 Step-down allocation method (related to Appendix) Mott Company has two service departments, Personnel and Administration, and two operating departments, Foundry and Assembly. The schedule below shows the costs in each service department and percentages of activity that each service department provides each of the other departments, both service and operating.

Department Providing Service	Costs of Department	Department Receiving Service			
		Personnel	Administration	Foundry	Assembly
Personnel	$200,000	0%	60%	10%	30%
Administration	$300,000	20%	0%	60%	20%

A member of the controller's staff made the following allocations.

	Foundry	Assembly
Personnel:		
$200,000 × (.10/.40)	$ 50,000	
$200,000 × (.30/.40)		$150,000
Administration:		
$300,000 × (.60/.80)	225,000	
$300,000 × (.20/.80)		75,000
Total	$275,000	$225,000

The controller is wondering whether it would make any difference to use the step-down method, instead of the direct method shown above.

Required

1. Allocate the service department costs using the step-down method, beginning with Personnel costs.
2. Explain why the controller would begin the step-down with Personnel costs.

10-13 Reciprocal allocation (continuation of 10-12)

Required

Do the allocation in 10-12 using the reciprocal method.

10-14 Allocations—actual versus budgeted costs Merion Turf Products produces lawn fertilizers and grass seed. The company's Research Department, which works to improve both types of products, had budgeted costs of $450,000, virtually all fixed. These costs were to be allocated to the two product lines based on the relative amounts of time spent on each. All of the scientists keep time sheets showing which projects they work on each month.

At year end the Research Department had actually spent $496,000 as a result of unanticipated cost increases and some inefficiencies in the department. The manager of the Fertilizer Department had budgeted $225,000 for allocated research costs but found that he was actually charged with $276,760. The final allocation was based on actual costs and actual relative time spent on work for his department. He was not happy with the situation, especially when he learned that the manager of the Grass Seed Department had canceled a major project, resulting in lower-than-budgeted research on grass seed.

Required

Suggest a way to allocate research costs that will not unduly penalize the managers of the Fertilizer and Grass Seed Departments.

10-15 Assignment of responsibility Klee Company is organized by function: sales, production, finance, and administration. The production manager is upset about her latest performance report (below). She contends that costs of about $8,000 were incurred solely because the sales manager ordered changes in production for rush orders from customers.

Performance Report—Production Department

	Budget	Actual	Variance (favorable)
Controllable costs:			
Materials	$ 80,000	$ 79,000	$(1,000)
Direct labor	160,000	162,000	2,000
Other labor	46,000	53,000	7,000
Idle time*	1,000	4,000	3,000
Other production costs	21,000	20,000	(1,000)
Totals	$308,000	$318,000	$10,000

* *Wages paid to workers while they are idle, as when machines are being reset because of a change from one product to another.*

The production manager argues that the $3,000 shown on the performance report as idle time was caused by changing the production process to meet special orders. In addition, she claims that about $5,000 in other labor was for costs incurred to make the necessary changes and for the overtime premium paid to workers to get the work finished in time to meet the deadlines given for rush orders.

Required
What is wrong and what do you recommend?

10-16 Transfer prices and goal congruence The controller of Calvert Company has set transfer prices for service departments, all of which used to be cost centers. One is for stenographic services. The charge is $18 per hour, based on total budgeted hours of available service and total budgeted costs for the stenographic pool. The manager of one operating department, a profit center, has obtained a price of $15 per hour for stenographers' time from an outside agency for a task that will take about 50 hours. The manager informs the controller and the manager of the stenographic pool of the outside price and is told to take it if she wishes; the transfer price will not be lowered.

Required
Comment on the position taken by the controller and the manager of the stenographic pool. (Budgeted costs for the pool are about 90% fixed.) Make a recommendation.

10-17 Set of performance reports Arcon, Inc., manufactures office equipment. The Raleigh Plant produces several models of copiers. The following schedule shows year-to-date controllable costs for the Assembly Department and for all others as a whole, in thousands of dollars.

	Assembly		All Others	
	Budget	Over (Under)	Budget	Over (Under)
Materials	$12.8	$1.1	$ 64.2	$3.2
Direct labor	28.9	(2.2)	256.8	4.3
Other controllable costs	15.3	1.8	102.2	(1.5)

There were $74,000 in budgeted costs controllable by the plant manager, but not by any of the department managers. Actual costs were $1,200 over budget. The Raleigh Plant is part of the Southeast region. Regions, like plants, and departments are cost centers. Budgeted costs of the other plants in the region totaled $3,265,200, actual costs were $12,300 over budget. Budgeted costs of $120,600 (actual were $1,300 over budget) were controllable by the regional manager, but not by the plant managers.

Required
Prepare a set of responsibility reports for the Assembly Department, the Raleigh Plant, and the Southeast region using the format of Exhibit 10-3.

10-18 Development of performance report Stratton Company is organized by functional areas: sales, production, finance, and administration. The Sales Department has product managers who are responsible for a particular product and who are evaluated based on the following typical performance report.

Activity Report—Product Zee May 19X4—Manager, J. Harrison		
Sales (30,000 units)		$300,000
Cost of goods sold		172,000
Gross profit		128,000
Other expenses:		
Advertising	$28,000	
Travel	17,000	
Depreciation	6,000	
Office expenses	19,000	
Administrative expense	23,000	93,000
Product profit		$ 35,000

The following additional information about the report is available.

(a) Because of problems in the production process, cost of goods sold is $11,000 higher than budgeted.

(b) Harrison authorized spending $16,000 on product advertising. The remainder of the advertising cost reported is an allocated share of general advertising costs incurred by the firm.

(c) Depreciation charges consist of the following: 20% on furniture and fixtures in Harrison's office and 80% for the building that houses all the firm's activities.

(d) Office expenses include $3,000 allocated from the expenses of the vice president for sales.

(e) Administrative expenses are allocated based on relative sales.

Required

Revise the performance report for product Zee to reflect the principle of controllability.

PROBLEMS

10-19 Cost allocation—direct method The schedule below shows the costs of the service departments of Winston Inc. and the percentages of service that the service departments provide to each other and to Winston's operating departments.

Department Providing Service	Costs of Department	Department Receiving Service			
		Purchasing	Administration	Trimming	Cutting
Purchasing	$280,000		20%	50%	30%
Administration	$300,000	30%		10%	60%

Required

Use the direct method to allocate the service department costs to the operating departments. Assignment 10-12 shows how to calculate the percentages.

10-20 *Cost allocation—step-down method (related to Appendix)* Use the information from the previous assignment to do a step-down allocation, beginning with the Administration Department.

10-21 *Cost allocation—reciprocal method (related to Appendix)* Use the information from 10-19 to do a reciprocal allocation.

10-22 *Performance reporting and allocations* Clark Company, a furniture outlet, allocates indirect costs to its two product lines based on sales. The income statement for 19X5 appears below.

	Indoor Furniture	Outdoor Furniture	Total
Sales	$350,000	$350,000	$700,000
Direct costs	180,000	180,000	360,000
Controllable profit	170,000	170,000	340,000
Indirect costs	150,000	150,000	300,000
Income	$ 20,000	$ 20,000	$ 40,000

In 19X6, price increases on indoor furniture increased sales of that line to $400,000. Prices of outdoor furniture were not changed, and sales remained at $350,000. Direct costs of each line were again $180,000, and total indirect costs were again $300,000.

Required

1. Prepare a product-line income statement for 19X6, allocating indirect costs based on sales.
2. Comment on the results. (Are they logical? Did the manager of outdoor furniture do a better job in 19X6 than in 19X5?)

10-23 *Responsibility for rush orders* Howard Company's sales manager, Luis Cavallari, often requests rush orders from the production department. Howard's production process requires a great deal of setup time whenever changes in the production mix are made. The production manager, Brad Givens, has complained about these rush orders, arguing that costs are much lower when the process runs smoothly. Cavallari argues that the paramount consideration is to keep the customer's goodwill and that, therefore, all sales orders should be made up as quickly as possible.

Required

1. Identify the issues creating the conflict.
2. Using the guidelines in Appendix B, write a memorandum to the two managers suggesting what steps might be taken to effect a satisfying solution.

10-24 *Performance measurement* Eleanor Chin, the sales manager of Warner Company, is evaluated on the basis of total sales. Exceeding the sales budget is considered good performance. The sales budget and cost data for 19X3 follow.

	Product			
	Alpha	Beta	Gamma	Total
Sales budget	$150,000	$300,000	$550,000	$1,000,000
Variable costs	75,000	135,000	165,000	375,000
Contribution margin	$ 75,000	$165,000	$385,000	$ 625,000

Actual sales for the year were:

Alpha	Beta	Gamma	Total
$500,000	$400,000	$200,000	$1,100,000

Actual prices were equal to budgeted prices, and variable costs were incurred as budgeted (per unit).

Required

1. Did Chin perform well? Support your answer with calculations.
2. Using the guidelines in Appendix B, write a memorandum to Warner's controller, George Karpinski, explaining what the changes in the firm's performance evaluation might contribute to goal congruence.

10-25 Behavioral problem Watson Company recently bought a copier with a capacity of 10,000 copies per day. Annual fixed costs of the copier are $24,000; the variable cost is $0.01 per copy. Previously, Watson had leased a similar copier with annual fixed costs of $14,000 and variable costs of $0.06 per copy. Watson allocates the fixed costs of the copier based on expected long-term use of the copier and the variable costs based on actual use.

Total copying had run about 8,000 per day with the old machine. The new copier is nearly always running at capacity, and people have complained that they cannot get copies within a reasonable time. Some managers have been forced to send material to outside copying services, which charge about $0.08 per copy.

Required

What seems to be happening, and what do you recommend, if anything?

10-26 Hospital allocations and decisions Blake Memorial Hospital is a full-service hospital with several departments. Departments that perform services directly for patients are called *revenue centers* and include the Medical, Surgical, and Emergency Departments. Other departments, such as Admissions, Patient Records, Laundry, and Housekeeping, are called *service centers.* Costs of service centers are allocated to revenue centers. Below is a schedule showing the percentages of costs allocated from two service centers to two revenue centers, together with the direct costs of each of the service centers.

		Revenue Center	
Service Center	Costs	Medical	Surgical
Admissions	$300,000	70%	30%
Records	$400,000	20%	80%

The hospital receives reimbursements from Blue Cross, Medicaid, and other third parties for services performed for some patients. The reimbursement contracts typically allow recovery of both direct and indirect costs. Such reimbursements amount to about 30% of total Medical Department costs and about 90% for surgical costs. Thus, at the present time, the hospital is reimbursed for $144,000 of its Admissions costs, calculated as follows:

Through medical reimbursements ($300,000 × 70% × 30%)	$ 63,000
Through surgical reimbursements ($300,000 × 30% × 90%)	81,000
Total	$144,000

The hospital administrator is considering some different procedures that will increase the cost of Records by $10,000, while reducing Admissions costs by $6,000. Obviously, the change would increase total cost, but the administrator is well aware of the differing reimbursement rates.

Required

1. Calculate the total reimbursement that the hospital now receives for the indirect costs of Admissions and Records.
2. Calculate the total reimbursement that the hospital will receive if the new procedures are adopted.
3. Comment on the effects of the procedural changes beyond Blake Memorial.

10-27 Allocations and expense reimbursement You need to take a business trip from your office in Atlanta to a branch in Los Angeles sometime in the next few weeks. You have also planned to play in a golf tournament near San Francisco. You manage to combine the trips so that you fly to Los Angeles, finish your business, then go to the tournament. Some airfares are:

Atlanta-Los Angeles each way	$380
Los Angeles-San Francisco each way	$105
Atlanta-San Francisco each way	$420

Because you will be staying over a weekend, you get a special excursion ticket that allows you to make the entire trip for $740. You spend three days working, two days playing golf. Your company reimburses your business expenses.

Required

1. How much airfare will you show on your expense account?
2. Suppose that you were your boss. How much airfare would you allow the company to reimburse?

10-28 Step-down allocation (related to Appendix) Walker Company has two operating departments—Machining and Assembly—and three service departments—Personnel, Data Processing, and General Administration. The controller wishes to allocate service department costs using the step-down method, beginning with Data Processing, then Personnel, and lastly, General Administration. She wants to use the following bases: Data Processing, number of transactions; Personnel, number of employees; General Administration, total direct costs (before any allocation of service department costs).

The controller has assembled the following data.

Department	Total Direct Costs	Number of Employees	Number of Data Processing Transactions
Data processing	$ 200,000	20	0
Personnel	150,000	30	20,000
General administration	300,000	100	30,000
Machining	2,000,000	300	40,000
Assembly	3,000,000	600	10,000

Required

Prepare a step-down allocation.

10-29 Performance report for a cost center Dominic Porter, the manager of the Casting Department of Western Foundries, was disturbed by the report that he received last month.

Monthly Cost Report—Casting Department	July, 19X6
Materials	$ 32,800
Direct labor	66,800
Indirect labor	2,380
Power	18,900
Maintenance	5,700
Other	9,350
Total	$135,930

The factory manager had commented unfavorably to Porter about power and maintenance costs, both of which were higher than in previous months. Both costs are mixed. The variable portions are relatively controllable by the department managers, but the fixed portions are not controllable at the departmental level. The amounts shown are allocations based on the department's use of the services each month. The Casting Department used 9,500 kilowatt-hours of power and 800 hours of maintenance service in July. The budgeted monthly costs of the two services are:

Power cost = $130,000 + $0.05 per kilowatt-hour
Maintenance cost = $24,000 + $0.80 per maintenance-hour

The Casting Department's long-term shares of the services are estimated at 10% for power and 15% for maintenance. All other costs on the report are controllable by the department manager.

Required

Prepare a new performance report for the Casting Department that shows controllable costs and noncontrollable costs separately and allocates fixed power and maintenance costs based on the department's long-term use of those services.

10-30 Ethics and allocations Tempest Foundry, a maker of heavy-duty machinery parts, now serves only commercial customers, but soon will begin doing work for the U.S. government. Cost-plus contracts are necessary because so much of the work is special-order parts, ones the company has not made before. Therefore, the company has no idea of what they will likely cost to manufacture.

The government's cost-plus contracts provide for the government to pay the cost of the work plus a profit based on a percentage of the cost of the work. The cost of work includes materials and labor, plus a "fair share" of overhead. The company will keep track of the materials and labor used on each government project.

Tempest's managers have been trying to decide how to allocate overhead costs between government and commercial business. They agree that they should, each month, allocate actual overhead costs to commercial and government business, but they are not sure what basis to use. One manager argues that they should base the allocations on labor time because government work is likely to be more labor-intensive than commercial work and will therefore be allocated more overhead. Another says that they should analyze overhead costs to see what activities drive them and use the drivers as the bases for allocation. A third argues that it really makes little difference and spending time on the issue is fruitless.

Required

Using the guidelines in Appendix B, prepare a memorandum to Tamara Vasilatos, the controller, discussing the issues and suggesting a solution.

10-31 Performance report in a service company Louis Wardlaw heads the Tax Department at Bryan & Cummings, a large firm of Certified Public Accountants. The firm also has an Audit Department and a Management Services Department. Wardlaw recently received the following performance report for his department.

	February	March
Revenues	$140,600	$148,400
Costs:		
Staff salaries	76,800	77,400
Travel and supplies	7,800	8,100
Occupancy and utilities	9,800	10,900
General office expense	15,400	21,800
Total costs	109,800	118,200
Income	$ 30,800	$ 30,200

Wardlaw thought that his department had done much better in March than in February and was surprised by the report. He talked to the firm's internal accountant, who had prepared the report, to gather additional information. Staff salaries, travel, and supplies are all direct to the department. Occupancy and utilities are allocated based on space occupied. In March, the lease on the firm's office expired and was renewed at a higher rent. General office expense is allocated to departments based on revenue. The Audit and Management Services Departments both experienced drops in revenue in March, resulting in a higher share going to the Tax Department.

Required

1. Revise the preceding report to show revenue, direct costs, controllable profit, allocated indirect costs, and income.

2. Did the Tax Department perform better in February than in March? Why or why not?

10-32 Compensation plan (CMA adapted) Parsons Company compensates its salespeople with commissions and a year-end bonus. The commission is 20% of a "net profit," which is computed as the normal selling price less manufacturing costs. (Such costs contain some allocated fixed overhead.) The profit is also reduced by any bad debts on sales written by individual salespeople. The granting of credit is the responsibility of the firm's credit department, and credit approval is required before sales are made.

Salespeople can give price reductions, which must be approved by the sales vice president. Commissions are not affected by such price concessions. The year-end bonus is 15% of commissions earned during the year provided that the individual salesperson has achieved the target sales volume. If the target is not reached, there is no bonus. The annual target volume is generally set at 105% of the previous year's sales.

Required

Using the guidelines in Appendix B, write a memorandum to Ralph Samson, vice president of sales, identifying the features of the compensation plan that are least and most likely to be effective in motivating salespeople to work in the firm's interests.

10-33 Selecting an allocation base Amelia Strelcyzyk, controller of Carter Brothers Discount Mart, is considering allocating indirect costs to its departments. She proposes to allocate annual building rent of $2,000,000 based on the floor space that each department occupies. Jennifer Bynum, manager of the Children's Department, objects to this basis. She contends that the basis should be the relative value of the space. Her department is on the second floor. Comparable second floor space rents for about $10 per square foot, while first floor space rents for about $15 per square foot.

The Children's Department occupies 20,000 square feet of the total 100,000 square feet on the second floor. The first floor also has 100,000 square feet.

Required

1. Determine the amount of cost that the Children's Department would be allocated using the controller's method.
2. Determine the amount of cost that the Children's Department would be allocated using the department manager's method.
3. Using the guidelines in Appendix B, write a memorandum to Ms. Strelczyk, giving and supporting your recommendation about which allocation method to use.

10-34 Allocations and decisions Cramer Company has several product lines, each controlled by a different manager. Each manager is evaluated partly on profit. The expenses charged to each line are the direct costs of the line plus 15% of sales. (The 15% covers costs not directly associated with the lines, such as salaries of the corporate staff, interest on corporate debt, and service functions like personnel, building security, and cafeteria. These costs are virtually all fixed.) The president of the company estimated that 15% would cover these expenses at budgeted sales of $6,000,000 for the coming year. Each year the percentage is adjusted based on budgeted costs and budgeted sales for the entire company.

The manager of the small appliances line has the opportunity to sell 20,000 units to a chain store at $30 each. Per-unit variable costs are $27, ignoring the 15% charge. There would be no incremental fixed costs associated with the order, and there is sufficient capacity to make the additional units.

Required

1. Given the existing plan for evaluating performance, will the manager of small appliances accept the order? Why or why not?
2. Is it in the company's best interests for the manager to accept the order? Why or why not?

10-35 Performance measures Below are five job titles and the measure by which performance in that job is judged. Comment on the usefulness of each in achieving goal congruence.

Job or Job Title	Performance Measure
(a) Director of the county's mental health program.	The number of patients released from treatment.
(b) Director of a program to reduce unemployment.	The number of jobs found for persons on the unemployment rolls, as a percentage of the total unemployed persons.
(c) Director of a regional program to rehabilitate substandard housing.	The number of homes now meeting local building codes that had previously been classified substandard.
(d) The operator of a particular machine.	The number of hours the machine is running.
(e) A salesperson.	The dollars of sales orders written divided by the number of customers visited.

10-36 Evaluation of compensation plans (AICPA adapted) Gibson Company was established some years ago to bring several new products to the market. Its founder, Gilbert Wilson, believed that once customers tried their products, they would become well accepted. For the first several years, Gibson grew at a rate Wilson considered to be satisfactory. In recent years, some problems have developed both in the firm's profitability and in the morale of and harmonious relationships among the firm's salespeople.

Since the company began, salespeople have been paid a base salary plus an 8% commission. The following data are available for two salespeople for the most recent year.

	Ronald McTavish	James Christy
Gross sales orders written	$250,000	$180,000
Commissions	20,000	14,400
Sales returns	17,500	9,000
Cost of goods sold—all variable	139,500	68,400
Discretionary expenses of salespersons (travel, entertainment, etc.)	19,200	21,500

Required

1. Determine which salesperson contributed more to the company's profit by preparing a performance report for each.

2. Using the guidelines in Appendix B, write a memorandum to Mr. Wilson recommending (and supporting) changes in Wilson's method of compensating its salespeople.

10-37 Allocations and ethics A slightly edited excerpt from an appeal for contributions from a charity appears below.

> The Fund's expenses for 1991 were $26,893,345. Of that amount, 21% was spent in support of research programs and 43% of expenses went in support of the Fund's public education programs in connection with fundraising appeals. Combined research and public education programs accounted for 64% of total expenses. Fundraising expenses were 22% of total expenses and administrative expenses were 14% of total expenses.

The mailing included five health tips (such as cut down on fats, do not smoke, and exercise regularly) that occupied about 15% of the mailing.

Required

1. To what categories given above do you think the charity allocated the costs of mailing? What sorts of costs might the charity have included as part of mailing costs?
2. With the information available, are you inclined to support the charity? Why or why not?

10-38 Allocation and behavior Brenner Company allocates common production costs such as depreciation, property taxes, payroll office, and factory accounting on the basis of the cost of materials used on jobs in each production department. Budgeted material costs for the coming year are $300,000, common production costs $750,000.

The manager of the Fabricating Department has developed a new process that requires 10% more materials than the old process, but 20% less labor time. Without the new process, she expects to incur materials costs of $60,000 and labor costs of $50,000 during the coming year.

Required

Determine the desirability of introducing the new process from the viewpoints of both the firm and the manager of the Fabricating Department. If your answers conflict, suggest a solution.

10-39 Performance reporting—alternative organizational structure (CMA adapted) Cranwell Company sells three products in a foreign market and a domestic market. An income statement for the first month of 19X2 shows the following.

Sales		$1,300,000
Cost of goods sold		1,010,000
Gross profit		290,000
Selling expenses	$105,000	
Administrative expenses	72,000	177,000
Income		$ 113,000

Data regarding the two markets and three products are given below.

	Products		
	A	B	C
Sales:			
Domestic	$400,000	$300,000	$300,000
Foreign	100,000	100,000	100,000
Total sales	$500,000	$400,000	$400,000
Variable production costs (percentage of sales)	60%	70%	60%
Variable selling costs (percentage of sales)	3%	2%	2%

Product A is made in a single factory that incurs fixed costs (included in cost of goods sold) of $48,000 per month. Products B and C are made in a single factory and require the same machinery. Monthly fixed production costs at that factory are $142,000.

Fixed selling expenses are joint to the three products, but $36,000 is direct to the domestic market and $38,000 to the foreign market. All administrative expenses are fixed. About $25,000 is traceable to the foreign market, $35,000 to the domestic market.

Required

1. Assume that Cranwell has separate managers responsible for each market. Prepare performance reports for the domestic and foreign markets.
2. Assume that Cranwell has separate managers responsible for each product. Prepare performance reports for the three products.

10-40 Cost allocations, transfer prices, and behavior Several top executives of Millard Company are discussing problems they perceive in the company's methods of cost allocation. For each of the costs discussed below, indicate what changes will help accomplish the stated objectives.

(a) Computer cost, which is 95% fixed, is allocated using a transfer price of $100 per hour of use. The executives believe that lower-level managers do not use the computer enough.

(b) Maintenance costs, which are budgeted at $10 per hour variable and $200,000 per year fixed, are allocated by dividing total incurred cost by total maintenance hours worked and distributing the resulting per-hour cost to operating departments according to the number of hours of maintenance work done. The executives believe that operating managers request maintenance work only when machinery is about to break down. Production has halted while repairs were made on critical machines. Operating managers have complained that the per-hour cost is too high.

(c) Millard has a consulting department that advises operating managers on various aspects of production and marketing. The costs of the department are fixed but discretionary and have been rising in recent years because of heavy demand for its services. The costs are not allocated because it was felt that managers should be encouraged to use the service. One executive commented that operating managers call the department to find out where to go for lunch.

10-41 Allocations and behavior R. A. Shore is a large mail-order company dealing in men's and women's clothing and accessories. Shore operates its six regional distribution centers as profit centers. Until now, each distribution center handled its own trucking requirements. Shore has just acquired a fleet of trucks, which are under the control of the traffic manager, who is based at central headquarters.

The traffic manager anticipates having to hire outside truckers because Shore's fleet is insufficient to meet peak demands. He wants the managers of the distribution centers to provide monthly estimates of their trucking needs, from which he will decide how much, if any, outside trucking to hire. For two reasons, explained below, costs will be higher than necessary if the estimates he receives are either too high or too low.

First, the typical agreement with an outside trucker provides for a payment of $1.20 per mile, but with a guarantee of 2,000 miles for a month. Thus, a trucker who drives 1,000 miles will be paid $2,400. The guarantees can add up to a substantial amount if the estimates are too high. Second, if the estimates are too low, the traffic manager must scramble to find additional truckers in the middle of the month, also adding to costs. Therefore, accurate estimates of trucking needs are desirable. The controller wants a cost allocation scheme that will encourage accuracy.

Required

1. Suppose the controller decides not to allocate trucking costs. Do you expect managers of the distribution centers to pay much attention to their monthly estimates of needs?
2. Answer the question in item 1 assuming that the controller decides to allocate all trucking costs, both for the owned fleet and for outsiders, based on mileage used by each center.
3. What would you do to encourage the managers of the distribution centers to act in Shore's best interests?

10-42 Allocations and managers' bonuses Katherine Grove, the owner of GroveMart, wants to pay her department managers bonuses totaling $7,500. Grove wants the $7,500 allocated based on the profit each department earns. In the following income statement, all indirect costs are allocated based on sales.

	Dry Goods	Housewares	Total
Sales	$250,000	$500,000	$750,000
Total direct costs	166,000	437,000	603,000
Controllable profit	84,000	63,000	147,000
Indirect costs (all fixed):			
Sales salaries	16,000	32,000	48,000
Other	8,000	16,000	24,000
Total indirect costs	24,000	48,000	72,000
Profit	$ 60,000	$ 15,000	$ 75,000

Some salespeople work in one department or the other, while some cover both departments. The manager of Housewares argues that the allocation of indirect sales salaries is inappropriate. He believes that the allocation should be based on the relative direct sales salaries of $60,000 for Dry Goods and $20,000 for Housewares. (These amounts are included in direct costs.) He says that the work of the salespeople is related to the total sales effort.

Required

1. Compute each manager's bonus given the existing allocations.
2. Prepare a new income statement allocating indirect sales salaries as suggested by the manager of Housewares. Compute each manager's bonus.
3. Comment on the results. Which method of allocation gives the better result?

4. How might Grove distribute the $7,500 to the managers in a reasonable way without getting into arguments over allocations?

10-43 Performance report Caldwell Department Store has three major lines—housewares, clothing, and sporting goods. The controller is developing performance analyses for the managers of the lines and has prepared the following income statement, in thousands of dollars.

	Housewares	Clothing	Sporting Goods	Total
Sales	$900	$1,200	$400	$2,500
Cost of goods sold	500	680	180	1,360
Gross profit	400	520	220	1,140
Other expenses:				
Sales	60	90	40	190
Advertising	45	60	20	125
Rent	40	40	20	100
Depreciation	20	16	12	48
General and administrative	90	120	40	250
Miscellaneous	60	85	32	177
Total expenses	315	411	164	890
Profit	$ 85	$ 109	$ 56	$ 250

You learn the following about the data in the above income statement:

(a) Cost of goods sold is direct.
(b) Salaries expense includes allocated salaries of $75,000 for employees whose work takes them into different departments. The controller used relative sales to make the allocations.
(c) Advertising is partly allocated. Each department is charged at standard market rates for newspaper space, radio time, and television time that its manager requests. The $50,000 cost of general advertising ordered by the sales vice president was allocated based on sales dollars.
(d) The rent allocation is based on floor space occupied. The three departments occupy 100,000 square feet. Sporting Goods is in the basement, the others on the first floor. Similar property in the city rents for $1.05 per square foot for first floor space, $0.80 for basement space. Rent on space occupied by the administrative offices is included in general and administrative expenses.
(e) Depreciation is all for furniture and fixtures within the departments.
(f) General and administrative expenses are allocated based on sales dollars.
(g) Miscellaneous expenses are partly separable, partly allocated. The allocated amounts by department are as follows: Housewares, $28,000; Clothing, $36,000; and Sporting Goods, $16,000.

Required

Prepare a new performance report using the principle of controllability. Include a column for unallocated costs, as well as one for each department.

10-44 Transfer prices and behavior All operating departments of Jacson Company are profit or investment centers, and some service departments are artificial profit centers. The Maintenance Department is an artificial profit center that charges $10 per hour for work it does for operating departments. The variable cost per hour is $4, and fixed costs are $40,000 per month.

The manager of Department A, an operating department, has just determined that some changes in the production process can be made. If the changes are made, maintenance requirements will drop from 2,100 hours per month to 1,600. However, the variable cost to produce a unit of product will increase from $6 to $7. Department A produces 4,000 units of product per month.

Required

1. Determine the change in monthly profit for Department A if the production process is changed.
2. Determine the change in profit of the Maintenance Department if Department A changes its production process.
3. Determine the effect of the change in Department A's production process on Jacson's monthly profit.
4. Suppose that the manager of Department A is prompted to study possible changes in the production process because the transfer price for maintenance work is to be raised to $12 per hour. The Maintenance Department expects a $1 increase in variable cost per hour and approval of other expenditures that will raise fixed costs by $8,000 per month. For the last several months, the Maintenance Department has shown a profit of $8,000, and the proposed new transfer price was designed to maintain that profit level.
   (a) How many hours of maintenance work per month are currently done by the Maintenance Department?
   (b) If the manager of Department A makes the change in the production process, what profit will Maintenance show for a month?

10-45 Cost allocation Galco Industries allocates indirect costs to departments and product lines using direct labor hours as the basis. The 19X5 allocations are based on 400,000 direct labor hours and $1,910,000 indirect costs. Data related to one product line, cleaners, and to all others as a group, for 19X5 follow.

	Totals	Cleaners	All Others
Direct labor hours	400,000	50,000	350,000

Galco's managers have become convinced that they need several bases to reflect the activities that drive their indirect costs. After careful study, the controller developed the following information regarding cost pools and activities that drive the pools.

Cost Driver	Amount of Activity	Amount of Related Indirect Costs
Labor hours	400,000 hours	$1,580,000
Recordkeeping	150,000 entries	180,000
Number of parts	4,000 parts	150,000
Total indirect costs		$1,910,000

Data related to one product line, cleaners, and to all others as a group, for 19X5 follow.

	Totals	Cleaners	All Others
Direct labor hours	400,000	50,000	350,000
Recordkeeping entries	150,000	6,000	144,000
Number of parts	4,000	100	3,900

Required

1. Allocate the indirect costs to cleaners and to the other products based on direct labor hours.
2. Allocate each group of costs separately to cleaners and to the group of others using the separate bases.
3. Galco sells 30,000 cases of cleaners annually. Its direct costs are $16.50 per unit. Separately calculate the total per-case costs using your results from part one and part two. Comment on the difference.

10-46 Performance report Budgeted and actual results for the carpet line of Glenn Products appear below, along with selected other data. Glenn makes a wide variety of products, with each line under a single manager.

Carpet Line, January 19X6 (in thousands of dollars)

	Budget	Actual	Over (Under)
Sales	$434.0	$446.4	$12.4
Cost of sales	262.0	279.1	17.1
Gross margin	172.0	167.3	(4.7)
Operating expenses	97.0	100.0	3.0
Profit	$ 75.0	$ 67.3	($ 7.7)

Other data:

1. The carpet line is manufactured in several plants, all of which make other products using fabric and other materials that go into carpets. The fixed costs of all of these factories, totaling about $8 million per month, are allocated to product lines based on relative variable manufacturing costs. Budgeted variable manufacturing costs for the carpet line were about 38% of sales, while actual costs were about 39% of sales because of some price reductions.
2. The carpet line had budgeted and actual fixed operating expenses traceable to its operations of $32,600. Variable operating expenses, both budgeted and actual, were 6% of sales. The remaining costs shown in the statement were allocated expenses common to the entire business of the firm. These costs are allocated based on relative sales.

Required

Prepare a report on the carpet line that identifies the responsibility of the manager in charge. Use the format of Exhibit 10-4 but include a column for actual results as well as for budgeted results and amounts over or under.

10-47 Cost allocations in a university Ed Cranston, the new dean of the School of Business at Midstate University, is concerned. It is only early February, and he has just received a report from the university's printing and duplicating service showing that the school has exceeded its budget for duplicating for the academic year. The report appears as follows.

Printing and Duplicating Department Statement of Budget and Charges for the School of Business, September-January

Annual Budget	Actual Charges	Over (Under)
$4,200	$4,350	$150

An enclosed note states that Ed must either stop using the service or obtain approval of a supplemental budget request from the university's chief fiscal officer. Ed pulls out his latest statement, from December, and finds that actual charges at that time were $1,830. Since the school was on vacation during a good part of January, he wonders how $2,520 could have been incurred in January.

He finds out that costs for the Printing and Duplicating Department in January were $6,300, of which $700 was for paper, $2,000 for salaries, $2,000 for machine rentals, and $1,600 general overhead (allocated share of all university utilities, depreciation, etc.). A total of 35,000 copies was made in January, a relatively low number because of the vacation. However, several faculty members in the School of Business had a substantial amount of printing done for scholarly papers that they were circulating to other professors throughout the country. The School of Business was responsible for 14,000 of the 35,000 copies. The $2,520 charge was computed by dividing total department costs for the month by the number of copies ($6,300/35,000) to arrive at a charge of $0.18 per copy. Ed also learns that during a typical month about $8,600 in cost is incurred and 150,000 copies are processed. Paper is the only variable cost.

Required

Evaluate the cost allocation system used and recommend changes if you think any are necessary.

10-48 Allocation of costs—distribution channels Weisner Company sells its products through wholesalers and retailers. Erica Stern is in charge of wholesale sales, and Ralph Pike manages retail sales. Frieda Weisner, president of the firm, has ordered an analysis of the relative profitability of the two channels of distribution to determine where emphasis should be placed. The following data show the operations for the last six months.

	Wholesalers	Retailers
Sales	$2,000,000	$3,000,000
Cost of sales—all variable	1,600,000	2,000,000
Sales commissions (3% of sales)	60,000	90,000
Managers' salaries	18,000	18,000
Advertising (allocated as a percentage of sales dollars)	12,000	18,000
Selling expenses—salespeople's expenses, delivery, order processing, credit checking (allocated on the basis of number of orders from each group)	80,000	160,000
General expenses (allocated as a percentage of sales dollars)	40,000	60,000
Total expenses	1,810,000	2,346,000
Income	$ 190,000	$ 654,000

The same products are sold to both wholesalers and retailers, but prices to wholesalers are about 20% less than those to retailers.

Required

1. Comment on the reasonableness of the allocation methods used.
2. Recast the statement based on the principle of controllability.
3. What further information would help in assigning costs to the responsible managers?

CASES

10-49 Allocations and behavior Clifford Electronics operates a single plant. Clifford allocates indirect costs to departments and then to product lines based on their direct labor content. Each department concentrates on one product line. The cost of an average unit of one of its major lines, made in Department Z, appears below. The data relate to a recent month when the company made 50,000 units of the product line.

Materials and components	$ 90
Direct labor at $12 per hour	24
Indirect costs at 500% of direct labor	120
Total cost	$234

The indirect cost rate of 500% of direct labor cost is based on actual total indirect costs divided by the $4,000,000 total company-wide labor cost for the most recent month. Because of the high combined labor and indirect costs, the department manager urged the Design Engineering Department to work on reducing the labor time in the product. The engineers did a great deal of redesigning that resulted in a 25% reduction in labor time over a six month period, largely by using costlier parts and components that required less time to assemble. The department manager was then surprised to see the following analysis for the sixth month of the program, when production was 50,000 units.

Materials and components	$ 95
Direct labor at $12	18
Indirect at 650% of direct labor	117
Total cost	$230

The manager was aghast at the results and could not understand why such a concentrated effort had shown so little payoff. The manager of engineering was also distressed at the results. The most disappointing aspect was the sharp increase in the indirect cost rate, and the manager decided to determine its cause. He learned that total labor hours for the company decreased about 10% over the six month period because other departments were also trying to reduce labor costs.

Required

1. Determine total indirect costs allocated to the product line in each month.
2. What reasons might there be for the disappointing results?

10-50 Allocations and behavior (continuation of 10-49) Sarah Torg, controller of Clifford Electronics, was well aware of the problems created by the company's use of direct labor to allocate all indirect costs. She did considerable analysis and developed the following plant-wide pools of average monthly indirect costs, as they related to particular cost drivers.

Activity	Amount of Activity	Amount of Related Indirect Costs
Labor cost	$ 3,480,000	$ 9,880,000
Recordkeeping	2,400,000 entries	840,000
Materials	$48,000,000 cost of materials	11,350,000
Engineering hours	4,000 hours	770,000
Total indirect costs		$22,840,000

Torg noted that using direct labor cost to allocate the indirect costs gave a rate of about 650%, as Department Z, experienced in a previous month. That is, $22,840,000/$3,480,000 = 656%. She wanted to see how the allocations would change using these four bases, instead of just direct labor. She collected the following data for the line described in the preceding assignment.

Labor cost	$ 900,000
Recordkeeping	400,000 entries
Cost of materials used	$4,750,000
Engineering hours	300 hours

Required

1. Calculate the rate per unit of activity for each group of indirect costs.
2. Use the rates calculated in part 1 to allocate indirect costs to Department Z, and determine the unit cost of the average product in Z's line using the new allocation.
3. Using the guidelines in Appendix B, write a memorandum to Ms. Torg commenting on the differences between the alternative allocation schemes.

10-51 Performance measurement in an automobile dealership In automobile dealerships the sales managers of new and used cars are commonly evaluated according to the profits on sales of new and used cars, respectively. Complicating such evaluations is the interrelationship that often exists between the actions taken by the two segments.

A new-car sales agreement may include some allowance for a traded-in used car. The trade-in allowance is often based on what the used-car manager is willing to pay the new-car manager for the car. For example, suppose that a customer wants to buy a new car that has a list price of $12,000 and trade in a used car. If there were no trade-in, the price of the car would be $11,200. If the used-car manager will give $3,500 for the used car to be traded in, the new-car salesperson could allow up to $4,300 to the customer, because the net price would still be satisfactory. The $7,700 cash paid ($12,000 list price – $4,300 allowed on the old car) is the same as the difference between the $11,200 desired price and the $3,500 that the used-car manager will pay for the car.

Sometimes the used-car manager will offer lower prices than at other times, say, if the used-car lot is full and sales are slow. If the used-car manager will pay only $2,800 for the car, the salesperson could give only a $3,600 trade-in allowance to obtain $11,200.

Required

1. Assuming that each manager is evaluated on profits in his respective area, what is the disadvantage of the system to the new-car manager? Is there a disadvantage to the used-car manager?

2. Suppose the dealership's policy provides that the new-car manager can try to sell the car to another used-car dealer if he is unhappy with the price offered by the used-car manager. In the second example, suppose the new-car manager believed that the trade-in automobile could be sold to another used-car dealer for $3,500. The $11,200 deemed acceptable for the new car would be obtained ($7,700 from the customer plus $3,500 from selling the trade-in), so this deal for the new car would be accepted despite the lower bid from the used-car manager. Does the system encourage the managers to act in the best interests of the total firm?

10-52 Home office allocations and decisions Worcester Manufacturing Company has 14 sales offices throughout the United States and Canada. Each sales office is a profit center, with the local manager able to set prices and offer special discounts to obtain customers. Many functions like checking credit worthiness of customers, billing, and others are centralized in the home office. A few years ago, Marquarite Campau, the president, decided to charge the sales offices for these functions. After some thought, she set the charge at 8% of revenue. Home office costs are almost all fixed.

The firm's factories bill the sales offices for goods at prices established annually. The charge includes both variable manufacturing costs and a margin to cover fixed costs. Variable manufacturing costs average about 40% of revenue at current prices.

Lee Mott, manager of the Miami office, has come to you for advice. She is considering a price reduction that she expects to add considerably to unit volume but is unsure of the effects on profit. She begins by showing you an income statement that reflects her expectations for the coming year without the price reduction.

Miami Office Budgeted Income Statement for 19X2

Sales		$2,400,000
Cost of sales		1,200,000
Gross margin		1,200,000
Salaries and commissions	$490,000	
Rent, utilities, insurance	86,000	
Home office charge	192,000	768,000
Profit		$ 432,000

Mott believes that it is possible to obtain the following increases in unit volume given the associated decreases in selling prices.

Decrease in Price	Increase in Unit Volume
5%	20%
10%	35%

Mott tells you that the only variable costs of running the office are the 15% commissions that salespeople earn. Of course, her "cost of sales" is variable also because it depends on unit volume, as is the home office charge because it depends on total revenue. Mott is evaluated on the profit that her office generates.

Required

1. Determine whether or not Mott should reduce prices, and if so, by how much.

2. Using the guidelines in Appendix B, write a memorandum to Ms. Mott giving and supporting your recommendation about which action (hold prices, reduce prices by 5%, reduce prices by 10%) is in Worcester's best interests.

10-53 Incurred costs and performance Weldon Oil Company operates a refinery in the northeastern United States. During the winter about 200 workers are employed as drivers of fuel-oil trucks to deliver oil for heating purposes. Drivers are paid $10 per hour. During the summer there is no need for their services as fuel-oil truck drivers, and they are given jobs in the refinery. These refinery jobs pay only $7 per hour. However, company policy is to pay the drivers their usual $10 rate.

The refinery manager is charged with the $10 wage paid to the drivers while they work in the refinery. The manager of fuel-oil distribution bears no charge except when the workers are delivering fuel oil. The refinery manager does not object to employing the drivers during the summer. Even with this addition to his regular work force he must hire students and other temporary employees in the summer. He does, however, object to the $10 charge in the summer, because he can obtain equally qualified (for those jobs) workers at $7 per hour and he must use the drivers as a matter of company policy.

Required

Using the guidelines in Appendix B, write a memorandum to Ms. Cohen, Weldon's controller, pointing out the problems by the firm's present cost-assignment policies and recommending an alternative approach for assigning the charges for drivers' wages during the summer.

11 divisional performance measurement

Responsibility accounting systems provide information that helps managers control operations and also helps higher-level managers evaluate performance. This chapter studies control and evaluation in investment centers, though much of the discussion also applies to profit centers. Investment centers are often large enough to be divisions of a large firm.[1] They are often relatively autonomous and act almost as independent firms. The use of investment centers allows their managers to be evaluated almost as if they were chief executive officers of firms.

Investment centers control all the major components of financial performance (revenues, costs, and investments). They can therefore be evaluated by more complete measures of performance than can cost centers or profit centers, which do not control all these elements. The more complete the performance measure the better. The measures described in this chapter are more complete than cost or profit measures.

DECENTRALIZATION

The term **decentralized** refers to companies that give managers broad authority. Companies that use investment centers are usually highly decentralized. Managers of such centers are responsible for and control revenues, expenses, and investment. In highly decentralized firms, operating units (usually called *divisions*) are almost autonomous; division managers are

1 *The term* division *can refer to any large operating unit of a firm, but in this chapter it refers to an investment center.*

Even decentralized companies must ensure that managers adhere to basic corporate policies. Little Caesar's, the pizza giant, is one of the most successful privately-owned companies in the U.S., in part because of its clear focus on objectives and means to achieving them. Founders and owners, Mike and Marion Ilitch, saw that Domino's had a significant advantage with its 30-minute guaranteed delivery, so they set out to dominate the carryout market. Little Caesar's offers two pizzas for the price of one, which entails that they be the lowest-cost producer.

The company emphasizes tight cost control in large and small ways. The company encourages franchisees to keep their offices in the store, not in a separate office building and to keep their books by hand for the first year. Marion Ilitch reviews the income statements of every one of the 1,000 stores that the company owns. (Franchisees own about 3,000 stores.) She believes that each store should stand on its own and that aggregated income statements, such as one statement for all stores in a particular city, might obscure important information.*

*"*Pizza Pizza and Tigers Too,*" Business Week, *September 14, 1992, 109.*

responsible for both production and marketing, as well as for functions such as personnel and accounting. Division managers also prepare and submit capital budgets to central headquarters for approval. However, as we noted in Chapter 10, control of long-term financing is usually retained at the highest level of management.

BENEFITS OF DECENTRALIZATION

Proponents of decentralizing argue that it promotes better decision making. They believe that the managers closest to an operation can make better decisions because they are better able to gather and evaluate information than are centrally located corporate managers. Managers at the scene can also act more quickly because they need not report to headquarters and wait for approval of their proposed actions.

In a modern business of any complexity, operating without delegating some authority to lower-level managers is impossible. Because of the interdependence of functional areas, conflicts between functional managers are inevitable. Hence, making some managers responsible for both revenues and costs is often wise. When the firm's chief executive is the only manager whose span of responsibility includes both conflicting functions, arbitration and settlement of disputes must necessarily take place at the top. Decentralization allows conflicts among managers of functional areas to be resolved at a lower level. Top management can also make better evaluations of managerial performance if the interdependencies and conflicts are resolved by managers responsible for profit and return on investment.

One benefit that flows from the increased ability to evaluate performance and fix responsibility is that top management need not make day-to-day decisions. With decentralization, top management can use the principle of management by exception when monitoring the activities of lower-level managers.

The degree of decentralization varies from company to company. Some very successful companies allow their managers very wide discretion. Dover Corporation, a diversified Fortune 500 company with 49 separate businesses, gives the manager of each business almost complete autonomy. Dover actually discourages the managers of these businesses from seeking advice from corporate headquarters. Neither does Dover require its businesses to buy from its sister businesses. Bed Bath & Beyond, a large household goods chain, allows local store managers to run the entire operation, experiment with different formats, change prices, and take other steps to meet competition.*

* Fortune, *December 14, 1992, 94-101.*

Decentralization is also advantageous to firms that operate in different industries. As firms widen their range of products, the need to give broad responsibility to division managers increases. A firm's president or other chief operating officer cannot be expected to be knowledgeable about a great many product lines, such as textiles, furniture, appliances, automobile supplies, movies, and sporting goods. Similarly, increased interest in international operations and markets has increased the need for knowledgeable on-site managers with decision-making authority.

There is considerable evidence that the broader responsibility accompanying decentralization increases motivation. Studies have shown that workers and managers alike tend to perform better as their responsibilities increase. In general, the least-motivated people are those who perform a single task again and again throughout the day. The effect of establishing manufacturing cells in companies using JIT is to broaden the responsibilities of workers that make up the cell. The term *job enlargement* is often applied to giving increased responsibility. People who do much of the work on a product, as opposed to doing only one small operation, and managers who control most of the factors that affect profitability, become more committed to their jobs—viewing their jobs as sources of satisfaction, not just as sources of income.

Managers of nearly autonomous divisions are well prepared for higher positions. Such managers appreciate all aspects of a company's operations. The chief executive of Container Corporation of America, in an annual report, commented on the advantages of decentralization:

> The corporate organization consists of over 21,000 men and women, working in plants and offices, laboratories, forests and paperboard mills in the U.S. and six other countries. Its 140 plants and mills operate as relatively independent businesses, under a management system that delegates authority and responsibility to local managers. This decentralized organization, which provides for successful development of local markets, also constitutes an environment which encourages individual self-development. One measure of its success, over the years, is that virtually all of the company's present senior management team is a product of this system.

PROBLEMS OF DECENTRALIZATION

Decentralization has its problems. The major one is that managers operating in nearly autonomous fashion might make decisions that harm the firm. Indeed, perhaps the most formidable problem of decentralization is achieving goal congruence while at the same time promoting and maintaining divisional autonomy. Decentralization can create other problems. In the early 1980s, Levi Strauss decentralized into divisions that each handled a product line. It reconsolidated because retailers were unhappy having to buy from several divisions instead of only one. Magna International, a leading auto-parts supplier, decentralized to extremes in the early 1980s. The company rewarded plant managers almost solely on profits and gave them near-complete freedom. Unlike most companies, Magna permitted plant managers to borrow money, build new factories, and sign long-term contracts. The plant managers added huge amounts of debt until the burden almost sank Magna in 1990, as the recession hit the company's sales.

Two managerial accounting issues are related to decentralization. First, there is the need to develop methods of evaluating performance that work to the benefit of the firm as a whole. Second, there is a need to develop transfer prices that, as far as possible, produce decisions that are in the best interests of the firm. We turn first to the problem of selecting performance measures for divisions.

MEASURES OF PERFORMANCE

INCOME

Although net income, the "bottom line," is the most widely examined (and least understood) financial datum, it is unsatisfactory for measuring the performance of divisions. First, net income considers interest and taxes, neither of which is normally under the control of divisional managers. Second, a division's expenses usually include some charges (allocations) for services provided by central headquarters. For example, much of the payroll work for divisions of Ford Motor Company is done by a single segment that bills units for its services. Third, any income figure tells only part of the story. A division that earns $10 million might be far less successful than one earning $3 million. The other part of the story is the investment that the manager uses to generate the income.

Although income is not the most useful performance measure, neither is it irrelevant. Indeed, the widely used performance measures that are discussed in this chapter all consider an income number. But the importance of income is as a part of other measures rather than as a measure in itself.

RETURN ON INVESTMENT (ROI)

Return on investment (ROI) is the general term used to describe a ratio of *some measure of income to some measure of investment.* In financial accounting you may have seen the ratio: net income divided by stockholders' equity, usually called *return on equity* (ROE). ROE is one type of ROI. Another is *return on assets* (ROA), usually measured as income before interest and taxes divided by total assets. Some firms use the term *return on capital employed,* or just *return on capital,* to designate the same ratio. For internal performance evaluation, managers generally use an ROI measure of the following form.

$$ROI = \frac{divisional\ income}{divisional\ investment}$$

Firms define and measure **divisional income** and **divisional investment** in different ways. We examine some of these ways shortly.

ROI is the most frequently used criterion for divisional performance measurement. It has a distinct advantage over divisional income as a performance measure, because companies usually have divisions of different sizes. A division earning $100,000 on an investment of $1,000,000 is more efficient than one earning the same profit on an investment of $5,000,000. ROI makes it possible to compare the *efficiency* of different-size divisions by relating output (*income*) to input (*investment*).

Some managers find it helpful to restate the ROI formula when they are looking for ways to improve operating performance. The restatement expands the basic formula (income ÷ investment) into two ratios.

$$ROI = \frac{income}{sales} \times \frac{sales}{investment}$$

The expanded version gives the same final answer because "sales" appears in the numerator of one factor and the denominator of the other and thus cancels out. But the expanded form helps to focus the manager's attention on the two components of ROI.

The first ratio, income ÷ sales, is the familiar **return on sales (ROS)** ratio introduced in Chapter 2. The second, sales ÷ investment, is **investment turnover.** This expanded version clearly shows that an increase in sales, by itself, will not increase ROI because sales cancels out. But a decrease in investment, with other factors remaining the same, will increase ROI (as will an increase in income with other factors held constant).

A manager can also determine the effect on ROI of a decision expected to change two factors. Suppose that ROS is now 15% and investment turnover is 2 times; ROI is 30% (15% × 2). If the manager is considering changing the product mix to items with lower margins and faster turnover, which will increase turnover to 2 1/2 times while reducing ROS to 10%, he or she could see that ROI will fall to 25% (10% × 2 1/2).

The values of the two components of ROI often give clues to the strategies used by companies or divisions. For example, a single company might operate both conventional department stores and discount stores. Both kinds of stores might earn the same ROI, but do so using very different strategies.

Assume the following data.

	Conventional Department Store Division	Discount Division
Sales	$2,000,000	$2,400,000
Divisional profit	240,000	192,000
Divisional investment	1,000,000	800,000
Return on sales	12%	8%
Investment turnover	2	3
Return on investment	24%	24%

The discount operations have a lower return on sales but a higher turnover.

While the advantages of ROI in considering relative sizes and alternative strategies are obvious, absolute size still matters in assessing a segment's contribution to the entity as a whole. Depending on the circumstances, a 12% ROI for a very large division might be making a greater contribution than a 40% ROI in another division. Recall from Chapter 8 that a company is wise to accept all proposed investments with expected returns greater than cost of capital. The same general principle is incorporated in evaluating divisions by using residual income as the performance measure.

RESIDUAL INCOME

Residual income (RI) is the income a division produces in excess of the **minimum required (desired, target) rate of return.** Top management establishes the minimum rate of return, which should be greater than cost of capital, as described in Chapter 8. Some companies set different minimum rates of return for different divisions to reflect differences in the risks associated with their businesses. A division in a risky industry such as fashion merchandise should earn higher returns than one in a more stable industry such as paper.

RI is computed as follows.

$$RI = income - (investment \times target\ ROI)$$

The parenthetical term is the profit that must be earned to satisfy the minimum requirements. It is the minimum required *dollar* return. Anything over that amount benefits the company. (Of course, *any* income benefits the company, but the minimum required ROI is needed simply to keep it going.) If the firm earns less than investors demand, they will invest their capital elsewhere and the firm will go out of business. The argument for using RI to evaluate divisional performance is that it measures the profit that the division provides to the firm over and above the minimum profit required for the amount invested.

RI has an important advantage over ROI as a measure of divisional performance. Applying it could show that a division with a higher ROI is less valuable *to the firm as a whole* than one with a lower ROI. Suppose that Division A produces a $200,000 income on an investment of $1,000,000, an ROI of 20%, while Division B earns $1,500,000 on an investment of $10,000,000, an ROI of 15%. Depending on the required ROI for the firm, the contributions of the divisions to the firm as a whole will appear quite different. Consider two possibilities: (1) required ROI is 10% and (2) required ROI is 18%. The RIs for each division are:

	1 Required ROI is 10%		2 Required ROI is 18%	
	Division A	Division B	Division A	Division B
Investment	$1,000,000	$10,000,000	$1,000,000	$10,000,000
Divisional income	$ 200,000	$ 1,500,000	$ 200,000	$ 1,500,000
Required minimum return (investment × minimum return)	100,000	1,000,000	180,000	1,800,000
Residual income	$ 100,000	$ 500,000	$ 20,000	($ 300,000)

If the minimum required ROI is 10%, Division B makes a greater contribution to the firm than does Division A despite Division B's lower ROI. In this situation we could say that Division B was more valuable to the firm. On the other hand, if the firm has an 18% minimum ROI, Division A contributes more and is more valuable under the RI criterion.

When using RI to evaluate divisional performance, the division rated highest is the one with the highest RI. Using RI to evaluate divisional performance is similar to using NPV to evaluate capital expenditures: The most desirable capital project is the one with the highest NPV *after* discounting future returns at the cost of capital (or the minimum required rate of return).

Because numbers for divisional income and divisional investment are needed to compute both RI and ROI, the same questions arise as to how those numbers should be computed. These questions are discussed later in the chapter.

BEHAVIORAL PROBLEMS

ROI VERSUS RI

In Chapter 8, we stated serious reservations about book rate of return as a capital budgeting technique. Nevertheless, we accept the use of book values for "investment," and book income for "return" in computing divisional ROI. The major reason for the inconsistency is that ROI is the most commonly used measure for evaluating divisional performance, and most users calculate ROI based on book amounts. In addition, over relatively long periods, book ROI may well approximate the IRR computed using cash flows. Accepting the drawbacks of using ROI based on book values, it is reasonable to say that a firm should expand if it can earn an ROI in excess of cost of capital.

As with all performance measures, the firm must be concerned about whether the measure accomplishes goal congruence. Unfortunately, using ROI to evaluate divisional performance can encourage managers to pass up projects that promise returns in excess of the minimum required return if the expected return is lower than the division's current ROI. Consider a division manager who expects an income of $300,000 on investment of $1,000,000 (ROI of 30%) and has an opportunity offering a $75,000 incremental profit on an incremental investment of $300,000 (ROI of 25% on the investment). Suppose further that the firm's minimum rate of return is 20%, and that the proposed new investment is in receivables and inventory and is recoverable at the end of the life of the investment.[2]

If the performance of the division (and its manager) is evaluated on the basis of ROI, the manager will be inclined to reject the new investment because ROI (now 30%) will fall, as can be seen in the following computations.

2 *Under these circumstances, the IRR on the new investment equals the book rate of return.*

Investment before new project		$1,000,000
Additional investment for the project		300,000
Total investment		$1,300,000
Divisional profit:		
Current	$300,000	
From new project	75,000	
Total divisional profit		$ 375,000
Divisional ROI after new investment		28.8%

From the *firm's* viewpoint, the proposed investment should be undertaken because it promises an ROI of 25% ($75,000 profit/$300,000 investment), which exceeds the 20% required minimum. Encouraging the division manager to make the decision that benefits the firm as well as the division requires an evaluation criterion which takes into account the minimum required return. The residual income approach to evaluation does this.

Using RI in the situation just described shows the following:

	Without New Project	With New Project
Divisional investment	$1,000,000	$1,300,000
Minimum required ROI	20%	20%
Divisional profit	$ 300,000	$ 375,000
Less minimum required	200,000	260,000
Residual income	$ 100,000	$ 115,000

A division manager evaluated on the basis of RI will undertake this project because performance improves. This should not be surprising because the 25% ROI exceeds the required 20%. The ROI criterion encourages maximizing the *ratio* of profit to investment. The RI criterion encourages maximizing total *dollars* of profit in excess of the minimum required dollar return.

Using ROI as the performance measure might also encourage a manager to make an investment that is poor from the standpoint of the firm, but desirable from the standpoint of the division because it raises a currently low ROI. Suppose a firm has a minimum required ROI of 20% and that a divisional manager currently expects income of $200,000 on an investment of $2,000,000, for a 10% ROI. How would the manager respond to an opportunity to increase income $15,000 by investing $100,000 in receivables and inventory (a 15% ROI on the investment)? Divisional ROI increases to 10.2%.

$$\textit{New ROI} = \frac{\$2{,}000{,}000 + \$15{,}000}{\$2{,}000{,}000 + \$100{,}000} = \frac{\$215{,}000}{\$2{,}100{,}000} = 10.2\%$$

Yet the proposed action actually generates negative residual income of $5,000 because a $100,000 investment requires income of $20,000 to meet the 20% minimum required rate of return. A manager being evaluated on the basis of ROI is encouraged to accept the investment. That is not the case if RI is the evaluation criterion because the already negative RI of $200,000 [$200,000 – ($2,000,000 × 20%)] grows to $205,000 if the investment proposal is accepted.

BOOK RESULTS AND DISCOUNTED CASH FLOWS

In the examples for the previous section, book ROI equaled the IRR on the proposed investment. That is seldom the case, especially with investments in plant and equipment. Few divisional managers have the authority to make large capital investments without getting approval from officers at the corporate level. Therefore, a divisional manager earning a low ROI probably would not be permitted to make a capital investment that would raise divisional ROI if its IRR was below cost of capital. But because they use *book* income and investment, *both* ROI and RI can prompt managers to avoid investments that would benefit the firm.

Consider the following example. A manager is considering a project that requires a $100,000 investment and provides pretax cash flows of $40,000 per year for five years. The company requires a minimum pretax ROI of 25%. The present value of the $40,000 stream of payments discounted at 25% is $107,560 ($40,000 × 2.689). Under the decision rules developed in Chapter 8, the investment is desirable because it has a positive NPV of $7,560 ($107,560 – $100,000). The book rates of return and RIs for the first two years of the investment are as follows, using the straight-line method of depreciation.

Year	Additional Cash Flow	Additional Depreciation	Increase in Book Income	Average Additional Investment [a]	ROI on Additional Investment	RI [b]
1	$40,000	$20,000	$20,000	$90,000	22.2%	($2,500)
2	$40,000	$20,000	$20,000	$70,000	28.6%	$2,500

a *Book value of investment at beginning of year plus book value at end of year, divided by two.*
b *Book income of $20,000 minus 25% required return on average additional investment.*

In the first year, book ROI is below the 25% required minimum and RI is negative. The division manager, seeing that undertaking the project will penalize performance in the first year, is not encouraged to accept the project.

Both ROI and RI rise over time unless income from the investment declines sharply. The cause of this pattern is the falling book investment (resulting from depreciation), and the pattern is more extreme if the firm uses an accelerated method of depreciation. Even if cash flows, and therefore book income, decline, the pattern of increasing ROI is likely to occur.

The rise in ROI based on book values is even more pronounced in more realistic situations where returns do not begin immediately or do not reach their peaks in the early years. Ordinarily some lead time is required—to build a plant, install machinery, test the operation, remove "bugs," and generally get the operation going. Incurring heavy startup costs is common in the opening of a new plant or even the remodeling of an existing one. The returns are likely to increase over the first few years as the plant gains efficiency. If a new product is involved, its sales in the first year or two may well be substantially lower than those in later years.

Thus, two factors work against the manager—lower income in early years and the natural tendency of ROI to rise as the book value of the investment falls because of depreciation charges. What can be done to encourage the manager to pursue worthwhile investments?

One way to avoid the first-year drop in ROI and thereby encourage managers to accept desirable investments is to leave the new investment out of the base for calculating ROI until the project is on-stream and running well. A version of this approach has been used by Burlington Industries, Inc., basing ROI calculations on investment at the end of the previous six months; this mitigates the effects of large amounts of construction in progress.[3] Of course, many major projects will take a relatively long time before they are running well.

Another approach is to amortize startup costs over several years instead of expensing them all in the first year of an investment's life. A third possibility, seldom observed in practice, is to base depreciation charges on budgeted income to be earned over several years; this results in lower depreciation in early years and higher charges in later years. Although top-level corporate managers might not object to leaving assets out of the base or to amortizing startup costs, there is not much support for increasing-charge depreciation. Perhaps the main reason for lack of interest in such depreciation methods is that they are almost never used in financial accounting.

Essentially, the problem just described is a conflict between the long and the short terms. As stated several times in this book, many actions that can help meet short-term goals are harmful in the long run. Such actions could reduce profits, ROI, and RI in the long term, but by then the manager might have been promoted to another job. Conversely, a manager who takes actions that benefit the division and firm in the long run, while hurting short-term performance, could be fired. The manager who takes over could well reap the benefits of the predecessor's good decisions. Obviously, then, it is unwise to evaluate divisions and their managers simply by reference to ROI, RI, or any other single quantitative measure. Qualitative factors must enter the evaluation process.

PROBLEMS IN MEASUREMENT

Whether ROI or RI is used as the evaluation criterion, a firm must determine what revenues, costs, and investments are to be included in the calculations. The determinations should be made along the lines of responsibility, with controllability as the principal criterion for including costs and investment. A division manager who is held responsible for earning returns (income) on investment should control the elements of both income and investment.

To compute the income for which the division's manager is responsible, we must identify variable costs and direct fixed costs. As discussed in Chapter 10, some companies also allocate common, indirect fixed costs for several reasons. If common fixed costs are allocated to divisions, they should be separated from direct fixed costs and clearly labeled as allocated. Opinions differ as to what to include in and how to measure divisional investment. As a start, investment includes at least those assets that are used only by a particular division.

3 *As reported by Donald R. Hughes, then assistant controller of Burlington Industries, Inc., in Thomas J. Burns, ed.,* The Behavioral Aspects of Accounting Data for Performance Evaluation *(Columbus, Ohio: College of Administrative Science, Ohio State University, 1970), 56.*

INVESTMENT

Under normal circumstances, most assets can readily be identified with specific divisions. Virtually all plant and equipment, for example, are under the control of divisions. Inventory and receivables, which are also investments, are generally under divisional control because the divisional manager controls production and credit terms. Cash may or may not be under divisional control. Division managers usually control some cash, but in many cases central headquarters receives payments directly from customers and pays bills submitted by the divisions.

Some assets are controlled only at the highest level of management. Central headquarters controls the headquarters building and equipment, investments in the securities of other firms, and such intangible assets as goodwill and organization costs.

Suppose we have analyzed the revenues, costs, and assets of Multiproducts, Inc., and have identified these by divisions as shown in Exhibit 11-1. The firm has three operating divisions, A, B, and C, and a central corporate office. The firm's minimum required ROI is 10%.

From the data in Exhibit 11-1 we can compute ROI and RI for each division and for the firm as a whole. The latter computation should be based on an investment defined as the total assets of the firm. Note that no performance measurement is given for unallocated assets.

Exhibit 11-1 Multiproducts, Inc. (in millions of dollars)

	Division				
	A	B	C	Unallocated	Total
Investment					
Cash	$ 20	$ 30	$ 60	$ 30	$ 140
Accounts receivable, net	60	80	90		230
Inventory	100	180	240		520
Prepaid expenses	10	10	20	20	60
Plant and equipment—net of depreciation	200	320	440	60	1,020
Investments	10	—	—	100	110
Total assets	$400	$620	$850	$210	$2,080
Income					
Sales	$100	$400	$700		$1,200
Variable costs	30	220	400		650
Contribution margin	70	180	300		550
Direct fixed costs	30	90	140		260
Divisional profit	$ 40	$ 90	$160		290
Common fixed costs					60
Income					$ 230

	Division A	Division B	Division C	Firm as a Whole
Computation of ROI				
Profit of the segment	$ 40	$ 90	$160	$ 230
Investment for the segment	400	620	850	2,080
ROI (profit/investment)	10%	14.5%	18.8%	11.1%
Computation of RI:				
Profit of the segment	$ 40	$ 90	$160	$ 230
Required return (investment × minimum return of 10%)	40	62	85	208
RI (profit – required return)	$—	$ 28	$ 75	$ 22

Amounts shown are in millions of dollars.

Although the firm's ROI is 11.1%, only one division earns so low a rate. Because of unallocated costs and assets, the company as a whole cannot earn the minimum required 10% ROI unless the divisions earn more than the required minimum. Note also that the combined RI of the divisions is partly consumed by the unallocated costs and assets, so that, although the divisions earn residual income of $103 million ($0 + $28 + $75), the firm earns only $22 million in excess of a 10% return on total assets.

When top management establishes an overall target ROI for the firm, it has two strategies available to encourage division managers to help achieve that target. One approach is to set divisional target ROI higher than the overall desired rate. Another is to allocate as much cost and investment as possible to divisions. Managers favoring the second strategy argue that divisional managers should be made aware of the substantial costs and investment involved in running the firm as a whole, which each of the divisions must work to offset. This argument was described in Chapter 10.

Another and perhaps more persuasive justification exists for following the strategy of allocating common costs and common assets to divisions. Corporate managers are interested in whether a division is earning returns comparable to those of independent firms in the same industry. If the division is to be treated more or less as an independent, autonomous entity, corporate managers argue that it should bear the costs and assets that an independent company requires. An independent firm must incur many costs, and maintain many assets, that a division often does not. For example, an independent firm performs research and development, while a division can often rely on a centrally administered R&D organization. Similarly, an independent firm must maintain some cash, while a division may rely on a centralized cash management function to meet its needs. To make reasonable comparisons between the division and an outside firm, then, corporate management might allocate central costs and assets to divisions (also reminding divisional managers of the needs met by the central administration).

Firms that allocate corporate costs among divisions do so in many ways. In some firms, central headquarters charges each division a management fee for services provided. For instance, divisions need financing, just as if they were separate firms; so, the charge reflects that service. The fee might be a percentage of revenue, total investment in the division, or some other base. One large firm charges each division 2% of gross sales.

Efforts to make division managers realize that they must consider the performance of the entire firm may be worthwhile, but the allocation of central costs and assets to divisions must be understood for what it is—an allocation. Whatever the allocation methods used, managers at both the divisional and corporate levels must be aware that allocations in no way change the nature of the costs or assets as indirect to the divisions and not controllable by the divisional managers.

LIABILITIES

There is seldom a satisfactory way to assign *all* liabilities to divisions. Some current liabilities (payables, accrued expenses) are readily associated with particular divisions. As a rule, divisions cannot issue long-term debt, and their managers are not responsible for it. Long-term debt results from financing decisions made at the highest level of management on the basis of the organization's overall needs and problems. Long-term debt could be allocated to divisions on the basis of relative investments in fixed assets and working capital, but there is little interest in doing so in practice. For performance measurement purposes, many firms include only those liabilities that are definitely (not arbitrarily) related to divisions, and define divisional investment as controlled assets minus divisional liabilities.

Using *any* liabilities in determining divisional investment naturally increases ROI, because the denominator (the investment base) decreases while the numerator (profit) remains the same. If we were to include liabilities in measuring investment in the example on page 450, the computations of ROI and RI are as follows, using assumed values for liabilities.

	Division			
	A	B	C	Firm as a Whole
Computation of ROI				
Profit of the segment	$ 40	$ 90	$160	$ 230
Total assets	400	620	850	2,080
Divisional liabilities (assumed)	60	170	310	540
Divisional investment	340	450	540	1,540
Unallocated liabilities (assumed)				730
Total investment	$340	$450	$540	$ 810
ROI	11.8%	20.0%	29.6%	28.4%
Computation of RI:				
Profit of the segment	$ 40	$ 90	$160	$ 230
Required return (investment above × minimum return of 10%)	34	45	54	81
RI	$ 6	$ 45	$106	$ 149

Amounts shown are in millions of dollars.

Both RI and ROI are higher for all divisions and for the firm as a whole when liabilities are included in the computations.

From a behavioral standpoint, the question whether to include liabilities is undecided. In favor of their inclusion is that most current liabilities are related to the operating level of the division and provide financing to it and to the firm. On the negative side, divisional managers could be encouraged to allow liabilities to rise too high in order to reduce investment and increase ROI. If divisional managers delay payments to suppliers, the credit rating of the firm as a whole might suffer. A reasonable compromise might be a corporate policy that allows managers to carry, say, trade payables up to the length of time specified by suppliers. Then, if a division had 40 days' purchases in accounts payable and suppliers offered 30-day credit, the division could not deduct the extra 10 days' worth of liabilities to determine divisional investment. Under this policy, the manager has no incentive to allow payables to extend beyond the suppliers' credit terms. (Note that divisional managers have no opportunity for delaying payments if cash disbursements are handled at the central headquarters.)

FIXED ASSETS

For all computations to this point, you have been given the amount of the investment in assets. In Exhibit 11-1, for example, the investments in cash, inventory, and fixed assets were given, but there was no mention of how these amounts were determined. There are many views about what values to use for fixed assets. Some of the valuation bases used are original (gross) cost, original cost less accumulated depreciation (often called *net cost,* or *net book value*), and current replacement cost. The basis used can have a significant effect on ROI and RI, and each basis has advantages and disadvantages.

The most popular basis by far is net book value. Its principal advantages are that it conforms to financial accounting practice and that it recognizes the decline in productivity that usually accompanies increasing age. Many believe it to be the most reasonable basis, given that divisional income includes depreciation expense. (It is argued that, if depreciation is recognized for determining income, it should also be recognized in computing investment.) The major disadvantage of net book value is that it gives, as shown earlier, rising ROI and RI over time.

Using gross (original) cost for valuing fixed assets overcomes the objection about rising ROI and RI. DuPont states its views as the following:

> Since plant facilities are maintained in virtually top condition during their working life, we believe it would be inappropriate to consider that operating management was responsible for earning a return on only the net operating investment. Furthermore, if depreciable assets were stated at net depreciated values, earnings in each succeeding period would be related to an ever-decreasing investment.[4]

Yet virtually all assets do lose productivity as they age, and continued use of gross cost ignores that decline. Moreover, the firm's investment in a fixed

4 *Frank R. Rayburn and Michael M. Brown, "Measuring and Using Return on Investment Information," in James Don Edwards and Homer A. Black, eds.,* The Managerial and Cost Accountant's Handbook *(Homewood, Illinois: Dow Jones-Irwin, 1979), 331. The authors were quoting from D. Solomons,* Divisional Performance: Measurement and Control *(Homewood, Illinois: Richard D. Irwin, 1965), 134-135, as modified by letter from E. I. DuPont dated August 8, 1978.*

asset *does* decline over time, as the firm recovers its investment through the cash flows that the asset produces.

Both gross and net book values suffer from the defect that they reflect costs the firm has already incurred, perhaps many years ago. Managers who have older assets generally have lower investment bases (either gross or net) than managers using similar assets that are newer and, in all likelihood, costlier. For this reason, many accountants and managers advocate valuing investments at replacement cost.

There are at least three ways to define replacement cost. Some consider replacement cost to be as the acquisition cost of new assets just like those currently in use. Others define replacement cost as the cost of acquiring assets of the same age and condition as those being used. Still another approach is to define replacement cost as the current cost of obtaining similar productive capacity or service. Under this interpretation, the emphasis is on how the firm currently would choose to accomplish a particular task. For example, suppose a company has a fleet of fork-lift trucks to move materials within its factory. The replacement cost of the fleet would be the cost of an automated conveyor system if the division would replace the fleet with such a system. Because managers should continuously evaluate the alternatives available for accomplishing tasks, we prefer the last interpretation (equivalent productive capacity) for evaluating divisional performance. There is, however, much disagreement on this point.

Whatever definition of replacement cost is adopted, its use eliminates the problems of different depreciation methods and also allows for changes in prices. Thus, managers are not penalized or rewarded simply because of the depreciation methods used or the ages of their assets. The normal accounting system does not automatically provide information about current replacement costs, and the practical difficulties and associated costs of determining replacement costs were long thought to be too great to warrant their development.[5] Despite the disadvantages, original cost less accumulated depreciation remains the most popular approach for valuing fixed assets.

THE SUBJECT OF EVALUATION—DIVISION OR MANAGER

As we stated in Chapter 10, it is important to distinguish between evaluating a division and evaluating its managers. ROI and RI give clues to where the firm might be wise to increase, maintain, or reduce investment; other things being equal, higher ROI and RI are desirable. However, for evaluating *managers* of divisions, both ROI and RI have drawbacks, depending on how the results for a division are interpreted. The critical issue is the standard used for comparison. With what should we compare a division's results?

There are several bases for comparison, including comparisons among divisions within the firm, with historical results in the same division, with

---

5 Beginning in 1979, the Securities and Exchange Commission and the Financial Accounting Standards Board required certain companies to report some replacement cost information in their external financial statements. As such information became available to those companies for internal *purposes at no additional cost, some firms might have elected to use the information for internal reporting. Requirements to provide replacement cost information were removed in 1986, and no evidence yet exists about the extent to which the affected companies used the information for internal purposes or continued to produce the information when it was no longer required.*

industry averages, and with budgets. Divisions within the firm can be ranked in terms of relative profitability. The ranking also might provide some insight into the relative contributions of the divisions. But such a ranking should *not* be used to rank the managers of the respective divisions, because different kinds of divisions *should* have different ROIs. For example, ROI is generally higher for units (divisions or firms) operating in consumer markets than for those selling mostly to other industrial firms. Both ROI and RI should be higher for divisions taking on high risks. (For example, a division in plant genetics, a very risky field, should do better than one making clothing.) The performance of a particular division manager must not be obscured by intrafirm comparisons that ignore the nature of the division. A mediocre manager might be able to earn a respectable ROI in a division operating in a growing industry. On the other hand, an excellent manager might be doing a great job to maintain an ROI of 5% in a division operating in a declining industry.

Comparing current results with historical results in the same division overcomes differences in results stemming from divisions being in different industries. If there is a change in managers, the relative performance of two managers can also be compared. On the other hand, historical comparisons suffer from the same objections as do intrafirm comparisons and should be interpreted carefully. That is, there is no way to tell whether historical experience is good or bad. Nevertheless, historical comparisons indicate relative improvement or decay.

Comparing divisional results with industry averages can be useful because differences among divisions resulting from differences in industry do not influence the comparison. A division (and its manager) can be seen as better or worse than the firms with which it competes. Such comparisons present their own problems, however, because, as noted earlier, a division should be expected to earn a higher ROI than an entire firm operating in the same industry. A division benefits from being part of a larger organization. As the trend to diversification continues, it becomes increasingly difficult to find companies to which the performance of a single division can be compared.[6]

Budgets developed with participation by divisional managers are valuable tools for assessing the performance of division managers. When managers participate and commit themselves to meeting budgeted goals, comparisons of actual and budgeted results are usually thought to be the best possible comparisons for evaluation purposes.

Exhibit 11-2 shows budgeted and actual statements of income and financial position for a division. Allocated costs are shown separately. The only assets shown are those controlled by the division's manager. The exhibit also shows why budgeted and actual ROI were not the same. The division earned more profit than budgeted, but its receivables and inventories climbed much higher than budgeted, resulting in a reduced ROI. This type of report gives more information than simple comparisons of ROI, RI, or both.

6 *Even if there are independent firms in essentially the same industry, it is no simple matter to compare them with a division. As Chapter 18 shows, comparisons among independent firms are not easy because of such factors as different accounting methods (first-in-first-out versus last-in-first-out is one example), different degrees of diversification, and different ages of plant assets.*

Exhibit 11-2 Divisional Performance Report (in millions of dollars)

	Budget	Actual	Variance
Sales	$573.0	$591.0	$18.0
Variable costs (perhaps detailed)	246.0	251.2	5.2
Contribution margin	327.0	339.8	12.8
Direct fixed costs	140.0	141.4	1.4
Divisional profit	187.0	198.4	11.4
Allocated costs	12.0	15.0	3.0
Profit	$175.0	$183.4	$ 8.4
Assets employed:			
Cash	$ 15.5	$ 17.0	$ 1.5
Receivables	110.0	141.0	31.0
Inventory	90.0	122.5	32.5
Fixed assets, net	450.0	453.4	3.4
Total assets employed	$665.5	$733.9	$68.4
ROI	26.3%	25.0%	1.3%

TRANSFER PRICES

A great deal of intrafirm buying and selling can occur in decentralized firms, which necessitates setting **transfer prices**. Some firms in the food industry have farming operations that supply their own processing plants as well as those of other firms. A textile mill might sell some of its cloth to divisions within the same firm for further processing and some to outsiders.

PRICING POLICIES

Transfer prices are important in evaluating performance because they are revenues to the selling division and costs to the buying division. We know from Chapter 10 that changes in transfer prices do not, in themselves, affect the firm's total profit. Total profit is affected only if individual managers change their operations because of a change in transfer prices. Because of their *potential* for promoting actions that might not be in the interest of the total firm, transfer prices are important factors in divisional performance measurement. The following examples explore some implications of several transfer-pricing policies.

1. *Actual cost with or without a markup for the selling division.* Basing prices on actual costs is unwise. The selling manager has no incentive to keep costs down. Worse, a price that is actual costs plus a percentage markup gives the selling manager more profit the higher costs go. The buying manager would naturally object that costs (and hence reported performance) are adversely affected.

2. *Budgeted cost, with or without a markup.* This method encourages the selling manager to keep costs down. If there is a markup, the selling division can earn a profit. The buying manager appreciates not having cost inefficiencies passed on from the selling division but prefers no markup at all. Thus, discussions center on budgeted cost and markup percentages.
3. *Market prices.* This method is generally considered the best. It puts both the buying and selling managers on an independent basis, provided that they are free to buy or sell on the outside as well as within the firm. Given this freedom, the managers are in the position of chief executives of autonomous firms. One difficulty in implementing this policy is that there might not be outside market prices available for the division's products, or the prices that are available might not be representative. For instance, available prices might reflect relatively small transactions, whereas the divisions deal in very large quantities. Under such circumstances, buying managers might contend that they should pay less because of the quantities bought. In many cases, the transfer price is less than the market price to reflect cost savings from dealing internally. For instance, suppose a division pays a 15% commission on outside sales, none on inside sales. The transfer price should be 85% of the market price to reflect that saving. Market prices might not be a good choice as a transfer price if the selling division is operating below capacity.
4. *Incremental cost.* Such prices are best, theoretically, when the selling division is operating below capacity. The manager of the selling division will object to this approach because it yields no profit to that division. Incremental cost can be as low as the variable cost of the goods or services, but might also include fixed costs that increase as a result of the transfer.
5. *Negotiated prices.* This method allows managers to bargain with each other and alleviates some problems that arise with other methods. If there are outside markets, a manager who is dissatisfied with the offered price can buy or sell in the outside market. A disadvantage is that managers with more power or better negotiating skills might prevail more often than is good for the company.

Despite our suggestion that market-based transfer prices are generally best, we hasten to point out that the autonomous division manager who is setting a transfer price must use judgment *and understand the information available.* Like the managers involved in making decisions discussed in earlier chapters, division managers must understand the concepts of contribution margin and incremental cost, and the implications of those concepts in light of the available alternatives.

For example, Chapter 5 presented the analysis underlying a decision whether to accept a special order at less than the normal price. Critical to that analysis was whether the firm had an alternative use for the facilities and whether the contribution margin covered any incremental fixed costs. The same principles apply when a division manager has to propose a selling price for an order from another division. When the selling division has excess capacity, its results (and the manager's reported performance) will be improved if the price is greater than variable costs and incremental fixed costs, and the manager should offer a transfer price accordingly. When the division's capacity can be fully used without taking the order, the selling manager should demand the market price less any costs saved by dealing internally. (An order might cause a division operating below capacity to lose regular sales. If the division is 4,000 units under capacity, an order for 5,000 will result in a loss of 1,000 at the regular price. The minimum acceptable transfer price is incremental cost for the first 4,000, market price for the last 1,000.)

In summary, if treated as the heads of autonomous units, division managers should be free to develop offers of transfer prices that reflect the cost structures of their divisions and the available alternatives. When the division is operating at full capacity, with some sales being made to customers outside the firm, a market-based transfer price is nearly always best. When the division is operating below capacity, a transfer price that falls between incremental cost and market price is usually best. Hence, division managers must understand the cost structures of their divisions and use that knowledge in setting transfer prices. If they have the freedom to negotiate prices, the resulting actions are likely to be in the firm's best interests. To see why this is true, let us consider an example.

ILLUSTRATIONS

Division A buys a component for its major product from an outside supplier for $13 per unit. The component is exactly like the product made by Division B, another division of the same firm, and the manager of A has asked B to supply the item at $13. Division B now sells its output to outside customers. The budgeted income statement for the coming year for Division B is shown below. Division A needs 6,000 units.

Budgeted Income Statement, Division B

Sales, 10,000 × $15	$150,000
Variable costs, 10,000 × $7	70,000
Contribution margin	80,000
Fixed costs	30,000
Income	$ 50,000

Let us assume, for simplicity, that Division B could make the component needed by A with no change in fixed costs and with the same variable cost per unit that it has now. How should the manager of B respond to the requested price? What price serves the best interests of the divisions and of the firm? The answer depends on the alternatives available to the manager of Division B, and on the manager's understanding of those alternatives and costs.

Suppose that Division B has a capacity of 11,000 units. If it accepts Division A's business, it loses 5,000 units of outside sales. (Capacity of 11,000 less 6,000 to Division A leaves 5,000 units available for sales to outsiders, a reduction of 5,000 from present sales of 10,000 units.) Below is a budgeted income statement for the division if a transfer takes place at $13, the price that A now pays to an outside supplier.

Budgeted Income Statement, Division B (Component Purchased Internally for $13)	
Sales to outsiders, 5,000 × $15	$ 75,000
Sales to A, 6,000 × $13	78,000
Total sales	153,000
Variable costs, 11,000 × $7	77,000
Contribution margin	76,000
Fixed costs	30,000
Income	$ 46,000

Because Division A is *already* paying $13 to an outside supplier, purchasing the component internally for that price would not change the division's income and its manager would be indifferent to the source of supply. The manager of Division B would not accept the $13 price, because divisional profit would decline by $4,000 (from $50,000 to $46,000). Is the manager's decision not to make the sale also in the best interest of the firm as a whole?

From the standpoint of the firm, the decision is a make-or-buy decision such as you studied in Chapter 5. That is, if Division B makes the component and sells it to Division A, the component is made by the firm; alternatively, the component could be bought from an outside supplier. We can, therefore, look at the decision from the point of view of the firm as we did in Chapter 5.

Lost contribution margin from outside sales by Division B [5,000 × ($15 – $7)]	$40,000
Savings of variable costs paid to outside supplier [6,000 × ($13 – $7)]	36,000
Loss to firm	($ 4,000)

The change in the firm's income (a $4,000 decline) equals the combined changes in the incomes of its divisions (no change for A, a $4,000 decline for B).

Now suppose that Division B can produce 20,000 (rather than 11,000 units) but that it can sell only 10,000 units to outsiders. If fixed costs will not be affected by producing additional units for sale to Division A, Division B's results will improve by selling to A at any price greater than B's variable cost of $7 per unit. For example, a budgeted income statement for Division B if the transfer takes place at as little as $8 per unit is below.

Budgeted Income Statement, Division B (Component Purchased Internally for $8)	
Sales to outsiders, 10,000 × $15	$150,000
Sales to A, 6,000 × $8	48,000
Total sales	198,000
Variable costs, 16,000 × $7	112,000
Contribution margin	86,000
Fixed costs	30,000
Income	$ 56,000

The manager of Division A will be happy to accept an $8 price, for that division's income will increase by $30,000 [6,000 units × ($13 – $8)]. Division B's manager *should* accept the $8 price because that division's income would improve by $6,000, the $1 contribution margin ($8 – $7) on the 6,000 additional units. If you understood the previous example, you should see that the firm's top managers also want the transfer to take place. The firm's total income would increase by $36,000, the combined changes in the incomes of its divisions ($30,000 + $6,000). Analyzing the situation as a make-or-buy decision, the company saves $36,000 in variable costs [6,000 × ($13 – $7)] by making the unit rather than buying it outside.

It would be unfortunate if the manager of Division B didn't understand the division's cost structure and considered the $8 price to be unacceptable. For example, suppose the manager had reviewed the original budgeted income statement and concluded that the cost was $10 per unit (variable costs of $70,000 plus fixed costs of $30,000, divided by the 10,000 units of planned production). The decision not to sell at $8 would, as indicated earlier, have been detrimental to Division A, to the firm, and to Division B.

As long as Division B has excess capacity, *any* price less than the market price of $13 and greater than B's variable costs of $7 is advantageous to both divisions and to the firm as a whole. Division A acquires the component at a lower price than it would have to pay to an outside supplier. Division B gains some contribution margin. And the firm benefits from having a lower total cost of the product (the $7 variable cost from Division B rather than the $13 outside price). Indeed, even a transfer price of $7 should be acceptable. Division B loses nothing and could gain by being able to retain good workers who might otherwise have left the area for other jobs, or by keeping good relations with suppliers who might be concerned about the low levels of B's orders for materials.

In summary, the major issue from the standpoint of the company as a whole is not the choice of a transfer price but whether the transfer should take place at all. For the company, the decision is a make-or-buy decision. For the buying division, the question is simply which supplier (sister division or outside firm) offers the lower price (assuming equal quality, delivery schedules, etc.). For the selling division, the decision is a special order decision, as in Chapter 5; the concern is whether the contribution margin from selling inside offsets the loss, if any, of contribution margin from lost outside sales. If the transfer is profitable from the standpoint of the company as a whole, the best transfer-pricing system is one that prompts the managers to make a decision in the best interests of the firm as a whole. Thus, setting transfer prices requires judgment and a full understanding of the circumstances and of the accounting information available.

MULTINATIONAL COMPANIES—SPECIAL PROBLEMS

Companies that operate in many countries are called *multinationals*. Some multinationals operate divisions in foreign countries, others set up separate, legal corporations. A division, or subsidiary corporation, that operates in France does business in French francs, not in dollars, and reports its financial results in francs. It pays French taxes and tariffs. Many U.S. companies are multinationals, as are many foreign companies such as British Petroleum, Toyota, and Unilever. Multinationals face special problems related both to evaluating performance and to transfer pricing.

Multinational companies have more complicated reporting needs than domestic companies. Besides the currency translation problems discussed in earlier chapters, there can be significant language barriers and little or no physical supervision of operations. These factors contribute to a heavy reporting load. Eastman Kodak says its managers receive 200 financial reports containing 1,300 documents per year.

With respect to evaluation, multinationals must cope with changes in exchange rates, which are the relationships of foreign currencies to dollars. For instance, the British pound sterling has over recent years been worth anywhere from $1.40 to $2.10 or so. One problem for performance evaluation is that the local manager in the foreign country does business in the foreign currency, but the multinational cares about the results in its home currency (dollars for U.S. multinationals). The trouble is that the local manager and the division can look good or bad in U.S. dollars simply because of changes in exchange rates, even though the local manager is not responsible for exchange rate fluctuations.

Consider the following division's monthly income statement in Xs, the currency of a foreign country.

	Division X
Sales	X3,000
Expenses	2,000
Income in local currency	X1,000

If an X was worth $10 during the month, the division would show $10,000 income for the month. Suppose that next month the division does exactly the same business and has the same income statement, but that the value of an X drops to $8. The division then shows $8,000 income, a 20% drop from last month even though it did the same business. Evaluating the manager's (or the division's) performance on the basis of reports using the currency of the home country penalizes him or her for a decline in the exchange rate (and gives undue credit when the rate rises). The question of translating foreign currency also vexes financial accounting.

The transfer pricing problem for multinationals is equally troublesome. Because different countries have different income tax rates, it is desirable, from the overall corporate point of view, to show higher profits in low-tax countries and lower profits in high-tax countries. One way to do so is through transfer prices. For example, suppose that Division A buys a product from Division B. The divisions are in different countries, but both use the same currency, denoted as T. Data appear below.

Selling price of Division A's product	T100
Variable cost, excluding transfer price	T20
Tax rate in Division A's country	20%
Variable cost of Division B's product	T30
Tax rate in Division B's country	60%

The income statements on the next page show the effects, including income taxes, of transferring 1,000 units of Division B's product at T30 and at T60.

Monsanto, a large chemical company, evaluates its managers on dollar results, so many of its foreign managers use hedges to be sure that their dollar results reflect their results in the foreign currency. In one example, Monsanto Agriculture Co. reduced prices in Britain to increase volume. The managers were worried that the British pound might drop against the U.S. dollar, so that their dollar results would suffer. They bought an option to buy dollars at a later date so that if the pound fell, they could gain enough on the option to offset the unfavorable effect on operating results of the pound's fall.*

Gregory J. Millman, "Currency Risk at Monsanto," Management Accounting, *April, 1991, 43.*

	Transfer at T30	
	Division A	Division B
Sales (1,000 × T100)	T100,000	
(1,000 × T30)		T30,000
Variable cost [1,000 × (T20 + T30)]	T50,000	
(1,000 × T30)		T30,000
Contribution margin	50,000	0
Income tax at 20% and 60%	T 10,000	0

	Transfer at T60	
	Division A	Division B
Sales (1,000 × T100)	T100,000	
(1,000 × T60)		T60,000
Variable cost [1,000 × (T20 + T60)]	80,000	
(1,000 × T30)		30,000
Contribution margin	20,000	30,000
Income tax at 20% and 60%	T 4,000	T18,000

Total income taxes are only T10,000 at the lower price, T22,000 at the higher price. (The corporation minimizes its total taxes if Division B *gives* the product to Division A, but the authorities in Division B's country would certainly not permit that.) If the corporation forces Division B to sell at a low price, it saves considerable taxes, but penalizes the performance of Division B and its manager. Of course, dictating the low transfer price also enhances the reported performance of Division A and its manager.

Similar problems arise with import duties, or tariffs, which are typically based on values reported for incoming goods. If a division is transferring goods to another that is located in a high-tariff country, a low transfer price reduces the tariff. Some countries also have export duties, though they are much less common than import duties. With high export duties, it is, of course, best to have a low transfer price.

Another area where income-shifting is tempting is in management fees and allocations of corporate costs. A corporation can shift income from a division (foreign country) to itself (home country) by charging a management fee. But the more costs charged to a division or subsidiary in a high-tax country and the less charged to those in low-tax countries, the lower the multinational's total tax bill. Here again, the reported performance of the local managers is influenced by corporate policies.

Besides the problems associated with portraying performance, some of the practices described above, if arbitrarily imposed, are unethical and in some countries illegal. Various authorities such as those responsible for collecting income taxes in the various countries will try to ensure that artificially high or low transfer prices are disallowed and that corporate charges reflect the services provided at the corporate level. Transfer prices and corporate fees are also of interest to the authorities in countries having significant currency restrictions. For example, Brazil permits currency to leave the country only in payment for goods. Brazil's policy makes it impossible to repatriate profits through management fees or allocations of corporate costs.

Transfer pricing entered the public arena in the 1992 presidential campaign when President Clinton argued that foreign-based multinationals were avoiding over $11 billion in annual taxes by manipulating transfer prices. (Many authorities believed that the correct amount was much less.) Early in 1993 the IRS issued new regulations that required companies to use pricing methods that accurately reflected business conditions, such as assets employed, functions performed, and risks taken by the subsidiaries or divisions. These regulations allowed more flexibility than older proposals that required that profits on intracompany business approximate profits on transactions with outsiders. Most authorities accept transfer prices that clearly represent arms-length transactions, those that would be the same if the buyer and seller were unrelated companies.

SUMMARY

The evaluation of investment centers requires determining which revenues, costs, and investments the manager can control. Commonly used performance measures are return on investment (ROI) and residual income (RI). ROI is the most popular measure, but RI is advantageous from a behavioral point of view. Use of either criterion requires answering difficult questions about which items to include in divisional income and investment and involves different opinions about how some items should be measured.

Intrafirm sales and purchases introduce the problem of transfer prices. Such prices can encourage managers to take actions that harm the firm as a whole. However, managers who are free to negotiate transfer prices are likely to make decisions that benefit both the divisions and the firm. Companies with divisions in countries using a different currency have special problems in evaluating the performance of those divisions. Such companies also have problems in setting transfer prices that take into consideration the different tax structures and currency restrictions of the countries in which their divisions operate.

KEY TERMS

decentralized
divisional income
divisional investment
investment turnover
minimum required (desired, target) rate of return
residual income (RI)
return on sales (ROS)
return on investment (ROI)
transfer prices

KEY FORMULAS

$$\text{Return on investment (ROI)} = \frac{\text{divisional income}}{\text{divisional investment}}$$

$$\text{Return on investment (ROI)} = \frac{\text{income}}{\text{sales}} \times \frac{\text{sales}}{\text{investment}}$$

$$\text{Return on sales (ROS)} = \frac{\text{income}}{\text{sales}}$$

$$\text{Investment turnover} = \frac{\text{sales}}{\text{investment}}$$

$$\text{Residual income (RI)} = \text{income} - (\text{investment} \times \text{target ROI})$$

REVIEW PROBLEM

The manager of the Bartram Division of United Products Company has given you the following information related to budgeted operations for the coming year, 19X5.

Sales (100,000 units at $5)	$500,000
Variable costs at $2 per unit	200,000
Contribution margin at $3 per unit	300,000
Fixed costs	120,000
Divisional profit	$180,000
Divisional investment	$800,000

The minimum required ROI is 20%.

Required

Consider each part independently.

1. Determine the division's expected ROI using the expanded second formula.
2. Determine the division's expected RI.
3. The manager has the opportunity to sell an additional 10,000 units at $4.50. Variable cost per unit would be the same as budgeted, but fixed costs would increase by $10,000. Additional investment of $50,000 would also be

required. If the manager accepts the special order, by how much and in what direction will RI change?

4. Bartram's budgeted volume includes 20,000 units that Bartram expects to sell to the Jeffers Division of United Products. However, the manager of Jeffers Division has received an offer from an outside firm to supply the 20,000 units at $4.20. If Bartram Division does not meet the $4.20 price, Jeffers will buy from the outside firm. Bartram could save $25,000 in fixed costs if it dropped its volume from 100,000 to 80,000 units.
   (a) Determine Bartram's profit assuming that it meets the $4.20 price.
   (b) Determine Bartram's profit if it fails to meet the price and loses the sales.
   (c) Determine the effect on the firm's total profit if Bartram meets the $4.20 price.
   (d) Determine the effect on the firm's total profit if Bartram does not meet the price.

ANSWER TO REVIEW PROBLEM

1. 22.5%

$$\frac{\text{Income}}{\text{sales}} \times \frac{\text{sales}}{\text{investment}} = \frac{\$180{,}000}{\$500{,}000} \times \frac{\$500{,}000}{\$800{,}000} = 0.36 \times 0.625 = 0.225 = 22.5\%$$

2. $20,000

Profit budgeted	$180,000
Minimum required return ($800,000 × 20%)	160,000
Residual income budgeted	$ 20,000

3. RI would increase by $5,000. This can be determined either by considering the changes in the variables or by preparing new data for total operations. Considering only the changes

Increase in sales (10,000 × $4.50)	$45,000
Increase in variable costs (10,000 × $2)	20,000
Increase in contribution margin	25,000
Increase in fixed costs	10,000
Increase in profit	15,000
Increase in minimum required return ($50,000 × 20%)	10,000
Increase in RI	$ 5,000

A new income statement and calculation of new total RI would show the following.

Sales ($500,000 + $45,000)	$545,000
Variable costs (110,000 × $2)	220,000
Contribution margin	325,000
Fixed costs ($120,000 + $10,000)	130,000
Divisional profit	195,000
Minimum required return ($850,000 × 20%)	170,000
Residual income	$ 25,000

The new $25,000 RI is $5,000 more than RI based on budgeted operations without the special order.

4. (a) $164,000. If Bartram accepts the lower price, revenue (and hence contribution margin) will be reduced by $0.80 per unit for 20,000 units. With no change in fixed costs, the $16,000 drop in contribution margin means a similar drop in profit. An income statement under the new assumption would show the following.

Sales [($5 × 80,000) + ($4.20 × 20,000)]	$484,000
Variable costs ($2 × 100,000)	200,000
Contribution margin	284,000
Fixed costs	120,000
Divisional profit	$164,000

(b) $145,000. If Bartram does not accept the lower price, the *full* contribution margin from sales to Jeffers will be lost. The avoidable fixed costs will be saved. The contribution margin lost would be $60,000 (20,000 units at $3), and the fixed costs saved would be $25,000. Hence, divisional profit would drop $35,000 ($60,000 – $25,000) to $145,000 ($180,000 budgeted profit – $35,000).

The answer could also be arrived at by reference to the income statement prepared in item a. The contribution margin lost would be $44,000 (20,000 × the lower contribution margin of $2.20), with fixed costs savings of $25,000. The net decline in profits would be $19,000 ($44,000 – $25,000), which, when subtracted from the $164,000 total profit shown in the income statement in item a, equals $145,000.

A third, somewhat longer, approach to the problem would be to prepare an income statement assuming the sales to Jeffers are not made. This approach, too, shows a new divisional profit of $145,000.

Sales ($5 × 80,000)	$400,000
Variable costs ($2 × 80,000)	160,000
Contribution margin	240,000
Fixed costs ($120,000 – $25,000)	95,000
Divisional profit	$145,000

(c) If you concluded that the firm's total profit would change as a result of the change in the transfer price, you have forgotten a very important point made in Chapter 10. Changes in transfer prices do not, in themselves, change total profit. Only if changes in transfer prices cause managers to change their operations and actions can total profit change. In this situation, the manager of Bartram Division had planned to sell to Jeffers Division and the income statement was budgeted accordingly. If he accepts the lower price, he will still be selling to Jeffers. Similarly, the manager of Jeffers Division had planned to buy from Bartram Division. He will still buy from Bartram Division, but at a lower price. The only thing that has changed is the transfer price. The reduction in the profit of Bartram Division (because of the lower contribution margin) will be exactly offset by the increased profit of Jeffers Division (because of that division's lower costs). Hence, the firm's total profit will not change.

(d) The firm would lose $19,000 if Jeffers bought its units from an outside supplier. From the point of view of the firm as a whole, the decision is basically a make-or-buy decision such as was discussed in Chapter 5. Consider, therefore, the two possible decisions, from the total firm's point of view.

	Decision	
	Buy from Outside Supplier	Make Product Inside (Bartram)
Purchase price (20,000 × $4.20)	$84,000	
Variable cost to produce (20,000 × $2)		$40,000
Avoidable fixed costs		25,000
Costs of each decision	$84,000	$65,000

As this analysis indicates, the decision to produce internally carries a $19,000 advantage.

Another approach to this problem is to consider the profits of the individual divisions and how those profits would differ from originally budgeted profits if a purchase were made from an outside supplier. If Jeffers can buy at $4.20 from either source, *its* profits will increase $16,000 (20,000 units × $0.80 saved) over what has been budgeted with an original transfer price of $5.00. For this reason, the manager of Jeffers would be eager to obtain the lower price. Now consider the position of the manager of Bartram Division, who has budgeted profits of $180,000. The profit of *his* division will decline $35,000 (budgeted profits of $180,000 – $145,000 profits, computed in item b) if he does not get the order from Jeffers. For this reason, the Bartram's manager should not want to lose the order from Jeffers. Putting these two changes in divisional profits together, we see that there will be a $19,000 loss (a $16,000 gain by Jeffers and a $35,000 loss by Bartram).

The important factor in this second approach is that if each division's manager evaluates his own situation properly, each will make a decision consistent with the good of the firm as a whole. The manager of Jeffers Division will wisely seek the lower price because it will increase his profits. The manager of Bartram Division will wisely consider the lower price because failing to do so will decrease his profit.

ASSIGNMENT MATERIAL

QUESTIONS FOR DISCUSSION

11-1 Alternative accounting methods Explain how various inventory cost-flow assumptions (last-in-first-out, first-in-first-out, weighted average) can affect the measurement of return on investment for a division.

11-2 Product-line reporting Financial analysts often express the desire that companies publish annual reports broken down by division or principal lines of activity. They have said they would like to see financial statements broken down by products, or perhaps separated into wholesale and retail business, or maybe separated into government and commercial business. What problems might arise from attempting to fulfill this desire for additional information? What recommendations might you make?

11-3 Types of responsibility centers Assume that the following multiple-choice question appeared on an examination covering this chapter and that the instructions were to select the single best answer.

Which of the following is true?

(a) All investment centers qualify as profit centers, but not all profit centers qualify as investment centers.
(b) All profit centers qualify as investment centers, but not all investment centers qualify as profit centers.
(c) All cost centers qualify as profit centers, but not all profit centers qualify as cost centers.
(d) All cost centers qualify as investment centers, but not all investment centers qualify as cost centers.

Forced to make a choice, most students would correctly select answer (a). If, however, only the first alternative were presented and the instructions were to indicate whether the statement was true or false, some of those same students might decide that the statement was false. What line of reasoning would those students present to justify their answer and how would you respond to their position?

EXERCISES

11-4 RI, ROI, and CVP analysis The following data refer to the DCB division of Mega Corporation. DCB sells one product.

Selling price	$10
Variable cost	$4
Total fixed costs	$200,000
Investment	$500,000

Required

Answer the following questions, considering each independently.

1. If the manager of DCB desires a 20% ROI, how many units must she sell?
2. If the division sells 60,000 units, what will ROI be?
3. The minimum desired ROI is 15%. If the division sells 60,000 units, what is RI?
4. The manager desires a 25% ROI and wishes to sell 50,000 units. What price must be charged?
5. The minimum desired ROI is 20% and RI is $30,000. What are sales, in units?

11-5 Comparison of ROI and RI, investment decisions The manager of Technic Division of Microprod, Inc., has developed the following schedule of investment opportunities. The schedule shows the amount to be invested and the expected annual profit. Currently, investment is $10,000,000 and profits are $2,500,000.

Investment Opportunity	Amount of Investment	Annual Profit
A	$ 500,000	$ 80,000
B	700,000	200,000
C	1,000,000	230,000
D	1,100,000	290,000
E	1,200,000	170,000

Required

1. The division manager wishes to maximize ROI. (a) Which projects will he select? (b) What ROI will he earn?
2. The manager wishes to maximize RI. Determine which projects he will select and the RI he will earn if the minimum desired ROI is (a) 15% and (b) 20%.
3. Assuming that the ROI on each project approximates the IRR discussed in this chapter and in Chapter 8, which policy (maximizing ROI or maximizing RI) is better for the firm? Assume that the minimum desired ROI equals cost of capital.

11-6 Basic transfer pricing Wharton Division of Tunney Industries manufactures furniture. Data on a sofa that Wharton makes appear below.

Selling price		$800
Variable costs:		
Fabric	$150	
Other variable costs	350	
Total variable costs		500
Contribution margin		$300
Expected volume		2,000 units

Wharton buys the fabric from an outside supplier. The manager of Wharton learns that Seagrave Division of Tunney makes a fabric that meets her requirements. Seagrave sells the fabric to outside customers for $180. Variable cost to Seagrave is $100. Wharton's manager offers to buy the fabric at $120.

Required

1. Seagrave has plenty of capacity to serve its outside customers and meet Wharton's needs. If Wharton buys 2,000 units from Seagrave at $120:
   (a) What will happen to Seagrave's income?
   (b) What will happen to Wharton's income?
   (c) What will happen to Tunney Industries' income?
2. Redo item 1 assuming that Seagrave has no excess capacity and will lose outside sales if it supplies Wharton.

11-7 Product line evaluation "My division as a whole is evaluated on ROI and RI, so why shouldn't I use those measures to evaluate my product lines?" The speaker was Lynn Cathcart, manager of the Household Products Division of General Enterprises, Inc. Cathcart provided the following data regarding the three major lines that the division handles.

	Cleaners	Disinfectants	Insect Sprays
Margin	20%	18%	25%
Turnover	2.5 times	2 times	1.8 times
Annual revenues, millions	$30	$10	$18

Required

1. For each product line, determine ROI, total investment, and annual profit.
2. The minimum required ROI is 30%. Determine RI for each product line.

11-8 Basic transfer pricing The Games Division of Toys-and-Stuff Inc. uses 100,000 batteries per year for its products. Currently, Games buys the batteries from an outside supplier for $1.40 each. Power Division of Toys-and-Stuff makes batteries of the type used by Games Division and sells them at $1.50 each. Power's variable cost to produce each battery is $0.90. Power Division has ample manufacturing capacity to serve its regular customers and also meet the needs of Games Division.

Required

Answer each of the following independently.

1. If Power agrees to supply the batteries at $1.20, what will be the effect on the incomes of each of the divisions and on Toys-and-Stuff as a whole?
2. Why might Power's manager accept an offer as low as $0.90 per battery from Games?
3. Repeat item 1 assuming, instead, that Power has no excess capacity and so would lose outside sales if it supplies the batteries to Games and then suggest the lowest per-battery price that Power's manager would probably accept under the revised conditions.
4. Repeat item 1 assuming, instead, that Power has only 40,000 units of excess capacity and so would lose outside sales of 60,000 units if it supplied the 100,000 batteries needed by Games.
5. Assume that Power has only 40,000 units of excess capacity and that the managers of the Games and Power Divisions agree on a price that would have no effect on the income of Power Division. What would that price be?

11-9 Components of ROI The following data refer to the three divisions of International Enterprises, Inc.

	Huge Division	Giant Division	Colossal Division
Sales	$2,000	$3,000	$5,000
Profit	500	300	300
Investment	2,500	2,000	1,500

Required

1. Compute ROI for each division, using the ratios of ROS and investment turnover.
2. Assume each division could increase its ROS by one percentage point with the same sales as are currently shown. Recompute ROI for each division and comment on the differences between the results here and those in item 1.

11-10 ROI and CVP analysis The following data refer to the operations of Martin Division of LND Enterprises.

Selling price per unit	$30
Variable cost per unit	$18
Fixed costs per year	$300,000
Investment	$900,000

Required

1. Determine the number of units that must be sold to achieve a 25% ROI.
2. The manager has been approached by a firm that wishes to buy 10,000 units per year at a reduced price. Current volume is 43,000 units. Accepting the special order will increase fixed costs by $30,000 and investment by $80,000.
   (a) Determine ROI without the special order.
   (b) Determine the lowest price at which the manager can sell the additional 10,000 units without reducing ROI.

11-11 Performance evaluation criteria Foster Company has four divisions. Operating data for 19X7 are, in thousands of dollars, as follows.

	A	B	C	D
Divisional profit	$ 3,000	$ 2,500	$ 6,000	$1,900
Assets employed	$18,000	$14,000	$42,000	$8,000

Required

1. Rank the divisions according to (a) ROI, (b) RI if the minimum required ROI is 10%, and (c) RI if the minimum required ROI is 15%.
2. What other information might be helpful in evaluating the divisions?

11-12 Basic RI relationships Grendel Division had RI of $2 million, investment of $25 million, and asset turnover of two times. The minimum required ROI was 20%.

Required

1. Determine Grendel's sales, profit, and ROS.
2. Determine the ROS that Grendel needs to raise its RI to $3 million, holding sales and investment constant.
3. With the ROS calculated in part 1, determine the sales required to earn $3 million RI, holding investment constant.

11-13 Transfer pricing—increased costs and sacrificed sales Division A of ABC Inc. has a capacity of 100,000 units and expects the following results for 19X8.

Sales (80,000 units at $7)	$560,000
Variable costs (at $3)	(240,000)
Fixed costs	(260,000)
Income	$ 60,000

Division B, another division of ABC, currently purchases 25,000 units of a part for one of its products from an outside supplier at $7 per unit. B's manager believes she could use a minor variation of A's product instead, and offers to buy the units from A at $6. The variation desired by B would cost A an additional $1 per unit and would increase A's annual fixed costs by $12,000. A's manager agrees to the deal offered by B's manager.

Required
Determine the amount and direction of the effect of the deal on the 19X8 income for Division A, for Division B, and for ABC as a whole.

11-14 Transfer prices and decisions Green Inc. consists of two divisions, Armonk and Braser. Armonk makes only one product, a chemical compound, at a variable manufacturing cost of $2.50 per gallon. The division sells both to outsiders (at $5 per gallon) and to Braser (at $4 per gallon). Braser spends $2 per gallon converting what it buys from Armonk into a product that it sells to outsiders at $9 per gallon. The budgeted income statements for Green and its divisions appear below.

	Armonk	Braser	Green
Sales to outsiders:			
Armonk (200,000 × $5)	$1,000,000		$1,000,000
Braser (60,000 × $9)		$ 540,000	540,000
Sales to Braser			
60,000 × $4	240,000		240,000
Total	1,240,000	540,000	1,780,000
Variable costs:			
$2.50 per gallon × 260,000	650,000		650,000
$4 paid to Armonk × 60,000		240,000	240,000
$2 per gallon × 60,000		120,000	120,000
Total variable costs	650,000	360,000	1,010,000
Contribution margin	590,000	180,000	770,000
Direct fixed costs	300,000	120,000	420,000
Division profit	$ 290,000	$ 60,000	350,000
Common costs			130,000
Income			$ 220,000

An outside supplier has offered to sell Braser 60,000 gallons of the needed chemical compound at $3.50 per gallon. Neither the outsider supplier nor Armonk is willing to supply anything less than Braser's total needs of 60,000 gallons.

Required
Answer each of the following independently.

1. If Armonk reduces the transfer price to $3.50 and Braser continues to buy from Armonk, what will happen to the incomes of each of the divisions and of Green Inc. as a whole?
2. If Armonk refuses to reduce the transfer price and Braser buys outside, what will happen to the incomes of each of the divisions and of Green Inc. as a whole? (Assume Armonk cannot increase its sales to outside customers.)
3. Assume that Armonk's capacity is 260,000 gallons and that, if Braser doesn't buy from Armonk, Armonk can increase its outside sales by 45,000 gallons. Should Armonk reduce its price to meet that offered by the outside supplier? (Consider the question from both Armonk's and Green's points of view.)

11-15 ***Range of transfer price*** Microtec Division of CR Industries makes a microchip that it presently sells only to outside companies. The Consumer Products Division of CR is bringing out a new oven that requires a sophisticated chip and has approached Microtec for a quotation. Microtec sells the chip for \$47 and incurs variable costs of \$12. It has excess capacity. The Consumer Products Division can acquire a suitable chip from outside the company for \$41.

Required

1. Determine the advantage to CR Industries as a whole for the Consumer Products Division to buy the chip from Microtec, as opposed to buying it outside.
2. Determine the minimum price that Microtec would accept for the chip.
3. Determine the maximum price that Consumer Products would pay Microtec for the chip.
4. How would your answers to each of the preceding items change if Microtec were working at capacity?

11-16 ***Basic ROI relationships*** Gandolf Division of Nationwide Motors had sales of \$30 million, ROI of 30%, and asset turnover of 3 times.

Required

1. Determine Gandolf's (a) investment, (b) profit, (c) ROS.
2. Suppose that by reducing its investment, Gandolf could increase its asset turnover to four without affecting sales or income. What will its ROI be?

11-17 ***ROI and RI relationships*** Fill in the blanks in the following schedule. Each case is independent of the others. In all cases, the minimum desired ROI is 20%.

	Case			
	A	B	C	D
Sales	\$400	\$____	\$400	\$700
Income	\$____	\$____	\$____	\$____
Investment	\$____	\$300	\$200	\$____
Margin	15%	8%	____%	6%
Turnover	____ times	3 times	____ times	____ times
ROI	30%	____%	____%	____%
RI	\$____	\$____	\$ 15	\$ 22

11-18 ***Relationships*** Fill in the blanks for each of the following independent situations. In all cases the minimum required ROI is 20%.

	(a) Income	(b) Investment	(c) ROI	(d) RI
1.	\$2,500	\$10,000	____	____
2.	\$5,400	____	30%	____
3.	____	\$20,000	30%	____
4.	____	\$25,000	____	\$1,000
5.	\$4,000	____	____	\$ 500
6.	____	____	30%	\$3,000

11-19 ***Transfer prices—pushing capacity*** For several years, ABC Division of Slavic Corp. has been selling some (currently 8,000 units) of its product to XYZ

Division of the same company at a price slightly below that charged to outside customers. Current income statements for the two divisions are as follows:

	ABC Division		XYZ Division	
Sales of ABC:				
To outsiders (80,000 at $5.50)		$440,000		
To XYZ (8,000 at $5.00)		40,000		
Sales of XYZ:				
To outsiders (8,000 at $65.00)				$520,000
Total sales		480,000		520,000
Variable costs:				
ABC (88,000 at $2.00)	$176,000			
XYZ (8,000 at $5.00)			$ 40,000	
XYZ (8,000 at $35)			280,000	
Total variable costs		176,000		320,000
Contribution margin		304,000		200,000
Direct fixed costs		230,000		95,000
Divisional profit		$ 74,000		$105,000

XYZ Division has received an offer from an outside supplier to sell 8,000 units such as those currently being purchased from ABC for $4.50.

Required

1. Assume that ABC's manager refuses to meet the outside supplier's price and cannot increase outside sales.
   (a) How will ABC's profit be affected if XYZ purchases the units from the outside supplier?
   (b) How will total profit of Slavic Corp. be affected if XYZ buys the units from the outside supplier?
2. Assume that ABC's manager doesn't want to meet the price offered by the outside supplier because she feels she's already giving XYZ a bargain. She says that meeting XYZ's needs is stretching her factory's capacity and that, while she couldn't make outside sales beyond the current level (80,000), her per-unit variable cost would drop to $1.85 for *all* units and her fixed costs would drop by $18,000 if she didn't sell to XYZ. How will total profit of Slavic Corp. be affected if XYZ accepts the offer from the outside supplier to provide 8,000 units at $4.50?

11-20 Transfer prices for service work The service department of an automobile dealership does two general kinds of work: (1) work on cars brought in by customers and (2) work on used cars purchased by the dealership for resale. The service manager is often evaluated on the basis of gross profit or some other dollar measure. Because of the evaluation measure, the prices to be charged to the used-car manager for reconditioning and repair work on cars bought for resale are particularly important. The used-car manager is also likely to be evaluated by his profits. Thus, he wants service work done as cheaply as possible. The service manager naturally wants the prices to be the same as those he charges outside customers.

Required

1. What possible transfer prices could be used, and what are their advantages and disadvantages?
2. What do you recommend?

11-21 ***Review of Chapters 10 and 11*** Tschebert Company has only two divisions, Tschett and Bert. Selected information about each follows.

	Tschett	Bert
Divisional sales	$1,600,000	$2,400,000
Divisional income	240,000	160,000
Divisional investment	1,000,000	800,000

Unallocated costs that are common to both divisions are $70,000 per year. Assets (net of liabilities) that are not associated with either division are $400,000.

Required

Answer the following questions. Note: The answers to most questions do not depend on the answers to previous questions.

1. What is the ROS for Tschett Division?
2. What is the investment turnover for Tschett Division?
3. What is the ROI for Tschett Division?
4. What is the ROI for the firm as a whole?
5. What is RI for Bert Division if Tschebert's minimum required ROI is 12%?
6. Suppose Tschebert's top managers decide to allocate common costs to its divisions on the basis of divisional sales.
   a. Determine Bert Division's ROI.
   b. Determine the ROI for the firm as a whole.
7. If Tschebert's top managers decide to allocate common costs on the basis of divisional investment, what will ROI be for the firm as a whole?

PROBLEMS

11-22 ***Performance evaluation criteria*** Hawthorne Company has two divisions, Hi and Lo. The firm evaluates divisional managers based on ROI. Budgeted data for the coming year are as follows:

	Hi	Lo	Total
Sales	$ 600,000	$ 300,000	$ 900,000
Expenses	300,000	200,000	500,000
Divisional profit	$ 300,000	$ 100,000	$ 400,000
Investment	$1,200,000	$1,000,000	$2,200,000

An investment opportunity is available to both divisions. It is expected to return $40,000 annually and requires an investment of $200,000.

Required

1. Given that the divisional managers are evaluated based on ROI, which, if either, of the managers will accept the project? Explain.
2. Assume that the managers are evaluated on residual income. If the minimum required ROI is 18%, which, if either, of the managers will accept the project? Explain.
3. If the minimum required ROI is 18%, is it in the firm's best interest for a division to accept the project? Explain.

11-23 *Components of ROI* The managers of two divisions of Diversified Company were recently discussing their operations. Fran Margin commented, "I get a good return on sales, about 20%, but my investment is a drag. Turnover last year was only 0.60 times." Florence Turns said, "My problem is margins; turnover is about 2.4 times, but return on sales is only 5%."

Required

1. Compute ROI for each division.
2. (a) Assume that Margin's division will maintain the same ROS. Determine the investment turnover required to achieve a 20% ROI.
   (b) Assume that Turns' division will maintain its turnover. Determine the ROS required to achieve a 20% ROI.

11-24 *Appropriate transfer prices* The Rohn Division of BLQ Industries expects the following results in 19X6, selling its product only to outside customers.

Sales (100,000 units at $8)	$800,000
Variable costs at $5	500,000
Contribution margin	300,000
Fixed costs	150,000
Profit	$150,000

Early in 19X6, the manager of Betts Division of BLQ asked the manager of Rohn to supply 20,000 units to Betts. Betts would modify the units at a variable cost of $4 and sell the resulting product for $11. Rohn Division has capacity of 110,000 units and will therefore lose 10,000 units in outside sales if it supplies the 20,000 to Betts. Rohn's fixed costs remain constant up to capacity.

Required

1. If Rohn does transfer 20,000 units to Betts, which modifies and sells them as described, what will happen to the profit of BLQ Industries as a whole?
2. What is the minimum transfer price that Rohn will accept from Betts for the 20,000 units?
3. What is the maximum transfer price that Betts will pay?
4. Redo item 1 assuming that Rohn's capacity is 150,000 units and that outside sales cannot increase over 100,000 units.

11-25 *ROI and RI on a special order* The Appliance Division of TVM Industries has the opportunity to sell 250,000 units of one of its principal lines to a large chain store at $24 per unit. Selected data follow.

Annual unit volume	1,700,000
Normal selling price	$40
Unit variable cost	$18
Annual fixed costs	$30,000,000
Divisional investment	$25,000,000

The manager of the Appliance Division expects a 50,000 unit decline in sales at the normal price if she supplies the chain. She also expects fixed costs to increase by $100,000 and investment to increase by $1,200,000 if she accepts the order.

Required

1. Determine whether the manager of the Appliance Division should accept the order, assuming that she is evaluated based on ROI.
2. Determine whether the manager of the Appliance Division should accept the order, assuming that she is evaluated based on RI and that the minimum required ROI is 20%.

11-26 Comprehensive review The following information relates to the Glove Division of Hand-and-Glove Company.

Selling price	$12
Variable cost, per unit	$ 8
Annual direct fixed costs, all unavoidable	$160,000
Total divisional investment	$500,000

Required

Answer each of the following numbered parts independently.

1. Assume Glove's current sales are 80,000 units.
   a. What is its ROI?
   b. What is its RI if the required ROI is 20%?
2. Suppose Hand-and-Glove expects a minimum ROI of 18%. How many units must Glove sell to earn an RI of $50,000?
3. If Glove's return on sales is 20% and ROI is 48%, what are its sales, in dollars?
4. Assume that Glove expects to produce and sell 80,000 but has the capacity to produce 100,000 units. The manager of Hand Division, which is currently buying 25,000 of a similar product from an outside supplier for $11, offers to buy the units from Glove only if Glove will supply the full 25,000 units needed.
   a. What is the maximum price that Hand's manager is likely to offer for the units?
   b. What is the minimum price that Glove's manager is likely to accept on a sale of 25,000 units to Hand Division?
   c. If Hand's manager offers $9 per unit and Glove's manager accepts the offer, what will be the amount and direction of the effect on the total income of Hand-and-Glove?

11-27 Transfer prices and required profit margins Johnna Roberts is the used-car manager of the Snappy Wheels automobile dealership. She is expected to earn a gross profit of 25% of sales in the used-car operation, and she is distressed by the firm's transfer pricing policy. Roberts is charged with the trade-in price she sets for a used car plus any reconditioning work. The charge for reconditioning is based on actual costs by the service department plus a one-third markup over cost (25% on sales). Roberts believes she is being unduly penalized by the one-third markup.

Ellen Black, the service manager, is held responsible for earning a 25% gross profit on sales. She argues that it would not be fair to force her to do reconditioning work any cheaper than the work she does on customers' cars.

Roberts has recently been approached by Joe Sharp, the owner of Sharp's Garage, an independent repair shop. Sharp offers to do reconditioning work for

Roberts at 20% over cost, the work to be done during Sharp's slack periods. The work will generally take about four days longer than work done by the service department, which has no excess capacity.

Required

Should Roberts take her reconditioning business to Sharp?

11-28 Make-or-buy and transfer pricing Lansing Enterprises, Inc. has three divisions, A, B, and C. One of the firm's products uses components made by A and B, with the final assembly done by C. One unit from A and one from B are required.

Data for the product are as follows.

Selling price (C division)	$100
Variable costs:	
A division	$ 32
B division	16
C division	14
Total variable costs	$ 62
Volume	1,000 units

Divisions A and B charge Division C $40 and $24, respectively, for each unit. Division C has been approached by an outside supplier who will sell the component now made by Division A at $35 per unit.

Required

1. Prepare partial income statements, down to contribution margin, for A, B, and C based on current operations.
2. Determine whether the offer from the outside supplier should be accepted. If A meets the outside price, C will continue to buy from A.
3. Suppose that A can sell its entire output of 1,000 units per year at $44 if it performs additional work on the component. The additional work will add $5 to variable cost per unit; fixed costs will be unchanged. Capacity of Division A is 1,000 units. Should A meet the outside supplier's price or allow C to buy from the outside supplier? Support with calculations. Is A's decision good for the company?

11-29 Goal congruence and motivation Rex Company manufactures furniture and related products. Tom Bills, manager of Rex's Redfern Division, has been seeking bids on a particular type of chair to be used in a new living room suite he wants to market. No division within the firm can supply the chair.

The lowest outside bid is $120 from Dorfman Chair Company. Wisner Chair Company has bid $130 and would purchase some of the materials from the Ronson Upholstery Division of Rex Company. The Ronson Division has excess capacity, would incur variable costs of $25 for the amount of material needed for one chair and would be paid $46 by Wisner. Bills knows that Wisner would buy the materials from Ronson and that Dorfman would not. Each division manager is evaluated on the basis of ROI.

Required

1. As manager of the Redfern Division, which bid would you accept, Dorfman's or Wisner's?

2. As Rex's president, which bid do you want to see accepted? Explain.
3. Using the guidelines in Appendix B, write a memorandum to Joan Blane, Rex's president, giving and explaining your recommendation about how this situation should be handled.

11-30 Performance of international division CWK Industries is a division of Martek, Inc. CWK operates in Hungary, where the currency is the forint (F). The information CWK used to develop its operating budgets for the first quarter of 19X7 appear below. The exchange rate is 50 forints per dollar.

Unit sales	1,000,000
Unit price	F200
Cost of sales percentage	40%
Operating expenses	F30,000,000 per month

Required

1. Prepare a budgeted income statement for the first quarter of 19X7, in forints.
2. Translate the budgeted income statement to dollars.

11-31 Performance of international division—continuation of 11-30 CWK's actual results for the first quarter of 19X7 appear below. After the budgets were prepared, the exchange rate quickly went to 60 forints per dollar and remained there over the quarter.

	CWK Division Income Statement First Quarter, 19X7
Sales, 1,044,000 × F200	F208,800,000
Cost of sales	84,000,000
Gross profit	124,800,000
Operating expenses	90,000,000
Income	F 34,800,000

Required

1. Translate the actual income statement to dollars.
2. Comment on the results. Did the managers of CWK perform well, badly, about as expected?

11-32 Divisional performance—interactions Acme Camera Company has two divisions, film and cameras. The manager of the Film Division, John Kretzmar, has just received a report from his laboratory indicating a breakthrough in a new type of film that produces much clearer pictures. The film can only be used in the X-40, a low-priced camera made by the Camera Division. The film currently sold for the X-40 has a variable cost per roll of $0.90 and sells for $3.00 per roll. The film currently sells 2 million rolls per year.

Kretzmar is confident that if he devoted his efforts and facilities to the production and sale of the new film he could sell 2.5 million rolls at $2.80 each. Additionally, he believes, on the basis of several market research studies, that if the Camera Division sold 200,000 more X-40s per year, sales of the new film could reach 4.8 million rolls. The variable cost of the new film is $0.80 per roll, additional fixed costs to produce it are $250,000 per year, and additional required investment totals $600,000.

Samantha Brewer, manager of the Camera Division, is not happy with the proposal that she increase production of X-40s. She argues that the camera has a contribution margin of only $6 and that she would have to increase her investment by $4,000,000 and her fixed costs by $500,000 in order to increase production by 200,000 units. She is virtually certain, as is Kretzmar, that the extra units could be sold, but she is also well aware that the Acme's minimum required ROI is 20%.

Required

1. Compute the change in RI for the Camera Division if production and sales of X-40s are increased by 200,000 units to show why Brewer is not eager to expand its production.
2. If the manager of the Camera Division will not increase production, what is the best action for the Film Division?
3. What is the best action for the firm as a whole?

11-33 RI, ROI, CVP analysis, and effects of decisions The following data refer to the Pratt Division of Standard National Company.

Selling price	$40
Variable costs	$24
Total fixed costs	$200,000
Investment	$800,000
Planned sales in 19X9	30,000 units

Required

Answer each of the following independently.

1. What is planned ROI for 19X9?
2. The minimum required ROI is 20% and the division manager wishes to maximize RI. A new customer wants to buy 10,000 units at $32 each. If the order is accepted, the division will incur additional fixed costs of $40,000 and will have to invest an additional $160,000 in various assets. Should the order be accepted?
3. The minimum desired ROI is 20% and the manager wishes to maximize RI. The division makes components for its product at a variable cost of $4. An outside supplier has offered to supply the 30,000 units needed at a cost of $5 per unit. The units that the supplier would provide are equivalent to the ones now being made and the supplier is reliable. If the component is purchased, fixed costs will decline by $20,000 and investment will drop by $40,000. Should the component be bought or made?
4. Again, minimum required ROI is 20% and the goal is maximizing RI. The manager is considering a new product. It will sell for $20, variable costs are $12, fixed costs will increase by $80,000, and sales are expected to be 15,000 units. What is the most additional investment that can be made without reducing RI?
5. Assume the same facts as in item 4 except that investment in the new product is $400,000 and that introducing the product will increase sales of the existing product by 2,000 units. What increase in unit sales of the existing product is needed to justify introducing the new product?

11-34 Corporate charges and behavior MST Company charges its operating divisions a percentage of sales to cover corporate expenses, which are virtually all fixed. The percentage is based on budgeted sales and budgeted corporate expenses and is predetermined for each year. In 19X6 the charge is 3%. The charge is included in calculating the profit of each division and its ROI, which is the basis for evaluating the performance of divisional managers.

Calco Division makes electronic equipment and has some excess capacity. Its manager has found a customer who will pay $10 million for a batch of product that has variable costs of $8.8 million. No incremental fixed costs are associated with the order. Accepting the order will require increased investment in receivables and inventories of about $5.1 million. The 3% charge is not included in the $8.8 million.

The divisional manager expects to earn $15.5 million on an investment of $70.5 million without the order.

Required

1. Should the divisional manager accept the order, acting in her own best interests?
2. Assuming that the minimum required ROI is 20%, is it to the firm's advantage to accept the order?

11-35 Performance measurement—athletic programs Haltom University is a medium-sized private university with a religious affiliation. Perhaps prompted by the prospect of declining college enrollment, a number of faculty members at Haltom have become increasingly concerned about the costs of the school's athletic program. The football program has been subjected to particular scrutiny. One professor assembled the following data and argues, based on these data, that football is clearly a drain on funds needed elsewhere in the university.

19X4 Football Program		
Revenue from ticket sales		$300,000
Revenue from concessions		25,000
Total revenue		325,000
Associated costs:		
Tuition for players on scholarship	$120,000	
Room rent in dormitories for players	22,000	
Board and incidentals for players	110,000	
Coaches' salaries	90,000	
Portion of salaries of athletic director, ticket office personnel, attendants, etc.	17,000	
Uniforms, equipment, etc.	10,000	
Total costs		369,000
Net loss on football program		($ 44,000)

Required

1. Comment on each item. Should it be included? If you are uncertain, state the conditions under which it should be included or excluded.
2. What other information do you want before reaching a decision on the desirability of the football program?

11-36 Transfer prices Following is a budgeted income statement for Superdivision of Weaver, Inc. The division sells both to outsiders and to a sister division.

	Intercompany Sales to Subdivision	Sales to Outsiders
Sales:		
100,000 units at $10		$1,000,000
50,000 units at $8	$400,000	
Variable costs ($4 per unit)	200,000	400,000
Contribution margin	200,000	600,000
Fixed costs ($300,000, allocated at $2 per unit)	100,000	200,000
Profit	$100,000	$ 400,000

Required

1. Subdivision can buy all of its requirements from an outside supplier at $7 per unit and will do so unless Superdivision meets the $7 price. Superdivision's manager knows that if the business of Subdivision is lost, Superdivision will not be able to increase sales to outsiders and fixed costs will not change. Should Superdivision meet the $7 price from the standpoint of (a) the firm and (b) Superdivision?
2. Superdivision meets the $7 price. It then is offered the opportunity to sell 60,000 units to a chain store at $7 each. The price of the 100,000 units now sold to outsiders will not be affected. However, Superdivision has capacity of 190,000 units. If Superdivision cannot fill all of the requirements of Subdivision, then Subdivision will have to buy *all* the units outside at $7. Should Superdivision accept the order, considering (a) the firm and (b) Superdivision?
3. Suppose now that Subdivision has received the offer from the outside supplier, who will provide as many units as Subdivision wants to buy at $7. Superdivision no longer has the opportunity to sell the 60,000 units to the chain store. The manager of Superdivision believes that reducing prices to outsiders could increase those sales greatly. Best estimates are that reducing the price to $9.20 would yield sales of 120,000 units; to $8.40, 150,000 units; and to $7.80, 170,000 units. Capacity is 190,000 units. Superdivision can sell any amount up to 50,000 units to Subdivision. Subdivision will buy units from the outside supplier as necessary. What should be done? How many units should Superdivision sell to outsiders, and how many units should it sell to Subdivision at $7?

11-37 ROI, RI, and investment decisions The manager of Brandon Division of Greene Industries has been analyzing her investment opportunities. The division currently has profits of $1,250,000 and investment of $5,000,000.

Investment Opportunity	Annual Profit	Amount of Investment
A	$300,000	$ 900,000
B	300,000	1,600,000
C	240,000	1,200,000
D	280,000	800,000
E	260,000	1,000,000

Required

1. Assume that the manager wishes to earn the highest ROI possible. Determine which projects will be selected and the ROI that will be earned.

2. Assume that the manager wishes to maximize RI. Determine which projects will be selected and the total RI that will be earned if the minimum required return is (a) 20% and (b) 28%.
3. Assume that the ROI on each project approximates the IRR discussed in Chapter 8 and that the minimum desired ROI approximates cost of capital. Determine which policy is better for the firm: maximizing ROI or maximizing RI.

11-38 Transfer pricing The Macron Division of 2M Company expects the following results in 19X6.

Sales (100,000 at $3)		$300,000
Variable costs	$120,000	
Fixed costs	150,000	270,000
Profit		$ 30,000

Sparkman Division of 2M Company wants to buy 30,000 units of Macron's product. Sparkman will incur an additional $0.80 per unit and sell the resultant new product for $4.50. Macron has capacity for 120,000 units.

Required

1. What will happen to 2M's profit if the transaction takes place at a transfer price of $1.50?
2. What will happen to the profit of each division if the transaction takes place at the $1.50 transfer price?
3. What is the minimum transfer price Macron will accept for the 30,000 units?

11-39 ROI and RI—capitalizing human resources Business Products Division of Data Systems Company develops software for business applications for mainframe computers and microcomputers. The division employs 350 people, of whom 320 are accounting and data processing professionals, the remainder clerks, secretaries, and editors. Because the division does no manufacturing, it has very low assets—about $500,000, consisting of microcomputers, office equipment, and an extensive library. The division earned $1,500,000 last year. The company controller believes that the 300% ROI ($1,500,000/$500,000) misstates the division's results because the asset base omits the costs of training professional employees. The division spent $750,000 last year (19X5) on such training, including sending employees to seminars and the startup time for new employees.

The controller realizes that GAAP do not condone capitalizing the costs of human assets. The controller thinks it would be interesting to see how the division would look if these costs were capitalized and amortized over five years. The following data is developed for the past four years (the division's entire life), in thousands of dollars.

Year	Book Profit	Training Cost	Book Assets
19X2	$ 110	$400	$220
19X3	520	500	270
19X4	960	600	420
19X5	1,500	750	500

Training costs are included as expenses in the book profit figures.

Required

1. Determine ROI for each year using the data given and applying GAAP.
2. Determine profit, investment, and ROI for each year using the controller's method. That is, capitalize training costs and amortize them over five years, beginning with the year of the expenditure.
3. Compare the results in items 1 and 2. Comment, including statements about the advantages and disadvantages of the controller's approach.

11-40 Transfer prices and goal congruence (CMA adapted) A. R. Oma Company manufactures a line of men's perfumes and aftershave lotions. The manufacturing process is a series of mixing operations with the adding of aromatic and coloring ingredients. The finished product is bottled and packed in cases of six bottles each.

The bottles are made by one division, which was bought several years ago. Management believes that the appeal of the product is partly due to the attractiveness of the bottles and so has spent a great deal of time and effort developing new types of bottles and new processes for making them.

The bottle division has been selling all of its output to the manufacturing division at market-based transfer prices. The price has been determined by asking other bottle manufacturers for bids on bottles of the appropriate size and in the required quantities. At present, the firm has the following bids.

Quantity, Cases of 6 Bottles	Price per Case	Total Price
2,000,000	$2.00	$ 4,000,000
4,000,000	1.75	7,000,000
6,000,000	1.6666	10,000,000

The bottle division has fixed costs of $1,200,000 per year and variable costs of $1 per case. Both divisions are investment centers, and their managers receive significant bonuses based on profitability, so the transfer price is of great interest to both of them.

The perfume manufacturing division has variable costs, excluding the cost of bottles, of $8 per case and fixed costs of $4,000,000 annually. The market research group has determined that the following price-volume relationships are likely to prevail during the coming year.

Sales Volume in Cases	Selling Price per Case	Total Revenue
2,000,000	$12.50	$25,000,000
4,000,000	11.40	45,600,000
6,000,000	10.65	63,900,000

The president, Miguel Enez, believes that the market-based transfer price should be used in pricing transfers. The bottle division has no outside sales potential because the firm does not wish to supply its highly appealing bottles to competitors.

Required

1. Of the three levels of volume given, determine which will provide the highest profit to the (a) bottle division, (b) perfume division, (c) firm as a whole.
2. Do the results in item 1 contradict your understanding of the effectiveness of market-based transfer prices? Explain why or why not.

3. Using the guidelines in Appendix B, write a memorandum to Mr. Enez giving and supporting your recommendation about the course of action that should be selected.

11-41 Transfer pricing (CMA adapted) The manager of the Arjay Division of National Industries, Inc. has the opportunity to supply a brake assembly to an aircraft manufacturer for $50. The manager is willing to accept the order if he can break even on it because he has excess capacity and will be able to keep skilled workers busy who would otherwise have to be laid off. Additionally, he believes there is a good chance of getting more business from the same firm at better prices.

Bradley Division of National Industries makes a part that is used in the brake assembly. Bradley is operating at capacity and producing the part at a variable cost of $4.25. Its selling price is $7.50 to outsiders. None of its output is currently being sold internally.

The manager of Arjay decides to offer Bradley a price that will result in breaking even on the order. He determines that the other costs involved in filling the order are as follows, per unit.

Parts purchased outside	$23
Other variable costs	14
Fixed overhead and administration	8
Total, before fitting	$45

He decides to offer the manager of Bradley $5 per fitting, which brings the total cost per unit to $50, the selling price of the assembly. The firm is decentralized and the managers are evaluated based on ROI.

Required

1. Determine whether the manager of Bradley is likely to accept the $5 offer.
2. Determine whether it is to the firm's advantage for Bradley to supply the part at $5.
3. As the controller of National Industries, what do you advise be done?

11-42 Budgeted and actual results Managers of divisions of Wycliff Company receive bonuses based on ROI. The bonuses constitute about 30% of total compensation of the average manager. Part of the bonus depends on whether the manager meets budgeted ROI.

F. C. Smith took over as general manager of the Poursh Division in late 19X1. Budgeted and actual results for 19X6 appear below, in thousands of dollars.

	Budget	Actual
Sales	$2,500	$2,480
Cost of sales	(1,250)	(1,310)
Operating expenses	(750)	(610)
Profit	$ 500	$ 560
Investment		
Current assets (50% of sales)	$1,250	$1,280
Current liabilities (40% of current assets)	(500)	(580)
Plant and equipment, net	1,800	1,770
Total investment	$2,550	$2,470
ROI	19.6%	22.6%

Smith received a sizable bonus. Smith commented on the results by saying that once he saw sales would not meet budget, he began to cut costs, especially in discretionary areas such as maintenance, employee training, and engineering. (Engineers were responsible for improving the quality of products and methods of manufacturing.) He also held off payments to suppliers, letting them finance more of the division's asset requirements.

Required

Discuss Smith's performance. Include in your discussion the long-term implications of the specific actions mentioned above and the ethical aspects of his actions.

11-43 *Divisional performance, cost allocations, and dropping a product line*
Sonya Rathman is the manager in charge of two product lines for Kingston Company. She has just received the following income statement for the three months ended March 31, 19X7. The statement shows Rathman's two product lines and the total results for the firm. There are 10 product lines in the firm.

	Product Line		
	A	B	Total Firm
Sales	$100,000	$200,000	$2,000,000
Separable expenses:			
Cost of sales	60,000	100,000	1,050,000
Selling and general	29,000	50,000	450,000
Total separable expenses	89,000	150,000	1,500,000
Common costs (allocated on basis of sales dollars)	15,000	30,000	300,000
Total expenses	104,000	180,000	1,800,000
Income (loss)	($ 4,000)	$ 20,000	$ 200,000

Rathman is disturbed by the showing of product line A. She believes that the line is contributing to the common costs of the firm and should be kept, but she is worried about the effect on her performance.

Required

1. Prepare an income statement assuming that product line A is dropped. Show the effects on both Rathman's and the firm's performance. All separable costs are avoidable. Be sure to reallocate common costs to product line B based on its relative percentage of the new sales for the firm. Round to the nearest $500.
2. Comment on the results. Does Rathman's performance look better if product line A is dropped? Is it better? Is the decision good for the firm?

11-44 *Developing divisional performance data* Dixon Company has three divisions, X, Y, and Z. The following data regarding operations and selected balance sheet elements have been prepared by the firm's accountant (in thousands of dollars).

	X	Y	Z
Sales	$2,000	$3,000	$5,000
Cost of goods sold	1,000	1,400	3,300
Gross profit	1,000	1,600	1,700
Selling and administrative expense	400	900	800
Income	$ 600	$ 700	$ 900
Current assets	$ 400	$ 700	$ 600
Current liabilities	$ 300	$ 200	$ 100
Fixed assets (net)	$2,250	$3,000	$3,750

After determining costs and assets directly traceable to the divisions, the accountant allocated the remainder in the following way.

(a) Common cost of goods sold of $1,800 was allocated based on sales dollars.
(b) Common selling and administrative costs of $1,000 were allocated on the basis of relative sales dollars.
(c) Common fixed assets of $3,000 were allocated on the basis of relative shares of directly assignable fixed assets of $1,500, $2,000, and $2,500, for X, Y, and Z, respectively.
(d) All current assets except cash (which is held and managed by corporate headquarters) are directly assignable. Cash of $200 is allocated based on sales.

Required

1. On the basis of the data developed by the firm, rank the divisions according to ROI on net assets and RI, with a 15% minimum required ROI.
2. Recast the statements, computing divisional profit and assets employed without allocations. Rank the divisions on the same bases as in item 1. Comment on the differences between your rankings.

11-45 Transfer pricing Westfall Division of Bailey Enterprises makes stereophonic speakers and sells them to other firms for use in complete systems. The division can make 45,000 speakers per year and cannot increase production because of shortages of specialized skilled labor. Data for the division's product follow.

Selling price		$80
Variable manufacturing costs	$48	
Variable selling costs	8	56
Contribution margin		$24

Westfall has just lost a customer and volume is projected at 40,000 speakers per year for the next several years. Another division of Bailey, Leakes Division, is interested in buying speakers from Westfall and putting them in sets to be sold through retail outlets. Leakes now buys speakers of somewhat higher quality than those made by Westfall at $84 each. The speakers are of better quality than the rest of the components of the set, so the manager of Leakes intends to reduce prices and predicts higher volume if she changes to the lower-quality speakers. Volume of the set in which the speakers are to be used is currently 3,500 per year. If the price were reduced from $680 to $600, volume is expected to be 4,500 units per year. Variable costs are currently $460 per set, including the $168 for two speakers now purchased outside. Leakes Division wants 9,000 speakers per year from Westfall and has offered $62 per speaker. Westfall will not incur variable selling expenses on speakers sold to Leakes.

Required

1. Determine whether it is in the firm's best interests if Westfall sold speakers to Leakes.
2. At the suggested transfer price, is it in the interests of each of the managers to have Westfall sell to Leakes?
3. Determine the limits on the transfer price—that is, the highest price that Leakes would be willing to pay and the lowest price that Westfall will accept.

11-46 Problems of market-based transfer prices Planton Division of Borgan Industries has developed an electronic measuring system that requires a sophisticated microprocessor. CLI Division makes such a microprocessor and currently sells it for $200 on the outside market. CLI incurs variable costs of $50 per unit. CLI has a lot of excess capacity. It now sells 30,000 units of the microprocessor per year and could make close to 40,000 units. However, increasing outside sales to 36,000 units would require reducing the selling price on all units to $160. Accordingly, CLI has been restricting output.

The manager of Planton received a bid of $200, the current market price, from CLI for the microprocessor and then analyzed data regarding expected volume at different selling prices. He intended to set the price of the measuring system at either $600 or $550 based on the following.

	Selling Price	
	$600	$550
Expected variable costs, per unit:		
Materials	$ 90	$ 90
Microprocessor from CLI	200	200
Labor and variable overhead	110	110
Total variable costs	400	400
Contribution margin	$ 200	$ 150
Expected volume	5,000 units	6,000 units

Required

1. At the $200 transfer price, what price will the manager of Planton Division set for the measuring system?
2. From the standpoint of the firm, which price is better, $600 or $550?
3. The manager of CLI Division knows that Planton will buy 5,000 microprocessors at the $200 price. What is the minimum price he will accept for 6,000 units—the price that gives him the same total contribution margin he could earn selling 5,000 at $200?
4. Will the transfer price you calculated in item 3 induce the manager of the Planton Division to try to sell 6,000 units of the measuring system at $550? Assume that the two managers have to agree on both the transfer price and the quantity to be taken. That is, the alternatives that the Platon manager faces are to (1) buy 5,000 microprocessors at $200 and (2) buy 6,000 at $175.

CASES

11-47 Divisional performance and accounting methods A division manager for McKy Company has been criticized for allowing ROI to fall in the past two years. She has explained that the division made some large investments on which a 30% before-tax ROI is expected. She argues that the use of straight-line depreciation is hurting ROI, on which her performance is evaluated. Below are comparative income statements and other data for the past three years.

	19X1	19X2	19X3
Sales	$2,200	$2,900	$3,800
Variable costs	1,200	1,500	1,800
Contribution margin	1,000	1,400	2,000
Discretionary costs	300	500	700
Committed costs (largely depreciation)	300	450	700
Total fixed costs	600	950	1,400
Divisional profit	$ 400	$ 450	$ 600
Invested capital (principally plant and equipment)	$1,000	$1,600	$2,400
ROI	40%	28%	25%
Capital expenditures	$ 200	$ 900	$1,500

Required

1. Explain why the falling ROI (in the years indicated) may not indicate poor performance.
2. What possible solutions are there?

11-48 Capital budgeting and performance evaluation Arnold Donald, manager of the Western Division of Global Enterprises, Inc., is considering an investment. He can save $10,000 in cash operating costs per year using a machine that costs $40,000 and has a ten-year life with no salvage value. Donald calculates the ROI in the first year as 15% [($10,000 – $4,000 depreciation)/$40,000]. He decides that the machine is not a wise investment because his current ROI is 20% and he is evaluated based on ROI. (Current income is $40,000 and investment is $200,000.)

The seller of the machine offers to lease it at $8,500 per year if Donald will accept a noncancellable lease for ten years. He asks your advice and specifically requests that you consider the effect of the lease on ROI.

The firm's minimum desired ROI before taxes is 12%, which approximates cost of capital.

Required

Using the guidelines in Appendix B, write a memorandum to Mr. Donald explaining his choices and the effects of each alternative from his standpoint and that of the firm.

11-49 National Automobile Company—introduction of a new model National Auto Company consists of four relatively autonomous divisions. In the past each division has concentrated on a relatively limited range of models designed to appeal to a particular segment of the automobile market. The Kalicak Division has been producing midsized cars for many years. They range in price (to dealers) from $4,000 to $5,200.

One day last August, Noel Mack, general manager of the Kalicak Division, was studying some reports prepared by the firm's Market Research Department at central headquarters. Mack had been considering for some time the possibility of bringing out a stripped-down version of the division's most popular model, the Panther. He had been hesitant to do so because he feared that sales of the higher-priced Panthers would suffer. The market research indicated, however, that lost sales of higher-priced versions would be negligible if a new Panther were introduced and priced to sell to the customer for about $4,100. The lowest price at retail now charged for a Panther is $4,550.

Mack was pleased at the results of the study and instructed his production manager to determine the costs of producing 80,000 units of the new model per year—the number of units that the study indicated could be sold. Mack also asked for information about additional investment in equipment, inventories, and receivables necessitated by the higher volume.

A few days later Mack had the additional information. The production manager estimated the cost per unit to be $3,600, composed of the following basic categories.

Variable costs	$3,000
Fixed costs	600
Total	$3,600

The fixed cost per unit included $10,000,000 in existing fixed costs that would be reallocated to the new model under a complicated formula used by the division's cost accounting department. The additional investment in equipment was $80,000,000 and in receivables and inventories about $30,000,000.

Mack was reasonably certain that the information he had gathered was as accurate as estimates are likely to be. He consulted with several large dealers and concluded that the model could be priced at $3,800 to dealers. Any higher price would force the dealers to charge more than $4,100, with a consequent decline in volume below the 80,000 per year target.

Like the other divisional managers, Mack is evaluated based on the residual income earned by his division. The minimum required return is 18%. Income taxes are ignored in determining residual income for the divisions.

Required

Determine whether the new Panther should be brought out.

11-50 National Automobile Company—interaction effects of decisions (continuation of 11-49) While mulling over his decision whether to introduce the new Panther model, Noel Mack was eating lunch with Deborah Diaz, general manager of the Hatfield Division, which specializes in compact and subcompact cars. Mack told Diaz about the study he had ordered and gave a general picture of the results, including the projection of 80,000 units of volume of the new model.

After lunch, Diaz called Hanna Joost, the chief of market research for the firm, and requested more information about the study. Joost said that the study indicated a potential decline in volume of 30,000 units of one of the Hatfield Division's best-selling higher-priced models if Kalicak brought out the new lower-priced model. Diaz asked why that information had not been included in the report given to Mack and was told that Mack had only asked for estimates in declines in volume of Kalicak Division cars. Diaz then immediately telephoned her production manager and sales manager. She informed them of the situation and demanded that they quickly collect information.

Several days later, the production manager informed Diaz that the model in question, which sold to retail dealers for $3,400, had unit costs of $2,900 at the division's current volume of 160,000 units per year. Fixed costs of $500 were included in the $2,900 figure. Diaz asked what savings in fixed costs might be expected if volume were to fall by 30,000 units and was told that the fixed cost per unit would rise to about $560, even though some fixed costs could be eliminated. Conversations with other managers revealed that the division's investment could be reduced by about $70,000,000 if volume fell as stated.

Diaz was visibly distressed by what she had heard. She was concerned with her division's interests, but realized that Mack had the right to operate in accordance with his best interests. She pondered the possibility of going to the firm's executive vice president for advice.

Required

1. Determine the effect on Hatfield of the introduction of the new Panther.
2. Determine the effect on the firm of the introduction of the new Panther.

11-51 ROI at Burlington Industries, Inc.[7] Burlington Industries, Inc. is a very large and widely diversified manufacturer of textiles and associated products. The organization consists of several largely autonomous divisions, the performances of which have been evaluated using, among other measures, ROI and dollar profit. Profit measures are before tax but after a special deduction called the Use of Capital Charge (UOCC). The minimum required ROI for a division is the weighted average of the minimum required ROIs for three different types or classes of assets. The classes are (1) accounts receivable less accounts payable, (2) inventories, and (3) fixed assets.

The central managers at Burlington have stated that the use of different required ROIs recognizes the different risks of the different types of investment. They feel that fixed assets, which are committed for relatively long periods and lack liquidity, should earn a higher ROI than assets committed for a shorter time. Receivables, which are turned into cash more quickly than are inventories, require a lower ROI. The minimum required ROIs for the three classes are 7% for receivables-less-payables, 14% for inventories, and 22% for fixed assets. These minimums are based on estimates of cost of capital and of relative investment in each class of assets for the firm as a whole.

The following data relate to a hypothetical division of Burlington, stated in thousands of dollars.

Sales	$23,450
Cost of sales	16,418
Selling and administrative expense	1,678
Other expenses, not including UOCC	1,025
Accounts receivable less accounts payable	2,540
Inventories	3,136
Net fixed assets	3,560

7 *This problem was adapted from material in a paper presented by Donald R. Hughes, then assistant controller of Burlington Industries, Inc., at a symposium at Ohio State University. The symposium's papers, and discussions of them, are in Thomas J. Burns, ed.,* The Behavioral Aspects of Accounting Data for Performance Evaluation *(Columbus, Ohio: College of Administrative Science, Ohio State University, 1970). We acknowledge gratefully the permission of Professor Burns to adapt the material.*

Required

1. Prepare an income statement for the hypothetical division. Use the same basis as is used by Burlington.
2. Compute ROI for the division and the weighted-average minimum required ROI.
3. Comment on the method used by Burlington. Does it seem to encourage desirable behavior on the part of managers? Is the use of different minimum ROIs a good idea?

12

control and evaluation of cost centers

This chapter applies the concepts of responsibility accounting to cost centers in manufacturing firms. We explain how managers set performance standards, how they use standards for performance evaluation, and what behavioral problems they encounter in using standards. We examine the role of standard costs for planning, with a major emphasis on developing standards for variable costs and interpreting variances from those standards. We also look at the use of standards in JIT operations.

COST CONTROL

All companies need to control costs and increase productivity because competition is now global, not only local. Chapter 6 described how companies use budgets to control costs while other chapters, especially Chapters 8 and 9, discussed increasing productivity. Eliminating non-value-adding activities is one way to increase productivity; another way is to develop or to buy better manufacturing technology.

Cost control is critically important for companies in mature industries where total demand for the product is not growing. Such companies cannot significantly increase profits unless they can produce at lower costs than their competitors. Recognition of this principle is evidenced in a recent annual report of Kellogg's, the giant cereal company. The report stated that the company used its leadership in manufacturing technology to control costs and increase productivity. In addition, its leadership allowed Kellogg to maintain the highest quality for its products. A company that does not make high-quality products will not prosper no matter how good its cost control.

This chapter is concerned primarily with measures of efficiency. We describe techniques for analyzing how well managers control the *acquisition* and *use* of resources and thereby how well they control costs.

STANDARDS AND STANDARD COSTS

A standard is a norm, a criterion by which performance is judged. One standard for effectiveness is producing a specified amount of product. One standard for efficiency is whether output was produced at budgeted cost. A **standard cost** is a per-unit cost that a company should incur to make a unit of product. Companies use standard costs for materials, direct labor, and overhead. In this chapter we deal only with variable overhead standards. Chapter 14 examines fixed overhead standards.

STANDARD PRICES AND STANDARD QUANTITIES

A standard cost has two components: a standard price, or rate, and a standard quantity. Both standards relate to the input factor (materials, direct labor, variable overhead). The standard price, or rate, is the amount that *should* be paid for one unit of the input factor: $2 per pound of materials, $8 per hour of direct labor, $4 variable overhead per machine hour. The standard quantity is the amount of the input factor that *should* be used to make a unit of product: three pounds of materials, 0.25 direct labor hours. Thus, if a unit of product should require 0.25 direct labor hours and the standard labor rate is $8 per hour, the standard direct labor cost per unit is $2 (0.25 hours × $8).

STANDARD COSTS AND BUDGETS

As early as Chapter 1 we described budgeting as the process of relating required resources (inputs) to planned results (outputs). Chapter 6 developed the principles of flexible budgets and flexible budget allowances. Recall that a flexible budget allowance is the amount of cost that should be incurred *given the actual level of activity*. In Chapter 6, activity could have been output (number of units produced) or input (number of labor or machine hours). Differences between the actual cost and the flexible budget allowance are *variances*.

The relationship of standard costs to flexible budgets is simple and direct: a standard cost is a per-unit expression of a flexible budget allowance *based on actual output*. Thus, with the standard quantity of labor of 0.25 hours per unit of product and the standard labor rate of $8 per hour, the standard cost for labor is $2 per unit of product. The flexible budget allowance for one unit is also $2. If the company makes 20,000 units, the flexible budget allowance for labor is $40,000 ($2 × 20,000). [Notice also that the total standard time to make 20,000 units is 5,000 hours (0.25 hours per unit × 20,000 units). Multiplying 5,000 total standard hours by the $8 standard rate gives the same $40,000 flexible budget allowance.] Now, if actual direct labor cost was

$42,200, a variance of $2,200 ($42,200 minus the flexible budget allowance of $40,000) would occur. In the pages that follow we show how to analyze that variance.

Establishing a flexible budget allowance that considers inputs rather than outputs is also possible. Remember that for any of the required input factors (for example, labor), two factors determine total cost: the quantity of the input used (the number of hours worked by laborers) and the cost of a unit of such input (the hourly wage paid to laborers). In the situation described above, if 5,100 hours of labor were used, the flexible budget allowance based on *input* is $40,800 ($8 per hour × 5,100 hours worked).

In this chapter, we use the term *total standard cost* to refer to the flexible budget allowances based on *output.* As we shall see, however, flexible budgets based on inputs are necessary in analyzing variances.

ILLUSTRATION OF STANDARD VARIABLE COST

Coulter, Inc., a manufacturer of wooden packing crates, uses standard variable costs to aid in planning and control. Careful study has determined that, if workers are producing at normal efficiency, the direct labor time per crate is one-half hour. Also given normal efficiency, 20 feet of lumber should be used per crate. Direct laborers are normally paid $6 per hour, and lumber costs $0.10 per foot. Additionally, variable overhead is expected to be incurred at the rate of $2 per direct labor hour. Using these data, we compute the standard variable cost of a crate as shown in Exhibit 12-1, which also shows actual results for a recent month. While this example is simplified, it illustrates all of the principles.

In practice, making the product might require several materials besides lumber and several kinds of direct labor at different rates. We use a single type of each factor to focus on the general concepts. The same reason prompts our use of a single measure of activity, hours of direct labor for variable overhead. We could use measures of activity other than labor hours for variable overhead. Selecting measures for overhead requires identifying the cost drivers for each overhead pool (see Chapter 3). In a highly automated

Exhibit 12-1 Standard Variable Costs

Cost Factor	Standard Quantity	×	Standard Price	=	Standard Cost
Materials	20 feet		$0.10		$2.00
Direct labor	1/2 hour		$6.00		3.00
Variable overhead	1/2 hour		$2.00		1.00
Total standard variable cost per rate					$6.00
Actual results:					
Crates produced	1,000				
Materials purchased (23,000 feet)	$2,415				
Materials used (19,500)					
Direct labor (480 hours at $6.10)	$2,928				
Variable overhead incurred	$ 980				

plant, some variable overhead is probably related to machine-hours or processing time, and some to the number and complexity of parts and components in each product. In most companies, several rates are used based on several factors. These might be determined by multiple regression analysis, as in the appendix to Chapter 3. The important thing is to find some reasonable way to develop overhead rates that can be translated into a variable overhead per unit of product. Again, for simplicity, we use a single figure for variable overhead which includes many costs, such as the variable portions of utilities, supplies, and payroll fringe benefits.

A standard variable cost per unit is a tool a manufacturer can use for planning, control, and performance evaluation. The standards can be used to plan for variable production costs at any level of production. When actual production is known, the standard cost per unit can be multiplied by the number of units produced to give the flexible budget allowance for that production level. Managers can compare actual costs with standard costs to evaluate performance. As we stated earlier, differences between standard and actual costs are **variances.**

VARIANCES

We begin the illustration of variance analysis with direct labor costs. With a single exception, the analysis to be shown here is the same for the other cost factors.

LABOR VARIANCES

Given that the company made 1,000 crates, what *should* direct labor cost be? The total standard direct labor cost, or flexible budget allowance, for 1,000 crates is $3,000, computed as follows, from data in Exhibit 12-1.

$$\begin{array}{ccccc} \textit{Total} & & \textit{actual} & & \textit{standard} \\ \textit{standard} & = & \textit{production} & \times & \textit{cost} \\ \textit{cost} & & \textit{(units)} & & \textit{per unit} \\ \$3{,}000 & = & 1{,}000 & \times & \$3.00 \end{array}$$

We could also have computed the flexible budget allowance for 1,000 crates by multiplying the 1,000 crates by the 0.50 standard hours, giving 500 standard hours allowed, which is then multiplied by the $6.00 standard rate. The calculation to be used is largely a matter of convenience. The term *standard hours allowed* describes the physical quantity of direct labor that should have been used to produce 1,000 units.

Direct laborers actually worked 480 hours during the month and earned $6.10 per hour, for $2,928 total actual cost. Actual costs were $72 less than standard (standard cost of $3,000 – $2,928 actual cost), producing a total variance of $72. But why? And who is responsible for the difference?

In some types of performance reporting (as in Chapter 10, for example), we made no distinction between variances in prices paid and in quantities used. However, it is likely that some managers control either prices or quantities, but not both. A supervisor is likely to be responsible only for the quantities of labor and materials used, not for wage rates or materials prices.

We want to isolate the type of variance so that we can identify the manager responsible for it. Here, we want to separate our $72 total variance into two components: (1) the difference due to price and (2) the difference due to quantity. Many terms are used to describe such variances. Price variances are sometimes called *rate, budget,* or *spending variances.* Quantity variances are sometimes called *use* or *efficiency variances.* The particular term you use is not important so long as you know which kind of variance is being referred to.

There are two common approaches to separating a total variance into its components. The first deals with total costs. We hold one of the factors constant (either price or quantity), and see what portion of the total variance is due to the effects of the other factor. The actual total labor cost can be separated as follows.

Actual input quantity	×	*actual rate for input factor*	=	*actual cost of input factor*
480 hours	×	*$6.10*	=	*$2,928*

To accomplish our objective we need a flexible budget allowance based on our *input* factor, labor. The budget allowance is computed below as $2,880—the number of hours actually worked times the standard wage rate.

Actual input quantity	×	*standard rate for input factor*	=	*budget allowance for actual quantity of input factor*
480 hours	×	*$6*	=	*$2,880*

The only difference between the two calculations is the rate used for the input factor. The input factor, circled in the calculations, is the same for both, 480 hours. Hence, the difference between the actual cost incurred ($2,928) and the flexible budget allowance ($2,880) is due to the difference between the standard wage rate and the actual wage rate. That $48 difference ($2,928 – $2,880) is the **labor rate variance,** and is *unfavorable* because the actual cost is greater than the flexible budget allowance for that quantity of input (480 hours).

The variance due to quantity is calculated in much the same way. We calculate the flexible budget allowance based on the actual *output* (1,000 units) as opposed to the actual input (480 hours). That budget allowance is $3,000.

Standard input quantity	×	*standard rate for input factor*	=	*budget allowance for actual quantity of output*
1,000 units × 1/2 hour per unit = 500 hours	×	*$6*	=	*$3,000*

Compare this formulation with the one immediately preceding it, where a budget allowance was computed for the *actual* quantity of the input factor, labor hours. Note that both calculations use the standard rate for the input factor, boxed in the calculations. The only difference between the two calculations is the quantity of input, labor hours. Hence, the $120 difference between the two budget allowances ($3,000 – $2,880) is due to the difference in the quantity of labor used. This difference is called the **labor efficiency variance** and is *favorable* because laborers worked fewer than the 500 standard hours allowed for 1,000 units of output. Our analysis shows that the $72 total variance can be explained as follows.

Labor rate variance	$ 48 unfavorable
Labor efficiency variance	120 favorable
Total labor variance	$ 72 favorable

These relationships are diagramed in Exhibit 12-2. The leftmost figure is actual cost, the middle figure is a flexible budget allowance based on input, and the right-hand figure is the budget allowance based on output. The chart can be used to determine the variance for any adjacent numbers: if the number to the right is larger than the one to the left, the variance is favorable; the variance is unfavorable if the opposite is true.

The labor efficiency variance should indicate how efficient direct laborers are when working on the product. Hence, the labor hours used to compute that variance should not include *idle time,* the time when laborers are not working. Including idle time in the computation could mask problems in production scheduling or some other function, or could label, as labor inefficiency, the cost of a manager's (or top management's) conscious decision not to lay off laborers when there is not enough work to keep them busy. Moreover, if idle time is included in the computation, a supervisor whose performance is evaluated by the size and direction of the efficiency variance could be prompted to take actions that are not in the firm's best interest. For example, the supervisor of laborers who would otherwise have idle time might assign them to making units and components not required by produc-

Exhibit 12-2 Labor Variances

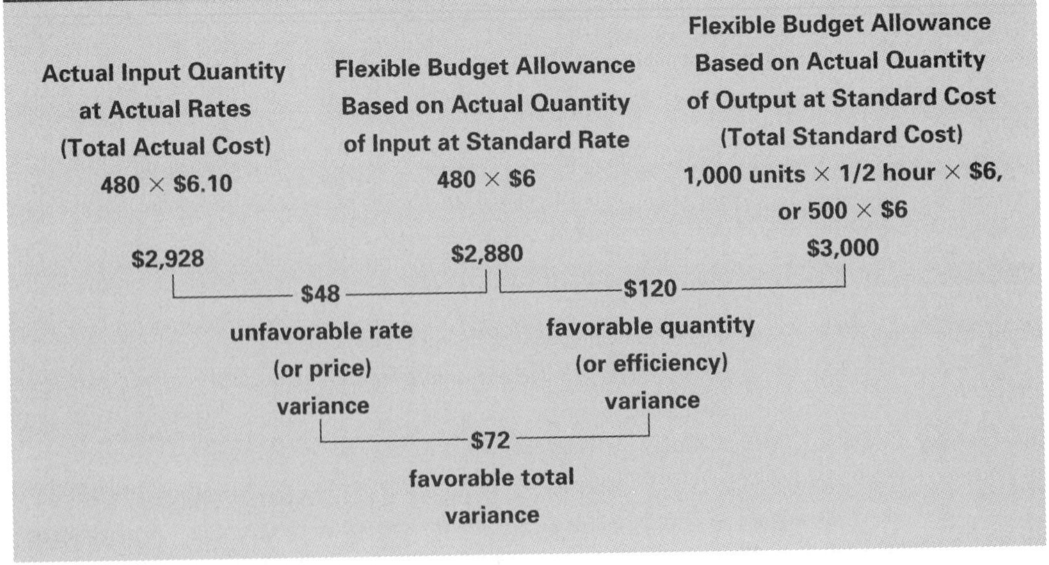

tion schedules, which means that the firm will incur unnecessary costs for storage, financing, insurance, taxes, etc. Such an action is obviously contrary to the efforts of many manufacturing companies today who are, as we have noted throughout this book, adopting JIT and other modern techniques that do not tolerate such production.

ALTERNATIVE COMPUTATION METHODS

We can also calculate variances by using the differences between the standard and actual figures for rate and quantity. The labor rate variance could be computed as follows.

$$\text{Labor rate variance} = \text{actual hours} \times \left(\text{standard rate} - \text{actual rate}\right)$$

$$-\$48 = 480 \times (\$6 - \$6.10)$$

Direct laborers were paid $0.10 per hour more than standard (an unfavorable occurrence) and earned this amount over 480 hours.

Using the same approach to calculate the labor efficiency variance:

$$\text{Labor efficiency variance} = \text{standard rate} \times \left(\text{standard hours} - \text{actual hours}\right)$$

$$\$120 = \$6 \times (500 \text{ hours} - 480 \text{ hours})$$

Employees worked 20 fewer hours than the standard for producing 1,000 units (a favorable occurrence).

When the number inside the parentheses (using these alternative formulations) is negative, as in the rate variance, the variance is unfavorable. When the number inside the parentheses is positive, as in the efficiency variance, the variance is favorable. Do not memorize these relationships. Rather, think of favorable variances as those giving lower total cost and vice versa.

You may use either or both methods. A minor difficulty with the alternative method is that sometimes the actual rate might require rounding. For example, if workers were paid $2,920 for 480 hours of work, the actual rate is $6.083333. . . . You would then have a small difference between the rate variance computed in this way and that computed using the method described earlier.

VARIABLE OVERHEAD VARIANCES

We used labor variances to illustrate the computations, but we could as easily have used variable overhead. The computations are the same, extending to the use of direct labor hours *if variable overhead is budgeted according to labor hours* (as they are in our example).

As shown in Exhibit 12-1, variable overhead costs for the month are $980. What are the variable overhead variances? Total standard variable overhead cost for 1,000 units of output is $1,000 ($1 standard cost per crate × 1,000 crates, or 500 standard direct labor hours at $2 standard rate per hour). So, we know that the total variance is $20 favorable (actual cost of $980 compared with a standard of $1,000).

Exhibit 12-3 shows that actual direct labor hours are used to determine the middle term (the flexible budget based on the actual quantity of input), and that standard labor hours are used to determine the right-hand term. (The right-hand term is also given by $1 standard variable overhead per unit × 1,000 units.) Both variable overhead variances, the **variable overhead budget variance** (or **spending variance**) and the **variable overhead efficiency variance,** are calculated in the same fashion as are the labor variances. Exhibit 12-3 shows the calculations.

If we based variable overhead on another activity, say machine hours, we would simply substitute actual and standard machine hours for actual and standard direct labor hours. We could also use more than one cost driver to assign variable overhead to a unit of product. Although the variable overhead budget variance is calculated in much the same way as the labor rate variance, it is not a rate variance in the sense of being the result of the prices paid for the input factor (overhead). For example, using more factory supplies than standard will show up in the variable overhead budget variance, not in the variable overhead efficiency variance.

The $20 budget variance can be computed using the alternative calculation method described earlier. However, because we were given only total overhead incurred, we must divide the total cost of $980 by the actual hours of 480 to determine the actual rate at which the variable overhead was incurred. That rate is about $2.0416 ($980/480). The format of the calculation is the same as for the computation of the direct labor variance.

Budget variance = *480 × ($2.00 – $2.0416) = - $19.97 (difference due to rounding)*

The $40 variable overhead efficiency variance can also be calculated using the standard rate per direct labor hour of $2 and the difference between the actual and standard hours.

Exhibit 12-3 Variable Overhead Variances

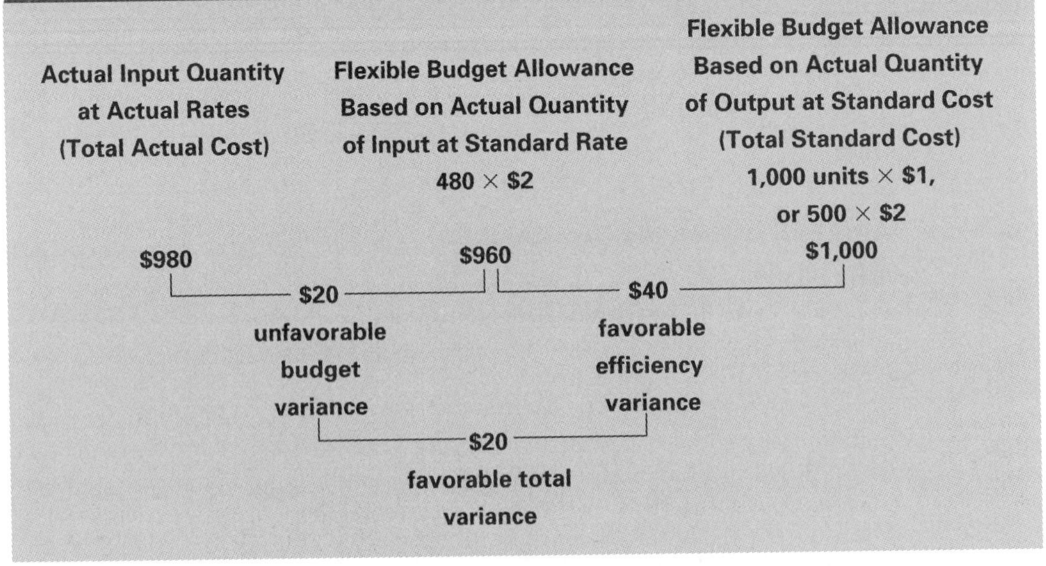

$$\textit{Efficiency variance} = \$2 \times (500 - 480) = \$40$$

When variable overhead standards are based on direct labor hours, the only difference in calculating labor and overhead variances is in the rates; that is, actual and standard direct labor hours are used both for labor and overhead. In fact, the variable overhead efficiency variance is then the result of using more or less labor than standard. Consider some of the costs that might be included in variable overhead. Payroll taxes, pensions, other fringe benefits, and many other costs will be incurred whenever employees work and regardless of whether they work efficiently or inefficiently. If the employee puts in an hour, the other costs follow. Hence, if there are inefficient labor hours (an unfavorable labor efficiency variance), there will be an unfavorable variable overhead variance, and vice versa. *As long as variable overhead is related to labor hours,* overhead efficiency variances do not indicate efficient (or inefficient) use of the factors making up variable overhead but rather the efficient (or inefficient) use of direct labor. Moreover, for parts of variable overhead that are related to some *other* measure of activity, such as machine time or cycle time (the time a product spends in the manufacturing process), the variable overhead efficiency variance will reflect the efficient or inefficient use of the related factor.

Of course, some elements of variable overhead may be related directly to the number of units produced, rather than to an input factor such as labor hours. For example, costs such as packaging materials (boxes, padding, lining) are directly related to units produced. Workers who pack the products should use standard quantities of these materials for each packaged product even if they work more or less efficiently than standard (take more or less time to package the product). If variable overhead contains significant amounts of such cost elements, the conventional calculations of variable overhead efficiency *and* budget variances are not appropriate for analysis and may be difficult for a manager to interpret.

It is important to identify the cost drivers to achieve the best possible estimates of cost. Suppose a considerable amount of overhead cost is driven by the number of components in a product, but the company uses direct labor hours. The company will have large, unexplainable variances because it is using the wrong driver. The choice of cost drivers for overhead is also important for behavioral reasons. Product designers, engineers, and other technical personnel whose responsibilities include cost reduction will naturally concentrate on high-cost factors. Thus, a company using direct labor to assign variable overhead will see these technical personnel working to reduce labor time. If direct labor does not drive significant amounts of overhead, the effort will be misplaced. The Tektronix example in Chapter 10 illustrates this point.

STANDARD COSTS AND ACTIVITY-BASED COSTING

We have referred to activity-based costing (ABC) in various contexts throughout the book. Its role in developing standards lies in determining which activities drive which costs. The objective is to achieve as accurate standard costs as possible. One result is better information about the cost and profitability of individual products.

Suppose that TGH Company has two principal overhead pools. One is driven by machine time and includes such costs as power, supplies, abrasive materials, and maintenance. The other pool is driven by the number of setups, or changeovers from making one product to another. These costs include such costs as wages of setup workers, supplies used in changeovers, and materials destroyed in testing machine settings and calibrations. The variable component of overhead related to machine hours is $6.00 per hour, related to setups is $140 per setup. Data and calculations for a 1,000 unit batch of TGH's products appear below.

Standard machine hours	1,500	
Rate per hour	$6.00	
Standard overhead related to machine hours		$ 9,000
Number of setups	20	
Rate per setup	$ 140	2,800
Total standard variable overhead		$11,800

Suppose that TGH made 10,000 units (10 batches) using 14,000 machine hours. Machine-hour driven variable overhead was $85,000, that driven by setups was $27,500. The number of setups was 210. The calculations of variances appear below.

Machine-driven

Actual Cost		Budget for Actual Use		Standard Cost
		14,000 × $6.00		10 × 1,500 × $6.00
$85,000		$84,000		$90,000
	$1,000 U		$6,000 F	
	Budget variance		Efficiency variance	

Part-driven

Actual Cost		Budget for Actual Use		Standard Cost
		210 × $140		10 × 20 × $140
$27,500		$29,400		$28,000
	$1,900 F		$1,400 U	
	Budget variance		Efficiency variance	

Of course, the company would also have materials and labor variances that it would calculate in the usual way.

MATERIALS VARIANCES

The material price variance is different from its counterparts in labor and variable overhead because materials, unlike labor, can be stored. What is purchased in one period is not necessarily used in that period, but the economic effect of paying more or less than standard price for materials occurs at the time of purchase. Consequently, the **material price variance** is calculated based on the quantity of materials *purchased,* not the quantity *used.* (The earlier that managers are aware of variances, the sooner they can take corrective action, so it makes sense to isolate the variance at the time of purchase rather than at the time of use.) The **material use variance** is calculated in the same way as are the labor and overhead efficiency variances.

The company in our earlier example (see Exhibit 12-1) bought 23,000 feet of lumber for $2,415. The average price was $0.105 ($2,415 ÷ 23,000). The standard price per foot of lumber is $0.10 (also from Exhibit 12-1). In calculating the material price variance, the flexible budget allowance is based on what you expect to pay for the quantity *purchased:* $2,300 (23,000 feet × $0.10 per foot). The material price variance is diagramed in Exhibit 12-4.

If we use the alternative formula, we must remember to use the actual quantity purchased, as follows.

$$\textit{Material price variance} = \textit{actual quantity purchased} \times \left(\textit{standard price} - \textit{actual price}\right)$$

$$-\$115 = 23{,}000 \times (\$0.10 - \$0.105)$$

The material use variance is calculated the same as the direct labor and variable overhead efficiency variances. The firm used 19,500 feet of lumber to make 1,000 crates. The standard quantity of lumber per crate is 20 feet (see Exhibit 12-1), so the total standard quantity for 1,000 crates is 20,000 feet. The standard cost of lumber for 1,000 crates is $2,000 (20,000 feet at $0.10 per foot, or 1,000 crates multiplied by the standard materials cost per crate of $2, as shown in Exhibit 12-1). The material use variance is diagramed in Exhibit 12-5.

Exhibit 12-4 Material Price Variance

Actual Quantity of Input Purchased, at Actual Prices	Flexible Budget Allowance for Actual Quantity of Input Purchased, at Standard Rate
	23,000 × $0.10
$2,415	$2,300

$115 unfavorable material price variance

Exhibit 12-5 Material Use Variance

Flexible Budget Allowance Based on Actual Quantity of Input Used, at Standard Rate	Flexible Budget Allowance Based on Actual Quantity of Output, at Standard Cost
19,500 × $0.10	1,000 × 20 × $0.10, or 1,000 × $2
$1,950	$2,000

$50 favorable material use variance

Alternatively, we can calculate the material use variance using the following formula.

$$\textit{Material use variance} = \textit{standard price} \times \left(\textit{standard quantity for output achieved} - \textit{actual quantity}\right)$$

$$\$50 = \$0.10 \times (20{,}000 - 19{,}500)$$

We were able to show labor and variable overhead variances in one schedule for each (see Exhibits 12-2 and 12-3, respectively). We cannot do that with materials variances because there are two middle terms, one based on units purchased, the other on units used. This is the only difference between materials variances and the other types of variance.

World-class manufacturers do not evaluate their purchasing functions solely on the basis of the prices they pay for materials and components. McKinsey & Co., a large consulting firm, reported a number of measures of performance for the purchasing function, some of which appear below.

	Typical Company	World-class Company
Agents per $100 million purchases	5.4	2.2
Purchasing costs as % of purchases	3.3%	0.8%
Time spent placing order, weeks	6	0.001
Percentage deliveries late	33%	2%
Percentage deliveries rejected	1.5%	0.0001%
Materials shortages, per year	400	4

Some of these measures relate to the cost of performing the purchasing function, while others relate to the quality of suppliers. It is important that companies reduce lead time of their suppliers because that fosters the JIT objective of reducing cycle time and inventory. Of course, quality measures are especially important for JIT companies.[1]

VARIANCES AND PERFORMANCE EVALUATION

Isolating variances is the first step toward providing information for performance evaluation. As we pointed out in Chapter 10, the relevant factors in evaluating the performance of an individual manager are those that the manager is responsible for and can control. Quantifying the effects of price and quantity differences is not the same thing as identifying the *causes* of, and the responsibility for, the differences. Knowing that laborers were paid more or less than the standard rate, or worked more or fewer than the standard hours, does not explain *why* these variances occurred.

Two issues complicate the interpretation of variances. First, variances signal nonstandard performance only if they are based on up-to-date standards that reflect current production methods and factor prices. Suppose that changing production methods to increase quality results in using more labor time. If the company does not change the standard labor time, it will have

1 *"Quality'"* Business Week, *November 30, 1992, 72.*

Advanced manufacturing is not as concerned with material price variances as is conventional manufacturing. JIT operations are much more concerned with the quality of a supplier's products and the supplier's ability to meet delivery requirements. Evaluating suppliers is an important activity. Such evaluations have benefited Copeland Electric, a subsidiary of Emerson Electric Co. The company evaluates the 10 factors listed below. The factors were selected from a list developed by representatives from purchasing, engineering, quality assurance, materials managements, and accounting. As you can see, some factors are quantifiable, such as whether the vendor meets delivery schedules, while others are more qualitative.

1. Dollar cost, actual prices versus expected prices
2. Quality costs, cost of deviations
3. Terms of sale, early payment discounts
4. Meets specifications, rejects
5. Meets expectations, monthly evaluation of events that might change rating
6. Quality assurance, vendor's capability to ensure quality
7. Delivery quality, actual delivery dates versus requested dates
8. Lead time, shorter the better
9. Administrative accuracy, accounting and receiving discrepancies
10. Support, quarterly assessment of vendor responsiveness to problems

Copeland assigns one to five points for each category, usually based on specific criteria. For instance, vendors who meet delivery dates within one day early or late receive five points, while those delivering more than 10 days early or five days late receive one point. Copeland's managers, as well as the vendors, believe the system has enhanced vendor performance. Both groups have also developed a better understanding of the importance of suppliers to Copeland's success.*

* *Michael A. Robinson and John E. Timmerman, "Vendor Analysis Supports JIT Manufacturing,"* Management Accounting, *December, 1987, 20-24.*

unfavorable labor efficiency variances. These variances are not the fault of the managers responsible for using labor; the fault lies with the standard. Modern companies are constantly trying to better their production methods. Issuing new standards every time a change occurs is costly, and frequent revisions of standards might cause the standards to lose their meaning. Accordingly, the decision to revise standards must compare the cost of making the revision with the expected benefits in the form of better control and performance evaluation.

Second, variances are not independent of one another. One variance may be directly related to others, either in the same or a different department. (We confronted a similar situation in Chapter 10, where the use of a particular cost-allocation scheme could cause one manager's actions to affect the reported performance of another.) For example, a purchasing manager could buy lower-quality materials at a favorable price. If the materials are hard to work with, labor time increases. Unfavorable labor and variable overhead efficiency variances in processing departments have the same cause as the favorable material price variance—the purchase of the substandard materials. Thus, knowing that there was a variance for some element of cost (materials, labor, or overhead) is not the same as knowing why the variance occurred or which manager was responsible for it.

INVESTIGATING VARIANCES

When variances occur, managers must decide whether (1) the amount of the variance is sufficient to warrant investigation; (2) there is a reasonable probability that finding the cause of the variance will lead to corrective action (some variances are not correctable); and (3) the cost of investigating the cause of the variance and correcting the problem will be less than the cost of a recurrence of the variance. As a general rule, a variance should be investigated if the inquiry is expected to lead to corrective action that will reduce costs by an amount greater than the cost of the inquiry.

Managers want to investigate only significant variances. Two criteria are generally used to evaluate significance: absolute size and percentage of standard cost. A variance of $5 is almost certainly not worth investigating, whereas a variance of $100 might be. If actual cost is $500 and standard cost is $400, the $100 variance is 25% of standard. This large variance percentage might well be worth investigating, whereas a $100 variance from a standard cost of $85,000 is almost certainly not. Thus, absolute size of a variance is probably less important than its percentage of standard cost.

The cost of investigating variances is difficult to determine. Managers with a fixed amount of time to spend on various tasks are wise to concentrate on variances that are likely to be correctable and whose correction may be expected to yield large savings. (There is a significant opportunity cost of managerial time.)

Many companies use **control charts** to decide when a particular variance should be investigated. These charts show past cost behavior patterns so that efforts will not be wasted investigating costs that normally show wide fluctuations. A control chart is shown in Exhibit 12-6.

The dots represent actual costs. The dotted lines represent the limits within which variances are not investigated. The lines could be set closer to or farther away from total standard cost. The closer the limits, the more variances will be investigated, and vice versa. The wide scattering of costs suggests high variances. A manager who believes that the production process is under adequate control and that the variances are unavoidable will set wide limits. A manager who thinks that most variances are caused by correctable factors will set narrow limits. There are many sophisticated ways of developing control charts which are studied in statistics courses.

Exhibit 12-6 Sample Control Chart

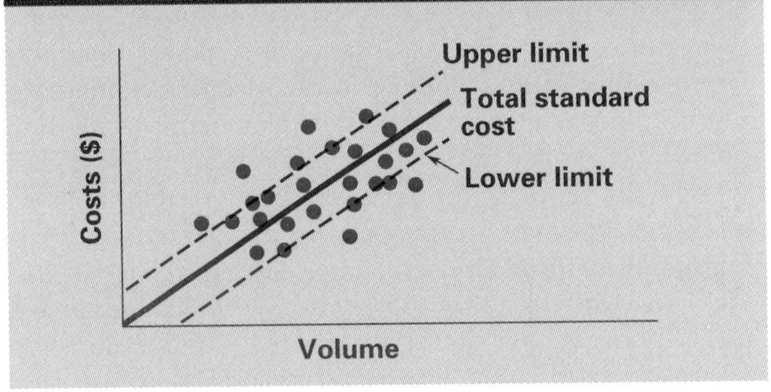

What should *not* be important in deciding whether to investigate a variance is whether the variance is favorable or unfavorable. Managers should avoid the tendency to believe that favorable variances can be left uninvestigated because they indicate that things are going better than expected. As we pointed out in the previous section, variances are not independent; so, a favorable variance in one area of responsibility might have unfavorable effects on another area. Moreover, favorable variances can be caused by actions that could harm the firm in the long run. For example, favorable variances in material prices or labor efficiency could stem from lessened concern for the quality of the finished products. When customers see reduced quality, the reputation and subsequent sales of the firm will be hurt. Short-run profits might increase because of lower costs (favorable variances), but long-run profits may suffer.

Because, as we suggested early in the chapter, standards can be useful for planning, one of the most important reasons for investigating variances is to detect bad standards. Variances can occur because of out-of-date standards. Variances can also result if standards are set at levels that are either too tight or too loose. If standards are used for planning and decision making, they must reflect current information about attainable performance.

SETTING STANDARDS—BEHAVIORAL PROBLEMS

ENGINEERING METHODS

Some companies develop standard quantities for materials and labor by carefully examining production methods and determining how much of an input factor is necessary to obtain a finished unit. In time-and-motion studies, which are often used to set labor standards, an industrial engineer analyzes the movements necessary to perform each task. For example, a worker might have to reach into a bin, pick up a part, place it on the workbench, drill two holes in specified places, then place the part into another bin. Each movement is timed. The total time required to perform the entire task becomes the standard time allowed. Similarly, industrial engineers study the characteristics of the product and its materials to determine how much material is required per unit. (Such studies also determine materials wasted through cutting and trimming.)

Engineering methods are also used to set standards for some overhead items, such as maintenance. Industrial engineers specify the components of a desirable maintenance program and estimate the costs of each component. A standard is then established that allows for specified maintenance expense per machine-hour used, with allowance for other maintenance that occurs because parts break or wear out.

Although some overhead items can be analyzed using engineering methods, it is usually difficult to analyze overhead by starting with a unit of product. Unlike materials and labor, most overhead costs are not directly related to single units of product. Large amounts of overhead are more likely to be related to large quantities of product, labor hours, machine hours or other cost drivers. Therefore, standards for elements of variable overhead are more often developed using the methods illustrated in Chapter 3: high-low, scatter diagram, and regression analysis.

MANAGERIAL ESTIMATES

Some firms rely on the judgment of the managers most closely associated with a task to determine quantities of input needed to produce a unit of product. Such managers understand current production conditions and specifications. This approach to setting standards is advantageous because, as we noted in Chapter 6, when managers participate in setting standards and budgets, they are more likely to commit to meeting them. There is, however, some reluctance to allow managers to set standards without guidance, as some higher-level managers believe that standards set in this way will include unnecessary slack (that is, standards will be too loose). Hence, standards, initially determined by managerial estimates, usually are carefully reviewed at higher levels of management.

However, even companies that can carefully engineer standards rely on the judgment of managers in establishing standards. Manufacturing managers understand that some factors are difficult to capture in engineering analyses. More important, as early as Chapter 6 we noted that managers who participate in setting goals (such as standards) are much more likely to commit themselves to achieving them.

The evidence is persuasive, but not conclusive, that performance also improves when workers participate in setting standards. The general idea of increasing employee involvement in managerial decisions extends to setting standards.

Product designers and managers developing standards should understand that cost reduction is not the only objective. Designing products that will be of high quality and manufacturability are important as well. These facets have become even more important for U.S. companies that want to do business in the European Community. Companies must usually demonstrate that their products meet the criteria of the International Standards Organization (ISO) of Geneva. For example, ISO 9000 requires companies to document each step their workers perform that affects the quality of the product. Companies applying for ISO certification must meet stringent requirements in 20 functional areas, ranging from design to employee training. ISO dispatches independent auditors to verify that companies follow required procedures.[2]

WHAT STANDARD—IDEAL, ATTAINABLE, OR HISTORICAL?

What level of performance ought to be considered in developing a standard? Should the standard be based on what can be done under the best possible conditions? Should it include allowances for waste, fatigue, and bottlenecks—that is, currently attainable performance? Should it be based on past performance, an historical measure?

An **ideal standard** can be attained only under *perfect* conditions. It assumes that laborers continuously work at the peak of their abilities; that materials always arrive at work stations on time; that tools never break; that maintenance on machines never stops production; that no one makes mistakes. In short, an ideal standard is not likely to be achieved under anything like normal working conditions.

2 Business Week, *"You Want EC Business? You Have Two Choices," October 19, 1992, 58.*

Some argue that ideal standards are best because the resulting variances alert managers to deviations from the ideal and motivate workers to do the best possible job. Whether ideal standards really do assist managers in these ways is questionable. Some evidence from the behavioral sciences suggests that motivation is reduced rather than increased by the use of ideal standards. Being unattainable goals, ideal standards can foster discouragement, lack of commitment to the goal, and distrust of higher levels of management. Frustrated managers and workers might even ignore standards they know to be unattainable.

Currently attainable performance as a standard is based on expectations about efficiency under *normal* working conditions. Such a standard allows for unavoidable losses of efficiency due to recurring problems that can never be eliminated. But currently attainable standards are not lax. Performance requirements are high, but they are attainable if everything goes reasonably well.

Research in the behavioral sciences indicates that managers and workers respond well to standards as goals when they have participated in setting the standards *and* when the standards are attainable. Such standards can also be useful for planning, whereas ideal standards cannot. (Managers who use ideal standards must make adjustments to *plan* accurately for expenses, pro forma financial statements, and cash flows.) Additionally, currently attainable standard costs are of more value than ideal standard costs for decision-making purposes. Acceptance of special orders, price reductions or increases, promotional campaigns, and other special decisions must be based on *expected* variable costs, not those that could be obtained only under ideal conditions.

Historical standards are based on experience. Using historical performance as a standard has serious drawbacks. Past inefficiencies are perpetuated as they become built into the standard. Changes in product design and work methods that drastically affect labor and materials requirements might be ignored. Historical achievements have no particular significance *except as they may aid in predicting the future.* (Compare this reservation with those expressed earlier—particularly in Chapters 5, 6, 7, and 11—about the usefulness of historical information for predicting the future.)

STANDARD COSTS AND PRODUCT LIFE CYCLE

It is important to use any managerial tool to its best advantage. Some work well in certain circumstances, poorly in others. One factor affecting how well standard costs are likely to work is the life-cycle stage of the product. Most products begin their lives with rapid sales growth, then mature and have stable sales, and finally decline.

Standard costs and variance analysis work best for mature, stable products such as clothing (except for high-fashion clothing). In the mature stage of product life, when price competition is important, cost control is one of the principal competitive weapons. Low costs allow a company to maintain its margin and to weather poor periods.

Products in growth stages are often highly differentiated and use rapidly changing technology. They compete on style or function, but not on price and the critical success factors are increasing volume and achieving high market share. Margins tend to be high, so that being a low cost producer contributes little to overall profitability.

This is not to say that standard costs have no place with growing products, only that they should not be emphasized at the expense of gaining volume and a secure share of the market.

VARIANCES AND COST CENTERS

Managers of cost centers typically receive reports like the one in Exhibit 12-7. Here, the number of units produced is less than the number budgeted, which could indicate that the manager was ineffective because she or he failed to meet the production goal. But failure to meet the production goal could also have been caused by a problem in a department that had previously worked on the product, in which case *this* manager cannot be held responsible for the shortfall in production. If the production shortfall is the manager's fault, then shortfalls also are likely to appear in any departments that subsequently work on the product. In any case, the cause of the production shortfall must be determined before this manager's performance can be evaluated.

The "actual" costs reported to the manager on the sample report have been adjusted to eliminate price variances. That is, the amounts in the *Actual* column for materials, labor, and supplies are actual quantities multiplied by standard prices. This approach is used when the manager controls only the quantities of each factor used.

Because calculating a variance does not explain its cause, performance reports usually contain a section for comments and explanations of variances. The department manager can then concentrate on those variances that need explanation and, if the cause of the variance is in that department, comment on the prospects for improvement. The sample performance report shows some noncontrollable costs clearly labeled as such and shown separately. Chapter 10 pointed out reasons for doing this.

In general, variable costs are controllable whereas many fixed costs are not, at least over short periods. Allocated costs are not controllable by the department to which they are allocated. Thus, depreciation on equipment in the machining department is direct to the department, but not controllable in the short run.

VARIANCES AND INCOME STATEMENTS

Typically, managers of profit or investment centers receive performance reports that show both revenues and expenses—that is, they receive some type of income statement. A manager responsible for both revenues and costs is concerned with variances related to both aspects of profit. The sample income statement in Exhibit 12-8 shows one format for reporting variances.

Note that the sample report does not show price and use variances separately. This particular income statement is a summary report and would be supported by one or more schedules showing the details of the variances. The number of supporting schedules, and the details on them, depend on

Exhibit 12-7 Departmental Performance Report

Month May 19X7

Department Machining **Manager** R. Jones

Date Delivered 6/4 **Date Returned** 6/6

	Budgeted	*Actual*	*Variance*
Production, in units (original budget 11,000 units)		9,000	2,000
Controllable costs, for actual production of 9,000 units:			
Materials, standard of $2 *	$18,000	$18,800	$800U ①
Labor, standard of $3 *	27,000	28,800	1,800U ①
Supplies, standard of $0.10 *	900	880	20F
Repairs	$1,100	$1,200	$100U
Indirect labor	900	900	0
Total controllable costs	$47,900	$50,580	$2,680U
Noncontrollable costs:			
Depreciation Machinery used in department	$1,500	$1,500	0
Heat and light (allocated)	200	220	20U
Other allocated costs	800	860	60U
Total noncontrollable costs	$2,500	$2,580	$80U
Total costs	$50,400	$53,160	$2,760U

***Actual costs are at standard prices.**

Comments and Explanations

① *Faulty materials required more time and created more waste.*

the level of the manager receiving the report: the higher the level, the less supporting detail. The general manager of a large division of a large company does not need to know about labor variances by cost center, only by plant. The sample report includes a budget variance relating to fixed manufacturing costs. Such variances are, as shown in the next section, identified for reporting purposes and analyzed for possible managerial action.

Exhibit 12-8 Sample Income Statement (thousands of dollars)

Sales		$14,345
Standard variable cost of sales		11,112
Standard variable manufacturing margin		3,233
Variances:		
Materials	$ 89U	
Direct labor	109U	
Variable overhead	6F	
Total		192U
Actual variable manufacturing margin		3,041
Variable selling and administrative expenses		871
Contribution margin		2,170
Fixed costs:		
Budgeted fixed manufacturing costs	1,045	
Budget variance—fixed manufacturing costs	15U	
Selling and administrative expenses	554	
Total fixed costs		1,614
Income		$ 556

One point that might not be obvious from the sample income statement is the difference in the quantity measures used for cost of sales and for calculating variances. Standard variable cost of sales is based on the number of units sold. On the other hand, variances are computed on the basis of the number of units produced. We shall see more income statements of this type in Chapter 14.

CONTROL OF FIXED COSTS

We know from earlier discussions that total cost per unit of product changes with a change in production because there is a fixed component in the total cost. As we discuss in Chapters 13 and 14, companies use per-unit fixed costs, including standard fixed costs, for product costing purposes. But for *control* purposes, the notion of a standard fixed cost per unit has little meaning. The total cost incurred for each element of fixed overhead is more relevant.

Fixed overhead includes many components, such as depreciation, property taxes, supervisory and managerial salaries, and the fixed components of mixed costs, such as maintenance and power. Each item is budgeted separately for the department that controls it.

There are two fixed cost variances. For the current purpose, the question of cost control, only the budget variance requires comment. The other variance is described in Chapter 14.

BUDGET VARIANCE

The **fixed overhead budget variance** is the difference between actual and budgeted fixed cost and is computed for each element of cost for a particular department. Budget variances occur for many reasons. There may have been changes in the prices for resources (a raise in salaries, an increase in property taxes); some discretionary costs, such as employee training or travel, might have been increased or decreased by managerial action; and quantities of resources used might have been greater or less than budgeted, as when more or fewer janitors were hired than were budgeted.

The major considerations in analyzing fixed cost budget variances are behavioral. Managers who are worried about exceeding their budget might postpone discretionary costs (such as employee training). On the other hand, managers might incur unnecessary costs if they fear that being below budget this period will lead to a budget cut for the next period.

Managers can manipulate some discretionary costs to achieve low *total* budget variances (total fixed costs incurred less total fixed costs budgeted). Focusing only on totals can obscure critical problems. Managers who scrimp on employee training or maintenance are improving short-run performance to the detriment of the long run. This type of undesirable action might escape notice if only the totals were considered.

There are different philosophies about budgeting fixed costs. There are advocates of tight budgets, loose budgets, and budgets based on currently attainable performance levels. Our preference is for the use of currently attainable budgets, with the persons whose budgets are being set participating in the determination of what is currently attainable. Likewise, the methods used in setting standard variable costs—historical analysis, engineering methods, and managerial judgment—can also be applied to the budgeting of fixed costs.

FIXED COSTS ON PERFORMANCE REPORTS

The cost-center performance report shown in Exhibit 12-7 does not distinguish between controllable variable costs and controllable fixed costs. Whereas materials and direct labor are usually variable, the other controllable items could be variable, fixed, or mixed. Exhibit 12-9 separates controllable costs into their fixed and variable components.

For planning, the manager wants to know whether a variance is likely to recur. It might be easier to plan for future variances if the fixed and variable controllable costs are separated. If a fixed cost is running $1,000 per month more or less than budgeted, and this variance is expected to continue, the manager can count on the variance being $1,000 per month. A direct labor efficiency variance of 10% of standard cost will be a different dollar amount in each month, depending on production. Thus, planning for future operations requires different analyses for the two kinds of costs—fixed and variable.

A PROBLEM AREA—SEPARATING FIXED AND VARIABLE COSTS

Some companies cannot determine separate budget variance for variable overhead and fixed overhead because they cannot determine how much of

Exhibit 12-9 Departmental Performance Report

Month May 19X7

Department Machining — Manager R. Jones

Date Delivered 6/4 — Date Returned 6/6

	Budgeted	Actual	Variance
Production, in units (original budget 11,000 units)		9,000	2,000
Controllable costs, for actual production of 9,000 units:			
Variable:			
Materials, standard of $2 *	$18,000	$18,800	$800U ①
Labor, standard of $3 *	27,000	28,800	1,800U ①
Supplies, standard of $0.10 *	900	880	20F
Total variable costs	$45,900	$48,480	$2,580U
Fixed:			
Repairs	$1,100	$1,200	$100U
Indirect labor	900	900	0
Total fixed costs	$2,000	$2,100	$100U
Total controllable costs	$47,900	$50,580	$2,680U
Noncontrollable costs:			
Depreciation Machinery used in department	$1,500	$1,500	0
Heat and light (allocated)	200	220	20U
Other allocated costs	800	860	60U
Total noncontrollable costs	$2,500	$2,580	$80U
Total costs	$50,400	$53,160	$2,760U

*Actual costs are at standard prices.

Comments and Explanations

① *Faulty materials required more time and created more waste.*

the *actual* overhead cost incurred is fixed and how much is variable. For example, a cost like electricity usually has both a fixed and a variable component. But it might not be possible to determine how much of the actual cost relates to the fixed component and how much to the variable component.

Suppose that electricity is budgeted using the following formula: Total cost = \$2,450 + (\$0.80 × machine hours). The fixed portion is for lighting; the variable portion is for machinery that is operated only when products are being made. Assume that the standard and actual cost per kilowatt-hour is \$0.03. Any difference between actual electricity cost and the flexible budget amount must then be caused by the quantity of electricity used. But, the firm's managers cannot tell how much electricity was used for machinery (the variable portion) and how much for other purposes (the fixed portion) unless there are separate meters for the machinery.

For a particular month, suppose that the standard machine hours per unit are two, production was 4,000 units, 8,100 machine hours were used (100 hours over standard), and actual electricity cost was \$9,210. The total standard hours allowed for production of 4,000 units are 8,000 (4,000 × 2). The total budgeted cost for electricity is \$8,850 [\$2,450 + (\$0.80 × 8,000 standard machine hours)]. Because we cannot, in the absence of separate meters, analyze the actual cost into its fixed and variable components, we cannot calculate separately the budget variances for the fixed and variable elements. In such cases, most firms calculate a single budget variance for the mixed cost as a whole. If we use the data in our example, the budget variance is

$$\begin{aligned} \textit{Total budget variance} &= \textit{actual cost} - \textit{flexible budget based on input} \\ &= \$9{,}210 - [(\$0.80 \times 8{,}100) + \$2{,}450] \\ &= \$9{,}210 - \$8{,}930 \\ &= \$280 \textit{ unfavorable variance} \end{aligned}$$

The variance is unfavorable because actual cost exceeds the budget allowance. We also know that actual machine hours were 100 over standard, so we know there is an \$80 unfavorable variable overhead efficiency variance.

Why might a firm not isolate the fixed and variable components of the actual cost? Why, for example, would the firm in the preceding example not install meters on its machines in order to determine how much electricity is related to machines and how much to lighting the factory? As stated in Chapter 10, the answer is usually that the cost to obtain the additional information exceeds the benefits. In this instance, the cost to install and maintain the meters might exceed the savings that could be achieved through better control. A fundamental principle of managerial accounting is that obtaining additional information is desirable only if the benefits exceed the costs.

STANDARD COSTS AND PERFORMANCE MEASURES IN JIT MANUFACTURING

Historically, conventional manufacturers have paid considerable attention to labor variances because direct labor was a significant proportion of total manufacturing cost and also drove much overhead cost. Today, direct labor is much less important, being about 10% to 20% of total manufacturing cost in many companies. Nor does direct labor drive as much overhead cost as it once did. Direct labor can be as little as 3%-5% of total cost in JIT operations and receives correspondingly less attention.

If overhead is based on direct labor, idle time of workers will be reflected in unfavorable labor efficiency variances and variable overhead efficiency variances. Some managers argue that labor efficiency variances can work against goal congruence because they encourage overproduction and the consequent build-up of inventory to keep workers busy. Moreover, many managers believe that reporting labor efficiency variances detracts from the main objective of rapid, smooth throughput of high-quality products. Some companies using JIT operations believe that the very idea of standards and standard costs conflicts with the JIT philosophy. They argue that standards stifle improvement because people who are given standards strive to meet them, which contrasts with the JIT principle of continual improvement. They also argue that variances concentrate on cost centers, small units in the company, whereas JIT operations emphasize factory-wide performance, preferring not to focus on individual areas.

Despite the reservations, some companies using JIT operations do use standards and variances much as do companies using conventional operations. Others use standards, but continually raise them to encourage improvement. JIT operations that do not use standards compare current period actual costs with prior period actual costs (or an average of actual costs for the past few periods) to gauge their improvement. Such comparisons are similar to variance calculations, with the prior period costs acting as the "standard."

Managers of JIT operations use many nonfinancial measures to evaluate performance. Measures used instead of, or along with, standard costs, include the following:

1. *Supplies of inventories* You already know that companies try to keep inventories low because they are costly to carry. Such measures as turnover and days supply of inventory help managers judge how efficiently they are operating. Inventory supply is often expressed as turnover, which is the days supply divided into 360 (or 365). Thus, a 10-day supply is the same as a turnover of 36 times. A company that can manufacture its products with only a 4-day supply of materials and components is doing better than one that requires a 12-day supply to keep its production lines running.
2. *Cycle time* This is the total time a company takes from receiving a customer's order through making the product, and shipping it to the customer. Time spent making the product is *value-adding time*, while the rest of the cycle time is not value-adding. So the closer cycle time is to manufacturing time, the less non-value-adding time.
3. *Setup time* This is the time it takes to change over from making one product to making another. Setting up is a non-value adding activity.
4. *Percentage of deliveries to customers made on-time* This indicates how well the company is meeting its commitments to customers.
5. *Quality measures* There are many ways to assess and measure quality. Some common ways are the percentage of defective units, number of warranty claims or customer complaints, and number of units reworked.
6. *Throughput measures* These indicate how much work a cell, a department, or an entire factory is doing. Measures of throughput include number of units finished, number of units finished divided by processing time available, and value-adding time divided by total time.

These measures, as well as others, are consistent with the objectives of JIT manufacturing. They can also be used by conventional manufacturers. AT&T's New River Valley Works utilizes the JIT philosophy with several product lines. A partial list of performance measures used on its Communications Transformer Line appears below.[3]

Measure	Goal
Number of defectives	0
Percentage of orders shipped on-time	100%
Manufacturing interval (cycle time)	5 hours
Supply of inventories	0.5 days
Cost of scrap	$1,500
Scrap as a percentage of output	1%
Number of line disruptions	0
Percentage of people cross-trained to do more than one job	100%

The plant is further along toward achieving some goals than others. We said earlier that people given ideal standards might not be motivated to work to achieve them. In a JIT environment, goals are not used as standards for monthly achievement, but rather as pinnacles of success.

Another study of measures of operating performance found the following measures, and percentages of companies using each.

Measure	Percentage using
Inventory supply	75%
Labor efficiency	73%
Physical scrap counts	72%
Cost of rework	72%
Materials use	61%
Customer delivery performance	55%
Machine utilization percentage	54%
Machine downtime	48%
Throughput rates	46%
Warranty costs	38%

The author found it interesting that so many companies tracked labor efficiency because, on average, labor costs for the companies were only 13% of total manufacturing cost.[4]

The emphasis that advanced manufacturers place on worker development benefits workers as well as companies. Because many foreign countries have lower wage rates than the U.S., U.S. companies will not be able to compete without upgrading worker skills. For example, Levi Strauss, maker of Levi's, now uses teams to produce an entire garment, replacing an assembly line where each worker did only a small part of the work. The company

3 *F. B. Green, Felix Amenkhienan, and George Johnson, "Performance Measures and JIT,"* Management Accounting, *February, 1991, 34.*

4 *James A. Hendricks, "Applying Cost Accounting to Factory Automation,"* Management Accounting, *December, 1988, 24.*

cut cycle time from six days to seven hours, so the company can switch products quickly and respond better to customer needs. Defects also dropped when the workers took over production of the entire garment.[5]

STANDARDS IN MULTIPRODUCT COMPANIES

So far we have dealt with companies making a single product. Multiproduct companies can also use standard costs. No conceptual problems are introduced simply because a company makes more than one product, but a practical question arises about the extent to which detailed information should be produced and the cost of obtaining the additional information.

Although it is seldom a problem for a multiproduct firm to develop standard costs, it can be difficult, even impossible, to isolate variances by product if the products are manufactured using the same facilities and the same workers, and the company cannot determine the *actual* use of materials and labor or machine time for *each* product. That is, the costs of materials and labor are traceable to production as a whole, but it might be very costly or impossible to keep track of materials and direct labor time used to make each product. In such cases, variances relate to all products as a group. It is desirable to keep track of materials and direct labor by product only if the cost of obtaining the information is less than the potential benefits of having that information.

Despite the difficulties of obtaining information about the actual costs of individual products, managers are interested in knowing such costs for planning and decision making. As a practical matter, a firm might occasionally keep track of materials and labor by product as a check on the standards. In addition, managers might suspect inappropriate standards and undertake an investigation if product mix appears to influence efficiency variances.

STANDARD COSTS FOR NONMANUFACTURING ACTIVITIES

Some firms have developed standard costs for nonmanufacturing activities. These activities have certain traits that render the development of standard costs difficult. For example, measuring output in nonmanufacturing activities is difficult. Rarely do homogeneous physical units flow out of the work done by the product design, legal, accounting, marketing, and general administration departments. There is seldom a definable measure of output because there is no standard product.

Costs associated with administrative work also tend to be more fixed than those of manufacturing. Consequently, it might be impossible to develop standard variable costs per unit of output even if an appropriate unit of output could be found. Therefore, administrative activities are usually controlled by static budgets, rather than by standard variable costs. Thus, the earlier discussion on control of fixed costs is applicable to nonmanufacturing activities, but the discussion on standard variable costs usually is not.

---

5 *"The Global Economy: Who Gets Hurt?"* Business Week, *August 10, 1992, 48.*

The difficulties notwithstanding, there have been and will continue to be attempts to develop standards for nonmanufacturing activities. For example, the number of typing strokes per page has been standardized by some organizations, as have the number of files processed and the number of books shelved. This is a challenging and important area of managerial accounting.

SUMMARY

Standard costs are a tool for planning, control, and evaluation of cost centers. Managers of cost centers, and their managers, receive information showing the efficiency of the operation.

The standard for each major element of product cost (materials, labor, and overhead) is a combination of two separate standards: one for the quantity of the factor used in the product, the other for the price of a unit of that factor. The total variance between budgeted and actual cost can be analyzed into one related to a difference in price and another related to a difference in the quantity of the factor used. Since a single manager is not usually responsible for both prices of resources and the quantity of resources used, separating total variances into price and use components assists in assigning responsibility. The separation is also helpful in planning future operations.

Because interdependencies exist among managerial functions, variances shown on the performance report for a manager cannot automatically be attributed to the good or bad performance of that manager. The causes of variances are not always easy to determine and include poor management in the department showing the variance or poor management in an entirely different department. The cause could also be a bad standard. JIT manufacturing might use other measures to evaluate operations.

KEY TERMS

control charts
currently attainable performance
fixed overhead budget variance
historical standards
ideal standard
labor efficiency variance
labor rate variance
material price variance
material use variance
standard cost
variable overhead budget (spending) variance
variable overhead efficiency variance
variances

KEY FORMULAS

$$\text{Total standard cost for input factor} = \text{actual production} \times \text{standard quantity of input factor per unit of production} \times \text{standard rate for input factor per unit of input}$$

$$\text{Actual cost for input factor} = \text{actual input quantity} \times \text{actual rate for input factor}$$

$$\text{Price variance} = \text{actual quantity of input acquired} \times \left(\text{standard price per unit of input} - \text{actual price per unit of input}\right)$$

$$\text{Quantity variance} = \text{standard price per unit of input} \times \left(\text{standard quantity of input required} - \text{actual quantity of input used}\right)$$

REVIEW PROBLEM

Baldwin Company makes cabinets. One model, the Deluxe, has the following requirements.

Materials	44 feet of wood at $0.20 per foot
Direct labor	4 hours at $7 per hour
Variable overhead	$5 per direct labor hour

During June 19X4 the firm made 1,200 Deluxe cabinets. Operating results were

Materials purchases	58,000 feet at $0.19	$11,020
Materials used	53,200 feet	
Direct labor	4,750 hours at $7.10	$33,725
Variable overhead		$23,900

Required
Compute the standard variable cost per Deluxe cabinet and the variances for June 19X4.

ANSWER TO REVIEW PROBLEM

Standard Variable Cost	
Materials (44 feet of wood at $0.20)	$ 8.80
Direct labor (4 hours at $7 per hour)	28.00
Variable overhead at $5 per direct labor hour	20.00
Total standard variable cost	$56.80

Materials Variances for June 19X4

Actual Cost of Materials Purchased		Budgeted Cost for 58,000 Feet
$0.19 × 58,000		$0.20 × 58,000
$11,020		$11,600
	$580 favorable material price variance	

Alternatively, 58,000 × ($0.20 – $0.19) = $580 favorable.

Budgeted Cost of Materials Used		Budgeted Cost for 1,200 Units
$0.20 × 53,200		$8.80 × 1,200
$10,640		$10,560
	$80 unfavorable material use variance	

Alternatively, $0.20 × [(1,200 × 44) – 53,200] = $80 unfavorable.

Labor Variances for June 19X4

Direct Labor Cost Incurred	Budgeted Cost for 4,750 Hours	Budgeted Cost for 1,200 Units
4,750 × $7.10	4,750 × $7	1,200 × $28
$33,725	$33,250	$33,600
$475 unfavorable labor rate variance		$350 favorable labor efficiency variance
	$125 unfavorable total labor variance	

Alternatively, the labor rate variance is:

4,750 × ($7 – $7.10) = –$475 unfavorable

The labor efficiency variance is:

$7 × [(1,200 × 4) – 4,750] = $7 × (4,800 – 4,750) = $350 favorable

Variable Overhead Variances

Actual Variable Overhead Incurred	Budgeted Variable Overhead for 4,750 Hours	Budgeted Variable Overhead for 1,200 Units
	4,750 × $5	1,200 × $20
$23,900	$23,750	$24,000
$150 unfavorable budget variance		$250 favorable efficiency variance
	$100 favorable total variance	

Alternatively, the budget variance could be computed by calculating the actual rate of about $5.032, subtracting it from the standard rate of $5, then multiplying by 4,750 hours.

4,750 × ($5 – $5.032) = –$152 unfavorable (difference due to rounding)

The efficiency variance is also given by:

$5 × (4,800 – 4,750) = $250 favorable

Note that because the variable overhead standard is based on direct labor hours, the only difference between the computation of the labor efficiency variance and the variable overhead efficiency variance is the rate used.

ASSIGNMENT MATERIAL

QUESTIONS FOR DISCUSSION

12-1 Budgeting and standards Budgeting aids managers in planning and control. Standard costs are useful for assisting in budgeting and for planning and control in general. What does the use of standard costs accomplish that budgeting does not?

12-2 Interpretation of variances For each of the following situations (a) indicate whether a variance is likely to occur; (b) state which variance(s) might be affected and in what direction; and (c) state whether an investigation should be undertaken and whether corrective action could be taken.

1. Wage rates have risen because a new union contract has been signed.
2. To increase safety, the plant manager has reduced the speeds at which forklifts carrying materials and semifinished products can be driven.
3. The firm sells its waste materials, chiefly metals, to a scrap dealer. Lately, revenue from waste sales has increased, while production has been steady.
4. Exceptionally heavy rainfall necessitates the drying out of materials that are stored outside.
5. The electric utility that supplies the company has been having difficulty with its generators. There are frequent blackouts and brownouts.
6. Many part-time workers are hired because of increases in production.

12-3 Revising standards State whether each of the following events calls for revising standards and, if so, which standard(s). If possible, state the direction of the revision. Assume that currently attainable performance is the basis for all standards.

1. Complaints from customers about dullness of a metallic finish on the product have induced the production manager to assign a worker to buff the surface.
2. The labor efficiency variance has consistently been unfavorable by 2% to 4%.
3. A new material that is more expensive than the old is being used. However, there is less waste and it is easier to handle.
4. The product is a wooden cabinet. Previously, a number of parts of the cabinet had been nailed together. Now those parts are being screwed together.
5. A strike at a supplier's plant has forced the purchase of some materials at higher prices from other sources.
6. Electricity rates have increased. The plant uses a great deal of electricity for machinery.
7. An overhead crane has been installed to speed the movement of semifinished product from one work station to another.

12-4 Effects of changed conditions Each of the following describes a change that occurred after standards had been set for the period and then lists three of the variances that were discussed in the chapter. For each item, select the variance most likely to be affected by the change and explain your choice.

1. To meet a shortage of workers in the face of a steady demand for the product, the firm decided to hire less experienced workers than it hired in the past.

   Variances: Material price variance, labor rate variance, labor efficiency variance.

2. Faced with the prospect of a shortage of the firm's normal materials, the firm decides to use a new, more expensive material that produces less waste and is easier to handle.

Variances: Labor rate variance, variable overhead budget variance, variable overhead efficiency variance.

3. Based on a suggestion from a worker, the process for assembling certain parts of the final product has been changed so that a single employee assembles six components. Before the change, two employees of the same department worked independently to assemble three components each and a third employee in that department put together the subassemblies produced by those two employees.

   Variances: Material use variance, labor efficiency variance, variable overhead spending variance.

12-5 Setting standards The controller of a large manufacturing company said: "In our company the standard cost is the true cost; actual cost is simply an aberration from true cost." Speculate on how the standards might have been set.

12-6 Responsibility for variances (CMA adapted) Phillips Company uses a standard cost system. Variances for each department are calculated and reported to the department manager. Reporting has two major purposes: evaluating performance, and improving operations.

Jack Smith was recently appointed manager of the Assembly Department. He has complained that the system does not work properly and discriminates against his department because of the current practice of calculating a variance for rejected units. The procedures for making this calculation are as follows: (1) all units are inspected at the end of the assembly operation; (2) rejected units are examined to see if the cause of rejection can be assigned to a particular department; (3) units that are rejected but cannot be identified with a particular department are totaled; (4) the unidentifiable rejects are apportioned to each department on the basis of the identifiable rejects. Thus, if a department had 20% of the identified rejects, it will also be charged with 20% of the unidentified rejects. The variance, then, is the sum of the identifiable rejects and the apportioned share of unidentified rejects.

Required

Write a memorandum to Henry Santos, Smith's supervisor, evaluating the validity of Smith's claim and making a recommendation for resolving the problem.

12-7 Significance of variances Ann Jackson, controller of Stone Company, was recently told by several production managers that "as long as total costs do not exceed budgeted costs, based on standard prices and quantities, there is no reason to do any investigating or analysis."

Required

Comment critically on the statement. Cite at least two reasons for rejecting it.

EXERCISES

12-8 Standard cost computations Blivet Company makes a plastic deck chair. It has established the standard prices and quantities for a finished unit as follows:

Materials	4 pounds at $1 per pound
Direct labor	3 hours at $8 per hour
Variable overhead	$6 per direct labor hour (DLH)

Blivet also has fixed overhead of $100,000 per year.

Required

Fill in the blanks in the following items.

1. The standard cost per unit of finished product is
   (a) _______ for materials.
   (b) _______ for direct labor.
   (c) _______ for variable overhead.
2. At 70,000 direct labor hours, total variable overhead cost should be _____.
3. At 90,000 direct labor hours, production should be _____ units.
4. If 100,000 pounds of materials are used, production should be _____ units.
5. At 60,000 direct labor hours, total materials used should be _____ pounds.
6. If 66,000 pounds of materials are used, total variable overhead cost should be _____ and total labor cost should be _____.

12-9 Fundamentals of standard costs and variances Bryant Company manufactures decorative statues. Each statue requires 20 pounds of special clay and two labor hours. The standard price of clay is $3 per pound. The standard direct labor rate is $9 per hour and the standard variable overhead rate is $6 per direct labor hour.

During November, Bryant manufactured 1,000 statues. It bought 25,000 pounds of clay for $71,800 and used 22,000 pounds. Bryant paid direct laborers $17,200 for 1,900 hours and incurred $12,500 in variable overhead.

Required

1. Determine the standard variable cost of a statue.
2. Determine all variable cost variances.

12-10 Basic material and labor variances Fergon Company makes a lamp shade and had the following budgeted and actual results in December.

	Budget	Actual
Unit production	10,000	11,000
Direct labor hours	20,000	21,700
Materials used, yards	40,000	43,200

The standard labor rate is $10 per hour, standard materials price is $2 per yard.

Required

Calculate the direct labor efficiency variance and the material use variance.

12-11 Basic variance relationships, materials Fill in the following blanks. You can work them in order, but you do not have to.

Standard materials cost per unit of product	$ 20
Material use variance	$ 2,000F
Standard material use for quantity produced, in pounds	23,600
Number of pounds of materials purchased	30,000
Material price variance	$ 3,000U
Standard price per pound of materials	$ 5
Standard pounds of materials per unit of product	_____
Units produced	_____
Number of pounds of materials used	_____
Amount paid for materials purchased	_____

12-12 ***Ethics and overhead assignment*** Ben Grayson, manager of a product line at FGH industries, was complaining about the calculation of standard costs. "My line has only three products. They are very simple and require no machine setups, no special quality control, little machine time, only direct labor and three or four kinds of materials. But some of the other lines we carry have products that require all manner of setup time, extra record keeping, more vendor analysis because they have many more materials and components. Most of them are also machine-intensive. It's just not fair for them to bear overhead based only on direct labor. I've talked to the controller, but she just tells me to do my job and she'll do hers."

Required

Comment on Grayson's complaints. Is the controller abiding by the IMA Standards reproduced in Exhibit 1-3? If not, why not?

12-13 ***Variance computations*** Below are the standard variable costs for one of Halsey Knitting's sweaters, the Highlander.

Materials, 2 pounds of yarn at $6 per pound	$12
Labor, 2 hours of labor at $8 per hour	16
Variable overhead, $3 per labor hour	6
	$34

Actual results in March follow.

Production	1,000 sweaters
Materials purchased and used	1,900 pounds for $12,100
Hours of labor worked	2,100 hours
Cost of labor	$16,300
Variable overhead incurred	$ 6,500

Required

Compute all variable cost variances.

12-14 *Comprehensive variance analysis* 4N Company makes industrial cleaners. Standard costs for Scumaway appear below, along with actual results for March.

Materials, 3 pounds at $4 per pound	$12
Direct labor at $10 per hour	30
Variable overhead at $6 per DLH	18
Total standard variable cost	$60

Actual results for March:

1. Production was 1,200 units.
2. Materials purchased were 3,200 pounds at $3.90 per pound.
3. The firm used 3,620 pounds of materials in production.
4. Direct laborers worked 3,800 hours at $10.10, earning $38,380.
5. Variable overhead was $22,000.

Required

Compute all variable cost variances.

12-15 *Evaluation in JIT manufacturing* Baskin Products recently implemented JIT principles and its controller is having difficulty in analyzing performance. She has collected the following statistics and asks you to tell her how each could help evaluate performance in the two months.

	July	September
Average processing time, hours	40	37
Average cycle time, days	31	24
Production, units	7,300	7,150
Maximum capacity, units	7,800	7,800
Defective units	91	67
Inventory of materials, days' supply	6	4
Inventory of in-process goods, days' supply	8	6
Inventory of finished goods, days' supply	3	4

Required

Use the data above to describe where Baskin is improving and where it is not. You might wish to calculate some ratios using these raw numbers.

12-16 *Revision of standard costs* Clarkson Company manufactures toys. One group of toys consists of small cars, each of which requires the same quantities of materials and direct labor. The cars are packaged and sold in batches of 50. The standard variable cost of a batch is given below.

Materials	$10.00
Direct labor (4 hours)	16.00
Variable overhead	12.00
Total standard variable cost	$38.00

The production supervisor is uncertain how to prepare the budget for the coming year. He tells you the following.

(a) Materials costs will be an average of 20% higher because of price increases.
(b) Laborers will get a 5% raise at the beginning of the year.
(c) Increased efficiency will reduce direct labor hours by 10%.
(d) The variable overhead rate will increase to $3.40 per direct labor hour.

Required

Prepare revised standard variable costs.

12-17 Relationships—labor variances Each of the independent situations given below relates to direct labor. Fill in the blanks.

	a	b	c	d
Units produced	2,000	______	3,000	______
Actual hours worked	4,800	4,200	______	______
Standard hours for production achieved	5,000	______	______	6,000
Standard hours per unit	______	0.5	2	3
Standard rate per hour	$ 6	$ 10	$ 4	______
Actual labor cost	______	$ 41,800	______	$ 24,500
Rate variance	$ 310U	______	$ 300U	$ 300F
Efficiency variance	______	$ 1,000U	$ 600F	$ 800U

12-18 Variance analysis Kuhn Car Products makes automobile antifreeze. Kuhn has developed the following formula for budgeting monthly factory overhead costs. Total overhead cost = $140,000 + ($10 × direct labor hours). Other data relating to the cost of a case of the product are given below.

Materials	4 gallons at $1.50 per gallon
Direct labor	20 minutes at $10 per hour

Last month Kuhn produced 12,000 cases and had the following costs.

Materials purchased	49,000 gallons	$ 73,000
Materials used	51,200 gallons	
Direct labor	3,920 hours	$ 38,750
Overhead		$188,500

Required

Compute the price and quantity variances for materials and direct labor and the total variance for overhead.

12-19 Performance reporting Paul Dickens, the president of your company, has asked you to investigate some unfavorable variances that occurred in one of the departments last month. You were given the following summary of the department's performance report.

	Budget	Actual	Variance
Production (in units)	2,000	2,500	500F
Costs (based on budgeted production):			
Direct labor	$6,000	$7,000	$1,000U
Supplies	400	650	250U
Repairs	1,000	1,200	200U
Power	800	1,100	300U
Total costs (all variable)	$8,200	$9,950	$1,750U

Required

1. Was performance poor?
2. Write a memorandum to Mr. Dickens recommending changes in the company's reporting.

12-20 ***Variances—relationships among costs*** Read the following in its entirety and then fill in the blanks.

1. Standard variable costs per unit:		
(a) Materials	4 pounds @ $____	$______
(b) Direct labor	____ hours @ $6.00	$12.00
(c) Variable overhead	$3 per DLH	$______
2. Production		8,000 units
3. Materials purchases	33,000 pounds	$62,000
4. Materials used, at standard prices	31,200 pounds	$______
5. Direct labor, actual	____ hours	$80,800
6. Material price variance		$ 4,000F
7. Material use variance		$______
8. Direct labor rate variance		$ 3,200F
9. Direct labor efficiency variance		$______
10. Variable overhead spending variance		$ 1,200U
11. Variable overhead efficiency variance		$______
12. Variable overhead, actual		$______

12-21 ***Standards—machine-hour basis*** Wilkens Company is highly automated and uses machine-hours to set standard variable costs. A unit requires two pounds of material costing $6 per pound and 12 minutes of machine time. The standard variable overhead rate is $10 per machine-hour. There is no direct labor; all workers are classified as indirect labor, and their wages are considered part of variable overhead.

During June, 23,000 units were produced using 5,200 machine-hours. Variable overhead costs were $50,300. Purchases of materials were 54,000 pounds for $318,000 and 45,000 pounds were used.

Required

1. Compute the standard variable cost of a unit of product.
2. Compute the variances for June.

PROBLEMS

12-22 ***Standards in a service function*** Graham Labs performs blood tests for local physicians. Dr. Graham, head of the company, has instituted a standard cost system to help control costs and measure employee efficiency. After extensive consultations with his employees, he developed the following standards for some high-volume tests.

Test	Standard Time (in minutes)
Blood sugar	12
Cell count	10
Others	6

The company's 12 lab technicians earn an average of $11 per hour, with a range of $10.25 to $11.50. During July, the first month the system was in effect, the lab had the following results.

Test	Number Performed
Blood sugar	4,500
Cell count	2,300
Others	5,400

Lab technicians earned $20,300 for 1,780 hours.

Required

Determine the labor rate variance and labor efficiency variance.

12-23 Investigation of variances The production manager of Knowles Company tells you that she exercises management by exception. She examines a performance report and calls for further analysis and investigation if a variance is greater than 10% of total standard cost or is more than $1,000. She is not responsible for any rate or price variances and is therefore concerned only with efficiency variances. During April, the following occurred.

1. Materials used: 4,520 gallons
2. Direct labor hours: 7,850
3. Production: 2,000 units

The standard cost of a unit is as follows.

Materials (2 gallons at $4)	$ 8
Direct labor (4 hours at $8)	32
Variable overhead ($6 per DLH)	24
Total standard variable cost	$64

Required

1. Compute the variances for which the production manager should be held responsible.
2. Determine which variances should be investigated according to her criteria.

12-24 Determining a base for cost standards The production manager of Wingate Company recently performed a study to see how many units of product could be made by a worker who had no interruptions, always had materials available as needed, made no errors, and worked at peak speed. He found that a worker could make 20 units in an hour under these ideal conditions. In the past, about 15 units per hour was the actual average output. However, some new materials handling equipment had recently been purchased and the manager is confident that an average of 18 units per hour could be achieved by nearly all workers.

All workers are paid $12 per hour. A month after the study was made, workers were paid $960,000 for 80,000 hours. Production was 1,410,000 units.

Required

1. Compute the standard labor cost per unit to the nearest $0.001 based on
   (a) historical performance
   (b) ideal performance
   (c) currently attainable performance
2. Compute the labor efficiency variance under each of the standards in item 1 and comment on the results.
3. Write a short memo to Barbara Wright, the production manager, stating which method of setting the standard you prefer for planning purposes and for control purposes.

12-25 Investigation of variances The supervisor of the Stamping Department is pleased with her performance this past month, which showed a favorable material use variance of $1,000. The following data relate to the stamping operation.

Units produced	2,000
Standard costs for materials:	
Libidinum, 3 pounds at $3	$ 9
Larezium, 2 pounds at $4	8
Total standard materials cost	$ 17

The operation used 5,000 pounds of libidinum and 4,500 pounds of larezium.

Required

1. Verify the amount of the material use variance.
2. Did the supervisor do a good job this month? What questions must be answered before coming to a conclusion about the manager's performance?

12-26 Determining standard costs Vernon Company makes its single product, Shine, by mixing the materials Dull and Buff in 500-pound batches in a 3:2 ratio (three pounds of Dull for each two pounds of Buff). The mixing is done by two laborers and takes three hours. The resulting mixture is boiled for four hours, which requires four workers. The mixture that comes out of the boiler yields four pounds of finished product for each five pounds of raw material, so that the 500 pounds of material mixed become 400 pounds of final product. (Evaporation during boiling reduces the volume.)

All laborers earn $6 per hour. Variable overhead is $3 per direct labor hour. Dull costs $2.80 per pound; Buff costs $2 per pound.

Required

Determine the standard variable cost per pound of Shine.

12-27 Standards and variances, two products Bascomb Company makes two coffee tables. Both go through essentially the same process, and the company does not keep records regarding the amounts of materials and labor used in making each model, only for the two models as a whole. Standard cost data are:

	Harcombe	Exeter
Materials:		
2 pounds at $4 per pound	$ 8	
3 pounds at $4 per pound		$12
Direct labor	16	24
Variable overhead	12	18
Total standard costs	$36	$54

All direct laborers earn $8 per hour, and the variable overhead rate is $6 per direct labor hour. The same materials are used in both models.

During March, the company had the following results.

Production	2,000 Harcombe, 1,500 Exeter
Materials purchased	9,000 pounds at $4.15 per pound
Materials used	8,900 pounds
Direct labor	8,750 hours at $7.95 per hour
Variable overhead	$55,500

Required

1. Compute all variable cost variances for production as a whole.
2. Can you compute variances for each model? If not, why not? Explain why you might want to isolate variances to the individual models?

12-28 Overhead rates, ABC, and pricing Darlene Bhada, controller of TGF Industries, was discussing the company's most recent operating results with Jill Simmons, the sales manager. Both were disappointed because a downward trend in profit was accelerating, even though sales were remaining about the same. Simmons said "Our major line is selling poorly because our competitors are undercutting our prices. I don't see how they do it! We have cut prices down to the bone. Fortunately, some of our minor lines are doing very well." Bhada replied that "The problem could be with our costs. Look at the standards for these representative products from the major line and one of the minor lines."

	Major Product	Minor Product
Materials	$25	$ 45
Direct labor at $12/hour	24	24
Variable overhead at $15/DLH	30	30
Total standard variable cost	$79	$ 99
Annual volume	80,000	4,000
Selling price	$90	$140

Bhada continued, "We have been revising our overhead rate by looking at the requirements of each product. I have divided our variable overhead costs into three pools and developed variable rates for each. My chief accountant has collected data for each product." The data Bhada referred to appear below.

Driver for Cost Pool	Variable Rate	Major Product	Minor Product
Direct labor	$2.00/DLH	2 DLH	2 DLH
Machine setups	$6/setup	1 setups	7 setups
Number of parts	$0.50/part	8 parts	18 parts

"Perhaps," Bhada went on, "we can get a better idea of our costs by incorporating this new information."

Required

1. Develop standard variable costs using the new information.
2. Write a memorandum to Ms. Bhada explaining the differences between your standard costs and the original standards as previously given. State why the company seems to be experiencing the results given previously.
3. In general, do you expect that high-volume or low-volume products are more likely to show higher overhead costs under ABC than under labor-based assignment? Why?

12-29 Input standards versus output standards Cassidy Company manufactures an industrial solvent. The company budgets manufacturing costs based on direct labor hours. The production manager is unable to interpret the report he has just received and asks for your assistance. The report contains the following data.

	Actual Cost at 10,000 Direct Labor Hours	Budgeted Cost for 10,000 Hours
Materials used at standard prices	$ 25,800	$ 24,000
Direct labor	68,300	68,000
Indirect labor	27,200	26,500
Other variable overhead	27,400	27,300
Total variable costs	$148,700	$145,800

Cassidy budgeted 50,000 gallons of production. Actual production was 51,000 gallons, which requires 10,200 direct labor hours at standard performance.

Required

For each component of cost, determine the variance due to efficiency (or inefficiency) and that due to spending or price.

12-30 Bases for standard costs and decisions Sewell Company uses very tight standards for determining standard costs. The production manager believes that the use of standards achievable only under ideal conditions helps to motivate employees by showing them how much improvement is possible and therefore giving them goals to achieve.

The sales manager has criticized the use of such high standards for performance and correspondingly low standard costs because it increases his difficulty in determining whether business at lower than normal prices should be accepted. In one specific instance, the sales manager was offered the opportunity to sell 4,000 units at $8.50, which is $4 below the normal selling price. He rejected the offer. The standard variable cost per unit of product is as follows.

Materials (3 pounds at $0.50)	$1.50
Direct labor (1/2 hour at $6 per hour)	3.00
Variable overhead ($4 per direct labor hour)	2.00
Total standard variable cost	$6.50

The sales manager was uncertain whether the order should have been accepted. He knew that the standards were never met. What bothered him was the extent to which they were not met. He asked his assistant to try to determine whether the order would have been profitable. The assistant developed the following information: material price and labor rate variances are negligible. However, during a normal month, when 10,000 units are produced, the material use variance, direct labor efficiency variance, and total variable overhead variance are about $2,000, $6,000, and $5,200, respectively, all unfavorable.

Required

1. Assuming that the experience of the month presented would have applied when the special order was being made up, should the order have been accepted?
2. Develop new standard variable costs based on currently attainable performance, assuming that the month described reflected currently attainable performance. Be sure to include both prices and quantities for each input factor.

12-31 Multiple products Cross Company manufactures three models of small plastic chairs. The standard material cost is $0.80 per pound, standard labor rate is $8.00 per hour, and standard variable overhead rate is $3.00 per direct labor hour. The standard quantities of each cost factor for each model appear below.

	Model 1	Model 2	Model 3
Materials, pounds	24	24	42
Direct labor hours	5	5	2

Actual results for March were

Production:	
Model 1	12,000
Model 2	16,000
Model 3	14,000
Materials purchased	1,400,000 pounds at $0.78
Materials used	1,275,000 pounds
Direct labor	173,000 hours for $1,365,200
Variable overhead	$497,000

Required

Determine the variable cost variances.

12-32 Standards and idle time Prescott Textiles manufactures a single kind of cloth in its Petzel Mill. The standard labor cost per 100 yards of cloth is $14.00, which is two standard labor hours at $7 per hour. In August, orders were slow and the mill turned out only 1,200,000 yards, well below the usual volume. Workers were paid for 29,000 hours. The company guarantees a 40-hour workweek to employees with five years of service. About 5,500 of the 29,000 hours were idle time, when eligible employees were paid, but had no work to do.

Required

1. Calculate the labor efficiency variance using the 29,000 hours actually worked.

2. Can you conclude from your answer to item 1 that the work force was inefficient in August? Why or why not? What do you recommend?

12-33 *Evaluation in JIT manufacturing* Crystal Enterprises has been using JIT principles for a short time and has been developing a variety of performance measures. Jill Rodriguez, the controller, recently received the following statistics and asks you to tell her how each could help evaluate performance.

Production in units	8,150
Number of defectives	240
Percentage of orders shipped on-time	88%
Manufacturing interval (cycle time)	36 hours
Supply of inventories	5 days
Cost of scrap	$4,600
Scrap as a percentage of output	3%
Number of line disruptions	5
Percentage of people cross-trained to do more than one job	65%

Required

Write a memorandum to Ms. Rodriguez telling her how each measure can help her evaluate operations. Use the guidelines in Appendix B.

12-34 *Analyzing results—sales and cost variances* Managers of Reed Blanket Company were disappointed at the shortfall in profit for 19X7, as shown in the income statements below. Amounts shown are in millions.

	Budgeted	Actual
Unit sales	10.0	10.8
Sales	$120.0	$122.1
Variable manufacturing costs:		
Materials	20.0	21.8
Direct labor	15.0	17.0
Variable overhead	5.0	5.2
Total variable costs	40.0	44.0
Contribution margin	80.0	78.1
Fixed costs:		
Manufacturing	50.0	50.8
Selling and administrative	20.0	19.9
Total fixed costs	70.0	70.7
Profit before taxes	$ 10.0	$ 7.4

Required

The president wants an analysis showing why profit fell short of budget. He wants you to determine the effects of the difference between budgeted and actual unit volume, budgeted and actual selling prices, and budgeted and actual costs for the volume achieved. Production equalled sales. Prepare such an analysis and be sure that it fully accounts for the difference between budgeted and actual profit.

12-35 Flexible and static budgets Marvel Manufacturing Company is managed by a family, none of whose members understand accounting. Ralph Marvel, one of the managers, was elated at the following performance report.

	Budget	Actual	Variance
Production	30,000	26,000	
Materials	$ 75,000	$ 72,000	$ 3,000F
Direct labor	45,000	40,000	5,000F
Variable overhead	90,000	86,000	4,000F
Fixed overhead	60,000	60,000	
Total	$270,000	$258,000	$12,000F

Marvel showed the report to Denise Wong, the newly hired assistant controller, saying that one did not need to understand accounting to see that coming in under budget was a good thing.

Required
As Wong, what would you say to Marvel?

12-36 Actual to actual comparisons—JIT Trivet Company operates a factory utilizing JIT operations. Results for two recent months appear below.

	June	May
Direct labor hours worked	21,500	20,200
Number of units produced	11,000	10,300
Rate paid to direct laborers	$7.20 per hour	$7.00 per hour
Price paid for materials	$0.96 per gallon	$0.98
Materials purchased and used in production	45,000 gallons	41,000 gallons
Variable overhead incurred	$85,800	$83,400
Unit cost	$25.80	$25.73

Required
The production manager wants to know if performance improved in June. Write a memorandum detailing the differences between May and June. Determine the differences in May and June costs resulting from changing input factory prices and changing efficiency.

12-37 Variance analysis—changed conditions Your firm makes a warm-up outfit with the following standard costs.

Materials (3 pounds at $4)	$12
Direct labor (2 hours at $8)	16
Variable overhead ($4 per DLH)	8
Total standard variable cost	$36

The standards have proved to be currently attainable and are generally met within small variances each month. In August the manufacturing vice president brought in a glowing report from the purchasing department. The company bought materials for $3.50 per pound. The new materials were different from the old but were of equal quality for the finished product. The materials bought during August were used in September with the following results.

Production scheduled	4,000 units
Actual production	3,700 units
Direct labor (8,350 hours)	$66,100
Variable overhead	$34,200
Materials used	12,300 pounds

Required

1. Compute all variances that you can.
2. Why might the variances have occurred?
3. Assuming that the experience of September will continue, should the company continue buying the new materials?

12-38 ***Economic cost of labor inefficiency*** Columbia Windows makes high-quality bay windows for houses. It sells to wholesalers who in turn sell to building contractors or homeowners. Some months of the year the company has trouble keeping up with demand and loses sales because customers are generally unwilling to wait and buy from a competitor. Direct labor time is constrained by the production process, so that the company can obtain a maximum of 280,000 direct labor hours per month. The typical product mix results in an average standard labor time of 14 hours per unit. The standard labor rate is $10 per hour, and the standard variable overhead rate is $8 per direct labor hour. Average materials cost is $82 per unit, and average selling price $620 per unit. Results for two recent months appear below. January is typically a slow month, June a busy one, with orders for over 22,000 units.

	January	June
Units produced	12,500	19,200
Actual labor hours	179,400	280,000

Materials costs were at standard. The actual labor rate equalled the standard rate, and variable overhead was incurred as budgeted for actual direct labor hours.

Required

1. Compute the labor efficiency variance and variable overhead efficiency variance for each month.
2. Do the variances for both months reflect the true cost to the firm of labor inefficiency? Why or why not?

12-39 ***Unit costs and total costs*** Wilton Matthews, the production manager of KRL Industries, was disturbed at the results for November (shown below). Budgeted production was 90,000 units, and actual production was 100,000 units.

	Budget for 90,000 Units	Actual for 100,000 Units
Materials	$ 288,000	$ 341,800
Direct labor	679,500	773,800
Variable overhead	339,750	391,300
Fixed overhead	850,000	860,700
Total costs	$2,157,250	$2,367,600
Cost per unit	$ 23.969	$ 23.676

Purchases of materials were about equal to use and were at 5% over standard prices. Labor rates were 2% over standard.

Matthews tells you that the 5% material price variance and 2% labor rate variance were the source of the unfavorable results, offering the following calculations to support his case.

Adjust budgeted costs to 100,000 units ($2,157,250 × 100/90)	$2,396,944
Material price variance ($288,000 × 100/90 × .05)	16,000
Labor rate variance ($679,500 × 100/90 × .02)	15,100
Total allowable costs	$2,428,044

"Look, these guys who prepare the reports can't hold me to a budget for 90,000 units when I put out 100,000. Besides, they charged me with variances that I am not responsible for, so I actually came in way under budget. Even with the stupid way they made up the report, you can see that my unit cost was below budget, but I *should* look even better."

Required

Matthews is responsible for materials and labor use and for all overhead costs. Determine whether his claim of good cost control is correct by calculating the total variances for which he is responsible. Calculate as many individual variances as you can.

12-40 Design change variances Grogan Company manufactures machine tools and often changes the design of a tool during the year to make it more suitable for customers. Grogan does not change the standards when it changes the design, which has caused some grumbling by production managers. The controller wants to be able to reconcile the year's actual results with the original budget and argues that changing standards during the year makes it virtually impossible to do so.

As a compromise, a production manager has suggested dividing the efficiency variances into two parts, one that captures the effects of design changes, the other to reflect efficiency in meeting the standard created by the revised design. The total efficiency variance will still be the difference between actual inputs at standard prices and the original standard inputs at standard prices.

The following data are representative of design changes.

	Original	Redesigned
Materials:		
6 feet at $3 per foot	$18.00	
7 feet at $3 per foot		$21.00
Direct labor:		
.60 hours at $10 per hour	6.00	
.55 hours at $10 per hour		5.50
Variable overhead at $7 per DLH	4.20	3.85
Totals	$28.20	$30.35

Production of the tool was 2,000 units, requiring 13,700 feet of materials and 1,180 direct labor hours.

Required

1. Determine the material, direct labor, and variable overhead efficiency variables, ignoring the redesign.
2. For each variance, determine how much resulted from the design change and how much from efficient or inefficient use of input factors.

12-41 Use of unit costs The supervisor of the machining department of Glenmills Company has just received the following performance report, which was prepared by the new cost accountant.

	Costs per Unit		
	Budget	Actual	Variance
Materials	$ 3.00	$ 2.96	($ 0.04)
Direct labor (1.5 hours per unit at standard)	6.00	6.084	0.084
Variable overhead:			
Indirect labor	2.40	2.48	0.08
Power	0.90	0.93	0.03
Fixed overhead	4.00	4.95 [a]	0.95
Totals	$16.30	$17.404	$1.104

a Actual cost incurred divided by actual production in units.

Budgeted production was 12,000 units, actual production was 10,000 units. Budgeted fixed overhead per unit is based on budgeted production. You learn that actual materials cost in the report is based on standard prices and that all other actual cost figures are based on actual prices and quantities.

The supervisor is not responsible for direct labor rates, which were $3.90 at actual cost. He is also not responsible for variable overhead spending variances, but he is responsible for fixed overhead budget variances.

Required

Prepare a new report including only those items for which the supervisor is responsible. (You may wish to use a different type of presentation from that shown above.)

12-42 Analysis of income statement The controller of Taylors Company has given you the following income statement.

Sales 20,000 × $20		$400,000
Standard variable cost of sales		240,000
Standard variable manufacturing margin		160,000
Variances:		
Materials	$ 6,000F	
Direct labor	4,000U	
Variable overhead	3,000U	1,000U
Actual variable manufacturing margin		159,000
Fixed costs:		
Budgeted manufacturing costs	75,000	
Fixed cost budget variance	2,000U	
Selling and administrative costs	40,000	117,000
Income before taxes		$ 42,000

The controller gives you additional data. Production was 22,000 units. Materials purchased were all made at standard price. Direct laborers averaged 0.85 hours per unit, which was 0.05 hours above the standard time. Actual direct labor cost was $144,800. The standard variable overhead rate is $2 per direct labor hour.

Required

Answer the following questions.

1. What was the direct labor efficiency variance?
2. What was the direct labor rate variance?
3. What was the standard materials cost per unit?
4. What was actual total variable overhead?
5. What was the variable overhead efficiency variance?
6. What was the variable overhead budget variance?
7. What was actual total fixed manufacturing cost?
8. If the standard materials price is $2 per pound, how many pounds are needed at standard to make a unit of product?
9. How many pounds of materials did the firm use?

12-43 Forecasting income Robyn Company had the following income statement in 19X7.

Sales (110,000 × $20)		$2,200,000
Standard variable cost of sales		880,000
Standard variable manufacturing margin		1,320,000
Variances:		
Materials	$ 2,400U	
Direct labor	1,800F	
Variable overhead	1,600F	1,000F
Actual variable manufacturing margin		1,321,000
Fixed costs:		
Manufacturing	560,000	
Selling and administrative	470,000	1,030,000
Income		$ 291,000

The details of standard cost were

Materials (0.50 pounds at $4 per pound)	$2.00
Direct labor (0.40 hours at $10 per hour)	4.00
Variable overhead at $5 per direct labor hour	2.00
Total standard variable cost	$8.00

The company's industrial engineers have redesigned the product so that (1) materials requirement should be 0.45 pounds and (2) direct labor hours should be 0.35. The company expects to produce 120,000 units in 19X8 and to sell 115,000. Materials costs will increase to $4.20 per pound. Each element of fixed cost should increase by 5%.

The managers and engineers expect to see materials use about 2% over the 0.45 pounds standard because it will take some time for workers to learn the new production methods. They also expect direct labor for the year to be 6% or so above standard for the same reason. They do want to use the 0.45 pounds and 0.35 hours as the standards, however, because they expect workers to operate at standard by mid-year. The standard variable overhead rate will increase by $0.20 per hour because of rising prices for input factors such as supplies and power. All elements not mentioned should be about the same as they were in 19X7.

Required

1. Determine the standard cost for the product for 19X8.
2. Prepare an income statement for 19X8 reflecting the manager's expectations, using the same format as the one for 19X7.

12-44 Relationships among data Dempsey Company uses standard variable costs. Variable overhead rate is based on direct labor hours. The following data are available for operations during April 19X4.

Total production	______
Actual labor cost	$61,600
Actual materials used	5,900 pounds
Actual variable overhead	$37,150
Standard labor cost per unit	$______
Standard materials cost per unit	$ 4.50
Standard variable overhead cost per unit	$______
Materials purchased (8,200 pounds)	$12,800
Material price variance	$ 500U
Labor rate variance	$ 2,500U
Variable overhead spending variance	$______F or U
Material use variance	$______F or U
Labor efficiency variance	$ 900F
Variable overhead efficiency variance	$______F or U
Direct labor hours worked	9,850 hours
Standard labor rate	$______
Standard direct labor hours per unit	5 hours
Variable overhead rate per DLH	$ 4

Required

Fill in the blanks. (*Hint:* You cannot do the parts in the order given.)

12-45 Standard costs—alternative raw materials Visodane, Inc. manufactures a household cleaner called Kleenall that is sold in 32-ounce (1/4 gallon) plastic bottles. The cleaner can be made using either of two basic raw materials—anaxohyde or ferodoxin. Their respective costs are $10 and $8 per pound. Whichever material is used is mixed with water and other chemical agents and is then cooked. The product is then bottled, and the bottles are packed into cartons of 20 bottles each.

Each batch is made with 1,200 gallons of water, costing $0.30 per 100 gallons. Chemical agents other than raw materials cost $120 per batch. If anaxohyde is used, 100 pounds are mixed with the water and chemical agents. If ferodoxin is used, 110 pounds are needed. Mixing takes three hours and requires three laborers.

The mixture is then cooked, for 80 minutes if anaxohyde is used and 90 minutes if ferodoxin is used. One worker is needed for the cooking process. With either raw material, the output of the cooking process is 1,000 gallons because of evaporation. Bottling and packing requires one laborer working two hours.

All laborers are paid $6 per hour. Variable overhead is based on the time required in each process because the high degree of mechanization makes direct labor a poor measure of activity for variable overhead. Overhead per hour is $30 for the mixing process, $120 for the cooking process, and $60 for the bottling and packing process. Bottles cost $0.04 each and the cartons cost $0.20 each.

Required

1. Compute the standard cost of a carton of 20 bottles of Kleenall, assuming (a) anaxohyde is used and (b) ferodoxin is used.
2. Suppose that each carton sells for $20 and that cooking time available each month is 1,000 hours. Which material should be used?

CASES

12-46 Developing standard costs (CMA adapted) The controller of Berman Detergents has asked for your help in preparing standard variable costs for its major product, Sudsaway. Berman has never used standard costs, and the controller believes that better control will be achieved if standards are used. She wants the standards to be based on currently attainable performance.

The following data are available for operations in 19X6.

Materials used (1,350,000 gallons at $0.80 per gallon)		$1,080,000
Direct labor (160,000 hours at $5.50 per hour)		880,000
Variable overhead:		
Indirect labor	$240,000	
Maintenance and repairs	80,000	
Packaging materials	370,000	
Other variable overhead	480,000	1,170,000
Total variable production costs		$3,130,000

During 19X6, 740,000 cases of Sudsaway were produced. Each case contains 12 bottles of 16 ounces each, a total of 1.5 gallons per case. During 19X6 the firm used an inferior raw material. During 19X7 the firm expects to pay $0.90 per gallon for a better material. Even with the better material, some shrinkage will occur during production. The controller expects that output of Sudsaway in gallons will be 90% of the raw material put into process.

The firm employed a number of inexperienced workers in 19X6. They worked about 48,000 of the total direct labor hours, which is about 12,000 more than standard hours. During 19X7 the controller expects all workers to be normally productive and to earn an average wage of $5.80.

According to the controller, variable overhead costs were under control during 19X6, given the excessive labor hours worked. Packaging materials were not affected by the excessive labor hours, being related to cases actually produced. Indirect laborers will receive a 10% wage increase early in 19X7.

Required

Prepare standard variable costs, by category of cost, for a case of Sudsaway.

12-47 Standard costs—joint products Sigmund Company buys a single raw material and processes it into two intermediate products, guild and stern. Both guild and stern are further processed into final products; neither can be sold at split-off.

The joint process is supervised by one manager; the additional processing of each product is supervised by separate managers. Based on currently attainable performance, it takes six workers three hours to process a one-ton batch of raw material into 800 pounds of guild and 1,000 pounds of stern. The remainder is worthless waste. The raw material costs $360 per ton. All laborers are paid $6 per hour, and variable overhead is $4 per direct labor hour.

Still based on currently attainable performance, it takes three workers five hours to complete the processing of an 800-pound batch of guild, and four workers three hours to complete a 1,000-pound batch of stern. When completed, guild sells for $0.75 per pound, stern for $0.90.

Required

Compute whatever standard costs you think might be helpful. Explain why you computed the ones you did.

12-48 Standard costs, variances, and evaluation (CMA adapted) Bergen Company manufactures a single product. Standard variable cost of a unit is given below.

Materials (1 pound plastic at $2)	$ 2.00
Direct labor (1.6 hours at $4)	6.40
Variable overhead	3.00
Total standard variable cost	$11.40

The variable overhead cost is not related to direct labor hours, but rather to units of product because production is thought to be the causal factor in the incurrence of the variable overhead elements. The elements of variable overhead, based on a yearly volume of 60,000 units of production, are as follows.

Indirect labor (30,000 hours at $4)	$120,000
Supplies, oil (60,000 gallons at $0.50)	30,000
Maintenance costs, variable portion (6,000 hours at $5 per hour)	30,000
Total budgeted variable overhead	$180,000

Fixed overhead is budgeted as follows, based on 60,000 units of product.

Supervision	$ 27,000
Depreciation	45,000
Other fixed overhead (includes fixed maintenance costs of $12,000)	45,000
Total budgeted fixed overhead	$117,000

During November, 5,000 units were produced and actual costs were as follows.

Materials (5,300 pounds used at $2)	$10,600
Direct labor (8,200 hours at $4.10)	33,620
Indirect labor (2,400 hours at $4.10)	9,840
Supplies (6,000 gallons of oil at $0.55)	3,300
Variable maintenance costs (490 hours at $5.30)	2,597
Supervision	2,475
Depreciation	3,750
Other fixed overhead (includes maintenance of $1,100)	3,600
Total	$69,782

Purchases of materials were 5,200 pounds at $2.10 per pound. The firm has divided responsibilities so that the purchasing manager is responsible for price variances for materials and oil and the production manager is responsible for all quantities of materials, labor (direct and indirect), supplies, and maintenance. The personnel manager is responsible for wage rate variances and the manager of the maintenance department is responsible for spending variances.

Required

1. Calculate the following variances.
   (a) material price
   (b) material use
   (c) direct labor rate
   (d) direct labor efficiency
   (e) total variable overhead
   (f) total fixed overhead
2. Prepare a report that details the overhead variances of each element by responsibility. (A convenient method is to list the managers across the top, and under each show the variances for which they are responsible.) You should account for all variable and fixed overhead variances. That is, the total of your answers to item 1 should be distributed to individual managers.

PART FOUR

product costing

Part Four deals with product costing—determining unit costs of manufactured products. Knowledge of product costing is important to nonaccounting managers because they receive reports that use the methods considered in Part Four. An understanding of cost behavior and of the significance of unit costs is particularly important in interpreting reports of manufacturers. Identifying cost drivers and developing activity-based costs is important because product costs are used for many managerial purposes such as pricing and evaluating the profitability of products and lines. Cost allocation is further considered together with some of its effects. The discussion of product costing methods also covers some behavioral problems. Thus, product costing has implications for control and performance evaluation.

13 introduction to product costing

This chapter and the next two chapters treat the highlights of product costing, introducing the basic approaches and cost accumulation methods. Product costing encompasses several areas, though its central focus is on determining the costs of manufactured products for inventory determination. Thus, the topics relate principally to manufacturers, although some of the material is relevant to other kinds of companies and to not-for-profit organizations. Because inventory determination is important for published financial statements, product costing is an important topic for financial reporting. Financial reporting is governed by GAAP, so manufacturers must adhere to them for their published financial statements. Of course, for internal reporting, manufacturers are not bound by GAAP and have more flexibility in preparing financial statements to meet their needs for planning and control.

There are many arcane issues in product costing and it is not our intent to make you into a competent cost accountant. Rather, because managers in manufacturing companies receive and interpret reports that use the principles we discuss here, it is important to understand those principles.

COST FLOWS

As early as Chapter 3, we saw that manufacturers incur costs for materials and components, for the labor required to turn materials into finished product, for the facilities needed for the manufacturing process, and for selling and administrative efforts. Selling and administrative costs are expensed in the period incurred and are **period costs**. Manufacturing costs are expensed when the product is sold (as cost of goods sold) and are called **product costs**. The accounting path followed by a product cost, from the time it is incurred to the time it becomes an expense, is called the *flow of costs*.

From your study of financial accounting you are familiar with the flow of product costs for a merchandising company. The cost of purchased products (including the purchase cost and freight-in) flows into inventory and then into cost of goods sold. For a manufacturing firm, the flow is basically the same—costs flow into inventory and then to cost of goods sold. But the situation is complicated by two factors noted in Chapters 3 and 6: (1) manufacturers typically have three types of inventory and (2) the cost associated with manufacturers' inventories includes more than the purchase price of materials needed in the manufacturing process.

Taking up the first factor, at any given time, a manufacturer might have three types of inventory.

1. **Finished goods inventory**, consisting of units that are ready for sale. This inventory is equivalent to what is called inventory by a merchandising concern.
2. **Work in process inventory**, consisting of semi-finished units (such as automobiles without windshields, doors, or engines). Reaching this semi-finished state requires not only materials but also labor and machinery. This inventory has no equivalent in a merchandising concern.
3. **Materials and components inventory**, consisting of the various materials (steel, glass, wood) and components (purchased switches, valves, handles) that go into a finished product but which have not been put into production. Here, again, there is no equivalent in a merchandising concern. We shall use the term *materials* for brevity, to refer to both materials and components.

Thus, the costs of a manufacturer flow into inventory and eventually to cost of goods sold. Also, the flow involves more than one type of inventory and involves costs other than purchase costs.

Manufactured inventories have three types of cost: materials, direct labor, and manufacturing overhead. Direct labor and overhead costs are necessary to transform or convert materials into finished products, a principle that we covered in Chapter 3. These costs all flow through inventory and eventually to cost of goods sold.

The flow of costs is shown in Exhibit 13-1. The costs of materials are first collected in the Materials account.[1] As materials are requisitioned for use in production, their costs flow to Work in Process Inventory.[2] The cost of labor is first collected in Direct Labor and then flows to Work in Process to show that work was done to transform materials to a semi-finished state. Manufacturing overhead costs are collected in a temporary account called Manufacturing Overhead, and then flow to Work in Process to reflect the role of such items as supervision, power, and depreciation in transforming

---

1 Many titles are used in practice to designate the same things. For instance, some companies use the title "Stores" to refer to the account that contains the cost of materials and purchased components.

2 To make it easier to follow the discussion, we capitalize the names of accounts, while using lowercase to denote the items themselves. Thus, "Work in Process Inventory" refers to the account, while "work in process" refers to the physical, semifinished product.

Exhibit 13-1 Flow of Costs in a Manufacturing Firm

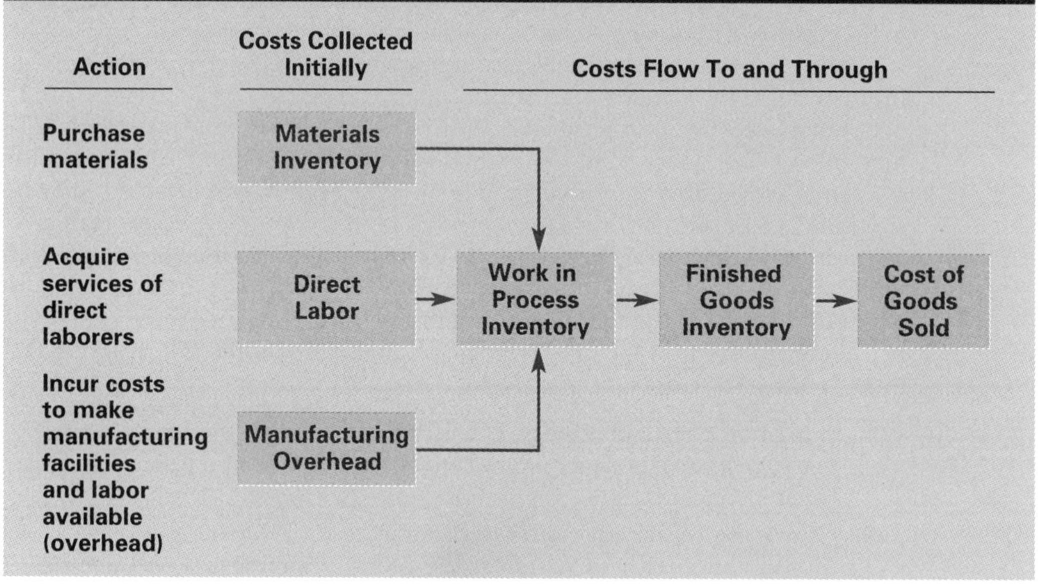

materials into finished product. Thus, Work in Process collects the costs of materials, labor, and manufacturing overhead. As goods are completed, their costs are transferred from Work in Process to Finished Goods. Finally, as goods are sold their costs are transferred from Finished Goods to Cost of Goods Sold.

The approach to collecting information about production differs depending on whether the company makes a single product or a variety of dissimilar products. Although they do not have inventory, some service companies can use the same basic technique. Banks provide examples of service companies that use product costing techniques extensively in developing and pricing their "products" (consumer loans, mortgages, and home equity loans are examples of products for banks). Like manufacturers, banks use such product cost information to achieve cost reductions.[3]

MANUFACTURING PROCESSES

Some companies make a single, homogeneous product in a more or less continuous process. Every pound of sugar, flour, or bulk chemical, every gallon of tomato juice is virtually the same as any other. In such cases, it makes perfect sense to calculate a unit cost by dividing total production costs by the number of units (pounds, gallons, etc.) produced. Thus, cost per unit is calculated as

$$\text{Cost per unit of product} = \frac{\text{total production costs}}{\text{total units processed}}$$

3 *Mona J. Gardner and Lucille E. Lammers, "Cost Accounting in Large Banks,"* Management Accounting, *April, 1988, 34.*

Managers of such companies can be satisfied with knowing the cost of an average unit. Such companies use process costing, which we discuss in Chapter 15.

At the other end of the spectrum are companies that rarely, if ever, make the same product twice. Construction companies never build *exactly* the same bridge, office building, or house twice. Each product is unique. A printer might work on 50 different books in a month, each with a different number of pages, type of ink, and quality of paper. Such companies typically produce several units, or batches, of product with each unit or batch differing from the others. Calculating an average cost for the period by using the equation above is senseless, because the units are so different. Yet the managers of such companies are keenly interested in the cost of each unit or batch. For, while they might not make the same product again, they will make similar ones—requiring similar amounts of materials, labor, and machine time—and therefore will want to use the costs on current jobs to estimate costs of future jobs. Such companies use job-order costing, which we will discuss later in this chapter.

Along the spectrum are many hybrids: most modern companies are mass producers or repetitive manufacturers. These companies produce many different products, so they cannot use the simple process costing formula given above. However, all of their products are relatively standard, so that each batch or unit of a particular product is much like every other. An automobile manufacturer is a good example. Such companies typically use standard costing, which we discuss in Chapter 14.

In addition to the three product costing methods just mentioned, there are two issues or choices that companies must make regarding their cost accounting. First is a choice that applies only to internal reporting.

ABSORPTION COSTING AND VARIABLE COSTING

For financial reporting and income tax purposes manufacturers must use **absorption costing** or **full costing**. Under absorption costing, inventory cost includes fixed manufacturing costs. From previous chapters, you know that expressing fixed costs as per-unit amounts can give misleading results, so why is absorption costing used?

Accounting systems provide information for managers, but they must also produce information for financial reporting and income tax returns. Both GAAP and income tax law require that the unit cost of manufactured products include all manufacturing costs, both variable and fixed. Therefore, inventories on the balance sheet, and cost of goods sold on the income statement, of a manufacturer must include both variable and fixed manufacturing costs. Accounting systems must produce absorption costing information to satisfy these external requirements.

Companies often use data required for external purposes for internal purposes. Managers who receive absorption costing reports must remember that per-unit costs include both variable and fixed manufacturing costs. These managers must understand how the information was developed and, more importantly, how to interpret that information.

Moreover, managers need to know the average total cost, including the fixed costs, of manufacturing a product or providing a service. Activity-based costing, which we introduced earlier in this book, determines the average cost of an activity, and ultimately of the products that the activity supports. For the most part, our objections to using unit fixed costs have had to do with short-term results, particularly short-term decision-making, as well as with the danger in projecting unit costs to different levels of activity. In the longer term, the distinction between fixed and variable costs becomes less critical because the company must periodically renew the commitments that give rise to fixed costs.

The idea that managers should have a reasonable idea of the costs of their manufactured products might seem obvious, but in former communist countries there was little need for cost information. "How do you determine the cost of a manufactured product?" was one question put to an American accountant who led a delegation of accountants to Minsk, in the former Soviet republic of Belarus. Soviet accounting aimed at providing information that was suitable for central planning and controlling of the economy. Factories did not need to earn profits, but to supply goods as specified by central planners.[4]

For internal purposes, a company is not bound by GAAP and so does not have to use absorption costing. **Variable costing** or **direct costing** is a technique that does not include fixed costs in calculating per-unit inventory cost. We consider absorption costing for the most part in this chapter and take up variable costing in Chapter 14.

JOB-ORDER COSTING

We begin with **job order costing**, which requires keeping track of the materials, labor, and perhaps machine time used on each job and then *applying*, *absorbing*, or *assigning* some amount of manufacturing overhead to each job. Tracing materials, labor, and machine time to specific jobs is usually straightforward; workers simply keep track of time and materials they use on each job and report them on forms designed for that purpose. But manufacturing overhead costs—such as heat, light, power, and machinery depreciation—cannot be traced directly to specific jobs. Rather, overhead costs are applied (assigned) to jobs indirectly, by determining *an overhead rate per unit of some input activity* with which total overhead seems to vary most closely. The measure could be direct labor hours, direct labor cost, machine hours, or some other measure. Managers use the techniques described in Chapter 3 to determine the activity with which total overhead is most closely associated. Historically, direct labor has been used more than any other base. More recently, companies with significant automation switched to machine hours.

Assigning overhead costs to one activity (a job) based on some other activity (like labor hours) is not a new concept. We introduced this idea in Chapter 3 and applied it in other chapters, most recently in Chapter 12, where we noted that variable overhead is usually related to an input factor such as labor time or machine time. We do the same in product costing. Many companies use several activity bases to apply overhead, as we noted in Chapter 3. Our basic example uses a single rate for simplicity. We cover multiple rates later in this chapter.

---

4 *Newton D. Becker, "Russia Faces a New Accounting World,"* The New Accountant, *December, 1992, 12.*

Caterpillar, the giant equipment manufacturer, is an example of a company that switched from direct labor to machine time a number of years ago. Because so much of its overhead (depreciation, tooling, maintenance, utilities, etc.) was machine-driven, Caterpillar developed the idea of an MBU (Machine Burden Unit) for some of its overhead costs years ago when most companies used direct labor only. Caterpillar now uses other cost drivers as well. Managers have found that they made much better decisions, especially in pricing. Caterpillar uses costing information for inventory valuation (financial accounting), operational controls such as tracking and managing costs and other operating characteristics, and product costing for long-term strategic decisions.

* *Lou F. Jones, "Product Costing at Caterpillar,"* Management Accounting, *February 1991, 34.*

Exhibit 13-2 contains the basic information for our illustration of job-order costing. (For now, ignore the lower part of the exhibit, which deals with budget information.) Farr Company manufactures electronic sensing devices to customer order. Three jobs (J-1, J-2, and J-3) were worked on in July. Farr uses machine hours to apply overhead.

Materials costs, direct labor costs, and machine hours in Exhibit 13-2 were determined from forms, prepared by employees, showing how much materials, labor time, and machine time were used. There are two commonly used methods of applying overhead to jobs: actual costing and normal costing. We shall illustrate both methods, and then discuss the effects of those procedures on the financial statements, particularly on the income statement.

ACTUAL COSTING

Under **actual costing**, all of the overhead incurred during a period is applied to the jobs worked on in that period. To assign all of the overhead costs to

Exhibit 13-2 Farr Company Data for July

Total overhead costs				$ 140,000
Total machine hours				7,000
	Job Number [a]			
Job Data	J-1	J-2	J-3	Total
Machine hours	2,000	1,000	4,000	7,000
Materials used	$20,000	$62,000	$30,000	$ 112,000
Direct labor cost	$20,000	$10,000	$40,000	$ 70,000
Budgeted data for year:				
Machine hours				100,000
Overhead costs, $1,200,000 + $5 per machine hour (MH)				$1,700,000

a Job J-1 was finished and sold in July. Job J-2 was finished, but not yet sold, and job J-3 was incomplete at the end of July.

jobs, we calculate the overhead rate by dividing total actual overhead by the total amount of the relevant input factor—machine hours here. In general form we have

$$\textit{Overhead rate} = \frac{\textit{total manufacturing overhead}}{\textit{total manufacturing activity}}$$

In this specific situation we have:

$$\textit{Overhead rate} = \frac{\$140{,}000}{7{,}000}$$
$$= \$20 \textit{ per machine hour}$$

We can now determine the total costs on the three jobs.

	Job Number		
	J-1	J-2	J-3
Overhead ($140,000):			
2,000 hrs. at $20	$40,000		
1,000 hrs. at $20		$20,000	
4,000 hrs. at $20			$ 80,000
Materials	20,000	62,000	30,000
Direct labor	20,000	10,000	40,000
Total cost of job	$80,000	$92,000	$150,000

Notice that all $140,000 of overhead cost is assigned to the three jobs ($40,000 + $20,000 + $80,000 = $140,000). Under actual costing, total overhead incurred is assigned to individual jobs.

What about the financial statements? Exhibit 13-2 states that job J-1 was sold in July, job J-2 was finished, but not sold, and job J-3 was not finished at the end of July. The cost of job J-1 would appear in the July income statement as Cost of Goods Sold (as we shall show later). The cost of job J-2 would appear in the July 31 balance sheet as Finished Goods Inventory and that of job J-3 would appear on the balance sheet as Work in Process Inventory.

Actual job-order costing is simple, but is not commonly used because it can produce misleading results. The reason is that overhead rates can fluctuate significantly from month to month. The differences in monthly rates are related to fixed overhead costs and there are two causes. First, activity (machine hours in our example) can differ from month to month because of seasonality or changes in the economy. Second, fixed overhead costs can fluctuate—heating is an obvious example. Although heating costs are higher in winter, to say that products made in the winter "cost more" is not useful. Let us illustrate this point using Farr Company data. Exhibit 13-2 shows that Farr's variable overhead cost is $5 per machine hour and that its fixed overhead averages $100,000 per month. Suppose that in May its fixed overhead is $100,000, but in December, because of seasonal cost factors, it is $110,000. Machine hours are 10,000 in May and 5,000 in December, again because of seasonal factors. Under actual job-order costing, the overhead rates for the two months are:

	May	December
Total overhead costs:		
$100,000 + (10,000 × $5)	$150,000	
$110,000 + (5,000 × $5)		$135,000
Machine hours	10,000	5,000
Overhead rate per machine hour	$ 15	$ 27

Suppose that Farr does two similar jobs in May and December, each requiring 100 machine hours at $10 per hour and $800 in materials. The total costs of the jobs are

	Job Done In	
	May	December
Materials	$ 800	$ 800
Labor (100 × $10)	1,000	1,000
Overhead, at $15 and $27	1,500	2,700
Total	$3,300	$4,500

Does the job done in December really cost $1,200 more than the one done in May? Is it likely that a customer will pay more for a job just because it was made in a slow month? Actually, customers often pay lower, not higher, prices in slow months, because companies need the business to keep their workers busy. Yet the profitability of the two jobs will appear different if they were sold at the same price, and this appearance might mislead a manager trying to develop a price quotation on a similar job. Most companies avoid this problem by using normal costing.

NORMAL COSTING

Normal costing uses the same overhead rate all year, smoothing the fluctuations of actual costing. The vehicle that accomplishes this smoothing is a **predetermined overhead rate**. A predetermined overhead rate is an overhead rate calculated in advance. The rate is not based on actual costs and activity, but rather on budgeted results. It is calculated as:

$$\frac{\textit{Predetermined}}{\textit{overhead rate}} = \frac{\textit{budgeted manufacturing overhead for year}}{\textit{budgeted production activity for year}}$$

Again, budgeted production activity can be expressed as direct labor hours, machine hours, or whatever other measure that managers think appropriate. The activity measures used in normal costing are the same as those used in actual costing; the difference is in the use of budgeted rather than actual figures.

Let us illustrate normal job-order costing with Farr Company, using the budgeted data at the bottom of Exhibit 13-2. The budget formula for overhead costs has the same form we saw in earlier chapters.

$$\begin{matrix}\textit{Budget} \\ \textit{allowance}\end{matrix} = \begin{matrix}\textit{fixed} \\ \textit{costs}\end{matrix} + \left(\begin{matrix}\textit{variable cost per} \\ \textit{unit of activity}\end{matrix} \times \begin{matrix}\textit{amount of} \\ \textit{activity}\end{matrix}\right)$$

Total budgeted overhead is $1,700,000, budgeted fixed costs of $1,200,000, plus $500,000 of variable cost ($5 variable overhead per machine hour × 100,000 budgeted machine hours). The predetermined overhead rate is $17 per machine hour ($1,700,000/100,000). This rate, multiplied by the number of hours worked on each job, gives the overhead costs of the jobs. Overhead assigned to jobs is called **applied** (or **absorbed**) **overhead.**

	Job Number		
	J-1	J-2	J-3
Overhead:			
2,000 hrs. @ $17	$34,000		
1,000 hrs. @ $17		$17,000	
4,000 hrs. @ $17			$ 68,000
Materials, as before	20,000	62,000	30,000
Direct labor, as before	20,000	10,000	40,000
Total cost of job	$74,000	$89,000	$138,000

There are several important points in this schedule. First, materials cost and direct labor cost are all the same as they were under actual costing. Only the overhead cost allocations are different. Differences in allocated overhead give the differences between the two costing methods.

The following analysis should help you understand the different treatments of overhead under actual costing and normal costing. Under actual costing, the overhead cost assigned to a particular job is:

$$\textit{Overhead assigned to job} = \textit{actual hours worked on job} \times \frac{\textit{total actual overhead}}{\textit{total actual hours}}$$

Under normal costing, the overhead assigned to a job is

$$\textit{Overhead assigned to job} = \textit{actual hours worked on job} \times \frac{\textit{total budgeted overhead}}{\textit{total budgeted hours}}$$

Thus, under actual costing, total actual overhead is assigned to all jobs. But under normal costing, total overhead assigned to jobs equals actual overhead only if total budgeted overhead equals total actual overhead and total actual hours equal total budgeted hours. (Offsetting differences could make the assignment come out even, but that is very unlikely.)

Which set of costs, actual or normal, is "correct"? There is no answer to this question, much as there is no answer to the question of whether first-in-first-out or last-in-first-out is the "correct" inventory cost flow assumption. Normal costing has the advantage of minimizing the effects of fluctuations in the overhead rate, and is therefore more popular than actual costing.

Normal costing nearly always shows a difference between actual overhead and applied overhead. The difference between actual overhead and applied overhead under normal costing is called misapplied overhead.

MISAPPLIED OVERHEAD

Let us look at the total overhead costs assigned under the two methods to jobs worked on in July.

	Overhead Applied to Jobs Using	
	Actual Costing	Normal Costing
Job J-1	$ 40,000	$ 34,000
Job J-2	20,000	17,000
Job J-3	80,000	68,000
Total	$140,000	$119,000

Note that you can also calculate total applied overhead by multiplying the predetermined overhead rate of $17 by the 7,000 total machine hours: $17 × 7,000 = $119,000.

We show $21,000 misapplied overhead ($140,000 – $119,000); the actual overhead is greater than applied overhead. When actual overhead is greater than applied overhead, the difference is called **underapplied** (or **underabsorbed**) **overhead**. When applied overhead is greater than actual overhead, we call the difference **overapplied** (or **overabsorbed**) **overhead**. Farr has $21,000 of underapplied overhead.

At first glance, misapplied overhead looks like the variances studied in Chapter 12. That is, if one views applied overhead as the "standard," any overapplication or underapplication appears to be analogous to favorable and unfavorable variable cost variances. But the analogy should not be carried too far. Remember that the predetermined overhead rate is based on both *budgeted* costs and *budgeted* production activity. Overapplied or underapplied overhead can result from actual costs being lower (a favorable variance) or higher (an unfavorable variance) than budgeted. Additionally, overapplied or underapplied overhead can result from a difference between actual activity and the activity level used to calculate the predetermined overhead rate.

OVERHEAD VARIANCES

To illustrate these two points, let us look more closely at the July results for Farr Company, when machine time totaled 7,000 hours. The budget formula for annual overhead cost is $1,200,000 of fixed costs plus $5 per machine hour for variable cost. With monthly fixed overhead budgeted at the average of $100,000 (one twelfth of the annual amount), July's budgeted and actual costs can be compared as below.

Actual costs, fixed and variable	$140,000
Budgeted costs [$100,000 + ($5 × 7,000 hours)]	135,000
Budget variance, unfavorable	$ 5,000

Farr incurred $5,000 more overhead cost than budgeted, an unfavorable **budget variance**. Calculating a budget variance is not new with this chapter. In this case, we cannot determine how much of this variance relates to fixed cost and how much to variable cost because we do not know the *actual* amounts of fixed and variable costs. This point was discussed in Chapter 12. But we *do* know now that $5,000 of the $21,000 underapplied overhead represents an unfavorable budget variance because actual costs were higher than budgeted costs.

Let us look at the other factor affecting the predetermined rate and, therefore, the amount of overhead applied. We know (again from Exhibit 13-2) that Farr planned to use 100,000 machine hours for the year, for a monthly average of 8,333 1/3 hours. But only 7,000 hours of machine time was used in July. The variance caused by a difference between actual hours of machine time and the budgeted hours used in the calculation of the predetermined rate that is used to apply overhead is called the **volume variance,** or the **idle capacity variance**, and is computed as follows.

Budgeted cost, as computed above	$135,000
Applied cost ($17 × 7,000 actual hours)	119,000
Volume variance, unfavorable	$ 16,000

Note that using budgeted cost in the calculation eliminates the effect of any budget variance. When applied overhead exceeds budgeted overhead, the volume variance is *said to be* favorable; when the opposite is true, the variance is *said to be* unfavorable. Hence, we have now identified two unfavorable variances that add up to the $21,000 difference between actual and applied overhead for the month.

The meaning of a budget variance is clear, but what does the volume variance mean? Does it have any economic significance? Very little, if any. Whether it is favorable or unfavorable is not good or bad per se, because it relates solely to the smoothing of fixed overhead and arises *only* because actual hours do not equal the monthly average of budgeted hours. To demonstrate this point more clearly, let us look further at the $17 predetermined overhead rate.

The budgeted overhead cost used in the calculation of the $17 predetermined overhead rate has both a fixed and a variable component. The variable portion of the rate is $5 per hour, so the fixed portion is $12. (Alternatively, budgeted fixed overhead is $1,200,000 and budgeted hours are 100,000, also giving a $12 fixed portion.) Now, look at the difference between actual hours (7,000) and the 8,333 1/3 monthly share of the hours budgeted for the year. The $16,000 volume variance is exactly that 1,333 1/3 hour difference multiplied by the $12 rate for fixed overhead. Perhaps this point is more easily seen if you recast the calculation of the volume variance and separate budgeted and applied costs into their variable and fixed components, as below.

	Variable Portion	Fixed Portion
Budgeted cost (7,000 hours × $5)	$35,000	$100,000
Applied cost:		
7,000 hours × $5	35,000	
7,000 hours × $12		84,000
Volume variance (1,333 1/3 hours × $12)	—	$ 16,000

The flexible budget allowance for variable costs depends on the actual level of activity. But because fixed costs are not expected to change with the level of activity, the budgeted amount is not affected when more (or fewer) hours are worked than were budgeted. Thus, what produces the volume variance is the difference between budgeted and actual production activity, the 1,333 1/3 hours.

We now have three different, but equivalent, formulas for calculating the volume variance.

$$\text{Volume variance} = \text{total budgeted manufacturing overhead} - \text{total applied manufacturing overhead}$$

$$= \text{total budgeted fixed manufacturing overhead} - \text{total applied fixed manufacturing overhead}$$

$$= \text{predetermined overhead rate for fixed costs} \times \left(\text{budgeted production volume} - \text{actual production volume} \right)$$

You should use whichever formula is most convenient in a given situation; they all give the same answer.

We can also use the graphical format shown in Chapter 12 to compute the overhead budget variance and volume variance.

Actual Overhead	Budgeted Overhead	Applied Overhead
	$100,000 + ($5 × 7,000)	$17 × 7,000
$140,000	$135,000	$119,000

$5,000 unfavorable budget variance (Actual Overhead − Budgeted Overhead)

$16,000 unfavorable volume variance (Budgeted Overhead − Applied Overhead)

$21,000 total underapplied overhead

Before leaving this topic we want to remind you that applying overhead is an accounting device. Managers should not expect to incur overhead at the rate used to apply it. Rather, they should expect to incur overhead according to the budget formula.

INCOME STATEMENTS, ACTUAL AND NORMAL COSTING

We have illustrated, using a job-order company, two methods for assigning overhead costs to product. We now look at how the two methods affect the income statement. Exhibit 13-3 shows the July income statement for Farr Company under the two methods. We assume that Farr had $40,000 of selling and administrative expenses and that, as stated earlier, job J-1 was completed and sold for $150,000. Costs accumulated on jobs J-2 and J-3 remain in inventory at the end of the month. In internal reports, many companies show additional detail about underapplied overhead, showing separately the budget and volume variances as computed earlier.

The most obvious and critical difference between the statements is the amount of income ($30,000 under actual costing and $15,000 under normal costing). What caused the $15,000 difference?

The difference between incomes under actual costing and normal costing lies in the treatment of overhead, not in the amount of overhead incurred, which is the same $140,000 regardless of the method used. The actual-costing income statement shows the actual overhead in a single amount; the normal-costing income statement shows the actual overhead in two amounts, $119,000 assigned to jobs, and $21,000 as a separate deduction.

Exhibit 13-3 Farr Company, Income Statements for July

		Normal Costing	Actual Costing
Sales		$150,000	$150,000
Normal cost of sales	$74,000 [a]		
Plus underapplied overhead	21,000		
Cost of sales		95,000	80,000 [b]
Gross profit		55,000	70,000
Selling and administrative expenses		40,000	40,000
Income		$ 15,000	$ 30,000
Details of cost of sales			
Cost of sales:			
Beginning inventories		$ 0	$ 0
Materials		112,000	112,000
Labor		70,000	70,000
Overhead		119,000	140,000
Total costs		301,000	322,000
Less ending inventory		227,000 [c]	242,000 [d]
Normal cost of sales		74,000	
Underapplied overhead		21,000	
Cost of sales		$ 95,000	$ 80,000

a Cost of job J-1
b Cost of job J-2
c Job J-2 ($89,000) + job J-3 ($138,000) = $227,000
d Job J-2 ($92,000) + job J-3 ($150,000) = $242,000

If you look closely at the statements you will see that the source of the $15,000 difference in income is the $15,000 difference in the ending inventories. The cost of job J-2 is $3,000 greater and that of J-3 is $12,000 greater under actual costing than under normal costing, and that difference occurs because more overhead is assigned to those jobs under actual costing. Remember that overhead was assigned at the actual rate under actual costing, but at a predetermined rate for normal costing, so that for a single period within the year such differences are very common. The difference in incomes, then, relates to the differences in overhead assigned to inventory.

We have shown underapplied overhead as an addition to normal cost of sales. Another possibility is to show an amount called normal gross margin, which is sales minus normal cost of sales. We would then have subtracted underapplied overhead from normal gross margin. Either approach can be used and income will be the same. The choice is a matter of preference. The income statement in Exhibit 13-4 shows the alternative format and also separates underapplied overhead into the budget variance and volume variance.

Exhibit 13-4 Farr Company Normal Costing Income Statement

Sales		$150,000
Normal cost of goods sold		74,000
Normal gross margin		76,000
Variances:		
Budget variance	$ 5,000U	
Volume variance	16,000U	21,000
Gross margin		55,000
Selling and administrative expenses		40,000
Income		$ 15,000

ACTIVITY-BASED OVERHEAD RATES

Our example used a single overhead rate, which implies that virtually all overhead is driven by machine hours—an unreasonable assumption for most manufacturers. As you know from previous chapters, companies using activity-based costing (ABC) identify cost drivers for each pool of costs. **Cost pools** might be departments, or pools related to such activities as materials use, labor time, or machine time. Some companies allocate such costs as purchasing, receiving, inspecting, and storing—costs associated with materials—to jobs based on the materials cost of each job. They also might recognize multiple cost drivers by using different rates for labor time and for machine time, even in a single department. For brevity, we shall refer to all of these as examples of *multiple rates*.

Using multiple rates often provides better information than does a single, plant-wide rate. But it is costlier to operate a system where overhead is applied differently from department to department, or on multiple bases. For instance, it is necessary not only to identify the cost drivers and pools, but to keep track of the amount of activity associated with each job, product, or other object of allocation. Keeping such records can be quite costly. Accordingly, using multiple rates is wise only when the expected benefits, in the form of better control and decision making, exceed the additional costs. It is no easy task to determine whether benefits exceed costs, for the benefits are not usually experienced in dollar terms. Nonetheless, managers must make judgments about benefits.

There are two general cases where multiple rates are better than a single, plant-wide rate. One is when overhead is related to more than one input factor. In our example, Farr applied overhead using machine hours, which reflects an automated, machine-intensive operation. However, a department with a low investment in machinery and many laborers would use labor hours to apply overhead. Another example of the same case is if some overhead is clearly related to materials, other overhead to labor or machine time;

here again, separate rates make sense. The other case is when the same input factor applies to all departments, but the overhead rates in the departments differ greatly from one to another.

We now show how activity-based overhead rates can improve pricing decisions. The data given below relate to Reinhart Company, which makes electrical equipment.

	Data for Cost Pool		
	Direct Labor	Machine Setups	Total
Budgeted overhead costs	$900,000	$300,000	$1,200,000
Budgeted direct labor hours	100,000		
Budgeted number of setups		1,500	
Rates	$9/hour	$200/setup	

If Reinhart uses only direct labor to apply overhead, it will calculate a rate of $12 per direct labor hour, which is total overhead of $1,200,000 divided by 100,000 direct labor hours. The $12 rate does not capture the differences between the two types of overhead, and using it could lead to poor decisions.

Suppose that Reinhart works on the following two jobs and sets prices at 120% of manufacturing costs, including overhead applied at the $12 rate.

	Job A	Job B
Direct labor hours	500	200
Materials cost	$10,000	$10,000
Direct labor cost at $10/hour	5,000	2,000
Overhead applied at $12/DLH	6,000	2,400
Total cost	$21,000	$14,400
Price at 120% of cost	$25,200	$17,280

If Job A requires two machine setups and Job B requires 20 setups, the cost of each job using the activity-based rates would be as follows.

	Job A	Job B
Materials cost	$10,000	$10,000
Direct labor cost at $10/hour	5,000	2,000
Overhead:		
Labor-related at $9/DLH	4,500	1,800
Setup-related at $200/setup	400	4,000
Total cost	$19,900	$17,800
Price at 120% of cost	$23,880	$21,360

Using the single, labor-based rate, Reinhart will charge lower prices for jobs requiring lots of setups. In fact, in the example shown, the $17,280 price for Job B does not cover its costs as calculated using the activity-based rates. If Reinhart has a competitor that has similar cost structure and uses activity-based rates, Reinhart will bid higher than the competitor on labor-intensive jobs and will lose much of that business to the competitor. Reinhart will obtain a great deal of setup-intensive business because it will underbid the competitor. The problem is that Reinhart will not cover its costs if it bids so low on setup-intensive jobs. Remember that the price also has to cover selling and administrative expenses as well as manufacturing costs.

Determining cost drivers for JIT manufacturing is in some respects easier than it is for conventional manufacturing. Costs that are indirect in a conventional manufacturing environment are often direct in a JIT environment. Activities such as materials handling, maintenance, and other support services are carried out by centrally-administered units in conventional manufacturing but are done by the workers in each manufacturing cell. The costs of these activities, which are direct to the output of a particular manufacturing cell, make product costing much simpler. We examine product costing in JIT environments in Chapter 15.

OVERHEAD APPLICATION AND COST MANAGEMENT

Companies that apply both fixed and variable overhead to products can experience problems in interpreting cost data. Such problems can lead to misuses of information and to dysfunctional behavior, especially if a company uses an inappropriate allocation basis. Many companies today, especially those that are adopting new manufacturing techniques such as just-in-time, flexible manufacturing, and computer-integrated manufacturing, are finding that labor costs are declining precipitously as percentages of total manufacturing cost. At the same time overhead costs are rising, both in absolute dollars and as a percentage of total manufacturing cost. The rise in overhead is a natural consequence of changing the manufacturing environment to one that requires more brainwork. Support personnel such as industrial engineers, mechanical engineers, electrical engineers, computer experts and highly skilled maintenance workers are more in demand.

A company whose cost structure is moving toward less labor and more overhead (which also means more fixed cost and less variable cost) can make serious errors if it allocates overhead using, say, direct labor hours or direct labor cost. Because overhead is rising while direct labor is falling, an overhead rate calculated using direct labor hours will become astronomically high (perhaps to hundreds of dollars per direct labor hour). Careful studies of cost drivers led many companies to use activity-based rates to direct attention to areas where cost control was most needed.

An instructive case in point concerns Tektronix's Portables, which we discussed briefly in Chapter 10.[5] The Portables Group had based its overhead allocations on direct labor, but direct labor had declined to less than 7% of total manufacturing cost, as low as 3% on newer products. Simultaneously, overhead costs were rising because the Group was introducing new manufacturing methods and operations had become increasingly technological. These two factors combined to make labor-based overhead rates extremely high. A serious consequence was that engineers and other manufacturing people believed that reducing labor time was the best way to reduce total costs because while labor cost *per se* was low, when an hour of direct labor was loaded with a huge overhead charge, the total *labor-related* cost loomed very large. Design engineers drove labor time down by using special parts

5 *John W. Jonez and Michael A. Wright "Material Burdening,"* Management Accounting, *August, 1987, 27-31.*

and other devices, but that did not have the desired effect. Overhead costs did not decline as labor declined: they continued to rise.

As Chapter 10 reported, The Group studied overhead costs and concluded that much of it related to materials and components. Costs of activities such as purchasing, receiving, inspecting, storage, and record keeping were significant. The Group changed its allocation procedures, using both materials and conversion activities (labor and machine time). The new allocation methods have contributed to better understanding and to greater potential for cost reduction.

For our purposes, the major point that comes out of this discussion is that the use of separate overhead rates is desirable when overhead is driven by more than one factor. Of course, it is important that the overhead costs be correctly classified into their pools, otherwise there is little gained by using activity-based rates.

SUMMARY

Product costing is determining costs of inventory and of cost of goods sold for manufacturing firms. For financial reporting and income tax purposes, manufacturers must use absorption costing, which requires that all manufacturing costs, variable and fixed, be included in unit cost.

In a manufacturing firm, costs flow through inventory accounts to cost of goods sold. Cost data are accumulated in various ways, depending on the manufacturing process. Companies that produce essentially identical products accumulate costs using process costing. Companies that seldom produce the same product accumulate costs using job-order costing.

Some companies compute product costs based on actual costs incurred. Others use a normal costing system, under which the firm applies overhead to products using a predetermined overhead rate based on budgeted manufacturing overhead and budgeted production activity. The rate is usually stated as a cost per unit of some input measure such as direct labor hours or machine hours. Predetermined overhead rates can be calculated for each department or for a factory as a whole.

Companies that use normal costing will almost always have a difference between actual overhead and overhead applied. The difference, called underapplied or overapplied overhead, can be reported in an income statement as an adjustment to either normal cost of sales or normal gross margin. Underapplied or overapplied overhead can be analyzed into a budget variance and a volume variance. The latter variance has little economic significance.

Activity-based overhead rates are useful for many companies because they can provide better information than a single, plant-wide rate, or departmental rates based on labor or machine time. Companies using such rates have found that they improved decision-making. An ABC system costs more to operate than a conventional system and so the benefits must be weighed against the additional costs.

KEY TERMS

absorption (or full) costing
actual costing
applied (or absorbed) overhead
budget variance
cost pools
finished goods inventory
idle capacity variance
job-order costing
materials and components inventory
normal costing
overapplied (overabsorbed) overhead
period costs
predetermined overhead rate
product costs
underapplied (underabsorbed) overhead
variable (or direct) costing
volume variance
work in process inventory

KEY FORMULAS

$$\text{Predetermined overhead rate} = \frac{\text{budgeted manufacturing overhead for year}}{\text{budgeted production activity for year}}$$

$$\begin{matrix}\text{Variable overhead}\\ \text{budget variance}\end{matrix} = \begin{matrix}\text{actual}\\ \text{variable}\\ \text{overhead}\end{matrix} - \begin{matrix}\text{flexible budget}\\ \text{allowance for actual}\\ \text{production activity}\end{matrix}$$

$$\begin{matrix}\text{Underabsorbed}\\ \text{(overabsorbed)}\\ \text{overhead}\end{matrix} = \begin{matrix}\text{actual}\\ \text{manufacturing}\\ \text{overhead}\end{matrix} - \begin{matrix}\text{applied}\\ \text{manufacturing}\\ \text{overhead}\end{matrix}$$

$$\begin{matrix}\text{Fixed overhead}\\ \text{budget}\\ \text{variance}\end{matrix} = \begin{matrix}\text{actual}\\ \text{fixed}\\ \text{overhead}\end{matrix} - \begin{matrix}\text{budgeted}\\ \text{fixed}\\ \text{overhead}\end{matrix}$$

$$\text{Volume variance} = \begin{matrix}\text{budgeted (fixed)}\\ \text{manufacturing}\\ \text{overhead}\end{matrix} - \begin{matrix}\text{applied (fixed)}\\ \text{manufacturing}\\ \text{overhead}\end{matrix}$$

$$\text{Volume variance} = \begin{matrix}\text{predetermined}\\ \text{overhead rate for}\\ \text{fixed overhead}\end{matrix} \times \left(\begin{matrix}\text{budgeted}\\ \text{volume}\end{matrix} - \begin{matrix}\text{actual}\\ \text{volume}\end{matrix}\right)$$

$$\text{Total overhead budget variance} = \begin{matrix}\text{actual}\\ \text{total overhead}\end{matrix} - \begin{matrix}\text{budgeted}\\ \text{total overhead}\end{matrix}$$

REVIEW PROBLEM

Boulder Company makes drill presses to customer order and uses job-order costing. The firm began the month of March with no inventories. During March, it worked on two jobs, for which data appear below.

	Job #15	Job #16
Materials used	$69,000	$45,000
Direct labor at $10 per hour	$35,000	$60,000

Boulder incurred factory overhead costs of $209,000. Budgeted monthly factory overhead is $150,000 + ($5 × direct labor hours). The firm uses a predetermined overhead rate based on 10,000 direct labor hours per month. Activity does not usually fluctuate much from one month to another.

Required

1. Calculate the predetermined overhead rate per direct labor hour.
2. Determine the amounts of overhead to apply to each job.
3. Determine the overhead budget variance and volume variance.
4. Suppose that job #15 was sold for $240,000 and job #16 remained in inventory. Selling and administrative expenses for March were $24,000. Prepare an income statement for March. Treat variances as adjustments to normal cost of sales.
5. Suppose now that the firm used actual costing, allocating overhead to jobs based on the actual overhead rate per direct labor hour. Determine the amounts of overhead applied to each job and prepare an income statement assuming the relevant data from item 4.

ANSWER TO REVIEW PROBLEM

1. $20.00 per direct labor hour, calculated as follows.

$$\text{Predetermined rate} = \frac{\text{total budgeted overhead}}{\text{total budgeted activity}}$$

$$= \frac{\$150{,}000 + (\$5 \times 10{,}000)}{10{,}000}$$

$$= \$20$$

The rate consists of $15 fixed and $5 variable. Because there is no significant fluctuation in activity during the year, it is reasonable to use the monthly rather than the annual figures to calculate the rate. In fact, with annual fixed overhead of $1,800,000 ($150,000 × 12) and 120,000 direct labor hours (10,000 × 12), we would have exactly the same result.

2.

	Job #15	Job #16	Total
Direct labor hours:			
$35,000/$10	3,500		
$60,000/$10		6,000	9,500
Overhead at $20 per hour	$70,000	$120,000	$190,000

3.

Actual Overhead	Budgeted Overhead	Applied Overhead
	$150,000 + ($5 × 9,500)	9,500 × $20
$209,000	$197,500	$190,000

$11,500 unfavorable budget variance (Actual Overhead to Budgeted Overhead)

$7,500 unfavorable volume variance (Budgeted Overhead to Applied Overhead)

$19,000 total underapplied overhead

4.

Sales		$240,000
Cost of sales:		
Normal cost of sales [a]	$174,000	
Variances:		
Budget variance	11,500 U	
Volume variance	7,500 U	
Cost of sales		193,000
Gross profit		47,000
Selling and administrative expenses		24,000
Income		$ 23,000

a Job #15, materials + direct labor + applied overhead = $69,000 + $35,000 + $70,000 = $174,000.

5. The problem here is simply to determine the actual overhead rate.

$$\text{Actual rate} = \frac{\text{actual overhead}}{\text{actual activity}} = \frac{\$209{,}000}{9{,}500 \text{ hours}} = \$22.00 \text{ per hour}$$

The applied amounts are

	Job #15	Job #15	Total
Direct labor hours	3,500	6,000	9,500
Overhead applied at $22 per hour	$77,000	$132,000	$209,000

All overhead goes to individual jobs, so there are no variances. The income statement would show the following, with job #15 costing $181,000 ($69,000 + $35,000 + $77,000).

Sales	$240,000
Cost of sales	181,000
Gross margin	59,000
Selling and administrative expense	24,000
Income	$ 35,000

The difference in incomes ($23,000 versus $35,000) arises from the differences in inventory. Under normal costing, as in item 2, overhead of $120,000 is applied to job #16, which is still in inventory. Under actual costing, as shown above, overhead of $132,000 is applied to job #16. The $12,000 difference in income under the two methods is explained by the $12,000 difference in the overhead assigned to the job remaining in inventory (job #16).

ASSIGNMENT MATERIAL

QUESTIONS FOR DISCUSSION

13-1 Interrelationships with earlier chapters What similarities and differences do you see between predetermined overhead rates and flexible expense budgets?

13-2 Absorbing overhead Business people sometimes make statements like: "Our overhead rates allow us to absorb overhead costs at 80% of capacity." What does this statement mean?

13-3 Overhead application "Underapplied overhead is a bad sign because the more overhead you apply, the lower your fixed cost per unit." Discuss this statement critically.

13-4 Actual and normal costing Suppose a company begins and ends a year with no inventories. Will there be any difference between its income computed using actual costing and using normal costing? Why or why not?

13-5 "What's normal about it?" A student sitting near you in class just asked this question. The student does not see how you can apply overhead using a predetermined rate, and went on to say: "If overhead cost per hour is $15 in one month and $6 the next, that's the way it goes. All this 'applying' business is a bookkeeping trick, but it doesn't make any sense in the real world." Comment on the statements.

13-6 Are cost accountants the villains? Mr. Robert Fox, executive vice president of Creative Output, a management consulting firm in Connecticut, was quoted as arguing that allowing cost accounting "to dictate the way a factory floor is organized and run" is harmful. Fox was further quoted as saying that

> The cost accounting system assigns part of overall costs of running the factory to each step in the manufacturing process. Each hour a machine is running, for instance, may be costed at a given amount. A foreman will then try to get as much material as he can through that machine . . . to keep the costs assigned to his particular work stations as low as possible.

Discuss the quotation. What does Mr. Fox mean and how must a company be applying overhead for the quotation to be correct?

EXERCISES

13-7 Basic actual job-order costing Brindley Furniture uses actual job-order costing, applying overhead to jobs based on direct labor hours. Brindley worked on two large orders in March.

	Job	
	M-1	M-2
Material cost	$80,000	$115,000
Direct labor cost	$70,000	$ 85,000
Direct labor hours	9,000	11,000

Actual overhead in March was $180,000.

Required

1. Determine the actual overhead rate for March.
2. Determine the amount of overhead to be applied to each job.
3. Determine the total cost of each job.

13-8 Basic normal job-order costing (extension of 13-7) Suppose now that Brindley uses normal costing, with a predetermined overhead rate of $10 per direct labor hour.

Required

1. Determine the amount of overhead to be applied to each job.
2. Determine the total cost of each job.
3. Determine the amount of overapplied or underapplied overhead for March.
4. Suppose that Brindley budgeted annual overhead using the formula: $1,500,000 + ($4 × direct labor hours). The predetermined overhead rate was based on 250,000 budgeted direct labor hours. Assuming that budgeted monthly fixed overhead is $125,000, what were the budget variance and volume variance?

13-9 Job-order costing income statements (extension of 13-7 and 13-8) Brindley Furniture's job M-1 was incomplete at the end of March, while job M-2 was sold for $600,000. Selling and administrative expenses were $150,000.

Required

1. Prepare an income statement for March using the results from 13-7.
2. Prepare an income statement for March using the results from 13-8. Show any misapplied overhead as an adjustment to normal cost of sales.

13-10 Job-order costing—income statement SBO Company uses normal job-order costing. Its predetermined overhead rate is based on the following data.

Variable overhead per direct labor hour	$ 2
Total budgeted fixed overhead	$600,000
Total budgeted direct labor hours	200,000

The company began 19X5 with no inventories. A summary of materials and direct labor cost for 19X5 appears below.

	Total	Jobs Sold	Jobs in Ending Inventories
Materials costs	$ 800,000	$ 700,000	$100,000
Direct labor cost	$1,800,000	$1,600,000	$200,000
Direct labor hours	180,000	160,000	20,000

Total sales were $6,000,000; selling and administrative expenses were $2,600,000. Total actual manufacturing overhead was $840,000.

Required

1. Compute the predetermined overhead rate for 19X5.
2. Prepare an income statement for 19X5 with overapplied or underapplied overhead shown as an adjustment to cost of sales.

13-11 Predetermined overhead rates For each of the following situations, fill in the missing data. The predetermined overhead rates are based on budgeted fixed costs and budgeted machine hours for the year. There is no variable overhead.

	(a) Fixed Overhead Rate	(b) Budgeted Fixed Overhead	(c) Budgeted Hours	(d) Actual Hours	(e) Fixed Overhead Applied
1.	______	$180,000	30,000	31,000	______
2.	$8	______	20,000	22,000	______
3.	______	$ 70,000	______	11,000	$ 77,000
4.	$4	$160,000	______	______	$172,000

13-12 Ethics and overhead application Milton Machine does considerable work for the U.S. government on cost-plus contracts. The typical cost-plus contract provides that the government will pay for materials, direct labor, and overhead. The government requires that overhead assigned to jobs be reasonable and in conformity with the company's usual methods. An allowance for profit is then added to the total cost to determine the price.

Milton has been using machine hours to apply overhead but its controller believes that the company should shift to labor hours. He explains, "Our government business could be a lot more profitable if we used labor time to apply overhead. Government business is much more labor-intensive than commercial business and would therefore shoulder more overhead."

Required

Comment on the controller's proposal.

13-13 Overhead relationships—variances Each of the following cases is independent. Fill in the blanks, being sure to indicate whether a variance is favorable or unfavorable. The amounts for "total budgeted overhead" are the flexible budget allowances for the actual level of activity for the period. In each case, the firm uses a single rate to apply both fixed and variable overhead.

Case	(a) Total Budgeted Overhead	(b) Total Actual Overhead	(c) Total Applied Overhead	(d) Budget Variance	(e) Volume Variance
1	$400,000	$402,000	$403,000	______	______
2	$600,000	______	$585,000	$6,000U	______
3	______	$310,000	______	$6,000U	$18,000F
4	$400,000	______	______	$6,000F	$10,000U

13-14 Job-order costing—assigning overhead Marquette Boatworks uses normal costing and its predetermined overhead rate is based on the following information. Monthly budgeted overhead = $800,000 + ($0.60 × direct labor cost). Monthly budgeted direct labor cost is $1,000,000. At the end of March, the following information was available.

	Total	Jobs Sold	Jobs in Ending Inventory of Work in Process	Jobs in Ending Inventory of Finished Goods
Materials cost	$ 630,000	$500,000	$ 70,000	$60,000
Direct labor cost	$1,010,000	$820,000	$100,000	$90,000

Actual overhead for the month was $1,388,000.

Required

1. Compute the predetermined overhead rate based on direct labor cost.
2. Determine cost of goods sold for the month.
3. Determine ending inventory of work in process.
4. Determine ending inventory of finished goods.
5. Determine overapplied or underapplied overhead.
6. Determine the volume variance.

13-15 Predetermined overhead rates—job-order costing Walton Company uses predetermined rates for fixed overhead, based on machine hours. The following data are available relating to 19X5.

Budgeted fixed factory overhead cost	$240,000
Budgeted machine hours	40,000
Actual fixed factory overhead cost incurred	$242,000
Actual machine hours used	39,000
Actual machine hours by job	

Job No.	Machine Hours Used on Job
12	8,000
13	14,000
14	7,000
15	10,000

Required

1. Compute the predetermined overhead rate.
2. Determine the overhead to be applied to each job.
3. Determine the budget variance and the volume variance.

13-16 Job order costing—activity-based overhead rates MFG Industries applies overhead to jobs using two rates—one based on the number of parts used on each job, the other based on machine hours for each job. Because of the high amounts of overhead associated with purchasing, receiving, storing, and issuing materials, the managers believe that simply using machine hours to allocate this overhead is inappropriate. Summary data for 19X5 follow.

	Budget	Actual
Part-related overhead	$ 240,000	$ 234,000
Machine-related overhead	$ 700,000	$ 697,000
Cost of materials used on jobs	$1,600,000	$1,582,000
Direct labor cost	$ 900,000	$ 869,000
Machine hours	100,000	98,000
Number of parts	1,000,000	1,040,000

Data related to jobs worked on in 19X5 follow.

			Jobs in Ending Inventory of	
	Total	Jobs Sold	Work in Process	Finished Goods
Materials cost	$1,582,000	$1,321,000	$82,000	$179,000
Direct labor cost	$ 869,000	$ 788,000	$33,000	$ 48,000
Machine hours	98,000	77,000	7,000	14,000
Number of parts	1,040,000	980,000	25,000	35,000

Sales were $3,890,000 and administrative expenses were $356,000.

Required

1. Compute the predetermined overhead rates for parts and for machine hours.
2. Determine the cost of jobs sold and the cost of each type of ending inventory.
3. Prepare an income statement showing misapplied overhead as an adjustment to normal cost of sales.

13-17 Basic job order costing Rehman Machinery, Inc. manufactures large custom drills. It uses a predetermined overhead rate of $4.20 per machine hour. During August, Rehman worked on three jobs. Data appear below.

	Z-101	K-221	K-341
Machine hours	2,280	930	2,910
Direct labor cost	$23,400	$14,200	$36,320
Materials cost	$24,570	$ 9,220	$26,245

Job Z-101 was completed and sold. The other jobs remained in inventory. Actual overhead for August was $25,210.

Required

1. Determine the overhead to be applied to each job.
2. Determine normal cost of sales and ending inventory.
3. Determine overapplied or underapplied overhead.

13-18 Comparison of actual and normal costing Riopelle Company uses actual job-order costing, assigning overhead to jobs based on direct labor cost. During March, Riopelle had the following activity.

	Jobs Worked on in March		
	M-1	M-2	M-3
Materials cost	$28,000	$41,000	$32,000
Direct labor cost	$24,000	$18,000	$28,000

Total actual overhead was $196,000; selling and administrative expenses were $28,000. Job M-1 was sold for $160,000. Jobs M-2 and M-3 were incomplete at the end of March.

Required

1. Determine the actual overhead rate per direct labor dollar.
2. Determine the overhead assigned to each job and the total cost of each job.
3. Prepare an income statement for March.
4. Suppose now that Riopelle uses normal costing. Its predetermined overhead rate is based on $2,100,000 budgeted overhead and $700,000 budgeted direct labor cost for the year. Calculate the predetermined overhead rate and redo items 2 and 3 using normal costing. Show any misapplied overhead as an adjustment to normal gross margin.

13-19 ***Graphical analysis of overhead*** The graph below shows the budgeted manufacturing overhead for Minich Company.

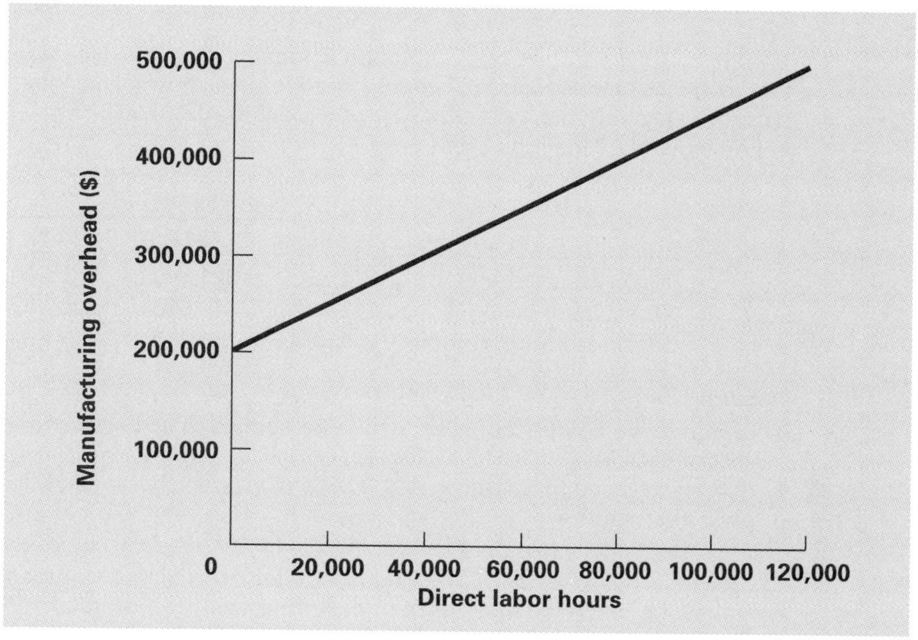

Required

1. Draw in the line that represents applied overhead for each of these two cases.
   (a) The predetermined overhead rate is $5 per direct labor hour.
   (b) The predetermined overhead rate is based on 100,000 direct labor hours.
2. Suppose that actual overhead equals budgeted overhead and that volume is 90,000 direct labor hours. What are the volume variances under each of the two cases from item 1?

13-20 ***Job order costing for a service business*** D. J. Grimm Co. is an engineering consulting firm that specializes in mining work. The company uses a job-order cost system to accumulate costs for each job. Data on operations for August appear below.

	Grand Bay Gold	Big Butte Copper	Flake River
Engineers' time, hours	200	350	150
Engineers' cost	$5,000	$7,300	$3,600
Other expenses	$2,000	$1,500	$1,200

Other expenses include travel, lodging, auto rentals, meals and other items that are charged to clients. Grimm applies overhead to jobs using a predetermined overhead rate. The rate is based on the following data.

Budgeted overhead cost	$6,400,000
Budgeted engineering hours	200,000

Required

1. Calculate the predetermined rate.
2. Using the rate calculated in part 1, determine the cost of each job worked on in August.

13-21 Basic job-order costing Kelton Company makes a wide variety of gear assemblies for industrial applications. The firm uses normal costing, with a predetermined overhead rate of $3.70 per machine hour. During March 19X6, Kelton worked on the jobs listed below.

	Job Number		
	311	312	313
Materials used on job	$15,260	$21,340	$ 8,890
Direct labor cost	$17,250	$13,550	$10,100
Machine hours	1,480	1,230	860

Required

1. Compute the amounts of overhead to be applied to each job and the total cost of each job.
2. Actual overhead for March was $12,980. What was overapplied or underapplied overhead?

13-22 Overhead application The controller of Williams Company received the following budgeted data for manufacturing overhead costs of 19X7.

	Fixed Amount	Variable Cost per Direct Labor Hour
Indirect labor	$ 47,800	$0.40
Supplies	25,300	0.15
Lubricants	7,700	0.10
Utilities	46,400	0.48
Repairs	21,000	0.17
Property taxes	6,000	0
Depreciation	32,000	0
Total	$186,200	$1.30

It is estimated that 70,000 direct labor hours will be worked in 19X7.

Required

1. Compute the predetermined fixed overhead rate per direct labor hour.
2. Assume that 67,000 direct labor hours are worked on jobs in 19X7.
   (a) How much fixed overhead will be applied?
   (b) How much variable overhead should be incurred? How much applied?
   (c) If actual overhead costs are $274,800, what are the budget variance and volume variance?

13-23 Overhead application Vavasour Company is a highly automated operation that measures its activity by machine hours. Its managers have budgeted machine hours for the coming year, 19X2, at 300,000. They budget annual manufacturing overhead as: total budgeted overhead = $600,000 + ($3 × machine hours). There were no beginning inventories.

Required

1. Compute the predetermined overhead rate for 19X2.
2. At the end of 19X2, the controller collected the following information.

Total manufacturing overhead incurred	$1,585,000
Total machine hours:	315,000
Machine hours on jobs sold	275,000
Machine hours on jobs in ending inventories	40,000

Determine the amounts of applied overhead in costs of goods sold and in ending inventories. Determine the amount of overapplied or underapplied overhead and break it down into the budget variance and volume variance.

PROBLEMS

13-24 Job order costing—activity-based overhead rates Billings Machines uses two rates to apply overhead to jobs. One rate is based on materials cost, the other on machine time. Billings has relatively high overhead that is related to buying, receiving, storing, and issuing materials; hence the managers believe that applying this overhead through the relative materials cost of jobs is appropriate. The data below relate to 19X4.

	Budget
Materials-related overhead	$ 640,000
Machine-related overhead	$1,100,000
Cost of materials used on jobs	$1,600,000
Machine hours	200,000

Data related to three jobs worked on in March follow.

	Job XT-56	Job XR-23	Job XY-67
Materials cost	$21,000	$82,000	$39,000
Direct labor cost	$16,000	$13,000	$18,000
Machine hours	8,500	4,500	2,900

Actual material-related overhead was $59,200 and actual machine-related overhead was $92,800.

Required

1. Compute the predetermined overhead rates for materials and for machine hours.
2. Determine the amount of overhead to be applied to each job and the total cost of each job.
3. Determine overapplied or underapplied overhead for each type of overhead.

13-25 Job-order costing—two departments Barton Machinery Company makes industrial robots to customer order. There are two departments,

Machining and Assembly. The Machining Department is highly mechanized, and the Assembly Department is labor intensive. Accordingly, the firm applies overhead using machine hours in the Machining Department and direct labor hours in the Assembly Department. Budgeted data for 19X6 appear below.

	Machining Department	Assembly Department
Total budgeted overhead	$720,000	$120,000
Machine hours	120,000	
Direct labor hours		60,000

During March Barton worked on two jobs.

	Job #1029	Job #1030
Materials used	$21,000	$32,000
Direct labor, Assembly Department, at $6 per hour	$12,000	$19,200
Machine hours in Machining Department	4,000	5,000

Required

1. Calculate the predetermined overhead rate for each department.
2. Calculate the overhead applied to each job and the total cost of each job.
3. Actual overhead in the Machining Department was $55,500, in the Assembly Department, $10,200. Calculate overapplied or underapplied overhead for each department.

13-26 Basic job-order costing Walker Company manufactures precision optical instruments to customers order. Walker uses normal costing and sets its predetermined overhead rate based on machine hours. For 19X4, the rate is $11.40 per hour, which is based on $3,192,000 budgeted overhead and 280,000 budgeted hours.

During January, the firm worked on three jobs.

	Job Number		
	M-101	R-12	Z-610
Materials used	$ 36,800	$ 74,200	$41,600
Direct labor cost	$122,200	$119,200	$77,300
Machine hours	8,800	8,200	7,200

Job M-101 was completed and sold while the other two remained in inventory at the end of January. Actual overhead incurred in January was $271,300.

Required

1. Determine the amount of overhead that should be applied to each job.
2. Determine normal cost of goods sold for January and ending inventory.
3. Determine overapplied or underapplied overhead for January.

13-27 Job costing in a service firm Juarez and Garcia is a firm of architectural engineers operating in a single office in a medium-sized city. The firm charges clients for the time that each person on the staff spends on the client's business, using a rate of 2 1/2 times the person's salary, based on an 1,800-hour working year. Thus, an architectural draftsperson earning a salary of $15,000 is charged out to clients at $21 per hour [($15,000/1,800) × 2.5 = $20.83, rounded to $21]. The rate is intended to cover all costs and to yield a profit.

Budgeted Results for 19X9	
Salaries of professional staff	$ 700,000
Salaries of support personnel (clerks, typists, etc.)	78,000
Other costs	680,000
Total expected costs	$1,458,000

The listed costs do not include salaries for Juarez and Garcia. Each partner expects to work about 1,200 chargeable hours at a rate of $60 per hour. About 80% of the professional staff's time is chargeable to clients, as well as about 40% of the support personnel's time. Nonchargeable time is for general firm business, professional activities (attending seminars and continuing-education programs), and business development.

Required

1. What total income will the partners earn if their estimates prove correct?
2. Suppose that two professional employees work on a design for a particular client. One earns $18,000 per year, the other $21,000, and each works 12 hours on this particular project. How much will the firm charge the client for the project assuming that neither the partners nor the support staff is involved in this project? (Round hourly rates to the nearest dollar.)

13-28 Overhead costs and pricing policy HortonWorks is a medium-sized machine shop that does custom work for industrial customers. Business is seasonal, with about four busy months, three slack months, and the rest about average. HortonWorks uses an actual job-order costing system, assigning overhead to jobs at the end of each month based on the labor cost of each job. Rae Horton, the owner, sets prices using the following format, with hypothetical data.

Estimated material cost	$32.50
Estimated labor cost	16.80
Subtotal	49.30
Allowance for overhead at 60%	29.58
Subtotal	78.88
Allowance for profit at 10%	7.89
Price	$86.77

Horton developed the formula based on experience and on the financial results of the past few years. Overhead has averaged about 60% of the sum of materials and labor costs, and a 10% profit is reasonable in the industry.

Horton has found that similar jobs seem to be more or less profitable depending on the month in which they are done. This bothers her, and she has begun to wonder whether her pricing policy is sensible.

Required

1. In which months, busy or slack, will jobs *appear* more profitable? Why?
2. Should Horton modify her pricing policy? What should she do?

13-29 Job-order costing The following data pertain to the March operations of Covera Machine Tool Company. The company ships jobs as it completes them, keeping no inventory of finished goods.

Jobs in beginning work in process:	
Materials	$237,670
Direct labor	$322,200
Factory overhead	$467,190
Materials put into process in March:	
To jobs in ending inventory	$228,310
To jobs finished and sold in March	$881,480
Direct labor for March:	
To jobs in ending work in process	$452,400
To jobs finished and sold in March	$892,880

The company uses normal costing and applies overhead at $1.50 per direct labor dollar. The materials and labor costs for jobs finished and sold include the cost to finish the beginning inventory of work in process.

The company had sales of $4,680,000 in March, selling and administrative expenses of $453,650.

Required

1. Determine the overhead cost in ending inventory of work in process and in cost of goods sold.
2. Overhead was overapplied by $18,430 in March. What was actual overhead?
3. Prepare an income statement for March, treating overapplied overhead as an adjustment to normal cost of sales.

13-30 Job order costing—comparison of overhead rates Rubenstein Machines uses a single overhead rate based on machine hours. One of its managers believes that the company could benefit from using two rates, one based on materials cost, the other on machine time. The manager believes that because Rubenstein has relatively high overhead related to buying, receiving, storing, and issuing materials, applying this overhead through the relative materials cost of jobs is appropriate. The data below relate to 19X4.

	Budget
Materials-related overhead	$ 480,000
Machine-related overhead	1,300,000
Total overhead	$1,780,000
Cost of materials used on jobs	$1,600,000
Machine hours	200,000

Data related to three jobs worked on in March follow.

	Job XT-56	Job XR-23	Job XY-67
Materials cost	$21,000	$82,000	$39,000
Direct labor cost	$16,000	$13,000	$18,000
Machine hours used	8,500	4,500	2,900

Actual materials-related overhead was $39,800 and actual machine-related overhead was $105,800.

Required

1. Compute the predetermined overhead rate per machine hour assuming that Rubenstein uses only machine hours to apply overhead, as it has been doing.

2. Determine the amount of overhead to be applied to each job and the total cost of each job.
3. Redo parts 1 and 2 using the two rates as suggested by the manager. Comment on the differences in job costs here and in part 2.

13-31 Job order costing for a service business D. J. Westlake Co. is a partnership of Certified Public Accountants that specializes in tax work. The company uses a job-order cost system to accumulate costs for each job it does for a particular client. Data on operations for June appear below.

	Walton Estate Planning	GHK, Inc Federal Return	All Other Jobs
Senior accountant time, hours	80	40	3,000
Junior accountant time, hours	20	150	12,000

Westlake pays senior accountants an average of $60,000 per year for an expected 2,000 hour year. It pays juniors an average of $30,000 per year for the same expected hours. Westlake uses the average hourly pay to determine the cost of accountants' time on jobs. Westlake also charges an hourly amount to cover overhead costs and provide a profit. The client is charged for the time and the combined overhead/profit rate. This year, the rate is based on the following data.

Budgeted overhead cost	$9,200,000
Budgeted profit	$ 800,000
Budgeted hours	200,000

Required

1. Calculate the rates Westlake will use for senior accountants' and junior accountants' time.
2. Calculate the predetermined rate that Westlake must use to cover its overhead costs and meet its profit objective.
3. Using that rate, determine the "cost" of each job worked on in June and the cost of "all other jobs."
4. How is Westlake's accounting different from that of a manufacturer? Does its method make sense?

13-32 Job-order costing, beginning inventory Wisconsin Machinery Company makes large industrial machines. It uses a job-order costing system applying overhead at $15 per direct labor hour. Direct laborers are paid $8 per hour. The following data relate to jobs worked on in March 19X4.

	4-22	4-23	4-24	4-25
Costs in beginning inventory:				
Materials	$ 34,000	$10,000	0	0
Direct labor	48,000	8,000	0	0
Overhead	90,000	15,000	0	0
Total	$172,000	$33,000	0	0
Costs incurred in March:				
Materials	$ 11,000	$46,000	$60,000	$ 9,000
Direct labor	$ 16,000	$32,000	$52,000	$12,000

Jobs 4-22, 4-23, and 4-24 were completed and sold. Job 4-25 was not finished at the end of March. Total overhead incurred during March was $212,000.

Required

1. Compute the amounts of overhead to be applied to each job.
2. Compute the amount of overapplied or underapplied overhead for March.
3. Compute cost of goods sold for March and the inventory at March 31.
4. Revenue from the three jobs sold was $860,000. Selling and administrative expenses for March were $180,000. Prepare an income statement for March.

13-33 CVP analysis for a job order company Brill Optics manufactures special lenses to customer order. Kim Brill, the owner, is trying to develop a profit plan and has collected the following budgeted data for 19X7.

Materials cost	$200,000
Labor cost (40,000 hours at $9 per hour)	360,000
Variable overhead	160,000
Fixed overhead	240,000
Selling and administrative expenses, all fixed	120,000

Brill has set a predetermined overhead rate of $10 per direct labor hour. She sets prices at 120% of total manufacturing cost, including applied overhead.

Required

1. What profit will Brill earn if operations meet her expectations?
2. Suppose that Brill is able to generate only 35,000 direct labor hours worth of work, a 12.5% decline. Materials and variable overhead also decline by 12.5%. Brill treats misapplied overhead as an adjustment to normal cost of sales. What profit will she earn, assuming prices were set using applied overhead?
3. What pricing policy, stated as a percentage of total manufacturing cost, will give Brill a $100,000 profit working 40,000 direct labor hours?

13-34 Costing and pricing in a hospital The controller of Prairie Memorial Hospital has recently decided to set prices for laboratory tests using a formula based on costs. She has analyzed each type of test as follows.

Class of Test	Time Required (minutes)	Number Performed in Average Year
I	12	38,000
II	15	17,000
III	30	9,000

Variable costs are negligible. The controller believes that because all lab technicians are salaried, it is best to treat their salaries as overhead costs. Total annual overhead costs are $960,000.

Required

1. Calculate a predetermined overhead rate per minute. Round to the nearest $0.001.
2. Determine the price for each class of test that will make the laboratory break even. Round prices to the nearest cent.
3. Suppose that the laboratory performs 37,000 Class I; 17,000 Class II; and 10,000 Class III tests. Total costs are $965,000. Determine profit or loss.

13-35 Overhead application and pricing decisions Grendel Company makes high-quality furniture. The company has just received an offer from a large wholesaler for a single batch of goods. The price is $25,000, which is about $10,000 less than normal. The sales manager is sure that existing sales would be unaffected by the special order and wants to accept the order if any profit can be made. The production manager provided the following estimates of cost for the order.

Materials	$ 6,000
Direct labor (3,000 hours)	9,000
Overhead	15,000
Total	$30,000

The production manager informed you that the overhead cost is based on the overhead application rate of $5 per direct labor hour. The rate includes both fixed and variable overhead and was based on 60,000 expected direct labor hours and $300,000 budgeted total overhead costs. The rate last year was $5.50, based on 50,000 direct labor hours and $275,000 total overhead costs. The production manager told you that the difference in rates is due to the difference in budgeted direct labor hours—the cost structure is the same this year as last year.

Required

1. Determine the incremental cost of the order. Should it be accepted?
2. What other factors should be considered in deciding whether to accept this special order?

13-36 Overhead rates and cost analysis Walton Machinery Company makes industrial machines. The firm has been operating well below capacity, and Latashia Williams, the sales manager, has been trying to increase orders. She recently received an offer to bid on a large press and submitted the specifications to Walton's cost estimators. Their estimate appears below.

Materials	$29,600
Direct labor at $9 per hour	19,800
Overhead at $12 per direct labor hour	26,400
Total manufacturing cost	75,800
Standard allowance for selling and administrative expenses, 10% of manufacturing cost	7,580
Total cost	83,380
Standard allowance for profit at 15% of total cost	12,507
Suggested price	$95,887

Williams told the executive vice president that this suggested price is not low enough to get the job. She said that the customer expected a price in the neighborhood of $75,000, which another company had already bid. The vice president called in the controller, who said that the overhead rate was about 60% variable, 40% fixed, and that variable selling and administrative expenses were negligible. The vice president was reluctant to meet the $75,000 price but agreed to think it over and get back to Williams.

Required
Write a memorandum to Ms. Williams indicating whether Walton should meet the $75,000 price.

13-37 Pricing policy and profits Sumter Milling is a job-order firm. It uses material supplied by its customers, so that virtually all of its manufacturing costs are direct labor and overhead. Jackie Wiggins, the controller, prepared the following data for use in establishing the company's pricing policy for the coming year.

Total budgeted direct labor hours	240,000
Total budgeted manufacturing costs	$4,800,000

Total budgeted manufacturing costs were developed using the formula:

$$\text{Total manufacturing costs} = \$1{,}200{,}000 + (\$15 \times \text{direct labor hours})$$

Total selling and administrative expenses are budgeted as: $800,000 + ($0.10 × revenue). The management of the company seeks an $880,000 profit.

Required
1. Determine the revenue Sumter must earn to achieve its profit objective.
2. Determine the price per direct labor hour Sumter must charge to achieve the objective.
3. Suppose that the company uses the pricing policy you developed and actually works 230,000 direct labor hours. What will its profit be?
4. Suppose that the company uses your pricing policy and works 250,000 hours. What will its profit be?

13-38 Overhead rates, ABC, and pricing Jarod Kane, controller, and Renee Poston, sales manager of Hicks Furniture, were discussing the company's dismal operating results. Poston said "Some of the products in our high-volume lines just are not selling. Our competitors prices are less than ours, but we are leaving almost no margin to cover selling and administrative expenses and provide a reasonable profit. However, some of our low-volume products are doing quite well, especially some of those we make in small jobs."

Kane had begun a study of the company's costs and thought that part of the problem might lie with the way it applied overhead to jobs. "Look," he said, "a job order of our high-volume chairs might be 200-300 units, while for some of the others, say an expensive sofa, a typical job size is more like 20. There have to be significant costs of making up many such small batches instead of a few large ones. After all, we have to do a cost estimate and start some paperwork for each job, workers have to log in their time, we have to track the job through the plant, and so on.

Plus, some of our costs are related to such activities as setting up machinery, moving materials and semi-finished product, packing up a shipment, and are typically made in large batches. My new assistant is completing the study I started and I expect to hear about the findings this afternoon." You, the new assistant, have accumulated the following information that you believe is accurate enough for preliminary analysis.

Costs and activities under current procedures

	Model 807 Chair	Model 5052 Table
Number in typical job order	200	30
Average cost per job:		
Materials	$24,000	$20,400
Direct labor at $10/hour	6,000	1,500
Overhead at $25/DLH	15,000	3,750
Total unit cost	$45,000	$25,650
Price at 120% of manufacturing cost	$54,000	$30,780

Activity-based data

Driver for Cost Pool	Total Cost in Pool	Annual Activity of Driver
Direct labor	$4,800,000	300,000
Machine setups	1,200,000	5,000
Number of parts/components	900,000	450,000
Number of record keeping transactions	400,000	400,000

Amounts of Cost Driver per Job

Model 807	Model 5052
600 DLH	150 DLH
1 setup	12 setups
400 parts	800 parts
200 transactions	500 transactions

Required

1. Calculate overhead rates for each cost driver and determine the cost and price of each model.
2. Write a memorandum to Mr. Kane explaining the differences between your costs and the original costs above. State why the company seems to be experiencing the operating results described by Poston.
3. In general, would you expect high-volume or low-volume products to show higher overhead costs under ABC than under labor-based assignment? Why?

13-39 Changing overhead rates Benson Electronics has been on a cost-cutting program designed to help it meet foreign competition. The cost of a typical unit of Benson's major product appears below.

Materials and components	$180
Direct labor	44
Overhead at 400% of direct labor	176
Total cost	$400

The overhead cost reflects actual overhead divided by actual labor hours at 50,000 units, the expected production level of the product. Benson's engineers did considerable redesigning of the product line to reduce labor cost. They introduced some custom-made components, which, though costlier than the existing components, were easier to assemble into the units. They also changed some job descriptions and rerouted product flow. The head of engineering understood that the changes would raise material/component costs by about $16, but would reduce labor cost by roughly $16 and therefore reduce overhead by about $64 at the 400% rate. The results in the first six months were not encouraging as the following unit cost calculation, which as before is based on actual overhead costs and direct labor for 50,000 units, shows.

Materials and components	$190
Direct labor	29
Overhead at 600% of direct labor	174
Total cost	$393

The heads of production and engineering, as well as the controller, were not happy with the results. A great deal of work had resulted in little net decrease in unit cost. The most disappointing aspect was the sharp increase in the overhead rate occasioned by the drop in direct labor.

Required

1. Determine total overhead before and after the cost-cutting program.
2. Suppose that the entire difference you found in part 1 is attributable to the component of overhead that varies with direct labor. Determine the variable component of overhead, with respect to direct labor. Can you now explain why costs did not fall as much as one might have thought?
3. What do you recommend?

13-40 Normal costing Boardman Company manufactures equipment used to cap bottles. The following data summarize 19X3 activities.

Beginning inventories of work in process and finished goods	$ 360,000
Materials put into process	2,240,000
Direct labor	1,780,000
Manufacturing overhead incurred	2,520,000
Selling and administrative expenses	880,000
Sales	7,960,000

The firm uses an overhead application rate of $1.40 per direct labor dollar, based on budgeted direct labor cost of $1,800,000 and the following formula for budgeting manufacturing overhead:

$$\text{Manufacturing overhead} = \$1{,}440{,}000 + (\$0.60 \times \text{direct labor cost})$$

At the end of the year, the controller prepared the following analysis of costs.

			Ending Inventory of	
	Total	Jobs Sold	Incomplete Jobs	Finished Jobs
Materials	$2,240,000	$1,890,000	$120,000	$230,000
Direct labor	$1,780,000	$1,480,000	$100,000	$200,000

Required

Prepare an income statement for the year, using normal costing and showing the budget variance and volume variance as separate adjustments to gross margin.

13-41 Overhead rate behavior Ned Clinton, controller of Walcott Industries, has been puzzled by the behavior of overhead rates. The company has been engaged in a program to reduce costs and the focus has been on direct labor and associated overhead costs. Because the average cost per direct labor hour (DLH) was in the $10.20-$10.40 range and the average overhead rate around $39 per DLH, Clinton expected savings in the area of $50 for reductions in DLH.

Clinton has been collecting data (see below) for the past few quarters to track the progress of the program. Output was about the same in each quarter, so the decreased labor hours represent improved performance.

Quarter	Direct Labor Hours	Direct Labor Cost	Overhead Cost	Actual Overhead per DLH
3rd 19X1	62,000	$634,500	$2,432,000	$39.23
4th 19X1	61,100	629,450	2,431,900	39.80
1st 19X2	61,200	630,180	2,431,200	39.74
2nd 19X2	58,300	601,100	2,428,800	41.66
3rd 19X2	55,400	569,900	2,427,200	43.81

Clinton was puzzled at the behavior of the overhead rate. He knew that overhead was not totally variable with direct labor, but thought that there surely should have been a considerable drop in overhead as direct labor hours declined.

Required

1. Using the high-low method, determine the component of overhead costs that varies with direct labor hours.
2. State why you think Clinton might have been incorrect in his estimates of the effects of reducing labor time and what he might do now.

13-42 Job-order costing and decisions Last month, Marchmont Furniture Company began work on custom-made chairs ordered by a retail store. When the work was nearly complete, the retailer went bankrupt and was not able to pay for the chairs. The sales manager of Marchmont immediately called other stores in an effort to sell the chairs. The original price was $210,000, but the best price the sales manager could get if the chairs were finished according to the original specifications was $140,000. This offer was from the Z-Store chain. Randle Company, which also operates a chain of stores, offered $158,000 for the chairs provided that different upholstery and trim were used. The sales manager talked to the production manager about the order and got the following information.

	Costs Accumulated to Date
Materials	$ 31,500
Direct labor (7,000 hours at $5)	35,000
Factory overhead at $10 per hour	70,000
Total accumulated costs	$136,500

The factory overhead rate includes $4 variable overhead and $6 fixed overhead. The additional work required to complete the chairs was estimated as follows by the production manager.

	Original Specifications	Randle's Specifications
Materials	$4,100	$9,000
Direct labor hours	800 hours	1,800 hours

Required

1. Using the firm's costing method, determine the total costs to be charged to the job assuming (a) the work is completed based on the original specifications and (b) the chairs are modified as required by Randle Company.
2. Determine which offer Marchmont should accept.

13-43 Job-order costing—service business Sofdat Inc. develops computer programs for businesses, hospitals, local governments, and other organizations. The company has been having difficulty analyzing the profitability of jobs and estimating costs for use in bidding.

The company has hired you to develop a job-order costing system. So far, you have decided that production costs should include the costs listed below.

Programmers' salaries	$480,000
Supervisors' salaries	120,000
Other costs of programming	240,000

You decide that the company should use normal costing, treating programmers' salaries as direct labor with each programmer having an hourly rate equaling her or his salary divided by the normal 2,000-hour working year. You also decide to treat the other two elements of cost as manufacturing overhead. You intend to use programming hours to set the predetermined overhead rate because programmers earn different salaries. Finally, you intend to treat the cost of idle programming time (actual salaries paid less salaries charged to jobs) and "excess cost" (amounts charged to jobs in excess of actual salaries paid) as part of overhead.

The president expects selling and administrative expenses to be $180,000. She also expects programmers to work about 24,000 hours, and you decide to use this figure to compute the predetermined overhead rate.

The president is interested in seeing how the system will operate and gives you the following information for a hypothetical month. There was no beginning inventory and sales were $170,000. All costs incurred were one twelfth of the estimated annual amounts given above. Jobs sold had a total of 1,350 programming hours and jobs in process at the end of the month had 450 programming hours, so that actual charged hours for the month were 1,800 (1,350 + 450). Information on programmers' salaries follows.

Salaries on jobs sold	$27,000
Salaries in ending inventory	$ 9,200

Idle time was $3,800 ($40,000 incurred – $27,000 – $9,200).

Required

1. Calculate the predetermined overhead rate per hour of programmer's time.
2. Determine the cost of ending inventory of jobs in process.

3. Determine overapplied or underapplied overhead cost for the month, including idle time.
4. Prepare an income statement for the month showing overapplied or underapplied overhead as a separate expense or negative expense.

13-44 Comparing actual and normal costing—seasonal business Barnett Company has used actual job-order costing for several years. At the end of each month, a clerk divides total manufacturing overhead cost incurred during the month by total direct labor cost for the month to get an overhead rate per labor dollar. He then applies overhead at this rate to each job worked on during the month. Because the company uses actual costing, there is no underapplied or overapplied overhead.

The president has been unhappy with this method because it results in widely differing overhead costs in different months. The work is highly seasonal, with the summer months very heavy and the winter months light. The president has asked you to show how normal costing differs from actual costing and has given you the following data regarding two similar jobs done in the past year.

	Job J-12	Job A-16
Materials cost	$10,410	$10,310
Direct labor	16,900	16,400
Overhead	40,560	29,520
Total	$67,870	$56,230

Job J-12 was done in January, when total overhead was $528,000 and total labor cost was $220,000. Job A-16 was done in August, when total overhead was $1,179,000 and total labor cost was $655,000. The firm budgets annual overhead using the formula:

$$\text{Total annual overhead} = \$3{,}200{,}000 + (\$1.20 \times \text{direct labor cost})$$

Total budgeted labor cost for the current year is $4,000,000.

Required

1. Develop the predetermined overhead rate based on total budgeted overhead and labor cost.
2. Determine the costs of the two jobs using the rate calculated in item 1.
3. Comment on the advantages of using predetermined overhead rates.

13-45 Activity-based overhead rates Percan Industries has been using a single overhead rate, but its managers have become convinced that they need several rates to reflect the activities with which overhead costs are associated. After careful study, the controller developed the following budgeted information regarding cost pools and activities that drive the pools.

Activity	Amount of Activity	Overhead Costs in Pool
Labor hours	400,000 hours	$1,580,000
Machine set-ups	1,600 set ups	$ 256,000
Record keeping	150,000 entries	$ 90,000

Data related to jobs worked on in 19X5 follow.

	Totals	Jobs Sold	Jobs in Ending Inventories
Materials cost	$2,582,000	$2,321,000	$261,000
Direct labor cost	$4,169,000	$3,788,000	$381,000
Direct labor hours	410,000	371,000	39,000
Machine set-ups	1,640	1,560	80
Entries	152,000	136,000	16,000

Actual overhead costs were, by pool: labor hour-based, $1,610,000; machine set-up-based, $262,800; and record keeping, $92,600.

Required

1. Compute the predetermined overhead rate for each activity.
2. Determine the amount of each type of overhead to apply to jobs sold and jobs still in inventory.
3. Determine the total cost of jobs sold and the cost of ending inventory.
4. Determine the amount of misapplied overhead for each cost pool.

13-46 Effects of separate overhead rates (extension of 13-45) One of the managers of Percan Industries says that the new system with its three overhead cost pools is more elaborate and costly than the company needs. He proposes to go back to the old basis, where all overhead was applied using labor hours. In trying to convince him of the wisdom of the separate rates, you pull out the following information about two products that the company manufactures regularly. The data are for typical-sized batches of each product. The company makes several models of each product, but they are all roughly the same. The company prices its products at 150% of total manufacturing cost.

	Product XT-12	Product JY-09
Materials costs	$260	$ 780
Labor cost	280	2,880
Direct labor hours	20	200
Machine set-ups	6	1
Record keeping entries	200	80

Required

1. Determine the cost and price of each product using the overhead rates you developed in the previous assignment.
2. Determine the cost and price of each product using a single overhead rate based on labor hours. Use the budgeted data from the previous assignment and remember to include all of the overhead cost, not just the labor-driven cost.
3. Comment on the results.

13-47 Analyzing overhead The president of your company has asked you some questions about overhead. You recently changed the accounting system from actual to normal costing, with some opposition from other managers who could not see the advantages. Although the president was not happy with the actual costing system, he is not convinced that normal costing is a significant improvement.

The specific questions he wants you to answer relate to determining whether or not costs are under control and what information he can get from the figures for underapplied and overapplied overhead. He gives you the following results from the most recent three months.

	March	April	May
Direct labor hours worked on jobs	14,000	8,000	5,000
Total overhead incurred	$71,000	$52,000	$51,000
Total overhead applied at $6 per direct labor hour	84,000	48,000	30,000
Underapplied (overapplied) overhead	($13,000)	$ 4,000	$21,000

The predetermined rate of $6 per hour was calculated using budgeted direct labor hours for the year of 120,000 and budgeted overhead of $480,000 fixed and $2.00 variable per direct labor hour. Budgeted fixed overhead is $40,000 for each of the three months shown above.

Required

Making any calculations you consider relevant, tell the president what he can learn using the above data.

13-48 Departmental versus plant-wide overhead rates Caldwell Company operates two departments, Grinding and Assembly, in a plant that makes optical devices such as binoculars and telescopes. Because nearly all of its products are made to customer order, Caldwell uses job-order costing. In the past, it has used a single overhead application rate based on total budgeted direct labor hours and total budgeted overhead. The rate for 19X8 was computed using the following data.

	Grinding Department	Assembly Department	Total
Total budgeted overhead	$1,200,000	$800,000	$2,000,000
Budgeted direct labor hours	200,000	50,000	250,000
Rate ($2,000,000/250,000)			$8

Budgeted overhead was based on the following formulas.

Grinding Department	$800,000 + ($2 × direct labor hours)
Assembly Department	$500,000 + ($6 × direct labor hours)

The firm bases its bid prices on total estimated cost including direct labor, materials, and overhead at $8 per direct labor hour. The controller has been thinking about changing to departmental rates and has collected the following data regarding two jobs recently completed. All direct laborers earn $10 per hour.

	Job 391	Job 547
Direct labor hours:		
Grinding	330	80
Assembly	30	180
Materials cost	$3,000	$2,500
Direct labor cost	3,600	2,600

The policy is to bid a price that is 150% of the total estimated manufacturing cost.

Required

1. Determine the overhead that the firm will apply to each job using the $8 plant-wide rate. Determine the total cost of each job. Assuming that the actual results for each job were also the estimated results that the firm used to set the bid prices, determine the price that the firm bid for each job.
2. Compute the predetermined overhead rate for each department.
3. Determine the amounts of overhead applied to each job, the total cost of each job, and the bid price for each job using the predetermined departmental overhead rates that you computed in item 2.
4. Comment on the differences in your results for the two jobs using the plant-wide rate and departmental rates. Do you recommend that the firm switch to departmental rates?

13-49 CVP analysis in a job-order firm Carthage Machine Works manufactures industrial machinery, principally small cutting equipment. Virtually all machines are custom made and Carthage uses job-order costing. The president has developed the following estimates for the coming year, 19X8.

Materials cost	$280,000
Direct labor hours	20,000
Direct labor wage rate	$9 per hour
Variable manufacturing overhead	80% of direct labor cost
Fixed manufacturing overhead	$200,000
Selling and administrative expenses	$ 70,000

The president tells you that her pricing policy is to charge the customer 125% of material cost plus a per-hour amount for direct labor. She wants to earn a profit of $60,000 before taxes in 19X8.

Required

1. Determine the price per direct labor hour the firm must charge to meet the target profit.
2. Suppose that the company adopts the per-hour charge you computed in item 1 and has the following results: material costs, $300,000; direct labor hours, 18,000. All overhead costs are incurred as expected (variable per unit of activity and fixed in total). Determine the profit that the company will earn.

13-50 Overhead application and cost control Guinn Print Shop had the following results in three recent months.

	April	May	June
Actual overhead costs	$25,000	$28,000	$34,000
Applied overhead costs	18,000	27,000	36,000

Arief Guinn, the owner, said that cost control was poor in April, better in May, and excellent in June. "We really need to overapply overhead because that reflects good cost control," he said.

Guinn budgets overhead as $2 variable per direct labor hour and $240,000 fixed per year. Monthly fixed overhead is budgeted at $20,000. Guinn uses 60,000 direct labor hours per year to set its predetermined overhead rate.

Required

1. Determine Guinn's predetermined overhead rate.
2. Determine the number of direct labor hours worked in each month.

3. Determine the budget variance for each month.
4. Explain to Mr. Guinn why his conclusions about cost control were, or were not, correct.

CASES

13-51 Cost justification The following material is taken from a column by Rowland Evans and Robert Novak that appeared in the July 8, 1976 *Knickerbocker News* (Albany, New York). At that time, the federal election laws required that candidates for the presidency limit spending before their parties' conventions to $13 million.

> When Treasury Secretary William Simon traveled to Raleigh, N.C., last Jan. 20 to address the state Chamber of Commerce and then a President Ford Committee (PFC) reception, the taxpayers' bill was $2,310. The reimbursement to Uncle Sam for the PFC for political expenses: $17.44. . . .
>
> The method used for Simon's Jan. 20 journey to North Carolina, an important primary state, is the model. The Air Force charged $2,310 for a Jetstar carrying Simon and seven others (including aides and Secret Service agents) to North Carolina. Since Simon occupied only one of eight seats, his share of the cost is $288.75. The 30 minutes spent at the PFC reception amounted to only 5 per cent of the portal-to-portal time from Washington. So, 5 percent of $288.75 is $14.44. Add $3 for the share of meals, and the cost to the PFC is $17.44.

Required

1. Suppose that you had been engaged as a consultant to former President Ronald Reagan, who was President Ford's opponent in that campaign for the Republican nomination. What would you say about the method used to determine the cost billed to the PFC? What other information would you seek?
2. Suppose that you were engaged as a consultant to the PFC. How would you defend the $17.44 charge?

13-52 What is cost?—consumer action Easy Ed Johnson's Belchfire Auto Agency advertises that it will sell cars at $50 over cost and that anyone who can prove that Johnson is making more than $50 on a sale will get a $5,000 prize. Phyllis Henley decides to disprove Johnson's claim. She obtains the following information from a consumer magazine.

Cost Data from Consumer Scoop—
Belchfire 8 with Standard Equipment

Invoice cost to dealer	$3,400
Commission to salesperson, basic rate per car	100
Variable cost of make-ready services (lubrication, washing, etc.)	40
Total cost to dealer	$3,540

Since Henley knows that Johnson has been selling this particular model for $3,900, she marches into the showroom and demands a $5,000 prize because she can "prove" that Johnson is selling this model at $360 over his cost. Johnson, with considerable aplomb, summons his accountant, who presents the following information to Henley.

Invoice cost to dealer	$3,400
Commission to salesperson, basic rate per car	100
Cost of make-ready services	120
General overhead	230
Total cost	$3,850

The accountant points out that Henley failed to consider the "real" costs of running a large automobile dealership. He states that the make-ready and general overhead costs are based on the total service department cost and total overhead costs divided by the number of cars sold last year (500). General overhead costs are virtually all fixed. Johnson pleasantly and politely offers his condolences to Henley for having failed to win the $5,000 and invites her back any time she wants to buy a car at $50 over cost.

Henley is not at all happy with her reception at Johnson's or the data provided by his accountant, and she decides to sue for the $5,000.

Required

Assume that Henley loses the case at the local level and appeals the decision to a higher court. The trial judge (original decision) agreed with the explanation of Easy Ed's accountant. Nevertheless, Henley argues that Easy Ed is defrauding the populace and owes her $5,000. Her lawyer has asked you to serve as an expert witness. What will your testimony be?

13-53 Determining product costs Renata Tomato Company processes and cans tomato paste. The company has the capability to can whole tomatoes as well, but has not done so for about a year because of lack of profitability. The firm has the capacity to process 5,000,000 pounds of tomatoes per month, whether for canning whole or making into paste.

The production manager and controller were recently discussing the production budget for the next several months. They agreed, on the basis of the information in the following schedule, that the firm should continue to process only tomato paste.

	Whole Tomatoes	Tomato Paste
Selling price per case	$6.00	$5.80
Variable costs:		
Tomatoes [a]	3.10	2.00
Direct labor	0.90	1.00
Variable overhead	1.80	2.00
Packaging	0.52	0.60
Total variable costs	6.32	5.60
Contribution margin	($0.32)	$0.20

a Whole tomatoes must be grade A tomatoes, which cost 15.5¢ per pound.

Paste is made from grade B tomatoes, which cost $0.08 per pound. There are 20 pounds of tomatoes in a case of whole tomatoes, 25 pounds in a case of paste.

A few days after the decision had been made to process only paste, the president received a call from a large tomato grower who offered to sell Renata as many pounds of tomatoes as it could use for the next six months. The price was to be $0.095 per pound, and the batches would be mixed A and B grades. The grower guaranteed that at least 40% of the tomatoes would be grade A.

The president told the production manager about the offer. The latter replied that it should cost $0.005 per pound to sort the tomatoes into the two grades, but that there would be no other additional costs if the offer were accepted. The firm's capacity to process 5,000,000 pounds per month would not be affected. The firm can sell all it can produce of either product.

The production and sales managers decided to investigate the probable effects of taking the offer. They agreed that it was profitable to can whole tomatoes if the price were much less than the current $0.155 per pound, but they were uncertain of the effects on the contribution margin of paste. They agreed to ask the controller to prepare a new analysis of relative profitability of the two products. The controller's analysis showed that paste was now a losing proposition, while whole tomatoes were extremely profitable. For the cost of tomatoes, the controller used $0.10 per pound, the purchase price plus additional sorting costs.

	Whole Tomatoes	Tomato Paste
Selling price per case	$6.00	$5.80
Variable costs:		
Tomatoes	2.00	2.50
Other variable costs	3.22	3.60
Total variable costs	5.22	6.10
Contribution margin	$0.78	($0.30)

The production manager and sales manager wondered about the wisdom of using the $0.10 per pound cost of tomatoes for both products. "After all," said the sales manager, "aren't we paying more for the grade A tomatoes and less for the grade B? It seems unreasonable to say that they cost the same." The controller said that other methods were possible, suggesting that the costs could also be assigned based on the ratios of costs of buying tomatoes already sorted. "If we did it that way," he said, "buying 2,000,000 pounds of grade A tomatoes at $0.155 would cost $310,000. The 3,000,000 grade B tomatoes would cost $240,000 at $0.08. The total cost is $550,000. The cost of grade B is thus about 43.6% of the total. So we could assign $218,000 ($500,000 × 43.6%) to the grade B tomatoes in the package deal. That gives a cost per pound of $0.07267. Doing the same with the grade A produce gives $0.141 per pound."

At this point the president entered the room and commented that it seemed to her that the firm was buying $240,000 worth of grade B tomatoes at $0.08 per pound and the rest of the purchase and sorting costs should be assigned to the grade A tomatoes. "That gives $260,000 to the grade A ($500,000 – $240,000), which is $0.13 per pound. Isn't that best?"

Required

1. Determine whether the firm should buy the unsorted tomatoes.
2. Discuss the appropriateness of the methods of determining the cost of tomatoes suggested by each of the managers and make a recommendation.

14 standard costing and variable costing

Chapter 12 showed how standards can be used to help control variable costs. Chapter 13 introduced absorption costing—the product costing method required for external reporting. Chapter 14 shows how standard costs can be used in product costing and presents an alternative to absorption costing, called variable costing, or direct costing. Variable costing excludes fixed production costs from inventory calculations and uses the familiar contribution margin format of the income statement. Variable costing is acceptable, and widely used, for internal reporting purposes. It can be used by job-order and process costers, and with actual, normal, or standard costing.

STANDARD COSTING

As Chapter 12 described, companies establish standard costs for materials, direct labor, and variable overhead. Large and medium-sized manufacturing companies use **standard costing** much more than they use actual or normal costing. One important reason is that standard costing integrates standard costs and variances into the company's records, so that variances are calculated as a normal part of record keeping. Having as much information as possible captured directly by the accounts is wise, because the information is more likely to be accurate and is easier to retrieve.

Under standard absorption costing, companies determine a standard fixed overhead cost per unit for each product. The resulting total standard cost per unit is used to calculate the cost of inventory and the cost of goods sold. Variances from standard are treated as expenses (or negative expenses if the variances are favorable) and reported separately in the income statement. Chapter 12 covered the determination of standards for variable production costs, so the only new problem is the development of a standard for fixed overhead. The concept of the predetermined overhead rate is useful here. We begin with a simple, one-product company. Such a company can determine a standard fixed cost per unit simply by dividing total budgeted fixed manufacturing overhead by some number of units of product. There is no need to use an input factor such as direct labor hours or machine hours, nor to develop activity-based measures because all resources are devoted to that one product.

Exhibit 14-1 presents data for SMP Company, which produces an automobile part. The company has standards for labor, materials, and variable overhead. To simplify the situation, we group all the standard variable costs into a single per-unit variable cost. Because you have already learned to analyze variable cost variances, we will not give data to identify each variable cost variance, but will only calculate total variable cost variances. Notice that variable selling and administrative expenses are incurred based on units sold, not on units produced.

CALCULATING A STANDARD FIXED COST

The **standard fixed cost per unit** depends, as did the predetermined overhead rate, on two things: (1) the choice of a measure of activity (e.g., number of units, direct labor hours, or machine hours) and (2) a level of activity (e.g., budgeted units or hours). Since we are dealing with a single-product company, the obvious measure of activity is units of product and we have a choice for the level of activity.

Under normal costing, we used budgeted activity to set the predetermined overhead rate. We can use that same level of activity, but we could also use two other levels: **normal activity** (or **normal capacity**) and **practical capacity**. Normal activity is the average activity expected or budgeted over

Exhibit 14-1 SMP Company, Operating Data for 19X5

Production in units	110,000
Sales in units, at $80 each	90,000
Ending inventory in units	20,000
Actual production costs:	
Variable	$2,255,000
Fixed	$3,200,000
Selling and administrative expenses:	
Variable at $5 per unit	$ 450,000
Fixed	$1,400,000
Standards and budgets:	
Budgeted fixed production costs	$3,000,000
Standard variable production costs	$20 per unit

the coming two to five years. The objective in using this activity level is to develop a standard fixed cost that reflects the company's expected long-term per-unit costs, not the cost for a single year (as budgeted activity reflects). Practical capacity is the maximum activity the company can achieve given the usual kinds of interruptions. Events such as strikes or severe shortages of materials are not considered usual. As with budgeted and normal activity, the measure of activity might be units of product, direct labor hours, or a set of activity-based measures. Standard costs based on practical capacity reflect the lowest *reasonable* long-term average fixed cost.

Suppose that the managers of SMP decided to set the standard per-unit fixed cost using normal capacity of 100,000 units. The standard is then $30 per unit, computed as follows:

Standard fixed cost per unit = $3,000,000/100,000 = $30 per unit

The total standard cost per unit is $50, consisting of the $20 standard variable cost per unit and the $30 standard fixed cost per unit. We shall use this standard fixed cost per unit to determine variances, and, if variances are not significant, the standard will also be used in external financial statements for the period.

VARIANCES

We first calculate variable manufacturing cost variances. Total variable cost variances are $55,000 unfavorable, calculated as follows.

Total actual variable production costs (Exhibit 14-1)	$2,255,000
Standard variable costs (110,000 × $20)	2,200,000
Unfavorable variable cost variances	$ 55,000

Fixed overhead variances follow the general pattern of Chapter 13. There is a budget variance and a volume variance.

The *total* fixed overhead variance (misapplied fixed overhead) is $100,000, computed as follows:

Total actual fixed overhead	$3,200,000
Fixed overhead applied (110,000 × $30)	3,300,000
Overapplied overhead	$ 100,000

The volume variance under standard costing is budgeted fixed overhead minus applied fixed overhead. (The volume variance under normal costing is calculated the same way, but applied overhead is based on inputs, not outputs.) The budget variance under standard costing is, just as under normal costing, actual fixed overhead minus budgeted fixed overhead.

Following is an analysis of fixed overhead variances using the diagram format introduced in Chapter 12. The budget variance is $200,000 unfavorable, and the volume variance is $300,000 favorable.

Actual fixed overhead		Budgeted fixed overhead		Applied fixed overhead 110,000 x $30
$3,200,000		$3,000,000		$3,300,000
	$200,000U budget variance		$300,000F volume variance	
		$100,000 overapplied overhead		

Exhibit 14-2 provides a graphical analysis of the same situation.

INCOME STATEMENTS

Using the standard cost per unit and the operating data from Exhibit 14-1, we can prepare an income statement for SMP Company for 19X5. Exhibit 14-3 shows the statement. As you can see, the format is similar to those used for actual and normal absorption costing in Chapter 13, which in turn were based on the typical income statement presentation used in financial accounting. That is, cost of sales is computed by adding the standard production costs for the year to the beginning inventory and then subtracting the ending inventory.

Exhibit 14-2 SMP Company, Fixed Overhead, 19X5

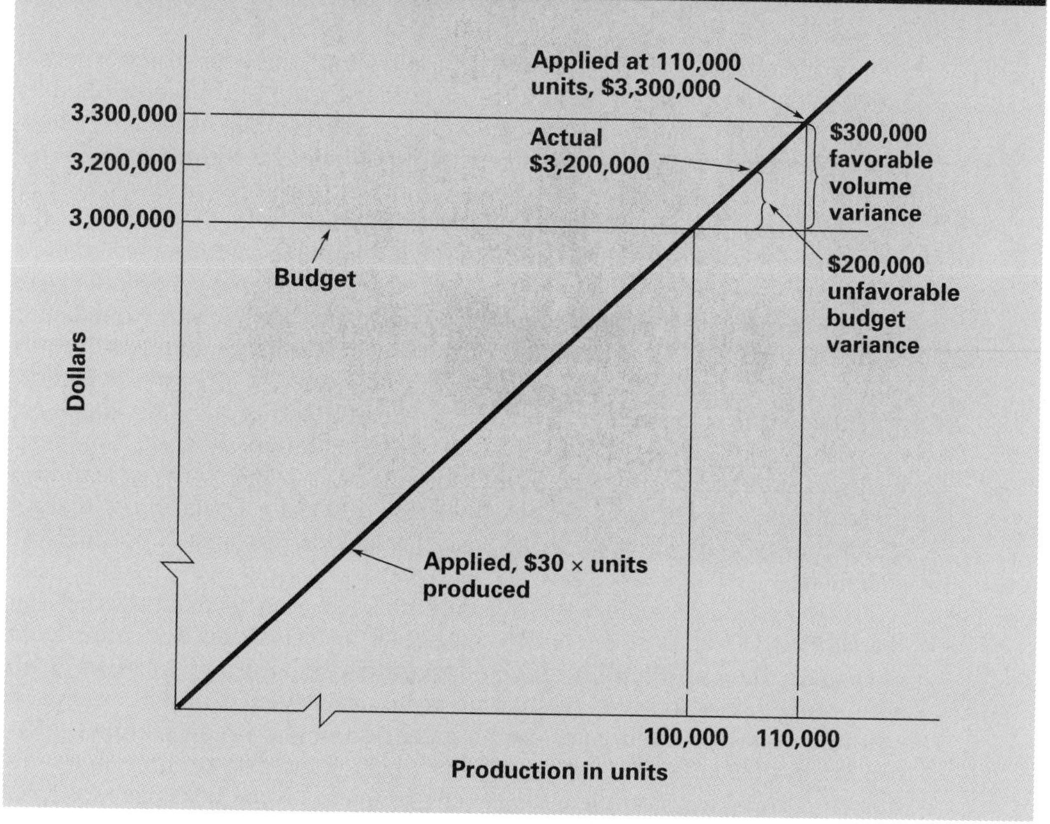

Exhibit 14-3 SMP Company, Income Statement for 19X5

Sales		$7,200,000
Standard cost of sales:		
Beginning inventory	$ 0	
Standard variable production costs (110,000 × $20)	2,200,000	
Applied fixed production costs (110,000 × $30)	3,300,000	
Cost of goods available for sale (110,000 × $50)	5,500,000	
Ending inventory (20,000 × $50)	1,000,000	
Standard cost of sales (90,000 × $50)		4,500,000
Standard gross margin		2,700,000
Variances:		
Fixed manufacturing cost budget variance	200,000U	
Fixed manufacturing cost volume variance	300,000F	
Variable manufacturing cost variances	55,000U	45,000F
Actual gross margin		2,745,000
Selling and administrative (S & A) expenses*		1,850,000
Profit		$ 895,000

* *Fixed costs of $1,400,000 plus variable costs of $450,000, 90,000 × $5*

Notice that the variable production costs and fixed production costs added to the beginning inventory are at standard cost per unit multiplied by unit production. *Under standard costing, all amounts in the calculation of standard cost of goods are standard cost per unit multiplied by the number of units.* This is true for the beginning inventory, applied production costs, cost of goods available for sale, and standard cost of goods sold. Therefore, if the standard cost of units in the beginning inventory is the same as the standard cost for the current year, *standard cost of sales is simply the per-unit standard cost multiplied by the number of units sold.* There is no need to show the details of the section for the standard cost of sales, as it equals the number of units sold times the standard cost per unit. Thus, we can also prepare an income statement such as the one in Exhibit 14-4, which does not show the details of the cost of goods sold section. Exhibit 14-4 also shows variances as adjustments to standard cost of goods sold instead of as adjustments to standard gross margin. You should see that the final results for actual gross margin and income will be the same regardless of where the variances appear in the statement.

Finally, please remember that we do not expect to *incur* fixed overhead at the standard fixed cost per unit—we expect to *incur* total budgeted fixed overhead. The application of fixed overhead to units of product is an accounting device to avoid fluctuating per-unit fixed costs under absorption costing. Standard fixed costs are an extension of the predetermined overhead rates of Chapter 13. Before we show how standards are used in a multiproduct company, complete the review problem on the next page to make sure you understand the basics of standard costing.

Exhibit 14-4 SMP Company, Income Statement for 19X5 (Alternative format)

Sales		$7,200,000
Cost of sales:		
Standard cost of sales (90,000 × $50)	$4,500,000	
Variances:		
Fixed manufacturing cost budget variance	200,000U	
Fixed manufacturing cost volume variance	300,000F	
Variable manufacturing cost variances	55,000U	
Cost of sales		4,455,000
Gross margin		2,745,000
S & A expenses *		1,850,000
Profit		$ 895,000

* *Fixed costs of $1,400,000 plus variable costs of $450,000, 90,000 × $5*

REVIEW PROBLEM

SMP continued to use the same standard costs for 19X6. Its operating data for 19X6 were as follows:

Production, in units	95,000
Sales, in units, at $80 each	100,000
Ending inventory, in units	15,000
Actual production costs:	
Variable	$1,881,000
Fixed	$2,950,000
Selling and administrative expenses:	
Variable at $5 per unit	$ 500,000
Fixed	$1,400,000
Standard variable production cost	$20 per unit
Budgeted fixed production costs	$3,000,000

Prepare income statements for 19X6, using the formats shown in Exhibits 14-3 and 14-4. The solution appears in Exhibit 14-5. This solution uses a slightly different format from that in Exhibit 14-3. Here we show variances as an adjustment to standard cost of goods sold instead of as an adjustment to standard gross margin. The choice is a matter of personal preference.

MULTIPLE PRODUCTS

Standard costing is very popular with *repetitive manufacturers*, companies that make many standard products. It can also be used by companies that make several products of different design. So long as the products are relatively standard, even a job-order company can use standard costing. Any company that can develop standards can use a standard costing system.

Exhibit 14-5 SMP Company, Income Statement for 19X6

Sales (100,000 × $80)		$8,000,000
Standard cost of sales:		
Beginning inventory (Exhibit 14-3)	$1,000,000	
Standard variable production costs (95,000 × $20)	1,900,000	
Applied fixed production costs (95,000 × $30)	2,850,000	
Cost of goods available for sale (115,000 × $50)	5,750,000	
Ending inventory (15,000 × $50)	750,000	
Standard cost of sales (100,000 × $50)	5,000,000	
Variances:		
Fixed manufacturing cost budget variance	50,000F	
Fixed manufacturing cost volume variance	150,000U	
Variable manufacturing cost variances	19,000F	
Cost of sales		5,081,000
Gross margin		2,919,000
S & A expenses*		1,900,000
Profit		$1,019,000

Variances:

Variable cost, $1,881,000 − ($20 × 95,000) = $19,000F

Fixed cost

Actual fixed overhead	Budgeted fixed overhead	Applied fixed overhead (95,000 x $30)
$2,950,000	$3,000,000	$2,850,000

$50,000F budget variance (actual vs. budgeted); $150,000U volume variance (budgeted vs. applied)

$100,000 total fixed overhead variances

* *Fixed costs of $1,400,000 plus variable costs of $500,000, 100,000 × $5*

Consider, for example, Richards Company, which makes two models of tables, Model 345 and Model 788. (If Richards made 500 types of tables and 300 of chairs, it could still use standard costing. We limit the number of products for calculational convenience.) Through engineering studies the company has determined that the standard materials and labor costs for making each model are as follows:

	Model 345	Model 788
Standard materials cost	$20	$60
Standard labor cost, at a standard rate of $10 per hour:		
3 hours × $10	$30	
5 hours × $10		$50

Richards budgets its factory overhead using a budget formula developed with regression analysis (see Chapter 3). The equation for the company is:

$$\textit{Annual factory overhead} = \$2{,}000{,}000 + (\$8 \times \textit{direct labor hours})$$

Richards can establish the standard variable overhead cost per unit of each model simply by multiplying the $8 variable overhead rate by the number of labor hours per unit of each model—a standard of $24 ($8 × 3 hours) for Model 345, and a standard of $40 ($8 × 5 hours) for Model 788. Establishing a standard fixed overhead cost for each model requires not only the standard hours for each model, but also a predetermined fixed overhead rate per labor hour.

Suppose that Richards uses normal capacity of 500,000 labor hours to set the predetermined overhead rate. The predetermined overhead rate for fixed overhead is $4 ($2,000,000/500,000). We can now determine the total standard cost for each model, as follows:

	Model 345	Model 788
Standard materials cost	$20	$ 60
Standard labor cost, at the standard labor rate of $10 per hour		
3 hours × $10	30	
5 hours × $10		50
Standard variable overhead, at the standard rate of $8 per hour		
3 hours × $8	24	
5 hours × $8		40
Standard fixed overhead, at the standard rate of $4 per hour		
3 hours × $4	12	
5 hours × $4		20
Total standard cost per unit	$86	$170

Richards will use these standard costs to report inventory and cost of goods sold, as well as for analyzing variances. Suppose that Richards makes 90,000 units of Model 345 and 42,000 units of Model 788. Total fixed overhead applied and the volume variance are:

Total fixed overhead applied:	
Model 345 (90,000 units × $12 standard fixed cost per unit)	$1,080,000
Model 788 (42,000 units × $20 standard fixed cost per unit)	840,000
Total applied fixed overhead	1,920,000
Budgeted fixed overhead	2,000,000
Volume variance, unfavorable	$ 80,000

COMPARISON OF STANDARD AND NORMAL COSTING

Although the normal-costing concept of a predetermined overhead rate is related to the idea of a standard fixed cost per unit, the results reported under the two types of costing systems are not the same. Remember that, under normal costing, *overhead is applied based on the actual level of the activity.* Under standard costing, *overhead is applied based on the number of units produced, or standard quantity of inputs used.* Let us see how the results differ in the case of Richards Company, using as an example the production activity given in the preceding section.

In the prior analysis, the volume variance was calculated by applying the standard fixed overhead cost per unit: this cost was based on standard labor hours per unit. The actual number of hours worked on each type of product was not needed. But assume that to produce the quantities stated above, Richards worked 280,000 hours making Model 345 tables and 205,000 hours making Model 788 tables, for a total of 485,000 hours. If Richards had been using normal costing with a predetermined fixed overhead rate of $4 per hour (the same as the rate used to determine the standard cost per unit), total fixed overhead applied would have been $1,940,000 (485,000 actual hours × $4 per hour), or $20,000 more than the overhead applied under standard costing ($1,920,000). Exhibit 14-6 shows these differences in overhead application and how they affect the reported volume variance.

Unless standard hours equal actual hours, normal costing and standard costing give different volume variances. The two systems will always give the same *budget* variance, because the budget variance is simply actual cost minus budgeted cost. But different volume variances arise because different amounts of fixed overhead are *applied* under the two methods. The difference in volume variances serves to remind you of what we said when introducing the concept of a volume variance in Chapter 13: the variance has little or no economic significance and reflects only the effect of using some activity level other than the actual level to determine the overhead application rate.

Exhibit 14-6 Comparison of Normal and Standard Costing

Normal Costing	
Total *actual* hours worked:	
Model 345	280,000
Model 788	205,000
Total actual hours	485,000
Predetermined overhead rate	$ 4
Total fixed overhead applied	$1,940,000
Budgeted fixed overhead	2,000,000
Volume variance—unfavorable	$ 60,000
Standard Costing	
Total *standard* hours for output level achieved:	
Model 345 (90,000 units × 3 hours per unit)	270,000
Model 788 (42,000 units × 5 hours per unit)	210,000
Total standard hours	480,000
Predetermined overhead rate	$ 4
Total fixed overhead applied equals the amount determined using units of product	$1,920,000
Budgeted fixed overhead	2,000,000
Volume variance—unfavorable	$ 80,000

We have presented several costing methods in this and previous chapters. The table below summarizes the similarities and differences among the three methods, actual costing, normal costing, and standard costing, showing the basis for determining *inventoriable* cost of a unit of product.

Cost Element	Actual Costing	Normal Costing	Standard Costing
Materials	actual cost	actual cost	standard cost
Direct labor	actual cost	actual cost	standard cost
Overhead	actual cost (actual input × actual rate)	applied cost (actual input × predetermined rate)	standard cost (actual output × standard cost)

The table shows that actual costing and normal costing differ only in the treatment of overhead, as explained in Chapter 13. Standard costing differs from both of the other methods in using standard rather than actual costs. As shown earlier, the only difference between standard costing and normal costing with respect to overhead is that applied overhead under standard costing is based on standard quantities of the input factor (or, what amounts to the same thing, on actual unit production), while overhead applied under normal costing is based on the actual quantities of input factors.

ACTIVITY-BASED COSTING

As early as Chapter 3 we began discussing the idea of activity-based costing (ABC), under which companies (and other organizations) associate overhead cost pools with their respective drivers and assign the costs in each overhead pool based on the relative use of drivers. Most recently, Chapters 12 and 13 used those concepts in applying overhead. ABC also applies to standard costing. The idea behind activity-based costing—to associate as much cost as possible with activities, and subsequently with products, to determine how much resource use is traceable to the product—is certainly applicable to standard costing. The objective is to get better information about the costs and profitability of individual products.

Suppose that ARG Company has two major types of overhead. Overhead related to materials, such as purchasing, inspection, warehousing, and handling is budgeted at $500,000. Overhead related to direct labor is $3,000,000 and the rate per direct labor hour is $4.00. (You already know how to make that calculation.) Material-related overhead is allocated based on the total number of component parts budgeted for use during a year. ARG makes two types of instruments. Data and calculations appear below.

	Portable Model	Table Model
Standard direct labor hours	8	12
Number of component parts	100	200
Budgeted production	6,000	2,000
Total budgeted component use	600,000	400,000
Overhead rate per component	$500,000/1,000,000 = $0.50	

	Portable Model	Table Model
Standard overhead costs:		
Material-related:		
Portable Model 100 × $0.50	$50	
Table Model 200 × $0.50		$100
Direct labor related:		
Portable Model 8 hours × $4	32	
Table Model 12 hours × $4		48
Total standard overhead	$82	$148

The $50 and $100 material-related overheads are treated just like any other overhead. The company applies both types of overhead, just as we did in Chapter 13. Misapplied overhead, budget variances and volume variances are calculated separately for each pool of overhead.

VARIABLE COSTING

Thus far, we have discussed only absorption costing systems. Such systems are required for financial reporting and for income tax purposes and are often used, as we mentioned earlier, for internal purposes also. However, throughout this book we have recommended internal reports using the contribution margin format, which treats all fixed costs as period costs. When this approach is applied to product costing, the result is called **variable costing (direct costing).**

Variable costing excludes fixed production costs from the unit costs of inventories, and treats *all* fixed costs as expenses in the period incurred. It is possible—and we think preferable—to use variable costing for internal reports. The flow of manufacturing costs using variable costing can easily be shown by a slight variation of the cost-flow figure presented in Chapter 13. Exhibit 14-7 depicts the difference in cost flows under variable and absorption costing systems.

Exhibit 14-7 Flow of Costs in a Manufacturing Firm

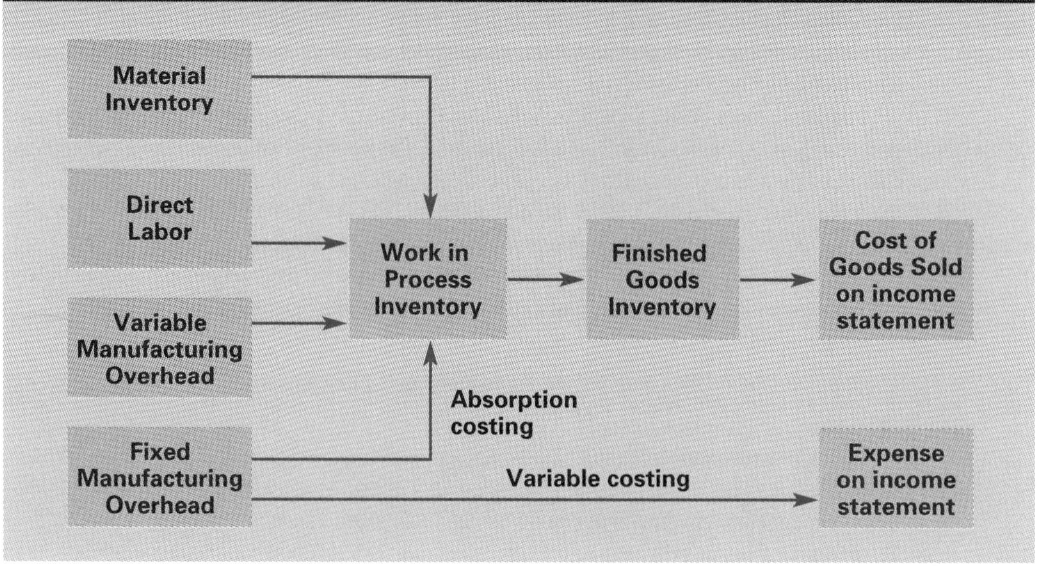

Exhibit 14-8 presents variable costing income statements using actual costing for SMP (the subject of our earlier example) for 19X5 and Exhibit 14-9 shows an actual costing income statement for 19X6. Except in job order costing, actual costing normally requires a cost-flow assumption. We do the unit-cost calculations using FIFO.

Exhibit 14-8 SMP Company, Income Statement for 19X5—Actual Variable Costing

Sales		$7,200,000
Variable cost of sales:		
Beginning inventory	$ 0	
Actual variable production costs	2,255,000	
Cost of goods available for sale	2,255,000	
Ending inventory *	410,000	
Variable cost of sales		1,845,000
Variable manufacturing margin		5,355,000
Variable S & A expenses		450,000
Contribution margin		4,905,000
Actual fixed costs:		
Manufacturing	3,200,000	
S & A	1,400,000	4,600,000
Profit		$ 305,000

** $2,255,000/110,000 = $20.50 unit cost, 20,000 units times $20.50 = $410,000.*

Exhibit 14-9 SMP Company, Income Statement for 19X6—Actual Variable Costing

Sales		$8,000,000
Variable cost of sales:		
Beginning inventory	$ 410,000	
Actual variable production costs	1,881,000	
Cost of goods available for sale	2,291,000	
Ending inventory *	297,000	
Variable cost of sales		1,994,000
Variable manufacturing margin		6,006,000
Variable S & A expenses		500,000
Contribution margin		5,506,000
Actual fixed costs:		
Manufacturing	2,950,000	
S & A	1,400,000	4,350,000
Profit		$1,156,000

** $1,881,000/95,000 = $19.80 unit cost, 15,000 units times $19.80 = $297,000.*

Variable costing can also be used with standard costs, as shown in Exhibits 14-10 and 14-11 for SMP for 19X5 and 19X6. We use the $20 per unit standard variable cost here. Note that there is no need to select a level of activity to calculate a predetermined fixed overhead rate because variable costing does not include fixed costs in the calculation of inventory cost per unit. The variable cost variances are the same as they are under standard absorption costing, and so is the fixed overhead budget variance. The volume variance does not appear under variable costing because no fixed overhead is applied to products. Note that we show total budgeted fixed manufacturing costs and the fixed overhead budget variance separately. Recall from Chapter 12 that companies calculate fixed overhead budget variances because they are economically significant. *A variable costing company recognizes fixed costs—it just does not inventory them.*

If you had been given the 19X5 information about SMP Company in an earlier chapter, say Chapter 3, you would probably have prepared an income statement like that in Exhibit 14-12.

The income statements in Exhibits 14-8 and 14-9 *appear* to be different from and more complex than statements you have seen in earlier chapters, but the only real difference is in the amount of detail on cost of sales. Whether you use the shortened format of Exhibit 14-12 or the expanded format of Exhibits 14-8 and 14-9, the incomes for the two years are the same and reflect an expensing of fixed costs in the year incurred. Without knowing it, you have been preparing variable costing income statements since Chapter 3.

Exhibit 14-10 SMP Company, Income Statement for 19X5—Standard Variable Costing

Sales		$7,200,000
Standard cost of sales:		
Beginning inventory	$ 0	
Standard variable production costs (110,000 × $20)	2,200,000	
Cost of goods available for sale (110,000 × $20)	2,200,000	
Ending inventory (20,000 × $20)	400,000	
Standard variable cost of sales (90,000 × $20)		1,800,000
Standard variable manufacturing margin		5,400,000
Variable manufacturing cost variances		55,000U
Variable manufacturing margin		5,345,000
Variable S & A expenses (90,000 × $5)		450,000
Contribution margin		4,895,000
Fixed costs:		
Budgeted fixed manufacturing costs	3,000,000	
Fixed manufacturing cost budget variance	200,000U	
S & A expenses	1,400,000	
Total fixed costs		4,600,000
Profit		$ 295,000

Exhibit 14-11 SMP Company, Income Statement for 19X6—Standard Variable Costing

Sales		$8,000,000
Standard cost of sales:		
Beginning inventory (20,000 × $20)	$ 400,000	
Standard variable production costs (95,000 × $20)	1,900,000	
Cost of goods available for sale (115,000 × $20)	2,300,000	
Ending inventory (15,000 × $20)	300,000	
Standard variable cost of sales (100,000 × $20)		2,000,000
Standard variable manufacturing margin		6,000,000
Variable manufacturing cost variances		19,000F
Variable manufacturing margin		6,019,000
Variable S & A expenses (100,000 × $5)		500,000
Contribution margin		5,519,000
Fixed costs:		
Budgeted fixed manufacturing costs	3,000,000	
Fixed manufacturing cost budget variance	50,000F	
S & A expenses	1,400,000	
Total fixed costs		4,350,000
Profit		$1,169,000

Exhibit 14-12 SMP Company, Income Statement for 19X5—Actual Variable Costing (Alternative Format)

Sales:	
90,000 × $80	$7,200,000
Variable costs:	
Manufacturing costs	
90,000 × $20.50*	1,845,000
S & A expenses	
90,000 × $5	450,000
Total variable costs at $25.50	2,295,000
Contribution margin	4,905,000
Fixed costs:	
Production	3,200,000
S & A expenses	1,400,000
Total fixed costs	4,600,000
Profit	$ 305,000

COMPARING VARIABLE AND ABSORPTION COSTING RESULTS

Compare the 19X5 and 19X6 results under variable costing (Exhibit 14-10 and 14-11) with the results under absorption costing for the same economic activity (see Exhibits 14-3 and 14-5). Absorption costing income is higher than variable costing income for 19X5 and lower for 19X6. Absorption costing income in 19X5 is higher because absorption costing transfers some of the fixed costs of 19X5 into 19X6 as part of the cost of the ending inventory of 20,000 units. Absorption costing income in 19X6 is lower because a similar shift of 19X6 costs (to 19X7) was smaller (fixed costs in an ending inventory of only 15,000 units) than the amount of fixed costs transferred in from 19X5.

In more general terms, the differences are traceable to the relationship between production and sales. Subject to a few technicalities, *when production exceeds sales, so that ending inventory is greater than beginning inventory, absorption costing gives a higher income than variable costing. When sales exceed production, absorption costing gives a lower income than variable costing.* The difference in incomes is due entirely to the fixed costs that are carried forward in inventory under absorption costing. Such costs are shown on the balance sheet as inventory and are expensed when the goods are sold. Exhibit 14-13 shows the amounts of fixed production costs expensed in each year under the two approaches, along with a reconciliation of the incomes under standard costing.

If the standard fixed cost *per unit* does not change from year to year, the difference between absorption costing income and income under variable costing can be computed directly by multiplying the standard fixed cost per unit by the change in units in inventory. Thus, we could have made the reconciliation shown in Exhibit 14-13 simply by using the formula:

$$\textit{Difference in incomes} = \left(\begin{array}{c}\textit{units in}\\ \textit{beginning}\\ \textit{inventory}\end{array} - \begin{array}{c}\textit{units in}\\ \textit{ending}\\ \textit{inventory}\end{array}\right) \times \begin{array}{c}\textit{standard}\\ \textit{fixed cost}\\ \textit{per unit}\end{array}$$

$$\textit{19X5 Difference} = (0 - 20{,}000) \times \$30 = (\$600{,}000)$$

$$\textit{19X6 Difference} = (20{,}000 - 15{,}000) \times \$30 = \$150{,}000$$

EVALUATION OF METHODS

We have already stated that we believe variable costing to be generally superior to absorption costing for internal reporting purposes. Not all managers, in accounting or elsewhere, agree with our position.

EXTERNAL REPORTING

Although arguments about the suitability of either method for external reporting are not germane to internal reporting, we mention some here to alert you to the principal justifications offered for absorption costing.[1]

---

1 For income tax reporting, the tax law, which can be extraordinarily complex, governs the determination of inventory and related costs of sales. We might point out that in a growing economy, inventories and costs will rise. Companies probably pay more taxes under absorption costing than they would under variable costing, which could be one reason why the government requires absorption costing.

Exhibit 14-13 Reconciliation of Incomes—Variable and Absorption Costing

	19X5	19X6
Comparison of reported income:		
Variable costing (Exhibit 14-10 and 14-11)	$ 295,000	$1,169,000
Absorption costing (Exhibits 14-3 and 14-5)	895,000	1,019,000
Difference to be explained	($ 600,000)	$ 150,000
Explanation of income difference:		
Fixed production costs in beginning inventory (transferred from prior year):		
0 units × $30	$ 0	
20,000 units × $30		$ 600,000
Fixed production costs incurred during the year	3,200,000	2,950,000
	3,200,000	3,550,000
Less fixed production costs in ending inventory (being transferred to a future year):		
20,000 units × $30	600,000	
15,000 units × $30		450,000
Total fixed costs expensed under absorption costing for the year	2,600,000	3,100,000
Total fixed costs expensed under variable costing—equal to total fixed costs incurred	3,200,000	2,950,000
Difference between fixed costs incurred and expensed for the year	($ 600,000)	$ 150,000

The matching concept, which you studied in financial accounting, holds that costs must be matched against related revenues or against the revenues of the periods that have benefited from the costs. As an example, the cost of a fixed asset is assigned, through depreciation, to the year of its life.

Fixed production costs "benefit" the firm in the sense that, without them, few firms could produce anything at all. Thus, having a factory building and equipment entails depreciation, property taxes, some level of maintenance, and other fixed costs. Moreover, many factory personnel, such as managers and supervisors, are salaried. Because these fixed costs are essential to the production of goods, one could argue that they should be expensed when the goods are sold, not when the goods are still in inventory. This argument is made by those favoring absorption costing.

Advocates of variable costing for financial reporting purposes counter by arguing that fixed production costs benefit production, but production as a whole, rather than any single unit of product. In other words, fixed costs provide the *capacity* to produce. Thus, once the firm is in business and producing goods, fixed production costs have done their job; they are not needed for this or that unit, only for production as a whole. Accordingly, the argument continues, considering fixed costs on a per-unit basis is inappropriate because fixed costs cannot be identified with individual units; fixed costs are joint to all the units produced. Controversy about the most appropriate method for external reporting purposes has raged for many years, and we do not expect it to stop in the foreseeable future.

INTERNAL REPORTING

Variable costing has an important advantage for internal reporting. It presents information in the form that is most useful for managers—the form needed for CVP analysis.

Separating fixed and variable costs and reporting contribution margin enable managers to perform the CVP analysis that cannot be done working directly with absorption costing statements. Managers cannot predict income for future periods using an absorption costing income statement for two reasons: (1) they must predict not only sales for that future period, but also production, and (2) they must break down the cost figures into their fixed and variable components (i.e., managers must develop the information that is already provided by variable costing.)

With variable costing, production has no influence on income. Managers can concentrate on the effects of changes in sales without having to allow for production. If sales fall from one period to another, variable costing income will also fall. Using absorption costing, income might well rise when sales fall if production is higher than sales. Most managers think of sales, not production, as the income-generating activity. Therefore, variable costing is more in tune with a manager's basic understanding of income than is absorption costing.

Variable costing offers another significant advantage because its income figure is not affected by production. Over the long run, production and sales for a given product will be about the same, and so both absorption costing and variable costing will give the same total income. Variable costing income represents an equilibrium in the sense that it shows what the company would earn over the long run if sales continue at the same level. Absorption costing income can be misleadingly high when production exceeds sales because the income cannot be maintained at the same level of sales. (You should not produce indefinitely in excess of sales unless sales are rising.)

Of course, absorption costing requires making allocations of fixed costs to units of product. We have consistently argued that allocations are unwise for managerial purposes because they obscure CVP relationships, can lead to poor decisions, and are not helpful in control and performance evaluation. Absorption costing can therefore be criticized because it requires allocations.

A multiple-product firm using absorption costing allocates fixed production costs to its products and to the individual units of each product. The many costs that are common to several products (depreciation on factory building, salary of plant manager, etc.) will thus be allocated first to products, and then to units of each product. Hence, statements prepared by product or by product line will contain two sets of allocations, making it extremely difficult to analyze the relative profitability of a product or a product line.

In summary, the information that managers need is provided much more directly by variable costing statements. Where absorption costing is used, a manager must recast statements to perform many of the analyses needed to plan, make decisions, control, and evaluate performance.

Advocates of absorption costing argue that variable costing may prompt managers to take a short-run approach to problems when a long-run approach is more desirable. Although they acknowledge the usefulness of variable costing information for specific short-run decisions (like the acceptance of special orders), they argue that concentrating on variable costs can be harmful in the long run. Their major objection is that if fixed costs are not treated as costs of product, managers might set prices too low to cover fixed costs and earn profits. They argue that managers who become accustomed to reports prepared using variable costing could come to ignore the fixed costs that might be the great bulk of production costs. In short, advocates of absorption costing argue that it is useful because it alerts managers to the need to cover both fixed and variable costs.

Advocates of variable costing offer two counterarguments. One is that even absorption costing does not include all costs as product costs. Selling and administrative costs are excluded from inventory under both costing methods. In many cases, these costs exceed production costs. In the same vein, when a standard fixed cost per unit is used, the amount of fixed cost included in product cost (and therefore in inventory) is decided in advance. Since fixed costs will probably be overapplied or underapplied, some of them will not be included in inventory.

The other counterargument is that it is unnecessary to allocate fixed costs to units in setting prices when the firm faces competition and cannot charge any price it chooses. For example, suppose a firm could analyze the expected volume-price relationships as suggested in Chapter 4 and select the best combination of price and expected volume. If a firm has discretion over prices and can expect to sell about the same volume no matter what price is charged, there is no harm in using a total cost per unit to set prices. However, firms in these circumstances are much less common than firms that face competition and therefore cannot charge any price they wish.

If absorption costing is to be used, it seems better to use a standard fixed cost per unit than an actual fixed cost per unit. When a standard fixed cost is used, the effect of production's being different from production used to set the standard is isolated in the volume variance. (The volume variance tells us what the effect is, but is not helpful for control purposes.) Using standard fixed costs might alleviate the problem of a manager's changing prices at frequent intervals, if only because total cost per unit will not change as production changes.

SUMMARY

Standard costing is a method of product costing that uses standard costs instead of actual or normal costs. One major benefit of standard costing is that it ties the accounting records to the calculations of the variances used for control purposes. Another benefit is that it simplifies record keeping for a firm that makes several products.

Standard absorption costing requires the calculation of a standard fixed cost per unit. Like normal costing, standard absorption costing yields a volume variance as well as a fixed overhead budget variance. But the volume variance, under either approach, is of little, if any, economic significance. Setting a standard fixed cost per unit requires selecting a level of activity, the most common of which are normal activity and practical capacity. The magnitude, and perhaps even the direction, of the volume variance will depend on the activity level chosen for setting the standard.

The required use of some type of absorption costing for external reporting has contributed to the internal distribution of, and the need for managers to understand, reports reflecting this approach to product costing. For internal managerial purposes, some firms use standard variable costing or even actual variable costing, which consider only variable production costs as product costs and treat fixed manufacturing costs as expenses in the period in which they are incurred. Variable costing is compatible with both CVP analysis and the contribution margin format of the income statement.

KEY TERMS

normal activity (normal capacity)
practical capacity
standard costing
standard fixed cost per unit
variable (direct) costing

KEY FORMULA

$$\text{Volume variance — standard costing} = \left(\begin{array}{c}\text{actual}\\ \text{units}\\ \text{produced}\end{array} - \begin{array}{c}\text{units at}\\ \text{selected}\\ \text{capacity}\end{array} \right) \times \begin{array}{c}\text{standard}\\ \text{fixed cost}\\ \text{per unit}\end{array}$$

REVIEW PROBLEM

In 19X7, SMP Company again used a $20 standard variable cost and $30 standard fixed cost based on $3,000,000 and 100,000 units. SMP produced 112,000 units and sold 102,000. It incurred all manufacturing costs as expected. Selling and administrative expenses were again $5 variable per unit and $1,400,000 fixed.

Required

1. Prepare an income statement using absorption costing.
2. Prepare an income statement using variable costing.

ANSWER TO REVIEW PROBLEM

1.

SMP Company, 19X7 Income Statement—Absorption Costing

Sales (102,000 × $80)		$8,160,000
Standard cost of sales:		
Beginning inventory (15,000 × $50)	$ 750,000	
Variable production costs (112,000 × $20)	2,240,000	
Fixed production costs (112,000 × $30)	3,360,000	
Cost of goods available (127,000 × $50)	6,350,000	
Ending inventory (25,000 × $50)	1,250,000	
Standard cost of goods sold (102,000 × $50)		5,100,000
Standard gross margin		3,060,000
Fixed cost volume variance, favorable		360,000
Actual gross margin		3,420,000
S & A expenses		1,910,000
Profit		$1,510,000

The volume variance can be computed in either of two ways. It is the difference between budgeted fixed production costs of $3,000,000 and applied fixed production costs of $3,360,000. Because applied costs exceeded budgeted costs, the variance is favorable. Volume variance is also the difference between the 112,000 units produced and the 100,000 units used to set the standard fixed cost, multiplied by the standard fixed cost (12,000 units × $30 = $360,000).

2.

SMP Company, 19X7 Income Statement—Variable Costing

Sales (102,000 × $80)		$8,160,000
Standard variable cost of sales:		
Beginning inventory (15,000 × $20)	$ 300,000	
Variable production costs (112,000 × $20)	2,240,000	
Cost of goods available (127,000 × $20)	2,540,000	
Ending inventory (25,000 × $20)	500,000	
Standard variable cost of sales (102,000 × $20)		2,040,000
Standard variable manufacturing margin		6,120,000
Variable S & A expenses		510,000
Contribution margin		5,610,000
Fixed costs:		
Production	$3,000,000	
S & A expenses	1,400,000	4,400,000
Profit		$1,210,000

As explained in the chapter, the $300,000 difference in income under the two methods results because of the fixed overhead costs in the beginning and ending inventories under absorption costing. The beginning inventory of 15,000 units included fixed overhead costs of $450,000 (15,000 × $30 standard fixed cost per unit) carried forward from 19X6. The ending inventory of 25,000 units includes fixed overhead costs of $750,000 (25,000 × $30) being carried forward to 19X8. The $300,000 difference in income occurs because the fixed costs being carried forward *from* 19X7 ($750,000) are greater than those carried forward *to* 19X7 ($400,000). That is, the income difference results from the *increase in inventory* or, described another way, because 19X7 production (112,000 units) was greater than 19X7 sales (102,000 units).

ASSIGNMENT MATERIAL

QUESTIONS FOR DISCUSSION

14-1 Variable and absorption costing "The trouble with variable costing is that I have to put all of the fixed costs on the income statement right away. With absorption costing I can put some of them into inventory where they belong and take care of them later when the products are sold." Discuss these statements critically.

14-2 Period costs—product costs The distinction between product costs and period costs is a major point of contention between the advocates of variable costing and those of absorption costing. Is the distinction important for decision making?

EXERCISES

14-3 Basic standard costing—absorption and variable Rath Company makes Zuds, a household cleaning product. Zuds sells for $15 per case and has a standard variable manufacturing cost of $5 per case. Fixed production costs are $600,000 per month; fixed selling and administrative expenses $350,000 per month. The firm began March 19X1 with no inventories and had the following activity in March and April.

	March	April
Production in cases	120,000	90,000
Sales in cases	100,000	100,000

The president wants two sets of monthly income statements: one showing monthly income using variable costing, the other showing monthly income using absorption costing with practical capacity of 120,000 cases per month used to set the standard fixed cost.

Required
Prepare income statements by month as the president requested. Use the format that shows the details of beginning and ending inventories and of production costs in the cost of goods sold section.

14-4 Standard costing income statements The following data pertain to the operations of Lindsey Corporation for 19X8.

Normal capacity	200 units
Practical capacity	300 units
Budgeted production	240 units
Actual production	250 units
Actual sales ($25 per unit)	240 units
Standard variable production cost per unit	$ 10
Fixed production costs—budgeted	$2,400

During 19X8 there were no variable cost variances and fixed costs incurred were equal to the budgeted amount. There were no beginning inventories and no selling or administrative expenses.

Required

1. Determine the standard cost per unit assuming that standard fixed cost is based on (a) normal capacity, (b) practical capacity, and (c) budgeted production.
2. Prepare income statements for each of the three bases computed in item 1.

14-5 Basic absorption costing Perry Industries manufactures disk drives for microcomputers. Data related to its best-selling model, which is the only one made in its Bristol plant, appear below.

Production:	
April	12,000 units
May	8,000 units
Sales:	
April	8,000 units
May	11,000 units
Standard variable manufacturing cost	$125
Standard fixed manufacturing cost	75
Total standard manufacturing cost	$200

Perry has set its standard fixed manufacturing cost based on normal activity of 10,000 drives per month and budgeted fixed manufacturing costs of $750,000 per month. There was no inventory at the beginning of April. The drive sells for $300. Selling and administrative expenses are $350,000 per month. All manufacturing costs were incurred as expected (variable per unit and total fixed) in both months.

Required

Prepare standard absorption costing income statements for April and for May.

14-6 Basic variable costing (continuation of 14-5) Using the data in the previous assignment, prepare standard variable costing income statements for Perry Industries for April and for May.

14-7 Effect of measure of activity (extension of 14-5) The president of Perry Industries has heard that some companies use practical capacity as the basis for determining standard fixed manufacturing costs. He asks you to show him how using Perry's practical capacity of 15,000 drives per month would affect the income statements you prepared for 14-5.

Required

Prepare the income statements that the president wants. Comment on the differences between these statements and the ones you prepared for 14-5.

14-8 Absorption costing TRS Company makes a cabinet that sells for $50. The standard variable manufacturing cost is $20, and the standard fixed manufacturing cost is $10, based on budgeted fixed costs of $1,000,000 and budgeted production of 100,000 units. During 19X6, the company produced 96,000 units and sold 90,000. Actual fixed manufacturing costs were $980,000, actual variable manufacturing costs were $1,930,000. Selling and administrative expenses were $1,350,000, all fixed. There were no beginning inventories.

Required

Prepare a standard absorption costing income statement.

14-9 Variable costing (extension of 14-8) Prepare an income statement for TRS using standard variable costing.

14-10 Standard fixed cost and volume variance The following data refer to the operations of Hinson Company for 19X8.

Normal capacity	240,000 units
Practical capacity	300,000 units
Actual production	250,000 units
Fixed costs—budgeted and actual	$600,000

Required

1. Compute the standard fixed cost per unit based on (a) normal capacity and (b) practical capacity.
2. Compute the volume variances for each of the methods given in item 1.

14-11 Relationships For each of the following independent situations, fill in the missing data. In all cases, the standard fixed cost per unit is based on normal capacity of 10,000 units.

	(a) Standard Fixed Cost per Unit	(b) Total Budgeted Fixed Costs	(c) Actual Production	(d) Volume Variance (Favorable)
1.	$____	$____	8,000	$8,000
2.	$ 3	$____	____	$6,000
3.	$____	$40,000	8,000	$____
4.	$____	$30,000	____	($7,500)

14-12 Effects of changes in production—standard variable costing The following data relate to Elliot Pencil Company's best-selling model.

Sales (30,000 cases at $10)	$300,000
Production costs:	
Variable costs, standard and actual	$4 per case
Fixed, budgeted and actual	$150,000

The company has no beginning inventories and no selling and administrative expenses.

Required

Prepare income statements using standard variable costing assuming the firm produced (a) 30,000 cases and (b) 31,000 cases. Show the details of the cost of sales section of the income statements.

14-13 Effects of change in production—standard absorption costing (extension of 14-12)

Required

Assume that Elliot Pencil company uses standard absorption costing with a standard fixed cost per case of $5 based on normal activity of 30,000 cases. Prepare income statements assuming that production is (a) 30,000 cases and (b) 31,000 cases. Show details of cost of sales.

14-14 "Now wait a minute here." The title of this problem is the statement your boss made when you showed him the results of completing item 1 of this assignment.

Hownet makes panes for greenhouse windows, selling them for $10 each. Standard variable manufacturing cost is $2 and total fixed manufacturing costs are $60,000. Normal volume is 10,000 units, so that the standard fixed cost per unit is $6. Your boss had asked you to determine the firm's gross profit (after any production variances) from selling 10,000 units. The company treats all variances as adjustments to standard gross margin. Being conscientious, you decided to check your results by preparing income statements down to actual gross margin under each of the following cases. There are no beginning inventories.

1. Sales are 10,000 units, production is 10,000 units.
2. Sales are 10,000 units, production is 10,001 units.
3. Sales are 10,001 units, production is 10,001 units.
4. Sales are 9,999 units, production is 10,001 units.

Required

1. Prepare the income statements.
2. Explain why your boss gave the response he did.
3. Tell your boss why the results came out as they did.

14-15 All fixed cost company Fixed Company was organized on January 1, 19X5, and began operations immediately. The balance sheet immediately after organization showed plant and equipment of $2,400,000 and common stock of $2,400,000. The plant is completely automated and makes its one product from air. Its only cost is $240,000 depreciation, based on a ten-year life and the straight-line method. During the first two years of operation the company had the following results.

	19X5	19X6
Units produced	140,000	100,000
Units sold	120,000	120,000

All sales were at $5 per unit and were for cash. The company uses a standard fixed cost of $2 per unit based on normal volume of 120,000 units. There were no cash disbursements in either year so that cash at the end of each year was $5 multiplied by cumulative sales.

Required

1. Prepare income statements for each year.
2. Prepare a balance sheet as of the end of each year.
3. Repeat items 1 and 2 using variable costing.

14-16 Interpreting results The president of Stockley Jellies, Inc. has been reviewing the income statements of the two most recent months. She is puzzled because sales rose and profits fell in March, and she asks you, the controller, to explain.

	February	March
Sales ($30 per case)	$540,000	$660,000
Standard cost of sales	270,000	330,000
Standard gross profit	270,000	330,000
Volume variance	40,000	(50,000)
Selling and administrative expenses	(150,000)	(150,000)
Income	$160,000	$130,000

The standard fixed cost per case is $10, based on normal capacity of 20,000 cases per month.

Required

1. Determine production in each month.
2. Explain the results to the president.
3. Prepare income statements using variable costing.

14-17 Income determination—absorption costing The following data apply to Malkovich Company's 19X4 operation.

Sales (80,000 units)	$1,600,000
Production	90,000 units
Variable costs of production, standard and actual	$ 900,000
Fixed production costs, budgeted and actual	$ 360,000
Selling and administrative costs	$ 250,000

Required

Prepare income statements for 19X4 using standard absorption costing with (1) 90,000 units and (2) with 100,000 units used to set the standard fixed cost.

14-18 Income determination—variable costing (extension of 14-17)

Required

Prepare an income statement for Malkovich for 19X4, using standard variable costing.

14-19 Relationships Fill in the blanks for each of the following independent situations. In all situations, selling price is $10, standard and actual variable manufacturing cost is $6, fixed production costs—budgeted and actual—are $100,000, and the volume used to set the standard fixed cost per unit is 50,000 units. There are no selling and administrative expenses.

Case	(a) Unit Sales	(b) Unit Production	(c) Income—Variable Costing	(d) Income—Absorption Costing
1	70,000	_____	$_____	$170,000
2	_____	_____	$90,000	$110,000
3	50,000	55,000	$_____	$_____

14-20 All-fixed company Earthcare, Inc., manufactures a single product from garbage. It sells for $3 per unit. The production process is automated and there are no variable costs. Earthcare production costs are $10,000 per month. Normal activity is 10,000 units per month, and the standard fixed cost per unit is $1. Earthcare has no selling and administrative expenses. Earthcare began May with no inventory. Its activity for May, June, and July is summarized below, in units.

	May	June	July
Production	11,000	10,000	9,000
Sales	9,000	10,000	11,000

Required

1. Prepare income statements for each of the three months using standard absorption costing. Show the details of the cost of sales calculations.
2. Prepare income statements for each of the three months using standard variable costing.

PROBLEMS

14-21 Standard costing—absorption and variable Corson Company makes shaving lotion and uses standard absorption costing. Standard labor and materials per case are

Materials (3 gallons at $4 per gallon)	$12
Direct labor (0.50 hour at $10 per hour)	5

Total annual manufacturing overhead is budgeted according to the formula: $500,000 + ($2 × direct labor hours). The company uses normal capacity of 25,000 direct labor hours (50,000 cases) to set the standard fixed cost.

Corson began 19X7 with no inventories. It produced 45,000 cases and sold 40,000 at $40 each. Selling and administrative expenses were $200,000. There were no variable cost variances, and fixed production costs were incurred as budgeted ($500,000).

Required

1. Determine the total standard cost per case.
2. Prepare an income statement for 19X7.
3. Prepare an income statement for 19X7 using variable costing.

14-22 Absorption costing and variable costing Gordon Soups, Inc. makes a variety of soups. Data related to its chicken gumbo appear below.

Selling price per case	$50
Variable manufacturing costs per case	$15
Fixed manufacturing costs per month	$300,000
Selling and administrative expenses, all fixed, per month	$ 80,000

Gordon uses standard absorption costing, basing its unit fixed cost on normal activity of 15,000 cases per month. In July, Gordon produced 16,000 cases and sold 14,000. There were 3,000 cases in beginning inventory at standard cost. All costs were incurred as expected.

Required

1. Determine the standard fixed cost per unit.
2. Prepare an income statement for July. Use the short form of the income statement but calculate cost of goods sold separately.
3. Prepare an income statement for July assuming that Gordon uses variable costing. Remember that inventory at the beginning of July will be at standard variable cost.

14-23 Absorption costing and variable costing—variances VCX Company uses standard absorption costing, basing its standard fixed cost on 200,000 units of product per year, and $600,000 annual budgeted fixed manufacturing overhead. Standard variable manufacturing cost is $6 per unit. Results for 19X6 appear below. There were no beginning inventories.

Unit production	190,000
Unit sales (at $20 per-unit price)	185,000
Actual variable manufacturing costs	$1,160,000
Actual fixed manufacturing costs	$ 580,000
Actual selling and administrative expenses, all fixed	$ 800,000

Required

1. Determine the standard fixed cost per unit and the total standard cost per unit.
2. Compute all variances.
3. Prepare an income statement for 19X6. Show any variances as adjustments to standard cost of sales.
4. Prepare an income statement using variable costing.

14-24 Budgeted income statements Morrison WinterSports manufactures several lines of skiing equipment. Its Riverdale Plant makes a single model, the M-80 ski. Budgeted data for 19X7 appear below.

Sales (36,000 pairs at $70)	$2,520,000	
Production		38,000 pairs
Standard variable cost	$15	
Standard fixed cost	25	
Total standard cost	$40	
Selling and administrative expenses:		
Fixed	$ 600,000	
Variable		$8 per pair

Morrison uses normal activity of 40,000 pairs per year and budgeted fixed manufacturing costs of $1,000,000 to set its standard fixed cost. There were no beginning inventories.

Required

1. Prepare a budgeted income statement using standard absorption costing.
2. Prepare a budgeted income statement using standard variable costing.

14-25 Analysis of results (extension of 14-24) The Riverdale Plant of Morrison WinterSports actually produced 42,000 pairs and sold 40,000. All costs were incurred as expected—fixed in total and variable per unit.

Required

1. Prepare an income statement using standard absorption costing.
2. Prepare an income statement using standard variable costing.
3. Which set of statements from this and the previous assignment, the absorption or the variable, gives better information for analyzing results?

14-26 Analysis of income statement—standard costs The income statement for Bourque Manufacturing Company for 19X6 appears below. The company has established the following standards for a unit of finished product.

Materials (10 pounds at $1)	$10
Direct labor (2 hours at $8)	16
Variable overhead ($1 per direct labor hour)	2
Fixed overhead	2
Total	$30

The fixed overhead standard is based on normal capacity of 20,000 units. During 19X6, 49,000 direct labor hours were worked and 238,000 pounds of materials were used.

Bourque Manufacturing Company,
Income Statement for 19X6

Sales (20,000 units at $40)		$800,000
Cost of goods sold—at standard		600,000
Standard gross profit		200,000
Variances:		
Materials	$3,000U	
Labor	3,000U	
Variable overhead	3,000U	
Fixed overhead:		
Spending variance	5,000F	
Volume variance	8,000F	4,000F
Gross profit		204,000
Selling and administrative expenses		130,000
Income		$ 74,000

Required

1. Based on the information provided, determine the following:
   (a) Number of units produced.
   (b) Material use variance.
   (c) Material price variance.
   (d) Direct labor efficiency variance.

(e) Direct labor rate variance.
(f) Variable overhead efficiency variance.
(g) Variable overhead spending variance.
(h) Fixed overhead incurred.

2. Prepare an income statement using standard variable costing.

14-27 Conversion of absorption-costing income statement from normal to practical capacity (extension of 14-26) The standard costs and the income statement for Bourque Manufacturing Company use a standard fixed cost per unit based on normal capacity of 20,000 units. Assume, instead, that Bourque bases its standard fixed cost per unit on its practical capacity of 25,000 units.

Required

1. Determine the standard fixed cost per unit.
2. Prepare an income statement for 19X6.

14-28 Reconciling incomes—absorption costing AFT Industries had the following budgeted income statement for March, 19X5, in thousands of dollars.

Sales	$4,210.0
Standard cost of sales	1,894.5
Standard gross margin	2,315.5
Selling and administrative expenses (all fixed)	1,800.0
Income	$ 515.5

The budgeted volume was 210.5 thousand units at a selling price of $20. Standard cost of sales was $9, of which $4 was fixed. The assistant who prepared the statement had no information about budgeted production, so assumed that it would be equal to normal activity of 220 thousand units per month, eliminating the volume variance.

AFT actually sold 212 thousand units and produced 215 thousand. Actual fixed production costs were $880 thousand, actual variable production costs were $1,075 thousand. Selling and administrative expenses were as budgeted.

Required

1. Prepare an income statement reflecting the actual results.
2. Does it make sense that actual income is less than budgeted income when actual sales were higher than budgeted sales? Write a memorandum to Lynn Massett, AFT's president, explaining why the actual results were different from budget. Use the guidelines in Appendix B.

14-29 Reconciling incomes—variable costing

Required

1. Use the information from the previous assignment to prepare budgeted and actual income statements for AFT Industries using variable costing.
2. Explain the difference between budgeted and actual income.

14-30 Analysis of income statements As chief financial analyst of Markem Enterprises, Inc., you have been asked by the president to explain the difference between the two income statements prepared for her consideration. One was prepared by the controller, the other by the sales manager. Both used the same data from last year's operations.

	Statement A	Statement B
Sales (10,000 units)	$1,000,000	$1,000,000
Cost of goods sold:		
Beginning inventory	0	0
Production costs	600,000	900,000
Ending inventory	(200,000)	(300,000)
Cost of goods sold	400,000	600,000
Gross profit	600,000	400,000
Other costs	500,000	200,000
Income	$ 100,000	$ 200,000

Variable costs of production, the only variable costs, are $40 per unit.

Required

1. Determine which statement was prepared using variable costing, which using absorption costing.
2. Determine (a) fixed production costs; (b) selling and administrative costs; (c) production in units; and (d) cost per unit of inventory for both statements.
3. Which statement do you think was prepared by which manager and why do you think so?

14-31 Conversion of income statement The manager of the Morgan Division of Rorshoot Industries has been on the job only a short time. The following income statement, for the third quarter of 19X7, is the first report she has received. She is having some difficulty understanding it because she is familiar only with variable costing, and she has asked you to convert the statement to a variable costing basis.

Sales		$1,324,000
Cost of sales		893,700
Gross profit		430,300
Operating expenses:		
Selling and administrative	$276,300	
Unabsorbed fixed overhead	21,600	297,900
Income		$ 132,400

From reviewing internal records you have determined the following:

1. Selling and administrative costs are all fixed.
2. The division sells its one product at $40 per unit.
3. Fixed manufacturing overhead is applied at $12 per unit.
4. There was no fixed overhead budget variance.
5. Production during the quarter was 38,200 units.

Required

Prepare an income statement using standard variable costing.

14-32 Effects of costing methods on balance sheet McPherson Company has a loan with a large bank. Among the provisions of the loan agreement are

(a) the current ratio must be at least 3 to 1 and (b) the ratio of debt to stockholders' equity must be no higher than 75%. The balance sheet at December 31, 19X4 follows.

Assets		Equities	
Cash and receivables	$ 460,000	Current liabilities	$ 200,000
Inventory (40,000 units at variable cost)	200,000	Long-term bank loan	300,000
Total current assets	660,000	Stockholders' equity	760,000
Fixed assets (net)	600,000		
Total assets	$1,260,000	Total equities	$1,260,000

Current ratio $660,000/$200,000 = 3.3/1
Debt/stockholders' equity $500,000/$760,000 = 65%

The budgeted income statement for 19X5 follows.

Sales (100,000 units)		$1,000,000
Variable cost of sales		500,000
Variable manufacturing margin		500,000
Other variable costs (variable with sales)		50,000
Contribution margin		450,000
Fixed costs:		
Manufacturing	$300,000	
Other	50,000	350,000
Income		$ 100,000

Budgeted production is 100,000 units. The company's president foresees substantial expenditures for fixed assets and intends to obtain a loan to finance these expenditures. He projects the following pro forma balance sheet for December 31, 19X5.

Assets		Equities	
Cash and receivables	$ 400,000	Current liabilities	$ 240,000
Inventory (40,000 units at variable cost)	200,000	Long-term bank loan	460,000
Total current assets	600,000	Stockholders' equity	860,000
Fixed assets (net)	960,000		
Total assets	$1,560,000	Total equities	$1,560,000

He sees that the firm will be in default on both provisions of the loan agreement. (Compute the current ratio and debt/stockholders' equity ratio to verify his finding.) Trying to resolve the problem, he lists the following points.

(a) Practical capacity is 150,000 units.
(b) The company might benefit by using absorption costing.

Required

1. Prepare the income statement and balance sheet using standard absorption costing, with production of 150,000 units used to set the standard fixed cost. Also assume production of 150,000 units. Assume that all increased production costs are paid in cash.
2. Is the company safely within the limits of the loan agreement?
3. Is the company better off using absorption costing?

14-33 CVP analysis and absorption costing The Baltic Division of Samar Industries manufactures large drill bits. The division had the following plans for the first quarter of 19X5.

Unit sales	80,000
Selling price	$40
Variable cost	$24
Fixed costs	$800,000

The divisional manager expected profit of $480,000 from these results. The actual income statement for the quarter appears below. The divisional manager was surprised to see that the targets for volume, price, and costs were met or exceeded, but that profit was less than anticipated.

Sales (82,000 units at $40)	$3,280,000
Standard cost of sales at $30	2,460,000
Standard gross margin	820,000
Production variances	(180,000)
Actual gross margin	640,000
Selling and administrative expenses	200,000
Profit	$ 440,000

The divisional manager was informed that all variable costs and 75% of fixed costs were for manufacturing. The division uses standard costing, with practical capacity of 100,000 units per quarter used to set the standard. Actual production was only 70,000 units in the first quarter of 19X5 because of a large supply of inventory left over from the previous period.

Required

1. Prepare an income statement using variable costing.
2. Tell the divisional manager how your income statement would be of more help to her than the one shown above.

14-34 Standard costing—activity-based overhead rates Cannon Industries applies overhead to products using two rates—one based on machine hours, the other on the number of component parts. The latter rate is used because of the high amounts of overhead associated with purchasing, receiving, storing, and issuing parts. The company does not classify any employees as direct labor because production is highly automated. Summary data for 19X5 follow.

Budget	
Parts-related overhead	$1,200,000
Machine-related overhead	$6,480,000
Machine hours	100,000
Total number of parts to be used	8,000,000

The overhead costs given above are largely fixed with respect to output. Data for product GT-1029 follow.

Component parts, 11 parts at average $2.50 price	$27.50
Machine time, 0.15 hours	

During March, 19X6, the company made 60,000 of model GT-1029, and no other products. Parts-related overhead was $105,300; machine-related overhead was $542,230. The managers expect both of these categories of cost to be incurred evenly throughout the year. Use of parts was at standard.

Required

1. Calculate the predetermined overhead rates for parts and for machine hours.
2. Determine the standard cost of product GT-1029.
3. Determine whatever variances you can.

14-35 Preparing income statements Bob Cransk, president of BC Company, has been receiving monthly reports like the one below since he founded the company 10 years ago. As BC's newly hired controller, you have been discussing the reports with Cransk, trying to decide whether to make any changes. (All numbers are in thousands of dollars.)

	March	February
Sales	$1,256.8	$1,452.4
Standard cost of sales	769.3	879.7
Production variances	7.3U	29.8U
Cost of sales	776.6	909.5
Gross margin	480.2	542.9
Selling and administrative expenses	406.4	412.6
Profit before taxes	$ 73.8	$ 130.3
Summary of variances:		
Materials	$8.4U	$ 7.1U
Direct labor	7.8U	6.9U
Overhead	8.9F	15.8U
Total	$7.3U	$29.8U

Cransk has told you that he is generally satisfied with the reports, but he is sometimes surprised because they seem to contradict what he believes from his knowledge of operations. He attributes some of his surprise to his lack of understanding of accounting principles.

"For example," he said, "February is a good month. March starts our slow season. I expected February to be a little better than it was, but it seemed okay. March showed better than I had thought it would. I know that our production affects income, so I sort of make mental adjustments for it, but I'd rather not have to."

A review of the records reveals that standard variable cost of sales was $580.5 in February and $510.3 in March. Total fixed manufacturing overhead was $305.2 in February and $299.8 in March. Budgeted fixed manufacturing overhead was $304.5 in both months. Variable overhead variances were $3.2 unfavorable in February, $2.3 unfavorable in March. Although there is some variation in selling and administrative expenses, they can be considered fixed.

Required

1. Prepare income statements for February and March using standard variable costing.

2. Tell Cransk how much of the variances in the income statements above are attributable to the use of absorption costing.

14-36 Incorporating variances into budgets Viner Company is developing its budgets for the coming year. The firm uses the standard costs shown below for its final product.

Materials (3 gallons at $3)	$ 9
Labor (4 hours at $5)	20
Variable overhead ($6 per DLH)	24
Total standard variable cost	$53

Budgeted fixed manufacturing costs are $300,000. Selling and administrative expenses, all fixed, are budgeted at $400,000. Generally, there is about a 10% variance over standard quantity for materials, but the materials usually cost 5% less than the standard price. Direct laborers will receive a 6% wage increase at the beginning of the year, and labor efficiency is expected to be 4% better than standard. An unfavorable variable overhead spending variance of 5% is expected. Sales for the year are budgeted at 20,000 units at $100; production schedules indicate planned production of 24,000 units. There are no beginning inventories. Purchases of materials are budgeted to be equal to expected materials use.

Required

1. Determine the expected variable cost variances for the year.
2. Prepare a budgeted income statement for the coming year using standard variable costing.

14-37 Costs and decisions "You're fired!!" was the way your boss, the controller of Saran Bathing Suit Company, greeted you this morning. His ire was based on the two income statements shown below. A few months ago you recommended accepting an offer from a national chain for 10,000 suits at $12 each. At that time, inventories were getting too high because of slow sales. Things have not improved noticeably since then. Your recommendation was based on the variable production costs of $10 per unit, which are the only variable costs. The total standard cost of $16 per suit includes $6 in fixed costs, based on normal production of 130,000 units.

Income Statements for 19X4

	If Special Order Had Not Been Accepted	Actual, with Special Order
Sales: 100,000 × $25	$2,500,000	$2,500,000
10,000 × $12		120,000
Total sales	2,500,000	2,620,000
Cost of sales at standard cost of $16	1,600,000	1,760,000
Standard gross profit	900,000	860,000
Volume variance (20,000 × $6)	120,000U	120,000U
Actual gross profit	780,000	740,000
Selling and administrative expenses	710,000	710,000
Income	$ 70,000	$ 30,000

"Your recommendation cost us $40,000! Now clean out your desk and leave."

Required

Write a memorandum to your boss, Mr. Beatty, that will get your job back.

14-38 Actual versus standard costs—multiple products Brennan Company makes luggage. For some time, its managers have been dissatisfied with the firm's cost information. Unit costs have fluctuated greatly and have not been useful for planning and control purposes.

Under the present system, unit costs are computed at the end of each month. The costs are determined by allocating all actual production costs for the month to the various models produced, with the allocation based on the relative materials costs of the various models.

The controller has decided to develop standard costs for product costing purposes. She has analyzed the materials and labor requirements for each model, based on what she believes to be currently attainable performance. The results of her analysis follow. (For simplicity, the problem is limited to three models.)

	Briefcase #108	Cosmetic Case #380	Two-Suiter #460
Materials costs	$12.00	$14.00	$18.00
Labor hours required	0.5	0.8	1.5

Workers all earn $8 per hour, and the firm usually works about 6,000 labor hours per month. The controller intends to use 6,000 hours to set the standard fixed cost per unit. Her analysis of monthly manufacturing overhead yielded the formula: $90,000 + ($7 × direct labor hours).

During April the firm had the following results. There were no inventories at April 1.

	#108	#380	#460
Production in units	3,000	2,500	1,200
Sales in units	2,400	1,800	1,000
Sales in dollars	$84,000	$90,000	$85,000

There were no variable cost variances and fixed production costs were $92,000.

Required

1. Compute the standard cost for each model.
2. Compute the ending inventory of finished goods.
3. Prepare an income statement for April. Selling and administrative expenses were $28,000.

14-39 Interim results, costing methods, and evaluation of performance Kleffman Company sells a product with a highly seasonal demand. The budgeted income statement for 19X7 is given below.

Sales (240,000 units)		$2,400,000
Cost of goods sold—at standard:		
Materials	$420,000	
Direct labor	540,000	
Manufacturing overhead	600,000	1,560,000
Gross profit—at standard		840,000
Selling and administrative expenses		420,000
Income before taxes		$ 420,000

Budgeted production is 240,000 units, the number used to set the standard fixed cost per unit. The controller has determined that materials, labor, 40% of manufacturing overhead ($240,000), and $120,000 of the selling and administrative expenses are variable. All fixed costs are incurred evenly throughout the year.

January and February are relatively slow months, each with only about 5% of annual sales. March is the first month of a busy period, and production in February is generally high in order to stock up for the anticipated increase in demand. The actual income statements for January and February 19X7 appear below.

	January	February
Sales (12,000 units)	$120,000	$120,000
Cost of goods sold—at standard	78,000	78,000
Gross profit—at standard	42,000	42,000
Manufacturing variances:		
Variable costs	3,000F	4,000U
Fixed cost—budget	2,000F	3,000U
Fixed cost—volume	9,000U	7,500F
Gross profit—actual	38,000	42,500
Selling and administrative expenses	31,000	31,000
Income	$ 7,000	$ 11,500

Although the president is pleased that performance improved in February, she has asked the controller why the two months showed different profits, since sales were the same. She also wonders why profits were not about 5% of the $420,000 budget, as each month's sales were 5% of the annual budget.

Required

1. Explain to the president why profits in January and February would be expected to be less than 5% of the budgeted annual profit, even though each month's sales were 5% of the budgeted annual amount.
2. Explain to the president why profits differed in the two months. Comment on the president's being pleased that "performance improved in February."

14-40 ***Income statements and balance sheets*** Arens Company makes a single product, a microwave oven that sells for $300. Standard variable cost of production is $180 per unit, and the only other variable cost is a 10% sales commission. Fixed production costs are $3,600,000 per year, incurred evenly throughout the year. Of that amount, $800,000 is depreciation and the remainder all require cash disbursements. Fixed selling and administrative expenses of $200,000 per month all require cash disbursements.

For inventory costing Arens uses a standard fixed cost of $45 per unit, based on expected annual production of 80,000 units. However, during 19X6 the firm experienced the following results, by six-month periods.

	January-June	July-December
Sales in units	30,000	40,000
Production in units	32,000	42,000

The firm sells for cash only and pays all of its obligations as they are incurred. Its balance sheet at December 31, 19X5, in thousands of dollars was as follows.

Assets		Equities	
Cash	$ 400		
Inventory (1,000 units)	225	Common stock	$3,000
Plant and equipment (net)	3,000	Retained earnings	625
Total assets	$3,625	Total equities	$3,625

During 19X6, all costs were incurred as expected, variable costs per unit and fixed costs in total.

Required

1. Prepare income statements (in thousands of dollars) for each of the two six-month periods and the year as a whole.
2. Prepare balance sheets as of June 30 and December 31, 19X6, in thousands of dollars.

14-41 Pricing dispute Calligeris Company manufactures brake linings for automobiles. Late in 19X2 the firm received an offer for 10,000 linings from Phelan Company. Phelan was unwilling to pay the usual price of $5 per lining but offered to buy at a price that would give Calligeris a $0.50 gross profit per lining.

Without consideration of the order, Calligeris expected the following income statement for the year.

Sales (100,000 linings at $5)		$500,000
Cost of goods sold at standard:		
Beginning inventory (20,000 at $4)	$ 80,000	
Variable production costs (100,000 units at $2.50)	250,000	
Fixed production costs at $1.50 per unit	150,000	
Cost of goods available for sale	480,000	
Ending inventory (20,000 at $4)	80,000	
Cost of goods sold at standard		400,000
Standard gross profit		100,000
Volume variance (20,000 at $1.50)	30,000F	
Selling and administrative expenses	50,000	20,000
Income		$ 80,000

The production manager decided that the order could be filled from inventory, so no additional production was planned. The firm shipped 10,000 linings to Phelan Company, billing that firm for 10,000 units at $4.50 per lining. No additional costs were incurred in connection with this order.

Required

1. Prepare an income statement for 19X2 assuming that the actual results for the year were as planned except that the additional sale was made to Phelan company. Do the results show that the firm earned the agreed gross profit?
2. Suppose that you were the controller of Phelan Company. Would you dispute the $4.50 price? If so, why? What price would you propose and why?

14-42 Predetermined overhead rates—multiple products The controller of Salmon Company has been developing a new costing system. He believes that the use of standard costs would reduce the cost of record keeping and simplify the firm's internal reporting to managers. He has asked your assistance and you have collected the following information relating to the firm's three products.

	Model 84	Model 204	Model 340
Variable production costs	$4	$7	$11
Direct labor hours required	0.50	0.80	1.50

The firm works 50,000 direct labor hours per year at its normal operating level, and the controller uses that figure to set the predetermined overhead rate. Budgeted fixed production costs are $300,000. Operating results for 19X4 appear below. There were no beginning inventories.

	Production in Units	Sales in Units	Sales in Dollars
Model 84	30,000	25,000	$250,000
Model 204	24,000	20,000	$280,000
Model 340	20,000	18,000	$450,000

All production costs were incurred as expected, variable costs per unit and total fixed costs. Selling and administrative expenses were $140,000.

Required

1. Compute standard fixed costs per unit for each model.
2. Compute the ending inventory in dollars for each model.
3. Prepare an income statement for 19X4.

14-43 Standard costs and pricing The controller of Carolina Mills has been discussing costs and prices with the treasurer. The controller wants to use 2,400,000 machine hours to set standard fixed costs, while the treasurer prefers to use 3,000,000 hours. The controller feels that the lower base will make it easier for the company to absorb its fixed overhead, but the treasurer is concerned that the company might set its prices too high to be competitive with other companies.

"Look," the treasurer said, "suppose we use our formula for budgeting total manufacturing costs, materials, labor, and overhead."

Total manufacturing cost = $7,680,000 + $4.25 per machine hour

"Now," she went on, "if we use your basis of 2,400,000 hours and our usual pricing formula, setting prices at 150% of total manufacturing cost, we will have higher prices than competition will permit, with consequent loss of volume."

The controller replied, "I can't agree with you. Your basis of 3,000,000 hours is very close to practical capacity, and we'd be taking the risk of having a significant amount of underabsorbed overhead that would really hurt our profits."

Required

1. Suppose that selling and administrative expenses are $6,200,000, all fixed. What profit will the company earn if it uses 2,400,000 hours to set standard fixed costs, sets prices using the formula given above, and sells output requiring 2,400,000 machine hours? (Assume no inventories.)
2. Repeat item 1 substituting 3,000,000 machine hours for 2,400,000 hours.
3. Is the real issue here the selection of the base for applying fixed overhead? Why or why not? What is the real concern?

14-44 Product costing methods and CVP analysis Tollgate Company expects to produce 190,000 units in 19X6. The firm uses a predetermined overhead rate for fixed overhead based on 210,000 units, which is normal capacity. Overabsorbed or underabsorbed overhead is shown separately in the income statement. The selling price is $16 per unit. At the expected level of production Tollgate expects the following costs.

Variable production costs	$1,330,000
Fixed production costs	630,000
Fixed selling and administrative costs	434,000

In addition, there are variable selling costs of $2 per unit. The firm had no inventory at the end of 19X5.

Required

1. Determine the break-even point assuming that variable costing is used.
2. Determine the number of units that must be sold to break even given that production will be 190,000 units. Assume absorption costing.
3. If your answers to the first two items differ, explain the difference, showing calculations.
4. Would your answer to item 2 be different if the firm had a beginning inventory of 10,000 units costed at the same per-unit amount that the firm will use in 19X6? Explain why or why not, with calculations.

14-45 Comprehensive review, budgeting, overhead application Ruland Company makes and sells a single product. The product sells for $20 and Ruland expects sales of 880,000 units in 19X5. The distribution of sales by quarters is expected to be 20%, 25%, 25%, and 30%. The firm expects the following costs in 19X6.

Manufacturing Costs

	Fixed	Variable per Unit
Materials (4 pounds at $0.80)	—	$3.20
Direct labor (0.5 hour at $5)	—	2.50
Maintenance	$ 46,000	0.20
Indirect labor	422,000	0.40
Supplies	316,000	0.05
Power	186,000	0.10
Depreciation	1,900,000	—
Supervision	310,000	—
Miscellaneous	320,000	0.05
Totals	$3,500,000	$6.50

Selling, General, and Administrative Expenses

	Fixed	Variable per Unit
Sales commissions		$2.00
Salaries and wages	$1,200,000	—
Other expenses, including interest	4,350,000	
Total	$5,550,000	$2.00

Budgeted production and purchases are

Quarter	Production (units)	Raw Material Purchases (pounds)
1	210,000	733,000
2	220,000	950,000
3	260,000	904,000
4	210,000	795,000
Total	900,000	3,382,000

Other information relating to Ruland's operation follows.

1. The firm uses a standard fixed cost of $3.50 per unit.
2. Sales are collected 60 days after sale.
3. Purchases of raw materials are paid for in the month after purchase.
4. Direct labor costs unpaid at the end of a quarter are about 10% of the cost incurred in that quarter. All other manufacturing costs requiring cash disbursements (all but depreciation) are paid as incurred, except for raw material purchases.
5. All selling and administrative expenses require cash disbursements and are paid as incurred except for salesperson's commissions. These are paid in the month after incurrence.
6. The firm has a 40% income tax rate. At year end, the amount of unpaid taxes is about 25% of the total expense for the year.
7. A dividend of $300,000 will be paid in 19X5.
8. Purchases of plant assets, all for cash, will total $2,100,000 in 19X5.
9. Assume that sales, production, and purchases of raw materials are spread evenly over the months of each quarter (one-third of quarter in each month of the quarter).

The balance sheet at the end of 19X4 appears as follows, in thousands of dollars.

Assets		Equities	
Cash	$ 840	Accounts payable (materials)	$ 240
Accounts receivable	2,800	Accrued commissions	120
Inventory—finished goods (146,000 units)	1,460	Accrued payroll (direct labor)	64
Inventory—materials (530,000 pounds)	424	Income taxes payable	80
Plant and equipment	16,200	Long-term debt	4,000
Accumulated depreciation	(8,400)	Common stock	7,000
		Retained earnings	1,820
Total	$13,324	Total	$13,324

Required

1. Prepare a budgeted income statement for 19X5.
2. Prepare a cash budget for 19X5 for the year as a whole, not by quarter.
3. Prepare a pro forma balance sheet for the end of 19X5.
4. Without preparing new statements, describe the differences that would occur in your prepared statements if the firm were using variable costing.

CASES

14-46 ***Costing methods and evaluation of performance*** Donita Boroff is the manager of the Wallace Division of Fizer Industries, Inc. She is one of several managers being considered for the presidency of the firm, as the current president is retiring in a year.

All divisions use standard absorption costing; normal capacity is the basis for application of fixed overhead. Normal capacity in the Wallace Division is 40,000 units per quarter, and quarterly fixed overhead is $500,000. Variable production cost is $50 per unit. Boroff has been looking at the report for the first three months of the year and is not happy with the results.

Wallace Division Income Statement for First Quarter

Sales (25,000 units)		$2,500,000
Cost of goods sold:		
Beginning inventory (10,000 units)	$ 625,000	
Production costs applied	1,562,500	
Total	$2,187,500	
Less ending inventory	625,000	1,562,500
Gross profit		937,500
Volume variance		(187,500)
Selling and general expenses		(500,000)
Income		$ 250,000

The sales forecast for the second quarter is 25,000 units. Boroff had budgeted second-quarter production at 25,000 units but changes it to 50,000 units, which is practical capacity for a quarter. The sales forecasts for each of the last two quarters of the year are also 25,000 units. Costs incurred in the second quarter are the same as budgeted, based on 50,000 units of production.

Required

1. Prepare an income statement for the second quarter.
2. Does the statement for the second quarter reflect Boroff's performance better than that for the first quarter? Can you make any suggestions for reporting in the future? Do you think Boroff should be seriously considered for the presidency of the firm? Why or why not?

14-47 ***Costing methods and performance evaluation*** Warren Progman, the new manager of the Oliver Division of General Products Company, was greatly displeased at the income statements that his controller, Hal Gannon, had been giving him. Progman had recently been placed in charge of the division because it had not been showing satisfactory results. Progman was upset because, although sales had risen in each of the last two months, profits had not kept pace. Income statements for the last three months are given below.

	March	April	May
Sales	$360,000	$440,000	$560,000
Cost of sales	198,000	264,000	381,000
Gross profit	162,000	176,000	179,000
Other expenses	142,000	150,000	162,000
Profit before taxes	$ 20,000	$ 26,000	$ 17,000

Progman asked Gannon why profits had declined when sales had increased and why a substantial increase in sales from March to April had produced only a small increase in profits. Gannon's reply was simply that operations had gone according to plans that Progman had set, and that the problems that Progman wanted to know about were due to the method of accounting for product costs and the relationships of sales to production.

Progman was unimpressed with this explanation and rather testily pointed out that he had been put in charge of the division to "turn it around." He was not about to let accounting conventions give corporate management second thoughts about placing him in charge. Gannon, who was fully aware of the claims Progman had made when being considered for the manager's job, had not liked Progman from the start. To the suggestion that accounting conventions were standing in the way of Progman's performance, Gannon replied only that the reports for all divisions were prepared from the same uniform accounting system and in the form required for corporate reporting. He told Progman that the reports were prepared using GAAP, which was necessary because the corporation was publicly held and had to issue reports to shareholders. He did not tell Progman that he believed the methods used by the firm for external reporting were inappropriate for internal purposes.

Later, at lunch with Theodora Holloway, the division's sales manager, Gannon related the conversation that he had had with Progman. Holloway, who had also wondered about the firm's accounting methods, asked Gannon why he didn't just explain the statements to Progman. "Not on your life," said Gannon. "I see no reason to help that braggart. Let *him* explain to the top brass why things aren't going the way he said they would if he were put in charge instead of me."

"Actually," Gannon continued, "what he's worried about just isn't a difficult problem. Cost of sales included both standard cost and the adjustment needed when production for the month did not equal the 25,000-unit volume that was used to set the standard fixed cost of $9 per unit. In fact, things have gone very well. We had no variances at all except for volume. Selling prices held very well at $20 per unit, and the division is doing much better now. But would I like to be there when the brass asks Progman why things are not going so well! Why, even production in April was right on target at 25,000 units budgeted."

Required

1. Explain the results in the three-month period. You may wish to compute standard fixed costs per unit and production in each month.
2. Prepare income statements for the three months using variable costing.

14-48 Costing methods and product profitability At a recent meeting, several of the managers of Cornwall Valve Company were discussing the firm's costing and pricing methods. Although there was general agreement that the methods should be helpful to managers in determining which products to emphasize, there was considerably less agreement on which methods would accomplish this.

The sales manager, Nado Oho, expressed his preference for product costs based on variable costs only. "I see no reason to charge a product with fixed costs. Contribution margin is, after all, the critical question in selecting the products to push."

"I just can't agree with you," said Perrie Emerson, the production manager. "If you'd just take a walk through the plant you'd be reminded that people and materials aren't the only things needed to produce one of our valves. There are tons of machinery that cost money too. Ignoring those costs can only get you into trouble, and it sure isn't very realistic anyway. You've *got* to consider the machine time required for each product, and that can only be accomplished by allocating the fixed production costs to products. Machine time is critical, and production costs should be allocated on a machine-hour basis."

To make this point, Emerson put an example on the conference room blackboard. "Look, let me show you. Let's take just three of our basic products that all require time in the grinding department. That department has a capacity of 1,000 machine hours a month, and the monthly fixed costs of the department are $10,000." Below is the schedule Emerson put on the board.

	101-27	101-34	101-56
Selling price	$9.00	$12.00	$17.40
Variable costs	5.00	6.00	8.40
Contribution margin	4.00	6.00	9.00
Fixed costs	1.00	1.25	2.50
Profit per unit	$3.00	$ 4.75	$ 6.50
Number of valves processed per hour	10	8	4

Emerson continued, "Now what I've done is compute a fixed cost per unit by dividing the $10 per hour fixed cost by the number of valves of each type that we can process in one hour. You can see that what I use the grinding machinery for *does* make a difference. It seems to me that this approach is much better at showing which products to emphasize. This shows that the 56 is the best bet and the 27 is the worst."

"But Perrie," said Oho, "we don't disagree. The 56 is a winner because it has the highest contribution margin, and we wouldn't push the 27 because it contributes the least. What are we arguing about?"

Emerson was not too happy about having her own example used to counter her argument. She admitted that, in the case she used, the relative rankings of the products were the same as they would be using the contribution margin approach. But she still felt that her method would be more valuable to the sales manager than a simple contribution margin approach, and she looked around the room for support.

"Well, now, it's nice to hear that you two are so interested in the information my staff has to offer," commented Joe Anderson, the controller. "But if you want to be realistic, let's consider something else. We're committed to making some of each of these valves, though not nearly enough to keep the grinding department operating at capacity. So the big decision isn't really which valve to produce and sell. What we really need to know is which one to produce after we've met the commitments we made. And the kicker is that we could probably sell all of whatever we produce. The way I see it, we have about 600 hours of grinding time available for discretionary production. So what do we do?"

Emerson continued to argue for her approach, and she specifically attacked the question of pricing. "The way we price our products just isn't rational; I know we could do better if we considered the fixed costs the way I said. We should be selling the 27s for $12.50 if we want to make them as profitable as the 56s, and we'd have to jack the price of 34s by $1.75 to equal the profit on the 56s. Okay, okay, I can see you're getting upset about the idea of such increases, Nado. I know the customers would be unhappy. But if we cater to their needs by producing these models, we ought to get a fair return for doing it."

Required

Determine which valve should be produced once the committed demand is satisfied. Criticize the analyses of the sales manager and the production manager, including their comments about pricing.

14-49 Budgeting, cash flow, product costing, motivation After almost two decades of profitable operations, Pennywise Company experienced its first loss in 19X6, and all internal reports during the first 11 months of 19X7 indicated a second losing year. At the meeting of the board of directors at the end of December 19X7, the members were given the first draft of the basic operating data for 19X7. (Exhibit 1 shows the basic data available to the directors at the meeting.) Public announcement of the data is made shortly after the directors' meeting.

Exhibit 1 Pennywise Company—Operating Data for 19X7

Part A: Condensed Statement of Income

Sales (1,200,000 units at $12 per unit)	$14,400,000
Cost of goods sold	11,760,000
Gross margin on sales	2,640,000
Selling and administrative expenses	3,630,000
Net operating loss for the year 19X7	($ 990,000)

Part B: Miscellaneous Operating Data

Normal operating capacity, in units	1,875,000
Fixed costs:	
Manufacturing	$ 6,000,000
Selling and administrative	$ 750,000
Variable costs, per unit:	
Manufacturing	$4.80
Selling and administrative	$2.40

The directors had maintained the dividend so as not to antagonize the stockholders or give the impression that the recent losses were any more than a temporary setback. Most of the directors had come to realize, by the end of 19X7, that future dividends were advisable only if the company returned to profitable operations. Consequently, the board members were willing to consider any plans which might help minimize inefficiencies, reduce costs, and build a profitable operation once again.

The chair of the board (and principal stockholder), Mr. Ira Hayes, had recently attended a conference sponsored by the National Association of Manufacturers on motivating personnel to better performance. Mr. Hayes was not particularly impressed with most of the discussions. He told the personnel manager, Ms. Gray: "Those speakers all seemed to concentrate on qualitative and nonquantifiable issues like working conditions and improving the general atmosphere to promote creativity and individuality. There was the usual lot of noise about implementing methods of 'participatory management,' and the like, and coordinating the efforts of the management team. But really, there wasn't much in the way of concrete suggestions."

Having been closely associated with the company since its founding by Mr. Hayes 16 years before, Ms. Gray was well acquainted with Mr. Hayes' feelings on the matter of motivation. As Mr. Hayes had said on many occasions, he was convinced that the surest (and easiest) way to really motivate people was to provide monetary incentives of some kind and then let them know exactly what measures would be used to assess their performance. In keeping with this philosophy, Mr. Hayes proposed, at the first board meeting in 19X8, that the company adopt a profit-sharing plan in which all employees could participate. The other members of the board were receptive to the idea and a committee was appointed to draw up a plan.

According to the plan devised by the committee, the company would set aside cash equal to a certain percentage of before-tax profits. The cash would be distributed to all employees on the basis of a preestablished formula. Or, more correctly, a set of such formulas was needed because the performances of employees in different areas of the company had to be measured in different ways. Mr. Ira Hayes Jr., the president, wanted to provide his own incentives to encourage better performance by sales and production personnel. He gave the sales and production manager, individually, several long and enthusiastic pep talks on expanding their respective areas to higher levels. He further authorized an expenditure for $450,000 on a national advertising program.

Production in the plant reached the normal capacity of 1,875,000 units for the year 19X8. At the board meeting in early 19X9, the president remarked: "Back in the black again. The field people did a great job pushing sales up by almost 17%." (Exhibit 2 shows the data presented to the board at that meeting.)

Exhibit 2 Pennywise Company—Operating Data for 19X8

Sales (1,406,250 units at $12)		$16,875,000
Cost of goods sold:		
Fixed costs	$ 6,000,000	
Variable costs (1,875,000 @ $4.80)	9,000,000	
	15,000,000	
Less: Ending inventory (468,750 units @ $8.00)	3,750,000	
		11,250,000
Gross margin on sales		5,625,000
Selling and administrative expenses:		
Fixed costs	1,200,000	
Variable costs (1,406,250 @ $2.40)	3,375,000	
		4,575,000
Operating profit before taxes and allowance for profit-sharing pool		1,050,000
Provision for profit-sharing pool		210,000
Operating profit before taxes		840,000
Provision for federal income taxes		420,000
Net income for the year 19X8		$ 420,000
Dividends to common stockholders ($0.20 per share)		$ 200,000

The board was pleased with the results of their new plan and with its apparent immediate effectiveness. There was, in fact, much optimistic talk at the meeting about the effect that the new plan would have on 19X9 operations, especially because the special sales campaign would probably not be repeated regularly. The board voted to continue the plan for at least one more year. After the vote, Mr. Hayes Jr. suggested that it would probably be good for employee relations if the board would announce soon when the pool for profit sharing would be distributed in cash to the employees because the dividend announcement had already been widely publicized. In an outer room, the sales manager, the production manager, and the controller were discussing the advantages and disadvantages of nepotism and of nonoperating management on the board of directors.

The questions following this paragraph are not designed to limit your discussion or specifically direct your analysis. Nor is there any particular significance to the order in which they are listed. You will find it worthwhile to answer the first one first because it may provide some clue as to how you might proceed. It is probably inefficient to answer each of the questions directly and in order because some are interrelated, but you may want to incorporate some comments about each of them in your answer.

1. What is the company's break-even point?
2. What is the company's system for implementing the management functions of planning and control?
3. Are profits likely to continue?
4. Has the profit-sharing plan contributed to efficiency? to cost reduction? to a return to profitable operations?
5. Should the board announce a cash distribution to employees relatively soon?

15 process costing and the cost accounting cycle

Chapter 13 introduced product costing—determining the cost of a unit of manufactured product. The emphasis in Chapter 13 was on job-order costing. However, the concepts (such as cost flows and application of overhead) apply to all types of manufacturing. Job-order costing is used by companies producing nonstandard products. Companies that make a single, homogeneous product use a cost accumulation method called **process costing**. The first part of this chapter discusses process costing.

We complete our study of product costing by illustrating the **cost accounting cycle**. The illustrations cover the journal entries and accounts employed in the three principal types of cost accumulation systems, job-order costing, process costing, and standard costing. Because they keep low inventories, ideally none, advanced manufacturers have fewer problems with product costing. We illustrate one way that they account for product costs.

PROCESS COSTING

Some examples of companies that can use process costing are makers of sugar, bricks, cement, and bulk chemicals. The essence of process costing is the accumulation of costs by process, or department, for a period of time. The firm calculates per-unit costs for goods passing through a process by dividing costs for the process by production for the period.

For internal reporting, a process-costing firm, like a job-order firm, can use either variable or absorption costing, as described in Chapter 14. We concentrate on absorption costing in this chapter. A process costing company can also use either actual costing or normal costing. Process costing firms can also use standard costs as Chapter 14 described.

Because process costers manufacture a single, homogeneous product, they can use the basic formula we described earlier:

$$\textit{unit cost} = \frac{\textit{production costs}}{\textit{production}}$$

The *key* to process costing is determining production, which depends on the treatment of units of work in process. At any given time and in any given process, some units are not completely through that process. Look at the data for our illustration in Exhibit 15-1. Note that the company finished 100,000 units in August, but also did 60% of the work on 5,000 units. What is production for the period? The 100,000 units finished? No, because the $206,000 cost incurred involved not only those 100,000 units, but also the partially-finished 5,000 units. Because some work is done on units in process at the end of a period, we cannot simply use the number of units *finished* as the denominator. Instead, we use **equivalent unit production** (or **equivalent production**) in the denominator, as we discuss shortly. To do so, we must select a cost flow assumption, typically either first-in-first-out or weighted average. We shall use the **weighted-average method** in this chapter. (We describe the FIFO method in Appendix at the end of this chapter.)

Recall from financial accounting that the weighted-average inventory method applied to a merchandiser combines the cost of the beginning inventory with the costs incurred during the period and also combines the units in the beginning inventory with those purchased during the period. The principle is the same for manufactured products.

EQUIVALENT UNIT PRODUCTION AND UNIT COST

Under the weighted-average method, equivalent unit production is the sum of (1) the units finished during the period, and (2) the equivalent whole units in the ending inventory of work in process.

The formula for weighted-average equivalent production is

$$\frac{\textit{Equivalent}}{\textit{production}} = \frac{\textit{units}}{\textit{completed}} + \left(\frac{\textit{units in}}{\textit{ending inventory}} \times \frac{\textit{percentage}}{\textit{complete}}\right)$$

Exhibit 15-1 Data for Ronn Company

	August	September
Production costs	$206,000	$191,400
Unit data:		
In process at beginning of month	0	5,000
Completed during month	100,000	90,000
In process at end of month	5,000	10,000
Percentage of completion for end-of-period work in process	60%	40%

In our example, the 5,000 units in process at the end of August are 3,000 *equivalent whole units*, which is the number of units multiplied by their percentage of completion (5,000 × 60%). So at the end of August there were 3,000 equivalent units and at the end of September there were 4,000 equivalent units (10,000 × 40%).

In our example, equivalent unit production for August is

Units completed	100,000
Equivalent units in ending inventory, 5,000 × 60%	3,000
Weighted-average equivalent unit production	103,000

The weighted-average unit cost formula is

$$\textit{Unit cost} = \frac{\textit{cost of beginning inventory + current period cost}}{\textit{weighted-average equivalent unit production}}$$

Because there is no beginning inventory for August, the numerator is simply production cost for August. The unit cost for August is therefore $2.00:

$$\$206{,}000/103{,}000 = \$2.00$$

ENDING INVENTORY AND TRANSFERS

We use the $2 unit cost for both the units completed and those in the ending inventory of work in process. Thus, $200,000 is transferred to Finished Goods Inventory (100,000 × $2) and $6,000 is left in Work in Process Inventory (5,000 × 60% × $2). Notice especially that the inventory of work in process reflects its equivalent whole units. That is, we do not multiply 5,000 *physical* units by the $2 unit cost because the 5,000 units are only 60% complete. We account for the total production costs of $206,000 in the schedule below. Such a schedule helps you to be sure that you are correct. The costs accounted for in the schedule should equal the beginning inventory of work in process plus the current period production costs. In August, there is no beginning work in process, so we account only for the $206,000 August production costs.

Cost of finished units transferred to finished goods (100,000 × $2 per unit)	$200,000
Cost of ending inventory (5,000 units × 60% × $2 unit cost)	6,000
Total production costs accounted for	$206,000

BEGINNING INVENTORY

Ronn began September with 3,000 equivalent units of work in process that have a cost of $6,000, as we just calculated. As the formula above showed, these units do not affect the *denominator* of the unit-cost calculation for September, but the $6,000 cost does. September equivalent production is

Units completed	90,000
Equivalent units in ending inventory, 10,000 × 40%	4,000
Weighted-average equivalent unit production	94,000

And unit cost is

$$\frac{\$6{,}000 + \$191{,}400}{94{,}000} = \$197{,}400/94{,}000 = \$2.10$$

The $2.10 is the *weighted-average cost,* which includes both the September results and the inventory carried over from August. The disposition of the costs follows.

Ending inventory of work in process	
10,000 × 40% × $2.10	$ 8,400
To finished goods inventory, 90,000 × $2.10	189,000
Total	$197,400

The sum of the cost of the beginning inventory and September production costs is $197,400, as we calculated just above. Therefore, the $197,400 cost in ending inventory and transferred to finished goods inventory accounts for those costs. The total costs from August and September were accounted for by the costs transferred out of the process plus the costs remaining in process. This calculation offers a check on your work. If the total costs accounted for as either transferred out or still in process do not equal the beginning inventory plus current period cost (with due regard for rounding errors), you have made an error.

Although no other conceptual problems arise under process costing, one common situation increases the number of calculations and another common situation requires special care. First is when the components of manufacturing cost (materials, labor or machine time, and overhead) are not equally complete. The second situation is when—as in most manufacturing companies—there is more than one department or process. The next two sections discuss these refinements.

MATERIALS AND CONVERSION COSTS

The Ronn Company example assumed that the same percentage-of-completion figure applied to all productive factors—materials, labor or machine time, and overhead. Such equality is quite unlikely because materials are usually put into process at an early stage while labor and overhead are added more or less continuously. Work in process inventories then usually include all (or nearly all) of the necessary materials, but less than the total required labor and overhead. For example, consider a company that manufactures sugar from sugar beets. At any given time, all of the beets in process are 100% complete with regard to materials: the beets must be in process before any work is done. But grinding beets into sugar takes time, so that the in-process beets are not complete with regard to time and overhead.

Converting raw materials into finished product requires labor and overhead—power, supplies, maintenance, and so on. Labor and overhead are both called **conversion costs**. Labor and overhead are generally assumed to have the same completion percentage. In a machine-driven department where labor is relatively insignificant, there might only be materials and overhead—no direct labor cost at all. For our example, all conversion costs are overhead.

Differing degrees of completion for materials and conversion costs do not change the general formula for computing unit costs; they only require calculating costs separately for materials and conversion costs. We shall illustrate the computations using the data for Borne Company in Exhibit 15-2.

As before, we use these unit costs to determine the cost of the ending inventory of work in process and the cost of the units transferred to finished goods inventory.

Ending inventory:	
Materials cost (5,000 units × 100% × $0.80)	$ 4,000
Conversion cost (5,000 units × 60% × $1.20)	3,600
Total cost of ending work in process inventory	$ 7,600
Transferred to finished goods:	
Materials cost (45,000 units × $0.80)	$36,000
Conversion cost (45,000 units × $1.20)	54,000
Total cost transferred to finished goods	$90,000

Taking advantage of the checkpoint presented in earlier sections, we can see that the total costs are fully accounted for through the transfer of completed units and the costs assigned to the ending inventory.

Total costs to be accounted for:	
Costs in beginning inventory ($4,000 + $5,600)	$ 9,600
Costs for current month ($36,000 + $52,000)	88,000
Total	$97,600
Total costs accounted for as:	
Cost of finished units transferred to finished goods	$90,000
Cost of ending inventory	7,600
Total	$97,600

Exhibit 15-2 Production Data for Borne Company for May

		Materials	Conversion Costs
Costs of beginning inventory		$ 4,000	$ 5,600
Production costs incurred in May		$36,000	$52,000
Unit data:			
Units completed	45,000		
Units in process at May 31	5,000		
Percentage of work complete		100%	60%
Equivalent production:			
Units completed		45,000	45,000
Equivalent units in ending inventory:			
5,000 × 100%		5,000	
5,000 × 60%			3,000
Equivalent unit production		50,000	48,000
Unit costs:		= $4,000 + $36,000 / 50,000	= $5,600 + $52,000 / 48,000
		= $0.80	= $1.20

Thus, the different percentages of completion for materials and conversion costs require only that we compute different amounts of equivalent production and separate total costs by type.

MULTIPLE PROCESSES

When a product moves from one process to another, its total cost must include the costs of all the processes. Suppose the manufacture of a particular product includes both a forming operation (cutting large blocks of some raw material into smaller blocks of roughly equal size) and a sanding operation (refining the shapes to common specifications). The cost of a unit transferred from sanding to finished goods includes the cost of both the forming and the sanding processes. The cost of a unit in process in the sanding department includes not only the cost of that operation but also the cost of the forming department.

To illustrate the implications of multiple processes, let us extend the example of Borne Company, for whom the basic production data for May are provided in Exhibit 15-2. Suppose that the 45,000 units completed in May were actually transferred to the finishing department. No materials are added during the finishing process, and overhead in that department is closely associated with labor hours worked. Operating data for May for the finishing process appear below. The department adds no materials, so all costs it incurs are for conversion.

Unit Data:	
On hand at beginning of June	0
Transferred in from prior department	45,000
Completed and transferred to finished goods	40,000
On hand at end of period (70% complete)	5,000
Cost Data:	
Beginning inventory	$ 0
Transferred in from prior department	$ 90,000
Department's conversion costs for June	$156,600

What is the cost of a unit transferred from the finishing process to finished goods inventory?

The first step, of course, is to calculate the equivalent production for the finishing process.

Units completed	40,000
Equivalent units in ending inventory, 5,000 × 70%	3,500
Weighted-average equivalent unit production	43,500

And unit cost is

$$\frac{\$0 + \$156{,}600}{43{,}500} = \$3.60$$

The cost of a unit transferred to finished goods is the $2.00 from the prior department plus $3.60 from the finishing department, a total of $5.60. The cost of the ending in-process inventory is a bit less simple because the units have all of the work done by the prior department, but only 70% of the work of the finishing department. The calculation therefore takes two steps.

Ending work in process:	
Conversion costs, 5,000 × 70% × $3.60	$12,600
Cost from prior department, 5,000 × 100% × $2.00	10,000
Ending work in process	$22,600

The total cost to be accounted for by the finishing department consists of the costs transferred in ($90,000), the costs in the beginning inventory (none), and the month's production costs ($156,600), or $246,600. That total is accounted for as follows:

Transferred to finished goods, 40,000 × $5.60	$224,000
Ending inventory of work in process, above	22,600
Total	$246,600

THE COST ACCOUNTING CYCLE

Chapter 13 presented an overview of the flow of manufacturing costs (Exhibit 13-1), noting that costs are first accumulated by object (materials, labor, and overhead) and are then passed on to Work in Process to Finished Goods and, ultimately, to Cost of Goods Sold.[1] Chapter 14 noted that the choice between absorption and variable costing determines whether fixed manufacturing costs are inventoried or assigned directly to expense. We have not yet described these cost flows in terms of accounts and journal entries.

The transition from a set of ideas to an accounting flow is not difficult. Exhibit 15-3, which is but a minor variation of similar figures in Chapters 13 and 14, translates cost flows to changes in specific *accounts*. Exhibit 15-3 also points out the critical difference between absorption and variable costing: the latter assigns fixed manufacturing overhead to expense in the period in which those costs are incurred. Absorption costing assigns fixed manufacturing costs to Work in Process; hence, they flow through Finished Goods and, ultimately, to Cost of Goods Sold. We shall concentrate our discussion of accounting entries on those relevant to absorption costing.

The two principal cost accumulation systems are process and job-order costing. Actual or normal costing can be used under either system, and standard costs can always be used by process costers, sometimes by job-order manufacturers. Despite the differences among the various combinations available, the journal entries to record the flow of costs differ little from one system to another, because, as Exhibit 15-3 shows, there is a limited number of places for costs to be collected or transferred. The first illustration is actual process costing, the second is a job-order company using normal costing. We also illustrate standard costing in a simple, process-costing setting in order to concentrate on the accounting issues peculiar to standard costing.

1 Following the pattern introduced in Chapter 13, we indicate the names of accounts by using capital letters, while using lowercase letters to denote the objects themselves. Thus, "Work in Process" refers to an account, while "work in process" refers to the physical, semifinished product.

Exhibit 15-3 Cost Accounting Cycle

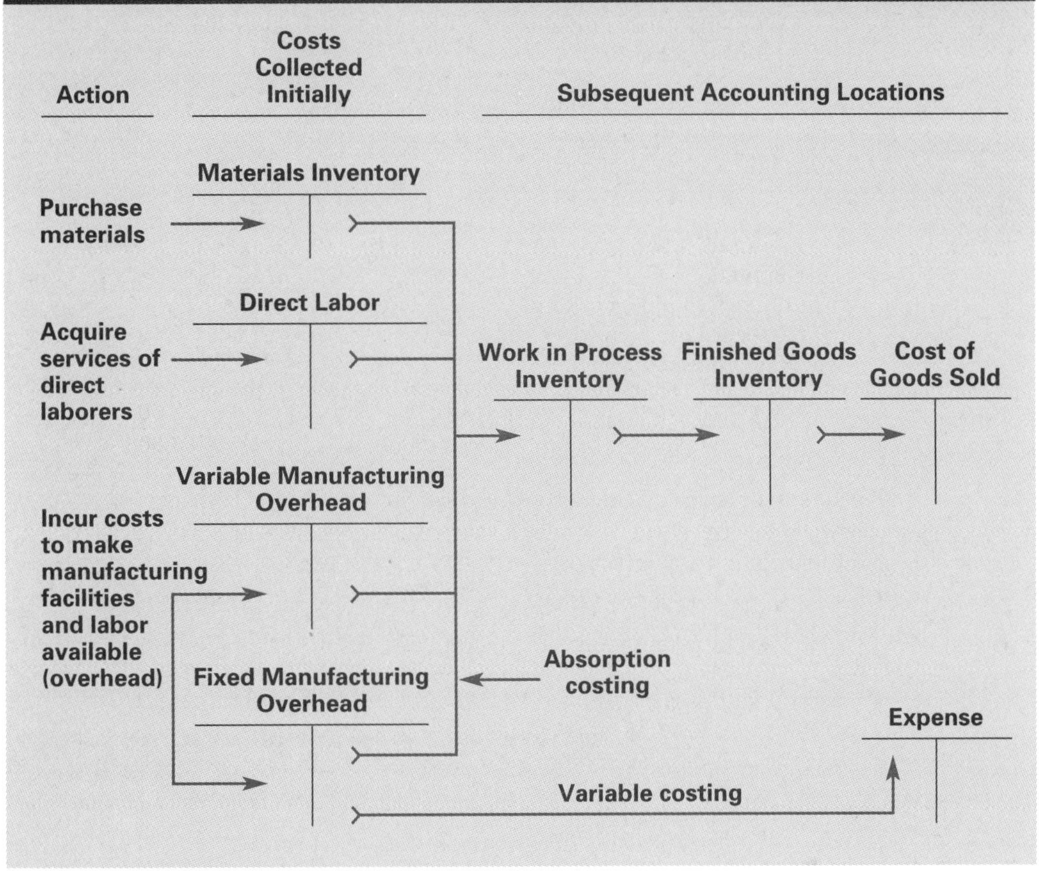

ILLUSTRATION OF ACTUAL PROCESS COSTING

Mason Company produces a special type of plywood. The manufacturing process requires sequential applications of layers of wood until the plywood reaches the required thickness. For simplicity, we assume that there were no beginning inventories of work in process. (The implications of beginning work in process inventories for the calculation of equivalent production were discussed on pages 640-641.) Mason had the following transactions in 19X5. (We omit explanations of the journal entries because the descriptions of the transactions serve the same purpose.)

Purchase of materials: Mason bought 1,400,000 feet of wood at $0.095 per foot.

1. Materials Inventory (1,400,000 × $0.095)	$133,000	
Cash or Accounts Payable		$133,000

Materials put into process: Mason used 1,300,000 feet of wood.

2. Work in Process (1,300,000 × $0.095)	$123,500	
Materials Inventory		$123,500

Direct labor incurred: Direct laborers earned $344,400 for 82,000 hours of work at $4.20 per hour.

3a. Direct Labor	$344,400	
Cash or Accrued Payroll		$344,400
3b. Work in Process Inventory	$344,400	
Direct Labor		$344,400

Overhead costs incurred: Mason incurred the following overhead costs. For brevity we list only a few individual items, lumping the bulk of overhead costs into the "Other" category. Overhead costs are first recorded by type of cost.

4. Indirect Labor	$ 84,000	
Supplies	12,000	
Other Variable Overhead	155,300	
Supervision	74,000	
Depreciation	96,000	
Other Fixed Overhead	291,000	
Accumulated Depreciation		$ 96,000
Cash, Accrued Payables		616,300

Overhead costs are not usually put directly into Work in Process Inventory. Instead, they are gathered into an account called Manufacturing Overhead or into two such accounts: one for variable overhead and one for fixed overhead.

5a. Variable Manufacturing Overhead	$251,300	
Indirect Labor		$ 84,000
Supplies		12,000
Other Variable Overhead		155,300
5b. Fixed Manufacturing Overhead	$461,000	
Supervision		$ 74,000
Depreciation		96,000
Other Fixed Overhead		291,000

The manufacturing overhead accounts are for convenience and are especially helpful when standard costing is used, as we shall show shortly. The amounts put into the manufacturing overhead accounts are now transferred to Work in Process Inventory.

5c. Work in Process Inventory	$251,300	
Variable Manufacturing Overhead		$251,300
Work in Process Inventory	$461,000	
Fixed Manufacturing Overhead		$461,000

Production: Mason finished 40,000 square yards of plywood. Another 3,000 square yards were still in process at the end of 19X5. These 3,000 square yards were two-thirds finished for both materials and conversion costs.

To transfer the cost of finished units to Finished Goods Inventory, we need the per-unit cost of production. Therefore, we need equivalent production, which is calculated as follows:

$$\textit{Equivalent production} = 40{,}000 + (3{,}000 \times 2/3) = 42{,}000 \textit{ square yards}$$

The 42,000 equivalent production is used to determine the cost per unit. At this point we have $1,180,200 in Work in Process Inventory, composed of the following costs. The numbers in parentheses refer to journal entries.

Materials (2)	$ 123,500
Direct labor (3b)	344,400
Variable overhead (5c)	251,300
Fixed overhead (5c)	461,000
Total	$1,180,200
Divided by equivalent production	42,000
Equals cost per unit	$ 28.10

The $28.10 cost per unit is used to transfer to Finished Goods Inventory.

6. Finished Goods Inventory (40,000 × $28.10)	$1,124,000	
Work in Process Inventory		$1,124,000

Sales: Mason sold 35,000 square yards at $40 each.

7a. Cash or Accounts Receivable (35,000 × $40)	$1,400,000	
Sales		$1,400,000
7b. Cost of Goods Sold (35,000 × $28.10)	$983,500	
Finished Goods Inventory		$983,500

Selling and administrative expenses: The firm incurred $340,000 in selling and administrative expenses.

8. Selling and Administrative Expenses	$340,000	
Cash, Accrued Payables		$340,000

At this point the accounts for direct labor, variable overhead, and fixed overhead all have zero balances. The other key accounts show the following:

Work in Process Inventory

	Debit	Credit	
(2)	$ 123,500		
(3b)	344,400		
(5c)	251,300	$1,124,000	(6)
(5c)	461,000		
	1,180,200	1,124,000	
Bal.	$ 56,200		

Finished Goods Inventory

	Debit	Credit	
(6)	$1,124,000	$983,500	(7b)
Bal.	$ 140,500		

Cost of Goods Sold

	Debit	Credit
(7b)	$ 983,500	

Materials Inventory

	Debit	Credit	
(1)	$ 133,000	$123,500	(2)
Bal.	$ 9,500		

An income statement for Mason Company is given in Exhibit 15-4.

Exhibit 15-4 Income Statement for Mason Company—Actual Process Costing

Sales (7a) [a]	$1,400,000
Cost of goods sold (7b)	983,500
Gross profit	416,500
Selling and administrative expenses (8)	340,000
Income	$ 76,500

a Figures in parentheses indicate journal entry numbers from the earlier illustrations.

ILLUSTRATION OF JOB-ORDER COSTING

Portland Mill Works makes industrial products that require work in two departments, stamping and assembly. The Stamping Department uses costly machinery and relatively little direct labor. Accordingly, the managers believe that machine hours (MH) is the appropriate measure of activity for applying overhead in that department. The Assembly Department is relatively labor intensive, with machinery limited to small devices. The managers use direct labor hours (DLH) as the measure of activity for applying overhead in that department.

The company has established predetermined overhead rates as shown below.

	Stamping Department	Assembly Department
Total budgeted overhead	$600,000	$250,000
Divided by budgeted levels of activity	200,000 MH	100,000 DLH
Equals predetermined overhead rates	$3.00 per MH	$2.50 per DLH

Exhibit 15-5 presents the actual results for the year, including the overhead applied for each department.

Exhibit 15-5 Portland Mill Works, Results for 19X6

Activity Data	Totals	Jobs Sold	Jobs in Ending Work in Process Inventory	Jobs in Ending Finished Goods Inventory
Machine hours in Stamping Department	210,000	190,000	7,000	13,000
Direct labor hours in Assembly Department	95,000	80,000	5,000	10,000
Cost Data				
Materials used	$ 650,000	$ 580,000	$30,000	$ 40,000
Direct labor	800,000	720,000	20,000	60,000
Applied overhead:				
Stamping Department at $3.00 [a]	630,000	570,000	21,000	39,000
Assembly Department at $2.50 [b]	237,500	200,000	12,500	25,000
Total costs	$2,317,500	$2,070,000	$83,500	$164,000
Actual Overhead				
Stamping	$ 608,000			
Assembly	244,000			
Total	$ 852,000			

a *Total, 210,000 × $3.00 = $630,000; jobs sold, 190,000 × $3.00 = $570,000, etc.*
b *Total, 95,000 × $2.50 = $237,500; jobs sold, 80,000 × $2.50 = $200,000, etc.*

We can calculate misapplied overhead as follows.

Total actual overhead ($608,000 + $244,000)	$852,000
Total applied overhead ($630,000 + $237,500)	867,500
Total overapplied overhead	$ 15,500

The journal entries and accounts of a job-order firm are similar in form to those of a process costing firm (or one that uses standard costs). Essentially, job-order costing is a specific identification method, so that transfers from Work in Process Inventory to Finished Goods Inventory and to Cost of Goods Sold are based on the particular jobs finished and sold. For Portland Mill Works, the following entries summarize our knowledge of the flows. All of the information comes from Exhibit 15-5.

Materials used

1. Work in Process Inventory	$ 650,000	
Materials Inventory		$ 650,000

Direct labor

2a. Direct Labor	$ 800,000	
Cash or Accrued Payroll		$ 800,000
2b. Work in Process Inventory	$ 800,000	
Direct Labor		$ 800,000

Overhead incurrence and application

3a. Factory Overhead—Stamping Department	$ 608,000	
Factory Overhead—Assembly Department	244,000	
Various Credits, Cash, Accrued Expenses, Accumulated Depreciation		$ 852,000
3b. Work in Process Inventory	$ 867,500	
Factory Overhead—Stamping Department		$ 630,000
Factory Overhead—Assembly Department		237,500

Completion of jobs

4. Finished Goods Inventory	$2,234,000	
Work in Process Inventory		$2,234,000

This entry is the total cost of all jobs completed during the year, which consists of the $2,070,000 cost of jobs sold plus the $164,000 cost of jobs still in Finished Goods Inventory at year end.

Cost of sales

5. Cost of Goods Sold	$2,070,000	
Finished Goods Inventory		$2,070,000

At this point, the various manufacturing overhead and inventory accounts appear as follows.

Factory Overhead—Stamping

	Debit	Credit	
(3a)	$ 608,000	$ 630,000	(3b)
		$ 22,000	Bal.

Factory Overhead—Assembly

	Debit	Credit	
(3a)	$ 244,000	$ 237,500	(3b)
Bal.	$ 6,500		

Work in Process Inventory

	Debit	Credit	
(1)	$ 650,000		
(2)	800,000		
(3b)	867,500	$2,234,000	(4)
	2,317,500	2,234,000	
Bal.	$ 83,500		

Finished Goods Inventory

	Debit	Credit	
(4)	$2,234,000	$2,070,000	(5)
Bal.	$ 164,000		

Cost of Goods Sold

	Debit	Credit
(5)	$2,070,000	

The amounts shown as ending balances in Cost of Good Sold and the two inventory accounts agree with the amounts shown in Exhibit 15-5. The balances of the factory overhead accounts represent the overapplied or underapplied overhead for the departments. The net overapplied overhead of $15,500 ($22,000 overapplied in stamping minus $6,500 underapplied in assembly) agrees with the misapplied overhead computed on page 649.

What happens to the balances representing misapplication (actual different from applied) of overhead? As Chapter 13 stated, there are two possibilities. The $15,500 can be shown in the income statement, as an adjustment either to cost of goods sold or to gross margin, or the company could convert to an actual costing basis by allocating the misapplied overhead to all the work done during the year.

ILLUSTRATION OF STANDARD COSTING

Our final illustration of the cost accounting cycle deals with standard costing systems. Virtually all such systems require that transfers of costs from Work in Process Inventory to Finished Goods Inventory be made at the total standard cost of units completed. But costs can be put into Work in Process Inventory in two ways: (1) put in actual quantities of inputs at standard prices or (2) put in standard quantities of inputs at standard prices. We shall illustrate the latter technique.

Data for one of DMV Company's products appear in Exhibit 15-6. For simplicity, we shall assume that the firm has no inventories of work in process—that it finishes the units it starts each day. With the information given, we can now calculate the several variances as shown in the following table.

One objective of a standard costing system is to isolate variances in the accounts as quickly as possible, instead of making separate calculations outside of the accounting system. Timely determination of variances helps in control because the sooner that managers know about variances, the sooner they can decide whether or not to investigate and possibly act.

Journal entries describing the events of March appear on page 662. Price variances are isolated when the cost is incurred, which is when the variance

Exhibit 15-6 DMV Company: Data for Illustration

Standard Costs	
Materials (3 pounds at $3 per pound)	$ 9
Direct labor (2 hours at $8 per hour)	16
Variable overhead at $6 per DLH	12
Fixed overhead [a]	20
Total standard cost	$ 57
Results for March 19X6	
Beginning inventory of finished units at standard cost (500 units × $57)	$ 28,500
Units produced in March	9,000
Units sold in March	9,200
Ending inventory of finished units	300
Costs in March	
Materials purchased (no beginning inventory)	$ 92,000
Materials used, 26,000 pounds	
Direct labor (19,000 hours × $8.20)	$155,800
Variable overhead	$112,000
Fixed overhead	$198,000

a Budgeted fixed overhead $200,000 per month/normal capacity of 10,000 units.

Materials Variances	
Price variance [($3 × 30,000 pounds) – $92,000]	$ 2,000 unfavorable
Use variance [(9,000 × 3 × $3) – (26,000 × $3)]	$ 3,000 favorable
Labor Variances	
Rate variance [($8.00 – $8.20) × 19,000 hours]	$ 3,800 unfavorable
Efficiency variance [(9,000 × 2 × $8) – (19,000 × $8)]	$ 8,000 unfavorable
Variable Overhead Variances	
Budget variance [($6 × 19,000) – $112,000]	$ 2,000 favorable
Efficiency variance [(18,000 – 19,000) × $6]	$ 6,000 unfavorable
Fixed Overhead Variances	
Budget variance ($200,000 – $198,000)	$ 2,000 favorable
Volume variance [(10,000 – 9,000) × $20]	$20,000 unfavorable

first becomes known, and quantity variances are isolated when costs are put into process. Thus, the entries putting costs into process are made at the end of the period, when production is known, because you must know production to determine the efficiency variances and fixed overhead volume variance. As we have said, there are other possible patterns, but they all share the essential characteristic of standard costing: all inventories appear at standard cost at the ends of periods.

Materials purchases

	Debit	Credit
1. Materials Inventory (30,000 pounds × $3)	$90,000	
Material Price Variance	2,000	
Cash or Accounts Payable		$92,000

Materials use

	Debit	Credit
2. Work in Process Inventory (27,000 pounds × $3)	$81,000	
Material Use Variance		$ 3,000
Materials Inventory (26,000 pounds × $3)		78,000

Direct labor

	Debit	Credit
3a. Direct Labor (19,000 × $8)	$152,000	
Direct Labor Rate Variance	3,800	
Cash or Accrued Payroll		$155,800
3b. Work in Process Inventory (18,000 × $8)	$144,000	
Direct Labor Efficiency Variance	8,000	
Direct Labor		$152,000

Variable overhead

	Debit	Credit
4a. Variable Manufacturing Overhead (19,000 × $6)	$114,000	
Variable Overhead Spending Variance		$ 2,000
Various Credits, Cash, Accrued Expenses		112,000
4b. Work in Process Inventory (18,000 × $6)	$108,000	
Variable Overhead Efficiency Variance	6,000	
Variable Manufacturing Overhead		$114,000

Fixed overhead

	Debit	Credit
5a. Fixed Manufacturing Overhead	$200,000	
Fixed Overhead Budget Variance		$ 2,000
Various Credits, Cash, Accumulated Depreciation		198,000
5b. Work in Process Inventory (9,000 × $20)	$180,000	
Fixed Overhead Volume Variance	20,000	
Fixed Manufacturing Overhead		$200,000

Completion of goods

	Debit	Credit
6. Finished Goods Inventory (9,000 × $57)	$513,000	
Work in Process Inventory		$513,000

Cost of sales

	Debit	Credit
7. Cost of Goods Sold (9,200 × $57)	$524,400	
Finished Goods Inventory		$524,400

The T-accounts for each type of inventory and for Cost of Goods Sold follow. The beginning balance in Finished Goods Inventory is the standard cost of the 500 units on hand at the beginning of March (from Exhibit 15-6).

The ending balance reflects the standard cost of the remaining 300 units (300 × $57 = $17,100). Materials Inventory shows the standard price of the 4,000 pounds in the ending inventory, which is the 30,000 pounds bought less the 26,000 used.

Work in Process Inventory

(2)	$ 81,000		
(3b)	144,000		
(4b)	108,000		
(5b)	180,000	$513,000	(6)
	$513,000	$513,000	

Finished Goods Inventory

3-1 Bal.	$ 28,500		
(6)	513,000	$524,400	(7)
	$541,500	$524,400	
3-31 Bal.	$ 17,100		

Materials Inventory

(1)	$ 90,000	$ 78,000	(2)
3-31 Bal	$ 12,000		

Cost of Goods Sold

(7)	$524,400	

What is the disposition of these account balances? As with misapplied overhead, there are usually two alternatives. The variances can be carried to the period's income statement as adjustments to either cost of goods sold or to gross margin. Or, they can be prorated among those accounts still containing the cost elements that gave rise to the variances. Thus, variances other than the material price variance could be prorated among Cost of Goods Sold, Finished Goods Inventory, and Work in Process Inventory. The proration of a material price variance also involves Material Inventory if materials were still on hand. As stated earlier, the need for proration depends on the magnitude of the variances and the ending inventories, since GAAP accept standard costs for financial reporting purposes as long as the income-statement results of using such costs do not differ materially from the results under actual costing. Unfortunately, what constitutes a "material" difference has never been defined to the satisfaction of all interested parties.

PRODUCT COSTING IN A JIT ENVIRONMENT

Because JIT inventory policies are characteristic of advanced manufacturing systems, firms using such systems have no significant work in process inventory and so have relatively few problems in accounting for that type of inventory. Some JIT operations might, however, have significant finished goods inventories, in which case product costing is still a concern. One technique used by such companies is **backflushing,** or **backflush costing**.

Backflushing requires relatively few entries during a period. There is no effort to keep Materials Inventory, Work in Process Inventory, or Finished Goods Inventory at their "correct" balances. Rather, companies using this technique maintain two inventory accounts, one for finished goods, and the other for both materials and work in process.

The following example shows one way to record events using a backflush system. Data for the example follow.

Beginning inventories	None
Materials and components purchased and put into process	$250,000
Labor and overhead costs incurred	$180,000
Units completed	40,000
Units sold	35,000

Because materials are put into process almost immediately after being received, there is no need for separate accounts for materials and work in process and material purchases are recorded in the following manner.

Materials and In-Process Inventory	$250,000	
Cash or Accounts Payable		$250,000

Conversion costs are collected in a single account as below.

Conversion Costs	$180,000	
Cash, Accounts Payable, Accumulated Depreciation, etc.		$180,000

The above two entries are made throughout the period as events require.

The average cost of production for the period is $10.75 [($250,000 + $180,000)/40,000]. At the end of the period, an entry is made to record the cost of the ending inventory of finished units and the cost of units sold.

Cost of Sales (35,000 × $10.75)	$376,250	
Finished Goods Inventory (5,000 × $10.75)	53,750	
Materials and In-Process Inventory		$250,000
Conversion Costs		180,000

The recording could also be done using standard costs, though JIT operations typically use actual rather than standard costs.

The pattern of entries shown above is not the only possibility. Some companies charge all costs to Finished Goods Inventory on the basis of reports of the number of units completed, and make a transfer of Cost of Sales only at month-end. Because backflush costing has the potential for reducing the information provided to managers during an accounting period, it is best suited to a firm with relatively stable levels of production activity and few in-process units.

FINAL COMPARATIVE COMMENTS

We have illustrated the cost accounting cycle in four situations. We showed a company that used actual process costing, a job-order firm that used normal costing, an operation that used standard costs, and finally, a JIT operation. At this point it is desirable to review briefly the many topics covered as part of our three-chapter discussion of product costing.

Any cost accounting system uses either variable costing or absorption costing, the difference being that only the latter assigns fixed manufacturing overhead to units of product. Any system must use either actual, normal, or standard costs. The nature of the manufacturing operation tends to separate cost accumulation systems into job order and process. Both types of firms could use either absorption or variable costing, and actual, normal, or standard costs. (Job-order cost systems are least likely to use standard costs because of the uniqueness of the products made on the various jobs.)

Yet, with all these possibilities, the only real differences among the various methods and systems lie in the valuation of inventories. That is, total fixed and variable manufacturing costs incurred in a particular period are facts, so the choice of a cost system does not change costs. The different techniques are simply different ways of assigning those costs to cost of goods sold and to inventories. *If a company has no inventories, all of the various approaches will give the same amount of income on the income statement.*

Thus, managers who must use accounting reports to help them in decision making must know the basis used for those reports and must understand the effects that any given method has on those reports.

SUMMARY

The type of manufacturing operation determines whether a company uses job-order or process costing. Calculating unit costs under process costing is complicated by incomplete units of inventory at the beginning or end of a period. The concept of equivalent production is used to resolve this complication, but the existence of beginning inventories requires further refinement of the concept to adopt a cost-flow assumption (weighted-average or first-in-first-out).

The flow of costs through a manufacturing firm can be accounted for in several ways regardless of whether a company uses job-order or process costing. Specifically, a company can use either actual or normal costing in the assignment of manufacturing overhead, or it can use standard costs. (In addition, of course, a firm could use either variable or absorption costing, but the latter is required for external reporting.)

The journal entries to record cost flows are quite similar for job-order and process costing. They are somewhat more complex when standard costs are used, because entries under standard costing must isolate variances into separate accounts.

KEY TERMS

backflushing (or backflush costing)
conversion costs
cost accounting cycle
equivalent unit product (equivalent production)
process costing
weighted-average

KEY FORMULAS

$$\text{Equivalent production—weighted average} = \text{units completed} + \left(\text{units in ending inventory} \times \text{percentage complete}\right)$$

$$\text{Equivalent production—first-in-first-out} = \text{units completed} + \left(\text{units in beginning inventory} \times \text{percentage complete}\right) - \left(\text{units in beginning inventory} \times \text{percentage complete in prior period}\right)$$

$$\text{Cost per unit—weighted average} = \frac{\text{cost of beginning inventory} + \text{costs incurred during the period}}{\text{equivalent production—weighted average}}$$

REVIEW PROBLEM—PROCESS COSTING

Stambol Manufacturing Company makes a chemical solvent and uses weighted-average process costing. Data for April 19X8 are as follows.

Beginning inventory of work in process	$ 6,000
Materials used	$485,000
Direct labor incurred	$648,000
Overhead incurred	$604,000
Gallons completed and sent to finished goods	800,000
Gallons in ending inventory (75% complete)	40,000

Required

1. Determine equivalent production and cost per unit.
2. Determine the cost of the ending inventory of work in process.
3. Prepare a T-account for Work in Process Inventory. Check the ending balance with your answer to item 2.
4. There was no inventory of finished product at the beginning of April. During April, 730,000 gallons were sold and 70,000 gallons remained in ending finished goods inventory. Determine the cost of goods sold and the cost of the ending inventory of finished product.

ANSWER TO REVIEW PROBLEM

1. Equivalent production and cost per unit.

Equivalent Production	
Gallons completed	800,000
Equivalent production in ending inventory (40,000 × 75%)	30,000
Equivalent production for April	830,000

Cost per Unit—Weighted Average	
Beginning inventory of work in progress	$ 6,000
Costs incurred:	
Materials	485,000
Direct labor	648,000
Overhead	604,000
Total	$1,743,000
Divided by equivalent production	830,000
Equals cost per unit	$ 2.10

2. Ending inventory of work in process is $63,000 (30,000 equivalent units × $2.10).
3.

Work in Process Inventory		
Beginning balance	$ 6,000	
Materials	485,000	
Direct labor	648,000	
Overhead	604,000	$1,680,000 transferred out (800,000 × $2.10)
	1,743,000	1,680,000
Ending balance	$ 63,000	

The $63,000 balance equals the answer to item 2.

4. Cost of goods sold is $1,533,000, 730,000 gallons multiplied by $2.10. Ending inventory of finished goods is $147,000, which is 70,000 gallons (800,000 – 730,000) multiplied by $2.10.

REVIEW PROBLEM—STANDARD COSTING

Mason Company, whose actual operations were accounted for in the chapter, has changed to standard costing. It developed the following standards per square yard of plywood.

Materials (30 feet of wood at $0.10 per foot)	$ 3
Direct labor (1 hour at $8 per hour)	8
Variable overhead ($6 per direct labor hour)	6
Fixed overhead*	9
Total standard cost	$26

** Based on budgeted fixed overhead of $450,000 and normal capacity of 50,000 square yards ($450,000/50,000 = $9 per square yard).*

Required

1. Using the actual results detailed in the chapter, calculate the variances from standard cost.
2. Prepare journal entries to record the events.
3. Prepare T-accounts for Work in Process Inventory, Finished Goods Inventory, Materials Inventory, and Cost of Goods Sold at standard.
4. Prepare an income statement for the year and contrast it with the one shown in Exhibit 15-4 that uses actual costing.

ANSWER TO REVIEW PROBLEM

1.

Materials Variances	
Price variance [1,400,000 feet × ($0.10 – $0.095)]	$ 7,000 favorable
Use variance [1,300,000 – (42,000 × 30 feet)] × $0.10	4,000 unfavorable

Direct Labor Variances	
Rate variance [41,000 hours × ($8.40 – $8)]	$16,400 unfavorable
Efficiency variance [41,000 hours – (42,000 × 1)] × $8	8,000 favorable

Variable Overhead Variances	
Spending variance [$251,300 – (41,000 × $6)]	$ 5,300 unfavorable
Efficiency variance [41,000 hours – (42,000 × 1)] × $6	6,000 favorable

Fixed Overhead Variances	
Budget variance ($461,000 – $450,000)	$11,000 unfavorable
Volume variance [(50,000 – 42,000) × $9]	72,000 unfavorable

2.

1. Materials Inventory (1,400,000 × $0.10)	$ 140,000	
Material Price Variance		$ 7,000
Cash or Accounts Payable		133,000
2. Work in Process (1,260,000 × $0.10)	$ 126,000	
Material Use Variance	4,000	
Materials Inventory		$ 130,000
3a. Direct Labor (41,000 × $8)	$ 328,000	
Direct Labor Rate Variance	16,400	
Cash		$ 344,400
3b. Work in Process Inventory (42,000 × 1 × $8)	$ 336,000	
Direct Labor Efficiency Variance		$ 8,000
Direct Labor		328,000
4a. Variable Manufacturing Overhead (41,000 hours × $6)	$ 246,000	
Variable Overhead Spending Variance	5,300	
Cash, Accrued Payables		$ 251,300
4b. Fixed Manufacturing Overhead (budget of $450,000)	$ 450,000	
Fixed Overhead Budget Variance	11,000	
Accumulated Depreciation		$ 96,000
Cash, Accrued Payables		365,000
5a. Work in Process Inventory (42,000 × $6)	$ 252,000	
Variable Overhead Efficiency Variance		$ 6,000
Variable Manufacturing Overhead		246,000
5b. Work in Process Inventory (42,000 × $9)	$ 378,000	
Fixed Overhead Volume Variance (8,000 × $9)	72,000	
Fixed Manufacturing Overhead		$ 450,000
6. Finished Goods Inventory (40,000 × $26)	$1,040,000	
Work in Process Inventory		$1,040,000
7a. Cash or Accounts Receivable (35,000 × $40 selling price)	$1,400,000	
Sales		$1,400,000

7b. Cost of Goods Sold (35,000 × $26)	$ 910,000	
Finished Goods Inventory		$ 910,000
8. Selling and Administrative Expenses	$ 340,000	
Cash, Accrued Payables		$ 340,000

3.

Work in Process Inventory

	Debit	Credit	
(2)	$ 126,000		
(3b)	336,000		
(5a)	252,000		
(5b)	378,000	$1,040,000	(6)
	1,092,000	1,040,000	
Bal.	$ 52,000		

Finished Goods Inventory

	Debit	Credit	
(6)	$1,040,000	$910,000	(7b)
Bal.	$ 130,000		

Materials Inventory

	Debit	Credit	
(1)	$ 140,000	$ 130,000	(2)
Bal.	$ 10,000		

Cost of Goods Sold

	Debit	Credit
(7b)	$ 910,000	

4.

Income Statements for Mason Company—Absorption Costing

	Actual Process Costing	Standard Process Costing	
Sales (7a)	$1,400,000		$1,400,000
Cost of goods sold (7b)	983,500		910,000
Gross profit	416,500		490,000
Manufacturing variances:			
Material price (1)		$ 7,000F	
Material use (2)		4,000U	
Direct labor rate (3a)		16,400U	
Direct labor efficiency (3b)		8,000F	
Variable overhead spending (4a)		5,300U	
Variable overhead efficiency (5a)		6,000F	
Fixed overhead budget (4b)		11,000U	
Fixed overhead volume (5b)		72,000U	87,700U
Actual gross profit			402,300
Less: Selling and administrative expenses (8)	340,000		340,000
Income	$ 76,500		$ 62,300

APPENDIX: PROCESS COSTING—THE FIFO METHOD

We stated in this chapter that there is a need to choose a cost-flow assumption (weighted average or first-in-first-out) when units are worked on in two periods. The need arises because the cost to work on a unit of product might change from one period to the next.

The illustration in the chapter used the weighted-average method. It is just as reasonable—and intuitively more appealing—to argue that the costs incurred in the current period apply only to that portion of the work done in the current period. This alternative leads to the use of the **first-in-first-out (FIFO)** method. Adopting this method changes the calculation of the unit cost for the current period, because it affects both the numerator and the denominator of the calculation of current-period unit cost. The numerator includes only the production costs of the current period, and the denominator includes only the work done during the current period.

ILLUSTRATION OF FIFO

To illustrate FIFO, let us return to the data used in this chapter to illustrate the weighted-average method. For your convenience, the data in Exhibit 15-1 are reproduced in Exhibit 15-7.

The company starts the month of August with no units in process. Hence, there is no need to know the cost flow assumption. The unit cost for August is computed, as shown in the chapter, by dividing the total manufacturing costs in August ($206,000) by the equivalent production in that month (103,000), for a unit cost of $2.00. That is, whatever work was done on whatever units were processed in August (started and finished during the month, or still unfinished at the end of the month), the total costs were $206,000. The cost of processing a *full* unit was $2.00 ($206,000/103,000).

The situation in September is different. In September, 90,000 units were completed and 10,000 were on hand, 40% complete. But of the 90,000 units completed, 5,000 units were 60% complete at the beginning of the period, so that the production costs for September apply to those beginning inventory units *only* to the extent of the 40% of the work done in September. Therefore, we calculate the cost of processing a unit of product in September by using *only* September's costs and an equivalent production figure that reflects *only* September's work. We already know that production costs in September were $191,400, so the task is to calculate an equivalent production related only to the September work. What we need is an equivalent production number that relates only to the work done in September. We can determine that number simply by backing out the work done in August from the weighted-average equivalent production computed for September. That is, if we start with the number of finished units (90,000 in September, in the present example), we need only subtract the amount of work done on some of those units *prior* to September. Thus, the calculation of equivalent production for September using the FIFO assumption is shown on the next page.

Exhibit 15-7 Data for Ronn Company

	August	September
Production costs	**$206,000**	**$191,400**
Unit data:		
In process at beginning of month	0	5,000
Completed during month	100,000	90,000
In process at end of month	5,000	10,000
Percentage of completion for end-of-period work in process	60%	40%

Units completed in September (90,000 × 100%)	90,000
Work done on units partially complete at the end of September (10,000 × 40%)	4,000
Weighted-average equivalent production	94,000
Less work done in August on units completed in September (5,000 units × 60%)	3,000
Equivalent production, FIFO	91,000

We can generalize this calculation in this way.

$$\text{Equivalent production—first-in-first-out} = \text{units completed} + \left(\text{units in ending inventory} \times \text{percent complete}\right) - \left(\text{units in beginning inventory} \times \text{percent cmplete in prior period}\right)$$

Under FIFO, equivalent production reflects only work done during the current period. Thus, the calculation of FIFO unit cost uses only the production costs for the period. The formula under FIFO is

$$\text{Unit cost—FIFO} = \frac{\text{production costs for the period}}{\text{equivalent production—FIFO}}$$

In the example, the unit cost is \$2.1033, September production costs of \$191,400 divided by equivalent production of 91,000 units. Because the unit cost determined for August was the same regardless of the cost-flow method, the total costs to be accounted for in September are the same as they were in the chapter and consist of

Costs of beginning inventory (5,000 units × 60% × \$2)	\$ 6,000
Production costs for September	191,400
Total cost to be accounted for	\$197,400

These costs either have been transferred to finished goods (for the completed units) or are associated with the units still in process. With the FIFO assumption, the cost relevant to the units in process at the end of the period is the unit cost for work done in September, or \$2.1033. The cost assigned to the ending inventory of 10,000 units that are 40% complete would be \$8,413 (10,000 × 40% × \$2.1033).

The costs transferred to finished goods can be determined by analyzing the units transferred.

Transfer of units that were in process at the beginning of the month:	
Cost from prior period, beginning inventory (5,000 × 60% × \$2)	\$ 6,000
Completion costs (5,000 × 40% × \$2.1033)	4,207
Total	10,207
Transfer of units started and completed in September [(90,000 – 5,000) × \$2.1033]	178,780
Total	\$188,987

Thus, the total cost of $197,400 can be accounted for as

Costs transferred to finished goods	$188,987
Costs in ending inventory	8,413
Total cost accounted for	$197,400

If you compare the FIFO results with the weighted-average results shown in the chapter, you will see that the unit cost for September under FIFO ($2.1033) is slightly higher than that under weighted average ($2.10). Hence, the total cost of the ending work in process under FIFO ($8,413) is slightly higher than that under weighted average ($8,400). The magnitude of the difference is a function of the illustrative data; you should not assume that the difference will always be so small.

WHY CHOOSE FIFO?

At the start of this appendix, we suggested that FIFO is intuitively appealing. This is so because the costs incurred in a given period are applicable only to the work done during that period. The method is also appealing because it supports a manager's interest in controlling costs. The per-unit cost given by the weighted-average method is not suitable for control purposes because it mixes performance of the current period with performance in prior periods.

Because the unit-cost calculation under FIFO uses (1) an equivalent production that includes only current work and (2) only the current period production costs, managers obtain performance data for different periods. From Chapter 12 we know that some companies establish *standard* costs for certain aspects of the manufacturing process, and that comparisons of actual costs with standards give managers useful information for control and performance evaluation. For a company that uses standard costs and process costing, FIFO is particularly useful because it does not intermingle actual costs from two periods.

ASSIGNMENT MATERIAL

QUESTIONS FOR DISCUSSION

15-1 "True" fixed cost Is there any meaning to the statement that there is a "true" fixed cost per unit of product? Discuss.

15-2 Kinds of standards If you were president of a manufacturing firm, which of the following income statements would you prefer to receive and why?

(a) One showing actual costs only.
(b) One showing standard costs and variances, with standard costs based on ideal standards.
(c) One showing standard costs and variances, with standard costs based on currently attainable standards.

EXERCISES

15-3 Basic process costing TUV Company uses weighted-average process costing. It makes its product from garbage and so has no material costs. The data following relate to July.

Beginning inventory	$ 3,200
Units completed in July	20,000 units
Units in ending work in process, 60% complete	4,000 units

Conversion costs incurred in July were $24,800.

Required

1. Determine equivalent production for July.
2. Determine the unit cost.
3. Determine the cost of the ending inventory of work in process.
4. Determine the cost of goods transferred to finished goods.

15-4 Job-order costing—journal entries Grimes Machine Shop had the following activity in March. Grimes uses actual job-order costing.

(a) The company used $4,960 in materials on jobs.
(b) Direct labor was $7,280.
(c) Factory overhead was $4,710.
(d) The cost of jobs finished was $12,500.
(e) The cost of jobs sold was $9,600.

Required

Prepare journal entries to record these events.

15-5 Basic process costing—weighted average The data below relate to the operations of Houston Milling Company for March. The company puts materials, labor, and overhead into process evenly throughout.

Beginning inventory, (5,000 units, 80% complete)	$ 4,400
Units completed in March	71,000 units
Ending inventory, 60% complete	15,000 units

Production costs incurred in March were $235,600. The company uses the weighted-average method.

Required

1. Compute equivalent production.
2. Compute unit cost.
3. Compute the cost of the ending inventory.
4. Compute the cost of units finished and transferred to finished goods inventory.

15-6 Basic process costing—FIFO (extension of 15-5, related to Appendix) Redo the previous assignment using the first-in-first-out method.

15-7 Journal entries—extension of 15-5 The following additional information about Houston Milling's March operations is available.

Materials purchases, on account	$ 85,000
Materials use	$ 78,000
Conversion costs:	
Direct labor	$ 52,000
Overhead	$105,600

Required
Prepare journal entries to account for Houston's March operations and show a T-account for Work in Process Inventory.

15-8 Journal entries—extension of 15-6 (Appendix) Refer to 15-6 and to the additional information in 15-7.

Required
Prepare journal entries to account for Houston's March operations and show a T-account for Work in Process Inventory.

15-9 Relationships—income, production, and volume variance Fosheim Company sells a single product at $10 per unit. There are no variable manufacturing costs, and fixed manufacturing costs are budgeted at $300,000. In 19X5 the company had a standard gross profit of $160,000, income of $58,000, and sales of 40,000 units. Selling and administrative expenses in 19X5 were $90,000, and fixed manufacturing costs were incurred as budgeted.

Required
1. Compute the standard fixed cost per unit.
2. Compute the volume variance for 19X5.
3. Determine how many units were produced in 19X5.
4. Determine what Fosheim would have shown as income in 19X5 if the company had used variable costing.

15-10 Relationships—income, sales, and volume variance In 19X3 Bishop Company sold 98,000 units of product. Variable cost per unit was $6, both standard and actual. The standard fixed manufacturing cost per unit is $8 and selling and administrative expenses were $200,000. Fixed manufacturing costs were incurred as budgeted. Income for 19X3 was $176,000 after considering an unfavorable volume variance of $16,000. There was no change in inventories over the year 19X3.

Required
1. Determine the selling price of a unit of product.
2. Determine the level of volume used to set the standard fixed cost per unit.
3. Determine the budgeted amount of fixed manufacturing costs.

15-11 Process costing—T-account Valley Manufacturing Company uses a process costing system. The following data apply to July 19X9. Percentages of completion are the same for materials and for conversion costs.

		Units
Beginning inventory, 20% complete		3,000
Finished during July		35,000
Ending inventory, 60% complete		5,000
Production costs:		
Cost in beginning inventory	$ 23,700	
Incurred during July	$766,700	

Required

1. Compute the cost per unit of the units finished during the period, using the weighted-average method.
2. Compute the amount of ending work in process inventory and transfers to finished goods.
3. Prepare a T-account for Work in Process Inventory.

15-12 Process costing (extension of 15-11, related to Appendix) Redo 15-11, using first-in-first-out.

15-13 Backflush costing Timmins Company has completed the transition to just-in-time manufacturing and is attempting to simplify its record keeping. The controller has given you the following data for January and asked what is the simplest, most direct way to record the events.

Beginning inventories	none
Units finished	100,000
Units sold	90,000
Materials purchased and used	$410,000
Direct labor and manufacturing overhead	$350,000

There was no ending inventory of materials or of work in process.

Required

Determine ending inventory and cost of goods sold.

15-14 Backflush costing, journal entries—continuation of 15-13

Required

Prepare journal entries for Timmins Company's January activity.

15-15 Process costing—two departments Berke Manufacturing Company makes a single product, a chemical called Argot. The product is made in two processes, mixing and boiling. The following data apply to May 19X7. There were no beginning inventories. Percentages of completion are the same for materials and for conversion costs.

	Mixing	Boiling
Barrels completed during May	70,000	70,000
Barrels on hand at May 31	9,000	
Percentage complete	60%	
Production costs incurred	$52,780	$42,000

Required

1. Compute the cost per barrel for each process.
2. Compute the amount of ending work in process inventory in the Mixing Department.

3. The firm had no finished product on hand at the beginning of May. Of the 70,000 gallons finished during May, 60,000 were sold. Compute cost of goods sold and ending inventory of finished goods.

15-16 Process costing Hittite Company makes a water-soluble paint. All materials are put into process and are then mixed for several hours. Data for July are

Unit Data	
Gallons completed in July	180,000
Gallons in ending inventory	30,000
Percentages complete:	
Materials	100%
Conversion costs	80%

Cost Data

	Materials	Conversion Costs
Beginning inventory	$ 3,240	$ 9,620
Incurred during July	$42,960	$127,060

Required

1. Using the weighted-average method, compute equivalent production for (a) materials and (b) conversion costs for the month of July.
2. Compute unit costs for each cost factor using the weighted-average method.
3. Prepare the journal entry to transfer the cost of finished gallons to Finished Goods Inventory.
4. Prepare a T-account for Work in Process Inventory.
5. Prove that your ending balance in Work in Process, from item 4, is correct.

PROBLEMS

15-17 Equivalent production and unit costs Borr Company manufactures a single type of fertilizer in a single process. Data for April are as follows.

Beginning inventory of work in process	5,000 pounds
Completed in April	150,000 pounds
Ending inventory of work in process	20,000 pounds
Cost of materials used in production	$366,150
Conversion costs incurred	$571,900
Costs in beginning inventory:	
Materials	$ 14,650
Conversion costs	$ 19,400

The inventories were 100% complete for materials. The beginning inventory was 75% complete for conversion costs, and the ending inventory was 60% complete. The company uses the weighted-average method.

Required

1. Determine equivalent production for materials and for conversion costs.
2. Determine unit costs for materials and for conversion costs.
3. Determine the cost of the ending inventory of work in process and the cost transferred to finished goods inventory.

15-18 Equivalent units and standard costs (related to Appendix) The production manager of Kneehi Company has just received his performance report for June 19X9. Among the data included are the following.

	Costs		
	Budget	Actual	Variance
Materials	$10,000	$11,500	$1,500U
Direct labor	20,000	21,300	1,300U
Variable overhead	15,000	15,400	400U
Fixed overhead	18,000	18,800	800U
Total	$63,000	$67,000	$4,000U

The budgeted amounts are based on 2,000 units, the number actually completed during June. The production manager is upset because 800 half-finished units are still in process at the end of June and are not counted as part of production for the month. However, at the beginning of June, 300 units were one-third complete.

Required

1. Compute equivalent unit production on a first-in-first-out basis.
2. Prepare a new performance report.

15-19 Costing methods and pricing The sales manager and the controller of Emerson Company were discussing the price to be set for a new product. They had accumulated the following data.

Variable costs	$8 per unit
Fixed costs	$80,000 per year

The sales manager had set a target volume of 10,000 units per year. He determined average fixed cost to be $8 per unit, bringing average total cost per unit to $16. The firm follows a policy of setting prices at 200% of cost, so the sales manager stated that the price should be $32 per unit.

The controller said that $32 seemed high, especially as competitors were charging only $30 for essentially the same product. The sales manager agreed, stating that perhaps only 8,000 units per year could be sold at $32. However, he was convinced that the price should be set at 200% of cost. He added that it was unfortunate that fixed costs were so high, because he felt that 10,000 units could definitely be sold if the price were $30, and probably 12,000 at $28. However, it would not be possible to achieve the desired markup at those prices.

Required

1. Point out the fallacies in the reasoning of the sales manager. (You might wish to show what would happen at the $32 price. Would the firm achieve the desired markup?)
2. Determine which price ($32, $30, $28) will give the highest profit.

15-20 ***Overhead rates, standard cost income statement*** The following data pertain to the operations of Dickson Company for 19X5.

Budgeted production		100,000 units
Actual production		90,000 units
Budgeted costs for 100,000 units:		
Materials	$ 400,000	
Direct labor	300,000	
Variable overhead	200,000	
Fixed overhead	300,000	
Actual costs:		
Materials	$ 350,000	
Direct labor	280,000	
Variable overhead	190,000	
Fixed overhead	320,000	
Administrative	400,000	
Actual sales (80,000 units)	$1,600,000	

There were no beginning inventories. Dickson uses a standard fixed cost based on budgeted production.

Required

Prepare a standard cost income statement. Show variances separately for each category of manufacturing cost.

15-21 ***Standard cost system—journal entries*** Watson Company makes a single product. Its standard cost is given below.

Materials (2 pounds at $4)	$ 8
Direct labor (3 hours at $5)	15
Variable overhead ($6 per direct labor hour)	18
Fixed overhead (based on normal capacity of 50,000 units)	10
Total standard cost	$51

At the beginning of 19X9 there were no inventories. During 19X9 the following events occurred.

(a) Materials purchases were 120,000 pounds for $455,000.
(b) Direct laborers were paid $790,000 for 151,000 hours of work.
(c) Variable overhead of $895,000 was incurred.
(d) Fixed overhead incurred was $490,000.
(e) Materials used were 95,000 pounds.
(f) Production was 48,000 units. All units started were finished.
(g) Sales were 45,000 units at $100 each.

Required

Prepare journal entries to record these events. Isolate variances as early as possible.

15-22 ***Process costing—journal entries*** Swanson Company makes a single type of pump on an assembly line. The firm uses process costing and applies manufacturing overhead at the rate of $12 per direct labor hour. Inventories at the beginning of 19X6 were as follows.

Raw materials	$ 34,000
Work in process	67,000
Finished goods	125,000

During 19X6 the following transactions took place.

1. Materials purchases were $286,000.
2. Wages earned by direct laborers for 35,000 hours were $289,000.
3. Raw materials costing $271,000 were put into process.
4. Other manufacturing costs incurred were

(a) Indirect labor	$ 46,000
(b) Supervision and other salaries	182,000
(c) Utilities and insurance	23,500
(d) Depreciation	72,000
(e) Other miscellaneous costs	112,000

5. Transfers from Work in Process to Finished Goods were $863,000.
6. Sales were $1,314,000.
7. Cost of goods sold was $818,000.
8. Selling and administrative expenses were $387,000.

Required

1. Prepare journal entries to record these events.
2. Determine the ending balance in each inventory account.
3. Prepare an income statement for 19X6.

15-23 Product costing and CVP analysis The president of Landry Company asked for your assistance in analyzing the firm's revenue and cost behavior. You gathered the following data relating to the firm's only product.

Selling price		$10
Variable costs:		
Production	$4	
Selling	2	6
Contribution margin		$ 4
Fixed production costs		$120,000 per month
Fixed selling and administrative expenses		$ 30,000 per month

You calculated the monthly break-even point as 37,500 units and the monthly sales required to earn the president's $8,000 target profit as 39,500 units.

Three months after you provided the analysis, the president called you. On your arrival at her office she gave you the following income statements.

	April	May	June
Sales	$380,000	$395,000	$420,000
Cost of goods sold	243,200	269,300	316,125
Gross profit	136,800	125,700	103,875
Selling and administrative costs	106,000	109,000	114,000
Profit (loss) before taxes	$ 30,800	$ 16,700	($ 10,125)

The president is extremely upset. She asks why your analysis does not hold, particularly because the production manager assured her that variable costs per unit and fixed costs in total were incurred as budgeted during the three months. The sales manager has also assured the president that selling prices were as expected.

After a few minutes you talk to the controller, who tells you the firm uses actual absorption costing and produced the following quantities of product during the three months: April, 50,000 units; May, 40,000 units; June, 32,000 units. There were no inventories on hand at the beginning of April.

Required

Explain the results to the president. Show calculations of the determination of cost of goods sold for each month.

15-24 ***Process costing*** Stockton Company makes a chemical spray that goes through two processes. Data for February are as follows.

	Mixing Department	Boiling Department
Gallons transferred to Boiling Department	75,000	
Gallons transferred to finished goods		68,000
Gallons on hand at end of month	9,000	15,000
Percent complete:		
Prior department costs	—	100%
Materials	100%	—[a]
Labor and overhead	60%	40%
Costs incurred during February:		
Materials	$18,480	—
Labor and overhead	$32,160	$25,900
Beginning inventories:		
Gallons	8,000	8,000
Costs:		
Materials	$ 1,680	—
Prior department costs	—	$ 6,350
Labor and overhead	$ 4,020	$ 2,220

a No material is added in this department.

Required

1. Determine the weighted-average equivalent production by cost category for each department.
2. Determine the per-unit cost by category for the Mixing Department.
3. Prepare the journal entry to record the transfer from the Mixing Department to the Boiling Department.
4. Determine the cost per unit by cost category for the Boiling Department.
5. Prepare the journal entry to record the transfer of product from the Boiling Department to Finished Goods.
6. Prepare the T-accounts for Work in Process for each department. Verify the ending inventory balances.

15-25 Process costing (related to Appendix, extension of 15-24) Assume that Stockton Company uses FIFO and that the beginning inventory in the Mixing Department was 60% complete as to materials and 70% complete as to conversion costs.

Required

1. Determine the FIFO equivalent production by cost category for the Mixing Department and the unit cost for each category.
2. Determine the total cost to be transferred to the Boiling Department.
3. Prepare a T-account for Work in Process in the Mixing Department and verify the ending inventory balance.

15-26 Standard costs—performance evaluation Topham Company is opening a new division to make and sell a single product. The product is to be made in a factory that has a practical capacity of 150,000 units per year. Production is expected to average 120,000 units after the first two years of operation. During the first two years, sales are expected to be 80,000 and 100,000, respectively, with production being 100,000 and 110,000 in those years.

The product is to sell for $20, with variable manufacturing costs of $8. Fixed production costs are expected to be $360,000 annually for the first several years. Selling and administrative costs, all fixed, are budgeted at $300,000 annually.

Dee Yost, controller of the firm, has suggested that the normal capacity of 120,000 units be used to set the standard fixed cost per unit. The other managers agree that Yost's idea is sound, and Roberto Martinez, the controller of the new division, is given the task of developing budgeted income statements based on the data given.

The operations of the first year are summarized as follows.

Sales (78,000 units)	$1,560,000
Production	115,000 units
Costs incurred:	
Variable production costs	$ 930,000
Fixed production costs	370,000
Selling and administrative costs	300,000

Required

1. Prepare a budgeted income statement based on the expected results in the first year of operations.
2. Prepare an income statement based on actual results.
3. Comment on the results. Was performance better than expected or worse? Explain.

15-27 Standard cost income statement—relationships and variances The income statement for Rider Company for 19X6 immediately follows.

Sales (200,000 units)		$2,000,000
Cost of sales:		
Materials	$300,000	
Direct labor	400,000	
Overhead	600,000	1,300,000
Standard gross profit		700,000
Manufacturing variances:		
Materials	$ 12,000U	
Direct labor	18,000F	
Variable overhead spending	4,000U	
Variable overhead efficiency	8,000F	
Fixed overhead budget	7,000F	
Other underabsorbed overhead	20,000U	3,000U
Actual gross profit		697,000
Selling and administrative expenses		600,000
Income		$ 97,000

Other data are as follows.

(a) There were no beginning inventories.

(b) Fixed overhead absorbed per unit is $2, based on budgeted production of 250,000 units, and budgeted fixed costs of $500,000.

(c) The standard direct labor rate is $4 per hour.

(d) Variable overhead standard cost is based on a rate of $2 per direct labor hour.

(e) Direct laborers worked 116,000 hours.

(f) The standard price for materials is $0.50 per pound.

(g) Materials purchases were 800,000 pounds at $3,000 over standard price.

Required

Determine the following:

1. Standard cost per unit, including standard prices and quantities for each element of cost.
2. Standard variable cost per unit.
3. Production for the year.
4. Ending inventory at standard cost.
5. Fixed overhead costs incurred.
6. Cost of materials purchased.
7. Material use variance.
8. Pounds of materials used in production.
9. Direct labor efficiency variance.
10. Direct labor rate variance.
11. Direct labor costs incurred.
12. Variable overhead costs incurred.
13. Amount by which income would have increased if one more unit had been sold, no more produced.
14. Amount by which income would have increased had one more unit been produced and sold.

15-28 Interpretation of standard cost statement The following income statement represents the operations of Chin Company for June. Variable manufacturing costs at standard are 50% of total standard manufacturing cost. Standard fixed cost per unit is based on normal activity of 30,000 units per month.

Chin Company
Income Statement for June, 19X4

Sales (20,000 units)		$200,000
Standard cost of sales		120,000
Standard gross profit		80,000
Manufacturing variances:		
Materials	$2,000U	
Direct labor	1,000F	
Overhead budget	1,000U	
		2,000U
		78,000
Volume variance		24,000U
Gross profit, actual		54,000
Selling and administrative costs		48,000
Income		$ 6,000

Required

Answer the following questions.

1. What are fixed and variable standard costs per unit?
2. What are monthly fixed manufacturing costs?
3. How many units were produced in June?
4. If beginning inventory of finished goods was $60,000 at standard cost, how much is ending inventory at standard cost? (*Hint:* Prepare an expanded cost-of-goods-sold section.)

15-29 Income statement for standard costing, practical capacity (extension of 15-28) Assume the same facts as in 15-28, except for the following.

(a) Production is 22,000 units.
(b) Total fixed production costs are $90,000.
(c) Chin bases its standard fixed cost per unit on its practical capacity of 40,000 units per month.
(d) There were no beginning inventories.

Required

Prepare a new income statement. (*Hint:* The standard fixed cost per unit will not be the same as that determined in 15-28.)

15-30 Standard costs, budgets, variances, journal entries The following data relate to the operations of Warner Company for 19X2.

Budgeted sales (100,000 units)	$1,000,000
Budgeted production	140,000 units
Budgeted costs:	
Materials (2 pounds per unit)	$ 210,000
Direct labor (1 hour per unit)	420,000
Variable overhead ($1 per direct labor hour)	140,000
Fixed overhead—manufacturing	300,000
Selling and administrative (all fixed)	180,000

The firm uses a standard cost system; the preceding production costs are based on standard cost per unit. Standard fixed cost per unit is based on

150,000 units of production at practical capacity. The inventory of finished goods at December 31, 19X1, is 13,000 units. There were no other inventories at December 31, 19X1.

Actual results for 19X2 are

Sales (95,000 units)	$950,000
Production	130,000 units
Materials purchased (250,000 pounds)	$192,500
Materials used	236,000 pounds
Direct labor (133,000 hours)	$402,000
Variable overhead	128,000
Fixed overhead	285,000
Selling and administrative expenses	175,000

Required

1. Prepare a budgeted income statement for 19X2.
2. Prepare all necessary journal entries to record events in 19X2. The production manager is responsible for all variances except material price and labor rate.
3. Prepare an income statement for 19X2.

15-31 Actual process costing, journal entries, and income statement Wilberforce Company uses actual process costing. The following data relate to its operations in July 19X7. There were no beginning inventories.

1. Materials purchases were $39,600 for 12,000 pounds ($3.30 per pound).
2. Payments to direct laborers were $28,850 for 7,300 hours of work.
3. Variable overhead costs incurred were $58,510.
4. Fixed overhead costs incurred were $86,500.
5. Materials use was 11,000 pounds.
6. Units completed totaled 7,200. At the end of July 19X7, units in process totaled 500 and were 40% complete.
7. Sales were 6,500 units at $50 per unit.
8. Selling and administrative expenses were $106,000.

Required

1. Prepare journal entries for July.
2. Prepare an income statement for July.

15-32 Standard process costing, journal entries, and income statement (extension of 15-31) The president of Wilberforce Company needs your assistance. She wants to know whether her firm could use standard costing and how it works. She believes that the following standards are appropriate.

Materials (1.5 pounds at $3.20)	$ 4.80
Direct labor (1 hour at $4)	4.00
Variable overhead at $8 per direct labor hour	8.00
Fixed overhead at $12 per direct labor hour	12.00
	$28.80

The president tells you that the $12 fixed overhead rate is based on normal capacity of 7,000 direct labor hours per month.

Required

1. Prepare journal entries for July using standard process costing.
2. Prepare an income statement for July using standard process costing.

15-33 Special order Western Corn Oil Company has found that its sales forecast for 19X6 was too high by about 40,000 cases of oil. Because the production budget was not revised, inventory is expected to be about 40,000 cases above normal at year end. In early December the sales manager was offered the opportunity to sell 25,000 cases at $4.80, well below the normal price of $8. Regular sales would not be affected by the order. He asked the controller for an analysis of the order and was given the partial income statement shown below. The controller said that because general and administrative expenses would not be affected, it was only necessary to determine the effect on gross profit.

Expected Income Statements

	Without Order	With Order
Sales	$2,400,000	$2,520,000
Standard costs of sales, $6 per case	1,800,000	1,950,000
Standard gross profit	600,000	570,000
Volume variance	(120,000)	(120,000)
Actual gross profit	$ 480,000	$ 450,000

The sales manager was puzzled and asked the controller about the volume variance. The controller replied that the volume variance related to production, not sales, and that production would not be increased because inventory was already too high. She said that the volume variance resulted because the firm used 400,000 cases on which to base the standard fixed cost, and actual production was expected to be only 340,000 cases.

Required

1. Determine whether the order should be accepted.
2. Prepare new partial income statements, using variable costing.
3. Prepare a new partial income statement assuming that production would be increased by 25,000 cases if the order were accepted.

15-34 Job-order costing—standards and variances Carlson Company makes a variety of furniture. The company has established the following standard variable costs for some of its high-volume models.

	Chair Model 803	Sofa Model 407
Materials:		
Wood	$ 24	$ 58
Fabric	46	92
Other	13	21
Total materials	83	171
Direct labor at $5 standard rate per hour	65	90
Variable overhead at $8 per direct labor hour	104	144
Total standard variable cost	$252	$405

During June the firm worked on two jobs. Order 82 was for 80 units of Model 803, and order 83 was for 50 units of Model 407. Both jobs were finished and sold for a total of $97,000.

Cost data are as follows.

Materials used, at standard prices:	
Wood	$ 4,855
Fabric	8,360
Other	2,090
Direct labor (2,050 hours × $5 per hour)	10,250
Variable overhead incurred	16,850

Fixed production costs were incurred as budgeted, $24,600. Selling and administrative expenses were $18,700. There were no material price variances.

Required

1. Determine the standard cost of each job order, by individual cost category.
2. Determine the following variances: material use, by type of material; direct labor efficiency; variable overhead spending; variable overhead efficiency.
3. Prepare an income statement for June using standard variable costing. Show the variances calculated in item 2 as a lump sum.

15-35 Comprehensive problem in costing methods The following data relate to Gagner Company operations for 19X5.

	Budgeted	Actual
Production (units)	200,000	180,000
Sales (units)	190,000	160,000
Direct materials	$400,000	$375,000
Direct labor	$600,000	$580,000
Variable overhead	$400,000	$395,000
Fixed overhead	$200,000	$208,000
Selling and administrative expenses	$700,000	$700,000

There were no beginning inventories; sales prices averaged $15 per unit; practical capacity is 250,000 units.

Required

1. Prepare income statements based on the following costing methods:
   (a) actual absorption costing.
   (b) standard absorption costing—fixed overhead based on budgeted production (show the total variance for each element of cost).
   (c) standard absorption costing using practical capacity as the fixed overhead allocation base.
   (d) standard variable costing.
   (e) actual variable costing.
2. Compare and contrast the results obtained in item 1.

15-36 Comprehensive problem in costing methods (extension of 15-35) Gagner Company now has data regarding operations for 19X6, during which selling prices again averaged $15 per unit. The following data relate to 19X6 activity.

	Budgeted	Actual
Production (units)	150,000	190,000
Sales (units)	140,000	200,000
Direct materials	$300,000	$400,000
Direct labor	$450,000	$590,000
Variable manufacturing overhead	$300,000	$410,000
Fixed manufacturing overhead	$200,000	$215,000
Selling and administrative expenses	$700,000	$720,000

Required

Prepare income statements for 19X6, using each of the methods listed in the previous assignment.

15-37 ***Standard costs and product profitability*** Tucumcary Office Products Company makes three sizes of file folders. The company has practical capacity of 50,000 machine hours per year and uses that figure to set standard fixed costs for each size of folder. At the beginning of 19X6 the controller had prepared the following data regarding the three sizes of folders (all data per carton of 50 folders).

	Two-Inch	Three-Inch	Four-Inch
Selling price	$17.00	$24.00	$31.00
Standard variable costs	8.00	11.00	16.00
Standard fixed costs	4.80	6.40	9.60
Total standard costs	12.80	17.40	25.60
Standard gross profit	$ 4.20	$ 6.60	$ 5.40
Expected sales in cartons	44,000	25,000	30,000
Machine hours required per carton	0.3	0.4	0.6

The sales manager has informed the controller that he has been approached by a large office supplies chain. The chain wants to buy 24,000 cartons of a six-inch folder and is willing to pay $40 per carton. The sales manager had discussed the offer with the production manager who stated that the folders could be made using the existing equipment. Variable costs per carton should be $19, and 0.8 machine hours should be required per carton.

Because the chain will take not fewer than 24,000 cartons, the sales manager was fairly sure that the firm did not have the capacity to fill the special order and still manufacture its other products in the volumes required by the expected sales. He therefore asked the controller to develop data on the proposed order and to decide which of the existing products should be partially curtailed. The controller then prepared the following analysis, which is incomplete because he was called away before finishing it. The sales manager was not sure how to proceed from this point and asked you to help him make the decision.

	Six-Inch Folder
Selling price	$40.00
Standard variable cost	19.00
Standard fixed cost	12.80
Total standard cost	31.80
Standard gross profit	$ 8.20

The controller also prepared the following analysis of budgeted profit for the year.

	Two-Inch	Three-Inch	Four-Inch	Total
Standard gross profit per carton	$ 4.20	$ 6.60	$ 5.40	
Expected volume	44,000	25,000	30,000	
Total expected gross profit—standard	$184,800	$165,000	$162,000	$511,800
Expected volume variance				140,800
Expected actual gross profit				371,000
Budgeted selling and administrative expenses, all fixed				327,000
Budgeted profit before taxes				$ 44,000

The firm generally manufactures about as many cartons of each size of folder as it sells. Because it rarely experiences differences between standard and actual machine hours for given levels of production, it computes its volume variance based on the difference between 50,000 hours and actual hours worked.

Required

Prepare an analysis for the sales manager showing him whether the special order should be accepted and for which products, if any, production and sales should be reduced.

15-38 ***Review problem*** Sally Ann Frocks is a manufacturer of dresses. Its relevant range is 1,500 to 5,000 dresses per month. For the month of May 19X5, it has prepared the following forecast.

Sales, 2,500 dresses @ $30 each
Variable manufacturing costs per dress:
  Materials, 3 yards @ $2 per yard
  Direct labor, 2 hours @ $0.50 per hour
  Variable overhead, $1 per DLH
Fixed manufacturing overhead, $3,000
Variable selling costs, commissions at 10% of sales
Fixed selling and administrative costs, $6,000
Inventories:
  May 1, 19X5 none
  May 31, 19X5 materials 500 yards, finished dresses 500

Normal capacity is 3,000 dresses per month, which is the basis for overhead application.

Required

Answer the following questions.

1. What is practical capacity?
2. What is budgeted production for May?
3. How many yards of materials should be purchased during May?
4. How many hours does it take to produce a dress?
5. What are total variable manufacturing costs per dress?
6. What are total manufacturing costs per dress?
7. What is contribution margin per dress?
8. What is the cost per dress if variable costing is used?
9. What is the cost per dress if actual absorption costing is used?

10. What is the cost to produce one additional dress?
11. What is the cost to produce and sell an additional dress?
12. What is the predetermined fixed overhead rate per direct labor hour?
13. What are total budgeted manufacturing costs for May?
14. Give a formula for total manufacturing costs in the range of 1,500 to 5,000 dresses per month.
15. What would the predetermined fixed overhead rate be per direct labor hour if practical capacity were used as the base?
16. What is budgeted income for May?
17. What is the break-even point, in dresses?
18. By how much could budgeted sales fall before a loss was incurred?
19. By how much would income increase for each unit sold above budgeted volume?

15-39 Process costing, second department (related to Appendix, extension of 15-25) The beginning inventory in the Boiling Department of Stockton Company was 50% complete as to conversion costs.

Required

Using the data from 15-24 and 15-25 and the above information, do the following.

1. Determine the FIFO equivalent production for conversion costs in the Boiling Department and the per-unit conversion cost.
2. Determine the total cost to be transferred from the Boiling Department to Finished Goods.
3. Prepare a T-account for Work in Process in the Boiling Department and verify the ending inventory balance.

15-40 Review of Chapters 12, 13, 14, and 15 ARC Industries makes fiberglass insulation, selling it for $20 per roll. The standard variable cost per roll is as follows.

Materials (25 pounds at $0.20 per pound)	$5
Direct labor (0.20 hour at $10 per hour)	2
Variable overhead at $5 per direct labor hour	1
Total standard variable cost per roll	$8

Budgeted fixed production costs are $1,500,000 per year.

ARC began 19X3 with no inventories. Actual results for 19X3 follow.

Sales (230,000 rolls)	$4,600,000
Production	260,000 rolls
Production costs:	
Materials purchased (7,000,000 pounds)	$1,425,000
Materials used	6,450,000 pounds
Direct labor (53,000 hours)	$ 520,000
Variable manufacturing overhead	$ 270,000
Fixed production overhead	$1,480,000
Selling and administrative costs, all fixed	$ 800,000

The firm uses actual absorption costing for most purposes, though it has established standard variable production costs. The treasurer wants to see how standard costing works for income determination and asks you to prepare income statements using the two approaches. One statement is to be a standard variable costing statement, the other a standard absorption costing statement, with 250,000 rolls used to set the standard fixed cost.

Required

1. Determine all variances from standard costs, including the fixed overhead budget and volume variances.
2. Prepare the income statements that the treasurer requested. On each, show the variances as a lump sum subtracted from the standard gross margin or contribution margin.

15-41 Review of Chapters 12, 13, 14, and 15 (extension of 15-40) During 19X4 ARC Industries produced 240,000 rolls and sold 250,000. The same standards and budgets in effect in 19X3 applied to 19X4, and the selling price remained at $20 per roll. Actual costs follow.

Materials purchased (6,200,000 pounds)	$1,210,000
Materials used	5,900,000 pounds
Direct labor (47,000 hours)	$ 475,000
Variable overhead	$ 240,000
Fixed production overhead	$1,510,000
Selling and administrative costs	$ 810,000

Required

Prepare income statements using the same bases as for 15-40. Again, calculate all variances and show the appropriate total as a lump sum on each statement.

quantitative methods and managerial accounting

Appendix A

We have stressed throughout this book that making decisions requires considering both quantitative and qualitative factors. Increases in the mathematical sophistication of managers and the availability of computers have resulted in refinements in the uses of quantifiable data in decision making. These refinements have usually been applied to complex situations, but the principles of the techniques are equally applicable in less complex cases.

Many managers do not fully understand all of the mathematics that underlie some of these quantitative techniques. Nevertheless, any manager, and most certainly a managerial accountant, should be familiar with these techniques, their uses, and their limitations. First, managers must be able to describe the problems and to specify the relevant information to the specialist who sets up and solves them. Second, managers must be able to comprehend what the specialist is saying and grasp the basics of the proposed solution. Third, managers must understand the limitations of a given technique, so that they can evaluate the applicability of a proposed technique to the problem at hand and suggest changes if the proposed solution appears to be ineffective.

QUANTITATIVE METHODS—AN OVERVIEW

The term *quantitative methods* describes sophisticated mathematical techniques for solving managerial problems. Other terms are *operations research, model building,* and *quantitative analysis.* You have used quantitative methods throughout this book. CVP analysis uses simple algebra; budgeting uses mathematically stated relationships among variables (collections on receivables are 40% of the current month's sales, 60% of the preceding month's sales); and capital budgeting uses present values.

Almost all of the quantitative techniques in this book require managers to state their expectations about the future. They predict prices, costs, demand, and so on. Often, the quantifiable factors are stated in equations [income = (sales price × units sold) − (variable costs × units sold) − fixed costs]. Operations research techniques and models work the same way. We determine which quantifiable factors are relevant to a decision, express relationships among those factors in equations, and solve the equations to obtain the answers. One major difference between operations research models and the techniques you have been using is the level of complexity. In one respect all quantitative methods are the same: a solution is only as good as the predictions about future conditions. If these predictions do not turn out to be true, the result will probably not be as expected.

STATISTICAL DECISION THEORY

We applied the **expected value** concept to sales forecasting in Chapter 6 when managers believed that several outcomes were possible and assigned probabilities to each of these outcomes. The concept is applicable to many other situations.

Suppose your company is considering alternative methods of acquiring computer time. There are three feasible choices.

(a) You can lease a computer for a flat rate of $5,500 per month, using as much time as you need.

(b) You can lease a computer for $2,000 per month plus $40 per hour of use.

(c) You can rent computer time from a service bureau for $80 per hour.

You have assessed the likelihood of your needs as follows.

(1) Event (Estimated Hours of Computer Time Needed per Month)	×	(2) Estimated Probability of Occurrence	=	(1) × (2) Expected Value
60		.25		15
100		.45		45
150		.30		45
		1.00		105

The expected value of required time is 105 hours. You can now compare the costs related to the three choices at 105 hours as follows.

Alternative	Cost
(a) Lease for $5,500 per month	$5,500
(b) Lease for $2,000 plus $40 per hour $2,000 + (105 hours × $40 per hour)	$6,200
(c) Buy time from the service bureau at $80 per hour (105 hours × $80 per hour)	$8,400

Renting the computer for $5,500 per month is the least-cost choice.

The costs of choices can also be directly associated with the probabilities of occurrence. You compute the **conditional values**, which are the monetary results of the events—computer costs at each level of use in this example—then multiply these values by the probabilities. You could compute the expected value of the cost for choice (b) as follows.

(1) Hours Required	(2) Probability	×	(3) Conditional Value [a]	=	(2) × (3) Expected Value
60	.25		$4,400		$1,100
100	.45		6,000		2,700
150	.30		8,000		2,400
	1.00				$6,200

a For example, $4,400 = $2,000 + ($40 × 60 hours).

The expected cost for choice (c) is computed as below.

Hours Required	Probability	×	Conditional Value	=	Expected Value
60	.25		$ 4,800		$1,200
100	.45		8,000		3,600
150	.30		12,000		3,600
	1.00				$8,400

Choice (a) has the same cost no matter what the required hours; so, the cost is 100% certain to be $5,500.

VARIANCE INVESTIGATION

Chapter 12 stated that a variance should be investigated when the expected savings from investigation exceed the cost of the investigation. The expected value framework is often helpful here as well.

Suppose a $300 variance has occurred and is expected to continue for six months if not corrected. An investigation to find its cause will cost nothing. The chances are about 80% that even after identifying the cause, the variance cannot be corrected. The expected values of the costs of investigating and of not investigating are summarized below.

Choice 1—Do Not Investigate	
Expected cost of $300 for six months	$1,800

Choice 2—Investigate

Event	Probability of Outcome	×	Conditional Value	=	Expected Value
Cause is correctable	.20		0		0
Cause is not correctable	.80		$1,800		$1,440
Total	1.00				$1,440

It is worthwhile to investigate the variance; it costs nothing to investigate, and there are potential savings of $1,800. The $360 ($1,800 – $1,440) difference between expected values has special significance. It is the maximum amount you would be willing to spend to investigate whether the variance can be corrected. This amount is called the **value of perfect information,** which is the difference between (1) the expected value of the best alternative, given the existing information, and (2) the expected value of alternatives when you know in advance what event will occur.

To confirm that $360 is the maximum you would pay to investigate the variance, suppose that it will cost $360 to investigate. What are the expected values (costs) of the two choices?

Choice 1—Do Not Investigate	
Cost of $300 for six months	$1,800

Choice 2—Investigate

Event	Probability of Outcome	×	Conditional Value	=	Expected Value
Cause is correctable	.20		$ 360 [a]		$ 72
Cause is not correctable	.80		2,160 [b]		1,728
Total	1.00				$1,800

a The cost to investigate will be incurred.
b The cost to investigate plus the cost of the continued variance will be incurred.

Thus, the expected cost of both choices is the same.

Let us modify the circumstances. The cost to investigate the variance is $200 and there is a 30% probability that the variance was caused by a random disturbance and will not continue beyond the first period. The usual expected value approach can be used under these circumstances also. The analysis follows.

Choice 1—Do Not Investigate

Event	Probability of Outcome	×	Conditional Value	=	Expected Value
Variance is random, will stop without action	.30		0		0
Variance will continue	.70		$1,800		$1,260
Total	1.00				$1,260

Choice 2—Investigate

Event	Probability of Outcome	×	Conditional Value	=	Expected Value
Variance is random, will stop without action	.30		$ 200		$ 60
A problem exists that can be corrected	.14 [a]		200		28
A problem exists that cannot be corrected	.56 [b]		2,000		1,120
Total	1.00				$1,208

a The 20% chance of being able to take corrective action now applies to only 70% of the cases. The probability thus becomes 70% × 20%, or 14%. (Remember the total probabilities must be 1.0.)
b Same reasoning as in above note except that the probability of there being an uncorrectable problem is 70% × 80%, or 56%.

Under the new conditions, the expected cost of investigating ($1,208) is still less than the expected cost of not investigating ($1,260). But the difference between the two choices is less ($52 as opposed to $360). This makes sense because not only is there a cost to investigate, but now there is a 30% chance that you do not have to do anything and the variance will stop.

Another approach to solving the problem is the **decision tree**, a commonly used device that offers a graphical representation of the problem. The decision tree for this decision, shown in Exhibit A-1, works essentially the same as the tabular format but has the advantage of allowing a step-by-step determination of probabilities when there are several possible events within other events (such as the 80%-20% probabilities within the 70% probability). Both approaches show that the expected cost of investigating is less than the expected cost of *not* investigating.

CAPITAL BUDGETING APPLICATION

Many investment opportunities could bring either high rewards (high net present values) or large losses (high negative net present values). Such opportunities are risky because they involve potential loss, but they can also be rewarding. (Chapter 2 discussed cost structure and risk; the substitution of fixed costs for variable costs could be either beneficial or disastrous, depending on future levels of sales.) Consider a manufacturer trying to decide whether to market a new toy.

Assume the following possibilities for net present value (NPV) in two circumstances: the toy sells well; the toy is a flop.

Exhibit A-1 Decision Tree

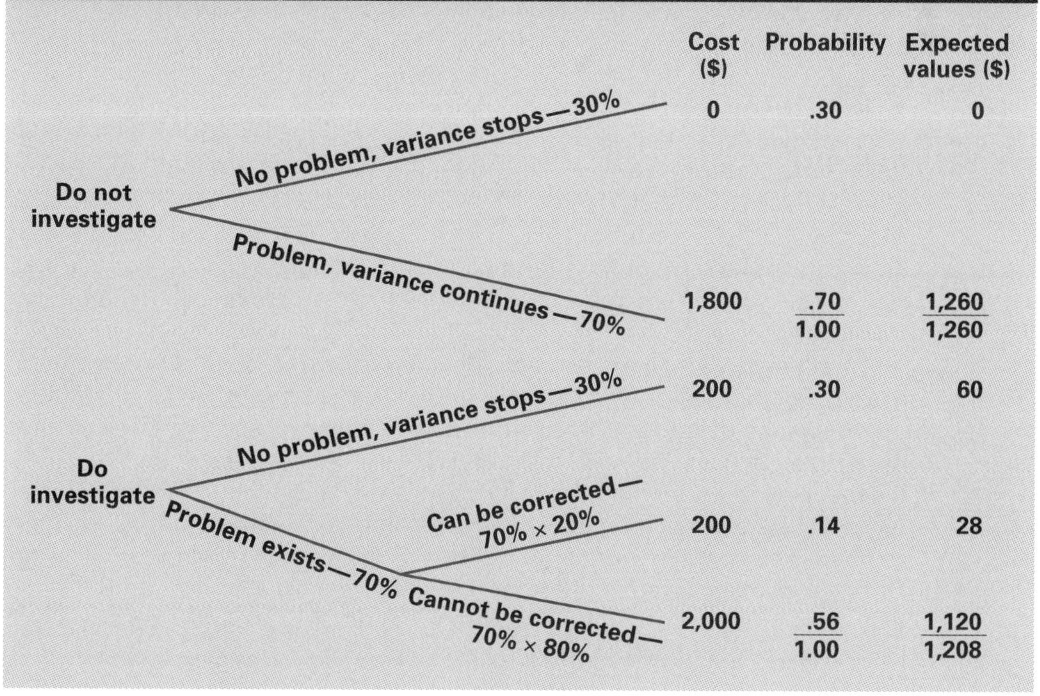

	Sells Well	Flops
NPV	$15,000,000	–$3,000,000

Suppose the marketing group believes there is a 60% chance of the toy's being a big seller and a 40% chance of its being a flop. What is the expected value?

	NPV	×	Probability of Occurrence	=	Expected Value
Sells well	$15,000,000		.60		$9,000,000
Flops	–3,000,000		.40		–1,200,000
Total			1.00		$7,800,000

The positive expected value of $7,800,000 strongly suggests that the investment is wise. However, it is important to managers that there is a 40% probability of a high negative NPV.

Relying solely on expected values is not always wise. Consider a simpler example. Suppose you were given the following choices: (1) take $10,000 now or (2) flip a coin, heads you get $40,000, tails you lose $20,000. Compute the expected values (assuming an honest coin, of course).

Choice 1—A certain gain of $10,000.
Choice 2—An expected value of $10,000, as indicated below.

Event	Probability	×	Conditional Value	=	Expected Value
Heads	.50		$40,000		$20,000
Tails	.50		–20,000		–10,000
	1.00				$10,000

The two choices appear equally valuable, since both have an expected value of $10,000. But unless you have a great deal of money, you probably would not select choice 2. The difficulty with relying solely on the expected value is that the concept is based on probabilities, and probability theory is based on mathematical laws that assume large numbers of occurrences. If you had 1,000 chances to play the coin flip game just described, it would not matter much whether you took the $10,000 or tossed the coin. You could expect to win about 500 times and to lose about 500 times. *But with only one try,* you do not have the laws of large numbers on your side. You therefore, have a 50% probability of losing $20,000, an event most people would shy away from.

Operations researchers incorporate such considerations into the simple expected value model by attaching *utilities* to the various outcomes. Utility represents the degree of "better-offness" or "worse-offness" associated with the events. By using utilities, operations researchers recognize that generally it detracts more from your well-offness to lose $20,000 than is added by winning $40,000. But assigning utilities to outcomes is a matter of judgment, and assigned values differ markedly depending on who is doing the choosing. Different managers make different decisions, even if they all use the same data. Some are more willing than others to accept risks. We consider this point in more detail in the following section.

PAYOFF TABLES

Managers use the expected value concept most often when they must make the same decision several times and have several available strategies with probabilities attached to the possible outcomes of each. A typical application is deciding how many units of a product to buy (or make) when there are given probabilities for sales and the unsold units are discarded or sold at substantial losses.

Suppose a florist must decide how many corsages to buy each week. All units must be bought in advance and no additional purchases are possible once the week has begun. Unsold corsages are discarded. The florist has estimated the demand as given below. (For computational simplicity we assume only three possible outcomes. Computers make it possible to analyze more realistic situations quickly.)

Demand in Units	Probability of Demand
4,000	20%
8,000	50%
12,000	30%

The variable cost per corsage is $6, and the selling price is $10.

Because the corsages are purchased in advance and discarded if unsold, the florist loses $6 on each unsold corsage. This is the trouble with a perishable good: buying (or making) more than can be sold brings a penalty of the variable cost of the unsold units (less any salvage value). *Perishability* is an economic concept, not a physical one. Corsages deteriorate rapidly; newspapers do not. But day-old newspapers do not sell any better than wilted flowers. High-fashion goods are another example of a perishable good in the economic sense.[1]

The approach to analyzing the purchasing decision for perishable goods is to prepare **payoff tables.** For each purchasing strategy, prepare a table of *conditional values* for each possible level of demand, without regard to the probabilities of each event. Then prepare a second table that shows the expected values (that is, considering the probabilities) of each strategy. (We could combine the tables, but that makes it much harder to follow the logic.) Exhibit A-2 shows the conditional values.

Each entry in the table is the contribution margin, or loss, from that particular combination of demand and purchases. Thus, if the firm *bought* 4,000 units, it would sell 4,000 units no matter what the demand because it could not buy any more even if it learned that buyers would demand 8,000 or

Exhibit A-2 Conditional Values of Strategies

	Strategy: Purchases of		
Event: Demand	4,000	8,000	12,000
4,000	$16,000	($ 8,000)	($32,000)
8,000	16,000	32,000	8,000
12,000	16,000	32,000	48,000

1 *Almost all goods are perishable to some extent, because a company can rarely guarantee that it can sell all that it makes or buys. The question is one of degree, and a florist is surely more vulnerable than a car dealer.*

12,000 units. Hence, if purchases are 4,000 units, the firm will earn $16,000 contribution margin by selling 4,000 units ($4 per unit × 4,000 units) and will lose nothing by having to discard units bought but not sold.

If the firm buys 8,000 units and can only sell 4,000, costs will be $48,000 (8,000 × $6) and revenues only $40,000 (4,000 × $10), for a loss of $8,000. Put another way, the firm earns $16,000 contribution margin on the 4,000 units sold but loses $6 per unit for the 4,000 unsold units discarded. If the firm did sell 8,000 units, it would earn revenues of $80,000, have costs of $48,000, and a contribution margin of $32,000 ($4 × 8,000). The same contribution margin would be earned if the firm could have sold 12,000 units but only sold 8,000, because only 8,000 were purchased.

The next step is to compute the expected value of each possible outcome, using the probabilities of demand. Exhibit A-3 summarizes the expected values.

Notice that the expected value of the strategy of purchasing 4,000 units ($16,000) is equal to the conditional value of each outcome: demand of 4,000, 8,000, and 12,000. This should not be surprising, because the firm can sell only 4,000 units if it buys only that many. The problem with that strategy is that the firm foregoes contribution margin if it could have sold more than 4,000 units.

Notice also that the outcomes, both conditional and expected values, of buying 12,000 units are more widely dispersed than the others. We would expect this because the more you buy and sell, the higher the profit, but the more you buy and do not sell, the lower the profit or higher the loss. Buying 12,000 is the riskiest strategy.

Using the expected value criterion, the florist would buy 8,000 units, the strategy with the highest expected value ($24,000). But remember that we are dealing with expectations; the actual values might be different from the ones expected. Most managers recognize how important the estimated probabilities are to the results and will perform "what if" analysis (the sensitivity analysis discussed in earlier chapters). For example, the manager might compute what happens if the probability of selling 12,000 units increases to 40%, with an offsetting decrease in the probability of selling 8,000 units, or might try several plausible combinations of probabilities. Using a microcomputer and one of the many available software packages, the manager could obtain information about many such combinations in just a few minutes.

Exhibit A-3 Expected Values of Strategies

		Strategy: Purchases of					
		4,000		8,000		12,000	
Demand	Probability	CV [a]	EV [b]	CV [a]	EV [b]	CV [a]	EV [b]
4,000	.20	$16,000	$ 3,200	($ 8,000)	($ 1,600)	($32,000)	($ 6,400)
8,000	.50	16,000	8,000	32,000	16,000	8,000	4,000
12,000	.30	16,000	4,800	32,000	9,600	48,000	14,400
Expected values			$16,000		$24,000		$12,000

a Conditional values from Exhibit A-2.
b Conditional value multiplied by probability.

Again, we stress the point that no quantitative method, from CVP analysis through expected value calculations, *tells* you what to do. It tells you only what will happen *if*—and "if" is a big word—all your predictions are correct. Accordingly, firms that continually make decisions about producing or purchasing perishable goods do this type of analysis often.

The value of perfect information can also be computed from payoff tables. In this application, it equals the difference between the contribution margin that would be earned if the firm knew how many units would be demanded and therefore purchased exactly that many, and the expected value of the strategy it would follow using only probabilities.

If the firm knew in advance how many corsages would be demanded, it would buy exactly that many and would have the following expected value of contribution margin, selling 4,000 units in 20% of the weeks, 8,000 units in 50% of the weeks, and 12,000 units in 30% of the weeks.

Sales	Contribution Margin, Conditional Value (Exhibit A-2)	Probability	Expected Value
4,000	$16,000	.20	$ 3,200
8,000	32,000	.50	16,000
12,000	48,000	.30	14,400
Expected value			$33,600

In this case, then, the value of perfect information is $9,600 ($33,600 – $24,000, the expected value of the strategy of buying 8,000 units each week). We can confirm the $9,600 value of knowing the level of demand by showing the expected sales for a ten-week period, following the strategy of buying 8,000 units each week and following the optimal strategy when the florist knows in advance what the week's demand will be.

During the ten-week period, the firm should sell 4,000 corsages twice (20% × 10 weeks); 8,000 corsages five times; and 12,000 corsages three times. Following the strategy of buying 8,000 each week, it would have losses of $8,000 twice and gains of $32,000 eight times. (As shown in Exhibit A-2, the company loses $8,000 when demand is 4,000 units and gains $32,000 when demand is 8,000.) Total contribution margin for the ten-week period is $240,000 [($32,000 × 8) – ($8,000 × 2)]. With perfect information, the florist buys and sells 4,000 corsages twice, 8,000 corsages five times, and 12,000 corsages three times. The contribution margin for the period is

Sales (in units)	Number of Weeks	×	Contribution Margin per Week	=	Total
4,000	2		$16,000		$ 32,000
8,000	5		32,000		160,000
12,000	3		48,000		144,000
Total					$336,000

The difference between the expected contribution margin with perfect information ($336,000) and using the optimal strategy without such information ($240,000) is $96,000, which is ten times—for ten weeks—the $9,600 calculated earlier as the value of perfect information.

In the real world it is impossible to obtain *perfect* information, but the concept is still valuable. *Some* additional information is almost always obtainable at a cost; test-marketing new products is an example of an effort to obtain more information. The questions are whether the information gained would result in a change in strategy, whether decisions would be better if the information were available, and whether the cost of obtaining the information is less than the benefits.

DEVELOPING PROBABILITIES

The probabilities used to compute expected values can be intuitive and judgmental, or they can be developed using more objective, sophisticated statistical techniques.

At one extreme, probabilities might be "best estimates" of experienced managers. There might be some historical basis for the estimates, as when managers develop rules through experience and believe that the current situation is similar to previous situations. For example, if a machine is not operating at peak efficiency, the manager might rely on several years of experience with similar machines to estimate a probability of about 60% that an internal part is wearing out, and 40% that some random factor is at work that will not continue.

In some cases, managers' estimates of probabilities are based on the presence or absence of external factors. Businesses that depend greatly on the weather provide good examples. A company that sells hot dogs and soft drinks at baseball parks might develop its sales probabilities based on weather forecasts. The hotter the day is expected to be, the more soft drinks the firm can expect to sell. Of course, the validity of the manager's estimates depends on the accuracy of the weather forecasts.

Managers often try to narrow the range of estimates by getting additional information and using statistical techniques to evaluate the information. Market research is one commonly used way to obtain additional information. A firm might be considering a new product that will require a nationwide advertising and promotional campaign. Because such campaigns are very costly, the company might test-market the product using a regional campaign. After the small-scale campaign is underway, the managers can analyze the results and gain a better perspective on probable nationwide sales. You might study some of these techniques in your courses in marketing and statistics.

Because probabilities are estimates, some managers react negatively to quantitative techniques that use them. Such managers argue that "sound business judgment" is better than quantitative analysis because the former does not require a lot of assumptions. But when a manager makes a decision, with or without the help of quantitative analysis, the decision *implies* some beliefs about the future. Consider a decision to set a production level without first estimating demand for the product. Such a decision implies *some* expectation about demand. Any manager who selects a particular course of action—say, ordering 4,000 corsages—is making assumptions about the future, whether or not those assumptions are specifically stated.

INVENTORY CONTROL MODELS

Chapters 6 and 7 showed that inventory policy is important and that a conflict exists between having too much inventory and having too little.

Merchandising companies must stock inventory to attract customers; manufacturers that do not use just-in-time methods must stock materials and components to avoid shutting down production. (We exclude JIT operations because, as you will recall, part of the JIT philosophy is the virtual elimination of all inventories.) Significant costs are incurred in carrying inventory, such as the opportunity cost of the money invested in it. Accordingly, managers try to minimize the investment in inventory, while at the same time keeping customers satisfied and production lines running smoothly. Inventory control models have been the subject of considerable research, and entire journals are devoted to them.

INVENTORY COSTS

Three kinds of costs are associated with inventory: (1) the costs of ordering and receiving inventory, called **ordering costs**, or **setup costs** for a manufacturer; (2) the costs of having inventory on hand, called **carrying costs;** and (3) the costs of *not* having enough inventory, called **stockout costs.** Examples of costs in each of these categories appear in Exhibit A-4.

Exhibit A-4 Inventory Costs

Costs of Ordering (including Receiving)

1. Processing orders
2. Form(s) used
3. Time spent (opportunity cost)
4. Order follow-up time
5. Unloading and inspection
6. Setting up machinery

Costs of Carrying Inventory

1. Cost of capital on investment
2. Space used
3. Wages of storage personnel
4. Personal property taxes
5. Fire and theft insurance
6. Record keeping
7. Risks of obsolescence and deterioration

Costs of Not Having Enough Inventory

1. Lost contribution margin from sales
   (a) Current sales are lost because customers could not get what they wanted.
   (b) Later sales might be lost because dissatisfied customers do not return and other customers do not come because of word-of-mouth notification that the selection is inadequate.
2. Bottlenecks in production because of lack of materials or components.

We want to minimize total inventory costs. A major difficulty is that the three types of costs are not independent. The more you order at one time, the lower the ordering costs. But the more you order, the higher your average inventory, so carrying costs increase. On the other hand, the higher your inventory, the less likely you are to lose sales (incur stockout costs).

Only incremental costs are relevant in determining the desired level of inventory. Hence, in any particular situation some of the costs listed in Exhibit A-4 might not be relevant. For example, a firm with large amounts of space for which there are no alternative uses has no incremental storage cost. If insurance premiums are based on the quantity of goods carried, they are relevant; if the premium is a flat amount no matter how much inventory is carried (unlikely, but possible), it is irrelevant.

Determining stockout costs can be especially difficult. These costs are opportunity costs and do not appear in accounting records. For this reason, they might be ignored or their significance downplayed, even though they are as real as, and might be far greater than costs that are recorded. When goods have a relatively high contribution margin, the cost of stockouts could greatly exceed the total costs of carrying inventory sufficient to ensure against stockouts.

Managers minimize costs in two stages: (1) they determine *when* to order, that is, how low to allow inventory to fall before ordering a new supply, and (2) they determine *how much* to order at a time. Ordering only as much as you need and at the right time minimizes costs.

WHEN TO ORDER—THE REORDER POINT

How low should inventory fall before more is ordered? The answer to this question is the **reorder point** and can be expressed in either units or dollars. In determining the reorder point, the goal is to minimize the total of stockout and carrying costs.

The reorder point depends on lead time, safety stock, and the expected daily use of inventory. **Lead time** is the number of working days between placing and receiving an order. **Safety stock** is the quantity of inventory that serves as a cushion in case an order comes in late or use is greater than expected during the lead time. The reorder point is computed as follows.

$$\textit{Reorder point} = \textit{safety stock} + (\textit{daily use} \times \textit{lead time})$$

Suppose that the lead time is ten days, daily use is 20 units, and no safety stock is considered necessary. The reorder point is 200 units (20 units × 10 days). *If* your predictions are accurate, you will not run out of inventory. As you use the last unit, the new units will have just come in. If the manager believes that a safety stock of 100 units is desirable, the reorder point is 300 units (200 + 100). Then, if the order arrives late or there is an unexpected need for more than 20 units on one or more days, there will be enough stock to last until the order is received. The behavior of inventory for this situation is depicted in Exhibit A-5. It is assumed in that graph that 800 units are ordered at a time.

Expected daily use is annual use divided by the number of working days a year. Suppose that records reveal the annual use to be $60,000, that there

Exhibit A-5 Behavior of Inventory Level

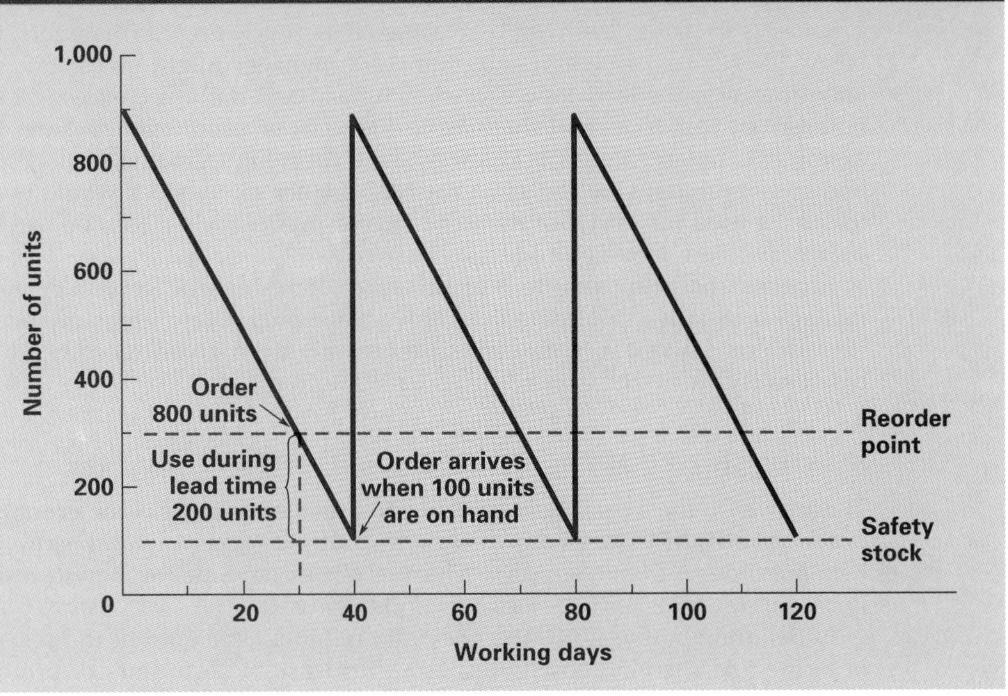

are 200 working days in the year, that lead time is 15 days, and that a safety stock of \$5,000 is desired. The reorder point in dollars is \$9,500, computed as below.

$$\textit{Reorder point} = \$5{,}000 + (\$300 \times 15) = \$9{,}500$$

DETERMINING SAFETY STOCK

One of the most critical aspects of inventory management is determining the level of safety stock. Stockout costs are most closely related to the amount of safety stock carried. Companies carry safety stock because of the uncertainties associated with the two factors that affect inventory use during the time between placing and receiving an order, namely, lead time and daily use. If both these factors are known, there is no reason to carry safety stock. (If lead time can then be driven down to a few hours, or minutes, rather than days, the company can carry only trivial amounts of inventory. This is the result that JIT operations strive to achieve.)

Suppose normal lead time is ten days but can be as long as 15 days. Suppose also average daily use is \$300 but can be as high as \$420. Using the averages, the reorder point before considering safety stock is \$3,000 (10 days × \$300). Using the extreme possibilities the reorder point is \$6,300 (15 days × \$420) and safety stock becomes, in effect, \$3,300 (\$6,300 – \$3,000). If we reorder when inventory is \$6,300, we are virtually certain never to run out. But the cost of carrying so much inventory might be prohibitive. Moreover, while we might expect occasionally to experience 15-day lead time or daily use of $420, seldom would we encounter both at the same time. So, a compromise is in order. We would select a safety stock greater than zero but below $3,300. To arrive at a compromise, a manager might investigate not only how *often* the lead time exceeds ten days and daily use exceeds $300, but also the importance of the item in the sales or production picture. For example, a higher safety stock is warranted for a high-volume, high-contribution-margin item. For the same reason, a higher safety stock would be set for a part used in several of the firm's major products than for one used in only a few, slow-moving products.

Because analyzing the flow of inventory items can be very expensive, managers usually make detailed analyses for only a few items of special importance. Low-cost, nonessential items might be given reorder points based solely on an experienced manager's intuition.

HOW MUCH TO ORDER—THE ECONOMIC ORDER QUANTITY

The answer to the question "how much to order at a time?" is the **economic order quantity (EOQ).** The firms in our examples do not manufacture the item but order it from a supplier. The analysis is the same for manufactured items, but the term *economic lot size* is normally used.

In determining the EOQ, the goal is to minimize the sum of the costs of ordering and carrying costs. Suppose a firm uses 12,000 units of product during a year. ("Uses" can mean either sells or uses in some other way, as supplies and raw materials are used.) The estimated incremental costs of carrying inventory are $0.60 per unit per year. The incremental cost of placing an order is estimated at $225 (including incremental clerical costs, forms, data processing, delivery, etc.).[2] If use is even throughout the year, we can calculate the EOQ by using the following formula. (The assumption that use is even throughout the year is critical to the EOQ model. The solution provided by the model will not produce the desired results if use varies significantly from month to month or week to week.)

$$EOQ = \sqrt{\frac{2CD}{k}}$$

where

C = incremental order cost;
D = number of units used in a year (annual demand);
k = annual carrying cost per unit.

Applying the formula to the example gives

$$EOQ = \sqrt{\frac{2 \times \$225 \times 12{,}000}{\$0.60}}$$
$$= 3{,}000 \text{ units}$$
$$\text{or 4 orders per year } (12{,}000/3{,}000)$$

2 *If we were dealing with a manufactured item, the costs to be considered would be those of setting up to make a batch of the product (for example, the idle time during the setup).*

The formula can also be used when the annual demand and the carrying costs are stated in dollars, instead of units. In our example, suppose that the purchase cost of a unit is $5, so that annual demand is $60,000 (12,000 × $5). Carrying costs are 12% of cost ($0.60/$5). The formula is

$$EOQ = \sqrt{\frac{2 \times \$225 \times \$60{,}000}{12\%}}$$
$$= \$15{,}000 \text{ (which is 3,000 units at \$5)}$$

Exhibit A-6 shows the costs associated with three order quantities. It should help you to understand the behavior of the two types of costs affected by the size of the order. Average inventory means the amount in excess of safety stock. (Remember that the carrying costs of safety stock are the same regardless of the order quantity and so are irrelevant in a decision of how many to order.) Average inventory is half of the order size because we assume even use throughout the year. The annual carrying cost is the per-unit amount multiplied by the average inventory.

Notice that at the EOQ, computed earlier as 3,000 units, total carrying costs equal total ordering costs. This is always true because of the relationships of these costs to order size.

Exhibit A-7 is a graphic presentation of the cost behavior reflected in Exhibit A-6. It shows the behavior of each group of costs and of total cost. Notice that the total-cost curve is relatively flat over the range near the EOQ. This means that modest errors in calculating the EOQ do not cost a great deal. Notice that, again, the EOQ is the point at which total carrying costs equal total ordering costs.

There is a relationship between the EOQ and JIT. If a company can reduce its setup (or ordering) cost to near-zero, then the EOQ approaches zero. This means that the company should make or buy one unit at a time, not large batches, so that average inventory is negligible. Thus, a very simplified way of looking at a JIT operation is that it has near-zero lead time which eliminates the need for safety stock, and near-zero setup costs, which makes the EOQ very small. Inventory control models therefore give a theoretical justification of how JIT operations are able to operate.

LINEAR PROGRAMMING

Chapter 5 noted that profits are maximized when the firm makes the combination of products that maximizes the contribution margin per unit of a

Exhibit A-6 Annual Incremental Inventory Costs for Selected Order Quantities

(a) Order Quantity	(b) Average Inventory (a)/2	(c) Orders per Year 12,000/(a)	(d) Annual Carrying Costs $0.60 × (b)	(e) Annual Ordering Costs $225 × (c)	(f) Total Annual Costs (d) + (e)
2,000	1,000	6	$ 600	$1,350	$1,950
3,000	1,500	4	900	900	1,800
4,000	2,000	3	1,200	675	1,875

Exhibit A-7 Behavior of Annual Inventory Costs

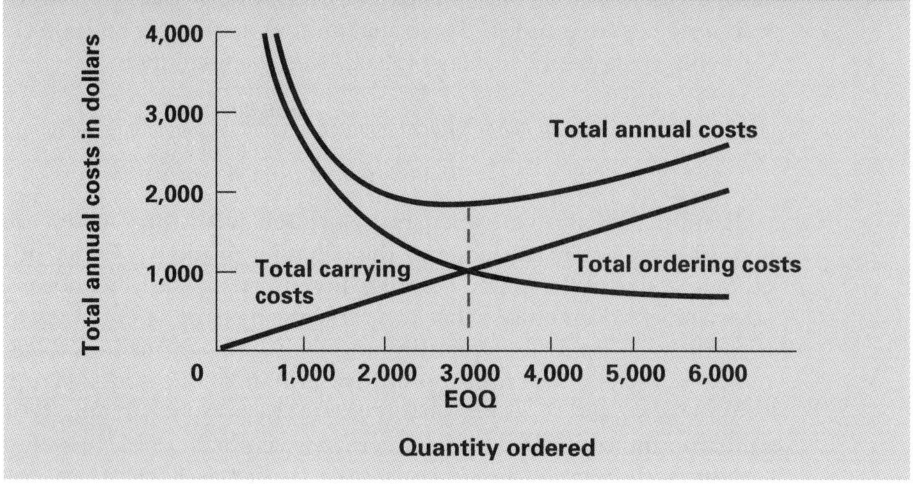

fixed resource. The example in that chapter involved only one fixed resource, but it is more likely that several resources will be fixed.

A multiproduct company that faces several constraints can use **linear programming** to determine the combination of products that maximizes profits. Linear programming can also be used to find the combination of input factors that minimizes the cost of an activity. A cattle feeder can determine the least-cost mix of various feeds to provide a specific level of nourishment. Or, a firm with several factories and warehouses can determine the least-cost way to move the required quantities of finished product from factories to warehouses.

The mathematics involved in linear programming is complex and is not detailed in this book. However, you should be able to recognize the kinds of problems that can be solved with linear programming, understand the formulation of the problem, and see what is being done when the problem is solved. Essentially, linear programming is the solving of a system of simultaneous linear equations. The system includes an *objective function* specifying what is to be maximized (usually contribution margin) or minimized (usually cost). The rest of the system's equations state the *constraints.*

A firm makes two products, *X* and *Y*. Both products require time in the Assembly Department and the Finishing Department. Data on the two products appear below.

	X	*Y*
Hours required in Assembly Department	2	4
Hours required in Finishing Department	3	2
Selling price	$65	$100
Variable cost	40	60
Contribution margin	$25	$ 40

Each week, 100 hours are available in the Assembly Department, and 90 hours in the Finishing Department. Using these data we can formulate the linear program in the following four steps.

Step 1.
Formulate the objective function, which in this case is to maximize total contribution margin per week.

$$\text{Maximize: contribution margin} = \$25X + \$40Y$$

where X and Y stand for the numbers of units of each product that will be produced.

Step 2.
Formulate the constraints as inequalities.

$$2X + 4Y \leq 100$$
$$3X + 2Y \leq 90$$

Each inequality describes the constraint of available time in a department. The first states that the hours spent assembling X (2 hours per unit) plus those spent assembling Y (4 hours per unit) cannot exceed (must be equal to or less than) 100, the available capacity of the Assembly Department. Similarly, the second inequality states that the hours used in finishing X (3 hours per unit) plus those spent in finishing Y (2 hours per unit) cannot exceed the 90 hours available in the Finishing Department.

Two other constraints are required—nonnegativity constraints.

$$X \geq 0$$
$$Y \geq 0$$

These constraints eliminate a solution that is mathematically possible but calls for negative production of a product.

The entire set of equations and inequalities appears below.

$$\text{Maximize: contribution margin} = \$25X + \$40Y$$

Subject to the constraints:

$$2X + 4Y \leq 100$$
$$3X + 2Y \leq 90$$
$$X \geq 0$$
$$Y \geq 0$$

Step 3.
Graph the lines representing constraints. The capacity constraints of the two departments are shown in Exhibit A-8. The nonnegativity constraints are implicit because we show only the upper right-hand quadrant of the graph, where production of both products is zero or positive.

The lines representing the capacity constraints can be drawn by determining the two extreme points. For example, the assembly constraint is $2X + 4Y \leq 100$. If only product X is made, maximum production is 50 units, which is 100/2. If only Y is made, maximum production is 25 units (100/4). Hence, the points on the axes are determined and the line is drawn to connect them. Each point on the line represents a possible combination of production. For

Exhibit A-8 Graphic Solution of Constraints on Capacity

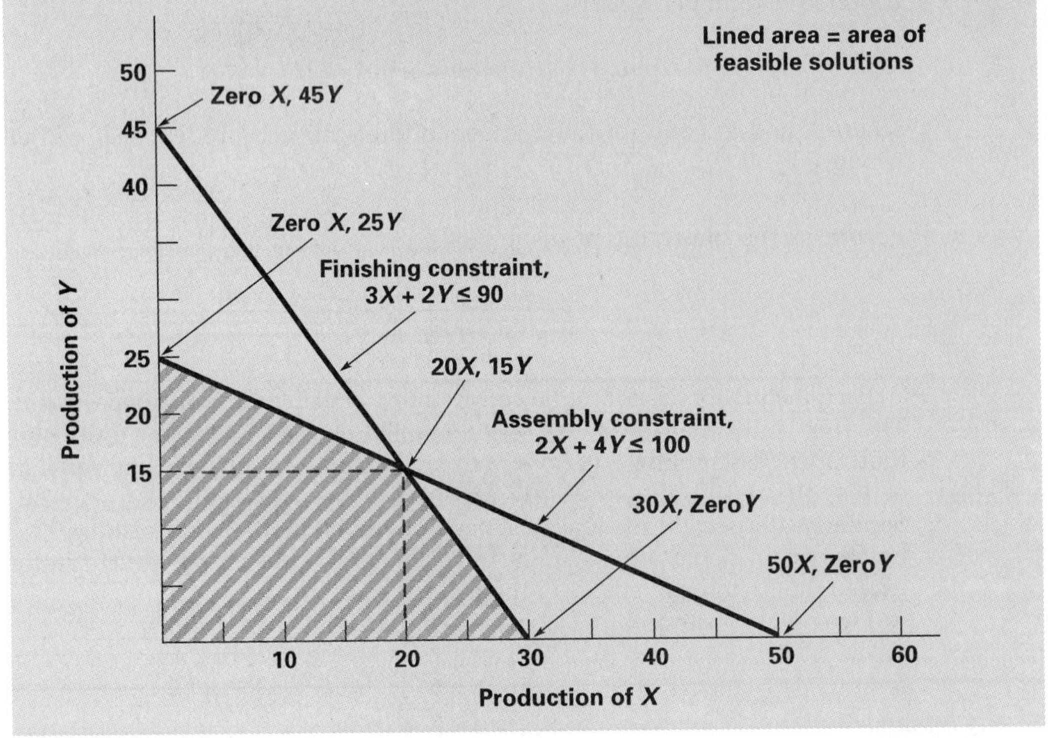

example, assembling 30 units of X requires 60 hours of assembly time. There would be 40 hours left (100 – 60) to assemble units of Y. In that time, 10 units of Y could be assembled.

The shaded area in the graph is the area of feasible solutions. All points within the shaded area are achievable combinations of production; all points outside the area are unachievable because they require more time than is available in one or the other department.

Step 4.

Determine the contribution margin at each of the corners in the area of feasible solutions. In linear programming an optimal solution always occurs at a corner, an intersection of two lines.[3] (The axes are considered to be lines.)

Corner		Contribution Margin		Total Contribution
X	Y	X	Y	Margin
0	0	$ 0	$ 0	$ 0
30	0	750	0	750
20	15	500	600	1,100
0	25	0	1,000	1,000

The corner 20X, 15Y produces the best solution.

3 Other solutions may also yield the best possible result, but none yields a better result than is achieved at an intersection.

It is often possible to solve for the intersections of constraints using simultaneous equations.[4] This enables you to find the intersection of two constraints without having to draw an accurate graph. Using our illustration, we turn the inequalities into equations.

$$(1)\ 2X + 4Y = 100$$
$$(2)\ 3X + 2Y = 90$$

Multiplying equation (2) by 2 and subtracting equation (1) we obtain

$$4X = 80$$
$$X = 20$$

Substituting 20 for X in equation (1) gives

$$40 + 4Y = 100$$
$$4Y = 60$$
$$Y = 15$$

Many other types of constraints are possible. Exhibit A-9 shows the graph when market conditions limit the sales of product X to 16 units per week. The formerly optimal solution of 20X, 15Y is no longer feasible. Two new corners have been created: 16X, zero Y and 16X, 17Y. Clearly, 16X and 17Y must be more desirable than 16X and zero Y. The question is now whether 16X, 17Y is better than zero X, 25Y, which was the second best solution in the original problem. At 16X, 17Y, total contribution margin per week is $1,080 [($25 × 16) + ($40 × 17)]. This is better than the $1,000 earned producing only 25 units of Y.

The constraint of the Finishing Department is no longer critical. It now lies completely outside the area of feasible solutions which means that the time in the Finishing Department will not be fully used. The Finishing Department will have eight hours of unused capacity because 16 units of X and 17 of Y can be finished in 82 hours.

$$3X + 2Y \leq 90$$
$$3 \times 16 = 48$$
$$2 \times 17 = \underline{34}$$
$$\text{Total} \quad 82$$

Managers would consider reducing the available capacity of the Finishing Department if they expected the constraint on sales of X to continue. They might also pursue opportunities to do finishing work for another company to use the capacity.

SENSITIVITY ANALYSIS

Sensitivity analysis, the testing of a solution to see how much it changes if one or more variables were to change, is, as we have seen throughout this

---

4 *The most widely used technique for solving large linear programming problems is called the* simplex method. *It requires finding solutions to a set of simultaneous equations until the optimal solution is found.*

Exhibit A-9 Linear Programming: Graphic Solution of Constraints on Capacity and on Sales of X

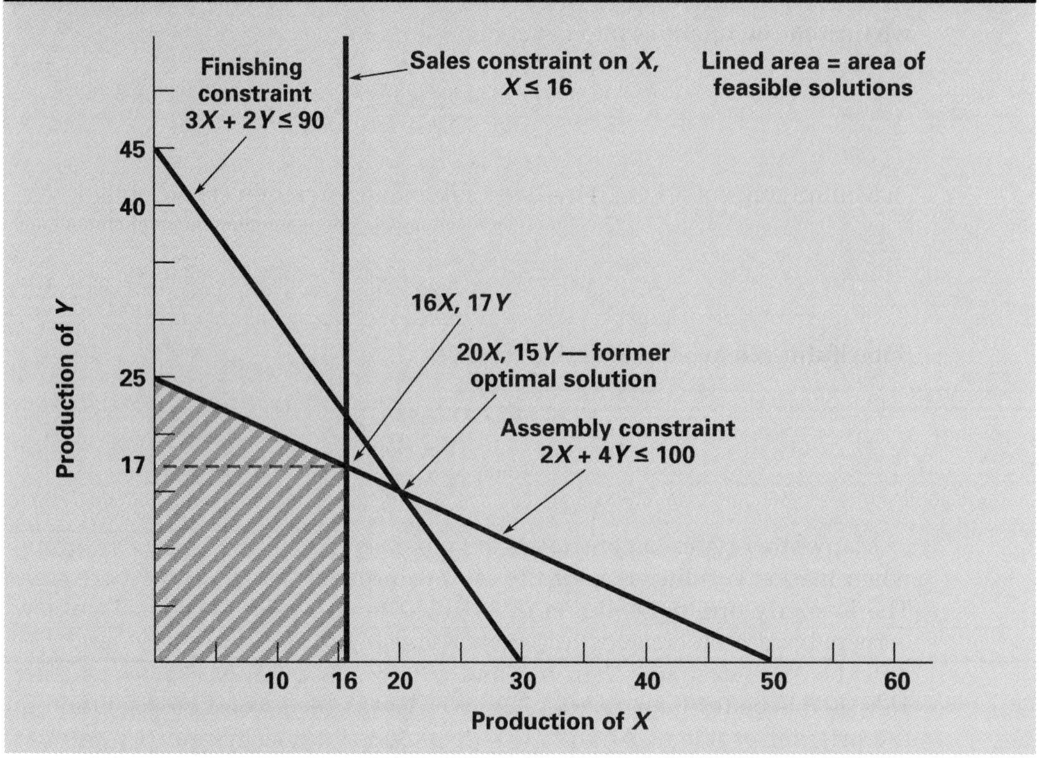

book, important in decision making. Let us consider the original situation when there was no constraint on the sales of product X. The sales manager might expect the price of X to fall, which would lower its contribution margin. Total contribution margin would also fall so long as the firm stayed with its original plan to produce 20 units of X and 15 of Y. At some point the drop in contribution margin would make it more profitable for the firm to produce 25 units of Y, none of X, than to continue with the original plan. That point is an indifference point, as described in Chapter 2.

The manager is interested in knowing how far the contribution margin of X has to fall before the company should stop producing it. The manager can determine that by finding what contribution margin from X in the 20X, 15Y combination equals the total contribution margin from zero X, 25Y. Using C to denote the contribution margin from a unit of X, the manager can frame the following equation.

Produce 25Y		*Produce 20X, 15Y*
$40 × 25	=	*(C × 20) + ($40 × 15)*
$1,000	=	*20C + $600*
C	=	*$20*

Consequently, if the contribution margin per unit of X falls below $20 (from $25), the firm would stop producing X and devote its facilities solely to making Y.

Similarly, a rise in the price and contribution margin per unit of Y would make the firm more likely to stop producing X and produce more of Y. The equation below states that when the contribution margin of 25 units of Y equals that of 15 units of Y plus 20 units of X, the firm will earn the same with either production mix. Here, C represents contribution margin per unit of Y.

$$C \times 25 = (C \times 15) + (\$25 \times 20)$$
$$C \times 25 = (C \times 15) + \$500$$
$$C \times 10 = \$500$$
$$C = \$50$$

If contribution margin of Y rises above \$50 per unit (from \$40), the firm will earn more total contribution margin producing 25Y, zero X, than 15Y, 20X.

Sensitivity analysis is repeatedly performing calculations that differ only in the values used for some of the variables. The availability of computers has significantly reduced the time required for such analyses.

SHADOW PRICES

Managers confronted with capacity constraints often wish to know whether it would be beneficial to add capacity in a particular department. They are interested in the value of adding, say, an hour per week of assembly time. The value of adding an hour of capacity is the additional contribution margin that could be earned. This amount is the **shadow price** of the resource.[5] A shadow price is an opportunity cost—the cost of *not* having an additional unit of capacity.

We shall calculate the shadow price of the assembly constraint using our original illustration in which there was no constraint on the sales of product X. To make it easier to show graphically, we shall add eight hours of capacity to the Assembly Department, rather than one hour. Exhibit A-10 shows the new assembly constraint. It also shows the former optimal solution, where the assembly constraint and finishing constraint lines intersected when capacity in the Assembly Department was 100 hours per week. Notice that the new corner, 18X, 18Y shows the firm making fewer units of X than before, but more units of Y.

Checking the new corners for the optimal solution, we have

Corner		Contribution Margin		Total Contribution Margin
X	*Y*	*X*	*Y*	
18	18	\$450	\$ 720	\$1,170
0	27	0	1,080	1,080

The new optimal solution of 18X, 18Y has a total contribution margin of \$1,170 per week. That is \$70 higher than the \$1,100 earned under the optimal

5 *Stated generally, a shadow price is the value of being able to relax a constraint by one unit. A unit could be an hour, or a unit of product. For example, in the illustration in which sales of X were limited to 16 units per week, a shadow price could be computed for that constraint. It would be the difference between contribution margin at 16X, 17Y and at the optimal solution if 17 units of X could be sold.*

Exhibit A-10 Linear Programming: Graphic Solution of Increased Assembly Capacity

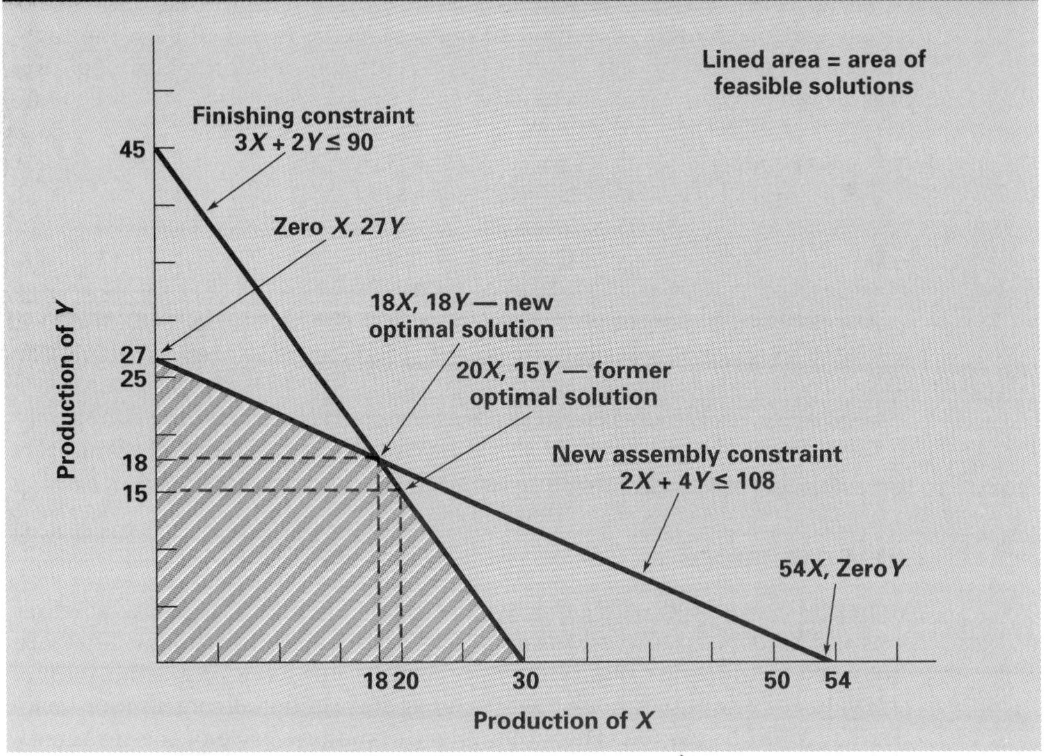

solution of 20X, 15Y when the Assembly Department had 100 available hours. *Therefore the firm would be willing to pay up to $70 per week to get an additional eight hours of assembly capacity.* The shadow price is $8.75, which is $70/8 hours. (Had we structured the example to add one hour instead of eight, we would have had contribution margin of $1,108.75 and a noninteger solution requiring production of fractional units of both products.) In linear programming, capacity is fixed for the planning period (a week, day, month, or year). In the long run the firm can add to capacity or reduce it. Shadow prices give an idea of the value of adding capacity and are important information for long-run planning.

LEARNING CURVES

Even before they faced serious competition from overseas companies, U.S. companies paid a great deal of attention to improving employee productivity and recognized that people generally need less time to do a task as they become more familiar with the task. For instance, airplane manufacturers long ago determined that the labor time required for each airplane of a given model declines as the workers learn.

The **learning curve** is a measure of increases in efficiency. The rate of performance improvement, expressed as a percentage, is called the *learning* *rate.* The most common form of the learning curve is expressed as follows: as output doubles, the *average* time to make a unit or batch of units drops to the learning rate percentage multiplied by the average time at the previous point. An example will clarify this relationship.

Northern Manufacturing is about to begin making a new product. The expected labor time for the first batch is 10 hours, and the expected learning rate is 80%. Exhibit A-11 illustrates the learning curve for Northern. The exhibit shows, for selected numbers of batches, both the average time per batch and the total time.

Notice that the exhibit shows results only at doubling points (2 is double 1, 4 is double 2, 8 is double 4). To determine the average time for some other number of batches, we can use the following formula.

$$Y = aX^b$$

where

Y = *average time for X number of batches;*
a = *the time required for the first batch (or unit);*
X = *total output (number of batches);*
b = *the learning exponent.*

The value of b is the logarithm of the learning rate (expressed as a decimal) divided by the logarithm of 2. (Because many calculators include both logarithm and exponentiation functions, using the formula is not difficult.) With the formula you can find the average time for any output level. For instance, in the above example, the value of b is about -.322. Thus, the per-batch average time for seven batches is

$$\begin{aligned} Y &= 10 \times 7^{-.322} \\ &= 10 \times .5344 \\ &= 5.344 \end{aligned}$$

We stress that the learning curve is expressed in terms of the per-batch *average* time for some total number of batches, not the *incremental* time to produce some number of additional batches. Thus, if we refer to Exhibit A-11, the second batch does not require eight hours; rather eight hours is the

Exhibit A-11 Examples of Expected Average and Total Times—80% Learning Curve

Total Output in Batches	Expected Average Time per Batch (hours)		Expected Total Time (hours) [a]	
1	10	(given)	10	
2	8	(10 × 80%)	16	(2 × 8)
4	6.4	(8 × 80%)	25.6	(4 × 6.4)
8	5.12	(6.4 × 80%)	40.96	(8 × 5.12)

a *Number of batches × average time per batch.*

per-batch average time to produce both of the first two batches. To find the incremental time for a batch, you must first find the total times for that number of batches and for one batch fewer. For Northern, we know from Exhibit A-11 that eight batches require 40.96 hours. Seven batches require 37.408 hours (7 × 5.344, the average time computed above using the formula). Hence, the eighth batch requires 3.552 hours (40.96 – 37.408).

You can also apply the learning curve directly to cost, rather than to time. For example, we could have said that labor and labor-related variable overhead costs were $10 for the first batch. In that case, the answers derived in the exhibit or from the formula would be expressed in dollars.

The learning curve is useful in planning and controlling. Managers can estimate labor time, and therefore labor and labor-related variable overhead costs, for specific quantities of output. They can then determine, by comparing actual time or cost with the estimated values, whether learning is as expected.

Suppose that CompuCom is considering a customer's offer to buy eight batches of a specialized microprocessor. (A batch could be 500, 1,000, or any other number of units, so long as all batches are the same size.) The customer has offered to pay $80,000 for the entire order. No incremental fixed costs are associated with the order. Materials and purchased components will cost $3,500 for each batch. (This portion of the cost is not subject to learning.) CompuCom estimates the cost of direct labor and labor-related variable overhead for the first batch at $3,000 and has usually experienced an 80% learning rate.

Suppose CompuCom's managers have decided not to accept the order unless they expect more than the $35,000 in contribution margin which the company could earn doing other business if the order is rejected. If the managers ignore the potential for lower costs because of learning, they would reject the order on the basis of the following analysis.

Revenues		$80,000
Variable costs:		
Materials and components (8 × $3,500)	$28,000	
Labor and labor-related overhead (8 × $3,000)	24,000	52,000
Expected contribution margin		$28,000

But, the order does have the desired profit potential if the learning factor is considered. The following schedule shows the expected costs of labor and labor-related variable overhead, based on the 80% learning rate and expected costs of the first batch.

Total Output in Batches	Expected Average Cost per Batch	Expected Total Cost [a]
1	$3,000 (given)	$ 3,000
2	2,400 ($3,000 × 80%)	4,800 (2 × $2,400)
4	1,920 ($2,400 × 80%)	7,680 (4 × $1,920)
8	1,536 ($1,920 × 80%)	12,288 (8 × $1,536)

a Number of batches × average cost per batch.

With this cost information, the order shows higher profit.

Revenues		$80,000
Variable costs:		
Materials and components (8 × $3,500)	$28,000	
Labor and labor-related overhead, previously given	12,288	40,288
Expected contribution margin		$39,712

Total expected contribution margin from the order is nearly $12,000 more than that shown by the analysis that ignores the cost reduction expected to result from learning and the order is more profitable than the available alternative (contribution margin of $35,000). The lesson here is that managers must study their firms' experiences for evidence of potential cost reductions as a result of learning and, where it exists, incorporate that potential into decision making.

SUMMARY

Managers use a variety of quantitative techniques to help them make decisions. Statistical decision theory enables managers to incorporate the effects of uncertainty. Inventory control models offer rational ways of evaluating inventory policies, including those associated with perishables. Linear programming helps managers decide how best to use existing resources. Shadow prices help managers to understand the significance of existing constraints and the potential gains from expanding capacity. Learning curves are useful in planning and controlling labor and labor-related costs.

Much of the information needed for using these techniques is supplied by managerial accountants. Managers and accountants must be aware of the objectives and information requirements of such techniques. The managerial accountant will sometimes have to assist in formulating the problem and must therefore understand the capabilities and limitations of the techniques available.

KEY TERMS

decision tree
carrying costs
conditional value
economic order quantity (EOQ)
expected value
lead time
learning curve
linear programming
ordering costs
payoff table
reorder point
safety stock
setup costs
shadow price
stockout costs
value of perfect information

KEY FORMULAS

$$\text{Economic order quantity} = \sqrt{\frac{(2 \times \text{incremental order cost} \times \text{annual demand})}{\text{annual carrying cost per unit}}}$$

Reorder point = safety stock + (daily use × lead time)

REVIEW PROBLEM—EXPECTED VALUES

In March, Grauger Company experienced an unfavorable cost variance of $2,000. Based on experience and judgment, the production manager believes there is a 40% probability that the variance was due to random causes and will not continue. A 60% probability exists that there is some difficulty in the production process and that the variance will continue at $2,000 per month for the next two months. Investigating the variance would cost $800. If the variance is investigated and something is wrong with the process, there is a 70% probability that corrective action could be taken and a 30% probability that nothing can be done.

Required

Determine the expected costs of investigating and of not investigating the variance.

ANSWER TO REVIEW PROBLEM

Expected Cost of Investigating

Event	Cost	Probability	Expected Value
Variance is random and will not continue	$ 800	.40	$ 320
Variance is caused by problem in process that can be corrected	800	.42 [a]	336
Variance is caused by problem that cannot be corrected	4,800 [b]	.18 [c]	864
Expected cost of investigating		1.00	$1,520

a 60% × 70%.
b $800 + (2 × $2,000).
c 60% × 30%.

Expected Cost of Not Investigating

Event	Cost	Probability	Expected Value
Variance is random	0	.40	0
Variance is caused by problem in process and will continue	$4,000	.60	$2,400
Expected cost of not investigating		1.00	$2,400

The variance should be investigated because the expected cost to investigate is less than that of not investigating.

REVIEW PROBLEM—INVENTORY CONTROL

The following data apply to one of Tebbetts Company's products.

Annual use	12,000 units
Annual carrying cost	\$0.80 per unit
Order cost	\$300 per order
Safety stock	500 units

There are 200 working days per year, and the lead time is 12 days.

Required

1. Determine the reorder point.
2. Determine the EOQ.

ANSWER TO REVIEW PROBLEM

1.

Safety stock	500
Use during lead time	
[12 × (12,000/200)]	720
Reorder point	1,220

2. 3,000 units.

$$\text{EOQ} = \sqrt{\frac{2 \times \$300 \times 12{,}000}{\$0.80}} = \sqrt{\frac{\$7{,}200{,}000}{\$0.80}} = \sqrt{9{,}000{,}000} = 3{,}000 \text{ units}$$

ASSIGNMENT MATERIAL

QUESTIONS FOR DISCUSSION

A-1 Optimum order size—changing conditions Explain the effect that each of the following tends to have on the optimum order size for a product.

(a) Leading banks have announced a reduction in the prime interest rate.
(b) The selling price of the product declines with no change in its purchase cost.
(c) The company moves to a high-crime, inner-city area.
(d) The city increases the personal property tax rate.
(e) There is a substantial increase in the demand for the product.
(f) The company changes from the straight-line method of depreciating its warehouse to the sum-of-the-years'-digits method.

A-2 Reorder point Indicate how each of the following factors, considered independently, influences the reorder point for inventory (relatively high, relatively low, or no effect). Explain your answers.

1. The company has low fixed costs and high variable costs (85% of sales).

2. A product is stored in expensive, custom-made freezers.
3. The product is ice cream, sold from a store in a large shopping center.
4. Your suppliers have had falling profits because of intense competition.
5. Your major supplier is having difficulties because two stockholder factions have been fighting for control.

EXERCISES

A-3 ***Inventory control*** Ridley Company uses 100,000 units of a particular raw material per year. The material is used evenly throughout the year. Order costs are $800 per order, and carrying costs are $10 per unit. The firm carries a safety stock of 2,000 units, has a lead time of 12 days, and works 200 days per year.

Required

1. Determine the reorder point.
2. Determine the EOQ.

A-4 ***Variance investigation*** Cole Company's controller has determined that it costs $600 to investigate a variance and that corrective action is possible in one out of four cases investigated. An unfavorable variance of $1,500 has occurred. The production process will be changed after next month, so that any savings will be for only one month if corrective action can be taken. Should the variance be investigated?

A-5 ***Inventory control*** Using the following data, determine the EOQ and the reorder point for Part No. 368. Round your computations to even units and dollars.

Cost per unit	$20
Use per year	6,000 units
Carrying costs	15% of cost
Order costs	$1,000 per order
Lead time	8 days
Safety stock	600 units
Working days per year	200

A-6 ***Basic learning curve*** Industrial engineers at Kemp Inc., a manufacturer of industrial presses, expect the first unit of a new model, the XZ-18, to require 4,000 direct labor hours. They also expect an 80% learning curve.

Required

1. Determine the average direct labor time and the total direct labor time to make four units of the XZ-18.
2. Determine the average direct labor time and the total direct labor time to make eight units of the XZ-18.

A-7 ***New products—expected values and risk*** The sales manager of Happy Toy Company is considering two new toys, a doll and a game. On the basis of market research and experience, she has formulated the following table.

	Doll		Game	
Event	Cash Flow	Probability	Cash Flow	Probability
Big success	$60,000	.2	$90,000	.3
Fair success	40,000	.5	50,000	.4
Flop	10,000	.3	(20,000)	.3

Required

1. Determine the expected value of cash flows associated with each new toy.
2. Which one would you select, and why?

A-8 Linear programming—formulation of problem Garson Company makes three products, A, B, and C. Their respective contribution margins are $60, $70, and $80. Each product goes through three processes: cutting, shaping, and painting. The numbers of hours required by each process for each product are as follows.

	Hours Required in Each Process		
Product	Cutting	Shaping	Painting
A	4	2	4
B	3	5	3
C	5	2	2

The following numbers of hours are available per month in each process: cutting, 8,000; shaping, 6,000; and painting, 4,000.

Required

Formulate the objective function and constraints to determine the optimal production policy.

A-9 Linear programming PQ Company makes two products.

	P	Q
Selling price	$50	$30
Variable costs	$25	$20
Labor hours required per unit:		
Grinding Department	3	1
Assembly Department	2	2

The firm has 900 hours of labor time available in the Grinding Department and 800 available in the Assembly Department.

Required

Determine the optimal product mix.

A-10 Learning curve Tallman Industries is bidding on a contract to make eight batches of landing gear assemblies for an aircraft company. Tallman's engineers expect direct labor and variable overhead for the first batch to be $50,000. Variable overhead is related to direct labor. Tallman usually achieves an 85% learning rate.

Required

1. Determine the expected average cost for direct labor and variable overhead for the eight batches.

2. Determine the expected total cost for direct labor and variable overhead for the eight batches.

A-11 Learning curve (extension of A-10) Tallman's managers expect the cost of materials and purchased components to be $25,000 per batch (not subject to learning). They also want an average contribution margin of $15,000 per batch.

Required

1. Determine the price that Tallman must bid to earn $15,000 average contribution margin per batch for eight batches.
2. Suppose now that the contract is for 16 batches. Redo item 1.
3. Suppose that the contract is still for eight batches, but that Tallman's managers believe that the learning rate will actually be 80%. Redo item 1.

A-12 Cost structure and probabilities The production manager of Omega Company is considering modifying one of her machines. The modification will add $10,000 per month to the cost of running the machine but will reduce variable operating costs by $0.20 per unit produced. The modification itself costs nothing, and the machine can be returned to its current operating method at any time.

The product made on the machine has an uncertain demand; the best estimates available are as follows.

Monthly Demand	Probability
25,000	.20
40,000	.40
60,000	.20
70,000	.20

Required

1. Determine the number of units that must be produced to justify the modification.
2. Determine the expected value of making the modification. Should it be made?

A-13 Payoff table Campus Program Company sells programs for football games. The owner has collected the following data regarding the pattern of sales.

Quantity Sold (cases)	Probability
400	.20
600	.60
700	.20

The owner is uncertain of the number of cases of programs to order. He must order one of the quantities given above. A case of programs sells for $300, and the purchase price is $100. Unsold programs are thrown away.

Required

Construct a payoff table to determine the number of cases of programs the firm should order.

A-14 Linear programming, formulation of problem Carter Company makes two models of its basic product. Data are as follows.

	X	Y
Selling price	$80	$100
Materials requirements, pounds	2	1
Labor time, hours	2	3

Materials cost $8 per pound and the combined labor and variable overhead rate is $12 per labor hour. The company has 400 pounds of materials and 500 hours of labor available. It can sell all of either model that it can make. Fixed costs are $2,000, of which $700 is depreciation. All fixed costs are unavoidable.

Required

Formulate the objective function and constraints.

A-15 Linear programming (extension of A-14) Refer to A-14.

Required

1. Determine the optimal mix.
2. Determine the shadow price of the labor constraint. Assume the addition of 20 hours of labor.

A-16 Sensitivity analysis The florist for whom you prepared the payoff table (Exhibit A-2) is not impressed. He has decided to order 4,000 corsages per week because he does not want to be stuck with unsold goods. Because you own a share of the business, you would like him to order 8,000 per week. In an effort to show him that he is being unduly conservative, you decide to show him how low the risk is by using more pessimistic probabilities. Because you would not order 12,000 corsages, you can lump together the probabilities of selling 8,000 and 12,000. (The contribution margin from ordering 8,000 corsages is the same whether demand is 8,000 or 12,000.)

Required

Determine the expected values of ordering 8,000 corsages with the following probabilities.

Case	Demand in Units	Probability of Demand
1	4,000	.30
	8,000	.70
2	4,000	.40
	8,000	.60
3	4,000	.50
	8,000	.50

A-17 Inventory control—sensitivity Morton Company sells a product with the following attributes.

Annual demand	10,000 units
Annual carrying cost per unit	$2
Order cost	$400

Required

1. Determine the EOQ. Determine the annual cost associated with this policy.

2. Suppose that the firm halves the order quantity, doubling the number of orders from the one you calculated in item 1. What is the cost of following the nonoptimal policy?

PROBLEMS

A-18 Expected values—a law firm The firm of Smith, Perez, and Jankowski has been approached by Hirt, who suffered a whiplash injury in an automobile accident. He wants the firm to represent him in a court suit, with the firm's fee being one third of the total judgment given by the court.

Jankowski estimates that 2,000 hours are needed to prepare and try the case, with the opportunity cost being $80 per hour. Based on experience with similar cases, she believes that the following judgments and associated probabilities are reasonable estimates on which to decide whether to accept the case.

Judgment for Hirt	Probability of Judgment
0	.40
$180,000	.20
$300,000	.30
$420,000	.10

Required

Determine whether the firm should accept the case.

A-19 Inventory control Blitzen Industries makes products in individual production runs, because all its products must go through one particular machine. Each time a new production run is set up, the firm incurs incremental costs of $1,500.

The cost to carry a unit of product A is $4 per year, including taxes, insurance, spoilage, and return on investment. Sales of product A are 24,000 units per year.

Required

1. Determine the number of units of A that should be made each run.
2. The company carries a safety stock of 800 units of A, the working year is 300 days, and production of a batch requires ten days. At what inventory level should a production run be made?

A-20 Learning curve in administrative work The Dean of Admissions at Mid-State University needs student help to process 6,400 application forms. She has found that a new student helper can process 20 forms the first day. The helpers usually achieve a 90% learning rate. The Dean plans to hire ten helpers, so each will process 640 forms. You may consider 20 forms to be a batch.

Required

Determine how many days it will take 10 new helpers to process the 6,400 forms.

A-21 Variance investigation DePardeu Company has just experienced a $3,000 unfavorable variance. The production supervisor believes that there is a

30% chance that the variance was a one-time thing and will not continue. She believes that if an investigation is made, the chance of correcting the variance is 60% and of not correcting it is 40%. It costs $800 to investigate a variance. The most that will be lost if the variance continues is $4,000.

Required

Determine whether to investigate the variance.

A-22 Linear programming Fast Class Company makes two products, the Fast and the Class. Fasts sell for $12 and have variable costs of $5. Classes sell for $14 and have variable costs of $6. Both products are put through two processes—cutting and forming. Each unit of Fast requires two hours of cutting and four hours of forming. Each unit of Class requires three hours of cutting and two of forming. The company has available 3,000 hours of cutting time and 2,400 hours of forming time per month. Fixed costs in cutting are $400, in forming are $300, all unavoidable.

Required

Determine the number of Fasts and Classes that should be produced each month.

A-23 Shadow prices and sensitivity analysis (extension of A-22) Refer to A-22.

Required

Consider each item independently.

1. Determine the shadow price of the forming constraint.
2. Determine the price of Fasts that would make the company indifferent between the current optimal mix (from A-22) and making all Fasts.
3. Determine the price of Classes that would make the company indifferent between the current optimal mix (from A-22) and making all Classes.

A-24 Product selection Henson Electronics is trying to decide which of three products to introduce. The managers think that only one should be brought out in order to concentrate promotional effort. Information about the products follows.

	Radio	Toaster	Coffee Maker
Selling price	$22	$37	$45
Variable cost	13	20	25
Contribution margin	$ 9	$17	$20
Sales forecasts, in units, with	25,000 (20%)	12,000 (10%)	15,000 (60%)
probabilities in parentheses	40,000 (40%)	19,000 (25%)	20,000 (20%)
	50,000 (30%)	25,000 (50%)	25,000 (20%)
	75,000 (10%)	38,000 (15%)	

Required

1. Compute the expected values of contribution margins for the three products.
2. Which product would you select, and why?

A-25 Expected value of hole-in-one The sponsors of the Eastern Open, a major golf tournament, have decided to give a new automobile to any player who gets a hole-in-one during the tournament. The car they have selected costs $22,000. One of the sponsors owns an insurance agency and offers to insure the tournament against a hole-in-one for $1,200. If the sponsors buy the policy and someone does get a hole-in-one, the insurance company will buy the car. Statistics show that a hole-in-one occurs about every 30 tournaments.

Required
Determine the expected value of *not* buying the insurance. Would you buy the insurance if you were a sponsor?

A-26 Learning curve in make-or-buy decision Barfield Company currently buys a component for one of its products at $22 per unit. Barfield needs 32,000 units of the component in the coming year. The product will be redesigned, so that the component will not be needed beyond the coming year. The production manager believes that Barfield could make the component with the following costs for the first batch of 1,000 units.

Materials	$13,000
Direct labor and variable overhead	15,000
Total variable cost	$28,000

There are no incremental fixed costs because Barfield could use existing equipment. The production manager expects an 85% learning rate on direct labor and variable overhead. Consider a batch to be 1,000 units.

Required
Determine whether Barfield should make or buy the component.

A-27 Make or buy Walters Company manufactures ceramic figurines. Sometimes the company subcontracts production of its designs to other companies, paying a set amount per piece. The chief designer has come up with a new item that most of the managers expect to be a best seller. Some of the managers are less sure and want to be as cautious as possible.

If Walters manufactures the item, it must lease additional space and machinery at a cost of $80,000 for the coming year. The lease could not be canceled for one year. Unit variable cost is $14, and the selling price is $36. Alternatively, the company could subcontract production. A local outlet has agreed to produce the item and sell it to Walters Company at $23.

Based on her experience with other, similar items, the company's sales manager has developed the following estimates of demand and probabilities for the new figurine.

Demand	Probability
7,000	.20
9,000	.30
12,000	.30
14,000	.20

Required
Determine the expected value of the profit on the figurine if Walters (a) makes it internally and (b) subcontracts it.

A-28 Inventory control—effects of errors in policy The purchasing manager of Kensington Company buys one of its principal products in batches of 2,000, basing the amount of the purchase on his judgment. Data for the product follows.

Order cost	$800
Carrying cost, annual per unit	$2
Annual demand	20,000

Required

1. Determine the EOQ.
2. Determine the cost to the firm of not following the optimal purchasing policy. That is, determine the difference between total costs under the existing policy and under the optimal policy.
3. Determine how high carrying costs must go to make the EOQ 2,000 units.
4. Determine the order costs that will make the EOQ 2,000 units, assuming that the carrying costs are $2.

A-29 Inventory control—determination of incremental costs Rankin Company currently has no stated inventory policy. The sales manager and controller have asked you to assist in preparing a policy. Two of the factors to be determined are the cost of carrying inventory and the cost of ordering. The following information pertains to the company's only product.

Cost per unit	$90	
Sales per year	15,000	units
Required return on investment	15%	
Insurance	$500	per year plus $1.70 per unit of average inventory
Taxes	$2	per unit of average inventory
Storage		The firm leases a warehouse that can hold 20,000 units. Rent is $1,000 per year
Costs of purchasing department:		
Salaries	$12,000	per year fixed, plus $50 per order
Forms, postage	$10	per order

In addition, each time an order is received, the company hires people from a local employment service to unload the order. On any size order, three people are hired at $30 each.

Required

Determine the EOQ. Be sure to determine which costs shown above are relevant to the analysis, which are not.

A-30 Special order decision—probabilities The sales manager of Schieren Company has been approached by a chain store that would like to buy 10,000 units of the firm's product. The sales manager believes that the order should be accepted because the price offered is $6 and variable costs of production are $5.

In a conversation with the production manager, the sales manager extracted the following information: (1) sufficient capacity exists to meet the special order; (2) prices for materials and wage rates are expected to increase by the time the order would be manufactured, but the amounts of the increases are not certain. The best estimates follow.

New Variable Cost	Probability
$5.20	.30
5.70	.40
6.60	.30

Required

1. Determine the expected contribution margin on the special order.
2. What other factors should be considered in reaching a decision?

A-31 Cost of investigating a variance Gilgenbach Company's production manager has been trying to decide whether a particular variable overhead variance should be investigated. The variance was $300 unfavorable this past month, and is expected to continue at the rate of $300 for five more months if nothing is done. The estimated cost to investigate the variance is $600, and the chances are four out of five that nothing can be done to correct the variance even if its cause can be isolated. If the variance is found to be correctable, the total savings, not considering the cost of the investigation, will be $1,500 (the total cost of the variance over the next five months).

Required

Determine whether the variance should be investigated.

A-32 Expected values and utilities The sales manager of Wonderland Toy Company has been studying a report prepared by a consultant. The company had asked the consultant to study the advisability of bringing out a new doll that would be quite different from anything on the market. The report indicated that there was considerable variation in sales expectations. The consultant concluded that there was about a 60% chance of selling 50,000 dolls and a 40% chance of selling only 10,000.

The doll's price is to be $24, with variable costs of $20. Incremental fixed costs, primarily for advertising, are $120,000.

The sales manager decided, on the basis of the expected value of profit, that the doll should be introduced, but the president of the firm was leery. The president felt that the doll was apt to lose money and that the company had had too many duds in recent years. After some discussion, the president decided that losing a dollar was twice as bad as earning a dollar was good. He instructed the sales manager to prepare a new analysis incorporating his utility, although he did not call it that.

Required

1. Prepare a schedule showing the expected value of profit without consideration of the president's views.
2. Prepare a new schedule in which the president's views are incorporated. Determine whether the doll should be brought out.

A-33 Variance investigation Mayan Company experienced an unfavorable variance of $2,000 in May. The production manager found, from past data, that 30% of the time a variance of this size is experienced, nothing is wrong with the process and the variance stops. When there is a problem, 60% of the time the variance continues for two additional months, at $2,000 per month, and 40% of the time it continues for three additional months, also at $2,000 per month.

Investigating the variance costs $800. If there is a problem with the production process, it can be corrected 40% of the time. The other 60% of the time nothing can be done. The 40% and 60% probabilities apply both to variances that would continue for two additional months and to those that would continue for three additional months. If the investigation has been done and the cause of the variance found to be correctable, correcting it costs an additional $600.

Required

1. Determine the expected cost of not investigating the variance.
2. Determine the expected cost of investigating the variance.

A-34 Variance investigation (CMA adapted) Cilla Company manufactures a line of women's handbags. A summary of Cilla's cutting department operations for May 19X5 showed a $16,000 unfavorable materials use variance.

Veronique Antek, the supervisor of the department, gathered the following information to assist her in deciding whether to investigate the variance.

Estimated cost to investigate the variance	$ 4,000
Estimated cost to make changes if the department is operating incorrectly	$ 8,000
Estimated savings if changes are made	$40,000
Estimated probability that the department is operating incorrectly	10%

Required

Determine whether Antek should investigate the variance.

A-35 Capital budgeting probabilities The following estimates have been prepared by the production manager of Hector Company. They relate to a proposed $60,000 investment in a machine that will reduce the cost of materials used by the firm. Cost of capital is 16%. Ignore taxes.

Annual Cash Savings		Useful Life	
Event	Probability	Event	Probability
$20,000	.30	9 years	.40
14,000	.30	8 years	.40
12,000	.40	6 years	.20

Required

1. Compute the expected values of annual cash savings and useful life. Determine whether the machine should be purchased.
2. The production manager wishes to see whether the machine would be a good investment if each of his most pessimistic estimates came true, but not both at the same time. Determine whether the investment would be desirable if (a) the useful life is the expected value computed in item 1 and annual cash flows are only $12,000; (b) the annual cash flows are equal to the expected value computed in item 1 and the useful life is only six years.

A-36 Expected values The managers of Hawkins Company are trying to decide how to operate in the coming year. The company rents a machine that performs essential operations on the product; the rental period is one year. The product sells for $10 per unit and has variable costs of $1.

Three machines are available; operating and other data are as follows,

Machine	Productive Capacity	Annual Rent
Standard	11,000 units	$50,000
DeLuxe	12,000 units	54,000
Super	13,000 units	55,500

The sales forecast for the coming year has been based on the 10,000 units sold the prior year; demand for the product is expected to increase, but the size of the increase is uncertain. The best estimates follow.

Sales in Units	Probability
11,000	.30
12,000	.50
13,000	.20

Required

Determine the best course of action for the company.

A-37 Inventory control—quantity discounts Alexander Company buys one of its principal products from Zephyr Company in batches of 2,000. The product costs Alexander $10, and annual demand is 20,000 units. Annual carrying costs are $1.60 per unit, which includes a required rate of return of 10% (all other carrying costs are related to units, not cost), and incremental ordering costs are $160 per order. The current batch size is the EOQ for this product.

Zephyr sells this product only to Alexander and has to set up a production run every time an order is received. There are no carrying costs because Zephyr maintains no inventory, and setup costs are $1,000 per production run. The production manager of Zephyr asked the sales manager whether it might not be a good idea to offer Alexander a price reduction if Alexander agreed to buy half as often, and double the usual quantity. After some discussion, they agreed to offer Alexander a $0.20 price reduction for buying in batches of 4,000 units or more.

Required

1. Compute the annual gain or loss to both Alexander and Zephyr if the price reduction is granted.
2. Suppose that Zephyr offers to supply all 20,000 units at a single time. Determine the lowest price per unit that Zephyr could charge and not reduce its income below the level it would earn supplying the product in batches of 4,000.
3. Determine whether Alexander should buy all of its annual requirements at once, at the price you computed in item 2. (Assume that Alexander would still get the $0.20 reduction if it decided to buy 4,000 units at a time.)

A-38 Payoff table *The Evening News* is a large metropolitan newspaper. The paper is sold through dealers who are charged $0.20 per copy that they sell. Unsold copies are returned to *The News* and full credit is given. The unsold copies are sold as wastepaper for $0.02 each. The variable cost of producing a paper is $0.10.

The News currently prints 500,000 papers each day. Management is considering a change and has asked for your help. A recent study showed the following results.

Papers Returned	Percentage of Time
100,000	20%
50,000	20%
0	60%

The study also indicated that when 500,000 copies were all sold, there were often more papers demanded. The best estimates are that 25% of the time

500,000 copies are demanded, 25% of the time 550,000 are demanded, and 10% of the time 600,000 papers could be sold if they were available.

Required

1. Determine the best strategy for *The Evening News.*
2. Determine the value of perfect information.

A-39 Linear programming, graphical solution Salinas Furniture Company makes two types of sofas, traditional and modern. Because of their different types of construction, they require different amounts of machine time and skilled labor time. The company has available, per week, 1,000 hours of skilled labor and 1,200 hours of machine time. The variable costs associated with skilled labor, including both wages and variable overhead, are $7 per hour; for machine time, the variable costs are $6 per hour. The firm can sell all of the modern sofas it can make, but only 200 traditional sofas per week.

Additional data on the two sofas are as follows.

	Traditional	Modern
Selling price	$240	$180
Materials costs (the only other variable cost)	$ 80	$ 60
Labor hours required, per unit	4	2
Machine hours required, per unit	3	4

The following figure plots the above constraints.

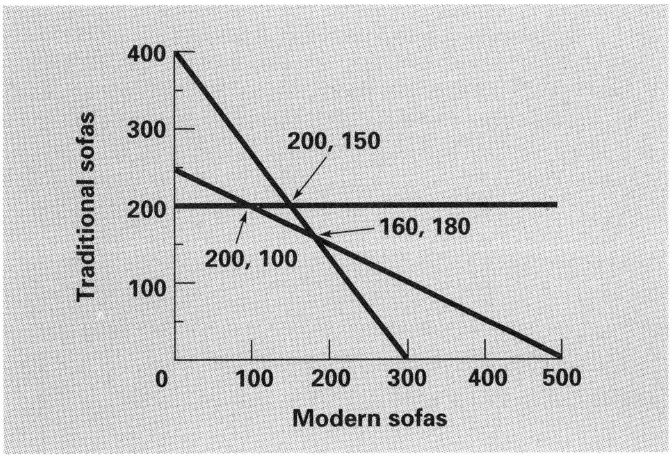

Required

1. Determine the number of each sofa that should be produced each week.
2. Assuming that the price of modern sofas remains constant, at what price for traditional sofas should the firm increase its production of traditional sofas and reduce that of modern sofas?

A-40 Expected values—capital budgeting Fleming Company plans to build a factory to manufacture a new product. The product and the factory are expected to have useful lives of ten years. No salvage value is expected for any of the components of the factory. The firm's marketing research staff has studied the potential demand for the product and has provided the following information.

Expected Annual Demand	Probability of Demand
200,000 units	60%
250,000 units	40%

The firm can build a factory with capacity of either 200,000 or 250,000 units. Data on the two possible factories are given below.

Capacity	Total Cost, All Depreciable Assets	Annual Fixed Costs Requiring Cash
200,000	$1,500,000	$300,000
250,000	1,800,000	380,000

The product will sell for $5 and have variable costs of $1. The tax rate is 40% and cost of capital is 16%. Straight-line depreciation is used for tax purposes.

Management has decided to base its decision on NPV. Whichever factory shows the greater favorable difference between the present value of the expected value of future cash flows and the required investment will be built.

Required

Prepare analyses of the expected values of future cash flows under the two investment possibilities. Determine which factory should be built.

A-41 Expected values (AICPA adapted) Wing Manufacturing Company makes a chemical compound, product X, that deteriorates rapidly. Any left unsold at the end of the month in which the firm makes it becomes worthless. The variable cost of manufacturing the product is $50 per pound and the selling price $80 per pound. The demand for the product, with associated probabilities, appears below.

Monthly Demand	Probability
8,000	.25
9,000	.60
10,000	.15

The management of Wing believes that it is necessary to supply all customers who order product X. Failing to do so would result, in the managers' judgment, in losing not only sales of product X, but also sales of other products. Wing has found a company that will sell product X to it at $80, plus $10 freight per pound. The managers want to develop a policy regarding production. Some argue that the high cost of obtaining additional amounts from the outside supplier makes it desirable to produce 10,000 pounds per month. Others argue that it is safer to produce less and to buy from the supplier as needed.

Required

Determine what production strategy maximizes the expected value of profit.

guidelines for preparing memoranda

Appendix B

Some assignments require you to write a memorandum about a specific problem. In most cases, such memoranda are short and focused on a few points. The general guidelines in this appendix regarding names, headings, supporting schedules, jargon, and environmental constraints apply to memoranda. In addition, other things to consider include:

1. Use proper memorandum format, including a heading, to whom the memorandum is addressed, who wrote the memorandum, the date, and the subject, as the following illustrates.

Illustration of Memorandum Format

```
                              MEMORANDUM

To:       John Jones, Controller
From:     Mary Smith, Smith & Co. Certified Public Accountants
Date:     January 19, 19X4
Subject:  Analysis of Plant Location

At your request, we evaluated alternative plant locations. We
have concluded that the Middleton location best suits your
needs.  Only the question of transportation charges remains. We
used the net present value of the cost savings from each alter-
native location to develop our analysis (exhibit attached).
```

2. Be direct and to the point. Do not use fancy words and avoid jargon as much as possible. Define your audience and make sure that you provide information in an understandable way. Take the viewpoint of the reader. What would you like to see if you were the reader?
3. Make your purpose clear. Executives are busy. If you do not grab their attention and hold it, they will scan your report with little interest or not read it at all. Make clear what response you would like from the reader.
4. Use the opening of your memorandum to establish a link between what you have been asked to do and your recommendations/conclusions. See the previous illustration. At the end of the memorandum tie things together. Also, end in such a way that the reader understands what you have done and is comfortable with your analysis.

GENERAL GUIDELINES

What follows are some guidelines for writing any report or memorandum. Some might not apply to a particular assignment, but they are generally useful.

AUDIENCE ANALYSIS

No writing assignment can be successful without your defining and analyzing your audience. Ask yourself these questions: Who will be reading this? What is my relationship with the reader? What do my readers know about the subject? Do my readers have strong feelings about this subject? Answering these questions will help you develop an audience profile to shape what you say and how you say it.

ANALYSIS VERSUS RESTATEMENT

Many students confuse analysis with restatement. Restatement is a summary of the facts in a situation. An analysis involves critical thinking and requires that you go beyond the facts to answer the following questions: What are the implications of this information? How does this information affect the present or future situation? What effect does this information have on my audience? By answering these questions, you are performing an analysis. All memoranda and cases require analysis; restatement is insufficient.

NAMES AND ABBREVIATIONS

The first time names of individuals and companies are used, they should be fully stated. Do not substitute "Co." for "Company," "Inc." for "Incorporated," or make any change in the name of a company. Define your abbreviations. For example, you could state, "In 1989, the situation at Federal Paper, Inc. (Federal) involved - . . . ." From that point, you could refer to the company as Federal. Once you have defined an abbreviation, use it consistently. If you want to abbreviate an individual's name, use the last name (e.g., Smith for Robin Smith) or use Ms. Smith. Your perspective will dictate how formal or informal to be with names.

SUPPORTING SCHEDULES

All supporting schedules, exhibits, graphs, and tables must be *labeled* and *referred to* in your analysis. Supporting materials can be called exhibits or tables and should be numbered in the order that they are referred to in the paper. All exhibits must have headings that describe their content.

We encourage you to generate material for exhibits and/or figures using programs such as Lotus 1-2-3. You will use such programs in your working career. However, be selective in what you include in exhibits. Consider your audience, role, and task; carefully format your exhibits, make sure they are properly titled, and provide appropriate references to sources. Finally, define all abbreviations.

USE OF JARGON

Avoid using jargon (topic or industry-specific terminology). You should be able to present your analyses without jargon, buzzwords, and cliches.

ENVIRONMENTAL CONSTRAINTS

Most assignments include constraints imposed by the internal or external environment. You should clearly state these constraints. They might affect your analysis.

ASSIGNMENTS

The assignments are glimpses of situations, some real, some not. Your knowledge is limited. The issues might or might not be clear. Ambiguity and uncertainty are characteristic of the real world. Nevertheless, you can see what problems are emerging and the kinds of decisions needed to solve them. Lack of information is not an excuse to avoid dealing with the issues.

READING THE ASSIGNMENT

Carefully read and reread the assignment. Get an overall understanding of the situation and supporting facts. When you reread the assignment, take notes about key facts, assumptions, and issues. Outline appropriate analytical techniques to help you gain additional information (e.g., CVP analysis, NPV analysis, transfer pricing). Examine the quantitative information for clues. Look at the assignment's questions for hints on how to approach your analysis.

First, avoid rushing to conclusions. You might overlook important information or distort it to fit a preconceived idea. Second, be sure that you fully understand the assignment before you try numerical analysis. Third, differentiate between facts, estimates, and assumptions or suppositions. As you read, ask yourself a broad range of questions: What are the problems and opportunities here? What information given will aid in solving these problems? What information is lacking? What is going on here? Why are these problems still unsolved? What is happening among the people in this organization? When you use an appropriate analytical technique, what will you learn? How sensitive is your analysis to changes? How probable are these changes? What assumptions and/or estimates do you have to make?

You should be very careful not to confuse the basic problem with its symptoms. For example, a decline in sales is probably a symptom of a problem, not the problem *per se*. Make sure you understand what background information is needed. Depending on the assignment, you might have to discuss factors inside the organization (management team, marketing issues, finances, etc.) and outside the organization (industry makeup, foreign competition, economic conditions, government regulations, etc.). The more a problem relates to strategic planning issues, the more important it is to identify the strengths and weaknesses of the company in relation to its internal and external environment.

In analyzing and planning how to respond to an assignment, do not be limited by the specific questions asked. Do not feel bound to address specific questions in lockstep. Remember that an assignment should be used as a springboard for any relevant issues that can usefully be brought into the analysis. Also, remember that you will write this response *after* having done all the supporting analysis. Thus, you should integrate your presentation. For example, if there are four sequential parts to an assignment, your answers to part 1 should not be presented as if you had not read and analyzed parts 2, 3, and 4.

Because an assignment extends the text in many instances, do not expect to always find specific text references or techniques for your analysis or solution. You might have to draw on ideas and/or techniques from several sources.

PERSPECTIVE OF WRITER AND READER

Take the detached role of a person observing the information and problem(s) who is analyzing and commenting on appropriate issues. Your audience is another person who is detached from the situation. Instructions should be clear about how much information your audience requires (how much background information is known and how much you should explain and/or summarize). If you are writing from the perspective of an outside consultant hired by a company or a member of management of a company, you are working with management to deal with appropriate issues. The assignment instructions or specific instructions from your instructor will let you know what perspective to take and for what audience. Knowing your audience should help you decide how much background information or explanation is appropriate.

HEADINGS

Headings provide transitions between sections and help the reader know where you are going. In addition, they provide a framework for your analysis and can help you write a more organized memorandum. They are valuable and you should use them whenever you change from one principal topic to another.

GENERAL WRITING GUIDELINES

The following guidelines for memoranda should be amended depending on your instructor and your assigned perspective (neutral, consultant, member of management).

Beginning/Introduction

The introduction to your analysis should include a statement of the problem(s) you have identified. You should state how you approached the analysis and solution to the problems and what courses of action you have identified. List the decisions you need to make. If you have made assumptions and/or estimates, state them clearly and justify them. If there is additional information that you could use to make a more informed decision, state what it is. Finally, include a brief summary of your conclusions (including actions recommended). Make sure that you use the specific evidence in the assignment to support your position.

The introduction sets the tone. Make sure that you build a sufficient foundation regarding the problems or issues, the facts, your approaches, etc. Make sure it is clear to the reader what you are doing and why.

Middle/Analysis

This is the heart of the memorandum, where you present your analyses and bases for your conclusions. What criteria are you using to select a course of action? What are the results of your analysis? Make sure to support your analysis. Do not make assertions without evidence or argument to support them. Here is where you need to spend the greatest amount of time and space. Your conclusions and recommendations should be clear and should logically follow your analysis. Finally, there must be a way to measure the consequences of your recommendations. Therefore, this section should:

1. Identify and explain courses of action open to the organization. Not all such courses of action are necessarily delineated in the assignment.
2. Clearly explain the criteria used to select the final course of action (increase profits, reduce risk, report only controllable costs). If criteria are mentioned in the assignment, you should evaluate them and justify their use. If no criteria are presented, you should develop realistic and applicable criteria through your analysis of the assignment's information and your knowledge from the course and from other courses.
3. Select a course of action. If appropriate, indicate how to implement your proposal.
4. Discuss means to measure the consequences of your recommendation(s). Establish standards by which the success or failure of your proposed course of action should be judged.

You should build a logical, integrated presentation, developing the ideas and issues within this section. Organization and the use of headings is very important. Everything should flow in a logical order; it should be clear how you have come to your conclusions and why you have made particular choices.

End/Conclusion

Your ending section should summarize your solutions. If there are unanswered questions, state them and indicate what you would do to resolve them. Give whatever recommendations you have. This final section should bring everything together in a natural end to the paper. There should be no surprises or new material; everything should continue logically from the previous sections and must be fully supported by discussion and facts presented earlier.

time value of money

Appendix C

Suppose you had the choice between receiving $10,000 now or one year from now. Suppose you are absolutely sure to receive $10,000 at either time. Virtually everyone would choose the first alternative. A dollar now is worth more than a dollar to be received in one year, or at any later date. This statement sums up an important principle: *money has a time value.* The reason that a dollar now is worth more than the certainty of a dollar to be received in the future is that you could invest the dollar now and have more than a dollar at the later date. It does not matter whether you expect inflation or deflation to change the purchasing power of money; you always prefer money now to the promise of *the same amount* of money later.

Many economic decisions involve investing money now in the hope of receiving *more* money later on. Any analysis of such decisions must consider the **time value of money**. Suppose you can invest $10,000 today with a promise that you will receive $10,800 at the end of one year. Should you make the investment? You know that to justify waiting for the money, the amount to be received should be larger than the amount available to you now. But how much larger? It depends on what else you could do with the cash you have to invest—the opportunities that are available.

Suppose your best alternative investment would earn 10% interest per year. If you invest $10,000 at 10% per year, you have $11,000 at the end of one year [$10,000 + ($10,000 × 10%)]. Comparing the two alternatives, you could have $11,000 at the end of the year as a result of a $10,000 investment now, or you could have $10,800 at the end of the year for a $10,000 investment now. You should choose the first alternative.

What happens when the time horizon is extended beyond one period? Suppose you can invest $10,000 today and receive $12,500 at the end of two years. Should you make the investment if the interest rate on another alternative is 10%? First determine how much you would have at the end of two years if you invested at a rate of 10%, as follows.

Now	You have $10,000
At the end of year 1	You have $11,000 [$10,000 + ($10,000 × 10%)]
At the end of year 2	You have $12,100 [$11,000 + ($11,000 × 10%)]

The interest earned in the second year is 10% of the total amount you have at the end of the first year, *not* 10% of the $10,000 you originally invested. This is **compound interest:** you earn the quoted interest rate both on the original amount invested and on the interest that you subsequently earn. The $12,100 you have at the end of two years is the **future value** of the $10,000 at a 10% interest rate. The $10,000 is the **present value** of $12,100 at a 10% interest rate.

By comparing the values of each available alternative at the end of the two years, you can see that you are better off to invest $10,000 now to receive $12,500 at the end of the two years. You could have only $12,100 by investing elsewhere. We show this by comparing the two values at the *end* of the investment term. The practice of comparing present values is more common.

PRESENT VALUE OF A SINGLE AMOUNT

To evaluate an opportunity to receive a single payment at some date in the future at some interest rate, we determine the present value of that choice. Instead of determining how much we would have at some future date if we invested $1 now, we want to know how much we would have to invest now to receive $1 at some future date. The preceding example showed that, at a 10% interest rate, an investment of $10,000 will accumulate to $12,100 at the end of two years. The present value of $12,100 two years from now at 10% is thus $10,000. The procedure to determine present values is called **discounting,** and the interest rate used is also called the **discount rate.** The amount of money to be received later is always a combination of the original investment (sometimes called *principal*) and the interest on that investment.

Formulas are available for determining the present value of a sum of money to be received in the future. Computer spreadsheets and many calculators have functions to find present and future values. You can also use tables to determine present values without the formulas. Suppose we want to find the present value of $1.21 to be received two years from now when we know that the interest rate is 10%. (We know already that the present value is $1, and this is the answer the table should give us.) Table A on page 740 shows the present value of $1 to be received at various times in the future and at various interest rates. Referring to the 10% column and the row for two periods, we find the factor .826. This means that the present value of $1 to be received two years from now is $0.826 when the interest rate is 10%. Because we expect to get $1.21 we multiply the factor by $1.21. This multiplication produces a present value of $0.99946, which is not significantly different from $1. (The slight difference is due to rounding in preparing the table.) The factors in Table A are generated by the following formula.

$$(1 + i)^{-n}$$

where

$$i = \text{the interest rate}$$
$$n = \text{the number of periods.}$$

Two characteristics of Table A are significant and should be understood. First, as you move down any column in Table A, the factors become smaller. You should expect this because the longer you must wait for a payment, the less it is worth now. If a dollar now is worth more than a dollar to be received in one year, then surely a dollar to be received one year later is worth more than one to come two years later. Second, the factors become smaller as you move across the table in any row. As the interest rate increases, the present value of the amount to be received in the future decreases. This should also be expected. The higher interest rate you can expect to earn on the sum invested now, the less you need to invest now to accumulate a given amount at the end of some number of years. In summary, the longer you have to wait for your money and the higher the interest rate you can earn, the less it is worth to you now to receive some specified amount at a future date.

PRESENT VALUE OF A STREAM OF EQUAL RECEIPTS

Sometimes it is necessary to compute the present value of a *series* of equal amounts to be received at the ends of a series of years. Such a stream is an **annuity** and describes, for example, bond interest received annually for a number of years. You can find the present value of an annuity by finding the present values of each component of the stream and adding them. For example, what is the present value of an annuity of $1 per year for four years at 10%?

Received at End of Year	Amount to Be Received	Present Value Factor (from Table A)	Present Value of Future Receipt
1	$1	.909	$0.909
2	$1	.826	0.826
3	$1	.751	0.751
4	$1	.683	0.683
Present value of annuity			$3.169

This procedure is cumbersome, especially if the annuity lasts for many years. You are multiplying the same number ($1) by several different numbers (the present value factors). From your study of mathematics, you know that the sum of these multiplications is equal to the product of the constant number ($1) and the sum of the different numbers. If you add up the present value factors (3.169) and multiply that sum by $1, you will get the same answer. (This can be verified at a glance because we are using an annuity of $1.)

Many practical situations deal with a series of equal receipts over several periods. These could be analyzed by using Table A and the lengthy procedure described above. But the task is made simpler by using a table like Table B on page 740, which adds the present value factors for you. Look at Table B in the column for 10% and the row for four periods. The factor is 3.170. This is the present value of a series of four $1 receipts when the interest rate is 10%. (The factor, 3.170, is rounded up from the sum of the factors given in Table A.)

The values shown in Table B are the cumulative sums of the factors from Table A (with an occasional rounding difference). The factor for an annuity for one period in Table B is the same as the factor for a single receipt in Table A, at the same interest rate. Try adding down Table A and checking each successive sum with the factor in Table B. The factors are generated by the formula,

$$\frac{1-(1+i)^{-n}}{i}$$

where

i = *the interest rate*
n = *the number of periods.*

All the factors in both tables relate to future receipts (or payments) of $1. When dealing with amounts other than $1, you multiply the factor by the number of dollars involved to compute the present value. But remember that you can use Table B only when all payments in the stream are equal.

STREAMS OF UNEQUAL AMOUNTS

What if the payments to be received in the future are *not* equal? You could use the factors from Table A, but that can be cumbersome. If *most* of the payments are equal, you can find the present value of the equal portions of each payment using Table B, then discount the remainder separately. We shall illustrate this method by modifying the previous example. Instead of receiving $1 per year for four years, you will receive $1 at the end of each of the first three years and $2 at the end of the fourth year.

From Table B we know that $1 per year for four years has a present value of $3.170 at 10%. That is the present value of the stream *except* for the extra $1 to be received at the end of year 4. Looking in Table A (for the present value of $1 to be received at the end of four years) we find that the extra $1 has a present value of $0.683. Adding the $0.683 to the $3.170, we obtain $3.853. We can check this by discounting each receipt separately.

Received at End of Year	Amount to Be Received	Present Value Factor (from Table A)	Present Value of Future Receipt
1	$1	.909	$0.909
2	$1	.826	0.826
3	$1	.751	0.751
4	$2	.683	1.366
Present value of this series of payments			$3.852*

**The difference ($0.001) is due to rounding.*

Suppose that only $0.60 is to be received at the end of the fourth year. We now have a stream of equal payments of $1 for three years, then a $0.60 payment at the end of the fourth year. Use Table B to find the present value of a stream of $1 payments for three years, then add to it the present value of $0.60 to be received at the end of four years (from Table A). The solution is as follows.

Present value of $1 per year for 3 years at 10% ($1 × 2.487)	$2.4870
Present value of $0.60 at end of year 4 at 10% ($0.60 × .683)	0.4098
Present value of this series of payments	$2.8968

COMPUTATIONS FOR PERIODS OTHER THAN YEARS

It is common practice to quote an annual interest rate. Nevertheless, many investments make payments more than once a year. For example, a savings bank might credit interest quarterly or even daily, and interest on most bonds is paid semiannually.

If interest is *compounded* more often than annually, the rate of interest actually earned is higher than the quoted interest rate. Suppose a savings bank pays 6% annual interest compounded semiannually. How much will you have at the end of a year if you deposit $1,000 today? You earn $30 for the first six months ($1,000 × 0.06 × 1/2). For the second six months, you earn interest on $1,030 ($1,000 + $30) and the interest earned is $30.90 ($1,030 × 0.06 × 1/2). Hence, at the end of the year you have $1,060.90. In effect, you earned at the rate of 6.09% per year, because the interest of $60.90 for one year is 6.09% of the $1,000 investment. The 6.09% is called the **effective interest rate** and must be distinguished from the quoted, or **nominal interest rate** of 6%. We could say that the investment is earning 3% *per period* (6% divided by the two compoundings per year). You are earning 3% on the investment at the beginning of each period. For any given nominal interest rate, the effective interest rate rises as the number of compoundings per year increases.

Compound interest tables such as Tables A and B are constructed on the basis of an interest rate *per period.* Therefore, you must be careful to determine the interest rate you should use in any given situation. If you want the present value of an amount to be received ten years from now using an *effective* rate of 10%, you look in Table A in the 10% column and the row for ten periods. (Remember that an effective rate is a rate per year.) If, on the other hand, you want the present value of an amount to be received ten years from now using a nominal interest rate of 10% compounded semiannually, you look in Table A in the *5% column* (10% divided by the number of compoundings per year) and the row for *20 periods* (10 years × the number of compoundings per year).

In most situations you know the nominal interest rate. Therefore, to complete the desired computation you convert the nominal rate to a rate per compounding period and revise the number of periods to take into account the compoundings. *When consulting the tables, the number of periods is the number of years times the number of compoundings per year, and the interest rate is the nominal annual rate divided by the number of compoundings per year.* Doing this you are stating the interest rate per compounding period.

One practical example involves applying almost every technique in this appendix. Suppose you can buy a bond that will mature in ten years. The bond carries a nominal interest rate of 6%, and interest is paid semiannually. You *want* to earn 10% compounded semiannually. How much would you be willing to pay for a bond with a face (maturity) value of $10,000?

First, you must recognize that your investment has two components. If you buy the bond you contract to receive (1) $10,000 ten years from now and (2) payments of $300 ($10,000 × 0.06 × 1/2) every six months for ten years. What is each of these components worth to you now? The price you would be willing to pay for the bond is the sum of the present values of the components.

To compute the price you would pay for the bond, you need the following.

1. The present value of $10,000 to be received ten years from now. You want to earn 10% compounded semiannually, so you refer to Table A for the present value factor for 20 periods (10 years × 2 compoundings) at 5% (10% divided by 2 compoundings). The factor is .377, so the present value you are looking for is $3,770 ($10,000 × .377).
2. The present value of an annuity of $300 to be received each six months for ten years. You want to earn 10% compounded semiannually, so you refer to Table B for the present value factor for 20 periods (10 years × 2 compoundings) at 5% (10% divided by 2 compoundings). The factor is 12.462, so the present value you are looking for is $3,739 ($300 × 12.462).

Thus, the price you would pay for this $10,000, 6% bond is $7,509 ($3,770 + $3,739). Note that the interest rate per period (5%) and the number of periods (20) are the same for both calculations. The bond is a single investment and earns a single rate of interest even though it provides both a single payment and an annuity.

USES AND SIGNIFICANCE OF PRESENT VALUES

Should you invest a sum of money now in order to receive a larger amount later (whether the amount comes in a single payment, a stream of payments or both)? Your decision should be based on the amounts of the cash to be invested and received later, the length of time over which the inflows are received, and the interest rate.

When the dollars to be received in the future are known, you can refer to the tables for an appropriate factor, multiply by the number of dollars to be received in the future, and compare that amount with the money that must be invested now to receive the amount or amounts in the future. If the result of the multiplication is greater than the amount to be invested now, the present value of the future returns is greater than the investment and the investment is desirable. Such an investment has a positive **net present value (NPV)**. If the result of the multiplication is smaller than the required investment, the opportunity is not desirable. (It has a negative NPV.)

The most common use of present value is to find values of future payments. In some situations, however, you want to find the interest rate earned by investing so many dollars now and receiving so many in the future. The procedures are discussed in the next section.

DETERMINING INTEREST RATES

When you wish to know the interest rate on an investment with known future receipts, you also use present value tables. The interest rate is also called the **discount rate,** the **time-adjusted rate of return,** or the **internal rate of return (IRR)**. The last term is the most common.

To find the present value of a stream of equal future receipts (annuity), you multiplied the annuity by a factor that incorporated both the length of the series of receipts and the interest rate being earned. This can be shown mathematically.

$$\textit{Present value of future receipt(s)} = \textit{amount of each future receipt} \times \textit{factor for discount rate and waiting period (present value factor)}$$

In previous examples, you were looking for the value to the left of the equal sign. In trying to find the interest rate on a given investment when you know the future receipts, you look for the interest rate that *equates* the present value of the future receipts with the investment required to produce those receipts. Using the preceding equation, you state that the value to the left of the equal sign is the investment required now. You know the amount of the future receipts, and you know one element in determining the factor required—the waiting period. You want the missing element in our equation—the interest rate, or IRR.

Suppose you can invest $3,791 today and receive $1,000 per year for five years beginning one year from now, and you want to know the interest rate you would be earning. Substituting in the preceding equation yields

$$\$3{,}791 = \$1{,}000 \times \textit{(the factor for the interest rate for five periods)}$$

The factor is 3.791, which is obtained by rearranging the equation to show

$$\textit{Present value factor for five periods} = \$3{,}791/\$1{,}000 = 3.791$$

The $1,000 payments are an annuity, so you can look in Table B for the factor in the five-period *row* that is closest to 3.791. That exact factor is found in the 10% column, so the investment yields a rate of return of 10%. (We can check this by multiplying $1,000 by 3.791, giving $3,791 as the present value.) In general terms, this basic equation can also be shown as

$$\textit{Present value factor} = \frac{\textit{present value of receipts (required investment)}}{\textit{periodic receipts}}$$

The basic formula can also be used with a single payment. Suppose you could receive $1,450 at the end of four years if you invested $1,000 today. The factor to look for in *Table A* is 0.690 (rounded), which is $1,000/$1,450. Looking across the four-period row in Table A, we come to .683 in the 10% column. The rate of return is therefore a bit less than 10%.

You can also use this modification of the basic equation if you know the receipts, the amount of investment (which is the present value), and the interest rate, but you want to know the length of time. Suppose you could invest $1,000 now and receive $300 per year, but the number of years is uncertain. If you want a 14% rate of return, you can compute the number of years over which you would have to receive the $300 payments.

$$\textit{Present value factor} = \frac{\$1{,}000}{\$300} = 3.333$$

This factor is for 14% and an unknown number of years. Therefore you look down the 14% column in Table B and find that 3.433 is the factor for five years. If you received five $300 annual payments you would earn slightly more than the desired 14%.

DETERMINING REQUIRED RECEIPTS

For some decisions you want to know the receipts, either single payment or annuity, needed to earn a particular interest rate (or IRR), given the necessary investment and the life of the receipts. The basic formula can be rearranged as follows.

$$\textit{Periodic receipt} = \frac{\textit{present value of receipts (required investment)}}{\textit{present value factor}}$$

Suppose you can invest $10,000 now expecting to receive $3,000 per year for six years. You would like to earn a 12% return. If you *do* receive $3,000 per year, your rate of return will be about 20% ($10,000/$3,000 = 3.33, which is close to the factor for 20% and six years). However, you are uncertain whether you *will* actually receive $3,000 and want to know the minimum annual receipt for six years that will give a 12% return.

$$\textit{Periodic receipt} = \frac{\$10{,}000}{\textit{4.111 (the factor for six years and 12\%)}} = \$2{,}432$$

Thus, if you receive at least $2,432 each year for the next six years you will earn at least a 12% return.

This method can also be applied to single payments; the only difference is the table to be used. Suppose you can invest $1,000 and receive a single payment at the end of five years. If you wish to earn a 14% return, you would have to receive $1,927 (rounded), which is $1,000/.519, the factor for a single payment at 14% at the end of five periods.

SUMMARY

Many decisions involve cash inflows and outflows at different times. Such situations require recognizing the time value of money. To evaluate a situation that involves cash flows occurring at different times, it is necessary to use the values of those flows at the same point in time.

Almost all managerial accounting decisions involving cash flows at different times use the present value of those flows as the point of analysis. The present value of a single cash flow at some time in the future can be computed manually or determined with the help of tables such as Table A. When several future cash flows are involved, it is usually easier to compute their present value by using tables such as Table B. Although tables such as Table B apply only when the individual amounts in the series of cash flows are equal, it is possible to deal with uneven cash flows by using Tables A and B.

The present value of a future cash flow (or a series of future cash flows) depends on the amount of the flow(s), the interest (discount) rate, and the length of the waiting period. Sometimes, the present value is known, but one of the other elements is not. The tables can also be used to determine the value of the unknown element.

Applications of the concept of present values include the computation of bond prices and the evaluation of other long-term investment opportunities. Chapters 8, 9, and Appendix A of this book include managerial decisions that must be analyzed using present values. The use of present values is not limited to accounting. You may apply your knowledge of present values in the study of economics, finance, and statistics.

KEY TERMS

annuity
compound interest
discounting
discount rate
effective interest rate
future value
internal rate of return (IRR)
net present value (NPV)
nominal interest rate
present value
time-adjusted rate of return
time value of money

KEY FORMULAS

$$\text{Present value of future receipts(s)} = \text{amount of each future receipt} \times \text{factor for discount rate and waiting period (present value factor)}$$

$$\text{Present value factor} = \frac{\text{present value of receipts (required investment)}}{\text{periodic receipts}}$$

$$\text{Periodic receipt} = \frac{\text{present value of receipts (required investment)}}{\text{present value factor}}$$

REVIEW PROBLEMS

1. Find the present value of the following sets of payments if the discount rate is (a) 10% and (b) 16%.

Received at End of Year	Amount i	ii	iii	iv
1	$1,000	$2,000	$1,500	$ 0
2	1,000	2,000	2,000	3,000
3	1,000	2,000	2,000	3,000
4	1,000	2,000	2,000	3,000
5		5,000		4,000

2. Find the discount rates for the following situations.

Case	Investment Required Now	Periodic Receipts	Number of Years for Receipts
i	$ 3,605	$1,000	5
ii	$12,300	$2,000	10
iii	$ 9,380	$3,000	5

3. Fill in the blanks for each of the following situations. All involve a single payment to be received at the end of the number of years given.

Case	Investment	Year in Which Payment to Be Received	Payment to Be Received	Interest Rate
i	$____	4	$4,000	14%
ii	$1,000	5	$1,464	____
iii	$3,000	__	$5,290	10%
iv	$5,000	7	_____	14%

4. Fill in the blanks for each of the following situations. All involve streams of equal annual payments. Round dollar calculations to the nearest $1.

Case	Investment	Annual Cash Payments	Number of Years Payments to be Received	Interest Rate
i	$_____	$1,000	10	14%
ii	$10,000	_____	8	10%
iii	$20,000	$5,000	__	8%
iv	$10,000	$2,000	8	____

ANSWERS TO REVIEW PROBLEMS

1. i. Stream of equal payments of $1,000 per year for four years.
   (a) At 10%—3.170 × $1,000 = $3,170
   (b) At 16%—2.798 × $1,000 = $2,798

   ii. Stream of four equal payments and larger amount at end of fifth year. We will discount the four equal payments and add the present value of the fifth one.

(a) At 10%—3.170 × $2,000	$6,340
(Table A, five years, 10%) .621 × $5,000	3,105
	$9,445
(b) At 16%—2.798 × $2,000	$5,596
(Table A, five years, 16%) .476 × $5,000	2,380
	$7,976

iii. Stream of unequal payments for four years. The easiest method is to find the present value of a $2,000 stream of payments for four years and subtract the present value of $500 at the end of one year.

(a) 10%—3.170 × $2,000	$6,340.00
(Table A, one year, 10%) .909 × $500	(454.50)
	$5,885.50
(b) At 16%—2.798 × $2,000	$5,596.00
(Table A, one year, 16%) .862 × $500	(431.00)
	$5,165.00

iv. Stream of unequal payments beginning at the end of year two. Although there are shortcuts, it is probably simplest to discount separately.

(a) At 10%

Received at End of Year	Amount to Be Received	Present Value Factor (From Table A)	Present Value of Future Receipt
1	0		
2	$3,000	.826	$2,478
3	$3,000	.751	2,253
4	$3,000	.683	2,049
5	$4,000	.621	2,484
Present value of this series			$9,264

(b) At 16% the present value is $7,712. Computations are similar to those for (a), except that the factors for 16% are used.

2. All of these problems require the use of Table B.

$$\frac{\text{Investment required}}{\text{periodic receipt}} = \text{the factor}$$

i.

$$\frac{\$3{,}605}{\$1{,}000} = 3.605 \text{ for five years} = 12\%$$

ii.

$$\frac{\$12{,}300}{\$2{,}000} = 6.15 \text{ for ten years; } 6.145 \text{ for } 10\% \text{ is the closest factor}$$

iii.

$$\frac{\$9{,}380}{\$3{,}000} = 3.126 \text{ for five years; closest factor is } 3.127 \text{ for } 18\%$$

3. All of these problems require the use of Table A.
   i. $2,368. $4,000 × .592 (the factor for 14% for four years)
   ii. About 8%. $1,000/$1,464 = .683, which is very close to .681, the factor for a single payment in five years at 8%.
   iii. About six years. $3,000/$5,290 = .567, which is very close to the 6-year factor at 10% (.564). In this case, you know the interest rate, so you are looking for the column with a factor that is closest to .567.
   iv. $12,500. $5,000/.400 (the factor for seven years at 14%)
4. All of these problems are solved by using Table B and the equation

   Present value = annual payment × present value factor

The present value, in each case, is the amount of the investment.

   i. $5,216. $1,000 × 5.216 (the factor for ten periods at 14%)

ii. $1,874. $10,000/5.335 (the factor for eight periods at 10%)
iii. About five years. $20,000/$5,000 = 4.0, which is the factor for 8% and an unknown number of years. Moving down the 8% column in Table B, we find 3.993, which is the closest factor to 4.0 under 8%.
iv. About 12%. $10,000/$2,000 = 5.0, which is the factor for eight years and an unknown interest rate. The closest factor in the 8-period row is 4.968, which is the factor for 12%. The true rate is slightly less than 12%.

ASSIGNMENT MATERIAL

C-1 Computations—present values Find the present value of the following sets of payments if the discount rate is as noted for each set.

Received at End of Year	Set A at 8%	Set B at 10%	Set C at 20%
1		$2,000	($3,000)
2		2,000	4,000
3		2,000	4,000
4		2,000	4,000
5		2,000	4,000
8	$10,000		

C-2 Missing factors Fill in the blanks for each of the following independent investment opportunities.

Case	Investment Required Now	Periodic Receipt	Number of Years of Receipt	Interest (Discount) Rate
A	$16,950	$3,000	10	__%
B	$16,775	______	10	8%
C	$______	$5,000	13	18%
D	$10,000	$2,500	__	24%

C-3 Computation of bond prices You are considering investing in some corporate bonds. Each bond is different, and because the companies are different, you believe you should earn a different rate of interest (effective interest rate) on each investment. The relevant data for each bond are provided below.

	Bond of Company		
	A	B	C
Face value	$10,000	$5,000	$20,000
Nominal (stated) interest rate	10%	8%	6%
Years to maturity	7	8	7
Interest paid	Annually	Annually	Semiannually
Desired interest rate	12%	10%	10%

Required
Compute the price you would pay for each bond.

C-4 Present values and rates of return The following information is available about two investments.

	A	B
Required investment now	$10,000	$20,000
Cash flows, annually for 7 years	$ 2,500	$ 4,700

Required

1. Compute the approximate IRR for each investment.
2. Compute the present value of each investment if the desired rate of return is 10%.
3. Determine the annual cash flows that would have to be received for each year in the 7-year period to make each investment provide a 16% return.
4. For each investment, determine the number of years that the stated annual cash flows would have to be received to make the investment provide a 20% return.

C-5 Present values—unusual timing Many situations involve cash flows occurring at or near the end of a period. Still others involve flows at or near the beginning of a period. Tables A and B can be used to deal with both types of situations. For each of the following situations, compute the present value of the cash flows described.

(a) A receipt of $5,000 four years from today; the interest rate is 9%.
(b) A receipt of $1,000 per year at the beginning of each of five years beginning today; the interest rate is 8%.
(c) A receipt of $10,000 per year for seven years, the first receipt to arrive exactly six years from today; the interest rate is 12%.

C-6 Relationships Fill in the blanks for each of the following investments.

	Case			
Item	1	2	3	4
a. Investment required now	______	$416,250	$32,280	______
b. Present value at desired rate of return	______	______	$31,080	$358,000
c. Annual cash receipt	$9,000	$125,000	______	$ 50,000
d. No. of years cash to be received	16	8	4	______
e. Desired rate of return	16%	14%	______	9%
f. Rate of return yielded	20%	______	18%	14%

Table A
Present Value of $1

Number of Periods	5%	6%	8%	9%	10%	12%	14%	16%	18%	20%	22%	24%	25%
	Interest Rates												
1	.952	.943	.926	.917	.909	.893	.877	.862	.847	.833	.820	.806	.800
2	.907	.890	.857	.842	.826	.797	.769	.743	.718	.694	.672	.650	.640
3	.864	.840	.794	.772	.751	.712	.675	.641	.609	.579	.551	.524	.512
4	.823	.792	.735	.708	.683	.636	.592	.552	.516	.482	.451	.423	.410
5	.784	.747	.681	.650	.621	.567	.519	.476	.437	.402	.370	.341	.328
6	.746	.705	.630	.596	.564	.507	.456	.410	.370	.335	.303	.275	.262
7	.711	.665	.583	.547	.513	.452	.400	.354	.314	.279	.249	.222	.210
8	.677	.628	.541	.502	.467	.404	.351	.305	.266	.233	.204	.179	.168
9	.645	.592	.500	.460	.424	.361	.308	.263	.225	.194	.167	.144	.134
10	.614	.558	.463	.422	.386	.322	.270	.227	.191	.162	.137	.116	.107
11	.585	.527	.429	.387	.350	.287	.237	.195	.162	.135	.112	.094	.086
12	.557	.497	.397	.355	.319	.257	.208	.168	.137	.112	.092	.076	.069
13	.530	.469	.368	.326	.290	.229	.183	.145	.116	.093	.075	.061	.055
14	.505	.442	.340	.299	.263	.205	.160	.125	.099	.078	.062	.049	.044
15	.481	.417	.315	.274	.239	.183	.140	.108	.084	.065	.051	.040	.035
16	.458	.394	.292	.251	.218	.163	.123	.093	.071	.054	.042	.032	.028
20	.377	.312	.215	.178	.149	.104	.073	.051	.037	.026	.019	.014	.012
30	.231	.174	.099	.075	.057	.033	.020	.012	.007	.004	.003	.002	.001

Table B
Present Value of $1 Annuity

Number of Periods	5%	6%	8%	9%	10%	12%	14%	16%	18%	20%	22%	24%	25%
	Interest Rates												
1	.952	.943	.926	.917	.909	.893	.877	.862	.847	.833	.820	.806	.800
2	1.859	1.833	1.783	1.759	1.736	1.690	1.647	1.605	1.566	1.528	1.492	1.457	1.440
3	2.723	2.673	2.577	2.531	2.487	2.402	2.322	2.246	2.174	2.106	2.042	1.981	1.952
4	3.546	3.465	3.312	3.240	3.170	3.037	2.914	2.798	2.690	2.589	2.494	2.404	2.362
5	4.329	4.212	3.993	3.890	3.791	3.605	3.433	3.274	3.127	2.991	2.864	2.745	2.689
6	5.076	4.917	4.623	4.486	4.355	4.111	3.889	3.685	3.498	3.326	3.167	3.020	2.951
7	5.786	5.582	5.206	5.033	4.868	4.564	4.288	4.039	3.812	3.605	3.416	3.242	3.161
8	6.463	6.210	5.747	5.535	5.335	4.968	4.639	4.344	4.077	3.837	3.619	3.421	3.329
9	7.108	6.802	6.247	5.996	5.759	5.328	4.946	4.607	4.303	4.031	3.786	3.566	3.463
10	7.722	7.360	6.710	6.418	6.145	5.650	5.216	4.833	4.494	4.192	3.923	3.682	3.571
11	8.306	7.887	7.139	6.805	6.495	5.988	5.453	5.029	4.656	4.327	4.035	3.776	3.656
12	8.863	8.384	7.536	7.160	6.814	6.194	5.660	5.197	4.793	4.439	4.127	3.851	3.725
13	9.394	8.853	7.904	7.487	7.103	6.424	5.842	5.342	4.910	4.533	4.203	3.912	3.780
14	9.899	9.295	8.244	7.786	7.367	6.628	6.002	5.468	5.008	4.611	4.265	3.962	3.824
15	10.380	9.712	8.559	8.061	7.606	6.811	6.142	5.575	5.092	4.675	4.315	4.001	3.859
16	10.838	10.106	8.851	8.313	7.824	6.974	6.265	5.669	5.162	4.730	4.357	4.033	3.887
20	12.462	11.470	9.818	9.129	8.514	7.469	6.623	5.929	5.353	4.870	4.460	4.110	3.954
30	15.372	13.765	11.258	10.274	9.427	8.055	7.003	6.177	5.517	4.979	4.534	4.160	3.995

statement of cash flows

Appendix D

An accounting information system must serve both financial and managerial accounting. Much of the information prepared for distribution outside the firm is used by the firm's managers. For example, data from income statements and balance sheets are used for performance measurement and budgeting.

A third statement commonly used in financial accounting is the statement of cash flows. This chapter discusses its content and development.

INTEREST IN CASH FLOWS

Profitability is but one of the factors important for the survival and growth of the firm. Also important are current and future inflows and outflows of cash. From Chapter 7 we know that managers develop cash budgets to anticipate potential shortages of cash needed for carrying out plans. (Will cash be available for planned operating levels? for capital expenditures? for dividends? for repaying debt?)

Managers are responsible for planning how and when cash will be obtained and used. When planned cash outflows are more than planned inflows, managers must decide what to do. At times, they obtain financing (through borrowing or issuing stock) or dispose of some existing investment (by selling some asset, or perhaps an entire segment of the business). At other times, they curtail planned activities by revising their plans for operations (e.g., dropping a special advertising campaign) or new investments (e.g., delaying acquisition of new machinery). Or, they might revise planned payments to financing sources (e.g., delay debt repayment or reduce dividends). Whatever they do, the managers' goal is to balance the cash available and the needs for cash.

Lenders, stockholders, suppliers, and other outsiders are also aware of the importance of planning and of decisions for balancing available cash and cash needs. They know that cash flows into the firm from operations, financing sources, and sales of fixed assets and other investments. They know that cash is used for operations, dividends, repayment of debt, and expansion. They are interested in cash flows and changes in cash because these reflect the firm's decisions for implementing its short-term and long-term plans for operations, investment, and financing. Stated more generally, outsiders are interested in information about the firm's **operating**, **investing**, and **financing activities** and the cash flows generated by those activities. The cash flow statement provides the interested reader with further information to assess managerial decisions and performance and prospects for future profit, payments to financing sources, and growth.

CASH FLOW STATEMENT

Because the cash flow statement is distributed outside the firm, its form and content are governed by official pronouncements on generally accepted accounting principles (GAAP).[1] As you might have guessed from the preceding discussion, the **cash flow statement** has three basic parts, which classify the firm's cash inflows and outflows as related to operating, investing, or financing activities. The following lists provide examples.

Operating flows: Inflows include cash received from customers, and for interest and dividends on investments. Outflows include cash paid for inventory, salaries and wages, taxes, and other expenses, including interest.

Investing flows: Inflows include receipts from sales of long-lived assets, such as property, plant, equipment, and patents and from sales of investments. Cash outlays to acquire these same types of assets, or to lend to others, are examples of investing outflows.

Financing flows: Inflows include cash received from long-term or short-term borrowing and from issuing stock. Dividends, purchases of treasury stock, and repayments of borrowings are examples of financing outflows.

Most cash flows are easy to classify. An important exception is interest payments. These cash outflows to providers of debt capital are included among the operating flows. Dividend payments to providers of equity capital are, however, reported among the financing flows. A major reason for this exception appears to be a desire to include all items affecting net income among operating cash flows. The Financial Accounting Standards Board (FASB) requires that cash paid for interest be reported separately.[2]

---

1 *The official pronouncement governing cash flow statements is Statement of Financial Accounting Standards Board, No. 95 (Stamford, Conn., Financial Accounting Standards Board, 1987). That Pronouncement is the source of statements in the chapter about GAAP requirements.*

2 *The same reasoning applies to interest and dividend revenues. However, the FASB required separate disclosure of these revenues only if a firm presents its operating cash flows using the "direct method." This method is discussed later.*

Beyond the basic classification scheme, a few other considerations affect the content and format of a cash flow statement. Before we present an example of a typical statement and illustrate its development, we discuss the three most important of these considerations.

DEFINING CASH

Cash is an extremely important asset, one the firm cannot get along without. Financial managers often invest cash in excess of immediate needs in highly liquid, income-producing securities such as government notes. In such cases, the firm's *immediately usable* funds include not only its cash but also those highly liquid securities (called **cash equivalents**).

To recognize the liquidity of short-term investments, GAAP require that the cash flow statement be based on the combination of cash and cash equivalents. That is, the amount reported as the net change in cash resulting from all types of activities equals the change in the sum of cash and cash equivalents. The practical implications of using the sum are that the cash relating to the purchases and sales of such securities will not be reported among the investing activities, and that the gain or loss from sales of the securities will be included among the operating cash flows.

REPORTING OPERATING CASH FLOWS

As stated above, both internal and external users of financial statements normally view the income statement as a report of a firm's operating activities. Now, reread the examples of operating cash flows provided earlier. Does the income statement report these inflows and outflows? Does reported net income equal the net cash flow from operating activities? The answer to both questions is "no."

From your study of financial accounting you know that the income statement is prepared using the accrual basis of accounting and does not necessarily reflect cash transactions relating to operations. (Studying comprehensive budgeting reinforces the distinction between accrual accounting, which is the basis for pro forma financial statements, and cash flows. Thus, desired information about operating cash flows is not available directly from an income statement.

To meet the need for information about cash flows relating to operating activities, two reporting approaches have achieved general acceptance and are permitted by the FASB. The first approach, called the **direct method**, separately reports operating cash inflows and outflows as described earlier. A reporting of operating cash flows under this approach resembles a cash budget showing receipts and disbursements for operations. The second approach, called the **indirect method**, reports only the net cash flow from operations, but does so by presenting reported net income and then adjusting that amount for the effects of *noncash* items that affected net income. Thus, the indirect approach neither reports inflows and outflows separately nor describes the major outflows. Rather, it reconciles reported income and net cash flows from operations. This calculation is often called a **reconciliation of net income and cash flow from operations**. We use the indirect method in the sample format and the illustration to be presented shortly, because you will have to understand the reconciliation approach whether or not the cash flow statement uses that method of presentation. The direct method will be illustrated later.

NONCASH TRANSACTIONS

Some significant operating, investing, and financing activities do not affect cash. For example, suppose a firm issues a ten-year note to buy machinery. Acquiring machinery is an investment; issuing the note is a financing activity. Alternatively, suppose the firm settles some of its long-term debt by issuing common stock. Both the issuance of stock and the reduction of debt affect the financing of the firm, but do not affect cash.

Although flows of cash (and cash equivalents) are important, a statement of operating, investing, and financing activities should not ignore such transactions as those listed above. Accordingly, *significant activities not involving cash must also be reported,* either in a separate schedule or in narrative form. Whichever alternative is adopted, great care must be taken to report these noncash transactions in a way that clearly reflects the net cash flow for each of the three major types of activities. For simplicity, we use the separate schedule approach in the sample format and basic illustration.

FORMAT OF THE STATEMENT

Exhibit D-1 shows a skeleton outline of a cash flow statement. It uses the indirect method of presenting operating cash flows and reports important noncash transactions in a separate schedule.

Note the descriptions of the net cash flow in each of the three major sections. Depending on the transactions during the year, the net flow in any section could be an inflow or an outflow and the description would be worded accordingly.

With this outline in mind, we shall illustrate the development of a cash flow statement.

ILLUSTRATION

The basis for our illustration is USL Corporation, a retailer whose financial statements are provided in Exhibits D-2 and D-3. Exhibit D-3 also includes information about some USL activities in 19X5. For convenience, in Exhibit D-3 we have shown the increase or decrease in each balance-sheet item.

The comparative balance sheets show that USL's cash decreased $174,500 and that there are no short-term investments that might qualify as cash equivalents. Our objective, then, is to develop a statement that shows how USL's operating, investing, and financing activities combined to produce that decrease. If the net result of all such activities during the current year was to decrease cash by $174,500, the changes in the *other* items in the balance sheet must also reflect the effects of such activities during the year. We will refer to these other changes as we develop the cash flow statement. Let us begin by determining cash flow from operations.

Exhibit D-1 Example Company, Statement of Cash Flows of 19X8

Net cash flow from operating activities:		
Net income	**xxx**	
Adjustments for noncash expenses, revenues, losses, and gains included in income:		
	(xxx)	
	xxx	
Net cash flow from (for) operating activities		**xxx**
Cash flows from investing activities:		
	xxx	
	(xxx)	
	xxx	
Net cash provided (used) by investing activities		**xxx**
Cash flows from financing activities:		
	xxx	
	(xxx)	
	xxx	
Net cash provided (used) by financing activities		**xxx**
Net increase (decrease) in cash		**xxx**
Cash balance, beginning of year		**xx**
Cash balance, end of year		**xxx**
Schedule of Noncash Investing and Financing Activities:		
	xxx	
	xxx	
	xxx	

Cash from Operations

We want to know net cash flow from operating activities. Using the indirect method, we must begin with net income, which was $229,500. (Note that in analyzing net income we are dealing with one of the two factors contributing to the net change in Retained Earnings. Dividends are the other factor.) Deriving net operating cash flow from net income is not difficult if you keep in mind the makeup of the income statement and the balance sheet. Look at Exhibit D-2 and ask yourself the following questions. Why might revenues on the income statement differ from cash collected from customers? Why would cost of goods sold and the various expenses differ from the cash disbursed for purchases and expenses? The answers to these questions give the content of the adjustments section of the cash flow statement.

Revenues Versus Cash Inflows Differences between sales and cash receipts occur for two reasons. First, early in the year cash was received from customers for sales made last year and included in last year's income statement. (This amount was the beginning balance of accounts receivable.) Second, for

Exhibit D-2 USL Corporation Combined Statement of Income and Retained Earnings for 19X5

Sales		$1,000,000
Cost of goods sold		
Beginning inventory	$100,000	
Purchases	540,000	
Cost of goods available for sale	640,000	
Less ending inventory	190,000	
Cost of goods sold		450,000
Gross profit		550,000
Expenses:		
Depreciation	56,000	
Interest	12,000	
Income taxes	123,700	
Other	128,800	
Total expenses		320,500
Net income		229,500
Retained earnings at the beginning of the year		190,000
		419,500
Dividends declared and paid during the year		30,000
Retained earnings at the end of the year		$ 389,500

Second, for some sales made late in the year, cash will not be collected until next year. (Amounts still due at year's end are accounts receivable at the end of the year.) Thus, net income reflects sales made this year regardless of the period in which cash was collected, while cash receipts reflect cash collected this year regardless of the period in which the sales were made. To move from the amount of net income to the cash flow for the year, we must (1) add the accounts receivable at the beginning of the year, and (2) subtract the accounts receivable at the end of the year. In the case of USL Corporation, we add $130,000 and subtract $272,000, or we can simply subtract the $142,000 increase in Accounts Receivable. This is the first adjustment on the statement. (You might want to look briefly now at the completed statement shown in Exhibit D-4.)

Cost of Sales Versus Cash Outflows Consider next why there would be a difference between cost of goods sold ($450,000) on the income statement and the amount of cash actually paid for merchandise. Two factors create a difference.

First, the beginning and ending inventories affect cost of goods sold for the year regardless of the year in which the firm pays for inventory. The beginning inventory increased cost of goods sold and so decreased net income; the ending inventory decreased cost of goods sold and so increased

Exhibit D-3 USL Corporation Balance Sheets as of December 31

	19X5	19X4	Increase (Decrease)
Assets			
Current assets:			
Cash	$ 185,500	$ 360,000	($174,500)
Accounts receivable, net	272,000	130,000	142,000
Inventory	190,000	100,000	90,000
Prepaid expenses	8,000	20,000	(12,000)
Total current assets	655,500	610,000	
Noncurrent assets:			
Plant and equipment, at cost	928,000	600,000	328,000
Les accumulated depreciation	215,000	160,000	55,000
Total noncurrent assets	713,000	440,000	
Total assets	$1,368,500	$1,050,000	
Equities			
Current liabilities:			
Short-term bank loan	$ 34,000	$ 50,000	(16,000)
Accounts payable	135,000	105,000	30,000
Accrued expenses—taxes	38,000	2,000	36,000
—wages	12,000	3,000	9,000
Total current liabilities	219,000	160,000	
Bonds payable, due 19X9	100,000	100,000	
Total liabilities	319,000	260,000	
Owners' equity:			
Common stock	660,000	600,000	60,000
Retained earnings	389,500	190,000	199,500
Total owners' equity	1,049,500	790,000	
Total equities	$1,368,500	$1,050,000	

Additional information:

The company issued common stock for $22,000 cash and $38,000 for new equipment.

USL obtained a new short-term bank loan for $80,000 and paid off a total of $96,000 on that loan and other loans.

The company sold equipment that had cost $10,000 and had $1,000 accumulated depreciation for $9,000.

The company bought new plant and equipment for $300,000 cash (in addition to that acquired by issuing stock).

net income. Thus, net income reflects the effects of inventories, while cash payments for merchandise have no relationship to whether the items were or are on hand. To remove from net income the effect of inventories, we must (1) add the beginning inventory, and (2) subtract the ending inventory. In USL's case, we add $100,000 and subtract $190,000, or we can simply subtract the $90,000 increase. This is the second adjustment in the statement in Exhibit D-4.

The second reason for a difference between cost of goods sold and cash outflows for merchandise is that cost of goods sold shows the merchandise purchases made this year regardless of when the purchased merchandise was paid for. From your knowledge of financial accounting you know two things. First, early in the year cash was paid for purchases made in the prior year. (This amount was the beginning balance in accounts payable.) Second, some purchases made late in the year will not be paid for until the next year. (Unpaid amounts at the year's end are the ending balance in accounts payable). Thus, the cost of goods sold as shown in this year's income statement can be higher or lower than cash payments for merchandise, depending on the relationship between the beginning and ending balance in Accounts Payable. To move from net income to the cash flow for the year, we must (1) subtract the accounts payable at the beginning of the year and (2) add the accounts payable at the end of the year. In the case of USL, we subtract $105,000 and add $135,000, or we can simply add the $30,000 increase. This is the third adjustment in Exhibit D-4.

Operating Expenses and Cash Outflows Finally, let us consider why other expenses shown on the income statement do not equal the cash disbursements. One reason for a difference is well known to you. The first expense listed, depreciation, requires no current disbursement of cash. Depreciation expense reduced net income without having any effect on cash flows this period. Hence, to remove from net income the effect of depreciation expense, we must add depreciation (in USL's case, $56,000) to net income. This is the fourth adjustment in Exhibit D-4.

There are two other reasons for the difference between the amounts shown in the income statement for various expenses and the cash payments for such expenses: accruals and prepayments. Let us consider accruals first.

In the early part of the year cash is paid to liquidate liabilities for expenses of the prior year (accrued expenses at the beginning of the year); in the latter part of the year expenses are incurred for which cash will not be disbursed until the next year (the ending balance of accrued expenses). Thus, the current year's income is reduced by this year's expenses regardless of the year in which the payments were made. To move from net income to cash flow for the year, we must (1) subtract the accrued expenses at the beginning of the year and (2) add the accrued expenses at the end of the year. In the case of USL, we subtract $2,000 and $3,000, the beginning balances in the two accrued expense accounts (for taxes and wages): then, we add $38,000 and $12,000, the ending balances of the same two accruals. For simplicity, we will add $36,000 and $9,000, the increases in the two accounts. These are the fifth and sixth adjustments in the completed cash flow statement.

Prepayments of expenses are similar to expense accruals in that the year in which cash is paid is not the year in which the expense affects net income. With prepayments, however, the cash flow occurs before the item appears in the income statement. Thus, the current year's income is reduced by some expenses paid for in the previous year (the beginning balance of prepaid expenses), but cash was paid this year for expenses that do not reduce income until next year (the ending balance of prepaid expenses). To move from net income to the cash flow for the year, we must (1) add the beginning-of-the-year prepayments and (2) subtract the end-of-year prepayments. USL will add $20,000 and subtract $8,000, or simply add the $12,000 decrease in Prepaid Expenses. This is the seventh and final adjustment in the cash flow statement and completes the reconciliation of the difference between USL's net income and its cash flow operations.

Investing and Financing Activities

Look again at the comparative balance sheets in Exhibit D-3. Every item on the balance sheet, except Bonds Payable, shows a change between the two years. We know already that the changes in Accounts Receivable, Inventory, Prepaid Expenses, Accounts Payable, two expense accruals, and part of the changes in Accumulated Depreciation and in Retained Earnings relate to operating activities. What brought about the other changes? Unless our investigation of these changes reveals some way in which they affected net income, they must be related to financing and investing activities.

The other flows are known from the additional information in Exhibit D-3. Notice that Exhibit D-4 shows the $38,000 common stock issuance for equipment in the schedule of noncash activities. We show the sale and purchase of equipment separately as well as the inflows and outflows for short-term debt.

We could have deduced some of these items from available information. For example, because retained earnings increased by $199,500 when net income was $229,500, we can be confident that dividends were $30,000. Similarly, we could also have deduced the sale of equipment by examining the changes in plant and equipment and accumulated depreciation. Because plant and equipment increased by $328,000 when we had purchases of new plant assets totaling $338,000 ($38,000 for stock, $300,000 for cash), we must have sold or retired plant assets with an original cost of $10,000. Because accumulated depreciation increased by $55,000 when depreciation expense was $56,000, the sold or retired assets must have had $1,000 accumulated depreciation. We sometimes need to do such analyses to determine inflows and outflows about which we have no information.

To summarize briefly, we started with comparative balance sheets for USL and noted that cash had decreased by $174,500. To explain that change, we analyzed the changes in all the other balance sheet accounts. The results of that analysis appear in the formal cash flow statement shown in Exhibit D-4, which is further discussed in the next section.

Cash Flow Statement

The cash flow statement in Exhibit D-4 provides a basis for further discussion. Consider first the adjustments to net income. If you reflect for a moment about the adjustments, you will recognize that the fourth, for depreciation, is quite different from the others.

The depreciation adjustment, required because depreciation expense appears on the income statement, has no relation to the operating cash inflows or outflows for the current period. The other six adjustments are

Exhibit D-4 USL Corporation, Statement of Cash Flows for 19X8

Net cash flow from operating activities:		
Net income	$229,500	
Adjustments for noncash expenses and revenues included in income:		
Increase in accounts receivable	(142,000)	
Increase in inventory	(90,000)	
Increase in accounts payable	30,000	
Depreciation for the year	56,000	
Increase in accrued taxes	36,000	
Increase in accrued wages	9,000	
Decrease in prepaid expense	12,000	
Net cash provided by operating activities		$140,500
Cash flows from investing activities:		
Purchase of plant and equipment	(300,000)	
Sales of equipment	9,000	
Net cash used by investing activities		(291,000)
Cash flows from financing activities:		
New short-term borrowing	80,000	
Repayment of short-term debt	(96,000)	
Proceeds from issuance of common stock	22,000	
Dividends on common stock	(30,000)	
Net cash used by financing activities		(24,000)
Net change (decrease) in cash		(174,500)
Cash balance, beginning of year		360,000
Cash balance, end of year		$185,500
Schedule of Noncash Investing and Financing Activities:		
Issuance of common stock to acquire new equipment	$38,000	

needed because of short-term timing differences between cash flows and appearance on the income statement. Once you understand the reasoning for the treatment of these other adjustments, you may find the following rules helpful.

1. Add to net income a decrease in an asset (or an increase in a liability) resulting from operating activities.
2. Subtract from net income an increase in an asset (or a decrease in a liability) resulting from operating activities

Note that the net change in cash, a decrease of $174,500, agrees with the decrease shown in the comparative balance sheets in Exhibit D-3. The two statements are thus linked, with the cash flow statement describing the cash inflows and outflows that contributed to the decline in cash, a balance sheet item. A link with the income statement is provided by using the indirect method to present cash flow from operations.

As we have shown, the information for a cash flow statement can be developed by analyzing the other financial statements and gathering some other information. Because the managers of the firm have access to information about its actual cash flows, the task is relatively easy. Without access to information about actual flows, the task is more difficult but not impossible. But for anyone—manager, stockholder, or creditor—presented with a cash flow statement, what is important is to understand its contents and implications; and that understanding begins with an understanding of how the statement is developed.

OPERATING FLOWS—SPECIAL CONSIDERATIONS

In developing USL's cash flow statement, we used the indirect method of presenting operating cash flows. We also used fairly common transactions. In this section we discuss and illustrate two important variations of these basic circumstances.

The Direct Method, Inflows and Outflows

Although the indirect method of reporting the cash flow from operating activities is acceptable, the FASB and many financial statement users prefer the direct method. Supporters of the direct method stress their interest in its separate disclosure of inflows and outflows. Of course, net operating cash flow is the same regardless of the method used to present information about it. Hence, the same items that reconcile net income with net operating cash flow under the indirect method also explain the differences between cash inflows and outflows for specific items included in the income statement.

Consider the three major income statement categories that affected net income for USL Corporation: sales, cost of goods sold, and other expenses. What is the difference between sales reported in the year's income statement and cash received during the year from customers? You answered that question already: the beginning and ending balances in Accounts Receivable. What is the difference between reported cost of goods sold and cash payments to acquire merchandise? The beginning and ending balances in Inventory and Accounts Payable. Finally, why are the expenses shown on the income statement different from the year's cash payments for operating expenses? Accruals, prepayments, and the noncash expense of depreciation.

Thus, the same type of analysis that produced the information needed to reconcile reported net income with net operating cash flow provides the information needed to present net operating cash flow under the direct method. The only difference is that, to develop the information about inflows and outflows separately, we adjust individual items in the income statement, rather than the net result of those items (net income). Let us determine the separate operating cash flows for USL using the information developed earlier. In each case we begin with the amount reported on the income statement (see Exhibit D-2) and compute the cash flow for that item.

Cash Receipts from Customers Reported sales were $1,000,000, but Accounts Receivable increased by $142,000. We can compute the cash received from customers as follows:

Sales		$1,000,000
Add Accounts Receivable, beginning of year (additional current cash collections)	$130,000	
Deduct Accounts Receivable, end of year (uncollected sales)	(272,000)	
Increase in Accounts Receivable		(142,000)
Cash receipts from customers		$ 858,000

Cash Payments to Merchandise Suppliers Cost of goods sold reported for the year was $450,000, but we know that this amount differed from cash payments to suppliers because of changes in Inventory and in Accounts Payable. To convert Cost of Goods Sold to cash payments to suppliers, we adjust for changes in these two balance-sheet items, as follows.

Cost of goods sold		$450,000
Add Inventory, end of year	$190,000	
Deduct Inventory, beginning of year	(100,000)	
Increase in Inventory		90,000
Add Accounts Payable, beginning of year	55,000	
Deduct Accounts Payable, end of year	(85,000)	
Increase in Accounts Payable		(30,000)
Cash payments to merchandise suppliers		$510,000

If you have trouble seeing why an increase in Inventory should be added to cost of goods sold to arrive at cash payments while an increase in Accounts Payable is subtracted, consider again how these items affect cost of goods sold and review our earlier explanation.

Cash Payments for Expenses From the earlier analysis we know that depreciation and the changes in Prepaid Expenses and two accrued expense accounts explain the difference between reported expenses and the cash flows for expenses. In response to the strongly expressed preferences of financial statement users, the FASB requires separate reporting of the cash paid for two expense items, interest and income taxes. (This requirement applies whether the direct or the indirect method is used to present operating cash flows.) Hence, although the same calculations apply to all the expenses, we have to separate these two items from other expenses. Accordingly, we can calculate the cash payments for expenses as shown below.

		Total	Interest	Income Taxes	Other
Expenses for the year		$325,000	$12,000	$123,700	$184,800
Eliminate effect of depreciation		(56,000)			(56,000)
Eliminate effect of change in Prepaid Expenses:					
Subtract beginning Prepaid Expenses	$20,000				(20,000)
Add ending Prepaid Expenses	8,000				8,000
Decrease in Prepaid Expenses		(12,000)			
Eliminate effect of change in accrued expenses:					
Add beginning accrued expenses	5,000			2,000	3,000
Deduct ending accrued expenses	50,000			(38,000)	(12,000)
Increase in accrued expenses		(45,000)			
Cash payments for expenses		$207,500	$12,000	$87,700	$107,800

Formal Presentation Exhibit D-5 shows the cash flow statement for USL Corporation using the direct method of presenting cash flow from operations. As you can see, the net cash flow from operations is the same as that shown in Exhibit D-4 when the indirect method was used. Note that, with the use of the direct method, the details of the computations (i.e., the descriptions of the adjustments) are not part of the presentation. Remember, however, that a reconciliation of net income and net cash flow from operations must also be provided.

Firms differ in the number and types of items reported separately. For example, some choose to highlight amounts paid for wages and fringe benefits, rent, or some other expense of major significance. USL's statement shows one item more than the required minimum detail for cash outflows, because it is acceptable to combine payments for merchandise with payments for other expenses.

In the next section we discuss a not uncommon circumstance that affects both the computation and the reporting of operating cash flows regardless of which reporting approach is followed.

Nonoperating Gains and Losses

One transaction that we included in the example is unlikely—the sale of plant and equipment at book value. There was no gain or loss on the sale to appear in the income statement, and we had only to report the proceeds as an inflow from investing activities. It is highly unlikely, however, that a noncurrent asset will be sold at exactly its book value. Thus, when a sale occurs, the resulting gain or loss is included in net income.

Reporting a gain or loss on the sale of an asset in no way changes the fact that the sale is an investing activity. The proceeds from the sale are still an inflow to be reported under investing activities. The complication presented

Exhibit D-5 USL Corporation, Statement of Cash Flows for 19X8

Net cash flow from operating activities:		
Cash receipts from customers	$858,000	
Cash payments to merchandise suppliers	(510,000)	
Interest paid	(12,000)	
Income taxes paid	(87,700)	
Cash paid for other expenses	(107,800)	
Net cash provided by operating activities		$140,500
Cash flows from investing activities:		
Purchase of plant and equipment	(300,000)	
Sales of equipment	9,000	
Net cash used by investing activities		(291,000)
Cash flows from financing activities:		
New short-term borrowing	80,000	
Repayment of short-term debt	(96,000)	
Proceeds from issuance of common stock	22,000	
Dividends on common stock	(30,000)	
Net cash used by financing activities		(24,000)
Net change (decrease) in cash		(174,500)
Cash balance, beginning of year		360,000
Cash balance, end of year		$185,500
Schedule of Noncash Investing and Financing Activities:		
Issuance of common stock to acquire new equipment	$38,000	

by such sales is that the resulting gains or losses do not reflect cash flow from operating activities and require adjustment.

For example, suppose a long-term investment that had cost $30,000 was sold for $45,000. Cash of $45,000 was provided by the sale, and that amount should be shown on the cash flow statement as an inflow from investing activities. But the income statement for the year includes the $15,000 gain on the sale. Hence, net income increased by $15,000 as a result of a nonoperating activity. Under either the direct or the indirect method of presenting operating cash flows, the $15,000 income effect of the sale has to be eliminated. (If the book value of the investment had been $60,000, so that a $15,000 loss, rather than a $15,000 gain, occurred on the sale, the cash inflow would still be $45,000, and the $15,000 loss on the sale would also have to be eliminated to arrive at the cash flow from operating activities.)

Thus, gains and losses from investing activities are adjustments in deriving operating cash flows from amounts reported in an income statement. In a cash flow statement that uses the indirect method of reporting flow from operating activities, losses appear as additions to net income and gains as subtractions.

Let's look at the logic of why gains and losses on sales of non-current assets do not directly affect cash. Suppose a company sells a plant asset that cost \$50,000 and has accumulated depreciation of \$30,000 (book value of \$20,000). First, suppose the sale is for \$24,000, giving a \$4,000 gain, then suppose it is for \$15,000, giving a \$5,000 loss. In journal entry form the sales show,

Sale for \$24,000		
Cash	\$24,000	
Accumulated depreciation	30,000	
Plant and equipment		\$50,000
Gain on sale		4,000
Sale for \$15,000		
Cash	\$15,000	
Accumulated depreciation	30,000	
Loss on sale	5,000	
Plant and equipment		\$50,000

The cash flow is the amount of cash received. The gain or loss is reported on the income statement. Because the gain or loss did not directly affect cash flow, it must be removed to determine cash provided by operations using the indirect method. Using the direct method, the gain or loss is simply not reported and no adjustment is needed.

CONCLUDING COMMENTS

Over the years, a common misconception has arisen that depreciation and similar expenses are inflows of cash. This misconception is understandable if we recognize that (1) the indirect method of computing operating cash flows has predominated in practice and (2) under that method depreciation is added to net income to arrive at cash flow from operations. As you know, depreciation neither increases nor decreases cash. It requires no current outlay of cash; rather, an outflow of cash occurs at the time the asset is acquired, and that outflow is reported as an investing activity.

In one sense, however, depreciation influences cash flows. Because depreciation is deductible for tax purposes, a firm's income tax payment—which *is* an operating cash flow—is lower than it would have been had there been no depreciation to deduct. Hence, net cash inflow from operations is higher than would be the case had there been no depreciation.

We should also point out that the cash flow statement provides information beyond a classified listing of the firm's cash flows. As we note in the next chapter, an understanding and evaluation of a firm's activities requires review of more than one year's financial statements. At this point we comment only briefly on insights that might be provided by review of the cash flow statements.

Consider the companies whose cash flow statements are provided in the chapter. Exhibits D-4 and D-5 show that USL Corporation spent more cash on investments than was made available from normal operations and traditional financing sources. Is this a good or bad sign? As you might expect, the answer is that it depends. A substantial net new investment in plant and equipment suggests expansion and the potential for growth in earnings. True, normal operating activities and financing sources didn't provide enough cash for USL's new investment. But USL's cash balance at the beginning of 19X8 was relatively large (about 34% of total assets), which might indicate that significant new financing was obtained in the preceding year. (Remember that a firm must plan in advance to meet cash needs for long-term capital investments.) Thus, review of the prior year's financial statements, particularly the cash flow statement, is necessary before drawing conclusions. To return to the ideas presented at the beginning of this chapter, perhaps the primary value of a cash flow statement is that it shows managers' current responses to planned short-term and long-term needs for cash.

SUMMARY

Information about flows of cash is important to both managers and external parties. Generally accepted accounting principles require a cash flow statement as part of a typical financial statement package. Some short-term investments qualify as cash equivalents.

A firm's activities can generally be classified as operating, investing, or financing activities. A formal cash flow statement reports a firm's cash flows under these three headings. Significant activities having no effect on current cash flows are also reported, either in narrative form or in a separate schedule of the cash flow statement.

Two approaches are acceptable for presenting information about cash flows relating to operating activities. One approach, the indirect method, reconciles net income with the net cash flow from operations. The indirect method does not report operating inflows and outflows separately. The preferred approach, the direct method, reports inflows and outflows separately but does not offer a direct link between the cash flow statement and reported net income. Cash flow statements prepared using either the direct or the indirect method will report the same net cash flow from operations, the same cash flows relating to investing and financing activities, and the same net change of cash, and will disclose the cash paid for interest and for income taxes. Statements using the direct method must also provide a reconciliation of net income to net cash flow from operations.

KEY TERMS

cash equivalents
cash flow statement
cash flow from operations
direct method
financing activities
indirect method
investing activities
operating activities
reconciliation of net income and cash flow from operations

REVIEW PROBLEM

Comparative balance sheets and a combined statement of income and retained earnings for Harold Company are given in Exhibits D-6 and D-7.

Exhibit D-6 Harold Company, Balance Sheets at December 31

	19X7	19X8	Change Increase (Decrease)
Assets			
Current assets:			
Cash	$ 205	$ 190	$15
Accounts receivable, net	420	430	(10)
Inventory	350	310	40
Total current assets	975	930	
Investments	120	160	(40)
Plant and equipment	2,500	2,250	250
Accumulated depreciation	(800)	(720)	80
Total assets	$2,795	$2,620	
Equities			
Current liabilities:			
Accounts payable	$ 210	$ 220	(10)
Accrued expenses—taxes	28	22	6
—interest	6	16	(10)
—other	31	32	(1)
Total current liabilities	275	290	
Long-term debt	100	250	(150)
Total liabilities	375	540	
Owners' equity:			
Common stock, no par value	1,800	1,800	1,600
Retained earnings	620	480	140
Total owners' equity	2,420	2,080	
Total equities	$2,795	$2,620	

The following additional information is also available to you.

1. Common stock was issued for $200 cash.
2. Investments costing $40 were sold at a gain of $30.
3. Equipment costing $30 and with accumulated depreciation of $20 was sold for $10.

Exhibit D-7 Harold Company, Combined Statement of Income and Retained Earnings for 19X7

Sales		$2,350
Cost of goods sold:		
Beginning inventory	$ 310	
Purchases	890	
Cost of goods available for sale	1,200	
Less ending inventory	350	
Cost of goods sold		850
Gross profit on sales		1,500
Operating expenses:		
Depreciation	100	
Other operating expenses	359	
Total operating expenses		459
Operating income		1,041
Other income and expense:		
Gain on sale of investment	30	
Interest expense	21	
Net other income		9
Income before taxes		1,050
Income tax expense		320
Net income		730
Retained earnings of December 31, 19X6		480
		1,210
Dividends declared and paid		590
Retained earnings at December 31, 19X7		$ 620

Required

1. Determine cash flow from operations using the indirect method.
2. Prepare a cash flow statement for 19X7.
3. Show the cash flow from operations using the direct method. Show separately the cash inflow from sales and the cash outflows for merchandise purchases, operating expenses, interest, and income taxes.

ANSWER TO REVIEW PROBLEM

1. To compute cash flow from operations we must determine the adjustments to net income. Review of the company's income statement reveals the need for three adjustments:
   (a) Depreciation, a noncash expense, has reduced income.
   (b) The sale of a long-term investment, a nonoperating transaction, has increased income.
   (c) The change in Inventory, which is not directly related to cash flows, has increased net income.

The change in Inventory (an increase) produced higher net income because the ending inventory (which reduced cost of goods sold and hence increased income) was greater than the beginning inventory (which increased cost of goods sold and hence decreased income).

We can then turn to the comparative balance sheets for any other facts that might cause the reported components of net income (revenues, cost of goods sold, and operating expenses and other income and expense) to differ from cash flows relating to operations. Review of the comparative balance sheets reveals the need for three additional adjustments:

(d) The change in Accounts Receivable means there is a difference between cash inflows from operations and reported revenues.

(e) The change in Accounts Payable means there is a difference between cash outflows for operations and the reported cost of goods sold because there is a difference between cash outflows for purchases and reported purchases.

(f) The change in various accrued expenses means that there is a difference between operating cash outflows for expenses and reported operating expenses, interest, and taxes.

Changes in the other balance-sheet items, though they may have affected cash, would not have given rise to operating cash flows. If such changes affected net income, their effects should be eliminated from net income as we compute the cash flow from operating activities. Let us look at the other balance-sheet changes.

A change in noncurrent investments is normally from an investing activity, a sale or purchase. A cash flow from such a change does not result from operations. We have already recognized that net income must be adjusted to remove the effect of the sale of investments on net income (adjustment (b) above). A change in plant and equipment is also an investing activity, a sale or purchase. The income statement shows no evidence that either type of investing activity affected net income. The only operations-related change in Accumulated Depreciation is the depreciation for the year, which has no effect on cash flow from operations. We have already identified an adjustment (a) to remove the effect of the depreciation expense from the net income.

The changes in long-term debt and common stock, whatever their causes, give rise to financing flows. Again, there is no evidence (such as a gain from retirement of debt) in the income statement that financing activities affected net income. The change in Retained Earnings is explained by net income, which we have already considered, and the payment of dividends, which is a financing activity.

Thus, we can compute the cash flow from operations by starting with net income and making the six adjustments (a) through (f).

Reconciliation of Net Income and Cash from Operations

Net income	$730
Adjustments for noncash expense, revenues, and gains:	
(a) Depreciation for the year	100
(b) Gain on sale of long-term investment	(30)
(c) Increase in inventory	(40)
(d) Decrease in various accounts receivable	10
(e) Decrease in accounts payable	(10)
(f) Decrease in various accrued expenses	(5)
Cash flow from operations	$755

2. In item 1, the information needed for one section of the statement, cash flow from operations, was developed. Our objective now is to find any nonoperating inflows or outflows of cash. For this information we refer again to the balance-sheet changes that did not affect cash flow from operations. The changes, already discussed briefly, are summarized below.

Item	Change Increase (Decrease)	Change Already Explained Increase (Decrease)
Investments	($40)	Sold item for $30 gain
Plant and equipment	250	($30)
Accumulated depreciation	80	80
Long-term debt	(150)	
Common stock	200	
Retained earnings	140	730

Let us examine each of these changes carefully.

The $40 decrease in Investments was the result of a sale that produced a gain of $30. Since the investments that were sold cost $40 (the amount of the balance-sheet decrease in Investments), the *proceeds* from the sale must have been $70. Hence, we have an investing cash inflow of $70 to be reported on the statement.

The normal reason for an increase in Plant and Equipment is a purchase of new equipment. But, we already know that during the year the company sold equipment that originally cost $30, thus reducing Plant and Equipment by $30. Thus, the purchases of new plant and equipment must have been enough to offset this decrease and produce a net increase in Plant and Equipment of $250, or $280 ($250 + $30). So we have two transactions: sale of equipment and purchase of equipment, both of which involve investing cash flows. The old equipment was sold for $10, and this amount should be reported as an investing cash inflow. The new equipment must have cost $280 and should be reported as an investing use of cash.

As we know, depreciation neither produces nor uses cash. Hence, the change in Accumulated Depreciation is not a cash inflow or outflow. We have already explained the $80 increase for the year. Accumulated Depreciation increased by $100 because of the current year's depreciation expense, as shown on the income statement. Accumulated Depreciation decreased by $20 because an asset on which depreciation of $20 had accumulated was sold. The net change is an increase of $80 (an increase of $100 offset by a decrease of $20). In our analysis of Plant and Equipment, we determined that an investing cash inflow of $10 should be reported in connection with the sale of equipment.

The normal reason for a decline in long-term debt is that some of the debt was repaid. Such a repayment is a financing outflow. Since we have no evidence to indicate some other reason for the decrease, we shall report the decline as a financing outflow in the amount of $150.

Common Stock increased by $200; the usual explanation for such a increase is that additional shares of stock were issued. This conclusion is confirmed by the information obtained at the beginning of the problem, and so we include among the financing inflows of cash the issuance of additional stock for $200.

The lower portion of Exhibit D-7 reports that the net change in Retained Earnings resulted from an increase because of net income and a decrease because of dividends. Net income is an operating source of cash, and we have already dealt with cash from operations. The payment of dividends should be reported on our statement as a $590 financing outflow of cash.

Having analyzed and explained all the changes in balance sheet accounts during the year, we now incorporate our conclusions into the cash flow statement, as shown in Exhibit D-8.

3. Calculating cash flow from operations under the direct method requires you to look at the individual sections of the income statement and apply the adjustments determined in item 1 to specific sections. Following Exhibit D-8 are the calculations of specific operating cash inflows or outflows.

Exhibit D-8 Harold Company, Cash Flow Statement for 19X7

Net cash flow from operating activities:		
Net income	$730	
Adjustments for noncash expenses, revenues, and gains:		
Decrease in accounts receivable	10	
Increase in inventory	(40)	
Decrease in accounts payable	(10)	
Depreciation for the year	100	
Decrease in various accrued expenses	(5)	
Gain on sale of long-term investment	(30)	
Net cash provided by operating activities		$ 755
Cash flows from investing activities:		
Acquisition of plant and equipment	(280)	
Sale of equipment	10	
Sale of investments	70	
Net cash used by investing activities		(200)
Cash flows from financing activities:		
Retirement of long-term debt	(150)	
Proceeds from issuance of common stock	200	
Dividends on common stock	(590)	
Net cash used by financing activities		(540)
Net increase in cash		15
Cash balance, beginning of year		190
Cash balance, end of year		$ 205

Computation of Cash Receipts from Customers

Sales		$2,350
Add Accounts Receivable, beginning of year (additional current cash collections)	$430	
Deduct Accounts Receivable, end of year (uncollected sales)	(420)	
Decrease in Accounts Receivable		(10)
Cash receipts from customers		$2,360

Cash Payments to Merchandise Suppliers

Cost of goods sold		$850
Eliminate effect of change in Inventory:		
Add Inventory, end of year	$350	
Deduct Inventory, beginning of year	(310)	
Increase in Inventory		40
Eliminate effect of change in Accounts Payable:		
Add Accounts Payable, beginning of year	220	
Deduct Accounts Payable, end of year	(210)	
Decrease in Accounts Payable		10
Cash payments to merchandise suppliers		$900

Cash Payments for Operating Expenses

	Operating	Interest	Taxes
Expenses for the year	$459	$21	$320
Eliminate effect of depreciation (noncash expense)	(100)		
Eliminate effect of change in accrued expenses:			
Add accrued expenses, beginning of year	32	16	22
Deduct accrued expenses, end of year	(31)	(6)	(28)
Cash payments for expenses	$360	$31	$314

We already know that the only other item to affect net income, the gain on sale of investments, resulted from an investing, rather than an operating activity. Hence, neither the gains nor the proceeds from the sale would be reported as a part of the cash flow from operations. If Harold Company used the direct method of reporting its cash flow from operations, that segment of its cash flow statement would appear as below.

Net cash flow from operating activities:	
Cash receipts from customers	$2,360
Cash payments to merchandise suppliers	(900)
Cash paid for interest	(31)
Cash paid for income taxes	(314)
Cash payments for operating expenses	(360)
Net cash provided by operating activities	$ 755

Note that the $755,000 cash provided by operating activities agrees with the amount shown in Exhibit D-8, where the indirect method of reporting was used.

ASSIGNMENT MATERIAL

QUESTIONS FOR DISCUSSION

D-1 Depreciation and cash It is often said that cash generated by operations consists of net income and depreciation. Explain why this statement is or is not true.

D-2 Net income and cash flow Walter Bryant started Bryant Machine Shop five years ago. The shop has been profitable and Mr. Bryant has been withdrawing cash in an amount equal to net income each year. He has taken out an amount equal to nearly half of his original investment of $80,000, most of which was used originally to purchase machinery. Mr. Bryant's customers pay cash on completion of work. He keeps very little inventory and pays his bills promptly, and he is puzzled because the cash balance keeps growing despite his withdrawals. Can you explain the increase in cash?

D-3 Net income and cash Suppose that a large retail chain and a railroad earned the same income. Which firm would you expect to show the higher cash provided by operations? Explain your answer.

D-4 Explanation of a cash flow statement You have provided the president of Ralston Company with a full set of financial statements, including a statement of cash flows. He understands everything except some of the adjustments in the operations section of the statement. He has three specific questions:

1. "Why do you subtract the increase in accounts receivable? We don't pay out cash for our accounts receivable, we collect it."
2. "You show the decrease in inventory as an addition. We sure didn't get any cash because our inventory decreased. In fact, the decrease means that we have less to sell next year and will have to spend more cash to replenish our supply. So why add it back to net income?"
3. "Our accrued expenses increased, and you showed this as an addition? Look, we had especially heavy payroll costs at the end of the year, and we paid them the third day of the new year. So it seems to me that we had to use more cash because of the increase, not less."

Required

Explain each of the items to the president.

D-5 "How am I doing?" Clyde Mackey, president of Mackey Enterprises has just received a copy of the company's 19X8 financial statements from the company's controller. "I give up," Mr. Mackey says. "For years you've been telling me that if I want to know how the business is doing I should look at the income statement, not our cash balance. Now you give me an income statement, but you also give me a statement that tells me what happened in the company's cash account. So which statement do I look at to find out how I'm doing?"

Required

Respond to Mr. Mackey's question.

EXERCISES

D-6 Cash receipts from customers Fill in the blanks in the following schedule.

Sales (shown in 19X8 income statement)	$800,000	$1,000,000	$_____	$910,000
Net Accounts Receivable:				
At beginning of 19X8	42,000	37,000	18,000	31,000
At end of 19X8	25,000	45,000	25,000	$_____
Cash collected from customers in 19X8	$_____	$_____	853,000	925,000

D-7 Cash payments to merchandise suppliers For each of the three cases given below, compute the cash paid in 19X7 to merchandise suppliers.

	Case A	Case B	Case C
Cost of goods sold (as reported in the 19X7 income statement)	$831,000	$595,000	$3,316,000
Merchandise inventory:			
Beginning of 19X7	215,000	142,000	846,000
End of 19X7	193,000	91,000	872,000
Accounts payable:			
Beginning of 19X7	21,000	22,000	78,000
End of 19X7	32,000	18,000	64,000
Cash paid to merchandise suppliers during 19X7	$_____	$_____	$_____

D-8 Relationships Fill in the blanks in the following schedule.

	Case A	Case B	Case C
Cost of goods sold (as reported in the 19X3 income statement)	$659,000	$431,000	$_____
Merchandise inventory:			
Beginning of 19X3	91,000	57,000	262,000
End of 19X3	84,000	71,000	245,000
Accounts payable:			
Beginning of 19X3	32,000	68,000	93,000
End of 19X3	41,000	$_____	85,000
Cash paid to merchandise suppliers during 19X3	$_____	$423,000	$2,824,000

D-9 Components of cash flow from operating activities Which of the following items would appear in the operations section of the cash flow statement for Washburn Company? Washburn uses the indirect method of presenting operating cash flows.

1. Depreciation expense for the year.
2. Increase in Dividends Payable.
3. Decrease in Income Taxes Payable.
4. Loss from sale of long-term investments
5. Decrease in Prepaid Insurance.
6. Increase in Inventory.
7. Proceeds from sale of long-term investments.
8. Increase in Accounts Receivable.
9. Amortization of patents covering Washburn's major product.
10. Payment for machinery to be used to produce Washburn's major product.

D-10 Classifying activities State how each of the following transactions is classified, as an operating, investing, or financing activity.

1. Sale of merchandise (an inventory item) for cash.
2. Sale of merchandise (an inventory item) on account.
3. Sale of a fully depreciated machine for cash.
4. Declaration of a cash dividend on common stock.
5. Payment of a previously declared cash dividend on common stock.
6. Purchase of merchandise (for resale) on credit.
7. Payment of cash for purchase made in item 6.
8. Payment of the premium on a three-year policy for theft insurance on the firm's inventory.
9. Acquisition of land by issuing a long-term note payable.
10. Payment of wages.
11. Purchase of 10,000 shares of the firm's common stock from some of its stockholders. The price paid is less than that at which the shares were originally issued.
12. Sale of 5,000 shares of treasury stock at a price in excess of that paid to acquire that stock.
13. Accrual of interest due on a 20-year mortgage note payable.
14. Conversion of some 20-year convertible bonds to common stock.
15. Payment of previously accrued wages and salaries for employees.

D-11 Reconciliation of net income and cash from operations Select from the following list those items that are relevant to a reconciliation of net income and cash from operations and prepare such a reconciliation.

Loss on sale of long-term investment	$43,000
Increase in accounts receivable	52,500
Increase in land	48,000
Increase in accrued expenses payable	6,800
Decrease in inventory	26,500
Decrease in accounts payable	112,000
Decrease in prepaid insurance	1,500
Increase in common stock	85,000
Net income	174,000

Depreciation expense	61,000
Decrease in cash	14,000
Cash received from sale of long-term investment	228,800
Cash provided by operations	148,300

D-12 Cash payments for operating expenses For each of the three cases given below, compute the cash paid in 19X7 for operating expenses.

	Case A	Case B	Case C
Operating expenses (according to the 19X7 income statement)	$476,900	$31,425	$4,150,000
Prepaid expenses:			
Beginning of 19X7	12,000	1,863	97,100
End of 19X7	9,300	1,541	105,400
Accrued expenses:			
Beginning of 19X7	21,200	3,260	57,800
End of 19X7	25,100	2,045	53,400
Cash paid in 19X7 for operating expenses	$______	$______	$______

D-13 Relationships Fill in the blanks in the following schedule.

	Case A	Case B	Case C
Operating expenses (according to the 19X7 income statement)	$927,400	$123,865	$______
Prepaid expenses:			
Beginning of 19X7	25,400	12,500	103,000
End of 19X7	19,300	$______	81,000
Accrued expenses:			
Beginning of 19X7	48,800	21,426	193,000
End of 19X7	51,100	24,382	242,000
Cash paid in 19X7 for operating expenses	$______	$118,416	$4,250,000

D-14 Cash from operations—indirect method In 19X9, Drew Company reported net income of $28,000. You also have the following information about 19X9.

1. Depreciation expense for the year was $109,000.
2. Increase in Accounts Receivable from 19X8 to 19X9 was $17,000.
3. Decrease in Inventory from 19X8 to 19X9 was $9,000.
4. Decrease in Accounts Payable from 19X8 to 19X9 was $14,000.
5. Increase in Accrued Expenses from 19X8 to 19X9 was $6,000.

Required

Compute cash flow from operations.

D-15 Effects of transactions Determine the effect, if any, of each transaction listed below on (a) net income and (b) cash. Show the amount of the change and its direction (+ or −).

1. Common stock was issued in exchange for equipment. The agreed price was $300,000.
2. A dividend payable in cash of $120,000 was declared, but not paid.
3. The dividend in item 2 was paid.
4. An account receivable of $10,000 was written off against the Allowance for Doubtful Accounts.
5. A customer who owed the firm $12,000 on account receivable gave the firm equipment with a fair market value of $12,000 in settlement of the receivable.
6. Interest payable was accrued in the amount of $14,000.
7. The interest payable in item 6 was paid.
8. The firm bought 100 shares of its own stock for the treasury. The cost was $4,600, paid in cash.
9. Inventory with a cost of $18,000 was written off as obsolete.
10. Plant assets that had cost $45,000 and were one-third depreciated were sold for $12,000 cash.

D-16 Classifying activities Indicate whether each of the following transactions would be classified as an operating, investing, or financing activity.

1. Cash collected on previously recorded credit sale of merchandise.
2. Sale of factory machinery for an amount of cash that exceeds the machine's book value.
3. Sale of factory machinery for an amount of cash that is less than the machine's book value.
4. Payment of cash for previously recorded credit purchase.
5. Payment of the premium on a three-year policy for theft insurance on the firm's inventory.
6. Acquisition of land by issuing common stock having a market value in excess of par.
7. Payment of wages.
8. Purchase of 10,000 shares of the firm's common stock from some of its stockholders. The price paid is in excess of the price at which the shares were originally issued.
9. Sale of 5,000 shares of treasury stock at a price in excess of that paid to acquire the stock.
10. Payment of previously accrued interest on a 5-year note payable.
11. Declaration and issuance of a 5% stock dividend on common stock.
12. Receipt of insurance proceeds as a result of destruction of company's factory buildings and machinery because of an earthquake. (The proceeds exceeded the book value of buildings and machinery destroyed.)

D-17 Analysis of noncurrent accounts The following data were taken from the records of Miller Mining Company.

	End of Year	
	19X6	19X5
Plant and equipment	$2,240,000	$1,980,000
Accumulated depreciation	(980,000)	(740,000)
Mineral properties, net of depletion	3,750,000	2,950,000

You have also determined that plant and equipment costing $240,000 and with accumulated depreciation of $90,000 was sold for $80,000 and that depletion expense related to mineral properties was $440,000. The only other transactions affecting the accounts shown were depreciation expense, purchases of plant and equipment, and purchases of mineral properties.

Required

1. Determine the amount of cash provided by sales of plant and equipment.
2. Determine the gain or loss to be added or subtracted in the reconciliation of net income to cash flow from operations.
3. Determine the amount of depreciation expense to be added to net income in the reconciliation of net income to cash flow from operations.
4. Determine the amount of cash paid to buy plant and equipment.
5. Determine the amount of cash paid to buy mineral properties.

D-18 Cash flow from operations—special situations (continuation of D-14) After more careful study of Drew Company's income statement for 19X9, you determine that the following items also affected net income.

1. Amortization of intangible assets, $22,000.
2. Loss of sale of plant assets, $3,000.
3. On one sale, for $24,000, the customer gave Drew Company a five-year note bearing interest at 9%.

Required

Recompute the cash provided by operations considering this additional information.

D-19 Statement preparation Below is a list of items that would appear in the cash flow statement for Collins Company for the year 19X8.

Net income for the year	$346,000
Dividends paid during the year	140,000
Proceeds from sale of a 10-year bond issue	350,000
Amortization of the company's patents	47,000
Depreciation expense	153,000
Cash received on sale of land	106,000
Decrease in inventory	17,000
Increase in accounts receivable	74,000
Gain on the sale of land	20,000
Decrease in accrued expenses	12,000
Cash purchase of new equipment	400,000
Cash purchase of a long-term investment	265,000
Increase in income taxes payable	6,000
Decrease in accounts payable	48,000
Purchase of land and buildings by giving a 20-year note	350,000

Required

Prepare a cash flow statement for 19X8 using all the items given. (Hint: The change in cash was an increase of $66,000.)

D-20 Converting cash flow to income Boyd Company uses the direct method of reporting cash flow from operations. Below is the operations sections of its cash flow statement for 19X7.

Cash receipts from customers		$917,000
Cash payments for:		
Merchandise for resale	$470,000	
Wages and salaries	160,000	
Income taxes	25,000	
Other operating expenses	120,000	
Total cash payments for operating activities		775,000
Cash provided by operations		$142,000

Other data taken from Boyd's records for 19X7 show the following.

1. Accounts receivable increased by $20,000.
2. Accounts payable decreased by $8,000.
3. Inventory remained constant at $50,000.
4. Accrued wages and salaries (the only accrued expense) increased by $3,000.
5. Depreciation expense was $55,000.

Required

Determine Boyd Company's reported net income for 19X7.

D-21 Reconciliation of net income and cash flow from operations (continuation of D-20) Using the data provided in D-20 prepare a reconciliation of net income and cash flow from operations.

D-22 Cash flow statement from comparative balance sheets Below are the balances of certain balance-sheet items for Lorelei Company at December 31, 19X5, and 19X6.

	December 31 19X5	December 31 19X6
Cash	$ 4,000	$23,000
Accounts receivable, net	5,000	9,000
Inventory	12,000	10,000
Long-term investments	2,000	—
Property, plant, and equipment	30,000	47,000
Totals	$53,000	$89,000
Accumulated depreciation on plant and equipment	$5,000	$8,000
Accounts payable	3,000	5,000
Notes payable, due in 1 year	4,000	3,000
Long-term notes payable	10,000	18,000
Common stock	25,000	29,000
Retained earnings	6,000	26,000
Totals	$53,000	$89,000

The following information is also available about the firm's transactions in 19X6.

1. Net income for the year was $27,000.
2. Depreciation on plant and equipment for the year was $3,000.
3. Long-term investments were sold during the year for $8,000.
4. Property, plant, and equipment costing $5,000 was purchased for cash.
5. Dividends of $7,000 were declared and paid.
6. Some equipment was purchased by giving a $12,000 long-term note.
7. The company liquidated a $4,000 long-term note payable by issuing capital stock to the holder of the note.

Required

Prepare a cash flow statement for 19X6. Use the indirect method to present operating cash flows.

PROBLEMS

D-23 Determining cash flow from operations With the information provided for each of the following cases, determine the cash provided (used) by operations.

	Case A	Case B
From the income statement:		
Sales	$1,850,000	$851,850
Cost of goods sold	925,000	436,200
Operating expenses, total	683,000	428,500
Depreciation expense (included in expense total)	73,000	128,000
From the balance sheet:		
Increase (decrease) in Accounts Receivable	25,000	(32,000)
Increase (decrease) in Prepaid Expenses	(12,000)	8,300
Decrease in inventory	37,000	24,500
Increase (decrease) in Accounts Payable	(68,000)	41,000
Increase in Accrued Expenses	17,000	6,400

D-24 Cash from operations—direct method (continuation of D-23) For each case in D-23, prepare the operations section of the cash flow statement using the direct method of presenting operating cash flows.

D-25 Distinguishing operating cash flows In 19X5, Bard Company reported net income of $168,600. The following facts are also known about the year's activities.

Increase in Inventory	$ 5,000
Decrease in Prepaid Expenses	400
Depreciation expense—company cars	31,000
Increase in Accounts Receivable	12,000
New short-term bank borrowings	45,000
Decrease in Dividends Payable	32,000
Amortization expense—patents	9,000
Decrease in Accounts Payable	4,000

Required

1. Compute the cash flow from operations for 19X5.
2. Explain how your answer in item 1 would change if you also knew that during 19X5 Bard sold some machinery for $2,800 cash, incurring a loss of $1,300.

D-26 Selecting relevant information Use the following information as necessary to compute cash flow from operations for the year.

Net income	$ 80
Increase in Accounts Receivable	12
Increase in Inventory	40
Decrease in Accrued Interest Receivable	3
Increase in Long-term Investments	135
Depreciation and amortization expense	161
Gain on sale of machinery and equipment	27
Proceeds from sale of machinery and equipment	198
Increase in Accounts Payable	74

D-27 Cash flow statement from transaction information Fisher Company began 19X4 with $18,000 cash. The following information is available for 19X4 activities.

1. Net income was $115,000.
2. Depreciation expense was $70,000.
3. Fisher retired bonds payable that were due in 19X9. The cash paid to retire the bonds was equal to their $60,000 book value.
4. Fisher paid $90,000 cash for new plant and equipment.
5. Fisher declared dividends of $18,000 to be paid in January of 19X5. Dividends payable at the end of 19X3 were $3,000.
6. One of Fisher's long-term investments in stock was written off as a loss in 19X4 because the company in which Fisher had invested went bankrupt. The book value of the investment was $30,000.
7. Accounts Receivable increased by $15,000 during the year.
8. Inventory increased by $26,000 during the year.
9. Prepaid Expenses decreased by $8,000 during the year.
10. During 19X4 Fisher sold, for $54,000 cash, a patent with a $38,000 book value.

Required

Prepare a cash flow statement for Fisher Company for 19X4.

D-28 Cash flows from transactions Transactions of Martin Company for 19X6 and other selected data are given below.

1. Sales, all on account, were $800,000.
2. Cost of goods sold was $360,000.
3. Depreciation expense was $60,000.
4. Other operating expenses, all paid in cash, were $210,000.
5. Equipment was purchased for $220,000 cash.
6. Long-term investments were sold at an $8,000 gain. They had cost $57,000.
7. Common stock was issued for cash of $150,000.

8. A building that had cost $80,000 and had accumulated depreciation of $72,000 was destroyed by fire. There was no insurance coverage.
9. Over the year, the following changes occurred in the current accounts.

Cash	+$ 17,000
Accounts receivable, net	+ 128,000
Prepaid expenses	+12,000
Inventory	+82,000
Accounts payable	+14,000

Required

1. Determine net income for 19X6.
2. Prepare a cash flow statement for 19X6.

D-29 Effects of transactions Explain how each of the following affects the 19X9 cash flow statement of Gray Company.

1. A long-term investment in the common stock of Black Company was sold for $183,000, which was $42,000 less than its book value at the date of sale.
2. At the beginning of 19X9, Gray had a patent with a book value of $180,000. On November 15, 19X9, Gray sold the patent for $98,000. Amortization expense (for 19X9) to the date of sale was $45,000.
3. On October 31, 19X9, Gray sold some of its equipment for $18,000. The book value of the equipment at the beginning of 19X9 was $13,000, and 19X9 depreciation on the equipment to the date of sale was $2,200.
4. On July 3, 19X9, when the market value of its common stock was $28 per share, Gray declared a 10% stock dividend on its 100,000 shares of outstanding $20 par-value stock. The dividend was distributed on October 1, 19X9.
5. On April 1, 19X9, Gray retired an outstanding issue of bonds, paying $103,500 in cash. The bonds had a book value at the date of retirement of $98,300. Amortization of discount on these bonds between January 1 and April 1 of 19X9 was $200.
6. On March 19, 19X9, Gray acquired new machinery valued at $460,000. Gray paid $85,000 in cash for this machinery and gave a five-year, 10% note for the difference.

D-30 Cash flow As you were walking down the hall to your office at Complan Company, you met the president of the firm. She was disturbed at the latest financial statements and wanted your help. She explained that the firm was faced with a serious shortage of cash even though profits were high and working capital increased. She showed you the following condensed financial statements. (All data are in thousands of dollars.)

Complan Company, Income Statements for 19X7

Sales	$6,720
Cost of sales	3,850
Gross profit	2,870
Operating expenses	2,140
Net income	$ 730

Complan Company, Balance Sheets as of December 31

	19X7	19X6	Change
Assets			
Cash	$ 25	$ 380	($355)
Accounts receivable, net	990	860	130
Inventory	1,445	1,200	245
Plant and equipment, net	3,850	3,370	480
Total	$6,310	$5,810	
Equities			
Accounts payable	$ 190	$ 280	($90)
Accrued expenses	110	200	(90)
Long-term debt	2,250	2,200	50
Common stock	2,080	2,080	0
Retained earnings	1,680	1,050	630
Total	$6,310	$5,810	

The president told you that it had been touch-and-go whether the firm would have enough cash to pay a $100,000 dividend that had been declared when the directors realized that the firm was having an excellent year. To pay the dividend, the firm had to increase its long-term borrowings by $50,000. "We made $730,000 and had depreciation expense of $150,000. We did buy $630,000 worth of plant assets, but I figured that our cash would stay about the same as it was last year. Look at this stuff and tell me what happened."

Required

Explain the results to the president.

D-31 Cash flow statement from comparative trial balances Below are the beginning and ending balances of the balance sheet accounts for Truitt Company for 19X3.

	Beginning of Year		End of Year	
	Dr.	Cr.	Dr.	Cr.
Cash	$36,000		$26,000	
Accounts receivable	50,000		60,000	
Allowance for bad debts		$10,000		$12,000
Inventory	70,000		85,000	
Buildings and equipment	190,000		240,000	
Patents	26,000		20,000	
Accounts payable		30,000		40,000
Accrued wages payable		4,000		5,000
Accumulated depreciation on buildings and equipment		96,000		100,000
10-year bonds payable		80,000		104,000
Premium on bonds payable		—		1,000
Treasury stock	—		4,000	
Common stock		100,000		135,000
Retained earnings		52,000		38,000
Total	$372,000	$372,000	$435,000	$435,000

The following information is also available about the firm's activities in 19X3.

1. Net income was $14,000.
2. Dividends of $8,000 were declared and paid.
3. A stock dividend was declared and distributed, and for this reason $20,000 was charged to Retained Earnings, which amount represented the par and market value of the stock issued in connection with the dividend.
4. Depreciation in the amount of $8,000 was recorded as expense this year.
5. Machinery costing $6,000 and having a book value of $2,000 was sold for $3,000 cash in 19X3.

Required

Prepare a cash flow statement for Truitt Company for 19X3. You may assume that any changes other than those described above are attributable to reasonable transactions with which you should be familiar.

D-32 Treatment of transactions Explain how each of the following transactions is reflected on a cash flow statement. Be specific.

1. Depreciation expense was $340,000.
2. A $110,000 dividend was declared late in the year and will be paid early next year.
3. Fixed assets costing $380,000 with accumulated depreciation of $170,000 were sold for $80,000 cash.
4. Long-term investments were written off because the firms issuing the securities were bankrupt. The write-off was $220,000.
5. The firm issued long-term debt in exchange for land. The value of the land was $640,000, which equaled the value of the debt.
6. Near the end of the year the firm sold a parcel of land for $300,000, which was $60,000 more than its cost. The buyer gave the firm a 5-year, 8% note for $300,000.
7. The firm paid $50,000 in settlement of a dispute relating to its income tax return of three years ago. The firm debited Retained Earnings for $50,000.

D-33 Statements from limited data The following changes in the balance sheet accounts for Rohmer Company occurred during 19X8.

	Change	
Account	Debit	Credit
Cash	$120	
Accounts receivable, net		$180
Inventory	120	
Plant and equipment	350	
Accumulated depreciation		90
Accounts payable	80	
Accrued expenses		30
Long-term debt	15	
Common stock		200
Retained earnings		185
Totals	$685	$685

The firm had net income of $225 and paid dividends of $40. No plant assets were sold or retired.

Required

Prepare a cash flow statement. In the absence of available information, make the most reasonable assumption about the cause of a change.

D-34 Classification of items in the cash flow statement A list of items follows, most of which appear on a cash flow statement for Brillan Company for 19X8. During the current year, cash increased by $101,000.

1. Dividends declared during the year were $125,000, but dividends actually paid in cash were $103,000.
2. An issue of 10-year bonds payable was sold for $275,000 cash.
3. Amortization of the company's franchise cost was $6,000.
4. Depreciation on the company's tangible fixed assets was $159,000.
5. Land was sold at a loss of $14,000; cash received for the sale was $74,000.
6. Decrease in Inventory was $6,000.
7. Increase in Accounts Receivable was $81,000.
8. Increase in Accrued Expenses Payable was $11,000.
9. Decrease in Income Taxes Payable was $24,000.
10. Increase in Accounts Payable was $51,000.
11. Decrease in Prepaid Expenses was $1,000.
12. Increase in Allowance to Reduce Short-term Investments to Lower-of-Cost-or-Market was $3,000.
13. Decrease in short-term bank borrowings (debt) was $13,000.
14. Cash paid for new equipment was $500,000.
15. Cash paid for a long-term investment was $158,000.
16. A ten-year note payable for $200,000 was given to acquire land and buildings.
17. Amortization of discount on the 10-year bond issue mentioned in item 2 was $2,000.
18. Cash received as dividend on stock held as a long-term investment and accounted for on the equity basis was $25,000.
19. Amortization of discount on a long-term investment in bonds was $3,000.
20. Cash received from sale of treasury stock was $6,000; the stock had cost the company $4,000.
21. Increase in credit balance of Deferred Taxes account was $4,000.
22. Brillan's portion of net income of company whose stock is mentioned in item 18 was $56,000.
23. Net income for the year was $402,000.

Required

Prepare a cash flow statement for Brillan Company for 19X8.

D-35 Comprehensive problem Comparative balance sheets and an income statement for RJM Company are given on page 776. All data are in millions of dollars.

Sales and other revenue includes a gain of $0.8 million on sale of investments. Amortization expense is related to intangible assets. Other expenses include losses of $1.3 million on sales and other disposals of equipment. These assets had cost $9.6 million and had accumulated depreciation of $3.6 million. Long-term debt and common stock were issued for cash.

Required

Prepare a cash flow statement for the year ended June 30, 19X7.

RJM Company, Balance Sheets as of June 30

	19X7	19X6
Assets		
Cash	$ 9.5	$ 28.7
Accounts receivable, net	125.8	88.6
Inventories	311.4	307.0
Prepayments	12.6	11.4
Total current assets	459.3	435.7
Investments	68.3	71.8
Plant and equipment	1,313.9	1,240.6
Accumulated depreciation	(753.1)	(687.4)
Intangible assets	42.5	46.2
Total assets	$1,130.9	$1,106.9
Equities		
Accounts payable	$ 62.6	$ 59.8
Taxes payable	32.4	29.6
Accrued expenses	38.9	52.6
Total current liabilities	133.9	142.0
Long-term debt	505.3	496.2
Common stock, no par value	384.2	377.4
Retained earnings	107.5	91.3
Total equities	$1,130.9	$1,106.9

RJM Company, Income Statement for 19X7

Sales and other revenues		$896.3
Expenses:		
Cost of goods sold	$493.2	
Depreciation	69.3	
Amortization	3.7	
Income taxes	85.0	
Other expenses	203.5	854.7
Net income		$ 41.6

D-36 Cash flow statement from comparative trial balances—comprehensive problem Below are the trial balances for Mesmer Company at the beginning and the end of 19X5.

The following data are available regarding Mesmer Company's 19X5 activities.

1. Net income was $70,000 including gains and losses on transactions relating to fixed assets and bond retirements.
2. Land costing $100,000 was purchased, paying 20% in cash and giving long-term notes payable for the remainder of the purchase price. The only other transaction related to land was a sale that produced a gain of $12,000.
3. Equipment that had originally cost $82,000 and had a book value of $23,000 was sold for $8,000 cash. Additional equipment was purchased for cash.
4. At the beginning of the year, bonds payable carrying an interest rate of 5% and a maturity value of $200,000 were sold for $190,000 cash. Very shortly

thereafter, the 6% bonds were purchased on the open market for $159,000 and retired.

5. During the year, a stock dividend was declared and issued and was appropriately accounted for by a charge against Retained Earnings for $27,500, the market value of the stock distributed in connection with the dividend. The market value was 10% higher than the par value for the shares issued. Cash dividends were declared and paid as usual.

	Beginning of Year		End of Year	
	Dr.	Cr.	Dr.	Cr.
Cash	$ 50,000		$ 60,000	
Accounts receivable	150,000		200,000	
Inventory	250,000		270,000	
Prepaid expenses	50,000		70,000	
Land	250,000		307,000	
Buildings and equipment	700,000		838,000	
Bond discount—5% bonds	—		8,000	
Allowance for bad debts		$ 25,000		$ 35,000
Accumulated depreciation		300,000		421,000
Accounts payable		170,000		220,000
Accrued expenses		105,000		115,000
Bonds payable:				
5% bonds		—		200,000
6% bonds		175,000		—
Bond premium—6% bonds		4,000		—
Long-term notes payable		—		80,000
Capital stock—par value		450,000		475,000
Paid-in capital in excess of par		81,000		83,500
Retained earnings		140,000		123,500
	$1,450,000	$1,450,000	$1,753,000	$1,753,000

Required

Prepare a cash flow statement for 19X5.

analyzing financial statements

Appendix E

From Chapter 2 we already know that managers often express target profits as a ratio of income to sales (return on sales). We have also seen that the ratio of income to total assets (or some other measure of return on investment) is commonly used in measuring divisional performance. The chapters on comprehensive budgeting stressed the development of pro forma financial statements and the cash squeeze that can accompany buildups of inventories and receivables. This chapter addresses the analysis of financial statements, including the calculation, interpretation, and evaluation of financial ratios.

Many people and organizations outside a company, such as suppliers and investors in debt or equity securities, are interested in a firm's activities. Banks that provide short-term loans, insurance companies that buy long-term bonds, brokerage firms that give (or sell) investment advice to their customers, mutual funds that buy stocks or bonds—all of these, and many other institutions, employ financial analysts to help make decisions about a business. Individual investors also perform financial analyses in making investing decisions. Our approach to analyzing financial statements is that of a financial analyst, who makes recommendations to investors after studying financial statements and other sources of information about a business. Because the analyst's recommendations can affect a firm's ability to obtain credit, sell stock, and secure new contracts, its managers must be aware of what concerns the financial analyst. But as we proceed, it should become obvious that managers and analysts share many of the same concerns.

PURPOSE AND APPROACH OF THE ANALYST

Like company managers, financial analysts base their decisions on expectations about the future. Thus, just as managers focus on forecasts, financial analysts concentrate on what the future holds. Analysts want to know what to expect from a firm—whether it will be able to pay its employees and suppliers, repay its loans, pay dividends on stock, or expand into new areas. Financial analysts, like the firm's managers, are concerned with the past only insofar as it can be considered a reliable guide to the future. For example, an impressive history of growth in net income and sales, financial stability, and capable management is overshadowed if the firm's major product becomes illegal (e.g., asbestos, the insecticide DDT) or obsolete (e.g., early types of computers and calculators). Nevertheless, like managers who use information such as a cost prediction formula based on past experience, analysts assume that what has held true in the past is likely to continue unless they have information that indicates otherwise, Hence, both analysts and the firm's managers must be continually alert for signs that the future will differ from the past.

In addition to having a common focus on the future, the firm's managers and financial analysts use many of the same analytical approaches. Because a firm's well-being often depends on investors' continued willingness to supply capital at reasonable rates, internal managers try to duplicate the analyses made financial analysts so they can see the firm as outsiders do. Managers review these analyses to see whether the firm's ratios are out of line with those of other firms in the industry or with what the managers believe to be the expectations of outsiders.

For obvious reasons, the internal manager has access to more information than the external analyst and can study ratios, and their underlying components, in more depth. For example, by using a technique described later in this chapter, an outsider might calculate the average age of a firm's accounts receivable. The internal manager could, however, obtain a more precise picture of the age of receivables by requesting a schedule of receivables that shows exactly how much of total receivables are under 30 days old, 31 to 60 days old, and so on. In effect, the external analyst obtains a general picture of the firm's operations and financial position, while the internal analyst is interested in, and can obtain information about, the details of that picture. This difference is consistent with the interests of the two analysts. The external analyst is interested in the firm as a whole, its prospects for the future, and the decisions by management as a team. The internal analyst is interested also in what specific actions can be taken by individual managers.

GENERAL METHODS OF ANALYSIS

Financial analysis consists of a number of interrelated activities. Among the most important are considerations of ratios and trends and the comparison of ratios and trends against some norms. (A norm is a standard for comparison, which could be an average value for a particular industry or for all firms in the economy.) Trends are of interest as clues to the future.

AREAS OF ANALYSIS

Different types of investors are interested in different aspects of a firm. Short-term creditors, such as suppliers and banks considering loans of relatively short duration (90 days or six months), are concerned primarily with the firm's short-term prospects. They want to know whether the firm will be able to pay its obligations in the near future. Banks, insurance companies, pension funds, and other investors considering relatively long-term commitments (e.g., ten-year loans) cannot ignore short-term prospects, but are more concerned with the long-term outlook. Even if such investors are satisfied that the firm has no short-term problems, they want to be reasonably sure that the firm has good prospects for long-term financial stability and can be expected to repay its longer-term loans with interest.

Stockholders, current and potential, are also interested in both the short-term and long-term prospects of the firm. But their interest goes beyond the company's ability to repay loans and make interest payments. Their concern is with profitability—the ability to earn satisfactory profits and pay dividends—and the likelihood that the market price of the stock will increase.

We have divided the discussion of these aspects of a firm's prospects into three major areas: liquidity, solvency, and profitability. For the most part we work with ratios. Apart from expressing relationships between two factors, ratios are useful because they facilitate comparisons among firms of different sizes.

SAMPLE FINANCIAL STATEMENTS

We shall use the comparative financial statements and the additional financial information about Graham Company shown in Exhibit E-1.

The analysis has actually begun in the exhibit because it shows the percentages of sales for each item on the income statement and the percentage of total assets or total equities for each balance sheet item. These percentage statements, or **common size statements**, can help an analyst to spot trends.

Two of the more important percentages on the income statement are the **gross profit ratio**, which is gross profit divided by sales, and **return on sales (ROS)**, which is net income divided by sales. These ratios for Graham in 19X6 are 38.5% and 7.9%, respectively. The gross profit ratio improved in 19X6 over 19X5, but ROS declined.

Financial analysts and internal managers are interested in ROS and the gross profit ratio because these ratios indicate how valuable a dollar of sales is to the firm. These ratios are not the same as the contribution margin ratio, but they do give a rough idea of the profit/sales relationship. A relatively low ROS, combined with a gross profit ratio that is normal for the industry, could indicate that operating expenses are higher than those of other firms. As we mention several times in this chapter, ratios provide clues or indicators, but they do not tell you that a firm is acting wisely or unwisely.

Balance-sheet ratios show whether the proportions of particular assets or liabilities are increasing or decreasing, and whether they are within reasonable bounds. We shall explore balance-sheet ratios in more detail later in the chapter.

Exhibit E-1 Graham Company, Balance Sheets as of December 31

	19X6		19X5	
	Dollars	Percent	Dollars	Percent
Current assets:				
Cash	$ 80,000	5.2%	$ 50,000	3.6%
Accounts receivable, net	180,000	11.6	120,000	8.7
Inventory	190,000	12.2	230,000	16.7
Total current assets	450,000	29.0	400,000	29.0
Plant and equipment—cost	1,350,000	87.1	1,150,000	83.3
Accumulated depreciation	(340,000)	(21.9)	(250,000)	(18.1)
Net plant and equipment	1,010,000	65.2	900,000	65.2
Other assets	90,000	5.8	80,000	5.8
Total assets	$1,550,000	100.0%	$1,380,000	100.0%
Current liabilities:				
Accounts payable	$ 110,000	7.1%	$ 105,000	7.6%
Accrued expenses	40,000	2.6	15,000	1.1
Total current liabilities	150,000	9.7	120,000	8.7
Long-term debt	600,000	38.7	490,000	35.5
Total liabilities	750,000	48.4	610,000	44.2
Common stock, 22,000 shares	220,000	14.2	220,000	15.9
Paid-in capital	350,000	22.6	350,000	25.4
Retained earnings	230,000	14.8	200,000	14.5
Total stockholders' equity	800,000	51.6	770,000	55.8
Total equities	$1,550,000	100.0%	$1,380,000	100.0%

Graham Company, Income Statements for the Years Ended December 31

	19X6		19X5	
	Dollars	Percent	Dollars	Percent
Sales	$1,300,000	100.0%	$1,080,000	100.0%
Cost of goods sold	800,000	61.5	670,000	62.0
Gross profit	500,000	38.5	410,000	38.0
Operating expenses[a]	280,000	21.6	210,000	19.4
Income before interest and taxes	220,000	16.9	200,000	18.6
Interest expense	48,000	3.7	42,000	3.9
Income before taxes	172,000	13.2	158,000	14.7
Income taxes at 40% rate	68,800	5.3	63,200	5.9
Net income	$ 103,200	7.9%	$ 94,800	8.8%

[a]*Including depreciation of $90,000 in 19X6 and $75,000 in 19X5.*

Graham Company, Cash Flow Statements for the Years ended December 31

	19X6	19X5
Net cash flow from operating activities:		
Collections from customers	$1,240,000	$1,075,000
Payments to suppliers	(755,000)	(656,400)
Payments for operating expenses	(182,000)	(143,600)
Interest paid	(44,000)	(39,000)
Taxes paid	(55,800)	(58,400)
Net cash provided by operating activities	203,200	177,600
Cash flows for investing activities:		
Purchase of plant and equipment	(200,000)	(97,000)
Sale of plant and equipment		12,000
Purchase of other assets	(10,000)	
Net cash used by investing activities	(210,000)	(85,000)
Cash flows from (for) financing activities:		
Proceeds from bond issue	110,000	
Repayment of short-term loans		(42,000)
Payment of dividends	(73,200)	(63,000)
Net cash from (for) financial activities	36,800	(105,000)
Increase (decrease) in cash	30,000	(12,400)
Cash balance, beginning of year	50,000	62,400
Cash balance, end of year	$ 80,000	$ 50,000

LIQUIDITY

Liquidity is a firm's ability to meet obligations due in the near future. The more liquid a firm, the more likely it is to be able to pay its employees, suppliers, and holders of its short-term notes payable. A company with excellent long-term prospects could fail to realize them because it was forced into bankruptcy when it could not pay its debts in the near term. Hence, while liquidity is most important to short-term creditors, it is also of concern to long-term creditors and stockholders.

WORKING CAPITAL AND THE CURRENT RATIO

Working capital, the difference between current assets and current liabilities, is a very rough measure of liquidity. Graham had the following amounts of working capital at the ends of 19X5 and 19X6.

	19X6	19X5
Current assets	$450,000	$400,000
Current liabilities	150,000	120,000
Working capital	$300,000	$280,000

Working capital is positive and increased. But this does not necessarily mean that the firm has adequate liquidity or became more liquid. Most analysts consider changes in working capital as only a very rough indication of changes in liquidity and supplement their analysis with several other calculations. Working capital is stated in absolute dollar terms and hence is greatly influenced by the size of the firm.

The **current ratio** is a measure of relative liquidity that takes into account differences in absolute size. It is used to compare firms with different total current assets and liabilities as well as to compare the same firm's liquidity from year to year.

$$\textit{Current ratio} = \frac{\textit{current assets}}{\textit{current liabilities}}$$

Graham has current ratios of 3.33 to 1 in 19X5 ($400,000/$120,000) and 3 to 1 in 19X6 ($450,000/$150,000). On the basis of the current ratio, we would say that the firm seemed to be less liquid at the end of 19X6. There is a very good reason for saying "seemed to be less liquid." One major problem that arises with any ratio, but especially the current ratio, is that of composition. The **composition problem** arises when one uses a total, such as total current assets (or current liabilities), that might mask information about the individual components. How soon will the current assets be converted into cash so that they can be used to pay current liabilities? How soon are the current liabilities due for payment? You already know that current assets normally are listed in order of liquidity from cash, the most liquid, to prepaid expenses. The analyst obtains a general idea of the magnitude of the composition problem by reviewing the common-size balance sheet to see how much of current assets are composed of relatively liquid items.

QUICK RATIO (ACID-TEST RATIO)

The **quick ratio**, or **acid-test ratio**, is cash plus accounts receivable plus marketable securities divided by current liabilities. It is similar to the current ratio, but includes only those assets that are cash or "near cash" (called **quick assets**). Hence, the ratio gives a stricter indication of short-term debt-paying ability than does the current ratio.

$$\textit{Quick ratio} = \frac{\textit{cash + marketable securities + receivables}}{\textit{current liablities}}$$

Graham had no marketable securities at the end of either year, so its quick ratios are as follows:

$$\textit{19X5} \quad \frac{\$50{,}000 + \$120{,}000}{\$120{,}000} = 1.42$$

$$\textit{19X6} \quad \frac{\$80{,}000 + \$180{,}000}{\$150{,}000} = 1.73$$

Graham seems to have increased its liquidity because its quick ratio increased. We could say that the firm was better able to meet current liabilities at the end of 19X6; but we would still like to know how soon its current liabilities have to be paid and how rapidly the firm can expect to turn its receivables and inventory into cash. The next section presents ratios that measure the liquidity of current assets.

WORKING CAPITAL ACTIVITY RATIOS

Two commonly used ratios provide information about the time within which the firm should realize cash from its receivables and inventories. And, although we cannot tell the time within which the firm must pay its various current liabilities simply by examining the financial statements, one commonly used ratio offers some insight into the company's bill-paying practices.

Accounts Receivable Turnover Accounts receivable turnover measures how rapidly the firm collects its receivables; in general, the higher the turnover the better.

$$\textit{Accounts receivable turnover} = \frac{\textit{credit sales}}{\textit{average receivables}}$$

In general, average receivables are defined as the beginning balance plus the ending balance, divided by 2. This simple averaging procedure is satisfactory so long as there are no extremely high or low points during the year (including the end of the year). If a firm has widely fluctuating receivable balances, it is better to use a monthly average. For illustrative purposes we assume that all of Graham's sales are on credit. Because we do not have the beginning balance for 19X5, we can only calculate the turnover of *average* receivables for 19X6 for Graham Company. (Some analysts do compute turnovers using end-of-year values.)

$$\frac{\$1{,}300{,}000}{(\$120{,}000 + \$180{,}000)/2} = \frac{\$1{,}300{,}000}{\$150{,}000} = 8.67 \textit{ times}$$

Some analysts make a related calculation called number of **days' sales in accounts receivable**. This figure indicates the average age of ending accounts receivable.

$$\textit{Day's sales in accounts receivable} = \frac{\textit{ending accounts receivable}}{\textit{average daily credit sales}}$$

Average daily sales is simply credit sales for the year divided by 365. For Graham Company, we have average daily credit sales of about $2,959 ($1,080,000/365) for 19X5 and about $3,562 ($1,300,000/365) for 19X6. Hence, days' sales in accounts receivable are

$$\textit{19X5} \quad \frac{\$120{,}000}{\$2{,}959} = 41 \textit{ days}$$

$$19X6 \quad \frac{\$180{,}000}{\$3{,}562} = 51 \text{ days}$$

On the average, then, Graham's accounts receivable were 41 days old at the end of 19X5 and 51 days old at the end of 19X6. The collection period has lengthened considerably in one year, but the period must be interpreted in light of the credit terms offered to customers. The faster customers pay, the better, but there are always trade offs. If a firm loses sales because of tight credit policies, the advantage of faster collection might be more than offset by the loss of profits from lower total sales. The increase in the average collection period might well be the result of a management decision to offer more liberal terms to stimulate sales.

We used Graham's total sales to compute the two receivables-related ratios because we assumed that all sales were on credit. An outside analyst seldom knows what portion of sales is on credit and uses total sales for lack of better information. The ratios so computed are not misleading as long as the proportions of cash and credit sales did not change significantly (another instance of "the composition problem"). An internal manager, of course, has access to information about the composition of total sales and could make a more precise calculation of the receivables ratios. Moreover, the internal manager is extremely interested in the precise patterns of customer payments, for cash budgeting and control purposes. Nevertheless, as a first step in the analysis, the internal manager is likely to use the same ratios as the external analyst.

Inventory Turnover The same type of analysis applies to the firm's inventory. Inventory turnover is calculated as follows.

$$\text{Inventory turnover} = \frac{\text{cost of goods sold}}{\text{average inventory}}$$

Again, average inventory is the sum of the beginning and ending balances divided by 2 unless the firm has much higher and lower inventories for significant portions of the year because of seasonal business. It is then better to use monthly figures to determine the average.

Graham's inventory turnover for 19X6 is about 3.8 times, calculated as follows:

$$\frac{\$800{,}000}{(\$230{,}000 + \$190{,}000)/2} = \frac{\$800{,}000}{\$210{,}000} = 3.8$$

Using only the year-end inventory for 19X5, turnover is 2.9 ($670,000/ $230,000).

This measure indicates the efficiency with which the firm uses its inventory. High inventory turnover is critical for many businesses, especially those that sell at relatively low markup (ratio of gross profit to cost) and depend on high sales volumes to earn satisfactory profits. For example, discount stores and food stores rely on quick turnover for profitability. Firms with very high markups, such as jewelry stores, do not need such rapid turnovers to be profitable.

As discussed in Chapters 6 and 9, and Appendix A showed, investment in inventory can be very expensive. Some costs—insurance, personal property taxes, interest on the funds tied up in inventory, and obsolescence—can be very high. Therefore, managers prefer to keep inventory as low as possible. The problem is that if inventory is too low, particularly in retail stores, sales might be lost because customers cannot find what they want.

Analysts will also sometimes calculate the number of **days' sales in inventory**, which is a measure of the supply that the firm maintains.

$$\textit{Days' sales in inventory} = \frac{\textit{ending inventory}}{\textit{average daily cost of goods sold}}$$

Average daily cost of goods sold is simply cost of goods sold for the year divided by 365. For Graham, this is $1,836 ($670,000/365) for 19X5 and $2,192 ($800,000/365) for 19X6. Days' sales in inventory are as follows.

$$\textit{19X5} \quad \frac{\$230{,}000}{\$1{,}836} = \textit{125 days}$$

$$\textit{19X6} \quad \frac{\$190{,}000}{\$2{,}192} = \textit{87 days}$$

The decline in days' sales in inventory could indicate a deliberate change in inventory policy, or perhaps just a temporary reduction of inventory because of heavier than expected sales near the end of the year.

As you may remember from your study of financial accounting, generally accepted accounting principles (GAAP) allow several formats for the income statement. Some formats do not show cost of goods sold, so that the outside analyst cannot compute inventory turnover using the approach just presented. In such cases, the analyst will use total sales as a substitute for cost of goods sold, even though sales and inventory are not measured in the same way. (Sales is measured in selling prices, while inventory is measured in cost prices.) The inventory turnover so derived is overstated—a unit costing $1 and sold for $2 will reflect two inventory turnovers when only one unit has been sold. If analysts recognize the overstatement in the calculation, they will not be misled by the results.

As you will recall from Chapter 13, a manufacturing firm has not one but three types of inventory: raw materials, work in process, and finished goods. The calculation of inventory turnover, as described above, relates to the finished goods inventory of a manufacturing firm, since only that inventory is measured on the same basis (full cost of a completed unit) as cost of goods sold. An internal analyst also should be able to compute the firm's **turnover of inventory of raw materials.**

$$\textit{Turnover of inventory of raw materials} = \frac{\textit{raw materials used in production}}{\textit{average raw materials inventory}}$$

An external analyst is seldom able to compute this second inventory turnover because externally available financial statements seldom provide sufficient information to determine the value of the numerator of the ratio.

Days' Purchases in Accounts Payable This ratio is of special concern to both creditors and the firm's managers.

$$\textit{Days' purchases in accounts payable} = \frac{\textit{ending accounts payable}}{\textit{average daily purchases}}$$

When a firm reports cost of goods sold in its income statement, the analyst can compute total purchases as follows.

$$\textit{Purchases} = \textit{cost of goods sold} + \textit{ending inventory} - \textit{beginning inventory}$$

For Graham, days' purchases in accounts payable is about 53 days.

$$\textit{Days' purchases in accounts payable} = \frac{\$110{,}000}{(\$800{,}000 + \$190{,}000 - \$230{,}000)/365}$$

$$= \frac{\$110{,}000}{\$2{,}082} = 52.8 \textit{ days}$$

We cannot compute the ratio for 19X5 because we do not know the beginning inventory for that year.

The value for 19X6, about 53 days, must be interpreted in light of the credit terms offered by suppliers. If normal terms require payment in 60 days, the 53 day value indicates no significant problem; if normal terms are cash in 30 days, the ratio suggests that a problem exists. Of course, it pays a company to take as long as possible to pay suppliers, so long as it does not incur high interest charges or damage its credit rating.

PROFITABILITY

Profitability can be measured in absolute dollar terms, such as net income, or by ratios. The most commonly used measures of profitability fall under the general heading of **return on investment (ROI)**. As described in Chapter 11, ROI is actually a family of ratios having the general form

$$\textit{Return on investment} = \frac{\textit{income}}{\textit{investment}}$$

External investors, especially stockholders and potential stockholders, are interested in the return that they can expect from their investments. Managers within the firm are concerned with earning satisfactory returns on the investments that they control. As a practical matter, then, different analysts and managers will define both income and investment differently when trying to measure the same basic relationships. In this section, we present some of the most often used alternative ways of looking at this basic relationship of accomplishment (return, income) to effort (investment).

RETURN ON ASSETS (ROA)

ROA is a measure of operating efficiency, of how well managers have used the assets under their control to generate income. The following ratio is one way to make the calculation.

$$\textit{Return on assets} = \frac{\textit{net income + interest + income taxes}}{\textit{average total assets}}$$

For Graham, ROA was about 15% for 19X6, calculated as follows.

$$\textit{Return on assets} = \frac{\$103{,}200 + \$48{,}000 + \$68{,}800}{(\$1{,}380{,}000 + \$1{,}550{,}000)/2}$$

$$= \frac{\$220{,}000}{\$1{,}465{,}000} = 15.0\%$$

Adding interest and income taxes back to net income is equivalent to using income before interest and income taxes. Remember that we are concerned with operations: Interest and, to some extent, income taxes depend on how the company finances its assets—how much debt it uses. Moreover, income taxes are affected by many matters not related to operations, which is another reason for adding them back. (Some of these nonoperating factors are the company's investments in securities and its use of tax benefits such as percentage depletion.) Some analysts add back only interest; others add back only the after-tax effect of interest. There are arguments to support several measures of the numerator in the ROA calculation. Choosing one alternative over another is a matter of both personal preference and of the particular objective.

Average total assets is normally the sum of the beginning and ending balance-sheet amounts divided by 2, although if significant fluctuations occur from month to month, it is better to use monthly data to determine the average. Some analysts use end-of-year assets in the denominator, some use beginning-of-year amounts, and still others use total assets minus current liabilities. (Analysts in the latter group argue that current liabilities are "automatic" sources of financing and typically relate to operating, rather than financing, decisions.) In this chapter, we use average total assets, with no consideration of current liabilities, but we caution you that this is a matter of choice and preference.

Both internal and external analysts can obtain the information for this ratio directly from publicly available financial statements, and can make direct comparisons with firms in the same industry.

RETURN ON COMMON EQUITY (ROE)

ROA is a measure of operating efficiency. Common stockholders are also concerned with the return on *their* investment, which is affected not only by operations but also by the amount of debt and preferred stock in the firm's capital structure.

ROE is computed as follows.

$$\textit{Return on common equity (ROE)} = \frac{\textit{net income} - \textit{dividends on preferred stock}}{\textit{average common stockholders' equity}}$$

In the absence of preferred stock, average common stockholders' equity is simply the sum of the beginning and ending amounts of stockholders' equity divided by 2. If there is preferred stock, preferred dividends must be subtracted from net income in the numerator, and the amount of total stockholders' equity attributable to preferred stock is subtracted in the denominator to obtain common stockholders' equity.

Graham Company has no preferred stock, but it does have debt. ROE for Graham in 19X6 is a bit over 13%.

$$\frac{\$103{,}200}{(\$770{,}000 + \$800{,}000)/2} = \frac{\$103{,}200}{\$785{,}000} = 13.1\%$$

Notice that Graham's ROE is less than its ROA. If a firm finances its assets solely with common stock, such a relationship will hold between ROE and ROA because ROE is computed using after-tax income. But debt holders do not participate in the earnings of the firm; they receive a stipulated, constant amount of interest. Hence, the firm can increase its ROE if it uses debt, provided that ROA is greater than the interest rate it must pay to debt holders. This method of using debt (or preferred stock) to increase ROE is called **leverage** or **trading on the equity**. Leverage increases both risk and the potential for greater return.

THE EFFECTS OF LEVERAGE

Suppose that a company having a 40% tax rate requires total assets of $1,000,000 to earn $180,000 per year before interest and income taxes, for an ROA of 18%. Three possible financing alternatives are: (1) all common stock; (2) $400,000 common stock and $600,000 in 7% bonds (interest expense of $42,000); and (3) $400,000 in common stock and $600,000 in 8% preferred stock (dividends of $48,000). The schedule below shows the differing effects of the three alternatives on ROE.

	(1) All Common Stock	(2) Debt and Common Stock	(3) Preferred Stock and Common Stock
Income before interest and taxes	$ 180,000	$180,000	$180,000
Interest expense at 7%	0	42,000	0
Income before taxes	180,000	138,000	180,000
Income taxes at 40%	72,000	55,200	72,000
Net income	108,000	82,800	108,000
Less preferred stock dividends	0	0	48,000
Earnings available for common stock	$ 108,000	$ 82,800	$ 60,000
Divided by common equity invested	$1,000,000	$400,000	$400,000
Equals return on common equity	10.8%	20.7%	15%

Note that dividends on preferred stock must be subtracted from net income to reach earnings *available for common stockholders* (because the preferred shareholders have a prior claim on the firm's earnings). Note also that, though the plans that include debt or preferred stock both result in lower earnings available for common equity, both produce a higher ROE than would be achieved if all common equity were used. That is, these two plans provide the benefits of leverage.

However, leverage works both ways. It is good for the common stockholder when earnings are high and bad when they are low. If in one year the firm earns only $60,000 before interest and taxes, it has the following results.

	(1) All Common	(2) $600,000 Debt	(3) $600,000 Preferred
Income before interest and taxes	$ 60,000	$ 60,000	$ 60,000
Interest expense	0	42,000	0
Income before taxes	60,000	18,000	60,000
Income taxes at 40%	24,000	7,200	24,000
Net income	36,000	10,800	36,000
Preferred stock dividends	0	0	42,000
Earnings available for common	$ 36,000	$ 10,800	($ 6,000)
Common equity invested	$1,000,000	$400,000	$400,000
Return on common equity	3.6%	2.7%	negative

As you can see, ROE is highest if all common equity is used, but the return is very low. Firms that have relatively stable revenues and expenses, like public utilities, can use considerable leverage. Leverage is very risky for firms in cyclical businesses like automobiles, aircraft, and construction, where income fluctuates greatly from year to year. A couple of bad years in a row could bring a heavily leveraged firm into bankruptcy. During the 1980's, leverage was so important in the acquisition of entire companies that the term leveraged buyout (LBO) became a standard part of financial discussions. Often such acquisitions were financed with high-yield bonds, called junk bonds because of their high risk.

EARNINGS PER SHARE (EPS)

Investors in common stock are less concerned with the total income of the firm than with their share of that income—their proportional interest in the firm represented by earnings per share (EPS). EPS is the most widely cited statistic in the financial press, business section of newspapers, and recommendations by brokerage firms and other investment advisers. In relatively simple cases, EPS is calculated below.

$$\textit{Earnings per share (EPS)} = \frac{\textit{net income} - \textit{dividends on preferred stock}}{\textit{weighted-average common shares outstanding}}$$

The weighted average of common shares outstanding is the best measure of the shares outstanding throughout the period when the income is earned.

If Graham Company had 22,000 shares outstanding all through 19X5 and 19X6, as well as at the ends of those years, its EPS figures are

$$\textit{19X5}\quad \frac{\$94{,}800 - 0}{22{,}000} = \frac{\$94{,}800}{22{,}000} = \$4.31$$

$$\textit{19X6}\quad \frac{\$103{,}200 - 0}{22{,}000} = \frac{\$103{,}200}{22{,}000} = \$4.69$$

EPS in 19X6 was $0.38 higher than in 19X5. This is an 8.8% growth rate, which can be calculated as follows.

$$\textit{Growth rate of EPS} = \frac{\textit{EPS current year} - \textit{EPS prior year}}{\textit{EPS prior year}}$$

$$= \frac{\$4.69 - \$4.31}{\$4.31} = 8.8\%$$

In general, the greater the growth that investors expect, the more they are willing to pay for the common stock. Of course, an increase in EPS does not always mean that the firm is growing; it might simply reflect a rebound from a particularly poor year. Growth rates should be calculated over a number of years, rather than for a single year as we have done here.

Some companies issue *convertible securities*, bonds and preferred stock that can be converted into common stock at the option of the owner. Conversion poses the problem of potential **dilution** (decreases) in EPS, because earnings have to be spread over a greater number of shares.[1] The calculation of EPS when dilution is possible can be extremely complex. We shall show a single, relatively simple, illustration. Assume that a firm has net income of $200,000, 80,000 common shares outstanding, and an issue of convertible preferred stock. The preferred stock pays dividends of $20,000 and is convertible into 30,000 common shares. Using the basic formula, EPS is $2.25.

$$\textit{EPS} = \frac{\$200{,}000 - \$20{,}000}{80{,}000} = \frac{\$180{,}000}{80{,}000} = \$2.25$$

In some cases the $2.25 is presented on the income statement and called *primary earnings per share*. Then, another EPS calculation, called *fully diluted earnings per share*, is made. Fully diluted EPS is calculated assuming that the convertible securities had been converted into common stock at the beginning of the year. Had this occurred, there would have been no preferred dividends, but an additional 30,000 common shares would have been outstanding for the entire year. We calculate fully diluted EPS by adding back the

1 The computation of EPS is governed by Accounting Principles Board Opinion No. 15 (New York: American Institute of Certified Public Accountants, 1969) and Unoficial Accounting Interpretations of APB Opinion No. 15 (New York: American Institue of Certified Public Acountants, 1970). Together, these two documents contain about 100 pages.

preferred dividends on the convertible stock to the $180,000 earnings available for common stock and adding 30,000 shares to the denominator.

$$\textit{Filly diluted EPS} = \frac{\$180{,}000 + \$20{,}000}{80{,}000 + 30{,}000} = \frac{\$200{,}000}{110{,}000} = \$1.82$$

PRICE-EARNINGS RATIO (PE)

The PE ratio is the ratio of the market price of a share of common stock to its earnings per share. The ratio indicates the amount investors are paying to buy a dollar of earnings. PE ratios of high-growth companies are often very high; those of low-growth or declining firms tend to be low. Assume that Graham's common stock sold at $60 per share at the end of 19X5 and $70 at the end of 19X6. The PE ratios are

$$\textit{Price-earnings ratio} = \frac{\textit{market price per share}}{\textit{earnings per share}}$$

$$19X5 \quad \frac{\$60}{\$4.31} = 14$$

$$19X6 \quad \frac{\$70}{\$4.69} = 14.9$$

The PE ratio increased from 19X5 to 19X6. This could have happened because EPS had been growing rather slowly until 19X6 and investors believed the growth rate would increase in the future. Such a situation justifies a higher PE ratio. It is also possible that PE ratios throughout the economy increased because of good economic news and expectations of good business conditions.

DIVIDEND YIELD AND PAYOUT RATIO

We have been viewing earnings available for common stockholders as the major return accruing to owners of common stock. However, investors do not "get" EPS. They receive dividends and, they hope, increases in the market value of their shares. The **dividend yield** is a measure of the current cash income that an investor can obtain per dollar of investment.

$$\textit{Dividend yield} = \frac{\textit{dividend per share}}{\textit{market price per share}}$$

Graham declared and paid dividends of $63,000 in 19X5 and $73,200 in 19X6 on 22,000 shares, giving dividends per share of $2.86 and $3.33 for 19X5 and 19X6, respectively. Given per-share market prices of $60 and $70 at the ends of 19X5 and 19X6, dividend yields are

$$19X5 \quad \frac{\$2.86}{\$60} = 4.77\%$$

$$\textit{19X6} \quad \frac{\$3.33}{\$70} = 4.76\%$$

The **payout ratio** is the ratio of dividends per share to earnings per share. For Graham, the payout ratio in 19X6 is 71% ($3.33/$4.69) and in 19X5 was 66% ($2.86/$4.31). In general, companies with high growth rates have relatively low dividend yields and payout ratios. Such companies are investing the cash that could be used for dividends. Investors who favor high-growth companies are not looking for dividends so much as for increases in the market price of the common stock. Because such hoped-for increases may or may not occur, investing in high-growth companies is generally riskier than investing in companies that pay relatively high, stable dividends.

SOLVENCY

Solvency refers to long-term safety, to the likelihood that the company will be able to pay its long-term liabilities. It is similar to liquidity but has a much longer time horizon. Both long-term creditors and stockholders are interested in solvency—long-term creditors because of a concern about receiving interest payments and a return of principal; stockholders because they cannot receive dividends and benefit from increased market prices unless the firm survives.

DEBT RATIO

One common measure of solvency is the **debt ratio**, which is calculated as follows.

$$\textit{Debt ratio} = \frac{\textit{total liabilities}}{\textit{total assets}}$$

This ratio measures the proportion of debt in the firm's capital structure. It is also called the debt-to-assets ratio. As with other ratios, variations provide much the same information. For example, some analysts calculate a *debt-to-equity ratio*, dividing total liabilities by stockholders' equity; others calculate a ratio of long-term liabilities to total assets or of long-term liabilities to fixed assets, such as property, plant, and equipment. The basic objective is the same with all of these variations: to determine the firm's degree of debt. The higher the proportion of debt in the capital structure, the riskier the firm. Firms in different industries can handle different percentages of debt. For example, public utilities typically have very high percentages of debt because they have stable cash flows, manufacturing firms somewhat less.

The debt ratios for Graham Company for 19X5 and 19X6 are

$$\textit{19X5} \quad \frac{\$610{,}000}{\$1{,}380{,}000} = 44.2\%$$

$$\textit{19X6} \quad \frac{\$750{,}000}{\$1{,}550{,}000} = 48.4\%$$

Notice that if we subtract the debt ratio from 1, we get the proportion of stockholders' equity in the capital structure. This is usually called the *equity ratio*. Like the debt ratio, it is a way of measuring solvency, but from a different standpoint.

Graham's debt ratio increased from 19X5 to 19X6, but we cannot tell whether it is near a dangerous level without knowing a good deal more. We can obtain some additional information by calculating the burden that interest expense places on the firm.

TIMES INTEREST EARNED

Times interest earned, or interest coverage, measures the extent to which operations cover interest expense. The higher the ratio, the more likely the firm will be able to continue meeting the interest payments.

$$\textit{Times interest earned} = \frac{\textit{income before interest and taxes}}{\textit{interest expense}}$$

Graham had interest coverage of 4.8 times in 19X5, but slipped to 4.6 times in 19X6.

$$\textit{19X5} \quad \frac{\$200{,}000}{\$42{,}000} = \textit{4.8 times}$$

$$\textit{19X6} \quad \frac{\$220{,}000}{\$48{,}000} = \textit{4.6 times}$$

We use income before interest and taxes because interest is a tax-deductible expense. Some analysts also add depreciation in the numerator. Reasoning that depreciation does not require cash payments, these analysts believe that the numerator in their ratio approximates the total amount of cash available to pay interest.

CASH FLOW TO TOTAL DEBT

A major study of ratios computed for actual companies showed that the single best ratio for predicting a firm's failure was the ratio of **cash flow to total debt**.[2] In that study, cash flow was defined as net income plus depreciation, amortization, and depletion, and total debt was defined as total liabilities plus preferred stock.

$$\textit{Cash flow to total debt} = \frac{\textit{net income + depreciation + amortization + depletion}}{\textit{total liabilities + preferred stock}}$$

Graham has no amortization or depletion and no preferred stock. Therefore, the values of the ratio are

2 See William H. Beaver, "Financial Ratios as Predictors of Failure," Empirical Research in Accounting, Selected Studies, 1966, Journal of Accounting Research, 1967, 71-111.

$$\textit{19X5} \quad \frac{\$94{,}800 + \$75{,}000}{\$610{,}000} = \frac{\$169{,}800}{\$610{,}000} = 27.8\%$$

$$\textit{19X6} \quad \frac{\$103{,}200 + \$90{,}000}{\$750{,}000} = \frac{\$193{,}200}{\$750{,}000} = 25.8\%$$

The research study drawing attention to this ratio was conducted before companies were required to provide a cash flow statement as part of the financial-statement package. Using the operating cash flow taken *directly* from Graham's cash flow statement, the ratios are

$$\textit{19X5} \quad \frac{\$177{,}600}{\$610{,}000} = 29.1\%$$

$$\textit{19X6} \quad \frac{\$203{,}200}{\$750{,}000} = 27.1\%$$

Though both versions of this solvency ratio show a decline, the decline does not seem serious. Nevertheless, comparison of the ratio with the industry average might indicate a potential problem.

Other uses of cash flow ratios are becoming popular, especially now that the cash flow statement is required for virtually all publicly-traded companies. Analysts use ratios to assess the adequacy of a company's cash flow. Brandt et al. propose a number of such ratios.[3]

RATIOS AND EVALUATION

Calculating ratios for the current year is only the starting point in analyzing a firm's operations and prospects. Comparisons are critical and many factors besides the magnitudes of the ratios must be considered.

Analysts should compare ratios with those from prior years, evaluate trends, and explore related ratios. (Is the company becoming more or less liquid? More or less profitable? Were changes in sales and ROA consistent with changes in turnovers of receivables and inventory?) Whenever possible, ratios should also be compared with those of similar firms and with those for the industry as a whole. (Are the firm's ratios consistent with, and moving in the same direction as, those for the industry? Are out-of-line ratios or trends explainable?)

Several factors make both inter-firm and industry comparisons difficult. Comparisons become more difficult as more and more companies diversify their operations. Some highly diversified companies operate in 15 or more different industries. A welcome trend in financial reporting is increased disclosure of data about the major segments of diversified companies. Such additional disclosure allows analysts to make comparisons that were not possible when only overall results were available.

---

3 *For an excellent discussion of cash flow ratios, see Lloyd Brandt, Jr., Joseph R. Danos, and J. Herman Brasseaux, "Financial Statement Analysis: Benefits and Pitfalls," The Financial Accountant, June 1989, 69-78.*

Even comparisons with fairly similar companies must be made with care because ratios can differ considerably when companies use different accounting methods. For example, differences in the accounting methods used to value inventory (e.g. FIFO and LIFO) can influence many ratios. If purchase prices have generally been rising, a LIFO firm will show a lower inventory, current ratio, ROS, and EPS, and a higher inventory turnover than a FIFO firm. The longer the price trend has continued and the longer the firm has used LIFO, the more marked the effects of the difference in inventory method. Consider too the effects of different depreciation methods on ratios. A firm using the sum-of-the-years'-digits method will show lower book values for its fixed assets than one using the straight-line method; and the differences will affect all ratios involving total assets, net income, or both.

Until 1977, profitability measures were significantly influenced by whether a firm acquired the use of fixed assets by issuing long-term debt or stock or by arranging long-term leases. To a great extent, the effects of this particular difference in financial arrangements were eliminated by the issuance of *Financial Accounting Standard No. 13*[4] but some differences still remain.

Even comparisons among similar companies using similar accounting methods can be misleading in the sense that a firm that shows up better than another in several measures of liquidity, profitability, or solvency might not be more successful, better, or stronger than another. For example, a company might be too liquid. Too much cash is not as bad as too little cash, but having excessive cash is unwise, because cash does not earn profits unless it is used for something. Faster turnover of inventory could be the result of unnecessarily low selling prices. A shorter collection period on receivables could result from highly restrictive credit policies. Hence, turnovers must be studied in relation to ROS and gross profit ratios, and to trends in the industry. In short, no single ratio, or group of ratios, should be considered in a vacuum.

Another factor to consider in evaluating a firm is the extent to which one or more ratios can be affected by a single transaction. For example, consider the effect of a large cash payment for a current liability. Such a payment reduces both cash and current liabilities, and has no effect on total working capital. Yet it can improve the current ratio. To illustrate, look at the ratios for Graham Company for 19X6 and assume that it paid current liabilities of $30,000 just before the end of that year. Its current assets before the payment would have been $480,000 ($450,000 + $30,000), and its current liabilities would have been $180,000 ($150,000 + $30,000), giving a current ratio of 2.67 to 1. This ratio is lower than the 3 to 1 we calculated earlier. Before the payment the acid-test ratio would have been 1.6 to 1 [($80,000 + $180,000 + $30,000)/($150,000 + $30,000)]. This is also lower than the ratio calculated earlier (1.73 to 1). Actions taken to improve ratios are called **window dress-**

4 *Financial Accounting Standards Board,* Statement of Financial Accounting Standards No. 13, Accounting for Leases *(Stanford, Connecticut: Financial Accounting Standards Board, 1976).*

ing. This particular type of window dressing is possible if the current ratio and acid-test ratio are greater than 1 to 1. If those ratios are less than 1 to 1, paying a current liability will reduce them, but window dressing is then possible by delaying payments of current liabilities.

Any evaluation based on ratios and comparisons of them must recognize the relative importance of the ratio to the particular industry. The nature of the product and of the production process, the degree of competition in the industry, and many other industry-related factors are relevant in interpreting a particular firm's liquidity, profitability, and solvency ratios. For example, consider the utility industry. Because a utility is a monopoly, the government unit granting the monopoly right also regulates many of the utility's actions. In most cases, the regulating authority both ensures and limits the profitability of the utility. Liquidity problems are unlikely for a utility because their cash flows are relatively stable, they need not build up inventories in advance because they sell a service, and because the collectibility of their accounts is increased by their ability to shut off a necessary service. For the same reasons, the investing public tolerates more leverage and a lower, but more stable, level of profitability in a utility.

All of the preceding considerations point out the need for understanding (1) the company being analyzed and (2) the industry in which the company operates. That a company's ratios differ from those in the past, or are in line or out of line with those of other companies in the industry, is not, per se, good or bad. (Knowing that, from 1980 to 1982, Chrysler Corporation improved its liquidity, profitability, and prospects for solvency, in relation to both its prior performance and to the average for the industry, does not change the fact that that entire industry performed poorly during that period.)

SUMMARY

Ratio analysis is used in making investment decisions. Analysts are concerned with trends in ratios and with whether a firm's ratios are in line with those of other firms in the same industry. Ratios can be classified into three major types: liquidity, profitability, and solvency.

Which ratios to use and which to emphasize depend on the type of decision to be made. Short-term creditors are primarily concerned with liquidity. Long-term creditors are concerned more with solvency than with liquidity and profitability, but the latter aspects are still important. Current and potential common stockholders are most concerned with profitability, but liquidity and solvency are still significant.

Ratio analysis must be used with care. Ratios provide information only in the context of a comparison. Comparisons must be made with other firms and with norms for the industry. Different accounting methods, such as LIFO and FIFO, sum-of-the-years'-digits depreciation and straight-line depreciation, can cause similar firms to show quite different ratios.

KEY TERMS

common size statements
composition problem
convertible securities
dilution (of earnings per share)
leverage (trading on the equity)
liquidity
quality of earnings
quick assets
return on investment
solvency
window dressing
working capital

KEY FORMULAS

Liquidity Ratios

$$\text{Current ratio} = \frac{\text{current assets}}{\text{current liabilities}}$$

$$\text{Quick ratio} = \frac{\text{cash} + \text{marketable securities} + \text{receivables}}{\text{current liabilities}}$$

$$\text{Accounts receivable turnover} = \frac{\text{credit sales}}{\text{average receivables}}$$

$$\text{Days' sales in accounts receivable} = \frac{\text{ending accounts receivable}}{\text{average daily credit sales}}$$

$$\text{Inventory turnover} = \frac{\text{cost of goods sold}}{\text{average inventory}}$$

$$\text{Days' sales in inventory} = \frac{\text{ending inventory}}{\text{average daily cost of goods sold}}$$

$$\text{Inventory turnover (raw materials)} = \frac{\text{raw materials used in production}}{\text{average raw materials inventory}}$$

$$\text{Days' purchases in accounts payable} = \frac{\text{ending accounts payable}}{\text{average daily purchases}}$$

Profitability Ratios

$$\text{Return on assets (ROA)} = \frac{\text{net income} + \text{interest} + \text{income taxes}}{\text{average total assets}}$$

$$\text{Return on common equity (ROE)} = \frac{\text{net income}}{\text{average common stockholders' equity}}$$

$$\text{Earnings per share (EPS)} = \frac{\text{net income} - \text{preferred stock dividends}}{\text{weighted-average common shares outstanding}}$$

$$\text{Price-earnings ratio} = \frac{\text{market price per share}}{\text{earnings per share}}$$

$$\text{Dividend yield} = \frac{\text{dividend per share}}{\text{market price per share}}$$

$$\text{Gross profit ratio} = \frac{\text{gross profit}}{\text{sales}}$$

$$\text{Return on sales (ROS)} = \frac{\text{net income}}{\text{sales}}$$

$$\text{Payout ratio} = \frac{\text{dividends per share}}{\text{earnings per share}}$$

Solvency Ratios

$$\text{Debt ratio} = \frac{\text{total liabilities}}{\text{total assets}}$$

$$\text{Times interest earned} = \frac{\text{income before interest and taxes}}{\text{interest expense}}$$

$$\text{Cash flow to debt} = \frac{\text{net income} + \text{depreciation} + \text{amortization} + \text{depletion}}{\text{total liabilities} + \text{preferred stock}}$$

REVIEW PROBLEM

Financial statements for Quinn Company are given below.

Quinn Company, Balance Sheets as of December 31

	19X7	19X6
Assets		
Cash	$ 180,000	$ 200,000
Accounts receivable, net	850,000	830,000
Inventory	620,000	560,000
Total current assets	1,650,000	1,590,000
Plant and equipment	7,540,000	6,650,000
Accumulated depreciation	(1,920,000)	(1,500,000)
Total assets	$7,270,000	$6,740,000
Equities		
Accounts payable	$ 220,000	$ 190,000
Accrued expenses	450,000	440,000
Total current liabilities	670,000	630,000
Long-term debt	1,000,000	950,000
Total liabilities	1,670,000	1,580,000
Common stock, no par value	4,000,000	4,000,000
Retained earnings	1,600,000	1,160,000
Total equities	$7,270,000	$6,740,000

Quinn Company, Income Statement for 19X7

Sales		$8,650,000
Cost of good sold		4,825,000
Gross profit		3,825,000
Operating expenses:		
Depreciation	$ 420,000	
Other operating expenses	2,135,000	2,555,000
Income before interest and taxes		1,270,000
Interest expense		70,000
Income before taxes		1,200,000
Income taxes at 30% rate		360,000
Net income		$ 840,000

Quinn Company, Cash Flow Statement for 19X7

Net cash flow from operating activities:		
Collections from customers		$8,630,000
Payments to suppliers		(4,855,000)
Payments for operating expenses		(2,163,000)
Interest paid		(72,000)
Taxes paid		(320,000)
Net cash provided by operating activities		1,220,000
Cash flows for investing activities—purchase of plant and equipment		(890,000)
Cash flows from (for) financing activities:		
Payment of dividends	($400,000)	
Proceeds from new long-term debt issue	50,000	
Net cash from (for) financing activities		(350,000)
Change in cash (decrease)		(20,000)
Cash balance, beginning of year		200,000
Cash balance, end of year		$ 180,000

There were 200,000 shares of common stock outstanding throughout the year. The market price of the stock at year end was $65. All sales are on credit.

Required

Compute the following ratios as of the end of 19X7 or for the year ended December 31, 19X7, whichever is appropriate.

1. Current ratio.
2. Quick ratio.
3. Accounts receivable turnover.
4. Days' credit sales in accounts receivable.
5. Inventory turnover.
6. Days' sales in inventory.
7. Days' purchases in accounts payable.
8. Gross profit ratio.
9. Return on sales (ROS).
10. Return on assets (ROA).
11. Return on equity (ROE).
12. Earnings per share (EPS).

13. Price-earnings ratio (PE).
14. Dividend yield.
15. Payout ratio.
16. Debt ratio.
17. Times interest earned.
18. Cash flow to debt ratio.

ANSWERS TO REVIEW PROBLEMS

1. Current ratio

$$\frac{\$1{,}650{,}000}{\$670{,}000} = 2.46 \text{ to } 1$$

2. Quick ratio

$$\frac{\$180{,}000 + \$850{,}000}{\$670{,}000} = 1.54 \text{ to } 1$$

3. Accounts receivable turnover

$$\frac{\$8{,}650{,}000}{(\$850{,}000 + \$830{,}000)/2} = 10.3 \text{ times}$$

4. Days' sales in accounts receivable

$$\frac{\$850{,}000}{\$8{,}650{,}000/365} = 36 \text{ days}$$

5. Inventory turnover

$$\frac{\$4{,}825{,}000}{(\$620{,}000 + \$560{,}000)/2} = 8.2 \text{ times}$$

6. Days' sales in inventory

$$\frac{\$620{,}000}{\$4{,}825{,}000/365} = 47 \text{ days}$$

7. Days' purchases in accounts payable

$$\frac{\$220{,}000}{(\$,825{,}000 + \$620{,}000 - \$560{,}000)/365} = 16.4 \text{ days}$$

8. Gross profit ratio

$$\frac{\$3{,}825{,}000}{\$8{,}650{,}000} = 44.2\%$$

9. ROS

$$\frac{\$840{,}000}{\$8{,}650{,}000} = 9.7\%$$

10. ROA

$$\frac{\$840{,}000 + \$70{,}000 + \$360{,}000}{(\$7{,}270{,}000 + \$6{,}740{,}000)/2} = 18.1\%$$

11. ROE

$$\frac{\$840{,}000}{(\$5{,}600{,}000 + \$5{,}160{,}000)/2} = 15.6\%$$

12. EPS

$$\frac{\$840,000}{200,000} = \$4.20$$

13. PE ratio

$$\frac{\$65}{\$4.20} = 15.5 \text{ times}$$

14. Dividend yield

$$\frac{\$2}{\$65} = 3.1\%$$

15. Payout ratio

$$\frac{\$2}{\$4.20} = 47.6\%$$

16. Debt ratio

$$\frac{\$1,670,000}{\$7,270,000} = 23.0\%$$

17. Times interest earned

$$\frac{\$1,270,000}{\$70,000} = 18 \text{ times}$$

18. Cash flow to debt ratio

$$\frac{\$840,000 + \$420,000}{\$1,670,000} = 75.5\%$$

ASSIGNMENT MATERIAL

QUESTIONS FOR DISCUSSION

E-1 Dividend yield Your friend bought stock in NMC Corporation five years ago for $20 per share. NMC is now paying a $5 dividend per share and the stock sells for $100. He says that the 25% dividend yield is an excellent return. How did he calculate the dividend yield? Is he correct?

E-2 Ratios and accounting methods LIFO Company uses the last-in-first-out method of inventory determination; FIFO Company uses first-in-first-out. They have virtually identical operations, physical quantities of inventory, sales, and fixed assets. What differences would you expect to find in ratios of the firms?

E-3 Ratios and operating decisions Bronson Company and Corman Company are in the same industry and have virtually identical operations. The only difference between them is that Bronson rents 60% of its plant and equipment on short-term leases, while Corman owns all of its fixed assets. Corman has long-term debt of 60% of the book value of its fixed assets, Bronson has none. The two firms show the same net income because Bronson's rent and depreciation are the same as Corman's depreciation and interest. What differences would you expect to find in the ratios of the two firms?

E-4 Ratios and accounting methods SYD Company uses sum-of-the-years'-digits depreciation. SL Company uses straight-line depreciation. Both firms have the same original cost of fixed assets. Their operations are also about the same. They are both growing rapidly, in sales, profits, and assets. What differences would you expect to find between the ratios of the two firms?

E-5 Liquidity You are the chief loan officer of a medium-size bank. Two firms have applied for short-term loans, but you can only grant one because of limited funds. Both firms have the same working capital and the same current ratio. They are in the same industry and their current ratios are well above the industry average. What additional information about their current positions would you seek?

E-6 Seasonality and ratios The following independent questions deal with seasonality in ratio analysis.

1. The inventory turnover of Robertson Toy Store, which does about half of its business in November and December, was computed at 22 times, based on the average of the beginning and ending inventories. The firm's fiscal year ends January 31. Does the turnover figure reflect the firm's activity?
2. The president of Skimpy Bathing Suit Company was bragging that his current ratio was 5 to 1 and his acid-test ratio 4 to 1. The ratios were computed on October 31st. Do you expect the firm to have such ratios throughout the year?
3. The accounts receivable turnover for Long Golf Ball Company, which sells golf balls only in the northeastern United States, was only 2 times. The computation was based on the receivables at June 30, 19X7, and June 30, 19X8. Does the firm seem to have problems collecting its accounts?

E-7 Price-earnings ratio Your friend says that his investment strategy is simple. He buys stocks with very low PE ratios. He reasons that he is getting the most for his money that way. Do you agree that this is a good strategy?

E-8 Relevance of ratios to industry The annual report of GTE (General Telephone and Electronics) Corporation for 1982 contained the normal complement of financial statements. The major sections and amounts in its balance sheet follow (listed in the order, and with the same major headings, as in the statement).

	December 31 1982	1981
	(in millions of dollars)	
Assets		
Property, plant, and equipment	$18,236	$16,927
Investments and other assets	561	506
Current assets	3,497	3,532
Totals	$22,294	$20,965
Shareholders' Equity and Liabilities		
Shareholders' equity	$ 5,816	$ 5,071
Minority interests in equity of subsidiaries	597	592
Preferred stock	744	701
Long-term debt	8,304	7,979
Reserves and deferred credits	3,251	2,912
Current liabilities	3,582	3,710
Totals	$22,294	$20,965

Required

Discuss the relevance of the three ratio groups to the analysis of a firm such as GTE.

E-9 Ratio variations The Financial Highlights section of the 1986 annual report of Motorola Inc. includes the values of the following ratios for 1985 and 1986.

1. Return on average invested capital (stockholders' equity) plus long-term and short-term debt, net of marketable securities.
2. Percent of total debt less marketable securities to total debt less marketable securities plus equity.

To which of the three general categories of ratios does each of these ratios belong? How would you explain why the components of these ratios differ from those given in the chapter?

EXERCISES

E-10 Effects of transactions Indicate the effects of each of the following transactions on the firm's (a) current ratio and (b) acid-test ratio. There are three possible answers: (+) increase, (−) decrease, and (0) no effect. Before each transaction takes place, both ratios are greater than 1 to 1.

	Effects on	
Transaction	(a) Current Ratio	(b) Acid-Test Ratio
Example: Purchase inventory for cash	0	−
1. Purchase inventory on account	______	______
2. Pay a current account payable	______	______
3. Borrow cash on a short-term loan	______	______
4. Purchase plant assets for cash	______	______
5. Borrow cash on a long-term loan	______	______
6. Collect an account receivable	______	______
7. Record accrued expenses payable	______	______
8. Sell a plant asset for cash at a profit	______	______
9. Sell a plant asset for cash at a loss	______	______
10. Buy marketable securities, for cash, for a short-term investment	______	______

E-11 Relationships Answer the questions for each of the following independent situations.

1. The current ratio is 2.5 to 1. Current liabilities are $120,000. What are current assets?
2. ROA is 18%; ROE is 20%. There is no preferred stock. Net income is $2 million, and average total assets are $16 million. What is average total stockholders' equity?

3. The current ratio is 3 to 1; the acid-test ratio is 1.8 to 1; and cash and receivables are $360,000. The only current assets are cash, receivables, and inventory.

   (a) What are current liabilities?
   (b) What is inventory?

4. Accounts receivable turnover is 6 times; inventory turnover is 5 times. Both accounts receivable and inventory have remained constant for several years. All sales are on credit. On January 1, 19X8, the firm bought inventory.

   (a) On the average, how long will it be before the new inventory is sold?
   (b) On the average, how long after the inventory is sold will cash be collected?

5. A firm had current assets of $200,000. It then paid a current liability of $40,000. After the payment, the current ratio was 2 to 1. What were current liabilities before the payment was made?
6. A firm normally has accounts receivable equal to 35 days' credit sales. During the coming year it expects credit sales of $730,000 spread evenly over the year. What should its accounts receivable be at the end of the year?

E-12 Leverage Balance Company is considering the retirement of $600,000 in 10% bonds payable. These bonds are the company's only interest-bearing debt. The retirement plan calls for the firm to issue 20,000 shares of common stock at a total price of $600,000 and use the proceeds to buy back the bonds. Stockholders' equity is now $1,000,000, with 25,000 shares of common stock outstanding (no preferred stock). The firm expects to earn $300,000 before interest and taxes in the coming year. The tax rate is 40%.

Required

1. Determine net income, EPS, and ROE for the coming year, assuming that the bonds are retired before the beginning of the coming year. Assume no change in stockholders' equity except for the new stock issue.
2. Determine net income, EPS, and ROE for the coming year, assuming that the bonds are not retired. Again, assume that year-end stockholders' equity will be the same as at the beginning of the year.
3. Is the proposed retirement wise? Why or why not?

E-13 Return on assets and return on equity Travis Toys, Inc., has annual sales of $22 million, and ROS of 6%. Interest expense is $0.8 million; total assets are $16 million; and the debt ratio is 60%. There is no preferred stock. Ignore taxes.

Required

1. Determine income, ROA, and ROE.
2. Suppose the firm could increase its ROS to 6.5% and keep the same level of sales. What would net income, ROA, and ROE be?
3. Suppose that Travis reduced its debt ratio to 40% by retiring debt. New common stock was issued to finance the retirement, keeping total assets at $16 million. Net income is $1.72 million because of lower interest expense that now totals $0.40 million. What are ROA and ROE?

E-14 Financing alternatives The founders of Marmex Company are trying to decide how to finance the firm. They have three choices:

1. Issue $2,000,000 in common stock.
2. Issue $1,200,000 in common stock and $800,000 in 10% bonds.

3. Issue $1,200,000 in common stock and $800,000 in 12% preferred stock.

Income before interest and taxes is expected to be $500,000. The tax rate is 40%.

Required

1. Compute net income, earnings available for common stock, and ROE for each financing choice.
2. Suppose that the tax rate increases to 60%. Redo item 1. Can you draw any conclusions about the effects of tax rates on the relative desirability of the three choices?

E-15 Effects of transactions Indicate the effects of each of the following transactions on the firm's (a) receivables turnover; (b) inventory turnover; (c) gross profit ratio. The possible answers are (+) increase, (−) decrease, and (0) no effect. Before each transaction takes place, the ratios are as follows: (a) receivable turnover of 8 times; (b) inventory turnover of 6 times; (c) gross profit ratio of 25%.

	Effects on		
Transaction	(a) Receivables Turnover	(b) Inventory Turnover	(c) Gross Profit Ratio
1. Purchase inventory on account	______	______	______
2. Sell merchandise, for cash, at the normal price	______	______	______
3. Sell a plant asset, at a profit, for some cash and a short-term note	______	______	______
4. Sell merchandise, on account, at a bargain (lower than normal) price	______	______	______
5. Receive merchandise returned by a customer for credit	______	______	______

E-16 Return on assets and equity Randolph Company has average total assets of $4,000,000 and a debt ratio of 30%. Interest expense is $120,000, and return on average total assets is 12%. The firm has no preferred stock. Ignore taxes.

Required

1. Determine income, average stockholders' equity, and ROE.
2. Suppose that sales have been $3,600,000 annually and are expected to continue at this level. If the firm could increase its ROS by one percentage point, what would be its income, ROA, and ROE?
3. Refer to the original data and your answers to item 1. Suppose that Randolph retires $600,000 in debt and therefore saves interest expense of $60,000 annually. The firm would issue additional common stock in the amount of $600,000 to finance the retirement. Total assets would remain at $4,000,000. What would be the income, ROA, and ROE?

E-17 Effects of transactionsreturns ratios Indicate the effects of each of the following transactions on the firm's (a) ROS, (b) ROA, and (c) EPS. There are three possible answers: (+) increase, (−) decrease, and (0) no effect. Before each transaction takes place, the ratios are as follows: (a) ROS, 10%; (b) ROA, 5%; (c) EPS, $0.25.

	Effects on (a) ROS	(b) ROA	(c) EPS
1. Sell a plant asset for cash, at twice the asset's book value	______	______	______
2. Declare and issue a stock dividend	______	______	______
3. Purchase inventory on account	______	______	______
4. Purchase treasury stock for cash	______	______	______
5. Acquire land by issuing common stock	______	______	______

E-18 Ratios The financial statements for Massin Company, a merchandising firm, appear below. The company has 200,000 common shares outstanding. The price of the stock is $21. Dividends of $0.80 per share were declared. The balance sheet at the end of 19X5 showed approximately the same amounts as that at the end of 19X6.

Massin Company, Income Statement for 19X6 (in thousands of dollars)

Sales		$3,200
Cost of goods sold		1,400
Gross profit		1,800
Operating expenses:		
Depreciation	$ 240	
Other	1,060	1,300
Income before interest and taxes		500
Interest expense		60
Income before taxes		440
Income taxes at 40% rate		176
Net income		$ 264

Massin Company, Balance Sheet as of December 31, 19X6
(in thousands of dollars)

Assets			Equities	
Cash		$ 200	Accounts payable	$ 210
Accounts receivable		400	Accrued expenses	280
Inventory		350		
Total current assets		950	Total current liabilities	490
Plant and equipment	$3,200		Long-term debt	680
Accumulated			Common stock	920
depreciation	1,200	2,000	Retained earnings	860
Total assets		$2,950	Total equities	$2,950

Required

Calculate the following ratios.

1. Current ratio.
2. Acid-test ratio.
3. Accounts receivable turnover.
4. Inventory turnover.
5. Days' purchases in accounts payable.
6. Gross profit ratio.

7. ROS.
8. ROA.
9. ROE.
10. EPS.
11. PE ratio.
12. Dividend yield.
13. Payout ratio.
14. Debt ratio.
15. Times interest earned.
16. Cash flow to debt.

PROBLEMS

E-19 Analyzing ROE (adapted from a paper by Professor William E. Ferrara) Chapter 11 introduced the idea of separating the components of ROI as follows.

$$\text{ROI} = \frac{\text{net income}}{\text{sales}} \times \frac{\text{sales}}{\text{investment}}$$

Applying this separation to the calculation of return on stockholders' equity, we could express ROE as

$$\text{ROE} = \frac{\text{net income}}{\text{sales}} \times \frac{\text{sales}}{\text{stockholders' equity}}$$

This separation is less enlightening that it might be, however, because net income combines the effects of financing choices (leverage) with the operating results. Letting total assets/stockholders' equity stand as a measure of financial leverage, we can also express return on stockholders' equity as follows.

$$\text{ROE} = \frac{\text{net income}}{\text{sales}} \times \frac{\text{sales}}{\text{total assets}} \times \frac{\text{total assets}}{\text{stockholders' equity}}$$

Sales and total assets cancel out, leaving the ratio net income/stockholders' equity. The three-factor expression allows the analyst to look at operations (margin x turnover, the first two terms) separately from financing (the last term).

The separation is not perfect because interest (financing expense) is included in calculating net income, but the expansion is adequate for many purposes. Thus, the product of the first two terms is a measure of operating efficiency, while the third is a measure of leverage and therefore of financial risk.

The following data summarize results for three companies.

Company Results (in thousands of dollars)

	A	B	C
Sales	$4,500	$6,000	$5,000
Net income	$ 450	$ 400	$ 480
Total assets	$4,500	$4,500	$4,400
Stockholders' equity	$3,000	$2,000	$4,000
ROE	15%	20%	12%

Required

Calculate ROE for each company using the three-factor expression and comment on the results. You should be able to draw tentative conclusions about the relative operating and financing results of the companies.

E-20 ***Current asset activity*** The treasurer of Billingsgate Company has asked for your assistance in analyzing the firm's liquidity. She provides the following data.

	19X6	19X5	19X4
Total sales (all credit)	$480,000	$440,000	$395,000
Cost of goods sold	320,000	290,000	245,000
Accounts receivable at year end	64,000	48,000	31,000
Inventory at year end	50,000	44,000	38,000
Accounts payable at year end	37,000	29,000	28,000

Required

1. Compute accounts receivable turnover for 19X5 and 19X6.
2. Compute days' credit sales in accounts receivable at the ends of 19X5 and 19X6.
3. Compute inventory turnover for 19X5 and 19X6.
4. Compute days' sales in inventory at the end of 19X5 and 19X6.
5. Compute days' purchases in accounts payable at the ends of 19X5 and 19X6.
6. Comment on the trends in the ratios. Do the trends seem to be favorable or unfavorable?

E-21 ***Constructing financial statements*** The following information is available concerning the Warnock Company's expected results in 19X7 (in thousands of dollars). Turnovers are based on year-end values.

Required

Fill in the blanks.

Return on sales	8%
Gross profit percentage	30%
Inventory turnover	4 times
Receivables turnover	5 times
Current ratio	3 to 1
Ratio of total debt to total assets	40%

Condensed Income Statement	
Sales	$800
Cost of sales	____
Gross profit	____
Operating expenses	____
Net income	$____

Condensed Balance Sheet			
Cash	$ 30	Current liabilities	$____
Receivables	____	Long-term debt	____
Inventory	____	Stockholders' equity	600
Plant and equipment	____		
Total	$____	Total	$____

E-22 ***Effects of transactions on ratios*** Indicate the effects of each of the following transactions on the firm's current ratio, acid-test ratio, and debt ratio. There are three possible answers: increase (+), decrease (−), and no effect (0). Before each transaction takes place, the current ratio is greater than 1 to 1 and the acid-test ratio is less than 1 to 1.

	Effects		
	Current Ratio	Acid-Test Ratio	Debt Ratio
Example: An account payable is paid.	+	−	−
1. Inventory is bought for cash.	______	______	______
2. A sale is made on account, with cost of sales being less than the selling price.	______	______	______
3. Long-term bonds are issued for cash.	______	______	______
4. Land is sold for cash at its book value.	______	______	______
5. Marketable securities being held as temporary investments are sold at a gain.	______	______	______
6. Common stock is issued in exchange for plant assets.	______	______	______
7. An account receivable is collected.	______	______	______
8. Long-term debt is issued for plant assets.	______	______	______
9. A dividend payable in cash is declared, but not paid.	______	______	______
10. The dividend in item 9 is paid.	______	______	______
11. A short-term bank loan is paid.	______	______	______
12. Depreciation expense is recorded.	______	______	______
13. Obsolete inventory is written off, with the debit to a loss account.	______	______	______

E-23 Comparisons of firms Condensed financial statements for Amex Company and Corex Company appear below. Both companies are in the same industry and use the same accounting methods. Balance-sheet data for both companies were the same at the end of 19X4 as at the end of 19X5.

Balance Sheets, End of 19X5 (in thousands of dollars)

	Amex Company	Corex Company
Assets		
Cash	$ 185	$ 90
Accounts receivable	215	170
Inventory	340	220
Plant and equipment (net)	850	810
Total assets	$1,590	$1,290
Equities		
Accounts payable	$ 150	$ 140
Other current liabilities	80	90
Long-term debt	300	500
Common stock	700	300
Retained earnings	360	260
Total equities	$1,590	$1,290

Income Statements for 19X5

		Amex Company		Corex Company
Sales		$3,050		$2,800
Cost of goods sold		1,400		1,350
Gross profit		1,650		1,450
Operating expenses:				
Depreciation	$ 280		$240	
Other	1,040	1,320	900	1,140
Income before interest and taxes		330		310
Interest expense		30		55
Income before taxes		300		255
Income taxes at 40% rate		120		102
Net income		$ 180		$ 153
Earnings per share		$ 0.90		$ 0.77
Dividends per share		$ 0.40		$ 0.20
Market price of common stock		$12.00		$11.50

Required

On the basis of the data given, answer the following questions.

1. Which company seems to be more liquid?
2. Which company seems to be more profitable?
3. Which company seems to be more solvent?
4. Which stock seems to be a better buy?

Support your answers with whatever calculations you believe appropriate?

E-24 ***Effects of transactions—selected ratios*** In the following exhibit, several transactions or events are listed in the left-hand column and the names of various ratios and the value of that ratio before the associated transaction are listed in the right-hand column. Indicate the effect of the transaction on the specified ratio. There are three possible answers: (+) increase, (−) decrease, and (0) no effect.

Transaction	Effect on Ratio	Ratio of Concern
1. Write off an uncollectible account receivable	______	Current ratio of 3 to 1
2. Sell merchandise, on account, at less than normal price	______	42 days' sales in accounts receivable
3. Borrow cash on a short-term loan	______	Acid-test ratio of 0.9 to 1
4. Write off an uncollectible account receivable	______	Return on sales of 18%
5. Sell treasury stock at a price greater than its cost	______	Return on equity of 20%
6. Acquire plant asset by issuance of long-term note	______	Debt ratio of 40%
7. Record accrued salaries payable	______	Times interest earned of 3.2

Transaction	Effect on Ratio	Ratio of Concern
8. Record depreciation on plant assets	______	Cash flow to debt ratio of 60%
9. Return inventory items to supplier, for credit	______	Inventory turnaover of 8 times
10. Acquire plant assset by issuance of common stock	______	Debt ratio of 60%

E-25 Construction of financial statements using ratios The following data are available for Wasserman Pharmaceutical Company as of December 31, 19X4, and for the year then ended.

Current ratio	3 to 1
Days' sales in accounts receivable	60 days
Inventory turnover	3 times
Debt ratio	40%
Current liabilities	$300,000
Stockholders' equity, all common stock	$1,200,000
Return on sales	8%
Return on common equity	15%
Gross profit ratio	40%

Wasserman has no preferred stock, no marketable securities, and no prepaid expenses. Beginning-of-year balance-sheet figures are the same as end-of-year figures. All sales are on credit and the only noncurrent assets are plant and equipment.

Required

Prepare a balance sheet as of December 31, 19X4, and an income statement for 19X4 in as much detail as you can with the available information. Round the calculation of average daily credit sales to the nearest dollar.

E-26 Dilution of EPS Boston Tarrier Company has been very successful in recent years, as shown by the income statement data given below. The treasurer of the firm is concerned because he expects holders of the firm's convertible preferred stock to exchange their shares for common shares early in the coming year. All of the company's preferred stock is convertible, and the number of common shares issuable on conversion is 300,000.

Boston Tarrier Company, Selected Income Statement Data

	19X6	19X5
Net income	$3,400,000	$2,600,000
Preferred stock dividends	800,000	800,000
Earnings available for common	$2,600,000	$1,800,000

Throughout 19X6 and 19X5 the firm had 500,000 shares of common stock outstanding.

Required

1. Compute primary EPS for 19X5 and 19X6.
2. Compute fully diluted EPS for 19X5 and 19X6.

E-27 Inventory turnover and return on equity Timmons Company is presently earning net income of $300,000 per year, which gives a 10% ROE. The president believes that inventory can be reduced with tighter controls on buying. Any reduction of inventory frees cash, which would be used to pay a dividend to stockholders. Thus, stockholders' equity would drop by the same amount as inventory.

Inventory turnover is 3 times per year. Cost of goods sold is running at $2,700,000 annually. The president hopes that turnover can be increased to 5 times. He also believes that sales, cost of goods sold, and net income will remain at their current levels.

Required

1. Determine the average inventory that the firm currently holds.
2. Determine the average inventory that would be held if turnover could be increased to 5 times per year.
3. Determine ROE if Timmons can increase turnover and reduce stockholders' equity by the amount of the reduction in investment in inventory.

E-28 Ratios—industry averages The president of Brewster Company has been concerned about its operating performance and financial strength. She has obtained, from a trade association, the averages of certain ratios for the industry. She gives you these ratios and the most recent financial statements of the firm. The balance-sheet amounts were all about the same at the beginning of the year as they are now.

Brewster Company, Balance Sheet as of December 31, 19X6
(in thousands of dollars)

Assets		Equities	
Cash	$ 860	Accounts payable	$ 975
Accounts receivable	3,210	Accrued expenses	120
Inventory	2,840	Taxes payable	468
Total current assets	6,910	Total current liabilities	1,563
Plant and equipment (net)	7,090	Bonds payable, due 19X9	6,300
		Common stock, no par	4,287
		Retained earnings	1,850
Total assets	$14,000	Total equities	$14,000

Brewster Company, Income Statement for 19X6
(in thousands of dollars)

Sales	$11,800
Cost of goods sold	7,350
Gross profit	4,450
Operating expenses, including $650 depreciation	2,110
Operating profit	2,340
Interest expense	485
Income before taxes	1,855
Income taxes at 40% rate	742
Net income	$ 1,113

Brewster has 95,000 shares of common stock outstanding, which gives earnings per share of $11.72 ($1,113,000/95,000). Dividends are $5 per share and the market price of the stock is $120. Average ratios for the industry are

Current ratio	3.8 to 1	Return on equity	17.5%
Quick ratio	1.9 to 1	Price-earnings ratio	12.3
Accounts receivable turnover	4.8 times	Dividend yield	3.9%
Inventory turnover	3.6 times	Payout ratio	38.0%
Return on sales	7.6%	Debt ratio	50.0%
Return on assets	17.6%	Times interest earned	6 times
		Cash flow to debt	25.0%

Required

1. Compute the ratios shown above for Brewster Company.
2. Prepare comments to the president indicating areas of apparent strength and weakness for Brewster Company in relation to the industry.

E-29 Generation of cash flows Humbert Company must make a $600,000 payment on a bank loan at the end of March 19X9. At December 31, 19X8 Humbert had cash of $95,000 and accounts receivable of $355,000.

Estimated cash payments required during the first three months of 19X9, exclusive of the payment to the bank, are $315,000. Humbert expects sales to be $810,000 in the three-month period, all on credit. Accounts receivable are normally equal to 40 days' credit sales.

Required

1. Determine the expected balance in accounts receivable at the end of March 19X9. Assume that the three-month period has 90 days.
2. Determine whether the firm will have enough cash to pay the bank loan on March 31, 19X9.

E-30 Evaluation of trends and comparison with industry Comparative balance sheets and income statements for Marcus Manufacturing Company appear below. Your boss, the chief financial analyst for Hanmattan Bank, has asked you to analyze trends in the firm's operations and financing and to make some comparisons with the averages for the same industry. The bank is considering the purchase of some shares of Marcus for one of its trust funds.

Marcus Manufacturing Company Balance Sheets as of December 31
(in thousands of dollars)

	19X7	19X6
Assets		
Cash	$ 170	$ 180
Accounts receivable	850	580
Inventory (finished goods)	900	760
Total current assets	1,920	1,520
Plant and equipment (net)	2,050	1,800
Total assets	$3,970	$3,320

	19X7	19X6
Equities		
Current liabilities	$ 812	$ 620
Long-term debt	1,640	1,300
Common stock	1,000	1,000
Retained earnings	518	400
Total equities	$3,970	$3,320

Marcus Manufacturing Company, Income Statements
(in thousands of dollars)

	19X7	19X6
Sales, all on credit	$4,700	$4,350
Cost of goods sold	2,670	2,460
Gross profit	2,030	1,890
Operating expenses	1,470	1,440
Income before interest and taxes	560	450
Interest expense	130	100
Income before taxes	430	350
Income taxes at 40% rate	172	140
Net income	$ 258	$ 210
Earnings per share	$2.58	$2.10
Market price of stock at year end	$32	$28
Dividends per share	$0.96	$0.80

Selected data from the 19X5 balance sheet include the following.

Accounts receivable	$510
Inventory (finished goods)	620
Total assets	2,940
Stockholders' equity	1,320

The following are averages for Marcus's industry.

Current ratio	2.7 to 1	Receivable turnover	8.5 times
Quick ratio	1.4 to 1	Inventory turnover	4.2 times
Debt ratio	52%	Return on assets	15%
Price-earnings ratio	11.5	Return on equity	13.5%
Dividend yield	4.5%	Return on sales	5.0%
Payout ratio	48.0%		

Required

Compute the above ratios for Marcus for 19X6 and 19X7 and comment on the trends in the ratio and on relationships to industry averages.

E-31 Trends in ratios As the chief investment officer of a large pension fund, you must make many investing decisions. One of your assistants has prepared the following ratios for MBI Corporation, a large multinational manufacturer.

	Industry Average All Years	19X7	Year 19X6	19X5
Current ratio	2.4	2.6	2.4	2.5
Quick ratio	1.6	1.55	1.6	1.65
Receivable turnover	8.1	7.5	7.9	8.3
Inventory turnover	4.0	4.3	4.2	4.0
Debt ratio	43.0%	38.0%	41.3%	44.6%
Return on assets	17.8%	19.1%	19.4%	19.5%
Return on equity	15.3%	15.1%	15.6%	15.9%
Price-earnings ratio	14.3	13.5	13.3	13.4
Times interest earned	8.3	9.7	9.5	8.9
Earnings per share growth rate	8.4%	7.1%	6.9%	7.0%

Required

What is your decision in the following cases? Give your reasons.

1. Granting a short-term loan to MBI.
2. Buying long-term bonds of MBI on the open market. The bonds yield 7%, which is slightly less than the average for bonds in the industry.
3. Buying MBI common stock.

E-32 Financial planning with ratios The treasurer of MaxiMart, Inc., a large chain of stores, has been trying to develop a financial plan. In conjunction with other managers, she has developed the following estimates, in millions of dollars.

	19X3	19X4	19X5	19X6
Sales	$100	$120	$150	$210
Fixed assets, net	80	95	110	125

In addition, for planning purposes she is willing to make the following estimates and assumptions about other results.

Cost of goods sold as a percentage of sales	60%
Return on sales	10%
Dividend payout ratio	30%
Turnovers based on year-end values:	
Cash and accounts receivable	4 times
Inventory	3 times
Required current ratio	3 to 1
Required ratio of long-term debt to stockholders' equity	50%

At the beginning of 19X3 the treasurer expects stockholders' equity to be $60 million and long-term debt to be $30 million.

Required

Prepare pro forma balance sheets and any supporting schedules you need for the end of each of the next four years. Determine how much additional common stock, if any, the firm will have to issue each year if the treasurer's estimates and assumptions are correct.

E-33 Leverage Mr. Harmon, treasurer of Stokes Company, has been considering two plans for raising $2,000,000 for plant expansion and modernization. One choice is to issue 9% bonds. The other is to issue 25,000 shares of common stock at $80 per share.

The modernization and expansion is expected to increase operating profit, before interest and taxes, by $320,000 annually. Depreciation of $200,000 is included in the $320,000. Condensed financial statements for 19X4 are given below.

Stokes Company Balance Sheet, as of December 31, 19X4

Assets		Equities	
Current assets	$ 3,200,000	Current liabilities	$ 1,200,000
Plant and equipment		Long-term debt, 7%	3,000,000
(net)	7,420,000	Stockholders' equity	7,290,000
Other assets	870,000		
Total assets	$11,490,000	Total equities	$11,490,000

Stokes Company Condensed Income, Statement for 19X4

Sales		$8,310,000
Cost of sales	$5,800,000	
Operating expenses	1,200,000	7,000,000
Operating profit		1,310,000
Interest expense		210,000
Income before taxes		1,100,000
Income taxes at 40% rate		440,000
Net income		$ 660,000
Earnings per share, based on 100,000 outstanding shares		$6.60
Dividends per share		$3.30

Mr. Harmon is concerned about the effects of issuing debt. The average debt ratio for companies in the industry is 42%. He believes that if this ratio is exceeded, the PE ratio of the stock will fall to 11 because of the potentially greater risk. If Stokes increases its common equity substantially by issuing new shares, he expects the PE ratio to increase to 12.5. He also wonders what will happen to the dividend yield under each plan. The firm follows the practice of paying dividends equal to 50% of net income.

Required

1. For each financing plan, calculate the debt ratio that the company would have after the securities (bonds or stocks) are issued.
2. For each financing plan, determine the expected net income in 19X5, expected EPS, and the expected market price of the common stock.
3. Calculate, for each financing plan, the dividend per share that Stokes would pay following its usual practice and the yield that would be obtained at the market prices from your answer to item 2.
4. Suppose that you now own 100 shares of Stokes Company. Which alternative would you prefer the firm to use? Why?

index

A

C

G

H

Q

R

S

W

Z

check figures

Chapter 1

1-4 $33,200 Taxes payable; $341,000 Total assets
1-5 (b) $96,000 Net cash provided
1-6 (2) $42,000 Cash; Total assets $458,000
1-7 $17,000 Net cash provided

Chapter 2

2-4 (1) $40,000 income; (2b) $400,000; (3a) 80,000 units
2-5 (1) $30,000 income; (2) $750,000; (3) $850,000
2-6 (1) $28,000 income; (2b) $800,000; (3) $10.67
2-7 (1) $18,000 income; (2) $850,000
2-8 (1b) $1,000,000; (2b) $1,200,000; (4) $35.33; (5) $35.93
2-9 (1b) $4,166,667; (2) $28.67; (3) $28.52
2-10 (1b) 75%; (2d) $78,000; (3b) 80%
2-18 (1) $10,500 income; (2b) $215,000; (3) $20.40
2-20 (1) $50,200 income; (2) 50,000 units; (3) $15.21
2-21 (1) $54,800 income; (2) 13,750 units; (3) $143.03
2-22 (1) 3,500 units for Alternative #2; (2) 6,000 units
2-24 (1) 11,111 units; (2a) $21; (3a) $22; (3b) $200,000
2-25 (1a) $25,000,000; (2) $27; (3) $21.20; (4) $32.56
2-26 (1) $250,000; (2) $370,000; (5) $18.50; (6) $18.33
2-28 (1) $55 per child; (2) 36 children
2-29 (1) a; (2) a; (3) 60,000 units; (4) $4
2-30 Variable cost per unit: March, $13; April, $13.40

2-31 (1) 60,000 units; (2) $8,000 increase in income
2-33 (1) 135,000; (2) $16; (3) $1 reduction
2-34 (1) $5,200 increase; (2) $39
2-35 (1) $200,000; (2) 56,667 hrs.
2-36 $24,300 total fixed costs
2-39 Total contribution margin, $1,816,000
2-41 (1) $8,200 loss; (2) $9.87 for residential
2-43 (1) $4,210,526 for Normal; (2) $1,320,000 income-to-the-producer for N
2-44 (1) $6,000 loss; (2) 12,000 units; (3) $5,000 reduction in loss
2-46 (1) $97,200 CM; (2b) $21
2-47 $700,000 sales = indifference point
2-48 (1) 14.97% or less; (2) $25,830; (3) about 34% of total attendance would have to buy a unit
2-49 (1) $2,960; (2) $196.11; (3) approx. 26.4%

Chapter 3

3-10 (1) Fixed component, selling = $5,900; (2) income = $13,400
3-13 (1) Fixed S&A expenses, $63,000; (2) June income = $99,000
3-14 (1c) $62,000; (2b) $7; (3a) 30,000 units
3-15 (1) 103,846 units; (2) $4.83; (3) $1,800 increase
3-16 (1) $80,000; (2) break-even = $533,333; (4) 5.55%
3-18 (1) Fixed cost = $294; (2) fixed cost = $364
3-19 (1) 400 sweaters; (2) $51.11; (3) 469 sweaters
3-22 $41,455 quarterly fixed costs + $9.232 per product
3-24 (1) 6.3%; (2) $7,622
3-25 (1) $63,930; (2) $23.93; (3) $4.97
3-26 (1) $293,138; (3) $106.0245
3-27 (3) 24,000 units; (5) 48,000 units; (6) $400,000; (7) 54,000 units; (8) 60,000 units; (9) $10.20; (10) $10.36
3-29 $3,020 better off to stay open
3-30 Blockbusters would prefer S in (1) and N in (2); Kirkwalker would prefer N in (1) and S in (2)
3-33 (1) $200,000; (2) $21; (3a) $22.50
3-34 $64,436 + $3.845 per part
3-36 (1) Hifixed is at break-even; (3) 100,000 units for both
3-37 (3) 260 if 300 units are purchased; 280 if 400 are purchased
3-39 (1) Basic labor cost per month = $12,800 until production exceeds 6,400; (3) 6,400 units to 12,800 units
3-41 (1) 53.33% of capacity; (2) 55.56% of capacity
3-43 (1) 40%; (2) $36,000
3-44 (2) Profit with monthly lease = $78,000
3-50 (1) $4 per unit; (2) $280,000; (3) 70,000 units
3-46 (1) 450,000 board ft. of good output sold to earn $4,500 income; (2) 80 loaves; (3) $.05 per board foot
3-47 Production costs: $5,225 + $7.75 per hr. (high-low); $5,397 + $7.50 per hr. (regression)
3-49 (1) $66.50 for #816; (2) $65 for #389

Chapter 4

4-4 Volume variance = $32,000U
4-6 (1) 60%; (3a) 62%; (3b) $46,000
4-8 (2) $6.85; (3) price variance = $4,650U
4-10 (1) 60%, $200,000; (2) $5.50, 21,818 units
4-11 (3a) 52%; (3c) 8,800 units; (4a) $9; (4c) 12,711 units
4-12 Volume variance = $187.2 thousand favorable

4-14	(2) $6,000 increase in income
4-16	(1a) $1.34; (1b) $1.33
4-17	(1) $22,000 F volume variance; (2) 16.5%; (3) $22,000
4-18	(1) 56,000 units (2) $128,800; (4) $15,000; (6) $11,200; (7) $41,280
4-19	Flavorsavers ($6,500 profit increase)
4-20	Price variance: $26,000U, senior staff; $38,000U, junior staff
4-21	Segment margin: housewares, $356.1; hardware, $707.8
4-22	$250
4-23	(1) 63,518; (3) $9,690 profit decrease; (4) $3.125; (5) 70,080
4-24	(1) Income of $4 million at $50 price; (2) $40 price
4-25	(1) $1.3 million; (2) $2.95 price
4-26	(2) 52%; (4) $2,019,231; (5a) $l,750,000; (5b) $2,187,500
4-27	(1) $210 loss; (2) $350; (3) $90 increase
4-28	(1) $210,000 Detergents margin; (2) paper products; (3) detergents
4-29	(1) $312,000 income; (2) $54,000 income increase
4-30	$65.8U volume variance
4-31	(1) $833,333; (2) $12.63
4-32	$13.2 long-term margin, suits
4-33	(3a) 48%; (3b) $416,667; (3c) $479,167; (4a) $400,000; (4b) $460,000; (5a) $10; (5c) 23,000 units
4-34	(1a) A, B, C; (1c) B, C, A
4-35	(1) $72,000 CM, saws; (2) 3,000 saws; (3) planned CM% = 37.3%
4-37	$800 profit advantage for Waters
4-38	(2) $450,000; (3) $150,000 more than that in part 2
4-39	(1) $4,090,700; (2) $4,210,500; (3) $4,050,900
4-40	$42
4-41	(2) 32.5%; (3) saucers, $5.25; (4a) $123,750; (5) Plan B
4-42	(1) Income drops $8,000; (2) savings = $16,000
4-43	(1) B's long-term margin = $60,000; (2) foreign's long-term margin = $45,000; (3) $2,200 profit increase; (4) at least $166,000
4-44	$26,600F price variance
4-45	(1) With best choice, lipstick CM = $2,400,000; mascara CM = $1,402,500; eyeliner CM = $904,000
4-46	(1) 443,183; (2) $77.50 for surgical; (3) $87 for medical
4-47	(1) Fixed cost = $28,000; (2) $46,667; (5) C = 4,200 units; (6) $6,000 income increase; (7) $29,000; (8a) 55.56%; (9) $20,000
4-48	(1) Eastern segment margin = $145.2
4-49	(1) $73,000; (2) $93,000; (4) income will be $6,855; (7) #3
4-50	(1) $58.5 million; (2) occupancy variance = $4.3 million unfavorable
4-51	Break-even sales = $233,645
4-52	$720F volume variance
4-53	(1) Volume variance: drill = $340U; saw = $240U

Chapter 5

5-8	(1) Doride profit = $65,000; (2) $564,000
5-9	(2) Supergadgets; (3) Price of Gadget's must rise to $12.33
5-10	(1) $10,000; (2) $65,000; (3) $46,000
5-13	(1) $222; (2) 9%; (3) $435
5-16	(1) Process M and O; (2) $140
5-17	(1) $140,000; (2) $40,000
5-18	(1) $1,050; (2) $1,140
5-19	(1) $5,000 income decrease; (2) $17.50; (3) 9,167 units
5-22	(1) $1,000,000; (2) $960,000 profit drop; (3) $80,000 profit increase; (4) $25,000 profit increase; (6) $7,500 profit increase
5-23	(1) $8,000 profit increase; (2) $10,000 profit increase; (3) $14

5-24 $25 drop in lunch profit
5-25 Costs: old method = $162,340, new method = $131,000
5-26 (1) Mashed; (2) $5,000; (3) 4.5 lbs.
5-28 Gain of $10,800
5-29 (1) Process Nyron; (2) gain from change = $30,000; (3) 66,667 lbs.
5-30 (2) Sunday profit = $302
5-31 (1) $67,500 income increase; (2) $46,000 income increase; (4) 26,866 shirts
5-32 (1) $546,600 cost to "make"; (2) 24,474 units; (3) $25.20
5-34 $256,000 advantage to operating the joint process
5-35 (1) Gross margin from calling on retailers = $4,320
5-36 (1) $60,000 income increase; (2) $16.25; (3) $120,000 income drop
5-39 $20,000 loss from new plan
5-40 (1) $2,480 incremental profit; (2) more than $3,980
5-42 (1) $200,000 income increase; (3) $200,000 loss of CM; (4) $93,000 gain
5-43 (2) $124,000 income with hardware
5-44 (1) $300,000 CM increase; (2) $30,000 profit increase; (3) $500,000
5-45 (1) 7,000 jars; (2) 8,000 jars
5-46 (1) $400,000; (2) $800,000; (6a) $660,000; (6c) $780,000
5-47 CM per 1,000 sq/ ft. of paneling = $45 in (1) and $31 in (2); (3) $86; (4) $2,700 gain from more veneer capacity
5-48 (1) $4,500 income drop; (2) $7.95
5-49 (1) 3 months; (2) $580,000 annual CM from holding 3 months
5-51 $15,800 profit reduction (cost)
5-52 $66,800 revenue from leased department; $38,516 incremental profit from in-house boutique

Chapter 6

6-10 (1) Income = $62,000; (2) Mar. purchases = $45,000
6-11 (1) Income = $36,000; (2) Feb. purchases = $72,000
6-14 (1a) Unit purchases: March, 2,100; April, 1,700
6-19 Income: May, $40,000; June, $92,500
6-23 Purchases = 228,000 lbs.
6-24 (1) Production = 18,000 (Apr.), 14,000 (May); April purchases = $552,000
6-25 Production = 8,00 (Feb.), 19,000 (Mar.); purchases = 45,000 lbs. (Jan.), 110,000 lbs. (Feb.)
6-26 Production = 14,300 (Sep.), 15,600 (Nov.); purchases = 71,900 lbs. (Sep.), 76,200 lbs. (Oct.)
6-27 (1) Production, Feb. = 1,900; (2) purchases, Jan. = $12,150
6-29 (1) 900 units; (2) $14,400; (3) $320; (4) $34,160; (5) 550 (6) $9,400; (7) 1,050 units; (8) $22,880
6-30 (1) Production, Feb. = 1,900; (2) purchases of Tacs, Feb. = 3,550
6-31 (2) $36,000 expected income
6-32 (1) Production: 160,000 (Feb.), 250,000 (Apr.); (3) smoothed production saves $184,000 in carrying costs and $270,000 of production costs
6-33 Mar. sales = 4,200; Mar. production = 4,800; July sales = 5,400
6-34 $141,200 revenues, May-Dec.; $84,200 total income
6-35 (1) Sales = $437,933 + $1,542 per thousand housing units built (from regression)
6-36 (1) Income: $100,000 (Jan.), $156,000 (Feb.); (2) production: 39,000 (Jan.), 25,000 (Feb.); (3) 19,000 Feb. purchases
6-38 (1) Medical-services, total room revenues, $1,176,000
6-39 (1) $14,000; (2) $20,000
6-40 Total cost: $627,000 (Case A); $669,000 (Case B)
6-41 (1) $8,000 total fixed costs
6-42 (1) Total costs, 4 mos. = $5,055; (2) Total costs, 4 mos. = $5,020; (3) Total costs, 4 mos. = $4,990

6-43 (2) Trogs
6-44 (1) Production: 3,400 (Apr.), 4,200 (Jun.); (2) May = $16,250, Jul. = $10,610; (3) Apr. purchases = $9,000 (blank iron), $520 (handles)
6-46 (1) 8 clerks; 13 hrs. idle time for typists; (2) $205U; (3) 840 orders
6-47 (1) $3,840,000 income for yr.; (2) July production = 18,240
6-48 (2) Income: $8,580 (Sept.), $19,020 (Nov.); (3) purchases of nuts, $16,000 (Oct. and Nov.); Sept. total purchases, $20,600
6-50 (1) $425 fixed component

Chapter 7

7-8 (1) Payments: $227,000 (May), $216,000 (June); (2) balance, end of June, $47,000
7-10 (1) Production: 2,350 (Feb.), 2,550 (Mar.); (2) disbursements: $51,900 (Jan.), $65,550 (Mar.)
7-11 (1) Receipts: $56,600 (Jan.), $70,000 (Mar.); (2) balance: $22,700 (end of Jan.), $21,400 (end of Mar.)
7-12 (1) Feb. receipts, $70,000; (2) Feb. payments, $70,000; (3) end-of-Feb. balance, $40,000
7-14 (1) Feb. receipts, $106,000; (2) Jan. payments, $85,000; (3) end-of-Mar. balance, $19,000
7-16 (1) $2,340; (2) $2,720; (3) $2,054
7-18 (1) Borrowing of $840, second quarter; (2) $430,000
7-20 (4) $36,000; (7) $57,000
7-21 $600,000 Jan. receipts; $530,000 Feb. payments
7-22 (1) Purchases: $54,000 (Jan.) $60,000 (Mar.); (2) Feb. receipts, $68,000; Mar. payments, $49,000; (3) $54,000 income
7-23 (1) $51,000; (2) $78,000; (3) $45,000; (4) $3,300; (5) $26,500; (8) $7,800; (9) $35,100; (10) $4,200
7-24 55.6 hrs. required in both Oct. and Nov.
7-25 (1)Income = $5,000; (2) total assets = $185,500, cash = $22,000
7-26 (2) Jan. purchases, $66,000; Feb. receipts, $84,000; Feb. payments, $77,600; (3) $472,100 total assets
7-28 (1) $33.5714 per $1,000; (2) $33.8834 per $1,000
7-29 (1) Production: 34,000 (Jan.), 30,000 (Mar.); cash balance, end of Feb., $48,200; (3) $85,000 monthly cash flow
7-30 $288,000 collections; $273,080 disbursements
7-31 Additional financing needed: $249.3 (19X5), $390.8 (19X6)
7-33 (2) Oct. ending cash, $22,400; (3) $362,800 total assets
7-34 $62,800 deficiency
7-35 Additional financing needs: $23.9 (19X6), $30.6 (19X7)
7-36 Feb. and Mar. purchases, $12,000; Feb. payments, $28,500
7-37 (1b) $527,600 Feb. payments; (1c) $69,800 final cash; (2) $2,855,800 total assets; $2,712,400 stockholders' equity
7-38 Payments: $623,904 (June), $865,424 (Aug.); $1,632,904 final cash
7-39 (1) $0.80; (4) $1,000; (8) $900; (9) $13,200
7-40 Borrow $85,000 (Apr.); invest $127,000 (June), $78,000 (July)
7-41 3/31 cash, $62,000; $2,944,000 total assets
7-42 $1,570,000 asset requirements
7-43 $692,000 asset requirements

Chapter 8

8-6 (1a) About 14%; (2a) $9,500; (2b) ($2,302)
8-7 (1) $2,220; (2) just under 16%
8-8 (1) $27,216; (2) present value of annual payments = $268,400; (4) (3) $2,298,755
8-9 (2) 6 yrs.; (3) $4,564; (4) 4 yrs.; (5) $1,937
8-10 (1) $26,800; (3) 2.5 yrs.; (4) 30%
8-11 (1) $12,535; (3) 2.817 yrs.; (4) 21%

8-12 (1) $107,400; (2) NPV increases $9,540
8-13 (1) $8,660; (2) nearly 20%; (4) about 27%
8-14 (1) ($2,326); (2) just over 12%; (4) 16%
8-15 (1a) A, B, C; (1b) C, B, A; (1c) B, C, A
8-16 $142
8-17 (a) $29,504; (b) 4.54 yrs.; (c) about 18%
8-18 (1) $80,730; (2) between 16% and 18%
8-19 (1e) $46,080; (2e) $86,700; (3c) 10%; (5c) 16%
8-20 (1) Book income, hand-fed, $165,000; (2) NPV, hand-fed, $263,610
8-21 (1) $2,070,000; (2) $472,000; (4) NPV increases $256,000
8-22 (1) $24,870
8-23 $955,000
8-24 NPV is negative $7,334
8-25 (1) $171,080 advantage to 10-year term
8-26 (1) ($1,434); (2) $2,920
8-27 (1) $166,000; (4) $19,878
8-28 $2,536.4 thousand
8-30 (1) NPV of $92,220 for desk; (3) between 12% and 14%
8-31 $205 NPV advantage of buying
8-32 (1) PV = $2,158,982
8-33 (1) $976,404; (2) lump-sum
8-34 (1) NPV = ($46,512); (2) NPV = $262,458
8-35 Maximum before-tax amount, $120,825
8-36 PV of savings, $118,642
8-37 (1) PV of future receipts, $25,893,400
8-38 (1) Income, labor intensive, $960,000; (3) NPV difference, $97,360
8-39 NPV = ($57,339)
8-40 (1) NPV about $3.16 million; (2) NPV about $16.10 million
8-41 Net annual cash flow is $47,000; IRR about 16%
8-42 (1) NPV = ($87,320); (2) $1.04037
8-43 NPV = $1,196,360
8-44 (1) NPV advantage of operating stand, $3,368
8-45 (2) $43.54; (4) about $38.90
8-46 NPV of accepting and expanding, ($10,742)
8-47 (1) NPV of $1,616,712

Chapter 9

9-6 B, C, A
9-7 (1) ($1,792); (2) $50,573; (4) NPV advantage of new, $18,038
9-8 (1) $64,800; (2) NPV = $4,031; (3) NPV increase of $1,656
9-9 (1) $52,432; (2) $63,387; (3) 16,156 units
9-10 NPV = $52,972
9-11 NPV = $2,992
9-12 NPV = $175,440
9-13 (1) 1.228 for semi-automatic
9-14 NPV about $16.72 million
9-15 (1) $65,250; (2a) $43,757; (3) $80,457; (5) 43,181 units
9-17 (1a) NPV for hand-fed is $351,900
9-18 Sales to yield 10%, hand-fed, $1,431,857
9-19 (1) NPV = ($11,867); (2) NPV = $26,473
9-20 (1) $68,000; (2) $54,452; (3) $32,692; (7) $126,663
9-21 (1f) $26,779; (2f) $14,685; (3e) 20%; (4f) $90,400
9-22 (2) ($2,589); (4) $56,883; (5) ($802); (7) $27,217
9-23 NPV = $82,954
9-24 NPV = $84,428

9-25 NPV = ($648)
9-26 Required pre-tax savings, $343,942
9-27 PV of after-tax savings from B = $43,015
9-28 (1) NPV = ($34,760); (2) just over 14%
9-29 NPV = $381.3 thousand
9-30 NPV for Polltrol = ($1,497,368)
9-31 (1) NPV = $38,825; (2) about 18%; (3) about $13,691
9-32 (1) $77,000; (2) $74,984; (3) ($2,016)
9-33 (1) 29,027 units; (2) 31,712 units
9-34 (1) About $4.04; (2) about $4.61; (3) about 11,515 units
9-35 (1) NPV to fight heart disease, $62,850
9-36 91) About 14%; (3) IRR highest at 9 years
9-37 $26,450 annual increase in after-tax cash flows
9-38 (1) 207,527 units
9-39 (1) NPV = $78,616; (2) $947,100 required revenue
9-40 (1) $19,900; (2) $26,866 PV of savings
9-41 (1) $17,591,288; (2) $16,250,627
9-42 About $1,221 thousand
9-43 (1) NPV = ($128,047)
9-44 $59,980 PV advantage of buying equipment
9-45 (1) $166,688 NPV favoring keeping Quickclean
9-46 (1) NPV = ($155,160); (2) $251,544 NPV of increased sales 1,110,000 units
9-47 (1) $268,800 NPV advantage of closing
9-48 PV of Rapidgo 350 is $92,779
9-49 (1) $4,253,555 PV of making; (2) about 63,831 units
9-50 NPV = $303,791
9-51 (1) PV = $48,185; (2) NPV = $57,328; (3) NPV = $53,461
9-52 NPV of Plan A, $497,400; NPV of Plan B, $353,400

Chapter 10

10-9 Dept B: $20,000 and $35,000
10-10 (1) Meat, $152,500; (2) meat, $170,000
10-11 Total variance is $590 under budget.
10-12 $335,000 allocated to Foundry
10-13 $184,091 allocated to Foundry
10-17 Over budget: Assembly Dept., $0.7, Raleigh Plant, $7.9; Southeast region, $21.5
10-18 Product profit = $88,800
10-19 $217,857 allocated to Trimming
10-20 $261,250 allocated to Trimming
10-21 $234,681 allocated to Trimming
10-22 (1) Income, outdoor furniture, $30,000
10-24 Alpha's CM is $250,000
10-26 (1) $456,000; (2) $460,920
10-28 $3,361,400 total cost for Assembly
10-29 Total controllable costs, $112,045
10-31 Controllable profit: $56,000 (Feb.), $62,900 (Mar.)
10-33 (1) $200,000; (2) $160,000
10-34 (1) $30,000 profit drop; (2) $60,000 profit increase
10-36 Incremental profit, McTavish, $53,800
10-39 (1) Margin, foreign, $30,000; (2) product profit, C, $152,000
10-42 Housewares bonus: (1) $1,500; (2) $3,500
10-43 Total unallocated expenses, $455,000
10-44 (1) $1,000 increase; (2) $3,000 decrease; (4a) 8,000 hrs.
10-45 (1) $238,750 allocated to cleaners; (2) $208,450 to cleaners; (3) per-case cost down $1.01

10-46 $212.9 actual product margin
10-48 (2) $370,000 unallocated costs
10-49 (1) $6.0 million before, $5.85 million after; (2) decline in unit cost of 1.7%
10-50 (2) New allocation to Z is $3,876,315
10-52 (1) $450,720 profit if 5% decrease

Chapter 11

11-4 (1) 50,000 units; (2) 32%; (4) $10.50; (5) 55,000 units
11-5 (1a) B and D; (1b) 25.34%; (2a) not E; (2b) B, C, D
11-6 (1a) $40,000 increase; (2b) $60,000 increase
11-7 Cleaners: (1) 50% ROI, $6 profit; (2) $2.4 RI
11-8 (1) total gain = $50,000; (3) total loss = $10,000; (5) $1.26
11-9 Giant: (1) 10% ROS, 15% ROI; (2) 11% ROS, 16.5% ROI
11-10 (1) $43,750; (2a) 24%; (2b) $22.92
11-11 (1a) D, B, A, C; (1b) C, A, B, D; (1c) D, B, A, C
11-12 (1) 14% ROS; (2) 16% ROS; (3) $57.1 million required sales
11-13 Total gain = $43,000
11-14 (1) no change in total income; (2) total income falls $60,000
11-15 (1) $29; (3) $41
11-16 (1a) $10 million; (1c) 10%; (2) 40%
11-17 A: $60 income, $20 RI; B: 24% ROI, $12 RI; C: $55 income, 27.5% RI
11-18 (1c) 25%; (2d) $1,800; (4a) $6,000; (5b) $17,500; (6a) $9,000
11-19 (1a) $24,000 decrease; (2) $10,000 increase
11-21 (3) 24%; (4) 15%; (5) $64,000; (6a) 14.75%; (7) 15%
11-22 (2) New RI: Hi = $88,000; Lo = ($76,000)
11-23 (1) 12% for Margin and 12% for Turn; (2b) 8.3%
11-24 (1) $10,000 increase; (2) $6.50; (3) $7; (4) $40,000 increase
11-25 (1) 25% ROI on order; (2) $60,000 RI on order
11-26 (1a) 32%; (2) 75,000 units; (3) $1,200,000; (4b) $8.80
11-28 (1) CM: B, $8,000; C, $22,000; (2) $3,000 loss; (3) $4,000 advantage to selling outside
11-30 Income = $600,000
11-31 (1) Income = $580,000
11-32 (1) Camera's RI down $100,000; (2) RI up $430,000 if Film invests; (3) RI up $4,930,000 if production increased and X-40s sold
11-33 (1) 35%; (2) RI up $8,000; (4) $200,000; (5b) 2,500 units
11-34 (1) 21.6% ROI if order accepted
11-36 (1) $150,000 advantage to intercompany sale; (2) $30,000 advantage to accepting order
11-37 (1) A and D; (2a) not B; (2b) A and D
11-38 (1) $57,000 increase; (2) $57,000 net gain; (3) $54,000
11-39 (2) ROI: 80% (19X2), 93% (19X4), 103% (19X5)
11-40 (1a) 6 million cases; (1c) 6 million cases
11-41 (2) $5.50 CM advantage of filling order
11-43 (1) Income: $18,500 (Randy), $189,000 (total)
11-44 (1) ROI: X, Z, Y; (2) 63% ROI for Y, 79% for Z
11-45 (1) Total CM up $88,000; (3) $68.45 maximum, $58.67 minimum
11-46 (1) $600; (2) $550; (3) $175
11-49 Added RI from new model is $6.2 million
11-50 (1) $10.2 million drop in RI
11-51 $2.929 million pre-tax profit; (2) 31.7% divisional ROI

Chapter 12

12-9 (1) $90; (2) $6,000U material use variance; $900F labor efficiency variance
12-13 $600F material use variance; $800U labor efficiency variance
12-14 $80F material use variance; $1,200U overhead efficiency variance

12-18 $4,800U material use; $8,500U total overhead variance
12-19 $300F total variance
12-20 (1a) $2 per lb.; (1c) $6 per unit; (5) 14,000 hrs.; (9) $12,000F; (11) $6,000F; (12) $43,200
12-21 (2) $6,000F material use; $6,000U variable overhead efficiency
12-23 (1) $2,080U material use variance; $1,200F labor efficiency variance
12-24 (2a) $168,000F; (2b) $114,000U; (2c) $19,530U
12-26 $3.595
12-27 (1) $1,350 material price variance, $2,000U labor efficiency variance
12-28 (1) $63 and $124
12-29 $1,320U material use variance; $530F indirect labor efficiency variance; $546F other variable overhead efficiency variance
12-30 (2) $7.82
12-31 $12,000U material use; $15,000U variable overhead efficiency
12-34 $6.4 million F sales volume variance; $0.8 million U variable cost variances; $0.7 million fixed cost variances
12-35 $16,000U variance from flexible budget for variable costs
12-37 $4,800U material use variance; $7,600U labor efficiency variance; total unfavorable variances, $17,000
12-38 (1) Total: $79,200U (Jan.), $201,600U (June)
12-39 $5,800U material use; $3,700U labor efficiency; $13,800U variable overhead variances total; $10,700U fixed overhead budget
12-40 (1) $5,100U material use; $200F labor efficiency; (2) $900F material use; $800U labor efficiency
12-41 $4,820U variance from flexible budget for 10,000 units
12-42 (1) $8,800U; (2) $4,800F; (3) $4; (8) 2 lbs.; (9) 41,000 lbs.
12-43 (1) $7.21; (2) $346,510 income; $4,536U material use variance; $25,200U labor efficiency variance
12-44 2,000 units produced; $150F material use variance
12-45 (1) $8.838 standard per-carton cost, using Anaxohyde
12-46 $4.19 total standard variable cost per case
12-48 (1a) $520U; (1c) $820U; (1e) $737U (total); (1f) $75U (total)

Chapter 13

13-7 (1) $9 per hr.; (3) $231,000 (M-1); $299,000 (M-2)
13-8 (2) $240,000 (M-1); (3) $20,000 over; (4) $25,000F, $5,000U
13-9 (1) $151,000 income; (2) $160,000 income, $20,000 overapplied overhead
13-10 (1) $5; (2) $360,000 income; $60,000 overapplied overhead
13-11 (1e) $186,000; (2e) $176,000; (3a) $7; (4d) 43,000 hrs.
13-13 (1d) $2,000U; (2b) $606,000; (3a) $304,000; (4d) $390,000
13-14 (1) $1.40; (3) $310,000; (5) $26,000 overapplied; (6) $8,000F
13-15 (2) $234,000 applied; (3) $2,000U budget var.; $6,000U volume var.
13-16 (1) $0.24 per part and $7 per machine hr.; (2) $2,883,200 cost of sales; (3) $655,400 income
13-17 (2) $57,546 cost of sales; (3) $494 overapplied overhead
13-18 (3) $119,200 cost of sales; $12,800 income; (4) $14,000 overapplied
13-21 (2) $229 overapplied
13-23 (2) $10,000 underapplied; $30,000F volume variance
13-24 (1) $0.40 per material dollar and $5.50 per machine hr.; (2) $144,250 total overhead applied
13-25 (3) Machining $1,500 underapplied; Assembly $200 overapplied
13-26 (2) $259,320 cost of sales; (3) $4,580 overapplied
13-29 (1) $1,806,510 cost of sales; (2) $1,999,490; (3) $18,430 overapplied overhead; $104,040 income
13-30 (1) $8.90; (3) overhead applied: $61,550 (XT-56), $53,850 (XR-23), $30,550 (XY-67)
13-31 (1) $30 for seniors; (2) $50 per hr.

13-32 (2) $42,000 underapplied; (3) $609,500 cost of sales
13-33 (1) $72,000; 92) $18,000; (3) $1,180,000 required revenue
13-34 (1) $0.979; (2) $14.69 Class II; (3) $13,180
13-35 (1) $22,500 incremental cost
13-36 $9,760 additional CM
13-37 (1) $7,200,000; (2) $30; (3) $760,000; (4) $1,000,000
13-38 (1) $49,008 price for 200 Model 807 chairs.
13-39 (1) $100,000 saving
13-40 $1,250,000 income; $12,000U budget variance; $28,000 underapplied
13-42 (1) $172,500 Randle's; (2) $4,100 CM advantage to Randle's
13-43 (2) $15,950; (3) $6,800 underapplied; (4) $100,950 income
13-44 (1) $2.00; (2) $59,510 (A-16)
13-45 (2) $1,796,650 cost of sales; (3) $7,905,650 cost of sales; (4) $9,500 overapplied labor-related overhead
13-46 (1) $1,699 cost (XT-12), $4,658 cost (JY-09); (2) $945 price (XT-12), $6,936 price (JY-09)
13-47 Underapplied: $4,000 (Apr.), $21,000 (May)
13-48 (1) $14,220 bid (391); (2) $6 per hr., grinding; (3) $13,590 bid (391)
13-49 (1) $29.20 per hr.; (2) $39,000
13-51 (2) 3,000 hrs. (Apr.), 4,500 hrs. (May); (3) $2,000U budget variance (June)
13-53 $2,000 monthly CM advantage to buying unsorted tomatoes

Chapter 14

14-3 March and April income: $50,000 variable costing; $150,000 March income, absorption costing
14-4 (1) $22, $18, $20; (2) $1,300 income, budgeted production
14-5 $600,000 Apr. income; $150,000U volume variance (May)
14-6 Income: $300,000 (Apr.); $825,000 (May)
14-7 Income: $500,000 (Apr.); $675,000 (May); $350,000U volume variance (May)
14-8 $410,000 income; $40,000U volume variance
14-9 $350,000 income
14-10 (1a) $2.50; (1b) $2; (2a) $25,000F; (2b) $100,000U
14-12 $30,000 income
14-13 Income: $30,000 (a), $35,000 (b)
14-14 (1) Actual gross margin: $20,000; $20,006; $20,008; $20,004
14-15 (1) $400,000 19X5 income; $40,000F volume variance; (2) $3,120,000 total assets, 19X6; (3) $2,760,000 total assets, 19X5
14-16 (1) 24,000 (Feb.), 15,000 (Mar.); (2) $200,000 Mar. income
14-17 Income: $230,000 (1), $226,000 (2)
14-19 (1b) 65,000; (2b) 57,500; (3d) $110,000
14-20 (1) $20,000 income (June); (2) income: $17,000 (May), $20,000 (June)
14-21 (1) $28; (2) $50,000U volume variance; (3) $180,000 income
14-22 (2) $20,000F volume variance; $150,000 income; (2) $110,000 income
14-23 (2) $30,000U volume variance; $20,000U variable cost variances; (3) income = $1,205,000
14-24 (1) $50,000U volume variance; $142,000 income; (2) $92,000 income
14-25 (1) $50,000F volume variance; $330,000 income; (2) $280,000 income
14-26 (1b) $2,000F; (1c) $5,000U; (1e) $5,000F; (1g) $2,000U
14-27 (2) $1,600U volume variance, $72,400 income
14-28 (1) $20,000U volume variance; $512,000 income
14-29 Income: $477,500 budgeted, $500,000 actual
14-31 $15 variable cost per unit; $71,200 income
14-32 (1) $630,000 end. inventory; $280,000 income; (2) 3.25 current ratio
14-33 (1) $512,000
14-34 (2) $38.87; (3) $1,000U volume variance (parts-related overhead)

14-35 (1) $21,800 Mar. income; (2) $6,500F volume variance, Mar.
14-36 (1) $21,600U material use var.; $27,648U labor rate var.; $27,648U variable overhead spending var.; (2) $217,224 income
14-38 (1) $38 for #380; (2) $55,400; (3) $10,500U volume variance
14-40 (1) $690,000 income, second 6 mos.; (2) $4,105,000 total assets at 12/31; $140,000 cash at 6/30
14-41 (1) $30,000F volume variance; $85,000 income
14-42 (1) $4.80 (204); (2) $47,200 (204); (3) $154,200 income; $85,200F volume variance
14-43 (1) $2,740,000; (2) $4,015,000
14-44 (1) 152,000 units; (2) 123,500 units; (4) same as (2)
14-45 (1) $350,000 underabsorbed overhead, $684,000 net income; (2) $17,391,100 disbursements; $328,900 balance at 12/31; (3) $13,758,500 total assets; $2,204,000 retained earnings; $1,660,000 finished goods inventory
14-46 (1) $125,000F volume variance; $562,500 income
14-47 (2) $61,000 loss in March; $89,000 income in May
14-49 Break-even point of 1,406,250 units for 19X7 cost structure; 19X8 profit even with higher fixed costs and volume below old break-even.

Chapter 15

15-3 (1) 22,400; (2) $1.25; (3) $3,000; (4) $25,000
15-5 (1) 80,000; (2) $3; (3) $27,000; (4) $213,000
15-6 (1) 76,000; (2) $3.10; (3) $27,900; (4) $212,100
15-9 (1) $6; (2) $12,000U; (3) 48,000; (4) $10,000
15-11 (1) $20.80; (3) $62,400 end. balance; $728,000 transferred
15-12 (1) $20.50; (2) $61,500 end. balance; $728,900 transferred
15-15 (1) $0.70 Mixing; (2) $3,780; (3) $78,000 cost of sales
15-16 (1) 210,000 (materials); (2) $0.22 (materials); (3) $160,200 transfers
15-17 (1) 170,000 (materials); (2) $2.24 (materials); (3) $883,500 transfers
15-18 (1) 2,300; (2) $2,750F total variance
15-19 (2) $240,000 CM at $28
15-20 $12 std. cost; $30,000U volume variance; $10,000U labor variance; $180,000 income
15-22 (1-5) $863,000 transferred; (2) $184,000 work-in-process balance; (3) $93,500 income; $15,500 underapplied overhead
15-23 Cost of sales: $269,300 (May), $316,125 (June)
15-24 (1) Equivalent units for conversion costs: 80,400 (Mixing), 74,000 (Boiling); (2) $0.24 for materials; (3) $51,750 transferred; (4) $73,440 transferred
15-25 (1) $0.43 (conversion costs); (2) $51,922
15-26 (1) $360,000 income; (2) $15,000U volume variance; $367,000 income
15-27 (1) $6.50; (2) $4.50; (3) 240,000; (5) $493,000; (6) $403,000; (7) $9,000U; (8) 738,000; (10) $2,000F; (12) $236,000; (14) $5.50
15-29 $4,500 income; $40,500U volume variance
15-30 (1) $50,000 income; $20,000U volume variance; (3) $22,000U total variances, $40,500 income
15-31 (1) $204,480 transferred to finished goods; (2) $34,400 income
15-32 (1) $207,360 transferred to finished goods; (2) $320F material use variance; $350F labor rate variance; $4,800F volume variance; $2,860F total variances; $34,660 income
15-33 (1) $20,000 CM on order; (3) $500,000 actual gross profit
15-34 (1) $20,250 (Job 83); (2) $115U total material use variance; $1,995U total variances; (3) $11,295 income
15-35 Income: $315,112 (1a); $298,000 (1c); $292,000 (1e)
15-36 Income: $576,888 (a); $587,000 (c); $588,684 (e)
15-37 $30 CM per machine hr. per 2-inch folder; approx. $244,005 gain from accepting order
15-38 (1) 5,000; (2) 3,000; (3) 9,500; (5) $9; (7) $18; (8) $9 (9) $10; (11) $12; (12) $1 per dress or $0.50 per hr.; (13) $30,000; (15) $0.30 per hr. or $0.60 per dress; (17) 500; (18) 2,000; (19) $18

15-39 (1) \$0.37; (2) \$73,788; (3) \$12,604 ending inventory

15-40 (1) \$10,000F material use variance; \$10,000U labor efficiency variance; \$60,000F volume variance; (2) \$455,000 income, variable costing; \$635,000 income, absorption costing

15-41 \$20,000F material use variance; \$10,000F labor efficiency variance; \$60,000U volume variance; \$735,000 income, variable costing; \$675,000 income, absorption costing

Appendix A

A-3 (1) 8,000; (2) 4,000

A-4 \$1,725 cost to investigate

A-5 2,000 EOQ; 840 reorder point

A-6 (1) 10,240 total; (2) 2,048 average

A-7 (1) \$35,000 for the doll; \$41,000 for the game

A-9 250 P and 150 Q

A-10 (1) \$30,706; (2) \$245,648

A-11 (1) \$70,700; (2) \$66,100; (3) \$65,600

A-12 (1) 50,000; (2) (\$600)

A-13 \$108,000 expected value, 600 cases

A-15 (1) 175 X and 50 Y; total CM of \$9,800; (2) \$18 per hr.

A-16 (1) \$20,000; (2) \$16,000; (3) \$12,000

A-17 (1) 2,000; (2) \$5,000

A-18 \$168,000 expected value

A-19 (1) 4,243; (2) 1,600

A-20 Between 18 and 19 days

A-21 \$1,920 cost of investigating

A-22 900 Classes, 150 Fasts

A-23 (1) \$0.625; (2) \$21; (3) \$16.50

A-24 \$410,550 CM for toaster; \$391,500 CM for radio

A-26 \$6,656 ave. cost for 32 batches; \$212,992 total cost for 32 batches

A-27 Expected value: to make = \$151,000; to subcontract = \$136,500

A-28 (1) 4,000; (2) \$2,000; (3) \$8; (4) \$200

A-29 \$17.20 per-unit carrying cost; \$150 per-order ordering cost

A-31 \$1,800 expected cost of investigation

A-32 (1) \$16,000 expected value of profit

A-33 (1) \$3,360; (2) \$2,984

A-34 \$4,800 expected cost to investigate; \$4,000 not to investigate

A-35 (1) \$15,000 savings, 8 yrs.; (2a) \$52,128 PV of savings

A-36 Expected value: \$49,000 (Std. Model); \$51,600 (Super Model)

A-37 (1) \$3,240 gain to Alexander; (2) \$9.60; (3) No

A-38 (1) 500,000 copies; (2) \$4,650

A-39 (1) \$82 CM from Modern; (2) \$290

A-40 \$372,000 expected value of annual cash flows for 250,000-unit factory; \$239,880 NPV for 200,000-unit factory

A-41 9,000 lbs.